Biological Psychology

11e

James W. Kalat
North Carolina State University

WADSWORTH
CENGAGE Learning™

Australia • Brazil • Japan • Korea • Mexico • Singapore • Spain • United Kingdom • United States

Biological Psychology, **Eleventh Edition**
James W. Kalat

Senior Publisher: Linda Schreiber-Ganster

Publisher: Jon-David Hague

Acquisitions Editor: Timothy Matray

Developmental Editors: Renee Deljon and Vicki Malinee

Assistant Editor: Paige Leeds

Editorial Assistant: Lauren Moody

Senior Media Editor: Lauren Keyes

Marketing Program Manager: Sean Foy

Senior Content Project Manager: Pat Waldo

Design Director: Rob Hugel

Senior Art Directors: Vernon Boes and Pam Galbreath

Manufacturing Planner: Karen Hunt

Rights Acquisitions Specialist: Roberta Broyer

Production Service: Megan Greiner, Graphic World Inc.

Text Designer: Lisa Buckley

Photo Researcher: Sarah Bonner, Bill Smith Group

Text Researcher: Karyn Morrison

Copy Editor: Graphic World Inc.

Illustrators: Graphic World Inc. and Argosy, Inc.

Cover Designer: Riezebos Holzbaur/ Brieanna Hattey

Cover Image: Argosy, Inc.

Compositor: Graphic World Inc.

For product information and technology assistance, contact us at **Cengage Learning Customer & Sales Support, 1-800-354-9706.**

For permission to use material from this text or product, submit all requests online at **www.cengage.com/permissions**. Further permissions questions can be e-mailed to **permissionrequest@cengage.com**

Library of Congress Control Number: 2011933697

ISBN-13: 978-1-111-83100-4
ISBN-10: 1-111-83100-9

Wadsworth
20 Davis Drive
Belmont, CA 94002-3098
USA

Cengage Learning is a leading provider of customized learning solutions with office locations around the globe, including Singapore, the United Kingdom, Australia, Mexico, Brazil, and Japan. Locate your local office at **www.cengage .com/global**

Cengage Learning products are represented in Canada by Nelson Education, Ltd.

To learn more about Wadsworth visit **www.cengage.com/Wadsworth**

Purchase any of our products at your local college store or at our preferred online store **www.CengageBrain.com**

Printed in the United States of America

1 2 3 4 5 6 7 15 14 13 12 11

About the Author

James W. Kalat (rhymes with ballot) is Professor of Psychology at North Carolina State University, where he teaches courses in introduction to psychology and biological psychology. Born in 1946, he received an AB degree summa cum laude from Duke University in 1968 and a PhD in psychology from the University of Pennsylvania in 1971. He is also the author of *Introduction to Psychology* (9th ed.) and co-author with Michelle Shiota of *Emotion* (2nd ed.). In addition to textbooks, he has written journal articles on taste-aversion learning, the teaching of psychology, and other topics. A remarried widower, he has three children, two stepsons, and four grandchildren.

To my wife's Uncle Josh on the
occasion of his 101st birthday. And
yes, this is a recent photo.

Brief Contents

Contents

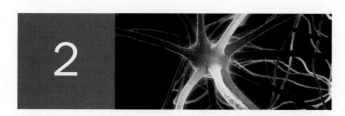

Anatomy of the Nervous System   84

Development and Plasticity
of the Brain   122

Vision   152

Other Sensory Systems   192

Movement   230

Wakefulness and Sleep   264

Internal Regulation 296

Reproductive Behaviors 326

Emotional Behaviors   354

The Biology of Learning and Memory   388

Cognitive Functions   420

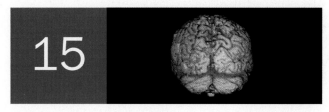

Mood Disorders and Schizophrenia   458

APPENDIX A

APPENDIX B

Preface

In the first edition of this text, published in 1981, I remarked, "I almost wish I could get parts of this text . . . printed in disappearing ink, programmed to fade within ten years of publication, so that I will not be embarrassed by statements that will look primitive from some future perspective." I would say the same thing today, except that I would like for the ink to fade faster. Biological psychology progresses rapidly, and many statements become out-of-date quickly.

The most challenging aspect of writing a text is selecting what to include and what to omit. It is possible to err on the side of too little information or too much. This field is full of facts, and it is unfortunately easy to get so bogged down in memorizing them that one loses the big picture. The big picture here is fascinating and profound: Your brain activity *is* your mind. I hope that readers of this book will remember that message even after they forget some of the details.

Each chapter is divided into modules; each module begins with an introduction and finishes with a summary. This organization makes it easy for instructors to assign part of a chapter per day instead of a whole chapter per week. Modules can also be covered in a different order. Indeed, of course, whole chapters can be taken in different orders.

I assume that the reader has a basic background in psychology and biology and understands such basic terms as *classical conditioning, reinforcement, vertebrate, mammal, gene, chromosome, cell,* and *mitochondrion.* I also assume familiarity with a high school chemistry course. Those with a weak background in chemistry or a fading memory of it may consult Appendix A.

▌ The Electronic Edition

Will electronic editions replace printed books? Should they? Maybe or maybe not, but electronic editions have some important advantages. The electronic edition of this text includes animations, videos, sounds, and many new and enhanced interactive try-it-yourself activities that a printed text cannot include. At various points, the student encounters Concept Checks in multiple-choice format. After the student clicks one of the answers, the electronic text reports whether the answer was right or wrong. If it was wrong, the text states the correct answer and explains why it is right and the other answer wrong. The electronic edition also offers the opportunity to access valuable websites. Also, the electronic edition is significantly less expensive than the printed text. Many students do opt for the electronic edition, if they know about it. Go to **www.cengagebrain.com** to obtain it.

▌ Changes in This Edition

The 11th edition of this textbook includes many changes in content to reflect the rapid progress in biological psychology. Here are a few noteworthy items:

Overall

- **The latest research in biological psychology.** This edition includes more than 500 new references—more than 80% of them from 2008 or later. New studies are presented on topics such as fMRI; tasters, supertasters, and nontasters; sensitivity of touch by gender; synesthesia; and oxytocin.
- **Many new and improved illustrations.** There are numerous new, updated, and revised figures, oftentimes in three dimensions, that further strengthen this text's ability to help students learn visually.
- **New topics and discussions.** The 11th edition includes the latest issues and controversies in the field, such as:
  - **Epigenetics.** This emerging field focuses on changes in gene expression without modification of the DNA sequence. Epigenetics may help explain differences between monozygotic twins, effects of prenatal environments, and more.
  - **Sleep as neuronal inhibition.** During sleep, spontaneous and evoked activities decline only slightly, but increased synaptic inhibition blocks spread to other areas. Because inhibition can be stronger in one area than in another, one brain area may be more awake than another. Sleepwalking is one example. Another is the experience of awakening but being temporarily unable to move.
  - **The emerging controversy about effectiveness of antidepressant drugs.** Antidepressant drugs appear to be no more effective than placebos for most patients, showing significant benefits only for those with severe depression. When they are effective, they probably work by releasing the neurotrophin BDNF, rather than by the more familiar mechanism of altering serotonin and dopamine release at the synapses.

▌ Chapter-by-Chapter

Chapter 1: The Major Issues

- Added introductory section in Module 1.1 that puts the mind–brain problem in a larger context of the mysteries of the universe.
- Most of the discussion of the mind–brain problem relocated to Chapter 14.
- Added new section about epigenetics to Module 1.2.
- Expanded information on the genetics of aging.

Chapter 2: Nerve Cells and Nerve Impulses

- Clearer explanation of the biochemical basis of the action potential.
- Modified Figures 2.14, 2.15, 2.17 and 2.19 in Module 2.2: The Nerve Impulse to more clearly show what is happening within the membrane.

Chapter 3: Synapses

- New Figure 3.5 shows how summation effects can depend on the order of stimuli.
- New Figures 3.9, 3.10, and 3.11 indicate how the synaptic wiring diagram controls responses.
- New Figure 3.22 illustrates a gap junction.
- Modified Figures 3.7, 3.13, 3.16, 3.17, 3.23 for clarity.
- Revised description of addiction, including discussion of tolerance and withdrawal and an expanded treatment of brain reorganization.

Chapter 4: Anatomy of the Nervous System

- Several revisions in the discussion about fMRI. An fMRI measurement showing increased activity in a certain area during a certain activity does not necessarily identify that area as specific to the activity. The best way to test our understanding is to see whether someone can use the fMRI results to guess what the person was doing, thinking, or seeing. Two studies successfully demonstrated that possibility.
- Reorganized, updated, and shortened description of research on brain size and intelligence.

Chapter 5: Development and Plasticity of the Brain

- Added new research that indicates new neurons form in adult primate cerebral cortex after brain damage (although we don't know how long they survive).
- Updated and revised discussion of musician's cramp.
- Added section covering how brain research possibly relates to behavioral changes in adolescence and old age.
- Many updates in the module on recovery from brain damage.

Chapter 6: Vision

- Revised section in Module 6.1: "Would the Brain Know What to do with Extra Color Information?"
- Reorganized Modules 6.2 and 6.3, so Module 6.2 now includes most of the material about development of the visual cortex, thus keeping all of the Hubel and Wiesel work together. Module 6.3 discusses the separate paths for processing in the visual cortex, with emphasis on human brain damage cases.
- Revised discussions on facial recognition and motion blindness.

Chapter 7: Other Sensory Systems

- Added interesting study that explains why women have more touch sensitivity than men (primarily due to having smaller fingers).
- New section on social pain, including the finding that Tylenol can relieve hurt feelings.
- Stronger evidence that temporal patterns of response in brain neurons code for different kinds of taste.
- New studies show that the difference between tasters and supertasters relates to the number of fungiform papillae on the tongue but not to the gene that differentiates tasters from nontasters.
- New study shows how synesthesia can result from cross-connections between axons of different sensory systems.

Chapter 8: Movement

- New study shows that people move more quickly when reacting to a stimulus than when making the same movement spontaneously. This result relates to the old Western movies in which the hero drew his gun second but still outgunned the bad guy who drew first. It says that outcome is at least plausible.
- Expanded and moved discussion of the antisaccade task (now defined) from first to second module.
- Updated and reorganized description of the cortical areas that plan movements before sending their output to the primary motor cortex.

Chapter 9: Wakefulness and Sleep

- Added figure showing circadian rhythms in people's mood.
- Revised discussion and revised figure concerning the role of the PER and TIM proteins in producing circadian rhythms.
- New section on sleep and the inhibition of brain activity makes the point that sleep can occur locally within the brain, such as during sleepwalking.
- Module 9.3 on functions of sleep and dreams has several points of reorganization and reordering of material.

Chapter 10: Internal Regulation

- New examples of behavioral relevance of body temperature.
- Added illustration showing seasonal variation in eating.
- Added mother's diet in pregnancy as a predisposing factor in obesity.
- Deleted the section on anorexia nervosa.

Chapter 11: Reproductive Behaviors

- Expanded and revised discussion of sex differences based on X and Y chromosomes that do not depend on sex hormones.

- Expanded and revised discussion of effects of prenatal hormones on children's play.
- Added research on the relationship between testosterone and seeking new sexual partners.
- More research added on oxytocin.

Chapter 12: Emotional Behaviors

- Added the "triple imbalance" hypothesis of aggressive behavior, which links aggression to high testosterone relative to cortisol and serotonin.
- Added section on individual differences in amygdala response and anxiety.
- Enhanced description of patient SM with bilateral amygdala damage. She shows no fear of snakes, spiders, or horror movies. Unfortunately, she wanders into dangerous situations without due caution.
- New section on anxiety disorders, especially panic disorder, and methods of coping with severe anxiety.

Chapter 13: The Biology of Learning and Memory

- Substituted the term *instrumental conditioning* for *operant conditioning.*
- Reorganized and expanded treatment of consolidation. Added the concept of reconsolidation.
- Updated the fact that patient H. M. has died.
- Substituted new figure to illustrate the Morris water maze.
- New section about the role of the basal ganglia.
- Updated discussion of Alzheimer's disease, particularly about the interactions between amyloid and tau.
- Added figure to illustrate long-term potentiation.
- New section "Improving Memory" concludes that, from a biological standpoint, there's not much we can do.

Chapter 14: Cognitive Functions

- Added information on a gene important for language learning.
- Revised and reorganized discussion about brain representation of language in bilingual people.
- Moved and condensed most of the material about the mind–brain problem from Chapter 1 to Module 14.3.
- Revised discussion of consciousness, incorporating much of what used to be in Chapter 1. It also includes the study using brain measurements to infer possible consciousness in a patient in a persistent vegetative state.
- Added section about attention.

Chapter 15: Mood Disorders and Schizophrenia

- Added distinction between early-onset and late-onset depression, evidently influenced by different genes.
- Included many failures to replicate Caspi's report of an interaction between a gene and stressful experiences.

- Increased emphasis on the role of BDNF and new learning in explaining antidepressant effects.
- Updated discussion and new research on the limited effectiveness of antidepressant drugs.
- Expanded discussion of the relative effectiveness of psychotherapy versus antidepressant drugs.
- Revised description of the diagnosis of schizophrenia.

A Comprehensive Teaching and Learning Package

Biological Psychology, **11th Edition,** is accompanied by an array of supplements developed to facilitate both instructors' and students' best experience inside as well as outside the classroom. All of the supplements continuing from the 10th edition have been thoroughly revised and updated; other supplements are new to this edition. Cengage Learning invites you to take full advantage of the teaching and learning tools available to you and has prepared the following descriptions of each.

Print Resources
Instructor's Resource Manual

This manual, updated and expanded for the 11th edition, is designed to help streamline and maximize the effectiveness of your course preparation. It provides chapter outlines and learning objectives; class demonstrations and projects, including lecture tips and activities, with handouts; a list of video resources, additional suggested readings and related websites, discussion questions designed to work both in class and on message boards for online classes; key terms from the text; and James Kalat's answers to the "Thought Questions" that conclude each module.

Test Bank for *Biological Psychology,* 11th Edition

Simplify testing and assessment using this printed selection of more than 3,500 multiple-choice, true/false, short answer, and essay questions, which have been thoroughly revised in this edition. All new questions are flagged as "New" to help instructors update their existing tests. This teaching resource includes separate questions for both a midterm and a comprehensive final exam.

Media Resources
PowerLecture™

The fastest, easiest way to build powerful, customized, media-rich lectures, PowerLecture provides a collection of book-specific PowerPoint lectures, and class tools to enhance the educational experience.

Psychology CourseMate

Biological Psychology, 11th Edition, includes Psychology Course-Mate, a complement to your textbook. Psychology CourseMate includes:

- An interactive eBook
- Interactive teaching and learning tools including:
  - quizzes
  - flashcards
  - videos
  - and more
- Engagement Tracker, a first-of-its-kind tool that monitors student engagement in the course

Go to login.cengage.com to access these resources.

WebTutor on Blackboard and WebCT

Jump-start your course with customizable, rich, text-specific content within your Course Management System:

- Jump-start—Simply load a WebTutor cartridge into your Course Management System.
- Customizable—Easily blend, add, edit, reorganize, or delete content.

- Content—Rich, text-specific content, media assets, quizzing, weblinks, discussion topics, interactive games and exercises, and more

Whether you want to web-enable your class or put an entire course online, WebTutor delivers. Visit webtutor.cengage.com to learn more.

eBook for *Biological Psychology*, 11th Edition

Available at **cengagebrain.com**, the PDF version of this book looks just like the printed text but also provides animations, videos, sounds, and interactive try-it-yourself activities. The Concept Checks offer multiple-choice questions with feedback about why incorrect answers were incorrect. It also has links to websites and a convenient menu of links to each chapter's main headings so that students can easily navigate from section to section. Using Acrobat's search feature, students may also search for key terms or other specific information in this version of the text.

Acknowledgments

Let me tell you something about researchers in this field: As a rule, they are amazingly cooperative with textbook authors. Many colleagues sent me comments, ideas, articles, and photos. I thank especially Bart Hoebel at Princeton University.

I have received an enormous number of letters and e-mail messages from students. Many included helpful suggestions; some managed to catch errors or inconsistencies that everyone else had overlooked. I thank especially Chenzhen Dai, Detroit Country Day School. I also received helpful comments from many of my students at N. C. State University, including Emily Diethelm, Lillian Martin, Lisa Price, and Sara Thompson.

I appreciate the helpful comments provided by instructors who reviewed the text, as well as those who participated in a survey that gave us valuable insights on the issues in this course:

Text Reviewers and Contributors:

- John Agnew, *University of Colorado at Boulder*
- John Dale Alden III, *Lipscomb University*
- Joanne Altman, *Washburn University*
- Kevin Antshel, *SUNY–Upstate Medical University*
- Ryan Auday, *Gordon College*
- Susan Baillet, *University of Portland*
- Teresa Barber, *Dickinson College*
- Christie Bartholomew, *Kent State University*
- Howard Bashinski, *University of Colorado*
- Bakhtawar Bhadha, *Pasadena City College*
- Chris Brill, *Old Dominion University*
- J. Timothy Cannon, *The University of Scranton*
- Lore Carvajal, *Triton College*
- Sarah Cavanagh, *Assumption College*
- Linda Bryant Caviness, *La Sierra University*
- Cathy Cleveland, *East Los Angeles College*
- Elie Cohen, *The Lander College for Men (Touro College)*
- Howard Cromwell, *Bowling Green State University*
- David Crowley, *Washington University*
- Carol DeVolder, *St. Ambrose University*
- Jaime L. Diaz-Granados, *Baylor University*
- Carl DiPerna, *Onondaga Community College*
- Francine Dolins, *University of Michigan–Dearborn*
- Timothy Donahue, *Virginia Commonwealth University*
- Michael Dowdle, *Mt. San Antonio College*
- Jeff Dyche, *James Madison University*
- Gary Felsten, *Indiana University–Purdue University Columbus*

- Erin Marie Fleming, *Kent State University*
- Laurie Fowler, *Weber State University*
- Deborah Gagnon, *Wells College*
- Jonathan Gewirtz, *University of Minnesota*
- Jackie Goldstein, *Samford University*
- Peter Green, *Maryville University*
- Jeff Grimm, *Western Washington University*
- Amy Clegg Haerich, *Riverside Community College*
- Christopher Hayashi, *Southwestern College*
- Suzane Helfer, *Adrian College*
- Alicia Helion, *Lakeland College*
- Jackie Hembrook, *University of New Hampshire*
- Phu Hoang, *Texas A&M International University*
- Richard Howe, *College of the Canyon*
- Barry Hurwitz, *University of Miami*
- Karen Jennings, *Keene State College*
- Craig Johnson, *Towson University*
- Robert Tex Johnson, *Delaware County Community College*
- Kathryn Kelly, *Northwestern State University*
- Shannon Kendey, *Hood College*
- Craig Kinsley, *University of Richmond*
- Philip Langlais, *Old Dominion University*
- Jerry Lee, *Albright College*
- Robert Lennartz, *Sierra College*
- Hui-Yun Li, *Oregon Institute of Technology*
- Cyrille Magne, *Middle Tennessee State University*
- Michael Matthews, *U.S. Military Academy (West Point)*
- Estelle Mayhew, *Rutgers University–New Brunswick*
- Daniel McConnell, *University of Central Florida*
- Maria McLean, *Thomas More College*
- Elaine McLeskey, *Belmont Technical College*
- Corinne McNamara, *Kennesaw State University*
- Brian Metcalf, *Hawaii Pacific University*
- Richard Mills, *College of DuPage*
- Daniel Montoya, *Fayetteville State University*
- Paulina Multhaupt, *Macomb Community College*
- Walter Murphy, *Texas A&M University–Central Texas*
- Joseph Nedelec, *Florida State University*
- Ian Norris, *Murray State University*
- Marcia Pasqualini, *Avila University*
- Susana Pecina, *University of Michigan–Dearborn*
- Linda Perrotti, *The University of Texas–Arlington*

- Terry Pettijohn, *The Ohio State University*
- Jennifer Phillips, *Mount St. Mary's University*
- Edward Pollak, *West Chester University*
- Brian Pope, *Tusculum College*
- Mark Prendergast, *University of Kentucky*
- Jean Pretz, *Elizabethtown College*
- Mark Prokosch, *Elon University*
- Adam Prus, *Northern Michigan University*
- Khaleel Razak, *University of California–Riverside*
- John Rowe, *Florida Gateway College*
- David Rudek, *Aurora University*
- Jeffrey Rudski, *Muhlenberg College*
- Karen Sabbah, *California State University–Northridge*
- Sharleen Sakai, *Michigan State University*
- Ron Salazar, *San Juan College*
- Shanon Saszik, *Northeastern University*
- Steven Schandler, *Chapman University*
- Sue Schumacher, *North Carolina A&T State University*
- Vicki Sheafer, *LeTourneau University*
- Timothy Shearon, *The College of Idaho*
- Stephanie Simon-Dack, *Ball State University*
- Steve Smith, *University of California–Santa Barbara*
- Suzanne Sollars, *University of Nebraska–Omaha*
- Gretchen Sprow, *University of North Carolina–Chapel Hill*
- Jeff Stowell, *Eastern Illinois University*
- Gary Thorne, *Gonzaga University*
- Chris Tromborg, *Sacramento City College and University of California–Davis*
- Lucy Troup, *Colorado State University*
- Joseph Trunzo, *Bryant University*
- Sandy Venneman, *University of Houston–Victoria*
- Beth Venzke, *Concordia University*
- Ruvanee Vilhauer, *Felician College*
- Jacquie Wall, *University of Indianapolis*
- Zoe Warwick, *University of Maryland–Baltimore County*
- Jon Weimer, *Columbia College*
- Rosalyn Weller, *The University of Alabama–Birmingham*
- Adam Wenzel, *Saint Anselm College*
- David Widman, *Juniata College*
- Steffen Wilson, *Eastern Kentucky University*
- Joseph Wister, *Chatham University*
- Jessica Yokley, *University of Pittsburgh*

My acquisitions editor, Timothy Matray, has been as helpful and supportive as he could possibly be. For this edition I worked with two developmental editors, Renee Deljon and Vicki Malinee, both of whom have my highest respect and appreciation. Pat Waldo supervised the production, a major task for a book like this one. As art directors and editors, Vernon Boes and Pam Galbreath's considerable artistic abilities helped to compensate for my complete lack. Bobbie Broyer and Karyn Morrison had charge of permissions, a major task for a book like this. Sarah Bonner was the photo manager; I hope you enjoy the new photos in this text as much as I do. I thank Lisa Buckley for the text design and Sandra Cannon for the indexes. I have been fortunate to have Sharon Baker as my copy editor. All of these people have been splendid colleagues, and I thank them immensely.

I thank my wife, Jo Ellen, for keeping my spirits high, and my department head, Douglas Gillan, for his support and encouragement. I especially thank my son Sam for many discussions and insightful ideas. Sam Kalat, coming from a background of biochemistry and computer science, has many original and insightful ideas about brain functioning.

I welcome correspondence from both students and faculty. Write: James W. Kalat, Department of Psychology, Box 7650, North Carolina State University, Raleigh, NC 27695–7801, USA. E-mail: james_kalat@ncsu.edu

James W. Kalat

The Major Issues

1

CHAPTER OUTLINE

MAIN IDEAS

1. Biological explanations of behavior fall into several categories, including physiology, development, evolution, and function.

2. Nearly all current philosophers and neuroscientists reject the idea that the mind exists independently of the brain. Still, the question remains as to how and why brain activity is connected to consciousness.

3. The expression of a given gene depends on the environment and on interactions with other genes.

4. Research with nonhuman animals yields important information, but it sometimes inflicts distress or pain on the animals. Whether to proceed with a given experiment can be a difficult ethical issue.

It is often said that Man is unique among animals. It is worth looking at this term "unique" before we discuss our subject proper. The word may in this context have two slightly different meanings. It may mean: Man is strikingly different—he is not identical with any animal. This is of course true. It is true also of all other animals: Each species, even each individual is unique in this sense. But the term is also often used in a more absolute sense: Man is so different, so "essentially different" (whatever that means) that the gap between him and animals cannot possibly be bridged—he is something altogether new. Used in this absolute sense the term is scientifically meaningless. Its use also reveals and may reinforce conceit, and it leads to complacency and defeatism because it assumes that it will be futile even to search for animal roots. It is prejudging the issue.

Niko Tinbergen (1973, p. 161)

OPPOSITE: It is tempting to try to "get inside the mind" of people and other animals, to imagine what they are thinking or feeling. In contrast, biological psychologists try to explain behavior in terms of its physiology, development, evolution, and function. *(Source: C. D. L. Wynne, 2004)*

Biological psychologists study the animal roots of behavior, relating actions and experiences to genetics and physiology. In this chapter, we consider three major issues: the relationship between mind and brain, the roles of nature and nurture, and the ethics of research. We also briefly consider career opportunities in this and related fields.

The Biological Approach to Behavior

Of all the questions that people ask, two stand out as the most profound and the most difficult. One of those questions deals with physics. The other pertains to the relationship between physics and psychology.

Philosopher Gottfried Leibniz (1714) posed the first question: "Why is there something rather than nothing?" It would seem that nothingness would be the default state. Evidently, the universe—or whoever or whatever created the universe—had to be self-created.

So… how did that happen?

That question is supremely baffling, but a subordinate question is more amenable to discussion: Given the existence of a universe, why this particular kind of universe? Could the universe have been fundamentally different? Our universe has protons, neutrons, and electrons with particular dimensions of mass and charge. It also contains less familiar types of particles, plus certain quantities of energy and poorly understood "dark matter" and "dark energy." The universe has four fundamental forces—gravity, electromagnetism, the strong nuclear force, and the weak nuclear force. What if any of these properties had been different?

Beginning in the 1980s, specialists in a branch of physics known as *string theory* set out to prove mathematically that this is the only possible way the universe could be. Succeeding in that effort would have been theoretically satisfying, but alas, as string theorists worked through their equations, they concluded that this is not the only possible universe. The universe could have taken a vast number of forms with different laws of physics. How vast a number? Imagine the number 1 followed by about 500 zeros. And that's the *low* estimate.

Of all those possible universes, how many could have supported life? Very few. Consider the following (Davies, 2006):

- If gravity were weaker, matter would not condense into stars and planets. If it were stronger, stars would burn brighter and use up their fuel too quickly for life to evolve.
- If the electromagnetic force were stronger, the protons within an atom would repel one another so strongly that atoms would burst apart.
- In the beginning was hydrogen. The other elements formed by fusion within stars. The only way to get

those elements out of stars and into planets (like Earth) is for a star to explode as a supernova and send its contents out into the galaxy. If the weak nuclear force were *either* a bit stronger *or* a bit weaker, a star could not explode. Also, during the first fraction of a second after the Big Bang that started the universe, if the weak force had been a bit stronger, the universe would consist of almost nothing but hydrogen. If the weak force had been a bit weaker, the universe would consist of almost nothing but helium.

- Because of the exact ratio of the electromagnetic force to the strong nuclear force, helium (element 2 on the periodic table) and beryllium (element 4) go into resonance within a star, enabling them to fuse easily into carbon, which is essential to life as we know it. (It's hard to talk about life as we don't know it.) If either the electromagnetic force or the strong nuclear force changed slightly (less than 1%), the universe would have almost no carbon.
- The electromagnetic force is 10^{40} times stronger than gravity. If gravity were a bit stronger than this, relative to the electromagnetic force, planets would not form. If it were a bit weaker, planets would consist of only gases, without any of the heavier elements that form surfaces… and bones and bodies.
- Have you ever wondered why water (H_2O) is a liquid? Other light molecules, such as carbon dioxide, nitric oxide, ozone, and methane are gases except at extremely low temperatures. In a water molecule, the two hydrogen ions form a 104.5° angle (Figure 1.1). As a result, one end of the water molecule has a slight positive charge and the other a slight negative charge. The difference is enough for water molecules to attract one another electrically. If they attracted one another a bit less, all water would be a gas (steam). But if water molecules attracted one another a bit more strongly, water would always be a solid (ice).

In short, the universe could have been different in many ways, and in nearly all of them, life as we know it would be

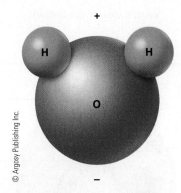

© Argosy Publishing Inc.

FIGURE 1.1 A water molecule
Because of the angle between hydrogen, oxygen, and hydrogen, one end of the molecule is more positive and the other is more negative. The exact amount of difference in charge causes one water molecule to attract another—just strongly enough to be a liquid, but not strongly enough to be a solid.

impossible. Why is the universe the way it is? Maybe it's just a coincidence. (Lucky for us, huh?) Or maybe intelligence of some sort guided the formation of the universe. That hypothesis obviously goes way beyond the reach of empirical science. A third possibility, popular among many physicists, is that a huge number of other universes (perhaps an infinite number) really *do* exist, and we of course know about only the kind of universe in which we could evolve. That hypothesis, too, goes way beyond the reach of empirical science, as we can't know about other universes.

Will we ever know why the universe is the way it is? Maybe not, but the question is so fascinating that thinking about it becomes irresistible.

At the start, I mentioned two profound but difficult questions. The second one is what philosopher David Chalmers (1995) calls the **hard problem**: Given this universe composed of matter and energy, why is there such a thing as consciousness? We can imagine how matter came together to form molecules, and how certain kinds of carbon compounds came together to form a primitive type of life, which then evolved into animals, and then animals with brains and complex behaviors. But why and how did brain activity become conscious? What is the relationship between mental experience and brain activity? This question is called the **mind–brain problem** or the **mind–body problem**.

That question is as baffling, and as fascinating, as the one about why there is something rather than nothing. So far, no one has offered a convincing explanation of consciousness. A few scholars have suggested that we do away with the concept of consciousness or mind altogether (Churchland, 1986; Dennett, 1991). That proposal seems to avoid the question, not answer it. Chalmers (2007) and Rensch (1977) proposed, instead, that we regard consciousness as a fundamental property of matter. A fundamental property is one

that cannot be reduced to something else. For example, mass is a fundamental property. We can't explain *why* matter has mass; it just does. Similarly, we can't explain why protons and electrons have charge. They just do. Maybe consciousness is like that.

Well, maybe, but it's an unsatisfying answer. First, consciousness isn't like other fundamental properties. Matter has mass all the time, and protons and electrons have charge all the time. As far as we can tell, consciousness occurs only in certain parts of certain kinds of nervous systems, and just some of the time—not when you are in a dreamless sleep, and not when you are in a coma. Besides, it's unsatisfying to call *anything* a fundamental property, even mass or charge. To say that mass is a fundamental property doesn't mean that there is no reason. It means that we have given up on finding a reason. And, in fact, string theorists have not given up. They are trying to explain mass and charge in terms of sub-sub-subatomic string-like items that compose everything. To say that consciousness is a fundamental property would mean that we have given up on explaining it. Perhaps we never will explain it, but it is too soon to give up. After we learn as much as possible about the nervous system, maybe someone will come up with a brilliant insight and understand what consciousness is all about. Even if not, the research teaches us much that is useful and interesting for other reasons. We will come to understand ourselves better, even if we don't fully understand our place in the cosmos.

Biological psychology is the study of the physiological, evolutionary, and developmental mechanisms of behavior and experience. It is approximately synonymous with the terms *biopsychology, psychobiology, physiological psychology,* and *behavioral neuroscience.* The term *biological psychology* emphasizes that the goal is to relate biology to issues of psychology. *Neuroscience* includes much that is relevant to behavior but also includes more detail about anatomy and chemistry.

Biological psychology is more than a field of study. It is also a point of view. It holds that we think and act as we do because of certain brain mechanisms, which we evolved because ancient animals with these mechanisms survived and reproduced better than animals with other mechanisms.

Much of biological psychology concerns brain functioning. Figure 1.2 offers a view of the human brain from the top (what anatomists call a *dorsal* view) and from the bottom (a *ventral* view). The labels point to a few important areas that will become more familiar as you proceed through this text. An inspection of a brain reveals distinct subareas. At the microscopic level, we find two kinds of cells: the *neurons* (Figure 1.3) and the *glia.* Neurons, which convey messages to one another and to muscles and glands, vary enormously in size, shape, and functions. The glia, generally smaller than neurons, have many functions but do not convey information over great distances. The activities of neurons and glia somehow produce an enormous wealth of behavior and experience. This book is about researchers' attempts to elaborate on that word "somehow."

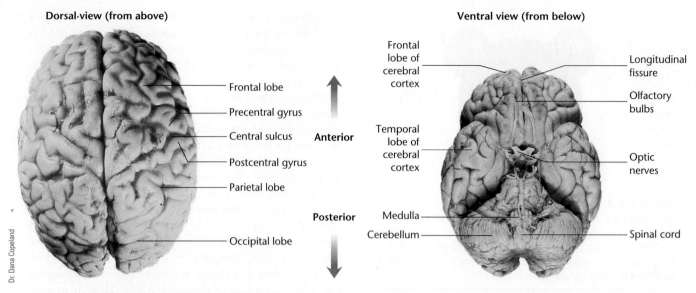

Dorsal·view (from above)

Frontal lobe
Precentral gyrus
Central sulcus
Postcentral gyrus
Parietal lobe
Occipital lobe

Anterior

Posterior

Ventral view (from below)

Frontal lobe of cerebral cortex
Temporal lobe of cerebral cortex
Medulla
Cerebellum

Longitudinal fissure
Olfactory bulbs
Optic nerves
Spinal cord

Dr. Dana Copeland

FIGURE 1.2 Two views of the human brain
The brain has an enormous number of divisions and subareas; the labels point to a few of the main ones on the surface of the brain.

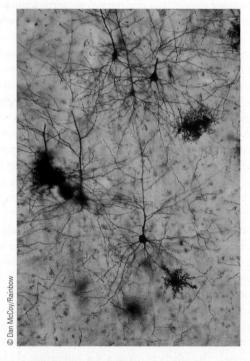

© Dan McCoy/Rainbow

FIGURE 1.3 Neurons, magnified
The brain is composed of individual cells called neurons and glia.

Biological Explanations of Behavior

Common-sense explanations of behavior often refer to intentional goals such as, "He did this because he was trying to . . ." or "She did that because she wanted to . . . ." But often, we have no reason to assume intentions. A 4-month-old bird migrat-

ing south for the first time presumably does not know why. The next spring, when she lays an egg, sits on it, and defends it from predators, again she doesn't know why. Even humans don't always know the reasons for their own behaviors. Yawning and laughter are two examples. You do them, but can you explain what they accomplish?

In contrast to common-sense explanations, biological explanations of behavior fall into four categories: physiological, ontogenetic, evolutionary, and functional (Tinbergen, 1951). A **physiological explanation** relates a behavior to the activity of the brain and other organs. It deals with the machinery of the body—for example, the chemical reactions that enable hormones to influence brain activity and the routes by which brain activity controls muscle contractions.

The term *ontogenetic* comes from Greek roots meaning the origin (or genesis) of being. An **ontogenetic explanation** describes how a structure or behavior develops, including the influences of genes, nutrition, experiences, and their interactions. For example, the ability to inhibit impulses develops gradually from infancy through the teenage years, reflecting gradual maturation of the frontal parts of the brain.

An **evolutionary explanation** reconstructs the evolutionary history of a structure or behavior. The characteristic features of an animal are almost always modifications of something found in ancestral species (Shubin, Tabin, & Carroll, 2009). For example, monkeys use tools occasionally, and humans evolved elaborations on those abilities that enable us to use tools even better (Peeters et al., 2009). Evolutionary explanations also call attention to features left over from ancestors that serve little or no function in the descendants. For example, frightened people get "goose bumps"—erections of the hairs—especially on their arms and shoulders. Goose bumps are useless to humans because our shoulder and arm hairs are so short and usually covered by clothing. In most other mammals, how-

Researchers continue to debate exactly what good yawning does. Yawning is a behavior that even people do without knowing its purpose.

Jane Burton/Nature Picture Library

FIGURE 1.4 A frightened cat with erect hairs
A functional explanation for the tendency for fear to erect the hairs is that it makes the animal look larger and more intimidating. An evolutionary explanation for human goose bumps is that we inherited the tendency from ancestors who had enough hair for the behavior to be useful.

ever, hair erection makes a frightened animal look larger and more intimidating (Figure 1.4). An evolutionary explanation of human goose bumps is that the behavior evolved in our remote ancestors and we inherited the mechanism.

A **functional explanation** describes *why* a structure or behavior evolved as it did. Within a small, isolated population, a gene can spread by accident through a process called *genetic drift*. For example, a dominant male with many offspring spreads all his genes, including some that helped him become dominant and other genes that were neutral or possibly disadvantageous. However, a gene that is prevalent in a large population presumably provided some advantage—at least in the past, though not necessarily today. A functional explanation identifies that ad-

ZITS   *BY JERRY SCOTT AND JIM BORGMAN*

Unlike all other birds, doves and pigeons can drink with their heads down. (Others fill their mouths and then raise their heads.) A physiological explanation would describe these birds' unusual pattern of nerves and throat muscles. An evolutionary explanation states that all doves and pigeons share this behavioral capacity because they inherited their genes from a common ancestor.

FIGURE 1.5 **A sea dragon, an Australian fish related to the seahorse, lives among kelp plants, looks like kelp, and usually drifts slowly and aimlessly, *acting* like kelp.** A functional explanation is that potential predators overlook a fish that resembles inedible plants. An evolutionary explanation is that genetic modifications expanded smaller appendages that were present in these fish's ancestors.

vantage. For example, many species have an appearance that matches their background (Figure 1.5). A functional explanation is that camouflaged appearance makes the animal inconspicuous to predators. Some species use their behavior as part of the camouflage. For example, zone-tailed hawks, native to Mexico and the southwestern United States, fly among vultures and hold their wings in the same posture as vultures. Small mammals and birds run for cover when they see a hawk, but they learn to ignore vultures, which pose no threat to a healthy animal. Because the zone-tailed hawks resemble vultures in both appearance and flight behavior, their prey disregard them, enabling the hawks to pick up easy meals (W. S. Clark, 2004).

To contrast the four types of biological explanation, consider how they all apply to one example, birdsong (Catchpole & Slater, 1995):

Type of Explanation	Example from Birdsong
Physiological	A particular area of a songbird brain grows under the influence of testosterone; hence, it is larger in breeding males than in females or immature birds. That brain area enables a mature male to sing.
Ontogenetic	In many species, a young male bird learns its song by listening to adult males. Development of the song requires a certain set of genes and the opportunity to hear the appropriate song during a sensitive period early in life.
Evolutionary	Certain pairs of species have similar songs. For example, dunlins and Baird's sandpipers, two shorebird species, give their calls in distinct pulses, unlike other shorebirds. The similarity suggests that the two evolved from a single ancestor.
Functional	In most bird species, only the male sings. He sings only during the reproductive season and only in his territory. The functions of the song are to attract females and warn away other males. As a rule, a bird sings loudly enough to be heard only in the territory he can defend. In short, birds evolved tendencies to sing in ways that improve their chances for mating.

Stop & Check

1. How does an evolutionary explanation differ from a functional explanation?

ANSWER

1. An evolutionary explanation states what evolved from what. For example, humans evolved from earlier primates and therefore have certain features that we inherited from those ancestors, even if the features are not useful to us today. A functional explanation states why something was advantageous and therefore evolutionarily selected.

Career Opportunities

If you want to consider a career related to biological psychology, you have a range of options relating to research and therapy. Table 1.1 describes some of the major fields.

A research position ordinarily requires a PhD in psychology, biology, neuroscience, or other related field. People with a master's or bachelor's degree might work in a research laboratory but would not direct it. Many people with a PhD hold college or university positions, where they perform some combination of teaching and research. Other individuals have pure research positions in laboratories sponsored by the government, drug companies, or other industries.

TABLE 1.1	**Fields of Specialization**
Specialization	**Description**
Research Fields	**Research positions ordinarily require a PhD. Researchers are employed by universities, hospitals, pharmaceutical firms, and research institutes.**
Neuroscientist	Studies the anatomy, biochemistry, or physiology of the nervous system. (This broad term includes any of the next five, as well as other specialties not listed.)
Behavioral neuroscientist (almost synonyms: psychobiologist, biopsychologist, or physiological psychologist)	Investigates how functioning of the brain and other organs influences behavior.
Cognitive neuroscientist	Uses brain research, such as scans of brain anatomy or activity, to analyze and explore people's knowledge, thinking, and problem solving.
Neuropsychologist	Conducts behavioral tests to determine the abilities and disabilities of people with various kinds of brain damage and changes in their condition over time. Most neuropsychologists have a mixture of psychological and medical training; they work in hospitals and clinics.
Psychophysiologist	Measures heart rate, breathing rate, brain waves, and other body processes and how they vary from one person to another or one situation to another.
Neurochemist	Investigates the chemical reactions in the brain.
Comparative psychologist (almost synonyms: ethologist, animal behaviorist)	Compares the behaviors of different species and tries to relate them to their habitats and ways of life.
Evolutionary psychologist (almost synonym: sociobiologist)	Relates behaviors, especially social behaviors, including those of humans, to the functions they have served and, therefore, the presumed selective pressures that caused them to evolve.
Practitioner Fields of Psychology	**In most cases, their work is not directly related to neuroscience. However, practitioners often need to understand it enough to communicate with a client's physician.**
Clinical psychologist	Requires PhD or PsyD. Employed by hospital, clinic, private practice, or college. Helps people with emotional problems.
Counseling psychologist	Requires PhD or PsyD. Employed by hospital, clinic, private practice, or college. Helps people make educational, vocational, and other decisions.
School psychologist	Requires master's degree or PhD. Most are employed by a school system. Identifies educational needs of schoolchildren, devises a plan to meet the needs, and then helps teachers implement it.
Medical Fields	**Practicing medicine requires an MD plus about 4 years of additional study and practice in a specialization. Physicians are employed by hospitals, clinics, medical schools, and in private practice. Some conduct research in addition to seeing patients.**
Neurologist	Treats people with brain damage or diseases of the brain.
Neurosurgeon	Performs brain surgery.
Psychiatrist	Helps people with emotional distress or troublesome behaviors, sometimes using drugs or other medical procedures.
Allied Medical Field	**These fields ordinarily require a master's degree or more. Practitioners are employed by hospitals, clinics, private practice, and medical schools.**
Physical therapist	Provides exercise and other treatments to help people with muscle or nerve problems, pain, or anything else that impairs movement.
Occupational therapist	Helps people improve their ability to perform functions of daily life, for example, after a stroke.
Social worker	Helps people deal with personal and family problems. The activities of a social worker overlap those of a clinical psychologist.

Fields of therapy include clinical psychology, counseling psychology, school psychology, medicine, and allied medical practice such as physical therapy. These fields range from neurologists (who deal exclusively with brain disorders) to social workers and clinical psychologists (who need to recognize possible signs of brain disorder so they can refer a client to a proper specialist).

Anyone who pursues a career in research needs to stay up to date on new developments by attending conventions, consulting with colleagues, and reading research journals, such as *Journal of Neuroscience, Neurology, Behavioral Neuroscience, Brain Research, Nature Neuroscience,* and *Archives of General Psychiatry.* But what if you are entering a field on the outskirts of neuroscience, such as clinical psychology, school psychology, social work, or physical therapy? In that case, you probably don't want to wade through technical journal articles, but you do want to stay current on major developments—at least enough to converse intelligently with medical colleagues. You can find much information in the magazine *Scientific American Mind* or at websites such as The Dana Foundation (http://www.dana.org).

Your Brain and Your Experience

The goal in this module has been to preview the kinds of questions biological psychologists hope to answer. In the next several chapters, we shall go through a great deal of technical information of the type you need to know before we can start applying it to interesting questions about why people do what they do and experience what they experience.

Biological psychologists are ambitious, hoping to explain as much as possible about psychology in terms of brain processes, genes, and the like. The guiding assumption is that the pattern of activity that occurs in your brain when you see a rabbit *is* your perception of a rabbit. The pattern that occurs when you feel fear *is* your fear. This is not to say, "your brain physiology controls you" any more than, "you control your brain." Rather, your brain *is* you! The rest of this book explores how far we can go with this guiding assumption.

SUMMARY

1. Two profound, difficult questions are why the universe is as it is (indeed why it exists at all), and why and how consciousness occurs. Regardless of whether these questions are answerable, they motivate research on related topics.   2

2. Biological psychologists try to answer four types of questions about any given behavior. Physiological: How does it relate to the physiology of the brain and other organs? Ontogenetic: How does it develop within the individual? Evolutionary: How did the capacity for the behavior evolve? Functional: Why did the capacity for this behavior evolve? (That is, what function does it serve?)   4

3. Biological explanations of behavior do not necessarily assume that the individual understands the purpose or function of the behavior.   4

4. Many careers relate to biological psychology, including various research fields, certain medical specialties, and counseling and psychotherapy.   6

KEY TERMS

Terms are defined in the module on the page number indicated. They're also presented in alphabetical order with definitions in the book's Subject Index/Glossary, which begins on page 561. Interactive flashcards and crossword puzzles are among the online resources available to help you learn these terms and the concepts they represent.

biological psychology   3

evolutionary explanation   4

functional explanation   5

hard problem   3

mind–body or mind–brain problem   3

ontogenetic explanation   4

physiological explanation   4

THOUGHT QUESTIONS

Thought questions are intended to spark thought and discussion. In most cases, there is no clearly right answer but several fruitful ways to think about the question.

1. Is consciousness useful? That is, what (if anything) can we do because of consciousness that we couldn't do otherwise?

2. What are the special difficulties of studying the evolution of behavior, given that behavior doesn't leave fossils (with a few exceptions such as footprints showing an animal's gait)?

Genetics and Behavior

Everything you do depends on both your genes and your environment. Consider facial expressions. A contribution of the environment is obvious: You smile more when the world is treating you well and frown when things are going badly. Does heredity influence your facial expressions? Researchers examined facial expressions of people who were born blind and therefore could not have learned to imitate facial expressions. The facial expressions of the people born blind were remarkably similar to those of their sighted relatives, as shown in Figure 1.6 (Peleg et al., 2006). These results suggest a major role for genetics in controlling facial expressions.

Controversies arise when we move beyond the generalization that both heredity and environment are important. For example, do differences in human intelligence depend mostly on genetic differences, environmental influences, or both about equally? Similar questions arise for sexual orientation, alcoholism, weight gain, and almost everything else that interests psychologists. This module should help you understand these controversies as they arise later in this text or elsewhere. We begin with a review of genetics, a field that has become more and more complicated as research has progressed.

Mendelian Genetics

Before the work of Gregor Mendel, a late-19th-century monk, scientists thought that inheritance was a blending process in which the properties of the sperm and the egg simply mixed, like two colors of paint.

Mendel demonstrated that inheritance occurs through **genes**, units of heredity that maintain their structural identity from one generation to another. As a rule, genes come in pairs because they are aligned along **chromosomes** (strands of genes) that also come in pairs. (As an exception to this rule, a male mammal has unpaired X and Y chromosomes with different genes.) Classically, a gene has been defined as a portion of a chromosome, which is composed of the double-stranded molecule **deoxyribonucleic acid (DNA)**. However, many genes do not have the discrete locations we once imagined (Bird, 2007). Sometimes several genes overlap on a stretch of chromosome. Sometimes a genetic outcome depends on parts of two or more chromosomes. In many cases,

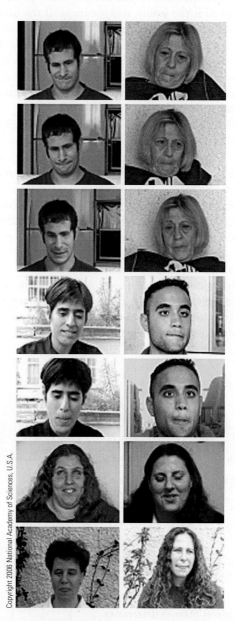

Copyright 2006 National Academy of Sciences, U.S.A.

FIGURE 1.6 Facial expressions by people born blind (left) and their sighted relatives (right)
The marked similarities imply a genetic contribution to facial expressions.

part of a chromosome alters the expression of other genes without coding for any protein of its own.

A strand of DNA serves as a template (model) for the synthesis of **ribonucleic acid** (**RNA**) molecules, a single-strand chemical. One type of RNA molecule—messenger RNA—serves as a template for the synthesis of protein molecules. DNA contains four "bases"—adenine, guanine, cytosine, and thymine—in any order. The order of those bases determines the order of corresponding bases along an RNA molecule—adenine, guanine, cytosine, and uracil. The order of bases along an RNA molecule in turn determines the order of amino acids that compose a protein. For example, if three RNA bases are, in order, cytosine, adenine, and guanine, then the protein adds the amino acid *glutamine*. If the next three RNA bases are uracil, guanine, and guanine, the next amino acid on the protein is *tryptophan*. In total, proteins consist of 20 amino acids, and the order of those amino acids depends on the order of DNA and RNA bases. It's an amazingly simple code, considering the complexity of body structures and functions that result from it.

Figure 1.7 summarizes the main steps in translating information from DNA through RNA into proteins. Some proteins form part of the structure of the body. Others serve as **enzymes**, biological catalysts that regulate chemical reactions in the body.

Anyone with an identical pair of genes on the two chromosomes is **homozygous** for that gene. An individual with an unmatched pair of genes is **heterozygous** for that gene. For example, you might have a gene for blue eyes on one chromosome and a gene for brown eyes on the other.

Genes are dominant, recessive, or intermediate. A **dominant** gene shows a strong effect in either the homozygous or heterozygous condition. A **recessive** gene shows its effects only in the homozygous condition. For example, a gene for brown eyes is dominant and a gene for blue eyes is recessive. If you have one gene for brown eyes and one for blue, the result is brown eyes. The gene for high sensitivity to the taste of phenylthiocarbamide (PTC) is dominant, and the gene for low sensitivity is recessive. Only someone with two recessive genes has trouble tasting it (Wooding et al., 2004). Figure 1.8 illustrates the possible results of a mating between people who are both heterozygous for the PTC-tasting gene. Because each has one high taste sensitivity gene—let's abbreviate it "T"—the parents can taste PTC. However, each parent transmits either a high taste sensitivity gene (T) or a low taste sensitivity gene (t) to a given child. Therefore, a child in this family has a 25% chance of two T genes, a 50% chance of the heterozygous Tt condition, and a 25% chance of being homozygous for the t gene.

▸ **Stop & Check**

2. Suppose you have high sensitivity to tasting PTC. If your mother can also taste it easily, what (if anything) can you predict about your father's ability to taste it?

3. Suppose you have high sensitivity to the taste of PTC. If your mother has low sensitivity, what (if anything) can you predict about your father's taste sensitivity?

ANSWERS

2. If your mother has high sensitivity to the taste of PTC, we can make no predictions about your father. You may have inherited a high-sensitivity gene from your mother, and because the gene is dominant, you need only one copy of the gene to taste PTC. **3.** If your mother has low sensitivity, you must have inherited your high-sensitivity gene from your father, so he must have high sensitivity.

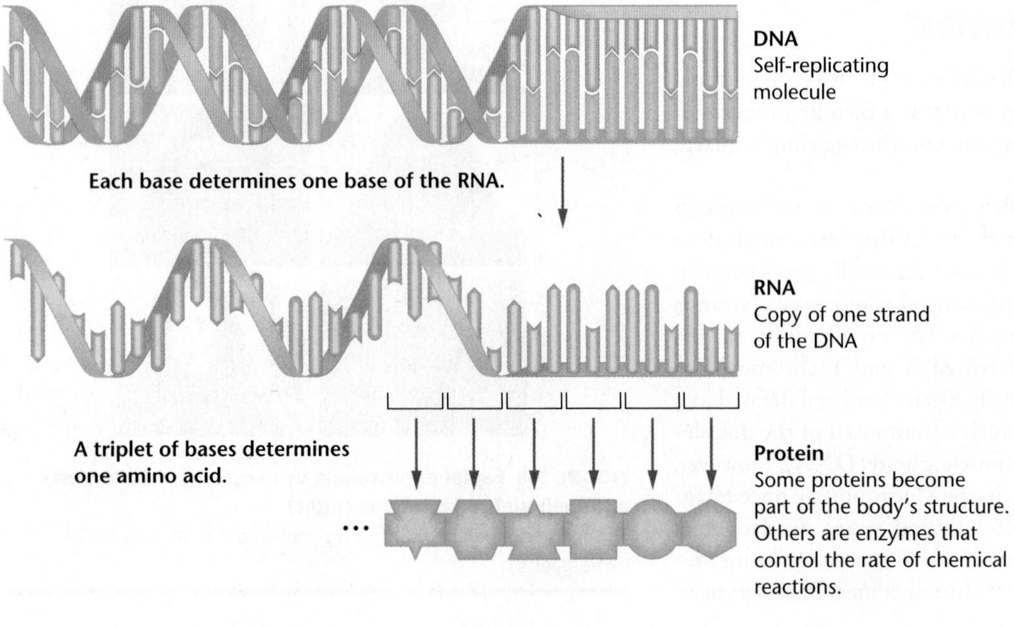

DNA
Self-replicating molecule

Each base determines one base of the RNA.

RNA
Copy of one strand of the DNA

A triplet of bases determines one amino acid.

Protein
Some proteins become part of the body's structure. Others are enzymes that control the rate of chemical reactions.

FIGURE 1.7 How DNA controls development of the organism
The sequence of bases along a strand of DNA determines the order of bases along a strand of RNA; RNA in turn controls the sequence of amino acids in a protein molecule.
(© Cengage Learning 2013)

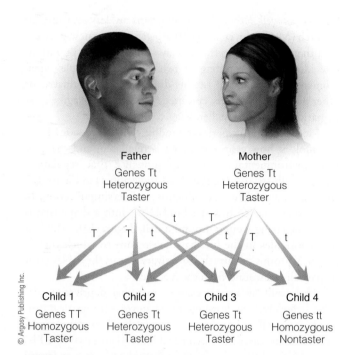

Father
Genes Tt
Heterozygous
Taster

Mother
Genes Tt
Heterozygous
Taster

Child 1
Genes TT
Homozygous
Taster

Child 2
Genes Tt
Heterozygous
Taster

Child 3
Genes Tt
Heterozygous
Taster

Child 4
Genes tt
Homozygous
Nontaster

© Argosy Publishing Inc.

FIGURE 1.8 Four equally likely outcomes of a mating between parents who are heterozygous for a given gene (Tt) A child in this family has a 25% chance of being homozygous for the dominant gene (TT), a 25% chance of being homozygous for the recessive gene (tt), and a 50% chance of being heterozygous (Tt).

However, an example like PTC or eye color can be misleading, because it implies that if you have a gene, it produces its outcome, period. It also implies that a single gene completely controls a characteristic. Even in the case of eye color that is not true. Researchers have identified at least ten genes that contribute to variations in eye color (Liu et al., 2010). At least 180 genes contribute to differences in people's height (Allen et al., 2010). Furthermore, it is also possible to have a gene and express it only partly—in some cells and not others, or under some circumstances and not others. Genes affecting behavior are particularly subject to multiple influences.

Sex-Linked and Sex-Limited Genes

The genes on the sex chromosomes (designated X and Y) are known as **sex-linked** genes. All other chromosomes are autosomal chromosomes, and their genes are known as **autosomal genes.**

In mammals, a female has two X chromosomes, whereas a male has an X and a Y. During reproduction, the female necessarily contributes an X chromosome, and the male contributes either an X or a Y. If he contributes an X, the offspring is female; if he contributes a Y, the offspring is male.

The Y chromosome is small. In humans, it has genes for only 27 proteins, far fewer than other chromosomes. However, the Y chromosome also has many sites that influence the functioning of genes on other chromosomes. The X chromosome has genes

for about 1,500 proteins (Arnold, 2004). Thus, when biologists speak of sex-linked genes, they usually mean X-linked genes.

An example of a human sex-linked gene is the recessive gene for red-green color vision deficiency. Any man with this gene on his X chromosome is red-green color deficient because he has no other X chromosome. A woman is color deficient only if she has that recessive gene on both of her X chromosomes. So, for example, if 8% of human X chromosomes contain the gene for color vision deficiency, then 8% of men will be color deficient, but less than 1% of women will be (.08 × .08).

Distinct from sex-linked genes are the **sex-limited genes,** which are present in both sexes, generally on autosomal chromosomes, but active mainly in one sex. Examples include the genes that control the amount of chest hair in men, breast size in women, amount of crowing in roosters, and rate of egg production in hens. Both sexes have those genes, but sex hormones activate them in one sex or the other.

Stop & Check

4. How does a sex-linked gene differ from a sex-limited gene?

5. Suppose someone identifies a "gene" for certain aspects of sexual development. In what ways might that statement be misleading?

ANSWERS

4. A sex-linked gene is on a sex chromosome (usually the X chromosome). A sex-limited gene could be on any chromosome, but it is activated by sex hormones and therefore shows its effects only in one sex or the other. **5.** The effect of a gene depends on other influences, as described in the previous section. In the case of a gene affecting sexual development, the gene is probably more active during adolescence than in childhood. Its effect might depend on diet, social influences, and so forth.

Genetic Changes

Genes change in several ways. One way is by **mutation,** a heritable change in a DNA molecule. Changing just one base in DNA to any of the other three types means that the mutant gene will code for a protein with a different amino acid at one location in the molecule. Given that evolution has already had eons to select the best makeup of each gene, a new mutation is rarely advantageous. Still, those rare exceptions are important. The human *FOXP2* gene differs from the chimpanzee version of that gene in just two bases, but those two mutations modified the human brain and vocal apparatus in several ways that facilitate language development (Konopka et al., 2009).

Another kind of mutation is a duplication or deletion. During the process of reproduction, part of a chromosome that should appear once might instead appear twice or not at all. When this process happens to just a tiny portion of a chromosome, we call it a microduplication or microdeletion. Many researchers believe that microduplications and microdeletions of brain-relevant genes are a possible explanation for schizophrenia (International Schizophrenia Consortium, 2008; Stefansson et al., 2008).

In addition to these permanent changes in genes, the field of **epigenetics** deals with changes in gene expression without modification of the DNA sequence. Although any gene is present in every cell of the body, it might be active only in certain types of cells, or only at a particular time of life, such as early in embryonic development. Some genes become more active during puberty, some become less active in old age, and some are more active at one time of day than another. Various experiences also can turn a gene on or off. For example, if a mother rat is malnourished during pregnancy, her offspring alter the expression of certain genes to conserve energy and adjust to a world in which food will presumably be hard to find. If in fact rich food becomes abundant later in life, those offspring are predisposed, because of their gene expression, to a high probability of obesity and heart disease (Godfrey, Lillycrop, Burdge, Gluckman, & Hanson, 2007). Rat pups with a low degree of maternal care early in life alter the expression of certain genes in a brain area called the hippocampus, resulting in high vulnerability to emotional stress reactions later in life (Harper, 2005; Weaver et al., 2004; Zhang et al., 2010). Changes in gene expression are also central to learning and memory (Feng, Fouse, & Fan, 2007) and to brain changes resulting from drug addiction (Sadri-Vakili et al., 2010; Tsankova, Renthal, Kumar, & Nestler, 2007). Although most of the research deals with rats or mice, similar mechanisms almost certainly apply to

humans as well, although human brains are less available for research (McGowan et al., 2009). Epigenetics is a new, growing field that will almost certainly play an increasingly important role in our understanding of behavior. For example, when monozygotic ("identical") twins differ in their psychiatric or other medical conditions, epigenetic differences are a likely explanation (Poulsen, Esteller, Vaag, & Fraga, 2007).

How could an experience modify gene expression? First, let's look at how gene expression is regulated, and then see how environmental factors can influence that regulation. Standard illustrations of the DNA molecule, as in Figure 1.7, show it as a straight line, which is an oversimplification. In fact, proteins called histones bind DNA into a shape that is more like string wound around a ball (Figure 1.9). The histone molecules in the ball have loose ends to which certain chemical groups can attach. To activate a gene, the DNA must be partially unwound from the histones.

The result of an experience—maternal deprivation, cocaine exposure, new learning, or whatever—brings new proteins into a cell or in other ways alters the chemical environment. In some cases the outcome adds acetyl groups ($COCH_3$) to the histone tails near a gene, causing the histones to loosen their grip on the DNA, and facilitating the expression of that gene. Removal of the acetyl group causes the histones to tighten their grip on the DNA, and turns the gene off. Another possible outcome is to add or remove methyl groups from DNA, usually at the promoter regions at the beginning of a gene. Adding methyl groups (CH_3) to promoters turns genes off, and removing them turns on a gene (Tsankova, Renthal, Kumar, & Nestler, 2007). Actually, the result is more compli-

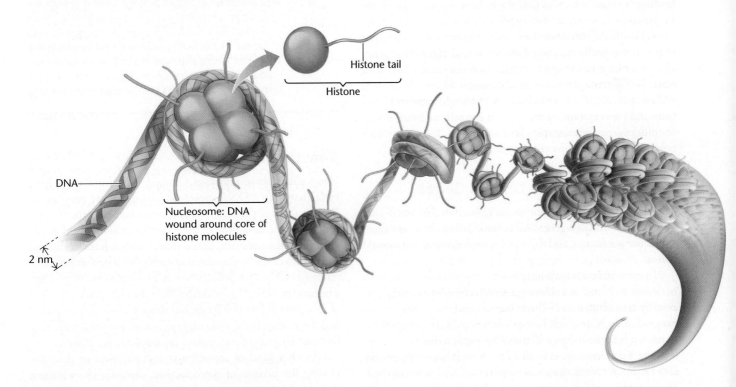

FIGURE 1.9 DNA bound into a ball shape by a histone protein
Chemicals that attach to a loose end of a histone molecule tighten or loosen its grip on DNA, exposing fewer or more genes to the possibility of being active. (© Cengage Learning 2013)

cated, as attaching a methyl or acetyl group affects different genes in different ways (Alter et al., 2008). The general point is that what you do at any moment not only affects you now, but also produces epigenetic effects that alter gene expression for longer periods of time. Furthermore, the line between "genetic" effects and "experiential" effects becomes blurrier than ever. Experiences act by altering the activity of genes.

> **Stop & Check**

6. How does an epigenetic change differ from a mutation?

7. How does adding a methyl or acetyl group to a histone protein alter gene activity?

ANSWERS

6. A mutation is a permanent change in part of a chromosome. An epigenetic change is an increase or decrease in the activity of a gene or group of genes. In some cases an epigenetic change lasts months or years, but it would not be passed on generation after generation. **7.** A methyl group tightens the histone molecule's grip on DNA, exposing fewer genes to possible activation. An acetyl group loosens the grip and increases gene activation.

Heredity and Environment

Suppose someone asks whether singing ability depends on heredity or environment. That question as stated is meaningless. Unless you had both heredity and environment, you couldn't sing at all. However, we can rephrase the question meaningfully: Do the observed *differences* among individuals depend more on *differences* in heredity or *differences* in environment? For example, if you sing better than someone else, the reason could be different genes, better training, or both.

To determine the contributions of heredity and environment, researchers rely mainly on two kinds of evidence. First, they compare **monozygotic** ("from one egg") twins and **dizygotic** ("from two eggs") twins. People usually call monozygotic twins "identical" twins, but that term is misleading, because identical twins often differ in important ways. Some are mirror images of each other. Also, for epigenetic reasons, certain genes may be activated more in one twin than the other (Raj, Rifkin, Andersen, & van Oudenaarden, 2010). Still, they have the same genes, whereas dizygotic twins do not. A stronger resemblance between monozygotic than dizygotic twins suggests a genetic contribution.

A second kind of evidence is studies of adopted children. Any tendency for adopted children to resemble their biological parents suggests a hereditary influence. If the variations in some characteristic depend largely on genetic differences, the characteristic has high **heritability**. Researchers sometimes also examine "virtual twins"—children of the same age, adopted at the same time into a single family. They grow up in the same environment from infancy, but without any genetic similarity. Any similarities in behavior can be attributed to environmental influences. However, the behavioral differ-

ences—which are in many cases substantial—suggest genetic influences (Segal, 2000).

New biochemical methods make possible a third kind of evidence: In some cases, researchers identify specific genes linked to a behavior. For example, certain genes are more common than average among people with depression. Identifying genes leads to further questions: *How much* is the gene associated with a condition? How does it produce its effect? Which environmental conditions moderate its effect? Can we find ways to undo the effects of an undesirable gene?

Researchers have found evidence for a significant heritability of almost every behavior they have tested (Bouchard & McGue, 2003). Examples include loneliness (McGuire & Clifford, 2000), neuroticism (Lake, Eaves, Maes, Heath, & Martin, 2000), television watching (Plomin, Corley, DeFries, & Fulker, 1990), social attitudes (Posner, Baker, Heath, & Martin, 1996), and speed of learning a second language (Dale, Harlaar, Haworth, & Plomin, 2010). About the only behavior anyone has tested that has *not* shown a significant heritability is religious affiliation—such as Protestant or Catholic (Eaves, Martin, & Heath, 1990).

Any estimate of the heritability of a particular trait is specific to a given population. Consider alcohol abuse, which has moderate heritability in the United States. Imagine a population somewhere in which some families teach very strict prohibitions on alcohol use, perhaps for religious reasons, and other families are more permissive. With such strong environmental differences, the genetic influences exert less effect, and heritability will be relatively low. Then consider another population where all families have the same rules, but people happen to differ substantially in genes that affect their reactions to alcohol. In that population, heritability will be higher. In short, estimates of heritability are never absolute. They apply to a particular population at a particular time.

> **Stop & Check**

8. What are the main types of evidence to estimate the heritability of some behavior?

9. Suppose someone determines the heritability of IQ scores for a given population. Then society changes in a way that provides the best possible opportunity for everyone within that population. Will heritability increase, decrease, or stay the same?

ANSWERS

8. One type of evidence is greater similarity between monozygotic twins than dizygotic twins. Another is resemblance between adopted children and their biological parents. A third is a demonstration that a particular gene is more common than average among people who show a particular behavior. **9.** Heritability will *increase*. Heritability estimates how much of the variation is due to differences in genes. If everyone has the same environment, then differences in environment cannot account for any remaining differences in IQ scores. Therefore, the differences in genes must account for the differences.

Environmental Modification

Even a trait with high heritability can be modified by environmental interventions. In a later chapter, we examine evidence that a certain gene increases the probability of violent behavior in people who were seriously maltreated during childhood. That is, the effect of a gene depends on the person's environment.

Consider also **phenylketonuria** (FEE-nil-KEET-uhn-YOOR-ee-uh), or **PKU**, a genetic inability to metabolize the amino acid phenylalanine. If PKU is not treated, phenylalanine accumulates to toxic levels, impairing brain development and leaving children mentally retarded, restless, and irritable. Approximately 1% of Europeans carry a recessive gene for PKU. Fewer Asians and almost no Africans have the gene (T. Wang et al., 1989).

Although PKU is a hereditary condition, environmental interventions can modify it. Physicians in many countries routinely measure the level of phenylalanine or its metabolites in babies' blood or urine. If a baby has high levels, indicating PKU, physicians advise the parents to put the baby on a strict low-phenylalanine diet to minimize brain damage (Waisbren, Brown, de Sonneville, & Levy, 1994). Our ability to prevent PKU provides particularly strong evidence that *heritable* does not mean *unmodifiable*.

A couple of notes about PKU: The required diet is difficult. People have to avoid meats, eggs, dairy products, grains, and especially aspartame (NutraSweet), which is 50% phenylalanine. Instead, they eat an expensive formula containing all the other amino acids. Physicians long believed that children with PKU could quit the diet after a few years. Later experience has shown that high phenylalanine levels damage teenage and adult brains, too. A woman with PKU should be especially careful during pregnancy and when nursing. Even a genetically normal baby cannot handle the enormous amounts of phenylalanine that an affected mother might pass through the placenta.

Stop & Check

10. What example illustrates the point that even if some characteristic is highly heritable, a change in the environment can alter it?

ANSWER

10. Keeping a child with the PKU gene on a strict low-phenylalanine diet prevents the mental retardation that the gene ordinarily causes. The general point is that sometimes a highly heritable condition can be modified environmentally.

How Genes Affect Behavior

A biologist who speaks of a "gene for brown eyes" does not mean that the gene directly produces brown eyes. The gene produces a protein that makes the eyes brown, assuming normal health and nutrition. If we speak of a "gene for alcoholism," we should not imagine that the gene itself causes alcoholism. Rather, it produces a protein that under certain circumstances increases the probability of alcoholism. It is important to specify these circumstances as well as we can.

Exactly how a gene increases the probability of a given behavior is a complex issue. Some genes control brain chemicals, but others affect behavior indirectly (Kendler, 2001). Suppose your genes make you unusually attractive. As a result, strangers smile at you and many people want to get to know you. Their reactions to your appearance may change your personality, and if so, the genes altered your behavior by altering your environment!

For another example, imagine a child born with genes promoting greater than average height, running speed, and coordination. The child shows early success at basketball, and soon spends more and more time playing basketball. Soon the child spends less time on other pursuits—including television, playing chess, collecting stamps, or anything else you might imagine. Thus the measured heritability of many behaviors might depend partly on genes that affect leg muscles. This is a hypothetical example, but it illustrates the point: Genes influence behavior in roundabout ways. We should not be amazed by reports that nearly every human behavior has some heritability.

The Evolution of Behavior

Evolution is a change over generations in the frequencies of various genes in a population. Note that, by this definition, evolution includes *any* change in gene frequencies, regardless of whether it helps or harms the species in the long run. We distinguish two questions about evolution: How *did* some species evolve, and how *do* species evolve? To ask how a species did evolve is to ask what evolved from what, basing our answers on inferences from fossils and comparisons of living species. For example, biologists find that humans are more similar to chimpanzees than to other species, and they infer a common ancestor. Biologists have constructed "evolutionary trees" that show the relationships among various species (Figure 1.10). As new evidence becomes available, biologists change their opinions of how closely any two species are related.

The question of how species *do* evolve is a question of how the process works, and that process is, in its basic outlines, a necessary outcome. Given what we know about reproduction, evolution *must* occur. The reasoning goes as follows:

- Offspring generally resemble their parents for genetic reasons. That is, "like begets like."

- Mutations, recombinations, and microduplications of genes introduce new heritable variations that help or harm an individual's chance of surviving and reproducing.

- Certain individuals successfully reproduce more than others do, thus passing on their genes to the next generation. Any gene that is associated with greater reproductive success will become more prevalent in later generations.

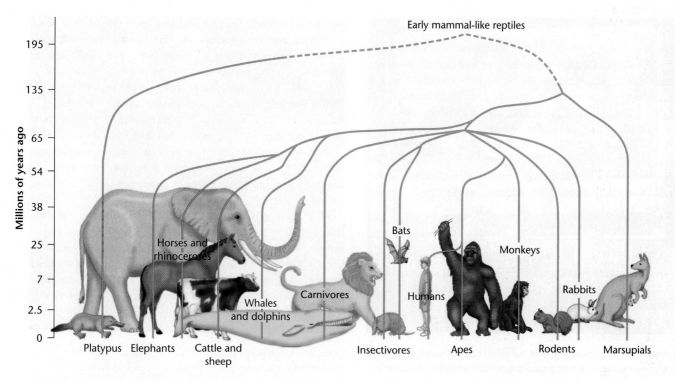

FIGURE 1.10 An evolutionary tree
Various groups of mammals branched off from common ancestors over millions of years. Evolutionary trees like this are inferences from fossils and detailed comparisons of living species. *(© Cengage Learning 2013)*

That is, the current generation of any species resembles the individuals that successfully reproduced in the past. You can witness and explore this principle with the interactive Try It Yourself activity "Genetic Generations."

Because plant and animal breeders have long known this principle, they choose individuals with a desired trait and make them the parents of the next generation. This process is called **artificial selection**, and over many generations, breeders have produced exceptional racehorses, hundreds of kinds of dogs, chickens that lay huge numbers of eggs, and so forth. Charles Darwin's (1859) insight was that nature also selects. If certain individuals are more successful than others in finding food, escaping enemies, attracting mates, or protecting their offspring, then their genes will become more prevalent in later generations. Given a huge amount of time, this process can produce the wide variety of life that we in fact encounter.

Common Misunderstandings About Evolution

Let's clarify the principles of evolution by addressing a few misconceptions.

- *Does the use or disuse of some structure or behavior cause an evolutionary increase or decrease in that feature?* You may have heard people say something like, "Because we hardly ever use our little toes, they get smaller and smaller in each succeeding generation." This idea is a carry-over of biologist Jean Lamarck's theory of evolution through the inheritance of acquired characteristics, known as **Lamarckian evolution**. According to this idea, if you exercise your arm muscles, your children will be born with bigger arm muscles, and if you fail to use your little toes, your children's little toes will be smaller than yours. However, biologists have found no mechanism for Lamarckian evolution to occur and no evidence that it does. Using or failing to use some body structure does not change the genes.

  (It is possible that people's little toes might shrink in future evolution but only if people with genes for smaller little toes manage to reproduce more than other people do.)

- *Have humans stopped evolving?* Because modern medicine can keep almost anyone alive, and because welfare programs in prosperous countries provide the necessities of life for almost everyone, some people assert that humans are no longer subject to the principle of "survival of the fittest." Therefore, the argument goes, human evolution has slowed or stopped.

The flaw in this argument is that evolution depends on reproduction, not just survival. If people with certain genes

Barry Lewis/Alamy Limited

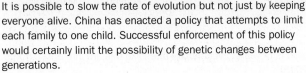

It is possible to slow the rate of evolution but not just by keeping everyone alive. China has enacted a policy that attempts to limit each family to one child. Successful enforcement of this policy would certainly limit the possibility of genetic changes between generations.

© F.J. Hierschel/Okapia/Photo Researchers

Sometimes, a sexual display, such as a peacock's spread of its tail feathers, improves reproductive success and spreads the associated genes. In a changed environment, this gene could become maladaptive. For example, if an aggressive predator with good color vision enters the range of the peacock, the bird's colorful feathers could seal its doom.

have more than the average number of children, their genes will spread in the population.

- *Does "evolution" mean "improvement"?* It depends on what you mean by "improvement." By definition, evolution improves **fitness**, which is operationally defined as *the number of copies of one's genes that endure in later generations.* If you have more children than average (and they survive long enough to also reproduce), you are evolutionarily fit, regardless of whether you are successful in any other way. You also increase your fitness by supporting your relatives, who share many of your genes and may spread them by their own reproduction. Any gene that spreads is, by definition, fit. However, genes that increase fitness at one time and place might be disadvantageous after a change in the environment. For example, the colorful tail feathers of the male peacock enable it to attract females but might become disadvantageous in the presence of a new predator that responds to bright colors. In other words, the genes of the current generation evolved because they were fit for *previous* generations. They may or may not be adaptive in the future.

- *Does evolution benefit the individual or the species?* Neither: It benefits the genes! In a sense, you don't use your genes to reproduce yourself. Rather, your genes

use *you* to reproduce *themselves* (Dawkins, 1989). Imagine a gene that causes you to risk your life to protect your children. If that gene enables you to leave behind more surviving children than you would have otherwise, then that gene will increase in prevalence within your population.

Stop & Check

11. Many people believe the human appendix is useless. Will it become smaller and smaller with each generation?

ANSWER **11.** No. Failure to need a structure does not make it smaller in the next generation. The appendix will shrink only if people with a gene for a smaller appendix reproduce more successfully than other people do.

Evolutionary Psychology

Evolutionary psychology concerns how behaviors evolved. The emphasis is on *evolutionary* and *functional* explanations—that is, the presumed genes of our ancestors and why natural selection might have favored genes that promote certain behaviors. The assumption is that any behavior characteristic of a species arose through natural selection and presumably provided some advantage, at least in ancestral times. Consider these examples:

- Some animal species have better color vision than others, and some have better peripheral vision. Presumably, species evolve the kind of vision they need for their way of life (see Chapter 6).

- Mammals and birds devote more energy to maintaining body temperature than to all other activities combined. We would not have evolved such an expensive mechanism unless it gave us major advantages (see Chapter 10).

- Bears eat all the food they can find, and small birds eat only enough to satisfy their immediate needs. Eating habits relate to different needs by different species (see Chapter 10).

On the other hand, some characteristics of a species have a less certain relationship to natural selection. Consider two examples:

- More men than women enjoy the prospect of casual sex with multiple partners. Theorists have related this tendency to the fact that a man can spread his genes by impregnating many women, whereas a woman cannot multiply her children by having more sexual partners (Buss, 1994). Are men and women prewired to have different sexual behaviors? We shall explore this controversial and uncertain topic in Chapter 11.

- People grow old and die, with an average survival time of 70 to 80 years under favorable circumstances. However, people vary in how rapidly they deteriorate in old age, and part of that variation is under genetic control. Researchers have identified several genes that are significantly more common among people who remain healthy and alert at ages 85 and beyond (Halaschek-Wiener et al., 2009; Poduslo, Huang, & Spiro, 2009; Puca et al., 2001). Why don't we all have those genes? Perhaps living many years after the end of your reproductive years is evolutionarily disadvantageous. Did we evolve a tendency to grow old and die in order to get out of the way and stop competing with our children and grandchildren? Curiously, a few species of turtles and deep-ocean fish continue reproducing throughout their lives, and they do not seem to "grow old." That is, so far as we can tell from limited samples, they are no more likely to die when they are 100 years old than when they are 50 or 20. One rockfish is known to have lived more than 200 years (Finch, 2009). Again, the idea is that old-age deterioration might be an evolved mechanism, and its presence or absence could be under genetic control.

To further illustrate evolutionary psychology, let's consider the theoretically interesting example of **altruistic behavior**, an action that benefits someone other than the actor. A gene that encourages altruistic behavior would help *other* individuals survive and spread *their* genes. Could a gene for altruism spread, and if so, how?

How common is altruism? It certainly occurs in humans (sometimes): We contribute to charities. We try to help people in distress. A student may explain something to a classmate who is competing for a good grade in a course. Some people donate a kidney to save the life of someone they didn't even know (MacFarquhar, 2009).

Among nonhumans, altruism is harder to find. Cooperation occurs, certainly. A pack of animals may hunt together or forage together. A flock of small birds may "mob" an owl or hawk to drive it away. But these examples are different from helping without any gain in return (Clutton-Brock, 2009). In one study, a chimpanzee could pull one rope to bring food into its own cage or a second rope that would bring food to itself and additional food to a familiar but unrelated chimpanzee in a neighboring cage. Most often, chimps pulled whichever rope happened to be on the right at the time—suggesting right-handedness—apparently indifferent to the welfare of the other chimpanzee, even when the other made begging gestures (Silk et al., 2005).

Even when animals do appear altruistic, they often have a selfish motive. When a crow finds food on the ground, it caws loudly, attracting other crows that will share the food. Altruism? Not really. A bird on the ground is vulnerable to attack by cats and other enemies. Having other crows around means more eyes to watch for dangers.

Also consider meerkats (a kind of mongoose). Periodically, one or another member of a meerkat colony stands and, if it sees danger, emits an alarm call that warns the others (Figure 1.11). Its alarm call helps the others (including its relatives), but the one who sees the danger first and emits the alarm call is the one most likely to escape (Clutton-Brock et al., 1999).

For the sake of illustration, let's suppose—without evidence—that some gene increases altruistic behavior. Could it spread within a population? One common reply is that most altruistic behaviors cost very little. True, but costing little is not good enough. A gene spreads only if the individuals with it reproduce more than those without it. Another common reply is that the altruistic behavior benefits the species. True again, but the rebuttal is the same. A gene that benefits the species but fails to help the individual dies out with that individual.

A more controversial hypothesis is *group selection*. According to this idea, altruistic groups survive better than less cooperative ones (Bowles, 2006; Kohn, 2008). Although this idea is certainly true, group selection would seem to be unstable. Imagine a highly successful altruistic group with one individual whose mutated gene leads to competitive, "cheating" behavior. If the uncooperative individual survives and reproduces more than others within the group, the uncooperative gene will spread, unless the group has a way to punish or expel an uncooperative member.

A better explanation is **kin selection**—selection for a gene that benefits the individual's relatives. A gene spreads if it

FIGURE 1.11 Sentinel behavior: altruistic or not?
As in many other prey species, meerkats sometimes show sentinel behavior in watching for danger and warning the others. However, the meerkat that emits the alarm is the one most likely to escape the danger.

causes you to risk your life to protect your children, who share many of your genes, including perhaps a gene for this kind of altruism. Natural selection can also favor altruism toward other relatives—such as brothers and sisters, cousins, nephews, and nieces (Dawkins, 1989; Hamilton, 1964; Trivers, 1985). In both humans and nonhumans, helpful behavior is more common toward relatives than toward unrelated individuals (Bowles & Posel, 2005; Krakauer, 2005).

Another explanation is **reciprocal altruism**, the idea that individuals help those who will return the favor. Researchers find that people are prone to help not only those who helped them but also people whom they observed helping someone else (Nowak & Sigmund, 2005). The idea is not just "you scratched my back, so I'll scratch yours," but "you scratched someone else's back, so I'll scratch yours." By helping others, you build a reputation for helpfulness, and others are willing to cooperate with you. This system works only if individuals recognize one another. Otherwise, an uncooperative individual can accept favors, prosper, and never repay the favors. In other words, reciprocal altruism requires an ability to identify individuals and remember them later. Perhaps we now see why altruism is more common in humans than in most other species.

At its best, evolutionary psychology leads to research that helps us understand a behavior. The search for a functional explanation directs researchers to explore species' different habitats and ways of life until we understand why they behave differently. However, this approach is criticized when its practitioners propose explanations without testing them (Schlinger, 1996).

> **Stop & Check**

12. What are two plausible ways for possible altruistic genes to spread in a population?

ANSWER **12.** Altruistic genes could spread because they facilitate care for one's kin or because they facilitate exchanges of favors with others (reciprocal altruism). Group selection may also work under some circumstances, especially if the cooperative group has some way to punish or expel an uncooperative individual.

MODULE 1.2 ■ IN CLOSING

Genes and Behavior

In the control of behavior, genes are neither all-important nor irrelevant. Certain behaviors have a high heritability, such as the ability to taste PTC. Many other behaviors are influenced by genes but also subject to strong influence by experience. Our genes and our evolution make it possible for humans to be what we are today, but they also give us the flexibility to change our behavior as circumstances warrant.

Understanding the genetics of human behavior is important but also especially difficult, because researchers have such limited control over environmental influences and *no* control over who mates with whom. Inferring human evolution is also difficult, partly because we do not know enough about the lives of our ancient ancestors.

Finally, we should remember that the way things *are* is not necessarily the same as the way they *should be*. For example, even if our genes predispose us to behave in a particular way, we can still decide to try to overcome those predispositions if they do not suit the needs of modern life.

SUMMARY

1. Genes are chemicals that maintain their integrity from one generation to the next and influence the development of the individual. A dominant gene affects development regardless of whether a person has pairs of that gene or only a single copy per cell. A recessive gene affects development only in the absence of the dominant gene. **9**

2. Genes can change by mutations, microduplications, and microdeletions. Gene expression can also change in a process called epigenetics, as chemicals activate or deactivate parts of chromosomes. **11**

3. Most behavioral variations reflect the combined influences of genes and environmental factors. Heritability is an estimate of the amount of variation that is due to genetic variation as opposed to environmental variation. **13**

4. Researchers estimate heritability of a human condition by comparing monozygotic and dizygotic twins and by comparing adopted children to their biological and adoptive parents. In some cases, they identify specific genes that are more common in people with one type of behavior than another. **13**

5. Even if some behavior shows high heritability for a given population, a change in the environment might significantly alter the behavioral outcome. **14**

6. Genes influence behavior directly by altering brain chemicals and indirectly by affecting other aspects of the body and therefore the way other people react to us. **14**

7. The process of evolution through natural selection is a necessary outcome, given what we know about reproduction: Mutations sometimes occur in genes, and individuals with certain sets of genes reproduce more successfully than others do. **14**

8. Evolution spreads the genes of the individuals who have reproduced the most. Therefore, if some characteristic is widespread within a population, it is reasonable to look for ways in which that characteristic is or has been adaptive. However, we cannot take it for granted that all common behaviors are the product of our genes. We need to distinguish genetic influences from learning. **16**

KEY TERMS

Terms are defined in the module on the page number indicated. They're also presented in alphabetical order with definitions in the book's Subject Index/Glossary, which begins on page 561. Interactive flashcards and crossword puzzles are among the online resources available to help you learn these terms and the concepts they represent.

altruistic behavior **17**
artificial selection **15**
autosomal genes **11**
chromosomes **9**
deoxyribonucleic acid
  (DNA) **9**
dizygotic **13**
dominant **10**
enzymes **10**

epigenetics **12**
evolution **14**
evolutionary psychology **16**
fitness **16**
genes **9**
heritability **13**
heterozygous **10**
homozygous **10**
kin selection **17**

Lamarckian evolution **15**
monozygotic **13**
mutation **11**
phenylketonuria (PKU) **14**
recessive **10**
reciprocal altruism **18**
ribonucleic acid (RNA) **10**
sex-limited genes **11**
sex-linked genes **11**

THOUGHT QUESTIONS

For what human behaviors, if any, are you sure that heritability would be extremely low?

Genetic differences probably account for part of the difference between people who age slowly and gracefully and others who grow old more rapidly and die younger. Given that the genes controlling old age have their onset long after people have stopped having children, how could evolution have any effect on such genes?

The Use of Animals in Research

Certain ethical disputes resist agreement. One is abortion. Another is the use of animals in research. In both cases, well-meaning people on each side of the issue insist that their position is proper and ethical. The dispute is not a matter of the good guys against the bad guys. It is between two views of what is good.

Research on laboratory animals is responsible for a great deal of what we know about the brain and behavior, as you will see throughout this book. That research ranges from mere observation of behavior to studies in which it is clear that no animal would volunteer, if it had a choice. How shall we deal with the fact that, on the one hand, we want more knowledge, and on the other hand, we want to minimize animal distress?

▮ Reasons for Animal Research

Given that most biological psychologists and neuroscientists are primarily interested in the human brain and human behavior, why do they study nonhumans? Here are four reasons.

1. *The underlying mechanisms of behavior are similar across species and sometimes easier to study in a nonhuman species.* If you want to understand a complex machine, you might begin by examining a simpler machine. We also learn about brain–behavior relationships by starting with

simpler cases. The brains and behavior of nonhuman vertebrates resemble those of humans in their chemistry and anatomy (Figure 1.12). Even invertebrate nerves follow the same basic principles as our own. Much research has been conducted on squid nerves, which are thicker than human nerves and therefore easier to study.

2. *We are interested in animals for their own sake.* Humans are naturally curious. We would love to know about life, if any, elsewhere in the universe. Similarly, we would like to understand how bats chase insects in the dark, how migratory birds find their way over unfamiliar territory, and how schools of fish manage to swim in unison. Whereas psychological researchers once concentrated heavily on rats, today they focus on a wider variety of species, relating the behaviors to each animal's habitat and way of life (Shettleworth, 2009).

3. *What we learn about animals sheds light on human evolution.* How did we come to be the way we are? What makes us different from chimpanzees and other primates? Why and how did primates evolve larger brains than other species? Researchers approach such questions by comparing species.

4. *Legal or ethical restrictions prevent certain kinds of research on humans.* For example, investigators insert electrodes

Animals are used in many kinds of research studies, some dealing with behavior and others with the functions of the nervous system.

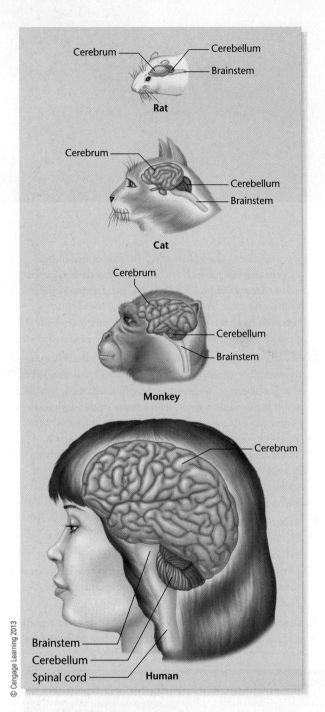

FIGURE 1.12 Brains of several species
The general plan and organization of the brain are similar for all mammals, even though the size varies from species to species.

© Cengage Learning 2013

into the brain cells of rats and other animals to determine the relationship between brain activity and behavior. They also inject chemicals, extract brain chemicals, and study the effects of brain damage. Such experiments answer questions that investigators cannot address in any other way, including some questions that are critical for medical progress. They also raise an ethical issue: If the research is unacceptable with humans, is it also unacceptable with other species?

13. Describe reasons biological psychologists conduct much of their research on nonhuman animals.

ANSWER

13. Sometimes the mechanisms of behavior are easier to study in a nonhuman species. We are curious about animals for their own sake. We study animals to understand human evolution. Certain procedures that might lead to important knowledge are illegal or unethical with humans.

The Ethical Debate

In some cases, researchers simply observe animals in nature as a function of different times of day, different seasons of the year, changes in diet, and so forth. These procedures raise no ethical problems. In other studies, however, including many discussed in this book, animals have been subjected to brain damage, electrode implantation, injections of drugs or hormones, and other procedures that are clearly not for their own benefit. Anyone with a conscience (including scientists) is bothered by this fact. Nevertheless, experimentation with animals has been critical to the medical research that led to methods for the prevention or treatment of polio, diabetes, measles, smallpox, massive burns, heart disease, and other serious conditions. Most Nobel prizes in physiology or medicine have been awarded for research conducted on nonhuman animals. The hope of finding methods to treat or prevent AIDS, Alzheimer's disease, stroke, and many other disorders depends largely on animal research. In many areas of medicine and biological psychology, research would progress slowly or not at all without animals.

Degrees of Opposition

Opposition to animal research ranges considerably in degree. "Minimalists" tolerate certain kinds of animal research but wish to prohibit others depending on the probable value of the research, the amount of distress to the animal, and the type of animal. (Few people have serious qualms about hurting an insect, for example.) They favor firm regulations on research. Researchers agree in principle, although they might differ in where they draw the line between acceptable and unacceptable research.

The legal standard emphasizes "the three Rs": *reduction* of animal numbers (using fewer animals), *replacement* (using computer models or other substitutes for animals, when possible), and *refinement* (modifying the procedures to reduce pain and discomfort). In the United States, every college or other institution that receives government research funds is required to have an Institutional Animal Care and Use Committee, composed of veterinarians, community representatives, and scientists, that evaluates proposed experiments, decides whether they are acceptable, and specifies procedures to minimize pain and discomfort. Similar regulations and committees govern research on human subjects. In addition, all research laboratories must abide by national laws requiring standards of cleanliness and animal care. Similar laws apply in other countries, and scientific journals accept publications only after researchers state that they followed all the laws and regulations. Professional organizations such as the Society for Neuroscience publish guidelines for the use of animals in research (see Appendix B). The following website of the National Institutes of Health's Office of Animal Care and Use describes U.S. regulations and advice on animal care: **http://oacu.od.nih.gov/index.htm**

In contrast to "minimalists," the "abolitionists" see no room for compromise. Abolitionists maintain that all animals have the same rights as humans. They regard killing an animal as murder, whether the intention is to eat it, use its fur, or gain scientific knowledge. Keeping an animal in a cage (presumably even a pet) is, in their view, slavery. Because animals cannot give informed consent to research, abolitionists insist it is wrong to use them in any way, regardless of the circumstances. According to one opponent of animal research, "We have no moral option but to bring this research to a halt. Completely.... We will not be satisfied until every cage is empty" (Regan, 1986, pp. 39–40). Advocates of this position sometimes claim that most animal research is painful and that it never leads to important results. However, for a true abolitionist, neither of those points really matters. Their moral imperative is that people have no right to use animals at all, even for highly useful, totally painless research.

The disagreement between abolitionists and animal researchers is a dispute between two ethical positions: "Never knowingly harm an innocent" and "Sometimes a little harm leads to a greater good." On the one hand, permitting research has the undeniable consequence of inflicting pain or distress. On the other hand, banning the use of animals for human purposes means a great setback in medical research as well as the end of animal-to-human transplants (e.g., transplanting pig heart valves to prolong lives of people with heart diseases).

It would be nice to say that this ethical debate has always proceeded in an intelligent and mutually respectful way. Unfortunately, it has not. Over the years, the abolitionists have sometimes advanced their cause through intimidation. Examples include vandalizing laboratories (causing millions of dollars of damage), placing a bomb under a professor's car, placing a bomb on a porch (intended for a researcher but accidentally placed on the neighbor's porch), banging on a researcher's children's windows at night, and inserting a garden hose through a researcher's window to flood the house (G. Miller, 2007a). Michael Conn and James Parker (2008, p. 186) quote a spokesperson for the Animal Defense League as follows: "I don't think you'd have to kill—assassinate—too many [doctors involved with animal testing]... I think for 5 lives, 10 lives, 15 human lives, we could save a million, 2 million, 10 million nonhuman lives." One researcher, Dario Ringach, finally agreed to stop his research on monkeys, if animal-rights extremists would stop harassing and threatening his children. He emailed them, "You win." In addition to researchers who quit in the face of attacks, many colleges and other institutions have declined to open animal research laboratories because of their fear of violence. Researchers have replied to attacks with campaigns such as the one illustrated in Figure 1.13.

Courtesy of the Foundation for Biomedical Research

FIGURE 1.13 In defense of animal research
For many years, opponents of animal research have been protesting against experimentation with animals. This ad represents a reply by supporters of such research.

The often fervent and extreme nature of the argument makes it difficult for researchers to express intermediate or nuanced views. Many remark that they really do care about animals, despite using them for research. Some neuroscientists are even vegetarians (Marris, 2006). But even admitting to doubts seems almost like giving in to intimidation. The result is extreme polarization that interferes with open-minded contemplation of the difficult issues.

> **Stop & Check**

14. How does the "minimalist" position differ from the "abolitionist" position?

ANSWER

14. A "minimalist" wishes to limit animal research to studies with little discomfort and much potential value. An "abolitionist" wishes to eliminate all animal research regardless of how the animals are treated or how much value the research might produce.

MODULE 1.3 ■ IN CLOSING

Humans and Animals

We began this chapter with a quote from Nobel Prize–winning biologist Niko Tinbergen, who argued that no fundamental gulf separates humans from other animal species. Because we are similar in many ways to other species, we learn much about ourselves from animal studies. Also because of that similarity, we identify with animals and we wish not to hurt them. Neuro-science researchers who decide to conduct animal research do not, as a rule, take this decision lightly. They want to minimize harm to animals, but they also want to increase knowledge. They believe it is better to inflict distress under controlled conditions than to permit ignorance and disease to inflict greater distress. In some cases, however, it is a difficult decision.

SUMMARY

1. Researchers study animals because the mechanisms are sometimes easier to study in nonhumans, because they are interested in animal behavior for its own sake, because they want to understand the evolution of behavior, and because certain kinds of experiments are difficult or impossible with humans.   **21**

2. The ethics of using animals in research is controversial. Some research does inflict stress or pain on animals; however, many research questions can be investigated only through animal research.   **22**

3. Animal research today is conducted under legal and ethical controls that attempt to minimize animal distress.   **22**

4. Use of intimidation and violence by certain animal-rights extremists interferes with open discussion of some difficult ethical issues.   **23**

CHAPTER 1 Interactive Exploration and Study

The **Psychology CourseMate** for this text brings chapter topics to life with interactive learning, study, and exam preparation tools, including quizzes and flashcards for the Key Concepts that appear throughout each module, as well as an interactive media-rich eBook version of the text that is fully searchable and includes highlighting and note-taking capabilities and interactive versions of the book's **Stop & Check** quizzes and **Try It Yourself Online** activities. The site also features **Virtual Biological Psychology Labs, videos,** and **animations** to help you better understand concepts—log on and learn more at **www.cengagebrain.com**, which is your gateway to all of this text's complimentary and premium resources, including the following:

Virtual Biological Psychology Labs

Explore the experiments that led to modern-day understanding of biopsychology with the Virtual Biological Psychology Labs, featuring a realistic lab environment that allows you to conduct experiments and evaluate data to better understand how scientists came to the conclusions presented in your text. The labs cover a range of topics, including perception, motivation, cognition, and more. You may purchase access at **www.cengagebrain.com**, or login at **login.cengagebrain.com** if an access card was included with your text.

Videos

Evolutionary Studies

Animations

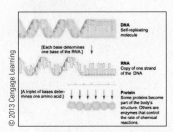

RNA, DNA, Proteins

Try It Yourself Online

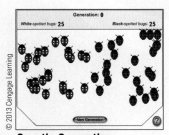

Genetic Generations

Suggestions for Further Exploration

Books

de Waal, F. (2005). *Our inner ape*. New York: Riverhead. An exploration of evolutionary psychology, especially with regard to how human behavior compares to that of related species.

Morrison, A. R. (2009). *An odyssey with animals: A veterinarian's reflections on the animal rights & welfare debate*. New York: Oxford University Press. A defense of animal research that acknowledges the difficulties of the issue and the competing values at stake.

Websites

The Psychology CourseMate for this text provides regularly updated links to relevant online resources for this chapter, such as the **Timeline of Animal Research Progress** and the **Dana Foundation for Brain Information**.

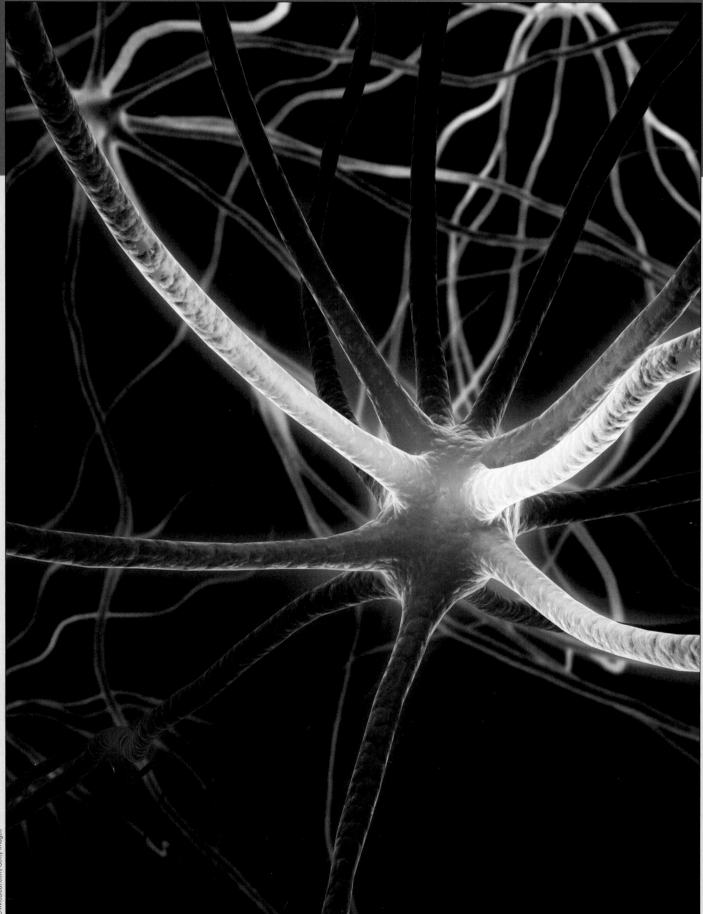

Nerve Cells and Nerve Impulses

2

MAIN IDEAS

1. The nervous system is composed of two kinds of cells: neurons and glia. Only the neurons transmit impulses from one location to another.

2. The larger neurons have branches, known as axons and dendrites, that can change their branching pattern as a function of experience, age, and chemical influences.

3. Many molecules in the bloodstream that can enter other body organs cannot enter the brain.

4. The action potential, an all-or-none change in the electrical potential across the membrane of a neuron, is caused by the sudden flow of sodium ions into the neuron and is followed by a flow of potassium ions out of the neuron.

5. Local neurons are small and do not have axons or action potentials. Instead, they convey information to nearby neurons by graded potentials.

OPPOSITE: An electron micrograph of neurons, magnified tens of thousands of times. The color is added artificially. For objects this small, it is impossible to focus light to obtain an image. It is possible to focus an electron beam, but electrons do not show color.

If you lived entirely alone, how long could you survive? If you are like most people, you have never hunted your own meat. Maybe you have occasionally caught your own fish. You have probably never grown enough fruits or vegetables to meet your needs. Could you build your own house? Have you ever made your own clothing? Of all the activities necessary for your survival, are there *any* that you could do entirely on your own, other than breathe? People can do an enormous amount together, but very little by themselves.

The cells of your nervous system are like that, too. Together they accomplish amazing things, but one cell by itself is helpless. We begin our study of the nervous system by examining single cells. Later, we examine how they act together.

Advice: Parts of this chapter and the next assume that you understand the basic principles of chemistry. If you have never studied chemistry, or if you have forgotten what you did study, read Appendix A.

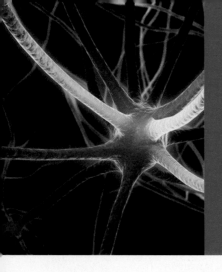

The Cells of the Nervous System

Y ou think of yourself—I assume—as a single individual. You don't think of your mental experience as being composed of pieces… but it is. Your experiences depend on the activity of a huge number of separate cells. The activity of one cell, by itself, accomplishes almost nothing and means almost nothing, but this vast array of cells working together constitutes *you*. Researchers are far from fully understanding how that happens, but the place to begin is by trying to understand what each cell does.

▌Anatomy of Neurons and Glia

The nervous system consists of two kinds of cells: neurons and glia. **Neurons** receive information and transmit it to other cells. Glia serve many functions that are difficult to summarize, and we shall defer that discussion until later in the chapter. According to one estimate, the adult human brain contains approximately 100 billion neurons (R. W. Williams & Herrup, 1988) (Figure 2.1). An accurate count would be more difficult than it is worth, and the exact number varies from person to person.

The idea that the brain is composed of individual cells is now so well established that we take it for granted. However, the idea was in doubt as recently as the early 1900s. Until then, the best microscopic views revealed little detail about the brain. Observers noted long, thin fibers between one neuron's cell body and another, but they could not see whether each fiber merged into the next cell or stopped before it (Albright, Jessell, Kandel, & Posner, 2001). Then, in the late 1800s, Santiago Ramón y Cajal used newly developed staining techniques to show that a small gap separates the tips of one neuron's fibers from the surface of the next neuron. The brain, like the rest of the body, consists of individual cells.

Cerebral cortex and associated areas:12 to 15 billion neurons

Cerebellum: 70 billion neurons

Spinal cord: 1 billion neurons

FIGURE 2.1 Estimated numbers of neurons in humans
Because of the small size of many neurons and the variation in cell density from one spot to another, obtaining an accurate count is difficult. *(Source: R. W. Williams & Herrup, 1988)*

APPLICATIONS AND EXTENSIONS

Santiago Ramón y Cajal, a Pioneer of Neuroscience

Two scientists are widely recognized as the main founders of neuroscience: Charles Sherrington, whom we shall discuss in Chapter 3, and the Spanish investigator Santiago Ramón y Cajal (1852–1934). Cajal's early career did not progress altogether smoothly. At one point, he was imprisoned in a solitary cell, limited to one meal a day, and taken out daily for public floggings—at the age of 10—for the crime of not paying attention during his Latin class (Cajal, 1901–1917/1937). (And *you* complained about *your* teachers!)

Cajal wanted to become an artist, but his father insisted that he study medicine as a safer way to make a living. He managed to combine the two fields, becoming an outstanding anatomical researcher and illustrator. His detailed drawings of the nervous system are still considered definitive today.

Before the late 1800s, microscopy revealed few details about the nervous system. Then the Italian investigator Camillo Golgi found a way to stain nerve cells with silver salts. This method, which completely stained some cells without affecting others at all, enabled researchers to examine the structure of a single cell. Cajal used Golgi's methods but applied them to infant brains, in which the cells are smaller and therefore easier to examine on a single slide. Cajal's research demonstrated that nerve cells remain separate instead of merging into one another.

Philosophically, we see the appeal of the old idea that neurons merge. We describe our experience as undivided, not the sum of separate parts, so it seems right that all the cells in the brain might be joined together as one unit. How the separate cells combine their influences is a complex and still mysterious process. ■

Bettmann/CORBIS

Santiago Ramón y Cajal
(1852–1934)

How many interesting facts fail to be converted into fertile discoveries because their first observers regard them as natural and ordinary things! . . . It is strange to see how the populace, which nourishes its imagination with tales of witches or saints, mysterious events and extraordinary occurrences, disdains the world around it as commonplace, monotonous and prosaic, without suspecting that at bottom it is all secret, mystery, and marvel. (Cajal, 1937, pp. 46-47).

The Structures of an Animal Cell

Figure 2.2 illustrates a neuron from the cerebellum of a mouse (magnified enormously, of course). Neurons have much in common with the rest of the body's cells. The surface of a cell is its **membrane** (or *plasma membrane*), a structure that separates the inside of the cell from the outside environment. It is composed of two layers of fat molecules that are free to flow around one another, as illustrated in Figure 2.3. Most chemicals cannot cross the membrane, but specific protein channels in the membrane permit a controlled flow of water, oxygen, sodium, potassium, calcium, chloride, and other important chemicals.

Except for mammalian red blood cells, all animal cells have a **nucleus**, the structure that contains the chromosomes. A **mitochondrion** (pl.: mitochondria) is the structure that performs metabolic activities, providing the energy that the cell requires for all other activities. Mitochondria require fuel and oxygen to function. **Ribosomes** are the sites at which the cell synthesizes new protein molecules. Proteins provide building materials for the cell and facilitate various chemical reactions. Some ribosomes float freely within the cell. Others are attached to the **endoplasmic reticulum**, a network of thin tubes that transport newly synthesized proteins to other locations.

The Structure of a Neuron

The most distinctive feature of neurons is their shape, which varies enormously from one neuron to another (Figure 2.4). Unlike most other body cells, neurons have long branching extensions. The larger neurons have these components: dendrites, a soma (cell body), an axon, and presynaptic terminals.

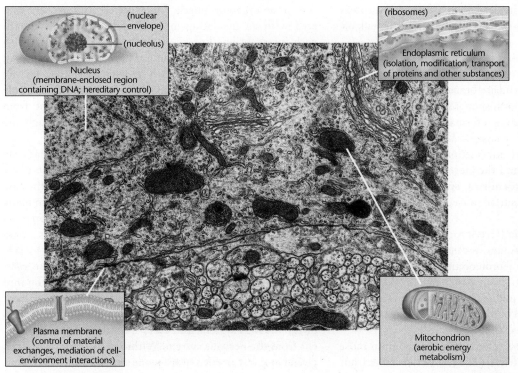

(nuclear envelope)

(nucleolus)

Nucleus
(membrane-enclosed region containing DNA; hereditary control)

(ribosomes)

Endoplasmic reticulum
(isolation, modification, transport of proteins and other substances)

Plasma membrane
(control of material exchanges, mediation of cell-environment interactions)

Mitochondrion
(aerobic energy metabolism)

FIGURE 2.2 An electron micrograph of parts of a neuron from the cerebellum of a mouse The nucleus, membrane, and other structures are characteristic of most animal cells. The plasma membrane is the border of the neuron. Magnification approximately x 20,000. (*Source: Micrograph courtesy of Dennis M. D. Landis*)

Phospholipid molecules   Protein molecules

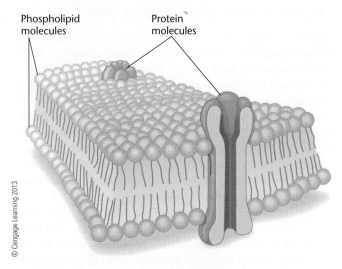

© Cengage Learning 2013

FIGURE 2.3 **The membrane of a neuron**
Embedded in the membrane are protein channels that permit certain ions to cross through the membrane at a controlled rate.

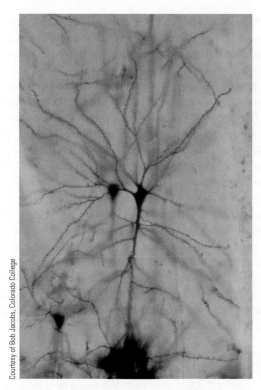

Courtesy of Bob Jacobs, Colorado College

FIGURE 2.4 **Neurons, stained to appear dark**
Note the small fuzzy-looking spines on the dendrites.

(The tiniest neurons lack axons, and some lack well-defined dendrites.) Contrast the motor neuron in Figure 2.5 and the sensory neuron in Figure 2.6. A **motor neuron** has its soma in the spinal cord. It receives excitation from other neurons through its dendrites and conducts impulses along its axon to a muscle. A **sensory neuron** is specialized at one end to be highly sensitive to a particular type of stimulation, such as light, sound, or touch. The sensory neuron shown in Figure 2.6 is a neuron conducting touch information from the skin to the spinal cord. Tiny branches lead directly from the receptors into the axon, and the cell's soma is located on a little stalk off the main trunk.

Dendrites are branching fibers that get narrower near their ends. (The term *dendrite* comes from a Greek root word meaning "tree." A dendrite branches like a tree.) The dendrite's surface is lined with specialized *synaptic receptors*, at which the dendrite receives information from other neurons. (Chapter 3 concerns synapses.) The greater the surface area of a dendrite, the more information it can receive. Some dendrites branch widely and therefore have a large surface area. Many also contain **dendritic spines**, the short outgrowths that increase the surface area available for synapses (Figure 2.7).

The **cell body**, or **soma** (Greek for "body"; pl.: somata), contains the nucleus, ribosomes, and mitochondria. Most of the metabolic work of the neuron occurs here. Cell bodies of neurons range in diameter from 0.005 mm to 0.1 mm in mammals and up to a full millimeter in certain invertebrates. Like the dendrites, the cell body is covered with synapses on its surface in many neurons.

The **axon** is a thin fiber of constant diameter, in most cases longer than the dendrites. (The term *axon* comes from

a Greek word meaning "axis.") The axon is the neuron's information sender, conveying an impulse toward other neurons or an organ or muscle. Many vertebrate axons are covered with an insulating material called a **myelin sheath** with interruptions known as **nodes of Ranvier** (RAHN-vee-ay). Invertebrate axons do not have myelin sheaths. An axon has many branches, each of which swells at its tip, forming a **presynaptic terminal**, also known as an *end bulb* or *bouton* (French for "button"). This is the point from which the axon releases chemicals that cross through the junction between one neuron and the next.

A neuron can have any number of dendrites. It has only one axon, but that axon may have branches far from the soma. Axons can be a meter or more in length, as in the case of axons from your spinal cord to your feet. That is, in many cases the length of an axon is enormous in comparison to its width—like that of a narrow highway that stretches across a continent.

Other terms associated with neurons are *afferent*, *efferent*, and *intrinsic*. An **afferent axon** brings information into a structure; an **efferent axon** carries information away from a structure. Every sensory neuron is an afferent to the rest of the nervous system, and every motor neuron is an efferent from the nervous system. Within the nervous system, a given neuron is an efferent from one structure and an afferent

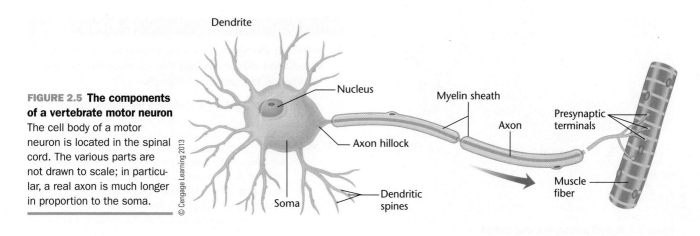

Dendrite

Nucleus

Myelin sheath

Axon hillock

Axon

Presynaptic terminals

Soma

Dendritic spines

Muscle fiber

© Cengage Learning 2013

FIGURE 2.5 The components of a vertebrate motor neuron
The cell body of a motor neuron is located in the spinal cord. The various parts are not drawn to scale; in particular, a real axon is much longer in proportion to the soma.

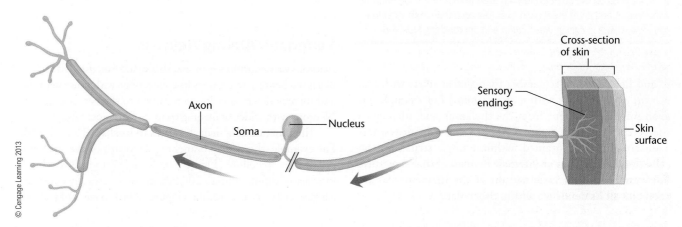

Axon

Soma

Nucleus

Cross-section of skin

Sensory endings

Skin surface

© Cengage Learning 2013

FIGURE 2.6 A vertebrate sensory neuron
Note that the soma is located on a stalk off the main trunk of the axon. (As in Figure 2.5, the various structures are not drawn to scale.)

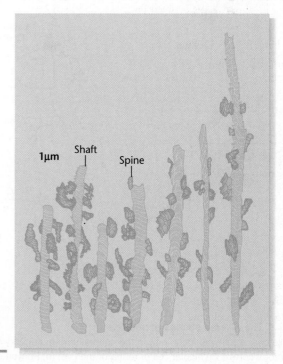

1μm Shaft Spine

FIGURE 2.7 Dendritic spines
The dendrites of certain neurons are lined with spines, short outgrowths that receive specialized incoming information. That information apparently plays a key role in long-term changes in the neuron that mediate learning and memory. *(Source: From K. M. Harris and J. K. Stevens, Society for Neuroscience, "Dendritic Spines of CA1 Pyramidal Cells in the Rat Hippocampus: Serial Electron Microscopy With Reference to Their Biophysical Characteristics."* Journal of Neuroscience, 9, *1989, 2982–2997. Copyright © 1989 Society for Neuroscience. Reprinted by permission.)*

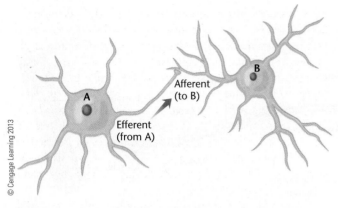

© Cengage Learning 2013

Afferent
(to B)

Efferent
(from A)

FIGURE 2.8 Cell structures and axons
It all depends on the point of view. An axon from A to B is an efferent axon from A and an afferent axon to B, just as a train from Washington to New York is exiting Washington and approaching New York.

to another. (You can remember that *efferent* starts with *e* as in *exit; afferent* starts with *a* as in *admit*.) For example, an axon might be efferent from the thalamus and afferent to the cerebral cortex (Figure 2.8). If a cell's dendrites and axon are entirely contained within a single structure, the cell is an **interneuron** or **intrinsic neuron** of that structure. For example, an intrinsic neuron of the thalamus has its axon and all its dendrites within the thalamus.

1. What are the widely branching structures of a neuron called? And what is the long thin structure that carries information to another cell called?

2. Which animal species would have the longest axons?

ANSWERS
1. The widely branching structures of a neuron are called *dendrites*, and the long thin structure that carries information to another cell is called an *axon*. 2. The longest axons occur in the largest animals. For example, giraffes and elephants have axons that extend from the spinal cord to the feet, nearly two meters away.

Variations Among Neurons

Neurons vary enormously in size, shape, and function. The shape of a given neuron determines its connections with other neurons and thereby determines its contribution to the nervous system. Neurons with wider branching connect with more targets.

The function of a neuron relates to its shape (Figure 2.9). For example, the widely branching dendrites of the Purkinje cell of the cerebellum (Figure 2.9a) enable it to receive a huge number of inputs—up to 200,000 in some cases. By contrast, certain cells in the retina (Figure 2.9d) have only short

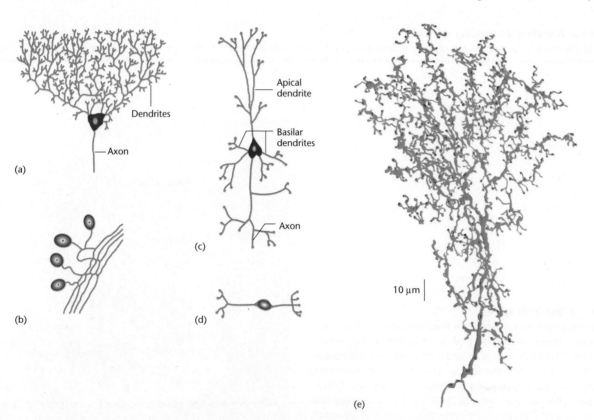

Dendrites

Axon

(a)

(b)

Apical dendrite

Basilar dendrites

Axon

(c)

(d)

10 μm

(e)

FIGURE 2.9 The diverse shapes of neurons
(a) Purkinje cell, a cell type found only in the cerebellum; (b) sensory neurons from skin to spinal cord; (c) pyramidal cell of the motor area of the cerebral cortex; (d) bipolar cell of retina of the eye; (e) Kenyon cell, from a honeybee. *(Source: Part e courtesy of R. G. Goss)*

branches on their dendrites and therefore pool input from only a few sources.

Glia

Glia (or neuroglia), the other major components of the nervous system, do not transmit information over long distances as neurons do, although they perform many other functions. The term *glia*, derived from a Greek word meaning "glue," reflects early investigators' idea that glia were like glue that held the neurons together (Somjen, 1988). Although that concept is obsolete, the term remains. Glia are smaller but more numerous than neurons (Figure 2.10).

The brain has several types of glia with different functions (Haydon, 2001). The star-shaped **astrocytes** wrap around the presynaptic terminals of a group of functionally related axons, as shown in Figure 2.11. By taking up ions released by axons and then releasing them back to axons, an astrocyte helps synchronize the activity of the axons, enabling them to send messages in waves (Angulo, Kozlov, Charpak, & Audinat, 2004; Antanitus, 1998). Astrocytes also remove waste material created when neurons die and control the amount of blood flow to each brain area (Mulligan & MacVicar, 2004). An additional function is that during periods of heightened activity in some brain areas, astrocytes dilate the blood vessels to bring more nutrients into that area (Filosa et al., 2006; Takano et al., 2006). Uncertainty surrounds another possible function: Neurons communicate by releasing certain transmitters, such as *glutamate*. After a neuron releases much glutamate, nearby glia cells absorb some of the excess. We know that the glia convert most of this glutamate into a related chemical, *glutamine*, and then pass it back to the neurons, which convert it back to glutamate, which they get ready for further release. (It's a recycling system.) The uncertain question is whether glia cells also release glutamate and other chemicals themselves. If so, they could be part of the brain's signaling system (Hamilton & Attwell, 2010).

Microglia, very small cells, also remove waste material as well as viruses, fungi, and other microorganisms. In effect, they function like part of the immune system (Davalos et al., 2005). **Oligodendrocytes** (OL-i-go-DEN-druh-sites) in the brain and spinal cord and **Schwann cells** in the periphery of the body are specialized types of glia that build the myelin sheaths that surround and insulate certain vertebrate axons. **Radial glia** guide the migration of neurons and their axons and dendrites during embryonic development. When embryological development finishes, most radial glia differentiate into neurons, and a smaller number differentiate into astrocytes and oligodendrocytes (Pinto & Götz, 2007).

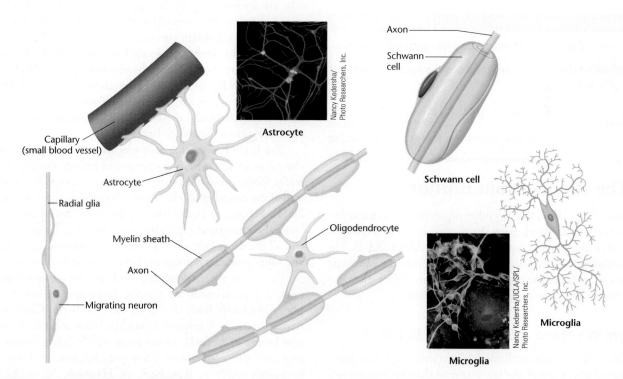

FIGURE 2.10 Shapes of some glia cells

Oligodendrocytes produce myelin sheaths that insulate certain vertebrate axons in the central nervous system; Schwann cells have a similar function in the periphery. The oligodendrocyte is shown here forming a segment of myelin sheath for two axons; in fact, each oligodendrocyte forms such segments for 30 to 50 axons. Astrocytes pass chemicals back and forth between neurons and blood and among neighboring neurons. Microglia proliferate in areas of brain damage and remove toxic materials. Radial glia (not shown here) guide the migration of neurons during embryological development. Glia have other functions as well. *(© Cengage Learning 2013)*

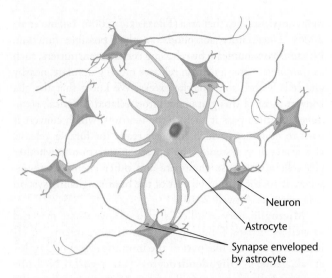

Neuron

Astrocyte

Synapse enveloped
by astrocyte

FIGURE 2.11 How an astrocyte synchronizes associated axons
Branches of the astrocyte (in the center) surround the presynaptic terminals of related axons. If a few of them are active at once, the astrocyte absorbs some of the chemicals they release. It then temporarily inhibits all the axons to which it is connected. When the inhibition ceases, all of the axons are primed to respond again in synchrony. (*Source: Based on Antanitus, 1998*)

Stop & Check

3. Identify the four major structures that compose a neuron.

4. Which kind of glia cell wraps around the synaptic terminals of axons?

ANSWERS

3. Dendrites, soma (cell body), axon, and presynaptic terminal. **4.** Astrocytes.

▌The Blood–Brain Barrier

Although the brain, like any other organ, needs to receive nutrients from the blood, many chemicals cannot cross from the blood to the brain (Hagenbuch, Gao, & Meier, 2002). The mechanism that excludes most chemicals from the vertebrate brain is known as the **blood–brain barrier**. Before we examine how it works, let's consider why we need it.

Why We Need a Blood–Brain Barrier

When a virus invades a cell, mechanisms within the cell extrude virus particles through the membrane so that the immune system can find them. When the immune system cells identify a virus, they kill it and the cell that contains it. In effect, a cell exposing a virus through its membrane says, "Look, immune system, I'm infected with this virus. Kill me and save the others."

This plan works fine if the virus-infected cell is, say, a skin cell or a blood cell, which the body replaces easily. However, with few exceptions, the vertebrate brain does not replace damaged neurons. To minimize the risk of irreparable brain damage, the body builds a wall along the sides of the brain's blood vessels. This wall keeps out most viruses, bacteria, and harmful chemicals.

"What happens if a virus does enter the nervous system?" you might ask. Certain viruses, such as the rabies virus, evade the blood–brain barrier, infect the brain, and lead to death. For several other viruses that enter the nervous system, microglia and other mechanisms attack the viruses or slow their reproduction without killing the neurons they invaded (Binder & Griffin, 2001). However, a virus that enters your nervous system probably remains with you for life. For example, the virus responsible for chicken pox and shingles enters spinal cord cells. No matter how effectively the immune system attacks that virus outside the nervous system, virus particles remain in the spinal cord, from which they can emerge decades later. The same is true for the virus that causes genital herpes.

How the Blood–Brain Barrier Works

The blood–brain barrier (Figure 2.12) depends on the endothelial cells that form the walls of the capillaries (Bundgaard, 1986; Rapoport & Robinson, 1986). Outside the brain, such cells are separated by small gaps, but in the brain, they are joined so tightly that virtually nothing passes between them.

"If the blood–brain barrier is such a good defense," you might ask, "why don't we have similar walls around our other organs?" The answer is that the barrier keeps out useful chemicals as well as harmful ones. Those useful chemicals include all fuels and amino acids, the building blocks for proteins. For the brain to function, it needs special mechanisms to get these chemicals across the blood–brain barrier.

The brain has several such mechanisms. First, *small uncharged molecules,* including oxygen and carbon dioxide, cross freely. Water crosses through special protein channels in the wall of the endothelial cells (Amiry-Moghaddam & Ottersen, 2003). Second, *molecules that dissolve in the fats of the membrane* also cross passively. Examples include vitamins A and D and all the drugs that affect the brain—from antidepressants and other psychiatric drugs to illegal drugs such as heroin.

For a few other chemicals, the brain uses **active transport,** a protein-mediated process that expends energy to pump chemicals from the blood into the brain. Chemicals that are actively transported into the brain include glucose (the brain's main fuel), amino acids (the building blocks of proteins), purines, choline, a few vitamins, iron, and certain hormones (Abbott, Rönnback, & Hansson, 2006; A. R. Jones & Shusta, 2007).

The blood–brain barrier is essential to health. In people with Alzheimer's disease or similar conditions, the endothelial cells lining the brain's blood vessels shrink, and harmful

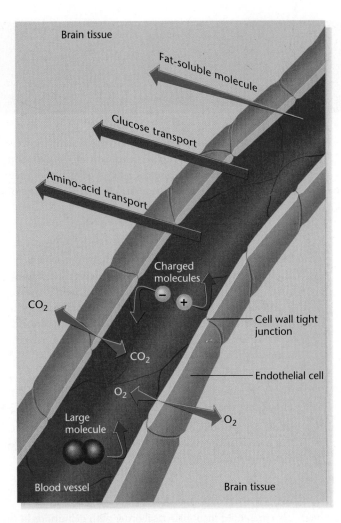

FIGURE 2.12 The blood–brain barrier
Most large molecules and electrically charged molecules cannot cross from the blood to the brain. A few small, uncharged molecules such as O_2 and CO_2 cross easily; so can certain fat-soluble molecules. Active transport systems pump glucose and certain amino acids across the membrane. (© Cengage Learning 2013)

chemicals enter the brain (Zipser et al., 2006). However, the barrier also poses a difficulty in medicine because it keeps out many medications. Brain cancers are difficult to treat because nearly all the drugs used for chemotherapy fail to cross the blood–brain barrier.

5. Identify one major advantage and one disadvantage of having a blood–brain barrier.

6. Which chemicals cross the blood–brain barrier passively?

7. Which chemicals cross the blood–brain barrier by active transport?

ANSWERS **5.** The blood–brain barrier keeps out viruses (an advantage) and also most nutrients (a disadvantage). **6.** Small, uncharged molecules such as oxygen, carbon dioxide, and water cross the blood–brain barrier passively. So do chemicals that dissolve in the fats of the membrane. **7.** Glucose, amino acids, purines, choline, certain vitamins, iron, and a few hormones.

Nourishment in Vertebrate Neurons

Most cells use a variety of carbohydrates and fats for nutrition, but vertebrate neurons depend almost entirely on **glucose,** a sugar. (Cancer cells and the testis cells that make sperm also rely overwhelmingly on glucose.) Because the metabolic pathway that uses glucose requires oxygen, neurons need a steady supply of oxygen (Wong-Riley, 1989). The brain uses about 20% of all the oxygen consumed in the body.

Why do neurons depend so heavily on glucose? Although neurons have the enzymes necessary to metabolize other fuels, glucose is practically the only nutrient that crosses the blood–brain barrier after infancy, except for *ketones* (a kind of fat), and ketones are seldom available in large amounts (Duelli & Kuschinsky, 2001).

Although neurons require glucose, glucose shortage is rarely a problem. The liver makes glucose from many kinds of carbohydrates and amino acids, as well as from glycerol, a breakdown product from fats. The only likely problem is an inability to *use* glucose. To use glucose, the body needs vitamin B_1, **thiamine**. Prolonged thiamine deficiency, common in chronic alcoholism, leads to death of neurons and a condition called *Korsakoff's syndrome*, marked by severe memory impairments (Chapter 13).

MODULE 2.1 ■ IN CLOSING

Neurons

What does the study of individual neurons tell us about behavior? One important principle is that our experience and behavior *do not* follow from the properties of any one neuron. Just as a chemist must know about atoms to make sense of compounds, a biological psychologist or neuroscientist must know about cells to understand the nervous system. However, the nervous system is more than the sum of the individual cells, just as water is more than the sum of oxygen and hydrogen. Our behavior emerges from the communication among neurons.

SUMMARY

1. Neurons receive information and convey it to other cells. The nervous system also contains *glia*. **28**

2. In the late 1800s, Santiago Ramón y Cajal used newly discovered staining techniques to establish that the nervous system is composed of separate cells, now known as neurons. **28**

3. Neurons contain the same internal structures as other animal cells. **29**

4. Neurons have four major parts: a cell body, dendrites, an axon, and presynaptic terminals. Their shapes vary greatly depending on their functions and their connections with other cells. **29**

5. Because of the blood–brain barrier, many molecules cannot enter the brain. The barrier protects the nervous system from viruses and many dangerous chemicals.
   The blood–brain barrier consists of an unbroken wall of cells that surround the blood vessels of the brain and spinal cord. A few small uncharged molecules, such as water, oxygen, and carbon dioxide, cross the barrier freely. So do molecules that dissolve in fats. **34**

6. Active transport proteins pump glucose, amino acids, and a few other chemicals into the brain and spinal cord. **34**

7. Adult neurons rely heavily on glucose, the only nutrient that can cross the blood–brain barrier. They need thiamine (vitamin B_1) to use glucose. **35**

KEY TERMS

Terms are defined in the module on the page number indicated. They're also presented in alphabetical order with definitions in the book's Subject Index/Glossary, which begins on page 561. Interactive flashcards and crossword puzzles are among the online resources available to help you learn these terms and the concepts they represent.

active transport **34**	glia **33**	nodes of Ranvier **30**
afferent axon **30**	glucose **35**	nucleus **29**
astrocytes **33**	interneuron **32**	oligodendrocytes **33**
axon **30**	intrinsic neuron **32**	presynaptic terminal **30**
blood–brain barrier **34**	membrane **29**	radial glia **33**
cell body (soma) **30**	microglia **33**	ribosomes **30**
dendrites **30**	mitochondrion **29**	Schwann cells **33**
dendritic spines **30**	motor neuron **30**	sensory neuron **30**
efferent axon **32**	myelin sheath **30**	thiamine **35**
endoplasmic reticulum **30**	neurons **28**	

THOUGHT QUESTION

Although heroin and morphine are similar in many ways, heroin exerts faster effects on the brain. What can we infer about those drugs with regard to the blood–brain barrier?

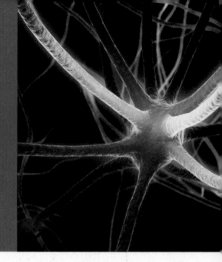

The Nerve Impulse

Think about the axons that convey information from your feet's touch receptors toward your spinal cord and brain. If the axons used electrical conduction, they could transfer information at a velocity approaching the speed of light. However, given that your body is made of water and carbon compounds instead of copper wire, the strength of the impulse would decay rapidly as it traveled. A touch on your shoulder would feel stronger than a touch on your abdomen. Short people would feel their toes more strongly than tall people could—if either could feel their toes at all!

The way your axons actually function avoids these problems. Instead of conducting an electrical impulse, the axon regenerates an impulse at each point. Imagine a long line of people holding hands. The first person squeezes the second person's hand, who then squeezes the third person's hand, and so forth. The impulse travels along the line without weakening because each person generates it anew.

Although the axon's method of transmitting an impulse prevents a touch on your shoulder from feeling stronger than one on your toes, it introduces a different problem: Because axons transmit information at only moderate speeds (varying from less than 1 meter/second to about 100 m/s), a touch on your shoulder will reach your brain *sooner* than will a touch on your toes. If you get someone to touch you simultaneously on your shoulder and your toe, you will not notice that your brain received one stimulus before the other, because the difference is small. In fact, if someone touches you on one hand and then the other, you won't be sure which hand you felt first, unless the delay between touches exceeds 70 milliseconds (ms) (S. Yamamoto & Kitazawa, 2001). Your brain is not set up to register small differences in the time of arrival of touch messages. After all, why should it be? You almost never need to know whether a touch on one part of your body occurred slightly before or after a touch somewhere else.

TRY IT
YOURSELF
ONLINE

In vision, however, your brain *does* need to know whether one stimulus began slightly before or after another one. If two adjacent spots on your retina—let's call them A and B—send impulses at almost the same time, an extremely small difference in timing indicates whether light moved from A to B or from B to A. To detect movement as accurately as possible, your visual system compensates for the fact that some parts of the retina are slightly closer to your brain than other parts are. Without some sort of compensation, simultaneous flashes arriving at two spots on your retina would reach your brain at different times, and you might perceive movement inaccurately. What prevents this illusion is the fact that axons from more distant parts of your retina transmit impulses slightly faster than those closer to the brain (Stanford, 1987)!

In short, the properties of impulse conduction in an axon are well adapted to the exact needs for information transfer in the nervous system. Let's examine the mechanics of impulse transmission.

The Resting Potential of the Neuron

Messages in a neuron develop from disturbances of the resting potential. Let's begin by understanding the resting potential.

All parts of a neuron are covered by a membrane about 8 nanometers (nm) thick (just less than 0.00001 mm), composed of two layers (an inner layer and an outer layer) of phospholipid molecules (containing chains of fatty acids and a phosphate group). Embedded among the phospholipids are cylindrical protein molecules through which various chemicals can pass (see Figure 2.3 on page 30). The structure of the membrane provides it with a combination of flexibility and firmness and controls the flow of chemicals between the inside and outside of the cell.

In the absence of any outside disturbance, the membrane maintains an **electrical gradient**, also known as **polarization**—a difference in electrical charge between the inside and outside of the cell. The neuron inside the membrane has a slightly negative electrical potential with respect to the outside, mainly because of negatively charged proteins inside the cell. This difference in voltage in a resting neuron is called the **resting potential.**

Researchers measure the resting potential by inserting a very thin *microelectrode* into the cell body, as Figure 2.13 shows. The diameter of the electrode must be as small as possible so that it enters the cell without causing damage. The most common electrode is a fine glass tube filled with a con-

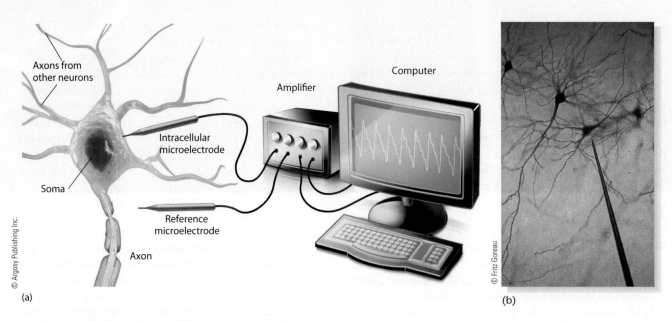

(a)

(b)

FIGURE 2.13 Methods for recording activity of a neuron
(a) Diagram of the apparatus and a sample recording. (b) A microelectrode and stained neurons magnified hundreds of times by a light microscope.

centrated salt solution and tapering to a tip diameter of 0.0005 mm or less. A reference electrode outside the cell completes the circuit. Connecting the electrodes to a voltmeter, we find that the neuron's interior has a negative potential relative to its exterior. A typical level is –70 millivolts (mV), but it varies from one neuron to another.

Forces Acting on Sodium and Potassium Ions

If charged ions could flow freely across the membrane, the membrane would depolarize. However, the membrane is **selectively permeable.** That is, some chemicals pass through it more freely than others do. Oxygen, carbon dioxide, urea, and water cross freely through channels that are always open. Most large or electrically charged ions and molecules do not cross the membrane at all. A few biologically important ions, such as sodium, potassium, calcium, and chloride, cross through membrane channels (or gates) that are sometimes open and sometimes closed. When the membrane is at rest, the sodium channels are closed, preventing almost all sodium flow, as shown on the right side of Figure 2.14. Certain kinds of stimulation can open the sodium channels, as in the center of that figure. When the membrane is at rest, potassium channels are nearly but not entirely closed, so potassium flows slowly. Stimulation opens them more widely also, as it does for sodium channels.

The **sodium–potassium pump,** a protein complex, repeatedly transports three sodium ions out of the cell while drawing two potassium ions into it. The sodium–potassium pump is an active transport that requires energy. As a result of the sodium–potassium pump, sodium ions are more than 10 times more concentrated outside the membrane than inside,

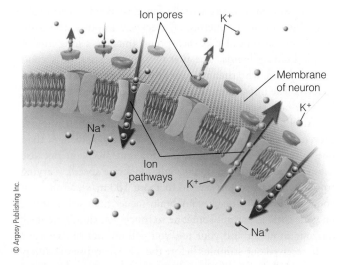

FIGURE 2.14 Ion channels in the membrane of a neuron
When a channel opens, it permits one kind of ion to cross the membrane. When it closes, it prevents passage of that ion.

and potassium ions are similarly more concentrated inside than outside.

The sodium–potassium pump is effective only because of the selective permeability of the membrane, which prevents the sodium ions that were pumped out of the neuron from leaking right back in again. When sodium ions are pumped out, they stay out. However, some of the potassium ions pumped into the neuron slowly leak out, carrying a positive charge with them. That leakage increases the electrical gradient across the membrane, as shown in Figure 2.15.

When the neuron is at rest, two forces act on sodium, both tending to push it *into* the cell. First, consider the electrical gradient. Sodium is positively charged and the inside of the cell is negatively charged. Opposite electrical charges attract, so the electrical gradient tends to pull sodium into the cell. Second, consider the **concentration gradient,** the difference in distribution of ions across the membrane. Sodium is more concentrated outside than inside, so just by the laws of probability, sodium is more likely to enter the cell than to leave it. (By analogy, imagine two rooms connected by a door. There are 100 cats in room A and only 10 in room B. Cats are more likely to move from A to B than from B to A. The same principle applies to the movement of ions across a membrane.) Given that both the electrical gradient and the concentration gradient tend to move sodium ions into the cell, sodium would move rapidly if it could. However, the sodium channels are closed when the membrane is at rest, and almost no sodium flows except for the sodium pushed *out of* the cell by the sodium–potassium pump.

Potassium is subject to competing forces. Potassium is positively charged and the inside of the cell is negatively charged, so the electrical gradient tends to pull potassium in. However, potassium is more concentrated inside the cell than outside, so the concentration gradient tends to drive it out. (Back to our cat analogy: Imagine some female cats tethered inside a room. Male cats can enter the room or leave through a narrow door. They are attracted to the female cats, but when the males get too crowded, some of them leave.)

If the potassium channels were wide open, potassium would have a small net flow out of the cell. That is, the electrical gradient and concentration gradient for potassium are almost in balance, but not quite. The sodium–potassium pump pulls more potassium into the cell as fast as it flows out of the cell, so the two gradients cannot get completely in balance.

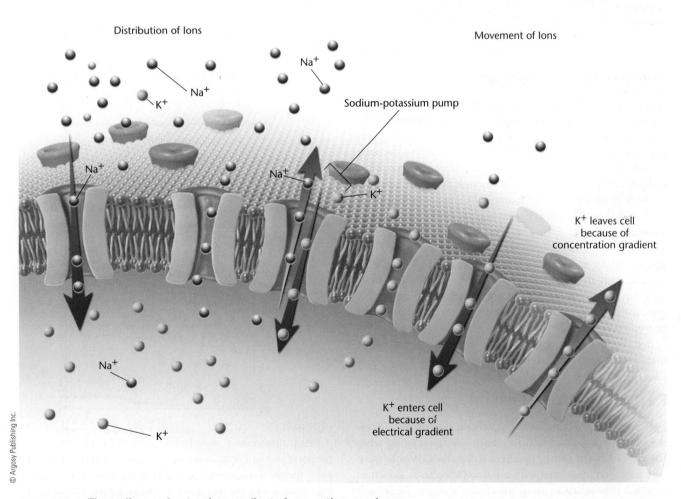

© Argosy Publishing Inc.

FIGURE 2.15 The sodium and potassium gradients for a resting membrane
Sodium ions are more concentrated outside the neuron. Potassium ions are more concentrated inside. Protein and chloride ions (not shown) bear negative charges inside the cell. At rest, very few sodium ions cross the membrane except by the sodium–potassium pump. Potassium tends to flow into the cell because of an electrical gradient but tends to flow out because of the concentration gradient. However, potassium gates retard the flow of potassium when the membrane is at rest.

The cell has negative ions, too. Negatively charged proteins inside the cell are responsible for the membrane's polarization. Chloride ions, being negatively charged, are mainly outside the cell. When the membrane is at rest, the concentration gradient and electrical gradient balance, so opening chloride channels produces little effect. However, chloride does have a net flow when the membrane's polarization changes.

Stop & Check

8. When the membrane is at rest, are the sodium ions more concentrated inside the cell or outside? Where are the potassium ions more concentrated?

9. When the membrane is at rest, what tends to drive the potassium ions out of the cell? What tends to draw them into the cell?

ANSWERS **8.** Sodium ions are more concentrated outside the cell; potassium is more concentrated inside. **9.** When the membrane is at rest, the concentration gradient tends to drive potassium ions out of the cell; the electrical gradient draws them into the cell. The sodium–potassium pump also draws them into the cell.

Why a Resting Potential?

The body invests much energy to operate the sodium–potassium pump, which maintains the resting potential. Why is it worth so much energy? The resting potential prepares the neuron to respond rapidly. As we shall see in the next section, excitation of the neuron opens channels that allow sodium to enter the cell rapidly. Because the membrane did its work in advance by maintaining the concentration gradient for sodium, the cell is prepared to respond vigorously to a stimulus.

Compare the resting potential of a neuron to a poised bow and arrow: An archer who pulls the bow in advance and then waits is ready to fire at the appropriate moment. The neuron uses the same strategy. The resting potential remains stable until the neuron is stimulated. Ordinarily, stimulation of the neuron takes place at synapses, which we consider in Chapter 3. In the laboratory, it is also possible to stimulate a neuron by inserting an electrode into it and applying current.

▌The Action Potential

Messages sent by axons are called **action potentials.** To understand action potentials, let's begin by considering what happens when the resting potential is disturbed. We can measure a neuron's potential with a microelectrode, as shown in Figure 2.13b. When an axon's membrane is at rest, the recordings show a negative potential inside the axon. If we now use another electrode to apply a negative charge, we can further increase the negative charge inside the neuron. The change is called **hyperpolarization,** which means increased polariza-

tion. When the stimulation ends, the charge returns to its original resting level. The recording looks like this:

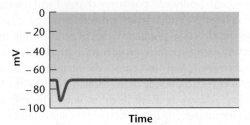

Now let's apply a current to **depolarize** the neuron—that is, reduce its polarization toward zero. If we apply a small depolarizing current, we get a result like this:

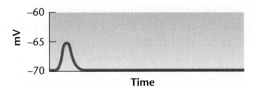

With a slightly stronger depolarizing current, the potential rises slightly higher but again returns to the resting level as soon as the stimulation ceases:

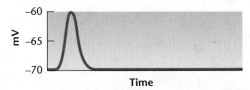

Now let's apply a still stronger current: Stimulation beyond the **threshold of excitation** produces a massive depolarization of the membrane. When the potential reaches the threshold, the membrane opens its sodium channels and permits sodium ions to flow into the cell. The potential shoots up far beyond the strength of the stimulus:

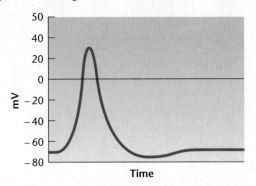

Any *subthreshold* stimulation produces a small response proportional to the amount of current. Any stimulation beyond the threshold, regardless of how far beyond, produces a big response like the one shown. That response, a rapid depolarization and then reversal of the usual polarization, is the action potential. The peak of the action potential, shown as +30 mV in this illustration, varies from one axon to another, but it is consistent for a given axon.

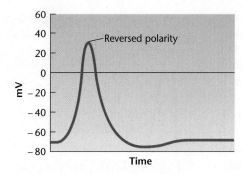

Stop & Check

10. What is the difference between a hyperpolarization and a depolarization?

11. What is the relationship between the threshold and an action potential?

ANSWERS

10. A hyperpolarization is an exaggeration of the usual negative charge within a cell (to a more negative level than usual). A depolarization is a decrease in the amount of negative charge within the cell. **11.** A depolarization that passes the threshold produces an action potential. One that falls short of the threshold does not produce an action potential.

The Molecular Basis of the Action Potential

The chemical events behind the action potential make sense if you remember these principles:

1. At the start, sodium ions are mostly outside the neuron and potassium ions are mostly inside.

2. When the membrane is depolarized, sodium and potassium channels in the membrane open.

3. At the peak of the action potential, the sodium channels close.

A neuron's membrane contains several types of cylindrical proteins, like the one in Figure 2.3, that can open or close. When one of these proteins is open, it allows a particular type of ion to cross the membrane. (Which ion crosses depends on the exact size and shape of the opening.) A protein that allows sodium to cross is called a sodium channel, one that allows potassium to cross is a potassium channel, and so forth. The ones regulating sodium and potassium are **voltage-gated channels**. That is, their permeability depends on the voltage difference across the membrane. At the resting potential, the sodium channels are closed (permitting no sodium to cross) and the potassium channels are almost closed (allowing only a little flow of potassium). As the membrane becomes depolarized, both the sodium and the potassium channels begin to open, allowing freer flow. At first, opening the potassium channels makes little difference, because the concentration gradient and electrical gradient are almost in balance anyway. However, opening the sodium channels makes a big difference, because both the electrical gradient and the concentration gradient tend to drive sodium ions into the neuron. When the depolarization reaches the threshold of the membrane, the sodium channels open wide enough for sodium to flow freely. Driven by both the concentration gradient and the electrical gradient, the sodium ions enter the cell rapidly, until the electrical potential across the membrane passes beyond zero to a reversed polarity, as shown in the following diagram:

Compared to the total number of sodium ions in and around the axon, less than 1% of them cross the membrane during an action potential. Even at the peak of the action potential, sodium ions continue to be far more concentrated outside the neuron than inside. Because of the persisting concentration gradient, sodium ions should still tend to diffuse into the cell. However, at the peak of the action potential, the sodium gates snap shut and resist reopening for the next millisecond.

Then what happens? Remember that depolarizing the membrane also opens potassium channels. At first, opening those channels made little difference. However, after so many sodium ions have crossed the membrane, the inside of the cell has a slight positive charge instead of its usual negative charge. At this point both the concentration gradient and the electrical gradient drive potassium ions out of the cell. As they flow out of the axon, they carry with them a positive charge. Because the potassium channels remain open after the sodium channels close, enough potassium ions leave to drive the membrane beyond its usual resting level to a temporary hyperpolarization. Figure 2.16 summarizes the key movements of ions during an action potential.

At the end of this process, the membrane has returned to its resting potential, but the inside of the neuron has slightly more sodium ions and slightly fewer potassium ions than before. Eventually, the sodium–potassium pump restores the original distribution of ions, but that process takes time. After an unusually rapid series of action potentials, the pump cannot keep up with the action, and sodium accumulates within the axon. Excessive buildup of sodium can be toxic to a cell. (Excessive stimulation occurs only under abnormal conditions, however, such as during a stroke or after the use of certain drugs. Don't worry that thinking too hard will explode your brain cells!)

Action potentials require the flow of sodium and potassium. **Local anesthetic** drugs, such as Novocain and Xylocaine, attach to the sodium channels of the membrane, preventing sodium ions from entering, and thereby stopping action potentials (Ragsdale, McPhee, Scheuer, & Catterall, 1994). When a dentist administers Novocain before drilling into one of your teeth, your receptors are screaming, "pain, pain, pain!" but the axons can't transmit the message to your brain, and so you don't feel it.

To explore the action potential further and try some virtual experiments on the membrane, use the online MetaNeuron program available through the Department of Neuroscience at the University of Minnesota: http://www2.neuroscience.umn.edu/eanwebsite/metaneuron.htm

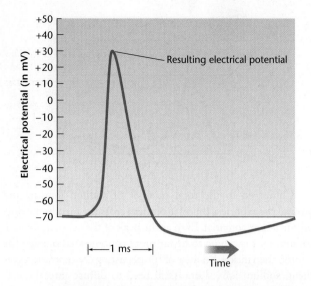

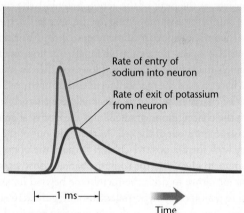

FIGURE 2.16 The movement of sodium and potassium ions during an action potential
Sodium ions cross during the peak of the action potential and potassium ions cross later in the opposite direction, returning the membrane to its original polarization. (© Cengage Learning 2013)

Stop & Check

12. During the rise of the action potential, do sodium ions move into the cell or out of it? Why?

13. As the membrane reaches the peak of the action potential, what brings the membrane down to the original resting potential?

ANSWERS

12. During the action potential, sodium ions move into the cell. The voltage-dependent sodium gates have opened, so sodium can move freely. Sodium is attracted to the inside of the cell by both an electrical and a concentration gradient. **13.** After the peak of the action potential, potassium ions exit the cell, driving the membrane back to the resting potential. Important note: The sodium–potassium pump is NOT responsible for returning the membrane to its resting potential. The sodium–potassium pump is too slow for this purpose.

The All-or-None Law

An action potential always starts in an axon and propagates without loss along the axon. However, once it starts, in many cases it "back-propagates" into the cell body and dendrites (Lorincz & Nusser, 2010). The cell body and dendrites do not conduct action potentials in the same way that axons do, but they passively register the electrical event happening in the nearby axon. This back-propagation is important in some neurons, as we shall see in Chapter 13: When an action potential back-propagates into a dendrite, the dendrite becomes more susceptible to the structural changes responsible for learning.

Here, we concentrate on the axon: When the voltage across an axon membrane reaches the threshold, voltage-gated sodium channels open wide enough to let sodium ions enter, and the incoming sodium depolarizes the membrane enough to produce an action potential. For a given neuron, all action potentials are approximately equal in amplitude (intensity) and velocity. More properly stated, the **all-or-none law** is that the amplitude and velocity of an action potential are independent of the intensity of the stimulus that initiated it, provided that the stimulus reaches the threshold. By analogy, imagine flushing a toilet: You have to make a press of at least a certain strength (the threshold), but pressing harder does not make the toilet flush faster or more vigorously.

Although the amplitude, velocity, and shape of action potentials are consistent over time for a given axon, they vary from one neuron to another. The earliest studies dealt with squid axons because squid have very thick axons that are easy to study. More recent studies of mammalian axons have found much variation in the types of protein channels and therefore in the characteristics of the action potentials (Bean, 2007).

The all-or-none law puts constraints on how an axon can send a message. To signal the difference between a weak stimulus and a strong stimulus, the axon can't send bigger or faster action potentials. All it can change is the timing. By analogy, suppose you agree to exchange coded messages with someone who can see your window when you flick the lights on and off. The two of you might agree, for example, to indicate some kind of danger by the frequency of flashes. (The more flashes, the more danger.) Much of the brain's signaling follows the principle that more frequent action potentials signal a greater intensity of stimulus.

You could also convey information by a rhythm.

Flash-flash . . .   [long pause] . . .   flash-flash

might mean something different from

Flash . . . [pause] . . . flash . . . [pause] . . . flash . . . [pause] . . . flash.

In some cases, the nervous system uses this kind of coding. For example, a taste axon shows one rhythm of responses for sweet tastes and a different rhythm for bitter tastes (Di Lorenzo, Leshchinskiy, Moroney, & Ozdoba, 2009).

The Refractory Period

While the electrical potential across the membrane is returning from its peak toward the resting point, it is still above the threshold. Why doesn't the cell produce another action potential during this period? (If it did, of course, it would go into a permanent repetition of one action potential after another.) Immediately after an action potential, the cell is in a **refractory period** during which it resists the production of further action potentials. In the first part of this period, the **absolute refractory period**, the membrane cannot produce an action potential, regardless of the stimulation. During the second part, the **relative refractory period**, a stronger than usual stimulus is necessary to initiate an action potential. The refractory period has two mechanisms: The sodium channels are closed, and potassium is flowing out of the cell at a faster than usual rate.

In most of the neurons that researchers have tested, the absolute refractory period is about 1 ms and the relative refractory period is another 2–4 ms. (To return to the toilet analogy, there is a short time right after you flush a toilet when you cannot make it flush again—an absolute refractory period. Then follows a period when it is possible but difficult to flush it again—a relative refractory period—before it returns to normal.)

Stop & Check

14. State the all-or-none law.

15. Does the all-or-none law apply to dendrites? Why or why not?

16. Suppose researchers find that axon A can produce up to 1,000 action potentials per second (at least briefly, with maximum stimulation), but axon B can never produce more than 100 per second (regardless of the strength of the stimulus). What could we conclude about the refractory periods of the two axons?

ANSWERS **14.** According to the all-or-none law, the size and shape of the action potential are independent of the intensity of the stimulus that initiated it. That is, every depolarization beyond the threshold of excitation produces an action potential of about the same amplitude and velocity for a given axon. **15.** The all-or-none law does not apply to dendrites because they do not have action potentials. **16.** Axon A must have a shorter absolute refractory period, about 1 ms, whereas B has a longer absolute refractory period, about 10 ms.

Propagation of the Action Potential

Up to this point, we have considered how the action potential occurs at one point on the axon. Now let us consider how it moves down the axon. Remember, it is important for axons to convey impulses without any loss of strength over distance.

In a motor neuron, an action potential begins on the **axon hillock**, a swelling where the axon exits the soma (Figure 2.5). During the action potential, sodium ions enter a point on the axon. Temporarily, that spot is positively charged in comparison with neighboring areas along the

axon. The positive ions flow within the axon to neighboring regions. The positive charges slightly depolarize the next area of the membrane, causing it to reach its threshold and open its voltage-gated sodium channels. Therefore, the membrane regenerates the action potential at that point. In this manner, the action potential travels along the axon, as in Figure 2.17.

The term **propagation of the action potential** describes the transmission of an action potential down an axon. The propagation of an animal species is the production of offspring. In a sense, the action potential gives birth to a new action potential at each point along the axon. As a result, the action potential is just as strong at the end of the axon as it was at the beginning.

Let's reexamine Figure 2.17 for a moment. What is to prevent the electrical charge from flowing in the direction opposite that in which the action potential is traveling? Nothing. In fact, the electrical charge does flow in both directions. Then what prevents an action potential near the center of an axon from reinvading the areas that it has just passed? The answer is that the areas just passed are still in their refractory period.

Let's review the action potential:

- When an area of the axon membrane reaches its threshold of excitation, sodium channels and potassium channels open.
- At first, the opening of potassium channels produces little effect.
- Opening sodium channels lets sodium ions rush into the axon.
- Positive charge flows down the axon and opens voltage-gated sodium channels at the next point.
- At the peak of the action potential, the sodium gates snap shut. They remain closed for the next millisecond or so, despite the depolarization of the membrane.
- Because the membrane is depolarized, voltage-gated potassium channels are open.
- Potassium ions flow out of the axon, returning the membrane toward its original depolarization.
- A few milliseconds later, the voltage-dependent potassium channels close.

All of this may seem like a lot to memorize, but it is not. Everything follows logically from the facts that voltage-gated sodium and potassium channels open when the membrane is depolarized and that sodium channels snap shut at the peak of the action potential.

The Myelin Sheath and Saltatory Conduction

In the thinnest axons, action potentials travel at a velocity of less than 1 m/s. Increasing the diameter brings conduction velocity up to about 10 m/s. At that speed, an impulse along an axon to or from a giraffe's foot takes about half a second. To increase the speed still more, vertebrate axons evolved a

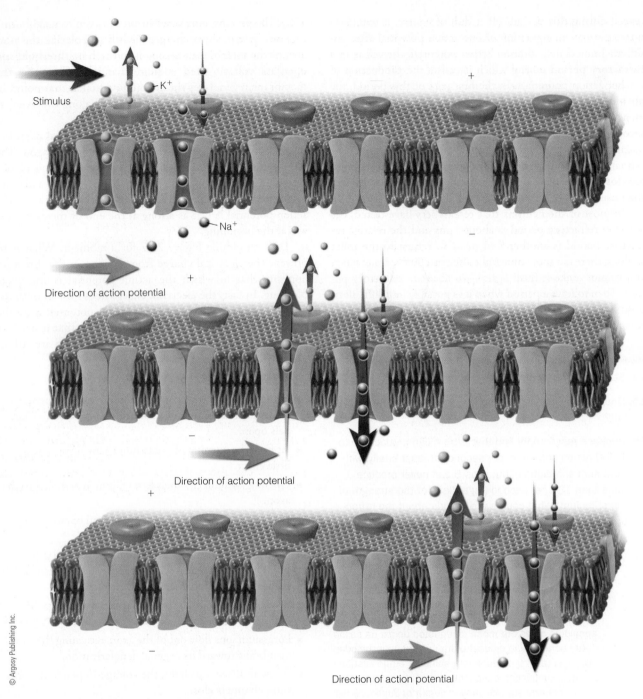

FIGURE 2.17 **Propagation of an action potential**
As an action potential occurs at one point on the axon, enough sodium enters to depolarize the next point to its threshold, producing an action potential at that point. In this manner the action potential flows along the axon. Behind each area of sodium entry, potassium ions exit, restoring the resting potential.

special mechanism: sheaths of **myelin,** an insulating material composed of fats and proteins.

Consider the following analogy. Suppose your job is to take written messages over a long distance without using any mechanical device. Taking each message and running with it would be reliable but slow, like the propagation of an action potential along an unmyelinated axon. If you tied each message to a ball and threw it, you could increase the speed, but your throws would not travel far enough. The best solution is to station people at moderate distances along the route and throw the message-bearing ball from person to person until it reaches its destination.

The same principle applies to **myelinated axons,** those covered with a myelin sheath. Myelinated axons, found only in vertebrates, are covered with layers of fats and proteins. The myelin sheath is interrupted periodically by short sections of axon called nodes of Ranvier, each one about 1 micrometer wide, as shown in Figure 2.18. In most cases, the action potential starts at the axon hillock, but in some cases it starts at the first node of Ranvier (Kuba, Ishii, & Ohmari, 2006).

Suppose an action potential starts at the axon hillock and propagates along the axon until it reaches the first myelin segment. The action potential cannot regenerate along the membrane between nodes because sodium channels are virtually absent between nodes (Catterall, 1984). After an action potential occurs at a node, sodium ions enter the axon and diffuse within the axon, pushing a chain of positive ions along the axon to the next node, where they regenerate the action potential (Figure 2.19). This flow of ions is considerably faster than the regeneration of an action potential at each point along the axon. The jumping of action potentials from node to node is referred to as **saltatory conduction,** from the Latin word *saltare,* meaning "to jump." (The same root shows up in the word *somersault.*) In addition to providing rapid conduction of impulses, saltatory conduction conserves energy: Instead of admitting sodium ions at every point along the axon and then having to pump them out via the sodium–potassium pump, a myelinated axon admits sodium only at its nodes.

In multiple sclerosis, the immune system attacks myelin sheaths. An axon that never had a myelin sheath conducts impulses slowly but steadily. An axon that has lost its myelin is not the same. After myelin forms along an axon, the axon loses its sodium channels under the myelin (Waxman & Ritchie,

1985). If the axon later loses its myelin, it still lacks sodium channels in the areas previously covered with myelin, and most action potentials die out between one node and the next. People with multiple sclerosis suffer a variety of impairments, ranging from visual impairments to poor muscle coordination.

Stop & Check

17. In a myelinated axon, how would the action potential be affected if the nodes were much closer together? How might it be affected if the nodes were much farther apart?

ANSWER **17.** If the nodes were closer, the action potential would travel more slowly. If they were much farther apart, the action potential would be faster if it could successfully jump from one node to the next. When the distance becomes too great, the current cannot diffuse from one node to the next and still remain above threshold, so the action potentials would stop.

▌Local Neurons

Axons produce action potentials. However, many small neurons have no axon. Neurons without an axon exchange information with only their closest neighbors. We therefore call them **local neurons.** Because they do not have an axon, they do not follow the all-or-none law. When a local neuron receives information from other neurons, it has a **graded potential,** a

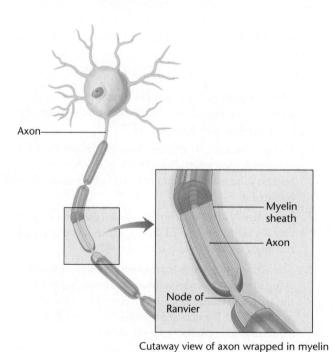

FIGURE 2.18 An axon surrounded by a myelin sheath and interrupted by nodes of Ranvier
The inset shows a cross-section through both the axon and the myelin sheath. Magnification approximately x 30,000. The anatomy is distorted here to show several nodes; in fact, the distance between nodes is generally at least 100 times as long as the nodes themselves. (© *Cengage Learning 2013*)

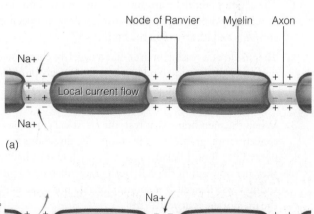

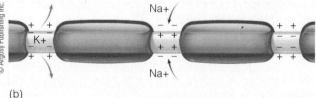

FIGURE 2.19 Saltatory conduction in a myelinated axon
An action potential at the node triggers flow of current to the next node, where the membrane regenerates the action potential. In reality, a myelin sheath is much longer than shown here, relative to the size of the nodes of Ranvier and to the diameter of the axon.

membrane potential that varies in magnitude in proportion to the intensity of the stimulus. The change in membrane potential is conducted to adjacent areas of the cell, in all directions, gradually decaying as it travels. Those various areas of the cell contact other neurons, which they excite or inhibit through synapses (which we consider in the next chapter).

Local neurons are difficult to study because it is almost impossible to insert an electrode into a tiny cell without damaging it. Most of our knowledge, therefore, has come from large neurons, and that bias in our research methods may have led to a misconception. Many years ago, all that neuroscientists knew about local neurons was that they were small. Given their focus on larger neurons, many scientists assumed that the small neurons were immature. As one textbook author put it, "Many of these [neurons] are small and apparently undeveloped, as if they

constituted a reserve stock not yet utilized in the individual's cerebral activity" (Woodworth, 1934, p. 194). In other words, the small cells would contribute to behavior only if they grew.

Perhaps this misunderstanding was the origin of that widespread, nonsensical belief that "they say we use only 10% of our brain." (Who are "they," incidentally?) Other origins have also been suggested for this belief. Regardless of how it started, it has been remarkably persistent, given its total lack of justification. Surely, it can't be true that someone could lose 90% of the brain and still behave normally. Nor is it true that only 10% of neurons are active at any given moment. The belief that we use only a small part of the brain became popular, presumably because people wanted to believe it. Eventually, people were simply quoting one another long after everyone forgot where the idea originated.

MODULE 2.2 ■ IN CLOSING

Neural Messages

In this chapter, we have examined what happens within a single neuron, as if each neuron acted independently. It does not, of course. All of its functions depend on communication with other neurons, which we will consider in the next chapter. We may as well admit from the start, however, that neural communication is amazing. Unlike human communication, in which a speaker sometimes presents a complicated

message to an enormous audience, a neuron delivers only an action potential—a mere on/off message—to only that modest number of other neurons that receive branches of its axon. At various receiving neurons, an "on" message can be converted into either excitation or inhibition (yes or no). From this limited system, all of our behavior and experience emerge.

SUMMARY

1. The action potential transmits information without loss of intensity over distance. The cost is a delay between the stimulus and its arrival in the brain.   37

2. The inside of a resting neuron has a negative charge with respect to the outside. Sodium ions are actively pumped out of the neuron, and potassium ions are pumped in.   37

3. When the membrane is at rest, the electrical gradient and concentration gradient act in competing directions for potassium, almost balancing out. Potassium ions have a slow net flow out of the cell. Both gradients tend to push sodium into the cell, but sodium ions do not cross while the membrane is at rest.   39

4. When the charge across the membrane is reduced, sodium and potassium channels begin to open. When the membrane potential reaches the threshold of the neuron, sodium ions enter explosively, suddenly reducing and reversing the charge across the membrane. This event is known as the action potential.   41

5. After the peak of the action potential, the membrane returns to its original level of polarization because of the outflow of potassium ions.   41

6. The all-or-none law: For any stimulus greater than the threshold, the amplitude and velocity of the action potential are independent of the size of the stimulus that initiated it.   42

7. Immediately after an action potential, the membrane enters a refractory period during which it is resistant to starting another action potential.   42

8. The action potential is regenerated at successive points along the axon as sodium ions flow through the core of the axon and stimulate the next point along the axon to its threshold. The action potential maintains a constant magnitude as it passes along the axon.   43

9. In axons that are covered with myelin, action potentials form only in the nodes that separate myelinated segments. Transmission in myelinated axons is faster than in unmyelinated axons.   43

KEY TERMS

Terms are defined in the module on the page number indicated. They're also presented in alphabetical order with definitions in the book's Subject Index/Glossary, which begins on page 561. Interactive flashcards and crossword puzzles are among the online resources available to help you learn these terms and the concepts they represent.

absolute refractory period   43

action potential   40

all-or-none law   42

axon hillock   43

concentration gradient   39

depolarize   40

electrical gradient   37

graded potentials   45

hyperpolarization   40

local anesthetic   41

local neurons   45

myelin   44

myelinated axons   44

polarization   37

propagation of the action potential   43

refractory period   43

relative refractory period   43

resting potential   37

saltatory conduction   45

selectively permeable   38

sodium–potassium pump   38

threshold   40

voltage-gated channels   41

THOUGHT QUESTIONS

1. Suppose the threshold of a neuron were the same as its resting potential. What would happen? At what frequency would the cell produce action potentials?

2. In the laboratory, researchers can apply an electrical stimulus at any point along the axon, making action potentials travel in both directions from the point of stimulation. An action potential moving in the usual direction, away from the axon hillock, is said to be traveling in the *orthodromic* direction. An action potential traveling toward the axon hillock is traveling in the *antidromic* direction. If we started an orthodromic action potential at the axon hillock and an antidromic action potential at the opposite end of the axon, what would happen when they met at the center? Why?

3. If a drug partly blocks a membrane's potassium channels, how does it affect the action potential?

CHAPTER 2 Interactive Exploration and Study

The **Psychology CourseMate** for this text brings chapter topics to life with interactive learning, study, and exam preparation tools, including quizzes and flashcards for the Key Concepts that appear throughout each module, as well as an interactive media-rich eBook version of the text that is fully searchable and includes highlighting and note-taking capabilities and interactive versions of the book's **Stop & Check** quizzes and **Try It Yourself Online** activities. The site also features **Virtual Biological Psychology Labs, videos,** and **animations** to help you better understand concepts—log on and learn more at **www.cengagebrain.com**, which is your gateway to all of this text's complimentary and premium resources, including the following:

Virtual Biological Psychology Labs

Explore the experiments that led to modern-day understanding of biopsychology with the Virtual Biological Psychology Labs, featuring a realistic lab environment that allows you to conduct experiments and evaluate data to better understand how scientists came to the conclusions presented in your text. The labs cover a range of topics, including perception, motivation, cognition, and more. You may purchase access at **www.cengagebrain.com**, or login at **login.cengagebrain.com** if an access card was included with your text.

Animations

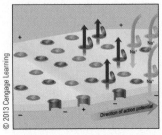

Propogation of the Action Potential

Also available—

- Parts of the Neuron
- Neuron Membrane at Rest
- Saltatory Conduction

Suggestions for Further Exploration

Websites

The Psychology CourseMate for this text provides regularly updated links to relevant online resources for this chapter, such as the **University of Minnesota's MetaNeuron Program.**

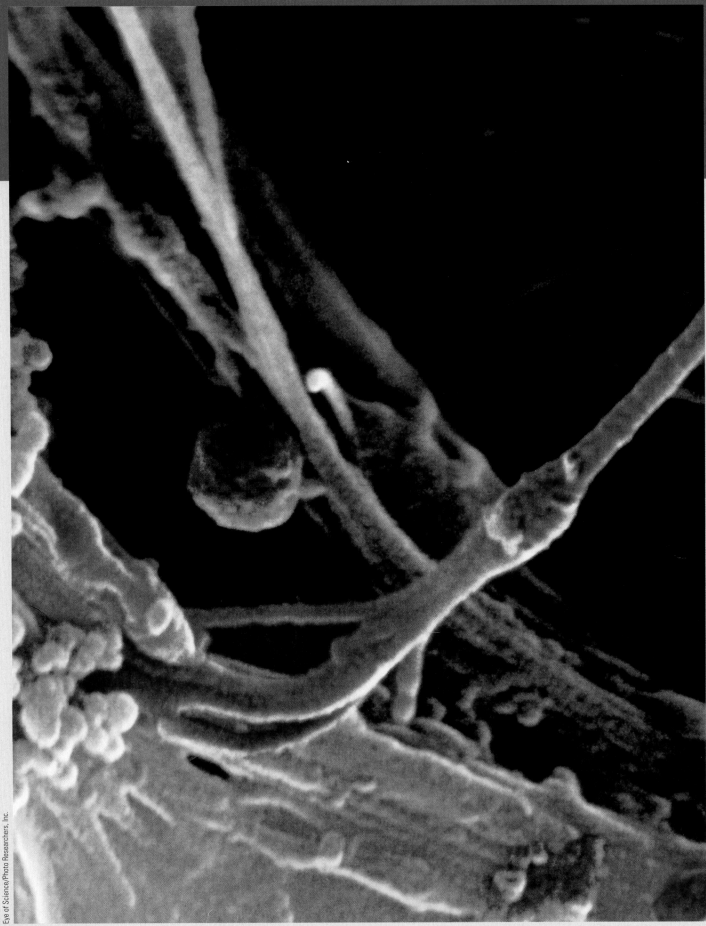

Synapses

CHAPTER OUTLINE

MAIN IDEAS

1. At a synapse, a neuron releases chemicals called neurotransmitters that excite or inhibit another cell.

2. In most cases, a single release of neurotransmitter produces only a subthreshold response in the receiving cell. This response summates with other subthreshold responses to determine whether or not the cell produces an action potential.

3. Transmission at synapses goes through many steps, and interference at any of them can alter the outcome.

4. Nearly all drugs that affect behavior or experience do so by acting at synapses.

5. Nearly all abused drugs increase the release of dopamine in certain brain areas.

6. Addiction changes certain brain areas, increasing the tendency to seek the addictive substance and decreasing the response to other kinds of reinforcement.

I f you had to communicate with someone without sight or sound, what would you do? Chances are, your first choice would be a touch code or a system of electrical impulses. You might not even think of passing chemicals back and forth. Chemicals are, however, the main way your neurons communicate. Neurons communicate by transmitting chemicals at specialized junctions called *synapses*.

OPPOSITE: This electron micrograph, with color added artificially, shows that the surface of a neuron is practically covered with synapses, the connections it receives from other neurons.

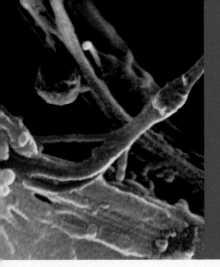

The Concept of the Synapse

n the late 1800s, Ramón y Cajal anatomically demonstrated a narrow gap separating one neuron from another. In 1906, Charles Scott Sherrington physiologically demonstrated that communication between one neuron and the next differs from communication along a single axon. He inferred a specialized gap between neurons and introduced the term **synapse** to describe it. Cajal and Sherrington are regarded as the great pioneers of modern neuroscience, and their nearly simultaneous discoveries supported each other: If communication between one neuron and another was special in some way, then there could be no doubt that neurons were anatomically separate from one another. Sherrington's discovery was an amazing feat of scientific reasoning, as he used behavioral observations to infer the major properties of synapses half a century before researchers had the technology to measure those properties directly.

The Properties of Synapses

Sherrington studied **reflexes**—automatic muscular responses to stimuli. In a leg flexion reflex, a sensory neuron excites a second neuron, which in turn excites a motor neuron, which excites a muscle, as in Figure 3.1. The circuit from sensory neuron to muscle response is called a **reflex arc**. If one neuron is separate from another, as Cajal had demonstrated, a reflex must require communication between neurons, and therefore, measurements of reflexes might reveal some of the special properties of that communication.

Sherrington strapped a dog into a harness above the ground and pinched one of the dog's feet. After a fraction of a second, the dog *flexed* (raised) the pinched leg and *extended* the other legs. Sherrington found the same reflexive movements after he made a cut that disconnected

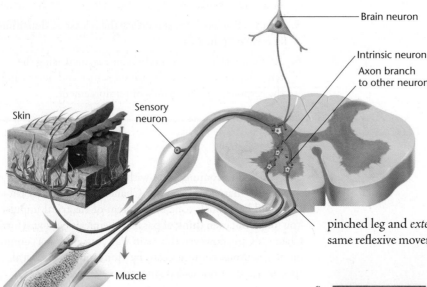

Brain neuron

Intrinsic neuron

Axon branch to other neurons

Skin

Sensory neuron

Muscle

FIGURE 3.1 A reflex arc for leg flexion
Anatomy has been simplified to show the relationship among sensory neuron, intrinsic neuron, and motor neuron. (© Argosy Publishing Inc.)

Reprinted with the permission of Cambridge University Press

Charles Scott Sherrington (1857–1952)

A rainbow every morning who would pause to look at? The wonderful which comes often or is plentifully about us is soon taken for granted. That is practical enough. It allows us to get on with life. But it may stultify if it cannot on occasion be thrown off. To recapture now and then childhood's wonder is to secure a driving force for occasional grown-up thoughts. (Sherrington, 1941, p. 104.)

the spinal cord from the brain. Evidently, the spinal cord controlled the flexion and extension reflexes. In fact, the movements were more consistent after he separated the spinal cord from the brain. (In an intact animal, messages descending from the brain modify the reflexes, making them stronger at some times and weaker at others.)

Sherrington observed several properties of reflexes suggesting special processes at the junctions between neurons: (a) Reflexes are slower than conduction along an axon. (b) Several weak stimuli presented at slightly different times or locations produce a stronger reflex than a single stimulus does. (c) When one set of muscles becomes excited, a different set becomes relaxed. Let's consider each of these points and their implications.

Speed of a Reflex and Delayed Transmission at the Synapse

When Sherrington pinched a dog's foot, the dog flexed that leg after a short delay. During that delay, an impulse had to travel up an axon from the skin receptor to the spinal cord, and then an impulse had to travel from the spinal cord back down the leg to a muscle. Sherrington measured the total distance that the impulse traveled from skin receptor to spinal cord to muscle and calculated the speed at which the impulse must have traveled to produce the response. He found that the speed of conduction through the reflex arc varied but was never more than about 15 meters per second (m/s). In contrast, previous research had measured action potential velocities along sensory or motor nerves at about 40 m/s. Sherrington concluded that some process was slowing conduction through the reflex, and he inferred that the delay must occur where one neuron communicates with another (Figure 3.2). This idea is critical, as it established the existence of synapses. Sherrington, in fact, introduced the term *synapse*.

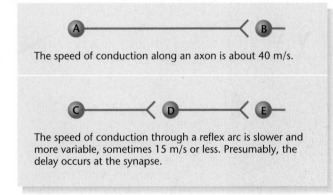

The speed of conduction along an axon is about 40 m/s.

The speed of conduction through a reflex arc is slower and more variable, sometimes 15 m/s or less. Presumably, the delay occurs at the synapse.

FIGURE 3.2 Sherrington's evidence for synaptic delay
An impulse traveling through a synapse in the spinal cord is slower than one traveling a similar distance along an uninterrupted axon. (© Cengage Learning 2013)

1. What evidence led Sherrington to conclude that transmission at a synapse is different from transmission along an axon?

ANSWER

1. Sherrington found that the velocity of conduction through a reflex arc was significantly slower than the velocity of an action potential along an axon. Therefore, some delay must occur at the junction between one neuron and the next.

Temporal Summation

Sherrington found that repeated stimuli within a brief time have a cumulative effect. He referred to this phenomenon as **temporal summation** (summation over time). A light pinch of the dog's foot did not evoke a reflex, but a few rapidly repeated pinches did. Sherrington surmised that a single pinch did not reach the threshold of excitation for the next neuron. The neuron that delivers transmission is the **presynaptic neuron**. The neuron that receives it is the **postsynaptic neuron**. Sherrington proposed that this subthreshold excitation in the postsynaptic neuron decays over time, but it can combine with a second excitation that follows it quickly. With a rapid succession of pinches, each adds its effect to what remained from the previous ones, until the combination exceeds the threshold of the postsynaptic neuron, producing an action potential.

Decades later, John Eccles (1964) attached microelectrodes to stimulate axons of presynaptic neurons while he recorded from the postsynaptic neuron. For example, after he had briefly stimulated an axon, Eccles recorded a slight depolarization of the membrane of the postsynaptic cell (point 1 in Figure 3.3).

Note that this partial depolarization is a graded potential. Unlike action potentials, which are always depolarizations, graded potentials may be either depolarizations (excitatory) or hyperpolarizations (inhibitory). A graded depolarization is known as an **excitatory postsynaptic potential** (**EPSP**). It results from a flow of sodium ions into the neuron. If an EPSP does not cause the cell to reach its threshold, the depolarization decays quickly.

When Eccles stimulated an axon twice, he recorded two EPSPs. If the delay between EPSPs was short enough, the second EPSP added to what was left of the first one (point 2 in Figure 3.3), producing temporal summation. At point 3 in Figure 3.3, a quick sequence of EPSPs combines to exceed the threshold and produce an action potential.

Spatial Summation

Sherrington also found that synapses have the property of **spatial summation**—that is, summation over space. Synaptic inputs from separate locations combine their effects on a neuron. Sherrington again began with a pinch too weak to

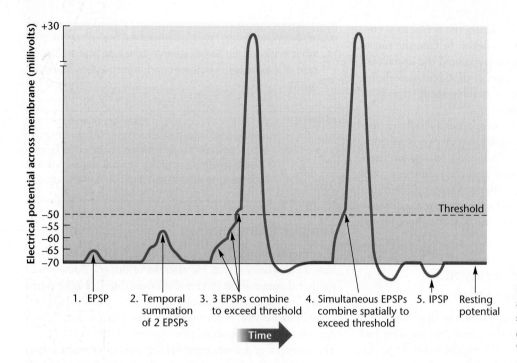

FIGURE 3.3 **Recordings from a postsynaptic neuron during synaptic activation** (© *Cengage Learning 2013*)

elicit a reflex. This time, instead of pinching one point twice, he pinched two points at once. Although neither pinch alone produced a reflex, together they did. Sherrington concluded that pinching two points activated separate sensory neurons, whose axons converged onto a neuron in the spinal cord. Excitation from either sensory axon excited that spinal neuron, but not enough to reach the threshold. A combination of excitations exceeded the threshold and produced an action potential (point 4 in Figure 3.3). Again, Eccles confirmed Sherrington's inference, demonstrating that EPSPs from several axons summate their effects on a postsynaptic cell (Figure 3.4).

Spatial summation is critical to brain functioning. Sensory input to the brain arrives at synapses that individually produce weak effects. However, each neuron receives many incoming axons that frequently produce synchronized responses (Bruno & Sakmann, 2006). Spatial summation ensures that a sensory stimulus stimulates neurons enough to activate them.

Temporal summation and spatial summation ordinarily occur together. That is, a neuron might receive input from several axons at approximately, but not exactly, the same time. Integrating these inputs provides complexity. As Figure 3.5

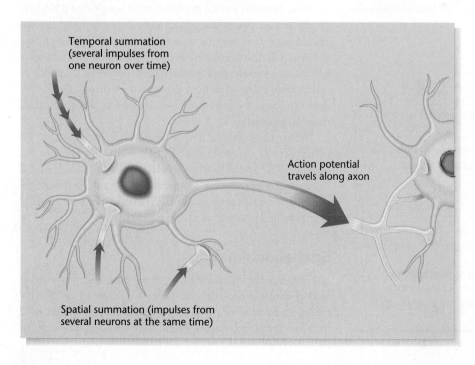

FIGURE 3.4 **Temporal and spatial summation** (© *Cengage Learning 2013*)

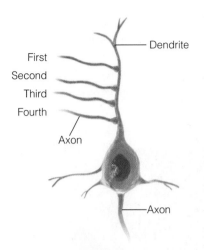
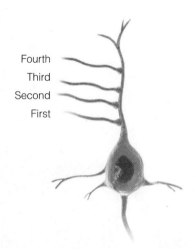

First
Second
Third
Fourth

Dendrite

Axon

Axon

Fourth
Third
Second
First

Summation in this direction
produces greater depolarization.

Summation in this direction
produces less depolarization.

FIGURE 3.5 Summation effects can depend on the order of stimuli. *(© Argosy Publishing Inc.)*

shows, a series of axons active in one order can have a different result from the same axons in a different order. For example, a neuron in the visual system could respond to light moving in one direction and not another (Branco, Clark, & Häusser, 2010).

Stop & Check

2. What is the difference between temporal summation and spatial summation?

ANSWER

2. Temporal summation is the combined effect of quickly repeated stimulation at a single synapse. Spatial summation is the combined effect of several nearly simultaneous stimulations at several synapses onto one neuron.

Inhibitory Synapses

When Sherrington vigorously pinched a dog's foot, the flexor muscles of that leg contracted, and so did the extensor muscles of the other three legs (Figure 3.6). Also, the dog relaxed the extensor muscles of the stimulated leg and the flexor muscles of the other legs. Sherrington's explanation assumed certain connections in the spinal cord: A pinch on the foot sends a message along a sensory neuron to an *interneuron* (an intermediate neuron) in the spinal cord, which in turn excites the motor neurons connected to the flexor muscles of that leg (Figure 3.7). Sherrington surmised that the interneuron also sends a message to block activity of motor neurons to the extensor muscles in the same leg and the flexor muscles of the three other legs.

Later researchers physiologically demonstrated the inhibitory synapses that Sherrington had inferred. At these synapses, input from an axon hyperpolarizes the postsynap-

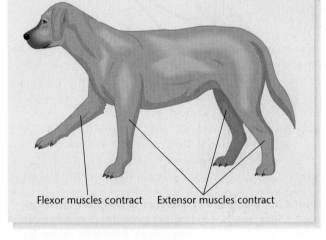

Flexor muscles contract   Extensor muscles contract

FIGURE 3.6 Antagonistic muscles
Flexor muscles draw an extremity toward the trunk of the body, whereas extensor muscles move an extremity away from the body. *(© Cengage Learning 2013)*

tic cell. That is, it increases the negative charge within the cell, moving it further from the threshold and decreasing the probability of an action potential (point 5 in Figure 3.3). This temporary hyperpolarization of a membrane—called an **inhibitory postsynaptic potential**, or **IPSP**—resembles an EPSP. An IPSP occurs when synaptic input selectively opens the gates for potassium ions to leave the cell (carrying a positive charge with them) or for chloride ions to enter the cell (carrying a negative charge).

Today, we take for granted the concept of inhibition, but at Sherrington's time, the idea was controversial, as no one could imagine a mechanism to accomplish it. Establishing the idea of inhibition was critical not just for neuroscience but for psychology as well.

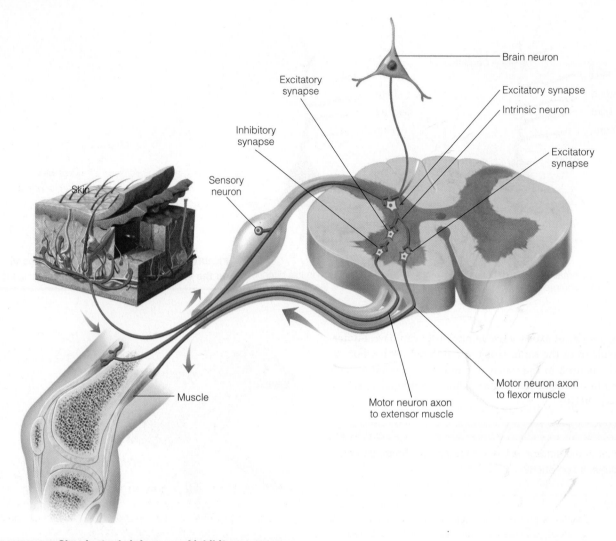

FIGURE 3.7 Sherrington's inference of inhibitory synapses
When a flexor muscle is excited, the probability of excitation decreases in the paired extensor muscle. Sherrington inferred that the interneuron that excited a motor neuron to the flexor muscle also inhibited a motor neuron connected to the extensor muscle. (© Argosy Publishing Inc.)

Stop & Check

3. What was Sherrington's evidence for inhibition in the nervous system?

4. What ion gates in the membrane open during an EPSP? What gates open during an IPSP?

5. Can an inhibitory message flow along an axon?

ANSWERS 3. Sherrington found that a reflex that stimulates a flexor muscle prevents contraction of the extensor muscles of the same limb. He therefore inferred that an axon sending an excitatory message for the flexor muscle also sent an inhibitory message for the extensor muscle. 4. During an EPSP sodium gates open. During an IPSP potassium or chloride gates open. 5. No. Only action potentials propagate along an axon. Inhibitory messages—IPSPs—decay over time and distance.

Relationship Among EPSP, IPSP, and Action Potentials

Sherrington's work opened the way to exploring the wiring diagram of the nervous system. Consider the neurons shown in Figure 3.8. When neuron 1 excites neuron 3, it also excites neuron 2, which inhibits neuron 3. The excitatory message reaches neuron 3 faster because it goes through just one synapse instead of two. The result is brief excitation (EPSP) in neuron 3, which stops quickly. You see how the inhibitory neurons, which are typically very small, can regulate the timing of activity.

The nervous system is full of complex patterns of connections, which produce an unending variety of responses. To see how the synaptic wiring diagram controls responses, consider Figures 3.9 through 3.11. In Figure 3.9, either the axon from cell A or the axon from cell B stimulates cell X enough to reach its threshold. Therefore cell X responds to

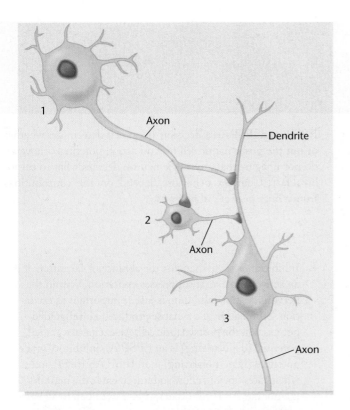

FIGURE 3.8 One of many possible wiring diagrams for synapses
Excitatory synapses are in green, and inhibitory synapses in red. In the circuit shown here, excitation would reach the dendrite before inhibition. (Remember, any transmission through a synapse produces a delay.) Therefore, the result would be brief excitation of the dendrite and then a stop. Inhibitory synapses serve many other functions, too. *(Based on Kullmann & Lamsa, 2007)*

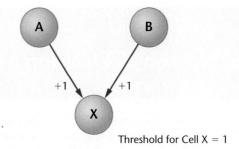

FIGURE 3.9 Wiring diagram for an "A or B" response
The axon from either A or B stimulates cell X enough to reach its threshold. *(© Cengage Learning 2013)*

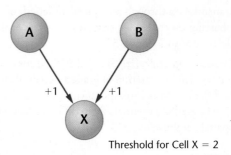

FIGURE 3.10 Wiring diagram for an "A and B" response
The axons from A and B stimulate cell X but neither one by itself reaches the threshold for X. The combination of both at the same time reaches the threshold. *(© Cengage Learning 2013)*

"A or B." In Figure 3.10, neither A nor B stimulates cell X enough to reach its threshold, but the two can summate to reach the threshold. (Remember spatial summation.) Therefore in this case cell X responds to "A and B." In Figure 3.11, cell X responds to "A and B if not C." With a little imagination, you can construct other possibilities. In reality, the possibilities are vast. Sherrington assumed—as did many people who have proposed mathematical models of the nervous system since then—that synapses simply produce on and off responses. In fact, synapses vary enormously in their duration of effects. Furthermore, many inputs interact in ways that are not quite additive. The effect of two synapses at the same time can be more than double the effect of either one, or less than double (Silver, 2010).

Most neurons have a **spontaneous firing rate**, a periodic production of action potentials even without synaptic input. In such cases, the EPSPs increase the frequency of action potentials above the spontaneous rate, whereas IPSPs decrease it. For example, if the neuron's spontaneous firing rate is 10 action potentials per second, a stream of EPSPs might increase the rate to 15 or more, whereas a preponderance of IPSPs might decrease it to 5 or fewer.

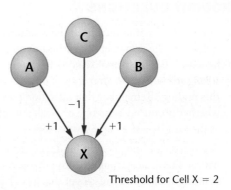

FIGURE 3.11 Wiring diagram for an "A and B if not C" response
The axons from A and B can combine to reach the threshold for X, but the axon from C can inhibit X enough to prevent a response. *(© Cengage Learning 2013)*

The Neuron as Decision Maker

Synapses are where the action is. Transmission along an axon merely sends information from one place to another. Synapses determine whether to send the message. The EPSPs and IPSPs reaching a neuron at a given moment compete with one another, and the net result is a complicated, not exactly algebraic summation of their effects. We could regard the summation of

EPSPs and IPSPs as a "decision" because it determines whether or not the postsynaptic cell fires an action potential. However, do not imagine that any single neuron decides what to eat for breakfast. Complex behaviors depend on the contributions from a huge network of neurons.

SUMMARY

1. The synapse is the point of communication between two neurons. Charles S. Sherrington's observations of reflexes enabled him to infer the properties of synapses. **52**

2. Because transmission through a reflex arc is slower than transmission through an equivalent length of axon, Sherrington concluded that some process at the synapses delays transmission. **53**

3. Graded potentials (EPSPs and IPSPs) summate their effects. The summation of graded potentials from stimuli at different times is temporal summation. The summation of graded potentials from different locations is spatial summation. **53**

4. Inhibition is more than just the absence of excitation; it is an active "brake" that suppresses excitation. Within the nervous system, inhibition is just as important as excitation. Stimulation at a synapse produces a brief graded potential in the postsynaptic cell. An excitatory graded potential (depolarizing) is an EPSP. An inhibitory graded potential (hyperpolarizing) is an IPSP. An EPSP occurs when gates open to allow sodium to enter the neuron's membrane. An IPSP occurs when gates open to allow potassium to leave or chloride to enter. **55**

5. The EPSPs on a neuron compete with the IPSPs; the balance between the two increases or decreases the neuron's frequency of action potentials. **56**

KEY TERMS

Terms are defined in the module on the page number indicated. They're also presented in alphabetical order with definitions in the book's Subject Index/Glossary, which begins on page 561. Interactive flashcards and crossword puzzles are among the online resources available to help you learn these terms and the concepts they represent.

excitatory postsynaptic potential (EPSP)   **53**
inhibitory postsynaptic potential (IPSP)   **55**
postsynaptic neuron   **53**
presynaptic neuron   **55**

reflex arc   **52**
reflexes   **52**
spatial summation   **53**
spontaneous firing rate   **57**

synapse   **52**
temporal summation   **53**

THOUGHT QUESTIONS

1. When Sherrington measured the reaction time of a reflex (i.e., the delay between stimulus and response), he found that the response occurred faster after a strong stimulus than after a weak one. Can you explain this finding? Remember that all action potentials—whether produced by strong or weak stimuli—travel at the same speed along a given axon.

2. A pinch on an animal's right hind foot excites a sensory neuron that excites an interneuron that excites the motor neurons to the flexor muscles of that leg. The interneuron also inhibits the motor neurons connected to the extensor muscles of the leg. In addition, this interneuron sends impulses that reach the motor neuron connected to the extensor muscles of the left hind leg. Would you expect the interneuron to excite or inhibit that motor neuron? (Hint: The connections are adaptive. When an animal lifts one leg, it must put additional weight on the other legs to maintain balance.)

3. Suppose neuron X has a synapse onto neuron Y, which has a synapse onto Z. Presume that no other neurons or synapses are present. An experimenter finds that stimulating neuron X causes an action potential in neuron Z after a short delay. However, she determines that the synapse of X onto Y is inhibitory. Explain how the stimulation of X might produce excitation of Z.

4. Figure 3.11 shows synaptic connections to produce a cell that responds to "A and B if not C." Construct a wiring diagram so that a cell responds to "A or B if not C." This is much trickier than it sounds. If you simply shift the threshold of cell X to 1, it will respond to "A if not C, or B if not C, or A and B even if C." Can you get X to respond to either A or B, but only if C is inactive? (Hint: You might need to introduce one or two additional cells on the way to X.)

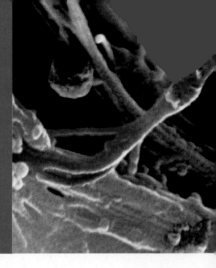

Chemical Events at the Synapse

Although Charles Sherrington accurately inferred many properties of the synapse, he was wrong about one important point: Although he knew that synaptic transmission was slower than transmission along an axon, he thought it was still too fast to depend on a chemical process and therefore concluded that it must be electrical. We now know that the great majority of synapses rely on chemical processes, which are much faster and more versatile than Sherrington or anyone else of his era would have guessed. Over the years, our concept of activity at synapses has grown in many ways.

The Discovery of Chemical Transmission at Synapses

A set of nerves called the sympathetic nervous system accelerates the heartbeat, relaxes the stomach muscles, dilates the pupils of the eyes, and regulates other organs. T. R. Elliott, a young British scientist, reported in 1905 that applying the hormone *adrenaline* directly to the surface of the heart, the stomach, and the pupils produces the same effects as those of the sympathetic nervous system. Elliott therefore suggested that the sympathetic nerves stimulate muscles by releasing adrenaline or a similar chemical.

However, Elliott's evidence was not convincing. Perhaps adrenaline merely mimicked effects that are ordinarily electrical in nature. At the time, Sherrington's prestige was so great that most scientists ignored Elliott's results and continued to assume that synapses transmitted electrical impulses. Otto Loewi, a German physiologist, liked the idea of chemical synapses but did not see how to demonstrate it more decisively. Then in 1920, he awakened one night with an idea. He wrote himself a note and went back to sleep. Unfortunately, the next morning he could not read his note. The following night he awoke at 3 A.M. with the same idea, rushed to the laboratory, and performed the experiment.

Loewi repeatedly stimulated a frog's vagus nerve, thereby decreasing the heart rate. He then collected fluid from that heart, transferred it to a second frog's heart, and found that the second heart also decreased its rate of beating, as shown in Figure 3.12. Then Loewi stimulated the accelerator nerve to the first frog's heart, increasing the heart rate. When he collected fluid from that heart and transferred it to the second frog's heart, its heart rate increased. That is, stimulating one nerve released something that

inhibited heart rate, and stimulating a different nerve released something that increased heart rate. He knew he was collecting and transferring chemicals, not loose electricity. Therefore, Loewi concluded, nerves send messages by releasing chemicals.

Loewi later remarked that if he had thought of this experiment in the light of day, he probably would not have tried it (Loewi, 1960). Even if synapses did release chemicals, his daytime reasoning went, they probably did not release much. Fortunately, by the time he realized that the experiment should not work, he had already completed it, and it did work. It earned him a Nobel Prize.

Despite Loewi's work, most researchers over the next three decades continued to believe that most synapses were electrical and that chemical synapses were the exception. Finally, in the 1950s, researchers established that chemical transmission predominates throughout the nervous system. That discovery revolutionized our understanding and led to research developing drugs for psychiatric uses (Carlsson, 2001). (A small number of electrical synapses do exist, however, as discussed at the end of this module.)

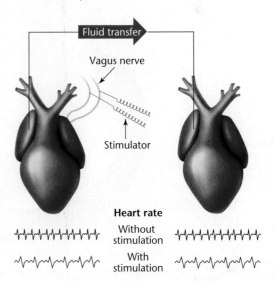

FIGURE 3.12 Loewi's experiment demonstrating that nerves send messages by releasing chemicals
Loewi stimulated the vagus nerve to one frog's heart, decreasing the heartbeat. When he transferred fluid from that heart to another frog's heart, he observed a decrease in its heartbeat. Why does he insist on doing this to me. (© Cengage Learning 2013)

Stop & Check

6. What was Loewi's evidence that neurotransmission depends on the release of chemicals?

ANSWER

6. When Loewi stimulated a nerve that increased or decreased a frog's heart rate, he could withdraw some fluid from the area around the heart, transfer it to another frog's heart, and thereby increase or decrease its rate also.

The Sequence of Chemical Events at a Synapse

Understanding the chemical events at a synapse is fundamental to understanding the nervous system. Every year, researchers discover more and more details about synapses, their structure, and how those structures relate to function. Here are the major events:

1. The neuron synthesizes chemicals that serve as neurotransmitters. It synthesizes the smaller neurotransmitters in the axon terminals and synthesizes neuropeptides in the cell body.

2. Action potentials travel down the axon. At the presynaptic terminal, an action potential enables calcium to enter the cell. Calcium releases neurotransmitters from the terminals and into the *synaptic cleft*, the space between the presynaptic and postsynaptic neurons.

3. The released molecules diffuse across the cleft, attach to receptors, and alter the activity of the postsynaptic neuron.

4. The neurotransmitter molecules separate from their receptors.

5. The neurotransmitter molecules may be taken back into the presynaptic neuron for recycling or they may diffuse away.

6. Some postsynaptic cells send reverse messages to control the further release of neurotransmitter by presynaptic cells.

Figure 3.13 summarizes these steps. Let's now consider each step in more detail.

Types of Neurotransmitters

At a synapse, a neuron releases chemicals that affect another neuron. Those chemicals are known as **neurotransmitters**. A hundred or so chemicals are believed or suspected to be neurotransmitters, as shown in Table 3.1 (Borodinsky et al., 2004). Here are the major categories:

amino acids acids containing an amine group (NH_2)

monoamines chemicals formed by a change in certain amino acids

acetylcholine (a one-member "family") a chemical similar to an amino acid, except that it includes an $N(CH_3)_3$ group instead of an NH_2

neuropeptides chains of amino acids

purines a category of chemicals including adenosine and several of its derivatives

gases nitric oxide and possibly others

The oddest transmitter is **nitric oxide** (chemical formula NO), a gas released by many small local neurons. (Do not confuse nitric oxide, NO, with nitrous oxide, N_2O, sometimes known as "laughing gas.") Nitric oxide is poisonous in large quantities and difficult to make in a laboratory. Yet, many neurons contain an enzyme that enables them to make it efficiently. One special function of nitric oxide relates to blood flow: When a brain area becomes highly active, blood flow to that area increases. How does the blood "know" which brain area has become more active? The message comes from nitric oxide. Many

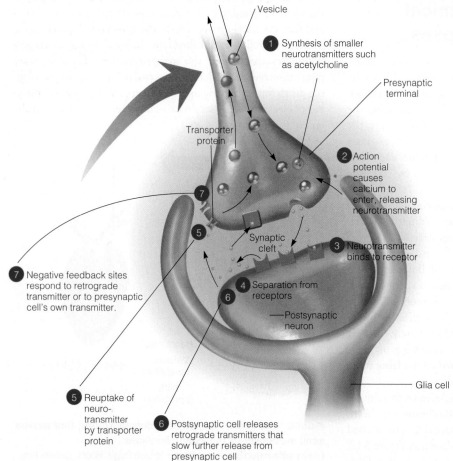

Vesicle

1 Synthesis of smaller neurotransmitters such as acetylcholine

Presynaptic terminal

Transporter protein

2 Action potential causes calcium to enter, releasing neurotransmitter

7

5

Synaptic cleft

3 Neurotransmitter binds to receptor

4 Separation from receptors

6

Postsynaptic neuron

7 Negative feedback sites respond to retrograde transmitter or to presynaptic cell's own transmitter.

Glia cell

5 Reuptake of neuro-transmitter by transporter protein

6 Postsynaptic cell releases retrograde transmitters that slow further release from presynaptic cell

FIGURE 3.13 Some major events in transmission at a synapse (© Argosy Publishing Inc.)

TABLE 3.1	Neurotransmitters
Amino Acids	glutamate, GABA, glycine, aspartate, maybe others
A Modified Amino Acid	acetylcholine
Monoamines (also modified from amino acids)	indoleamines: serotonin catecholamines: dopamine, norepinephrine, epinephrine
Neuropeptides (chains of amino acids)	endorphins, substance P, neuropeptide Y, many others
Purines	ATP, adenosine, maybe others
Gases	NO (nitric oxide), maybe others

© Cengage Learning 2013

neurons release nitric oxide when they are stimulated. In addition to influencing other neurons, nitric oxide dilates the nearby blood vessels, thereby increasing blood flow to that brain area (Dawson, Gonzalez-Zulueta, Kusel, & Dawson, 1998).

Stop & Check

7. What does a highly active brain area do to increase its blood supply?

ANSWER

7. In a highly active brain area, many stimulated neurons release nitric oxide, which dilates the blood vessels in the area and thereby increases blood flow to the area.

Synthesis of Transmitters

Neurons synthesize nearly all neurotransmitters from amino acids, which the body obtains from proteins in the diet. Figure

3.14 illustrates the chemical steps in the synthesis of acetylcholine, serotonin, dopamine, epinephrine, and norepinephrine. Note the relationship among epinephrine, norepinephrine, and dopamine—compounds known as **catecholamines**, because they contain a catechol group and an amine group, as shown here:

© Cengage Learning 2013

Each pathway in Figure 3.14 begins with substances found in the diet. Acetylcholine, for example, is synthesized from choline, which is abundant in milk, eggs, and peanuts. The amino acids phenylalanine and tyrosine, present in proteins, are precursors of dopamine, norepinephrine, and epinephrine. Remember from Chapter 2 that people with phenylketonuria lack the enzyme that converts phenylalanine to tyrosine. They can get tyrosine from their diet, but they need to minimize intake of phenylalanine.

The amino acid *tryptophan*, the precursor to serotonin, crosses the blood–brain barrier by a special transport system that it shares with other large amino acids. The amount of tryptophan in the diet controls the amount of serotonin in the brain (Fadda, 2000), so your serotonin levels rise after you eat foods

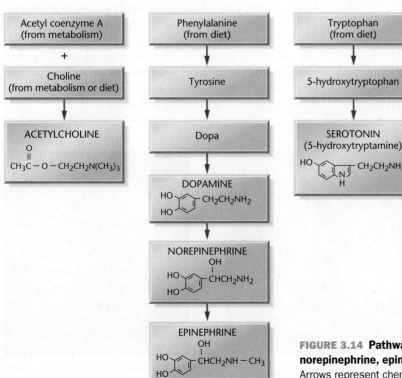

FIGURE 3.14 Pathways in the synthesis of acetylcholine, dopamine, norepinephrine, epinephrine, and serotonin
Arrows represent chemical reactions. (© *Cengage Learning 2013*)

richer in tryptophan, such as soy, and fall after something low in tryptophan, such as maize (American corn). However, tryptophan has to compete with other, more abundant large amino acids, such as phenylalanine, that share the same transport system. One way to increase tryptophan entry to the brain is to decrease consumption of phenylalanine. Another is to eat carbohydrates. Carbohydrates increase the release of the hormone *insulin*, which takes several competing amino acids out of the bloodstream and into body cells, thus decreasing the competition against tryptophan (Wurtman, 1985).

Stop & Check

8. Name the three catecholamine neurotransmitters.

ANSWER   **8.** Epinephrine, norepinephrine, and dopamine

Storage of Transmitters

Most neurotransmitters are synthesized in the presynaptic terminal, near the point of release. The presynaptic terminal stores high concentrations of neurotransmitter molecules in **vesicles**, tiny nearly spherical packets (Figure 3.15). (Nitric oxide is an exception to this rule. Neurons release nitric oxide as soon as they form it instead of storing it.) The presynaptic terminal also maintains many neurotransmitter molecules outside the vesicles.

It is possible for a neuron to accumulate excess levels of a neurotransmitter. Neurons that release serotonin, dopamine, or norepinephrine contain an enzyme, **MAO (monoamine oxidase)**, that breaks down these transmitters into inactive chemicals. We shall return to MAO in the discussion on depression, because several antidepressant drugs inhibit MAO.

Release and Diffusion of Transmitters

At the end of an axon, the action potential itself does not release the neurotransmitter. Rather, the depolarization opens voltage-dependent calcium gates in the presynaptic terminal. Within 1 or 2 milliseconds (ms) after calcium enters the presynaptic terminal, it causes **exocytosis**—release of neurotransmitter in bursts from the presynaptic neuron into the synaptic cleft that separates one neuron from another. An action potential often fails to release any transmitter, and even when it does, the amount varies (Craig & Boudin, 2001).

After its release from the presynaptic cell, the neurotransmitter diffuses across the synaptic cleft to the postsynaptic membrane, where it attaches to a receptor. The neurotransmitter takes no more than 0.01 ms to diffuse across the cleft, which is only 20 to 30 nanometers (nm) wide. Remember, Sherrington did not believe chemical processes could be fast enough to account for the activity at synapses. He did not imagine such a narrow gap through which chemicals could diffuse so quickly.

Although the brain as a whole uses many neurotransmitters, no single neuron releases them all. For many years, investigators believed that each neuron released just one neurotransmitter, but later researchers found that many, perhaps most, neurons release a combination of two or more transmitters (Hökfelt, Johansson, & Goldstein, 1984). Still later researchers found that at least one kind of neuron releases different transmitters from different branches of its axon: Motor neurons in the spinal cord have one branch to the muscles, where they release acetylcholine, and another branch to other spinal cord neurons, where they release both acetylcholine and glutamate (Nishimaru, Restrepo, Ryge, Yanagawa, & Kiehn, 2005). If one kind of neuron can release different transmitters at different branches, maybe others can, too.

Why does a neuron release a combination of transmitters instead of just one? The combination makes the neuron's message more complex, such as brief excitation followed by slight but prolonged inhibition (P. Jonas, Bischofberger, & Sandkühler, 1998).

Although a neuron releases only a limited number of neurotransmitters, it may receive and respond to many neurotransmitters at different synapses. For example, at various locations on its membrane, it might have receptors for glutamate, serotonin, acetylcholine, and others.

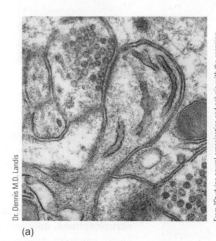
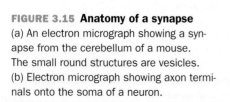
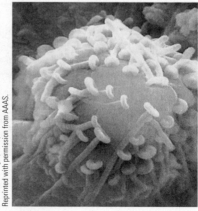

FIGURE 3.15 Anatomy of a synapse
(a) An electron micrograph showing a synapse from the cerebellum of a mouse. The small round structures are vesicles.
(b) Electron micrograph showing axon terminals onto the soma of a neuron.

Dr. Dennis M.D. Landis

From "Studying neural organization and aplysia with the scanning electron micrograph", by E.R. Lewis, et al., Science 1969, 165:1142. Reprinted with permission from AAAS.

(a)   (b)

9. When the action potential reaches the presynaptic terminal, which ion must enter the presynaptic terminal to evoke release of the neurotransmitter?

ANSWER

9. Calcium

Activating Receptors of the Postsynaptic Cell

Sherrington's concept of the synapse was simple: Input produced excitation or inhibition—in other words, on/off. When Eccles recorded from individual cells, he happened to choose cells that produced only brief EPSPs and IPSPs—again, just on/off. The discovery of chemical transmission at synapses didn't change that, at first. Researchers discovered more and more neurotransmitters and wondered, "Why does the nervous system use so many chemicals, if they all produce the same type of message?" Eventually they found that the messages are more complicated and more varied.

The effect of a neurotransmitter depends on its receptor on the postsynaptic cell. When the neurotransmitter attaches to its receptor, the receptor may open a channel—exerting an *ionotropic* effect—or it may produce a slower but longer effect—a *metabotropic* effect.

Ionotropic Effects

At one type of receptor, neurotransmitters exert **ionotropic** effects, corresponding to the brief on/off effects that Sherrington and Eccles studied. Imagine a paper bag that is twisted shut at the top. If you untwist it, the opening grows larger so that something can go into or come out of the bag. An ionotropic receptor is like that. When the neurotransmitter binds to an ionotropic receptor, it twists the receptor enough to open its central channel, which is shaped to let a particular type of ion pass through. In contrast to the sodium and potassium channels along an axon, which are voltage-gated, the channels controlled by a neurotransmitter are **transmitter-gated** or **ligand-gated channels**. (A *ligand* is a chemical that binds to another chemical.) That is, when the neurotransmitter attaches, it opens a channel.

Ionotropic effects begin quickly, sometimes within less than a millisecond after the transmitter attaches (Lisman, Raghavachari, & Tsien, 2007). The effects decay with a half-life of about 5 ms. They are well suited to conveying visual information, auditory information, and anything else that needs to be updated as quickly as possible.

Most of the brain's excitatory ionotropic synapses use the neurotransmitter *glutamate*. In fact, glutamate is the most abundant neurotransmitter

in the nervous system. Most of the inhibitory ionotropic synapses use the neurotransmitter GABA (gamma-amino-butyric acid), which opens chloride gates, enabling chloride ions, with their negative charge, to cross the membrane into the cell more rapidly than usual. Glycine is another common inhibitory transmitter, found mostly in the spinal cord (Moss & Smart, 2001). Acetylcholine, another transmitter at many ionotropic synapses, is excitatory in most cases. Figure 3.16a shows an acetylcholine receptor (hugely magnified, of course), as it would appear if you were looking down at it from within the synaptic cleft. Its outer portion (red) is embedded in the neuron's membrane; its inner portion (purple) surrounds the sodium channel. When the receptor is at rest, the inner portion coils together tightly enough to block sodium passage. When acetylcholine attaches as in Figure 3.16b, the receptor folds outward, widening the sodium channel (Miyazawa, Fujiyoshi, & Unwin, 2003).

Metabotropic Effects and Second Messenger Systems

At other receptors, neurotransmitters exert **metabotropic** effects by initiating a sequence of metabolic reactions that are slower and longer lasting than ionotropic effects (Greengard, 2001). Metabotropic effects emerge 30 ms or more after the release of the transmitter (North, 1989). Typically, they last

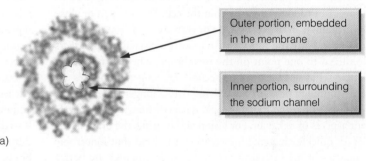

Outer portion, embedded in the membrane

Inner portion, surrounding the sodium channel

(a)

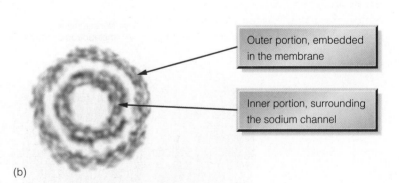

Outer portion, embedded in the membrane

Inner portion, surrounding the sodium channel

(b)

FIGURE 3.16 The acetylcholine receptor
(a) A cross-section of the receptor at rest, as viewed from the synaptic cleft. The membrane surrounds it. (b) A similar view after acetylcholine has attached to the side of the receptor, opening the central channel wide enough for sodium to pass through. *(Source: From A. Miyazawa, Y. Fujiyoshi, and N. Unwin. "Structure and gating mechanism of the acetylcholine receptor pore," Nature, 423, pp. 949–955)* *(© Argosy Publishing Inc.)*

up to a few seconds, but sometimes longer. Whereas most ionotropic effects depend on either glutamate or GABA, metabotropic synapses use many neurotransmitters, including dopamine, norepinephrine, and serotonin. . . and sometimes glutamate and GABA too.

Apologies if you find this analogy silly, but it might help clarify metabotropic synapses: Imagine a large room. You are outside the room holding a stick that goes through a hole in the wall and attaches to the hinge of a cage. If you shake the stick, you open that cage and release an angry dog. The dog runs around waking up all the rabbits in the room, which then scurry around causing all kinds of further action. A metabotropic receptor acts a little like that. When a neurotransmitter attaches to a metabotropic receptor, it bends the receptor protein that goes through the membrane of the cell. The other side of that receptor is attached to a **G protein**—that is, a protein coupled to guanosine triphosphate (GTP), an energy-storing molecule. Bending the receptor protein detaches that G protein, which is then free to take its energy elsewhere in the cell, as shown in Figure 3.17 (Levitzki, 1988; O'Dowd, Lefkowitz, & Caron, 1989). The result of that G protein is increased concentration of a second messenger, such as cyclic adenosine monophosphate (cyclic AMP), inside the cell. Just as the "first messenger" (the neurotransmitter) carries information to the postsynaptic cell, the **second messenger** communicates to many areas within the cell. It may open or close ion channels in the membrane or activate a portion of a chromosome. Note the contrast: An ionotropic synapse has effects localized to one point on the membrane, whereas a metabotropic synapse, by way of its second messenger, influences activity in much or all of the cell and over a longer time.

Ionotropic and metabotropic synapses contribute to different aspects of behavior. For vision and hearing, the brain needs rapid, quickly changing information, the kind that ionotropic synapses bring. In contrast, metabotropic synapses are better suited for more enduring effects such as taste (Huang et al.,

2005), smell, and pain (Levine, Fields, & Basbaum, 1993), where the exact timing isn't important anyway. Metabotropic synapses are also important for many aspects of arousal, attention, pleasure, and emotion—again, functions that arise more slowly and last longer than a visual or auditory stimulus.

The brain has a great variety of metabotropic receptors. Even for just serotonin, the brain has at least seven families of receptors, and some of those families include several kinds of receptors. Receptors differ in their chemical properties, responses to drugs, and roles in behavior. Because of this variation in properties, it is possible to devise drugs with specialized effects on behavior. For example, the serotonin receptor type 3 mediates nausea, and the drug *ondansetron* that blocks this receptor helps cancer patients undergo treatment without nausea.

Neuropeptides

Researchers often refer to neuropeptides as **neuromodulators,** because they have several properties that set them apart from other transmitters (Ludwig & Leng, 2006). Whereas the neuron synthesizes most other neurotransmitters in the presynaptic terminal, it synthesizes neuropeptides in the cell body and then slowly transports them to other parts of the cell. Whereas other neurotransmitters are released at the axon terminal, neuropeptides are released mainly by dendrites, and also by the cell body and the sides of the axon. Whereas a single action potential can release other neurotransmitters, neuropeptide release requires repeated stimulation. However, after a few dendrites release a neuropeptide, the released chemical primes other nearby dendrites to release the same neuropeptide also, including dendrites of other cells. That is, neurons containing neuropeptides do not release them often, but when they do, they release substantial amounts. Furthermore, unlike other transmitters that are released immediately adjacent to their receptors, neuropeptides diffuse widely, affecting many neurons in their region of the brain. In that way they resemble hormones. Because many of them exert their effects by altering gene activity, their effects are

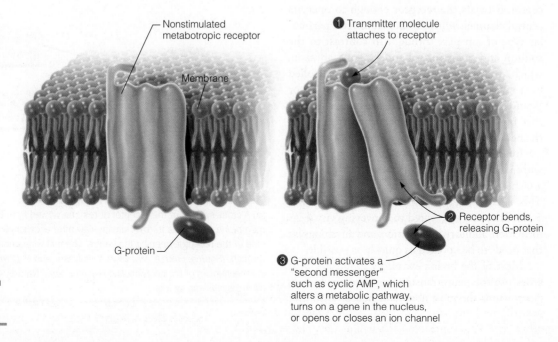

FIGURE 3.17
Sequence of events at a metabotropic synapse, using a second messenger within the postsynaptic neuron
(© Argosy Publishing Inc.)

Nonstimulated metabotropic receptor

Membrane

G-protein

❶ Transmitter molecule attaches to receptor

❷ Receptor bends, releasing G-protein

❸ G-protein activates a "second messenger" such as cyclic AMP, which alters a metabolic pathway, turns on a gene in the nucleus, or opens or closes an ion channel

TABLE 3.2	Distinctive Features of Neuropeptides	
	Neuropeptides	**Other Neurotransmitters**
Place synthesized	Cell body	Presynaptic terminal
Place released	Mostly from dendrites, also cell body and sides of axon	Axon terminal
Released by	Repeated depolarization	Single action potential
Effect on neighboring cells	They release the neuropeptide too	No effect on neighbors
Spread of effects	Diffuse to wide area	Effect mostly on receptors of the adjacent postsynaptic cell
Duration of effects	Many minutes	Generally less than a second to a few seconds

© Cengage Learning 2013

long-lasting, in the range of 20 minutes or more. Neuropeptides are important for hunger, thirst, intense pain, and other long-term changes in behavior and experience. Table 3.2 summarizes differences between other neurotransmitters and neuropeptides.

For almost any rule about the nervous system, one can find exceptions. One general rule is that a neuron delivers neuropeptides that diffuse to receptors throughout a wide area, but it delivers other transmitters only in small amounts directly adjacent to their receptors. Here is an exception: **A neurogliaform cell**—a kind of neuron that is shaped more like a glia cell—releases huge amounts of GABA all at once, forming a "cloud" that spreads to a large number of neurons in the area, producing widespread inhibition (Oláh et al., 2009).

| Stop & Check |

10. How do ionotropic and metabotropic synapses differ in speed and duration of effects?

11. What are second messengers, and which type of synapse relies on them?

12. How are neuropeptides special compared to other transmitters?

ANSWERS **10.** Ionotropic synapses act more quickly and more briefly. **11.** At metabotropic synapses, the neurotransmitter attaches to its receptor and thereby releases a chemical (the second messenger) within the postsynaptic cell, which alters metabolism or gene expression of the postsynaptic cell. **12.** Neuropeptides are released only after prolonged stimulation, but when they are released, they are released in large amounts by all parts of the neuron, not just the axon terminal. Neuropeptides diffuse widely, producing long-lasting effects on many neurons.

Hormones

A **hormone** is a chemical that is secreted by cells in one part of the body and conveyed by the blood to influence other cells. A neurotransmitter is like a telephone signal: It

conveys a message from the sender to the intended receiver. Hormones function more like a radio station: They convey a message to any receiver tuned in to the right station. Neuropeptides are intermediate. They are like hormones, except that they diffuse only within the brain, and the blood doesn't carry them to other parts of the body. Figure 3.18 presents the major **endocrine** (hormone-producing) **glands**. Table 3.3 lists some important hormones and their principal effects.

Hormones are particularly useful for coordinating long-lasting changes in multiple parts of the body. For example, birds that are preparing for migration secrete hormones that change their eating and digestion to store extra energy for a long journey. Among the various types of hormones are **protein hormones** and **peptide hormones**, composed of chains of amino acids. (Proteins are longer chains and peptides are shorter.) Protein and peptide hormones attach to membrane receptors, where they activate a second messenger within the cell—exactly like a metabotropic synapse. In fact, many chemicals serve as both neurotransmitters and hormones.

Just as circulating hormones modify brain activity, hormones secreted by the brain control the secretion of many other hormones. The **pituitary gland**, attached to the hypo-

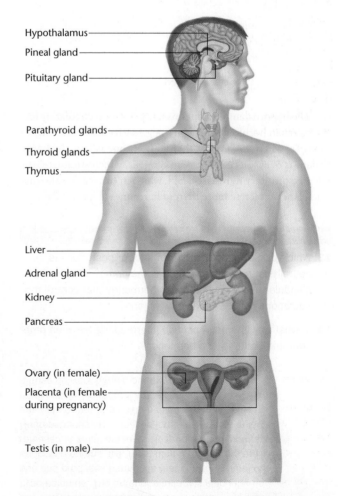

Hypothalamus
Pineal gland
Pituitary gland
Parathyroid glands
Thyroid glands
Thymus
Liver
Adrenal gland
Kidney
Pancreas
Ovary (in female)
Placenta (in female during pregnancy)
Testis (in male)

FIGURE 3.18 Location of some major endocrine glands (Source: Starr & Taggart, 1989)

thalamus (Figure 3.19), consists of two distinct glands, the **anterior pituitary** and the **posterior pituitary**, which release different sets of hormones (Table 3.3). The posterior pituitary, composed of neural tissue, can be considered an extension of the hypothalamus. Neurons in the hypothalamus synthesize the hormones **oxytocin** and **vasopressin** (also known as antidiuretic hormone), which migrate down axons to the posterior pituitary, as shown in Figure 3.20. Later, the posterior pituitary releases these hormones into the blood.

The anterior pituitary, composed of glandular tissue, synthesizes six hormones, although the hypothalamus controls their release (Figure 3.20). The hypothalamus secretes **releasing hormones,** which flow through the blood to the anterior pituitary. There they stimulate or inhibit the release of the following hormones:

Adrenocorticotropic hormone (ACTH)	Controls secretions of the adrenal cortex
Thyroid-stimulating hormone (TSH)	Controls secretions of the thyroid gland
Prolactin	Controls secretions of the mammary glands
Somatotropin, also known as growth hormone (GH)	Promotes growth throughout the body
Gonadotropins Follicle-stimulating hormone (FSH) Luteinizing hormone (LH)	Control secretions of the gonads

The hypothalamus maintains fairly constant circulating levels of certain hormones through a negative feedback system. For example, when the level of thyroid hormone is low, the hypothalamus releases *TSH-releasing hormone*, which stimulates the anterior pituitary to release TSH, which in turn causes the thyroid gland to secrete more thyroid hormones (Figure 3.21).

Stop & Check

13. Which part of the pituitary—anterior or posterior—is neural tissue, similar to the hypothalamus? Which part is glandular tissue and produces hormones that control the secretions by other endocrine organs?

14. In what way is a neuropeptide intermediate between other neurotransmitters and hormones?

ANSWERS

13. The posterior pituitary is neural tissue, like the hypothalamus. The anterior pituitary is glandular tissue and produces hormones that control several other endocrine organs. 14. Most neurotransmitters are released in small amounts close to their receptors. Neuropeptides are released into a brain area in larger amounts or not at all. When released, they diffuse more widely. Hormones are released into the blood for diffuse delivery throughout the body.

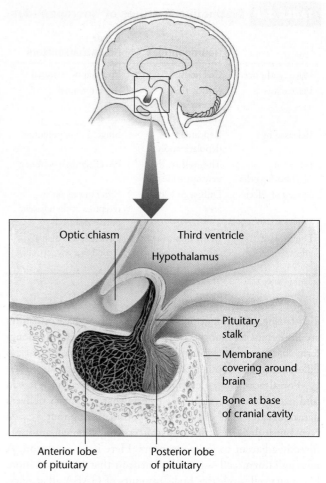

FIGURE 3.19 Location of the hypothalamus and pituitary gland in the human brain *(Source: Starr & Taggart, 1989)*

Optic chiasm
Third ventricle
Hypothalamus
Pituitary stalk
Membrane covering around brain
Bone at base of cranial cavity
Anterior lobe of pituitary
Posterior lobe of pituitary

Inactivation and Reuptake of Neurotransmitters

A neurotransmitter does not linger at the postsynaptic membrane. If it did, it might continue exciting or inhibiting the receptor. Various neurotransmitters are inactivated in different ways.

After acetylcholine activates a receptor, it is broken down by the enzyme **acetylcholinesterase** (a-SEE-til-ko-lih-NES-teh-raze) into two fragments: acetate and choline. The choline diffuses back to the presynaptic neuron, which takes it up and reconnects it with acetate already in the cell to form acetylcholine again. Although this recycling process is highly efficient, it takes time, and the presynaptic neuron does not reabsorb every molecule it releases. A sufficiently rapid series of action potentials at any synapse can deplete the neurotransmitter faster than the presynaptic cell replenishes it, thus slowing or interrupting transmission (G. Liu & Tsien, 1995).

Serotonin and the catecholamines (dopamine, norepinephrine, and epinephrine) do not break down into inactive fragments at the postsynaptic membrane. They simply detach from the receptor. At that point, the next step varies. In

TABLE 3.3	Partial List of Hormone-Releasing Glands	
Organ	**Hormone**	**Hormone Functions**
Hypothalamus	Various releasing hormones	Promote or inhibit release of various hormones by pituitary
Anterior pituitary	Thyroid-stimulating hormone (TSH)	Stimulates thyroid gland
	Luteinizing hormone (LH)	Increases production of progesterone (female), testosterone (male); stimulates ovulation
	Follicle-stimulating hormone (FSH)	Increases production of estrogen and maturation of ovum (female) and sperm production (male)
	ACTH	Increases secretion of steroid hormones by adrenal gland
	Prolactin	Increases milk production
	Growth hormone (GH), also known as somatotropin	Increases body growth, including the growth spurt during puberty
Posterior pituitary	Oxytocin	Controls uterine contractions, milk release, certain aspects of parental behavior, and sexual pleasure
	Vasopressin (also known as antidiuretic hormone)	Constricts blood vessels and raises blood pressure, decreases urine volume
Pineal	Melatonin	Increases sleepiness, influences sleep–wake cycle, also has a role in onset of puberty
Thyroid	Thyroxine } Triiodothyronine }	Increases metabolic rate, growth, and maturation
Parathyroid	Parathyroid hormone	Increases blood calcium and decreases potassium
Adrenal cortex	Aldosterone	Reduces secretion of salts by the kidneys
	Cortisol, corticosterone	Stimulates liver to elevate blood sugar, increase metabolism of proteins and fats
Adrenal medulla	Epinephrine, norepinephrine	Similar to effects of sympathetic nervous system
Pancreas	Insulin	Increases entry of glucose to cells and increases storage as fats
	Glucagon	Increases conversion of stored fats to blood glucose
Ovary	Estrogens	Promote female sexual characteristics
	Progesterone	Maintains pregnancy
Testis	Androgens	Promote sperm production, growth of pubic hair, and male sexual characteristics
Liver	Somatomedins	Stimulate growth
Kidney	Renin	Converts a blood protein into angiotensin, which regulates blood pressure and contributes to hypovolemic thirst
Thymus	Thymosin (and others)	Support immune responses
Fat cells	Leptin	Decreases appetite, increases activity, necessary for onset of puberty

certain brain areas, the presynaptic neuron takes up most of the released neurotransmitter molecules intact and reuses them. This process, called **reuptake**, occurs through special membrane proteins called **transporters**. Individuals vary in the activity of certain transporters. Genetic variations in serotonin transporters relate to individual differences in anxiety (Murphy et al., 2008). Transporters also differ in their abundance from one brain area to another. Dopamine transporters in the caudate nucleus are highly efficient, and reuptake accounts for nearly all of the released dopamine. In other brain areas, fewer transporters are present, and reup-

take is slower. If dopamine is released rapidly in those areas, it accumulates and an enzyme called **COMT** (catechol-o-methyltransferase) breaks down the excess into inactive chemicals that cannot stimulate the dopamine receptors. Those breakdown products wash away and eventually show up in the blood and urine. In the prefrontal cortex, COMT breaks down about half of the released dopamine (Yavich, Forsberg, Karayiorgou, Gogos, & Männistö, 2007). A consequence is that neurons in that area easily diminish their supply of dopamine, and they cannot release dopamine rapidly for long.

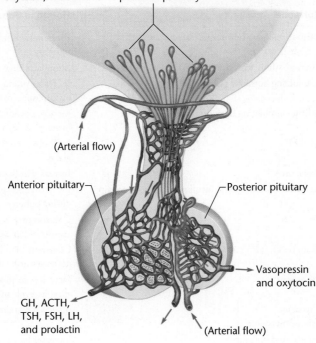

Hypothalamus secretes releasing hormones and inhibiting hormones that control anterior pituitary. Also synthesizes vasopressin and oxytocin, which travel to posterior pituitary.

(Arterial flow)

Anterior pituitary

Posterior pituitary

Vasopressin and oxytocin

GH, ACTH, TSH, FSH, LH, and prolactin

(Arterial flow)

FIGURE 3.20 Pituitary hormones
The hypothalamus produces vasopressin and oxytocin, which travel to the posterior pituitary (really an extension of the hypothalamus). The posterior pituitary releases those hormones in response to neural signals. The hypothalamus also produces releasing hormones and inhibiting hormones, which travel to the anterior pituitary, where they control the release of six hormones synthesized there. *(© Cengage Learning 2013)*

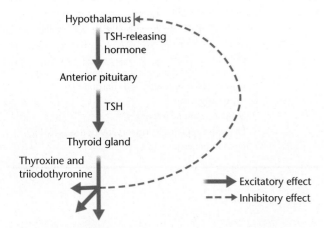

Hypothalamus

TSH-releasing hormone

Anterior pituitary

TSH

Thyroid gland

Thyroxine and triiodothyronine

→ Excitatory effect
- - → Inhibitory effect

FIGURE 3.21 Negative feedback in the control of thyroid hormones
The hypothalamus secretes a releasing hormone that stimulates the anterior pituitary to release TSH, which stimulates the thyroid gland to release its hormones. Those hormones in turn act on the hypothalamus to decrease its secretion of the releasing hormone. *(© Cengage Learning 2013)*

The neuropeptides are neither inactivated nor reabsorbed. They simply diffuse away. Because these large molecules are resynthesized slowly, a neuron can temporarily exhaust its supply.

Stop & Check

15. What happens to acetylcholine molecules after they stimulate a postsynaptic receptor?

16. What happens to serotonin and catecholamine molecules after they stimulate a postsynaptic receptor?

ANSWERS

15. The enzyme acetylcholinesterase breaks acetylcholine molecules into two smaller molecules, acetate and choline, which are then reabsorbed by the presynaptic terminal. **16.** Most serotonin and catecholamine molecules are reabsorbed by the presynaptic terminal. Some of their molecules are broken down into inactive chemicals, which then diffuse away.

Negative Feedback from the Postsynaptic Cell

Suppose someone often sends you an e-mail message and then, worried that you might not have received it, sends it again and again. To prevent cluttering your inbox, you might add a system that provides an automatic answer, "Yes, I got your message. Don't send it again."

A couple of mechanisms in the nervous system serve that function. First, many presynaptic terminals have receptors sensitive to the same transmitter they release. These receptors are known as **autoreceptors**—receptors that respond to the released transmitter by inhibiting further synthesis and release. That is, they provide negative feedback (Kubista & Boehm, 2006).

Second, some postsynaptic neurons respond to stimulation by releasing special chemicals that travel back to the presynaptic terminal, where they inhibit further release of the transmitter. Nitric oxide is one such transmitter. Two others are *anandamide* and *2-AG* (*sn*-2 arachidonylglycerol). We shall discuss them further in the next module, as we consider drug mechanisms. Here, the point is that postsynaptic neurons have ways to control or limit their own input.

Electrical Synapses

At the start of this module, you learned that Sherrington was wrong to assume that synapses convey messages electrically. Well, he wasn't completely wrong. A few special-purpose synapses operate electrically. Electrical transmission is faster than even the fastest chemical transmission, and electrical synapses have evolved in cases where exact synchrony between two cells is important. For example, some of the cells that control your rhythmic breathing are synchronized by electrical synapses. (It's important to inhale on the left side at the same time as on the right side.)

At an electrical synapse, the membrane of one neuron comes into direct contact with the membrane of another, as shown in Figure 3.22. This contact is called a **gap junction**. Fairly large pores of the membrane of one neuron line up pre-

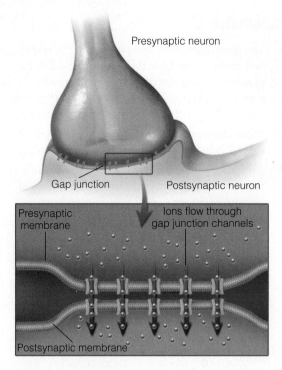

FIGURE 3.22 A gap junction for an electrical synapse
(© Argosy Publishing Inc.)

cisely with similar pores in the membrane of the other cell. These pores are large enough for sodium and other ions to pass readily, and unlike the other membrane channels we have considered, these pores remain open constantly. Therefore, whenever one of the neurons is depolarized, sodium ions from that cell can pass quickly into the other neuron and depolarize it, too. As a result, the two neurons act almost as if they were in fact a single neuron. A major point to note here is that the nervous system has a great variety of types of synapses, serving a similar variety of functions.

MODULE 3.2 ■ IN CLOSING

Neurotransmitters and Behavior

Synapses are the building blocks of behavior. They determine which messages get transmitted, and where, and for how long. One of the guiding assumptions of biological psychology is that much of the difference in behavior between one person and another relates to activity at the synapses. For example, people with greater amounts of dopamine release tend to be more impulsive and more inclined to seek immediate pleasure (Buckholtz et al., 2010). The drugs that help control Parkinson's disease, anxiety, schizophrenia, and other disorders act at synapses, suggesting that these disorders reflect excesses or deficits of certain transmitters. Perhaps even normal personality differences also depend on variations in synapses. From quantitative variations in synapses come many rich variations in behavior.

SUMMARY

1. The great majority of synapses operate by transmitting a neurotransmitter from the presynaptic cell to the postsynaptic cell. Otto Loewi demonstrated this point by stimulating a frog's heart electrically and then transferring fluids from that heart to another frog's heart.   **59**

2. Many chemicals are used as neurotransmitters. Most are amino acids or chemicals derived from amino acids.   **60**

3. An action potential opens calcium channels in the axon terminal, and the calcium enables release of neurotransmitters.   **62**

4. At ionotropic synapses, a neurotransmitter attaches to a receptor that opens the gates to allow a particular ion, such as sodium, to cross the membrane. Ionotropic effects are fast and brief. At metabotropic synapses, a neurotransmitter activates a second messenger inside the postsynaptic cell, leading to slower but longer lasting changes.   **63**

5. Neuropeptides diffuse widely, affecting many neurons for a period of minutes. Neuropeptides are important for hunger, thirst, and other slow, long-term processes.   **64**

6. Hormones are released into the blood to affect receptors scattered throughout the body. Their mechanism of effect resembles that of a metabotropic synapse.   **65**

7. After a neurotransmitter (other than a neuropeptide) has activated its receptor, many of the transmitter molecules reenter the presynaptic cell through transporter molecules in the membrane. This process, known as reuptake, enables the presynaptic cell to recycle its neurotransmitter.   **66**

8. Postsynaptic neurons have mechanisms to inhibit further release of the neurotransmitter from the presynaptic neuron.   **69**

KEY TERMS

Terms are defined in the module on the page number indicated. They're also presented in alphabetical order with definitions in the book's Subject Index/Glossary, which begins on page 561. Interactive flashcards and crossword puzzles are among the online resources available to help you learn these terms and the concepts they represent.

acetylcholine   **60**
acetylcholinesterase   **66**
amino acids   **60**
anterior pituitary   **66**
autoreceptors   **69**
catecholamines   **61**
COMT   **67**
endocrine glands   **65**
exocytosis   **62**
gap junction   **69**
G protein   **64**
gases   **60**
hormone   **65**

ionotropic effects   **63**
ligand-gated channels   **63**
MAO   **62**
metabotropic effects   **63**
monoamines   **60**
neurogliaform cell   **65**
neuromodulators   **64**
neuropeptides   **60**
neurotransmitters   **60**
nitric oxide   **60**
oxytocin   **66**
peptide hormones   **65**
pituitary gland   **65**

posterior pituitary   **66**
protein hormones   **65**
purines   **60**
releasing hormones   **66**
reuptake   **67**
second messenger   **64**
transmitter-gated
    channels   **63**
transporters   **67**
vasopressin   **66**
vesicles   **62**

THOUGHT QUESTION

Suppose axon A enters a ganglion (cluster of neurons) and axon B leaves on the other side. An experimenter who stimulates A shortly thereafter records an impulse traveling down B. We want to know whether B is just an extension of axon A or whether A formed an excitatory synapse on some neuron in the ganglion, whose axon is axon B. How could an experimenter determine the answer? You should be able to think of more than one good method. Presume that the anatomy within the ganglion is so complex that you cannot simply trace the course of an axon through it.

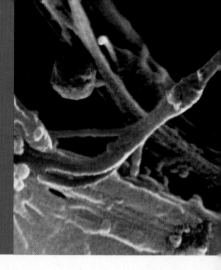

Synapses, Drugs, and Addictions

Did you know that your brain is constantly making chemicals resembling opiates? It also makes its own marijuana-like chemicals, and it has receptors that respond to cocaine and LSD. Nearly every drug with psychological effects acts at the synapses. (The exceptions are Novocain and related anesthetic drugs that block sodium channels in the membrane instead of acting at synapses.) By studying the effects of drugs, we learn more about the drugs and also about synapses. This module deals mainly with abused drugs. Later chapters will consider antidepressants, antipsychotic drugs, and other psychiatric medications.

Most of the commonly abused drugs derive from plants. For example, nicotine comes from tobacco, caffeine from coffee, opiates from poppies, and cocaine from coca. We might wonder why our brains respond to plant chemicals. An explanation is more apparent if we put it the other way: Why do plants produce chemicals that affect our brains? Nearly all neurotransmitters and hormones are the same in humans as in other species (Cravchik & Goldman, 2000). So if a plant evolves a chemical to attract bees, repel caterpillars, or whatever, that chemical is likely to affect humans also.

▌Drug Mechanisms

Drugs either facilitate or inhibit transmission at synapses. A drug that blocks a neurotransmitter is an **antagonist**, whereas a drug that mimics or increases the effects is an **agonist**. (The term *agonist* is derived from a Greek word meaning "contestant." The term *agony* derives from the same root. An *antagonist* is an "anti-agonist," or member of the opposing team.) A *mixed agonist–antagonist* is an agonist for some effects of the neurotransmitter and an antagonist for others or an agonist at some doses and an antagonist at others.

Drugs influence synaptic activity in many ways. As in Figure 3.23, which illustrates a dopamine synapse, a drug can increase or decrease the synthesis of the neurotransmitter, cause it to leak from its vesicles, increase its release, decrease its reuptake, block its breakdown into inactive chemicals, or act on the postsynaptic receptors.

Investigators say that a drug has an **affinity** for a receptor if it binds to it, like a key into a lock. Affinities vary from strong to weak. A drug's **efficacy** is its tendency to activate the receptor. A drug that binds to a receptor but fails to stimulate it has a high affinity but low efficacy.

The effectiveness and side effects of drugs vary from one person to another. Why? Most drugs affect several kinds of receptors. People vary in their abundance of each kind of receptor. For example, one person might have a relatively large number of dopamine type D_4 receptors and relatively few D_1 or D_2 receptors, whereas someone else has the reverse (Cravchik & Goldman, 2000).

Stop & Check

17. Is a drug with high affinity and low efficacy an agonist or an antagonist?

ANSWER

17. It is an antagonist because, by occupying the receptor, it blocks out the neurotransmitter.

▌A Survey of Abused Drugs

Let's consider some commonly abused drugs. In the process, we learn about synapses as well as drugs.

What Abused Drugs Have in Common

Despite many differences among abused drugs, they share certain effects on dopamine and norepinephrine synapses. The story behind the discovery of the brain mechanisms begins with a pair of young psychologists who were trying to answer a different question.

James Olds and Peter Milner (1954) wanted to test whether stimulation of a certain brain area might influence which direction a rat turns. When they implanted their electrode, they missed the intended target and instead hit an area called the septum. To their surprise, when the rat received the brain stimulation, it sat up, looked around, and sniffed, as if reacting to a favorable stimulus. Olds and Milner later placed rats in boxes where they could press a lever to produce electrical **self-stimulation of the brain** (Figure 3.24). With electrodes in the septum and certain other places, rats sometimes pressed as often as 2,000 times per hour (Olds, 1958).

71

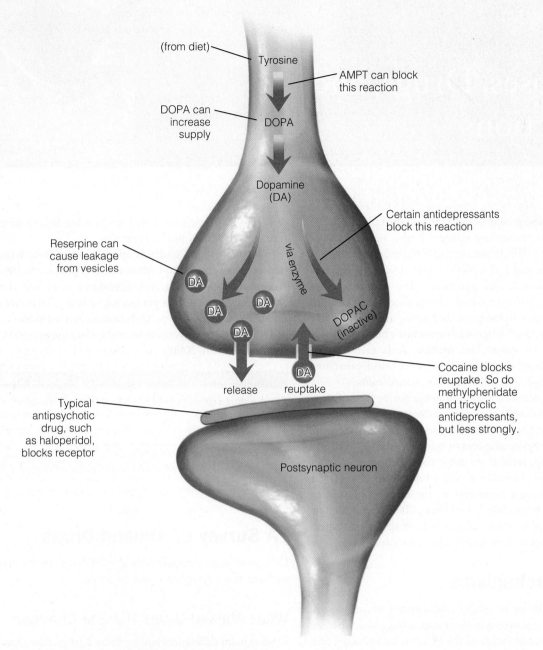

(from diet) Tyrosine

AMPT can block this reaction

DOPA can increase supply → DOPA

Dopamine (DA)

Certain antidepressants block this reaction

Reserpine can cause leakage from vesicles

via enzyme

DA DA DA DA DA

DOPAC (inactive)

DA

release reuptake

Cocaine blocks reuptake. So do methylphenidate and tricyclic antidepressants, but less strongly.

Typical antipsychotic drug, such as haloperidol, blocks receptor

Postsynaptic neuron

FIGURE 3.23 Effects of some drugs at dopamine synapses
Drugs can alter any stage of synaptic processing, from synthesis of the neurotransmitter through release and reuptake. *(© Argosy Publishing Inc.)*

Later researchers found many brain areas that rats would work to stimulate. All those areas had axons that directly or indirectly increase the release of dopamine or norepinephrine in the **nucleus accumbens**, as illustrated in Figure 3.25 (Wise, 1996).

The nucleus accumbens is central to reinforcing experiences of all types. Sexual excitement also stimulates this area (Damsma, Pfaus, Wenkstern, Philips, & Fibiger, 1992; Lorrain, Riolo, Matuszewich, & Hull, 1999), and so does the taste of sugar (Roitman, Wheeler, Wightman, & Carelli, 2008). If you simply imagine something pleasant, you activate your nucleus accumbens (Costa, Lang, Sabatinelli, Versace, &

Bradley, 2010). Gambling activates this area for habitual gamblers (Breiter, Aharon, Kahneman, Dale, & Shizgal, 2001), and video game playing activates it for habitual video game players (Ko et al., 2009; Koepp et al., 1998). People with major depression show much less than normal response in the nucleus accumbens, corresponding to the fact that they show little motivation and report getting little joy out of life (Pizzagalli et al., 2009).

Reinforcement has two components that psychologists call "wanting" and "liking" (Berridge & Robinson, 1995, 1998). Ordinarily, you want something that you like, but wanting (motivation) is not always the same as liking (pleasure). You might

FIGURE 3.24 **A rat pressing a lever for self-stimulation of its brain**

want medicine but not enjoy it. You might know you would enjoy an extremely rich, fattening dessert, but you don't want it. If you narrowly miss out on the opportunity for some prize or award, you might work extra hard at the next opportunity to get it, indicating that you *want* it, even if the prize itself doesn't bring you great pleasure (Litt, Khan, & Shiv, 2010). Recordings from individual cells in rats suggest that small parts of the nucleus accumbens respond to pleasure (liking), but larger areas respond to motivation—that is, wanting (Peciña, 2008).

Like sex, food, and other reinforcing experiences, addictive drugs strongly activate the nucleus accumbens by releasing dopamine or norepinephrine (Caine et al., 2007; Weinshenker & Schroeder, 2007). The liking-wanting distinction

is important here, because people addicted to a drug show an overwhelming, all-consuming drive to obtain the drug, even though it no longer provides much pleasure. We shall continue an exploration of addiction later in this module.

Stop & Check

18. What do drug use, sex, gambling, and video game playing have in common?

ANSWER

18. They increase the release of dopamine in the nucleus accumbens.

Stimulant Drugs

Stimulant drugs increase excitement, alertness, and activity, while elevating mood and decreasing fatigue. Both **amphetamine** and **cocaine** stimulate dopamine synapses in the nucleus accumbens and elsewhere by increasing the presence of dopamine in the presynaptic terminal. Recall reuptake: The presynaptic terminal ordinarily reabsorbs released dopamine through a protein called the **dopamine transporter.** Amphetamine and cocaine inhibit the transporter, thus decreasing reuptake and prolonging the effects of released dopamine (Beuming et al., 2008; Schmitt & Reith, 2010; Zhao et al., 2010). Amphetamine has similar effects on the serotonin and norepinephrine transporters. Methamphetamine has effects similar to those of amphetamine, but stronger.

Thus, stimulant drugs increase the accumulation of dopamine in the synaptic cleft. However, the excess dopamine in the synapse washes away faster than the presynaptic cell makes more to replace it. A few hours after taking a stimulant

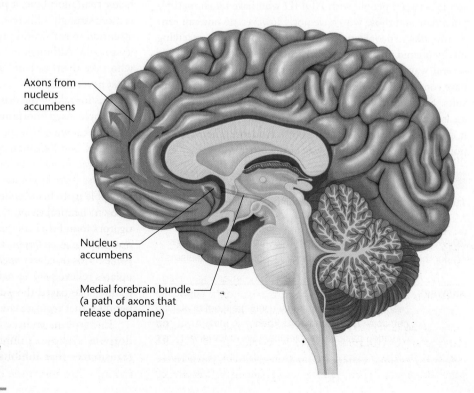

FIGURE 3.25 **Location of the nucleus accumbens in the human brain**
Nearly all abused drugs, as well as a variety of other highly reinforcing or addictive activities, increase dopamine release in the nucleus accumbens. *(© Cengage Learning 2013)*

Axons from nucleus accumbens

Nucleus accumbens

Medial forebrain bundle (a path of axons that release dopamine)

drug, a user has a deficit of the transmitters and enters a withdrawal state, marked by reduced energy, reduced motivation, and mild depression.

Stimulant drugs produce varied behavioral effects. Low doses enhance attention, and low doses of amphetamine are sometimes used as a treatment for attention deficit disorder (ADHD), a condition marked by impulsiveness and poor control of attention. However, higher doses of stimulant drugs impair attention and learning (Stalnaker et al., 2007). A study of pairs of human twins, in which one twin abused cocaine or amphetamine and the other did not, found that the twin abusing stimulant drugs showed attentional problems that lingered for a year after quitting the drugs (Toomey et al., 2003). By altering blood flow, cocaine also increases the risk of stroke and epilepsy (Strickland, Miller, Kowell, & Stein, 1998).

Methylphenidate (Ritalin), another stimulant drug, is also prescribed for people with attention-deficit hyperactivity disorder. Methylphenidate and cocaine block the reuptake of dopamine in the same way at the same brain receptors. The differences between the drugs relate to dose and time course. Cocaine users typically sniff it or inject it to produce a rapid rush of effect on the brain. People taking methylphenidate pills experience a gradual increase in the drug's concentration over an hour or more, followed by a slow decline. Therefore, methylphenidate does not produce the sudden rush of excitement that is common with cocaine. However, someone who injects methylphenidate experiences effects similar to cocaine's, including the risk of addiction.

You might wonder whether the use of methylphenidate in childhood makes people more likely to abuse drugs later. This is not an easy question to investigate. Overall, people with ADHD are more likely than other people to use and abuse tobacco, alcohol, and many other drugs. The needed comparison is between people with ADHD who have taken methylphenidate and those who have not. However, no one can randomly assign people to these two groups. Those receiving methylphenidate probably differ from those not receiving it in several ways. Bearing these difficulties in mind, researchers have conducted a few studies, and have found inconclusive results. Some studies suggest that using methylphenidate increases the risk of later drug abuse, and other studies find that it decreases the risk (Golden, 2009). Evidently the risk does not change enormously, one way or the other.

![Stop & Check]

19. How do amphetamine and cocaine influence dopamine synapses?

20. Why is methylphenidate generally less disruptive to behavior than cocaine is despite the drugs' similar mechanisms?

ANSWERS

19. They interfere with reuptake of released dopamine. **20.** The effects of a methylphenidate pill develop and decline in the brain much more slowly than do those of cocaine.

Nicotine

Nicotine, a compound present in tobacco, stimulates a family of acetylcholine receptors, conveniently known as *nicotinic receptors*. Nicotinic receptors are abundant on neurons that release dopamine in the nucleus accumbens, so nicotine increases dopamine release there (Levin & Rose, 1995; Pontieri, Tanda, Orzi, & DiChiara, 1996). Nicotine increases dopamine release in mostly the same cells that cocaine stimulates (Pich et al., 1997). Animals with larger numbers of nicotine receptors show enhanced behavioral responses to rewarding situations and novel stimuli (Fagen, Mitchum, Vezina, & McGehee, 2007). That is, nicotine enhances reward.

One consequence of repeated exposure to nicotine is that receptors in the nucleus accumbens become more sensitive to nicotine (Changeux, 2010). However, they become less responsive than usual to other kinds of reinforcement (Epping-Jordan, Watkins, Koob, & Markou, 1998). The same pattern emerges with cocaine and other addictions: enhanced response to the drug and decreased reward by anything else.

![Stop & Check]

21. How does nicotine affect dopamine synapses?

ANSWER

21. Nicotine excites acetylcholine receptors on neurons that release dopamine and thereby increases dopamine release.

Opiates

Opiate drugs are derived from, or chemically similar to those derived from, the opium poppy. Familiar opiates include morphine, heroin, and methadone. Because heroin enters the brain faster than morphine, it produces a bigger rush of effects and is more strongly addictive. Opiates relax people, decrease their attention to real-world problems, and decrease their sensitivity to pain. Although opiates are frequently addictive, people who take them as painkillers under medical supervision almost never abuse them. Addiction depends on the person, the reasons for taking the drug, the dose, and the social setting.

People used morphine and other opiates for centuries without knowing how the drugs affected the brain. Then Candace Pert and Solomon Snyder found that opiates attach to specific receptors in the brain (Pert & Snyder, 1973). It was a safe guess that vertebrates had not evolved such receptors just to enable us to become drug addicts; the brain must produce its own chemical that attaches to these receptors. Soon investigators found that the brain produces certain neuropeptides now known as *endorphins*—a contraction of *endogenous morphines*. This discovery was important because it indicated that opiates relieve pain by acting on receptors in the brain. This finding also paved the way for the discovery of other neuropeptides that regulate emotions and motivations.

Endorphins indirectly activate dopamine release. Endorphin synapses inhibit neurons that release GABA, a transmitter that inhibits the firing of dopamine neurons

(North, 1992). By inhibiting an inhibitor, the net effect is to increase dopamine release. However, endorphins also have reinforcing effects independent of dopamine. Researchers managed to develop mice with an almost complete lack of dopamine in the nucleus accumbens. These mice show a preference for places in which they received morphine (Hnasko, Sotak, & Palmiter, 2005). Evidently endorphins have rewarding effects on their own, as well as effects that depend on dopamine.

> **Stop & Check**

22. How do opiates influence dopamine synapses?

ANSWER
22. Opiates stimulate endorphin synapses, which inhibit neurons that inhibit release of dopamine. By inhibiting an inhibitor, opiates increase the release of dopamine.

Marijuana

Marijuana leaves contain the chemical Δ^9-**tetrahydrocannabinol** (Δ^9-**THC**) and other **cannabinoids** (chemicals related to Δ^9-THC). Cannabinoids have been used medically to relieve pain or nausea, to combat glaucoma (an eye disorder), and to increase appetite. Purified THC (under the name *dronabinol*) has been approved for medical use in the United States, although marijuana itself has not—except in certain states, where state law and federal law conflict.

Common psychological effects of marijuana include an intensification of sensory experience and an illusion that time has slowed down. Studies have reported impairments of memory and cognition, especially in new users and heavy users. (Moderate users develop partial tolerance.) The observed memory impairments in heavy users could mean either that marijuana impairs memory or that people with memory impairments are more likely to use marijuana. However, former users show improved memory after 4 weeks of abstention from the drug (Pope, Gruber, Hudson, Huestis, & Yurgelun-Todd, 2001). That improvement implies that marijuana use had impaired their memory.

Investigators could not explain marijuana's effects until 1988, when researchers finally found the brain's cannabinoid receptors (Devane, Dysarz, Johnson, Melvin, & Howlett, 1988). Cannabinoid receptors are among the most abundant receptors in many areas of the mammalian brain (Herkenham, 1992; Herkenham, Lynn, de Costa, & Richfield, 1991), although they are scarce in the medulla, the area that controls breathing and heartbeat. Consequently, even large doses of marijuana do not stop breathing or heartbeat. In contrast, opiates have strong effects on the medulla, and opiate overdoses are life threatening.

Just as the discovery of opiate receptors in the brain led to finding the brain's endogenous opiates, investigators identified two brain chemicals that bind to cannabinoid receptors—**anandamide** (from the Sanskrit word *ananda*, meaning "bliss") (Calignano, LaRana, Giuffrida, & Piomelli, 1998;

DiMarzo et al., 1994) and the more abundant *sn-2* arachidonylglycerol, abbreviated **2-AG** (Stella, Schweitzer, & Piomelli, 1997).

Cannabinoid receptors are peculiar in being located on the *presynaptic* neuron. When certain neurons are depolarized, they release anandamide or 2-AG as retrograde transmitters that travel back to the incoming axons and inhibit further release of either glutamate (Kreitzer & Regehr, 2001; R. I. Wilson & Nicoll, 2002) or GABA (Földy, Neu, Jones, & Soltesz, 2006; Oliet, Baimoukhametova, Piet, & Bains, 2007). In effect, anandamide and 2-AG tell the presynaptic cell, "The postsynaptic cell got your message. You don't need to send it again." The cannabinoids in marijuana attach to these same presynaptic receptors, again telling them, "The cell got your message. Stop sending it." The presynaptic cell, unaware that it hadn't sent any message at all, stops sending. In short, the chemicals in marijuana decrease both excitatory and inhibitory messages from many neurons.

Why are marijuana's effects—at least some of them—pleasant or habit forming? Remember that virtually all abused drugs increase the release of dopamine in the nucleus accumbens. Cannabinoids do so indirectly. One place in which they inhibit GABA release is the ventral tegmental area of the midbrain, a major source of axons that release dopamine in the nucleus accumbens. By inhibiting GABA there, cannabinoids decrease inhibition (and therefore increase activity) of the neurons that release dopamine in the nucleus accumbens (Cheer, Wassum, Heien, Phillips, & Wightman, 2004).

Researchers have tried to explain some of marijuana's other effects. Cannabinoids relieve nausea by inhibiting serotonin type 3 synapses (5-HT$_3$), which are known to be important for nausea (Fan, 1995). Cannabinoid receptors are abundant in areas of the hypothalamus and hippocampus that influence feeding, and stimulation of these receptors increases the rewarding value of a meal (Massa et al., 2010).

The report that "time passes more slowly" under marijuana's influences is harder to explain, but whatever the reason, we can demonstrate it in rats as well: Consider a rat that has learned to press a lever for food on a fixed-interval schedule, where only the first press of any 30-second period produces food. With practice, a rat learns to wait after each press before it starts pressing again. Under the influence of marijuana, rats press sooner after each reinforcer. For example, instead of waiting 20 seconds, a rat might wait only 10 or 15. Evidently, the 10 or 15 seconds *felt like* 20 seconds; time was passing more slowly (Han & Robinson, 2001).

> **Stop & Check**

23. What are the effects of cannabinoids on neurons?

ANSWER
23. Cannabinoids released by the postsynaptic neuron attach to receptors on presynaptic neurons, where they inhibit further release of both glutamate and GABA.

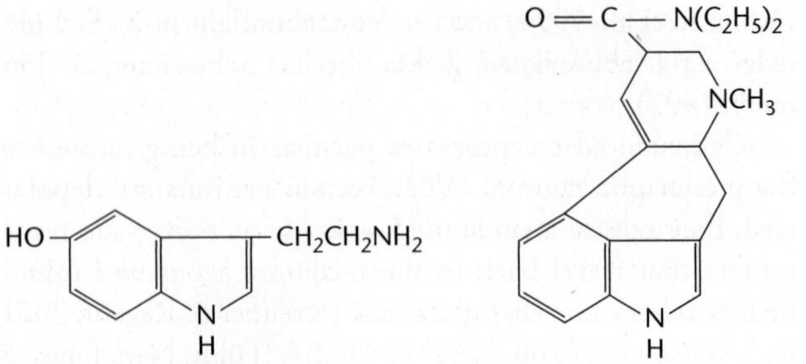

O = C — N(C$_2$H$_5$)$_2$

NCH$_3$

HO — CH$_2$CH$_2$NH$_2$

N
H
Serotonin

N
H
LSD

FIGURE 3.26 Resemblance of the neurotransmitter serotonin to LSD, a hallucinogenic drug (© Cengage Learning 2013)

Hallucinogenic Drugs

Drugs that distort perception are called **hallucinogenic drugs**. Many hallucinogenic drugs, such as lysergic acid diethylamide (LSD), chemically resemble serotonin (Figure 3.26). They attach to serotonin type 2A (5-HT$_{2A}$) receptors and provide stimulation at inappropriate times or for longer than usual durations. (Why and how the inappropriate stimulation of those receptors leads to distorted perceptions is an unanswered question.)

The drug methylenedioxymethamphetamine (MDMA, or "ecstasy") is a stimulant at low doses, increasing the release of dopamine and producing effects similar to amphetamine or cocaine. At higher doses, it also releases serotonin, altering perception and cognition like hallucinogenic drugs. Many people use MDMA at dance parties to increase their energy levels and pleasure. However, after the effects wear off, users experience

lethargy and depression. One of the effects is increased body temperature, occasionally to life-threatening levels.

Many studies on rodents and monkeys have found that repeated large injections of MDMA damage neurons that contain serotonin. One reason is that increased body temperature harms neurons. Another reason is that certain metabolites of MDMA are directly toxic to neurons (Capela et al., 2009).

The amount of risk to human users is not entirely clear. Most animal studies use larger doses than what most people take. Still, researchers have found that many repeated users show indications of long-term loss of serotonin receptors, persisting depression, anxiety, and impaired learning and memory (Capela et al., 2009). Gradual recovery occurs over a period of months. Those deficits may or may not be effects of MDMA itself, as most people who use MDMA also use a variety of other drugs (Hanson & Luciana, 2010).

Table 3.4 summarizes the effects of some commonly abused drugs.

> **Stop & Check**

24. If incoming serotonin axons were destroyed, LSD would still have its full effects. However, if incoming dopamine axons were destroyed, amphetamine and cocaine would lose their effects. Explain the difference.

ANSWER

24. Amphetamine and cocaine act by increasing the net release of dopamine and other transmitters. If those neurons were damaged, amphetamine and cocaine would be ineffective. In contrast, LSD directly stimulates the receptor on the postsynaptic membrane.

TABLE 3.4	Summary of Some Drugs and Their Effects	
Drugs	**Main Behavioral Effects**	**Main Synaptic Effects**
Amphetamine	Excitement, alertness, elevated mood, decreased fatigue	Blocks reuptake of dopamine and several other transmitters
Cocaine	Excitement, alertness, elevated mood, decreased fatigue	Blocks reuptake of dopamine and several other transmitters
Methylphenidate (Ritalin)	Increased concentration	Blocks reuptake of dopamine and others, but gradually
MDMA ("ecstasy")	Low dose: stimulant Higher dose: sensory distortions	Releases dopamine Releases serotonin, damages axons containing serotonin
Nicotine	Mostly stimulant effects	Stimulates nicotinic-type acetylcholine receptor, which (among other effects) increases dopamine release in nucleus accumbens
Opiates (e.g., heroin, morphine)	Relaxation, withdrawal, decreased pain	Stimulates endorphin receptors
Cannabinoids (marijuana)	Altered sensory experiences, decreased pain and nausea, increased appetite	Excites negative-feedback receptors on presynaptic cells; those receptors ordinarily respond to anandamide and 2AG
Hallucinogens (e.g., LSD)	Distorted sensations	Stimulates serotonin type 2A receptors (5-HT$_{2A}$)

▌Alcohol and Alcoholism

We treat alcohol separately because alcohol is the most common of the abused drugs and the research on it is extensive. People in most of the world have used alcohol throughout history. In moderate amounts, it relaxes people and decreases anxiety (Gilman, Ramchandani, Davis, Bjork, & Hommer, 2008), although people who quit alcohol often experience an increase in anxiety (Pandey et al., 2008). In larger amounts, alcohol causes health problems, impairs judgment, and ruins lives. **Alcoholism** or **alcohol dependence** is the habitual use of alcohol despite medical or social harm.

Alcohol affects neurons in several ways. It facilitates response at the GABA$_A$ receptor, the brain's main inhibitory site. It also blocks activity at the glutamate receptors, the brain's main excitatory site (Tsai et al., 1998). Both the GABA effect and the glutamate effect lead to a decrease in brain activity. From a behavioral standpoint, people sometimes describe alcohol as a stimulant, but that is only because alcohol decreases activity in brain areas responsible for inhibiting risky behaviors (Tu et al., 2007). Alcohol also increases stimulation at dopamine receptors in the nucleus accumbens (Chaudhri, Sahuque, & Janak, 2009).

Genetics

Studies of twins and adoptees confirm a strong influence of genetics on vulnerability to alcoholism (Ducci & Goldman, 2008). Heredity has a stronger role in some cases of alcoholism than others. Researchers distinguish two types of alcoholism, although not everyone fits neatly into one type or the other. People with **Type I** (or **Type A**) **alcoholism** develop alcohol problems gradually, usually after age 25, and may or may not have relatives with alcohol abuse. Those with **Type II** (or **Type B**) **alcoholism** have more rapid onset, usually before age 25. Most are men, and most have close relatives with alcohol problems (J. Brown, Babor, Litt, & Kranzler, 1994; Devor, Abell, Hoffman, Tabakoff, & Cloninger, 1994).

Genes influence the likelihood of alcoholism in various ways, most of which are not specific to alcohol. For example, many genes that affect alcohol have similar effects on nicotine intake (Lè et al., 2006). One identified gene controls variations in the dopamine type 4 receptor, one of the five known types of dopamine receptor. The type 4 receptor has two common forms, *short* and *long*. The long form is less sensitive, and people with the long form report stronger than average cravings for additional alcohol after having one drink (Hutchison, McGeary, Smolen, & Bryan, 2002). Researchers believe that people with less sensitive receptors seek more alcohol to compensate for receiving less than normal reinforcement.

Another key gene controls COMT, an enzyme that breaks down dopamine after its release. Some people have a less active form of this enzyme and others have a more active form. The more active form breaks down more dopamine and therefore tends to decrease reinforcement. People with that gene tend, on average, to be more impulsive—to choose immediate rewards instead of bigger rewards later. This gene is common

among people with the impulsive form of alcoholism (Boettiger et al., 2007). Other genes influence alcohol use by their effects on risk-taking behavior (Fils-Aime et al., 1996; Virkkunen et al., 1994), responses to stress (Choi et al., 2004; Kreek, Nielsen, Butelman, & LaForge, 2005), and reactions to anxiety-provoking situations (Pandey et al., 2008).

Prenatal environment also contributes to the risk for alcoholism. A mother who drinks alcohol during pregnancy increases the probability that her child will develop alcoholism later, independently of how much she drinks as the child is growing up (Baer, Sampson, Barr, Connor, & Streissguth, 2003). Experiments with rats have also shown that prenatal exposure to alcohol increases alcohol consumption after birth (March, Abate, Spear, & Molina, 2009). All of these biological forces interact, of course, with stressful experiences, opportunities for alcohol use, and other environmental factors.

▶ **Stop & Check**

25. Which type of alcoholism—Type I or Type II—has a stronger genetic basis? Which type has earlier onset?

26. Name at least two ways a gene could influence alcoholism.

ANSWERS **25.** Type II has a stronger genetic basis and earlier onset. **26.** Genes can influence alcoholism by producing less sensitive dopamine receptors, faster breakdown of dopamine by the enzyme COMT, greater risk-taking behavior, and altered responses to stress. Of course, other possibilities not mentioned in this section also exist.

Risk Factors

Are some people more likely than others to develop an alcohol problem? If we can identify those people, perhaps psychologists could intervene early to prevent alcoholism. We don't know whether early intervention would help, but it is worth a try.

To identify people at risk, one strategy is to study huge numbers of people for years: Measure as many factors as possible for a group of children or adolescents, years later determine which of them developed alcohol problems, and then see which early factors predicted the onset of alcoholism. Such studies find that alcoholism is more likely among those who were described in childhood as impulsive, risk-taking, easily bored, sensation-seeking, and outgoing (Dick, Johnson, Viken, & Rose, 2000; Legrand, Iacono, & McGue, 2005).

Other research follows this design: First, identify young men who are not yet problem drinkers. Compare those whose fathers were alcoholics to those who have no close relative with an alcohol problem. Because of the strong familial tendency toward alcoholism, researchers expect that many of the sons of alcoholics are future alcoholics themselves. (Researchers focus on men instead of women because almost all Type II alcoholics are men. They study sons of fathers with alcoholism instead of mothers to increase the chance of seeing genetic instead of prenatal influences.) The idea is that any behavior more common in the sons of alcoholics is probably a predictor of future alcoholism (Figure 3.27).

Here are the findings:

- Sons of alcoholics show *less* than average intoxication after drinking a moderate amount of alcohol. They report feeling less drunk, show less body sway, and register less change on an EEG (Schuckit & Smith, 1996; Volavka et al., 1996). Presumably, someone who begins to feel tipsy after a drink or two stops, whereas one who "holds his liquor well" continues drinking, perhaps enough to impair his judgment. A follow-up study found that sons of alcoholics who report low intoxication after moderate drinking have a probability greater than 60% of developing alcoholism (Schuckit & Smith, 1997). Low response to alcohol predicts later alcohol abuse, even after controlling for other variables, such as age of first alcoholic drink (Trim, Schuckit, & Smith, 2009). Similar results have been reported for women (Eng, Schuckit, & Smith, 2005).

- Alcohol decreases stress for most people, but it decreases it even more for sons of alcoholics (Levenson, Oyama, & Meek, 1987).

- Sons of alcoholics have some brain peculiarities, including a smaller than normal amygdala in the right hemisphere (Hill et al., 2001). These young men were not yet alcohol abusers, so the brain abnormality represents a predisposition to alcoholism, not a result of it.

27. What are two ways sons of alcoholics differ behaviorally, on average, from sons of nonalcoholics?

ANSWER

27. Sons of alcoholics show less intoxication, including less body sway, after drinking a moderate amount of alcohol. They also show greater relief from stress after drinking alcohol.

Addiction

Addiction poses a paradox: Nearly everyone with an addiction recognizes that the habit does more harm than good. As the addiction progresses, the pleasures become weaker while the costs and risks increase. And yet the person remains preoccupied, unable to quit. When we talk about addiction, we think mainly of alcohol and other drugs, but the same principles apply to gambling, overeating, or excessive video game playing. In each case, the person finds it difficult to quit a habit that has become clearly disadvantageous. Why?

Tolerance and Withdrawal

As an addiction develops, many of its effects, especially the enjoyable effects, decrease. That decrease is called **tolerance**. Because of tolerance, heroin users raise their amount and fre-

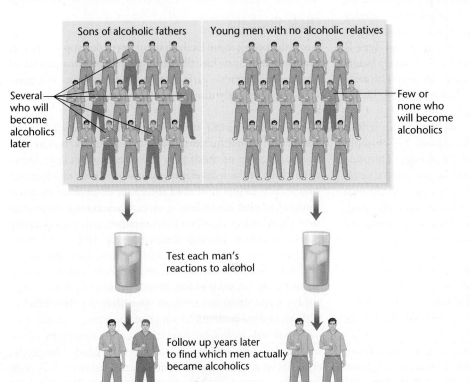

FIGURE 3.27 **Design for studies of predisposition to alcoholism** Sons of alcoholic fathers are compared to other young men of the same age and same current drinking habits. Any behavior that is more common in the first group is presumably a predictor of later alcoholism. (© Cengage Learning 2013)

quency of use to greater and greater levels, eventually taking amounts that would kill other people. Drug tolerance, a complex phenomenon, is to a large extent learned. For example, rats that consistently receive opiates or other drugs in a distinctive location show more tolerance in that location than elsewhere (Cepeda-Benito, Davis, Reynoso, & Harraid, 2005; Siegel, 1983). Evidently they learn to suppress their responses when they know what to expect.

As the body comes to expect the drug, at least under certain circumstances, it reacts strongly when the drug is absent. The effects of drug cessation are called **withdrawal**. The withdrawal symptoms after someone quits heroin or other opiates include anxiety, sweating, vomiting, and diarrhea. Symptoms of alcohol withdrawal include irritability, fatigue, shaking, sweating, and nausea. In severe cases, alcohol withdrawal progresses to hallucinations, convulsions, fever, and cardiovascular problems. Nicotine withdrawal leads to irritability, fatigue, insomnia, headache, and difficulty concentrating. Even habitual video game players (those who average more than 4 hours per day) show distress symptoms during a period of abstinence.

One explanation that theorists have advanced to explain addiction is that it is an attempt to avoid withdrawal symptoms. However, that cannot be the whole explanation. Ex-smokers sometimes report strong cravings months or years after quitting.

A modified explanation is that someone with an addiction learns to use the substance to cope with stress. In one study, researchers gave rats an opportunity to press a lever to inject themselves with heroin. Then they withdrew the opportunity for the drug. Midway through the withdrawal period, some of the rats had an opportunity to self-administer heroin again, while others went through withdrawal without heroin. Later, when rats went through withdrawal a second time, all the rats had an opportunity to press a lever to try to get heroin, but this time, the lever was inoperative. Although both groups of rats pressed the lever, those that had self-administered heroin during the previous withdrawal state pressed far more frequently (Hutcheson, Everitt, Robbins, & Dickinson, 2001). Evidently, receiving an addictive drug during a withdrawal period is a powerful experience. In effect, the user—rat or human—learns that the drug relieves the distress caused by drug withdrawal. That learning can generalize to other situations, so that the user craves the drug during other kinds of distress.

Stop & Check

28. Someone who is quitting an addictive substance for the first time is strongly counseled not to try it again. Why?

ANSWER

28. Taking an addictive drug during the withdrawal period is likely to lead to a habit of using the drug to relieve other kinds of distress.

Cravings in Response to Cues

Another hypothesis is that a drug user learns to associate cues with a drug. Later, even after a long period of abstinence, exposure to those cues triggers a renewed craving. Both humans and rats during abstention from a drug show heightened seeking of the drug (i.e., craving) after a reminder of the drug. For example, seeing a lit cigarette triggers a craving in smokers (Hutchison, LaChance, Niaura, Bryan, & Smolen, 2002), a video of cocaine use triggers cravings in cocaine users (Volkow et al., 2006), and the sight of a popular video game triggers a craving in a habitual excessive video game player (Thalemann et al., 2007). A drug-related cue increases activity in the nucleus accumbens and several related areas (Gloria et al., 2009). However, after an instruction to inhibit the craving, people are capable of decreasing this arousal (Volkow et al., 2010).

Brain Reorganization

Although escape from withdrawal symptoms and conditioned responses to cues are important, they seem insufficient to explain the way an addiction completely dominates someone's life. Somehow, the addiction hijacks a person's motivations. It changes the brain so that other kinds of reinforcing experiences become less powerful, less able to compete with the drug.

Recall epigenesis from Chapter 1: Certain events change the expression of genes. Cocaine provides a strong example of that principle. Cocaine increases the activity of certain genes that control changes in dendrites within the nucleus accumbens. The result restructures the nucleus accumbens so that the drug stimulates more dendrites, and other events stimulate fewer (Mameli et al., 2009; Maze et al., 2010). Even sexual stimulation becomes less rewarding. A similar process happens with heroin. In one study, rats had opportunities each day to press levers for heroin and for self-stimulation of the brain. Over 23 days, they took larger amounts of heroin, and became less responsive to the rewarding brain stimulation (Kenny, Chen, Kitamura, Markou, & Koob, 2006).

Furthermore, cocaine induces changes that impair extinction. Ordinarily, if an animal or person learns a response for a reinforcer, and then reinforcement ceases, responding declines through the process called extinction. You can think of extinction as learning to withhold the response. Repeated drug use impairs extinction of the drug-seeking response, so that even if the drug becomes much less reinforcing, the responding persists (Noonan, Bulin, Fuller, & Eisch, 2010).

Stop & Check

29. When addiction develops, how does the nucleus accumbens change its response to the addictive activity and to other reinforcements?

ANSWER

29. The nucleus accumbens becomes selectively sensitized, increasing its response to the addictive activity and decreasing its response to other reinforcing activities.

Medications to Combat Substance Abuse

Many people who wish to overcome substance abuse join Alcoholics Anonymous, Narcotics Anonymous, or similar organizations, and others see psychotherapists. For those who do not respond well to those approaches, several medications are available.

Medications to Combat Alcohol Abuse

After someone drinks ethyl alcohol, enzymes in the liver metabolize it to *acetaldehyde*, a poisonous substance. An enzyme, acetaldehyde dehydrogenase, then converts acetaldehyde to *acetic acid*, a chemical that the body uses for energy:

$$\text{Ethyl alcohol} \xrightarrow{} \text{Acetaldehyde} \xrightarrow[\text{dehydrogenase}]{\text{Acetaldehyde}} \text{Acetic acid}$$

People with a weaker gene for acetaldehyde dehydrogenase metabolize acetaldehyde more slowly. If they drink much alcohol, they accumulate acetaldehyde, which produces flushing of the face, increased heart rate, nausea, headache, abdominal pain, impaired breathing, and tissue damage. More than a third of the people in China and Japan have a gene that slows acetaldehyde metabolism. Probably for that reason, alcohol abuse has historically been uncommon in those countries (Luczak, Glatt, & Wall, 2006) (Figure 3.28).

The drug *disulfiram*, which goes by the trade name **Antabuse**, antagonizes the effects of acetaldehyde dehydrogenase by binding to its copper ion. Its effects were discovered by accident. The workers in one rubber-manufacturing plant found that when they got disulfiram on their skin, they developed a rash (L. Schwartz & Tulipan, 1933). If they inhaled it, they couldn't drink alcohol without getting sick. Soon therapists tried using disulfiram as a drug, hoping that alcoholics would associate alcohol with illness and stop drinking.

Most studies find that Antabuse is moderately effective (Hughes & Cook, 1997). When it works, it supplements the

FIGURE 3.28 **Robin Kalat (the author's teenage daughter) finds an alcohol vending machine in Tokyo in 1998**

alcoholic's own commitment to stop drinking. By taking a daily pill and imagining the illness that could follow a drink of alcohol, the person reaffirms a decision to abstain. In that case, it doesn't matter whether the pill really contains Antabuse or not, because someone who never drinks does not experience the illness (Fuller & Roth, 1979). Those who drink in spite of taking the pill become ill, but often they quit taking the pill instead of quitting alcohol. Antabuse treatment is more effective if friends make sure the person takes the pill daily (Azrin, Sisson, Meyers, & Godley, 1982). A related idea is to have people drink alcohol and then take a drug that produces nausea, thereby forming a learned aversion to the taste of the alcohol. That procedure has been quick and highly effective in the occasions when people have tried it, although its use has never become popular (Revusky, 2009).

Another medication is naloxone (trade name Revia), which blocks opiate receptors and thereby decreases the pleasure from alcohol. Like Antabuse, naloxone is moderately effective. It works best with people who are strongly motivated to quit, and it is more effective for Type II alcoholics (with a family history of alcoholism) than Type I alcoholics (Krishnan-Sarin, Krystal, Shi, Pittman, & O'Malley, 2007).

> **Stop & Check**
>
> **30.** Who would be likely to drink more alcohol—someone who metabolizes acetaldehyde to acetic acid rapidly or one who metabolizes it slowly?
>
> **31.** How does Antabuse work?
>
> **ANSWERS**
>
> **30.** People who metabolize it rapidly would be more likely to drink alcohol because they suffer fewer unpleasant effects. **31.** Antabuse blocks the enzyme that converts acetaldehyde to acetic acid and therefore makes people sick if they drink alcohol. Potentially, it could teach people an aversion to alcohol, but more often, it works as a way for the person to make a daily recommitment to abstain from drinking.

Medications to Combat Opiate Abuse

Heroin is an artificial substance invented in the 1800s as a supposedly safer alternative for people who were trying to quit morphine. Some physicians at the time recommended that people using alcohol switch to heroin (S. Siegel, 1987). They abandoned this idea when they discovered how addictive heroin is.

Still, the idea has persisted that people who can't quit opiates might switch to a less harmful drug. **Methadone** (METH-uh-don) is similar to heroin and morphine but has the advantage that it can be taken orally. (If heroin or morphine is taken orally, stomach acids break down most of it.) Methadone taken orally gradually enters the blood and then the brain, so its effects rise slowly, avoiding the "rush" experience. Because it is metabolized slowly, the withdrawal symptoms are also gradual. Furthermore, the user avoids the risk of an injection with a possibly infected needle.

Buprenorphine and levomethadyl acetate (LAAM), similar to methadone, are also used to treat opiate addiction. LAAM has the advantage of producing a long-lasting effect so that the person visits a clinic three times a week instead of daily. People using any of these drugs live longer and healthier, on average, than heroin or morphine users, and they are far more likely to hold a job (Vocci, Acri, & Elkashef, 2005). However, these drugs do not end the addiction. They merely satisfy the craving in a less dangerous way.

Stop & Check

32. Methadone users who try taking heroin experience little effect from it. Why?

ANSWER

32. Because methadone is already occupying the endorphin receptors, heroin cannot add much stimulation to them.

MODULE 3.3 ■ IN CLOSING

Drugs and Behavior

In studying the effects of drugs, researchers have gained clues that may help combat drug abuse. They have also learned much about synapses. For example, the research on cocaine called attention to the importance of reuptake transporters, and the research on cannabinoids led to increased understanding of the retrograde signaling from postsynaptic cells to presynaptic cells.

However, from the standpoint of understanding the physiology of behavior, much remains to be learned. For example, research has identified dopamine activity in the nucleus accumbens as central to reinforcement and addiction, but ... well, *why* is dopamine activity in that location reinforcing? Stimulation of 5-HT_{2A} receptors produces hallucinations, but again we ask, "Why?" In neuroscience or biological psychology, answering one question leads to new ones, and the deepest questions are usually the most difficult.

SUMMARY

1. A drug that increases activity at a synapse is an agonist; one that decreases activity is an antagonist. Drugs act in many ways, varying in their affinity (tendency to bind to a receptor) and efficacy (tendency to activate it).   **71**

2. Reinforcing brain stimulation, reinforcing experiences, and self-administered drugs increase the activity of axons that release dopamine in the nucleus accumbens.   **72**

3. Activity in the nucleus accumbens probably contributes more to "wanting" than to "liking," although it has a role in both. Addiction is based heavily on "wanting," as the amount of pleasure declines during addiction.   **72**

4. Amphetamine, cocaine, and methylphenidate act by blocking the reuptake transporters and therefore decreasing the reuptake of dopamine and serotonin after their release.   **73**

5. Nicotine excites acetylcholine receptors, including the ones on axon terminals that release dopamine in the nucleus accumbens.   **74**

6. Opiate drugs stimulate endorphin receptors, which inhibit the release of GABA, which would otherwise inhibit the release of dopamine. Thus, the net effect of opiates is increased dopamine release.   **74**

7. At certain synapses in many brain areas, after glutamate excites the postsynaptic cell, the cell responds by releasing endocannabinoids that inhibit further release of both glutamate and GABA by nearby neurons. Chemicals in marijuana mimic the effects of these endocannabinoids.   **75**

8. Hallucinogens act by stimulating certain kinds of serotonin receptors.   **76**

9. Compared to Type I alcoholism, Type II alcoholism starts faster and sooner, is usually more severe, and affects more men than women. Genes influence alcoholism in several ways, including effects on impulsiveness, responses to stress, and overall calmness.   **77**

10. Risk factors for alcoholism, in addition to a family history, include feeling low intoxication after moderate drinking and experiencing much relief from stress after drinking.   **77**

11. People with an addiction learn to use an addictive habit to cope with stress.   **79**

12. Addiction is associated with sensitization of the nucleus accumbens so that it responds more strongly to the addictive activity and less to other kinds of reinforcement.   **79**

13. Ethyl alcohol is metabolized to acetaldehyde, which is then metabolized to acetic acid. People who, for genetic reasons, are deficient in that second reaction tend to become ill after drinking and therefore are unlikely to drink heavily.   **80**

14. Antabuse, a drug sometimes used to treat alcohol abuse, blocks the conversion of acetaldehyde to acetic acid.   **80**

15. Methadone and similar drugs are sometimes offered as a substitute for opiate drugs. The substitutes have the advantage that if taken orally, they satisfy the cravings without severely interrupting the person's ability to carry on with life.   **80**

KEY TERMS

Terms are defined in the module on the page number indicated. They're also presented in alphabetical order with definitions in the book's Subject Index/Glossary, which begins on page 561. Interactive flashcards and crossword puzzles are among the online resources available to help you learn these terms and the concepts they represent.

affinity   71
agonist   71
alcoholism (alcohol
   dependence)   77
amphetamine   73
anandamide   75
Antabuse   80
antagonist   71
cannabinoids   75
cocaine   73

Δ^9-tetrahydrocannabinol
   (Δ^9-THC)   75
dopamine transporter   73
efficacy   71
hallucinogenic drugs   76
methadone   80
methylphenidate   74
nicotine   74
nucleus accumbens   72
opiate drugs   74

self-stimulation of the
   brain   71
stimulant drugs   73
2-AG   75
tolerance   78
Type I (Type A)
   alcoholism   77
Type II (Type B)
   alcoholism   77
withdrawal   79

THOUGHT QUESTIONS

1. People who take methylphenidate (Ritalin) for control of attention-deficit disorder often report that, although the drug increases their arousal for a while, they feel a decrease in alertness and arousal a few hours later. Explain.

2. The research on sensitization of the nucleus accumbens has dealt with addictive drugs, mainly cocaine. Would you expect a gambling addiction to have similar effects? How could someone test this possibility?

CHAPTER 3 Interactive Exploration and Study

The **Psychology CourseMate** for this text brings chapter topics to life with interactive learning, study, and exam preparation tools, including quizzes and flashcards for the Key Concepts that appear throughout each module, as well as an interactive media-rich eBook version of the text that is fully searchable and includes highlighting and note taking capabilities and interactive versions of the book's **Stop & Check** quizzes and **Try It Yourself Online** activities. The site also features **Virtual Biological Psychology Labs, videos,** and **animations** to help you better understand concepts—logon and learn more at **www.cengagebrain.com**, which is your gateway to all of this text's complimentary and premium resources, including the following:

Virtual Biological Psychology Labs

Explore the experiments that led to modern-day understanding of biopsychology with the Virtual Biological Psychology Labs, featuring a realistic lab environment that allows you to conduct experiments and evaluate data to better understand how scientists came to the conclusions presented in your text. The labs cover a range of topics, including perception, motivation, cognition, and more. You may purchase access at **www.cengagebrain.com**, or login at **login.cengagebrain.com** if an access card was included with your text.

Videos

Understanding Addiction

Animations

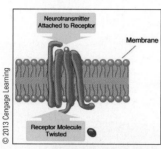

Metabotropic Demonstration

Also available—

- Post-synaptic Potentials
- Synaptic Activation
- Transmitter Release Demo
- Release of Neurotransmitter
- Cholinergic Synapse
- Acetylcholinesterase Inhibits Acetylcholine
- Opiates

Suggestions for Further Exploration

Books

McKim, W. A. (2007). *Drugs and behavior* (6th ed.). Upper Saddle River, NJ: Prentice Hall. Concise, informative text on drugs and drug abuse.

Websites

The Psychology CourseMate for this text provides regularly updated links to relevant online resources for this chapter, such as **The Endocrine Society** and **Nucleus Accumbens.**

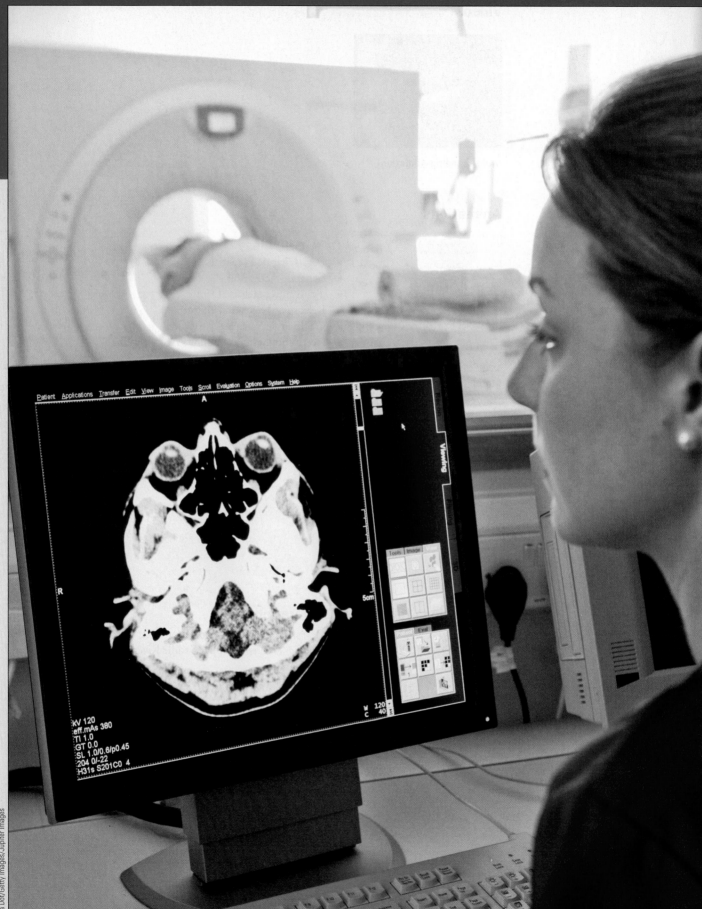

Anatomy of the Nervous System

4

MAIN IDEAS

1. Each part of the nervous system has specialized functions. Damage to different areas results in different behavioral deficits.

2. The cerebral cortex, the largest structure in the mammalian brain, elaborately processes sensory information and provides fine control of movement.

3. As research has identified the different functions of different brain areas, a new question has arisen: How do the areas work together to produce unified experience and behavior?

4. It is difficult to conduct research on the functions of the nervous system. Conclusions come from multiple methods and careful behavioral measurements.

Trying to learn **neuroanatomy** (the anatomy of the nervous system) from a book is like trying to learn geography from a road map. A map can tell you that Mystic, Georgia, is about 40 km north of Enigma, Georgia. Similarly, a book can tell you that the habenula is about 4.6 mm from the interpeduncular nucleus in a rat's brain (proportionately farther in a human brain). But these little gems of information will seem both mysterious and enigmatic unless you are concerned with that part of Georgia or that area of the brain.

This chapter does not provide a detailed road map of the nervous system. It is more like a world globe, describing the large, basic structures (analogous to the continents) and some distinctive features of each.

The first module introduces key neuroanatomical terms and outlines overall structures of the nervous system. In the second module, we concentrate on the structures and functions of the cerebral cortex, the largest part of the mammalian central nervous system. The third module deals with the main methods that researchers use to discover the behavioral functions of brain areas.

Be prepared: This chapter contains a huge number of new terms. You should not expect to memorize all of them at once, and you should review this chapter repeatedly.

OPPOSITE: New methods allow researchers to examine living brains.

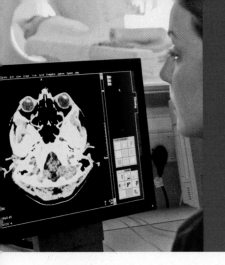

Structure of the Vertebrate Nervous System

Your nervous system consists of many substructures, a huge number of neurons, and an even huger number of synapses. How do all the parts work together to make one behaving unit? Does each neuron have an independent function? Or does the brain operate as an undifferentiated whole?

The answer is, "something between those extremes." Consider an analogy to human society: Each individual has a special role, such as teacher, farmer, or nurse, but no one performs any function without the cooperation of many other people. Similarly, each brain area and each neuron has a specialized role, but they also depend on the cooperation of other areas.

Terminology to Describe the Nervous System

For vertebrates, we distinguish the central nervous system from the peripheral nervous system (Figure 4.1). The **central nervous system (CNS)** is the brain and the spinal cord. The **peripheral nervous system (PNS)** connects the brain and spinal cord to the rest of the body. Part of

the PNS is the **somatic nervous system**, which consists of the axons conveying messages from the sense organs to the CNS and from the CNS to the muscles. The axons to the

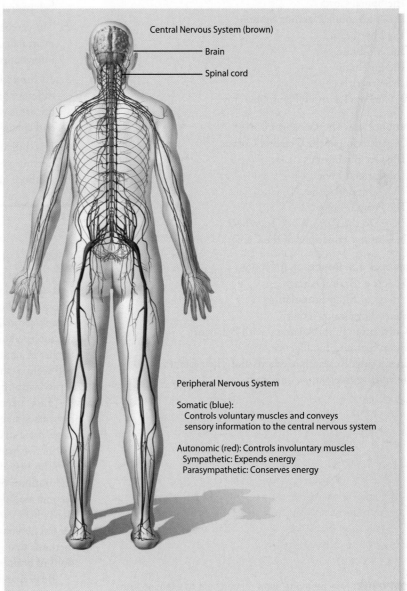

Central Nervous System (brown)

Brain

Spinal cord

Peripheral Nervous System

Somatic (blue):
Controls voluntary muscles and conveys sensory information to the central nervous system

Autonomic (red): Controls involuntary muscles
Sympathetic: Expends energy
Parasympathetic: Conserves energy

FIGURE 4.1 The human nervous system
The central nervous system consists of the brain and spinal cord. The peripheral nervous system is the nerves outside the brain and spinal cord. (© Argosy Publishing Inc.)

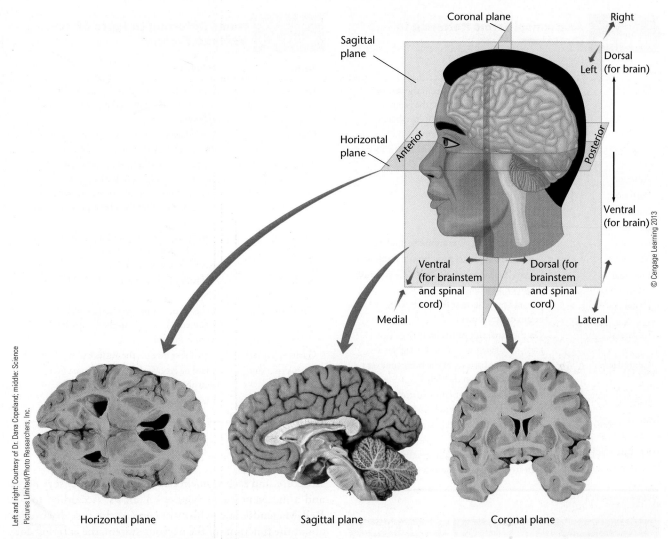

Left and right: Courtesy of Dr. Dana Copeland; middle: Science Pictures Limited/Photo Researchers, Inc.

© Cengage Learning 2013

FIGURE 4.2 Terms for anatomical directions in the nervous system
In four-legged animals, dorsal and ventral point in the same direction for the head as they do for the rest of the body. However, humans' upright posture has tilted the head, so the dorsal and ventral directions of the head are not parallel to those of the spinal cord.

muscles are an extension from cell bodies in the spinal cord, so part of each cell is in the CNS and part is in the PNS. Another part of the PNS, the **autonomic nervous system**, controls the heart, intestines, and other organs. The autonomic nervous system has some of its cell bodies within the brain or spinal cord and some in clusters along the sides of the spinal cord.

To follow a map, you must understand *north, south, east,* and *west.* Because the nervous system is three-dimensional, we need more terms to describe it. As Figure 4.2 and Table 4.1 indicate, **dorsal** means toward the back and **ventral** means toward the stomach. (One way to remember these terms is that a *ventri*loquist is literally a "stomach talker.") In a four-legged animal, the top of the brain is dorsal (on the same side as the animal's back), and the bottom of the brain

is ventral (on the stomach side). The same would be true for you if you got down on your knees and crawled. However, when humans evolved upright posture, the position of the head changed relative to the spinal cord. For convenience, we still apply the terms *dorsal* and *ventral* to the same parts of the human brain as other vertebrate brains. Consequently, the dorsal–ventral axis of the human brain is at a right angle to the dorsal–ventral axis of the spinal cord. Figure 4.2 also illustrates the three ways of taking a plane through the brain, known as horizontal, sagittal, and coronal (or frontal).

Table 4.2 introduces additional terms that are worth learning. Tables 4.1 and 4.2 require careful study and review. After you think you have mastered the terms, check yourself with the following.

TABLE 4.1	Anatomical Terms Referring to Directions
Term	**Definition**
Dorsal	Toward the back, away from the ventral (stomach) side. The top of the brain is considered dorsal because it has that position in four-legged animals.
Ventral	Toward the stomach, away from the dorsal (back) side
Anterior	Toward the front end
Posterior	Toward the rear end
Superior	Above another part
Inferior	Below another part
Lateral	Toward the side, away from the midline
Medial	Toward the midline, away from the side
Proximal	Located close (approximate) to the point of origin or attachment
Distal	Located more distant from the point of origin or attachment
Ipsilateral	On the same side of the body (e.g., two parts on the left or two on the right)
Contralateral	On the opposite side of the body (one on the left and one on the right)
Coronal plane	A plane that shows brain structures as seen from the front (or frontal plane)
Sagittal plane	A plane that shows brain structures as seen from the side
Horizontal plane	A plane that shows brain structures as seen from above (or transverse plane)

© Cengage Learning 2013

TABLE 4.2	Terms Referring to Parts of the Nervous System
Term	**Definition**
Lamina	A row or layer of cell bodies separated from other cell bodies by a layer of axons and dendrites
Column	A set of cells perpendicular to the surface of the cortex, with similar properties
Tract	A set of axons within the CNS, also known as a projection. If axons extend from cell bodies in structure A to synapses onto B, we say that the fibers "project" from A onto B.
Nerve	A set of axons in the periphery, either from the CNS to a muscle or gland or from a sensory organ to the CNS
Nucleus	A cluster of neuron cell bodies within the CNS
Ganglion	A cluster of neuron cell bodies, usually outside the CNS (as in the sympathetic nervous system)
Gyrus (pl.: gyri)	A protuberance on the surface of the brain
Sulcus (pl.: sulci)	A fold or groove that separates one gyrus from another
Fissure	A long, deep sulcus

© Cengage Learning 2013

Stop & Check

1. What does *dorsal* mean, and what is its opposite?

2. What term means *toward the side, away from the midline*, and what is its opposite?

3. If two structures are both on the left side of the body, they are _____ to each other. If one is on the left and the other is on the right, they are _____ to each other.

4. The bulges in the cerebral cortex are called _____ . The grooves between them are called _____ .

ANSWERS

1. Dorsal means toward the back, away from the stomach side. Its opposite is ventral. 2. lateral; medial 3. ipsilateral; contralateral 4. gyri; sulci. If you have trouble remembering sulcus, think of the word *sulk*, meaning "to pout" (and therefore lie low).

▋ The Spinal Cord

The **spinal cord** is the part of the CNS within the spinal column. The spinal cord communicates with all the sense organs and muscles except those of the head. It is a segmented structure, and each segment has on each side a sensory nerve and a motor nerve, as Figure 4.3 shows. According to the **Bell-Magendie law**, which was one of the first discoveries about the functions of the nervous system, the entering dorsal roots (axon bundles) carry sensory information, and the exiting ventral roots carry motor information. The axons to and from the skin and muscles are the peripheral nervous system. The cell bodies of the sensory neurons are in clusters of neurons outside the spinal cord, called the **dorsal root ganglia**. (*Ganglia* is the plural of *ganglion*, a cluster of neurons. In most cases, a neuron cluster outside the CNS is called a ganglion, and a cluster inside the CNS is called a nucleus.) Cell bodies of the motor neurons are inside the spinal cord.

In the cross-section through the spinal cord shown in Figures 4.4 and 4.5, the H-shaped **gray matter** in the center of the cord is densely packed with cell bodies and dendrites. Many neurons of the spinal cord send axons from the gray matter to the brain or other parts of the spinal cord through the **white matter**, which consists mostly of myelinated axons.

Each segment of the spinal cord sends sensory information to the brain and receives motor commands from the brain. All that information passes through tracts of axons in the spinal cord. If the spinal cord is cut at a given segment, the brain loses sensation from that segment and below. The brain also loses motor control over all parts of the body served by that segment and the lower ones.

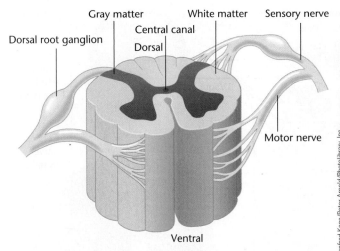

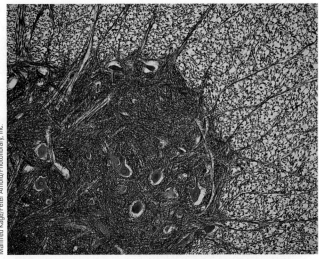

FIGURE 4.3 Diagram of a cross-section through the spinal cord
The dorsal root on each side conveys sensory information to the spinal cord; the ventral root conveys motor commands to the muscles. (© Cengage Learning 2013)

FIGURE 4.5 A section of gray matter of the spinal cord (lower left) and white matter surrounding it
Cell bodies and dendrites reside entirely in the gray matter. Axons travel from one area of gray matter to another in the white matter.

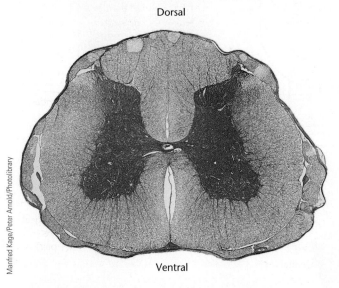

FIGURE 4.4 Photo of a cross-section through the spinal cord
The H-shaped structure in the center is gray matter, composed largely of cell bodies. The surrounding white matter consists of axons. The axons are organized in tracts; some carry information from the brain and higher levels of the spinal cord downward, while others carry information from lower levels upward.

❚ The Autonomic Nervous System

The autonomic nervous system consists of neurons that receive information from and send commands to the heart, intestines, and other organs. It has two parts: the sympathetic and parasympathetic nervous systems (Figure 4.6). The **sympathetic nervous system**, a network of nerves that prepare the organs for vigorous activity, consists of chains of ganglia just to the left and right of the spinal cord's central regions

(the thoracic and lumbar areas). These ganglia are connected by axons to the spinal cord. Sympathetic axons prepare the organs for "fight or flight"—increasing breathing and heart rate and decreasing digestive activity. Because the sympathetic ganglia are closely linked, they often act as a single system "in sympathy" with one another, although various events activate some parts more than others. The sweat glands, the adrenal glands, the muscles that constrict blood vessels, and the muscles that erect the hairs of the skin have only sympathetic, not parasympathetic, input.

The **parasympathetic nervous system** facilitates vegetative, nonemergency responses. The term *para* means "beside" or "related to," and parasympathetic activities are related to, and generally the opposite of, sympathetic activities. For example, the sympathetic nervous system increases heart rate, but the parasympathetic nervous system decreases it. The parasympathetic nervous system increases digestive activity, whereas the sympathetic nervous system decreases it. Although the sympathetic and parasympathetic systems produce contrary effects, both are constantly active to varying degrees, and many stimuli arouse parts of both systems.

The parasympathetic nervous system is also known as the craniosacral system because it consists of the cranial nerves and nerves from the sacral spinal cord (Figure 4.6). Unlike the ganglia in the sympathetic system, the parasympathetic ganglia are not arranged in a chain near the spinal cord. Rather, long *preganglionic* axons extend from the spinal cord to parasympathetic ganglia close to each internal organ. Shorter *postganglionic* fibers then extend from the parasympathetic ganglia into the organs themselves. Because the parasympathetic ganglia are not linked to one another, they act more independently than the sympathetic ganglia do. Parasympathetic activity decreases heart rate, increases digestive rate, and, in general, conserves energy.

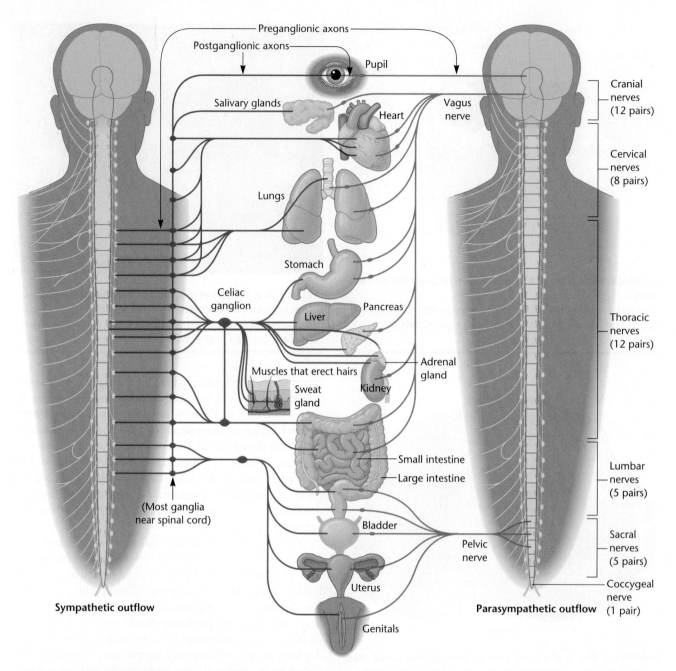

FIGURE 4.6 The sympathetic nervous system (red lines) and parasympathetic nervous system (blue lines)
Note that the adrenal glands and hair erector muscles receive sympathetic input only. *(Starr & Taggart, 1989)*

The parasympathetic nervous system's postganglionic axons release the neurotransmitter acetylcholine. Most of the postganglionic synapses of the sympathetic nervous system use norepinephrine, although a few, such as those that control the sweat glands, use acetylcholine. Because the two systems use different transmitters, certain drugs excite or inhibit one system or the other. For example, over-the-counter cold remedies exert most of their effects by blocking parasympathetic activity or increasing sympathetic activity. Because the flow of sinus fluids is a parasympathetic response, drugs that block the parasympathetic system inhibit sinus flow. The side effects of cold remedies stem from their pro-sympathetic, anti-parasympathetic activities: They increase heart rate and inhibit salivation and digestion.

> **Stop & Check**
>
> **5.** Sensory nerves enter which side of the spinal cord, dorsal or ventral?
>
> **6.** Which functions are controlled by the sympathetic nervous system? Which are controlled by the parasympathetic nervous system?

ANSWERS

5. Dorsal **6.** The sympathetic nervous system prepares the organs for vigorous fight-or-flight activity. The parasympathetic system increases vegetative responses such as digestion.

APPLICATIONS AND EXTENSIONS

Goose Bumps

Erection of the hairs, known as "goose bumps" or "goose flesh," occurs when we are cold. What does it have to do with the fight-or-flight functions associated with the sympathetic nervous system? Part of the answer is that we also get goose bumps when we are frightened. You have heard the expression, "I was so frightened my hairs stood on end." You may also have seen a frightened cat erect its fur. Human body hairs are so short that erecting them accomplishes nothing, but a cat with erect fur looks bigger. A frightened porcupine erects its quills, which are just modified hairs (Richter & Langworthy, 1933). The behavior that makes the quills so useful—their erection in response to fear—evolved before the quills themselves did. ∎

TABLE 4.3	Major Divisions of the Vertebrate Brain	
Area	**Also Known as**	**Major Structures**
Forebrain	Prosencephalon ("forward-brain")	
	Diencephalon ("between-brain")	Thalamus, hypothalamus
	Telencephalon ("end-brain")	Cerebral cortex, hippocampus, basal ganglia
Midbrain	Mesencephalon ("middle-brain")	Tectum, tegmentum, superior colliculus, inferior colliculus, substantia nigra inferior colliculus, substantia nigra
Hindbrain	Rhombencephalon (literally, "parallelogram-brain")	Medulla, pons, cerebellum
	Metencephalon ("afterbrain")	Pons, cerebellum
	Myelencephalon ("marrow-brain")	Medulla

© Cengage Learning 2013

▌The Hindbrain

The brain has three major divisions: the hindbrain, the midbrain, and the forebrain (Figure 4.7 and Table 4.3). Some neuroscientists prefer these terms with Greek roots: rhombencephalon (hindbrain), mesencephalon (midbrain), and prosencephalon (forebrain). You may encounter these terms in other reading.

The **hindbrain**, the posterior part of the brain, consists of the medulla, the pons, and the cerebellum. The medulla and pons, the midbrain, and certain central structures of the forebrain constitute the **brainstem** (Figure 4.8).

The **medulla**, or medulla oblongata, is just above the spinal cord and can be regarded as an enlarged extension of the spinal cord into the skull. The medulla controls vital reflexes—including breathing, heart rate, vomiting, salivation, coughing, and sneezing—through the **cranial nerves**, which control sensations from the head, muscle movements in the head, and much of the parasympathetic output to the or-

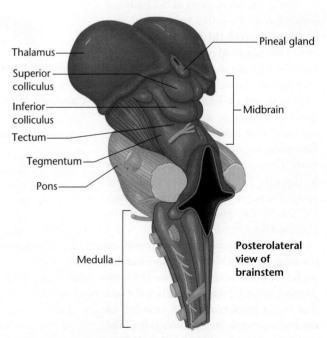

FIGURE 4.8 The human brainstem
This composite structure extends from the top of the spinal cord into the center of the forebrain. The pons, pineal gland, and colliculi are ordinarily surrounded by the cerebral cortex. (© Cengage Learning 2013)

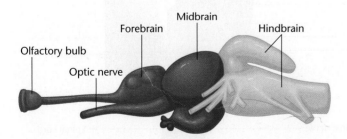

FIGURE 4.7 Three major divisions of the vertebrate brain
In a fish brain, as shown here, the forebrain, midbrain, and hindbrain are clearly visible as separate bulges. In adult mammals, the forebrain grows and surrounds the entire midbrain and part of the hindbrain. (© Cengage Learning 2013)

TABLE 4.4	The Cranial Nerves
Number and Name	**Major Functions**
I. Olfactory	Smell
II. Optic	Vision
III. Oculomotor	Control of eye movements; pupil constriction
IV. Trochlear	Control of eye movement
V. Trigeminal	Skin sensations from most of the face; control of jaw muscles for chewing and swallowing
VI. Abducens	Control of eye movements
VII. Facial	Taste from the anterior two thirds of the tongue; control of facial expressions, crying, salivation, and dilation of the head's blood vessels
VIII. Statoacoustic	Hearing; equilibrium
IX. Glossopharyngeal	Taste and other sensations from throat and posterior third of the tongue; control of swallowing, salivation, throat movements during speech
X. Vagus	Sensations from neck and thorax; control of throat, esophagus, and larynx; parasympathetic nerves to stomach, intestines, and other organs
XI. Accessory	Control of neck and shoulder movements
XII. Hypoglossal	Control of muscles of the tongue

Cranial nerves III, IV, and VI are coded in red to highlight their similarity: control of eye movements. Cranial nerves VII, IX, and XII are coded in green to highlight their similarity: taste and control of tongue and throat movements. Cranial nerve VII has other important functions as well. Nerve X (not highlighted) also contributes to throat movements, although it is primarily known for other functions.
© Cengage Learning 2013

gans. Some of the cranial nerves include both sensory and motor components, whereas others have just one or the other. Damage to the medulla is frequently fatal, and large doses of opiates are life-threatening because they suppress activity of the medulla.

Just as the lower parts of the body are connected to the spinal cord via sensory and motor nerves, the receptors and muscles of the head and organs connect to the brain by 12 pairs of cranial nerves (one of each pair on the right side and one on the left), as shown in Table 4.4. Each cranial nerve originates in a *nucleus* (cluster of neurons) that integrates the sensory information, regulates the motor output, or both. The cranial nerve nuclei for nerves V through XII are in the medulla and pons. Those for cranial nerves I through IV are in the midbrain and forebrain (Figure 4.9).

The **pons** lies anterior and ventral to the medulla. Like the medulla, it contains nuclei for several cranial nerves. The term *pons* is Latin for "bridge," reflecting the fact that in the pons, axons from each half of the brain cross to the opposite side of the spinal cord so that the left hemisphere controls the muscles of the right side of the body and the right hemisphere controls the left side.

The medulla and pons also contain the reticular formation and the raphe sys-

tem. The **reticular formation** has descending and ascending portions. The descending portion is one of several brain areas

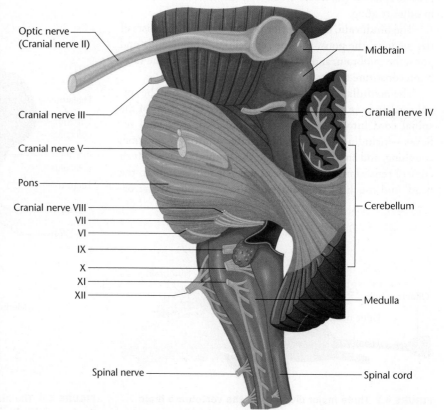

FIGURE 4.9 Cranial nerves II through XII
Cranial nerve I, the olfactory nerve, connects directly to the olfactory bulbs of the forebrain. (*Based on Braus, 1960*)

that control the motor areas of the spinal cord. The ascending portion sends output to much of the cerebral cortex, selectively increasing arousal and attention in one area or another (Guillery, Feig, & Lozsádi, 1998). The **raphe system** also sends axons to much of the forebrain, modifying the brain's readiness to respond to stimuli (Mesulam, 1995).

The **cerebellum** is a large hindbrain structure with many deep folds. It has long been known for its contributions to the control of movement (Chapter 8), and many older textbooks describe the cerebellum as important for "balance and coordination." True, people with cerebellar damage are clumsy and lose their balance, but the functions of the cerebellum extend far beyond balance and coordination. People with damage to the cerebellum have trouble shifting their attention back and forth between auditory and visual stimuli (Courchesne et al., 1994). They have much difficulty with timing, including sensory timing. For example, they are poor at judging whether one rhythm is faster than another.

The Midbrain

As the name implies, the **midbrain** is in the middle of the brain, although in adult mammals it is dwarfed and surrounded by the forebrain. The midbrain is more prominent in birds, reptiles, amphibians, and fish. The roof of the midbrain is called the **tectum**. (*Tectum* is the Latin word for "roof." The same root occurs in the geological term *plate tectonics*.) The swellings on each side of the tectum are the **superior colliculus** and the **inferior colliculus** (Figures 4.8 and 4.10). Both are important for sensory processing—the inferior colliculus for hearing and the superior colliculus for vision.

Under the tectum lies the **tegmentum**, the intermediate level of the midbrain. (In Latin, *tegmentum* means a "covering," such as a rug on the floor. The tegmentum covers several other midbrain structures, although it is covered by the tectum.) The tegmentum includes the nuclei for the third and fourth cranial nerves, parts of the reticular formation, and extensions of the pathways between the forebrain and the spinal cord or hindbrain. Another midbrain structure, the **substantia nigra**, gives rise to a dopamine-containing pathway that facilitates readiness for movement (Chapter 8).

The Forebrain

The **forebrain** is the most prominent part of the mammalian brain. It consists of two cerebral hemispheres, one on the left and one on the right (Figure 4.11). Each hemisphere is organized to receive sensory information, mostly from the contralateral (opposite) side of the body, and to control muscles,

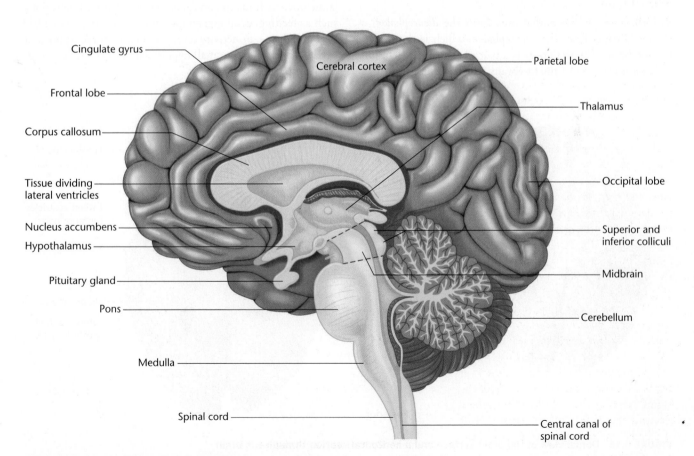

FIGURE 4.10 A sagittal section through the human brain
(After Nieuwenhuys, Voogd, & vanHuijzen, 1988)

mostly on the contralateral side, by way of axons to the spinal cord and the cranial nerve nuclei.

The outer portion is the cerebral cortex. (*Cerebrum* is a Latin word meaning "brain." *Cortex* is a Latin word for "bark" or "shell.") Under the cerebral cortex are other structures, including the thalamus, which is the main source of input to the cerebral cortex. The basal ganglia are a set of structures important for certain aspects of movement. A number of other interlinked structures, known as the **limbic system**, form a border (or *limbus*, the Latin word for "border") around the brainstem. These structures are particularly important for motivations and emotions, such as eating, drinking, sexual activity, anxiety, and aggression. The limbic system includes the olfactory bulb, hypothalamus, hippocampus, amygdala, and cingulate gyrus of the cerebral cortex. Figure 4.12 shows the positions of these structures in three-dimensional perspective. Figures 4.10 and 4.13 show coronal (from the front) and sagittal (from the side) sections through the human brain. Figure 4.13 also includes a view of the ventral surface of the brain.

In describing the forebrain, we begin with the subcortical areas. The next module focuses on the cerebral cortex. In later chapters, we return to each of these areas as they become relevant.

Thalamus

The thalamus and hypothalamus form the *diencephalon*, a section distinct from the *telencephalon*, which is the rest of the forebrain. The **thalamus** is a pair of structures (left and right) in the center of the forebrain. The term derives from a Greek word meaning "anteroom," "inner chamber," or "bridal bed." It resembles two avocados joined side by side, one in the left hemisphere and one in the right. Most sensory information goes first to the thalamus, which processes it and sends output to the cerebral cortex. An exception to this rule is olfactory information, which progresses from the olfactory receptors to the olfactory bulbs and then directly to the cerebral cortex.

Many nuclei of the thalamus receive their input from a sensory system, such as vision, and transmit information to a single area of the cerebral cortex, as in Figure 4.14. The cerebral cortex sends information back to the thalamus, prolonging and magnifying certain kinds of input at the expense of others, thereby focusing attention on particular stimuli (Komura et al., 2001).

Hypothalamus

The **hypothalamus** is a small area near the base of the brain just ventral to the thalamus (Figures 4.10 and 4.12). It has widespread connections with the rest of the forebrain and the midbrain. The hypothalamus contains a number of distinct nuclei, which we examine in Chapters 10 and 11. Partly through nerves and partly through hypothalamic hormones, the hypothalamus conveys messages to the pituitary gland, altering its release of hormones. Damage to any hypothalamic nucleus leads to abnormalities in motivated behaviors, such as feeding, drinking, temperature regulation, sexual behavior, fighting, or activity level. Because of these important behavioral effects, the small hypothalamus attracts much research attention.

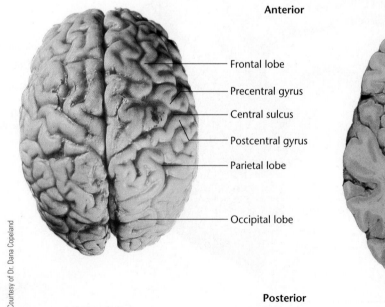

Anterior

Frontal lobe

Precentral gyrus

Central sulcus

Postcentral gyrus

Parietal lobe

Occipital lobe

Posterior

Courtesy of Dr. Dana Copeland

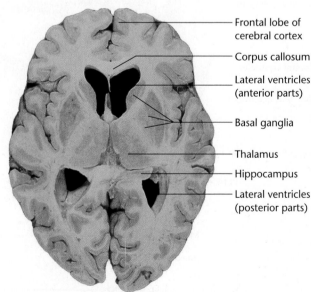

Frontal lobe of cerebral cortex

Corpus callosum

Lateral ventricles (anterior parts)

Basal ganglia

Thalamus

Hippocampus

Lateral ventricles (posterior parts)

FIGURE 4.11   Dorsal view of the brain surface and a horizontal section through the brain

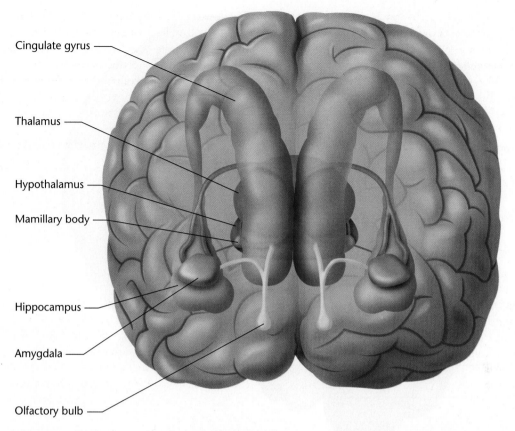

FIGURE 4.12 **The limbic system is a set of subcortical structures that form a border (or limbus) around the brainstem**
(© Cengage Learning 2013)

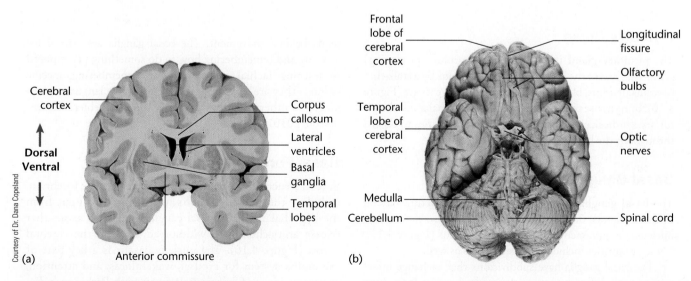

FIGURE 4.13 **Two views of the human brain**
(a) A coronal section. Note how the corpus callosum and anterior commissure provide communication between the left and right hemispheres. **(b)** The ventral surface. The optic nerves (cut here) extend from the eyes to the brain.

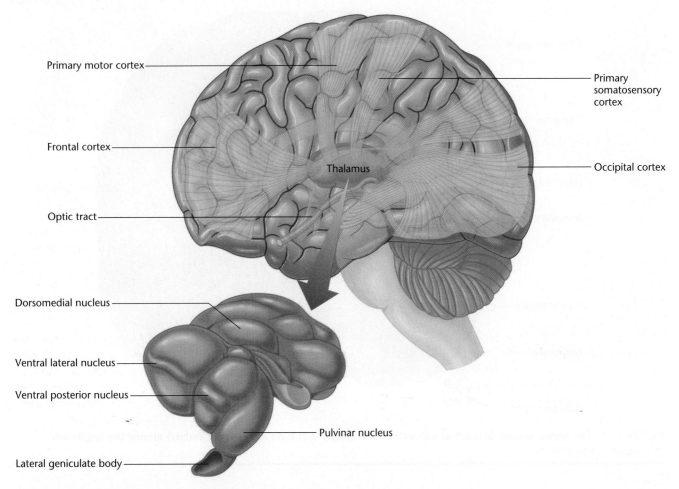

FIGURE 4.14 **Routes of information from the thalamus to the cerebral cortex**
Each thalamic nucleus projects its axons to a different location in the cortex. *(After Nieuwenhuys, Voogd, & vanHuijzen, 1988)*

Pituitary Gland

The **pituitary gland** is an endocrine (hormone-producing) gland attached to the base of the hypothalamus by a stalk that contains neurons, blood vessels, and connective tissue (Figure 4.10). In response to messages from the hypothalamus, the pituitary synthesizes hormones that the blood carries to organs throughout the body.

Basal Ganglia

The **basal ganglia**, a group of subcortical structures lateral to the thalamus, include three major structures: the caudate nucleus, the putamen, and the globus pallidus (Figure 4.15). Some authorities include other structures as well.

The basal ganglia have subdivisions that exchange information with different parts of the cerebral cortex. It has long been known that damage to the basal ganglia impairs movement, as in conditions such as Parkinson's disease and Huntington's disease. However, the role of the basal ganglia ex-

tends beyond movement. The basal ganglia are critical for learning and remembering how to do something (as opposed to learning factual information or remembering specific events). They are also important for attention, language, planning, and other cognitive functions (Stocco, Lebiere, & Anderson, 2010).

Basal Forebrain

Several structures lie on the ventral surface of the forebrain, including the **nucleus basalis**, which receives input from the hypothalamus and basal ganglia and sends axons that release acetylcholine to widespread areas in the cerebral cortex (Figure 4.16). The nucleus basalis is a key part of the brain's system for arousal, wakefulness, and attention, as we consider in Chapter 9. Patients with Parkinson's disease and Alzheimer's disease have impairments of attention and intellect because of inactivity or deterioration of their nucleus basalis.

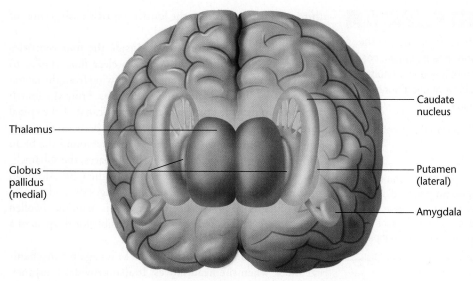

Thalamus

Globus pallidus (medial)

Caudate nucleus

Putamen (lateral)

Amygdala

FIGURE 4.15 **The basal ganglia**
The thalamus is in the center, the basal ganglia are lateral to it, and the cerebral cortex is on the outside. *(After Nieuwenhuys, Voogd, & vanHuijzen, 1988)*

Hippocampus

The **hippocampus** (from the Latin word meaning "seahorse," a shape suggested by the hippocampus) is a large structure between the thalamus and the cerebral cortex, mostly toward the posterior of the forebrain, as shown in Figure 4.12. We consider the hippocampus in more detail in Chapter 12. The gist of that discussion is that the hippocampus is critical for storing certain kinds of memories, especially memories for individual events. People with hippocampal damage have trouble storing new memories, but they do not lose all the memories they had before the damage occurred.

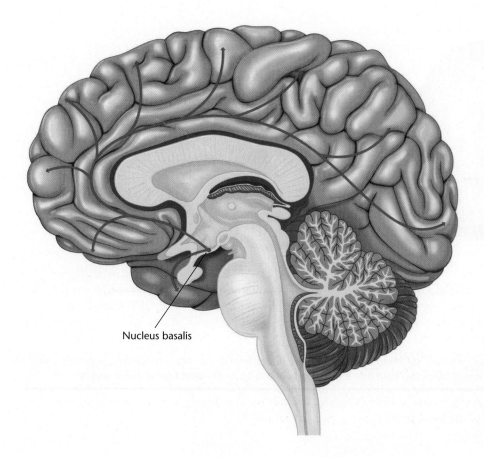

Nucleus basalis

FIGURE 4.16 **The basal forebrain**
The nucleus basalis and other structures in this area send axons throughout the cortex, increasing its arousal and wakefulness through release of the neurotransmitter acetylcholine. *(After Woolf, 1991)*

Stop & Check

7. Of the following, which are in the hindbrain, which in the midbrain, and which in the forebrain: basal ganglia, cerebellum, hippocampus, hypothalamus, medulla, pituitary gland, pons, substantia nigra, superior and inferior colliculi, tectum, tegmentum, thalamus?

8. Which area is the main source of input to the cerebral cortex?

ANSWERS

8. Thalamus.

7. Hindbrain: cerebellum, medulla, and pons. Midbrain: substantia nigra, superior and inferior colliculi, tectum, and tegmentum. Forebrain: basal ganglia, hippocampus, hypothalamus, pituitary, and thalamus.

▌The Ventricles

The nervous system begins its development as a tube surrounding a fluid canal. The canal persists into adulthood as the **central canal**, a fluid-filled channel in the center of the spinal cord, and as the **ventricles**, four fluid-filled cavities within the brain. Each hemisphere contains one of the two large lateral ventricles (Figure 4.17). Toward their posterior, they connect to the third ventricle, positioned at the midline, separating the left thalamus from the right thalamus. The third ventricle connects to the fourth ventricle in the center of the medulla.

Cells called the *choroid plexus* inside the four ventricles produce **cerebrospinal fluid (CSF)**, a clear fluid similar to blood plasma. CSF fills the ventricles, flowing from the lateral ventricles to the third and fourth ventricles. From the fourth ventricle, some of it flows into the central canal of the spinal cord, but more goes into the narrow spaces between the brain and the thin **meninges**, membranes that surround the brain and spinal cord. In one of those narrow spaces, the subarachnoid space, the blood gradually reabsorbs the CSF. Although the brain has no pain receptors, the meninges do, and meningitis—inflammation of the meninges—is painful. Swollen blood vessels in the meninges are responsible for the pain of a migraine headache (Hargreaves, 2007).

Cerebrospinal fluid cushions the brain against mechanical shock when the head moves. It also provides buoyancy. Just as a person weighs less in water than on land, cerebrospinal fluid helps support the weight of the brain. It also provides a reservoir of hormones and nutrition for the brain and spinal cord.

If the flow of CSF is obstructed, it accumulates within the ventricles or in the subarachnoid space, increasing pressure on the brain. When this occurs in infants, the skull bones spread, causing an overgrown head. This condition, known as *hydrocephalus* (HI-dro-SEFF-ah-luss), is usually associated with mental retardation.

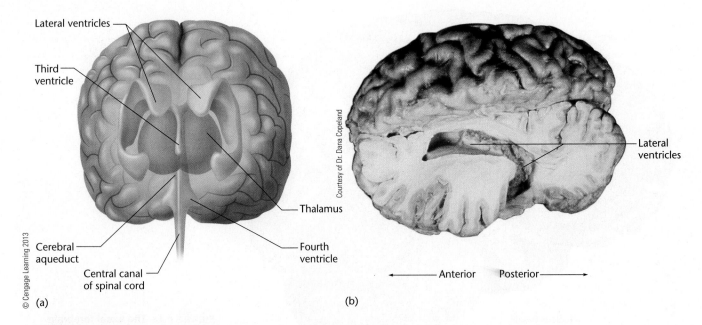

Courtesy of Dr. Dana Copeland

© Cengage Learning 2013

(a)

(b)

FIGURE 4.17 The cerebral ventricles

(a) Diagram showing positions of the four ventricles. **(b)** Photo of a human brain, viewed from above, with a horizontal cut through one hemisphere to show the position of the lateral ventricles. Note that the two parts of this figure are seen from different angles.

MODULE 4.1 ■ IN CLOSING

Learning Neuroanatomy

The brain is a complex structure. This module has introduced a great many terms and facts. Do not be discouraged if you have trouble remembering them. It will help to return to this module to review anatomy as you encounter structures again in later chapters. Gradually, the material will become more familiar.

It helps to see the brain from different angles and perspectives. Check this fantastic website, The Whole Brain Atlas, which includes detailed photos of both normal and abnormal human brains: **http://www.med.harvard.edu/AANLIB/ home.html**

SUMMARY

1. The vertebrate nervous system has two main divisions, the central nervous system and the peripheral nervous system. **86**

2. Each segment of the spinal cord has a sensory nerve and a motor nerve on both the left and right sides. Spinal pathways convey information to the brain. **88**

3. The sympathetic nervous system (one of the two divisions of the autonomic nervous system) activates the body's internal organs for vigorous activities. The parasympathetic system (the other division) promotes digestion and other nonemergency processes. **89**

4. The central nervous system consists of the spinal cord, the hindbrain, the midbrain, and the forebrain. **91**

5. The hindbrain consists of the medulla, pons, and cerebellum. The medulla and pons control breathing, heart rate, and other vital functions through the cranial nerves. The cerebellum contributes to movement and timing short intervals. **91**

6. The cerebral cortex receives its sensory information (except for olfaction) from the thalamus. **94**

7. The subcortical areas of the forebrain include the thalamus, hypothalamus, pituitary gland, basal ganglia, and hippocampus. **94**

8. The cerebral ventricles contain fluid that provides buoyancy and cushioning for the brain. **98**

KEY TERMS

Terms are defined in the module on the page number indicated. They're also presented in alphabetical order with definitions in the book's Subject Index/Glossary, which begins on page 561. Interactive flashcards and crossword puzzles are among the online resources available to help you learn these terms and the concepts they represent.

autonomic nervous system 87	hindbrain 91	raphe system 93
basal ganglia 96	hippocampus 97	reticular formation 93
Bell-Magendie law 88	hypothalamus 94	somatic nervous system 86
brainstem 91	inferior colliculus 93	spinal cord 88
central canal 98	limbic system 94	substantia nigra 93
central nervous system (CNS) 86	medulla 91	superior colliculus 93
	meninges 98	sympathetic nervous system 89
cerebellum 93	midbrain 93	
cerebrospinal fluid (CSF) 98	neuroanatomy 85	tectum 93
cranial nerves 91	nucleus basalis 96	tegmentum 93
dorsal 87	parasympathetic nervous system 89	thalamus 94
dorsal root ganglia 88	peripheral nervous system (PNS) 86	ventral 87
forebrain 93	pituitary gland · 96	ventricles 98
gray matter 88	pons 92	white matter 88

THOUGHT QUESTION

The drug phenylephrine is sometimes prescribed for people suffering from a sudden loss of blood pressure or other medical disorders. It acts by stimulating norepinephrine syn-apses, including those that constrict blood vessels. One common side effect of this drug is goose bumps. Explain why. What other side effects might be likely?

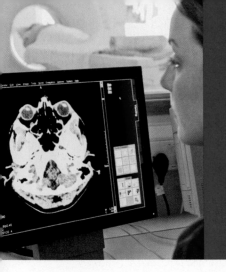

The Cerebral Cortex

The most prominent part of the mammalian brain is the **cerebral cortex**, consisting of the cellular layers on the outer surface of the cerebral hemispheres. The cells of the cerebral cortex are gray matter, and their axons extending inward are white matter (Figure 4.13). Neurons in each hemisphere communicate with neurons in the corresponding part of the other hemisphere through two bundles of axons, the **corpus callosum** (Figures 4.10, 4.11, and 4.13) and the smaller **anterior commissure** (Figure 4.13). Several other commissures (pathways across the midline) link subcortical structures.

If we compare mammalian species, we see differences in the size of the cerebral cortex and the degree of folding (Figure 4.18). The cerebral cortex constitutes a higher percentage of the brain in **primates**—monkeys, apes, and humans—than in other species of comparable size. Figure 4.19 shows the size of the cerebral cortex in comparison to the rest of the brain for insectivores and two suborders of primates (Barton & Harvey, 2000). Figure 4.20 compares species in another way (D. A. Clark, Mitra, & Wang, 2001). The investigators arranged the insectivores and primates from left to right in terms of what percentage of their brain was devoted to the forebrain, which includes the cerebral cortex. They also inserted tree shrews, a species often considered intermediate. Note that as the proportion devoted to the forebrain increases, the relative sizes of

the midbrain and medulla decrease. Curiously, the cerebellum occupies a remarkably constant percentage—approximately 13% of any mammalian brain (D. A. Clark et al., 2001). That is, the cerebellum maintains an almost constant proportion to the whole brain. (Why? No one knows.)

Organization of the Cerebral Cortex

The microscopic structure of the cells of the cerebral cortex varies from one cortical area to another and correlates with differences in function. Much research has been directed toward understanding the relationship between structure and function.

In humans and most other mammals, the cerebral cortex contains up to six distinct **laminae**, layers of cell bodies that are parallel to the surface of the cortex and separated from each other by layers of fibers (Figure 4.21). The laminae vary in thickness and prominence from one part of the cortex to another, and a given lamina may be absent from certain areas. Lamina V, which sends long axons to the spinal cord and other distant areas, is thickest in the motor cortex, which has the greatest control of the muscles. Lamina IV, which receives axons from the various sensory nuclei of the thalamus, is

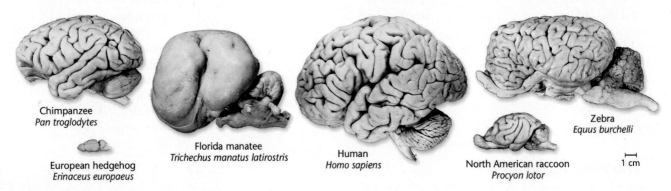

FIGURE 4.18 Comparison of mammalian brains
The human brain is the largest of those shown, although whales, dolphins, and elephants have still larger brains. All mammals have the same brain subareas in the same locations. *(From the University of Wisconsin—Madison Comparative Mammalian Brain Collection, Wally Welker, Curator. Project supported by the Natural Science Foundation.)*

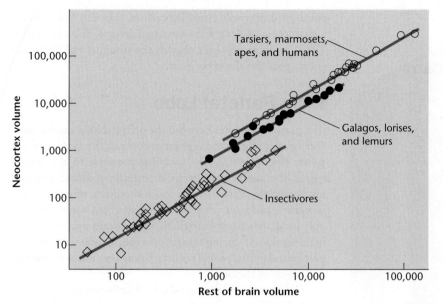

FIGURE 4.19 Relationship between volume of the cortex and volume of the rest of the brain
For each of the three groups, cortical volume increases quite predictably as a function of the volume of the rest of the brain. However, the lines for the two primate groups are displaced upward. *(Fig. 1, p. 1055 in R. A. Barton & R. H. Harvey, "Mosaic evolution of brain structure in mammals." Nature, 405, p. 1055–1058. Reprinted with permission from Nature. Copyright © 2000 Macmillan Magazine Limited.)*

prominent in all the primary sensory areas (visual, auditory, and somatosensory) but absent from the motor cortex.

The cells of the cortex are also organized into **columns** of cells perpendicular to the laminae. Figure 4.22 illustrates the idea of columns, although in nature they are not so straight. The cells within a given column have similar properties to one another. For example, if one cell in a column responds to touch on the palm of the left hand, then the other cells in that column do, too. If one cell responds to a horizontal pattern of light at a particular location, then other cells in the column respond to the same pattern in nearby locations.

We now turn to some specific parts of the cortex. Researchers make fine distinctions among areas of the cerebral cortex based on the structure and function of cells. For convenience, we group these areas into four *lobes* named for the skull bones that lie over them: occipital, parietal, temporal, and frontal.

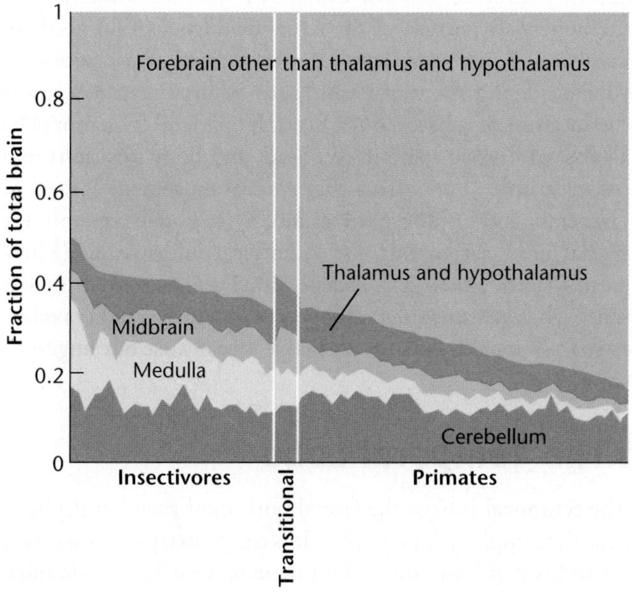

FIGURE 4.20 Relative sizes of five brain components in insectivores and primates
The forebrain composes a larger percentage of primate than insectivore brains. Note also the near constant fraction devoted to the cerebellum. *(Fig. 1, p. 189 in D. A. Clark, P. P. Mitra, & S. S-H. Wong, "Scalable architecture in mammalian brains." Nature, 411, pp. 189–193. Reprinted with permission from Nature. Copyright © 2001 Macmillan Magazine Limited.)*

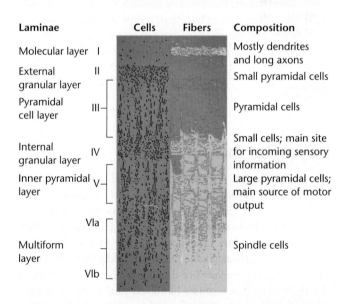

FIGURE 4.21 The six laminae of the human cerebral cortex
(From S. W. Ranson & S. L. Clark, The Anatomy of the Nervous System, 1959. Copyright © 1959 W. B. Saunders Co. Reprinted by permission.)

Surface of cortex

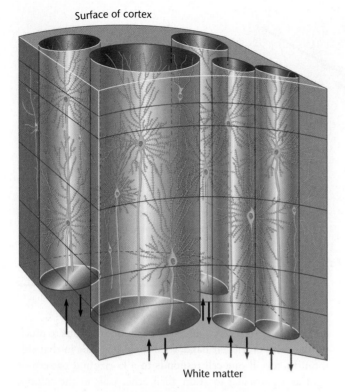

White matter

FIGURE 4.22 Columns in the cerebral cortex
Each column extends through several laminae. Neurons within a given column have similar properties. For example, in the somatosensory cortex, all the neurons within a given column respond to stimulation of the same area of skin. *(© Cengage Learning 2013)*

Stop & Check

9. If several neurons of the visual cortex all respond best when the retina is exposed to horizontal lines of light, then those neurons are probably in the same _____ .

ANSWER   uɯnloɔ **·6**

The Occipital Lobe

The **occipital lobe**, at the posterior (caudal) end of the cortex (Figure 4.23), is the main target for visual information. The posterior pole of the occipital lobe is known as the *primary visual cortex*, or *striate cortex*, because of its striped appearance in cross-section. Destruction of any part of the striate cortex causes *cortical blindness* in the related part of the visual field. For example, extensive damage to the striate cortex of the right hemisphere causes blindness in the left visual field (that is, the left side of the world from the viewer's perspective). A person with cortical blindness has normal eyes and pupillary reflexes, but no conscious visual perception and no visual imagery (not even in dreams). People who suffer eye damage become blind, but if they have an intact occipital

cortex and previous visual experience, they can still imagine visual scenes and can still have visual dreams (Sabo & Kirtley, 1982). In short, the eyes provide the stimulus and the visual cortex provides the experience.

The Parietal Lobe

The **parietal lobe** lies between the occipital lobe and the **central sulcus**, one of the deepest grooves in the surface of the cortex (Figure 4.23). The area just posterior to the central sulcus, the **postcentral gyrus**, or *primary somatosensory cortex*, receives sensations from touch receptors, muscle-stretch receptors, and joint receptors. Brain surgeons sometimes use only local anesthesia (anesthetizing the scalp but leaving the brain awake). If during this process they lightly stimulate the postcentral gyrus, people report tingling sensations on the opposite side of the body.

The postcentral gyrus includes four bands of cells parallel to the central sulcus. Separate areas along each band receive simultaneous information from different parts of the body, as shown in Figure 4.24a (Nicolelis et al., 1998). Two of the bands receive mostly light-touch information, one receives deep-pressure information, and one receives a combination of both (Kaas, Nelson, Sur, Lin, & Merzenich, 1979). In effect, the postcentral gyrus represents the body four times.

Information about touch and body location is important not only for its own sake but also for interpreting visual and auditory information. For example, if you see something in the upper-left portion of the visual field, your brain needs to know which direction your eyes are turned, the position of your head, and the tilt of your body before it can determine the location of whatever you see. The parietal lobe monitors all the information about eye, head, and body positions and passes it on to brain areas that control movement (Gross & Graziano, 1995). The parietal lobe is essential not only for spatial information but also numerical information (Hubbard, Piazza, Pinel, & Dehaene, 2005). That overlap makes sense when you consider all the ways in which numbers relate to space—including the fact that we initially use our fingers to count.

The Temporal Lobe

The **temporal lobe** is the lateral portion of each hemisphere, near the temples (Figure 4.23). It is the primary cortical target for auditory information. The human temporal lobe—in most cases, the left temporal lobe—is essential for understanding spoken language. The temporal lobe also contributes to complex aspects of vision, including perception of movement and recognition of faces. A tumor in the temporal lobe may give rise to elaborate auditory or visual hallucinations, whereas a tumor in the occipital lobe ordinarily evokes only simple sensations, such as flashes of light. When psychiatric patients report hallucinations, brain scans detect extensive activity in the temporal lobes (Dierks et al., 1999).

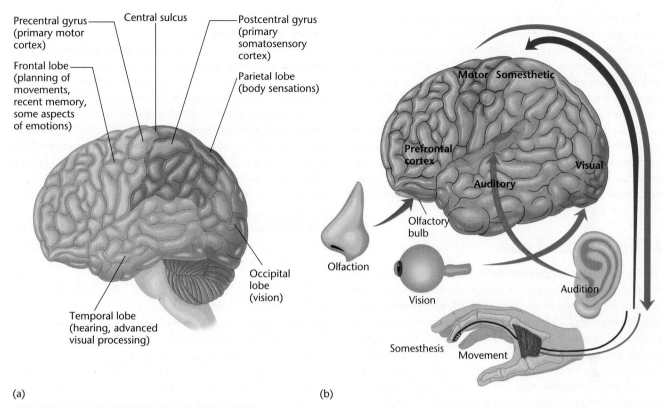

FIGURE 4.23 Areas of the human cerebral cortex
(a) The four lobes: occipital, parietal, temporal, and frontal. **(b)** The primary sensory cortex for vision, hearing, and body sensations; the primary motor cortex; and the olfactory bulb, a noncortical area responsible for the sense of smell. *(Part b: T. W. Deacon, 1990)*

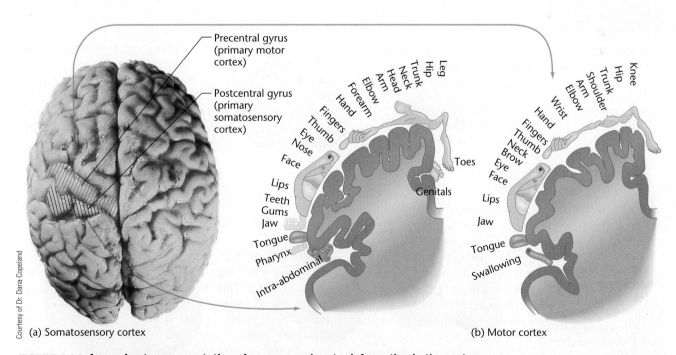

FIGURE 4.24 Approximate representation of sensory and motor information in the cortex
(a) Each location in the somatosensory cortex represents sensation from a different body part. **(b)** Each location in the motor cortex regulates movement of a different body part. *(After Penfield & Rasmussen, 1950)*

The temporal lobes are also important for emotional and motivational behaviors. Temporal lobe damage can lead to a set of behaviors known as the **Klüver-Bucy syndrome** (named for the investigators who first described it). Previously wild and aggressive monkeys fail to display normal fears and anxieties after temporal lobe damage (Klüver & Bucy, 1939). They put almost anything they find into their mouths and attempt to pick up snakes and lighted matches (which intact monkeys consistently avoid). Interpreting this behavior is difficult. For example, a monkey might handle a snake because it is no longer afraid (an emotional change) or because it no longer recognizes what a snake is (a cognitive change). We explore these issues in Chapter 12.

▌The Frontal Lobe

The **frontal lobe**, containing the primary motor cortex and the prefrontal cortex, extends from the central sulcus to the anterior limit of the brain (Figure 4.23). The posterior portion of the frontal lobe just anterior to the central sulcus, the **precentral gyrus**, is specialized for the control of fine movements, such as moving one finger at a time. Separate areas are responsible for different parts of the body, mostly on the contralateral (opposite) side but also with slight control of the ipsilateral (same) side. Figure 4.24b shows the traditional map of the precentral gyrus, also known as the *primary motor cortex*. However, the map is only an approximation. For example, within the arm area, there is no one-to-one relation-

ship between brain location and specific muscles (Graziano, Taylor, & Moore, 2002).

The most anterior portion of the frontal lobe is the **prefrontal cortex**. In general, the larger a species' cerebral cortex, the higher the percentage of the prefrontal cortex it occupies (Figure 4.25). For example, it forms a larger portion of the cortex in humans and the great apes than in other species (Semendeferi, Lu, Schenker, & Damasio, 2002). The dendrites in the prefrontal cortex have up to 16 times as many dendritic spines (Figure 2.7) as neurons in other cortical areas (Elston, 2000). As a result, the prefrontal cortex integrates an enormous amount of information.

Stop & Check

10. Which lobe of the cerebral cortex includes the primary auditory cortex?

11. Which lobe of the cerebral cortex includes the primary somatosensory cortex?

12. Which lobe of the cerebral cortex includes the primary visual cortex?

13. Which lobe of the cerebral cortex includes the primary motor cortex?

ANSWERS

10. Temporal lobe 11. Parietal lobe 12. Occipital lobe 13. Frontal lobe

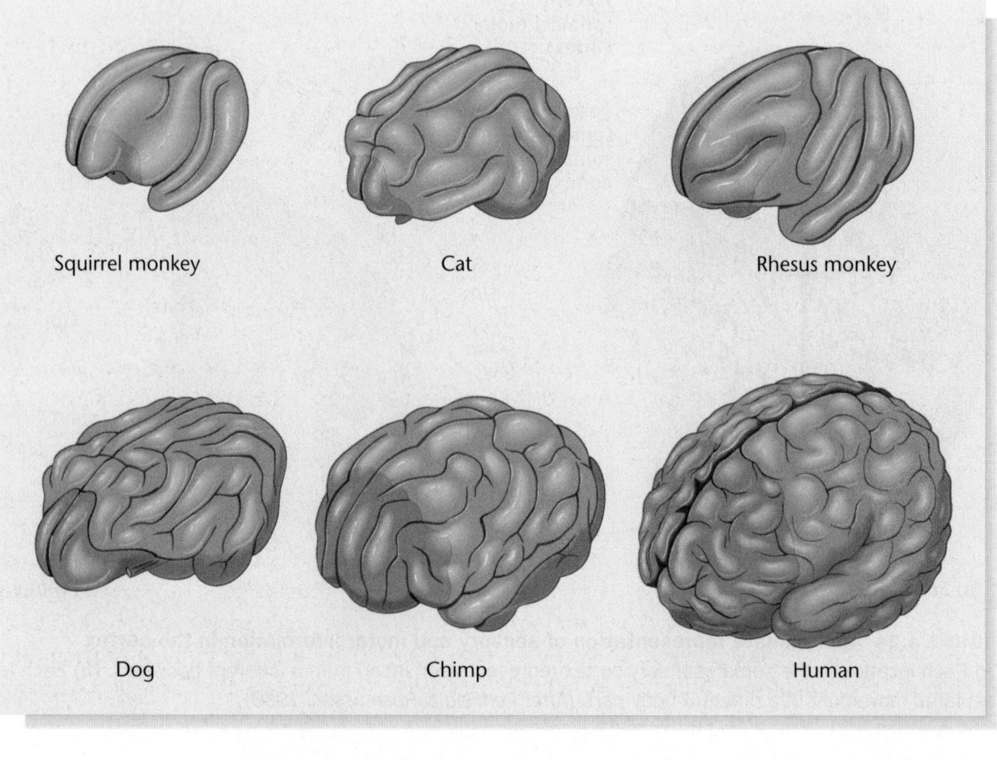

FIGURE 4.25 Species differences in prefrontal cortex
Note that the prefrontal cortex (blue area) constitutes a larger proportion of the human brain than of these other species. (*After Fuster, 1989*)

Squirrel monkey

Cat

Rhesus monkey

Dog

Chimp

Human

The Rise and Fall of Prefrontal Lobotomies

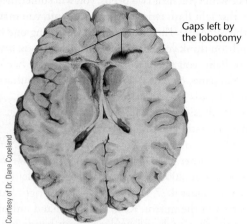

Courtesy of Dr. Dana Copeland

Gaps left by the lobotomy

A horizontal section of the brain of a person who had a prefrontal lobotomy many years earlier. The two holes in the frontal cortex are the visible results of the operation.

You may have heard of the infamous procedure known as **prefrontal lobotomy**—surgical disconnection of the prefrontal cortex from the rest of the brain. The surgery consisted of damaging the prefrontal cortex or cutting its connections to the rest of the cortex. Lobotomy began with a report that damaging the prefrontal cortex of laboratory primates made them tamer without noticeably impairing their sensations or coordination. A few physicians reasoned loosely that the same operation might help people who suffered from severe, untreatable psychiatric disorders.

In the late 1940s and early 1950s, about 40,000 prefrontal lobotomies were performed in the United States (Shutts, 1982), many of them by Walter Freeman, a medical doctor untrained in surgery. His techniques were crude, even by the standards of the time, using such instruments as an electric drill and a metal pick. He performed many operations in his office or other nonhospital sites. (Freeman carried his equipment in his car, which he called his "lobotomobile.")

At first, Freeman and others limited the technique to people with severe schizophrenia, for which no effective treatment was available at the time. Later, Freeman lobotomized people with less serious disorders, including some whom we would consider normal by today's standards. After drug therapies became available in the mid-1950s, lobotomies quickly dropped out of favor.

Among the common consequences of prefrontal lobotomy were apathy, a loss of the ability to plan and take initiative, memory disorders, distractibility, and a loss of emotional expressions (Stuss & Benson, 1984). People with prefrontal damage lost their social inhibitions, ignoring the rules of polite, civilized conduct. They often acted impulsively because they failed to calculate adequately the probable outcomes of their behaviors.

Modern View of the Prefrontal Cortex

The prefrontal cortex is a complex structure. Different parts of it, even a few millimeters apart from one another, perform significantly different functions (Gilbert, Henson, & Simons, 2010). One major function is working memory, the ability to remember recent events, such as where you parked your car or what you were talking about before being interrupted (Goldman-Rakic, 1988). People with damage to the prefrontal cortex have trouble on the **delayed-response task**, in which they see or hear something, and then have to respond to it after a delay.

The prefrontal cortex is also important for making decisions and planning movements, especially for behaviors that depend on the context (E. Miller, 2000). For example, if the phone rings, do you answer it? It depends: You would in your own home, but probably not in someone else's. If you see a good friend from a distance, do you shout out a greeting? Yes in a public park, but not in a library. People with prefrontal cortex damage often fail to adjust to their context, so they behave inappropriately or impulsively.

Stop & Check

14. What are the functions of the prefrontal cortex?

ANSWER

14. The prefrontal cortex is especially important for working memory (memory for what is currently happening) and for planning actions based on the context.

How Do the Parts Work Together?

How do various brain areas combine to produce integrated behavior and the experience of a single self? Consider the sensory areas of the cerebral cortex. The visual area, auditory area, and somatosensory area are in different locations, only weakly connected with one another. When you hold your radio or iPod, how does your brain know that the object you see is also what you feel and what you hear?

The question of how various brain areas produce a perception of a single object is known as the **binding problem**, or *large-scale integration* problem. In an earlier era, researchers thought that various kinds of sensory information converged onto what they called the association areas of the cortex (Figure 4.26). Their guess was that those areas "associate" vision with hearing, hearing with touch, or current sensations with memories of previous experiences. Later research found that the association areas perform advanced processing on a particular sensory system, such as vision or hearing, but few cells combine one sense with another. Discarding the idea that various senses converge in the association areas called attention to the binding problem. If different sensory paths don't converge, then how do we know that something we see is also what we hear or feel?

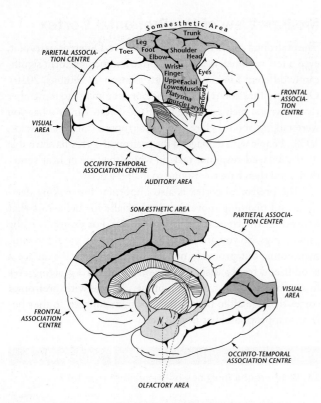

FIGURE 4.26 An old, somewhat misleading view of the cortex
Note the designation "association centre" in this illustration of the cortex from an old introductory psychology textbook (Hunter, 1923). Today's researchers are more likely to regard those areas as "additional sensory areas."

Although we cannot fully explain binding, we know what is necessary for it to occur: It occurs if you perceive two sensations as happening at the same time and in the same place. For example, when a skilled ventriloquist makes the dummy's mouth move at the same time as his or her own speech, in nearly the same place, you perceive the sound as coming from the dummy. As part of this illusion, the visual stimulus alters the response of the auditory cortex, so that the sound really does seem to come from the same location as the dummy's mouth (Bonath et al., 2007). In contrast, when you watch a foreign-language film that was poorly dubbed and the lips do not move at the same time as the speech, you perceive that the words did *not* come from those lips.

Applying these principles, researchers arranged a camera to video someone's back and sent the pictures to a three-dimensional display mounted to the person's head. The person viewed his or her own back, apparently 2 meters in front. Then someone stroked the participant's back, so that the person simultaneously felt the touch and saw the action, apparently 2 meters in front. After a while, the person had what you might call an "out of body" experience, perceiving the body as being 2 meters in front of its real position. When asked, "please return to your seat," the person walked to a spot displaced from the actual seat, as if he or she had actually been moved forward (Lenggenhager, Tadi, Metzinger, & Blanke, 2007).

Here is a demonstration you can try: If you see a light flash once while you hear two beeps, you will sometimes think you saw the light flash twice. If the tone is soft, you may experience the opposite: The tone beeps twice during one flash of light, and you think you heard only one beep. If you saw three flashes of light, you might think you heard three beeps (Andersen, Tiippana, & Sams, 2004). The near simultaneity of lights and sounds causes you to bind them and perceive an illusion. You can experience this phenomenon with the Online Try It Yourself activity "Illustration of Binding."

TRY IT YOURSELF ONLINE

Here is another great demonstration to try (I. H. Robertson, 2005). Position yourself parallel to a large mirror, as in Figure 4.27, so that you see your right hand and its reflection in the mirror. Keep your left hand out of sight. Now repeatedly clench and unclench both hands in unison. Wiggle your fingers, touch your thumb to each finger, and so forth, in each case doing the same thing with both hands at the same time. At each moment you will feel your left hand doing the same thing you see the hand in the mirror doing, which (being the mirror image of your right hand) looks like your left hand. After 2 or 3 minutes, you may start to feel that the hand in the mirror is your own left hand. Some people feel that they have three hands—the right hand, the real left hand, and the apparent left hand in the mirror!

TRY IT YOURSELF

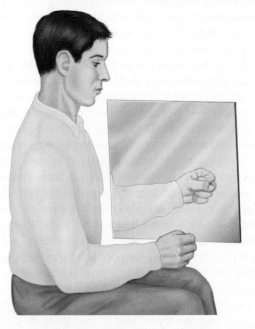

FIGURE 4.27 An illusion to demonstrate binding
Clench and unclench both hands while looking at your right hand and its reflection in the mirror. Keep your left hand out of sight. After a couple of minutes, you may start to experience the hand in the mirror as being your own left hand.
(© Cengage Learning 2013)

So binding depends on perceiving two or more aspects of a stimulus as coming from approximately the same location. People with damage to the parietal cortex have trouble locating objects in space—that is, they are not sure where anything is—and they often fail to bind objects. For example, if they see a display such as

they might report seeing a green triangle and a red square instead of a red triangle and a green square (L. Robertson, Treisman, Friedman-Hill, & Grabowecky, 1997; Treisman, 1999; R. Ward, Danziger, Owen, & Rafal, 2002; Wheeler & Treisman, 2002).

Even people with intact brains sometimes make mistakes of this kind if the displays are flashed very briefly or while they are distracted (Holcombe & Cavanagh, 2001; Lehky, 2000). You can experience this failure of binding with the Online Try It Yourself activity "Failure of Binding."

Stop & Check

15. What is meant by the binding problem, and what is necessary for binding to occur?

ANSWER

15. The binding problem is the question of how the brain combines activity in different brain areas to produce unified perception and coordinated behavior. Binding requires identifying the location of an object and perceiving sight, sound, and other aspects of a stimulus as being simultaneous. When the sight and sound appear to come from the same location at the same time, we bind them as a single experience.

MODULE 4.2 ■ IN CLOSING

Functions of the Cerebral Cortex

The human cerebral cortex is so large that we easily slip into thinking of it as "the" brain. In fact, only mammals have a true cerebral cortex, and many animals produce impressive and complex behaviors without a cerebral cortex.

What, then, is the function of the cerebral cortex? The primary function seems to be one of elaborating sensory material.

Even fish, which have no cerebral cortex, can see, hear, and so forth, but they do not recognize and remember all the complex aspects of sensory stimuli that mammals do. The cerebral cortex takes information and analyzes it in great detail.

SUMMARY

1. Although brain size varies among mammalian species, the overall organization is similar. **100**

2. The cerebral cortex has six laminae (layers) of neurons. A given lamina may be absent from certain parts of the cortex. For example, the lamina responsible for sensory input is absent from the motor cortex. The cortex is organized into columns of cells arranged perpendicular to the laminae. **100**

3. The occipital lobe of the cortex is primarily responsible for vision. Damage to part of the occipital lobe leads to blindness in part of the visual field. **102**

4. The parietal lobe processes body sensations. The postcentral gyrus contains four separate representations of the body. **102**

5. The temporal lobe contributes to hearing, complex aspects of vision, and processing of emotional information. **102**

6. The frontal lobe includes the precentral gyrus, which controls fine movements. It also includes the prefrontal cortex, which contributes to memories of recent stimuli and planning of movements. **104**

7. The prefrontal cortex is important for working memory and for planning actions that depend on the context. **105**

8. The binding problem is the question of how we connect activities in different brain areas, such as sights and sounds. The various brain areas do not all send their information to a single central processor. **105**

9. Binding requires perceiving that two aspects of a stimulus (such as sight and sound) occurred at the same place at the same time. **106**

KEY TERMS

Terms are defined in the module on the page number indicated. They're also presented in alphabetical order with definitions in the book's Subject Index/Glossary, which begins on page 561. Interactive flashcards and crossword puzzles are among the online resources available to help you learn these terms and the concepts they represent.

anterior commissure **100**	delayed-response task **105**	postcentral gyrus **104**
binding problem **105**	frontal lobe **104**	prefrontal cortex **104**
central sulcus **102**	Klüver-Bucy syndrome **104**	prefrontal lobotomy **105**
cerebral cortex **100**	laminae **100**	primates **100**
columns **101**	occipital lobe **102**	temporal lobe **102**
corpus callosum **100**	parietal lobe **102**	

THOUGHT QUESTION

When monkeys with Klüver-Bucy syndrome pick up lighted matches and snakes, we do not know whether they are displaying an emotional deficit or an inability to identify the object. What kind of research method might help answer this question?

Research Methods

Imagine yourself trying to understand a large, complex machine. You could begin by describing the appearance and location of the machine's parts. That task could be formidable, but it is easy compared to discovering what each part does.

Similarly, describing the structure of the brain is difficult enough, but the real challenge is to discover how it works. Throughout the text, we shall consider many research methods as they become relevant. However, most methods fall into a few categories. This module provides an overview of those categories and the logic behind them:

1. *Examine the effects of brain damage.* After damage or temporary inactivation, what aspects of behavior are impaired?

2. *Examine the effects of stimulating a brain area.* Ideally, if damaging some area impairs a behavior, stimulating that area should enhance the behavior.

3. *Record brain activity during behavior.* We might record changes in brain activity during fighting, sleeping, finding food, solving a problem, or any other behavior.

4. *Correlate brain anatomy with behavior.* Do people with some unusual behavior also have unusual brains? If so, in what way?

▌Effects of Brain Damage

In 1861, French neurologist Paul Broca found that a patient who had lost the ability to speak had damage in part of his left frontal cortex. Additional patients with loss of speech also showed damage in and around that area, now known as *Broca's area*. This discovery revolutionized neurology, as many other physicians at the time doubted that different brain areas had different functions at all.

Since then, researchers have made countless reports of behavioral impairments after brain damage. Brain damage can produce an inability to recognize faces, an inability to perceive motion, a shift of attention to the right side of the body and world, increased or decreased hunger, changes in emotional responses, memory impairments, and a host of other highly specialized effects.

Some of the most interesting results come from humans with brain damage, but human studies have their limitations. Few people have damage confined to just one brain area, and no two people have exactly the same damage. Therefore researchers often turn to producing carefully localized damage in laboratory animals. An **ablation** is a removal of a brain area, generally with a surgical knife. However, surgical removal is difficult for tiny structures far below the surface of the brain. In that case, researchers make a **lesion**, meaning damage. To damage a structure in the interior of the brain, researchers use a **stereotaxic instrument**, a device for the precise placement of electrodes in the brain (Figure 4.28). By consulting a stereotaxic atlas (map) of some species' brain, a researcher aims an electrode at the desired position relative to certain landmarks on the skull. Then the researcher anesthetizes an animal, drills a small hole in the skull, inserts the electrode (which is insulated except at the tip), lowers it to the target, and passes an

James W. Kalat

FIGURE 4.28 A stereotaxic instrument for locating brain areas in small animals
Using this device, researchers can insert an electrode to stimulate, record from, or damage any point in the brain.

electrical current just sufficient to damage that area. For example, researchers have made lesions in parts of the hypothalamus to explore their contributions to eating and drinking. After the death of the animal, someone takes slices of its brain, applies stains, and verifies the actual location of the damage.

Suppose a researcher makes a lesion and reports some behavioral deficit. You might ask, "How do we know the deficit wasn't caused by anesthetizing the animal, drilling a hole in its skull, and lowering an electrode to this target?" (Good question.) To test this possibility, an experimenter produces a *sham lesion* in a control group, performing all the same procedures except for passing the electrical current. Any behavioral difference between the two groups must result from the lesion and not the other procedures.

Besides lesions, several other procedures can inactivate various brain structures or systems. In the *gene-knockout approach*, researchers use biochemical methods to direct a mutation to a particular gene that is important for certain types of cells, transmitters, or receptors (Joyner & Guillemot, 1994).

Transcranial magnetic stimulation, the application of an intense magnetic field to a portion of the scalp, temporarily inactivates neurons below the magnet (Walsh & Cowey, 2000). This procedure enables researchers to study a given individual's behavior with the brain area active, then inactive, and then active again. Figure 4.29 shows the apparatus. For example, one study found that when transcranial magnetic stimulation temporarily silenced people's visual cortex, they had no conscious perception of visual stimuli, but could nevertheless direct their eye movements toward a light. This result suggests that the visual cortex is necessary for conscious perception, but not for all visually guided movements (Ro, Shelton, Lee, & Chang, 2004).

After any kind of brain damage or inactivation, the problem for psychologists is to specify the exact behavioral deficit. By analogy, suppose you cut a wire in a television and the picture disappeared. You would know that this wire is necessary for the picture, but you would not know why. Similarly, if you damaged a brain area and the animal stopped eating, you wouldn't know why. Did it lose its hunger? Its ability to taste food? Its ability to find the food? Its ability to move at all? You would need many further behavioral tests to narrow down the possibilities.

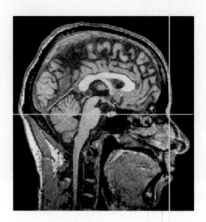

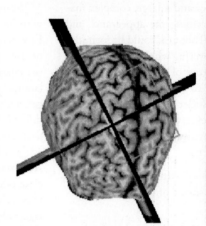

FIGURE 4.29 **Apparatus for magnetic stimulation of a human brain** Procedure is known as transcranial magnetic stimulation, or TMS. *(Reprinted from "Brain Mapping: The Methods," 2e, 2002, Toga et al., pp. 691–705, 2002, with permission from Elsevier.)*

> **Stop & Check**

16. What is the difference between a lesion and an ablation?

ANSWER

16. A lesion is damage to a structure. An ablation is removal of the structure. For example, a blood clot might produce a lesion, whereas surgery could produce an ablation.

▌Effects of Brain Stimulation

If brain damage impairs some behavior, stimulation should increase it. Researchers can insert electrodes to stimulate brain areas in laboratory animals. A new technique, *optogenetics*, enables researchers to turn on activity in targeted neurons by a device that shines a laser light within the brain (Buchen, 2010).

With humans, the choices are more limited. Occasionally researchers insert electrodes into the brain of someone who already has the brain exposed in preparation for brain surgery. In other cases, they use a less invasive (and less precise) method, applying a magnetic field to the scalp to stimulate the brain areas beneath it (Fitzgerald, Brown, & Daskalakis, 2002). Whereas intense transcranial magnetic stimulation inactivates the underlying area, a brief, mild application stimulates it.

A limitation of any stimulation study is that complex behaviors and experiences depend on a temporal pattern of activity across many brain areas, not just a general increase of activity in one, so an artificial stimulation produces artificial responses. For example, electrically or magnetically stimulating the visual cortex produces reports of flashing points of light, not the sight of any recognizable object. It is easier to discover which brain area is responsible for vision (or movement or whatever) than to discover how it produces a meaningful pattern.

Stop & Check

17. How do the effects of brief, mild magnetic stimulation differ from those of longer, more intense stimulation?

18. Why does electrical or magnetic stimulation of the brain seldom produce complex, meaningful sensations or movements?

ANSWERS

17. Brief, mild magnetic stimulation on the scalp increases activity in the underlying brain areas, whereas longer, more intense stimulation blocks it. **18.** Meaningful sensations and movements require a pattern of precisely timed activity in a great many cells, not just a burst of overall activity diffusely in one area.

▮ Recording Brain Activity

Suppose damage to some brain area impairs a behavior (eating, for example) and stimulation of that area increases the behavior. We can further confirm the connection if we demonstrate that the activity of that area increases during occurrences of the behavior. With laboratory animals, researchers insert electrodes to record brain activity, or they use more recent methods that record the activity of many individual neurons at the same time (Kerr & Denk, 2008).

Studies of human brains almost always use noninvasive methods—that is, methods that record from outside the skull without inserting anything. A device called the **electroencephalograph (EEG)** records electrical activity of the brain through electrodes—ranging from just a few to more than a hundred—attached to the scalp (Figure 4.30). Electrodes glued to the scalp measure the average activity at any moment for the population of cells under the electrode. The output is then amplified and recorded. This device can record spontaneous brain activity or activity in response to a stimulus, in which case we call the results **evoked potentials** or **evoked responses**. In one study, researchers recorded evoked potentials from young adults as they watched pictures of nudes of both sexes. Men reported high arousal by the female nudes, while women reported neutral feelings to both the males and females, but both men's and women's brains showed strong evoked potentials to the opposite-sex nudes (Costa, Braun, & Birbaumer, 2003). That is, evoked potentials sometimes reveal information that self-reports do not.

A **magnetoencephalograph (MEG)** is similar, but instead of measuring electrical activity, it measures the faint magnetic fields generated by brain activity (Hari, 1994). Like an EEG, an MEG recording identifies the approximate location of activity to within about a centimeter. However, an

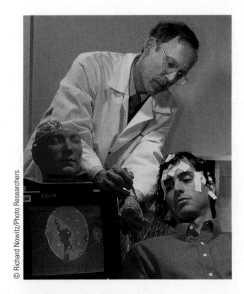

FIGURE 4.30 Electroencephalography
An electroencephalograph records the overall activity of neurons under various electrodes attached to the scalp.

MEG has excellent temporal resolution, showing changes from 1 millisecond to the next.

Figure 4.31 shows an MEG record of brain responses to a brief tone heard in the right ear. The diagram represents a human head as viewed from above, with the nose at the top (Hari, 1994). Researchers using an MEG can identify the times at which various brain areas respond and thereby trace a wave of brain activity from its point of origin to all the other areas that process it (Salmelin, Hari, Lounasmaa, & Sams, 1994).

Another method, **positron-emission tomography (PET)**, provides a high-resolution image of activity in a living brain by recording the emission of radioactivity from injected chemicals. First, the person receives an injection of glucose or some other chemical containing radioactive atoms. When a radioactive atom decays, it releases a positron that immediately collides with a nearby electron, emitting two gamma rays in exactly opposite directions. The person's head is surrounded by a set of gamma ray detectors (Figure 4.32). When two detectors record gamma rays at the same time, they identify a spot halfway between those detectors as the point of origin of the gamma rays. A computer uses this information to determine how many gamma rays are coming from each spot in the brain and therefore how much of the radioactive chemical is located in each area (Phelps & Mazziotta, 1985). The areas showing the most radioactivity are the ones with the most blood flow and, therefore, presumably, the most brain activity. For an example of a PET study, we shall see in Chapter 9 how PET identified the brain areas that become active during a certain stage of sleep.

Ordinarily, PET scans use radioactive chemicals with a short half-life, made in a device called a cyclotron. Because cyclotrons are large and expensive, PET scans are available only at research hospitals. Furthermore, PET requires ex-

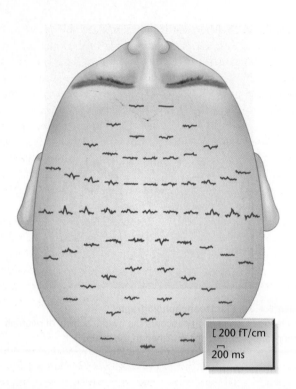

FIGURE 4.31 **A result of magnetoencephalography, showing responses to a tone in the right ear**
The nose is shown at the top. For each spot on the diagram, the display shows the changing response over a few hundred ms following the tone. (Note calibration at lower right.) The tone evoked responses in many areas, with the largest responses in the temporal cortex, especially on the left side. *(Reprinted from* Neuroscience: From the Molecular to the Cognitive, *by R. Hari, 1994, p. 165, with kind permission from Elsevier Science—NL, Sara Burgerhartstraat 25, 1055 KV Amsterdam, The Netherlands.)*

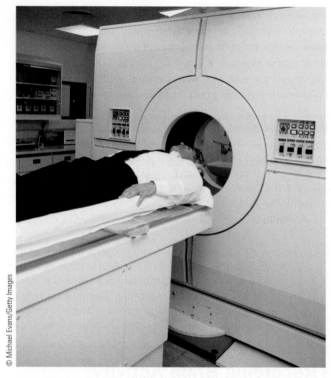

FIGURE 4.32 **A PET scanner**
A person engages in a cognitive task while attached to this apparatus that records which areas of the brain become more active and by how much.

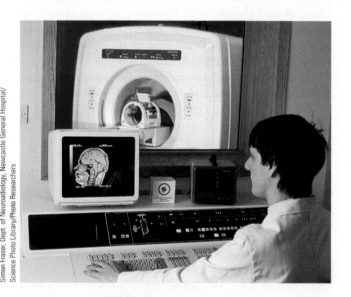

FIGURE 4.33 **An fMRI scan of a human brain**
An fMRI produces fairly detailed photos at rates up to about one per second. *(Wagner et al., 1998)*

posing the brain to radioactivity. For most purposes, PET scans have been replaced by **functional magnetic resonance imaging (fMRI)**, which is less expensive and less risky. Standard MRI scans record the energy released by water molecules after removal of a magnetic field. (The text provides more details about this method later.) An fMRI is a modified version of MRI based on hemoglobin (the blood protein that binds oxygen) instead of water (Detre & Floyd, 2001). Hemoglobin with oxygen reacts to a magnetic field differently than hemoglobin without oxygen. Researchers set the fMRI scanner to detect hemoglobin with and without oxygen (Viswanathan & Freeman, 2007). When a brain area becomes more active, two relevant changes occur: First, blood vessels dilate to allow more blood flow to the area. Second, as the brain area uses oxygen, the percentage of hemoglobin without oxygen increases. An fMRI scan records both of these processes (Sirotin, Hillman, Bordier, & Das, 2009). An fMRI image has a spatial resolution of 1 or 2 mm (almost as good as standard MRI) and temporal resolution of about a second (Figure 4.33).

An fMRI while you were, for example, reading would mean nothing without a comparison to something else. Researchers would record your brain activity while you were reading and during a comparison task and then subtract the brain activity during the comparison task to determine which areas are more active during reading. As a comparison task, for example, researchers might ask you to look at a page written in a language you do not understand. That task would activate visual areas just as the reading task did, but it presumably would not activate the language areas of your brain. Figure 4.34 illustrates the idea.

Here is one example of an fMRI study: Researchers asked which brain areas become more active when your "mind wanders." Several brain areas, including the posterior cingulate cortex, consistently show increased activity during times when people have no particular task (M. F. Mason et al., 2007). Later, when researchers watched people's performance on a task requiring constant attention, they saw performance decline whenever activity increased in these mind-wandering areas (Weissman, Roberts, Visscher, & Woldorff, 2006). Evidently, the non-task-related activity interferes with the brain processes necessary for vigilance.

Interpreting fMRI results is a complex task. Suppose researchers find that some area becomes more active while people process emotional information. Later, during some other activity, that area again becomes active. Can we therefore assume that the person is undergoing an emotional experience? Not necessarily. A given area may have many functions, and we have to be cautious about equating one area with one function.

The best way to test our understanding is this: If we think we know what a given fMRI pattern means, we should be able to use that pattern to identify what someone is doing or thinking. In other words, we should be able to use it to read someone's mind, to a limited degree. In one study, researchers used fMRI to record activity in the visual cortex as people looked at 1,750 photographs. Then they showed 120 new photographs similar to one or more of the original ones, and analyzed the fMRI results with a computer. In most cases they were able to use the fMRI results to guess which of the new photographs the person was seeing. Accuracy was high if they recorded the fMRI response several times to each photo, but even with a single trial, they usually identified either the correct photo or something similar (Kay, Naselaris, Prenger, & Gallant, 2008).

In another study, researchers used fMRI to monitor people's intentions. In each trial, a participant was to decide freely whether to "add" or "subtract," without telling anyone. After a delay, a pair of numbers appeared on the screen (to be added or subtracted, depending on the person's decision), and then an array of four numbers. At that point the person was to point to the correct answer as quickly as possible. In the example shown in Figure 4.35, if the person had decided to add, the correct answer would be 89 (upper right) and if the decision was to subtract, the answer would be 23 (lower left). A key point is that the numbers and their positions were unpredictable. During the delay, the person could think "add" or "subtract" but could not choose a particular position of response. The fMRI recordings from the prefrontal cortex enabled researchers to predict people's behaviors with 71% accuracy (Haynes et al., 2007).

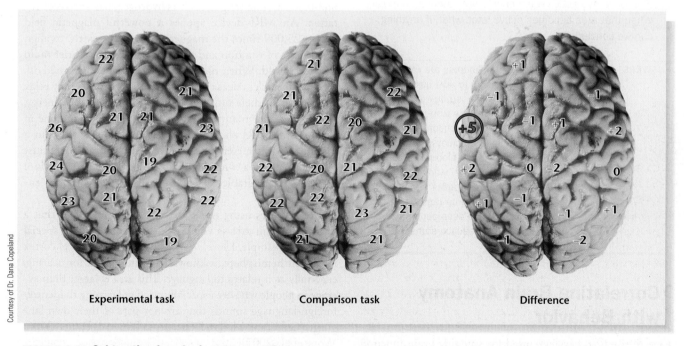

Courtesy of Dr. Dana Copeland

Experimental task   **Comparison task**   **Difference**

FIGURE 4.34 Subtraction for a brain scan procedure
Numbers on the brain at the left show hypothetical levels of arousal during some task, measured in arbitrary units. The brain at the center shows activity during the same brain areas during a comparison task. The brain at the right shows the differences. The highlighted area shows the largest difference. In actual data, the largest increases in activity would be one or two tenths of a percent.

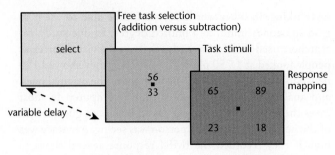

FIGURE 4.35 Procedure for monitoring people's intentions
People decided silently whether to add or subtract. After a delay, they saw two numbers. After applying either addition or subtraction, they chose the correct answer among four choices. An fMRI during the delay could predict whether the person was about to add or subtract. *(From Haynes, J.-D., Katsuyuki, S., Rees, G., Gilbert, S., Frith, C., & Passingham, R. E. (2007). Reading hidden intentions in the human brain.* Current Biology, *17, 323-328.)*

How far can this procedure go? At this point we can read people's minds in only this very limited way. It would be hazardous to guess how far the procedure might or might not develop in the future. The main point is that trying to read people's minds (in a limited way) tests how well we understand what the brain recordings mean.

Stop & Check

19. What does fMRI measure?

20. Suppose someone demonstrates that a particular brain area becomes active when people are listening to music. When that area becomes active later, what, if anything, can we conclude?

ANSWERS

19. It measures changes in blood flow to the brain. It detects an increase in blood flow to a brain area immediately after an increase in brain activity, and it also detects a slightly slower increase in the percentage of hemoglobin lacking oxygen. **20.** Without further evidence, we should not draw any conclusion. Perhaps the person is listening to music again, but this area may perform functions other than listening to music. A good test of how well we understand the area would be to find out whether we can use fMRI recordings to guess which type of music someone is hearing (or whether they are listening at all).

Correlating Brain Anatomy with Behavior

One of the first ways ever used for studying brain function sounds easy: Find someone with unusual behavior and then look for unusual features of the brain. In the 1800s, Franz Gall observed some people with excellent verbal memories who had protruding eyes. He inferred that verbal memory depended on brain areas behind the eyes that had pushed the eyes forward. Gall then examined the skulls of people with other talents or personalities. He assumed that bulges and depressions on their skull corresponded to the brain areas below them. His process of relating skull anatomy to behavior is known as **phrenology**. One of his followers made the phrenological map in Figure 4.36.

One problem with phrenologists was their uncritical use of data. In some cases, they examined just one person with a behavioral quirk to define a brain area presumably responsible for it. Another problem was that skull shape has little relationship to brain anatomy. The skull is thicker in some places than others and thicker in some people than others.

Today, researchers examine detailed brain anatomy in detail in living people. One method is **computerized axial tomography**, better known as a **CT** or **CAT scan** (Andreasen, 1988). A physician injects a dye into the blood (to increase contrast in the image) and then places the person's head into a CT scanner like the one shown in Figure 4.37a. X-rays are passed through the head and recorded by detectors on the opposite side. The CT scanner is rotated slowly until a measurement has been taken at each angle over 180 degrees. From the measurements, a computer constructs images of the brain. Figure 4.37b is an example. CT scans help detect tumors and other structural abnormalities.

Another method is **magnetic resonance imaging (MRI)** (Warach, 1995), based on the fact that any atom with an odd-numbered atomic weight, such as hydrogen, has an axis of rotation. An MRI device applies a powerful magnetic field (about 25,000 times the magnetic field of the earth) to align all the axes of rotation and then tilts them with a brief radio frequency field. When the radio frequency field is turned off, the atomic nuclei release electromagnetic energy as they relax and return to their original axis. By measuring that energy, MRI devices form an image of the brain, such as the one in Figure 4.38. MRI shows anatomical details smaller than a millimeter in diameter. One drawback is that the person must lie motionless in a confining, noisy apparatus. The procedure is usually not suitable for children or anyone who fears enclosed places.

Researchers using these methods sometimes find that a particular brain area is enlarged in people who have special skills. For example, *Heschl's gyrus*, part of the temporal cortex in the left hemisphere, is known to be important for hearing, especially as it relates to language. This area is larger than average in people who are especially good at learning to identify foreign-language sounds that are not part of their own language (Golestani, Molko, Dehaene, LeBihan, & Pallier, 2006; Wong et al., 2007).

Table 4.5 summarizes various methods of studying brain-behavior relationships.

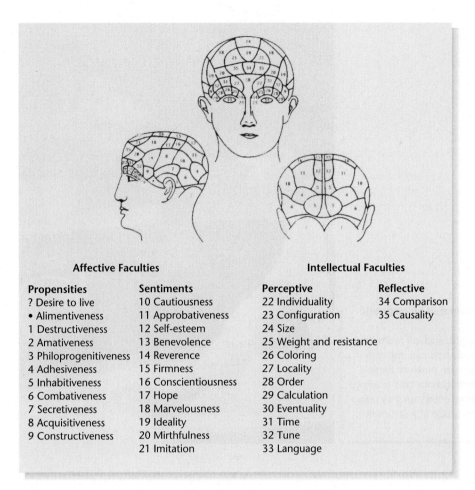

Affective Faculties

Propensities	Sentiments
? Desire to live	10 Cautiousness
• Alimentiveness	11 Approbativeness
1 Destructiveness	12 Self-esteem
2 Amativeness	13 Benevolence
3 Philoprogenitiveness	14 Reverence
4 Adhesiveness	15 Firmness
5 Inhabitiveness	16 Conscientiousness
6 Combativeness	17 Hope
7 Secretiveness	18 Marvelousness
8 Acquisitiveness	19 Ideality
9 Constructiveness	20 Mirthfulness
	21 Imitation

Intellectual Faculties

Perceptive	Reflective
22 Individuality	34 Comparison
23 Configuration	35 Causality
24 Size	
25 Weight and resistance	
26 Coloring	
27 Locality	
28 Order	
29 Calculation	
30 Eventuality	
31 Time	
32 Tune	
33 Language	

FIGURE 4.36 A phrenologist's map of the brain
Neuroscientists today also try to localize functions in the brain, but they use more careful methods and they study such functions as vision and hearing, not "secretiveness" and "marvelousness." *(From Spurzheim, 1908)*

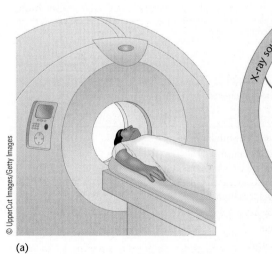

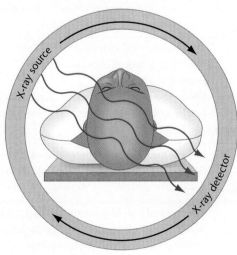

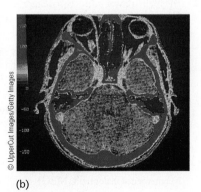

(a) (b)

FIGURE 4.37 CT scanner
(a) A person's head is placed into the device and then a rapidly rotating source sends X-rays through the head while detectors on the opposite side make photographs. A computer then constructs an image of the brain. **(b)** A view of a normal human brain generated by computerized axial tomography (CT scanning).

© Will and Demi McIntyre/Photo Researchers

FIGURE 4.38 A view of a living brain generated by magnetic resonance imaging
Any atom with an odd-numbered atomic weight, such as hydrogen, has an inherent rotation. An outside magnetic field can align the axes of rotation. A radio frequency field can then make all these atoms move like tiny gyros. When the radio frequency field is turned off, the atomic nuclei release electromagnetic energy as they relax. By measuring that energy, we can obtain an image of a structure such as the brain without damaging it.

TABLE 4.5

Examine Effects of Brain Damage

Study victims of stroke, etc.	Used with humans; each person has different damage
Lesion	Controlled damage in laboratory animals
Ablation	Removal of a brain area
Gene-knockout	Effects wherever that gene is active (e.g., a receptor)
Transcranial magnetic stimulation	Intense application temporarily inactivates a brain area

Examine Effects of Stimulating a Brain Area

Stimulating electrodes	Invasive; used with laboratory animals, seldom with humans
Transcranial magnetic stimulation	Brief, mild application activates underlying brain area

Record Brain Activity During Behavior

Record from electrodes in brain	Invasive; used with laboratory animals, seldom humans
Electroencephalograph (EEG)	Records from scalp; measures changes by ms, but with low resolution of location of the signal
Evoked potentials	Similar to EEG but in response to stimuli
Magnetoencephalograph (MEG)	Similar to EEG but measures magnetic fields
Positron emission tomography (PET)	Measures changes over both time and location but requires exposing brain to radiation
Functional magnetic resonance imaging (fMRI)	Measures changes over about 1 second, identifies location within 1–2 mm, no use of radiation

Correlate Brain Anatomy with Behavior

Computerized axial tomography (CAT)	Maps brain areas, but requires exposure to X-rays
Magnetic resonance imaging (MRI)	Maps brain areas in detail, using magnetic fields

21. Researchers today sometimes relate differences in people's behavior to differences in their brain anatomy. How does their approach differ from that of phrenologists?

ANSWER

21. Phrenologists drew conclusions based on just one or a few people with some oddity of behavior. Today's researchers compare groups statistically. Also, today's researchers examine the brain itself, not the skull.

Brain Size and Intelligence

Let's consider in more detail a specific example of correlating brain structure with behavior: What is the relationship between brain size and intelligence? It seems natural to assume that bigger brains are better, but maybe it's not that simple.

In the 1800s and early 1900s, several societies arose whose members agreed to donate their brains after death for research into whether the brains of eminent people were unusual in any way. No conclusion resulted. The brains of the eminent varied considerably, as did those of less eminent people. If brain anatomy was related to intellect in any way, the relation wasn't obvious (Burrell, 2004). Still, the idea lingers: Even if brain size isn't strongly related to intelligence, shouldn't it have *some* relationship?

Comparisons Across Species

All mammalian brains have the same organization, but they differ greatly in size. You can examine a variety of mammalian brains at the Comparative Mammalian Brain Collections website: **http://www.brainmuseum.org/sections/index.html**

Do variations in brain size relate to animal intelligence? We humans like to think of ourselves as the most intelligent animals—after all, we get to define what intelligence means! However, humans do not have the largest brains. Sperm whales' brains are eight times larger than ours, and elephants' are four times larger. Perhaps, many people suggest, intelli-

gence depends on brain-to-body ratio. Figure 4.39 illustrates the relationship between logarithm of body mass and logarithm of brain mass for various vertebrates (Jerison, 1985). Note that the species we regard as most intelligent—such as, ahem, ourselves—have larger brains in proportion to body size than do the species we consider less impressive, such as frogs.

However, brain-to-body ratio has problems also: Chihuahuas have the highest brain-to-body ratio of all dog breeds, not because they were bred for intelligence but because they were bred for small bodies (Deacon, 1997). Squirrel monkeys, which are also very thin, have a higher brain-to-body ratio than humans. (And with the increasing prevalence of human obesity, our brain-to-body ratio is declining!) The elephant-nose fish (Figure 4.40), which you might keep in an aquarium, has a 3% brain-to-body ratio compared to 2% for humans (Nilsson, 1999). So neither total brain mass nor brain-to-body ratio puts humans in first place.

A further problem is that we lack a clear definition of animal intelligence (Macphail, 1985). No test could fairly compare elephants, chimpanzees, and dolphins; each species is intelligent in its own way. Given that studies of brain and behavior in nonhumans are not helping, let's abandon that effort and turn to humans.

FIGURE 4.40 An elephant-nose fish
The brain of this odd-looking fish weighs 0.3 g (0.01 ounce), which is 3% of the weight of the whole fish—a vastly higher percentage than most other fish and higher even than humans. What this fish does with so much brain, we don't know, but it may relate to the fish's unusual ability to detect electrical fields.

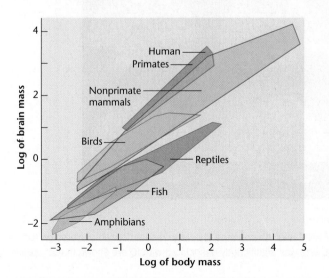

FIGURE 4.39 Relationship of brain mass to body mass across species
Each species is one point within one of the polygons. In general, log of body mass is a good predictor of log of brain mass. Note that primates in general and humans in particular have a large brain mass in proportion to body mass. (*Adapted from Jerison, 1985*)

> **Stop & Check**

22. Why are both brain size and brain-to-body ratio unsatisfactory ways of estimating animal intelligence?

ANSWER 22. If we consider ourselves to be the most intelligent species, we are confronted with the fact that we have neither the largest brains nor the highest brain-to-body ratios. Brain-to-body ratio depends on selection for thinness as well as selection for brain size. Furthermore, animal intelligence is undefined, so we cannot determine what correlates with it.

Comparisons Among Humans

For many years, studies of human brain size and intelligence found correlations barely above zero. However, a low correlation between two variables can mean either that they are unrelated or that they were measured poorly. Most early studies measured skull size instead of brain size. Today, using more accurate measurements based on MRI scans, most studies find a moderate positive correlation between brain size and IQ, typically around .3 (McDaniel, 2005).

Presumably certain brain areas are more important than others for intelligence. Several researchers have looked for particular brain areas that might be larger in people who score higher on intelligence tests. Many areas emerged as important, but the areas identified were not exactly the same from one study to the next (Colom et al., 2009; Frangou, Chitins, & Williams, 2004; Haier et al., 2009; Karama et al., 2009). In one case, investigators used MRI to measure the size of gray matter and white matter areas throughout the brains of 23 young adults from one university campus and 24 middle-aged or older adults from another campus. In Figure 4.41, the areas highlighted in red showed a statistically significant correlation with IQ, and those highlighted in yellow showed an even stronger correlation. Note the differences between the two samples, even though the procedures were the same for both (Haier, Jung, Yeo, Head, & Alkire, 2004).

The discrepancies point out some of the problems with this type of research: If we record from all brain areas during some task, it is like testing hundreds of hypotheses at the same time. The evidence will confirm some of them, just by chance. (The protection against this kind of error is to try to replicate the results, but if results vary across experiments, we need to beware.) Also, a given task may activate different areas in different people simply because they approached the task in different ways. That is, a given task—even an intelligence test—may be in fact a different task for different people.

> **Stop & Check**

23. Why do recent studies show a stronger relationship between brain size and IQ than older studies did?

ANSWER 23. The use of MRI greatly improves the measurement of brain size, in comparison to measurements based on the skull.

Comparisons of Men and Women

Now for the most confusing part: If we examine intelligence test scores and brain size for just men, or for just women, we find a moderate positive correlation. If we combine results for men and women, the correlation declines. Men on average have larger brains than women but equal IQs (Gilmore et al., 2007; Willerman, Schultz, Rutledge, & Bigler, 1991; Witelson, Beresh, & Kigar, 2006). Even if we take into account differences in height, men's brains remain larger (Ankney, 1992).

Although male and female brains differ, on average, behavioral differences, when carefully measured, are smaller than most people expect (Hyde, 2005). For example, vastly more men than women become grand masters in chess. Does that fact indicate a difference in abilities? No. Boys and girls start at an equal level in playing chess and progress at equal rates. Apparently the only reason more men reach the highest level is that vastly more boys

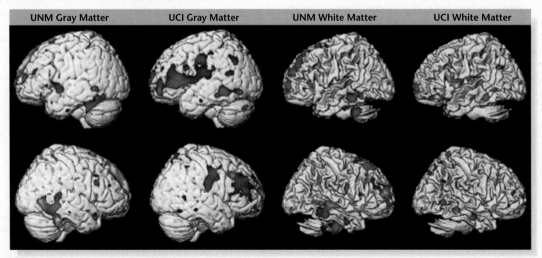

Adapted from NeuroImage, 23, Haier, R.J., Jung, R.E, Yeo, R.A., Head, K., & Alkire, M.T., Structural brain variation and general intelligence, pp. 425-433, Copyright 2004 with permission from Elsevier.

FIGURE 4.41 Cortical areas whose size correlated with IQ
The top row shows the left hemisphere; the bottom row shows the right. UNM and UCI columns show the results for two universities (University of New Mexico and University of California at Irvine). Areas whose size was significantly associated with IQ are shown in red; areas with the strongest relationship are shown in yellow.

than girls *start* playing chess (Chabris & Glickman, 2006). The difference pertains to interests, not abilities.

Many people believe that men tend to be better than women at mathematics. That may have been true in the past, and it still is true today in countries where men have much greater status than women, but in countries where men and women have roughly equal opportunities, their performance on math tests is about equal (Guiso, Monte, Sapienza, & Zingales, 2008). In the United States, girls on average do at least as well as boys in all math courses from elementary school through college, except for certain aspects of geometry, such as the items in Figure 4.42 (Hyde, Lindberg, Linn, Ellis, & Williams, 2008; Spelke, 2005). Even that difference may reflect differences in interests rather than ability. From an early age, most boys spend more time on activities related to angles and distances. In one study, young women who spent 10 hours playing action video games significantly improved on the kind of item shown in Figure 4.42 (Feng, Spence, & Pratt, 2007).

How can we explain why men and women are equal in intellect, but men have larger brains? One potentially relevant factor pertains to relative amounts of gray matter (cell bodies) and white matter (axons). Women average more and deeper sulci on the surface of the cortex, especially in the frontal and parietal areas (Luders et al., 2004). Consequently, the surface area of the cortex is almost equal for men and women. Because the surface is lined with neurons (gray matter), the sexes have about the same number of neurons, despite differences in brain volume (Allen, Damasio, Grabowski, Bruss, & Zhang, 2003). This idea would provide a convincing explanation *if* intelligence depended only on gray matter. However, the research points to important contributions from both gray matter and white matter (Chiang et al., 2009; Narr et al., 2007; van Leeuwen et al., 2009). We are left, then, with the apparent conclusion that women's brains and men's brains differ structurally but accomplish the same thing, presumably because they are organized differently. However, until we can expand on what we mean by "organized differently," it is not very satisfying.

In short, the data do not support any simple summary of the relationship between brain size and intelligence. Progress will

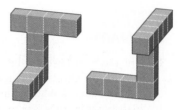

Can the set of blocks on the left be rotated to match the set at the right?

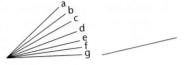

Which of the lines at the left has the same angle as the one at the right?

FIGURE 4.42 Spatial perception tasks
For the first question, the correct answer is *no*.
For the second question, the correct answer is *e*.
On average, men answer more quickly or more accurately than women, but women who spend 10 hours playing video games narrow the gap. (© *Cengage Learning 2013*)

probably depend on more detailed measurements of specific intellectual abilities and more detailed brain measurements. That is, how do the anatomy, chemistry, and other features of specific brain areas relate to specific aspects of behavior? In the rest of this text, we concentrate on those questions.

Stop & Check

24. In which way do men and women differ most—intellectual performance, total gray matter, or total white matter?

ANSWER

24. Men have more white matter, and therefore larger brains. However, men and women are about equal in gray matter and intellectual performance.

MODULE 4.3 ■ IN CLOSING

Research Methods and Their Limits

Why do we need so many research methods? It is because few studies conclusively establish one theory or another. Far more often, researchers gradually accumulate evidence that points in a particular direction, until eventually that view becomes dominant. Even in those rare cases when a single study appears to have been decisive, researchers often identify it as decisive only in retrospect, after many additional studies confirmed the finding.

The reason we need so many methods is that almost any study has limitations. Results often depend on what seem like minor details of procedure. Even when several studies using the same method produce similar results, the possibility remains that the method itself has a hidden flaw. Therefore, scientists prefer whenever possible to compare results from widely different methods. The more types of evidence point to a given conclusion, the greater our confidence.

SUMMARY

1. One way to study brain-behavior relationships is to examine the effects of brain damage. If someone suffers a loss after some kind of brain damage, then that area contributes in some way to that behavior. **109**

2. If stimulation of a brain area increases some behavior, presumably that area contributes to the behavior. **110**

3. Researchers try to understand brain-behavior relationships by recording activity in various brain areas during a given behavior. Many methods are available, including EEG, MEG, and fMRI. **111**

4. People who differ with regard to some behavior sometimes also differ with regard to their brain anatomy. MRI is one modern method of imaging a living brain. However, correlations between behavior and anatomy should be evaluated cautiously. **114**

5. Research using modern methods to measure brain size suggests a moderate positive relationship between brain size and intelligence, although many puzzles and uncertainties remain. **117**

6. Men and women are equal in IQ scores, despite men's having larger brains. **118**

KEY TERMS

Terms are defined in the module on the page number indicated. They're also presented in alphabetical order with definitions in the book's Subject Index/Glossary, which begins on page 561. Interactive flashcards and crossword puzzles are among the online resources available to help you learn these terms and the concepts they represent.

ablation **109**

computerized axial tomography (CT or CAT scan) **114**

electroencephalograph (EEG) **111**

evoked potentials or evoked responses **111**

functional magnetic resonance imaging (fMRI) **112**

lesion **109**

magnetic resonance imaging (MRI) **114**

magnetoencephalograph (MEG) **111**

phrenology **114**

positron-emission tomography (PET) **111**

stereotaxic instrument **109**

transcranial magnetic stimulation **110**

THOUGHT QUESTION

Certain unusual aspects of brain structure were observed in the brain of Albert Einstein (M. C. Diamond, Scheibel, Murphy, & Harvey, 1985; Witelson, Kigar, & Harvey, 1999).

One interpretation is that he was born with certain specialized brain features that encouraged his scientific and intellectual abilities. What is an alternative interpretation?

CHAPTER 4 Interactive Exploration and Study

The **Psychology CourseMate** for this text brings chapter topics to life with interactive learning, study, and exam preparation tools, including quizzes and flashcards for the Key Concepts that appear throughout each module, as well as an interactive media-rich eBook version of the text that is fully searchable and includes highlighting and note taking capabilities and interactive versions of the book's **Stop & Check** quizzes and **Try It Yourself Online** activities. The site also features **Virtual Biological Psychology Labs**, **videos**, and **animations** to help you better understand concepts—logon and learn more at **www.cengagebrain.com**, which is your gateway to all of this text's complimentary and premium resources, including the following:

Virtual Biological Psychology Labs

Explore the experiments that led to modern-day understanding of biopsychology with the Virtual Biological Psychology Labs, featuring a realistic lab environment that allows you to conduct experiments and evaluate data to better understand how scientists came to the conclusions presented in your text. The labs cover a range of topics, including perception, motivation, cognition, and more. You may purchase access at **www.cengagebrain.com**, or login at **login.cengagebrain.com** if an access card was included with your text.

Videos

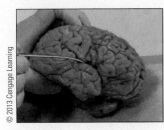

© 2013 Cengage Learning

Structures of the Brain, Part 1

Also available—

- Structures of the Brain, Part 2
- Magnetic Stimulation of the Brain
- Research with Brain Scans
- Politics and the Brain
- Visual Mind Reading

Animations

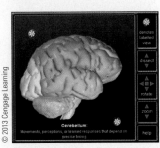

© 2013 Cengage Learning

Interactive 3D Brain

Also available—

- Interactive Left Hemisphere Function
- Interactive Sagittal Section: Right Hemisphere #1
- Interactive Sagittal Section: Right Hemisphere #2
- Interactive Sagittal Section: Right Hemisphere #3
- Interactive Brain Puzzle
- Interactive Cortex Puzzle
- Interactive Sensory Cortex
- Structures of the Brain

Suggestions for Further Exploration

Books

Burrell, B. (2004). *Postcards from the brain museum.* New York: Broadway Books. Fascinating history of the attempts to collect brains of successful people and try to relate their brain anatomy to their success.

Klawans, H. L. (1988). *Toscanini's fumble and other tales of clinical neurology.* Chicago: Contemporary Books. Description of illustrative cases of brain damage and their behavioral consequences.

Websites

The Psychology CourseMate for this text provides regularly updated links to relevant online resources for this chapter, such as the **Whole Brain Atlas** and **Comparative Mammalian Brain Collections.**

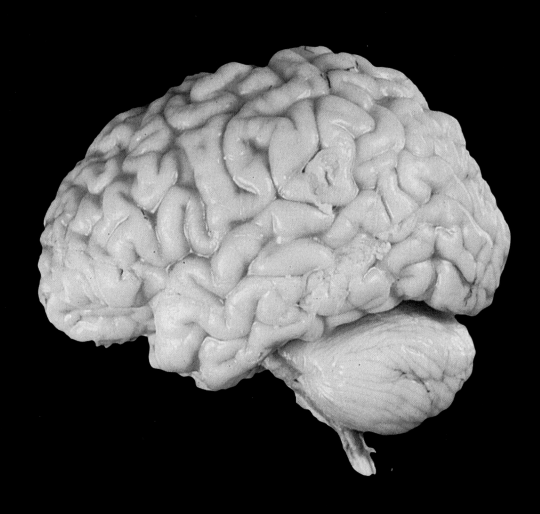

Development and Plasticity of the Brain

MAIN IDEAS

1. Neurons begin by migrating to their proper locations and developing axons, which extend to their targets by following chemical pathways.

2. The nervous system forms far more neurons than it needs and then eliminates those that do not establish suitable connections or receive sufficient input. It also forms excess synapses and discards the less active ones.

3. Experiences alter brain anatomy. Plasticity is greatest early in life but continues throughout life.

4. Many mechanisms contribute to recovery from brain damage, including restoration of undamaged neurons to full activity, regrowth of axons, readjustment of surviving synapses, and behavioral adjustments.

"Some assembly required." Have you ever bought a package with those ominous words? Sometimes, all you have to do is attach a few parts, but other times, you face page after page of barely comprehensible instructions.

The human nervous system requires an enormous amount of assembly, and the instructions are different from those for the objects we assemble from a kit. Instead of, "Put this piece here and that piece there," the instructions are, "Put these axons here and those dendrites there, and then wait to see what happens. Keep the connections that work the best and discard the others. Continue making new connections and keeping only the successful ones."

Therefore, we say that the brain's anatomy is *plastic*. It changes rapidly in early development and continues changing throughout life.

OPPOSITE: An enormous amount of brain development has already occurred by the time a person is 1 year old.

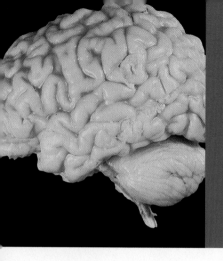

Development of the Brain

Think of all the things you can do that you couldn't have done a few years ago—analyze statistics, read a foreign language, write brilliant critiques of complex issues, and so on. Have you developed these new skills because of brain growth? Many of your dendrites have grown new branches, but your brain as a whole is the same size.

Now think of all the things that 1-year-old children can do that they could not do at birth. Have *they* developed their new skills because of brain growth? To a large extent, yes, although the results depend on experiences as well. Brain development depends on experience in complex ways that blur the distinction between learning and maturation. In this module, we consider how neurons develop, how their axons connect, and how experience modifies development.

Maturation of the Vertebrate Brain

The human central nervous system begins to form when the embryo is about 2 weeks old. The dorsal surface thickens and then long thin lips rise, curl, and merge, forming a neural tube that surrounds a fluid-filled cavity (Figure 5.1). As the tube sinks under the surface of the skin, the forward end enlarges and differentiates into the hindbrain, midbrain, and forebrain (Figure 5.2). The rest becomes the spinal cord. The fluid-filled cavity within the neural tube becomes the central canal of the spinal cord and the four ventricles of the brain, containing the cerebrospinal fluid (CSF). At birth, the average human brain weighs about 350 grams (g). By the end of the first year, it weighs 1,000 g, close to the adult weight of 1,200 to 1,400 g.

Growth and Development of Neurons

Neuroscientists distinguish these processes in the development of neurons: proliferation, migration, differentiation, myelination, and synaptogenesis. **Proliferation** is the production of new cells. Early in development, the cells lining the ventricles of the brain divide. Some cells remain where they are (as *stem cells*), continuing to divide. Others become primitive neurons and glia that begin migrating to other locations. Neuron proliferation is similar among vertebrates, differing mainly in the number of cell divisions. Human brains differ from chimpanzee brains mainly because human neurons continue proliferating longer (Rakic, 1998; Vrba, 1998).

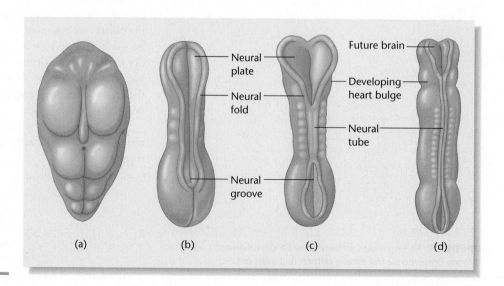

FIGURE 5.1 Early development of the human central nervous system
The brain and spinal cord begin as folding lips surrounding a fluid-filled canal. The stages shown occur at approximately age 2 to 3 weeks. (© Cengage Learning 2013)

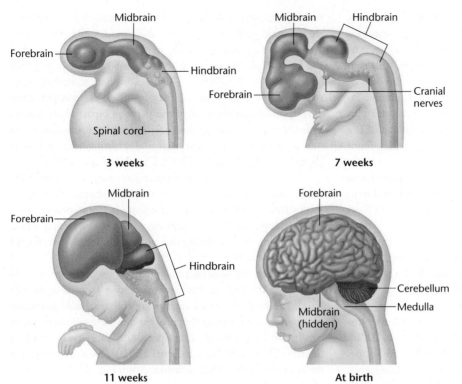

Midbrain
Forebrain
Hindbrain
Spinal cord
3 weeks

Midbrain   Hindbrain
Forebrain
Cranial nerves
7 weeks

Midbrain
Forebrain
Hindbrain
11 weeks

Forebrain
Cerebellum
Medulla
Midbrain (hidden)
At birth

FIGURE 5.2 Human brain at four stages of development
Chemical processes develop the brain to an amazing degree even before the start of any experience with the world. Further changes continue throughout life. (© *Cengage Learning 2013*)

After cells have differentiated as neurons or glia, they **migrate** (move). Some neurons migrate much faster than others, and a few of the slowest don't reach their final destinations until adulthood (Ghashghaei, Lai, & Anton, 2007). Some neurons move radially from the inside of the brain to the outside, some move tangentially along the surface of the brain, and some move tangentially and then radially (Nadarajah & Parnavelas, 2002). Chemicals known as *immunoglobulins* and *chemokines* guide neuron migration. A deficit in these chemicals leads to impaired migration, decreased brain size, decreased axon growth, and mental retardation (Berger-Sweeney & Hohmann, 1997; Crossin & Krushel, 2000; Tran & Miller, 2003). The brain has many kinds of immunoglobulins and chemokines, presumably reflecting the complexity of brain development.

At first, a primitive neuron looks like any other cell. Gradually, the neuron **differentiates**, forming its axon and dendrites. The axon grows first. In many cases, a migrating neuron tows its growing axon along like a tail (Gilmour, Knaut, Maischein, & Nüsslein-Volhard, 2004), allowing its tip to remain at or near its target. In other cases, the axon needs to grow toward its target, finding its way through a jungle of other cells and fibers. After the migrating neuron reaches its destination, its dendrites begin to form.

A later and slower stage of neuronal development is **myelination**, the process by which glia produce the insulating fatty sheaths that accelerate transmission in many vertebrate axons. Myelin forms first in the spinal cord and then in the hindbrain, midbrain, and forebrain. Unlike the rapid prolifer-

ation and migration of neurons, myelination continues gradually for decades (Benes, Turtle, Khan, & Farol, 1994).

The final stage is **synaptogenesis**, or the formation of synapses. Although this process begins before birth, it continues throughout life, as neurons form new synapses and discard old ones. However, the process generally slows in older people, as does the formation of new dendritic branches (Buell & Coleman, 1981; Jacobs & Scheibel, 1993).

Stop & Check

1. Which develops first, a neuron's axon or its dendrites?

ANSWER   1. The axon forms first.

New Neurons Later in Life

Can the adult vertebrate brain generate new neurons? The traditional belief, dating back to Cajal's work in the late 1800s, was that vertebrate brains formed all their neurons in embryological development or early infancy at the latest. Beyond that point, neurons could modify their shape, but the brain could not develop new neurons. Later researchers found exceptions.

The first were the olfactory receptors, which, because they are exposed to the outside world and its toxic chemicals, have a half-life of only 90 days. **Stem cells** in the nose remain immature throughout life. Periodically, they divide, with one cell remaining immature while the other differentiates to replace a dying olfactory receptor. It grows its axon back to the appropriate site in the brain (Gogos, Osborne, Nemes, Mendelsohn, & Axel, 2000; Graziadei & deHan, 1973). Later researchers also found a similar population of stem cells in the interior of the brain. They sometimes divide to form "daughter" cells that migrate to the olfactory bulb and transform into glia cells or neurons (Gage, 2000). The newly formed neurons are necessary for maintaining the olfactory bulb. Any procedure that prevents their formation leads to a gradual shrinkage of the olfactory bulbs, because neurons die without replacement (Imayoshi et al., 2008).

New neurons also form in an area of the songbird brain necessary for singing. This area loses neurons in fall and winter and regains them the next spring (mating season) (Nottebohm, 2002; Wissman & Brenowitz, 2009).

Stem cells also differentiate into new neurons in the adult hippocampus of birds (Smulders, Shiflett, Sperling, & DeVoogd, 2000) and mammals (Song, Stevens, & Gage, 2002; van Praag et al., 2002). The hippocampus is an important area for memory formation. Blocking the formation of new neurons (such as by exposing the hippocampus to X-rays) impairs new memories (Clelland et al., 2009; Meshi et al., 2006).

In general, animals learn most easily when they are young. As they grow older, their neurons become less changeable. Newly formed neurons of the hippocampus go through a stage when they are highly changeable, like those of youth (Ge, Yang, Hsu, Ming, & Song, 2007; Schmidt-Hieber, Jonas, & Bischofberger, 2004). During this period, they integrate into new circuits that represent new memories (Kee, Teixeira, Wang, & Frankland, 2007; Ramirez-Amaya, Marrone, Gage, Worley, & Barnes, 2006). More of the newly formed neurons survive during times of new learning (Tashiro, Makino, & Gage, 2007). A supply of new neurons keeps the hippocampus "young" for learning new tasks. It is also possible that incorporating clusters of new neurons into a single new circuit may be a way of labeling memories that formed at a given time. It might lead to a recollection that certain events happened at the same time (Aimone, Wiles, & Gage, 2006).

Possible formation of new neurons in the mature primate cerebral cortex has been controversial. The best evidence against their formation came from a clever study using a radioactive isotope of carbon, ^{14}C. The concentration of ^{14}C in the atmosphere, compared to other isotopes of carbon, was nearly constant over time until the era of nuclear bomb testing, which released much radioactivity. That era ended with the test ban treaty of 1963. The concentration of ^{14}C peaked in 1963 and has been declining since then. If you examine, for example, tree rings, you will find that a ring that formed in 1963 has the ^{14}C content typical of 1963, a ring that formed in 1990 has the ^{14}C content typical of 1990, and so forth. Researchers examined the carbon in the DNA of various human cells. Every cell keeps its DNA molecules until it dies. When researchers examined people's skin cells, they found a concentration of ^{14}C corresponding to the year in which they did the test. That is, skin cells turn over rapidly, and all of your skin cells are less than a year old. When they examined skeletal muscle cells, they found a ^{14}C concentration corresponding

to 15 years ago, indicating that skeletal muscles are replaced slowly, making the average cell 15 years old. Cells of the heart are, on average, almost as old as the person, indicating that the body replaces no more than 1% of heart cells per year (Bergmann et al., 2009). When researchers examined neurons in the cerebral cortex, they found a ^{14}C concentration corresponding to the year of the person's birth. These results indicate that the mammalian cerebral cortex forms few or no new neurons after birth, at least under normal circumstances (Spalding, Bhardwaj, Buchholz, Druid, & Frisén, 2005).

Are you surprised to learn that your cortex may not have made any new neurons since you were born? Researcher Pasko Rakic (2008, p. 894) commented, "Some people seem to be disappointed by this finding, as if it is a bad thing. I find it fascinating that… during our prolonged lifespan we always use the same cells."

However, the situation may be different after brain damage. After damage to the sensory axons from a monkey's hand, the cerebral cortex on the contralateral side gradually reorganizes, and during this process new neurons do form, as confirmed by chemicals that specifically label newly formed neurons (Vessal & Darian-Smith, 2010). New neurons also form in the cortex after a stroke (Ohira et al., 2010). Most of the newly formed neurons are small ones with inhibitory functions. How long they survive is not yet known.

Stop & Check

2. In which brain areas do new neurons form in adults?

3. What evidence indicated that new neurons seldom or never form in the adult cerebral cortex?

ANSWERS **2.** Olfactory receptors, neurons in the hippocampus, and neurons in the song-producing areas of certain bird species. **3.** The ^{14}C concentration in the DNA of cerebral cortex neurons corresponds to the level during the year the person was born, indicating that all or nearly all of those neurons are as old as the person is.

Pathfinding by Axons

If you asked someone to run a cable from your desk to another desk across the room, your directions could be simple. But imagine asking someone to run a cable to somewhere on the other side of the country. You would have to give detailed instructions about how to find the right city, building, and desk. The developing nervous system faces a similar challenge because it sends axons over great distances. How do they find their way?

Chemical Pathfinding by Axons

A famous biologist, Paul Weiss (1924), conducted an experiment in which he grafted an extra leg to a salamander and then waited for axons to grow into it. (Unlike mammals, salamanders and other amphibians accept transplants of extra limbs and generate new axon branches to the extra limbs. Much research requires finding the right species to study.) After the axons reached the muscles, the extra leg moved in synchrony with the normal leg next to it.

Weiss dismissed the idea that each axon found its way to exactly the correct muscle in the extra limb. He suggested instead that the nerves attached to muscles at random and then sent a variety of messages, each one tuned to a different muscle. The muscles were like radios tuned to different stations: Each muscle received many signals but responded to only one. (The 1920s were the early days of radio, and it was an appealing analogy to think the nervous system might work like a radio. In the 1600s, Descartes thought the nervous system worked like a hydraulic pump, the most advanced technology of the time. Today many people think the nervous system works like a computer, our own most advanced technology.)

Specificity of Axon Connections

Later evidence supported the interpretation that Weiss had rejected: The salamander's extra leg moved in synchrony with its neighbor because each axon found exactly the correct muscle.

Roger Sperry, a former student of Weiss, performed a classic experiment that showed how sensory axons find their way to their correct targets. The principle is the same as for axons finding their way to muscles. First Sperry cut the optic nerves of some newts. (Note the importance of choosing the right species: A cut optic nerve grows back in newts and other amphibians, but not in mammals or birds.) The damaged optic nerve grew back and connected with the *tectum*, which is amphibians' main visual area (Figure 5.3), thereby reestablishing normal vision.

Roger W. Sperry
(1913–1994)

When subjective values have objective consequences... they become part of the content of science.... Science would become the final determinant of what is right and true, the best source and authority available to the human brain for finding ultimate axioms and guideline beliefs to live by, and for reaching an intimate understanding and rapport with the forces that control the universe and created man. (Sperry, 1975, pp. 432-433)

Then Sperry (1943) cut the optic nerve and rotated the eye by 180 degrees. When the axons grew back to the tectum, which area would they contact? The axons from what had originally been the dorsal portion of the retina (which was now ventral) grew back to the area responsible for vision in the dorsal retina. Axons from other parts of the retina also grew back to their original targets. The newt now saw the world upside down and backward, responding to stimuli in the sky as if they were on the ground and to stimuli on the left as if they were on the right (Figure 5.4). Each axon regenerated to the same place where it had originally been, presumably by following a chemical trail.

Chemical Gradients

The next question was: How specific is the axon's aim? The current estimate is that humans have only about 30,000 genes total—far too few to provide a specific target for each

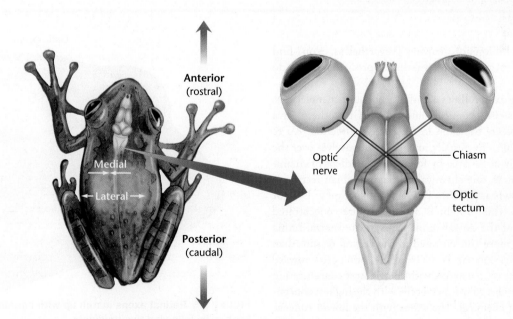

FIGURE 5.3 Connections from eye to brain in a frog
The optic tectum is a large structure in fish, amphibians, reptiles, and birds. Its location corresponds to the midbrain of mammals, but its function is analogous to what the cerebral cortex does in mammals. Note: Connections from eye to brain are different in humans, as described in Chapter 14. *(Source: After Romer, 1962)*

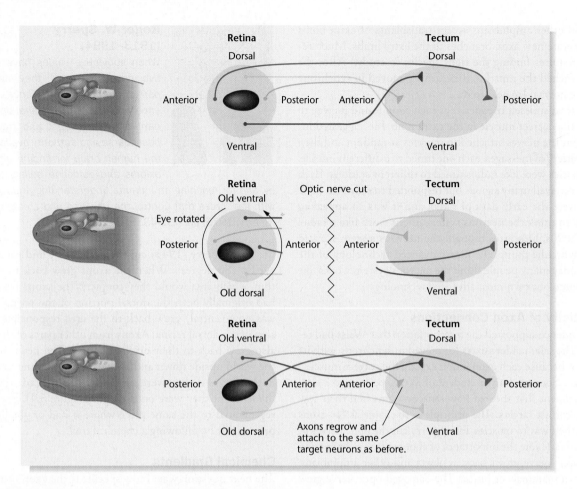

FIGURE 5.4 Sperry's experiment on nerve connections in newts
After he cut the optic nerve and inverted the eye, the axons grew back to their original targets, not to the targets corresponding to the eye's current position. (© Cengage Learning 2013)

of the brain's billions of neurons. Nevertheless, axons find their correct targets with remarkable precision. How do they do it?

A growing axon follows a path of cell–surface molecules, attracted by some chemicals and repelled by others, in a process that steers the axon in the correct direction (Yu & Bargmann, 2001). Eventually, axons sort themselves over the surface of their target area by following a gradient of chemicals. For example, one chemical in the amphibian tectum is a protein known as TOP_{DV} (TOP for *to*pography; DV for *do*rsoventral). This protein is 30 times more concentrated in the axons of the dorsal retina than of the ventral retina and 10 times more concentrated in the ventral tectum than in the dorsal tectum. As axons from the retina grow toward the tectum, the retinal axons with the greatest concentration of TOP_{DV} connect to the tectal cells with the highest concentration of that chemical. The axons with the lowest concentration connect to the tectal cells with the lowest concentration. A similar gradient of another protein aligns the axons along the anterior–posterior axis (J. R. Sanes, 1993) (Figure 5.5). By analogy, you could think of men lining up from tallest to shortest, pairing up with women who lined up from tallest to shortest.

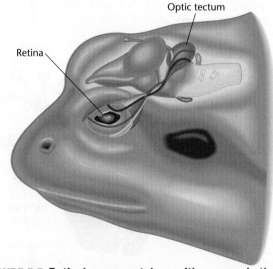

FIGURE 5.5 Retinal axons match up with neurons in the tectum by following two gradients
The protein TOP_{DV} is concentrated mostly in the dorsal retina and the ventral tectum. Axons rich in TOP_{DV} attach to tectal neurons that are also rich in that chemical. A second protein directs axons from the posterior retina to the anterior portion of the tectum (© Cengage Learning 2013)

Stop & Check

4. What was Sperry's evidence that axons grow to a specific target instead of attaching at random?

5. If all cells in an amphibian's tectum produced the same amount of TOP$_{DV}$, what would be the effect on the attachment of axons?

ANSWERS **4.** Sperry found that if he cut a newt's eye and inverted it, axons grew back to their original targets, even though the connections were inappropriate to their new positions on the eye. **5.** Axons would attach haphazardly instead of arranging themselves according to their dorsoventral position on the retina.

Competition Among Axons as a General Principle

When axons initially reach their targets, chemical gradients steer them to approximately their correct location, but it would be hard to imagine that they achieve perfect accuracy. Instead, each axon forms synapses onto many cells in approximately the correct location, and each target cell receives synapses from many axons. Over time, each postsynaptic cell strengthens some synapses—presumably the most appropriate ones—and eliminates others (Hua & Smith, 2004). This adjustment depends on the pattern of input from incoming axons (Catalano & Shatz, 1998). For example, one part of the thalamus receives input from many retinal axons. During embryological development, long before the first exposure to light, repeated waves of spontaneous activity sweep over the retina from one side to the other. Consequently, axons from adjacent areas of the retina send almost simultaneous messages to the thalamus. Each thalamic neuron selects a group of axons that are simultaneously active. In this way, it finds receptors from adjacent regions of the retina (Meister, Wong, Baylor, & Shatz, 1991). It then rejects synapses from other locations.

These results suggest a general principle, called **neural Darwinism** (Edelman, 1987). In the development of the nervous system, we start with more neurons and synapses than we can keep. Synapses form with only approximate accuracy, and then a selection process keeps some and rejects others. The most successful axons and combinations survive, and the others fail. The principle of competition among axons is an important one, although we should use the analogy with Darwinian evolution cautiously. Mutations in the genes are random events, but neurotrophins steer new axonal branches and synapses in the right direction.

Stop & Check

6. If axons from the retina were prevented from showing spontaneous activity during early development, what would be the probable effect on development of the lateral geniculate?

ANSWER **6.** The axons would attach based on a chemical gradient but could not fine-tune their adjustment based on experience. Therefore, the connections would be less precise.

Determinants of Neuronal Survival

Getting the right number of neurons for each area of the nervous system is more complicated than it might seem. Consider an example. The sympathetic nervous system sends axons to muscles and glands. Each ganglion has enough axons to supply the muscles and glands in its area, with no axons left over. How does the match come out so exact? Long ago, one hypothesis was that the muscles sent chemical messages to tell the sympathetic ganglion how many neurons to form. Rita Levi-Montalcini was largely responsible for disconfirming this hypothesis.

Levi-Montalcini's early life would seem most unfavorable for a scientific career. She was a young Italian Jewish woman

Carla J. Shatz

The functioning of the brain depends upon the precision and patterns of its neural circuits. How is this amazing computational machine assembled and wired during development? The biological answer is so much more wonderful than anticipated! The adult precision is sculpted from an early imprecise pattern by a process in which connections are verified by the functioning of the neurons themselves. Thus, the developing brain is not simply a miniature version of the adult. Moreover, the brain works to wire itself, rather than assembling itself first and then flipping a switch, as might happen in the assembly of a computer. This kind of surprise in scientific discovery opens up new vistas of understanding and possibility and makes the process of doing science infinitely exciting and fascinating. (Shatz, personal communication)

Carla J. Shatz

Rita Levi-Montalcini

Many years later, I often asked myself how we could have dedicated ourselves with such enthusiasm to solving this small neuroembryological problem while German armies were advancing throughout Europe, spreading destruction and death wherever they went and threatening the very survival of Western civilization. The answer lies in the desperate and partially unconscious desire of human beings to ignore what is happening in situations where full awareness might lead one to self-destruction.

Erich Hartmann/Magnum Photos New York

during the Nazi era. World War II destroyed the Italian economy, and almost everyone at the time discouraged women from scientific or medical careers. She had to spend several years in hiding during the war, but she spent those years conducting research on development of the nervous system, as she described in her autobiography (Levi-Montalcini, 1988) and a later interview with Moses Chao (2010). She developed a love for research and eventually discovered that the muscles do not determine how many axons *form*; they determine how many *survive*.

Initially, the sympathetic nervous system forms far more neurons than it needs. When one of its neurons forms a synapse onto a muscle, that muscle delivers a protein called **nerve growth factor** (**NGF**) that promotes the survival and growth of the axon (Levi-Montalcini, 1987). An axon that does not receive NGF degenerates, and its cell body dies. That is, each neuron starts life with a "suicide program": If its axon does not make contact with an appropriate postsynaptic cell by a certain age, the neuron kills itself through a process called **apoptosis**,[1] a programmed mechanism of cell death. (Apoptosis is distinct from *necrosis*, which is death caused by an injury or a toxic substance.) NGF cancels the program for apoptosis; it is the postsynaptic cell's way of telling the incoming axon, "I'll be your partner. Don't kill yourself."

The brain's system of overproducing neurons and then applying apoptosis enables the CNS to match the number of incoming axons to the number of receiving cells. When the sympathetic nervous system begins sending axons toward the muscles and glands, it doesn't know the exact size of the muscles or glands. It makes more neurons than necessary and discards the excess. In fact, all areas of the developing nervous system make far more neurons than will survive into adulthood. Each brain area has a period of massive cell death, becoming littered with dead and dying cells (Figure 5.6). This loss of cells is a natural part of development. In fact, loss of cells in a particular brain area often indicates maturation. For example, teenagers lose cells in parts of the prefrontal cortex while showing increased neuronal activity in those areas (Sowell, Thompson, Holmes, Jernigan, & Toga, 1999). Maturation of successful cells is linked to simultaneous loss of less successful ones. Another example is the visual cortex of people born blind. Contrary to what you might guess, the visual cortex is *thicker* than average in people born blind. A likely explanation is that in the absence of visual experience, the visual cortex is unable to prune out the ineffective and inappropriate synapses (Jiang et al., 2009).

Nerve growth factor is a **neurotrophin**, meaning a chemical that promotes the survival and activity of neurons. (The word *trophin* derives from a Greek word for "nourishment.") In addition to NGF, the nervous system responds to *brain-derived neurotrophic factor* (BDNF) and several other neurotrophins (Airaksinen & Saarma, 2002). Neurotrophins are

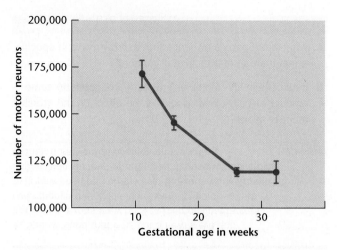

FIGURE 5.6 **Cell loss during development of the nervous system**
The number of motor neurons in the spinal cord of human fetuses is highest at 11 weeks and drops steadily until about 25 weeks. If an axon fails to make a synapse, its cell dies. *(Source: From N. G. Forger and S. M. Breedlove, Motoneuronal death in the human fetus.* Journal of Comparative Neurology, *264, 1987, 118–122. Copyright © 1987 Alan R. Liss, Inc. Reprinted by permission of N. G. Forger.)*

not necessary for survival of brain neurons, but they are essential for growth of axons and dendrites, formation of new synapses, and learning (Alleva & Francia, 2009; Pascual et al., 2008; Rauskolb et al., 2010). Remember the term BDNF, because it becomes important again in Chapter 15 on depression and schizophrenia.

For an immature neuron to avoid apoptosis and survive, it needs to receive neurotrophins not only from its target cells but also from incoming axons. In one study, researchers examined mice with a genetic defect that prevented all release of neurotransmitters. The brains initially assembled normal anatomies, but then neurons started dying rapidly (Verhage et al., 2000). When neurons release neurotransmitters, they also release neurotrophins. Neurons that fail to receive neurotransmitters also fail to receive neurotrophins, and so they die (Poo, 2001).

Stop & Check

7. What process ensures that the spinal cord has the right number of axons to innervate all the muscle cells?

8. What class of chemicals prevents apoptosis?

9. At what age does a person have the greatest number of neurons—before birth, during childhood, during adolescence, or during adulthood?

ANSWERS   before birth.
nerve growth factor **9.** The neuron number is greatest
not make lasting synapses. **8.** Neurotrophins, such as
it needs and discards through apoptosis those that do
7. The nervous system builds far more neurons than

---

[1]Apoptosis is based on the Greek root *ptosis* (meaning "dropping"), which is pronounced TOE-sis. Therefore, most scholars insist that the second *p* in *apoptosis* should be silent, a-po-TOE-sis. Others argue that *helicopter* is also derived from a root with a silent *p* (*pteron*), but we pronounce the *p* in *helicopter*, so we should also pronounce the second *p* in *apoptosis*. Be prepared for either pronunciation.

The Vulnerable Developing Brain

According to Lewis Wolpert (1991), "It is not birth, marriage, or death, but gastrulation, which is truly the most important time of your life." (Gastrulation is one of the early stages of embryological development.) Wolpert's point was that if you mess up in early development, you have problems from then on. Actually, if you mess up during gastrulation, your life is over.

The early stages of brain development are critical. A mutation in one identified gene leads to any of a wide variety of defects in brain development (Bilgüvar et al., 2010). The developing brain is also highly vulnerable to malnutrition, toxic chemicals, and infections that would produce only mild problems at later ages. For example, impaired thyroid function produces lethargy in adults but mental retardation in infants. (Thyroid deficiency was common in the past because of iodine deficiency. It is rare today because table salt is fortified with iodine.) A fever is a mere annoyance to an adult, but it impairs neuron proliferation in a fetus (Laburn, 1996). Low blood glucose decreases an adult's pep, but before birth, it impairs brain development (C. A. Nelson et al., 2000).

The infant brain is highly vulnerable to damage by alcohol. Children of mothers who drink heavily during pregnancy are born with **fetal alcohol syndrome**, a condition marked by hyperactivity, impulsiveness, difficulty maintaining attention, varying degrees of mental retardation, motor problems, heart defects, and facial abnormalities (Figure 5.7). Even in milder cases, those who were exposed to prenatal alcohol show impairments in learning, memory, language, and attention (Kodituwakku, 2007).

The mechanism of fetal alcohol syndrome relates partly to apoptosis: Remember that to prevent apoptosis, a neuron must receive neurotrophins from the incoming axons as well as from its own axon's target cell. Alcohol suppresses the release of glutamate, the brain's main excitatory transmitter, and enhances activity of GABA, the main inhibitory transmitter. Consequently, many neurons receive less excitation and neurotrophins than normal, and they undergo apoptosis (Ikonomidou et al., 2000). Alcohol also impairs brain development by altering the migration pattern of small neurons (Cuzon, Yeh, Yanagawa, Obata, & Yeh, 2008).

Prenatal exposure to other substances can be dangerous, too. On average, children of mothers who use cocaine or smoke cigarettes during pregnancy have an increased risk of attention-deficit disorder and other behavioral deficits (B. L. Thompson, Levitt, & Stanwood, 2009). Children whose mother used antidepressant drugs during pregnancy have increased risk of heart problems (Thompson et al., 2009). Because these are correlational studies, we cannot be sure of cause and effect. Mothers who smoke or use cocaine tend to be of lower socioeconomic status, less educated, and so forth, so the effect of smoking is probably smaller than the results suggest (Thapar et al., 2003).

Finally, the immature brain is highly responsive to influences from the mother. If a mother rat is exposed to stressful experiences, she becomes more fearful, she spends less than the

AP Images

FIGURE 5.7 Child with fetal alcohol syndrome
Note the facial pattern. Many children exposed to smaller amounts of alcohol before birth have behavioral deficits without facial signs.

usual amount of time licking and grooming her offspring, and her offspring become permanently more fearful in a variety of situations (Cameron et al., 2005). Analogously, the children of impoverished and abused women have, on average, increased problems in both their academic and social lives. The mechanisms in humans are not exactly the same as those in rats, but the overall principles are similar: Stress to the mother changes her behavior in ways that change her offspring's behavior.

Stop & Check

10. Anesthetic drugs increase inhibition of neurons, blocking most action potentials. Why would we predict that exposure to anesthetics might be dangerous to the brain of a fetus?

ANSWER

10. Prolonged exposure to anesthetics might produce effects similar to fetal alcohol syndrome. Fetal alcohol syndrome occurs because alcohol increases inhibition and therefore increases apoptosis of developing neurons.

Differentiation of the Cortex

Neurons in different brain areas differ in shape and chemistry. When and how does a neuron "decide" which kind of neuron it is going to be? It is not a sudden decision. Immature neurons experimentally transplanted from one part of the developing cortex to another develop the properties characteristic of their new location (S. K. McConnell, 1992). However, neurons transplanted at a slightly later stage develop some new properties while retaining some old ones (Cohen-Tannoudji, Babinet, & Wassef, 1994). It is like the speech of immigrant children: Those who enter a country when very young master the correct pronunciation, whereas older children retain an accent.

In one fascinating experiment, researchers explored what would happen to the immature auditory portions of the brain if they received input from the eyes instead of the ears. Ferrets—mammals in the weasel family—are born so immature that their optic nerves (from the eyes) have not yet reached the thalamus. On one side of the brain, researchers damaged the superior colliculus and the occipital cortex, the two main targets for the optic nerves. On that side, they also damaged the auditory input. Therefore, the optic nerve could not attach to its usual target, and the auditory area of the thalamus lacked its usual input. As a result, the optic nerve attached to what is usually the auditory area of the thalamus. What would you guess happened? Did the visual input cause auditory sensations, or did the auditory areas of the brain turn into visual areas?

The result, surprising to many, was this: What would have been auditory thalamus and cortex reorganized, developing some (but not all) of the characteristic appearance of visual areas (Sharma, Angelucci, & Sur, 2000). But how do we know whether the animals treated that activity as vision? Remember that the researchers performed these procedures on one side of the brain. They left the other side intact. The researchers presented stimuli to the normal side of the brain and trained the ferrets to turn one direction when they heard something and the other direction when they saw a light, as shown in Figure 5.8. After the ferrets learned this task well, the researchers presented a light that the rewired side could see. The result: The ferrets turned the way they had been taught to turn when they saw something. In short, the rewired temporal cortex, receiving input from the optic nerve, produced visual responses (von Melchner, Pallas, & Sur, 2000).

Stop & Check

11. In the ferret study, how did the experimenters determine that visual input to the auditory portions of the brain actually produced a visual sensation?

ANSWER 11. They trained the ferrets to respond to stimuli on the normal side, turning one direction in response to sounds and the other direction to lights. Then they presented light to the rewired side and saw that the ferret again turned in the direction it had associated with lights.

Fine-Tuning by Experience

The blueprints for a house determine its overall plan, but because architects can't anticipate every detail, construction workers often have to improvise. The same is true for your nervous system. Because of the unpredictability of life, our brains have evolved the ability to remodel themselves (within limits) in response to our experience (Shatz, 1992).

Experience and Dendritic Branching

Decades ago, researchers doubted that adult neurons substantially changed their shape. We now know that axons and den-

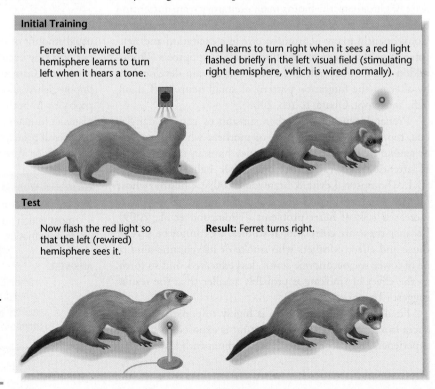

Initial Training

Ferret with rewired left hemisphere learns to turn left when it hears a tone.

And learns to turn right when it sees a red light flashed briefly in the left visual field (stimulating right hemisphere, which is wired normally).

Test

Now flash the red light so that the left (rewired) hemisphere sees it.

Result: Ferret turns right.

FIGURE 5.8 A ferret with rewired temporal cortex
First, the normal (right) hemisphere is trained to respond to a red light by turning to the right. Then, the rewired (left) hemisphere is tested with a red light. The fact that the ferret turns to the right indicates that it regards the stimulus as light, not sound. (© Cengage Learning 2013)

drites continue to modify their structure throughout life. Dale Purves and R. D. Hadley (1985) developed a method of injecting a dye that enabled them to examine the structure of a living neuron at different times, days to weeks apart. They found that some dendritic branches extended between one viewing and another, whereas others retracted or disappeared (Figure 5.9). About 6% of dendritic spines appear or disappear within a month (Xu, Pan, Yang, & Gan, 2007). The gain or loss of spines means a turnover of synapses, which relates to learning (Yang, Pan, & Gan, 2009).

Experiences guide the neuronal changes. Let's start with a simple example. Decades ago, it was typical for a laboratory rat to live alone in a small gray cage. Imagine by contrast a group of rats in a larger cage with a few objects to explore. Researchers called this an enriched environment, but it was enriched only in contrast to the deprived experience of a typical rat cage. A rat in the more stimulating environment developed a thicker cortex, more dendritic branching, and improved learning (Greenough, 1975; Rosenzweig & Bennett, 1996). An enriched environment enhances sprouting of axons and dendrites in many other species also (Coss, Brandon, & Globus, 1980) (Figure 5.10). As a result of this research, most rats today are kept in a more enriched environment than was typical in the past.

We might suppose that the neuronal changes in an enriched environment depend on new and interesting experiences, and many of them do. For example, after practice of particular skills, the connections relevant to those skills proliferate, while other connections retract. Nevertheless, much of the enhancement produced by the enriched environment is due to physical activity. Using a running wheel enhances growth of axons and dendrites, even for rats in isolation (Pietropaolo, Feldon, Alleva, Cirulli, & Yee, 2006; Rhodes et al., 2003; van Praag, Kempermann, & Gage, 1999). Activity also improves learning and memory (Van der Borght, Havekes, Bos, Eggen, & Van der Zee, 2007).

Can we extend these results to humans? Could we, for example, improve people's intelligence by giving them a more enriched environment? It's not that easy. Educators have long oper-

ated on the assumption that training children to do something difficult will enhance their intellect in general. Long ago, British schools taught children Greek and Latin. Today it might be Shakespeare's plays or advanced math, but in any case, the idea is to teach one thing and hope students get smarter in other ways, too. The psychological term is "far transfer." (*Near transfer* is training on one task and finding improvement on a very similar task.) In general, far transfer is weak and hard to demonstrate. Most attempted interventions to improve people's memory and reasoning produce only small benefits (Hertzog, Kramer, Wilson, & Lindenberger, 2009). Many companies offer computer programs designed to "train your brain." How well do they work? In one careful evaluation, researchers studied more than 11,000 people who did the computer-guided exercises several times a week for 6 weeks. At the end of that time, participants had improved substantially on the tasks the computer trained them to do, but they showed no sign of improvement on other cognitive tasks (Owen et al., 2010). That is, they showed no far transfer. This is not to say that *no* training method has benefits. For example, certain complex video games improve people's attention patterns (Boot, Kramer, Simons, Fabiani, & Gratton, 2008; Hertzog et al., 2009). But your brain isn't like a muscle, where you could exercise it to be bigger and stronger.

Similarly, many people advise old people to do crossword puzzles or Sudoku puzzles to "exercise their brains." Many correlational studies show that people who engage in such activities remain mentally alert longer than others do, but we cannot conclude cause and effect. Perhaps working puzzles helps keep the brain active, but the other interpretation is that people who already have active brains are more likely than average to work puzzles. Experimental studies suggest that practicing crossword puzzles doesn't help people remember where they left their keys, what time they were planning to meet someone for lunch, or anything else other than crossword puzzles (Salthouse, 2006).

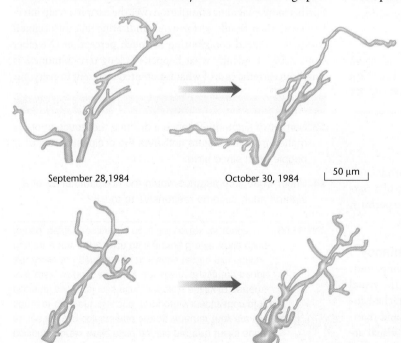

September 28,1984   October 30, 1984   50 μm

October 3,1984   November 2, 1984

FIGURE 5.9 Changes in dendritic trees of two neurons
During a month, some branches elongated and others retracted. The shape of the neuron is in flux even during adulthood. *(Source: Reprinted from "Changes in Dendritic Branching of Adult Mammalian Neurons Revealed by Repeated Imaging in Situ," by D. Purves and R. D. Hadley, Nature, 315, p. 404–406. Copyright © 1985 Macmillan Magazines, Ltd. Reprinted by permission of D. Purves and Macmillan Magazines, Ltd.)*

Richard Coss

(a)   (b)

FIGURE 5.10 **Effect of a stimulating environment**
(a) A jewel fish reared in isolation develops neurons with fewer branches. (b) A fish reared with others has more neuronal branches.

One of the best-documented ways to maintain intellectual vigor in old age is the same thing that works so well for laboratory animals—physical activity. Experimental studies, in which older people were randomly assigned to daily aerobic exercise or sedentary activities, confirm that the physical activity enhances both cognitive processes and brain anatomy (Rosano et al., 2010; P. J. Smith et al., 2010).

Stop & Check

12. An enriched environment promotes growth of axons and dendrites. What is known to be one important reason for this effect?

ANSWER

12. Animals in an enriched environment are more active, and their exercise enhances growth of axons and dendrites.

Effects of Special Experiences

Attempts to enhance overall brain development produce at best modest effects. However, prolonged experience of a particular type profoundly enhances the brain's ability to perform the same function again.

Brain Adaptations in People Blind Since Infancy

What happens to the brain if one sensory system is impaired? Recall the experiment on ferrets, in which axons of the visual system, unable to contact their normal targets, attached instead to the brain areas usually devoted to hearing and managed to convert them into more or less satisfactory visual areas (p. 132). Might anything similar happen in the brains of people born deaf or blind?

People often say that blind people become better than usual at touch and hearing, or that deaf people develop a finer sense of touch and vision. Those statements are true in a way, but we need to be more specific. Being blind does not change the touch receptors in the fingers or the receptors in the ears. However, it increases attention to touch and sound, and the brain adapts to that attention.

In several studies, investigators asked sighted people and people blind since infancy to feel Braille letters or other objects and say whether two items were the same or different. On average, blind people performed more accurately than sighted people, as you would guess. More surprisingly, PET and fMRI scans indicated substantial activity in the occipital cortex of blind people while they performed these tasks (Burton et al., 2002; Sadato et al., 1996, 1998). Evidently, touch information activated this cortical area, which is ordinarily devoted to vision alone. In people blind since birth or early childhood, auditory stimuli also produce increased responses in what are usually visual areas of the cortex (Gougoux et al., 2009; Wan, Wood, Reutens, & Wilson, 2010).

To double-check this conclusion, researchers asked blind and sighted people to perform the same kind of task during temporary inactivation of the occipital cortex. As discussed in Chapter 4, intense magnetic stimulation on the scalp temporarily inactivates neurons beneath the magnet. Applying this procedure to the occipital cortex of people who are blind interferes with their ability to identify Braille symbols, whereas it does not impair touch perception in sighted people. In short, blind people, unlike sighted people, use the occipital cortex to help identify what they feel (L. G. Cohen et al., 1997).

Similar changes can occur even in adulthood, to a limited extent. Researchers blindfolded healthy sighted adults for five days while they learned Braille. By the end of that time, the participants' occipital cortex became responsive to touch stimuli. Furthermore, magnetic stimulation over the occipital scalp interfered with their Braille performance, indicating that the occipital cortex was indeed contributing to touch perception (Merabet et al., 2008). Evidently what happens in long-term blindness is simply an extreme case of what is potentially present in everyone.

Stop & Check

13. Name two kinds of evidence indicating that touch information from the fingers activates the occipital cortex of people blind since birth.

14. Under what circumstance would the occipital cortex of a sighted adult become responsive to touch?

ANSWERS

13. First, brain scans indicate increased activity in the occipital cortex while blind people perform tasks such as feeling two objects and saying whether they are the same or different. Second, temporary inactivation of the occipital cortex blocks blind people's ability to perform that task, without affecting the ability of sighted people. 14. A sighted person who practices tactile discrimination for a few days, such as learning Braille while blindfolded, begins to use the occipital cortex for touch.

Learning to Read

If you learn to read, and then spend a few hours every day reading, does your brain change? Ordinarily, this hypothesis is difficult to test, because children learn to read while their brains are changing in many ways already. Also, in most countries, nearly all children are learning to read. Experimenters took advantage of an unusual opportunity: In Colombia, many children became guerrilla fighters instead of going to school, but many of them returned to society as adults. Of those, some were taught to read and others were not. Researchers found several differences between the brains of those who learned to read in adulthood and those who did not. Those who learned had more gray matter (presumably expanded neuron cell bodies and dendrites) in five gyri of the cerebral cortex, and greater thickness in part of the corpus callosum (Carreiras et al., 2009).

Music Training

People who develop expertise in any area spend enormous amounts of time practicing, and it seems reasonable to look for corresponding changes in their brains. Of the various kinds of expertise, which would you want to examine? Researchers' favorite choice has been musicians, for two reasons. First, we have a good idea of where in the brain to look for changes—the brain areas responsible for hearing and finger control. Second, serious musicians are numerous and easy to find. Almost any big city has an orchestra, and so do most universities. Most orchestra members have been practicing for hours every day for years.

One study used magnetoencephalography (MEG, described in Chapter 4) to record responses of the auditory cortex to pure tones. The responses in professional musicians were about twice as strong as those in nonmusicians. An examination of their brains, using MRI, found that one area of the temporal cortex in the right hemisphere was about 30% larger in professional musicians (Schneider et al., 2002). Other studies found enhanced responses of subcortical brain structures

to musical sounds and speech sounds, compared to nonmusicians (Herdener et al., 2010; Lee, Skoe, Kraus, & Ashley, 2009; Musacchia, Sams, Skoe, & Kraus, 2007). These brain changes help musicians attend to key sounds in tonal languages. For example, in Chinese, *nián* (with a rising tone) means year, and *niàn* (with a falling tone) means study. Musicians learn to recognize these differences faster than other people do (Wong, Skoe, Russo, Dees, & Kraus, 2007).

According to a study using MRI, gray matter of several brain areas was thicker in professional musicians than in amateurs and thicker in amateurs than in nonmusicians, as shown in Figure 5.11 (Gaser & Schlaug, 2003). The most strongly affected areas related to hand control and vision (which is important for reading music). A related study on stringed instrument players found that a larger than normal section of the postcentral gyrus in the right hemisphere was devoted to representing the fingers of the left hand, which they use to control the strings (Elbert, Pantev, Wienbruch, Rockstroh, & Taub, 1995). The area devoted to the left fingers was largest in those who began their music practice early and therefore also continued for more years.

These results suggest that practicing a skill reorganizes the brain to maximize performance of that skill. However, an alternative hypothesis is that brain characteristics that people were born with attract them to one occupation or another. Phoneticians—people who specialize in analyzing details of speech, including regional accents—are more likely than other people to have certain features of the auditory cortex that are known to form before birth (Golestani, Price, & Scott, 2011). Might it also be the case that inborn brain features attract certain people to music? One way to address that question is with a longitudinal study. Researchers examined 15 6-year-olds who were beginning piano lessons and 16 other children not taking music lessons. At the start of training, neither brain scans nor cognitive tests showed any significant difference between the two groups. After 15 months, the trained group performed better

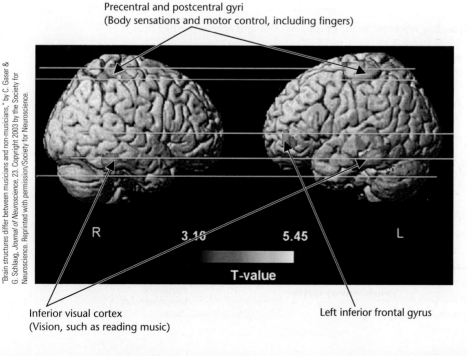

Precentral and postcentral gyri
(Body sensations and motor control, including fingers)

R   3.18   5.45   L

T-value

Inferior visual cortex
(Vision, such as reading music)

Left inferior frontal gyrus

FIGURE 5.11 Brain correlates of music practice
Areas marked in red showed thicker gray matter among professional keyboard players than in amateurs and thicker among amateurs than in nonmusicians. Areas marked in yellow showed even stronger differences in that same direction.

on measures of rhythm and melody discrimination, and they showed enlargements of brain areas responsible for hearing and hand movements, similar to those seen in adult musicians (Hyde et al., 2009a, 2009b). These results imply that the brain differences are the result of musical training, not the cause.

Another issue is whether music training produces bigger effects if it begins early in life, while the brain is more easily modified. Several studies have found major differences between young adults who started music training in childhood and those who began as teenagers. However, those studies do not separate the effects of age at starting from those of total years of practice. A later study compared people who started music training before age 7 with people who started later but continued for just as many years. The result was that those who started younger showed an advantage on several tasks (Watanabe, Savion-Lemieux, & Penhune, 2007).

Stop & Check

15. Which brain area shows expanded representation of the left hand in people who began practicing stringed instruments in childhood and continued for many years?

ANSWER

15. Postcentral gyrus (somatosensory cortex) of the right hemisphere

When Brain Reorganization Goes Too Far

If playing music—or practicing anything else—expands a relevant brain area, the change is good, right? Usually it is, but not always. As mentioned, when people play piano or string instruments many hours a day for years, the representation of the hand increases in the somatosensory cortex. Imagine the normal representation of the fingers in the cortex:

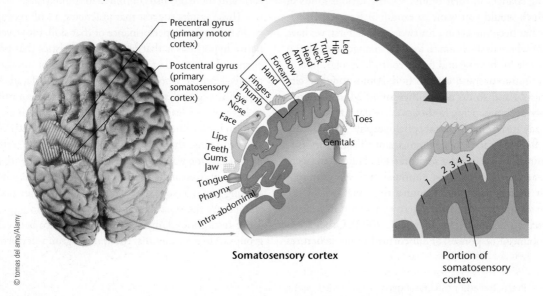

Somatosensory cortex

Portion of somatosensory cortex

With extensive musical practice, the expanding representations of the fingers might spread out like this:

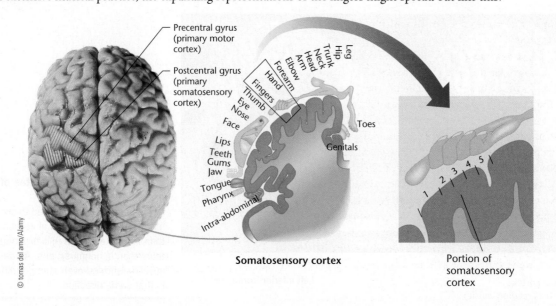

Somatosensory cortex

Portion of somatosensory cortex

Or the representations of all fingers could grow from side to side without spreading out so that representation of each finger overlaps that of its neighbor:

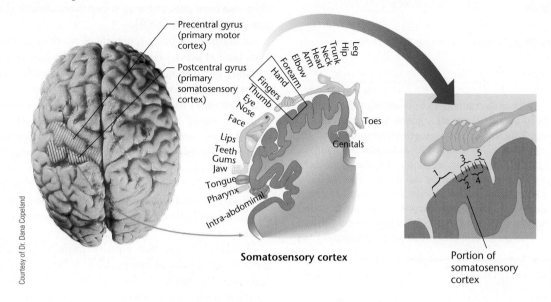

Precentral gyrus (primary motor cortex)

Postcentral gyrus (primary somatosensory cortex)

Leg
Hip
Trunk
Neck
Head
Arm
Elbow
Forearm
Hand
Fingers
Thumb
Eye
Nose
Face
Lips
Teeth
Gums
Jaw
Tongue
Pharynx
Intra-abdominal
Toes
Genitals

Somatosensory cortex

Portion of somatosensory cortex

Courtesy of Dr. Dana Copeland

In some cases, the latter process does occur, such that stimulation on one finger excites mostly the same cortical areas as another finger (Byl, McKenzie, & Nagarajan, 2000; Elbert et al., 1998; Lenz & Byl, 1999; Sanger, Pascual-Leone, Tarsy, & Schlaug, 2001; Sanger, Tarsy, & Pascual-Leone, 2001). If you can't clearly feel the difference between one finger and another, it is difficult to move them independently. Furthermore, the motor cortex changes also. Representation of the middle fingers expands, overlapping and displacing representation of the index finger and little finger. As a result, the person has trouble controlling the index finger and little finger. One or more fingers may go into constant contraction (Beck et al., 2008; Burman, Lie-Nemeth, Brandfonbrener, Parisi, & Meyer, 2009). This condition, known as "musician's cramp" or more formally as **focal hand dystonia**, is often a career ender for a musician. Some people who spend all day writing develop the same problem, in which case it is known as "writer's cramp."

Previously, physicians assumed that musician's cramp or writer's cramp was in the hands themselves, in which case the treatment would be hand surgery or injection of some drug into the hand. Now that we have identified brain reorganization as the problem, the approach is to find an appropriate type of retraining. Here is one promising possibility: Researchers gave periodic bursts of vibration stimuli to various hand muscles, in random sequence, instructing people with musician's cramp to attend carefully to the stimuli and any changes in their vibration frequency. A mere 15-minute treatment produced improvement in finger sensations and use, which lasted up to 24 hours (Rosenkranz, Butler, Williamson, & Rothwell, 2009). Further development of this technique or something similar may help people with this disorder.

© tomas del amo/Alamy

Someone with musician's cramp or writer's cramp has difficulty moving one finger independently of others. One or more fingers may twitch or go into a constant contraction.

➤ **Stop & Check**

16. What change in the brain is responsible for musician's cramp?

17. What procedure is most promising for treating musician's cramp?

ANSWERS

[answers printed upside-down:]

16. Extensive practice of violin, piano, or other instruments causes expanded representation of the fingers in the somatosensory cortex, as well as displacement of representation of one or more fingers in the motor cortex. If the sensory representation of two fingers overlaps too much, the person cannot feel them separately or move them separately. **17.** The most promising treatment so far is training the person to attend to specific sensations in the hand. The training is intended to reorganize the brain representation.

Brain Development and Behavioral Development

Behavior changes as people grow older. How much of that change has to do with the brain? Let's consider adolescence and old age.

Adolescence

Adolescents are widely regarded as impulsive and prone to seek immediate pleasure. Neither of those characteristics is unique to adolescents, as children are even more impulsive and eager for immediate pleasure. Still, on average, adolescents differ in these regards from adults. Impulsiveness is a problem if it leads to risky driving, drinking, sex, spending sprees, and so forth.

Impulsiveness means a difficulty inhibiting an impulse. Here is a simple way to measure it: Hold your hands to the left and right of someone's head. Instruct the person that when you wiggle a finger, he or she should look at the *other* hand. Before age 5 to 7 years, most children find it almost impossible to look away from the wiggling finger. They are "impulsive" in that they do not inhibit their strong tendency to look at a moving object. Similarly, if a face suddenly appears on one side of a screen, people find it difficult to look in the opposite direction (Morand, Grosbras, Caldara, & Harvey, 2010). Looking away from a powerful attention-getter is called the **antisaccade task**. A saccade is a voluntary eye movement, and an antisaccade is a voluntary eye movement away from the normal direction.

TRY IT YOURSELF

Ability to perform this task improves sharply between ages 7 to 11, and then gradually improves during the teenage years, depending on areas of the prefrontal cortex that mature slowly (Michel & Anderson, 2009; Munoz & Everling, 2004).

As you might guess, children with attention-deficit hyperactivity disorder (ADHD), who tend to be impulsive in other ways, also have difficulty with the antisaccade task (Loe, Feldman, Yasui, & Luna, 2009).

In addition to being more impulsive than adults, adolescents (and children) tend to "discount the future," preferring a smaller pleasure now over a larger one later. Which would you prefer, $100 now or $125 a year from now? What about $100 now vs. $150 a year from now? $175? How much bigger would the payoff have to be next year to make you willing to wait? Adolescents are more likely to choose an immediate reward than are older adults, in a variety of situations (Steinberg et al., 2009). However, to be fair, the situation is not the same for people of different ages. Most adolescents have little cash on hand and need the money right now. Most older adults are more financially secure and can afford to wait for a higher reward.

Adolescents are not equally impulsive in all situations. In an argument before the U.S. Supreme Court, the American Psychological Association (APA) took the position that adolescents are mature enough to make their own decisions about a possible abortion. Later, the APA took the position that an adolescent who commits murder is too immature to be held to the same legal standard as an adult. Was the APA flip-flopping about adolescent maturity, based on the political decisions they favored? Could be, but the argument is more defensible than it might sound at first. According to the research, most adolescents make reasonable, mature decisions when they have time to consider their options carefully. However, they are impulsive when making quick decisions, especially in the face of peer pressure (Luna, Padmanabhan, & O'Hearn, 2010; Reyna & Farley, 2006).

Many studies have found that adolescent brains show stronger responses than older adults when anticipating rewards, and weaker responses in the areas of the prefrontal cortex responsible for inhibiting behaviors (Geier, Terwilliger, Teslovich, Velanova, & Luna, 2010; Luna, et al., 2010). But should we conclude that adolescents are impulsive *because* their prefrontal cortex is less active? Maybe, but not necessarily. Consider this analogy: Imagine a college professor who has spent the afternoon sitting at his desk writing this chapter. If you monitored his leg muscles you would find that they had a low activity level all afternoon. Would you conclude that he sat working on writing this chapter *because* his leg muscles were inactive? I assume you would not. If those leg muscles were *incapable* of moving, they would help explain why someone spent an afternoon at a computer. But when someone simply fails to use healthy leg muscles, monitoring their activity explains nothing. Similarly, if we found that certain parts of the adolescent prefrontal cortex are *incapable* of strong activity, we may have an explanation for impulsive behavior. But most research simply reports that adolescents' prefrontal cortex *is* relatively inactive in certain situations, and that result is not sufficient to explain the behavior.

> **Stop & Check**

18. Under what circumstances are adolescents most likely to make an impulsive decision?

19. When people claim that adolescents make risky decisions because of a lack of inhibition, which brain area do they point to as being responsible for inhibition?

ANSWERS

18. Adolescents are most likely to make an impulsive decision when they have to decide quickly in the presence of peer pressure. **19.** The prefrontal cortex

Old Age

Many studies confirm that, on average, people's memory and reasoning fade beyond age 60, if not sooner. In old age, neurons alter their synapses more slowly (Gan, Kwon, Feng, Sanes, & Lichtman, 2003; Grutzendler, Kasthuri, & Gan, 2002). The thickness of the temporal cortex shrinks by about half a percent per year, on average (Fjell et al., 2009). The volume of the hippocampus also gradually declines, and certain aspects of memory decline in proportion to the loss of hippocampus (Erickson et al., 2010). The frontal cortex begins thinning at age 30 (Brans et al., 2010)!

Nevertheless, most chief executives of major corporations, world political leaders, college presidents, and so forth are over 60 years old. Is this a problem? Should we fire them and replace them with 25-year-olds?

Much of the research underestimates older people, for several reasons. First, people vary. Some people deteriorate markedly, but others show little sign of loss in either behavior or brain anatomy well into old age. If we take an average, it appears that everyone is decaying a little each year, but averages can be misleading. Second, as people grow older, they may be slower in many intellectual activities, but they have a greater base of knowledge and experience. On certain kinds of questions, older people do significantly better than younger people (Queen & Hess, 2010). Third, many older people find ways to compensate for any losses. In one study, a certain memory task activated the right prefrontal cortex in young adults and in older adults who did poorly on the task. For older people who did well, the task activated the prefrontal cortex of *both* hemispheres (Cabeza, Anderson, Locantore, & McIntosh, 2002). That is, high-performing older adults activate more brain areas to make up for less efficient activity.

> **Stop & Check**

20. What is one way in which older adults compensate for less efficient brain functioning?

ANSWER

20. Many of them compensate by activating additional brain areas.

MODULE 5.1 ■ IN CLOSING

Brain Development

Considering the number of ways in which abnormal genes and chemicals can disrupt brain development, let alone the possible varieties of abnormal experience, it is a wonder that any of us develop normally. Evidently, the system has enough margin for error that we can function even if all of our connections are not quite perfect. Development can go wrong in many ways, but somehow, the system usually manages to work.

SUMMARY

1. In vertebrate embryos, the central nervous system begins as a tube surrounding a fluid-filled cavity. Developing neurons proliferate, migrate, differentiate, myelinate, and generate synapses. Neuron proliferation varies among species mainly by the number of cell divisions. Migration depends on a large number of chemicals that guide immature neurons to their destinations.   **124**

2. Even in adults, new neurons can form in the olfactory system, the hippocampus, and the song-producing brain areas of some bird species. Although controversy persists, new neurons apparently also form in the adult primate cerebral cortex following damage to the nervous system. How long such neurons survive is not known.   **125**

3. Growing axons find their way close to the right locations by following chemicals. Then they array themselves over a target area by following chemical gradients.   **126**

4. After axons reach their targets based on chemical gradients, the postsynaptic cell adjusts the connections

based on experience, accepting certain combinations of axons and rejecting others. This kind of competition among axons continues throughout life. **129**

5. Initially, the nervous system develops far more neurons than will actually survive. Some axons make synaptic contacts with cells that release to them nerve growth factor or other neurotrophins. The neurons that receive neurotrophins survive, and the others die in a process called apoptosis. **129**

6. The developing brain is vulnerable to chemical insult. Many chemicals that produce only mild, temporary problems for adults can permanently impair early brain development. **131**

7. At an early stage of development, the cortex is sufficiently plastic that visual input can cause what would have been the auditory cortex to develop different properties and now respond visually. **132**

8. Enriched experience leads to greater branching of axons and dendrites, partly because animals in enriched environments are more active than those in deprived environments. However, this enrichment effect has been demonstrated in comparison to a standard laboratory environment that is extremely deprived. **132**

9. Specialized experiences can alter brain development, especially early in life. For example, in people who are born blind, representation of touch and hearing expands in areas usually reserved for vision. **134**

10. Extensive practice of a skill expands the brain's representation of sensory and motor information relevant to that skill. For example, the representation of fingers expands in people who regularly practice musical instruments. **135**

11. Although expanded representation in the brain is ordinarily a good thing, it can be harmful if carried too far. Some musicians and others who use their hands many hours each day develop brain changes that interfere with their ability to feel or use one finger independently of the others. **136**

12. Compared to adults, adolescents tend to be impulsive and centered more on present pleasures than future prospects. Research demonstrates increased response of their brain to anticipated pleasures, and decreased activity in the prefrontal cortex, responsible for inhibiting behavior tendencies. However, it is not clear that these brain phenomena explain the behaviors. **138**

13. On average, people in old age show declining memory and reasoning, and shrinkage of certain brain areas. However, these averages do not apply to all individuals or all situations. Many older people compensate for inefficiency of certain brain functions by recruiting activity in additional brain areas. **139**

KEY TERMS

Terms are defined in the module on the page number indicated. They're also presented in alphabetical order with definitions in the book's Subject Index/Glossary, which begins on page 561. Interactive flashcards and crossword puzzles are among the online resources available to help you learn these terms and the concepts they represent.

antisaccade task **138**

apoptosis **130**

differentiates **125**

fetal alcohol syndrome **131**

focal hand dystonia **137**

migrate **125**

myelination **125**

nerve growth factor (NGF) **130**

neural Darwinism **129**

neurotrophin **130**

proliferation **124**

stem cells **125**

synaptogenesis **125**

THOUGHT QUESTION

Biologists can develop antibodies against nerve growth factor (i.e., molecules that inactivate nerve growth factor). What would happen if someone injected such antibodies into a developing nervous system?

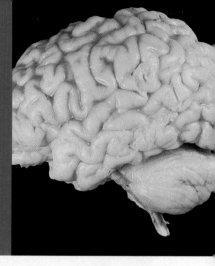

Plasticity After Brain Damage

An American soldier who suffered a wound to the left hemisphere of his brain during the Korean War was at first unable to speak at all. Three months later, he could speak in short fragments. When he was asked to read the letterhead, "New York University College of Medicine," he replied, "Doctors—little doctors." Eight years later, when someone asked him again to read the letterhead, he replied, "Is there a catch? It says, 'New York University College of Medicine'" (Eidelberg & Stein, 1974).

Almost all survivors of brain damage show behavioral recovery to some degree. Some of the mechanisms rely on the growth of new branches of axons and dendrites, similar to the mechanisms of brain development discussed in the first module. Understanding the process leads to better therapies for people with brain damage and contributes to our understanding of brain functioning.

Brain Damage and Short-Term Recovery

The possible causes of brain damage include tumors, infections, exposure to radiation or toxic substances, and degenerative conditions such as Parkinson's disease and Alzheimer's disease. In young people, the most common cause is **closed head injury**, a sharp blow to the head resulting from an accident or assault that does not puncture the brain. The effects of closed head injury depend on severity and frequency. Many, probably most, children and young adults sustain at least a mild blow to the head from falling off a bicycle or similar accident, from which they recover within a few days. Repeated head injuries, common in certain sports, are more worrisome (Shaughnessy, 2009). After a severe head injury, recovery is slow and often incomplete (Forsyth, Salorio, & Christensen, 2010).

One cause of damage after closed head injury is the rotational forces that drive brain tissue against the inside of the skull. Another cause is blood clots that interrupt blood flow to the brain (Kirkpatrick, Smielewski, Czosnyka, Menon, & Pickard, 1995).

APPLICATIONS AND EXTENSIONS

How Woodpeckers Avoid Concussions

Speaking of blows to the head, have you ever wondered how woodpeckers manage to avoid giving themselves concussions? If you repeatedly banged your head into a tree at 6 or 7 meters per second (about 15 miles per hour), you would quickly harm yourself.

Using slow-motion photography, researchers found that woodpeckers usually start with a couple of quick preliminary taps against the wood, much like a carpenter lining up a nail with a hammer. Then the birds make a hard strike in a straight line, keeping a rigid neck. They almost completely avoid rotational forces and whiplash (May, Fuster, Haber, & Hirschman, 1979).

The researchers suggested that football helmets, race car helmets, and so forth would give more protection if they extended down to the shoulders to prevent rotation and whiplash. They also suggest that if you see a crash about to happen, you should tuck your chin to your chest and tighten your neck muscles.

Reducing the Harm from a Stroke

A common cause of brain damage, especially in older people, is temporary interruption of normal blood flow to a brain area during a **stroke**, also known as a **cerebrovascular accident**. The more common type of stroke is **ischemia** (iss-KEE-me-uh), the result of a blood clot or other obstruction in an artery. The less common type is **hemorrhage** (HEM-oh-rage), the result of a ruptured artery. Effects of strokes vary from barely noticeable to immediately fatal. Figure 5.12 shows the brains of three people: one who died immediately after a stroke, one who survived long after a stroke, and a bullet wound victim. For a good collection of information about stroke, visit the website of the National Stroke Association at http://www.stroke.org/.

In ischemia, the neurons deprived of blood lose much of their oxygen and glucose supplies. In hemorrhage, they are

141

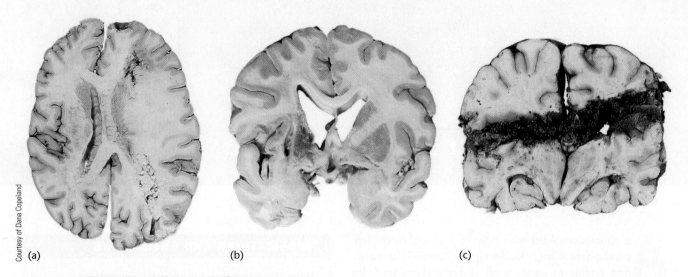

Courtesy of Dana Copeland

(a)   (b)   (c)

FIGURE 5.12 Three damaged human brains
(a) Brain of a person who died immediately after a stroke. Note the swelling on the right side. (b) Brain of someone who survived for a long time after a stroke. Note the cavities on the left side, where many cells were lost. (c) Brain of a person who suffered a gunshot wound and died immediately.

flooded with blood and excess oxygen, calcium, and other chemicals. Both ischemia and hemorrhage lead to many of the same problems, including **edema** (the accumulation of fluid), which increases pressure on the brain and the probability of additional strokes (Unterberg, Stover, Kress, & Kiening, 2004). Both ischemia and hemorrhage also impair the sodium–potassium pump, leading to an accumulation of sodium inside neurons. The combination of edema and excess sodium provokes excess release of the transmitter glutamate (Rossi, Oshima, & Attwell, 2000), which overstimulates neurons: Sodium and other ions enter the neurons faster than the sodium–potassium pump can remove them. The excess positive ions block metabolism in the mitochondria and kill the neurons (Stout, Raphael, Kanterewicz, Klann, & Reynolds, 1998). As neurons die, microglia cells proliferate, removing the products of dead neurons and supplying neurotrophins that promote survival of the remaining neurons (Lalancette- Hébert, Gowing, Simard, Weng, & Kriz, 2007).

Immediate Treatments

As recently as the 1980s, hospitals had little to offer to a stroke patient. Today, prospects are good for ischemia if physicians act quickly. A drug called **tissue plasminogen activator (tPA)** breaks up blood clots (Barinaga, 1996). To get significant benefit, a patient should receive tPA within 3 hours after a stroke, although slight benefits are possible during the next several hours. Emergency wards have improved their response times, but the limiting factor is that most stroke victims don't get to the hospital quickly enough (Evenson, Foraker, Morris, & Rosamond, 2009).

It is difficult to determine whether someone has had an ischemic or hemorrhagic stroke. Given that tPA is useful for

ischemia but could only make matters worse in a hemorrhage, what is a physician to do? An MRI scan distinguishes between the two kinds of stroke, but MRIs take time, and time is limited. The usual decision is to give the tPA. Hemorrhage is less common and usually fatal anyway, so the risk of making a hemorrhage worse is small compared to the hope of alleviating ischemia.

What other treatments might be effective shortly after a stroke? Given that strokes kill neurons by overstimulation, one approach has been to decrease stimulation by blocking glutamate synapses, blocking calcium entry, or other means. Many such techniques have shown benefits in laboratory animals (e.g., Sun et al., 2009), but so far none has produced much benefit in humans. It is fair to object that they haven't been given a fair try. Nearly all of the clinical studies have used small doses (to avoid side effects such as hallucinations), and nearly all have given the treatments 12 or more hours after a stroke, despite evidence from laboratory animals that the treatments are effective only within the first 3 to 6 hours (Ginsberg, 2008).

The most effective known method of preventing brain damage after strokes in laboratory animals is to cool the brain. Cooling slows a variety of harmful processes. People can be cooled safely to about 34–35° C (93–95° F). What matters is temperature at the core of the body, so it is possible to keep the skin warm enough to prevent shivering, while cooling the interior of the body. This procedure has shown much promise, and additional research is under way (Ginsberg, 2008; Steiner, Ringleb, & Hacke, 2001).

Another procedure might surprise you: Exposure to cannabinoids (the chemicals found in marijuana) minimizes the damage caused by strokes in laboratory animals. You might wonder how anyone thought of trying such a thing. Research-

(a)   (b)

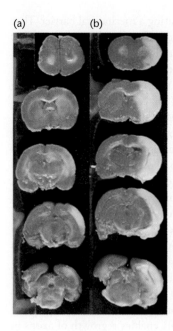

FIGURE 5.13 Effects of a cannabinoid on stroke damage
Row (a) shows slices through the brains of 5 rats treated with a high dose of a cannabinoid shortly after a stroke. Row (b) shows slices for rats not treated with cannabinoids. The white areas on the right of each brain show the extent of the damage. *(From Schomacher, M., Müller, H. D., Sommer, C., Schwab, S., & Schäbitz, W.-R. (2008). Endocannabinoids mediate neuroprotection after transient focal cerebral ischemia.* Brain Research, *1240, 213–220.)*

ers had a theoretical rationale: As mentioned in Chapter 3, cannabinoids decrease the release of glutamate. If excessive glutamate is one of the reasons for cell loss, then cannabinoids might be helpful. They do, in fact, minimize the damage after a stroke, as shown in Figure 5.13, although the explanation is not yet clear (Schomacher, Müller, Sommer, Schwab, & Schäbitz, 2008). In addition to putting the brakes on glutamate, cannabinoids exert anti-inflammatory effects and alter brain chemistry in other ways that might protect against damage. So far, physicians have made only limited attempts to apply cannabinoids to human stroke patients, and again the limiting factor is that the chemicals are effective only within the first few hours after a stroke. In fact, the research on laboratory animals indicates that cannabinoids are most effective if taken shortly *before* the stroke. It would be difficult to apply that advice in humans!

> **Stop & Check**

21. What are the two kinds of stroke, and what causes each kind?

22. Why is tPA not helpful in cases of hemorrhage?

23. If one of your relatives has a stroke and a well-meaning person offers a blanket, what should you do?

ANSWERS

21. The more common form, ischemia, is the result of an occlusion of an artery. The other form, hemorrhage, is the result of a ruptured artery. **22.** The drug tPA breaks up blood clots, and hemorrhage results from a ruptured blood vessel, not a blood clot. **23.** Refuse the blanket. Recovery will be best if the stroke victim remains cold.

▌ Later Mechanisms of Recovery

After the first days following brain damage, many of the surviving brain areas increase or reorganize their activity (Nishimura et al., 2007). In some cases, one area more or less takes over the function of another, damaged area. For example, after damage to the connections from one brain hemisphere to the leg on the opposite side of the body, the hemisphere on the same side increases its connections to that leg (Ghosh et al., 2009). In other cases, surviving brain areas do not take over the functions of the damaged area, but they compensate in various ways.

Increased Brain Stimulation

A behavioral deficit after brain damage reflects more than just the cells that died. After damage to any brain area, other areas that have lost part of their normal input become less active. For example, shortly after damage in one brain hemisphere, its input to the other hemisphere declines, and therefore the other hemisphere shows deficits also (van Meer et al., 2010). Recovery from a stroke depends largely on increasing activity for the opposite side of the brain (Takatsuru et al., 2009).

Diaschisis (di-AS-ki-sis, from a Greek term meaning "to shock throughout") refers to the decreased activity of surviving neurons after damage to other neurons. If diaschisis contributes to behavioral deficits following brain damage, then increased stimulation should help. Researchers studied one man who had been in a "minimally conscious state" for 6 years, showing almost no activity or response to stimulation. Electrical stimulation of his central thalamus led to substantial improvements, including self-feeding and some intelligible speech (Schiff et al., 2007).

Stimulant drugs also promote recovery. In a series of experiments, D. M. Feeney and colleagues measured the behavioral effects of cortical damage in rats and cats. Depending on the location of the damage, the animals showed impairments in movement or depth perception. Injecting amphetamine significantly enhanced both behaviors, and animals that practiced the behaviors under the influence of amphetamine showed long-lasting benefits. Injecting a different drug to block dopamine synapses impaired behavioral recovery (Feeney & Sutton, 1988; Feeney, Sutton, Boyeson, Hovda, & Dail, 1985; Hovda & Feeney, 1989; Sutton, Hovda, & Feeney, 1989). Stimulant drugs may be helpful after other kinds of brain damage, too, and not just strokes (Huey, Garcia, Wassermann, Tierney, & Grafman, 2008).

Although amphetamine is too risky for use with human patients, other stimulant drugs are more promising (Whyte et al., 2005). A related idea is to use drugs that block the release of GABA, the brain's main inhibitory neurotransmitter. As with amphetamine, GABA blockers are effective in promoting recovery after stroke in laboratory animals (Clarkson, Huang, MacIsaac, Mody, & Carmichael, 2010).

Stop & Check

24. After someone has had a stroke, would it be best (if possible) to direct stimulant drugs to the cells that were damaged or somewhere else?

ANSWER 24. It is best to direct the amphetamine to the cells that had been receiving input from the damaged cells. Presumably, the loss of input has produced diaschisis.

Regrowth of Axons

Although a destroyed cell body cannot be replaced, damaged axons do grow back under certain circumstances. A neuron of the peripheral nervous system has its cell body in the spinal cord (for motor neurons) or in a ganglion near the spinal cord (for sensory neurons). In either case, the axon extends into one of the limbs. A crushed axon grows back toward the periphery at a rate of about 1 mm per day, following its myelin sheath to the original target. If the axon is cut instead of crushed, the myelin on the two sides of the cut may not line up correctly, and the regenerating axon may not have a sure path to follow. In that case, a motor nerve may attach to the wrong muscle, as Figure 5.14 illustrates.

Within a mature mammalian brain or spinal cord, damaged axons do not regenerate, or do so only slightly (Schwab, 1998). However, in many kinds of fish, axons do regenerate across a cut in the spinal cord and restore nearly normal functioning (Bernstein & Gelderd, 1970; Rovainen, 1976; Scherer, 1986; Selzer, 1978). Why do damaged CNS axons regenerate so much better in fish than in mammals? Can we find ways to improve axon regeneration in mammals?

Several problems limit axon regeneration in mammals. First, a cut in the nervous system causes a scar to form (thicker

in mammals than in fish), creating a mechanical barrier. That scar tissue is beneficial immediately after the damage, but it blocks regrowth of axons later (Rolls, Shechter, & Schwartz, 2009). Second, neurons on the two sides of the cut pull apart. Third, the glia cells that react to CNS damage release chemicals that inhibit axon growth (Yiu & He, 2006).

These problems are formidable, but hope remains. Researchers developed a way to build a protein bridge, providing a path for axons to regenerate across a scar-filled gap. When they applied this technique to hamsters with a cut in the optic nerve, many axons from the eye grew back and established synapses, enabling most hamsters to regain partial vision (Ellis-Behnke et al., 2006). Also, injecting neurotrophins at appropriate locations helps axons grow and establish normal synapses (Alto et al., 2009). A third possibility: Infant axons grow under the influence of a protein called mTOR (which stands for mammalian Target Of Rapamycin). As the individual matures, mTOR levels decrease and axons in the spinal cord lose their capacity for regrowth. Deleting a gene responsible for inhibiting mTOR enables regrowth of axons in the adult spinal cord (Liu et al., 2010). So far, these methods have been tried only in laboratory animals, and we don't know about their feasibility with humans.

Axon Sprouting

Ordinarily, the surface of dendrites and cell bodies is covered with synapses, and a vacant spot doesn't stay vacant for long. After a cell loses input from an axon it secretes neurotrophins that induce other axons to form new branches, or **collateral sprouts**, that take over the vacant synapses (Ramirez, 2001) (Figure 5.15). In the area near the damage, new synapses form at a high rate, especially for the first 2 weeks (C. E. Brown, Li, Boyd, Delaney, & Murphy, 2007).

Is collateral sprouting helpful or harmful? It depends on whether the sprouting axons convey information similar to those that they replace. For example, the hippocampus receives much input from an area called the entorhinal cortex. If the entorhinal cortex is damaged in one hemisphere, then axons from the entorhinal cortex of the other hemisphere sprout, take over the vacant synapses, and largely restore behavior (Ramirez, Bulsara, Moore, Ruch, & Abrams, 1999; Ramirez, McQuilkin, Carrigan, MacDonald, & Kelley, 1996). However, if the entorhinal cortex is damaged in both hemispheres, then axons from other locations sprout into the vacant synapses, conveying different information. Under those conditions, the sprouting interferes with behavior and prevents recovery (Ramirez, 2001; Ramirez et al., 2007).

Here is another example where sprouting is either useless or harmful: Imagine a stroke that damages the axons bringing information from the upper-left visual field—that is, everything that appears to the viewer as being in the upper left. Suppose this stroke does not damage the visual cortex. Now the area of visual cortex that used to receive input from the upper left has lost its input, and axons represent-

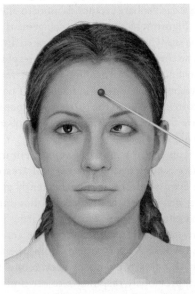
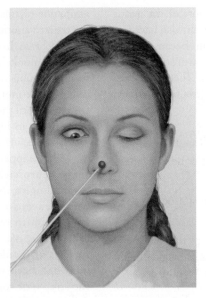
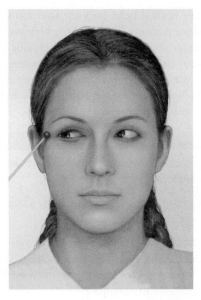

FIGURE 5.14 What can happen if damaged axons regenerate to incorrect muscles
Damaged axons to the muscles of the patient's right eye regenerated but attached incorrectly. When she looks down, her right eyelid opens wide instead of closing like the other eyelid. Her eye movements are frequently misaimed, and she has trouble moving her right eye upward or to the left. *(© Cengage Learning 2013)*

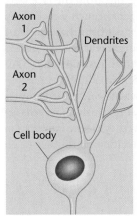
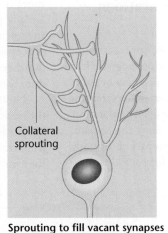

At first   **Loss of an axon**   **Sprouting to fill vacant synapses**

FIGURE 5.15 Collateral sprouting
A surviving axon grows a new branch to replace the synapses left vacant by a damaged axon. *(© Cengage Learning 2013)*

ing another part of the visual field—the lower left—sprout into the vacant synapses. As that happens, a stimulus that should look as shown here on the left begins to look like the stimulus on the right (Dilks, Serences, Rosenau, Yantis, & McCloskey, 2007):

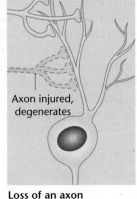

Denervation Supersensitivity

Neurons make adjustments to maintain a nearly constant level of arousal. After learning strengthens one set of synapses, other synapses weaken. (If this didn't happen, every time you learned something your brain would get more and more aroused.) Something similar happens after certain kinds of brain damage: If most of the axons that transmit dopamine to some brain area die or become inactive, the remaining dopamine synapses become more responsive, more easily stimulated. This process of enhanced response is known as **denervation supersensitivity** or *receptor supersensitivity* (Kostrzewa, Kostrzewa, Brown, Nowak, & Brus, 2008).

Denervation supersensitivity helps compensate for decreased input. In some cases, it enables people to maintain nearly normal behavior even after losing most of the axons in some pathway (Sabel, 1997). However, it can also have unpleasant consequences, such as chronic pain. Because spinal injury damages many axons, postsynaptic neurons develop increased sensitivity to the remaining ones. Therefore, even mild input produces enhanced responses (Hains, Everhart, Fullwood, & Hulsebosch, 2002).

Stop & Check

25. Is collateral sprouting a change in axons or dendritic receptors?

26. Is denervation supersensitivity a change in axons or dendritic receptors?

27. Many people with schizophrenia take drugs that block dopamine synapses. After prolonged use, the side effects include frequent involuntary movements. What is one possible explanation?

ANSWERS

25. Axons 26. Dendritic receptors 27. Denervation supersensitivity. The decreased input may have led to hyperresponsive receptors.

Reorganized Sensory Representations and the Phantom Limb

If a brain area loses a set of incoming axons, we can expect some combination of increased response (denervation supersensitivity) by the remaining axons and collateral sprouting by other axons that ordinarily attach to some other target. Let's imagine how these processes might apply in the case of an amputation.

Reexamine Figure 4.24: Each section along the somatosensory cortex receives input from a different part of the body. Within the area marked "fingers" in that figure, a closer ex-

amination reveals that each subarea responds more to one finger than to another. Figure 5.16 shows the arrangement for a monkey brain. In one study, experimenters amputated finger 3 of an owl monkey. The cortical cells that previously responded to information from finger 3 lost their input. Soon various cells became more responsive to finger 2, finger 4, or part of the palm, until the cortex developed the pattern of responsiveness shown in Figure 5.16b (Kaas, Merzenich, & Killackey, 1983; Merzenich et al., 1984).

What happens if an entire arm is amputated? For many years, neuroscientists assumed that the cortical area corresponding to that arm would remain permanently silent, because axons from other cortical areas could not sprout far enough to reach the area representing the arm. Then came a surprise. Investigators recorded from the cerebral cortices of monkeys whose sensory nerves from one forelimb had been cut 12 years previously. They found that the stretch of cortex previously responsive to the limb was now responsive to the face (Pons et al., 1991). After loss of sensory input from the forelimb, the axons representing the forelimb degenerated, leaving vacant synaptic sites at several levels of the CNS. Evidently, axons representing the face sprouted into those sites in the spinal cord, brainstem, and thalamus (Florence & Kaas, 1995; E. G. Jones & Pons, 1998). Or perhaps axons from the face were already present but became stronger through denervation supersensitivity. Brain scan studies confirm that the same processes occur with humans. Reorganization also occurs in other brain areas that respond to skin sensations (Tandon, Kambi, Lazar, Mohammed, & Jain, 2009).

Now consider what happens when something activates the neurons in a reorganized cortex. Previously, those cells responded to arm stimulation, but now they receive information from the face. Does it feel like stimulation on the face or on the arm?

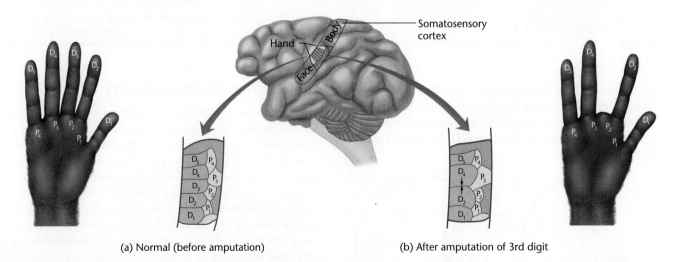

(a) Normal (before amputation)   (b) After amputation of 3rd digit

FIGURE 5.16 Somatosensory cortex of a monkey after a finger amputation
Note that the cortical area previously responsive to the third finger (D₃) becomes responsive to the second and fourth fingers (D₂ and D₄) and part of the palm (P₃). *(Redrawn from the Annual Review of Neuroscience, Vol. 6, © 1983, by Annual Reviews, Inc. Reprinted by permission of Annual Reviews, Inc. and Jon H. Kaas.)*

The answer: It feels like the arm (K. D. Davis et al., 1998). Physicians have long noted that many people with amputations experience a **phantom limb**, a continuing sensation of an amputated body part. That experience can range from occasional tingling to intense pain. It is possible to have a phantom hand, foot, or anything else that has been amputated. The phantom sensation might last days, weeks, or a lifetime (Ramachandran & Hirstein, 1998).

Until the 1990s, no one knew what caused phantom pains, and most believed that the sensations came from the stump of the amputated limb. Some physicians performed additional amputations, removing more of the limb in a futile attempt to eliminate the phantom sensations. Modern methods have demonstrated that phantom limbs develop only if the relevant portion of the somatosensory cortex reorganizes and becomes responsive to alternative inputs (Flor et al., 1995). For example, suppose axons representing the face come to activate the cortical area previously devoted to an amputated hand. A touch on the face now produces a facial sensation but it also produces a sensation in the phantom hand. Figure 5.17 shows a map of which face area stimulates sensation in which part of the phantom hand, for one person (Agliori, Smania, Atzei, & Berlucchi, 1997).

Note in Figure 4.24 that the part of the cortex responsive to the feet is adjacent to the part responsive to the genitals. Two patients with foot amputations felt a phantom foot during sexual arousal! One reported feeling orgasm in the phantom foot as well as the genitals—and enjoyed it intensely (Ramachandran & Blakeslee, 1998). Evidently, the representation of the genitals had spread into the cortical area responsible for foot sensation.

Is there any way to relieve a painful phantom sensation? In some cases, yes. Amputees who learn to use an artificial arm report that their phantom sensations gradually disappear (Lotze et al., 1999). They start attributing sensations to the artificial arm, and in doing so, they displace abnormal connections from the face. Similarly, a study of one man found that after his hands were amputated, the area of his cortex that usually responds to the hands partly shifted to face sensitivity, but after he received hand transplants, his cortex gradually shifted back to hand sensitivity (Giraux, Sirigu, Schneider, & Dubernard, 2001). Another patient had a hand amputated at age 19; 35 years later, a new hand was grafted in its place. Within months, he was starting to feel normal sensations in that hand (Frey, Bogdanov, Smith, Watrous, & Breidenbach, 2008). Evidently the brain areas that start off as hand areas, face areas, or whatever retain those properties even after decades without normal input.

© Argosy Publishing Inc.

FIGURE 5.17 Sources of phantom sensation for one person
Stimulation in the areas marked on the cheek produced phantom sensations of digits 1 (thumb), 2, 4, and 5. Stimulation on the shoulder also evoked phantom sensations of digits 1, 2, 3, and 5. *(Based on Figure 5.29 from* Phantoms in the Brain *by V. S. Ramachandran, M.D., PhD, and Sandra Blakeslee. Copyright © 1998 by V. S. Ramachandran and Sandra Blakeslee. Reprinted by permission of HarperCollins Publishers and authors.)*

Andy Manis/AP Photo

Amputees who feel a phantom limb are likely to lose those phantom sensations if they learn to use an artificial arm or leg.

28. What is responsible for the phantom limb experience?

ANSWER   ⱯⱯⱯ *(answer printed upside down)* **28.** Synapses that used to receive input from the now-amputated part become vacant. Axons representing another part of the body take over those synapses. Now stimulation of this other part activates the synapses associated with the amputated area, but that stimulation feels like the amputated area.

Learned Adjustments in Behavior

So far, the discussion has focused on anatomical changes. In fact, much recovery from brain damage is based on learning.

If you can't find your keys, perhaps you accidentally dropped them into the trash (so they are gone forever), or perhaps you absentmindedly put them in an unusual place (where you will find them if you keep looking). Similarly, someone with brain damage may have lost some ability totally or may be able to find it with enough effort. Much recovery from brain damage depends on learning to make better use of the abilities that were spared. For example, if you lose your peripheral vision, you learn to move your head from side to side to compensate (Marshall, 1985).

Sometimes, a person or animal with brain damage appears unable to do something but is in fact not trying. Consider an animal that incurred damage to the sensory nerves linking a forelimb to the spinal cord, as in Figure 5.18. The animal no longer feels the limb, although the motor nerves still connect to the muscles. We say the limb is **deafferented** because it has lost its afferent (sensory) input. A monkey with a deafferented limb does not spontaneously use it for walking, picking up objects, or any other voluntary behaviors (Taub & Berman, 1968). At first investigators assumed that a monkey *can't* use a deafferented limb. In a later experiment, however, they cut the afferent nerves of both forelimbs. Despite this more extensive damage, the monkey used both deafferented

limbs to walk, climb, and pick up food. Apparently, a monkey fails to use a deafferented forelimb only because walking on three limbs is easier than using an impaired limb. When it has no choice but to use its deafferented limbs, it does.

Now consider a rat with damage to its visual cortex. Before the damage, it learned to approach a white card instead of a black card for food, but after the damage, it approaches one card or the other randomly. Has it completely forgotten the discrimination? Evidently not, because it can more easily relearn to approach the white card than learn to approach the black card (T. E. LeVere & Morlock, 1973) (Figure 5.19). Thomas LeVere (1975) proposed that a lesion to the visual

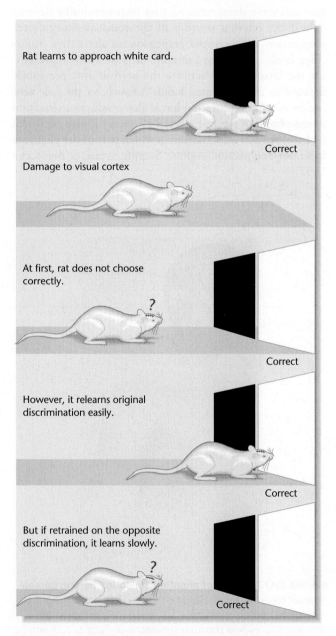

FIGURE 5.19 Memory impairment after cortical damage
Brain damage impairs retrieval but does not destroy the memory. *(Source: Based on T. E. LeVere & Morlock, 1973)*

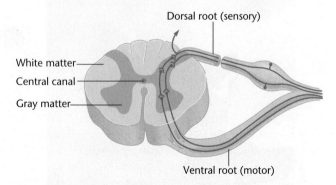

FIGURE 5.18 Cross-section through the spinal cord
A cut through the dorsal root (as shown) deprives the animal of touch sensations from part of the body but leaves the motor nerves intact. *(© Cengage Learning 2013)*

cortex does not destroy the memory trace but merely impairs the rat's ability to find it. As the animal recovers, it regains access to misplaced memories.

Similarly, therapy for people with brain damage focuses on encouraging them to practice skills that are impaired but not lost. Treatment begins with careful evaluation of a patient's abilities and disabilities. Such evaluations are the specialty of neuropsychologists, who develop tests to try to pinpoint the problems. For example, someone who has trouble carrying out spoken instructions might be impaired in hearing, memory, language, muscle control, or alertness. After identifying the problem, a neuropsychologist might refer a patient to a physical therapist or occupational therapist, who helps the patient practice the impaired skills. Therapists get their best results if they start soon after a patient's stroke, and animal researchers find the same pattern. In one study, rats with damage to the parietal cortex of one hemisphere showed poor coordination of the contralateral forepaw. Some of the rats received experiences designed to encourage them to use the impaired limb. Those who began practice 5 days after the damage recovered better than those who started after 14 days, who in turn recovered better than those who started after 30 days (Biernaskie, Chernenko, & Corbett, 2004). As other kinds of evidence have confirmed, the brain has increased plasticity during the first days after damage.

One important note is that behavior recovered after brain damage is effortful, and its recovery is precarious. A person with brain damage who appears to be functioning normally is working harder than usual. The recovered behavior deteriorates markedly after drinking alcohol, physical exhaustion, or other kinds of stress that would minimally affect most other people (Fleet & Heilman, 1986). It also deteriorates in old age (Corkin, Rosen, Sullivan, & Clegg, 1989).

Stop & Check

29. Suppose someone has suffered a spinal cord injury that interrupts all sensation from the left arm. Now he or she uses only the right arm. Of the following, which is the most promising therapy: electrically stimulate the skin of the left arm, tie the right arm behind the person's back, or blindfold the person?

ANSWER

29. Tie the right arm behind the back to force the person to use the impaired arm instead of only the normal arm. Stimulating the skin of the left arm would accomplish nothing, as the sensory receptors have no input to the CNS. Blindfolding would be either irrelevant or harmful (by decreasing the visual feedback from left-hand movements).

MODULE 5.2 ■ IN CLOSING

Brain Damage and Recovery

The mammalian body is well equipped to replace lost blood cells or skin cells but poorly prepared to deal with lost brain cells. Even the responses that do occur after brain damage, such as collateral sprouting of axons or reorganization of sensory representations, are not always helpful. It is tempting to speculate that we failed to evolve mechanisms to recover from brain damage because, through most of our evolutionary history, an individual with brain damage was not likely to survive long enough to recover. Today, many people with brain and spinal cord damage survive for years, and we need continuing research on how to improve their lives.

SUMMARY

1. Brain damage has many causes, including blows to the head, obstruction of blood flow to the brain, or a ruptured blood vessel in the brain. Strokes kill neurons largely by overexcitation. **141**

2. During the first 3 hours after an ischemic stroke, tissue plasminogen activator (tPA) can reduce cell loss by breaking up the blood clot. Theoretically, it should also be possible to minimize cell loss by preventing overexcitation of neurons, but so far, procedures based on this idea have been ineffective. Cooling the brain or providing cannabinoids can reduce cell loss. **142**

3. When one brain area is damaged, other areas become less active than usual because of their loss of input. Stimulant drugs can help restore normal function of these undamaged areas. **143**

4. After an area of the CNS loses its usual input, other axons begin to excite it as a result of either sprouting or denervation supersensitivity. In some cases, this abnormal input produces odd sensations such as the phantom limb. **144**

5. Many individuals with brain damage are capable of more than they show because they avoid using skills that have become impaired or difficult. **148**

KEY TERMS

Terms are defined in the module on the page number indicated. They're also presented in alphabetical order with definitions in the book's Subject Index/Glossary, which begins on page 561. Interactive flashcards and crossword puzzles are among the online resources available to help you learn these terms and the concepts they represent.

cerebrovascular accident **141**

closed head injury **141**

collateral sprouts **144**

deafferented **148**

denervation supersensitivity **145**

diaschisis **143**

edema **142**

hemorrhage **141**

ischemia **141**

phantom limb **147**

stroke **141**

tissue plasminogen activator (tPA) **142**

THOUGHT QUESTIONS

1. Ordinarily, patients with advanced Parkinson's disease (who have damage to dopamine-releasing axons) move very slowly if at all. However, during an emergency (e.g., a fire in the building), they may move rapidly and vigorously. Suggest a possible explanation.

2. Drugs that block dopamine synapses tend to impair or slow limb movements. However, after people have taken such drugs for a long time, some experience involuntary twitches or tremors in their muscles. Based on material in this chapter, propose a possible explanation.

CHAPTER 5 Interactive Exploration and Study

The **Psychology CourseMate** for this text brings chapter topics to life with interactive learning, study, and exam preparation tools, including quizzes and flashcards for the Key Concepts that appear throughout each module, as well as an interactive media-rich eBook version of the text that is fully searchable and includes highlighting and note taking capabilities and interactive versions of the book's **Stop & Check** quizzes and **Try It Yourself Online** activities. The site also features **Virtual Biological Psychology Labs, videos,** and **animations** to help you better understand concepts—logon and learn more at **www.cengagebrain.com**, which is your gateway to all of this text's complimentary and premium resources, including the following:

Virtual Biological Psychology Labs

Explore the experiments that led to modern-day understanding of biopsychology with the Virtual Biological Psychology Labs, featuring a realistic lab environment that allows you to conduct experiments and evaluate data to better understand how scientists came to the conclusions presented in your text. The labs cover a range of topics, including perception, motivation, cognition, and more. You may purchase access at **www.cengagebrain.com**, or login at **login.cengagebrain.com** if an access card was included with your text.

Videos

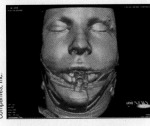

Traumatic Brain Damage

Also available—

- Brain Development in Childhood and Adolescence
- Waking from a Coma
- Brain Regrowth
- Stroke Robots

Animations

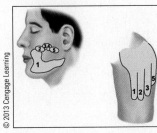

Phantom Limb

Also available—

- Sperry Experiment

Suggestions for Further Exploration

Books

Levi-Montalcini, R. (1988). *In praise of imperfection.* New York: Basic Books. Autobiography by the discoverer of nerve growth factor.

Ramachandran, V. S., & Blakeslee, S. (1998). *Phantoms in the brain.* New York: Morrow. One of the most thought-provoking books ever written about human brain damage, including the phantom limb phenomenon.

Websites

The Psychology CourseMate for this text provides regularly updated links to relevant on-line resources for this chapter, such as the **National Stroke Association** and instructions on how to experience an illusion similar to the phantom limb.

Vision

MAIN IDEAS

1. Each sensory neuron conveys a particular type of experience. For example, anything that stimulates the optic nerve is perceived as light.

2. Vertebrate vision depends on two kinds of receptors: cones, which contribute to color vision, and rods, which do not.

3. Every cell in the visual system has a receptive field, an area of the visual world that can excite or inhibit it.

4. Neurons of the visual system establish approximately correct connections and properties through chemical gradients that

are present before birth. However, visual experience can fine-tune or alter those properties, especially early in life.

5. After visual information reaches the brain, concurrent pathways analyze different aspects, such as shape, color, and movement.

6. Localized brain damage can produce surprisingly specific deficits, such as impaired ability to recognize faces or movement.

Several decades ago, a graduate student taking his final oral exam for a PhD in psychology was asked, "How far can an ant see?" He turned pale. He did not know the answer, and evidently he was supposed to. He tried to remember everything he knew about insect vision. Finally, he gave up and admitted he did not know.

With an impish grin, the professor told him, "Presumably, an ant can see 93 million miles—the distance to the sun." Yes, this was a trick question. However, it illustrates an important point: How far an ant sees, or how far you see, depends on how far the light travels before it strikes the eyes. You do not send out "sight rays." That principle is far from intuitive. It was not known until the Arab philosopher Ibn al-Haythem (965–1040) demonstrated that light rays bounce off any object in all directions, but we see only those rays that strike the retina perpendicularly (Gross, 1999).

Even today, a distressingly large number of college students believe they send out sight rays from their eyes when they see (Winer, Cottrell, Gregg, Fournier, & Bica, 2002). That view represents a profound misunderstanding. Here is one of the most important principles to remember from this text: When you see a tree, for example, your perception is not in the tree. It is in your brain. You perceive something only when it alters your brain activity. Even if you did send out rays from your eyes—and you don't—when they struck some object, you wouldn't know about it, unless they bounced back and returned to your eyes.

The sensory systems do not match our common-sense notions. In this chapter, we consider the visual system, the aspect of psychology for which our biological understanding has advanced the furthest.

OPPOSITE: Later in this chapter, you will understand why this prairie falcon has tilted its head.

Visual Coding

Imagine that you are a piece of iron. So there you are, sitting around doing nothing, as usual, when along comes a drop of water. What will be your perception of the water? Yes, of course, a bar of iron doesn't have a brain, and it wouldn't have any perception at all. But let's ignore that inconvenient fact and imagine what it would be like if a bar of iron could perceive the water. From the standpoint of a piece of iron, water is above all *rustish*.

Now return to your perspective as a human. You know that rustishness is not really a property of water itself but of how it reacts with iron. The same is true of human perception. When you see grass as *green*, the green is no more a property of grass than rustish is a property of water. Green is the experience that results when the light bouncing off grass reacts with the neurons in your brain. Greenness is in us—just as rust is in the piece of iron.

General Principles of Perception

Every animal is surrounded by objects that it needs to know about. You perceive an object when it emits or reflects energy that stimulates receptors that transmit information to your brain. How does your brain make sense of that information? The 17th-century philosopher René Descartes believed that the brain's representation of a stimulus resembled the stimulus. According to him, the nerves from the eye would project a pattern of impulses arranged like a picture, right side up. In fact, he was wrong. Your brain encodes the information in a way that doesn't resemble what you see. When a computer stores a representation of a triangle, for example, it stores it as a series of 0s and 1s. If you examine that sequence of 0s and 1s, it will not look like a triangle. Similarly, your brain stores a representation of a triangle in terms of altered activity in many neurons, and if you examine those neurons, you will see nothing that looks like a triangle. Your brain codes the information in terms of which neurons respond, their amount of response, and the timing of their responses.

One aspect of coding is *which* neurons are active. Impulses in certain neurons indicate light, whereas impulses in others indicate sound. In 1838, Johannes Müller described this insight as **the law of specific nerve energies**. Müller held that whatever excites a particular nerve establishes a special kind of energy unique to that nerve. In modern terms, the brain somehow interprets the action potentials from the auditory nerve as sounds, those from the olfactory nerve as odors, and so forth. Admittedly, that word "somehow" glosses over a deep mystery.

Here is a demonstration: If you rub your eyes, you may see spots or flashes of light even in a totally dark room. You applied mechanical pressure, which excited visual receptors in your eyes. Anything that excites those receptors is perceived as light. (If you try this demonstration, first remove any contact lenses. Shut your eyelids and rub gently.)

TRY IT YOURSELF

Another aspect of coding is the amount of response—that is, how many action potentials a neuron sends per unit of time. Much of sensory coding depends on the frequency of firing. For example, when pain axons fire many action potentials per second, you feel intense pain. Fewer per second would produce less pain.

Stop & Check

1. If someone electrically stimulated the auditory receptors in your ear, what would you perceive?

2. If it were possible to flip your entire brain upside down, without breaking any of the connections to sense organs or muscles, what would happen to your perceptions of what you see, hear, and so forth?

ANSWERS

1. Because of the law of specific nerve energies, you would perceive it as sound, not as shock. (Of course, a strong enough shock would spread far enough to excite pain receptors also.) 2. Your perceptions would not change. The way visual or auditory information is coded in the brain does not depend on the physical location within the brain. Seeing something as "on top," or "to the left" depends on which neurons are active but does not depend on the physical location of those neurons.

The Eye and Its Connections to the Brain

Light enters the eye through an opening in the center of the iris called the **pupil** (Figure 6.1). It is focused by the lens (adjustable) and cornea (not adjustable) and projected onto the **retina**, the rear surface of the eye, which is lined with visual receptors. Light from the left side of the world strikes the right half of the retina, and vice versa. Light from above strikes the bottom half of the retina, and light from below strikes the top half. The inversion of the image poses no problem for the nervous system. Remember, the visual system does not duplicate the image. It codes it by various kinds of neuronal activity.

Route Within the Retina

If you were designing an eye, you would probably send the receptors' messages directly back to the brain. In the vertebrate retina, however, messages go from receptors at the back of the eye to **bipolar cells**, located closer to the center of the eye. The bipolar cells send their messages to **ganglion cells**, located still closer to the center of the eye. The ganglion cells' axons join together and travel back to the brain (Figures 6.2 and 6.3). Additional cells called *amacrine cells* get information from bipolar cells and send it to other bipolar, amacrine, and ganglion cells. Various types of amacrine cells refine the input to ganglion cells, enabling them to respond specifically to shapes, movements, or other visual features (S. Fried, Münch, & Werblin, 2002; Sinclair, Jacobs, & Nirenberg, 2004; Wässle, 2004).

One consequence of this anatomy is that light passes through the ganglion cells and bipolar cells en route to the receptors. However, these cells are transparent, and light passes through them without distortion. A more important consequence is the *blind spot*. The ganglion cell axons form the **optic nerve**, which exits through the back of the eye. The point at which it leaves (which is also where the blood vessels enter and leave) is the **blind spot** because it has no receptors. You can demonstrate your own blind spot with Figure 6.4. Close your

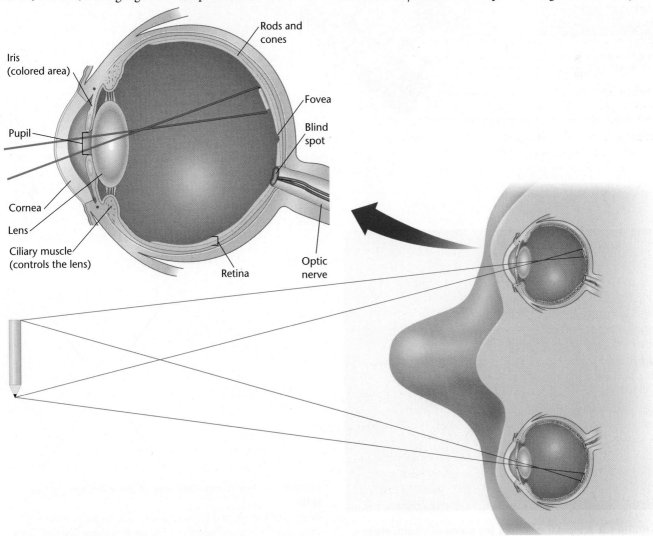

FIGURE 6.1 Cross-section of the vertebrate eye
An object in the visual field produces an inverted image on the retina. The optic nerve exits the eyeball on the nasal side (the side closer to the nose). *(© Cengage Learning 2013)*

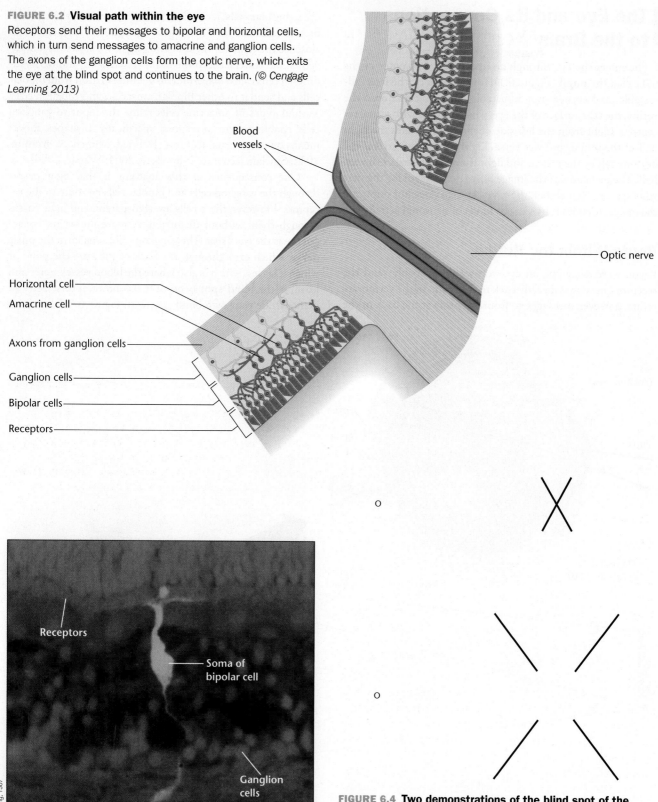

FIGURE 6.2 Visual path within the eye
Receptors send their messages to bipolar and horizontal cells, which in turn send messages to amacrine and ganglion cells. The axons of the ganglion cells form the optic nerve, which exits the eye at the blind spot and continues to the brain. (© Cengage Learning 2013)

Blood vessels

Optic nerve

Horizontal cell

Amacrine cell

Axons from ganglion cells

Ganglion cells

Bipolar cells

Receptors

Receptors

Soma of bipolar cell

Ganglion cells

Dowling, 1987

FIGURE 6.3 A bipolar cell from the retina of a carp, stained yellow
Bipolar cells get their name from the fact that a fibrous process is attached to each end (or pole) of the neuron.

FIGURE 6.4 Two demonstrations of the blind spot of the retina
Close your left eye and focus your right eye on the o in the top part. Move the page toward you and away, noticing what happens to the x. At a distance of about 25 cm (10 in.), the x disappears. Now repeat this procedure with the bottom part. At that same distance, what do you see? (© Cengage Learning 2013)

left eye and focus your right eye on the top o. Then move the page forward and back. When the page is about 25 cm (10 in.) away, the x disappears because its image strikes the blind spot.

Now repeat with the lower part of the figure. When the page is again about 25 cm away from your eyes, what do you see? The *gap* disappears! When the blind spot interrupts a straight line or other regular pattern, your brain fills in the gap.

In everyday life, you never notice your blind spot, for two reasons. First, your brain fills in the gap, as you just experienced. Second, anything in the blind spot of one eye is visible to the other eye. Use Figure 6.4 again to locate the blind spot in your right eye. Then close your right eye and open the left one. You will see the spot that the right eye couldn't see.

Stop & Check

3. What makes the blind spot of the retina blind?

ANSWER

3. The blind spot has no receptors because it is occupied by exiting axons and blood vessels.

Fovea and Periphery of the Retina

When you look at details such as letters on this page, you fixate them on the central portion of your retina, especially the **fovea** (meaning "pit"), a tiny area specialized for acute, detailed vision (Figure 6.1). Because blood vessels and ganglion cell axons are almost absent near the fovea, it has nearly unimpeded vision. The tight packing of receptors also aids perception of detail.

More important for perceiving detail, each receptor in the fovea connects to a single *bipolar cell*, which in turn connects to a single *ganglion cell*, which has an axon to the brain. The ganglion cells in the fovea of humans and other primates are called **midget ganglion cells** because each is small and responds to just a single cone. As a result, each cone in the fovea is connected to the brain with a direct route that registers the exact location of the input. Because the midget ganglion cells provide 70% of the input to the brain, our vision is dominated by what we see in the fovea (Nassi & Callaway, 2009).

You have heard the expression "eyes like a hawk." Many birds' eyes occupy most of the head, compared to only 5% of the head in humans. Furthermore, many bird species have two foveas per eye, one pointing ahead and one pointing to the side (Wallman & Pettigrew, 1985). The extra foveas enable perception of detail in the periphery.

Hawks and other predatory birds have a greater density of visual receptors on the top half of their retinas (looking down) than on the bottom half (looking up). That arrangement is adaptive because predatory birds spend most of their day soaring high in the air looking down. However, to look up, the bird must turn its head, as in Figure 6.5 (Waldvogel, 1990). Conversely, many prey species such as rats have most of their receptors on the bottom half of the retina (Lund, Lund, & Wise, 1974). As a result, they see above better than below.

Chase Swift Photography

FIGURE 6.5 **A consequence of how receptors are arranged on the retina**
One owlet has turned its head almost upside down to look up. Birds of prey have many receptors on the upper half of the retina, enabling them to see down in great detail during flight. But they see objects above themselves poorly, unless they turn their heads. Take another look at the prairie falcon at the start of this chapter. It is not a one-eyed bird; it is a bird that has tilted its head. Do you now understand why?

Toward the periphery of the retina, more and more receptors converge onto bipolar and ganglion cells, as shown in Figure 6.6. As a result, the brain cannot detect the exact location or shape of a peripheral light source (Rossi & Roorda, 2010). However, the summation enables perception of fainter lights in the periphery. In short, foveal vision has better *acuity* (sensitivity to detail), and peripheral vision has better sensitivity to dim light.

In the periphery, your ability to detect detail is limited by interference from other nearby objects (Pelli & Tillman, 2008). In the displays below, focus on the x. For the first display, you can probably identify the letter to the right. For the second display, you probably cannot read that same letter in the same location, because of interference from the neighboring letters.

    X   T

    X   ATE

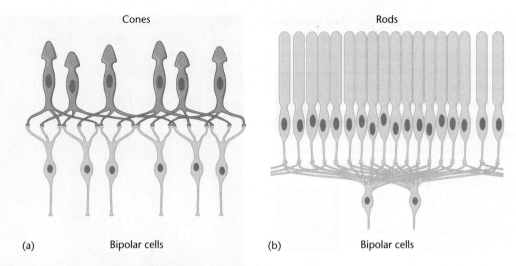

Cones

Rods

(a) Bipolar cells

(b) Bipolar cells

FIGURE 6.6 Convergence of input onto bipolar cells
In the fovea, each bipolar cell receives excitation from just one cone (and inhibition from a few surrounding cones), and relays its information to a single midget ganglion cell. In the periphery, input from many rods converges onto each bipolar cell, resulting in higher sensitivity to faint light and low sensitivity to spatial location. *(© Cengage Learning 2013)*

Visual Receptors:
Rods and Cones

The vertebrate retina contains two types of receptors: rods and cones (Figure 6.7). The **rods**, which are abundant in the periphery of the human retina, respond to faint light but are not useful in daylight because bright light bleaches them. **Cones**, which are abundant in and near the fovea, are less active in dim light, more useful in bright light, and essential for color vision. Because of the distribution of rods and cones, you have good color vision in the fovea but not in the periphery. Table 6.1 summarizes the differences between foveal and peripheral vision.

Although rods outnumber cones by about 20 to 1 in the human retina, cones provide about 90% of the brain's

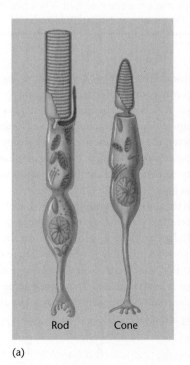

Rod   Cone

(a)

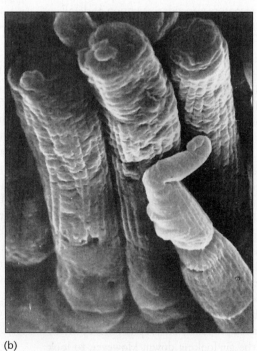

(b)

FIGURE 6.7 Structure of rod and cone
(a) Diagram of a rod and a cone. (b) Photo of rods and a cone, produced with a scanning electron microscope. Magnification x 7000. *(Reprinted from* Brain Research, 15 (2), *E. R. Lewis, Y. Y. Zeevi and F. S. Werblin, "Scanning electron microscopy of vertebrate visual receptors," 1969, by permission of Elsevier)*

TABLE 6.1 | **Human Foveal and Peripheral Vision**

Characteristic	Foveal Vision	Peripheral Vision
Receptors	Cones	Proportion of rods increases toward periphery
Convergence of input	Each ganglion cell excited by a single cone	Each ganglion cell excited by many receptors
Brightness sensitivity	Distinguishes among bright lights; responds poorly to dim light	Responds well to dim light; poor for distinguishing among bright lights
Sensitivity to detail	Good detail vision because each cone's own ganglion cell sends a message to the brain	Poor detail vision because many receptors converge their input onto a given ganglion cell
Color vision	Good (many cones)	Poor (few cones)

© Cengage Learning 2013

input (Masland, 2001). Remember the midget ganglion cells: In the fovea, each cone has its own line to the brain. In the periphery (mostly rods), each receptor shares a line with tens or hundreds of others. Overall, 120 million rods and 6 million cones converge onto 1 million axons in the optic nerve, on average. A 20 : 1 ratio of rods to cones may sound high, but the ratio is much higher in species that are active at night. South American oilbirds, which live in caves and emerge only at night, have about 15,000 rods per cone. As a further adaptation to detect faint lights, their rods are packed three deep throughout the retina (G. Martin, Rojas, Ramírez, & McNeil, 2004).

The average of one million axons in the optic nerve doesn't apply to everyone. Some people have two or three times as many axons from the eyes to the brain as others do. They also have more cells in their visual cortex (Andrews, Halpern, & Purves, 1997; Stevens, 2001; Sur & Leamey, 2001) and greater ability to detect brief, faint, or rapidly changing visual stimuli (Halpern, Andrews, & Purves, 1999). Heightened visual responses are valuable in many activities, especially in sports that require aim. Researchers find that top performers in tennis, squash, and fencing show faster than average brain responses to visual stimuli. Speed is only about average for top athletes in rowing or cycling, where strength is important but quick reactions are not (Nakata, Yoshie, Miura, & Kudo, 2010). Part of the difference among individuals in their visual sensitivity is due to the number of axons from the retina, which is probably established early in life. However, extensive practice can also change visual sensitivity. Extensive practice at action video games increases people's ability to detect subtle visual details (Li, Polat, Makous, & Bavelier, 2009).

Both rods and cones contain **photopigments**, chemicals that release energy when struck by light. Photopigments consist of 11-*cis*-retinal (a derivative of vitamin A) bound to proteins called *opsins*, which modify the photopigments' sensitivity to different wavelengths of light. Light converts 11-*cis*-retinal to all-*trans*-retinal, thus releasing energy that activates second messengers within the cell (Q. Wang, Schoenlein, Peteanu, Mathies, & Shank, 1994). (The light is absorbed in this process. It does not continue to bounce around the eye.)

Stop & Check

4. You sometimes find that you can see a faint star on a dark night better if you look slightly to the side of the star instead of straight at it. Why?

5. If you found a species with a high ratio of cones to rods in its retina, what would you predict about its way of life?

ANSWERS 4. If you look slightly to the side, the light falls on an area of the retina with more rods and more convergence of input. 5. We should expect this species to be highly active during the day and seldom active at night.

Color Vision

Visible light consists of electromagnetic radiation within the range from less than 400 nm (nanometer, or 10^{-9} m) to more than 700 nm. We perceive the shortest visible wavelengths as violet. Progressively longer wavelengths are perceived as blue, green, yellow, orange, and red (Figure 6.8). We call these wavelengths "light" only because the receptors in our eyes are tuned to detecting them. Ultraviolet radiation (shorter wavelengths) produces suntans and sometimes skin cancers, but we don't see it. However, many species of birds, fish, and insects have visual receptors sensitive to these short wavelengths. For them, ultraviolet radiation is a kind of light (Stevens & Cuthill, 2007). Of course, we can't know what it looks like to them, but it certainly affects their behavior. In some species of birds, the male and female look alike to us, but different to birds, because the male reflects more ultraviolet light.

The Trichromatic (Young-Helmholtz) Theory

People distinguish red, green, yellow, blue, orange, pink, purple, greenish-blue, and so forth. Presuming that we don't have a separate receptor for every possible color, how many types do we have?

The first person to advance our understanding on this question was an amazingly productive man named Thomas Young (1773–1829). Young was the first to start deciphering the Rosetta stone. He also founded the modern wave theory of light, defined energy in its modern form, founded the calculation of annuities, introduced the coefficient of elasticity,

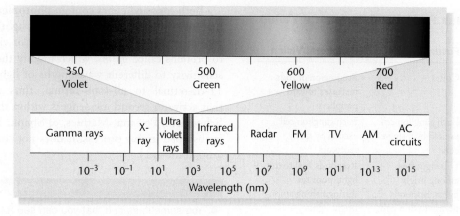

FIGURE 6.8 A beam of light separated into its wavelengths
Although the wavelengths vary as a continuum, we perceive distinct colors. (© Cengage Learning 2013)

discovered much about the anatomy of the eye, and made major contributions to other fields (Martindale, 2001). Previous scientists thought they could explain color by understanding the physics of light. Young recognized that color required a biological explanation. He proposed that we perceive color by comparing the responses across a few types of receptors, each of which was sensitive to a different range of wavelengths.

This theory, later modified by Hermann von Helmholtz, is now known as the **trichromatic theory** of color vision, or the **Young-Helmholtz theory**. According to this theory, we perceive color through the relative rates of response by three kinds of cones, each one maximally sensitive to a different set of wavelengths. (*Trichromatic* means "three colors.") How did Helmholtz decide on the number three? He found that people

could match any color by mixing appropriate amounts of just three wavelengths. Therefore, he concluded that three kinds of receptors—we now call them cones—are sufficient to account for human color vision.

Figure 6.9 shows wavelength-sensitivity functions for the *short-wavelength, medium-wavelength,* and *long-wavelength* cone types. Each cone responds to a broad range of wavelengths but to some more than others.

According to the trichromatic theory, we discriminate among wavelengths by the ratio of activity across the three types of cones. For example, light at 550 nm excites the medium-wavelength and long-wavelength receptors about equally and the short-wavelength receptor almost not at all. This ratio of responses among the three cones determines a

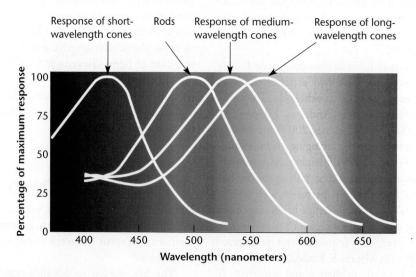

FIGURE 6.9 Responses of rods and three kinds of cones
Note that each kind responds somewhat to a wide range of wavelengths but best to wavelengths in a particular range. (*Adapted from Bowmaker & Dartnall, 1980*)

perception of yellow-green. More intense light increases the activity of all three cones without much change in their ratio of responses. As a result, the light appears brighter but still the same color. When all three types of cones are equally active, we see white or gray. Think about this example of coding: The perception depends on the frequency of response in one cell *relative to* the frequency of another cell.

The response of any one cone is ambiguous. For example, a low response rate by a middle-wavelength cone might indicate low-intensity 540 nm light or brighter 500 nm light or still brighter 460 nm light. The nervous system determines the color and brightness of the light by comparing the responses of different types of cones. (Consequently, mice, because they have only one kind of cone, are colorblind.)

Given the desirability of seeing all colors in all locations, we might suppose that the three kinds of cones would be equally abundant and evenly distributed. In fact, they are not. Long- and medium-wavelength cones are far more abundant than short-wavelength (blue) cones. Consequently, it is easier to see tiny red, yellow, or green dots than blue dots (Roorda & Williams, 1999). Try this: Look at the dots in the following display, first from close and then from greater distances. You probably will notice that the blue dots look blue when close but appear black from a greater distance. The other colors are still visible when the blue is not.

Although the short-wavelength (blue) cones are about evenly distributed across the retina, the other two kinds are

distributed haphazardly, with big differences among individuals (Solomon & Lennie, 2007). Figure 6.10 shows the distribution of short-, medium-, and long-wavelength cones in two people's retinas, with colors artificially added to distinguish them. Note the patches of all medium- or all long-wavelength cones. Some people have more than 10 times as many of one kind as the other. Surprisingly, these variations produce only small differences in people's color perceptions (Solomon & Lennie, 2007).

In the retina's periphery, cones are so scarce that you have no useful color vision (Diller et al., 2004; P. R. Martin, Lee, White, Solomon, & Rütiger, 2001). Try this: Get someone to put a colored dot on the tip of your finger without telling you the color. A spot of colored ink will do. While keeping your eyes straight ahead, slowly move your finger from behind your head into your field of vision and gradually toward your fovea. At what point do you see the color? Certainly you see your finger before you see the color. The smaller the dot, the farther you have to move it into your **visual field**—that is, the part of the world that you see—before you can identify the color.

The Opponent-Process Theory

The trichromatic theory is incomplete as a theory of color vision. For example, try the following demonstration: Pick a point in the top portion of Figure 6.11—such as the tip of the nose—and stare at it under a bright light, without moving your eyes, for a minute. (The brighter the light and the longer you stare, the stronger the effect.) Then look at a plain white surface, such as a wall or a blank sheet of paper. Keep your eyes steady. You will see a **negative color afterimage**, a replacement of the red you had been staring at with green, green with red, yellow and blue with each other, and black and white with each other.

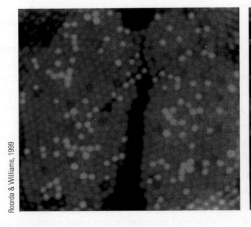
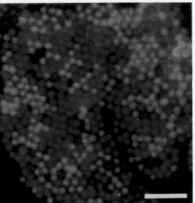

FIGURE 6.10 Distribution of cones in two human retinas
Investigators artificially colored these images of cones from two people's retinas, indicating short-wavelength cones with blue, medium-wavelength cones with green, and long-wavelength cones with red. Note the difference between the two people, the scarcity of short-wavelength cones, and the patchiness of the distributions. *(Reprinted by permission from Macmillan Publishers Ltd: Nature, "The arrangement of the three cone classes in the living human eye," Roorda & Williams, 1999)*

FIGURE 6.11 Stimulus for demonstrating negative color afterimages
Stare at a point on the face under bright light for about a minute and then look at a white field. You should see a negative afterimage.

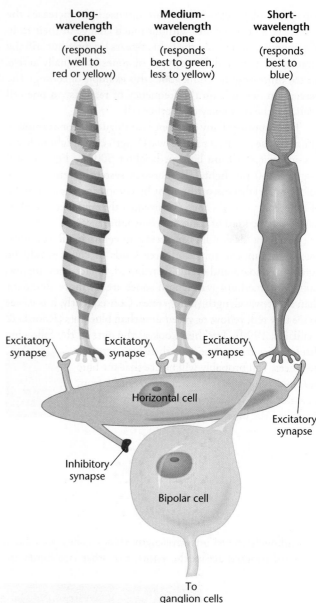

FIGURE 6.12 Possible wiring for one bipolar cell
Short-wavelength light (which we see as blue) excites the bipolar cell and by way of the horizontal cell also inhibits it. However, the excitation predominates, so blue light produces net excitation. Red, green, and yellow light inhibit this bipolar cell through the horizontal cell. The strongest inhibition is from yellow light, which stimulates both the long- and medium-wavelength cones. Therefore, we can describe this bipolar cell as excited by blue and inhibited by yellow. (© Cengage Learning 2013)

To explain this and related phenomena, Ewald Hering, a 19th-century physiologist, proposed the **opponent–process theory:** We perceive color in terms of opposites (Hurvich & Jameson, 1957). That is, the brain has a mechanism that perceives color on a continuum from red to green, another from yellow to blue, and another from white to black.

Here is a hypothetical mechanism: The bipolar cell diagrammed in Figure 6.12 is excited by the short-wavelength (blue) cone and inhibited by a mixture of the long-wavelength and medium-wavelength cones. An increase in this bipolar cell's activity produces the experience *blue,* and a decrease produces the experience *yellow.* If short-wavelength (blue) light stimulates this cell long enough, the cell becomes fatigued. If we now remove the short-wavelength light, the cell responds less than its baseline level, and therefore produces an experience of *yellow.* This example is a special kind of coding, in

which an increase in response produces one perception, and a decrease produces a different perception.

Although that explanation of negative color after images is appealingly simple, it cannot be the whole story. Try this: Stare at the x in the following diagram for a minute or more under a bright light and then look at a white page.

TRY IT YOURSELF

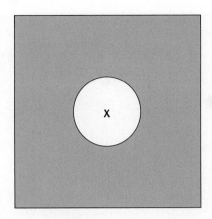

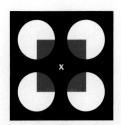

FIGURE 6.13 An afterimage hard to explain in terms of the retina
Stare at the x under bright light for a minute and then look at a white surface. Many people report an alternation between two afterimages, one of them based on the illusion of a red square. *(Reprinted by permission from "Afterimage of perceptually filled-in surface," Figure 1A, p. 1678 (left hand) by S. Shimojo, Y. Kamitani, and S. Nishida in* Science, 293, 1677–1680. Copyright 2001 American Association for the Advancement of Science.)*

For the afterimage of the surrounding area, you saw red, as the theory predicts. But what about the circle inside? Theoretically, you should see a gray or black afterimage (the opposite of white), but in fact, if you used a bright enough light, you saw a green afterimage.

Here is another demonstration: First, look at Figure 6.13. Note that although it shows four red quarter circles, you have the illusion of a whole red square. (Look carefully to convince yourself that it is an illusion.) Now stare at the x in Figure 6.13 for at least a minute under bright lights. Then look at a white surface.

TRY IT YOURSELF

People usually report that the afterimage fluctuates. Sometimes, they see four green quarter circles:

And sometimes, they see a whole green square (Shimojo, Kamitani, & Nishida, 2001):

If you see a whole green square, it is the afterimage of an illusion! The red square you "saw" wasn't really there. This demonstration suggests that afterimages depend on the whole context, not just the light on individual receptors. The cerebral cortex must be responsible, not the bipolar or ganglion cells.

Stop & Check

6. Suppose a bipolar cell receives excitatory input from medium-wavelength cones and inhibitory input from all three kinds of cones. When it is highly excited, what color would one see? When it is inhibited, what color perception would result?

ANSWER

6. Excitation of this cell should yield a perception of green under normal circumstances. Inhibition would produce the opposite sensation, red.

The Retinex Theory

The trichromatic theory and the opponent–process theory cannot easily explain **color constancy**, the ability to recognize colors despite changes in lighting (Kennard, Lawden, Morland, & Ruddock, 1995; Zeki, 1980, 1983). If you wear green-tinted glasses or replace your white light bulb with a green one, you still identify bananas as yellow, paper as white, and so forth. Your brain compares the color of one object with the color of another, in effect subtracting a certain amount of green from each.

To illustrate, examine the top part of Figure 6.14 (Purves & Lotto, 2003). Although different colors of light illuminate the two scenes, you easily identify the squares as red, yellow, blue, and so forth. Note the result of removing context. The bottom part shows the squares that looked red in the top part. Without the context that indicated yellow light or blue light, those on the left look orange and those on the right look purple. (For this reason, we should avoid talking about the "color" of a wavelength of light. A certain wavelength of light can appear as different colors depending on the background.)

Similarly, our perception of the brightness of an object requires comparing it with other objects. Examine Figure 6.15 (Purves, Shimpi, & Lotto, 1999). You see what appears to have a gray top and a white bottom. Now cover the border between the top and the bottom with your fingers. You will notice that the top of the object has exactly the same brightness as the bottom! For additional examples like this, visit the website of Dale Purves, Center for Cognitive Neuroscience, Duke University, at http://www.purveslab.net.

TRY IT YOURSELF

To account for color and brightness constancy, Edwin Land proposed the **retinex theory** (a combination of the words *retin*a and cor*tex*): The cortex compares information from various parts of the retina to determine the brightness and color for each area (Land, Hubel, Livingstone, Perry, & Burns, 1983).

(a)

(b)

(c)

FIGURE 6.14 Effects of context on color perception
In each block, we identify certain tiles as looking red. However, after removal of the context, those that appeared red on the left now look orange; those on the right appear purple. (*Why we see what we do, by D. Purves and R. B. Lotto, Figure 6.10, p. 134. Copyright 2003 Sinauer Associates, Inc. Reprinted by permission.*)

FIGURE 6.15 Brightness constancy
In the center of this figure, do you see a gray object above and a white object below? Place a finger over the border between them and then compare the objects. (*From "An Empirical Explanation of Cornsweet Effect," by D. Purves, A. Shimpi, & R. B. Lotto, in Journal of Neuroscience, 19, 8542–8551. Copyright 1999 by the Society for Neuroscience.*)

Dale Purves and colleagues have expressed a similar idea in more general terms: Whenever we see anything, we make an inference. For example, when you look at the objects in Figures 6.14 and 6.15, you ask yourself, "On occasions when I have seen something that looked like this, what was it really?" You go through the same process for perceiving shapes, motion, or anything else (Lotto & Purves, 2002; Purves & Lotto, 2003). That is, visual perception requires a reasoning process, not just retinal stimulation.

Stop & Check

7. When a television set is off, its screen appears gray. When you watch a program, parts of the screen appear black, even though more light is actually showing on the screen than when the set was off. What accounts for the black perception?

8. Figure 6.9 shows 500 nm light as blue and 550 nm light as yellow. Why should we nevertheless not call them "blue light" and "yellow light"?

ANSWERS

7. The black experience arises by contrast with the other brighter areas. The contrast occurs by comparison within the cerebral cortex, as in the retinex theory of color vision. **8.** Color perception depends not just on the wavelength of light from a given spot but also the light from surrounding areas. As in Figure 6.14, the context can change the color perception.

Color Vision Deficiency

Encyclopedias describe many examples of discoveries in astronomy, biology, chemistry, and physics, but what great discoveries can you think of in psychology? One of the first was colorblindness, better described as **color vision deficiency**. (Complete colorblindness, perception of only black and white, is rare.) Before color vision deficiency was discovered in the 1600s, people assumed that vision copies the objects we see (Fletcher & Voke, 1985). They assumed that everyone saw objects the same way. Investigators *discovered* that it is possible to have otherwise satisfactory vision without seeing color. That is, color depends on what our brains do with incoming light. It is not a property of the light itself.

For genetic reasons, some people lack one or two of the types of cones. Some have three kinds of cones, but one kind is abnormal (Nathans et al., 1989). In red-green color deficiency, the most common form of color deficiency, people have trouble distinguishing red from green because their long- and medium-wavelength cones have the same photopigment instead of different ones. The gene causing this deficiency is on the X chromosome. About 8% of men are red-green colorblind compared with less than 1% of women (Bowmaker, 1998). Women with one normal gene and one color-deficient gene—and that includes all women with a red-green color deficient father—are slightly less sensitive to red and green than the average for other people (Bimler & Kirkland, 2009).

APPLICATIONS AND EXTENSIONS

Would the Brain Know What to do with Extra Color Information?

Suppose a red-green deficient adult suddenly developed all three types of normal cones. Would the brain start seeing in full color? What if mice—which ordinarily have only one kind of cone and therefore no color vision—developed a second kind of cone. Would they start seeing in color? If a person added a fourth kind of cone, could the brain use the information to see things differently than other people do with three kinds of cones?

The answers are apparently yes, yes, and yes. Evidently, the brain adapts to use the information it receives. First, the mice: Ordinarily, mice have only one kind of cone, which helps them see differences of brightness but not color. Researchers genetically engineered some mice to have an additional kind of cone. These mice showed behavioral evidence of color vision (Jacobs, Williams, Cahill, & Nathans, 2007).

We don't know what would happen if red-green color-deficient people added a third kind of cone, but we do know what would happen for monkeys. Researchers took adult monkeys that were red-green color deficient from birth and used gene therapy to add a third kind of cone to their retinas. They quickly learned to discriminate red from green (Mancuso et al., 2009).

Finally, what about people with a fourth kind of cone? How could that happen? It happens only in women. The gene controlling the long-wavelength cone receptor varies, causing slight differences in responses to different wavelengths (Stockman & Sharpe, 1998). The gene controlling this receptor is on the X chromosome, and so—because men have only one X chromosome—men have only one type of long-wavelength receptor. For women, one X chromosome in each cell is activated and the other is inhibited, apparently at random. Therefore, women who have both kinds of long-wavelength genes produce two kinds of long-wavelength cones (Neitz, Kraft, & Neitz, 1998). Several studies have found that women with two kinds of long-wavelength receptors draw slightly finer color distinctions than other people do. That is, they see color differences between two objects that seem the same to other people (Jameson, Highnote, & Wasserman, 2001). This effect is small, however, and emerges only with careful testing. ■

Stop & Check

9. Most people can use varying amounts of three colors to match any other color that they see. Who would be an exception to this rule, and how many colors would they need?

ANSWER

9. Red-green color-deficient people would need only two colors. Women with four kinds of cones might need four.

Visual Receptors

I remember once explaining to my then-teenage son a newly discovered detail about the visual system, only to have him reply, "I didn't realize it would be so complicated. I thought the light strikes your eyes and then you see it." As you should now be starting to realize—and if not, the rest of the chapter should convince you—vision requires complicated processing. If you tried to equip a robot with vision, you would quickly discover that shining light into its eyes accomplishes nothing, unless its visual detectors are connected to devices that identify the useful information and use it to select the proper action. We have such devices in our brains, and they produce the amazing results that we call vision.

SUMMARY

1. According to the law of specific nerve energies, the brain interprets any activity of a given sensory neuron as representing the sensory information to which that neuron is tuned. **154**

2. Sensory information is coded so that the brain can process it. The coded information bears no physical similarity to the stimuli it describes. **154**

3. Light passes through the pupil of a vertebrate eye and stimulates the receptors lining the retina at the back of the eye. **155**

4. The axons from the retina loop around to form the optic nerve, which exits from the eye at a point called the blind spot. **155**

5. Visual acuity is greatest in the fovea, the central area of the retina. Because so many receptors in the periphery converge their messages to their bipolar cells, our peripheral vision is highly sensitive to faint light but poorly sensitive to detail. **157**

6. The retina has two kinds of receptors: rods and cones. Rods are more sensitive to faint light; cones are more useful in bright light. Rods are more numerous in the periphery of the eye. Cones are more numerous in the fovea. **158**

7. People vary in the number of axons from the retina to the brain. Those with more axons show a greater ability to detect brief, faint, or rapidly changing stimuli. **159**

8. Light stimulates the receptors by triggering a molecular change in 11-*cis*-retinal, releasing energy and thereby activating second messengers within the cell. **159**

9. According to the trichromatic (or Young-Helmholtz) theory of color vision, color perception begins with a given wavelength of light stimulating a distinctive ratio of responses by the three types of cones. **160**

10. According to the opponent-process theory of color vision, visual system neurons beyond the receptors themselves respond with an increase in activity to indicate one color of light and a decrease to indicate the opposite color. The three pairs of opposites are red-green, yellow-blue, and white-black. **161**

11. According to the retinex theory, the cortex compares the responses from different parts of the retina to determine brightness and color. **163**

12. For genetic reasons, certain people are unable to distinguish one color from another. Red-green color-blindness is the most common type. **165**

13. If genes are modified to provide extra color input to the brain, the brain makes use of that information, increasing its color perception. **165**

KEY TERMS

Terms are defined in the module on the page number indicated. They're also presented in alphabetical order with definitions in the book's Subject Index/Glossary, which begins on page 561. Interactive flashcards and crossword puzzles are among the online resources available to help you learn these terms and the concepts they represent.

bipolar cells   **155**
blind spot   **155**
color constancy   **163**
color vision deficiency   **165**
cones   **158**
fovea   **157**
ganglion cells   **155**

law of specific nerve energies   **154**
midget ganglion cells   **157**
negative color afterimage   **161**
opponent–process theory   **162**
optic nerve   **155**
photopigments   **159**
pupil   **155**

retina   **155**
retinex theory   **164**
rods   **158**
trichromatic theory
(or Young-Helmholtz
theory)   **160**
visual field   **161**

THOUGHT QUESTION

How could you test for the presence of color vision in a bee? Examining the retina does not help because invertebrate receptors resemble neither rods nor cones. It is possible to train bees to approach one visual stimulus and not another. However, if you train bees to approach, say, a yellow card and not a green card, you do not know whether they solved the problem by color or by brightness. Because brightness is different from physical intensity, you cannot assume that two colors equally bright to humans are also equally bright to bees. How might you get around the problem of brightness to test color vision in bees?

How the Brain Processes Visual Information

Vision is complicated. We shall go through it in some detail, for two reasons. First, without vision and other senses, you would have no more mental experience than a tree does. Everything in psychology starts with sensations. Second, neuroscientists have developed a relatively detailed understanding of vision. Examining the mechanisms of vision gives us some idea what it means to explain something in biological terms. It provides a model of what we would like to accomplish eventually for motivation, emotion, and other psychological processes.

An Overview of the Mammalian Visual System

Let's begin with a general outline of the anatomy of the mammalian visual system. The rods and cones of the retina make synapses with **horizontal cells** and bipolar cells (Figures 6.2 and 6.16). The horizontal cells make inhibitory contact onto bipolar cells, which in turn make synapses onto *amacrine cells* and ganglion cells. All these cells are within the eyeball.

The axons of the ganglion cells form the optic nerve, which leaves the retina and travels along the lower surface of the brain. The optic nerves from the two eyes meet at the optic chiasm (Figure 6.17a), where, in humans, half of the axons from each eye cross to the opposite side of the brain. As shown in Figure 6.17b, information from the nasal half of each eye (the side closer to the nose) crosses to the contralateral hemisphere. Information from the temporal half (the side toward the temporal cortex) goes to the ipsilateral hemisphere. The percentage of crossover varies from one species to another depending on the location of the eyes. In species with eyes far to the sides of the head, such as rabbits and guinea pigs, nearly all axons cross to the opposite side.

Most ganglion cell axons go to the **lateral geniculate nucleus**, part of the thalamus. (The term *geniculate* comes from the Latin root *genu*, meaning "knee." To *genuflect* is to bend the knee. The lateral geniculate looks a little like a knee, if you use some imagination.) A smaller number of axons go to the superior colliculus and other areas, including part of the hypothalamus that controls the waking–sleeping sched-

ule. The lateral geniculate, in turn, sends axons to other parts of the thalamus and the occipital cortex. The cortex returns many axons to the thalamus, so the thalamus and cortex constantly feed information back and forth (Guillery, Feig, & van Lieshout, 2001).

Stop & Check

10. Where does the optic nerve start and where does it end?

ANSWER

10. It starts with the ganglion cells in the retina. Most of its axons go to the lateral geniculate nucleus of the thalamus; some go to the hypothalamus and superior colliculus.

Processing in the Retina

At any instant, the rods and cones of your two retinas combined send a quarter of a billion messages. You couldn't possibly attend to all of that at once, and you don't need to. You need to extract the meaningful patterns. To understand how the wiring diagram of your retina highlights those patterns, let's explore one example in detail: lateral inhibition.

Lateral inhibition is the retina's way of sharpening contrasts to emphasize the borders of objects. For analogy, suppose 15 people stand in a line. At first, each holds one cookie. Now someone hands 5 extra cookies to the 5 people in the middle of the line, but then each of those 5 people has to throw away one of his or her own cookies, and throw away one cookie from the person on each side. Presuming that you want as many cookies as possible, where is the best place to be? You don't want to be in the middle of the group who receive cookies, because after gaining 5 you would have to throw away one of your own and lose one to each of your neighbors (a total loss of 3). But if you're either the first or last person to receive a cookie, you'll throw one away and lose one to just one neighbor (a total loss of 2). The worst place to be is right before or after the group receiving cookies. You would receive none, and lose the one you already had. The result is a sharp contrast at the border between those receiving cookies and those not.

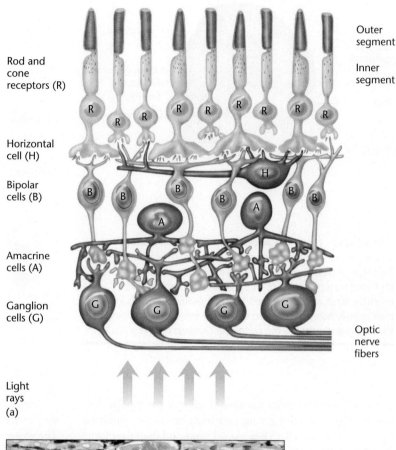

Rod and cone receptors (R)

Outer segment

Inner segment

Horizontal cell (H)

Bipolar cells (B)

Amacrine cells (A)

Ganglion cells (G)

Optic nerve fibers

Light rays
(a)

FIGURE 6.16 The vertebrate retina
(a) Diagram of the neurons of the retina. The top of the figure is the back of the retina. The optic nerve fibers group together and exit through the back of the retina, in the "blind spot" of the eye. *(Based on "Organization of the Primate Retina," by J. E. Dowling and B. B. Boycott, Proceedings of the Royal Society of London, B, 1966, 166, pp. 80–111. Used by permission of the Royal Society of London and John Dowling.)* (b) Cross-section in the periphery of the retina. A slice closer to the fovea would have a greater density of ganglion cells. *(Source: Ed Reschke.)*

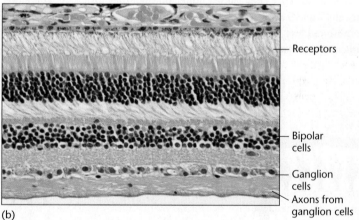

Receptors

Bipolar cells

Ganglion cells

Axons from ganglion cells

(b)

The analogy isn't perfect, but something similar happens in the retina. The receptors send messages to excite the closest bipolar cells (like giving them cookies) and also send messages to slightly inhibit them and the neighbors to their sides (like subtracting cookies).

Actually, light striking the rods and cones *decreases* their spontaneous output. However, they have *inhibitory* synapses onto the bipolar cells, and therefore, light on the rods or cones decreases their inhibitory output. A decrease in inhibition means net excitation, so to double negatives, we'll think of the output as excitation of the bipolar cells. In the fovea, each cone attaches to just one bipolar cell. We'll consider that simple case.

In the following diagram, the green arrows represent excitation. Receptor 8, which is highlighted, excites bipolar cell 8, as indicated by the thicker green arrow. It also excites a horizontal cell, which *inhibits* the bipolar cells, as shown by red arrows. Because the horizontal cell spreads widely, excitation of any receptor inhibits the surrounding bipolar cells. Because the horizontal cell is a *local cell*, with no axon and no action potentials, its depolarization decays with distance. The horizontal cell inhibits bipolar cells 7 through 9 strongly, bipolars 6 and 10 a bit less, and so on. Bipolar cell 8 shows net excitation, because the excitatory synapse outweighs the effect of the horizontal cell's inhibition. (It's like gaining some cookies

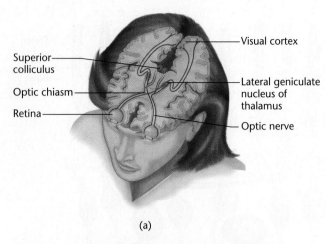

(a)

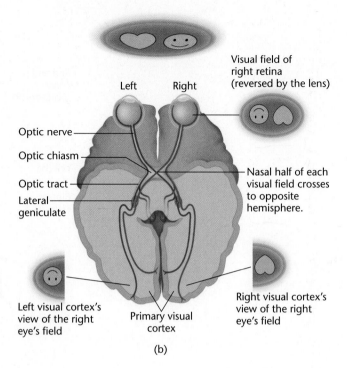

(b)

FIGURE 6.17 **Major connections in the visual system**
(a) Part of the visual input goes to the thalamus and from there to the visual cortex. Another part goes to the superior colliculus. (b) Axons from the retina maintain their relationship to one another—what we call their *retinotopic organization*—throughout their journey from the retina to the lateral geniculate and then from the lateral geniculate to the cortex. (© Cengage Learning 2013)

and then losing a smaller number.) However, the bipolar cells to the sides (laterally) get no excitation but some inhibition by the horizontal cell. (They gained none and then they lost.) Bipolar cells 7 and 9 are strongly inhibited, and bipolars 6 and 10 are inhibited less. In this diagram, the thickness of the arrow indicates the amount of excitation or inhibition.

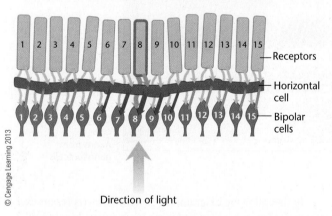

Now imagine that light excites receptors 6–10. These receptors excite bipolar cells 6–10 and the horizontal cell. Bipolar cells 6–10 all receive the same amount of excitation. Bipolar cells 7, 8, and 9 are inhibited by input on both sides, but bipolar cells 6 and 10 are inhibited from one side and not the other. That is, the bipolar cells in the middle of the excited area are inhibited the most, and those on the edges are inhibited the least. Therefore, bipolar cells 6 and 10 respond *more* than bipolars 7–9. That is, the ones on the edges get the greatest net excitation.

Next, consider bipolar cells 5 and 11. What excitation do they receive? None. However, the horizontal cell inhibits them. Therefore, receiving inhibition but no excitation, they respond less than bipolar cells that are farther from the area of excitation.

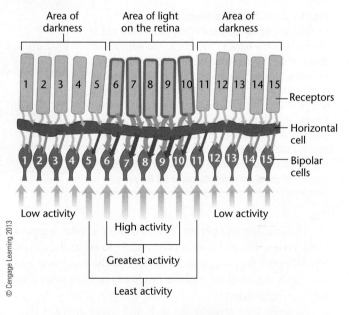

These results illustrate **lateral inhibition**, the reduction of activity in one neuron by activity in neighboring neurons (Hartline, 1949). Lateral inhibition heightens contrast. When light falls on a surface, as shown here, the bipolars just inside the border are most excited, and those outside the border respond the least.

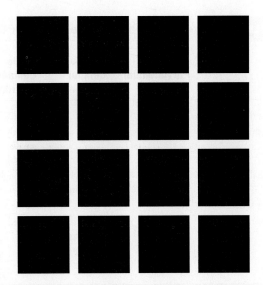

FIGURE 6.18 An illustration of lateral inhibition
Do you see dark diamonds at the "crossroads"? (© Cengage Learning 2013)

Stop & Check

11. When light strikes a receptor, does the receptor excite or inhibit the bipolar cells? What effect does it have on horizontal cells? What effect does the horizontal cell have on bipolar cells?

12. If light strikes only one receptor, what is the net effect (excitatory or inhibitory) on the nearest bipolar cell that is directly connected to that receptor? What is the effect on bipolar cells to the sides? What causes that effect?

13. Examine Figure 6.18. You should see grayish diamonds at the crossroads among the black squares. Explain why.

ANSWERS decreased compared to that in the arms. sides. Therefore, the response in the crossroads is each neuron is maximally inhibited by input on all four above and below or left and right). In the crossroads, maximally inhibited by input on two of its sides (either retina that look at the long white arms, each neuron is its all bipolar cells in the area. **13.** In the parts of your that the receptor excites a horizontal cell, which inhib- inhibition for the nearest bipolar cell. For surrounding bipolar cells, it produces only inhibition. The reason is in the surround. **12.** It produces more excitation than polar cell that was excited plus additional bipolar cells horizontal cell. The horizontal cell inhibits the same bi- **11.** The receptor excites both the bipolar cells and the

Further Processing

Each cell in the visual system of the brain has a **receptive field**, which is the area in visual space that excites or inhibits it. The receptive field of a receptor is simply the point in space

from which light strikes the cell. Other visual cells derive their receptive fields from the connections they receive. This concept is important, so let's spend a little time with it. Suppose you keep track of the events on one city block. We'll call that your receptive field. Someone else keeps track of events on the next block, and another person on the block after that. Now suppose that everyone responsible for a block on your street reports to a supervisor. That supervisor's receptive field is the whole street, because it includes reports from each block on the street. The supervisors for several streets report to the neighborhood manager, whose receptive field is the whole neighborhood. The neighborhood manager reports to a district chief, and so on.

The same idea applies to vision and other sensations. A rod or cone has a tiny receptive field in space to which it is sensitive. A small group of rods or cones connect to a bipolar cell, with a receptive field that is the sum of those of the cells connected to it. Several bipolar cells report to a ganglion cell, which therefore has a still larger receptive field, as shown in Figure 6.19. The receptive fields of several ganglion cells converge to form the receptive field at the next level, and so

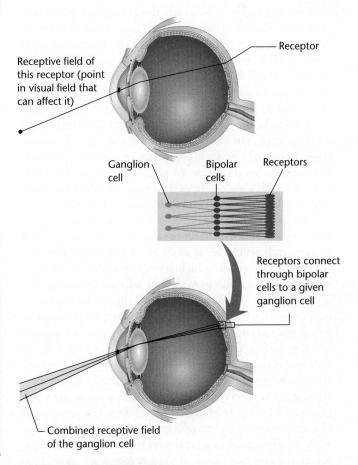

FIGURE 6.19 Receptive fields
The receptive field of any neuron in the visual system is the area of the visual field that excites or inhibits it. Receptors have tiny receptive fields and later cells have progressively larger receptive fields. (© Cengage Learning 2013)

on. However, unlike the neighborhood manager example, receptive fields in the visual system include both excitation and inhibition.

To find a cell's receptive field, an investigator records from the cell while shining light in various locations. If light from a particular spot excites the neuron, then that location is part of the neuron's excitatory receptive field. If it inhibits activity, the location is in the inhibitory receptive field.

The receptive field of a ganglion cell has a circular center with an antagonistic doughnut-shaped surround. That is, light in the center of the receptive field might be excitatory, with the surround inhibitory, or the opposite.

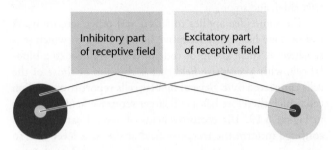

Primate ganglion cells fall into three categories: parvocellular, magnocellular, and koniocellular (Nassi & Callaway, 2009). The **parvocellular neurons**, with small cell bodies and small receptive fields, are mostly in or near the fovea. (Parvocellular means "small celled," from the Latin root *parv*, meaning "small.") The **magnocellular neurons**, with larger cell bodies and receptive fields, are distributed evenly throughout the retina. (Magnocellular means "large celled," from the Latin root *magn*, meaning "large." The same root appears in *magnify*.) The **koniocellular neurons** have small cell bodies, similar to the parvocellular neurons, but they occur throughout the retina. (Koniocellular means "dust celled," from the Greek root meaning "dust." They got this name because of their granular appearance.)

The parvocellular neurons, with their small receptive fields, are well suited to detect visual details. They also respond to color, each neuron being excited by some wavelengths and inhibited by others. The high sensitivity to detail and color relates to the fact that parvocellular cells are located mostly in and near the fovea, which has many cones. The magnocellular neurons, with larger receptive fields, respond strongly to movement and large overall patterns, but they do not respond to color or fine details. Magnocellular neurons are found throughout the retina, including the periphery, where we are sensitive to movement but not color or details. Koniocellular neurons have several functions, and their axons terminate in several locations (Hendry & Reid, 2000). The existence of so many kinds of ganglion cells implies that the visual system analyzes information in several ways from the start. Table 6.2 summarizes the three kinds of primate ganglion cells.

Axons from the ganglion cells form the optic nerve, which proceeds to the optic chiasm, where half of the axons (in humans) cross to the opposite hemisphere. Most of the axons go to the lateral geniculate nucleus of the thalamus. Cells of the lateral geniculate have receptive fields that resemble those

	Parvocellular Neurons	Magnocellular Neurons	Koniocellular Neurons
Cell bodies	Smaller	Larger	Small
Receptive fields	Smaller	Larger	Mostly small; variable
Retinal location	In and near fovea	Throughout the retina	Throughout the retina
Color sensitive	Yes	No	Some are
Respond to	Detailed analysis of stationary objects	Movement and broad outlines of shape	Varied

TABLE 6.2 **Three Kinds of Primate Ganglion Cells**

© Cengage Learning 2013

of the ganglion cells—an excitatory or inhibitory central portion and a surrounding ring with the opposite effect. After the information reaches the cerebral cortex, the receptive fields become more complicated.

Stop & Check

14. As we progress from bipolar cells to ganglion cells to later cells in the visual system, are receptive fields ordinarily larger, smaller, or the same size? Why?

15. What are the differences between the magnocellular and parvocellular systems?

ANSWERS

14. They become larger because each cell's receptive field is made by inputs converging at an earlier level. 15. Neurons of the parvocellular system have small cell bodies with small receptive fields, are located mostly in and near the fovea, and are specialized for detailed and color vision. Neurons of the magnocellular system have large cell bodies with large receptive fields, are located in all parts of the retina, and are specialized for perception of large patterns and movement.

The Primary Visual Cortex

Most visual information from the lateral geniculate nucleus of the thalamus goes to the **primary visual cortex** in the occipital cortex, also known as **area V1** or the *striate cortex* because of its striped appearance. If you close your eyes and imagine seeing something, activity increases in area V1 in a pattern similar to what happens when you actually see that object (Kosslyn & Thompson, 2003; Stokes, Thompson, Cusack, & Duncan, 2009). Although we do not know whether conscious visual perception occurs *in* area V1, area V1 is apparently necessary for it. People with damage to area V1 report no conscious vision, no visual imagery, and no visual images in their dreams (Hurovitz, Dunn, Domhoff, & Fiss, 1999). In contrast, adults who lose vision because of eye damage continue to have visual imagery and visual dreams.

Some people with damage to area V1 show a surprising phenomenon called **blindsight**, the ability to respond in limited ways to visual information without perceiving it consciously. Within the damaged part of their visual field, they have no awareness of visual input, not even to distinguish between bright sunshine and utter darkness. Nevertheless, they might be able to point accurately to something in the area where they cannot see, or move their eyes toward it, while insisting that they are "just guessing" (Bridgeman & Staggs, 1982; Weiskrantz, Warrington, Sanders, & Marshall, 1974). Some blindsight patients can reach for an object they cannot see, avoiding obstacles in the way (Striemer, Chapman, & Goodale, 2009). Some can identify an object's color, direction of movement, and approximate shape, again while insisting that they are just guessing (Radoeva, Prasad, Brainard, & Aguirre, 2008). Some can identify or copy the emotional expression of a face that they insist they do not see (Gonzalez Andino, de Peralta Menendez, Khateb, Landis, & Pegna, 2009; Tamietto et al., 2009).

The research supports two explanations for these puzzling contradictions: First, in many cases, small islands of healthy tissue remain within an otherwise damaged visual cortex, not large enough to provide conscious perception but enough to support limited visual functions (Fendrich, Wessinger, & Gazzaniga, 1992; Radoeva et al., 2008). Second, the thalamus sends visual input to several other brain areas besides V1, including parts of the temporal cortex. After V1 damage, the connections to these other areas strengthen enough to produce certain kinds of experience (such as "I guess something is moving to the left") despite a lack of conscious visual perception (Bridge, Thomas, Jbabdi, & Cowey, 2008; Cowey & Stoerig, 1995; Gonzalez Andino et al., 2009; Moore, Rodman, Repp, & Gross, 1995). Impairing the input from the thalamus to other cortical areas abolishes blindsight (Schmid et al., 2010).

Blindsight is a fascinating demonstration of how much brain activity can take place without consciousness. In any case, the conclusion remains that conscious visual perception requires activity in area V1.

Stop & Check

16. If you were in a darkened room and researchers wanted to "read your mind" just enough to know whether you were having visual fantasies, what could they do?

17. What is an example of an unconscious visually guided behavior?

ANSWERS **16.** Researchers could use fMRI, EEG, or other recording methods to see whether activity was high in your primary visual cortex. **17.** In blindsight, someone can point toward an object or move the eyes toward the object, despite insisting that he or she sees nothing.

Simple and Complex Receptive Fields

In the 1950s, David Hubel and Torsten Wiesel (1959) recorded from cells in cats' and monkeys' occipital cortex while shining light patterns on the retina (Methods 6.1). At first, they presented dots of light, using a slide projector and a screen, but they found little response by cortical

David Hubel

Brain science is difficult and tricky, for some reason; consequently one should not believe a result (one's own or anyone else's) until it is proven backwards and forwards or fits into a framework so highly evolved and systematic that it couldn't be wrong. (Hubel, personal communication)

Torsten Wiesel

Neural connections can be modulated by environmental influences during a critical period of postnatal development.... Such sensitivity of the nervous system to the effects of experience may represent the fundamental mechanism by which the organism adapts to its environment during the period of growth and development. (Wiesel, 1982, p. 591)

methods 6.1

Microelectrode Recordings

David Hubel and Torsten Wiesel pioneered the use of microelectrode recordings to study the properties of individual neurons in the cerebral cortex. With this method, investigators begin by anesthetizing an animal and drilling a small hole in the skull. Then they insert a thin electrode—either a fine metal wire insulated except at the tip or a narrow glass tube containing a salt solution and a metal wire. They direct the electrode either next to or into a single cell and then record its activity while they present various stimuli, such as patterns of light. Researchers use the results to determine what kinds of stimuli do and do not excite the cell.

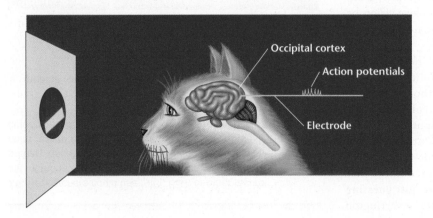

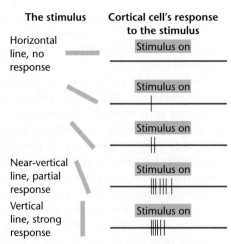

FIGURE 6.20 Responses of a cat's simple cell to a bar of light
This cell responds best to a vertical line in a particular location. Other simple cells respond to lines at other orientations. (*Right, from D. H. Hubel and T. N. Wiesel, "Receptive fields of single neurons in the cat's striate cortex,"* Journal of Physiology, 148, *1959, 574–591. Copyright © 1959 Cambridge University Press. Reprinted by permission.*)

cells. They wondered why cells were so unresponsive, when they knew the occipital cortex was essential for vision. Then they noticed a big response while they were moving a slide into place. They quickly realized that the cell was responding to the edge of the slide and had a bar-shaped receptive field, rather than a circular receptive field like cells in the retina and lateral geniculate (Hubel & Wiesel, 1998). Their research, for which they received a Nobel Prize, has often been called "the research that launched a thousand microelectrodes" because it inspired so much further research. By now, it has probably launched a million microelectrodes.

Hubel and Wiesel distinguished several types of cells in the visual cortex. Figure 6.20 illustrates the receptive field of a **simple cell**. A simple cell has a receptive field with fixed excitatory and inhibitory zones. The more light shines in the excitatory zone, the more the cell responds. The more light shines in the inhibitory zone, the less the cell responds. In Figure 6.20, the receptive field is a vertical bar. Tilting the bar slightly decreases the cell's response because light then strikes inhibitory regions as well. Moving the bar left, right, up, or down also reduces the response. Most simple cells have bar-shaped or edge-shaped receptive fields. More of them respond to horizontal or vertical orientations than to diagonals. That disparity makes sense, considering the importance of horizontal and vertical objects in our world (Coppola, Purves, McCoy, & Purves, 1998).

Unlike simple cells, **complex cells**, located in areas V1 and V2, do not respond to the exact location of a stimulus. A complex cell responds to a pattern of light in a particular orientation (e.g., a vertical bar) anywhere within its large receptive field (Figure 6.21). It responds most strongly to a moving stimulus—for example, a vertical bar moving horizontally. The best way to classify a cell as simple or complex is to present the stimulus in several locations. A cell that responds to a stimulus in only one location is a simple cell. One that responds equally throughout a large area is a complex cell.

End-stopped, or **hypercomplex**, cells resemble complex cells with one exception: An end-stopped cell has a strong in-

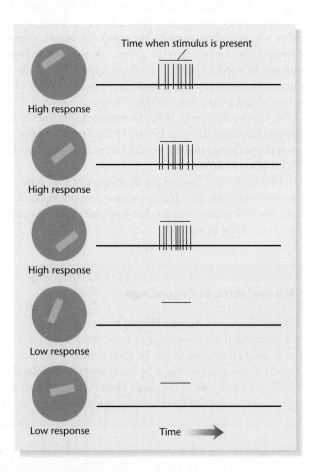

FIGURE 6.21 The receptive field of a complex cell
Like a simple cell, its response depends on a bar of light's angle of orientation. However, a complex cell responds the same for a bar in any location within a large receptive field. (*© Cengage Learning 2013*)

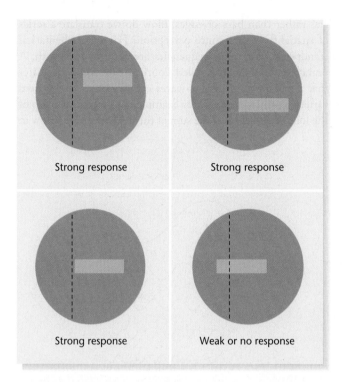

FIGURE 6.22 The receptive field of an end-stopped cell
The cell responds to a bar in a particular orientation (in this case, horizontal) anywhere in its receptive field, provided the bar does not extend into a strongly inhibitory area. (© Cengage Learning 2013)

hibitory area at one end of its bar-shaped receptive field. The cell responds to a bar-shaped pattern of light anywhere in its broad receptive field, provided the bar does not extend beyond a certain point (Figure 6.22). Table 6.3 summarizes the properties of simple, complex, and end-stopped cells.

Stop & Check

18. How could a researcher determine whether a given neuron in the visual cortex is simple or complex?

ANSWER

18. First identify a stimulus, such as a horizontal line, that stimulates the cell. Then present the stimulus in a different location. If the cell responds only in one location, it is a simple cell. If it responds in several locations, it is a complex cell.

The Columnar Organization of the Visual Cortex

Cells having similar properties are grouped together in the visual cortex in columns perpendicular to the surface (Hubel & Wiesel, 1977) (Figure 4.22). For example, cells within a given column might respond to only the left eye, only the right eye, or both eyes about equally. Also, cells within a given column respond best to lines of a single orientation. Curiously, although cells within a column have similar properties, they do not consistently fire at the same time (Ecker et al., 2010).

Figure 6.23 shows what happens when an investigator lowers an electrode through the visual cortex and records from each cell along the way. Each red line represents a neuron and shows the angle of orientation of its receptive field. In electrode path A, the first series of cells are all in one column and show the same orientation preferences. However, after passing through the white matter, the end of path A invades

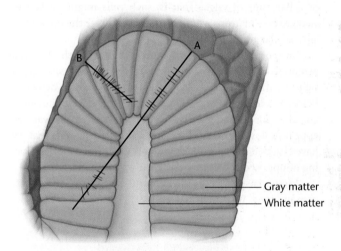

FIGURE 6.23 Columns of neurons in the visual cortex
When an electrode passes perpendicular to the surface of the cortex (first part of line A), it encounters a sequence of neurons responsive to the same orientation of a stimulus. (The colored lines show the preferred stimulus orientation for each cell.) When an electrode passes across columns (B, or second part of A), it encounters neurons responsive to different orientations. Column borders are drawn here to emphasize the point; no such borders are visible in the real cortex. (Hubel, 1963)

TABLE 6.3	Cells in the Primary Visual Cortex		
Characteristic	**Simple Cells**	**Complex Cells**	**End-Stopped Cells**
Location	V1	V1 and V2	V1 and V2
Binocular input	Yes	Yes	Yes
Size of receptive field	Smallest	Medium	Largest
Receptive field	Bar- or edge-shaped, with fixed excitatory and inhibitory zones	Bar- or edge-shaped, without fixed excitatory or inhibitory zones	Same as complex cell but with strong inhibitory zone at one end

two columns with different preferred orientations. Electrode path B, which is not perpendicular to the surface of the cortex, crosses through three columns and encounters cells with different properties. In short, the cells within a given column process similar information.

19. What do cells within a column of the visual cortex have in common?

ANSWER

19. They respond best to lines in the same orientation. Also, they are similar in their preference for one eye or the other, or both equally.

Are Visual Cortex Cells Feature Detectors?

Given that neurons in area V1 respond strongly to bar- or edge-shaped patterns, we might suppose that the activity of such a cell *is* (or at least is necessary for) the perception of a bar, line, or edge. That is, such cells might be **feature detectors**—neurons whose responses indicate the presence of a particular feature.

Supporting the idea of feature detectors is the fact that prolonged exposure to a given visual feature decreases sensitivity to that feature, as if it fatigued the relevant detectors. For example, if you stare at a waterfall for a minute or more and then look away, the rocks and trees next to the waterfall appear to flow upward. This *waterfall illusion* suggests that you have fatigued the neurons that detect downward motion, leaving unopposed the detectors for the opposite motion.

However, later researchers found that a cortical cell that responds well to a single bar or line

responds even more strongly to a sine wave grating of bars or lines:

Many cortical neurons respond best to a particular spatial frequency and hardly at all to other frequencies (DeValois, Albrecht, & Thorell, 1982). Most visual researchers therefore believe that neurons in area V1 detect spatial frequen-

cies rather than bars or edges. How do we translate a series of spatial frequencies into perception? From a mathematical standpoint, sine wave frequencies are easy to work with. A branch of mathematics called Fourier analysis demonstrates that a combination of sine waves can produce an unlimited variety of other patterns. For example, the graph at the top of the following display is the sum of the five sine waves below it:

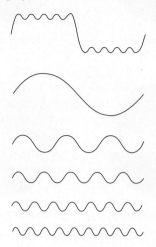

Therefore, a series of spatial frequency detectors, some sensitive to horizontal patterns and others to vertical patterns, could represent any possible display. Still, we perceive the world as objects, not sine waves. It is not clear how the visual cortex puts together all its information to perceive objects, but it does, presumably because of interactions between the primary visual cortex and other brain areas. When people view an incomplete or ambiguous drawing of a face, the response in the cortex resembles its usual response to a face only when the person *perceives* it as a face (Hsieh, Vul, & Kanwisher, 2010). That is, even at the early stages of perception, the brain's activity corresponds to what the person perceives and not just the physical pattern of light and dark.

20. What is a feature detector?

ANSWER

20. It is a neuron that detects the presence of a particular aspect of an object, such as a shape or a direction of movement.

Development of the Visual Cortex

How do cells in the visual cortex develop their properties? Are they born that way? Suppose you had lived all your life in the dark. Then today, for the first time, you came out into the light and looked around. Would you understand anything?

Unless you were born blind, you did have this experience—on the day you were born! At first, presumably you had no idea what you were seeing. Within months, however, you began to recognize faces and crawl toward your favorite toys. How did you learn to make sense of what you saw?

In a newborn mammal, many of the normal properties of the visual system develop normally at first, even without visual experience (Lein & Shatz, 2001; Rakic & Lidow, 1995; Shatz, 1996; White, Coppola, & Fitzpatrick, 2001). However, the brain needs visual experience to maintain and fine-tune its connections.

Deprived Experience in One Eye

What would happen if a young animal could see with one eye but not the other? For cats and primates—which have both eyes pointed in the same direction—most neurons in the visual cortex receive **binocular** input (stimulation from both eyes). When a kitten opens its eyes, at about age 9 days, each neuron responds to areas in the two retinas that focus on approximately the same point in space (Figure 6.24). Most cells in the visual cortex respond to both eyes, although generally better to one eye than the other. However, innate mechanisms cannot make the connections exactly right because the exact distance between the eyes varies from one kitten to another, and changes over age. Therefore, experience is necessary for fine-tuning.

If an experimenter sutures one eyelid shut for a kitten's first 4 to 6 weeks of life, synapses in the visual cortex gradually become unresponsive to input from the deprived eye (Rittenhouse, Shouval, Paradiso, & Bear, 1999). After the deprived eye is opened, the kitten does not respond to it. A later period of deprivation also weakens the responses to the deprived eye,

but in older and older monkeys, the effect becomes weaker and weaker (Wiesel, 1982; Wiesel & Hubel, 1963).

Deprived Experience in Both Eyes

If *both* eyes were kept shut for the first few weeks, what would you expect? You might guess that the kitten would become blind, but it does not. When just one eye is open, the synapses from the open eye inhibit the synapses from the closed eye (Maffei, Nataraj, Nelson, & Turrigiano, 2006). If neither eye is active, no axon outcompetes any other. For at least 3 weeks, the kitten's cortex remains responsive to visual input, although most cells become responsive to just one eye or the other and not both (Wiesel, 1982). If the eyes remain shut still longer, the cortical responses start to become sluggish and lose their well-defined receptive fields (Crair, Gillespie, & Stryker, 1998). Also, as mentioned in Chapter 5, the visual cortex eventually starts responding to auditory and touch stimuli.

For each aspect of visual experience, researchers identify a **sensitive period**, when experiences have a particularly strong and enduring influence (Crair & Malenka, 1995; T. L. Lewis & Maurer, 2005; Tagawa, Kanold, Majdan, & Shatz, 2005). The sensitive period ends with the onset of certain chemicals that stabilize synapses and inhibit axonal sprouting (Pizzorusso et al., 2002; Syken, GrandPre, Kanold, & Shatz, 2006). However, even long after the sensitive period, a prolonged experience— such as a full week without visual stimulation to one eye— produces a measurable effect on the visual cortex (Sato & Stryker, 2008). Cortical plasticity is greatest in early life, but it never ends.

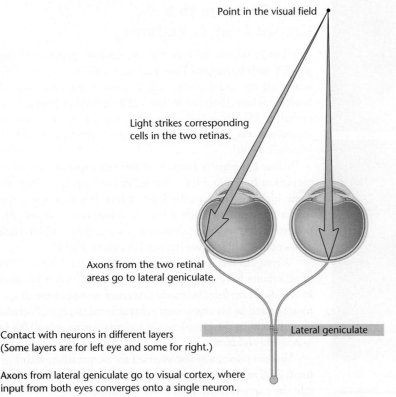

Point in the visual field

Light strikes corresponding cells in the two retinas.

Axons from the two retinal areas go to lateral geniculate.

Contact with neurons in different layers (Some layers are for left eye and some for right.)

Lateral geniculate

Axons from lateral geniculate go to visual cortex, where input from both eyes converges onto a single neuron.

FIGURE 6.24 Anatomical basis for binocular vision in cats and primates
Light from a point in the visual field strikes points in each retina. Those two retinal areas send their axons to separate layers of the lateral geniculate, which in turn send axons to a single cell in the visual cortex. That cell is connected (via the lateral geniculate) to corresponding areas of the two retinas. (*© Cengage Learning 2013*)

21. What is the effect of closing one eye early in life? What is the effect of closing both eyes?

ANSWER

21. If one eye is closed during early development, the cortex becomes unresponsive to it. If both eyes are closed, cortical cells remain somewhat responsive for several weeks and then gradually become sluggish and unselective in their responses.

Uncorrelated Stimulation in the Two Eyes

Most neurons in the human visual cortex respond to both eyes—specifically, to approximately corresponding areas of both eyes. By comparing the inputs from the two eyes, you achieve stereoscopic depth perception.

Stereoscopic depth perception requires the brain to detect **retinal disparity**, the discrepancy between what the left and right eyes see. Experience fine-tunes binocular vision, and abnormal experience disrupts it. Imagine a kitten with weak or damaged eye muscles so that its eyes do not point in the same direction. Both eyes are active, but no cortical neuron consistently receives messages from one eye that match messages

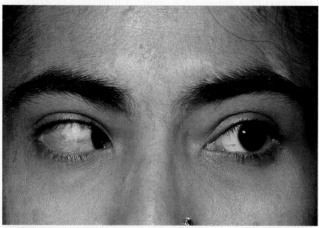

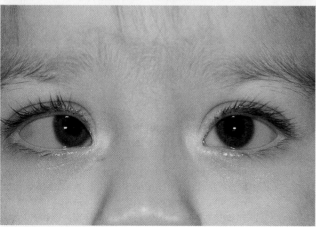

Two examples of lazy eye.

from the other eye. Each neuron in the visual cortex becomes responsive to one eye or the other and few neurons respond to both (Blake & Hirsch, 1975; Hubel & Wiesel, 1965). The behavioral result is poor depth perception.

A similar phenomenon occurs in humans. Certain children are born with **strabismus** (or strabismic amblyopia), also known as "lazy eye," a condition in which the eyes do not point in the same direction. Generally, these children attend to one eye and not the other. The usual treatment is to put a patch over the active eye, forcing attention to the other one. That procedure works to some extent, especially if it begins early (T. L. Lewis & Maurer, 2005). However, many children refuse to wear an eye patch for as long as necessary, and it often fails to establish stereoscopic depth perception.

A promising therapy for lazy eye is to ask a child to play action video games that require attention to both eyes. Good performance requires increasing attention to exactly the kind of input we want to enhance. Preliminary results have been encouraging, even with children who failed to respond to the usual eye patch technique (Cleary, Moody, Buchanan, Stewart, & Dutton, 2009).

22. What early experience is necessary to maintain binocular input to the neurons of the visual cortex?

ANSWER

22. To maintain binocular responsiveness, cortical cells must receive simultaneous activity from both eyes fixating on the same object at the same time.

Early Exposure to a Limited Array of Patterns

If a kitten spends its entire early sensitive period wearing goggles with horizontal lines painted on them (Figure 6.25), nearly all its visual cortex cells become responsive only to horizontal lines (Stryker & Sherk, 1975; Stryker, Sherk, Leventhal, & Hirsch, 1978). Even after months of later normal experience, the cat does not respond to vertical lines (D. E. Mitchell, 1980).

What happens if human infants are exposed mainly to vertical or horizontal lines instead of both equally? They become more sensitive to the kind of line they have seen. You might wonder how such a bizarre thing could happen. No parents would let an experimenter subject their child to such a procedure, and it never happens in nature. Right?

Wrong. In fact, it probably happened to you! About 70% of all infants have **astigmatism**, a blurring of vision for lines in one direction (e.g., horizontal, vertical, or one of the diagonals), caused by an asymmetric curvature of the eyes. Normal growth reduces the prevalence of astigmatism to about 10% in 4-year-old children.

You can informally test yourself for astigmatism with Figure 6.26. Do the lines in some direction look faint? If so, rotate the page. You will notice that the appearance of the lines

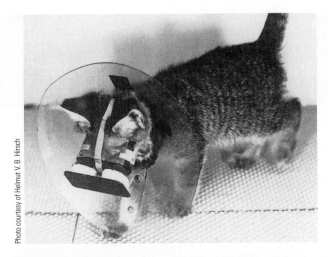

FIGURE 6.25 Procedure for restricting a kitten's visual experience
For a few hours a day, the kitten wears goggles that show just one stimulus, such as horizontal stripes or diagonal stripes. For the rest of the day, the kitten stays with its mother in a dark room without the mask.

FIGURE 6.26 An informal test for astigmatism
Do the lines in one direction look darker or sharper than the other lines do? If so, notice what happens when you rotate the page. If you wear corrective lenses, try this demonstration both with and without your lenses. (© Cengage Learning 2013)

depends on their position. If you wear corrective lenses, try this demonstration with and without them. If you see a difference in the lines only without your lenses, then the lenses have corrected your astigmatism.

Impaired Infant Vision and Long-Term Consequences

The existence of a sensitive period for the visual cortex means that after you pass that period, your visual cortex won't change as much or as fast. If an infant has a problem early, we need to fix it early. For example, cataracts (cloudy spots on the lenses) on one or both eyes during infancy cause visual deprivation, and a delay in surgically repairing the cataracts limits future vision.

The impairment is more extreme if the cataracts remain until later in life. Researchers found two people in India who had dense cataracts at birth and surgical correction at ages 7 and 12 years. At first they were nearly blind, but gradually improved (Ostrovsky, Meyers, Ganesh, Mathur, & Sinha, 2009). One of their lingering problems is displayed below. If asked, "How many objects are there?" most people say two, but those with early cataracts say three. Other people who lived even longer with cataracts also made some recovery but continued to find it difficult to recognize objects. Whereas most adults see objects and know almost immediately what they are, people who lived most of their lives with cloudy vision find it always difficult to guess what the objects are (Fine, Smallman, Doyle, & MacLeod, 2002; Fine et al., 2003). The visual expertise that most of us take for granted depends on years of practice.

Stop & Check

23. What causes astigmatism?

24. Why is it important to correct astigmatism early?

ANSWERS even after the astigmatism is corrected. **23.** Astigmatism results when the eyeball is not quite spherical. As a result, the person sees one direction of lines more clearly than the other. **24.** If the visual cortex sees one kind of line better than another, it becomes more responsive to the kind it sees well and less sensitive to the other. That tendency could persist

Understanding Vision by Understanding the Wiring Diagram

Your eyes are bombarded with a complex pattern of light emanating from every source in front of you. Out of all this, your brain needs to extract the most useful information. The nervous system from the start identifies the borders between one object and another through lateral inhibition. It identifies lines and their locations by simple and complex cells in

the primary visual cortex. Researchers have gone a long way toward mapping out the excitatory and inhibitory connections that make these cells possible. The visual experiences you have at any moment are the result of an awe-inspiring complexity of connections and interactions among a huge number of neurons.

SUMMARY

1. The optic nerves of the two eyes join at the optic chiasm, where half of the axons from each eye cross to the opposite side of the brain. Most of the axons then travel to the lateral geniculate nucleus of the thalamus, which communicates with the visual cortex.   **168**

2. Lateral inhibition is a mechanism by which stimulation in any area of the retina suppresses the responses in neighboring areas, thereby enhancing the contrast at light–dark borders.   **168**

3. Lateral inhibition in the vertebrate retina occurs because receptors stimulate bipolar cells and also stimulate the much wider horizontal cells, which inhibit both the stimulated bipolar cells and those to the sides.   **169**

4. Each neuron in the visual system has a receptive field, an area of the visual field to which it is connected. Light in the receptive field excites or inhibits the neuron depending on the light's location, wavelength, movement, and other properties.   **171**

5. The mammalian vertebrate visual system has a partial division of labor. In general, the parvocellular system is specialized for perception of color and fine details; the magnocellular system is specialized for perception of depth, movement, and overall patterns.   **172**

6. After damage to area V1, people report no vision, even in dreams. However, some kinds of response to light (blindsight) can occur after damage to V1 despite the lack of conscious perception.   **172**

7. Within the primary visual cortex, neuroscientists distinguish simple cells, which have fixed excitatory and inhibitory fields, and complex cells, which respond to a light pattern of a particular shape regardless of its exact location.   **173**

8. Neurons within a column of the primary visual cortex have similar properties, such as responding to lines in the same orientation.   **175**

9. Neurons sensitive to shapes or other visual aspects may or may not act as feature detectors. In particular, cells of area V1 are highly responsive to spatial frequencies, even though we are not subjectively aware of spatial frequencies in our visual perception.   **176**

10. The cells in the visual cortex of infant kittens have nearly normal properties. However, experience is necessary to maintain and fine-tune vision. For example, if a kitten has sight in one eye and not in the other during the early sensitive period, its cortical neurons become responsive only to the open eye.   **177**

11. Cortical neurons become unresponsive to axons from the inactive eye mainly because of competition with the active eye. If both eyes are closed, cortical cells remain somewhat responsive to visual input, although that response becomes sluggish and unselective as the weeks of deprivation continue.   **177**

12. Abnormal visual experience has a stronger effect during an early sensitive period than later in life.   **177**

13. To develop good stereoscopic depth perception, a kitten or human child must have experience seeing the same object with corresponding portions of the two eyes early in life. Otherwise, each neuron in the visual cortex becomes responsive to input from just one eye.   **178**

14. If a kitten sees only horizontal or vertical lines during its sensitive period, most of the neurons in its visual cortex become responsive to such lines only. For the same reason, a young child with astigmatism may have decreased responsiveness to one kind of line or another.   **178**

15. Some people have cataracts removed in adulthood. Vision recovers partly, but not completely.   **179**

KEY TERMS

Terms are defined in the module on the page number indicated. They're also presented in alphabetical order with definitions in the book's Subject Index/Glossary, which begins on page 561. Interactive flashcards and crossword puzzles are among the online resources available to help you learn these terms and the concepts they represent.

astigmatism **178**	horizontal cells **168**	receptive field **171**
binocular **177**	koniocellular neurons **172**	retinal disparity **178**
blindsight **173**	lateral geniculate nucleus **168**	sensitive period **177**
complex cells **174**	lateral inhibition **170**	simple cell **174**
end-stopped (or hypercomplex)	magnocellular neurons **172**	strabismus **178**
cells **174**	parvocellular neurons **172**	
feature detectors **176**	primary visual cortex (or area V1) **172**	

THOUGHT QUESTIONS

1. After a receptor cell is stimulated, the bipolar cell receiving input from it shows an immediate strong response. A fraction of a second later, the bipolar's response decreases, even though the stimulation from the receptor cell remains constant. How can you account for that decrease? (Hint: What does the horizontal cell do?)

2. A rabbit's eyes are on the sides of its head instead of in front. Would you expect rabbits to have many cells with binocular receptive fields—that is, cells that respond to both eyes? Why or why not?

3. Would you expect the cortical cells of a rabbit to be just as sensitive to the effects of experience as are the cells of cats and primates? Why or why not?

Parallel Processing in the Visual Cortex

If you were working on an important project for some business or government, you might receive information on a "need-to-know" basis. For example, if you were told to carry a particular package, you would need to know how heavy it is and whether it is fragile, but you might not need to know much about the object in the package. Someone else who is keeping track of the finances would need to know how much the object costs, but wouldn't need to know anything else. A third person might open the package and check to make sure the color matched the specifications, before handing it on to someone else with a different concern.

Similarly, different parts of the brain's visual system get information on a need-to-know basis. Cells that are helping your hand muscles reach out to an object need to know the size and location of the object, but they don't need to know about color. They might need to know a little about shape, but not in great detail. Cells that help you recognize people's faces need to be extremely sensitive to details of shape, but they don't pay much attention to location or direction of movement.

It is natural to assume that anyone who sees something sees everything about it—its shape, color, location, and movement. Ordinarily, a person as a whole does see all of those aspects, but each individual area of the visual cortex does not. The principle behind vision is counterintuitive: When you see something, one part of your brain sees its shape, another sees color, another detects location, and another perceives movement (Livingstone, 1988; Livingstone & Hubel, 1988; Zeki & Shipp, 1988). Neuroscientists have identified at least 80 brain areas that contribute to vision in different ways (Nassi & Callaway, 2009). Consequently, after localized brain damage it is possible to see certain aspects of an object and not others.

▍The "What" and "Where" Paths

The primary visual cortex (V1) sends information to the **secondary visual cortex** (area V2), which processes the information further and transmits it to additional areas, as shown in Figure 6.27. The connections in the visual cortex are reciprocal. For example, V1 sends information to V2, and V2 returns information to V1. From V2, the information branches out in several directions for specialized processing.

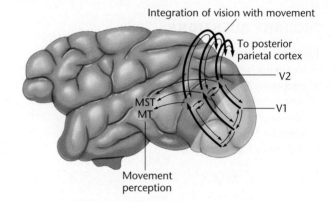

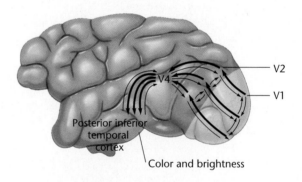

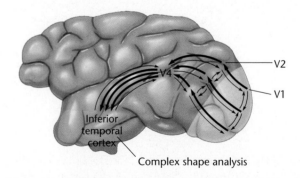

FIGURE 6.27 Visual pathways in the monkey cerebral cortex After processing in areas V1 and V2 of the occipital cortex, information branches in several directions into the parietal cortex and temporal cortex. *(Based on DeYoe, Felleman, Van Essen, & McClendon, 1994; Ts'o & Roe, 1995; Van Essen & DeYoe, 1995)*

One important distinction is between the ventral stream and the dorsal stream. The **ventral stream** through the temporal cortex is called the "what" pathway, because it is specialized for identifying and recognizing objects. The **dorsal stream** through the parietal cortex is the "where" pathway, because it helps the motor system locate objects. Don't imagine a 100% division of labor. The two streams communicate, and each participates to some extent in perceiving both shape and location (Farivar, 2009). Nevertheless, damaging one stream or the other will produce different deficits.

People with damage to the dorsal stream (parietal cortex) seem in most ways to have normal vision. They can read, recognize faces, and describe objects in detail. They would probably pass the vision test for a driver's license in most states. But although they know *what* things are, they don't know *where* they are (Goodale, 1996; Goodale, Milner, Jakobson, & Carey, 1991). (They would make terrible drivers!) They can't accurately reach out to grasp an object. While walking, they can describe what they see, but they bump into objects, oblivious to their location. Although they can describe from memory what their furniture looks like, they cannot remember how it is arranged in rooms of their house (Kosslyn et al., 2001). Sometimes they are not sure where certain parts of their body are (Schenk, 2006).

In contrast, people with damage to the ventral stream see "where" but not "what." One man had a stroke that damaged much of his temporal cortex while sparing his parietal cortex. He could not read, recognize faces, or identify objects by sight. (He could still identify objects by touch or smell, and he could recognize people by the sound of their voice.) He could make no sense of a television program except from the sound, as if he were listening to the radio. Nevertheless, he could take a walk, accurately going around obstacles in his way. He could reach out to grab objects, and he could reach out to shake hands. In short, he could see where objects were, even though he had trouble identifying what they were (Karnath, Rüter, Mandler, & Himmelbach, 2009).

→ **Stop & Check**

25. Suppose someone can describe an object in detail but stumbles and fumbles when trying to walk toward it and pick it up. Which is probably damaged, the dorsal path or the ventral path?

ANSWER

25. The inability to guide movement based on vision implies damage to the dorsal path.

▎Detailed Analysis of Shape

In module 6.2 we encountered simple and complex cells of the primary visual cortex (V1). As visual information goes from the simple cells to the complex cells and then to other brain areas, the receptive fields become more specialized. In the secondary visual cortex (V2), many cells still respond best to lines, edges, and sine wave gratings, but some cells respond selectively to circles, lines that meet at a right angle, or other complex pat-

terns (Hegdé & Van Essen, 2000). In later parts of the visual system, receptive properties become still more complex.

The Inferior Temporal Cortex

Cells in the **inferior temporal cortex** (Figure 6.27) respond to identifiable objects. Examine Figure 6.28. Researchers measured responses in monkeys' inferior temporal cortex to several kinds of transformations. A cell that responded to a particular stimulus would respond almost equally to its negative image or mirror image but not to a physically similar stimulus in which the "figure" now appeared to be part of the "background" (Baylis & Driver, 2001). That is, cells in the temporal cortex respond according to what the viewer perceives, not what the stimulus is physically. Cells that respond to the sight of a particular object continue responding about the same way despite changes in its position, size, and angle. Presumably these cells somehow learn to recognize all the different views as being the same object (Li & DiCarlo, 2008).

As we might expect, damage to the shape pathway of the cortex leads to specialized deficits. An inability to recognize objects despite otherwise satisfactory vision is called **visual agnosia** (meaning "visual lack of knowledge"). It usually results from damage in the temporal cortex. Someone might be able to point to visual objects and slowly describe them but fail to recognize what they are. For example, one patient, when shown a key, said, "I don't know what that is. Perhaps a file or a tool of some sort." When shown a stethoscope, he said that

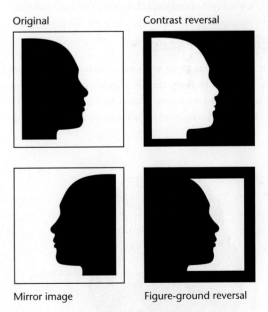

Original   Contrast reversal

Mirror image   Figure-ground reversal

FIGURE 6.28 Transformations of a drawing
In the inferior temporal cortex, cells that respond strongly to the original respond about the same to the contrast reversal and mirror image but not to the figure–ground reversal. Note that the figure–ground reversal resembles the original in terms of the pattern of light and darkness, but it is not perceived as the same object. *(Based on Baylis & Driver, 2001)*

it was "a long cord with a round thing at the end." When he could not identify a smoker's pipe, the examiner told him what it was. He then replied, "Yes, I can see it now," and pointed out the stem and bowl of the pipe. Then the examiner asked, "Suppose I told you that the last object was not really a pipe?" The patient replied, "I would take your word for it. Perhaps it's not really a pipe" (Rubens & Benson, 1971).

Within the brain areas specialized for perceiving shape, are there further specializations for particular types of shapes? Researchers used fMRI to record brain activity as people viewed pictures of many objects. Of the various types of objects, most did not activate one brain area more than another. That is, the brain does not have a specialized area for seeing flowers, fish, birds, clothes, food, or rocks. However, three types of objects do produce specific responses. One part of the parahippocampal cortex (next to the hippocampus) responds strongly to pictures of places, and not so strongly to anything else. Part of the *fusiform gyrus* of the inferior temporal cortex, especially in the right hemisphere (Figure 6.29), responds strongly to faces, much more than to anything else. And an area close to this face area responds more strongly to bodies than to anything else (Downing, Chan, Peelen, Dodds, & Kanwisher, 2005; Kanwisher, 2010). The brain is amazingly adept at detecting biological motion— the kinds of motion produced by people and animals. If you attach glow-in-the-dark dots to someone's elbows, knees, hips, shoulders, and a few other places, then when that person moves in an otherwise dark room, you perceive a moving person, even though you are actually watching only a few spots of light. You can view a wonderful demonstration at the Bio Motion Lab at http://www.biomotionlab.ca/Demos/BMLwalker.html.

Recognizing Faces

Much research has dealt with how the brain recognizes faces. Facial recognition is extremely important. For civilization to succeed, we have to know whom to trust and whom to distrust, and that distinction requires us to recognize people that we haven't seen in months or years. Someday you may attend a high school or college reunion and reunite with people you haven't seen in decades. You will recognize many of them (even if you forget their names), despite the fact that they have gained weight, become bald, or dyed their hair (Bruck, Cavanagh, & Ceci, 1991). Computer programmers who have tried to build machines to recognize faces have discovered the difficulty of this task that seems so easy for people.

Human newborns come into the world predisposed to pay more attention to faces than other stationary displays (Figure 6.30). That tendency supports the idea of a built-in face recognition module. However, the infant's concept of "face" is not like an adult's. Experimenters recorded infants' times of gazing at one face or the other, as shown in Figure 6.31. Newborns showed a strong preference for a right-side-up face over an upside-down face, regardless of whether the face was realistic (left pair) or distorted (central pair). When confronted with two right-side-up faces (right pair), they showed no significant preference between a realistic one and a distorted one (Cassia, Turati, & Simion, 2004). Evidently, a newborn's concept of "face" requires the eyes to be on top, but the face does not have to be realistic.

Developing good facial recognition requires practice, and as with other learning, it occurs best during early life. In one study, investigators examined 14 people who had been born with cataracts in both eyes but had them repaired at ages 2–6 months. Although they developed nearly normal vision, they had subtle lingering problems in recognizing slight differences between one face and another (Le Grand, Mondloch, Maurer, & Brent, 2001). The ability to recognize faces continues developing gradually all the way into adolescence (Mondloch, Maurer, & Ahola, 2006). Precision is best for faces similar to familiar faces. Your brain learns the "average" of the faces it sees and then detects small deviations from that average (Leopold, Bondar, & Giese, 2006). This mechanism underlies the phe-

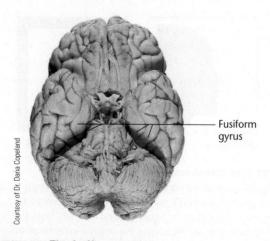

FIGURE 6.29 The fusiform gyrus
Many cells here are especially active during recognition of faces.

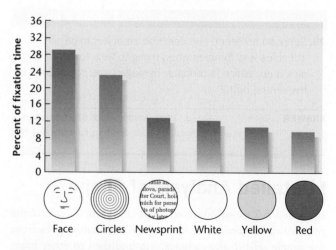

FIGURE 6.30 Amount of time infants spend looking at patterns
Even in the first 2 days after birth, infants look more at faces than at most other stimuli. *(Based on Fantz, 1963)*

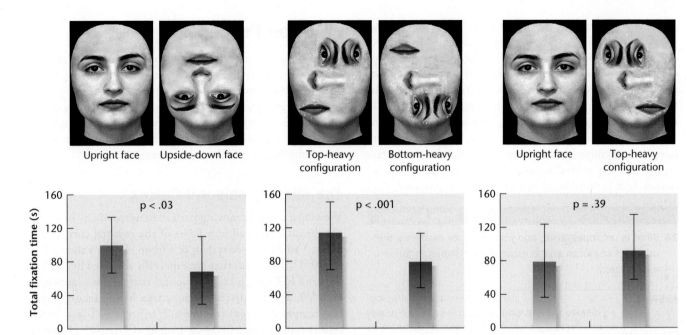

| Upright face | Upside-down face | | Top-heavy configuration | Bottom-heavy configuration | | Upright face | Top-heavy configuration |

FIGURE 6.31 How infants divided their attention between faces
A right-side-up face drew more attention than an upside-down one, regardless of whether the faces were realistic (left pair) or distorted (central pair). They divided their attention about equally between two right-side-up faces (right pair), even though one was realistic and the other was distorted. *(From "Can a nonspecific bias toward top-heavy patterns explain newborns' face preference?" by V. M. Cassia, C. Turati, & F. Simion, 2004. Psychological Science, 15, 379–383.)*

nomenon that most people recognize the faces of their own ethnic group better than those of other people. With enough practice, you could become adept at recognizing any kind of face, even nonhuman faces (Pascalis et al., 2005).

Face recognition depends on several brain areas, including parts of the occipital cortex, the anterior temporal cortex, the prefrontal cortex, and the **fusiform gyrus** of the inferior temporal cortex, especially in the right hemisphere (Kriegeskorte, Formisano, Sorger, & Goebel, 2007; McCarthy, Puce, Gore, & Allison, 1997; Ó Scalaidhe, Wilson, & Goldman-Rakic, 1997; Steeves et al., 2009) (Figure 6.29). Damage to any of these areas leads to **prosopagnosia** (PROSS-oh-pag-NOH-see-ah), meaning inability to recognize faces. Some individuals are poor throughout life at recognizing faces, because they were born with a shortage of connections to and from the fusiform gyrus (Grueter et al., 2007; C. Thomas et al., 2009). Oliver Sacks, famous for writing about other people's neurological problems, is one such case himself. In his words (Sacks, 2000, p. 37), "I have had difficulty recognizing faces for as long as I can remember. I did not think too much about this as a child, but by the time I was a teen-ager, in a new school, it was often a cause of embarrassment…. My problem with recognizing faces extends not only to my nearest and dearest but also to myself. Thus, on several occasions I have apologized for almost bumping into a large bearded man, only to realize that the large bearded man was myself in a mirror. The opposite situation once occurred at a restaurant. Sitting at a sidewalk table, I turned toward the restaurant window and began grooming my beard, as I often

do. I then realized that what I had taken to be my reflection was not grooming himself but looking at me oddly."

People with prosopagnosia can read, so visual acuity is not the problem. They recognize people's voices, so their problem is not memory (Farah, Wilson, Drain, & Tanaka, 1998). Furthermore, if they feel clay models of faces, they are worse than other people at determining whether two clay models are the same or different (Kilgour, de Gelder, & Lederman, 2004). Their problem is not vision in general, but something that relates specifically to faces.

When people with prosopagnosia look at a face, they can describe whether the person is old or young, male or female, but they cannot identify the person. (You would have a similar difficulty if you viewed faces quickly, upside-down.) One patient was shown 34 photographs of famous people and had a choice of two identifications for each. By chance alone, he should have identified 17 correctly; in fact, he got 18. He remarked that he seldom enjoyed watching movies or television programs because he had trouble keeping track of the characters. Curiously, his favorite movie was *Batman*, in which the main characters wore masks much of the time (Laeng & Caviness, 2001).

Much research has focused on the fusiform gyrus, because it responds so much more strongly to faces than to anything else. It responds strongly to a face viewed from any angle, as well as line drawings and anything else that looks like a face (Caldara & Seghier, 2009; Kanwisher & Yovel, 2006). But is it a built-in module for recognizing faces? Or does it respond to any visual stimulus at which we develop expertise? For example, some people become experts at recognizing cars, identifying bird species, or judging dogs at dog shows. The more someone develops one of these types of expertise, the more those stimuli activate the fusiform gyrus (Tarr & Gauthier, 2000), and damage to the fusiform gyrus impairs those types of expertise (Farah, 1990). However, even in people with extreme levels of expertise, many cells in the fusiform gyrus respond much more vigorously to faces than anything else (Kanwisher & Yovel, 2006). So face recognition may indeed be special. Isn't it interesting that we have evolved a special brain mechanism for this purpose?

Stop & Check

26. What is prosopagnosia, and what does its existence tell us about separate shape recognition systems in the visual cortex?

ANSWER

26. Prosopagnosia is the inability to recognize faces. Its existence implies that the cortical mechanism for identifying faces is different from the mechanism for identifying other complex stimuli.

Color Perception

Although neurons in many parts of the visual system show some response to changes in color, one brain area is particularly important, known as area V4 (Hadjikhani, Liu, Dale, Cavanagh, & Tootell, 1998; Zeki, McKeefry, Bartels, & Frackowiak, 1998). Recall the demonstration in Figure 6.14: The apparent color of an object depends not only on the light reflected from that object, but also how it compares with objects around it. The responses of cells in V4 correspond to the *apparent* or *perceived* color of an object, which depends on the total context (Brouwer & Heeger, 2009; Kusunoki, Moutoussis, & Zeki, 2006). After damage to area V4, people do not become colorblind, but they lose color constancy. Color constancy is the ability to recognize something as being the same color despite changes in lighting. If you entered a room with green lighting, or if you wore red-tinted sunglasses, you would nevertheless accurately identify the color of all the objects in the room. Your brain would in effect subtract a little green or red from all the objects to construct their natural colors. Both monkeys and people with damage to area V4 lose this ability. If they are trained to reach for a yellow object, they may not be able to find it if the overhead lighting is changed (Rüttiger et al., 1999; Wild, Butler, Carden, & Kulikowski, 1985).

Stop & Check

27. Area V4 is important for color constancy. What is color constancy?

ANSWER

27. It is the ability to recognize the color of an object despite changes in the lighting.

Motion Perception

Throughout our evolutionary history, moving objects have been worthy of immediate attention. A moving object might be a possible mate, something you could hunt and eat, or something that wants to eat you. If you are going to respond, you need to identify what the object is, but you also need to see where it is going, and how fast. The brain is set up to make those calculations quickly and efficiently.

The Middle Temporal Cortex

Viewing a complex moving pattern activates many brain areas spread among all four lobes of the cerebral cortex (Sunaert, Van Hecke, Marchal, & Orban, 1999; Vanduffel et al., 2001). Two areas that are especially activated by motion are **area MT** (for middle temporal cortex), also known as **area V5**, and an adjacent region, **area MST** (medial superior temporal cortex) (Figure 6.27). Areas MT and MST receive input mostly from the magnocellular path (Nassi & Callaway, 2006), which detects overall patterns, including movement over large areas of the visual field. Given that the magnocellular path is color-insensitive, MT is also color-insensitive.

Most cells in area MT respond selectively when something moves at a particular speed in a particular direction (Perrone & Thiele, 2001). They detect acceleration or deceleration as well as the absolute speed (Schlack, Krekelberg, & Albright, 2007), and they respond to motion in all three dimensions (Rokers, Cormack, & Huk, 2009). Area MT also responds to photographs that imply movement, such as a photo of people running (Kourtzi & Kanwisher, 2000).

Cells in the dorsal part of area MST respond best to more complex stimuli, such as the expansion, contraction, or rotation of a large visual scene, as illustrated in Figure 6.32. That kind of experience occurs when you move forward or backward or tilt your head. These two kinds of cells—the ones that record movement of single objects and the ones that record movement of the entire background—converge their messages onto neurons in the ventral part of area MST, where cells respond to an object that moves *relative to its background* (K. Tanaka, Sugita, Moriya, & Saito, 1993) (Figure 6.33).

Cells with such properties are critical for judging the motion of objects. When you move your head or eyes from left to right, everything in your visual field moves across your retina as if the world itself had moved right to left. (Go ahead and try it.) Yet the world seems stationary because nothing moved relative to anything else. Most neurons in area MST are silent during eye movements (Thiele, Henning, Kubischik, & Hoffmann, 2002). However, they respond briskly if something moves relative to the background. In short, MST neurons enable you to distinguish between the result of eye movements and the result of object movements.

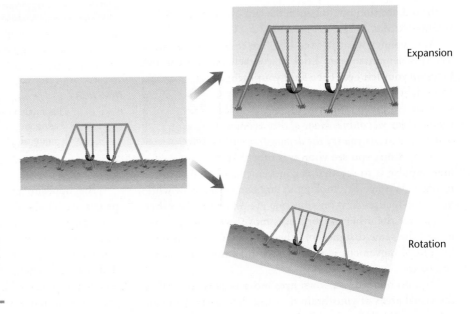

Expansion

Rotation

FIGURE 6.32 Stimuli that excite the dorsal part of area MST
Cells here respond if a whole scene expands, contracts, or rotates. That is, they respond if the observer moves forward or backward or tilts his or her head. *(© Cengage Learning 2013)*

FIGURE 6.33 Stimuli that excite the ventral part of area MST
Cells here respond when an object moves relative to its background. They therefore react either when the object moves or when the object is steady and the background moves. *(© Cengage Learning 2013)*

Motion Blindness

Given that areas MT and MST respond strongly to moving objects, and only to moving objects, what would happen after damage to these areas? The result is **motion blindness**, ability to see objects but impairment at seeing whether they are moving or, if so, which direction and how fast (Marcar, Zihl,

& Cowey, 1997). People with motion blindness are somewhat better at reaching for a moving object than at describing its motion (Schenk, Mai, Ditterich, & Zihl, 2000). However, in all aspects of dealing with visual motion, they are far behind other people.

People with full color vision can imagine what it would be like to be color deficient. It is much more difficult to imagine being motion blind. If something is moving, and you see it, how could you fail to see that it is moving? Because this experience seems so odd, neurologists for many years resisted the idea of motion blindness. Several patients were reported who apparently lost their motion vision as a result of brain damage, but most scientists ignored or disbelieved those reports. After the discovery of area MT, first from monkey research, researchers saw a mechanism whereby motion blindness could (and should) occur. They then became more amenable to the reports of motion blindness in people with brain damage.

Motion perception is a severe impairment. One patient with motion blindness reported that she felt uncomfortable when people walked around because they "were suddenly here or there but I have not seen them moving." She could not cross a street without help: "When I'm looking at the car first, it seems far away. But then, when I want to cross the road, suddenly the car is very near." Pouring coffee became difficult. The flowing liquid appeared to be frozen and unmoving, so she did not stop pouring until the cup overfilled (Zihl, von Cramon, & Mai, 1983).

You wonder what it would be like to be motion blind. Try this demonstration: Look at yourself in a mirror and focus on your left eye. Then shift your focus to your right eye. (*Please do this now.*) Did you see your eyes move? No, you did not. (*I said to try this. I bet you didn't. None of this section will make sense unless you try the demonstration!*)

TRY IT YOURSELF

Why didn't you see your eyes move? Your first impulse is to say that the movement was too small or too fast. Wrong. Try looking at someone else's eyes while he or she focuses first on your one eye and then the other. You *do* see the other person's eyes move, even though they moved the same distance and the same speed as your own. So an eye movement is neither too small nor too fast for you to see.

You do not see your own eyes move because several of the visual areas of your brain decrease their activity during voluntary eye movements, known as **saccades**. (They don't decrease activity while your eyes are following a moving object.) The brain areas that monitor saccades tell certain parts of the visual cortex, "We're about to move the eye muscles, so take a rest for the next split second." Neural activity and blood flow in the visual cortex begin to decrease 75 ms before the eye movement and remain suppressed during the movement (Burr, Morrone, & Ross, 1994; Paus, Marrett, Worsley, & Evans, 1995; Vallines & Greenlee, 2006). Suppression is particularly strong in area MT, responsible for motion detection, and the "where" path of the parietal cortex. The areas responsible for shape and color detection remain at nearly normal activity (Bremmer, Kubischik, Hoffmann, & Krekelberg, 2009). In short, during a voluntary eye movement, you become temporarily motion blind. Perhaps now you understand a little better what people with motion blindness experience all the time.

Stop & Check

28. Under what circumstance does someone with an intact brain become motion blind, and what accounts for the motion blindness?

ANSWER

28. People become motion blind shortly before and during a saccade (voluntary eye movement), because of suppressed activity in several brain areas, including area MT.

The opposite of motion blindness also occurs: Some people are blind *except* for the ability to detect which direction something is moving. How could someone see movement without seeing the object that is moving? Area MT gets some input directly from the lateral geniculate nucleus of the thalamus. Therefore, even after extensive damage to area V1 (enough to produce blindness), area MT still has enough input to permit motion detection (Sincich, Park, Wohlgemuth, & Horton, 2004). Again, we try to imagine this person's experience. What would it be like to see motion without seeing the objects that are moving? (Their answers don't help. When they say which direction something is moving, they insist they are just guessing.) The general point is that different areas of your brain process different kinds of visual information, and it is possible to develop many kinds of disability.

Stop & Check

29. What symptoms occur after damage limited to area MT? What may occur if MT is intact but area V1 is damaged?

ANSWER

29. Damage in area MT can produce motion blindness. If area MT is intact but area V1 is damaged, the person may be able to report motion direction despite no conscious identification of the moving object.

MODULE 6.3 ■ IN CLOSING

Different Aspects of Vision

Anatomists have identified at least 80 brain areas responsible for vision, each with specialized functions. We have discussed areas responsible for detecting location, shape, faces, color, and movement. Many of the visual areas have yet to be fully explored. Why do we have so many visual areas? We can only infer that the brain, like a human society, benefits from specialization. Life works better if some people become experts at repairing cars, some at baking cakes, some at delivering babies, some at moving pianos, and

so forth, than if each of us had to do everything for ourselves. Similarly, your visual system works better because visual areas specialize in a particular task without trying to do everything.

A related question: How do we put it all together? When you watch a bird fly by, you perceive its shape, color, location, and movement all at once. So it seems, anyway. How do you do that? This is the binding problem, as discussed in Chapter 4. Answering that question remains a major challenge.

SUMMARY

1. The ventral stream in the cortex is important for shape perception ("what"), and the dorsal stream is specialized for localizing visual perceptions and integrating them with action ("where"). **182**

2. The inferior temporal cortex detects objects and recognizes them despite changes in position, size, and so forth. After damage to this area, people experience visual agnosia, a difficulty in recognizing the objects they see. **183**

3. A circuit including the fusiform gyrus of the temporal cortex is specialized for recognizing faces. People with impairments anywhere in this circuit experience prosopagnosia, a difficulty in recognizing faces despite nearly normal vision in other regards. **184**

4. Area V4 is important for color constancy, the ability to perceive the color of an object despite changes in the lighting. **186**

5. The middle temporal cortex (including areas MT and MST) is specialized for detecting the direction and speed of a moving object. People with damage in this area experience motion blindness, an impairment in their ability to perceive movement. **186**

6. People with an intact brain experience a brief period of motion blindness beginning about 75 ms before a voluntary eye movement and continuing during the eye movement. **188**

KEY TERMS

Terms are defined in the module on the page number indicated. They're also presented in alphabetical order with definitions in the book's Subject Index/Glossary, which begins on page 561. Interactive flashcards and crossword puzzles are among the online resources available to help you learn these terms and the concepts they represent.

dorsal stream **183**

fusiform gyrus **185**

inferior temporal cortex **183**

motion blindness **187**

MST **186**

MT (or area V5) **186**

prosopagnosia **185**

saccade **185**

secondary visual cortex **182**

ventral stream **183**

visual agnosia **183**

THOUGHT QUESTIONS

1. The visual system has specialized areas for perceiving faces, bodies, and places, but not other kinds of objects. Why might we have evolved specialized areas for these functions but not others?

2. Why is it advantageous to become motion blind during voluntary eye movements? That is, why might we have evolved this mechanism?

CHAPTER 6 Interactive Exploration and Study

The **Psychology CourseMate** for this text brings chapter topics to life with interactive learning, study, and exam preparation tools, including quizzes and flashcards for the Key Concepts that appear throughout each module, as well as an interactive media-rich eBook version of the text that is fully searchable and includes highlighting and note taking capabilities and interactive versions of the book's **Stop & Check** quizzes and **Try It Yourself Online** activities. The site also features **Virtual Biological Psychology Labs, videos,** and **animations** to help you better understand concepts—logon and learn more at **www.cengagebrain.com**, which is your gateway to all of this text's complimentary and premium resources, including the following:

Virtual Biological Psychology Labs

Explore the experiments that led to modern-day understanding of biopsychology with the Virtual Biological Psychology Labs, featuring a realistic lab environment that allows you to conduct experiments and evaluate data to better understand how scientists came to the conclusions presented in your text. The labs cover a range of topics, including perception, motivation, cognition, and more. You may purchase access at **www.cengagebrain.com**, or login at **login.cengagebrain.com** if an access card was included with your text.

Animations

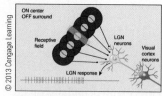

Retinal Fields

Also available—

- The Retina
- Visual Transduction

Try It Yourself Online

Brightness Contrast

Also available—

- Blind Spot
- Virtual Reality Eye
- Motion Aftereffect

Suggestions for Further Exploration
Books

Purves, D., & Lotto, R. B. (2003). *Why we see what we do: An empirical theory of vision.* Sunderland, MA: Sinauer Associates. Discussion of how our perception of color, size, and other visual qualities depends on our previous experience with objects and not just on the light striking the retina.

Sacks, O. (2010). *Mind's Eye.* New York: Alfred Knopf. Case histories of brain-damaged people who lost the ability to recognize faces, the ability to read, the ability to find their way around, and other specific visual abilities.

Websites

 The Psychology CourseMate for this text provides regularly updated links to relevant online resources for this chapter, such as the following:

Seeing, hearing, and smelling the world
Excellent explanation of the sensory systems
http://www.hhmi.org/senses/

Webvision
A detailed treatment of the retina and vision
http://webvision.med.utah.edu/

Studies from the Dale Purves Lab
Fascinating demonstrations of how our perception of color, shape, and other features depend on an object's context.
http://www.purveslab.net

Bio Motion Lab
Delightful demonstration of how highly prepared we are to detect biological motion, even from minimal stimuli
http://www.biomotionlab.ca-Demos/BMLwalker.html

Sensation and Perception Tutorials
Very engaging demonstrations
http://psych.hanover.edu/Krantz/sen_tut.html

Other Sensory Systems

7

CHAPTER OUTLINE

MAIN IDEAS

1. Our senses have evolved to give us information we can use rather than complete information about the world.

2. Each sensory system has receptors tuned to specific types of energy.

3. As a rule, the activity in a single sensory neuron is ambiguous by itself. The meaning depends on the pattern across a population of neurons.

OPPOSITE: The sensory world of bats—which find insects by echolocation—must be very different from that of humans.

According to a Native American saying, "A pine needle fell. The eagle saw it. The deer heard it. The bear smelled it" (Herrero, 1985). Different species are sensitive to different kinds of information. The ears of the green tree frog, *Hyla cinerea*, are highly sensitive to sounds at two frequencies—900 and 3000 hertz (Hz, cycles per second)—which are prominent in the adult male's mating call (Moss & Simmons, 1986). Mosquitoes have a specialized receptor that detects the odor of human sweat—and therefore helps them find us and bite us (Hallem, Fox, Zwiebel, & Carlson, 2004). Bats locate insects by emitting sonar waves at 20,000 to 100,000 Hz, well above the range of adult human hearing (Griffin, Webster, & Michael, 1960), and then locating the insects from the echoes. Curiously, some moths jam the signals by emitting similar high-frequency calls of their own (Corcoran, Barber, & Conner, 2009).

Humans, too, have important sensory specializations. Our sense of taste alerts us to the bitterness of poisons (Richter, 1950; Schiffman & Erickson, 1971) but does not respond to substances such as cellulose that neither help nor harm us. Our olfactory systems are unresponsive to gases that we don't need to detect (e.g., carbon dioxide) but highly responsive to the smell of rotting meat. This chapter concerns how our sensory systems process biologically useful information.

Audition

Evolution has been described as "thrifty." After it has solved one problem, it modifies that solution for other problems instead of starting from scratch. For example, imagine a gene for visual receptors in an early vertebrate. Make a duplicate of that gene, modify it slightly, and presto: The new gene makes receptors that respond to different wavelengths of light, and color vision becomes possible. In this chapter, you will see more examples of that principle. Various sensory systems have their specializations, but they also have much in common.

▌ Sound and the Ear

The human auditory system enables us to hear not only falling trees but also the birds singing in the branches and the wind blowing through the leaves. Many people who are blind learn to click their heels as they walk and use the echoes to locate obstructions. Our auditory systems are well adapted for detecting and interpreting many kinds of information.

Physics and Psychology of Sound

Sound waves are periodic compressions of air, water, or other media. When a tree falls, the tree and the ground vibrate, setting up sound waves in the air that strike the ears. Sound waves vary in amplitude and frequency. The **amplitude** of a sound wave is its intensity. A bolt of lightning produces sound waves of great amplitude. **Loudness** is a sensation related to amplitude but not identical to it. For example, a rapidly talking person sounds louder than slow music of the same physical amplitude. If you complain that television advertisements are louder than the program, one reason is that the people in the advertisements talk faster.

The **frequency** of a sound is the number of compressions per second, measured in Hz. **Pitch** is the related aspect of perception. Higher frequency sounds are higher in pitch. Figure 7.1 illustrates the amplitude and frequency of sounds. The height of each wave corresponds to amplitude, and the number of waves per second corresponds to frequency.

Most adult humans hear sounds ranging from about 15 Hz to somewhat less than 20,000 Hz. Children hear higher frequencies than adults, because the ability to perceive high

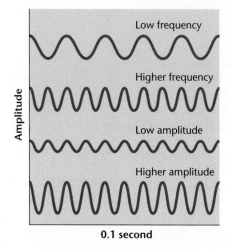

FIGURE 7.1 Four sound waves
The top line represents five sound waves in 0.1 second, or 50 Hz—a low-frequency sound that we experience as a low pitch. The other three lines represent 100 Hz. The vertical extent of each line represents its amplitude or intensity, which we experience as loudness. (© Cengage Learning 2013)

frequencies decreases with age and exposure to loud noises (B. A. Schneider, Trehub, Morrongiello, & Thorpe, 1986).

Structures of the Ear

Rube Goldberg (1883–1970) drew cartoons of complicated, far-fetched inventions. For example, a person's tread on the front doorstep would pull a string that raised a cat's tail, awakening the cat, which would then chase a bird that had been resting on a balance, which would swing up to strike a doorbell. The functioning of the ear is complex enough to resemble a Rube Goldberg device, but unlike Goldberg's inventions, the ear actually works.

Anatomists distinguish the outer ear, the middle ear, and the inner ear (Figure 7.2). The outer ear includes the **pinna**, the familiar structure of flesh and cartilage attached to each side of the head. By altering the reflections of sound waves, the pinna helps us locate the source of a sound. We have to learn to use that information because each person's pinna is

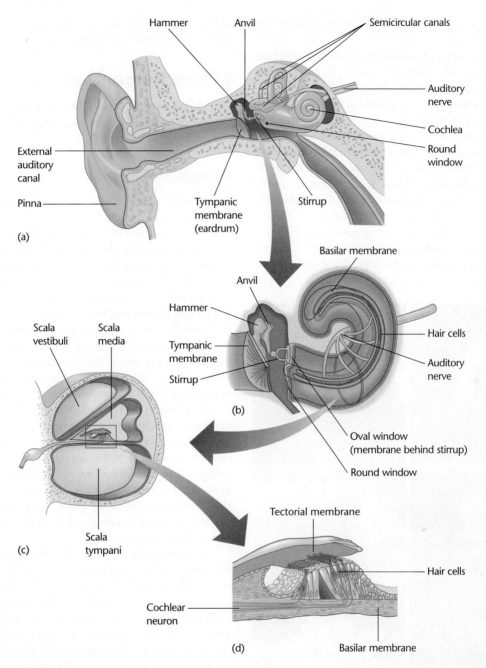

FIGURE 7.2 Structures of the ear

When sound waves strike the tympanic membrane in (a), they vibrate three tiny bones—the hammer, anvil, and stirrup—that convert the sound waves into stronger vibrations in the fluid-filled cochlea (b). Those vibrations displace the hair cells along the basilar membrane in the cochlea. (c) A cross-section through the cochlea. (d) A close-up of the hair cells. *(© Cengage Learning 2013)*

shaped differently from anyone else's (Van Wanrooij & Van Opstal, 2005). Rabbits' large movable pinnas enable them to localize sound sources even more precisely.

After sound waves pass through the auditory canal (Figure 7.2), they strike the **tympanic membrane**, or eardrum, in the middle ear. The tympanic membrane vibrates at the same frequency as the sound waves that strike it. The tympanic membrane connects to three tiny bones that transmit the vibrations to the **oval window**, a membrane of the inner ear. These bones

are sometimes known by their English names (hammer, anvil, and stirrup) and sometimes by their Latin names (malleus, incus, and stapes). The tympanic membrane is about 20 times larger than the footplate of the stirrup, which connects to the oval window. As in a hydraulic pump, the vibrations of the tympanic membrane transform into more forceful vibrations of the smaller stirrup. The net effect converts the sound waves into waves of greater pressure on the small oval window. This transformation is important because more force is required to move the viscous fluid behind the oval window than to move the eardrum, which has air on both sides.

The inner ear contains a snail-shaped structure called the **cochlea** (KOCK-lee-uh, Latin for "snail"). A cross-section through the cochlea, as in Figure 7.2c, shows three long fluid-filled tunnels: the scala vestibuli, scala media, and scala tympani. The stirrup makes the oval window vibrate at the entrance to the scala vestibuli, thereby setting in motion the fluid in the cochlea. The auditory receptors, known as **hair cells**, lie between the basilar membrane of the cochlea on one side and the tectorial membrane on the other (Figure 7.2d). Vibrations in the fluid of the cochlea displace the hair cells. A hair cell responds within microseconds to displacements as small as 10^{-10} meter (0.1 nanometer, about the diameter of an atom), thereby opening ion channels in its membrane (Fettiplace, 1990; Hudspeth, 1985). Figure 7.3 shows electron micrographs of the hair cells

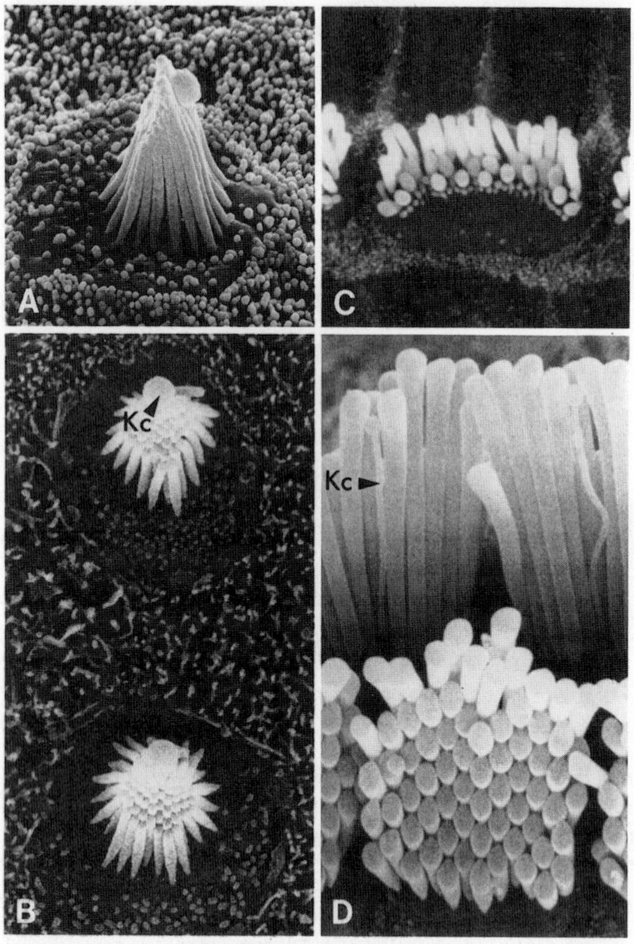

FIGURE 7.3 Hair cells from three species
(a, b) Hair cells from a frog sacculus, an organ that detects ground-borne vibrations. (c) Hair cells from the cochlea of a cat. (d) Hair cells from the cochlea of a fence lizard. Kc = kinocilium, one of the components of a hair bundle. *(From "The cellular basis of hearing: The biophysics of hair cells," by A. J. Hudspeth, Science 1985, 230: 4727, 745–752. Reprinted with permission from AAAS.)*

of three species. The hair cells excite the cells of the auditory nerve, which is part of the eighth cranial nerve.

Pitch Perception

Our ability to understand speech or enjoy music depends on our ability to differentiate among sounds of different frequencies. How do we do it?

Frequency and Place

Recall from Chapter 6 that two of the main ways of coding sensory information are which cells are active and how frequently they fire. Those same principles apply to perception of pitch.

According to the **place theory**, the basilar membrane resembles the strings of a piano in that each area along the membrane is tuned to a specific frequency. (If you sound a note with a tuning fork near a piano, you vibrate the piano string tuned to that note.) According to this theory, each frequency activates the hair cells at only one place along the basilar membrane, and the nervous system distinguishes among frequencies based on which neurons respond. The downfall of this theory is that the various parts of the basilar membrane are bound together too tightly for any part to resonate like a piano string.

According to the **frequency theory**, the basilar membrane vibrates in synchrony with a sound, causing auditory nerve axons to produce action potentials at the same frequency. For example, a sound at 50 Hz would cause 50 action potentials per second in the auditory nerve. The downfall of this theory in its simplest form is that the refractory period of a neuron, though variable, is typically about $^1/_{1,000}$ second, so the maximum firing rate of a neuron is about 1000 Hz, far short of the highest frequencies we hear.

The current theory is a modification of both theories. For low-frequency sounds (up to about 100 Hz—more than an octave below middle C in music, which is 264 Hz), the basilar membrane vibrates in synchrony with the sound waves, in accordance with the frequency theory, and auditory nerve axons generate one action potential per wave. Soft sounds activate fewer neurons, and stronger sounds activate more. Thus, at low frequencies, the frequency of impulses identifies the pitch, and the number of firing cells identifies loudness.

Because of the refractory period of the axon, as sounds exceed 100 Hz, it becomes harder for a neuron to continue firing in synchrony with the sound waves. At higher frequencies, it might fire on every second, third, fourth, or later wave. Its action potentials are phase-locked to the peaks of the sound waves (i.e., they occur at the same phase in the sound wave), as illustrated here:

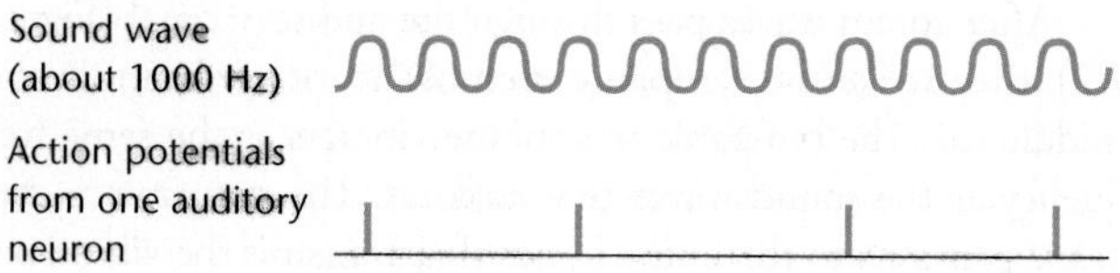

Sound wave (about 1000 Hz)

Action potentials from one auditory neuron

Other auditory neurons also produce action potentials that are phase-locked with peaks of the sound wave, but they can be out of phase with one another:

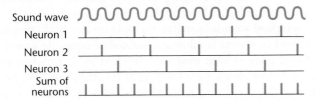

If we consider the auditory nerve as a whole, we find that with a tone of a few hundred Hz, each wave excites at least a few auditory neurons. According to the **volley principle** of pitch discrimination, the auditory nerve as a whole produces volleys of impulses for sounds up to about 4,000 per second, even though no individual axon approaches that frequency (Rose, Brugge, Anderson, & Hind, 1967). For this principle to work, auditory cells must time their responses quite precisely, and the evidence says that they do (Avissar, Furman, Saunders, & Parsons, 2007). However, beyond about 4000 Hz, even staggered volleys of impulses can't keep pace with the sound waves.

Most human hearing takes place below 4000 Hz, the approximate limit of the volley principle. For comparison, the highest key on a piano is 4224 Hz. When we hear very high frequencies, we use a mechanism similar to the place theory. The basilar membrane varies from stiff at its base, where the stirrup meets the cochlea, to floppy at the other end of the cochlea, the apex (von Békésy, 1956) (Figure 7.4). The hair cells along the basilar membrane have different properties based on their location, and they act as tuned resonators that vibrate only for sound waves of a particular frequency. The highest frequency sounds vibrate hair cells near the base, and lower frequency sounds vibrate hair cells farther along the membrane (Warren, 1999). Actually, the mechanisms of hearing are more complex, especially at frequencies over 4000. The responses depend on many physical parameters of the cochlea, including stiffness, friction, and the properties of the hair cells (Tomo, de Monvel, & Fridberger, 2007).

People vary in their sensitivity to pitch. For almost any other aspect of behavior, people's performances follow a "normal curve," with continuous variation. However, for pitch perception, a fair number of people are not part of the normal distribution. An estimated 4% of people have *amusia*, impaired detection of frequency changes (commonly called "tone-deafness") (Hyde & Peretz, 2004). They are not completely tone-deaf any more than colorblind people are completely insensitive to color, but they have trouble detecting a change in sound frequency less than about 10%, whereas other people can detect a change of less than 1% (Loui, Alsop, & Schlaug, 2009). They have trouble recognizing tunes, can't tell whether someone is singing off-key, and do not detect a "wrong" note in a melody. As you might guess, most people

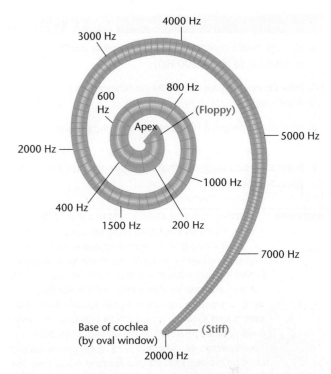

FIGURE 7.4 Basilar membrane of the human cochlea
High-frequency sounds excite hair cells near the base. Low-frequency sounds excite cells near the apex. (© Cengage Learning 2013)

with amusia have trouble singing even simple, familiar songs (Bella, Giguere, & Peretz, 2009).

Many relatives of a person with amusia have the same condition, so it probably has a genetic basis (Peretz, Cummings, & Dube, 2007). Given that pitch perception depends on the auditory cortex, we might expect to find a thinner than average auditory cortex. In fact, amusia is associated with a thicker than average auditory cortex in the right hemisphere but fewer than average connections from the auditory cortex to the frontal cortex (Hyde et al., 2007; Loui et al., 2009).

Absolute pitch (or "perfect pitch") is the ability to hear a note and identify it—for example, "That's a C sharp." People's accuracy on this task is either high or low. Intermediates are rare. Genetic predisposition may contribute (Theusch, Basu, & Gitschier, 2009), but the main determinant is early and extensive musical training. Not everyone with musical training develops absolute pitch, but almost everyone with absolute pitch had extensive musical training (Athos et al., 2007). Absolute pitch is more common among people who speak tonal languages, such as Vietnamese and Mandarin Chinese (Deutsch, Henthorn, Marvin, & Xu, 2006). In those languages, the meaning of a sound depends on its pitch, and therefore, people learn from infancy to pay close attention to slight changes of pitch.

STOP & CHECK

1. Through which mechanism do we perceive low-frequency sounds (up to about 100 Hz)?

2. How do we perceive middle-frequency sounds (100 to 4000 Hz)?

3. How do we perceive high-frequency sounds (above 4000 Hz)?

4. What evidence suggests that absolute pitch depends on special experiences?

ANSWERS

1. At low frequencies, the basilar membrane vibrates in synchrony with the sound waves, and each responding axon in the auditory nerve sends one action potential per sound wave. **2.** At intermediate frequencies, no single axon fires an action potential for each sound wave, but different axons fire for different waves, and so a volley (group) of axons fires for each wave. **3.** At high frequencies, the sound causes maximum vibration for the hair cells at one location along the basilar membrane. **4.** Absolute pitch occurs almost entirely among people who had early musical training and is also more common among people who speak tonal languages, which require greater attention to pitch.

The Auditory Cortex

As information from the auditory system passes through subcortical areas, axons cross over in the midbrain to enable each hemisphere of the forebrain to get most of its input from the opposite ear (Glendenning, Baker, Hutson, & Masterton, 1992). The information ultimately reaches the **primary auditory cortex (area A1)** in the superior temporal cortex, as shown in Figure 7.5.

The organization of the auditory cortex strongly parallels that of the visual cortex (Poremba et al., 2003). For example, just as the visual system has a "what" pathway and a "where" pathway, the auditory system has a "what" pathway sensitive to patterns of sound in the anterior temporal cortex, and a "where" pathway sensitive to sound location in the posterior temporal cortex and the parietal cortex (Lomber & Malhotra, 2008). The superior temporal cortex includes areas important for detecting visual motion and the motion of sounds. Just as patients with damage in area MT become motion blind, patients with damage in parts of the superior temporal cortex become motion deaf. They hear sounds, but they do not detect that a source of a sound is moving (Ducommun et al., 2004).

Just as the visual cortex is active during visual imagery, area A1 is important for auditory imagery. It becomes active when people view short silent videos that suggest sound—such as someone playing a piano, or a glass vase shattering on the ground (K. Meyer et al., 2010). That is, A1 responds to imagined sounds as well as real ones. In one study, people listened to several familiar and unfamiliar songs. At various points, parts of each song were replaced by 3- to 5-second gaps. When people were listening to familiar songs, they reported that they heard "in their heads" the notes or words that belonged in the gaps. That experience was accompanied by activity in area A1. During similar gaps in the unfamiliar songs, they did not hear anything in their heads, and area A1 showed no activation (Kraemer, Macrae, Green, & Kelley, 2005).

Also like the visual system, the auditory system requires experience for full development. Just as rearing an animal in the dark impairs visual development, rearing one in constant noise impairs auditory development (Chang & Merzenich, 2003). In people who are deaf from birth, the axons leading from the auditory cortex develop less than in other people (Emmorey, Allen, Bruss, Schenker, & Damasio, 2003).

However, the visual and auditory systems differ in this respect: Whereas damage to area V1 leaves someone blind, damage to area A1 does not produce deafness. People with damage to the primary auditory cortex hear simple sounds reasonably well, unless the damage extends into subcortical brain areas (Tanaka, Kamo, Yoshida, & Yamadori, 1991). Their main deficit is in the ability to recognize combinations or sequences of

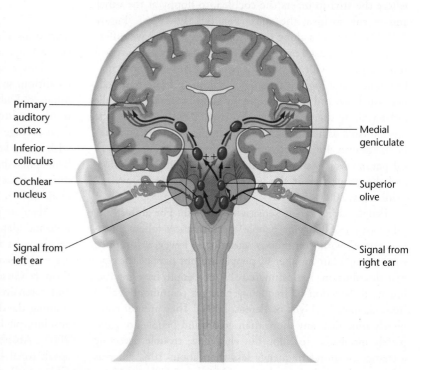

FIGURE 7.5 Route of auditory impulses from the receptors in the ear to the primary auditory cortex
The cochlear nucleus receives input from the ipsilateral ear only (the one on the same side of the head). All later stages have input from both ears. (© Cengage Learning 2013)

sounds, like music or speech. Evidently, the cortex is not necessary for all hearing, only for advanced processing of it.

When researchers record from cells in the primary auditory cortex while playing pure tones, they find that each cell has a preferred tone, as shown in Figure 7.6. Note the gradient from one area of the cortex responsive to lower tones up to areas responsive to higher and higher tones. The auditory cortex provides a kind of map of the sounds. Researchers call it a *tonotopic* map.

In alert, waking animals, each cell in area A1 responds to its preferred sound and hardly responds at all to other sounds (X. Wang, Lu, Snider, & Liang, 2005). Properties vary from one cell to another. Some cells are tuned sharply to a single tone, and others respond also to some neighboring tones. Some respond only briefly, and others show a more sustained response (de la Rocha, Marchetti, Schiff, & Reyes, 2008). Most cells respond best to a complex sound, such as a dominant tone and several harmonics (Barbour & Wang, 2003; Griffiths, Uppenkamp, Johnsrude, Josephs, & Patterson, 2001; Penagos, Melcher, & Oxenham, 2004; Wessinger et al., 2001). For example, for a tone of 400 Hz, the harmonics are 800 Hz, 1200 Hz, and so forth. We experience a tone with harmonics as "richer" than one without them.

Surrounding the primary auditory cortex are additional auditory areas. Just as the visual system starts with cells that respond to simple lines and progresses to cells that detect faces and other complex stimuli, the same is true for the auditory system. Cells outside area A1 respond best to what we might call auditory "objects"—sounds such as animal cries, machinery noises, music, and other identifiable, meaningful sounds (Gutschalk, Patterson, Scherg, Uppenkamp, & Rupp, 2004; Zatorre, Bouffard, & Belin, 2004).

5. How is the auditory cortex like the visual cortex?

6. What is one way in which the auditory and visual cortices differ?

7. What kinds of sounds most strongly activate the auditory cortex?

ANSWERS

5. Any of the following: (a) Both vision and hearing have "what" and "where" pathways. (b) Areas in the superior temporal cortex analyze movement of both visual and auditory stimuli. Damage there can cause motion blindness or motion deafness. (c) The visual cortex is essential for visual imagery, and the primary auditory cortex is essential for auditory imagery. (d) Both the visual and auditory cortices need normal experience early in life to develop normal sensitivities. **6.** Damage to the primary visual cortex leaves someone blind, but damage to the primary auditory cortex merely impairs perception of complex sounds without making the person deaf. **7.** Each cell in the primary auditory cortex has a preferred frequency. Many or most cells respond best to complex sounds that include harmonics. Outside the primary auditory cortex, most cells respond to "auditory objects" that mean something.

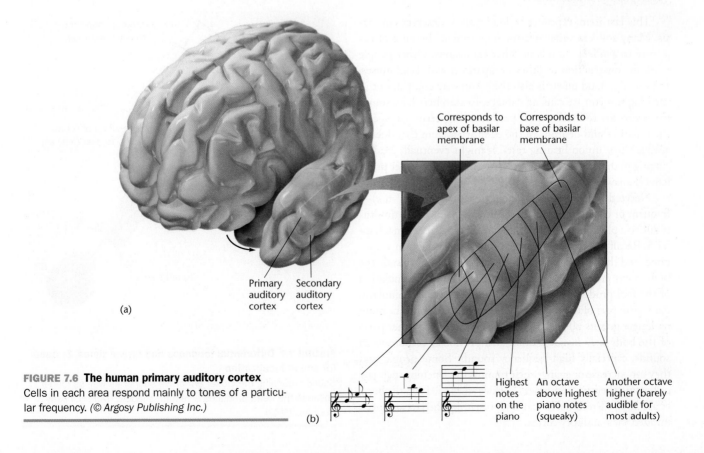

Corresponds to apex of basilar membrane

Corresponds to base of basilar membrane

(a)

Primary auditory cortex

Secondary auditory cortex

Highest notes on the piano

An octave above highest piano notes (squeaky)

Another octave higher (barely audible for most adults)

(b)

FIGURE 7.6 The human primary auditory cortex
Cells in each area respond mainly to tones of a particular frequency. (© Argosy Publishing Inc.)

Hearing Loss

Most hearing-impaired people respond at least slightly to loud noises. We distinguish two categories of hearing impairment: conductive deafness and nerve deafness.

Diseases, infections, or tumorous bone growth can prevent the middle ear from transmitting sound waves properly to the cochlea. The result is **conductive deafness**, or **middle-ear deafness**. It is sometimes temporary. If it persists, it can be corrected either by surgery or by hearing aids that amplify the stimulus. Because people with conductive deafness have a normal cochlea and auditory nerve, they hear their own voices, which can be conducted through the bones of the skull directly to the cochlea, bypassing the middle ear. Because they hear themselves clearly, they may blame others for talking too softly.

Nerve deafness, or **inner-ear deafness**, results from damage to the cochlea, the hair cells, or the auditory nerve. It can occur in any degree and may be confined to one part of the cochlea, in which case someone hears certain frequencies and not others. Nerve deafness can be inherited (A. Wang et al., 1998), or it can develop from a variety of disorders (Cremers & van Rijn, 1991; Robillard & Gersdorff, 1986), including:

- Exposure of the mother to rubella (German measles), syphilis, or other diseases or toxins during pregnancy
- Inadequate oxygen to the brain during birth
- Deficient activity of the thyroid gland
- Certain diseases, including multiple sclerosis and meningitis
- Childhood reactions to certain drugs, including aspirin
- Exposure to loud noises

This last item, exposure to loud noises, deserves emphasis. Many soldiers suffer hearing impairments because of exposure to artillery sounds or other explosions. Other people work in construction or other occupations with loud noises. Exposure to loud music is also risky. You may enjoy it, but in the long run you are causing damage. Researchers have found that exposure to loud sounds produces long-term damage to the synapses and neurons of the auditory system that doesn't always show up on hearing tests. It might eventually lead to ringing in the ears, extreme sensitivity to noise, or other problems (Kujawa & Liberman, 2009).

Nerve deafness often produces **tinnitus** (tin-EYE-tus)— frequent or constant ringing in the ears. In some cases, tinnitus is due to a phenomenon like phantom limb, discussed in Chapter 5. Recall the example in which someone has an arm amputated, and then the axons reporting facial sensations invade the brain areas previously sensitive to the arm so that stimulation of the face produces a sensation of a phantom arm. Similarly, damage to part of the cochlea is like an amputation: If the brain no longer gets its normal input, axons representing other parts of the body may invade a brain area previously responsive to sounds, especially high-frequency sounds. Some people find they can increase or change their tinnitus by clenching their jaw or tensing their neck muscles (Lockwood et al., 1998; Roberts et al., 2010). Presumably, axons representing the jaw and neck invaded their auditory cortex.

Sound Localization

You are walking alone when suddenly you hear a loud noise. You want to know what produced it (friend or foe), but equally, you want to know where it came from (so you can do something about it). Sound localization is less accurate than visual localization, but nevertheless impressive. You can identify a sound's direction even if it occurs just briefly and while you are turning your head (Vliegen, Van Grootel, & Van Opstal, 2004). Owls localize sound well enough to capture mice in the dark.

Determining the direction and distance of a sound requires comparing the responses of the two ears. One cue for location is the difference in intensity between the ears. For high-frequency sounds, with a wavelength shorter than the width of the head, the head creates a *sound shadow* (Figure 7.7), making the sound louder for the closer ear. In adult humans, this mechanism produces accurate sound localization for frequencies above 2000 to 3000 Hz and less accurate localizations for progressively lower frequencies. Another method is

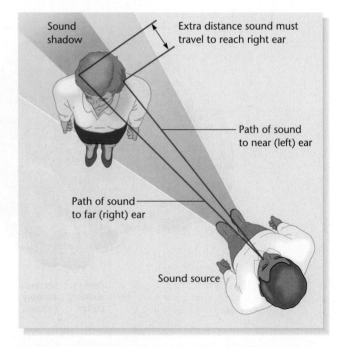

FIGURE 7.7 Differential loudness and arrival times as cues for sound localization
Sounds reaching the closer ear arrive sooner as well as louder because the head produces a "sound shadow." *(After Lindsay & Norman, 1972)*

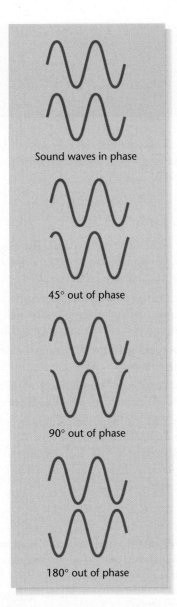

FIGURE 7.8 Sound waves in phase or out of phase
Sound waves that reach the two ears in phase are perceived as coming from directly in front of (or behind) the hearer. The more out of phase the waves, the farther the sound source is from the body's midline. *(© Cengage Learning 2013)*

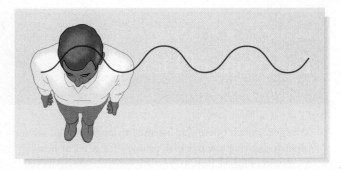

FIGURE 7.9 Phase differences as a cue for sound localization
A sound coming from anywhere other than straight ahead or straight behind reaches the two ears at different phases of the sound wave. The difference in phase is a signal to the sound's direction. With high-frequency sounds, the phases become ambiguous. *(© Cengage Learning 2013)*

the difference in *time of arrival* at the two ears. A sound coming from directly in front of you reaches both ears at once. A sound coming directly from the side reaches the closer ear about 600 microseconds (μs) before the other. Sounds coming from intermediate locations reach the two ears at delays between 0 and 600 μs. Time of arrival is most useful for localizing sounds with a sudden onset. Most birds' alarm calls increase gradually in loudness, making them difficult for a predator to localize.

A third cue is the *phase difference* between the ears. Every sound wave has phases with two consecutive peaks 360 degrees apart. Figure 7.8 shows sound waves that are in phase and 45 degrees, 90 degrees, or 180 degrees out of phase. If a sound originates to the side of the head, the sound wave strikes the two ears out of phase, as shown in Figure 7.9. How

much out of phase depends on the frequency of the sound, the size of the head, and the direction of the sound. Phase differences provide information that is useful for localizing sounds with frequencies up to about 1500 Hz in humans.

In short, humans localize low frequencies by phase differences and high frequencies by loudness differences. We localize a sound of any frequency by its time of onset if it occurs suddenly enough. We localize most speech sounds by their time of onset. All of these methods require learning, because the distance between the two ears changes during childhood as the head grows larger. Readjusting sound localization is a slow process (Kumpik, Kacelnik, & King, 2010).

What would happen if someone became deaf in one ear? At first, as you would expect, all sounds seem to come directly from the side of the intact ear. (Obviously, that ear hears a sound louder and sooner than the other ear because the other ear doesn't hear it at all.) Eventually, however, people learn to interpret loudness cues when they hear familiar sounds in a familiar location. They infer that louder sounds come from the side of the intact ear and softer sounds come from the opposite side. Their accuracy does not match that of people with two ears, but it becomes helpful under some conditions (Van Wanrooij & Van Opstal, 2004).

STOP & CHECK

9. Which method of sound localization is more effective for an animal with a small head? Which is more effective for an animal with a large head? Why?

ANSWER

9. An animal with a small head localizes sounds mainly by differences in loudness because the ears are not far enough apart for differences in onset time to be very large. An animal with a large head localizes sounds mainly by differences in onset time because its ears are far apart and well suited to noting differences in phase or onset time.

MODULE 7.1 ■ IN CLOSING

Functions of Hearing

We spend much of our day listening to language, and we sometimes forget that the original, primary function of hearing has to do with simpler but extremely important issues: What do I hear? Where is it? Is it coming closer? Is it a potential mate, a potential enemy, potential food, or something irrelevant? The organization of the auditory system is well suited to resolving these questions.

SUMMARY

1. Sound waves vibrate the tympanic membrane. Three tiny bones convert these vibrations into more forceful vibrations of the smaller oval window, setting in motion the fluid inside the cochlea. Waves of fluid inside the cochlea stimulate the hair cells that send messages to the brain. **194**

2. We detect the pitch of low-frequency sounds by the frequency of action potentials in the auditory system. At intermediate frequencies, we detect volleys of responses across many receptors. We detect the pitch of the highest frequency sounds by the area of greatest response along the basilar membrane. **196**

3. The auditory cortex resembles the visual cortex in many ways. Both have a "what" system and a "where" system. Both have specialized areas for detecting motion, and therefore, it is possible for a person with brain damage to be motion blind or motion deaf. The visual cortex is essential for visual imagery, and the auditory cortex is essential for auditory imagery. **198**

4. Each cell in the primary auditory cortex responds best to a particular frequency of tones, although many respond better to complex tones than to a single frequency. **199**

5. Areas bordering the primary auditory cortex analyze the meaning of sounds. **199**

6. Deafness may result from damage to the nerve cells or to the bones that conduct sounds to the nerve cells. **200**

7. We localize high-frequency sounds according to differences in loudness between the ears. We localize low-frequency sounds on the basis of differences in phase. If a sound occurs suddenly, we localize it by time of onset in the two ears. **200**

KEY TERMS

Terms are defined in the module on the page number indicated. They're also presented in alphabetical order with definitions in the book's Subject Index/Glossary, which begins on page 561. Interactive flashcards and crossword puzzles are among the online resources available to help you learn these terms and the concepts they represent.

amplitude **194**
cochlea **196**
conductive deafness (middle-ear deafness) **200**
frequency **194**
frequency theory **196**
hair cells **196**

loudness **194**
nerve deafness (inner-ear deafness) **200**
oval window **195**
pinna **194**
pitch **194**
place theory **196**

primary auditory cortex (area A1) **198**
tinnitus **200**
tympanic membrane **195**
volley principle **197**

THOUGHT QUESTIONS

1. Why do you suppose that the human auditory system evolved sensitivity to sounds in the range of 20 to 20,000 Hz instead of some other range of frequencies?

2. The text explains how we might distinguish loudness for low-frequency sounds. How might we distinguish loudness for a high-frequency tone?

The Mechanical Senses

If you place your hand on the surface of your radio, you feel the same vibrations that you hear. If you practiced enough, could you learn to "hear" the vibrations with your fingers? No, they would remain just vibrations. If an earless species had enough time, might its vibration detectors evolve into sound detectors? Yes! In fact, our ears evolved in just that way. Much of evolution consists of taking something that evolved for one purpose and modifying it for another purpose.

The *mechanical senses* respond to pressure, bending, or other distortions of a receptor. They include touch, pain, and other body sensations, as well as vestibular sensation, which detects the position and movement of the head. Audition is also a mechanical sense because the hair cells are modified touch receptors. We considered it separately because of its complexity and importance.

▌ Vestibular Sensation

Try to read a page while you jiggle your head up and down or back and forth. You will find that you can read it fairly easily. Now hold your head steady and jiggle the page up and down, back and forth. Suddenly, you can hardly read it at all. Why?

TRY IT YOURSELF

When you move your head, the vestibular organ adjacent to the cochlea monitors movements and directs compensatory movements of your eyes. When your head moves left, your eyes move right. When your head moves right, your eyes move left. Effortlessly, you keep your eyes focused on what you want to see (Brandt, 1991). When you move the page, however, the vestibular organ cannot keep your eyes on target.

Sensations from the vestibular organ detect the direction of tilt and the amount of acceleration of the head. We are seldom aware of our vestibular sensations except under unusual conditions, such as riding a roller coaster. They are nevertheless critical for guiding eye movements and maintaining balance. Astronauts, of course, become acutely aware of the *lack* of vestibular sensation while in orbit. Mice with an impairment of vestibular sensation frequently lose their balance and fall down. They cannot swim or float because they are often upside down (Mariño et al., 2010).

The vestibular organ, shown in Figure 7.10, consists of the *saccule*, *utricle*, and three semicircular canals. Like the hearing receptors, the vestibular receptors are modified touch receptors. Calcium carbonate particles called *otoliths* lie next to the hair cells. When the head tilts in different directions, the otoliths push against different sets of hair cells and excite them (Hess, 2001).

The three **semicircular canals**, oriented in perpendicular planes, are filled with a jellylike substance and lined with hair cells. Acceleration of the head at any angle causes the jellylike substance in one of these canals to push against the hair cells. Action potentials initiated by cells of the vestibular system travel through part of the eighth cranial nerve to the brainstem and cerebellum. (The eighth cranial nerve contains both an auditory component and a vestibular component.)

For the vestibular organ, as far as we can tell, the ideal size is nearly constant, regardless of the size of the animal. Whales are 10 million times as massive as mice, but their vestibular organ is only 5 times as large (Squires, 2004).

STOP & CHECK

10. People with damage to the vestibular system have trouble reading street signs while walking. Why?

ANSWER

10. The vestibular system enables the brain to shift eye movements to compensate for changes in head position. Without feedback about head position, a person would not be able to correct the eye movements, and the experience would be like watching a jiggling book page.

▌ Somatosensation

The **somatosensory system**, the sensation of the body and its movements, is not one sense but many, including discriminative touch (which identifies the shape of an object), deep pressure, cold, warmth, pain, itch, tickle, and the position and movement of joints.

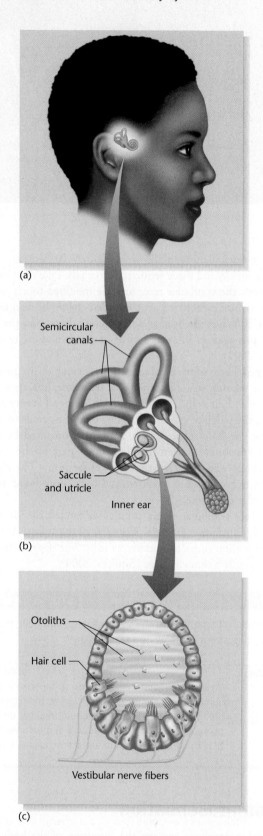

(a)

Semicircular canals

Saccule and utricle

Inner ear

(b)

Otoliths

Hair cell

Vestibular nerve fibers

(c)

FIGURE 7.10 Structures for vestibular sensation
(a) Location of the vestibular organs. (b) Structures of the vestibular organs. (c) Cross-section through a utricle. Calcium carbonate particles, called otoliths, press against different hair cells depending on the tilt and acceleration of the head. (© Cengage Learning 2013)

Somatosensory Receptors

The skin has many kinds of somatosensory receptors, including those listed in Figure 7.11. Table 7.1 lists the probable functions of these and other receptors (Iggo & Andres, 1982; Paré, Smith, & Rice, 2002). Others (not in the table) respond to deep stimulation, joint movement, or muscle movements.

A touch receptor may be a simple bare neuron ending (e.g., many pain receptors), a modified dendrite (Merkel disks), an elaborated neuron ending (Ruffini endings and Meissner's corpuscles), or a bare ending surrounded by other cells that modify its function (Pacinian corpuscles). Stimulation of a touch receptor opens sodium channels in the axon, thereby starting an action potential (Price et al., 2000).

Consider the **Pacinian corpuscle**, which detects sudden displacements or high-frequency vibrations on the skin (Figure 7.12). Inside its outer structure is the neuron membrane. The onion-like outer structure provides mechanical support that resists gradual or constant pressure. It thereby insulates the neuron against most touch stimuli. However, a sudden or vibrating stimulus bends the membrane, enabling sodium ions to enter, depolarizing the membrane (Loewenstein, 1960).

Merkel disks respond to light touch, such as if someone gently strokes your skin or if you feel an object (Maricich et al., 2009). Suppose you feel objects with thin grooves like these, without looking at them, and try to feel whether the grooves go left to right or up and down:

The experimenter varies the width of the grooves to find what are the narrowest grooves you can discern. On average, women can detect grooves about 1.4 mm apart, whereas men need the grooves to be about 1.6 mm apart. As sex differences go, this one is not particularly important, so your first question might be, "Who cares?" If you get past that question, your second question might be *why* men and women differ. Unlike many sex differences, this one is easy to explain. It reflects the fact that, on average, women have smaller fingers. Apparently they have the same number of Merkel disks compacted into a smaller area. If you compare men and women who have the same finger size, their touch sensitivity is the same (Peters, Hackeman, & Goldreich, 2009).

Certain chemicals stimulate the receptors for heat and cold. The heat receptor responds to **capsaicin**, the chemical that makes jalapeños and similar peppers taste hot. Szechuan peppers also stimulate the heat receptors and, in addition, stimulate certain touch receptors that give a tingling sensation (Bautista et al., 2008). Menthol and mint stimulate the coolness receptor (McKemy, Neuhausser, & Julius, 2002). So advertisements mentioning "the cool taste of menthol" are literally correct. Mice deficient in this receptor show little response to cold and fail to seek a warmer place when they become cold (Bautista et al., 2007).

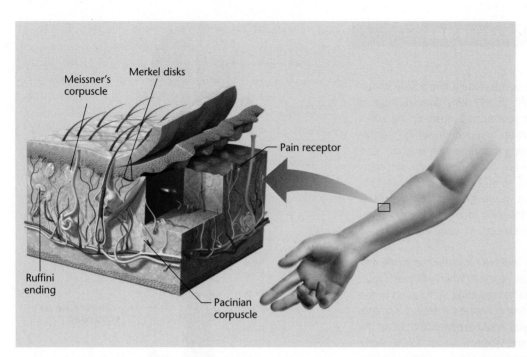

FIGURE 7.11 Sensory receptors in the skin
Different receptor types respond to different stimuli, as described in Table 7.1. (© Argosy Publishing Inc.)

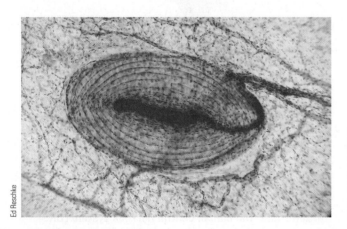

FIGURE 7.12 A Pacinian corpuscle
Pacinian corpuscles are receptors that respond best to sudden displacement of the skin or to high-frequency vibrations. The onion-like outer structure provides a mechanical support to the neuron inside it so that a sudden stimulus can bend it but a sustained stimulus cannot.

TABLE 7.1 Somatosensory Receptors and Probable Functions

Receptor	Location	Responds to
Free nerve ending (unmyelinated or thinly myelinated axons)	Near base of hairs and elsewhere in skin	Pain, warmth, cold
Hair-follicle receptors	Hair-covered skin	Movement of hairs
Meissner's corpuscles	Hairless areas	Sudden displacement of skin; low-frequency vibration (flutter)
Pacinian corpuscles	Both hairy and hairless skin	Sudden displacement of skin; high-frequency vibration
Merkel's disks	Both hairy and hairless skin	Light touch
Ruffini endings	Both hairy and hairless skin	Stretch of skin
Krause end bulbs	Mostly or entirely in hairless areas, perhaps including genitals	Uncertain

APPLICATIONS AND EXTENSIONS

Tickle

The sensation of tickle is interesting but poorly understood. Why does it exist at all? Why do you laugh if someone rapidly fingers your armpit, neck, or the soles of your feet? Chimpanzees respond to similar sensations with bursts of panting that resemble laughter. And yet tickling is unlike humor. Most people do not enjoy being tickled for long—if at all—and certainly not by a stranger. If a joke makes you laugh, you are more likely than usual to laugh at the next joke. But being tickled doesn't change your likelihood of laughing at a joke (C. R. Harris, 1999).

Why can't you tickle yourself? It is for the same reason that you can't surprise yourself. When you touch yourself, your brain compares the resulting stimulation to the "expected" stimulation and generates a weaker somatosensory response than you would experience from an unexpected touch (Blakemore, Wolpert, & Frith, 1998). Actually, some people can tickle themselves—a little—if they tickle the right side of the body with the left hand or the left side with the right hand. Try it. Also, you might be able to tickle yourself as soon as you wake up, before your brain is fully aroused. See whether you can remember to try that the next time you awaken. ■

TRY IT YOURSELF

Input to the Central Nervous System

Information from touch receptors in the head enters the central nervous system (CNS) through the cranial nerves. Information from receptors below the head enters the spinal cord and passes toward the brain through the 31 spinal nerves (Figure 7.13), including 8 cervical nerves, 12 thoracic nerves, 5 lumbar nerves, 5 sacral nerves, and 1 coccygeal nerve. Each spinal nerve has a sensory component and a motor component.

Each spinal nerve *innervates* (connects to) a limited area of the body called a **dermatome** (Figure 7.14). For example, the third thoracic nerve (T3) innervates a strip of skin just above the nipples as well as the underarm area. But the borders between dermatomes are less distinct than Figure 7.14 implies. Each dermatome overlaps one third to one half of the next dermatome.

The sensory information traveling through the spinal cord follows well-defined pathways toward the brain. The touch path has separate types of axons conveying deep touch and light touch (Löken, Wessberg, Morrison, McGlone, & Olausson, 2009). The pain path has different sets of axons conveying sharp pain, slow burning pain, and painfully cold sensations (Abrahamsen et al., 2008; Craig, Krout, & Andrew, 2001). That is, the nervous system codes the differences among these sensations in terms of which cells are

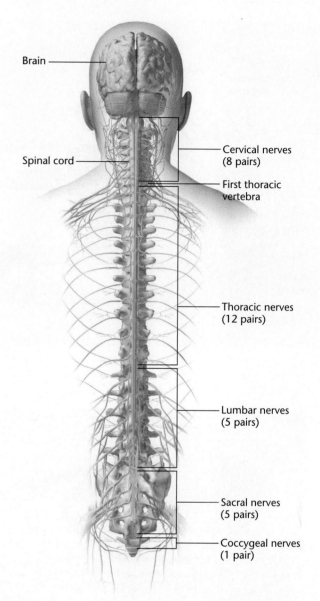

Brain

Spinal cord

Cervical nerves (8 pairs)

First thoracic vertebra

Thoracic nerves (12 pairs)

Lumbar nerves (5 pairs)

Sacral nerves (5 pairs)

Coccygeal nerves (1 pair)

FIGURE 7.13 The human central nervous system (CNS) Spinal nerves from each segment of the spinal cord exit through the correspondingly numbered opening between vertebrae. *(© Argosy Publishing Inc.)*

active. One patient had an illness that destroyed all the myelinated somatosensory axons from below his nose but spared his unmyelinated axons. He still felt temperature, pain, and itch, which depend on the unmyelinated axons. However, he had no sense of touch below the nose. Curiously, if someone lightly stroked his skin, he experienced a vague sense of pleasure. Recordings from his brain indicated no arousal of his primary somatosensory cortex but increased activity in the insular cortex, which is the secondary somatosensory cortex. The insular cortex responds to light touch as well as a variety of other pleasant emotional experiences (Björnsdotter, Löken, Olausson, Vallbo, & Wessberg, 2009). That is, he experienced

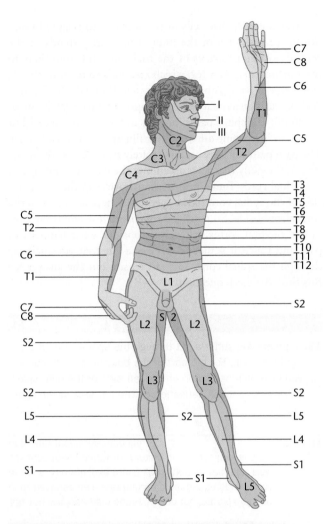

experiences. When weak, brief stimuli are applied to the fingers, people are conscious of only those that produce a certain level of arousal in the primary somatosensory cortex (Palva, Linkenkaer-Hansen, Näätäen, & Palva, 2005). If someone touches you quickly on two nearby points on the hand, you will probably have an illusory experience of a single touch midway between those two points. When that happens, the activity in the primary somatosensory cortex corresponds to that midway point (Chen, Friedman, & Roe, 2003). In other words, the activity corresponds to what you experience, not what has actually stimulated your receptors.

Another demonstration of that principle is called the *cutaneous rabbit illusion*. If someone taps you very rapidly six times on the wrist and then three times near the elbow, you will have a sensation of something like a rabbit hopping from the wrist to the elbow, with an extra, illusory, stop in between. The primary somatosensory cortex also responds as if you had been tapped in the intermediate location (Blankenburg, Ruff, Deichmann, Rees, & Driver, 2006). Unfortunately, you cannot easily try this yourself. For the illusion to work, you need all nine taps (six on the wrist and three near the elbow) within about four tenths of a second.

Damage to the somatosensory cortex impairs body perceptions. A patient with Alzheimer's disease who had damage in the somatosensory cortex had trouble putting her clothes on correctly. Also she could not point correctly in response to such directions as "show me your elbow," although she pointed correctly to objects in the room. When told to touch her elbow, her most frequent response was to feel her wrist and arm and suggest that the elbow was probably around there, somewhere (Sirigu, Grafman, Bressler, & Sunderland, 1991).

FIGURE 7.14 **Dermatomes innervated by the 31 sensory spinal nerves**
Areas I, II, and III of the face are not innervated by the spinal nerves but instead by three branches of the fifth cranial nerve. Although this figure shows distinct borders, the dermatomes actually overlap one another by about one third to one half of their width. *(© Cengage Learning 2013)*

the pleasurable, sensual aspects of touch even though he had no conscious detection of the touch itself.

The various areas of the somatosensory thalamus send their impulses to different areas of the primary somatosensory cortex, located in the parietal lobe. Two parallel strips in the somatosensory cortex respond mostly to touch on the skin. Two other parallel strips respond mostly to deep pressure and movement of the joints and muscles (Kaas, 1983). In short, various aspects of body sensation remain at least partly separate all the way to the cortex. Along each strip of somatosensory cortex, different subareas respond to different areas of the body. That is, the somatosensory cortex acts as a map of body location, as shown in Figure 4.24 on page 103.

Just as conscious vision depends on the primary visual cortex, the primary somatosensory cortex is essential for touch

STOP & CHECK

11. In what way is somatosensation several senses instead of one?

12. What evidence suggests that the somatosensory cortex is essential for the conscious perception of touch?

ANSWERS the primary somatosensory cortex. those touch stimuli that produce sufficient arousal in skin stimulation. **12.** People are conscious of only touch, heat, and so forth, and different parts of the somatosensory cortex respond to different kinds of **11.** We have several types of receptors, sensitive to

▌Pain

Pain, the experience evoked by a harmful stimulus, directs your attention toward a danger and holds your attention. The prefrontal cortex, which is important for attention, typically responds only briefly to any new light, sound, or touch. With pain, it continues responding as long as the pain lasts (Downar, Mikulis, & Davis, 2003).

Have you ever wondered why morphine decreases pain after surgery but not during the surgery itself? Or why some people seem to tolerate pain so much better than others? Or why even the slightest touch on sunburned skin is so painful? Research on pain addresses these and other questions.

Pain Stimuli and Pain Paths

Pain sensation begins with the least specialized of all receptors, a bare nerve ending (Figure 7.11). Some pain receptors also respond to acids, heat, or cold. Capsaicin, the chemical found in hot peppers such as jalapeños, also stimulates the receptors for painful heat. Capsaicin can produce burning or stinging sensations on many parts of your body, as you may have experienced if you ever touched the insides of hot peppers and then rubbed your eyes.

The axons carrying pain information have little or no myelin and therefore conduct impulses relatively slowly, in the range of 2 to 20 meters per second (m/s). The thicker and faster axons convey sharp pain. The thinner ones convey duller pain, such as postsurgical pain. Although pain messages reach the brain more slowly than other sensations, the brain processes pain information rapidly. Motor responses to pain are faster than motor responses to touch stimuli (Ploner, Gross, Timmerman, & Schnitzler, 2006).

Pain axons release two neurotransmitters in the spinal cord. Mild pain releases the neurotransmitter glutamate, whereas stronger pain releases both glutamate and **substance P** (Cao et al., 1998). Mice that lack receptors for substance P react to a severe injury as if it were a mild injury (DeFelipe et al., 1998). That is, without substance P, they do not detect the increased intensity.

The pain-sensitive cells in the spinal cord relay information to several sites in the brain. One path extends to the ventral posterior nucleus of the thalamus and from there to the somatosensory cortex, which responds to painful stimuli, memories of pain (Albanese, Duerden, Rainville, & Duncan, 2007), and signals that warn of impending pain (Babiloni et al., 2005). The spinal paths for pain and touch are parallel, but with one important difference, as illustrated in Figure 7.15: The pain pathway crosses immediately from receptors on one side of the body to a tract ascending the contralateral side of the spinal cord. Touch information travels up the ipsilateral side of the spinal cord to the medulla, where it crosses to the contralateral side. So pain and touch reach neighboring sites in the cerebral cortex. However, consider what happens to pain and touch if someone receives a cut that goes halfway through the spinal cord. You can reason out the answer for this Stop & Check question.

STOP & CHECK

13. Suppose you suffer a cut through the spinal cord on the right side only. For the part of the body below that cut, will you lose pain sensation on the left side or the right side? Will you lose touch sensation on the left side or the right side?

ANSWER

13. You will lose pain sensation on the left side of the body because pain information crosses the spinal cord at once. You will lose touch sensation on the right side because touch pathways remain on the ipsilateral side until they reach the medulla.

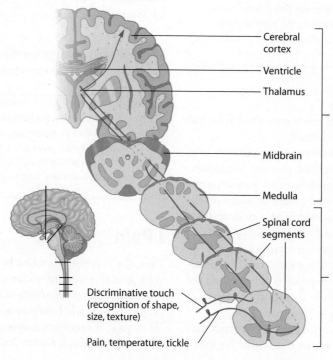

FIGURE 7.15 Spinal pathways for touch and pain

Pain information crosses to the contralateral side of the spinal cord at once, whereas touch information does not cross until the medulla. Touch and pain sensations from the right side of the body (not shown in the figure) are the mirror image of what you see here.
(© Cengage Learning 2013)

Cerebral cortex

Ventricle

Thalamus

From medulla to cerebral cortex, both touch and pain are represented on the contralateral side.

Midbrain

Medulla

Spinal cord segments

In spinal cord, information from one side of the body travels on ipsilateral side for touch and contralateral side for pain.

Discriminative touch (recognition of shape, size, texture)

Pain, temperature, tickle

Painful stimuli also activate a path that goes through the reticular formation of the medulla and then to several of the central nuclei of the thalamus, the amygdala, hippocampus, prefrontal cortex, and cingulate cortex (Figure 7.16). These areas react not to the sensation but to its emotional associations (Hunt & Mantyh, 2001). If you watch someone—especially someone you care about—experiencing pain, you experience a "sympathetic pain" that shows up mainly as activity in your cingulate cortex (Singer et al., 2004). A hypnotic suggestion to feel no pain decreases the responses in the cingulate cortex without much effect on the somatosensory cortex (Rainville, Duncan, Price, Carrier, & Bushnell, 1997). That is, someone responding to a hypnotic sensation still feels the painful sensation but reacts with emotional indifference. People with damage to the cingulate gyrus still feel pain, but it no longer distresses them. They return to normal activity and a more cheerful mood, despite chronic pain (Foltz & White, 1962).

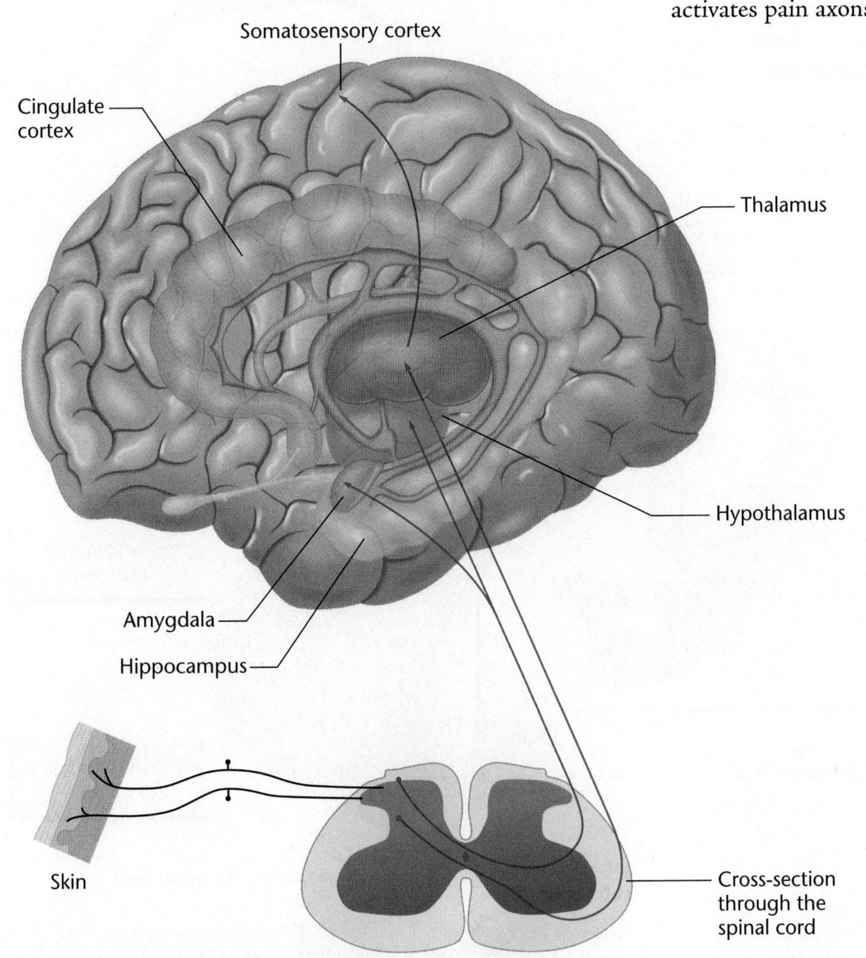

FIGURE 7.16 **Pain messages in the human brain**
A pathway to the thalamus, and from there to the somatosensory cortex, conveys the sensory aspects of pain. A separate pathway to the hypothalamus, amygdala, and cingulate cortex produces the emotional aspects. *(Hunt & Mantyh, 2001)*

Labels: Somatosensory cortex; Cingulate cortex; Thalamus; Hypothalamus; Amygdala; Hippocampus; Skin; Cross-section through the spinal cord

STOP & CHECK

14. How do jalapeños produce a hot sensation?

15. What would happen to a pain sensation if glutamate receptors in the spinal cord were blocked? What if substance P receptors were blocked?

ANSWERS

14. Jalapeños and other hot peppers contain capsaicin, which stimulates receptors that are sensitive to pain, acids, and heat. **15.** Blocking glutamate receptors would eliminate weak to moderate pain. (However, doing so would not be a good strategy for killing pain. Glutamate is the most abundant transmitter, and blocking it would disrupt practically everything the brain does.) Blocking substance P receptors makes intense pain feel mild.

Ways of Relieving Pain

Insensitivity to pain is dangerous. People with a gene that inactivates pain axons suffer repeated injuries and generally fail to learn to avoid dangers. One boy with this condition performed street theater in Pakistan by thrusting a knife through his arm or walking on burning coals. He died at age 14 by falling off a roof (Cox et al., 2006). Nevertheless, although we wouldn't want to eliminate pain, it would be good to hold it under control.

Opioids and Endorphins

After pain has alerted you to a danger, continuing pain messages are unnecessary. The brain puts the brakes on prolonged pain by **opioid mechanisms**—systems that respond to opiate drugs and similar chemicals. Candace Pert and Solomon Snyder (1973) discovered that opiates bind to receptors found mostly in the spinal cord and the **periaqueductal gray area** of the midbrain. Later researchers found that opiate receptors act by blocking the release of substance P (Kondo et al., 2005; Reichling, Kwiat, & Basbaum, 1988) (Figures 7.17 and 7.18).

The discovery of opiate receptors was exciting because it was the first evidence that opiates act on the nervous system rather than on the injured tissue. Furthermore, it implied that the nervous system must have its own opiate-type chemicals. The transmitters that attach to the same receptors as morphine are known as **endorphins**—a contraction

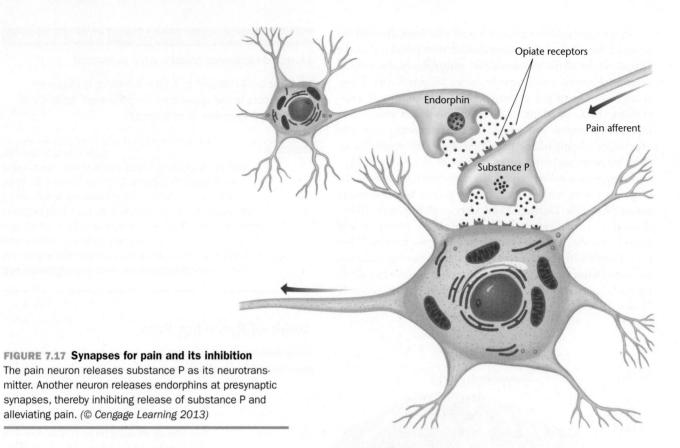

FIGURE 7.17 Synapses for pain and its inhibition
The pain neuron releases substance P as its neurotransmitter. Another neuron releases endorphins at presynaptic synapses, thereby inhibiting release of substance P and alleviating pain. *(© Cengage Learning 2013)*

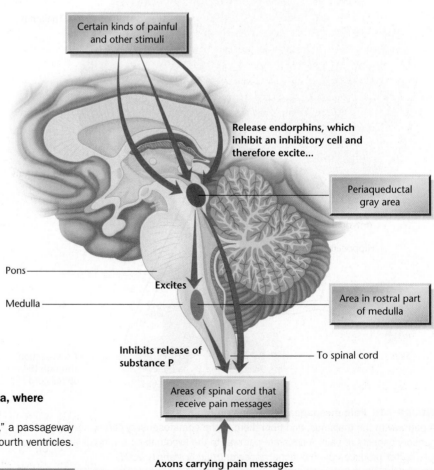

FIGURE 7.18 The periaqueductal gray area, where electrical stimulation relieves pain
Periaqueductal means "around the aqueduct," a passageway of cerebrospinal fluid between the third and fourth ventricles. *(© Cengage Learning 2013)*

of *endogenous morphines*. The brain produces several kinds of endorphins, which tend to relieve different types of pain, such as the pain from a cut and the pain from a burn (Scherrer et al., 2009).

Inescapable pain is especially potent at stimulating endorphins and inhibiting further pain (Sutton et al., 1997). Presumably, the evolutionary function is that continued intense pain accomplishes nothing when escape is impossible. Endorphins are also released during sex and when you listen to thrilling music that sends a chill down your spine (A. Goldstein, 1980). Those experiences tend to decrease pain. An enjoyable meal also decreases pain sensitivity (Foo & Mason, 2009), probably by releasing dopamine rather than endorphins (Schweinhardt, Seminowicz, Jaeger, Duncan, & Bushnell, 2009).

The discovery of endorphins provided physiological details for the gate theory, proposed decades earlier by Ronald Melzack and P. D. Wall (1965). The gate theory was an attempt to explain why some people withstand pain better than others and why the same injury hurts worse at some times than others. According to the **gate theory**, spinal cord neurons that receive messages from pain receptors also receive input from touch receptors and from axons descending from the brain. These other inputs can close the "gates" for the pain messages—and we now see that they do so at least partly by releasing endorphins. Although some details of Melzack and Wall's gate theory turned out to be wrong, the general principle is valid: Nonpain stimuli modify the intensity of pain. You have no doubt noticed this principle yourself. When you have an injury, you can decrease the pain by gently rubbing the skin around it or by concentrating on something else.

Morphine does not block the sharp pain of the surgeon's knife. For that, you need a general anesthetic. Instead, morphine blocks the slower, duller pain that lingers after surgery. Larger diameter axons, unaffected by morphine, carry sharp pain. Thinner axons convey dull postsurgical pain, and morphine does inhibit them (Taddese, Nah, & McCleskey, 1995).

Placebos

People also experience pain relief from placebos. A **placebo** is a drug or other procedure with no pharmacological effects. In many experiments, the experimental group receives the potentially active treatment, and the control group receives a placebo. Placebos have little effect for most medical conditions, but they often relieve pain (Hróbjartsson & Gøtzsche, 2001). People who receive placebos do not just *say* the pain decreased; scans of the brain and spinal cord also show a decreased response to pain (Eippert, Finsterbusch, Binget, & Büchel, 2009). However, a placebo's effects are mainly on emotional response to pain, not on the sensation itself. That is, a placebo decreases the response in the cingulate cortex but not the somatosensory cortex (Petrovic, Kalso, Petersson, & Ingvar, 2002; Wager et al., 2004).

Do placebos decrease pain just by increasing relaxation? No. In one study, people were given injections of capsaicin (which produces a burning sensation) into both hands and

both feet. They were also given a placebo cream on one hand or foot and told that it was a powerful painkiller. People reported decreased pain in the area that got the placebo but normal pain on the other three extremities (Benedetti, Arduino, & Amanzio, 1999). If placebos were simply producing relaxation, the relaxation should have affected all four extremities. Placebos relieve pain partly by increasing the release of opiates (Wager, Scott, & Zubieta, 2007) and partly by increasing release of dopamine (Schweinhardt et al., 2009).

In contrast, antiplacebos or *nocebos* (suggestions that the pain will increase) worsen pain by increasing anxiety. Antianxiety drugs weaken the effects of nocebos (Benedetti, Amanzio, Vighetti, & Asteggiano, 2006).

Cannabinoids and Capsaicin

Cannabinoids—chemicals related to marijuana—also block certain kinds of pain. Unlike opiates, cannabinoids act mainly in the periphery of the body rather than the CNS. Researchers found that if they deleted the cannabinoid receptors in the peripheral nervous system while leaving them intact in the CNS, cannabinoids lost most of their ability to decrease pain (Agarwal et al., 2007).

Another approach to relieving pain uses capsaicin. As mentioned, capsaicin produces a painful burning sensation by releasing substance P. However, it releases substance P faster than neurons resynthesize it, leaving the cells less able to send pain messages. Also, high doses of capsaicin damage pain receptors. Capsaicin rubbed onto a sore shoulder, an arthritic joint, or other painful area produces a temporary burning sensation followed by a longer period of decreased pain. However, do not try eating hot peppers to reduce pain in, say, your legs. The capsaicin you eat passes through the digestive system without entering the blood. Therefore, eating it will not relieve your pain—unless your tongue hurts (Karrer & Bartoshuk, 1991).

> **STOP & CHECK**
>
> **16.** Why do opiates relieve dull pain but not sharp pain?
>
> **17.** How do the pain-relieving effects of cannabinoids differ from those of opiates?
>
> **ANSWERS** **16.** Endorphins block messages from the thinnest pain fibers, conveying dull pain, but not from thicker fibers, carrying sharp pain. **17.** Unlike opiates, cannabinoids exert most of their pain-relieving effects in the peripheral nervous system, not the CNS.

Sensitization of Pain

In addition to mechanisms for decreasing pain, the body has mechanisms that increase pain. If you have ever been sunburned, you know how painful even a light touch can be on that sunburned skin. Damaged or inflamed tissue, such as sunburned skin, releases histamine, nerve growth factor, and other chemicals that help repair the damage but also magnify the responses of nearby heat and pain receptors (Chuang et al., 2001; Devor, 1996; Tominaga et al., 1998). Nonsteroidal anti-inflammatory drugs, such as ibuprofen, relieve pain by reducing the release of chemicals from damaged tissues (Hunt & Mantyh, 2001).

Some people suffer chronic pain long after an injury has healed. As we shall see in Chapter 13, a barrage of stimulation to a neuron can "potentiate" its synaptic receptors so that they respond more vigorously to the same input in the future. That mechanism is central to learning and memory, but unfortunately, pain activates the same mechanism. A barrage of painful stimuli potentiates the cells responsive to pain so that they respond more vigorously to similar stimulation in the future (Ikeda et al., 2006; Seal et al., 2009; Walters, 2009). The painful stimuli also release chemicals that decrease the release of GABA (an inhibitory transmitter) from nearby neurons (Knabl et al., 2008; Pernía-Andrade et al., 2009). In effect, the brain learns how to feel pain, and it gets better at it.

Therefore, to prevent chronic pain, it helps to limit pain from the start. Suppose you are about to undergo major surgery. Which approach is best?

A. Start taking morphine before the surgery.

B. Begin morphine soon after awakening from surgery.

C. Postpone the morphine as long as possible and take as little as possible.

Perhaps surprisingly, the research supports answer A: Start the morphine before the surgery (Coderre, Katz, Vaccarino, & Melzack, 1993). Allowing pain messages to bombard the brain during and after the surgery increases the sensitivity of the pain nerves and their receptors (Malmberg, Chen, Tonagawa, & Basbaum, 1997). People who begin taking morphine before surgery need less of it afterward.

Social Pain

Sometimes you might complain that someone hurt your feelings. After a romantic breakup, you might say you feel emotional pain. Many languages use the word for "hurt" or "pain" when referring to social disappointments and frustrations. Is this just an expression, or is emotional distress really like pain?

Hurt feelings do resemble physical pain in important regards. Imagine yourself in this experiment: You sit in front of a computer screen, playing a virtual ball-tossing game with two other people your own age. You "catch" a ball and then "throw" it to one of the others, who then tosses it back to someone. Unbeknownst to you, the other two have been paid to play certain roles. At first they throw it to you a fair share of times, but before long they start passing it back and forth between the two of them, leaving you out. Not much is at stake here, but still you might have hurt feelings from being left out. Experimenters monitored people's brain activity during this task and found significantly increased activity in the cingulate

cortex when someone felt left out (Eisenberger, Lieberman, & Williams, 2003). Recall that the cingulate cortex responds to the emotional aspect of pain.

Hurt feelings are like real pain in another way: You can relieve hurt feelings with the pain-relieving drug acetaminophen (Tylenol®)! Researchers repeated the virtual ball-tossing study, but gave some participants acetaminophen and the others a placebo. Those taking acetaminophen showed much less response in the cingulate cortex and other emotionally responsive areas. The researchers also asked college students to keep daily records about hurt feelings and social pain, while some took daily acetaminophen pills and others took a placebo. Those taking acetaminophen reported fewer cases of hurt feelings, and the frequency of hurt feelings declined over days as they continued taking the pills (De Wall et al., 2010). In short, hurt feelings are a great deal like being literally *hurt*. (And the next time someone says you hurt their feelings, just tell them to quit complaining and take a Tylenol!)

▶ **STOP & CHECK**

18. How do ibuprofen and other nonsteroidal anti-inflammatory drugs decrease pain?

19. Why is it preferable to start taking morphine before an operation instead of waiting until later?

20. In what ways are hurt feelings similar to physical pain?

ANSWERS

18. Anti-inflammatory drugs block the release of chemicals from damaged tissues, which would otherwise magnify the effects of pain receptors. 19. The morphine will not decrease the sharp pain of the surgery itself. However, it will decrease the barrage of pain stimuli that might sensitize pain neurons. 20. Hurt feelings activate the cingulate cortex, just as physical pain does. Also, acetaminophen relieves hurt feelings as well as physical pain.

Itch

Have you ever wondered, "What is itch, anyway? Is it a kind of pain? A kind of touch? Or something else altogether?" The answer is that it is a separate kind of sensation. Researchers have identified special receptors for itch (Y.-G. Sun et al., 2009) and special spinal cord paths conveying itch.

You have at least two kinds of itch. They feel about the same, but the causes are different. First, when you have mild tissue damage—such as when your skin is healing after a cut—your skin releases histamines that dilate blood vessels and produce an itching sensation. Second, contact with certain plants, especially cowhage (a tropical plant with barbed hairs), also produces itch. Antihistamines block the itch that histamines cause but not the itch that cowhage causes. Conversely, rubbing the skin with capsaicin relieves the itch that cowhage causes, but it has little effect on the itch that histamine causes (Johanek et al., 2007).

A particular spinal cord path conveys itch sensation (Andrew & Craig, 2001). Some of its axons respond to histamine itch and some to cowhage itch. However, these axons respond to heat as well, not just itch (S. Davidson et al., 2007). Itch axons activate certain neurons in the spinal cord that produce a chemical called *gastrin-releasing peptide*. Blocking that peptide has been shown to decrease scratching in mice without affecting their responses to pain (Sun & Chen, 2007).

The itch pathways are slow to respond, and when they do, the axons transmit impulses at the unusually slow velocity of only half a meter per second. At that rate, an action potential from your foot needs 3 or 4 seconds to reach your head. Imagine the delay for a giraffe or an elephant. You might try lightly rubbing some sandpaper or rough leaves against your ankle. Note how soon you feel the touch sensation and how much more slowly you notice the itch.

TRY IT YOURSELF

Itch is useful because it directs you to scratch the itchy area and remove whatever is irritating your skin. Vigorous scratching produces mild pain, and pain inhibits itch (Davidson, Zhang, Khasabov, Simone, & Giesler, 2009). Opiates, which decrease pain, increase itch (Andrew & Craig, 2001). This inhibitory relationship between pain and itch is the strongest evidence that itch is not a type of pain.

This research helps explain an experience that you may have noticed. When a dentist gives you Novocain before drilling a tooth, part of your face becomes numb. An hour or more later, as the drug's effects start to wear off, you may feel an itchy sensation in the numb portion of your face. But when you try to scratch it, you feel nothing because the touch and pain sensations are still numb. Evidently, the effects of Novocain wear off faster for itch than for touch and pain axons. The fact that you can feel itch at this time is evidence that it is not just a form of touch or pain. It is interesting that scratching the partly numb skin does not relieve the itch. Evidently, scratching has to produce some pain to decrease the itch.

STOP & CHECK

21. Do opiates increase or decrease itch sensations?

22. Suppose someone suffers from constant itching. What kinds of drugs might help relieve it?

ANSWERS

21. Opiates increase itch by blocking pain sensations. (Pain decreases itch.) **22.** Two kinds of drugs might help—antihistamines or capsaicin—depending on the source of the itch. Also, drugs that block gastrin-releasing peptide might help.

MODULE 7.2 ■ IN CLOSING

The Mechanical Senses

The mechanical senses alert you to many sorts of important information, from heat to cold and from pain to gentle, pleasant touch. The system consists of many types of receptors, separate spinal paths, and separate processing in the brain. Yet we perceive all this information together—for instance, when you feel the shape and temperature of an object.

You also integrate touch with other senses. For example, suppose someone touches you so lightly that you don't feel it. If at the same time you see a picture of someone touching you in just that way, you do feel it (Serino, Pizzoferrato, & Làdavas, 2008). All the senses combine to give a unified experience.

SUMMARY

1. The vestibular system detects the position and acceleration of the head and adjusts body posture and eye movements accordingly.   **203**

2. The somatosensory system depends on a variety of receptors that are sensitive to different kinds of stimulation of the skin and internal tissues.   **203**

3. The brain maintains several parallel somatosensory representations of the body.   **207**

4. Activity in the primary somatosensory cortex corresponds to what someone is experiencing, even if it is illusory and not the same as the actual stimulation.   **207**

5. Injurious stimuli excite pain receptors, which are bare nerve endings. Some pain receptors also respond to acids, heat, and capsaicin. Axons conveying pain stimulation to the spinal cord and brainstem release glutamate in response to moderate pain. They release both glutamate and substance P for stronger pain.   **208**

6. Painful information takes two routes to the brain. A route leading to the somatosensory cortex conveys the sensory information, including location in the body. A route to the cingulate cortex conveys the unpleasant emotional aspect. **208**

7. Opiate drugs attach to the brain's endorphin receptors. Endorphins decrease pain by blocking release of substance P and other transmitters from pain neurons. Both pleasant and unpleasant experiences release endorphins. **209**

8. A harmful stimulus may give rise to a greater or lesser degree of pain depending on other current and recent stimuli. According to the gate theory of pain, other stimuli can close certain gates and block the transmission of pain. **211**

9. Placebos decrease pain, especially the emotional aspect of pain. They do so partly by increasing opiate release. **211**

10. Chronic pain bombards pain synapses with repetitive input, and increases their responsiveness to later stimuli through a process like learning. Morphine is most effective as a painkiller if it is used promptly. Allowing the nervous system to be bombarded with prolonged pain messages increases the overall sensitivity to pain. **211**

11. Hurt feelings are like pain. They activate the cingulate cortex, as physical pain does, and acetaminophen relieves both hurt feelings and physical pain. **212**

12. Skin irritation releases histamine, which excites a spinal pathway responsible for itch. The axons of that pathway transmit impulses very slowly. They can be inhibited by pain messages. **212**

KEY TERMS

Terms are defined in the module on the page number indicated. They're also presented in alphabetical order with definitions in the book's Subject Index/Glossary, which begins on page 561. Interactive flashcards and crossword puzzles are among the online resources available to help you learn these terms and the concepts they represent.

capsaicin **208**
dermatome **206**
endorphins **209**
gate theory **211**

opioid mechanisms **209**
Pacinian corpuscle **204**
periaqueductal gray area **209**
placebo **211**

semicircular canals **203**
somatosensory system **203**
substance P **208**

THOUGHT QUESTION

How could you determine whether hypnosis releases endorphins?

The Chemical Senses

Suppose you had the godlike power to create a new species of animal, but you could equip it with only one sensory system. Which sense would you give it?

Your first impulse might be to choose vision or hearing because of their importance to humans. But an animal with only one sensory system is not going to be much like humans, is it? (And if you had only vision, and never tasted or felt pain or touch, would you have any idea what those visual stimuli meant?) To have any chance of survival, your animal will have to be small, slow, and probably one-celled. What sense will be most useful to such an animal?

Most theorists believe that the first sensory system of the earliest animals was a chemical sensitivity (G. H. Parker, 1922). A chemical sense enables a small animal to find food, avoid certain kinds of danger, and even locate mates.

Now imagine that you have to choose one of your senses to lose. Which one will it be? Most of us would not choose to lose vision, hearing, or touch. Losing pain sensitivity can be dangerous. You might choose to sacrifice your smell or taste.

Curious, isn't it? If an animal is going to survive with only one sense, it almost has to be a chemical sense, and yet to humans, with many other well-developed senses, the chemical senses seem dispensable. Perhaps we underestimate their importance.

▌Chemical Coding

Suppose you run a bakery and need to send messages to your supplier down the street. Suppose further you can communicate only by ringing three large bells on the roof of your bakery. You would have to work out a code.

One possibility would be to label the three bells: The high-pitched bell means, "I need flour." The medium-pitched bell calls for sugar, and the low-pitched bell calls for eggs. The more you need something, the faster you ring the bell. We shall call this system the *labeled-line* code because each bell has a single unchanging label. Of course, you can use it for only flour, sugar, or eggs.

Another possibility would be to set up a code that depends on a relationship among the bells. Ringing the high and medium bells equally means that you need flour. The medium

and low bells together call for sugar. The high and low bells call for eggs. Ringing all three together means you need vanilla extract. Ringing mostly the high bell while ringing the other two bells slightly means you need hazelnuts. And so forth. We call this the *across-fiber pattern* code because the meaning depends on the pattern across bells.

A sensory system could theoretically use either type of coding. In a system relying on the **labeled-line principle**, each receptor would respond to a limited range of stimuli, and the meaning would depend entirely on which neurons are active. In a system relying on the **across-fiber pattern principle**, each receptor responds to a wider range of stimuli, and a given response by a given axon means little except in comparison to what other axons are doing (R. P. Erickson, 1982).

In color perception, we encountered a good example of an across-fiber pattern code. For example, the perception of green requires stronger response by the medium-wavelength cones than the long- and short-wavelength cones. In auditory pitch perception, a given receptor responds best to a certain high-frequency tone, but it also responds in phase with a number of low-frequency tones (as do all the other receptors). Each receptor also responds to white noise (static) and to various mixtures of tones. Similarly, each taste and smell stimulus excites several kinds of neurons, and the meaning of a particular response by a particular neuron depends on the context of responses by other neurons. In short, nearly all perceptions depend on the pattern across an array of axons.

> **STOP & CHECK**

23. Of the following, which one uses an across-fiber pattern code?
(a) flipping a light switch
(b) playing a piano
(c) dialing a telephone number

ANSWER

23. Dialing a telephone number is an example of an across-fiber pattern code, because the result depends on the combination of numbers. No one of its numbers by itself has a clear meaning.

▮Taste

Taste results from stimulation of the **taste buds**, the receptors on the tongue. When we talk about the taste of food, we generally mean flavor, which is a combination of taste and smell. Whereas other senses remain separate throughout the cortex, taste and smell axons converge onto many of the same cells in an area called the endopiriform cortex (W. Fu, Sugai, Yoshimura, & Onoda, 2004). That convergence enables taste and smell to combine their influences on food selection.

Taste Receptors

The receptors for taste are not true neurons but modified skin cells. Like neurons, taste receptors have excitable membranes and release neurotransmitters to excite neighboring neurons, which in turn transmit information to the brain. Like skin cells,

however, taste receptors are gradually sloughed off and replaced, each one lasting about 10 to 14 days (Kinnamon, 1987).

Mammalian taste receptors are in taste buds located in **papillae** on the surface of the tongue (Figure 7.19). A given papilla may contain up to 10 or more taste buds (Arvidson & Friberg, 1980), and each taste bud contains about 50 receptor cells.

In adult humans, taste buds lie mainly along the edge of the tongue. You can demonstrate this principle as follows: Soak a small cotton swab in sugar water, saltwater, or vinegar. Then touch it lightly on the center of your tongue, not too far toward the back. If you get the position right, you will experience little or no taste. Then try it again on the edge of your tongue and notice the taste.

TRY IT YOURSELF

Now change the procedure a bit. Wash your mouth out with water and prepare a cotton swab as before. Touch the soaked portion to one edge of your tongue and then slowly

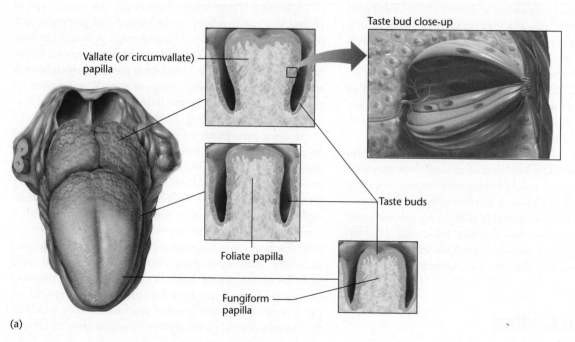

(a)

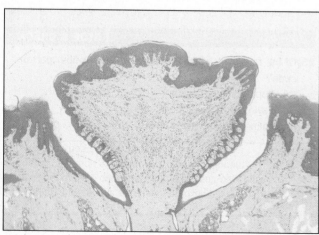

(b)

FIGURE 7.19 The organs of taste
(a) The tip, back, and sides of the tongue are covered with taste buds. Taste buds are located in papillae. (© *Argosy Publishing Inc.*) (b) Photo showing cross-section of a taste bud. Each taste bud contains about 50 receptor cells. (*SIU/Peter Arnold, Inc.*)

stroke it to the center of your tongue. It will seem as if you are moving the taste to the center of your tongue. In fact, you are getting only a touch sensation from the center of your tongue. You attribute the taste you had on the side of your tongue to every other spot you stroke (Bartoshuk, 1991).

How Many Kinds of Taste Receptors?

Traditionally, people in Western society have described sweet, sour, salty, and bitter as the "primary" tastes. However, some tastes defy categorization in terms of these four labels (Schiffman & Erickson, 1980; Schiffman, McElroy, & Erickson, 1980). How could we determine how many kinds of taste we have?

Further behavioral evidence for separate types of taste receptors comes from studies of the following type: Soak your tongue for 15 seconds in a sour solution, such as unsweetened lemon juice. Then try tasting some other sour solution, such as dilute vinegar. You will find that the second solution tastes less sour than usual. Depending on the concentrations of the lemon juice and vinegar, the second solution may not taste sour at all. This phenomenon, called **adaptation**, reflects the fatigue of receptors sensitive to sour tastes. Now try tasting something salty, sweet, or bitter. These substances taste about the same as usual. In short, you experience little **cross-adaptation**—reduced response to one taste after exposure to another (McBurney & Bartoshuk, 1973). Evidently, the sour receptors are different from the other taste receptors. Similarly, you can show that salt receptors are different from the others and so forth.

TRY IT YOURSELF

Although we have long known that people have at least four kinds of taste receptors, several types of evidence suggest a fifth also, which is glutamate, as in monosodium glutamate (MSG). The tongue has a glutamate receptor that resembles the brain's glutamate receptors (Chaudhari, Landin, & Roper, 2000). Recall the idea that evolution is "thrifty": After something evolves for one purpose, it can be modified for other purposes. Glutamate tastes somewhat like unsalted chicken broth. The English language had no word for this taste, so English-speaking researchers adopted the Japanese word *umami*.

In addition to the fact that different chemicals excite different receptors, they produce different rhythms of action potentials. For other senses we assume—rightly or wrongly—that what matters is the number of action potentials per unit of time. In taste, the temporal pattern is also important, perhaps more important. Figure 7.20 shows the responses of one brain neuron to five-second presentations of sucrose (sweet), NaCl (salty), HCl (sour), and quinine (bitter). This neuron responded to all four, but with different patterns over time. For example, its response to NaCl faded rapidly, whereas the response to sucrose took longer to start and then remained steady (Di Lorenzo, Chen, & Victor, 2009). Do these patterns actually code

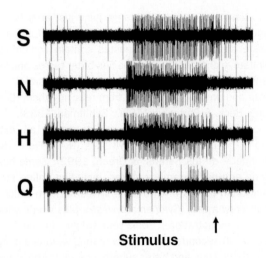

Stimulus

FIGURE 7.20 Responses of a cell in a rat brain to four tastes Each taste was presented for 5 seconds, marked by the Stimulus line at the bottom. Responses persisted until the tongue was washed with water, at the point marked by the arrow. The four lines represent S = sucrose (sweet), N = NaCl, table salt (salty), H = HCl, hydrochloric acid (sour), and Q = quinine (bitter). *(From "Quality time: Representation of a multidimensional sensory domain through temporal coding," by P. M. Di Lorenzo, J.-Y. Chen, & J. D. Victor, Journal of Neuroscience 2009, 29: 9227–9238.)*

taste experiences? Yes. Researchers stimulated rats' brain cells responsive to taste with an electrical pattern matching that for quinine. The rats backed away from whatever they were drinking at the time, reacting as if they were tasting something bitter (Di Lorenzo, Leshchinskiy, Moroney, & Ozdoba, 2009). Electrical stimulation at other temporal patterns did not cause this reaction.

APPLICATIONS AND EXTENSIONS

Chemicals that Alter the Taste Buds

One way to identify taste receptor types is to find procedures that alter one receptor but not others. For example, chewing a miracle berry (native to West Africa) gives little taste itself but temporarily changes sweet receptors. Miracle berries contain a protein—miraculin—that modifies sweet receptors, enabling acids to stimulate them (Bartoshuk, Gentile, Moskowitz, & Meiselman, 1974). If you try miracle berry extracts (available online), anything acidic will taste sweet in addition to its usual sour taste for the next half hour. Some people use these extracts as diet aids, so they can get sweet tastes without the calories.

But don't overdo it. A colleague and I once spent an evening experimenting with miracle berries. We drank straight lemon juice, sauerkraut juice, even vinegar. All tasted extremely sweet, but we awoke the next day with mouths full of ulcers.

Have you ever drunk orange juice just after brushing your teeth? How could something so wonderful suddenly taste so bad? Most toothpastes contain sodium lauryl sulfate, a chemical that intensifies bitter tastes and weakens sweet ones, apparently by coating the sweet receptors and preventing anything from reaching them (DeSimone, Heck, & Bartoshuk, 1980; Schiffman, 1983).

Another taste-modifying substance is an extract from the plant *Gymnema sylvestre* (R. A. Frank, Mize, Kennedy, de los Santos, & Green, 1992). Some health-food and herbal-remedy stores, including online stores, sell dried leaves of *Gymnema sylvestre*, from which you can brew a tea. (*Gymnema sylvestre* pills won't work for this demonstration.) Soak your tongue in the tea for about 30 seconds and then try tasting various substances. Salty, sour, and bitter substances taste the same as usual, but sugar becomes tasteless. Candies taste sour, bitter, or salty. (Those tastes were already present, but you barely noticed them because of the sweetness.) Curiously, the artificial sweetener aspartame (NutraSweet®) loses only some, not all, of its sweetness, implying that it stimulates an additional receptor besides the sugar receptor (Schroeder & Flannery-Schroeder, 2005). Note: Anyone with diabetes should avoid this demonstration because *Gymnema sylvestre* also alters sugar absorption in the intestines. Also note: One side effect of this demonstration is greenish bowel movements for the next few days. Don't panic if you notice that little souvenir of your experience. ∎

TRY IT YOURSELF

& Woodbury, 1994; Tomchik, Berg, Kim, Chaudhari, & Roper, 2007).

Bitter taste used to be a puzzle because bitter substances include a long list of dissimilar chemicals. Their only common factor is that they are to some degree toxic. What receptor could identify such a diverse set of chemicals? The answer is that we have not one bitter receptor but a family of 25 or more (Adler et al., 2000; Behrens, Foerster, Staehler, Raguse, & Meyerhof, 2007; Matsunami, Montmayeur, & Buck, 2000).

One consequence of having so many bitter receptors is that we detect a great variety of dangerous chemicals. The other is that because each type of bitter receptor is present in small numbers, we can't detect very low concentrations of bitter substances.

STOP & CHECK

24. Suppose you find a new, unusual-tasting food. How could you determine whether we have a special receptor for that food or whether we taste it with a combination of the other known taste receptors?

25. Although the tongue has receptors for bitter tastes, researchers have not found neurons in the brain itself that respond more strongly to bitter than to other tastes. Explain, then, how it is possible for the brain to detect bitter tastes.

26. If someone injected into your tongue a chemical that blocks the release of second messengers, how would it affect your taste experiences?

ANSWERS

24. You could test for cross-adaptation. If the new taste cross-adapts with others, then it uses the same receptors. If it does not cross-adapt, it may have a receptor of its own. Another possibility would be to find some procedure that blocks this taste without blocking other tastes. 25. Two possibilities: First, bitter tastes produce a distinctive temporal pattern of responses in cells sensitive to taste. Second, even if no one cell responds strongly to bitter tastes, the pattern of responses across many cells may be distinctive. Analogously, in vision, no cone responds primarily to purple, but we nevertheless recognize purple by its pattern of activity across a population of cones. 26. The chemical would block your experiences of sweet, bitter, and umami but should not prevent you from tasting salty and sour.

Mechanisms of Taste Receptors

The saltiness receptor is simple. Recall that a neuron produces an action potential when sodium ions cross its membrane. A saltiness receptor, which detects the presence of sodium, simply permits sodium ions on the tongue to cross its membrane. Chemicals that prevent sodium from crossing the membrane weaken salty tastes (DeSimone, Heck, Mierson, & DeSimone, 1984; Schiffman, Lockhead, & Maes, 1983). Sour receptors detect the presence of acids (Huang et al., 2006).

Sweetness, bitterness, and umami receptors resemble the metabotropic synapses discussed in Chapter 3 (He et al., 2004; Lindemann, 1996). After a molecule binds to one of these receptors, it activates a G-protein that releases a second messenger within the cell. Although each receptor detects just one kind of taste, several receptors feed into the next set of cells in the taste system. So, beyond the receptors, each neuron responds to two or more kinds of taste, and taste depends on a pattern of responses across fibers, not a system of pure labeled lines (R. P. Erickson, diLorenzo,

Taste Coding in the Brain

Information from the receptors in the anterior two thirds of the tongue travels to the brain along the chorda tympani, a branch of the seventh cranial nerve (the facial nerve). Taste information from the posterior tongue and the throat travels along branches of the ninth and tenth cranial nerves. What do you suppose would happen if someone anesthetized your chorda tympani? You would no longer taste anything in the anterior part of your tongue, but you probably would not notice, because you would still taste with the posterior part. However, the probability is about 40% that you would experience taste "phantoms," analogous to the phantom limb experience discussed in Chapter 5 (Yanagisawa, Bartoshuk, Catalanotto, Karrer, & Kveton, 1998). That is, you might experience taste even when nothing was on your tongue. Evidently, the inputs from the anterior and posterior parts of your tongue interact in complex ways.

The taste nerves project to the **nucleus of the tractus solitarius (NTS)**, a structure in the medulla (Travers, Pfaffmann, & Norgren, 1986). From the NTS, information branches out, reaching the pons, the lateral hypothalamus, the amygdala, the ventral-posterior thalamus, and two areas of the cerebral cortex (Pritchard, Hamilton, Morse, & Norgren, 1986; Yamamoto, 1984). One of these areas, the somatosensory cortex, responds to the touch aspects of tongue stimulation. The other area, known as the insula, is the primary taste cortex. Curiously, each hemisphere of the cortex receives input mostly from the ipsilateral side of the tongue (Aglioti, Tassinari, Corballis, & Berlucchi, 2000; Pritchard, Macaluso, & Eslinger, 1999). In contrast, each hemisphere receives mostly contralateral input for vision, hearing, and touch. A few of the major connections are illustrated in Figure 7.21. One connection from the insula goes to a small portion of the frontal cortex,

which maintains memories of recent taste experiences (Lara, Kennerley, & Wallis, 2009).

Individual Differences in Taste

A demonstration sometimes used in biology laboratory classes is to taste phenythiocarbamide (PTC) or 6-*n*-propylthiouracil (PROP). Most people—referred to as tasters—taste low concentrations as bitter, but many people—referred to as *nontasters*—fail to taste it except at high concentrations. One identified dominant gene controls most of the variance, although other genes contribute as well (Kim et al., 2003).

Researchers have collected extensive data about the percentage of nontasters in different populations, as shown in Figure 7.22 (Guo & Reed, 2001). The figure shows no obvious relationship between tasting PTC and cuisine. For example, nontasters are common in India, where the cuisine is spicy, and also in Britain, where it is relatively bland.

In the 1990s, researchers discovered that people with low sensitivity to bitter substances are also less sensitive than average to other tastes. People at the opposite extreme, known as **supertasters**, have the highest sensitivity to all tastes and mouth sensations (Drewnowski, Henderson, Shore, & Barratt-Fornell, 1998). Supertasters tend to have strong food preferences. On average, they like their favorite foods more than other people, and avoid their least-favorite foods more. Most

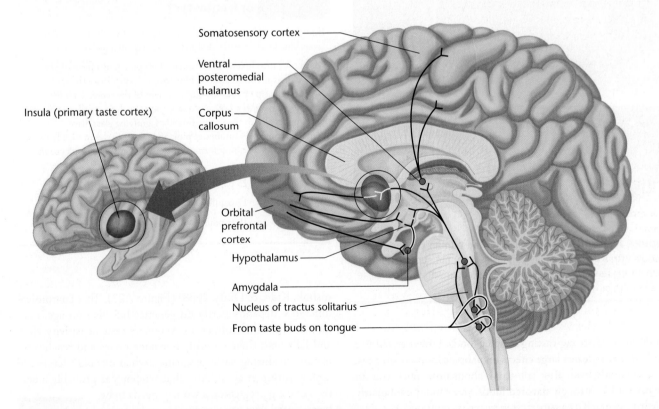

Somatosensory cortex

Ventral posteromedial thalamus

Insula (primary taste cortex)

Corpus callosum

Orbital prefrontal cortex

Hypothalamus

Amygdala

Nucleus of tractus solitarius

From taste buds on tongue

FIGURE 7.21 Major routes of impulses related to taste in the human brain
The thalamus and cerebral cortex receive impulses from both the left and the right sides of the tongue. *(Based on Rolls, 1995)*

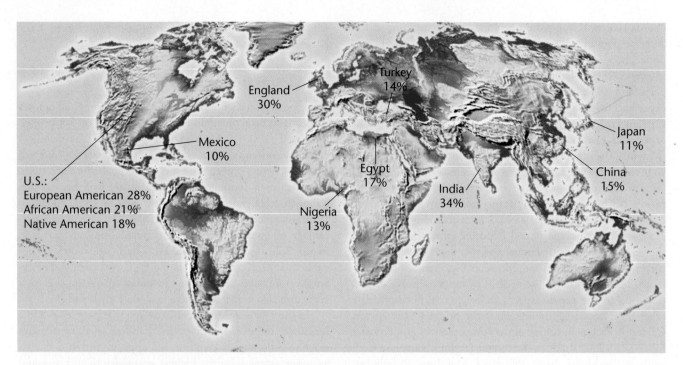

FIGURE 7.22 Percentage of nontasters in several human populations
Most of the percentages are based on large samples, including more than 31,000 in Japan and 35,000 in India. (© Cengage Learning 2013. Based on Guo & Reed, 2001)

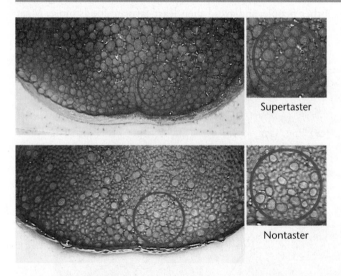

FIGURE 7.23 Fungiform papillae on the human tongue
People with a greater density of papillae (top) are supertasters, with strong reactions to intense tastes. People with fewer papillae are tasters or nontasters (bottom).

TABLE 7.2	Are You a Supertaster, Taster, or Nontaster?

Equipment: $\frac{1}{4}$-inch hole punch, small piece of wax paper, cotton swab, blue food coloring, flashlight, and magnifying glass

Make a $\frac{1}{4}$-inch hole with a standard hole punch in a piece of wax paper. Dip the cotton swab in blue food coloring. Place the wax paper on the tip of your tongue, just right of the center. Rub the cotton swab over the hole in the wax paper to dye a small part of your tongue. With the flashlight and magnifying glass, have someone count the number of pink, unstained circles in the blue area. They are your fungiform papillae. Compare your results to the following averages:

Supertasters: 25 papillae

Tasters: 17 papillae

Nontasters: 10 papillae

© Cengage Learning 2013

of them avoid strong-tasting or spicy foods. However, culture and familiarity exert large effects on people's food preferences. Consequently, even after you think about how much you do or do not like strongly flavored foods, you cannot confidently identify yourself as a supertaster, taster, or nontaster.

The difference between tasters and supertasters depends on the number of *fungiform papillae* near the tip of the tongue, with supertasters having the largest number (Hayes, Bar-

toshuk, Kidd, & Duffy, 2008) (Figure 7.23). That anatomical difference depends partly on genetics but also on age, hormones, and other influences. Women's taste sensitivity rises and falls with their monthly hormone cycles and reaches its maximum during early pregnancy, when estradiol levels are high (Prutkin et al., 2000). That tendency is probably adaptive: During pregnancy, a woman needs to be more careful than usual to avoid harmful foods.

If you would like to classify yourself as a taster, nontaster, or supertaster, follow the instructions in Table 7.2.

TRY IT YOURSELF

27. What causes supertasters to be more sensitive to tastes than other people are?

ANSWER

27. They have more taste buds near the tip of the tongue.

Olfaction

Olfaction, the sense of smell, is the response to chemicals that contact the membranes inside the nose. For most mammals, olfaction is critical for finding food and mates and for avoiding dangers. For example, rats and mice show an immediate, unlearned avoidance of the smells of cats, foxes, and other predators. Mice that lack certain olfactory receptors fail to avoid danger, as illustrated in Figure 7.24 (Kobayakawa et al., 2007).

Consider also the star-nosed mole and water shrew, two species that forage along the bottom of ponds and streams for worms, shellfish, and other edible invertebrates. We might assume that olfaction would be useless under water. However, these animals exhale tiny air bubbles onto the ground and then inhale them again. By doing so, they can follow an underwater trail well enough to track their prey (Catania, 2006).

A water shrew

We marvel at feats like this or at the ability of a bloodhound to find someone by following an olfactory trail through a forest, and we assume that we could never do anything like that. Of course, we can't follow an olfactory trail while standing upright, with our noses far above the ground! But what if you got down on your hands and knees and put your nose to the ground? Researchers blindfolded 32 young adults, made them wear gloves, and then asked them to try to follow a scent trail across a field. The scent was chocolate oil. (They decided to use something that people care about.) Most of the participants succeeded and improved their performance with practice. Figure 7.25 shows one example (Porter et al., 2007). So our olfaction is better than we might guess, if we give it a fair chance (even if it still doesn't compare to bloodhounds).

Olfaction is especially important for our food selection. Much of what we call "taste" or "flavor" is really the odor of the food. Try holding your nose while you eat, and notice how much flavor you lose.

Olfaction also plays an important, easily overlooked role in social behavior. If you were exposed to the smells of other people (with no other information about them), and you rated their desirability as a potential romantic partner, you would probably prefer people who smell a little different from yourself and your family members (Havlicek & Roberts, 2009). Women generally show this tendency more strongly than men do (Herz & Inzlicht, 2002). Avoiding a mate who smells like your brother or sister reduces the chance of inbreeding. It also increases the probability that your children will have a wide variety of immunities, because chemicals from the immune system contribute to body odors. Curiously, when women start taking contraceptive pills, their preference for a different-smelling mate decreases (Roberts, Gosling, Carter, & Petrie, 2008). One speculation is that a woman who cannot become pregnant (at that moment) no longer faces the risk of inbreeding.

FIGURE 7.24 The result of losing one type of olfactory receptor
Normal mice innately avoid the smell of cats, foxes, and other predators. This cat had just finished a large meal. (*Kobayakawa et al., 2007*)

FIGURE 7.25 A person following a scent trail
Most people successfully followed a trail with only their nose to
guide them. *(Reprinted by permission from Macmillan Publishers
Ltd. From:* Nature Neuroscience, 10, 27–29. *"Mechanisms of scent-
tracking in humans." J. Porter et al., 2007.)*

Olfactory Receptors

The neurons responsible for smell are the **olfactory cells**,
which line the olfactory epithelium in the rear of the nasal air
passages (Figure 7.26). In mammals, each olfactory cell has
cilia (threadlike dendrites) that extend from the cell body into
the mucous surface of the nasal passage. Olfactory receptors
are located on the cilia.

How many kinds of olfactory receptors do we have? Researchers answered the analogous question for color vision
in the 1800s but took much longer for olfaction. Linda Buck
and Richard Axel (1991) identified a family of proteins in
olfactory receptors, as shown in Figure 7.27. Like metabotropic neurotransmitter receptors, each of these proteins
traverses the cell membrane seven times and responds to a
chemical outside the cell (here an odorant molecule instead
of a neurotransmitter) by triggering changes in a G-protein
inside the cell. The G-protein then provokes chemical activities that lead to an action potential. The best estimate is
that humans have several hundred olfactory receptor proteins, whereas rats and mice have about a thousand types
(X. Zhang & Firestein, 2002). Correspondingly, rats distinguish among odors that seem the same to humans (Rubin
& Katz, 2001).

Although each chemical excites several types of receptors, the most strongly excited receptor inhibits the activity of
other ones in a process analogous to lateral inhibition (Oka,
Omura, Kataoka, & Touhara, 2004). The net result is that a
given chemical produces a major response in one or two kinds
of receptors and weak responses in a few others.

> **STOP & CHECK**

28. How do olfactory receptors resemble metabotropic neurotransmitter receptors?

ANSWER

28. Like metabotropic neurotransmitter receptors, an
olfactory receptor acts through a G-protein that triggers further events within the cell.

Implications for Coding

We have only three kinds of cones and five kinds of taste receptors, so researchers were surprised to find so many kinds
of olfactory receptors. That diversity makes possible narrow
specialization of functions. To illustrate, because we have only
three kinds of cones, each cone contributes to every color perception. Each olfactory receptor responds to only a few stimuli.
The response of one receptor might mean, "a fatty acid with a
straight chain of three to five carbon atoms." The response of
another might mean, "either a fatty acid or an aldehyde with a
straight chain of five to seven carbon atoms" (Araneda, Kini,
& Firestein, 2000; Imamura, Mataga, & Mori, 1992; Mori,
Mataga, & Imamura, 1992). The combined activity of those
two receptors identifies a chemical precisely.

The question may have occurred to you, "Why did evolution go to the bother of designing so many olfactory receptor
types? After all, color vision gets by with just three types of
cones." The main reason is that light energy can be arranged
along a single dimension—wavelength. Olfaction processes
airborne chemicals that do not range along a single continuum.

Messages to the Brain

When an olfactory receptor is stimulated, its axon carries
an impulse to the olfactory bulb (Figure 4.12). Although
the receptors sensitive to a particular chemical are scattered
haphazardly in the nose, their axons find their way to the
same target cells in the olfactory bulb, such that chemicals of
similar smell excite neighboring areas, and chemicals of different smell excite more separated areas (Uchida, Takahashi,
Tanifuji, & Mori, 2000). A slight change in a smell produces
a striking change in which cells are active, whereas a change
in smell intensity produces much less change (Niessing &
Friedrich, 2010). That is, cells of the olfactory bulb code the
identity of smells.

The olfactory bulb sends axons to the olfactory area of
the cerebral cortex. A complex substance such as a food activates a scattered population of cells (Lin, Shea, & Katz, 2006;

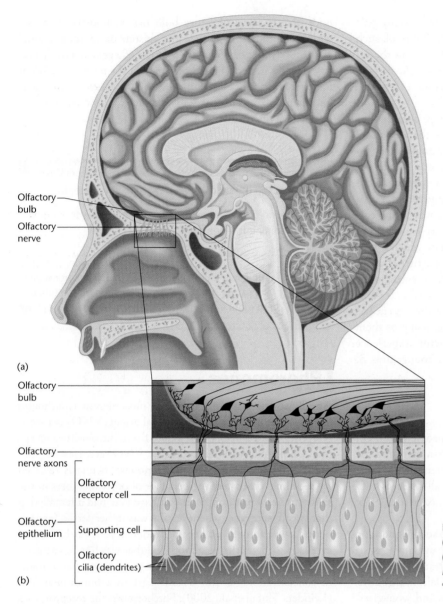

Olfactory bulb

Olfactory nerve

(a)

Olfactory bulb

Olfactory nerve axons

Olfactory receptor cell

Olfactory epithelium

Supporting cell

Olfactory cilia (dendrites)

(b)

FIGURE 7.26 Olfactory receptors
(a) Location of receptors in nasal cavity.
(b) Close-up of olfactory cells. (© Cengage Learning 2013)

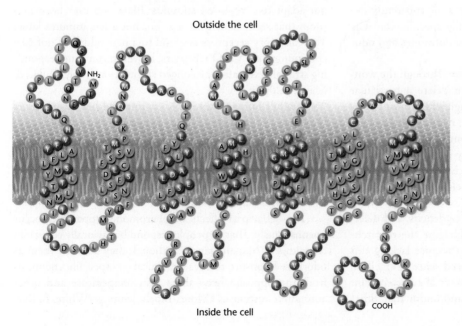

Outside the cell

Inside the cell

FIGURE 7.27 One of the olfactory receptor proteins

This protein resembles the synaptic receptor protein in Figure 3.17 on page 64. It responds to a chemical outside the cell and triggers activity of a G-protein inside the cell. Different olfactory receptors differ slightly in their structure. Each of the little circles in this diagram represents one amino acid of the protein. The light green circles represent amino acids that are the same in most of the olfactory receptor proteins. The dark green circles represent amino acids that vary.

(© Argosy Publishing Inc. Based on Buck & Axel, 1991)

Rennaker, Chen, Ruyle, Sloan, & Wilson, 2007). Many cells give their greatest response to a particular kind of food, such as berries or melons (Yoshida & Mori, 2007). As in the olfactory bulb, chemicals that smell similar to us evoke activity in neighboring cells (Howard, Plailly, Grueschow, Haynes, & Gottfried, 2009).

Olfactory receptors are vulnerable to damage because they are exposed to the air. Unlike your receptors for vision and hearing, which remain with you for a lifetime, an olfactory receptor has an average survival time of just over a month. At that point, a stem cell matures into a new olfactory cell in the same location as the first and expresses the same receptor protein (Nef, 1998). Its axon then has to find its way to the correct target in the olfactory bulb. Each olfactory neuron axon contains copies of its olfactory receptor protein, which it uses like an identification card to find its correct partner (Barnea et al., 2004; Strotmann, Levai, Fleischer, Schwarzenbacher, & Breer, 2004). However, if the entire olfactory surface is damaged at once by a blast of toxic fumes so that the system has to replace all the receptors at the same time, many of them fail to make the correct connections, and olfactory experience does not fully recover (Iwema, Fang, Kurtz, Youngentob, & Schwob, 2004).

Individual Differences

In olfaction, as with almost anything else, people differ. On average, women detect odors more readily than men, and the brain responses to odors are stronger in women than in men. Those differences occur at all ages and in all cultures that have been tested (Doty, Applebaum, Zusho, & Settle, 1985; Yousem et al., 1999).

In addition, if people repeatedly attend to some faint odor, young adult women gradually become more and more sensitive to it, until they can detect it in concentrations one ten-thousandth of what they could at the start (Dalton, Doolittle, & Breslin, 2002). Men, girls before puberty, and women after menopause do not show that effect, so it apparently depends on female hormones. We can only speculate on why we evolved a connection between female hormones and odor sensitization.

Finally, consider this surprising study: Through the wonders of bioengineering, researchers can delete a particular gene. One gene controls a channel through which most potassium passes in the membranes of certain neurons of the olfactory bulb. Potassium, you will recall from Chapter 2, leaves a neuron after an action potential, thereby restoring the resting potential. With no particular hypothesis in mind, researchers tested what would happen if they deleted that potassium channel in mice.

Ordinarily, deleting any gene leads to deficits, and deleting an important gene is often fatal. Imagine the researchers' amazement when they found that the mice lacking this potassium channel had a greatly enhanced sense of smell. In fact, you could say they have a superpower: They detect faint smells, less than one-thousandth the minimum that other

mice detect. Their olfactory bulb has an unusual anatomy, with more numerous but smaller clusters of neurons (Fadool et al., 2004). Exactly how the deletion of a gene led to this result remains uncertain, and presumably, the mice are deficient in some other way, or evolution would have deleted this gene long ago. Still, it is a remarkable example of how a single gene can make a huge difference.

> **STOP & CHECK**

29. What is the mean life span of an olfactory receptor?

30. What kind of person becomes most sensitive to a smell after sniffing it repeatedly?

ANSWERS

29. Most olfactory receptors survive a little more than a month before dying and being replaced. **30.** Young adult women become highly sensitive to a smell after sniffing it repeatedly.

▌ Pheromones

An additional sense is important for most mammals, although less so for humans. The **vomeronasal organ** (**VNO**) is a set of receptors located near, but separate from, the olfactory receptors. Unlike olfactory receptors, the VNO receptors are specialized to respond only to **pheromones**, chemicals released by an animal that affect the behavior of other members of the same species. For example, if you have ever had a female dog that wasn't neutered, whenever she was in her fertile (estrus) period, even though you kept her indoors, your yard attracted every male dog in the neighborhood that was free to roam.

Each VNO receptor responds to just one pheromone, in concentrations as low as one part in a hundred billion (Leinders-Zufall et al., 2000). Furthermore, the receptor does not adapt to a repeated stimulus. Have you ever been in a room that seems smelly at first but not a few minutes later? Your olfactory receptors respond to a new odor but not to a continuing one. VNO receptors, however, continue responding strongly even after prolonged stimulation (Holy, Dulac, & Meister, 2000).

In adult humans, the VNO is tiny and has no receptors (Keverne, 1999; Monti-Bloch, Jennings-White, Dolberg, & Berliner, 1994). It is vestigial—that is, a leftover from our evolutionary past. Nevertheless, part of the human olfactory mucosa contains receptors that resemble other species' pheromone receptors (Liberles & Buck, 2006; Rodriguez, Greer, Mok, & Mombaerts, 2000).

The behavioral effects of pheromones apparently occur unconsciously. That is, people respond behaviorally to certain chemicals in human skin even though they describe them as odorless. Exposure to these chemicals—especially chemicals from the opposite sex—alters skin temperature and other autonomic responses (Monti-Bloch, Jennings-White, & Berliner, 1998) and increases activity in the hypothalamus (Savic, Berglund, Gulyas, & Roland, 2001). The smell of a woman's sweat—especially if the woman was near her time of ovulation—increases a man's testosterone secretions (Miller & Maner, 2010). The smell of male sweat causes women to increase their release of cortisol (Wyart et al., 2007). Cortisol is a stress hormone, so the implication is that women are not altogether charmed by the smell of a sweaty man.

The best-documented effect of a human pheromone relates to the timing of women's menstrual cycles. Women who spend much time together find that their menstrual cycles become more synchronized, unless they are taking birth-control pills (McClintock, 1971; Weller, Weller, Koresh-Kamin, & Ben-Shoshan, 1999; Weller, Weller, & Roizman, 1999). To test whether pheromones are responsible for the synchronization, researchers exposed young volunteer women to the underarm secretions of a donor woman. In two studies, most of the women exposed to the secretions became synchronized to the donor's menstrual cycle (Preti, Cutler, Garcia, Huggins, & Lawley, 1986; Russell, Switz, & Thompson, 1980).

Another study dealt with the phenomenon that a woman in an intimate relationship with a man tends to have more regular menstrual periods than women not in an intimate relationship. According to one hypothesis, the man's pheromones promote this regularity. In the study, young women who were not sexually active were exposed daily to a man's underarm secretions. (Getting women to volunteer for this study wasn't easy.) Gradually, over 14 weeks, most of these women's menstrual periods became more regular than before (Cutler et al., 1986). In short, human body secretions probably do act as pheromones, although the effects are more subtle than in most other mammals.

STOP & CHECK

31. What is one major difference between olfactory receptors and those of the vomeronasal organ?

ANSWER

31. Olfactory receptors adapt quickly to a continuous odor, whereas receptors of the vomeronasal organ continue to respond. Also, vomeronasal sensations are apparently capable of influencing behavior even without being consciously perceived.

Synesthesia

Finally, let's consider something that is not one sense but a combination: **Synesthesia** is the experience some people have in which stimulation of one sense evokes a perception of that sense and another one also. In the words of one person, "To me, the taste of beef is dark blue. The smell of almonds is pale orange. And when tenor saxophones play, the music looks like a floating, suspended coiling snake-ball of lit-up purple neon tubes" (Day, 2005, p. 11).

No two people have quite the same synesthetic experience. Even when two people within the same family have synesthesia, one might see the letter J as green, while another insists that it is purple. Or one might see each letter as having a color, and another says each taste feels like a particular shape on the tongue (Barnett et al., 2008).

Various studies attest to the reality of synesthesia. People reporting synesthesia have increased amounts of gray matter in certain brain areas and altered connections to other areas (Jäncke, Beeli, Eulig, & Hänggi, 2009; Rouw & Scholte, 2007; Weiss & Fink, 2009). They also show behavioral peculiarities that would be hard to pretend. Try to find the 2 among the 5s in each of the following displays:

```
555555555555   555555555555   555555555555
555555555555   555555555555   552555555555
555555525555   555555555555   555555555555
555555555555   555555555525   555555555555
```

One person with synesthesia was able to find the 2 consistently faster than other people, explaining that he just looked for a patch of orange! However, he was slower than other people to find an 8 among 6s because both 8 and 6 look blue to him (Blake, Palmeri, Marois, & Kim, 2005). Another person had trouble finding an A among 4s because both look red but could easily find an A among 0s because 0 looks black (Laeng, Svartdal, & Oelmann, 2004). Oddly, however, someone who sees the letter P as yellow had no trouble finding it when it was printed (in black ink) on a yellow page. In some way, he sees the letter both in its real color (black) *and* its synesthetic color (Blake et al., 2005).

In another study, people were asked to identify as quickly as possible the shape formed by the less common character in a display like this:

```
TTTTTTT
TTTTTTT
TTCCCTTT
TTCCCTTT
TTTTTTT
TTTTTTT
```

Here, the correct answer is "rectangle," the shape formed by the Cs. People who perceive C and T as different colors find the rectangle faster than the average for other people. However, they do not find it as fast as other people would find the rectangle in this display, where the Cs really are in color:

```
TTTTTTT
TTTTTTT
TTCCCTTT
TTCCCTTT
TTTTTTT
TTTTTTT
```

What causes synesthesia? It clusters in families, suggesting a genetic predisposition (Barnett et al., 2008), but people are certainly not born with a letter-to-color or number-to-color synesthesia. (Children take a few years to learn the letters and numbers.) A study of 6- and 7-year-olds found some degree of synesthesia in about 10%—a considerably higher percentage than previous estimates for adults—but also found that the condition was incompletely developed at that age. Some reported colors for a few of the letters or numbers but not others. When they were retested a year later, many showed more complete and more consistent synesthesia (Simner, Harrold, Creed, Monro, & Foulkes, 2009). The implication is that synesthesia develops gradually over time.

When people misperceive a stimulus—as in an illusion—the synesthetic experience corresponds to what the person *thought* the stimulus was, not what it actually was (Bargary, Barnett, Mitchell, & Newell, 2009). This result implies that the phenomenon occurs in the cerebral cortex, not in the receptors or their first connections to the nervous system. Furthermore, for some people, the idea of a word triggers a synesthetic experience before they have thought of the word itself. One person who could not think of "castanets" said it was on the tip of the tongue . . . not sure what the word was, but it tasted like tuna (Simner & Ward, 2006). One man with color vision deficiency reports synesthetic colors that he does not see in real life. He calls them "Martian colors" (Ramachandran, 2003). Evidently, his brain can see all the colors, even though his cones cannot send the messages.

One hypothesis is that some of the axons from one cortical area branch into another cortical area. We don't know whether that is the best explanation in all cases, but it does apply to at least some. One woman suffered damage to the somatosensory area of her right thalamus. Initially she was, as expected, insensitive to touch in her left arm and hand. Over a year and a half, she gradually recovered part of her touch sensation. However, during that period, the somatosensory area of her right cortex was receiving little input. Some axons from her auditory system invaded the somatosensory cortex. As a result, she developed an unusual auditory-to-touch synesthesia. Many sounds cause her to feel an intense tingling sensation in her left arm and hand (Beauchamp & Ro, 2008; Naumer & van den Bosch, 2009).

STOP & CHECK

32. If someone reports seeing a particular letter in color, in what way is it different from a real color?

ANSWER

32. Someone who perceives a letter as yellow (when it is actually in black ink) can nevertheless see it on a yellow page.

MODULE 7.3 ■ IN CLOSING
Different Senses as Different Ways of Knowing the World

Ask the average person to describe the current environment, and you will probably get a description of what he or she sees and hears. If nonhumans could talk, most species would start by describing what they smell. A human, a dog, and a snail may be in the same place, but the environments they perceive are very different.

We sometimes underestimate the importance of taste and smell. People who lose their sense of taste say they no longer

enjoy eating and find it difficult to swallow (Cowart, 2005). Many people who lose the sense of smell feel permanently depressed. Taste and smell can't compete with vision and hearing for telling us about what is happening in the distance, but they are essential for telling us about what is right next to us or about to enter our bodies.

SUMMARY

1. Sensory information can be coded in terms of either a labeled-line system or an across-fiber pattern system. **215**

2. Taste receptors are modified skin cells inside taste buds in papillae on the tongue. **216**

3. We have receptors sensitive to sweet, sour, salty, bitter, and umami (glutamate) tastes. Taste is coded by the relative activity of different kinds of cells but also by the rhythm of responses within a given cell. **217**

4. Salty receptors respond simply to sodium ions crossing the membrane. Sour receptors respond to a stimulus by blocking potassium channels. Sweet, bitter, and umami

receptors act by a second messenger within the cell, similar to the way a metabotropic neurotransmitter receptor operates. **218**

5. Mammals have about 25 kinds of bitter receptors, enabling them to detect harmful substances that are chemically unrelated to one another. However, a consequence of so many bitter receptors is that we are not highly sensitive to low concentrations of any one bitter chemical. **218**

6. Part of the seventh cranial nerve conveys information from the anterior two thirds of the tongue. Parts of the

ninth and tenth cranial nerves convey information from the posterior tongue and the throat. The two nerves interact in complex ways. **218**

7. Some people, known as supertasters, have more fungiform papillae than other people do and are more sensitive to a variety of tastes. **219**

8. Olfactory receptors are proteins, each of them highly responsive to a few related chemicals and unresponsive to others. Vertebrates have hundreds of olfactory receptors, each contributing to the detection of a few related odors. **222**

9. Olfactory neurons in the cerebral cortex respond to complex patterns, such as those of a food. **222**

10. Olfactory neurons survive only a month or so. When the brain generates new cells to replace them, the new

ones become sensitive to the same chemicals as the ones they replace, and they send their axons to the same targets. **224**

11. In most mammals, each vomeronasal organ (VNO) receptor is sensitive to only one chemical, a pheromone. A pheromone is a social signal. Humans also respond somewhat to pheromones, although our receptors are in the olfactory mucosa, not the VNO. **224**

12. Some people experience synesthesia, a sensation in one modality after stimulation in another one. For example, someone might see purple neon tubes while listening to saxophones. In some cases, the explanation is that axons from one sense have invaded brain areas responsible for a different sense. **225**

KEY TERMS

Terms are defined in the module on the page number indicated. They're also presented in alphabetical order with definitions in the book's Subject Index/Glossary, which begins on page 561. Interactive flashcards and crossword puzzles are among the online resources available to help you learn these terms and the concepts they represent.

across-fiber pattern
   principle **215**
adaptation **217**
cross-adaptation **217**
labeled-line principle **215**

nucleus of the tractus solitarius
   (NTS) **219**
olfaction **221**
olfactory cells **222**
papillae **216**

pheromones **224**
supertasters **219**
synesthesia **225**
taste bud **216**
vomeronasal organ
   (VNO) **224**

THOUGHT QUESTIONS

1. In the English language, the letter t has no meaning out of context. Its meaning depends on its relationship to other letters. Indeed, even a word, such as *to*, has little meaning except in its connection to other words. So is language a labeled-line system or an across-fiber pattern system?

2. Suppose a chemist synthesizes a new chemical that turns out to have an odor. Presumably, we do not have a specialized receptor for that chemical. Explain how our receptors detect it.

CHAPTER 7 Interactive Exploration and Study

The **Psychology CourseMate** for this text brings chapter topics to life with interactive learning, study, and exam preparation tools, including quizzes and flashcards for the Key Concepts that appear throughout each module, as well as an interactive media-rich eBook version of the text that is fully searchable and includes highlighting and note taking capabilities and interactive versions of the book's **Stop & Check** quizzes and **Try It Yourself Online** activities. The site also features **Virtual Biological Psychology Labs, videos,** and **animations** to help you better understand concepts—logon and learn more at **www.cengagebrain.com**, which is your gateway to all of this text's complimentary and premium resources, including the following:

Virtual Biological Psychology Labs

Explore the experiments that led to modern-day understanding of biopsychology with the Virtual Biological Psychology Labs, featuring a realistic lab environment that allows you to conduct experiments and evaluate data to better understand how scientists came to the conclusions presented in your text. The labs cover a range of topics, including perception, motivation, cognition, and more. You may purchase access at **www.cengagebrain.com**, or login at **login.cengagebrain.com** if an access card was included with your text.

Videos

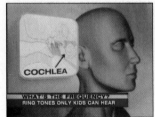

Ringtones and the Cochlea

Animations

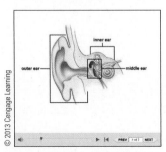

Learning Module: Hearing

Also available—

- Interactive Hearing Process Puzzle
- Sound Intensities

Suggestions for Further Exploration

Books

Pert, C. B. (1997). *Molecules of emotion.* New York: Simon & Schuster. Autobiographical statement by the woman who, as a graduate student, first demonstrated the opiate receptors.

Robertson, L. C., & Sagiv, N. (2005). *Synesthesia: Perspectives from cognitive neuroscience.* Oxford, England: Oxford University Press. A review of research on this fascinating phenomenon.

Thernstrom, M. (2010). *The Pain Chronicles.* New York: Farrar, Straus and Giroux. Why can some people withstand terrible injuries with little apparent pain? Why do others suffer endlessly? This book explores these and other questions about pain.

Websites

The Psychology CourseMate for this text provides regularly updated links to relevant online resources for this chapter, such as sites where you can test yourself for absolute pitch or (at the other extreme) tone-deafness. Other sites discuss hearing loss, pain, and olfaction.

Movement

8

MAIN IDEAS

1. Movements vary in sensitivity to feedback, skill, and variability in the face of obstacles.

2. Many brain areas contribute to movement control in different ways.

3. The role of conscious decisions is uncertain for the control of movement.

4. Brain damage that impairs movement also impairs cognitive processes. That is, control of movement is inseparably linked with cognition.

Before we get started, please try this: Get out a pencil and a sheet of paper, and put the pencil in your nonpreferred hand. For example, if you are right-handed, put it in your left hand. Now, with that hand, draw a face in profile—that is, facing one direction or the other but not straight ahead. *Please do this now before reading further.*

TRY IT
YOURSELF

If you tried the demonstration, you probably notice that your drawing is more childlike than usual. It is as if part of your brain stored the way you used to draw as a young child. Now, if you are right-handed and therefore drew the face with your left hand, why did you draw it facing to the right? At least I assume you did, because more than two thirds of right-handers drawing with their left hand draw the profile facing right. They revert to the pattern shown by young children. Up to about age 5 or 6, children drawing with the right hand almost always draw people and animals facing left, but when using the left hand, they almost always draw them facing right. But *why?* They say, "it's easier that way," but *why* is it easier that way? We have much to learn about the control of movement and how it relates to perception, motivation, and other functions.

OPPOSITE: Ultimately, what brain activity accomplishes is the control of movement—a far more complex process than it might seem.

The Control of Movement

Why do we have brains? Plants survive just fine without them. So do sponges, which are animals, even if they don't act like them. But plants don't move, and neither do sponges. A sea squirt (a marine invertebrate) has a brain during its infant stage, during which it swims, but when it transforms into an adult, it attaches to a surface, becomes a stationary filter feeder, and digests its own brain, as if to say, "Now that I've stopped traveling, I won't need this brain thing anymore." Ultimately, the purpose of a brain is to control behaviors, and behaviors are movements.

"But wait," you might reply. "We need brains for other things, too, don't we? Like seeing, hearing, finding food, talking, understanding speech . . ."

Well, what would be the value of seeing and hearing if you couldn't do anything? Finding food or chewing it requires movement, and so does talking. Understanding speech wouldn't do you much good unless you could do something about it. A great brain without muscles would be like a computer without a monitor, printer, or other output. No matter how powerful the internal processing, it would be useless.

❚ Muscles and Their Movements

All animal movement depends on muscle contractions. Vertebrate muscles fall into three categories (Figure 8.1): **smooth muscles**, which control the digestive system and other organs; **skeletal**, or **striated**, **muscles**, which control movement of the body in relation to the environment; and **cardiac muscles** (the heart muscles), which have properties intermediate between those of smooth and skeletal muscles.

Each muscle is composed of many fibers, as Figure 8.2 illustrates. Although each muscle fiber receives information from only one axon, a given axon may innervate more than one muscle fiber. For example, the eye muscles have a ratio of about one axon per three muscle fibers, and the biceps muscles of the arm have a ratio of one axon to more than a hundred fibers (Evarts, 1979). This difference allows the eye to move more precisely than the biceps.

A **neuromuscular junction** is a synapse between a motor neuron axon and a muscle fiber. In skeletal muscles, every axon releases acetylcholine at the neuromuscular junction, and acetylcholine always excites the muscle to contract. A deficit of acetylcholine or its receptors impairs movement. Each muscle makes just one movement, contraction. There is no message causing relaxation; the muscle simply relaxes when it receives no message to contract. There is also no message to move a muscle in the opposite direction. Moving a leg or arm back and forth requires opposing sets of muscles, called **antagonistic muscles**. At your elbow, for example, your **flexor** muscle brings your hand toward your shoulder and your **extensor** muscle straightens the arm (Figure 8.3).

▶ STOP & CHECK

1. Why can the eye muscles move with greater precision than the biceps muscles?

2. Which transmitter causes a skeletal muscle to contract?

ANSWERS **1.** Each axon to the biceps muscles innervates about a hundred fibers; therefore, it is not possible to change the movement by a small amount. In contrast, an axon to the eye muscles innervates only about three fibers. **2.** Acetylcholine. And remember that a muscle's only movement is to contract.

Adult sea squirts attach to a surface, never move again, and digest their own brains.

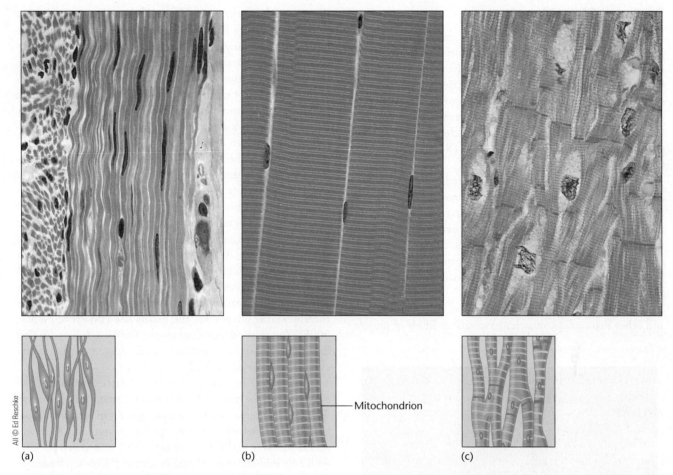

(a)   (b)   (c)

FIGURE 8.1 Vertebrate muscles

(a) Smooth muscle, found in the intestines and other organs, consists of long, thin cells. (b) Skeletal, or striated, muscle consists of long cylindrical fibers with stripes. (c) Cardiac muscle, found in the heart, consists of fibers that fuse together at various points. Because of these fusions, cardiac muscles contract together, not independently. *(Illustrations after Starr & Taggart, 1989)*

FIGURE 8.2 An axon branching to innervate several muscle fibers

Movements can be more precise where each axon innervates only a few fibers, as with eye muscles, than where it innervates many fibers, as with biceps muscles.

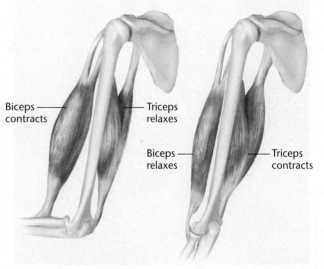

FIGURE 8.3 Antagonistic muscles

The biceps of the arm is a flexor. The triceps is an extensor. *(© Argosy Publishing Inc.)*

Fast and Slow Muscles

Imagine you are a small fish. Your only defense against bigger fish, diving birds, and other predators is your ability to swim away (Figure 8.4). Your temperature is the same as the water around you, and muscle contractions, being chemical processes, slow down in the cold. So when the water gets cold, presumably you will move slowly, right? Strangely, you will not. You will have to use more muscles than before, but you will swim at about the same speed (Rome, Loughna, & Goldspink, 1984).

A fish has three kinds of muscles: red, pink, and white. Red muscles produce the slowest movements, but they do not fatigue. White muscles produce the fastest movements, but they fatigue rapidly. Pink muscles are intermediate in speed and rate of fatigue. At high temperatures, a fish relies mostly on red and pink muscles. At colder temperatures, the fish relies more and more on white muscles, maintaining its speed but fatiguing faster.

All right, you can stop imagining you are a fish. Human and other mammalian muscles have various kinds of muscle

Tui De Roy/Minden Pictures

FIGURE 8.4 Temperature and movement
Fish are "coldblooded," but many of their predators (e.g., this pelican) are not. At cold temperatures, each fish muscle contracts more slowly than usual, but a fish compensates by using more muscles.

fibers mixed together, not in separate bundles as in fish. Our muscle types range from **fast-twitch fibers** with fast contractions and rapid fatigue to **slow-twitch fibers** with less vigorous contractions and no fatigue (Hennig & Lømo, 1985). We rely on our slow-twitch and intermediate fibers for nonstrenuous activities. For example, you could talk for hours without fatiguing your lip muscles. You might walk for a long time, too. But if you run up a steep hill at full speed, you switch to fast-twitch fibers, which fatigue rapidly.

Slow-twitch fibers do not fatigue because they are **aerobic**—they use oxygen during their movements. You can think of them as "pay as you go." Prolonged use of fast-twitch fibers results in fatigue because the process is **anaerobic**—using reactions that do not require oxygen at the time but need oxygen for recovery. Using them builds up an *oxygen debt*. Imagine yourself bicycling. At first your activity is aerobic, using your slow-twitch fibers. However, your muscles use glucose, and after a while your glucose supplies begin to dwindle. Low glucose activates a gene that inhibits the muscles from using glucose, thereby saving glucose for the brain's use (Booth & Neufer, 2005). You start relying more on the fast-twitch muscles that depend on anaerobic use of fatty acids. As you continue bicycling, your muscles gradually fatigue.

People vary in their percentages of fast-twitch and slow-twitch fibers, for reasons based on both genetics and training. The Swedish ultramarathon runner Bertil Järlaker built up so many slow-twitch fibers in his legs that he once ran 3,520 km (2,188 miles) in 50 days (an average of 1.7 marathons per day) with only minimal signs of pain or fatigue (Sjöström, Friden, & Ekblom, 1987). Contestants in the Primal Quest race have to walk or run 125 km, cycle 250 km, kayak 131 km, rappel 97 km up canyon walls, swim 13 km in rough water, ride horseback, and climb rocks over 6 days in summer heat. To endure this ordeal, contestants need many adaptations of their muscles and metabolism (Pearson, 2006). In contrast, competitive sprinters have more fast-twitch fibers and other adaptations for speed instead of endurance (Andersen, Klitgaard, & Saltin, 1994; Canepari et al., 2005).

STOP & CHECK

3. In what way are fish movements impaired in cold water?

4. Duck breast muscles are red ("dark meat"), whereas chicken breast muscles are white. Which species probably can fly for a longer time before fatiguing?

5. Why is an ultramarathoner like Bertil Järlaker probably not impressive at short-distance races?

ANSWERS

3. Although a fish can move rapidly in cold water, it must rely on white muscles that fatigue easily.
4. Ducks can fly great distances, as they often do during migration. The white muscle of a chicken breast has the power necessary to get a heavy body off the ground, but it fatigues rapidly. Chickens seldom fly far.
5. An ultramarathoner builds up large numbers of slow-twitch fibers at the expense of fast-twitch fibers. Therefore, endurance is great, but maximum speed is not.

Muscle Control by Proprioceptors

As you are walking along on a bumpy road, you occasionally set your foot down a little too hard or not quite hard enough. You adjust your posture and maintain your balance without even thinking about it. How do you do that?

A baby is lying on its back. You playfully tug its foot and then let go. At once, the leg bounces back to its original position. How and why?

In both cases, proprioceptors control the movement (Figure 8.5). A **proprioceptor** (from the Latin *proprius*, meaning one's own) is a receptor that detects the position or movement of a part of the body—in these cases, a muscle. Muscle proprioceptors detect the stretch and tension of a muscle and send messages that enable the spinal cord to adjust its signals. When a muscle is stretched, the spinal cord sends a reflexive signal to contract it. This **stretch reflex** is *caused* by a stretch; it does not *produce* one.

One kind of proprioceptor is the **muscle spindle**, a receptor parallel to the muscle that responds to a stretch (Merton, 1972; Miles & Evarts, 1979). Whenever the muscle spindle is stretched, its sensory nerve sends a message to a motor neuron in the spinal cord, which in turn sends a message back to the muscles surrounding the spindle, causing a contraction. Note that this reflex provides for negative feedback: When a muscle and its spindle are stretched, the spindle sends a message that results in a muscle contraction that opposes the stretch.

When you set your foot down on a bump on the road, your knee bends a bit, stretching the extensor muscles of that leg. The sensory nerves of the spindles send action potentials to the motor neuron in the spinal cord, and the motor neuron sends action potentials to the extensor muscle. Contracting the extensor muscle straightens the leg, adjusting for the bump on the road.

A physician who asks you to cross your legs and then taps just below the knee is testing your stretch reflexes (Figure 8.6). The tap stretches the extensor muscles and their spindles, resulting in a message that jerks the lower leg upward. The same reflex contributes to walking; raising the upper leg reflexively moves the lower leg forward in readiness for the next step.

Golgi tendon organs, also proprioceptors, respond to increases in muscle tension. Located in the tendons at opposite ends of a muscle, they act as a brake against an excessively vigorous contraction. Some muscles are so strong that they could damage themselves if too many fibers contracted at once. Golgi tendon organs detect the tension that results during a muscle contraction. Their impulses travel to the spinal cord, where they excite interneurons that inhibit the motor neurons. In short, a vigorous muscle contraction inhibits further contraction by activating the Golgi tendon organs.

TRY IT YOURSELF

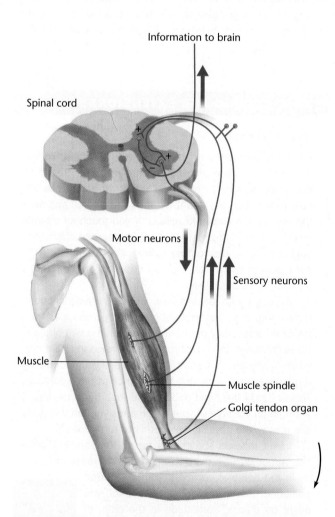

FIGURE 8.5 Two kinds of proprioceptors regulate muscle contractions
When a muscle is stretched, nerves from the muscle spindles transmit impulses that lead to contraction of the muscle. Contraction of the muscle stimulates the Golgi tendon organ, which acts as a brake or shock absorber to prevent a contraction that is too quick or extreme. (© Argosy Publishing Inc.)

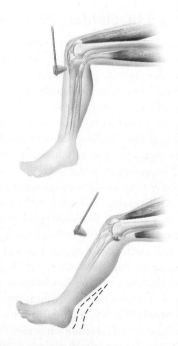

FIGURE 8.6 The knee-jerk reflex
This is one example of a stretch reflex. (© Argosy Publishing Inc.)

The proprioceptors not only control important reflexes but also provide the brain with information. Here is an illusion that you can try: Find a small, dense object and a larger, less dense object that weighs the same as the small one. For example, you might try a lemon and a hollowed-out orange, with the peel pasted back together so it appears to be intact. Drop one of the objects onto someone's hand while he or she is watching. (Watching is essential.) Then remove it and drop the other object onto the same hand. Most people report that the small one felt heavier. The reason is that with the larger object, people set themselves up with an expectation of a heavier weight. The actual weight displaces their proprioceptors less than expected and therefore yields the perception of a lighter object.

STOP & CHECK

6. If you hold your arm straight out and someone pulls it down slightly, it quickly bounces back. Which proprioceptor is responsible?

7. What is the function of Golgi tendon organs?

ANSWERS

6. The muscle spindle. 7. Golgi tendon organs respond to muscle tension and thereby prevent excessively strong muscle contractions.

Units of Movement

Movements include speaking, walking, threading a needle, and throwing a basketball while off balance and evading two defenders. Different kinds of movement depend on different kinds of control by the nervous system.

Voluntary and Involuntary Movements

Reflexes are consistent automatic responses to stimuli. We generally think of reflexes as *involuntary* because they are insensitive to reinforcements, punishments, and motivations. The stretch reflex is one example. Another is the constriction of the pupil in response to bright light.

Few behaviors are purely voluntary or involuntary, reflexive or nonreflexive. Even walking includes involuntary components. When you walk, you automatically compensate for the bumps and irregularities in the road. You also swing your arms automatically as an involuntary consequence of walking.

Try this: While sitting, raise your right foot and make clockwise circles. Keep your foot moving while you draw the number 6 in the air with your right hand. Or just move your right hand in counterclockwise circles. You will probably reverse the direction of your foot movement. It is difficult to make voluntary clockwise and counterclockwise movements on the same side of the body at the same time. Curiously, it is not at all difficult to move your left hand in one direction while moving the right foot in the opposite direction.

Even when a reaction to a stimulus is not a reflex, it differs from a spontaneous behavior. Many old Western movies included a gunfight between the hero and the villain. Always the villain drew his gun first, but the hero was faster, and even though he started later, he won the draw. Researchers wondered, is that realistic? Could someone draw second and still win? The answer is yes, sometimes. When you react to a stimulus, you move faster than when your action is spontaneous. In one experiment, two people had a competition. While watching each other, they had to wait an unpredictable period of time—if they acted too soon, the results didn't count—and then press three buttons in a particular order (analogous to drawing a gun and shooting). So, each person sometimes initiated the action and sometimes reacted after seeing the other person act, but the one who completed the action sooner was the winner. On average, when people were reacting to the other person's act, they made the movements 9% faster. Usually that difference was not enough to make up for starting second, but it illustrates the point that we move faster in response to a stimulus than when we decide on our own (Welchman, Stanley, Schomers, Miall, & Bülthoff, 2010).

APPLICATIONS AND EXTENSIONS

Infant Reflexes

Infants have several reflexes not seen in adults. For example, if you place an object firmly in an infant's hand, the infant grasps it (the **grasp reflex**). If you stroke the sole of the foot, the infant extends the big toe and fans the others (the **Babinski reflex**). If you touch an infant's cheek, the infant turns toward the stimulated cheek and begins to suck (the **rooting reflex**). The rooting reflex is not a pure reflex, as its intensity depends on the infant's arousal and hunger level.

Although such reflexes fade with age, the connections remain intact, not lost but suppressed by messages from the brain, especially the frontal cortex. If the cerebral cortex is damaged, the infant reflexes are released from inhibition. A physician who strokes the sole of your foot during a physical exam is looking for evidence of brain damage. This is hardly the most dependable test, but it is easy. If a stroke on the sole of your foot makes you fan your toes like a baby, the physician proceeds to further tests.

Infant reflexes sometimes return temporarily if alcohol, carbon dioxide, or other chemicals decrease the activity in the cerebral cortex. If you notice that someone has drunk too much alcohol, you might try placing something in the palm of the person's hand to see whether you can elicit a grasp reflex.

Infants and children also show certain *allied reflexes* more strongly than adults. If dust blows in your face, you reflexively close your eyes and mouth and

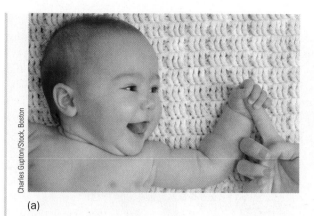

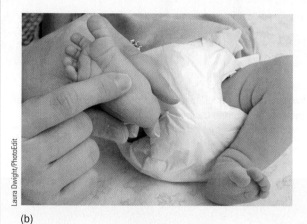

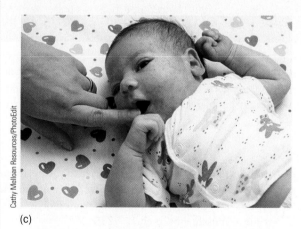

Three reflexes in infants but ordinarily not in adults:
(a) grasp reflex, (b) Babinski reflex, and (c) rooting reflex

An infant monkey's grasp reflex enables it to cling to the mother while she travels.

Movements Varying in Sensitivity to Feedback

The military distinguishes ballistic missiles from guided missiles. A ballistic missile is launched like a thrown ball: Once it is launched, no one can change its aim. A guided missile detects the target and adjusts its trajectory to correct its aim.

Similarly, some movements are ballistic, and others are corrected by feedback. A **ballistic movement** is executed as a whole: Once initiated, it cannot be altered. Reflexes are ballistic, for example. However, most behaviors are subject to feedback correction. For example, when you thread a needle, you make a slight movement, check your aim, and then readjust. Similarly, a singer who holds a single note hears any wavering of the pitch and corrects it.

Sequences of Behaviors

Many of our behaviors consist of rapid sequences, as in speaking, writing, dancing, or playing a musical instrument. Some of these sequences depend on **central pattern generators**—neural mechanisms in the spinal cord that generate rhythmic patterns of motor output. Examples include the mechanisms that generate wing flapping in birds, fin movements in fish, and the "wet dog shake." Although a stimulus may activate a central pattern generator, it does not control the frequency of the alternating movements. For example, cats scratch themselves at a rate of three to four strokes per second. Cells in the lumbar segments of the spinal cord generate this rhythm, and they continue doing so even if they are isolated from the brain or if the muscles are paralyzed (Deliagina, Orlovsky, & Pavlova, 1983).

A fixed sequence of movements is called a **motor program**. For example, a mouse periodically grooms itself by sitting up, licking its paws, wiping them over its face, closing

probably sneeze. These reflexes are *allied* in the sense that each of them tends to elicit the others. If you suddenly see a bright light—as when you emerge from a dark theater on a sunny afternoon—you reflexively close your eyes, and you may also close your mouth and perhaps sneeze. Many children and some adults react this way (Whitman & Packer, 1993). ■

its eyes as the paws pass over them, licking the paws again, and so forth (Fentress, 1973). Once begun, the sequence is fixed from beginning to end. By comparing species, we begin to understand how a motor program can be gained or lost through evolution. For example, if you hold a chicken above the ground and drop it, its wings extend and flap. Even chickens with featherless wings make the same movements, though they fail to break their fall (Provine, 1979, 1981). Chickens, of course, still have the genetic programming to fly. On the other hand, ostriches, emus, and rheas, which have not used their wings for flight for millions of generations, have lost the genes for flight movements and do not flap their wings when dropped (Provine, 1984). (You might pause to think about the researcher who found a way to drop these huge birds to test the hypothesis.)

Do humans have any built-in motor programs? Yawning is one example (Provine, 1986). A yawn includes a prolonged open-mouth inhalation, often accompanied by stretching, and a shorter exhalation. Yawns are consistent in duration, with a mean of just under 6 seconds. Certain facial expressions are also programmed, such as smiles, frowns, and the raised-eyebrow greeting.

Gerry Ellis/Minden Pictures

Nearly all birds reflexively spread their wings when dropped. However, emus—which lost the ability to fly through evolutionary time—do not spread their wings.

MODULE 8.1 ■ IN CLOSING

Categories of Movement

Charles Sherrington described a motor neuron in the spinal cord as "the final common path." He meant that regardless of what sensory and motivational processes occupy the brain, the final result is either a muscle contraction or the delay of a muscle contraction. A motor neuron and its associated muscle participate in a great many different kinds of movements, and we need many brain areas to control them.

SUMMARY

1. Vertebrates have smooth, skeletal, and cardiac muscles. **232**

2. All nerve–muscle junctions rely on acetylcholine as their neurotransmitter. **232**

3. Skeletal muscles range from slow muscles that do not fatigue to fast muscles that fatigue quickly. We rely on the slow muscles most of the time, but we recruit the fast muscles for brief periods of strenuous activity. **234**

4. Proprioceptors are receptors sensitive to the position and movement of a part of the body. Two kinds of proprioceptors, muscle spindles and Golgi tendon organs, help regulate muscle movements. **235**

5. Some movements, especially reflexes, proceed as a unit, with little if any guidance from sensory feedback. Other movements, such as threading a needle, are guided and redirected by sensory feedback. **237**

KEY TERMS

Terms are defined in the module on the page number indicated. They're also presented in alphabetical order with definitions in the book's Subject Index/Glossary, which begins on page 561. Interactive flashcards and crossword puzzles are among the online resources available to help you learn these terms and the concepts they represent.

aerobic 234

anaerobic 234

antagonistic muscles 232

Babinski reflex 236

ballistic movement 237

cardiac muscles 232

central pattern generators 237

extensor 232

fast-twitch fibers 234

flexor 232

Golgi tendon organ 235

grasp reflex 236

motor program 237

muscle spindle 235

neuromuscular junction 232

proprioceptor 235

reflexes 236

rooting reflex 236

skeletal (striated) muscles 232

slow-twitch fibers 234

smooth muscles 232

stretch reflex 235

THOUGHT QUESTION

Would you expect jaguars, cheetahs, and other great cats to have mostly slow-twitch, nonfatiguing muscles in their legs or mostly fast-twitch, quickly fatiguing muscles? What kinds of animals might have mostly the opposite kind of muscles?

Brain Mechanisms of Movement

Why do we care how the brain controls movement? One goal is to help people with spinal cord damage or limb amputations. Suppose we could listen in on their brain messages and decode what movements they would like to make. Then biomedical engineers might route those messages to muscle stimulators or robotic limbs. Sound like science fiction? Not really. Researchers implanted an array of microelectrodes into the motor cortex of a man who was paralyzed from the neck down (Figure 8.7). They determined which neurons were most active when he intended various movements and then attached them so that, when the same pattern arose again, the movement would occur. Then he could, just by thinking, turn on a television, control the channel and volume, move a robotic arm, open and close a robotic hand, and so forth (Hochberg et al., 2006). Similarly, researchers have attached electrodes to cells in monkey brains, enabling the monkeys to control mechanical arms or the monkeys' own paralyzed arms (Moritz, Perlmutter, & Fetz, 2008; Velliste, Perel, Spalding, Whitford, & Schwartz, 2008). Further progress will depend on both the technology and advances in understanding the brain mechanisms of movement.

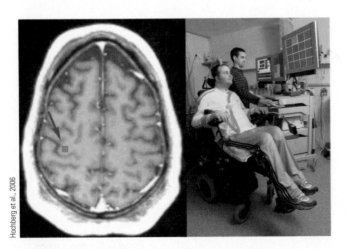

FIGURE 8.7 Paralyzed man with an electronic device implanted in his brain
Left: The arrow shows the location where the device was implanted. Right: Seated in a wheelchair, the man uses brain activity to move a cursor on the screen. *(From Macmillan Publishing Ltd./Hochberg, Serruya, Friehs, Mukand, et al. (2006). Nature, 442, 164–171)*

Controlling movement depends on many brain areas, as illustrated in Figure 8.8. Don't get too bogged down in details of the figure at this point. We shall attend to each area in due course.

The Cerebral Cortex

Since the pioneering work of Gustav Fritsch and Eduard Hitzig (1870), neuroscientists have known that direct electrical stimulation of the **primary motor cortex**—the precentral gyrus of the frontal cortex, just anterior to the central sulcus (Figure 8.9)—elicits movements. The motor cortex does not send messages directly to the muscles. Its axons extend to the brainstem and spinal cord, which generate the impulses that control the muscles. The cerebral cortex is particularly important for complex actions such as talking or writing. It is less important for coughing, sneezing, gagging, laughing, or crying (Rinn, 1984). Perhaps the lack of cerebral control explains why it is hard to perform such actions voluntarily.

Figure 8.10 (which repeats part of Figure 4.24) indicates which area of the motor cortex controls which area of the body. For example, the brain area shown next to the hand is active during hand movements. In each case, the brain area controls a structure on the opposite side of the body. However, don't read this figure as implying that each spot in the motor cortex controls a single muscle. The region responsible for any finger overlaps the regions responsible for other fingers (Sanes, Donoghue, Thangaraj, Edelman, & Warach, 1995). Furthermore, the output of a given neuron influences movements of the hand, wrist, and arm, and not just a single muscle (Vargas-Irwin et al., 2010).

For many years, researchers studied the motor cortex in laboratory animals by stimulating neurons with brief electrical pulses, usually less than 50 milliseconds (ms) in duration. The results were brief, isolated muscle twitches. Later researchers found different results when they lengthened the pulses to half a second. Instead of twitches, they elicited complex movement patterns. For example, stimulation of one spot caused a monkey to make a grasping movement with its hand, move its hand to just in front of the mouth, and open its mouth—as if it were picking up something and getting ready to eat it (Graziano, Taylor, & Moore, 2002). Repeated stimulation of this same spot elicited the same result each time, regardless of the

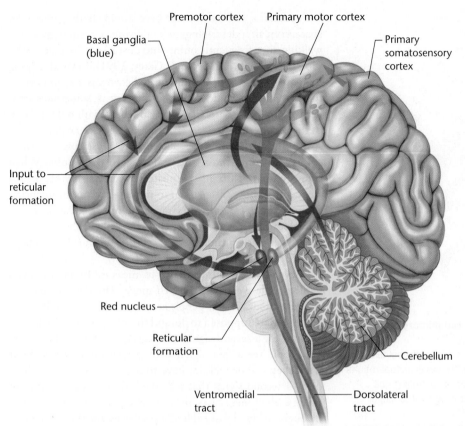

FIGURE 8.8 Motor control in mammals
Motor neurons in the medulla and spinal cord control muscle contractions. Pathways from the primary motor cortex, other cortical areas, midbrain, and medulla control those motor neurons.
(© Cengage Learning 2013)

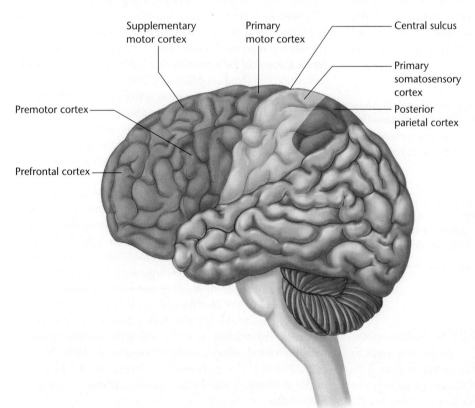

FIGURE 8.9 Principal motor areas of the human cortex
Cells in the premotor cortex and supplementary motor cortex are active during the planning of movements.
(© Cengage Learning 2013)

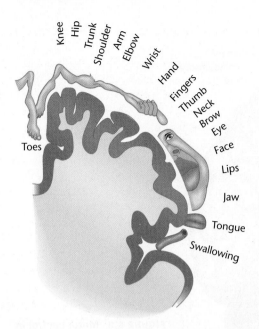

FIGURE 8.10 Coronal section through the primary motor cortex

Stimulation at a point in the primary motor cortex is most likely to evoke movements in the body area shown. However, actual results are less precise: For example, individual cells controlling one finger may be intermingled with cells controlling another finger. *(Adapted from Penfield & Rasmussen, 1950)*

initial position of the monkey's hand. That is, the stimulation produced a certain *outcome*, not a particular *muscle movement*. The motor cortex orders an outcome and leaves it to the spinal cord and other areas to find the right combination of muscles (S. H. Scott, 2004).

STOP & CHECK

8. What evidence indicates that cortical activity represents the "idea" of the movement and not just the muscle contractions?

ANSWER

8. Activity in the motor cortex leads to a particular outcome, such as movement of the hand to the mouth, regardless of what muscle contractions are necessary given the hand's current location.

Planning a Movement

The primary motor cortex is important for making movements but not for planning them. One of the first areas to become active is the **posterior parietal cortex** (Figure 8.9). This area keeps track of the position of the body relative to the world (Snyder, Grieve, Brotchie, & Andersen, 1998). People

with posterior parietal damage have trouble finding objects in space, even after describing their appearance accurately. When walking, they frequently bump into obstacles (Goodale, 1996; Goodale, Milner, Jakobson, & Carey, 1991). Beyond helping to control aim, the posterior parietal cortex is also important for planning movements. Brain surgery is sometimes conducted on people who are awake and alert, with only the skin of their scalp anesthetized. (The brain itself has no pain receptors.) During the course of such surgery, physicians can briefly stimulate certain brain areas and record the results. When they stimulate parts of the posterior parietal cortex, people frequently report an *intention* to move—such as an intention to move the left hand. After more intense stimulation at the same locations, people report that they believe they *did* make the movement—although, in fact, they did not (Desmurget et al., 2009).

Several studies used fMRI to measure brain responses while people were preparing to move. The details vary, but the general idea is that people see a first signal that tells them what they are supposed to do, and then they have to wait a few seconds for a second signal that says it is time for the action. Or people see a first signal with partial information about what they will or will not have to do, and then after a short delay a second signal that tells them more precisely what to do. In each of these cases, the posterior parietal cortex is active throughout the delay, evidently preparing for the movement. It is less active during a delay when no movement will be required (Hesse, Thiel, Stephan, & Fink, 2006; Lindner, Iyer, Kagan, & Andersen, 2010).

The prefrontal cortex and the **supplementary motor cortex** are also important for planning and organizing a rapid sequence of movements (Shima, Isoda, Mushiake, & Tanji, 2007; Tanji & Shima, 1994). If you have a habitual action, such as turning left when you get to a certain corner, the supplementary motor cortex is essential for inhibiting that habit when you need to do something else (Isoda & Hikosaka, 2007).

The **premotor cortex** is most active immediately before a movement. It receives information about the target to which the body is directing its movement, as well as information about the body's current position and posture (Hoshi & Tanji, 2000). Both kinds of information are, of course, necessary to direct a movement toward a target.

The **prefrontal cortex**, which is also active during a delay before a movement, stores sensory information relevant to a movement. It is also important for considering the probable outcomes of possible movements (Tucker, Luu, & Pribram, 1995). If you had damage to this area, many of your movements would be illogical or disorganized, such as showering with your clothes on or pouring water on the tube of toothpaste instead of the toothbrush (M. F. Schwartz, 1995). Interestingly, this area is inactive during dreams, and the actions we dream about doing are often as illogical as those of people with prefrontal cortex damage (Braun et al., 1998; Maquet et al., 1996). If you do something absent-minded first thing in the morning, it may be that your prefrontal cortex is not fully awake.

9. How does the posterior parietal cortex contribute to movement? The premotor cortex? The supplementary motor cortex? The prefrontal cortex?

ANSWER

9. The posterior parietal cortex is important for perceiving the location of objects and the position of the body relative to the environment. It is also active for planning a movement. The premotor cortex and supplementary motor cortex are also active in preparing a movement shortly before it occurs. The prefrontal cortex stores sensory information relevant to a movement and considers possible outcomes of a movement.

Mirror Neurons

Of discoveries in neuroscience, one of the most exciting to psychologists has been **mirror neurons**, which are active both during preparation for a movement and while watching someone else perform the same or a similar movement (Rizzolatti & Sinigaglia, 2010). Mirror neurons were first reported in the premotor cortex of monkeys (Gallese, Fadiga, Fogassi, & Rizzolatti, 1996) and later in other areas and other species, including humans (Dinstein, Hasson, Rubin, & Heeger, 2007; Kilner, Neal, Weiskopf, Friston, & Frith, 2009). These neurons are theoretically exciting because of the idea that they may be important for understanding other people, identifying with them, and imitating them. For example, mirror neurons in part of the frontal cortex become active when people smile or see someone else smile, and they respond especially strongly in people who report identifying strongly with other people (Montgomery, Seeherman, & Haxby, 2009). Many researchers have speculated that people with autism—who fail to form strong social bonds—might lack mirror neurons. However, one study using fMRI found normal mirror neuron responses in autistic people (Dinstein et al., 2010), so we need to look elsewhere to explain autism.

Mirror neurons are activated not only by seeing an action but also by any reminder of the action. Certain cells respond to hearing an action as well as seeing or doing it (Kohler et al., 2002; Ricciardi et al., 2009). Other cells respond to either doing an action or reading about it (Foroni & Semin, 2009; Speer, Reynolds, Swallow, & Zacks, 2009). Cells in the insular cortex become active when you feel disgusted, see something disgusting, or see someone else show a facial expression of disgust (Wicker et al., 2003).

The possibilities are exciting, but before we speculate too far, an important question remains: Do mirror neurons *cause* imitation and social behavior, or do they *result from* them? Put another way, are we born with neurons that respond to the sight of a movement and also facilitate the same movement? If so, they could be important for social learning. However, another possibility is that we learn to identify with others and learn which visible movements correspond to movements of our own. Then seeing others' actions reminds us of our own and activates brain areas responsible for those actions. In that case, mirror neurons are not responsible for imitation or socialization (Heyes, 2010).

The answer may be different for different cells and different movements. Some newborn infants imitate a few facial movements, especially tongue protrusion, as shown in Figure 8.11. That result implies built-in mirror neurons that connect the sight of a movement to the movement itself (Meltzoff & Moore, 1977). However, consider another case. Researchers identified mirror neurons that responded both when people moved a certain finger, such as the index finger, and when they watched someone else move the same finger. Then they asked people to watch a display on the screen and move their index finger whenever the hand on the screen moved the little finger. They were to move their little finger whenever the hand on the screen moved the index finger. After some practice, these "mirror" neurons turned into "counter-mirror" neurons that responded to movements of one finger by that person and the sight of a different finger on the screen (Catmur, Walsh, & Heyes, 2007). In other words, at least some—maybe most—mirror neurons develop their responses by learning.

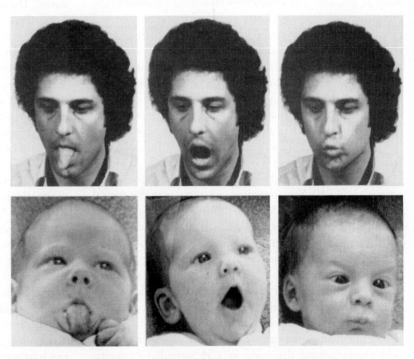

FIGURE 8.11 **Infants in their first few days imitate certain facial expressions**
These actions imply built-in mirror neurons. *(From A. N. Meltzoff & M. K. Moore. "Imitation of facial and manual gestures by human neonates." Science, 1977, 198, 75–78. Used by permission of Andrew N. Meltzoff, PhD.)*

STOP & CHECK

10. When expert pianists listen to familiar, well-practiced music, they imagine the finger movements, and the finger area of their motor cortex becomes active, even if they are not moving their fingers (Haueisen & Knösche, 2001). If we regard those neurons as another kind of mirror neuron, what do these results tell us about the origin of mirror neurons?

ANSWER

10. These neurons must have acquired these properties through experience. That is, they did not enable pianists to copy what they hear; they developed after pianists learned to copy what they hear.

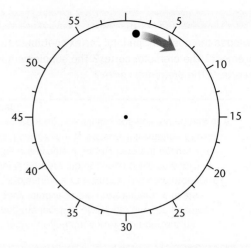

FIGURE 8.12 Procedure for Libet's study of conscious decision and movement
The participant was to make a spontaneous decision to move the wrist and remember where the light was at the time of that decision. *(From "Time of conscious intention to act in relation to onset of cerebral activities (readiness potential): The unconscious initiation of a freely voluntary act," by B. Libet et al., in* Brain, 106, *623–642. Reprinted by permission of Oxford University Press.)*

Conscious Decisions and Movements

Where does conscious decision come into all of this? Each of us has the feeling, "I consciously decide to do something, and then I do it." That sequence seems so obvious that we might not even question it, but research on the issue has found results that surprise most people.

Imagine yourself in the following study (Libet, Gleason, Wright, & Pearl, 1983). You are instructed to flex your wrist whenever you choose. You don't choose which movement to make, but you choose the time freely. You should not decide in advance when to move but let the urge occur as spontaneously as possible. The researchers take three measurements. First, they attach electrodes to your scalp to record evoked electrical activity over your motor cortex. Second, they attach a sensor to record when your hand starts to move. The third measurement is your self-report: You watch a clocklike device, as shown in Figure 8.12, in which a spot of light moves around the circle every 2.56 seconds. You are to watch that clock. Do not decide in advance that you will flex your wrist when the spot on the clock gets to a certain point. However, when you do decide to move, note where the spot of light is at that moment, and remember it so you can report it later.

The procedure starts. You think, "Not yet . . . not yet . . . not yet . . . NOW!" You note where the spot was at that critical instant and report, "I made my decision when the light was at the 25 position." The researchers compare your report to their records of your brain activity and your wrist movement. On average, people report that their decision to move occurred about 200 ms before the actual movement. (Note: It's the *decision* that occurred then. People *report* the decision later.) For example, if you reported that your decision to move occurred at position 25, your decision preceded the movement by 200 ms, so the movement began at position 30. (Remember, the light moves around the circle in 2.56 seconds.) However, your motor cortex produces a kind of activity called a **readiness potential** before any voluntary movement, and, on average, the readiness potential begins at least 500 ms before the movement. In this example, it would start when the light was at position 18, as illustrated in Figure 8.13.

Results varied among individuals, but most were similar. The key point is that the brain activity responsible for the movement apparently began *before* the person's conscious decision! The results seem to indicate that your conscious decision does not cause your action. Rather, you become conscious of the decision after the process leading to action has already been under way for about 300 ms.

As you can imagine, this experiment has been controversial. The result itself has been replicated in several laboratories, so the facts are solid (e.g., Lau, Rogers, Haggard, & Passingham, 2004; Trevena & Miller, 2002). One objection is that perhaps people cannot accurately report the time they become conscious of something. However, when people are asked to report the time of a sensory stimulus, or the time that they made a movement (instead of the decision to move), their estimates are usually within 30–50 ms of the correct time (Lau et al., 2004; Libet et al., 1983). That is, they cannot report the exact time when something happens, but they are close.

Nevertheless, it could easily be that we are less accurate at reporting the time of a conscious decision than the time of a sensory stimulus. After all, we often need to know when something happened, but we seldom need to know exactly when we made a decision. Do people know when they made a decision? Or are they guessing? Suppose we repeat Libet's experiment with one change: When you make your movement, you hear a sound, which you naturally assume is simultaneous with your movement. Sometimes it is, but sometimes it is delayed by a fraction of a second after your movement. On occasions when it is delayed, your reported time of making a conscious decision is also delayed! Apparently your report of when you made your decision depends on when you

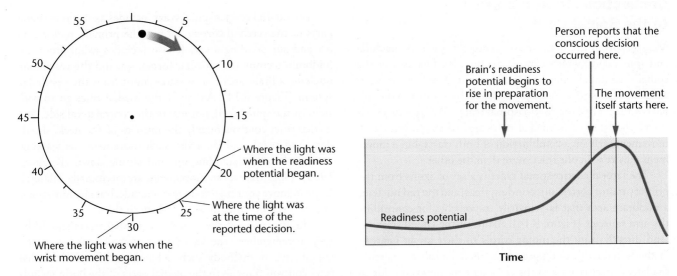

FIGURE 8.13 Results from study of conscious decision and movement
On average, the brain's readiness potential began at least 300 ms before the reported decision, which occurred 200 ms before the movement. *(From "Time of conscious intention to act in relation to onset of cerebral activities (readiness potential): The unconscious initiation of a freely voluntary act," by B. Libet et al., in Brain, 106, 623–642. Reprinted by permission of Oxford University Press.)*

think the movement occurred (Banks & Isham, 2009; Rigori, Brass, & Sartori, 2010). If your report of when you decided is little more than a guess, then Libet's results become difficult to interpret.

However, let's consider one more experiment: You watch a screen that displays letters of the alphabet, one at a time, changing every half-second. In this case you choose not just when to act, but which of two acts to do. The instruction is to decide at some point whether to press a button on the left or one on the right, press it immediately, and remember what letter was on the screen at the moment when you decided which button to press. Meanwhile, the researchers record activity from your cortex. The result: People usually report a letter they saw within one second of making the response. Remember, the letters changed only twice a second, so it wasn't possible to determine the time of decision with great accuracy. However, it wasn't necessary, because parts of the frontal and parietal cortices showed activity specific to the left or right hand *7 to 10 seconds* before the response (Soon, Brass, Heinze, & Haynes, 2008). That is, someone monitoring your cortex could, in this situation, predict which choice you were going to make a few seconds before you were aware of making the decision. Remember the issue about whether people accurately know when they made a decision, or whether they are just guessing. It's reasonable to assume that people's guesses might be wrong by half a second or so. But are they wrong by 7 to 10 seconds?

These studies suggest that what we identify as a "conscious" decision might be more the perception of an ongoing process than the cause of it. If so, we return to the issues raised in Chapter 1: What is the role of consciousness? Does it serve a useful function, and if so, what?

None of these results deny that you make a *voluntary* decision. The implication, however, is that your voluntary decision is, at first, unconscious. Your decision to do something develops gradually and builds up to a certain strength before it becomes conscious. Evidently, "voluntary" is not synonymous with "conscious."

Does brain activity always start 7–10 seconds before a movement? Of course not. If you see or hear something that calls for an action—such as a pedestrian darting into the road while you are driving—you respond within a split second. Recall the study in Module 8.1, in which people respond more quickly when they see someone else acting than when they initiate a similar action themselves. Only spontaneous actions require slow deliberation.

STOP & CHECK

11. Explain the evidence that someone's conscious decision to move does not cause the movement.

12. On what basis are some researchers skeptical of this evidence?

ANSWERS

11. Researchers recorded responses in people's cortex that predicted the upcoming response. Those brain responses occurred earlier than the time people reported as "when they made the decision." **12.** The studies assume that people accurately report the times of their intentions. However, people's reports are influenced by events after the movement, and therefore we cannot be confident of their accuracy.

Connections from the Brain to the Spinal Cord

Messages from the brain must eventually reach the medulla and spinal cord, which control the muscles. Diseases of the spinal cord impair the control of movement in various ways, as listed in Table 8.1. Paths from the cerebral cortex to the spinal cord are called the **corticospinal tracts**. We have two such tracts, the lateral and medial corticospinal tracts. Nearly all movements rely on a combination of both tracts, but a movement may rely on one tract more than the other.

The **lateral corticospinal tract** is a set of axons from the primary motor cortex, surrounding areas, and the **red nucleus**, a midbrain area that is primarily responsible for controlling the arm muscles (Figure 8.14). Axons of the lateral tract extend directly from the motor cortex to their target neurons in the spinal cord. In bulges of the medulla called *pyramids*, the lateral tract crosses to the contralateral (opposite) side of the spinal cord. (For that reason, the lateral tract is also called the pyramidal tract.) It controls movements in peripheral areas, such as the hands and feet.

Why does each hemisphere control the contralateral side instead of its own side? We do not know, but all vertebrates and many invertebrates have this pattern. In newborn humans, the immature primary motor cortex has partial control of both ipsilateral and contralateral muscles. As the contralateral control improves over the first year and a half of life, it displaces the ipsilateral control, which gradually becomes weaker. In some children with cerebral palsy, the contralateral path fails to mature, and the ipsilateral path remains relatively strong. The resulting competition causes clumsiness (Eyre, Taylor, Villagra, Smith, & Miller, 2001).

The **medial corticospinal tract** includes axons from many parts of the cerebral cortex, not just the primary motor cortex and surrounding areas. It also includes axons from the midbrain tectum, the reticular formation, and the **vestibular nucleus**, a brain area that receives input from the vestibular system (Figure 8.14). Axons of the medial tract go to *both* sides of the spinal cord, not just to the contralateral side. The medial tract controls mainly the muscles of the neck, shoulders, and trunk and therefore such movements as walking, turning, bending, standing up, and sitting down (Kuypers, 1989). Note that these movements are necessarily bilateral. You can move your fingers on just one side, but any movement of your neck or trunk must include both sides.

The functions of the lateral and medial tracts should be easy to remember: The lateral tract controls muscles in the lateral parts of the body, such as hands and feet. The medial tract controls muscles in the medial parts of the body, including trunk and neck.

Figure 8.14 compares the lateral and medial corticospinal tracts. Figure 8.15 compares the lateral tract to the spinal pathway bringing touch information to the cortex. Note that both paths cross in the medulla and that the touch information arrives at brain areas side by side with those areas responsible for motor control. Touch is obviously essential for movement. You have to know what your hands are doing now in order to control their next action.

Suppose someone suffers a stroke that damages the primary motor cortex of the left hemisphere. The result is a loss of the lateral tract from that hemisphere and a loss of movement control on the right side of the body. Eventually, depending on the location and amount of damage, the

TABLE 8.1	**Disorders of the Spinal Cord**	
Disorder	**Description**	**Cause**
Paralysis	Lack of voluntary movement in part of the body.	Damage to spinal cord, motor neurons, or their axons.
Paraplegia	Loss of sensation and voluntary muscle control in both legs. Reflexes remain. Although no messages pass between the brain and the genitals, the genitals still respond reflexively to touch. Paraplegics have no genital sensations, but they can still experience orgasm (Money, 1967).	Cut through the spinal cord above the segments attached to the legs.
Quadriplegia	Loss of sensation and muscle control in all four extremities.	Cut through the spinal cord above the segments controlling the arms.
Hemiplegia	Loss of sensation and muscle control in the arm and leg on one side.	Cut halfway through the spinal cord or (more commonly) damage to one hemisphere of the cerebral cortex.
Tabes dorsalis	Impaired sensation in the legs and pelvic region, impaired leg reflexes and walking, loss of bladder and bowel control.	Late stage of syphilis. Dorsal roots of the spinal cord deteriorate.
Poliomyelitis	Paralysis.	Virus that damages cell bodies of motor neurons.
Amyotrophic lateral sclerosis	Gradual weakness and paralysis, starting with the arms and later spreading to the legs. Both motor neurons and axons from the brain to the motor neurons are destroyed.	Unknown.

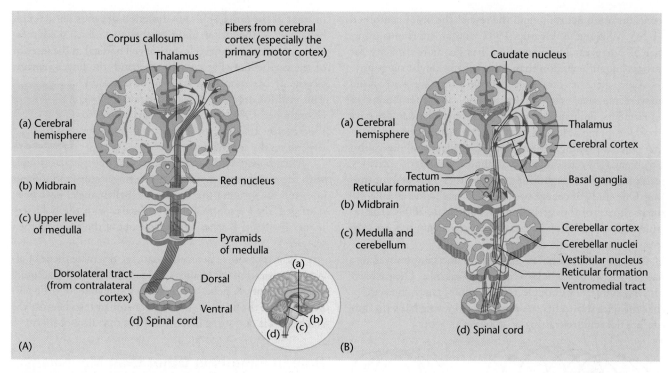

FIGURE 8.14 The lateral and medial corticospinal tracts
The lateral tract (A) crosses from one side of the brain to the opposite side of the spinal cord and controls precise and discrete movements of the extremities, such as hands, fingers, and feet. The medial tract (B) controls trunk muscles for postural adjustments and bilateral movements such as standing, bending, turning, and walking. (© Cengage Learning 2013)

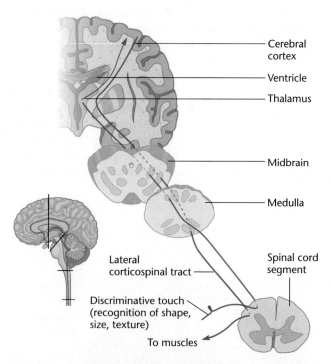

FIGURE 8.15 The touch path and the lateral corticospinal tract
Both paths cross in the medulla so that each hemisphere has access to the opposite side of the body. The touch path goes from touch receptors toward the brain; the corticospinal path goes from the brain to the muscles. (© Cengage Learning 2013)

person may regain some muscle control from spared axons in the lateral tract. If not, using the medial tract can approximate the intended movement. For example, someone with no direct control of the hand muscles might move the shoulders, trunk, and hips in a way that repositions the hand.

STOP & CHECK

13. What kinds of movements does the lateral tract control? The medial tract?

ANSWER

13. The lateral tract controls detailed movements in the periphery on the contralateral side of the body. (For example, the lateral tract from the left hemisphere controls the right side of the body.) The medial tract controls trunk movements bilaterally.

The Cerebellum

The term *cerebellum* is Latin for "little brain." Decades ago, most texts described the function of the cerebellum as "balance and coordination." Well, yes, people with cerebellar damage do lose balance and coordination, but that description understates the importance of this structure. The cerebellum contains more neurons than the rest of the brain combined (R. W. Williams & Herrup, 1988) and an enormous number of synapses. The cerebellum has far more capacity for processing information than its small size might suggest.

One effect of cerebellar damage is trouble with rapid movements that require aim, timing, and alternations of movements. For example, people with cerebellar damage have trouble tapping a rhythm, clapping hands, pointing at a moving object, speaking, writing, typing, or playing a musical instrument. They are impaired at almost all athletic activities, except those like weightlifting that do not require aim or timing. One study of college basketball players found an enlargement of part of the cerebellum (I. Park et al., 2009). The results did not indicate whether that enlargement was a cause or result of their athletic skill.

People with cerebellar damage are normal, however, at a *continuous* motor activity (Spencer, Zelaznik, Diedrichsen, & Ivry, 2003). For example, they can draw continuous circles, like the ones shown here. Although the drawing has a rhythm, it does not require starting or stopping an action.

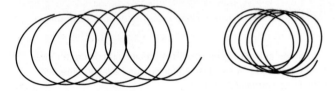

Here is a quick way to test someone's cerebellum: Ask the person to focus on one spot and then to move the eyes quickly to another spot. Saccades (sa-KAHDS)—ballistic eye movements from one fixation point to another—depend on impulses from the cerebellum and the frontal cortex to the cranial nerves. Someone with cerebellar damage has difficulty programming the angle and distance of eye movements (Dichgans, 1984). The eyes make many short movements until, by trial and error, they eventually find the intended spot.

In the *finger-to-nose test*, the person is instructed to hold one arm straight out and then, at command, to touch his or her nose as quickly as possible. A normal person does so in three steps. First, the finger moves ballistically to a point just in front of the nose. This *move* function depends on the cerebellar cortex (the surface of the cerebellum), which sends messages to the deep **nuclei** (clusters of cell bodies) in the interior of the cerebellum (Figure 8.16). Second, the finger remains steady at that spot for a fraction of a second. This *hold* function depends on the nuclei alone (Kornhuber, 1974). Finally, the finger moves to the nose by a slower movement that does not depend on the cerebellum.

After damage to the cerebellar cortex, a person has trouble with the initial rapid movement. The finger stops too soon or goes too far, striking the face. If cerebellar nuclei have been damaged, the person may have difficulty with the hold segment: The finger reaches a point in front of the nose and then wavers.

The symptoms of cerebellar damage resemble those of alcohol intoxication: clumsiness, slurred speech, and inaccurate eye movements. A police officer testing someone for drunkenness may use the finger-to-nose test or similar tests because the cerebellum is one of the first brain areas that alcohol affects.

Role in Functions Other than Movement

The cerebellum is not only a motor structure. In one study, functional MRI measured cerebellar activity while people performed several tasks (Gao et al., 1996). When they simply lifted objects, the cerebellum showed little activity. When they felt things with both hands to decide whether they were the same or different, the cerebellum was much more active. The cerebellum responded even when the experimenter rubbed an object across an unmoving hand. That is, the cerebellum responded to sensory stimuli even in the absence of movement.

What, then, is the role of the cerebellum? Masao Ito (1984) proposed that a key role is to establish new motor programs that enable one to execute a sequence of actions as a whole. Inspired by this idea, many researchers reported evidence that cerebellar damage impairs motor learning. Richard Ivry and his colleagues emphasized the importance of the cerebellum for behaviors that depend on

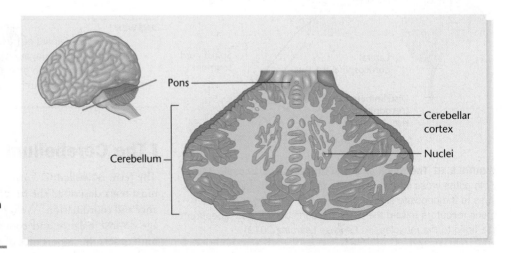

FIGURE 8.16 Location of the cerebellar nuclei relative to the cerebellar cortex
In the inset at the upper left, the line indicates the plane shown in detail at the lower right.
(© Cengage Learning 2013)

Pons
Cerebellum
Cerebellar cortex
Nuclei

Masao Ito

Brains seem to be built on several principles such that numerous neurons interact with each other through excitation and inhibition, that synaptic plasticity provides memory elements, that multilayered neuronal networks bear a high computational power and that combination of neuronal networks, sensors and effectors constitutes a neural system representing a brain function. Thus, Hebbian tradition has provided a very successful paradigm in modern neuroscience, but we may have to go beyond it in order to understand the entire functions of brains. (personal communication)

precise timing of short intervals (from about a millisecond to 1.5 seconds). Any sequence of rapid movements obviously requires timing. Many perceptual and cognitive tasks also require timing—for example, judging which of two visual stimuli is moving faster or listening to two pairs of tones and comparing the delays between them.

People who are accurate at one kind of timed movement, such as tapping a rhythm with a finger, tend also to be good at other timed movements, such as tapping a rhythm with a foot, and at judging which visual stimulus moved faster and which delay between tones was longer. People with cerebellar damage are impaired at all of these tasks but unimpaired at controlling the force of a movement or at judging which tone is louder (Ivry & Diener, 1991; Keele & Ivry, 1990). In short, the cerebellum is important mainly for tasks that require timing.

The cerebellum also appears critical for certain aspects of attention. For example, in one experiment, people were told to keep their eyes fixated on a central point. At various times, they would see the letter E on either the left or right half of the screen, and they were to indicate the direction in which it was oriented (E, Ǝ, ⊔, or ⊓) without moving their eyes. Sometimes, they saw a signal telling where the letter would be on the screen. For most people, that signal improved their performance even if it appeared just 100 ms before the letter. For people with cerebellar damage, the signal had to appear nearly a second before the letter to be helpful. Evidently, people with cerebellar damage need longer to shift their attention (Townsend et al., 1999).

STOP & CHECK

14. What kind of perceptual task would be most impaired by damage to the cerebellum?

ANSWER ·ƃuᴉɯᴉʇ ǝʇɐɹnɔɔɐ uo puǝdǝp ʇɐɥʇ sʞsɐʇ lɐnʇdǝɔɹǝd sɹᴉɐdɯᴉ ɯnllǝqǝɹǝɔ ǝɥʇ oʇ ǝƃɐɯɐ□ **.41**

Cellular Organization

The cerebellum receives input from the spinal cord, from each of the sensory systems by way of the cranial nerve nuclei, and from the cerebral cortex. That information eventually reaches the **cerebellar cortex**, the surface of the cerebellum (Figure 8.17).

Figure 8.17 shows the types and arrangements of neurons in the cerebellar cortex. The figure is complex, but concentrate on these main points:

- The neurons are arranged in a precise geometrical pattern, with multiple repetitions of the same units.
- The **Purkinje** (pur-KIN-jee) **cells** are flat (two-dimensional) cells in sequential planes, parallel to one another.
- The **parallel fibers** are axons parallel to one another and perpendicular to the planes of the Purkinje cells.
- Action potentials in parallel fibers excite one Purkinje cell after another. Each Purkinje cell then transmits an inhibitory message to cells in the *nuclei of the cerebellum* (clusters of cell bodies in the interior of the cerebellum) and the vestibular nuclei in the brainstem, which in turn send information to the midbrain and the thalamus.
- Depending on which and how many parallel fibers are active, they might stimulate only the first few Purkinje cells or a long series of them. Because the parallel fibers' messages reach different Purkinje cells one after another, the greater the number of excited Purkinje cells, the greater their collective *duration* of response. That is, if the parallel fibers stimulate only the first few Purkinje cells, the result is a brief message to the target cells; if they stimulate more Purkinje cells, the message lasts longer. The output of Purkinje cells controls the timing of a movement, including both its onset and offset (Thier, Dicke, Haas, & Barash, 2000).

STOP & CHECK

15. How are the parallel fibers arranged relative to one another and to the Purkinje cells?

16. If a larger number of parallel fibers are active, what is the effect on the collective output of the Purkinje cells?

ANSWERS ·ǝsuodsǝɹ ɟo uoᴉʇɐɹnp ɹᴉǝɥʇ ǝsɐǝɹɔuᴉ sllǝɔ ǝɾuᴉʞɹnꓱ ǝɥʇ 'ǝʌᴉʇɔɐ ǝɯoɔǝq sɹǝqᴉɟ lǝllɐɹɐd ɟo ɹǝqɯnu ɹǝƃɹɐl ɐ sⱯ **.61**
·sllǝɔ ǝɾuᴉʞɹnꓱ ǝɥʇ ɟo sǝuɐld ǝɥʇ oʇ ɹɐlnɔᴉpuǝdɹǝd puɐ ɹǝɥʇouɐ ǝuo oʇ lǝllɐɹɐd ǝɹɐ sɹǝqᴉɟ lǝllɐɹɐd ǝɥꓕ **.51**

▌ The Basal Ganglia

The term **basal ganglia** applies collectively to a group of large subcortical structures in the forebrain (Figure 8.18). (*Ganglia* is the plural of *ganglion*, so *ganglia* is a plural noun.) Various authorities differ in which structures they include as part of

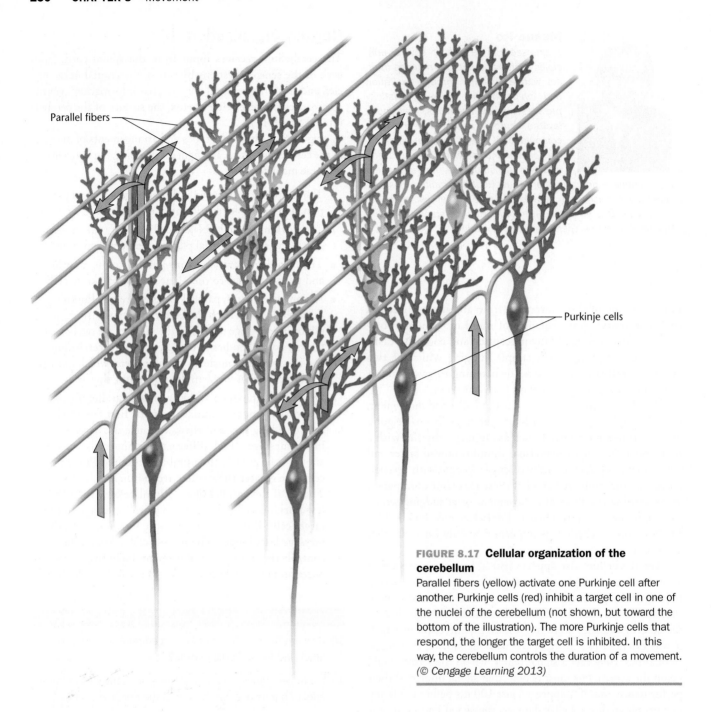

Parallel fibers

Purkinje cells

FIGURE 8.17 Cellular organization of the cerebellum
Parallel fibers (yellow) activate one Purkinje cell after another. Purkinje cells (red) inhibit a target cell in one of the nuclei of the cerebellum (not shown, but toward the bottom of the illustration). The more Purkinje cells that respond, the longer the target cell is inhibited. In this way, the cerebellum controls the duration of a movement. *(© Cengage Learning 2013)*

the basal ganglia, but everyone includes at least the **caudate nucleus**, the **putamen** (pyuh-TAY-men), and the **globus pallidus**. Input comes to the caudate nucleus and putamen, mostly from the cerebral cortex. Output from the caudate nucleus and putamen goes to the globus pallidus and from there mainly to the thalamus, which relays it to the cerebral cortex, especially its motor areas and the prefrontal cortex (Hoover & Strick, 1993).

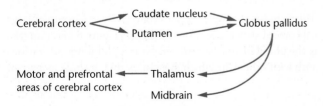

Most of the output from the globus pallidus to the thalamus releases GABA, an inhibitory transmitter, and neurons in the globus pallidus show much spontaneous activity. Thus, the globus pallidus is constantly inhibiting the thalamus. Input from the caudate nucleus and putamen tells the globus pallidus which movements to *stop inhibiting*. With extensive damage to the globus pallidus, as in people with Huntington's disease (which we shall consider later), the result is decreased inhibition and therefore involuntary, jerky movements.

In effect, the basal ganglia select a movement by ceasing to inhibit it. This circuit is particularly important for self-initiated behaviors. For example, a monkey in one study was trained to move one hand to the left or right to receive food. On trials when it heard a signal indicating exactly when to move, the basal ganglia showed little activity. However, on

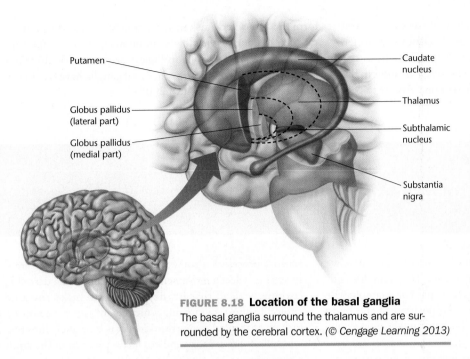

FIGURE 8.18 **Location of the basal ganglia**
The basal ganglia surround the thalamus and are surrounded by the cerebral cortex. (© Cengage Learning 2013)

Labels in figure: Putamen, Globus pallidus (lateral part), Globus pallidus (medial part), Caudate nucleus, Thalamus, Subthalamic nucleus, Substantia nigra

evant neurons in the motor cortex increase their firing rates (D. Cohen & Nicolelis, 2004). After prolonged training, the movement patterns become more consistent from trial to trial, and so do the patterns of activity in the motor cortex. In engineering terms, the motor cortex increases its signal-to-noise ratio (Kargo & Nitz, 2004).

The basal ganglia are critical for learning new habits (Yin & Knowlton, 2006). For example, when you are first learning to drive a car, you have to think about everything you do. Eventually, you learn to signal for a left turn, change gears, turn the wheel, and change speed all at once. If you try to explain exactly what you do, you will probably find it difficult. People with basal ganglia damage are impaired at learning motor skills and at converting new movements into smooth, "automatic" responses (Poldrack et al., 2005; Willingham, Koroshetz, & Peterson, 1996).

other trials, the monkey saw a light indicating that it should start its movement in not less than 1.5 seconds and finish in not more than 3 seconds. Therefore, the monkey had to choose its own starting time. Under those conditions, the basal ganglia were highly active (Turner & Anderson, 2005).

In another study, people used a computer mouse to draw lines on a screen while researchers used PET scans to examine brain activity. Activity in the basal ganglia increased when people drew a new line but not when they traced a line already on the screen (Jueptner & Weiller, 1998). Again, the basal ganglia seem critical for initiating an action but not when the action is directly guided by a stimulus.

> **STOP & CHECK**

18. What kind of learning depends most heavily on the basal ganglia?

ANSWER   18. The basal ganglia are essential for learning motor habits that are difficult to describe in words.

> **STOP & CHECK**

17. Why does damage to the basal ganglia lead to involuntary movements?

ANSWER   17. Output from the basal ganglia to the thalamus releases the inhibitory transmitter GABA. Ordinarily, the basal ganglia produce steady output, inhibiting all movements or all except the ones selected at the time. After damage to the basal ganglia, the thalamus, and therefore the cortex, receive less inhibition. Thus, they produce unwanted actions.

▌ Brain Areas and Motor Learning

Of all the brain areas responsible for control of movement, which are important for learning new skills? The apparent answer is all of them.

Neurons in the motor cortex adjust their responses as a person or animal learns a motor skill. At first, movements are slow and inconsistent. As movements become faster, rel-

▌ Inhibition of Movements

Finally, consider the situation in which you need to restrain yourself from following some strong impulse. One example—not a particularly important one for its own sake, but a good one for psychologists to study—is the **antisaccade task**. A saccade is a voluntary eye movement from one target to another. Suppose you are staring straight ahead when something to one side or the other moves. You have a strong tendency to look toward the moving object. In the antisaccade task, you are supposed to look in the *opposite* direction. You can try it yourself: Hold one hand to the left of someone's head and the other hand to the right. When you wiggle a finger, the person is instructed to look at the *other* hand. Or have someone do the same for you. Most people agree that it is easier to look at the finger that moved than the other finger.

TRY IT YOURSELF

Before age 5 to 7 years, most children find it almost impossible to ignore the wiggling finger and look the other way. Ability to perform this task smoothly improves all the way to late adolescence. Performing this task well requires sustained activity in parts of the prefrontal cortex and basal ganglia *before* seeing the wiggling finger (Velanova, Wheeler, & Luna, 2009; Watanabe & Munoz, 2010). That is, as the brain prepares itself, it sets itself to be ready to inhibit the unwanted action and substitute a different one. Ability to per-form the antisaccade task matures slowly because the prefrontal cortex is one of the slowest brain areas to reach maturity. Many adults who have neurological or psychiatric disorders affecting the prefrontal cortex or basal ganglia have trouble on this task (Munoz & Everling, 2004).

MODULE 8.2 ■ IN CLOSING

Movement Control and Cognition

It is tempting to describe behavior in three steps—first we perceive, then we think, and finally we act. The brain does not handle the process in such discrete steps. For example, the posterior parietal cortex monitors the position of the body relative to visual space and thereby helps guide movement. Thus, its functions are sensory, cognitive, and motor. The cerebellum has traditionally been considered a major part of the motor system, but it is now known to be important in timing sensory processes. People with basal ganglia damage are slow to start or select a movement. They are also often described as cognitively slow; that is, they hesitate to make any kind of choice. In short, organizing a movement is not something we tack on at the end of our thinking. It is intimately intertwined with all of our sensory and cognitive processes. The study of movement is not just the study of muscles. It is the study of how we decide what to do.

SUMMARY

1. The primary motor cortex is the main source of brain input to the spinal cord. The spinal cord contains central pattern generators that control the muscles. **240**

2. The primary motor cortex produces patterns representing the intended outcome, not just the muscle contractions. **240**

3. Areas near the primary motor cortex—including the prefrontal, premotor, and supplementary motor cortices—are active in detecting stimuli for movement and preparing for a movement. **242**

4. Mirror neurons in various brain areas respond to both a self-produced movement and an observation of a similar movement by another individual. Although some neurons may have built-in mirror properties, at least some of them acquire these properties by learning. Their role in imitation and social behavior is potentially important but as yet speculative. **243**

5. When people identify the instant when they formed a conscious intention to move, their time precedes the actual movement by about 200 ms but follows the start of motor cortex activity by about 300 ms. These results suggest that what we call a conscious decision is our perception of a process already under way, not really the cause of it.

However, it is not clear how accurately people can report the time of a conscious decision. **244**

6. The lateral tract, which controls movements in the periphery of the body, has axons that cross from one side of the brain to the opposite side of the spinal cord. The medial tract controls bilateral movements near the midline of the body. **246**

7. The cerebellum is critical for rapid movements that require accurate aim and timing. **247**

8. The cerebellum has multiple roles in behavior, including sensory functions related to perception of the timing or rhythm of stimuli. **248**

9. The cells of the cerebellum are arranged in a regular pattern that enables them to produce outputs of precisely controlled duration. **249**

10. The basal ganglia are a group of large subcortical structures that are important for selecting and inhibiting particular movements. Damage to the output from the basal ganglia leads to jerky, involuntary movements. **249**

11. The learning of a motor skill depends on changes occurring in both the cerebral cortex and the basal ganglia. **251**

KEY TERMS

Terms are defined in the module on the page number indicated. They're also presented in alphabetical order with definitions in the book's Subject Index/Glossary, which begins on page 561. Interactive flashcards and crossword puzzles are among the online resources available to help you learn these terms and the concepts they represent.

antisaccade task   251

basal ganglia   249

caudate nucleus   250

cerebellar cortex   249

corticospinal tracts   246

globus pallidus   250

lateral corticospinal tract   246

medial corticospinal tract   246

mirror neurons   243

nuclei of the cerebellum   248

parallel fibers   249

posterior parietal cortex   242

prefrontal cortex   242

premotor cortex   242

primary motor cortex   240

Purkinje cells   249

putamen   250

readiness potential   244

red nucleus   246

supplementary motor cortex   242

vestibular nucleus   246

THOUGHT QUESTION

Human infants are at first limited to gross movements of the trunk, arms, and legs. The ability to move one finger at a time matures gradually over at least the first year. What hypothesis would you suggest about which brain areas controlling movement mature early and which areas mature later?

Movement Disorders

If you have damage in your spinal cord, peripheral nerves, or muscles, you can't move, but cognitively, you are the same as ever. In contrast, brain disorders that impair movement also impair mood, memory, and cognition. We consider two examples: Parkinson's disease and Huntington's disease.

Parkinson's Disease

The main symptoms of **Parkinson's disease** (also known as *Parkinson disease*) are rigidity, muscle tremors, slow movements, and difficulty initiating physical and mental activity (M. T. V. Johnson et al., 1996; Manfredi, Stocchi, & Vacca, 1995; Pillon et al., 1996). It strikes about 1% to 2% of people over age 65. In addition to the motor problems, patients are slow on cognitive tasks, such as imagining events or actions, even when they don't have to do anything (Sawamoto, Honda, Hanakawa, Fukuyama, & Shibasaki, 2002). A loss of olfaction is often an early symptom, and sometimes the first symptom (Wattendorf et al., 2009). Depression and memory loss are also common symptoms, beginning early in the course of the disease (Ouchi et al., 1999).

People with Parkinson's disease are not paralyzed or weak. The basal ganglia have cells specialized for learning to start or stop a voluntary sequence of motions (Jin & Costa, 2010). Those cells are impaired in Parkinson's disease, and the result is a difficulty with spontaneous movements in the absence of stimuli to guide their actions. Parkinsonian patients sometimes walk surprisingly well when following a parade, when walking up a flight of stairs, or when walking across lines drawn at one-step intervals (Teitelbaum, Pellis, & Pellis, 1991).

Causes

The immediate cause of Parkinson's disease is the gradual progressive death of neurons, especially in the substantia nigra, which sends dopamine-releasing axons to the caudate nucleus and putamen. People with Parkinson's disease lose these axons and therefore dopamine.

The connections from the substantia nigra to the cerebral cortex are complex. The main route, known as the direct pathway, is as follows: Axons from the substantia nigra release dopamine that excites the caudate nucleus and putamen. The caudate nucleus and putamen inhibit the globus pallidus, which in turn inhibits parts of the thalamus. For people with Parkinson's disease, decreased output from the substantia nigra means less excitation of the caudate nucleus and putamen, and therefore less inhibition of the globus pallidus. The globus pallidus, freed from inhibition, increases its (inhibitory) output to the thalamus. So the net result is decreased activity in the thalamus, and therefore also in parts of the cerebral cortex, as shown in Figure 8.19 (Wichmann, Vitek, & DeLong, 1995; Yin & Knowlton, 2006). In summary, a loss of dopamine activity in the substantia nigra leads to less stimulation of the motor cortex and slower onset of movements (Parr-Brownlie & Hyland, 2005).

Researchers estimate that the average person over age 45 loses substantia nigra neurons at a rate of almost 1% per year. Most people have enough to spare, but some people start with fewer or lose them faster. If the number of surviving substantia nigra neurons declines below 20%–30% of normal, Parkinsonian symptoms begin (Knoll, 1993). Symptoms become more severe as the cell loss continues.

In the late 1990s, the news media excitedly reported that researchers had located a gene that causes Parkinson's disease. That report was misleading. Researchers had found families in which people sharing a particular gene all developed Parkinson's disease with onset before age 50 (Shimura et al., 2001). Since then, several other genes have been found that also lead to early-onset Parkinson's disease (Bonifati et al., 2003; Singleton et al., 2003; Valente et al., 2004). However, these genes are not linked to later-onset Parkinson's disease, which is far more common. Several other genes are linked to late-onset Parkinson's disease (Gao et al., 2009; Maraganore et al., 2005; E. R. Martin et al., 2001; W. K. Scott et al., 2001), but each of these genes has only a small impact. For example, one gene occurs in 82% of the people with Parkinson's disease and in 79% of those without it.

A study of twins highlighted the difference between early- and late-onset Parkinson's disease. If you have a monozygotic twin who develops early-onset Parkinson's disease, you are almost certain to get it, too. However, if your twin develops Parkinson's disease after age 50, your

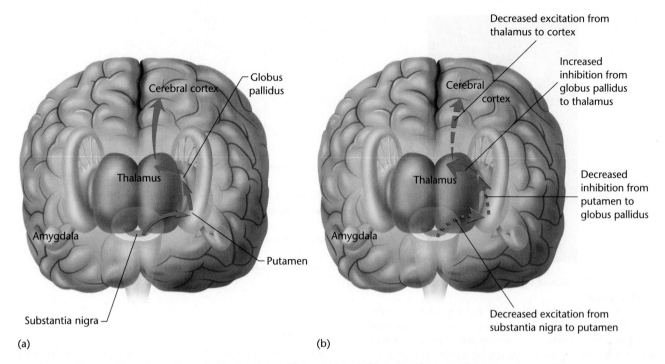

FIGURE 8.19 **Connections from the substantia nigra: (a) normal and (b) in Parkinson's disease**
Excitatory paths are shown in green; inhibitory are in red. Decreased excitation from the substantia nigra decreases inhibition from the putamen, leading to increased inhibition from the globus pallidus. The net result is decreased excitation from the thalamus to the cortex. *(Based on Yin & Knowlton, 2006)*

risk is about the same *regardless* of whether your twin is monozygotic or dizygotic (Tanner et al., 1999). Equal concordance for both kinds of twins implies low heritability. A later study of 132 Parkinson's patients over age 50 who had a twin found that only three of the twins also had Parkinson's disease (Wirdefeldt et al., 2008). These results imply that genes only weakly influence the risk of late-onset Parkinson's disease.

STOP & CHECK

19. Do monozygotic twins resemble each other more than dizygotic twins do for early-onset Parkinson's disease? For late-onset? What conclusion do these results imply?

ANSWER

19. Monozygotic twins resemble each other more than dizygotic twins do for early-onset Parkinson's disease, but not for late-onset. The conclusion is that early-onset Parkinson's disease has higher heritability than the late-onset condition.

What environmental influences might be relevant? An accidental discovery implicated exposure to toxins (Ballard, Tetrud, & Langston, 1985). In northern California in 1982, several young adults developed symptoms of Parkinson's disease after using a drug similar to heroin. Before the in-

vestigators could alert the community to the danger, many other users had developed symptoms ranging from mild to fatal (Tetrud, Langston, Garbe, & Ruttenber, 1989). The substance responsible for the symptoms was **MPTP**, a chemical that the body converts to **MPP$^+$**, which accumulates in, and then destroys, neurons that release dopamine[1] (Nicklas, Saporito, Basma, Geller, & Heikkila, 1992). Postsynaptic neurons react to the loss of input by increasing their number of dopamine receptors, as shown in Figure 8.20 (Chiueh, 1988).

No one supposes that Parkinson's disease often results from using illegal drugs. A more likely hypothesis is that people are sometimes exposed to hazardous chemicals in herbicides and pesticides (Figure 8.21), many of which damage cells of the substantia nigra (Hatcher, Pennell, & Miller, 2008). Parkinson's disease is more common than average among farmers and others who have had years of exposure to herbicides and pesticides (T. P. Brown, Rumsby, Capleton, Rushton, & Levy, 2006).

What else might influence the risk of Parkinson's disease? Researchers compared the lifestyles of people who did and didn't develop the disease. One factor that stands out consistently is cigarette smoking and coffee drinking: People

[1]The full names of these chemicals are 1-methyl-4 phenyl-1,2,3,6-tetrahydropyridine and 1-methyl-4-phenylpyridinium ion. (Let's hear it for abbreviations.)

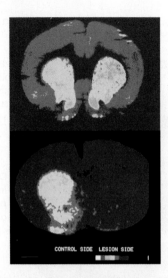

FIGURE 8.20 **Results of injecting MPP⁺ into one hemisphere of the rat brain**
The autoradiography above shows D_2 dopamine receptors; the one below shows axon terminals containing dopamine. Red indicates the highest level of activity, followed by yellow, green, and blue. Note that the MPP⁺ greatly depleted the number of dopamine axons and that the number of D_2 receptors increased in response to this lack of input. However, the net result is a great decrease in dopamine activity. *(From "Dopamine in the extrapyramidal motor function: A study based upon the MPTP-induced primate model of Parkinsonism," by C. C. Chiueh, 1988,* Annals of the New York Academy of Sciences, 515, p. 223. Reprinted by permission.)*

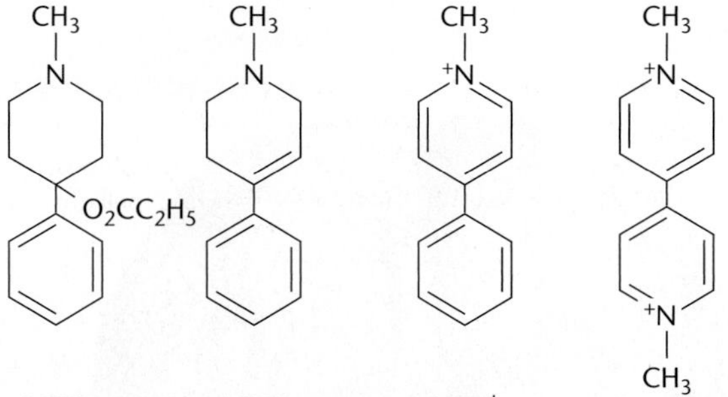

FIGURE 8.21 **Chemical structures of MPPP, MPTP, MPP⁺, and paraquat**
Exposure to paraquat and similar herbicides and pesticides may increase the risk of Parkinson's disease. *(© Cengage Learning 2013)*

who smoke cigarettes or drink coffee have less chance of developing Parkinson's disease (Ritz et al., 2007). (Read that sentence again.) One study took questionnaire results from more than a thousand pairs of young adult twins and compared the results to medical records decades later. Of the twins who had never smoked, 18.4% developed Parkinson's disease. In contrast, 13.8% of the smokers developed the disease, as did only 11.6% of the heaviest smokers (Wirdefeldt, Gatz, Pawitan, & Pedersen, 2005). A study of U.S. adults compared coffee drinking in middle-aged adults to their medical histories later in life. Drinking coffee decreased the risk of Parkinson's disease, especially for men (Ascherio et al., 2004). Needless to say, smoking cigarettes increases the risk of lung cancer and other diseases more than it decreases the risk of Parkinson's disease. Coffee has less benefit for decreasing Parkinson's disease, but it's safer than smoking. Animal research indicates that decaffeinated coffee works just as well as regular coffee, and nicotine-free tobacco works as well as full tobacco, so the effective chemicals are something other than caffeine and nicotine (Trinh et al., 2010). How these chemicals decrease the risk of Parkinson's disease is unknown.

In short, Parkinson's disease probably results from a mixture of causes. What they have in common is damage to the mitochondria. When a neuron's mitochondria begin to fail—because of genes, toxins, infections, or whatever—a chemical called α-synuclein clots into clusters that damage neurons containing dopamine (Dawson & Dawson, 2003). Dopamine-containing neurons are especially vulnerable to damage (Zeevalk, Manzino, Hoppe, & Sonsalla, 1997).

> **STOP & CHECK**
>
> **20.** How does MPTP exposure influence the likelihood of Parkinson's disease? What are the effects of cigarette smoking?
>
> **ANSWER** **20.** Exposure to MPTP can induce symptoms of Parkinson's disease. Cigarette smoking is correlated with decreased prevalence of the disease.

L-Dopa Treatment

If Parkinson's disease results from a dopamine deficiency, then a logical goal is to restore the missing dopamine. A dopamine pill would be ineffective because dopamine does not cross the blood–brain barrier. **L-dopa**, a precursor to dopamine, does cross the barrier. Taken as a daily pill, L-dopa reaches the brain, where neurons convert it to dopamine. L-dopa is the main treatment for Parkinson's disease.

However, L-dopa is disappointing in several ways. First, it is ineffective for some patients, especially those in the late stages of the disease. Second, L-dopa does not prevent the continued loss of neurons. Third, L-dopa produces unpleasant side effects such as nausea, restlessness, sleep problems, low blood pressure, repetitive movements, hallucinations, and delusions.

21. How does L-dopa relieve the symptoms of Parkinson's disease?

22. In what ways is L-dopa treatment disappointing?

ANSWERS

21. L-dopa enters the brain, where neurons convert it to dopamine, thus increasing the supply of a depleted neurotransmitter. **22.** L-dopa is ineffective for some people and has only limited benefits for most others. It does not stop the loss of neurons. It has unpleasant side effects.

Other Therapies

Given the limitations of L-dopa, researchers have sought alternatives and supplements. The following possibilities show promise (Chan et al., 2007; Kreitzer & Malenka, 2007; Leriche et al., 2009; Siderowf & Stern, 2003; Wu & Frucht, 2005):

- Antioxidant drugs to decrease further damage
- Drugs that directly stimulate dopamine receptors
- Drugs that inhibit glutamate or adenosine receptors
- Drugs that stimulate cannabinoid receptors
- Gene therapy: Using a virus to transfer into the brain a gene that increases dopamine synthesis
- Neurotrophins to promote survival and growth of the remaining neurons
- Drugs that decrease apoptosis (programmed cell death) of the remaining neurons
- High-frequency electrical stimulation of the globus pallidus or the subthalamic nucleus

High-frequency electrical stimulation is especially effective for blocking tremors and enhancing movement. However, it also leads to depressed mood by inhibiting serotonin release (Temel et al., 2007). By scrambling activity in the subthalamic nucleus, it leads to impulsive decision making (M. J. Frank, Samanta, Moustafa, & Sherman, 2007).

A potentially exciting strategy has been "in the experimental stage" since the 1980s. In a pioneering study, M. J. Perlow and colleagues (1979) injected the chemical 6-OHDA (a chemical modification of dopamine) into rats to damage the substantia nigra of one hemisphere, producing Parkinson's-type symptoms on the opposite side of the body. After the movement abnormalities stabilized, the experimenters removed the substantia nigra from rat fetuses and transplanted them into the damaged brains. Most recipients recovered much of their normal movement within four weeks. Control animals that suffered the same brain damage without receiving grafts showed little or no recovery. This is only a partial brain transplant, but still, the Frankensteinian implications are striking.

If such surgery works for rats, might it also for humans? The procedure itself is feasible. Perhaps because the blood–brain barrier protects the brain from foreign substances, the immune system is less active in the brain than elsewhere (Nicholas & Arnason, 1992), and physicians can give drugs to further suppress rejection of the transplanted tissue. However, only immature cells transplanted from a fetus can make connections, and simply making connections is not enough. In laboratory research, the recipient animal still has to relearn the behaviors dependent on those cells (Brasted, Watts, Robbins, & Dunnett, 1999). In effect, the animal has to practice using the transplanted cells.

Ordinarily, scientists test any experimental procedure extensively with laboratory animals before trying it on humans, but with Parkinson's disease, the temptation was too great. People in the late stages have little to lose and are willing to try almost anything. The obvious problem is where to get the donor tissue. Several early studies used tissue from the patient's own adrenal gland. Although that tissue is not composed of neurons, it produces and releases dopamine. Unfortunately, the adrenal gland transplants seldom produced much benefit (Backlund et al., 1985).

Another possibility is to transplant brain tissue from aborted fetuses. Fetal neurons transplanted into the brains of Parkinson's patients sometimes survive for years and make synapses with the patient's own cells. However, the operation is difficult and expensive, requiring brain tissue from four to eight aborted fetuses. One way to decrease the need for aborted fetuses is to grow cells in tissue culture, genetically alter them so that they produce large quantities of L-dopa, and then transplant them into the brain (Ljungberg, Stern, & Wilkin, 1999; Studer, Tabar, & McKay, 1998). That idea is particularly attractive if the cells grown in tissue culture are **stem cells**, immature cells that are capable of differentiating into a wide variety of other cell types. Researchers are developing methods to modify adult cells into stem cells so that they might take a patient's own cells and make them suitable for transplants into the brain (Park et al., 2008).

Unfortunately, the results so far with either fetal tissue or stem cells show only modest benefits at best (Freed et al., 2001; Olanow et al., 2003). One limitation is that surgeons usually limit this procedure to aged patients in an advanced stage of the disease. Animal studies find that transplants work best if the damaged area is small and the surrounding cells are healthy (Breysse, Carlsson, Winkler, Björklund, & Kirik, 2007). By the time people reach the stage where surgery seems worth a try, it may be too late to do much good.

The research on brain transplants has suggested yet another possibility for treatment. In several experiments, the transplanted tissue failed to survive, or differentiated into cells other than dopamine cells, but the recipient showed behavioral recovery anyway (Redmond et al., 2007). In many cases, the transplanted tissue releases neurotrophins that stimulate axon and dendrite growth in the recipient's own brain. Providing neurotrophins may be a useful therapy if researchers can find a way to deliver them to the appropriate brain areas (Lindholm et al., 2007). (Neurotrophins do not cross the blood–brain barrier.)

STOP & CHECK

23. What are some possible treatments for Parkinson's disease other than L-dopa?

ANSWER 23. Possible treatments include antioxidants, drugs that stimulate dopamine receptors, drugs that block glutamate or adenosine receptors, transferring a gene into the brain to increase dopamine synthesis, neurotrophins, drugs that decrease apoptosis, high-frequency electrical stimulation of the globus pallidus, and transplants of neurons or stem cells.

Huntington's Disease

Huntington's disease (also known as *Huntington disease* or *Huntington's chorea*) is a severe neurological disorder that strikes about 1 person in 10,000 in the United States (A. B. Young, 1995). Motor symptoms usually begin with arm jerks and facial twitches. Then tremors spread to other parts of the body and develop into writhing (M. A. Smith, Brandt, & Shadmehr, 2000). (*Chorea* comes from the same root as *choreography*. The rhythmic writhing of chorea resembles dancing.) Gradually, the tremors interfere more and more with walking, speech, and other voluntary movements. The ability to learn and improve new movements is especially limited (Willingham et al., 1996). The disorder is associated with gradual, extensive brain damage, especially in the caudate nucleus, putamen, and globus pallidus but also in the cerebral cortex (Tabrizi et al., 1999) (Figure 8.22).

People with Huntington's disease also suffer psychological disorders, including depression, sleep disorders, memory impairment, anxiety, hallucinations and delusions, poor judgment,

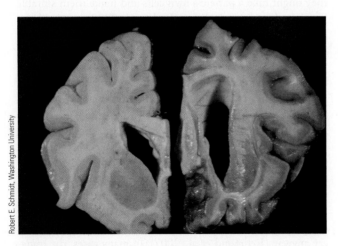

FIGURE 8.22 Brain of a normal person (left) and a person with Huntington's disease (right)
The angle of cut through the normal brain makes the lateral ventricle look larger in this photo than it actually is. Even so, note how much larger it is in the patient with Huntington's disease. The ventricles expand because of the loss of neurons.

Robert E. Schmidt, Washington University

alcoholism, drug abuse, and sexual disorders ranging from complete unresponsiveness to indiscriminate promiscuity (Shoulson, 1990). Deficits in memory and reasoning usually precede the motor symptoms (Robins Wahlin, Lundin, & Dear, 2007). Occasionally, individuals in the early stages of Huntington's disease are misdiagnosed as having schizophrenia.

Huntington's disease most often appears between the ages of 30 and 50, although onset can occur at any time from early childhood to old age. Once the symptoms emerge, both the psychological and the motor symptoms grow progressively worse and culminate in death.

Heredity and Presymptomatic Testing

Huntington's disease results from a dominant gene on chromosome #4. As a rule, a mutant gene that causes the loss of a function is recessive. The fact that the Huntington's gene is dominant implies that it produces the gain of some undesirable function.

Imagine that as a young adult you learn that your mother or father has Huntington's disease. In addition to your grief about your parent, you know that you have a 50% chance of getting the disease yourself. Would you want to know in advance whether or not you were going to get the disease? Knowing the answer might help you decide whether to have children, whether to enter a career that required many years of education, and so forth. However, getting bad news might not be easy to handle.

In 1993, researchers located the gene for Huntington's disease on chromosome number 4, a spectacular accomplishment for the technology available at the time (Huntington's Disease Collaborative Research Group, 1993). Now an examination of your chromosomes can reveal with almost perfect accuracy whether or not you will get Huntington's disease.

The critical area of the gene includes a sequence of bases C-A-G (cytosine, adenine, guanine), which is repeated 11 to 24 times in most people. That repetition produces a string of 11 to 24 glutamines in the resulting protein. People with up to 35 C-A-G repetitions are considered safe from Huntington's disease. Those with 36 to 38 might get it, but probably not until old age. People with 39 or more repetitions are likely to get the disease, unless they die of other causes earlier. The more C-A-G repetitions someone has, the earlier the probable onset of the disease, as shown in Figure 8.23 (U.S.–Venezuela Collaborative Research Project, 2004). In short, a chromosomal examination can predict not only whether a person will get Huntington's disease but also approximately when.

The graph shows a considerable amount of variation in age of onset, especially for those with fewer C-A-G repeats. The variation probably depends partly on stressful experiences, diet, and other influences. It also depends on additional genes. Variant forms of genes controlling glutamate receptors do not produce Huntington's disease by themselves, but they influence the age of onset of symptoms (Andresen et al., 2007).

Figure 8.24 shows comparable data for Huntington's disease and seven other neurological disorders. Each of them relates to an extended sequence of C-A-G repeats in a gene. In

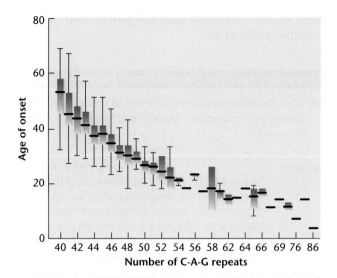

FIGURE 8.23 Relationship between C-A-G repeats and age of onset of Huntington's disease
For each number of C-A-G repeats, the graph shows the age of onset. The green bars show the range that includes the middle 50% of observations, from the 75th percentile to the 25th percentile. The vertical lines show the full range of observations. *(From the U.S.–Venezuela Collaborative Research Project, 2004. Proceedings of the National Academy of Sciences, USA, 101, 3498–3503.)*

each case, people with more repeats have an earlier onset of disease (Gusella & MacDonald, 2000). Those with a smaller number will be older when they get the disease, if they get it at all. Recall a similar fact about Parkinson's disease: Several genes have been linked to early-onset Parkinson's disease, but the late-onset condition is less predictable and probably depends on environmental factors more than genes. As discussed elsewhere in this book, genetic factors are clearly important for early-onset Alzheimer's disease, alcoholism, depression, and schizophrenia. For people with later onset, the role of genetics is weaker or less certain.

Identification of the gene for Huntington's disease led to the discovery of the protein that it codes, which has been designated **huntingtin**. Huntingtin occurs throughout the human body, although its mutant form produces no known harm outside the brain. Within the brain, it occurs inside neurons, not on their membranes. The mutant form impairs neurons in several ways. In the early stages of the disease, it increases neurotransmitter release, sometimes causing overstimulation of the target cells (Romero et al., 2007). Later, the protein forms clusters that impair the neuron's mitochondria (Panov et al., 2002). It also impairs the transport of chemicals down the axon (Morfini et al., 2009).

Identifying the abnormal huntingtin protein and its cellular functions has enabled investigators to search for drugs

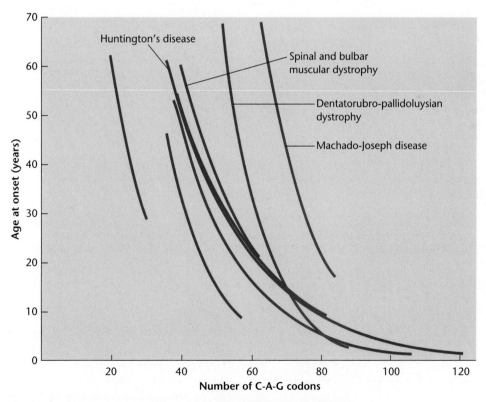

FIGURE 8.24 Relationship between C-A-G repeats and age of onset of eight diseases
The x axis shows the number of C-A-G repeats; the y axis shows the mean age at onset of disease. The various lines represent Huntington's disease and seven others. The four unlabeled lines are for four different types of spinocerebellar ataxia. The key point is that for each disease, the greater the number of repeats, the earlier the probable onset of symptoms. *(Reproduced by permission from "Molecular genetics: Unmasking polyglutamine triggers in neurogenerative disease," by J. F. Gusella and M. E. MacDonald, Figure 1, p. 111 in Neuroscience, 1, pp. 109–115, copyright 2000 Macmillan Magazines, Ltd.)*

that reduce the harm. Researchers have developed strains of mice with the same gene that causes Huntington's disease in humans. Research on these mice has found certain promising drugs. Several drugs block the glutamine chains from clustering (Sánchez, Mahlke, & Yuan, 2003; X. Zhang, Smith, et al., 2005). Another drug interferes with the RNA that enables expression of the huntingtin gene (Harper et al., 2005). Neurotrophins are effective if injected into the brain, although that is not an option for humans. (Neurotrophins do not cross the blood–brain barrier.) A more promising option is drugs that stimulate the brain to make more neurotrophins itself (Dunbar, Sandstrom, Rossignol, & Lescaudron, 2006). Another approach focuses on sleep. Mice with the Huntington's disease mutation, like people with the same mutation, show disrupted circadian patterns and poor sleep as well as impairments in learning and memory. Giving them a daily sleeping pill improved their sleep, learning, and memory (Pal-

lier et al., 2007). A similar approach with humans could improve the quality of life.

STOP & CHECK

24. What procedure enables physicians to predict who will or will not get Huntington's disease and to estimate the age of onset?

ANSWER

24. Physicians can count the number of consecutive repeats of the combination C-A-G on one gene on chromosome 4. If the number is fewer than 36, the person will not develop Huntington's disease. For repeats of 36 or more, the larger the number, the more certain the person is to develop the disease and the earlier the probable age of onset.

MODULE 8.3 ■ IN CLOSING

Heredity and Environment in Movement Disorders

Parkinson's disease and Huntington's disease show that genes influence behavior in different ways. Someone who examines the chromosomes can predict almost certainly who will and who will not develop Huntington's disease and with moderate accuracy predict when. A gene has also been identified for early-onset Parkinson's disease, but for the late-onset version, environmental influences appear to be more important. In later chapters, especially Chapter 15, we shall discuss other instances in which genes increase the risk of certain disorders, but we will not encounter anything with such a strong heritability as Huntington's disease.

SUMMARY

1. Parkinson's disease is characterized by impaired initiation of activity, slow and inaccurate movements, tremors, rigidity, depression, and cognitive deficits. **254**

2. Parkinson's disease is associated with the degeneration of dopamine-containing axons from the substantia nigra to the caudate nucleus and putamen. **254**

3. A gene has been identified that is responsible for early-onset Parkinson's disease. Heredity plays a smaller role in the more common form of Parkinson's disease, with onset after age 50. **254**

4. The chemical MPTP selectively damages neurons in the substantia nigra and leads to the symptoms of Parkinson's disease. Some cases of Parkinson's disease may result in part from exposure to toxins. **255**

5. The most common treatment for Parkinson's disease is L-dopa, which crosses the blood–brain barrier and enters neurons that convert it into dopamine. However, the effectiveness of L-dopa varies, and it produces unwelcome side effects. **256**

6. Many other treatments are in use or at least in the experimental stage. The transfer of immature neurons into a damaged brain area seems to offer great potential, but so far, it has provided little practical benefit. **257**

7. Huntington's disease is a hereditary condition marked by deterioration of motor control as well as depression, memory impairment, and other cognitive disorders. **258**

8. By examining a gene on chromosome 4, physicians can determine whether someone is likely to develop Huntington's disease later in life. The more C-A-G repeats in the gene, the earlier is the likely onset of symptoms. **258**

9. The gene responsible for Huntington's disease alters the structure of a protein, known as huntingtin. The altered protein interferes with functioning of the mitochondria. **259**

KEY TERMS

Terms are defined in the module on the page number indicated. They're also presented in alphabetical order with definitions in the book's Subject Index/Glossary, which begins on page 561. Interactive flashcards and crossword puzzles are among the online resources available to help you learn these terms and the concepts they represent.

huntingtin **259**
Huntington's disease **258**

L-dopa **256**
MPP$^+$ **255**
MPTP **255**

Parkinson's disease **254**
stem cells **257**

THOUGHT QUESTIONS

1. Haloperidol is a drug that blocks dopamine synapses. What effect would it be likely to have in someone suffering from Parkinson's disease?

2. Neurologists assert that if people lived long enough, sooner or later everyone would develop Parkinson's disease. Why?

CHAPTER 8 Interactive Exploration and Study

The **Psychology CourseMate** for this text brings chapter topics to life with interactive learning, study, and exam preparation tools, including quizzes and flashcards for the Key Concepts that appear throughout each module, as well as an interactive media-rich eBook version of the text that is fully searchable and includes highlighting and note taking capabilities and interactive versions of the book's **Stop & Check** quizzes and **Try It Yourself Online** activities. The site also features **Virtual Biological Psychology Labs, videos,** and **animations** to help you better understand concepts—logon and learn more at **www.cengagebrain.com**, which is your gateway to all of this text's complimentary and premium resources, including the following:

Virtual Biological Psychology Labs

© 2013 Cengage Learning

Explore the experiments that led to modern-day understanding of biopsychology with the Virtual Biological Psychology Labs, featuring a realistic lab environment that allows you to conduct experiments and evaluate data to better understand how scientists came to the conclusions presented in your text. The labs cover a range of topics, including perception, motivation, cognition, and more. You may purchase access at **www.cengagebrain.com**, or login at **login.cengagebrain.com** if an access card was included with your text.

Videos

© 2013 Cengage Learning

Mu Rhythms = Alpha Brainwaves

Mirror Neurons

Animations

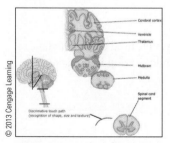
© 2013 Cengage Learning

Paths of Touch and Motor Control

Also available—
- Withdrawal Reflex
- Crossed Extensor Reflex
- Cellular Organization of the Cerebellum

Suggestions for Further Exploration

Books

Klawans, H. L. (1996). *Why Michael couldn't hit*. New York: Freeman. A collection of fascinating sports examples related to the brain and its disorders.

Lashley, K. S. (1951). The problem of serial order in behavior. In L. A. Jeffress (Ed.), *Cerebral mechanisms in behavior* (pp. 112–136). New York: Wiley. This classic article in psychology is a thought-provoking appraisal of what a theory of movement should explain.

Websites

The Psychology CourseMate for this text provides regularly updated links to relevant online resources for this chapter, such as sites for Parkinson's disease and Huntington's disease.

Wakefulness and Sleep

9

MAIN IDEAS

1. The brain generates a wake–sleep cycle of approximately 24 hours even in an unchanging environment.

2. Sleep progresses through various stages that differ in brain activity, heart rate, and other aspects. A stage known as paradoxical or REM sleep is light in some ways and deep in others.

3. Areas in the brainstem and forebrain control arousal and sleep. Localized brain damage can produce prolonged sleep or wakefulness.

4. Because sleep depends on inhibition of brain activity, sometimes one brain area is awake while another is asleep, as in the case of sleepwalking.

5. Sleep can be impaired in many ways.

6. We need sleep and REM sleep, although much about their functions remains uncertain.

A nyone deprived of sleep suffers. But if life evolved on another planet with different conditions, could animals evolve life without a need for sleep? Imagine a planet that doesn't rotate on its axis. Some animals evolve adaptations to live in the light area, others in the dark area, and still others in the twilight zone separating light from dark. There would be no need for any animal to alternate active periods with inactive periods on any fixed schedule and perhaps no need for prolonged inactive periods. If you were the astronaut who discovered these sleepless animals, you might be surprised.

Now imagine that astronauts from that planet set out on their first voyage to Earth. Imagine *their* surprise to discover animals like us with long inactive periods resembling death. To someone who hadn't seen sleep before, it would seem mysterious indeed. For the purposes of this chapter, let's adopt their perspective and ask why animals as active as we are spend one third of our lives doing so little.

OPPOSITE: Rock hyraxes at a national park in Kenya.

Rhythms of Waking and Sleeping

Y ou are probably not amazed to learn that your body spontaneously generates its own rhythm of wakefulness and sleep. Psychologists of an earlier era strongly resisted that idea. When behaviorism dominated experimental psychology during the mid-1900s, many psychologists believed that every behavior could be traced to external stimuli. For example, alternation between wakefulness and sleep must depend on something in the outside world, such as changes in light or temperature. Research as early as that of Curt Richter (1922) implied that the body generates its own cycles of activity and inactivity, but it took a huge amount of research to convince the skeptics. The idea of self-generated rhythms was a major step toward viewing animals as active producers of behaviors.

▌Endogenous Cycles

An animal that produced its behavior entirely in response to current stimuli would be at a serious disadvantage. Animals often need to anticipate changes in the environment. For example, migratory birds start flying toward their winter homes before their summer territory becomes too cold. A bird that waited for the first frost would be in trouble. Similarly, squirrels begin storing nuts and putting on extra layers of fat in preparation for winter long before food becomes scarce.

Animals' readiness for a change in seasons comes partly from internal mechanisms. Changes in the light–dark pattern of the day tell a migratory bird when to fly south for the winter, but what tells it when to fly back north? In the tropics, the temperature and amount of daylight are nearly the same throughout the year. Nevertheless, a migratory bird flies north at the right time. Even if it is kept in a cage with no clues to the season, it becomes restless in the spring, and if it is released, it flies north (Gwinner, 1986). Evidently, the bird generates a rhythm that prepares it for seasonal changes. We refer to that rhythm as an **endogenous circannual rhythm**. (*Endogenous* means "generated from within." *Circannual* comes from the Latin words *circum*, for "about," and *annum*, for "year.")

Animals also produce **endogenous circadian rhythms** that last about a day. (*Circadian* comes from *circum*, for "about," and *dies*, for "day.") If you go without sleep all night—as most college students do, sooner or later—you feel sleepier and sleepier as the night goes on, but as morning arrives, you feel more alert, not less. The light from the sun helps you feel less sleepy, but also your urge to sleep depends partly on the time of day, not just how long you have been awake (Babkoff, Caspy, Mikulincer, & Sing, 1991).

Figure 9.1 represents the activity of a flying squirrel kept in total darkness for 25 days. Each horizontal line represents one 24-hour day. A thickening in the line represents a period of activity. Even in this unchanging environment, the animal generates a consistent rhythm of activity and sleep. Depending on the individual and the details of the procedure, the self-generated cycle may be slightly shorter than 24 hours, as in Figure 9.1, or slightly longer (Carpenter & Grossberg, 1984).

Humans also generate wake–sleep rhythms, and we find it difficult to sleep on anything far from a 24-hour schedule. We can modify it a little. If we ever send astronauts to Mars, they will have to adjust to the Martian day, which lasts about 24 hours and 39 minutes of Earth time. Researchers have found that people can adjust to that schedule without much difficulty (Scheer, Wright, Kronauer, & Czeisler, 2007). Circadian rhythms may be the least of our problems if we travel to Mars. However, more severe departures from a 24-hour schedule pose difficulties. Naval personnel on U.S. nuclear-powered submarines are cut off from sunlight for months at a time, living under faint artificial light. In many cases, they live on a schedule of 6 hours of work alternating with 12 hours of rest. Even though they sleep (or *try* to sleep) on this 18-hour schedule, their bodies generate rhythms of alertness and body chemistry that average about 24.3 to 24.4 hours (Kelly et al., 1999).

Circadian rhythms affect much more than just waking and sleeping. We have circadian rhythms in our eating and drinking, urination, secretion of hormones, sensitivity to drugs, and other variables. For example, although we ordinarily think of human body temperature as 37° C, normal temperature fluctuates over the course of a day from

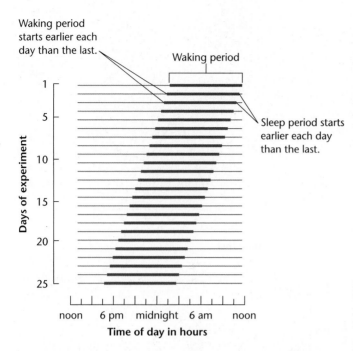

Waking period starts earlier each day than the last.

Waking period

Sleep period starts earlier each day than the last.

FIGURE 9.1 Activity record of a flying squirrel kept in constant darkness
The thickened segments indicate periods of activity as measured by a running wheel. Note that this free-running activity cycle lasts slightly less than 24 hours. *(From "Phase Control of Activity in a Rodent," by P. J. DeCoursey,* Cold Spring Harbor Symposia on Quantitative Biology, *1960, 25, 49–55. Reprinted by permission of Cold Spring Harbor and P. J. DeCoursey.)*

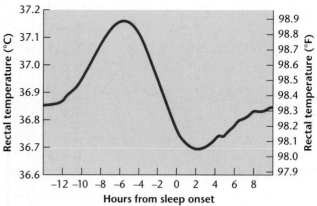

FIGURE 9.2 Mean rectal temperatures for nine adults
Body temperature reaches its low for the day about 2 hours after sleep onset; it reaches its peak about 6 hours before sleep onset. *(From "Sleep-Onset Insomniacs Have Delayed Temperature Rhythms," by M. Morris, L. Lack, and D. Dawson,* Sleep, *1990, 13, 1–14. Reprinted by permission.)*

a low near 36.7° C during the night to almost 37.2° C in late afternoon (Figure 9.2). We also have circadian rhythms in mood. In one study, young adults recorded their mood every two hours throughout the day. Although the results varied among individuals, most showed increases in positive mood (happiness) from waking until late afternoon, and then a slight decline from then to bedtime. In a follow-up study, the same investigators kept young adults awake for 30 consecutive hours, starting at either 10 a.m. or 5 p.m., in a laboratory setting with constant levels of light and temperature. Regardless of whether people started this procedure at 10 a.m. or 5 p.m., most reported their most pleasant mood around 5 p.m. and their least pleasant mood at around 5 a.m. (Murray et al., 2009). These results suggest a biologically driven circadian rhythm in our emotional well-being (Figure 9.3).

Circadian rhythms differ among individuals. Some people ("morning people," or "larks") awaken early, quickly become productive, and become less alert as the day progresses. Others ("evening people," or "owls") warm up more slowly, both literally and figuratively, reaching their peak in the late afternoon or evening. They tolerate staying up all night better than morning people do (Taillard, Philip, Coste, Sagaspe, & Bioulac, 2003).

Not everyone falls neatly into one extreme or the other, of course. A convenient way to compare people is to ask, "On holidays and vacations when you have no obligations, what time is the middle of your sleep?" For example, if you sleep from 1 a.m. until 9 a.m. on those days, your middle is 5 a.m. As Figure 9.4 shows, people differ by age. As a child, you almost certainly went to bed early and woke up early. As you entered adolescence, you started staying up later and waking up later, when you had the opportunity. The mean preferred time of going to sleep gets later and later until about age 20 and then starts a gradual reversal (Roenneberg et al., 2004).

Do people older than 20 learn to go to bed earlier because they have jobs that require them to get up early? Maybe, but two facts point instead to a biological explanation. First, in Figure 9.4, note how the shift continues gradually over decades. If people were simply adjusting to their jobs, we might expect a sudden shift in the early 20s and then steadiness until retirement. Second, a similar trend occurs in rats: Older rats reach their best performance shortly after awakening, whereas younger rats tend to improve performance as the day progresses (Winocur & Hasher, 1999, 2004).

STOP & CHECK

1. What evidence indicates that humans have an internal biological clock?

ANSWER   **1.** People who have lived in an environment with a light–dark schedule much different from 24 hours fail to follow that schedule and instead become wakeful and sleepy on about a 24-hour basis.

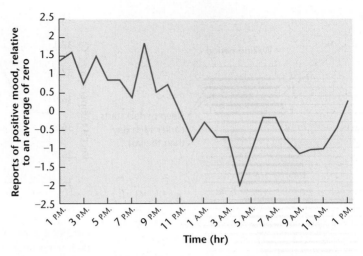

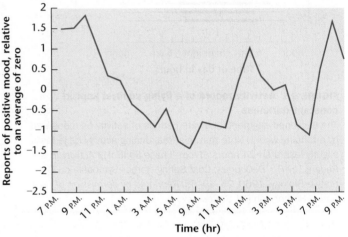

FIGURE 9.3 Reported positive mood over time
During 30 hours in an unchanging laboratory environment, the average young adult reported the most pleasant mood in the late afternoon or early evening, and the least pleasant mood around 5 to 7 a.m. The pattern was similar for those who started the procedure in the morning (above) or in the evening (below). *(From Murray, G., Nicholas, C. L., Kleiman, J., Dwyer, R., Carrington, M. J., Allen, N. B., et al. (2009). Nature's clocks and human mood: The circadian system modulates reward motivation.* Emotion, *9, 705–716.)*

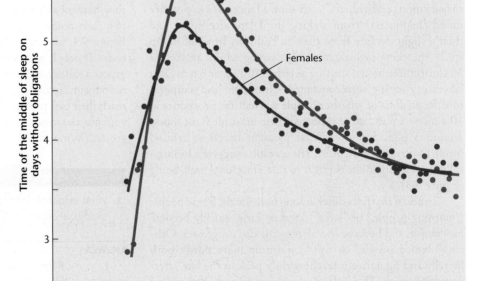

FIGURE 9.4 Age differences in circadian rhythms
People reported the time of the middle of their sleep, such as 3 a.m. or 5 a.m., on days when they had no obligations. *(Reprinted from T. Roenneberg et al., "A Marker for the End of Adolescence," Current Biology, 14, R1038–R1039.) Figure 1, copyright 2004, with permission from Elsevier.)*

Setting and Resetting the Biological Clock

Our circadian rhythms generate a period close to 24 hours, but they are not perfect. We readjust our internal workings daily to stay in phase with the world. Sometimes, we misadjust them. On weekends, when most of us are freer to set our own schedules, we expose ourselves to lights, noises, and activity at night and then awaken late the next morning. By Monday morning, when the clock indicates 7 a.m., the biological clock within us may say 5 a.m., and we stagger off to work or school without much pep (Moore-Ede, Czeisler, & Richardson, 1983).

Although circadian rhythms persist without light, light is critical for resetting them. Without something to reset your circadian rhythm, it would gradually drift away from the correct time. The stimulus that resets the circadian rhythm is referred to by the German term **zeitgeber** (TSITE-gay-ber), meaning "time-giver." Light is the dominant zeitgeber for land animals (Rusak & Zucker, 1979). (The tides are important for many marine animals.) In addition to light, other zeitgebers include exercise (Eastman, Hoese, Young-stedt, & Liu, 1995), arousal of any kind (Gritton, Sutton, Martinez, Sarter, & Lee, 2009), meals, and the temperature of the environment (Refinetti, 2000). Social stimuli—that is, the effects of other people—are weak zeitgebers, unless they induce exercise or other vigorous activity (Mistlberger & Skene, 2004). These additional zeitgebers merely supplement or alter the effects of light. On their own, their effects are weak. For example, people who are working in Antarctica during the constant darkness of an Antarctic winter try to maintain a 24-hour rhythm, but they drift away from it. Different people generate different rhythms, until they find it more and more difficult to work together (Kennaway & Van Dorp, 1991). Astronauts in Earth orbit face a special problem: As they orbit the Earth, a 45-minute period of daylight alternates with 45 minutes of darkness. If they retreat from the flight deck to elsewhere in the spacecraft, they have constant dim light. As a result, they are never fully alert during their wakeful periods and they sleep poorly during their rest periods (Dijk et al., 2001). On long trips, many of them experience depression, irritability, and impaired performance (Mallis & DeRoshia, 2005).

Even when we try to set our wake–sleep cycles by the clock, sunlight has its influence. Consider what happens when we shift to daylight savings time in spring. You set your clock to an hour later, and when it shows your usual bedtime, you dutifully go to bed, even though it seems an hour too early. The next morning, when the clock says it is 7 a.m. and time to get ready for work, your brain registers 6 a.m. Most people remain inefficient and ill-rested for days after the shift to daylight savings time. The adjustment is especially difficult for people who were already sleep-deprived, including most college students (Lahti et al., 2006; Monk & Aplin, 1980).

Particularly impressive evidence for the importance of sunlight comes from a study in Germany. The sun time at the eastern end of Germany differs by about half an hour from that at the western edge, even though everyone is on the same clock time. Researchers asked adults for their preferred times of awakening and going to sleep and determined for each person the midpoint of those values. (For example, if on weekends and holidays you prefer to go to bed at 12:30 a.m. and awaken at 8:30 a.m., your sleep midpoint is 4:30 a.m.) Figure 9.5 shows the results. People at the eastern edge have a sleep midpoint about 30 minutes earlier than those at the west, corresponding to the fact that the sun rises earlier at the eastern edge (Roenneberg, Kumar, & Merrow, 2007). The data shown here apply to people in towns and cities with populations under 300,000. People in larger cities show a less consistent trend, presumably because they spend more time indoors with less exposure to the sun.

What about blind people, who need to set their circadian rhythms by zeitgebers other than light? The results vary. Some do set their circadian rhythms by noise, temperature, meals, and activity. However, others who are not sufficiently sensitive to these secondary zeitgebers produce circadian rhythms that are a little longer than 24 hours. When their cycles are in phase with the clock, all is well, but when they drift out of phase, they experience insomnia at night and sleepiness during the day (Sack & Lewy, 2001).

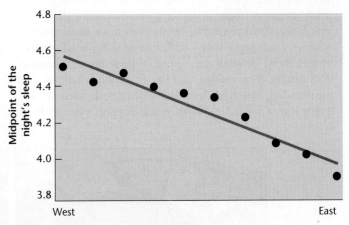

FIGURE 9.5 Sun time competes with social time
On days when people have no obligation to awaken at a particular time, they awaken about half an hour earlier at the eastern edge of Germany than at the western edge. Points along the y axis represent the midpoint between the preferred bedtime and the preferred waking time. Data are for people living in towns and cities with populations less than 300,000. *(From Roenneberg, T., et al. (2007). "The human circadian clock entrains to sun time." Current Biology, 17, R44–R45. Reprinted by permission of the Copyright Clearance Center.)*

2. Why do people at the eastern edge of Germany awaken earlier than those at the western edge on their weekends and holidays?

ANSWER 2. The sun rises about half an hour earlier at the eastern edge than at the western edge. Evidently, the sun controls waking–sleeping schedules even when people follow the same clock time for their work schedule.

Jet Lag

A disruption of circadian rhythms due to crossing time zones is known as **jet lag**. Travelers complain of sleepiness during the day, sleeplessness at night, depression, and impaired concentration. All these problems stem from the mismatch between internal circadian clock and external time (Haimov & Arendt, 1999). Most people find it easier to adjust to crossing time zones going west than east. Going west, we stay awake later at night and then awaken late the next morning, already partly adjusted to the new schedule. We *phase-delay* our circadian rhythms. Going east, we *phase-advance* to sleep earlier and awaken earlier (Figure 9.6). Most people find it difficult to go to sleep before their body's usual time and difficult to wake up early the next day.

Adjusting to jet lag is often stressful. Stress elevates blood levels of the adrenal hormone *cortisol*, and many studies have shown that prolonged elevations of cortisol damage neurons in the hippocampus, a brain area important for memory. One study examined flight attendants who had spent the previous 5 years making flights across 7 or more time zones—such as Chicago to Italy—with mostly short breaks (fewer than 6 days) between trips. Most of these flight attendants had smaller than average volumes of the hippocampus and surrounding structures, and they showed some memory impairments (Cho, 2001). These results suggest a danger from repeated adjustments of the circadian rhythm, although the problem here could be air travel itself. (A good control group would have been flight attendants who flew long north–south routes.)

Shift Work

People who sleep irregularly—such as pilots, medical interns, and shift workers in factories—find that their duration of sleep depends on when they go to sleep. When they have to sleep in the morning or early afternoon, they sleep only briefly, even if they have been awake for many hours (Frese & Harwich, 1984; Winfree, 1983).

People who work on a night shift, such as midnight to 8 a.m., sleep during the day. At least they try to. Even after months or years on such a schedule, many workers adjust incompletely. They continue to feel groggy on the job, they sleep poorly during the day, and their body temperature continues to peak when they are sleeping in the day instead of while they are working at night. In general, night–shift workers have more accidents than day–shift workers.

Working at night does not reliably change the circadian rhythm because most buildings use artificial lighting in the range of 150–180 lux, which is only moderately effective in resetting the rhythm (Boivin, Duffy, Kronauer, & Czeisler, 1996). People adjust best to night work if they sleep in a very dark room during the day and work under very bright lights at night, comparable to the noonday sun (Czeisler et al., 1990).

Mechanisms of the Biological Clock

How does the body generate a circadian rhythm? Curt Richter (1967) introduced the concept that the brain generates its own rhythms—a biological clock—and he reported that the biological clock is insensitive to most forms of interference.

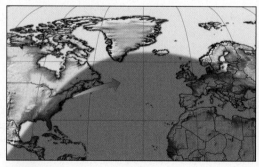
(a) Leave New York at 7 P.M.

(b) Arrive in London at 7 A.M., which is 2 A.M. in New York

FIGURE 9.6 **Jet lag**
Eastern time is later than western time. People who travel six time zones east fall asleep on the plane and then must awaken when it is morning at their destination but night back home. (© *Cengage Learning 2013*)

Blind or deaf animals generate circadian rhythms, although they slowly drift out of phase with the external world. The circadian rhythm remains surprisingly steady despite food or water deprivation, X-rays, tranquilizers, alcohol, anesthesia, lack of oxygen, most kinds of brain damage, or the removal of endocrine organs. Even an hour or more of induced hibernation often fails to reset the biological clock (Gibbs, 1983; Richter, 1975). Evidently, the biological clock is a hardy, robust mechanism.

The Suprachiasmatic Nucleus (SCN)

The biological clock depends on part of the hypothalamus, called the **suprachiasmatic** (soo-pruh-kie-as-MAT-ik) **nucleus**, or **SCN**. It gets its name from its location just above ("supra") the optic chiasm (Figure 9.7). The SCN provides the main control of the circadian rhythms for sleep and body temperature (Refinetti & Menaker, 1992), although several other brain areas generate local rhythms (Granados-Fuentes, Tseng, & Herzog, 2006). After damage to the SCN, the body's rhythms become erratic.

The SCN generates circadian rhythms itself in a genetically controlled, unlearned manner. If SCN neurons are disconnected from the rest of the brain or removed from the body and maintained in tissue culture, they continue to produce a circadian rhythm of action potentials (Earnest, Liang, Ratcliff, & Cassone, 1999; Inouye & Kawamura, 1979). Even a single isolated SCN cell can maintain a circadian rhythm, although interactions among cells sharpen the accuracy of the rhythm (Long, Jutras, Connors, & Burwell, 2005; Yamaguchi et al., 2003).

A mutation in one gene causes hamsters' SCN to produce a 20-hour instead of 24-hour rhythm (Ralph & Menaker, 1988). Researchers surgically removed the SCN from adult hamsters and transplanted SCN tissue from hamster fetuses into the adults. When they transplanted SCN tissue from fetuses with a 20-hour rhythm, the recipients produced a 20-hour rhythm. When they transplanted tissue from fetuses with a 24-hour rhythm, the recipients produced a 24-hour rhythm (Ralph, Foster, Davis, & Menaker, 1990). That is, the rhythm followed the pace of the donors, not the recipients. Again, the results show that the rhythms come from the SCN itself.

Curt P. Richter
(1894–1988)
I enjoy research more than eating.

3. What evidence strongly indicates that the SCN produces the circadian rhythm itself?

ANSWER 3. SCN cells produce a circadian rhythm of activity even if they are kept in cell culture isolated from the rest of the body. Also, when hamsters received transplanted SCN neurons, their circadian rhythm followed the pattern of the donor animals.

How Light Resets the SCN

The SCN is located just above the optic chiasm. Figure 9.7 shows the position in the human brain. The relationship is similar in other mammals. A small branch of the optic nerve, known as the *retinohypothalamic path*, extends directly from the retina to the SCN. Axons of that path alter the SCN's settings.

Most of the input to that path, however, does not come from normal retinal receptors. Mice with genetic defects that destroy nearly all their rods and cones nevertheless reset their biological clocks in synchrony with the light (Freedman et al., 1999; Lucas, Freedman, Muñoz, Garcia-Fernández, & Foster, 1999). Also, consider blind mole rats (Figure 9.8). Their eyes are covered with folds of skin and fur. They have neither eye muscles nor a lens with which to focus an image. They have fewer than 900 optic nerve axons compared with 100,000 in hamsters. Even a bright flash of light evokes no startle response and no measurable change in brain activity. Nevertheless, light resets their circadian rhythms (de Jong, Hendriks, Sanyal, & Nevo, 1990).

The surprising explanation is that the retinohypothalamic path to the SCN comes from a special population of retinal ganglion cells that have their own photopigment, called *melanopsin*, unlike the ones found in rods and cones (Hannibal, Hindersson, Knudsen, Georg, & Fahrenkrug, 2001; Lucas, Douglas, & Foster, 2001). These special ganglion cells receive some input from rods and cones (Gooley et al., 2010; Güler et al., 2008), but even if they do not receive that input, they respond directly to light (Berson, Dunn, & Takao, 2002). These special ganglion cells are located mainly near the nose, not evenly throughout the retina (Visser, Beersma, & Daan, 1999). (That is, they see toward the periphery.) They respond to light slowly and turn off slowly when the light ceases (Berson et al., 2002). Therefore, they respond to the overall average amount of light, not to instantaneous changes in light. The average intensity over a period of minutes or hours is, of course, exactly the information the SCN needs to gauge the time of day.

Note a couple of consequences: First, many people who are blind because of damage to the rods and cones nevertheless have enough input to the melanopsin-containing ganglion cells to entrain their waking and sleeping cycle to the local pattern of sunlight. Second, it was formerly puzzling that bright

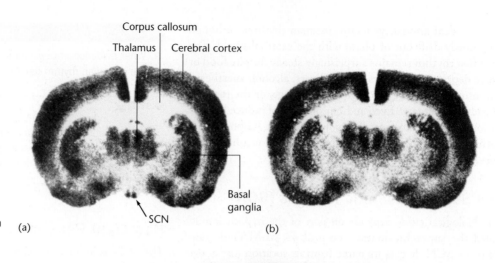

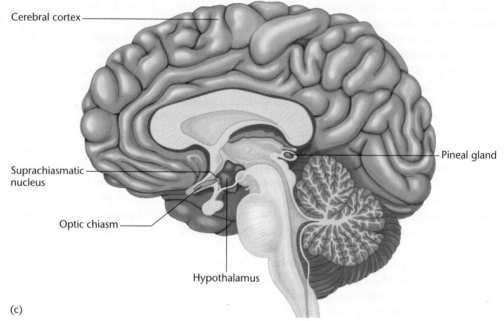

FIGURE 9.7 The suprachiasmatic nucleus (SCN) of rats and humans The SCN is located at the base of the brain, as seen in these coronal sections through the plane of the anterior hypothalamus. Each rat was injected with radioactive 2-deoxyglucose, which is absorbed by the most active neurons. A high level of absorption of this chemical produces a dark appearance on the slide. Note the greater activity in SCN neurons of a rat injected during the day (a) than in one injected at night (b). (From "Suprachiasmatic nucleus: Use of 14C-labeled deoxyglucose uptake as a functional marker," by W. J. Schwartz & H. Gainer, *Science*, 1977, 197: 1089–1091. Reprinted by permission from AAAS/American Association for the Advancement of Science.) (c) A sagittal section through a human brain showing the location of the SCN and the pineal gland. (© Cengage Learning 2013)

light aggravates migraine headaches even for many blind people. The explanation is that the melanopsin-containing ganglion cells send input to the posterior thalamus, which is part of the pathway producing pain in migraines (Noseda, et al., 2010). Someone with no input to the visual cortex, and therefore no conscious vision, can nevertheless have light-sensitive excitation in the thalamus.

STOP & CHECK

4. How does light reset the biological clock?

ANSWER

4. A branch of the optic nerve, the retinohypothalamic path, conveys information about light to the SCN. The axons comprising that path originate from special ganglion cells that respond to light by themselves, even if they do not receive input from rods or cones.

FIGURE 9.8 A blind mole rat Although blind mole rats are blind in other regards, they reset their circadian rhythms in response to light.

The Biochemistry of the Circadian Rhythm

The suprachiasmatic nucleus produces the circadian rhythm, but how? Research on production of the circadian rhythm began with insects. Studies on the fruit fly *Drosophila* found several genes responsible for a circadian rhythm (X. Liu et al., 1992; Sehgal, Ousley, Yang, Chen, & Schotland, 1999). Two of these genes, known as *period* (abbreviated *per*) and *timeless* (*tim*), produce the proteins PER and TIM. The concentration of these two proteins, which promote sleep and inactivity, oscillates over a day, based on feedback interactions among several sets of neurons. Early in the morning, the messenger RNA levels responsible for producing PER and TIM start at low concentrations. As they increase during the day, they increase synthesis of the proteins, but the process takes time, and so the protein concentrations lag hours behind, as shown in Figure 9.9. As the PER and TIM protein concentrations increase, they feed back to inhibit the genes that produce the messenger RNA molecules. Thus, during the night, the PER and TIM concentrations are high, but the messenger RNA concentrations are declining (Nitabach & Taghert, 2008). By the next morning, PER and TIM protein levels are low, the flies awaken, and the cycle is ready to start again. Because the feedback cycle takes about 24 hours, the flies generate a circadian rhythm even in an unchanging environment. However, in addition to the automatic feedback, light activates a chemical that breaks down the TIM protein, thereby increasing wakefulness and synchronizing the internal clock to the external world (Ashmore & Sehgal, 2003).

Why do we care about flies? The reason is that analyzing the mechanism in flies told researchers what to look for in humans and other mammals. Mammals have three versions of the PER protein and several proteins closely related to TIM and the others found in flies (Reick, Garcia, Dudley, & McKnight, 2001; Zheng et al., 1999). Mutations in the genes producing PER proteins lead to alterations of sleep schedules. People with a particular PER mutation have been found to have a circadian rhythm shorter than 24 hours, as if they were moving about a time zone west every day (C. R. Jones et al., 1999). They consistently get sleepy early in the evening and awaken early in the morning (Toh et al., 2001; Xu et al., 2005). Most people look forward to days when they can stay up late. People with the altered gene look forward to times when they can go to bed early. Most people with this sleep abnormality suffer from depression (Xu et al., 2005). As we see again in Chapter 15, sleep impairments and depression are closely linked. Another PER mutation has been identified that is more common but less intrusive. People with this gene are normal in most regards except that their alertness deteriorates substantially if they are deprived of a good night's sleep (Dijk & Archer, 2010).

> **STOP & CHECK**
>
> **5.** How do the proteins TIM and PER relate to sleepiness in *Drosophila*?
>
> **ANSWER**
>
> **5.** The proteins TIM and PER remain low during most of the day and begin to increase toward evening. They reach high levels at night, promoting sleep. They also feed back to inhibit the genes that produce them, so that their level declines toward morning.

Melatonin

The SCN regulates waking and sleeping by controlling activity levels in other brain areas, including the **pineal gland** (PIN-ee-al; Figure 9.7), an endocrine gland located just posterior to the thalamus (Aston-Jones, Chen, Zhu, & Oshinsky, 2001; von Gall et al., 2002). The pineal gland releases the hormone **melatonin**, which influences both circadian and circannual rhythms (Butler et al., 2010). The pineal gland secretes melatonin mostly at night, making us sleepy at that time. When people shift to a new time zone and start following a

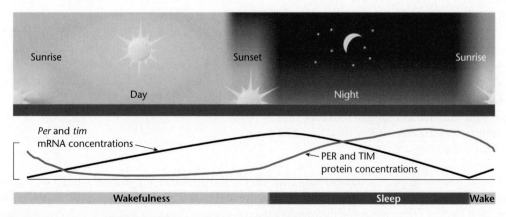

FIGURE 9.9 Feedback between proteins and genes to control sleepiness
In fruit flies *(Drosophila)*, the concentrations of the mRNA levels for PER and TIM oscillate over a day, and so do the proteins that they produce. *(© Cengage Learning 2013)*

new schedule, they continue to feel sleepy at their old times until the melatonin rhythm shifts (Dijk & Cajochen, 1997). People who have pineal gland tumors sometimes stay awake for days at a time (Haimov & Lavie, 1996).

Melatonin secretion starts to increase about 2 or 3 hours before bedtime. Taking a melatonin pill in the evening has little effect on sleepiness because the pineal gland produces melatonin at that time anyway. However, people who take melatonin at other times become sleepy within 2 hours (Haimov & Lavie, 1996). Melatonin pills are sometimes helpful when people travel across time zones or for other reasons need to sleep at an unaccustomed time.

Melatonin also feeds back to reset the biological clock through its effects on receptors in the SCN (Gillette & McArthur, 1996). A moderate dose of melatonin (0.5 mg) in the afternoon phase-advances the clock. That is, it makes the person get sleepy earlier in the evening and wake up earlier the next morning. A single dose of melatonin in the morning has little effect (Wirz-Justice, Werth, Renz, Müller, & Kräuchi, 2002), although repeated morning doses can phase-delay the clock, causing the person to get sleepy later than usual at night and awaken later the next morning.

MODULE 9.1 ■ IN CLOSING

Sleep–Wake Cycles

Unlike an electric appliance that stays on until someone turns it off, the brain periodically turns itself on and off. Sleepiness is not a voluntary or optional act. We have biological mechanisms that prepare us to wake at certain times and sleep at other times, even if we would prefer different schedules.

SUMMARY

1. Animals, including humans, have circadian rhythms—internally generated rhythms of activity and sleep lasting about 24 hours, even in an unchanging environment. It is difficult to adjust to a sleep schedule much different from 24 hours. **266**

2. Some people are most alert early in the morning, and others become more alert later in the day. On average, people show their greatest preference for staying awake late and sleeping late the next morning when they are about 20 years old. **267**

3. Although the biological clock continues to operate in constant light or constant darkness, the onset of light resets the clock. Even when people set their waking and sleeping times by the clock, the timing of sunrise strongly influences their circadian rhythm. **268**

4. It is easier for most people to follow a cycle longer than 24 hours (as when traveling west) than to follow a cycle shorter than 24 hours (as when traveling east). **270**

5. If people wish to work at night and sleep during the day, the best way to shift the circadian rhythm is to have bright lights at night and darkness during the day. **270**

6. The suprachiasmatic nucleus (SCN), a part of the hypothalamus, generates the body's circadian rhythms for sleep and temperature. **271**

7. Light resets the biological clock by a branch of the optic nerve that extends to the SCN. Those axons originate from a special population of ganglion cells that respond directly to light in addition to receiving some input from rods and cones. **272**

8. The genes controlling the circadian rhythm are almost the same in mammals as in insects. Circadian rhythms result from a feedback cycle based on genes that produce the proteins PER and TIM, and the ability of those proteins to inhibit the genes that produce them. **273**

9. The SCN controls the body's rhythm partly by directing the release of melatonin by the pineal gland. The hormone melatonin increases sleepiness; if given at certain times of the day, it can also reset the circadian rhythm. **274**

KEY TERMS

Terms are defined in the module on the page number indicated. They're also presented in alphabetical order with definitions in the book's Subject Index/Glossary, which begins on page 561. Interactive flashcards and crossword puzzles are among the online resources available to help you learn these terms and the concepts they represent.

THOUGHT QUESTIONS

1. Why would evolution have enabled blind mole rats to synchronize their SCN activity to light, even though they cannot see well enough to make any use of the light?

2. If you travel across several time zones to the east and want to use melatonin to help reset your circadian rhythm, at what time of day should you take it? What if you travel west?

Stages of Sleep and Brain Mechanisms

Suppose you buy a new radio. After you play it for 4 hours, it suddenly stops. You wonder whether the batteries are dead or whether the radio needs repair. Later, you discover that this radio always stops after playing for 4 hours but operates again a few hours later even without repairs or a battery change. You begin to suspect that the manufacturer designed it this way, perhaps to prevent you from listening to the radio all day. Now you want to find the device that turns it off whenever you play it for 4 hours. You are asking a new question. When you thought that the radio stopped because it needed repairs or new batteries, you did not ask which device turned it off.

Similarly, if we think of sleep as something like wearing out a machine, we do not ask which part of the brain produces it. But if we think of sleep as a specialized state evolved to serve particular functions, we look for the mechanisms that regulate it.

Sleep and Other Interruptions of Consciousness

Let's start with some distinctions. Sleep is a state that the brain actively produces, characterized by decreased response to stimuli. In contrast, **coma** (KOH-muh) is an extended period of unconsciousness caused by head trauma, stroke, or disease. It is possible to awaken a sleeping person but not someone in a coma. A person in a coma has a low level of brain activity throughout the day, and little or no response to stimuli, including those that are ordinarily painful. Any movements that occur are purposeless and not directed toward anything. Typically, someone in a coma either dies or begins to recover within a few weeks.

Someone in a **vegetative state** alternates between periods of sleep and moderate arousal, although even during the more aroused state, the person shows no awareness of surroundings. Breathing is more regular, and a painful stimulus produces at least the autonomic responses of increased heart rate, breathing, and sweating. The person does not speak, respond to speech, or show any purposeful activity. However, people in this state probably have some cognitive activity (Guérit, 2005). A **minimally conscious state** is one

stage higher, with occasional, brief periods of purposeful actions and a limited amount of speech comprehension. A vegetative or minimally conscious state can last for months or years.

Brain death is a condition with no sign of brain activity and no response to any stimulus. Physicians usually wait until someone has shown no sign of brain activity for 24 hours before pronouncing brain death, at which point most people believe it is ethical to remove life support.

Stages of Sleep

Nearly every scientific advance comes from new or improved measurements. Researchers did not even suspect that sleep has different stages until they accidentally measured them. The electroencephalograph (EEG), as described in Chapter 4, records an average of the electrical potentials of the cells and fibers in the brain areas nearest each electrode on the scalp (Figure 9.10). If half the cells in some area increase their electrical potentials while the other half decrease, they cancel out. The EEG record rises or falls when most cells do the same thing at the same time. You might compare it to a record of the noise in a crowded sports stadium: It shows only slight fluctuations until some event gets everyone yelling at once. The EEG enables brain researchers to compare brain activity at different times during sleep.

Figure 9.11 shows data from a **polysomnograph**, a combination of EEG and eye-movement records, for a college student during various stages of sleep. Figure 9.11a presents a period of relaxed wakefulness for comparison. Note the steady series of **alpha waves** at a frequency of 8 to 12 per second. Alpha waves are characteristic of relaxation, not of all wakefulness.

In Figure 9.11b, sleep has just begun. During this period, called stage 1 sleep, the EEG is dominated by irregular, jagged, low-voltage waves. Overall brain activity is less than in relaxed wakefulness but higher than other sleep stages. As Figure 9.11c shows, the most prominent characteristics of stage 2 are sleep spindles and K-complexes. A **sleep spindle** consists of 12- to 14-Hz waves during a burst that lasts at least half a second. Sleep spindles result from oscillating interactions between cells in the thalamus and the cortex. A **K-complex** is a

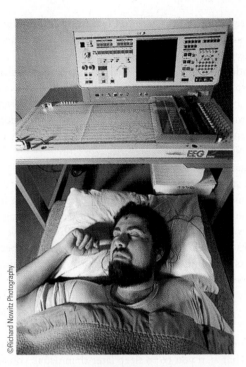

FIGURE 9.10 Sleeping person with electrodes in place on the scalp for recording brain activity
The printout above his head shows the readings from each electrode.

sharp wave associated with temporary inhibition of neuronal firing (Cash et al., 2009).

In the succeeding stages of sleep, heart rate, breathing rate, and brain activity decrease, while slow, large-amplitude waves become more common (Figures 9.11d and e). By

stage 4, more than half the record includes large waves of at least a half-second duration. Stages 3 and 4 together constitute **slow-wave sleep (SWS)**.

Slow waves indicate that neuronal activity is highly synchronized. In stage 1 and in wakefulness, the cortex receives a great deal of input, much of it at high frequencies. Nearly all neurons are active, but different populations of neurons are active at different times. Thus, the EEG is full of short, rapid, choppy waves. By stage 4, however, sensory input to the cerebral cortex is greatly reduced, and the few remaining sources of input can synchronize many cells.

STOP & CHECK

6. What do long, slow waves on an EEG indicate?

ANSWER

6. Long, slow waves indicate a low level of activity, with much synchrony of response among neurons.

Paradoxical or REM Sleep

Many discoveries occur when researchers stumble upon something by accident and then notice that it might be important. In the 1950s, French scientist Michel Jouvet was trying to test the learning abilities of cats after removal of the cerebral cortex. Because decorticate mammals don't do much, Jouvet recorded slight movements of the muscles and EEGs from the hindbrain. During certain periods of apparent sleep, the cats' brain activity was relatively high, but their neck muscles were completely relaxed. Jouvet (1960) then recorded the same phenomenon in normal, intact cats and named it **paradoxical**

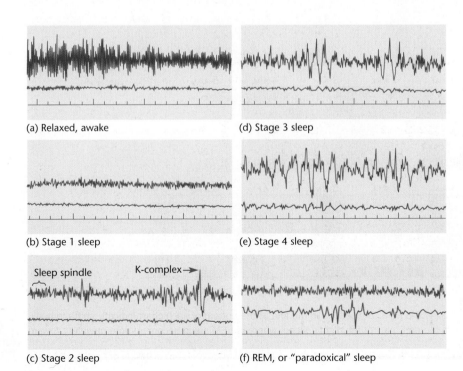

(a) Relaxed, awake

(b) Stage 1 sleep

(c) Stage 2 sleep   Sleep spindle   K-complex

(d) Stage 3 sleep

(e) Stage 4 sleep

(f) REM, or "paradoxical" sleep

FIGURE 9.11 Polysomnograph records from a college student
For each of these records, the top line is the EEG from one electrode on the scalp. The middle line is a record of eye movements. The bottom line is a time marker, indicating 1-second units. Note the abundance of slow waves in stages 3 and 4. *(Records provided by T. E. LeVere)*

sleep because it is deep sleep in some ways and light in others. (The term *paradoxical* means "apparently self-contradictory.")

Meanwhile, in the United States, Nathaniel Kleitman and Eugene Aserinsky were observing eye movements of sleeping people as a means of measuring depth of sleep, assuming that eye movements would stop during sleep. At first, they recorded only a few minutes of eye movements per hour because the recording paper was expensive and they did not expect to see anything interesting in the middle of the night anyway. When they occasionally found periods of eye movements in people who had been asleep for hours, the investigators assumed that something was wrong with their machines. Only after repeated careful measurements did they conclude that periods of rapid eye movements occur during sleep (Dement, 1990). They called these periods **rapid eye movement (REM) sleep** (Aserinsky & Kleitman, 1955; Dement & Kleitman, 1957a) and soon realized that REM sleep was synonymous with what Jouvet called *paradoxical sleep*. Researchers use the term *REM sleep* when referring to humans but often prefer the term *paradoxical sleep* for nonhumans because many species lack eye movements.

During paradoxical or REM sleep, the EEG shows irregular, low-voltage fast waves that indicate increased neuronal activity. In this regard, REM sleep is light. However, the postural muscles of the body, including those that support the head, are more relaxed during REM than in other stages. In this regard, REM is deep sleep. REM is also associated with erections in males and vaginal moistening in females. Heart rate, blood pressure, and breathing rate are more variable in REM than in stages 2 through 4. In short, REM sleep com-

bines deep sleep, light sleep, and features that are difficult to classify as deep or light. Consequently, it is best to avoid the terms *deep* and *light* sleep.

In addition to its steady characteristics, REM sleep has intermittent characteristics such as facial twitches and eye movements, as shown in Figure 9.11f. The EEG record is similar to that for stage 1 sleep, but notice the difference in eye movements. The stages other than REM are known as **non-REM (NREM) sleep.**

When you fall asleep, you start in stage 1 and slowly progress through stages 2, 3, and 4 in order, although loud noises or other intrusions can interrupt the sequence. After about an hour of sleep, you begin to cycle back from stage 4 through stages 3, 2, and then REM. The sequence repeats, with each cycle lasting about 90 minutes. (Some people have inferred that because a cycle lasts 90 minutes, you need to sleep at least 90 minutes to get any benefit. No evidence supports that claim.)

Early in the night, stages 3 and 4 predominate. Toward morning, REM occupies an increasing percentage of the time. Figure 9.12 shows typical sequences. The amount of REM depends on time of day more than how long you have been asleep. That is, if you go to sleep later than usual, you still increase your REM at about the same time that you would have ordinarily (Czeisler, Weitzman, Moore-Ede, Zimmerman, & Knauer, 1980).

Shortly after the discovery of REM, researchers believed it was almost synonymous with dreaming. William Dement and Nathaniel Kleitman (1957b) found that people who were awakened during REM reported dreams 80% to 90% of the time. Later research, however, found that people also some-

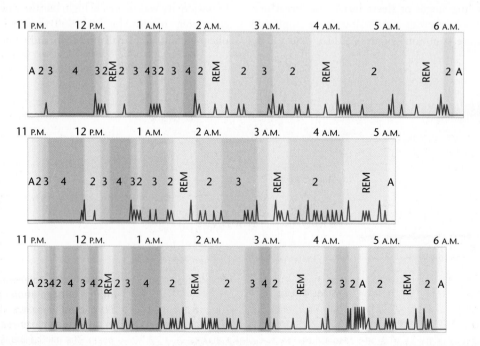

FIGURE 9.12 Sleep stages on three nights
Columns indicate awake (A) and sleep stages 2, 3, 4, and REM. Deflections in the line at the bottom of each chart indicate shifts in body position. Note that stage 4 sleep occurs mostly in the early part of the night's sleep, whereas REM sleep becomes more prevalent toward the end. *(Based on Dement & Kleitman, 1957a)*

William C. Dement

The average person would not, at first blush, pick watching people sleep as the most apparent theme for a spine-tingling scientific adventure thriller. However, there is a subtle sense of awe and mystery surrounding the "short death" we call sleep.

times report dreams when awakened from NREM sleep. REM dreams are more likely than NREM dreams to include striking visual imagery and complicated plots, but not always. Some people continue to report dreams despite an apparent lack of REM (Solms, 1997). In short, REM and dreams usually overlap, but they are not the same thing.

> **STOP & CHECK**

7. How can an investigator determine whether a sleeper is in REM sleep?

8. During which part of a night's sleep is REM most common?

ANSWERS

7. Examine EEG pattern and eye movements. **8.** REM becomes more common toward the end of the night's sleep.

Brain Mechanisms of Wakefulness and Arousal

Recall from Chapter 1 the distinction between the "easy" and "hard" problems of consciousness. The easy problems include such matters as, "Which brain areas increase overall alertness, and by what kinds of transmitters do they do so?" As you are about to see, that question may be philosophically easy, but it is scientifically complex.

Brain Structures of Arousal and Attention

After a cut through the midbrain separates the forebrain and part of the midbrain from all the lower structures, an animal enters a prolonged state of sleep for the next few days. Even after weeks of recovery, the wakeful periods are brief. We might suppose a simple explanation: The cut isolated the brain from the sensory stimuli that come up from the medulla and spinal cord. However, if a researcher cuts each individual tract that enters the medulla and spinal cord, thus depriving the brain of the sensory input, the animal still has normal periods of wakefulness and sleep. Evidently, the midbrain does more than just relay sensory information; it has its own mechanisms to promote wakefulness.

A cut through the midbrain decreases arousal by damaging the **reticular formation**, a structure that extends from the medulla into the forebrain. Some neurons of the reticular formation have axons ascending into the brain, and some have axons descending into the spinal cord. Those with axons descending into the spinal cord form part of the medial tract of motor control, as discussed in Chapter 8. In 1949, Giuseppe Moruzzi and H. W. Magoun proposed that those with ascending axons are well suited to regulate arousal. The term *reticular* (based on the Latin word *rete*, meaning "net") describes the widespread connections among neurons in this system. One part of the reticular formation that contributes to cortical arousal is known as the **pontomesencephalon** (Woolf, 1996). (The term derives from *pons* and *mesencephalon*, or "midbrain.") These neurons receive input from many sensory systems and generate spontaneous activity of their own. Their axons extend into the forebrain, as shown in Figure 9.13, releasing acetylcholine and glutamate, which excite cells in the hypothalamus, thalamus, and basal forebrain. Consequently, the pontomesencephalon maintains arousal during wakefulness and increases it in response to new or challenging tasks (Kinomura, Larsson, Gulyás, & Roland, 1996). Stimulation of the pontomesencephalon awakens a sleeping individual or increases alertness in one already awake, shifting the EEG from long, slow waves to short, high-frequency waves (Munk, Roelfsema, König, Engel, & Singer, 1996). However, subsystems within the pontomesencephalon control different sensory modalities, so a stimulus sometimes arouses one part of the brain more than others (Guillery, Feig, & Lozsádi, 1998).

The **locus coeruleus** (LOW-kus ser-ROO-lee-us; literally, "dark blue place"), a small structure in the pons, is usually inactive, especially during sleep, but it emits bursts of impulses in response to meaningful events, especially those that produce emotional arousal (Sterpenich et al., 2006). Axons from the locus coeruleus release norepinephrine widely throughout the cortex, so this tiny area has a huge influence. Anything that stimulates the locus coeruleus strengthens the storage of recent memories (Clayton & Williams, 2000) and increases wakefulness (Berridge, Stellick, & Schmeichel, 2005).

The hypothalamus has several axon pathways that influence arousal. One pathway releases the neurotransmitter *histamine* (J.-S. Lin, Hou, Sakai, & Jouvet, 1996), which produces excitatory effects throughout the brain (Haas & Panula, 2003). Cells releasing histamine are active during arousal and alertness. As you might guess, they are less active when you are getting ready for sleep and when you have just awakened in the morning (K. Takahashi, Lin, & Sakai, 2006). Antihistamine drugs, often used for allergies, counteract this transmitter and produce drowsiness. Antihistamines that do not cross the blood–brain barrier avoid that side effect.

Another pathway from the hypothalamus, mainly from the lateral and posterior nuclei of the hypothalamus, releases a peptide neurotransmitter called either **orexin** or **hypocretin**. For simplicity, this text will stick to the term orexin, but if you find the term hypocretin in other reading, it means the same

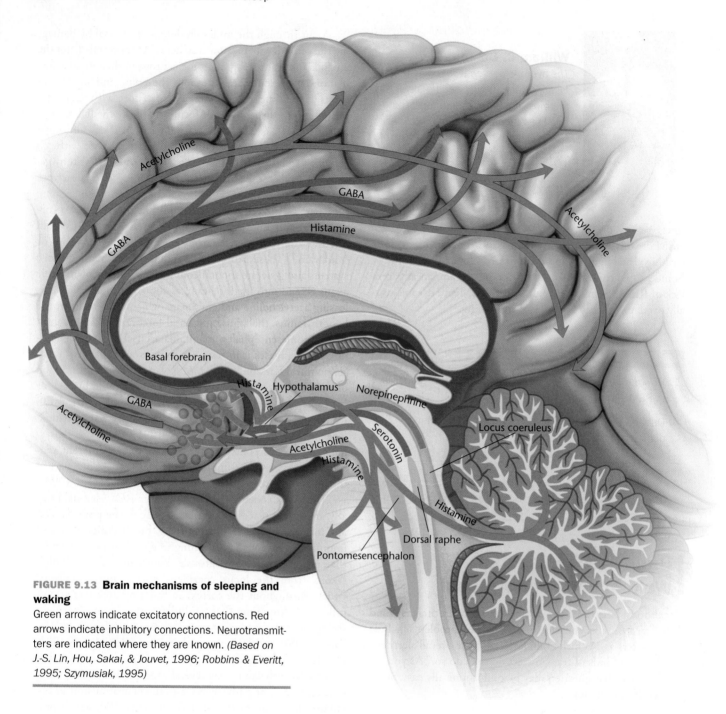

FIGURE 9.13 Brain mechanisms of sleeping and waking
Green arrows indicate excitatory connections. Red arrows indicate inhibitory connections. Neurotransmitters are indicated where they are known. *(Based on J.-S. Lin, Hou, Sakai, & Jouvet, 1996; Robbins & Everitt, 1995; Szymusiak, 1995)*

thing. The axons releasing orexin extend to the basal forebrain and other areas, where they stimulate neurons responsible for wakefulness (Sakurai, 2007). Orexin is not necessary for waking up, but it is for *staying* awake. That is, most adult humans stay awake for roughly 16–17 hours at a time, even when nothing much is happening. Staying awake depends on orexin, especially toward the end of the day (Lee, Hassani, & Jones, 2005). A study of squirrel monkeys found that orexin levels rose throughout the day and remained high when the monkeys were kept awake beyond their usual sleep time. As soon as the monkeys went to sleep, the orexin levels dropped

(Zeitzer et al., 2003). Mice lacking orexin fail to sustain activities, such as running in a running wheel, and therefore fall asleep at times when normal mice would remain alert (Anaclet et al., 2009). Drugs that block orexin receptors increase sleep (Brisbare-Roch et al., 2007), and procedures that increase orexin (e.g., a nasal spray of orexin) lead to increased wakefulness and alertness (Deadwyler, Porrino, Siegel, & Hampson, 2007; Prober, Rihel, Ohah, Sung, & Schier, 2006).

Other pathways from the lateral hypothalamus regulate cells in the **basal forebrain** (an area just anterior and dorsal to the hypothalamus). Basal forebrain cells provide axons that extend throughout the thalamus and cerebral cortex (Figure 9.13). Some of these axons release acetylcholine, which is excitatory and tends to increase arousal (Mesulam, 1995; Szymusiak, 1995). Acetylcholine is released during wakefulness and REM sleep, but not during slow-wave sleep (Hassani, Lee, Henny, & Jones, 2009). During wakefulness, its release sharpens attention—that is, it increases the accurate, reliable detection of sensory stimuli (Goard & Dan, 2009).

Table 9.1 summarizes the effects of some key brain areas on arousal and sleep.

![gray arrow banner] **STOP & CHECK**

9. Why do most antihistamines make people drowsy?

10. What would happen to the sleep–wake schedule of someone who lacked orexin?

ANSWERS

9. Two paths from the hypothalamus—one to the basal forebrain and one to the pontomesencephalon—use histamine as their neurotransmitter to increase arousal. Antihistamines that cross the blood-brain barrier block those synapses. **10.** Someone without orexin would alternate between brief periods of waking and sleeping.

Sleep and the Inhibition of Brain Activity

Figure 9.13 shows axons (in red) that lead to the release of GABA, the brain's main inhibitory transmitter. GABA is responsible for sleep. During sleep, body temperature and metabolic rate decrease slightly, as does the activity of neurons, but by less than we might expect. Spontaneously active neurons continue to fire at close to their usual rate, and neurons in the brain's sensory areas continue to respond to sounds and other stimuli. Nevertheless, we are unconscious. The reason is that GABA inhibits synaptic activity. When a neuron is active, the increased GABA levels cut the activity short and prevent axons from spreading stimulation to other areas (Massimini et al., 2005). Connections from one brain area to another become weaker (Esser, Hill, & Tononi, 2009). When stimulation doesn't spread, you don't become conscious of it. (Chapter 14 elaborates on that point.)

Because sleep depends on GABA-mediated inhibition, it can be local within the brain (Krueger et al., 2008). That is, you might have substantial inhibition in one brain area and not so much in another. Ordinarily, different brain areas wake up or go to sleep at almost the same time, but not necessarily. The most extreme case of this principle occurs in dolphins and other aquatic mammals. At night, they need to be alert enough to surface for a breath of air. They have evolved the ability to sleep on one side of the brain at a time. That is, the two hemispheres take turns sleeping, always leaving one awake enough to control swimming and breathing (Rattenborg, Amlaner, & Lima, 2000).

Thinking of sleep as a local phenomenon helps make sense of some otherwise puzzling phenomena. Take, for instance, sleepwalking. Almost by definition, a sleepwalker is awake in one part of the brain and asleep in another. Another example is lucid dreaming. During lucid dreaming, someone is dreaming but aware of being asleep and dreaming. Evidently some brain area is more awake than usual during dreaming. Another example: Have you ever had the experience of waking up but finding that you can't move your arms or legs? During REM sleep, cells in the pons send messages that inhibit the motor neurons that control the body's large muscles. A cat with damage to those cells moves around awkwardly during REM sleep, as if it were acting out its dreams (Morrison, Sanford, Ball, Mann, & Ross, 1995) (Figure 9.14). Ordinarily, when you awaken from a REM period, those cells in the pons shut off and you regain muscle control. But occasionally most of the brain wakes up while the pons remains in REM. The result is your experience of being temporarily unable to move—a very unsettling experience, if you don't understand it.

TABLE 9.1	**Brain Structures for Arousal and Sleep**	

Structure	Neurotransmitter(s) It Releases	Effects on Behavior
Pontomesencephalon	Acetylcholine, glutamate	Increases cortical arousal
Locus coeruleus	Norepinephrine	Increases information storage during wakefulness, suppresses REM sleep
Basal forebrain		
Excitatory cells	Acetylcholine	Excites thalamus and cortex; increases learning, attention; shifts sleep from NREM to REM
Inhibitory cells	GABA	Inhibits thalamus and cortex
Hypothalamus (parts)	Histamine	Increases arousal
(parts)	Orexin	Maintains wakefulness
Dorsal raphe and pons	Serotonin	Interrupts REM sleep

FIGURE 9.14 A cat with a lesion in the pons, wobbling about during REM sleep
Cells of an intact pons send inhibitory messages to the spinal cord neurons that control the large muscles. *(From Morrison, A. R., Sanford, L. D., Ball, W. A., Mann, G. L., & Ross, R. J., "Stimulus-elicited behavior in rapid eye movement sleep without atonia," Behavioral Neuroscience, 109, 972–979, 1995. Published by APA and reprinted by permission.)*

STOP & CHECK

11. What would happen to the sleep–wake schedule of someone who took a drug that blocked GABA?

12. Someone who has just awakened sometimes speaks in a loose, unconnected, illogical way. How could you explain this finding?

ANSWERS 11. Someone who took a drug that blocks GABA would remain awake. (Tranquilizers put people to sleep by facilitating GABA.) 12. People often awaken from a REM period, because REM is abundant toward morning when people usually awaken. Different brain areas don't wake up all at once. Shortly after awakening, parts of the brain may still be in a REM-like state, and thinking may have an illogical, dream-like quality.

▌Brain Function in REM Sleep

Researchers interested in the brain mechanisms of REM decided to use a PET scan to determine which areas increased or decreased in activity during REM. Although that research might sound simple, a PET scan requires injecting a radioactive chemical. Imagine trying to give sleepers an injection without awakening them. Further, a PET scan yields a clear image only if the head remains motionless during data collection. If the person tosses or turns even slightly, the image is worthless.

To overcome these difficulties, researchers in two studies persuaded young people to sleep with their heads firmly attached to masks that did not permit any movement. They also inserted a cannula (plastic tube) into each person's arm so that they could inject radioactive chemicals at various times during the night. So imagine yourself in that setup. You have a cannula in your arm and your head is locked into position. Now try to sleep.

Because the researchers foresaw the difficulty of sleeping under these conditions (!), they had their participants stay awake the entire previous night. Someone who is tired enough can sleep even under trying circumstances. (Maybe.)

Now that you appreciate the heroic nature of the procedures, here are the results. During REM sleep, activity increased in the pons (which triggers the onset of REM sleep) and the limbic system (which is important for emotional responses). Activity decreased in the primary visual cortex, the motor cortex, and the dorsolateral prefrontal cortex but increased in parts of the parietal and temporal cortex (Braun et al., 1998; Maquet et al., 1996).

REM sleep is associated with a distinctive pattern of high-amplitude electrical potentials known as **PGO waves**, for pons-geniculate-occipital (Figure 9.15). Waves of neural activity are detected first in the pons, shortly afterward in the lateral geniculate nucleus of the thalamus, and then in the occipital cortex (D. C. Brooks & Bizzi, 1963; Laurent, Cespuglio, & Jouvet, 1974). Each animal maintains a nearly constant amount of PGO waves per day. During a prolonged period of REM deprivation in laboratory animals, PGO waves begin to emerge during sleep stages 2 to 4 and even during wakefulness, often in association with strange behaviors, as if the animal were hallucinating. At the end of the deprivation period, when an animal is permitted to sleep without interruption, the REM periods have an unusually high density of PGO waves.

REM sleep apparently depends on a relationship between the neurotransmitters serotonin and acetylcholine. Injections of the drug *carbachol*, which stimulates acetylcholine synapses, quickly move a sleeper into REM sleep (Baghdoyan, Spotts, & Snyder, 1993). Note that acetylcholine is important for both wakefulness and REM sleep, states of brain arousal. Serotonin and norepinephrine interrupt REM sleep (Boutrel, Franc, Hen, Hamon, & Adrien, 1999; Singh & Mallick, 1996).

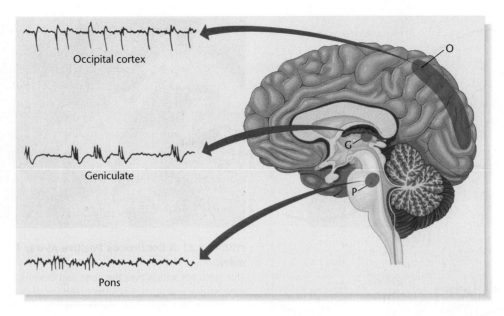

FIGURE 9.15 PGO waves

PGO waves start in the pons (P) and then show up in the lateral geniculate (G) and the occipital cortex (O). Each PGO wave is synchronized with an eye movement in REM sleep. *(© Cengage Learning 2013)*

▌Sleep Disorders

How much sleep is enough? Different people need different amounts. Most adults need about 7 ¹/₂ to 8 hours of sleep per night, but some have been known to get by with less than 3 hours per night, without unpleasant consequences (H. S. Jones & Oswald, 1968; Meddis, Pearson, & Langford, 1973). Among people who ordinarily get the more typical 7 ¹/₂ to 8 hours of sleep, some are better than others at withstanding a temporary lack of sleep. People who tolerate sleep deprivation relatively well are usually "evening people," who like to waken late and stay up late. They tend to show greater than average levels of brain arousal, as indicated by fMRI (Caldwell et al., 2005).

The best gauge of **insomnia**—inadequate sleep—is how someone feels the following day. If you feel tired during the day, you are not sleeping enough at night. Causes of insomnia include noise, uncomfortable temperatures, stress, pain, diet, and medications. Insomnia can also be the result of epilepsy, Parkinson's disease, brain tumors, depression, anxiety, or other neurological or psychiatric conditions. Some children suffer insomnia because they are milk-intolerant, and their parents, not realizing the intolerance, give them milk to drink right before bedtime (Horne, 1992). One man suffered insomnia until he realized that he dreaded going to sleep because he hated waking up to go jogging. After he switched his jogging time to late afternoon, he slept without difficulty. In short, try to identify the reasons for your sleep problems before you try to solve them.

Some cases of insomnia relate to shifts in circadian rhythms (MacFarlane, Cleghorn, & Brown, 1985a, 1985b). Ordinarily, people fall asleep while their temperature is declining and awaken while it is rising, as in Figure 9.16a. Someone whose rhythm is *phase-delayed*, as in Figure 9.16b, has trouble falling asleep at the usual time, as if the hypothalamus thinks it isn't late enough (Morris et al., 1990). Someone whose rhythm is *phase-advanced*, as in Figure 9.16c, falls asleep easily but awakens early.

Another cause of insomnia is, paradoxically, the use of tranquilizers as sleeping pills. Although tranquilizers help people fall asleep, repeated use causes dependence and an inability to sleep without the pills (Kales, Scharf, & Kales, 1978). Similar problems arise when people use alcohol to get to sleep.

Sleep Apnea

One type of insomnia is **sleep apnea**, impaired ability to breathe while sleeping. People with sleep apnea have breathless periods of a minute or so from which they awaken gasping for breath. They may not remember all their awakenings, although they certainly notice the consequences—sleepiness during the day, impaired attention, depression, and sometimes heart problems. People with sleep apnea have multiple brain areas that appear to have lost neurons, and consequently, they show deficiencies of learning, reasoning, attention, and impulse control (Beebe & Gozal, 2002; Macey et

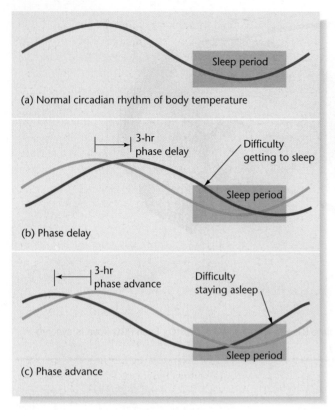

(a) Normal circadian rhythm of body temperature

3-hr phase delay

Difficulty getting to sleep

Sleep period

(b) Phase delay

3-hr phase advance

Difficulty staying asleep

Sleep period

(c) Phase advance

FIGURE 9.16 Insomnia and circadian rhythms
A delay in the circadian rhythm of body temperature is associated with onset insomnia. An advance is associated with termination insomnia. *(© Cengage Learning 2013)*

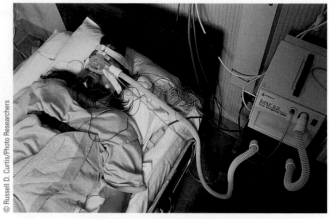

© Russell D. Curtis/Photo Researchers

FIGURE 9.17 A Continuous Positive Airway Pressure (CPAP) mask
The mask fits snugly over the nose and delivers air at a fixed pressure, strong enough to keep the breathing passages open.

> **STOP & CHECK**

13. What kinds of people are most likely to develop sleep apnea?

ANSWER

13. Sleep apnea is most common among people with a genetic predisposition, old people, and overweight middle-aged men.

al., 2002). These correlational data do not tell us whether the brain abnormalities led to sleep apnea or sleep apnea led to the brain abnormalities. However, research with rodents suggests the latter: Mice that are subjected to frequent periods of low oxygen (as if they hadn't been breathing) lose some neurons and impair others, especially in areas responsible for alertness (Zhu et al., 2007). Sleep impairments may be responsible for cognitive loss not only in people with sleep apnea but also in some with Alzheimer's disease.

Sleep apnea results from several causes, including genetics, hormones, and old-age deterioration of the brain mechanisms that regulate breathing. Another cause is obesity, especially in middle-aged men. Many obese men have narrower than normal airways and have to compensate by breathing frequently or vigorously. During sleep, they cannot keep up that rate of breathing. Furthermore, their airways become even narrower than usual when they adopt a sleeping posture (Mezzanotte, Tangel, & White, 1992).

People with sleep apnea are advised to lose weight and avoid alcohol and tranquilizers (which impair the breathing muscles). Medical options include surgery to remove tissue that obstructs the trachea (the breathing passage) or a mask that covers the nose and delivers air under enough pressure to keep the breathing passages open (Figure 9.17).

Narcolepsy

Narcolepsy, a condition characterized by frequent periods of sleepiness during the day (Aldrich, 1998), strikes about 1 person in 1,000. It sometimes runs in families, but many cases emerge in people with no affected relatives. No gene for narcolepsy has been identified, and many people with narcolepsy have no close relatives with the disease. Narcolepsy has four main symptoms, although not every patient has all four. Each of these symptoms can be interpreted as an intrusion of a REM-like state into wakefulness:

1. Gradual or sudden attacks of sleepiness during the day.

2. Occasional cataplexy—an attack of muscle weakness while the person remains awake. Cataplexy is often triggered by strong emotions, such as anger or great excitement. (One man suddenly collapsed during his own wedding ceremony.)

3. Sleep paralysis—an inability to move while falling asleep or waking up. Other people may experience sleep paralysis occasionally, but people with narcolepsy experience it more frequently.

4. Hypnagogic hallucinations—dreamlike experiences that the person has trouble distinguishing from reality, often occurring at the onset of sleep.

The cause relates to the neurotransmitter orexin. People with narcolepsy lack the hypothalamic cells that produce and release orexin (Thanickal et al., 2000). Why they lack them is unknown, but one possibility is an autoimmune reaction, in which the immune system attacks part of the body—in this case, cells with orexin (Hallmayer et al., 2009). Recall that orexin is important for maintaining wakefulness. Consequently, people lacking orexin alternate between short waking periods and short sleepy periods, instead of staying awake throughout the day. Dogs that lack the gene for orexin receptors have symptoms much like human narcolepsy, with frequent alternations between wakefulness and sleep (L. Lin et al., 1999). The same is true for mice that lack orexin (Hara, 2001; Mochizuki et al., 2004).

As discussed in Chapter 8, people with Huntington's disease have widespread damage in the basal ganglia. In addition, most lose neurons in the hypothalamus, including the neurons that make orexin. As a result, they have problems staying awake during the day and difficulty staying asleep at night (Morton et al., 2005).

Theoretically, we might imagine combating narcolepsy with drugs that restore orexin. Perhaps eventually, such drugs will become available. Currently, the most common treatment is stimulant drugs, such as methylphenidate (Ritalin), which enhance dopamine and norepinephrine activity.

STOP & CHECK

14. What is the relationship between orexin and narcolepsy?

ANSWER

14. Orexin is important for staying awake. Therefore, people or animals lacking either orexin or the receptors for orexin develop narcolepsy, characterized by bouts of sleepiness during the day.

Periodic Limb Movement Disorder

Another sleep disorder is **periodic limb movement disorder**, characterized by repeated involuntary movement of the legs and sometimes the arms (Edinger et al., 1992). Many people, perhaps most, experience an occasional involuntary kick, especially when starting to fall asleep. Leg movements are not a problem unless they become persistent. In some people, mostly middle-aged and older, the legs kick once every 20 to 30 seconds for minutes or hours, mostly during NREM sleep. Frequent or especially vigorous leg movements may awaken the person or his or her partner. In some cases, tranquilizers help suppress the movements (Schenck & Mahowald, 1996).

REM Behavior Disorder

For most people, the major postural muscles are relaxed and inactive during REM sleep. However, people with **REM be-havior disorder** move around vigorously during their REM periods, apparently acting out their dreams. They frequently dream about defending themselves against attack, and they may punch, kick, and leap about. Most of them injure themselves or other people and damage property (Olson, Boeve, & Silber, 2000).

REM behavior disorder occurs mostly in older people, especially older men with brain diseases such as Parkinson's disease (Olson et al., 2000). Presumably, the damage includes the cells in the pons that send messages to inhibit the spinal neurons that control large muscle movements.

Night Terrors and Sleepwalking

Night terrors are experiences of intense anxiety from which a person awakens screaming in terror. A night terror is more severe than a nightmare, which is simply an unpleasant dream. Night terrors occur during NREM sleep and are more common in children than adults. Dream content, if any, is usually simple, such as a single image.

Sleepwalking runs in families and occurs mostly in children. Most people who sleepwalk, and many of their relatives, have one or more additional sleep difficulties, such as chronic snoring, disordered sleep breathing, bedwetting, and night terrors (Cao & Guilleminault, 2010). The causes of sleepwalking are not well understood, but it is more common when people are sleep deprived or under unusual stress (Zadra & Pilon, 2008). It is most common during stage 3 or 4 sleep early in the night and is usually not accompanied by dreaming. (It does not occur during REM sleep, when the large muscles are completely relaxed.) Sleepwalking is usually harmless but not always. One teenage girl walked out of her house, climbed a crane, and went back to sleep on a support beam. Fortunately, a pedestrian saw her and called the police. Sleepwalkers have been known to eat, rearrange furniture, fall off balconies, and drive cars—while disregarding lanes and traffic lights. Unlike wakeful actions, the deeds of sleepwalkers are poorly planned and not remembered. Evidently, parts of the brain are awake and other parts are asleep (Gunn & Gunn, 2007). Incidentally, contrary to common sayings, it is not dangerous to awaken a sleepwalker. It is not particularly helpful either, but it is not dangerous.

An analogous condition is sleep sex or "sexsomnia," in which sleeping people engage in sexual behavior, either with a partner or by masturbation, and do not remember it afterward. Sexsomnia poses a threat to romances and marriages. As one woman said, "After getting married a few years ago, my husband told me I was masturbating in my sleep. I was mortified, thinking back to all the slumber parties as a girl, and then when I was older and my little sister stayed the night at my house! How many others might have witnessed and not said anything? My new marriage is on the rocks, since I'm having such good sex in my sleep, I have NO desire while I'm awake. This is killing my relationship with my husband." (Mangan, 2004, p. 290)

MODULE 9.2 ■ IN CLOSING

Stages of Sleep

Chemists divide the world into different elements, biologists divide life into different species, and physicians distinguish one disease from another. Similarly, psychologists try to recognize the most natural or useful distinctions among types of behavior or experience. The discovery of different stages of sleep was a major landmark in psychology because researchers found a previously unrecognized distinction that is both biologically and psychologically important. It also demonstrated that external measurements—in this case, EEG recordings—can be used to identify internal experiences. We now take it largely for granted that an electrical or magnetic recording from the brain can tell us something about a person's experience, but it is worth pausing to note what a surprising discovery that was in its time.

SUMMARY

1. During sleep, brain activity decreases, but a stimulus can awaken the person. Someone in a coma cannot be awakened. A vegetative state or minimally conscious state can last months or years, during which the person shows only limited responses. Brain death is a condition without brain activity or responsiveness of any kind. **276**

2. Over the course of about 90 minutes, a sleeper goes through stages 1, 2, 3, and 4 and then returns through stages 3 and 2 to a stage called REM. REM is characterized by rapid eye movements, more brain activity than other sleep stages, complete relaxation of the trunk muscles, irregular breathing and heart rate, penile erection or vaginal lubrication, and an increased probability of vivid dreams. **276**

3. REM sleep or paradoxical sleep is a condition marked by more cortical activity than other sleep, complete relaxation of the body's postural muscles, and an increased probability of dreaming. **277**

4. The brain has multiple systems for arousal. The pontomesencephalon and parts of the hypothalamus control various cell clusters in the basal forebrain that send axons releasing acetylcholine throughout much of the forebrain. **279**

5. The locus coeruleus is active in response to meaningful events. It facilitates attention and new learning; it also blocks the onset of REM sleep. **279**

6. Orexin is a peptide that maintains wakefulness. Cells in the lateral and posterior nuclei of the hypothalamus release this peptide. **279**

7. During sleep, enhanced release of GABA limits neuronal activity and blocks the spread of activation. Sometimes this suppression is stronger in one brain area than another. That is, sleep can occur in one brain area and not another at a given time. **281**

8. REM sleep is associated with increased activity in a number of brain areas, including the pons and limbic system. Activity decreases in the prefrontal cortex, the motor cortex, and the primary visual cortex. **282**

9. REM sleep begins with PGO waves, which are waves of brain activity transmitted from the pons to the lateral geniculate to the occipital lobe. **282**

10. People with sleep apnea have long periods without breathing while they sleep. Many have indications of neuronal loss, probably as a result of decreased oxygen while they sleep. **283**

11. People with narcolepsy have attacks of sleepiness during the day. Narcolepsy is associated with a deficiency of the peptide neurotransmitter orexin. **284**

KEY TERMS

Terms are defined in the module on the page number indicated. They're also presented in alphabetical order with definitions in the book's Subject Index/Glossary, which begins on page 561. Interactive flashcards and crossword puzzles are among the online resources available to help you learn these terms and the concepts they represent.

alpha waves **276**
basal forebrain **280**
brain death **276**
coma **276**
insomnia **283**
K-complex **276**
locus coeruleus **279**
minimally conscious state **276**
narcolepsy **284**

night terrors **285**
non-REM (NREM) sleep **278**
orexin (or hypocretin) **279**
paradoxical sleep **277**
periodic limb movement disorder **285**
PGO waves **282**
polysomnograph **276**
pontomesencephalon **279**
rapid eye movement (REM) sleep **278**

REM behavior disorder **285**
reticular formation **279**
sleep apnea **283**
sleep spindle **276**
slow-wave sleep (SWS) **277**
vegetative state **276**

THOUGHT QUESTION

When cats are deprived of REM sleep, longer periods of deprivation—up to about 25 days—are associated with greater rebound of REM when they can sleep uninterrupted. However, REM deprivation for more than 25 days produces no additional rebound. Speculate on a possible explanation. (Hint: Consider what happens to PGO waves during REM deprivation.)

Why Sleep? Why REM? Why Dreams?

Why do you sleep? "That's easy," you reply. "I sleep because I get tired." Well, yes, but you are not tired in the sense of muscle fatigue. You need almost as much sleep after a day of sitting around the house as after a day of intense physical or mental activity (Horne & Minard, 1985; Shapiro, Bortz, Mitchell, Bartel, & Jooste, 1981). Furthermore, you could rest your muscles just as well while awake as while asleep. (In fact, if your muscles ache after strenuous exercise, you probably find it difficult to sleep.)

You feel tired at the end of the day because inhibitory processes in your brain force you to become less aroused and less alert. That is, we evolved mechanisms to force us to sleep. Why?

❚ Functions of Sleep

Sleep serves many functions. During sleep, we rest our muscles, decrease metabolism, rebuild proteins in the brain (Kong et al., 2002), reorganize synapses, and strengthen memories (Sejnowski & Destexhe, 2000). People who don't get enough sleep have trouble concentrating and become more vulnerable to illness, especially mental illness (Wulff, Gatti, Wettstein, & Foster, 2010). We all have moments when our attention lapses and we fail to notice important stimuli. Those periods are longer and more frequent after a sleepless night. Furthermore, people who have had enough sleep notice their lapses and jar themselves into increased arousal. People who are sleep-deprived fail to do so (Chee et al., 2008). Inadequate sleep is a major cause of accidents by workers and poor performance by college students. Driving while sleep deprived is comparable to driving under the influence of alcohol (Falleti, Maruff, Collie, Darby, & McStephen, 2003).

People working in Antarctica during the winter sleep poorly and feel depressed (Palinkas, 2003). Even one night of sleeplessness activates the immune system (Matsumoto et al., 2001). That is, you react to sleep deprivation as if you were ill. With more prolonged sleep deprivation, people report dizziness, tremors, and hallucinations (Dement, 1972; L. C. Johnson, 1969).

Clearly, we need to sleep. Is there, however, one primary or original reason?

Sleep and Energy Conservation

Even if we identified what seems to be the most important function of sleep for humans today, it might not be the function for which sleep originally evolved. By analogy, consider computers: People use computers today to write papers, send e-mail, search the Internet, play video games, store and display photographs, play music, and find a date. Someone who didn't know the history might not guess that computers were built originally for mathematical calculations.

Similarly, sleep probably started with a simple function to which evolution added others later. Even bacteria have circadian rhythms of activity and inactivity (Mihalcescu, Hsing, & Leibler, 2004). What benefit of sleep applies to species with little or no nervous system?

A likely hypothesis is that sleep's original function—and still an important one—is to save energy (Kleitman, 1963; Siegel, 2009; Webb, 1974). Nearly every species is more efficient at some times of day than at others. Those with good vision are more efficient in the day. Those that rely on olfaction instead of vision are more efficient at night, when their predators cannot see them. Sleep conserves energy during the inefficient times, when activity would be wasteful and possibly dangerous. NASA's Rover spacecraft, built to explore Mars, had a mechanism to make it "sleep" at night to conserve its batteries. During sleep, a mammal's body temperature decreases by 1° or 2° C, enough to save a significant amount of energy. Muscle activity decreases, saving more energy. Animals increase their sleep duration during food shortages, when energy conservation is especially important (Berger & Phillips, 1995).

Sleep is therefore in some ways analogous to hibernation. Hibernation is a true need. A ground squirrel that is prevented from hibernating can become as disturbed as a person who is prevented from sleeping. However, the function of hibernation is simply to conserve energy while food is scarce.

If one of the main functions of sleep is to shut down activity at times of relative inefficiency, we might expect to find little or no sleep in species that are equally effective at all times of day. Indeed, that expectation appears to be confirmed. Certain fish have evolved for life in a cave where "day" and "night" have no meaning, because light is always absent and temperature is virtually constant. Observers report that these fish apparently never sleep (Kavanau, 1998).

Several other species turn off their need for sleep under certain circumstances (Siegel, 2009). After a dolphin or whale gives birth, both mother and baby stay awake 24 hours a day for the first couple of weeks while the baby is especially vulnerable. Neither shows any sign of harm from sleep deprivation. Migratory birds face a different kind of problem. During a week or two in fall and spring, they forage for food during the day and do their migratory flying at night. (Flying at night makes sense, because it is cooler then.) That schedule leaves little time for sleep. They apparently decrease their need for sleep at this time. If a bird is kept in a cage during the migration season, it flutters around restlessly at night, sleeping only one third its usual amount. It compensates to some extent with many brief periods of drowsiness (less than 30 seconds each) during the day (Fuchs, Haney, Jechura, Moore, & Bingman, 2006). Still, it is getting very little sleep, while remaining alert and performing normally on learning tasks. If the same bird is deprived of sleep during other seasons of the year, its performance suffers (Rattenborg et al., 2004). Exactly how a bird or a mother dolphin decreases its sleep need is unknown, but the fact that it is possible fits with the idea that sleep is primarily a way to conserve energy, rather than a way to fulfill a function that one could not fulfill in other ways.

Animal species vary in their sleep habits in ways that make sense if we ask how many hours the animal needs to be awake, and therefore how long it can afford to spend conserving energy (Allison & Cicchetti, 1976; Campbell & Tobler, 1984). Grazing animals that need to eat for many hours per day get less sleep than carnivores (meat eaters) that can satisfy their nutritional needs with a single meal. Animals that need to be on the alert for predators get little sleep, whereas the predators themselves sleep easily. Insect-eating bats are active in the early evening, when moths and similar insects are most abundant, and then they sleep the rest of the day (Figure 9.18).

Here's another bit of miscellaneous trivia about animal sleep: Swifts are small, dark birds that chase insects. They get all the nutrition and water they need from the insects. When a baby European swift first takes off from its nest, how long would you guess its first flight lasts, until it comes to land again?

The answer: up to 2 years. Except during treacherous storms, it doesn't come down until it is old enough to mate and build a nest. In the meantime, it spends both days and nights in the air. At night it heads into the wind, sticks out its wings, glides, and presumably sleeps—although confirming sleep would require measuring the EEG of a small bird in flight. It picks an altitude where the air is not too cold, accepts the risk of being blown a great distance, and awakens the next morning to resume its chase of flying insects (Bäckman & Alerstam, 2001).

STOP & CHECK

15. What kind of animal tends to get more than the average amount of sleep?

16. What might one predict about the sleep of fish that live deep in the ocean?

ANSWERS **15.** Predators get much sleep, and so do species that are unlikely to be attacked during their sleep (such as armadillos). **16.** The deep ocean, like a cave, has no light and no difference between day and night. These fish might not need to sleep because they are equally efficient at all times of day and have no reason to conserve energy at one time more than another.

APPLICATIONS AND EXTENSIONS

Hibernation

Hibernating animals decrease their body temperature to only slightly above that of the environment (except that they don't let it go low enough for their blood to freeze). Brain activity declines to almost nothing, neuron cell bodies shrink, and dendrites lose almost one fourth of their branches, replacing them when body temperature increases (von der Ohe, Darian-Smith, Garner, & Heller, 2006). A few curious facts about hibernation:

1. Hibernation occurs in certain small mammals, such as ground squirrels and bats. Bears' hibernation differs from that of small animals. Bears lower their body temperature from 37° to 33° C and maintain a lowered but steady metabolic rate throughout hibernation. Even after awakening from hibernation, their metabolic rate recovers slowly (Toien et al., 2011).

2. Hamsters also hibernate. If you keep your pet hamster in a cool, dimly lit place during the winter, and it appears to have died, make sure that it is not just hibernating before you bury it!

3. Hibernating animals other than bears come out of hibernation for a few hours every few days, raising their body temperature to about normal. However, they spend most of this nonhibernating time asleep (B. M. Barnes, 1996).

4. Hibernation retards the aging process. Hamsters that spend longer times hibernating have proportionately longer life expectancies than other hamsters do (Lyman, O'Brien, Greene, & Papafrangos, 1981). Hibernation is also a period of relative invulnerability to infection and trauma. Procedures that would ordinarily damage the brain, such as inserting a needle into it, produce little if any harm during hibernation (F. Zhou et al., 2001). ■

Much sleep per day

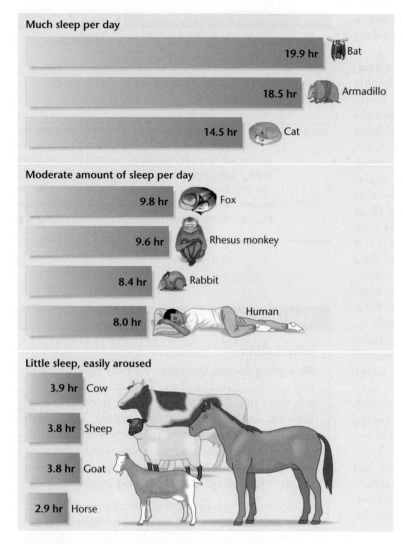

19.9 hr	Bat
18.5 hr	Armadillo
14.5 hr	Cat

Moderate amount of sleep per day

9.8 hr	Fox
9.6 hr	Rhesus monkey
8.4 hr	Rabbit
8.0 hr	Human

Little sleep, easily aroused

3.9 hr	Cow
3.8 hr	Sheep
3.8 hr	Goat
2.9 hr	Horse

FIGURE 9.18 Hours of sleep per day for various species
Generally, predators and others that are safe when they sleep tend to sleep a great deal. Animals in danger of being attacked while they sleep spend less time asleep. *(© Cengage Learning 2013)*

Alan Williams/Alamy

A European swift

Sleep and Memory

Another apparent function of sleep is improved memory. Young adults deprived of a night's sleep show deficits on memory tasks (Yoo, Hu, Gujar, Jolesz, & Walker, 2007). In contrast, if people learn something and then go to sleep, or even take a nap, their memory often improves beyond what it was before the sleep (Hu, Stylos-Allan, & Walker, 2006; Korman et al., 2007). That is, we see not just an absence of forgetting but also a gain of memory. The amount of improvement varies from one study to another and from one type of learning task to another (Cai & Rickard; Cai, Shuman, Gorman, Sage, & Anagnostaras, 2009; Doyon et al., 2009). Still, it appears that reviewing something right before you go to sleep is an excellent idea.

Sleep enhances memory of some events more than others. In one study, people viewed 50 objects making a sound (such as a cat meowing) in various locations on a computer screen. Then they took a nap, during which they heard some of those sounds again. After the nap, they were tested on their memory for the location of each object on the screen. They showed enhanced memory for the objects whose sounds they heard during the nap (Rudoy, Voss, Westerberg, & Paller, 2009). Evidently the sounds reminded them of the information, and the brain then processed that information again.

Sleep also helps people reanalyze their memories: In one study, people who had just practiced a complex task were more likely to perceive a hidden rule (an "aha" experience) after a period of sleep than after a similar period of wakefulness (Wagner, Gais, Haider, Verleger, & Born, 2004). Another study found that a nap that included REM sleep enhanced performance on certain kinds of creative problem solving (Cai, Mednick, Harrison, Kanady, & Mednick, 2009).

How does sleep enhance memory? Researchers recorded activity in the hippocampus during learning, and then recorded from the same locations during sleep, using microelectrodes within cells for laboratory animals and electrodes on the scalp for humans. The results: Patterns that occurred during sleep resembled those that occurred during learning, except that they were more rapid during sleep. Furthermore, the amount of hippocampal activity during sleep correlated highly with the subsequent improvement in performance (Derégnaucourt, Mitra, Fehér, Pytte, & Tchernichovski, 2005; Euston, Tatsuno, & McNaughton, 2007; Huber, Ghilardi, Massimini, & Tononi, 2004; Ji & Wilson, 2007; Maquet et al., 2000; Peigneux et al., 2004). These results suggest that the brain replays its daily experiences during sleep. However, further research found that the sleeping brain replays its experience backward as often as forward, and that it sometimes replays less common experiences more often than more common ones (Gupta, van der Meer, Touretzky, & Redish, 2010). Also, the hippocampus replays recently learned patterns during quiet waking periods, not just during sleep (Karlsson & Frank, 2009). So the role of hippocampal replay during sleep is less clear than it once appeared to be.

One way for sleep to strengthen memory is by weeding out the less successful connections. In Chapter 13, we shall examine the phenomenon of long-term potentiation, the ability of new experiences to strengthen synaptic connections. Suppose that every time you learn something, your brain strengthened certain synapses without making adjustments elsewhere. As you learned more and more, you would have more and more brain activity. By middle age, your brain might be burning with constant activity. To prevent runaway overactivity, your brain compensates for strengthening some synapses by weakening others, mostly during sleep (Liu, Faraguna, Cirelli, Tononi, & Gao, 2010; Vyazovskiy, Cirelli, Pfister-Genskow, Faraguna, & Tononi, 2008). Weakening synapses during sleep emphasizes the ones that were strengthened during wakefulness.

Another aspect of sleep's contribution to memory relates to sleep spindles. Recall that sleep spindles are waves of activity, about 12–14 Hz, that occur mostly during stage 2 sleep. They indicate an exchange of information between the thalamus and cerebral cortex. In both rats and humans, sleep spindles increase in number after new learning (Eschenko, Mölle, Born, & Sara, 2006). Most people are fairly consistent in their amount of spindle activity from one night to another, and the amount of spindle activity correlates more than .7 with nonverbal tests of IQ (Fogel, Nader, Cote, & Smith, 2007). Who would have guessed that brain waves during sleep could predict IQ scores?

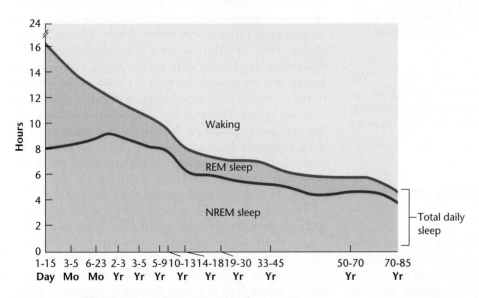

FIGURE 9.19 Sleep patterns for people of various ages
REM sleep occupies about 8 hours a day in newborns but less than 2 hours in most adults. The sleep of infants is not quite like that of adults, however, and the criteria for identifying REM sleep are not the same. *(From "Ontogenetic Development of Human Sleep-Dream Cycle," by H. P. Roffwarg, J. N. Muzio, and W. C. Dement, Science, 152, 1966, 604–609. Copyright 1966 AAAS. Reprinted by permission.)*

> **STOP & CHECK**
>
> **17.** Does sleep improve memory by strengthening or weakening synapses?
>
> ANSWER   **17.** The evidence so far points to weakening the synapses that were not strengthened during the day. Weakening these less relevant synapses enables the strengthened ones to stand out by contrast.

Functions of REM Sleep

An average person spends about one third of his or her life asleep and about one fifth of sleep in REM, totaling about 600 hours of REM per year. Presumably, REM serves a biological function. But what is it?

One way to approach this question is to compare the people or animals with more REM to those with less. REM sleep is widespread in mammals and birds, indicating that it is part of our ancient evolutionary heritage. Some species, however, have far more than others. As a rule, the species with the most total sleep hours also have the highest percentage of REM sleep (J. M. Siegel, 1995). Cats spend up to 16 hours a day sleeping, much or most of it in REM sleep. Rabbits, guinea pigs, and sheep sleep less and spend little time in REM.

Figure 9.19 illustrates the relationship between age and REM sleep for humans. The trend is the same for other mammalian species. Infants get more REM and more total sleep than adults do, confirming the pattern that more total sleep predicts a higher percentage of REM sleep. Among adult humans, those who sleep 9 or more hours per night have the highest percentage of REM sleep, and those who sleep 5 or fewer hours have the lowest percentage. This pattern implies that although REM is no doubt important, NREM is more tightly regulated. That is, the amount of NREM varies less among individuals and among species.

One hypothesis is that REM is important for memory storage, especially for weakening the inappropriate connections (Crick & Mitchison, 1983). REM and non-REM sleep may be important for consolidating different types of memories. Depriving people of sleep early in the night (mostly non-REM sleep) impairs verbal learning, such as memorizing a list of words, whereas depriving people of sleep during the second half of the night (more

REM) impairs consolidation of learned motor skills (Gais, Plihal, Wagner, & Born, 2000; Plihal & Born, 1997).

However, many people take antidepressant drugs that severely decrease REM sleep, without incurring memory problems (Rasch, Pommer, Diekelmann, & Born, 2009). Research on laboratory animals indicates that these drugs sometimes even enhance memory (Parent, Habib, & Baker, 1999).

Another hypothesis sounds odd because we tend to imagine a glamorous role for REM sleep: David Maurice (1998) proposed that REM just shakes the eyeballs back and forth enough to get sufficient oxygen to the corneas of the eyes. The corneas, unlike the rest of the body, get oxygen directly from the surrounding air. During sleep, because they are shielded from the air, they deteriorate slightly (Hoffmann & Curio, 2003). They do get some oxygen from the fluid behind them (see Figure 6.2), but when the eyes are motionless, that fluid becomes stagnant. Moving the eyes increases the oxygen supply to the corneas. According to this view, REM is a way of arousing a sleeper just enough to shake the eyes back and forth, and the other manifestations of REM are just byproducts. This idea makes sense of the fact that REM occurs mostly toward the end of the night's sleep, when the fluid behind the eyes would be the most stagnant. It also makes sense of the fact that individuals who spend more hours asleep devote a greater percentage of sleep to REM. (If you don't sleep long, you have less need to shake up the stagnant fluid.) However, as mentioned, many people take antidepressants that restrict REM sleep. They are not known to suffer damage to the cornea.

> **STOP & CHECK**

18. What kinds of individuals get more REM sleep than others? (Think in terms of age, species, and long versus short sleepers.)

ANSWER

18. Much REM sleep is more typical of the young than the old, of individuals who get much sleep than those who get little, and of species that sleep much of the day.

Biological Perspectives on Dreaming

Dream research faces a special problem: All we know about dreams comes from people's self-reports, and researchers have no way to check the accuracy of those reports. In fact, we forget most dreams, and even when we do remember them, the details fade quickly.

The Activation-Synthesis Hypothesis

According to the **activation-synthesis hypothesis**, a dream represents the brain's effort to make sense of sparse and distorted information. Dreams begin with periodic bursts of spontaneous activity in the pons—the PGO waves previously described—that activate some parts of the cortex but not others. The cortex combines this haphazard input with whatever other activity was already occurring and does its best to synthesize a story that makes sense of the information (Hobson & McCarley, 1977; Hobson, Pace-Schott, & Stickgold, 2000; McCarley & Hoffman, 1981). Sensory stimuli, such as sounds in the room, occasionally get incorporated into a dream, although usually they do not (Nir & Tononi, 2010).

Consider how this theory handles a couple of common dreams. Most people have had occasional dreams of falling or flying. Well, while you are asleep, you lie flat, unlike your posture for the rest of the day. Your brain in its partly aroused condition feels the vestibular sensation of your position and interprets it as flying or falling. Have you ever dreamed that you were trying to move but couldn't? Most people have. An interpretation based on the activation-synthesis theory is that during REM sleep (which accompanies most dreams), your motor cortex is inactive and your major postural muscles are virtually paralyzed. That is, when you are dreaming, you really *can't* move, you feel your lack of movement, and thus, you dream of failing to move.

One criticism is that the theory's predictions are vague. If we dream about falling because of the vestibular sensations from lying down, why don't we *always* dream of falling? If we dream we can't move because our muscles are paralyzed during REM sleep, why don't we *always* dream of being paralyzed?

The Clinico-Anatomical Hypothesis

An alternative view of dreams has been labeled the **clinico-anatomical hypothesis** because it was derived from clinical studies of patients with various kinds of brain damage (Solms, 1997, 2000). Like the activation-synthesis theory, this theory emphasizes that dreams begin with arousing stimuli that are generated within the brain combined with recent memories and any information the brain is receiving from the senses. However, the clinico-anatomical hypothesis puts less emphasis on the pons, PGO waves, or REM sleep. It regards dreams as thinking that takes place under unusual conditions, similar to mind-wandering during everyday life (Domhoff, 2011).

One of those conditions is that the brain is getting little information from the sense organs, and the primary visual and auditory areas of the cortex have lower than usual activity, so other brain areas are free to generate images without constraints or interference. Also, the primary motor cortex is suppressed, as are the motor neurons of the spinal cord, so arousal cannot lead to action. Activity is suppressed in the prefrontal cortex, which is important for working memory (memory of very recent events). Consequently, we not only forget most dreams after we awaken, but we also lose track of what has been happening within a dream, and sudden scene changes are common. We also lose a sense of volition—that is, planning (Hobson, 2009). It seems that events just happen, without any intention on our part.

Meanwhile, activity is relatively high in the inferior (lower) part of the parietal cortex, an area important for visuospatial perception. Patients with damage here have problems binding body sensations with vision. They also report no dreams. Fairly high activity is also found in the areas of visual cortex outside V1. Those areas are presumably important for the visual imagery that accompanies most dreams. Finally, activity is high in the hypothalamus, amygdala, and other areas important for emotions and motivations (Gvilia, Turner, McGinty, & Szymusiak, 2006).

So the idea is that either internal or external stimulation activates parts of the parietal, occipital, and temporal cortex. The arousal develops into a hallucinatory perception, with no sensory input from area V1 to override it. This idea, like the activation-synthesis hypothesis, is hard to test because it does not make specific predictions about who will have what dream and when.

STOP & CHECK

19. What is a key point of disagreement between the activation-synthesis hypothesis and the clinico-anatomical hypothesis?

ANSWER

19. The activation-synthesis hypothesis puts much more emphasis on the importance of the pons.

Our Limited Self-Understanding

Without minimizing how much we do understand about sleep, it is noteworthy how many basic questions remain. What is the function of REM sleep? Does dreaming have a function, or is it just an accident? Our lack of knowledge about activities that occupy so much of our time underscores a point about the biology of behavior: We evolved tendencies to behave in certain ways that lead to survival and reproduction. The behavior can serve its function even when we do not fully understand that function.

SUMMARY

1. One important function of sleep is to conserve energy at a time when the individual would be less efficient. Animal species vary in their sleep per day depending on their feeding habits and how much danger they face while asleep. **288**

2. In addition to saving energy, sleep serves other functions, including enhancement of memory. **290**

3. REM sleep occupies the greatest percentage of sleep in individuals and species that sleep the most total hours. **291**

4. According to the activation-synthesis hypothesis, dreams are the brain's attempts to make sense of the information reaching it, based mostly on haphazard input originating in the pons. **292**

5. According to the clinico-anatomical hypothesis, dreams originate partly with external stimuli but mostly from the brain's own motivations, memories, and arousal. The stimulation often produces peculiar results because it does not have to compete with normal visual input and does not get organized by the prefrontal cortex. **292**

KEY TERMS

Terms are defined in the module on the page number indicated. They're also presented in alphabetical order with definitions in the book's Subject Index/Glossary, which begins on page 561. Interactive flashcards and crossword puzzles are among the online resources available to help you learn these terms and the concepts they represent.

activation-synthesis hypothesis **292**

clinico-anatomical hypothesis **292**

THOUGHT QUESTION

Why would it be harder to deprive someone of just NREM sleep than just REM sleep?

CHAPTER 9   Interactive Exploration and Study

The **Psychology CourseMate** for this text brings chapter topics to life with interactive learning, study, and exam preparation tools, including quizzes and flashcards for the Key Concepts that appear throughout each module, as well as an interactive media-rich eBook version of the text that is fully searchable and includes highlighting and note-taking capabilities and interactive versions of the book's **Stop & Check** quizzes and **Try It Yourself Online** activities. The site also features **Virtual Biological Psychology Labs, videos,** and **animations** to help you better understand concepts—logon and learn more at **www.cengagebrain.com**, which is your gateway to all of this text's complimentary and premium resources, including the following:

Virtual Biological Psychology Labs

Explore the experiments that led to modern-day understanding of biopsychology with the Virtual Biological Psychology Labs, featuring a realistic lab environment that allows you to conduct experiments and evaluate data to better understand how scientists came to the conclusions presented in your text. The labs cover a range of topics, including perception, motivation, cognition, and more. You may purchase access at **www.cengagebrain.com**, or login at **login.cengagebrain.com** if an access card was included with your text.

Animations

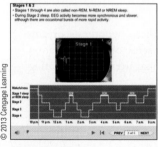

Sleep Rhythms

Also available—

- Cellular Clock
- Electroencephalography
- Pathways of Sleep and Waking
- Learning Module: Sleep Patterns

Suggestions for Further Exploration

Books

Dement, W. C. (1992). *The sleepwatchers*. Stanford, CA: Stanford Alumni Association. Fascinating, entertaining account of sleep research by one of its leading pioneers.

Foster, R. G., & Kreitzman, L. (2004). *Rhythms of life*. New Haven, CT: Yale University Press. Nontechnical discussion of research on circadian rhythms.

Moorcroft, W. H. (2003). *Understanding sleep and dreaming*. New York: Kluwer. Excellent review of the psychology and neurology of sleep and dreams.

Refinetti, R. (2005). *Circadian physiology* (2nd ed.). Boca Raton, FL: CRC Press. Marvelous summary of research on circadian rhythms and the relevance to human behavior.

Websites

The Psychology CourseMate for this text provides regularly updated links to relevant online resources for this chapter, including sites on sleep, dreams, and sleep disorders.

Internal Regulation

10

CHAPTER OUTLINE

MAIN IDEAS

1. Many physiological and behavioral processes maintain a near constancy of certain body variables. They anticipate needs as well as react to them.

2. Mammals and birds maintain constant body temperature as a way of staying ready for rapid muscle activity at any temperature of the environment. They use both behavioral and physiological processes to maintain temperature.

3. Thirst mechanisms respond to the osmotic pressure and total volume of the blood.

4. Hunger and satiety are regulated by many factors, including taste, stomach distension, the availability of glucose to the cells, and chemicals released by the fat cells. Many brain peptides help regulate feeding and satiety.

OPPOSITE: All life on Earth requires water, and animals drink it wherever they can find it.

What is life? You could define life in many ways depending on whether your purpose is medical, legal, philosophical, or poetic. Biologically, the necessary condition for life is *a coordinated set of chemical reactions*. Not all chemical reactions are alive, but all life has well-regulated chemical reactions.

Every chemical reaction in a living body takes place in a water solution at a rate that depends on the identity and concentration of molecules in the water and the temperature of the solution. Our behavior is organized to keep the right chemicals in the right proportions and at the right temperature.

Temperature Regulation

ere's an observation that puzzled biologists for years: When a small male garter snake emerges from hibernation in early spring, it emits female pheromones for the first day or two. The pheromones attract larger males that swarm all over him, trying to copulate. Presumably, the tendency to release female pheromones must have evolved to provide the small male some advantage. But what? Biologists speculated about ways in which this pseudo-mating experience might help the small male attract real females. The truth is simpler: A male that has just emerged from hibernation is so cold that it has trouble slithering out of its burrow. The larger males emerged from hibernation earlier and already had a chance to warm themselves in a sunny place. When the larger males swarm all over the smaller male, they warm him and increase his activity level (Shine, Phillips, Waye, LeMaster, & Mason, 2001).

Here are more behaviors that make sense in terms of temperature regulation:

- Have you ever noticed gulls, ducks, or other large birds standing on one leg (Figure 10.1)? Why do they do that, when balancing on two legs would seem easier? The answer is they stand this way in cold weather. Tucking a leg under the body keeps it warm (Ehrlich, Dobkin, & Wheye, 1988).
- Vultures sometimes defecate onto their own legs. Are they just careless slobs? No. They defecate onto their legs on hot days so that the evaporating excretions will cool their legs (Ehrlich et al., 1988).
- Toucans are tropical birds with huge bills (Figure 10.2). For many years biologists puzzled about the function of those huge, clumsy bills. The answer is temperature regulation (Tattersall, Andrade, & Abe, 2009). While flying on hot days, a toucan directs more blood flow to the beak, where the passing air cools it. At night the toucan tucks its bill under a wing to prevent undue loss of heat.
- Most lizards live solitary lives, but Australian thick-tailed geckos sometimes form tight huddles. Why? They live in an environment with rapid temperature fluctuations. They huddle only when the environmental temperature is falling rapidly. By huddling,

they gain insulation and prevent a rapid drop in body temperature (Shah, Shine, Hudson, & Kearney, 2003).

- The Japanese giant hornet sometimes invades bee colonies, kills one or more bees, and takes them to feed to its larvae. When one of these hornets invades a hive of Japanese honeybees, the bees form a tight swarm of more than 500, surrounding the hornet in a tiny ball. Why? The combined body heat of all those bees raises the temperature to a level that kills the hornet, although bees can survive it (Ono, Igarashi, Ohno, & Sasaki, 1995).
- Migratory birds do most of their migratory flying at night. Why? The nights are cooler. A bird flying in midday

© F1online digitale Bildagentur GmbH/Alamy

FIGURE 10.1 Why do birds sometimes stand on one foot? Like many other puzzling behaviors, this one makes sense in terms of temperature regulation. Holding one leg next to the body keeps it warm.

FIGURE 10.2 Why do toucans have such huge bills?
They use their bills to radiate heat when they need to cool the
body. They cover the bill at night to decrease heat loss.

**FIGURE 10.3 Difficulties of temperature regulation for a
newborn rodent**
A newborn rat has no hair, thin skin, and little body fat. If left
exposed to the cold, it becomes inactive.

would overheet and frequently have to stop for a drink,
often in places where fresh water is difficult to find.

- Decades ago, psychologists found that infant rats appeared deficient in certain aspects of learning, eating,
and drinking. Later results showed that the real problem
was temperature control. Researchers generally test animals at room temperature, about 20°–23° C (68°–73° F),
which is comfortable for adult humans but dangerously
cold for an isolated baby rat (Figure 10.3). In a warmer
room, infant rats show abilities that we once assumed
required more brain maturity (Satinoff, 1991).

- Certain studies found that female rats learned best during their fertile period (estrus). In other studies, they
learned best a day or two before their fertile period (proestrus). The difference depends on temperature. Rats
in estrus do better in a cooler environment, presumably
because they are generating so much heat on their own.
Rats in proestrus do better in a warmer environment
(Rubinow, Arseneau, Beverly, & Juraska, 2004).

The point is that temperature affects behavior in many
ways that we easily overlook. Temperature regulation is more
important than you might have guessed.

Homeostasis and Allostasis

Physiologist Walter B. Cannon (1929) introduced the term
homeostasis (HO-mee-oh-STAY-sis) to refer to temperature regulation and other biological processes that keep body
variables within a fixed range. The process resembles the thermostat in a house with heating and cooling systems. Someone
sets the minimum and maximum temperatures on the ther-

mostat. When the temperature in the house drops below the
minimum, the thermostat triggers the furnace to provide heat.
When the temperature rises above the maximum, the thermostat turns on the air conditioner.

Similarly, homeostatic processes in animals trigger physiological and behavioral activities that keep certain variables
within a set range. In many cases, the range is so narrow
that we refer to it as a **set point**, a single value that the body
works to maintain. For example, if calcium is deficient in
your diet and its concentration in the blood begins to fall
below the set point of 0.16 g/L (grams per liter), storage
deposits in your bones release additional calcium into the
blood. If the calcium level in the blood rises above 0.16 g/L,
you store part of the excess in your bones and excrete the
rest. Similar mechanisms maintain constant blood levels of
water, oxygen, glucose, sodium chloride, protein, fat, and
acidity (Cannon, 1929). Processes that reduce discrepancies from the set point are known as **negative feedback**.
Much of motivated behavior can be described as negative
feedback: Something causes a disturbance, and behavior
proceeds until it relieves the disturbance.

The body's set points change from time to time (Mrosovsky, 1990). For example, many animals (including most humans) increase their body fat in fall and decrease it in spring.
Your body maintains a higher temperature during the day than
at night, even if room temperature stays constant. To describe
these dynamic changes, researchers use the term **allostasis**
(from the Greek roots meaning "variable" and "standing"),
which means the adaptive way in which the body changes its
set points depending on the situation (McEwen, 2000). As you
will see throughout this chapter, much of that control depends
on cells in the hypothalamus.

STOP & CHECK

1. How does the idea of allostasis differ from homeostasis?

ANSWER

1. Homeostasis is a set of processes that keep certain body variables within a fixed range. Allostasis is an adjustment of that range, increasing it or decreasing it as circumstances change.

Controlling Body Temperature

If you were to list your strongest motivations in life, you might not think to include temperature regulation, but it has a high priority biologically. An average young adult expends about 2,600 kilocalories (kcal) per day. Where do you suppose all that energy goes? It is not to muscle movements or mental activity. Most of it goes to **basal metabolism**, the energy used to maintain a constant body temperature while at rest. Maintaining your body temperature requires about twice as much energy as do all other activities *combined* (Burton, 1994).

Amphibians, reptiles, and most fish are **poikilothermic** (POY-kih-lo-THER-mik, from Greek roots meaning "varied heat"). That is, their body temperature matches the temperature of their environment. A few large fish, including sharks and tuna, are exceptions to this rule, maintaining their core body temperature well above that of the surrounding water most of the time (Bernal, Donley, Shadwick, & Syme, 2005). Poikilothermic animals lack physiological mechanisms of temperature regulation, such as shivering and sweating. The informal term is "coldblooded," but that term is misleading because poikilothermic animals remain warm most of the day by choosing an appropriate location. A desert lizard moves between sunny areas, shady areas, and burrows to maintain a fairly steady body temperature. However, behavioral methods do not enable animals to maintain the same degree of constancy that mammals and birds have.

Mammals and birds are **homeothermic** (from Greek roots meaning "same heat"), except that certain species become poikilothermic during hibernation. Homeothermic animals use physiological mechanisms to maintain a nearly constant body temperature despite changes in the temperature of the environment. Homeothermy is costly, especially for small animals. An animal *generates* heat in proportion to its total mass, but it *radiates* heat in proportion to its surface area. A small mammal or bird, such as a mouse or hummingbird, has a high surface-to-volume ratio and therefore radiates heat rapidly. Such animals need much fuel each day to maintain their body temperature.

To cool ourselves when the air is warmer than body temperature, we have only one physiological mechanism—evaporation. Humans sweat to expose water for evaporation. For species that don't sweat, the alternatives are licking themselves and panting. As water evaporates, it cools the body. However, if the air is humid as well as hot, the moisture does not evaporate. Furthermore, you endanger your health if you cannot drink enough to replace the water you lose by sweating. If you sweat without drinking, you start becoming dehydrated (low on water). You then protect your body water by decreasing your sweat, despite the risk of overheating (Tokizawa, Yasuhara, Nakamura, Uchida, Crawshaw, & Nagashima, 2010).

Several physiological mechanisms increase your body heat in a cold environment. One is shivering. Any muscle contractions, such as those of shivering, generate heat. Second, decreased blood flow to the skin prevents the blood from cooling too much. A third mechanism works well for most mammals, though not humans: When cold, they fluff out their fur to increase insulation. (We humans also fluff out our "fur" by erecting the tiny hairs on our skin—"goose bumps." Back when our remote ancestors had a fuller coat of fur, that mechanism did some good.)

We also use behavioral mechanisms, just as poikilothermic animals do. In fact, we prefer to rely on behavior when we can. The more we regulate our temperature behaviorally, the less energy we need to spend physiologically (Refinetti & Carlisle, 1986). Finding a cool place on a hot day is much better than sweating (Figure 10.4). Finding a warm place on a cold day is much smarter than shivering. Here are a few other behavioral mechanisms of temperature regulation:

- Put on more clothing or take it off. This human strategy accomplishes what other mammals accomplish by fluffing out or sleeking their fur.
- Become more active to get warmer or less active to avoid overheating.
- To get warm, huddle with others. If you are waiting at a bus stop on a cold day, you might feel shy about suggesting to a stranger that you hug each other to keep warm. Other species have no such inhibitions (Figure 10.5). Spectacled eiders (in the duck family) spend their winters in the Arctic Ocean, which is mostly covered with ice. When more than 150,000 eiders crowd together, they not only keep warm but also maintain a big hole in the ice where they can dive for fish (Weidensaul, 1999).

FIGURE 10.4 One way to cope with the heat
On a hot day, wouldn't you do the same?

AP Photo/Sun-Journal, Ken Love

FIGURE 10.5 Behavioral regulation of body temperature
An emperor penguin chick is poorly insulated against Antarctic winter temperatures, but when chicks huddle together, they pool their heat. The cold ones on the outside push their way inward, and the warm ones on the inside drift outward. The process is so effective that a cluster of penguin chicks has to move frequently to prevent melting a hole in the ice.

APPLICATIONS AND EXTENSIONS

Surviving in Extreme Cold

If the atmospheric temperature drops below 0° C (32° F), you maintain your body temperature by shivering, shifting blood flow away from the skin, and so forth. However, a poikilothermic animal, which by definition takes the temperature of its environment, is vulnerable. If its body temperature drops below the freezing point of water, ice crystals form. Because water expands when it freezes, ice crystals would tear apart blood vessels and cell membranes, killing the animal.

Companies will freeze a dead body with the prospect that future technologies can restore the person to life.

Amphibians and reptiles avoid that risk by burrowing or finding other sheltered locations. However, some frogs, fish, and insects survive through winters in northern

Canada where even the underground temperature approaches −40° C (which is also −40° F). How do they do it? Some insects and fish stock their blood with glycerol and other antifreeze chemicals at the start of the winter (Liou, Tocilj, Davies, & Jia, 2000). Wood frogs actually do freeze, but they have several mechanisms to reduce the damage. They start by withdrawing most fluid from their organs and blood vessels and storing it in extracellular spaces. Therefore, ice crystals have room to expand when they form, without tearing blood vessels or cells. Also, the frogs have chemicals that cause ice crystals to form gradually, not in chunks. Finally, they have such extraordinary blood-clotting capacity that they quickly repair any blood vessels that do rupture (Storey & Storey, 1999).

As you may have heard, some people have had their bodies frozen after death in hopes that scientists will discover a cure for their disease *and* a way to bring a frozen body back to life. If you had enough money, would you choose this route to possible life after death?

At present, the chances don't look good. The wood frogs that survive after freezing begin by dehydrating their organs and blood vessels. Unless you underwent similar dehydration—before dying!—ice crystals will tear up blood vessels and cell membranes throughout your body. Repairing all those membranes sounds close to impossible. ∎

The Advantages of Constant High Body Temperature

As mentioned, we spend about two thirds of our total energy maintaining body temperature (basal metabolism). A poikilothermic animal, with a much lower level of basal metabolism, needs far less fuel. If we didn't maintain a constant, high body temperature, we could eat less and spend less effort finding food. Given the substantial costs of maintaining our body temperature, it must provide an important advantage, or we would not have evolved these mechanisms. What is that advantage?

For the answer, think back to Chapter 8: As the water gets colder, a fish has to recruit more and more fast-twitch muscle fibers to remain active, at the risk of rapid fatigue. Birds and mammals keep their muscles warm at all times, regardless of air temperature, and therefore stay constantly ready for vigorous activity. In other words, we eat a great deal to support our high metabolism so that even when the weather is cold, we can still run as fast and far as we need to.

Why did mammals evolve a body temperature of 37° C (98° F) instead of some other value? From the standpoint of muscle activity, we gain an advantage by being as warm as possible. A warmer animal has warmer muscles and therefore runs faster with less fatigue than a cooler animal. When a reptile has a choice of environments at different temperatures, it usually chooses to warm itself to 37°–38° C (Wagner & Gleeson, 1997).

If warmer is better, why not heat ourselves to an even higher temperature? First, maintaining a higher temperature requires more fuel and energy. Second, and more importantly, beyond about 40° or 41° C, proteins begin to break their bonds and lose their useful properties. Birds' body temperatures are in fact about 41° C (105° F).

It is possible to evolve proteins that are stable at higher temperatures; indeed, odd microscopic animals called thermophiles survive in boiling water. However, to do so, they need many extra chemical bonds to stabilize their proteins. The enzymatic properties of a protein depend on its flexibility, so making proteins rigid enough to withstand high temperatures makes them inactive at more moderate temperatures (Feller, 2010). In short, our body temperature of 37° C is a trade-off between the advantages of high temperature for rapid movement and the disadvantages of high temperature for protein stability.

Reproductive cells require a cooler environment than the rest of the body (Rommel, Pabst, & McLellan, 1998). Birds lay eggs and sit on them, instead of developing them internally, because the birds' internal temperature is too hot for an embryo. Similarly, in most male mammals, the scrotum hangs outside the body, because sperm production requires a cooler temperature than the rest of the body. A man who wears his undershorts too tight keeps his testes too close to the body, overheats them, and produces fewer healthy sperm cells. Preg-

nant women are advised to avoid hot baths and anything else that might overheat a developing fetus.

STOP & CHECK

2. What is the primary advantage of maintaining a constant high body temperature?

3. Why did mammals evolve a temperature of 37° C (98° F) instead of some other temperature?

ANSWERS

2. A constant high body temperature keeps the animal ready for rapid, prolonged muscle activity even in cold weather. **3.** Animals gain an advantage in being as warm as possible and therefore as fast as possible. However, proteins lose stability at temperatures much above 37° C (98° F).

Brain Mechanisms

The physiological changes that defend body temperature—such as shivering, sweating, and changes in blood flow to the skin—depend on areas in and near the hypothalamus (Figure 10.6), mainly the anterior hypothalamus and the preoptic area,

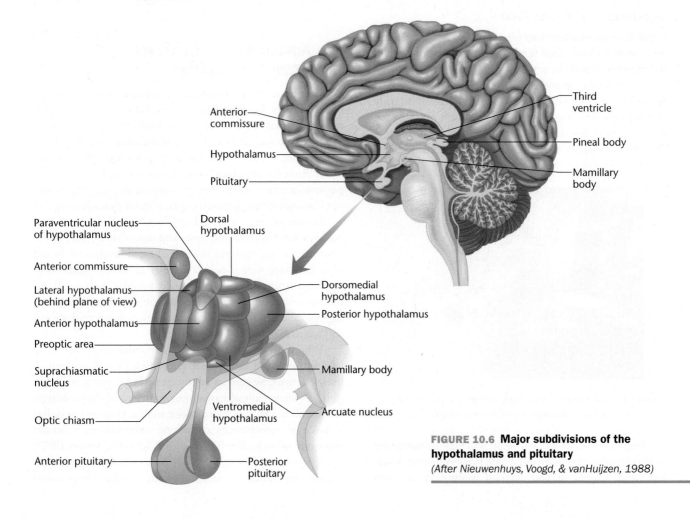

FIGURE 10.6 **Major subdivisions of the hypothalamus and pituitary**
(After Nieuwenhuys, Voogd, & vanHuijzen, 1988)

which is just anterior to the anterior hypothalamus. (It is called *preoptic* because it is near the optic chiasm, where the optic nerves cross.) Because of the close relationship between the preoptic area and the anterior hypothalamus, researchers often treat them as a single area, the **preoptic area/anterior hypothalamus**, or **POA/AH**. The POA/AH and a couple other hypothalamic areas send output to the hindbrain's raphe nucleus, which controls the physiological mechanisms (Yoshida, Li, Cano, Lazarus, & Saper, 2009).

The POA/AH monitors body temperature partly by monitoring its own temperature (D. O. Nelson & Prosser, 1981). If an experimenter heats the POA/AH, an animal pants or sweats, even in a cool environment. If the same brain area is cooled, the animal shivers, even in a warm room. An animal also reacts to a heated or cooled POA/AH by pressing a lever or doing other work for cold air or hot air reinforcements (Satinoff, 1964). That is, the animal acts as if it feels hot when its hypothalamus is hot, and it acts as if it feels cold when its hypothalamus is cold. Given that the hypothalamus is well insulated on the interior of the head, this mechanism makes sense. If the hypothalamus is hot or cold, the rest of the interior of the body probably is, too. Cells of the POA/AH also receive input from temperature receptors in the skin and spinal cord. The animal shivers most vigorously when both the POA/AH and the other receptors are cold. It sweats or pants most vigorously when both are hot.

The POA/AH is not the only brain area that detects temperature, but it is the primary area for controlling physiological mechanisms of temperature regulation, such as sweating or shivering. Separate populations of cells within the POA/AH and a couple other hypothalamic areas regulate different aspects of temperature regulation, such as shivering and changes in blood flow. Therefore, tiny localized damage can impair one aspect of temperature regulation and not others (McAllen, Tanaka, Ootsuka, & McKinley, 2010). After damage to all of the POA/AH, mammals can still regulate body temperature but only by the same behavioral mechanisms that a lizard might use, such as seeking a warmer or colder location (Satinoff & Rutstein, 1970; Van Zoeren & Stricker, 1977).

Fever

Bacterial and viral infections generally cause fever, an increase in body temperature. The fever is not part of the illness; it is part of the body's defense against the illness. When bacteria, viruses, fungi, or other intruders invade the body, they mobilize *leukocytes* (white blood cells) to attack them. The leukocytes release small proteins called **cytokines** that attack the intruders. Cytokines also stimulate the vagus nerve, which sends signals to the hypothalamus (Ek et al., 2001; Leon, 2002), increasing the release of chemicals called prostaglandins. Stimulation of a particular kind of prostaglandin receptor in one nucleus of the hypothalamus is necessary for fever. If you didn't have those receptors, illnesses would not give you a fever (Lazarus et al., 2007). Two children have been found with mutations of a particular gene, resulting in a failure to develop fevers, even in the presence of pneumonia (Hanada, et al., 2009).

A fever represents an increased set point for body temperature. Just as you shiver or sweat when your body temperature goes below or above its usual 37° C, when you have a fever of, say, 39° C, you shiver or sweat whenever your temperature deviates from that level. Moving to a cooler room does not lower your fever. Your body just works harder to keep its temperature at the feverish level.

Because newborn rabbits have an immature hypothalamus, they do not shiver in response to infections. If they are given a choice of environments, however, they select a spot warm enough to raise their body temperature (Satinoff, McEwen, & Williams, 1976). That is, they develop a fever by behavioral means. Fish and reptiles with an infection also choose a warm-enough environment, if they can find one, to produce a feverish body temperature (Kluger, 1991). Again, the point is that fever is something the animal does to fight an infection.

Does fever do any good? Certain types of bacteria grow less vigorously at high temperatures than at normal mammalian body temperatures. Also, fever enhances activity of the immune system (Skitzki, Chen, Wang, & Evans, 2007). Other things being equal, developing a moderate fever probably increases an individual's chance of surviving a bacterial infection (Kluger, 1991). However, a fever above about 39° C (103° F) in humans does more harm than good, and a fever above 41° C (109° F) is life-threatening (Rommel et al., 1998).

STOP & CHECK

4. What evidence do we have that the POA/AH controls body temperature?

5. How can an animal regulate body temperature after damage to the POA/AH?

ANSWERS

4. Direct cooling or heating of the POA/AH leads to shivering or sweating. Also, damage there impairs physiological control of temperature. 5. It can regulate temperature through behavior, such as by finding a warmer or cooler place.

STOP & CHECK

6. What evidence indicates that fever is an adaptation to fight illness?

ANSWER

6. The body will shiver or sweat to maintain its elevated temperature. Also, fish, reptiles, and immature mammals with infections use behavioral means to raise their temperature to a feverish level. Furthermore, a moderate fever inhibits bacterial growth and increases the probability of surviving a bacterial infection.

Combining Physiological and Behavioral Mechanisms

One theme of this module has been the redundancy of mechanisms. Your body has various physiological mechanisms to maintain constant body temperature, including shivering, sweating, and changes in blood flow. You also rely on behavioral mechanisms, such as finding a cooler or warmer place, adding or removing clothing, and so forth. Redundancy reduces your risk: If one mechanism fails, another mechanism comes to your rescue. It is not, however, a true redundancy in the sense of two mechanisms doing exactly the same thing. Each of your mechanisms of temperature regulation solves a different aspect of the problem in a different way. We shall see this theme again in the discussions of thirst and hunger.

SUMMARY

1. It is easy to overlook the importance of temperature regulation. Many seemingly odd animal behaviors make sense as ways to heat or cool the body. **298**

2. Homeostasis is a tendency to maintain a body variable near a set point. Temperature, hunger, and thirst are almost homeostatic, but the set point changes in varying circumstances. **299**

3. A high body temperature enables a mammal or bird to move rapidly and without fatigue even in a cold environment. **301**

4. From the standpoint of muscle activity, the higher the body temperature, the better. However, as temperatures exceed 41° C, protein stability decreases, and more energy is needed to maintain body temperature. Mammalian body temperature of 37° C is a compromise between these competing considerations. **301**

5. The preoptic area and anterior hypothalamus (POA/AH) are critical for temperature control. Cells there monitor both their own temperature and that of the skin and spinal cord. **302**

6. Even homeothermic animals rely partly on behavioral mechanisms for temperature regulation, especially in infancy and after damage to the POA/AH. **303**

7. A moderate fever helps an animal combat an infection. **303**

KEY TERMS

Terms are defined in the module on the page number indicated. They're also presented in alphabetical order with definitions in the book's Subject Index/Glossary, which begins on page 561. Interactive flashcards and crossword puzzles are among the online resources available to help you learn these terms and the concepts they represent.

allostasis **299**

basal metabolism **300**

cytokines **303**

homeostasis **299**

homeothermic **300**

negative feedback **299**

poikilothermic **300**

preoptic area/anterior hypothalamus (POA/AH) **303**

set point **299**

THOUGHT QUESTION

Speculate on why birds have higher body temperatures than mammals.

MODULE 10.2

Thirst

Water constitutes about 70% of the mammalian body. Because the concentration of chemicals in water determines the rate of all chemical reactions in the body, the water must be regulated within narrow limits. The body also needs enough fluid in the circulatory system to maintain normal blood pressure. People sometimes survive for weeks without food, but not without water.

Mechanisms of Water Regulation

Different species have different strategies for maintaining water. Beavers and other species that live in rivers or lakes drink plenty of water, eat moist foods, and excrete dilute urine. In contrast, gerbils and other desert animals don't need to drink at all. They gain water from their food and they have many adaptations to avoid losing water, including the ability to excrete dry feces and concentrated urine. Unable to sweat, they avoid the heat of the day by burrowing under the ground. Their highly convoluted nasal passages minimize water loss when they exhale.

We humans vary our strategy depending on circumstances. If you cannot find enough to drink or if the water tastes bad, you conserve water by excreting more concentrated urine and decreasing your sweat, somewhat like a gerbil, although not to the same extreme. Your posterior pituitary (Figure 10.6) releases the hormone **vasopressin** that raises blood pressure by constricting blood vessels. (The term *vasopressin* comes from *vascular pressure*.) The increased pressure helps compensate for the decreased blood volume. Vasopressin is also known as **antidiuretic hormone (ADH)** because it enables the kidneys to reabsorb water from urine and therefore make the urine more concentrated. (*Diuresis* means "urination.") You also increase secretion of vasopressin while you are sleeping to preserve body water at a time when you cannot drink (Trudel & Bourque, 2010).

In most cases, our strategy is closer to that of beavers: We drink more than we need and excrete the excess. (However, if you drink extensively without eating, as many alcoholics do, you may excrete enough body salts to harm yourself.) Most of our drinking is with meals or in social situations, and most people seldom experience intense thirst.

Osmotic Thirst

We distinguish two types of thirst. Eating salty foods causes *osmotic* thirst, and losing fluid by bleeding or sweating induces *hypovolemic* thirst.

The combined concentration of all *solutes* (molecules in solution) in mammalian body fluids remains at a nearly constant level of 0.15 M (molar). (Molarity is a measure of the number of particles per unit of solution, regardless of the size of each particle. A 1.0 M solution of sugar and a 1.0 M solution of sodium chloride have the same number of molecules per liter.) This fixed concentration of solutes can be regarded as a set point, similar to the set point for temperature. Any deviation activates mechanisms that restore the concentration of solutes to the set point.

Osmotic pressure is the tendency of water to flow across a semipermeable membrane from the area of low solute concentration to the area of higher concentration. A semipermeable membrane is one through which water can pass but solutes cannot. The membrane surrounding a cell is almost a semipermeable membrane because water flows across it freely and various solutes flow either slowly or not at all between the *intracellular fluid* inside the cell and the *extracellular fluid* outside it. Osmotic pressure occurs when solutes are more concentrated on one side of the membrane than on the other.

If you eat something salty, sodium ions spread through the blood and the extracellular fluid but do not cross the membranes into cells. The result is a higher concentration of solutes (including sodium) outside the cells than inside. The resulting osmotic pressure draws water from the cells into the extracellular fluid. Certain neurons detect their own loss of water and then trigger **osmotic thirst**, which helps restore the normal state (Figure 10.7). The kidneys also excrete more concen-

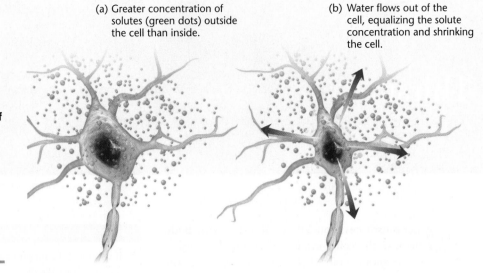

(a) Greater concentration of solutes (green dots) outside the cell than inside.

(b) Water flows out of the cell, equalizing the solute concentration and shrinking the cell.

FIGURE 10.7 The consequence of a difference in osmotic pressure (a) Suppose a solute such as NaCl is more concentrated outside the cell than inside. (b) Water flows by osmosis out of the cell until the concentrations are equal. Neurons in certain brain areas detect their own dehydration and trigger thirst. (© Argosy Publishing Inc.)

trated urine to rid the body of excess sodium and maintain as much water as possible.

How does the brain detect osmotic pressure? It gets part of the information from receptors around the third ventricle (Figure 10.8). Of all brain areas, those around the third ventricle have the leakiest blood–brain barrier (Simon, 2000). A weak blood–brain barrier would be harmful for most neurons, but it helps cells monitor the contents of the blood. The areas important for detecting osmotic pressure and the salt content of the blood include the **OVLT** (organum vasculosum laminae terminalis) and the **subfornical organ** (**SFO**) (Hiyama, Watanabe, Okado, & Noda, 2004). The OVLT receives input from receptors in the brain itself and from receptors in the digestive tract, enabling the brain to anticipate an osmotic need before the rest of the body experiences it (Bourque, 2008).

Receptors in the OVLT, the subfornical organ, the stomach, and elsewhere relay their information to several parts of the hypothalamus, including the **supraoptic nucleus** and the **paraventricular nucleus** (**PVN**), which control the rate at which the posterior pituitary releases vasopressin. Receptors also relay information to the **lateral preoptic area** and surrounding parts of the hypothalamus, which control drinking (Saad, Luiz, Camargo, Renzi, & Manani, 1996).

After osmotic pressure triggers thirst, how do you know when to stop drinking? You do *not* wait until water has restored normal osmotic pressure for the receptors in the brain. The water you drink has to be absorbed through the digestive system and then pumped through the blood to the brain. That process takes 15 minutes or so, and if you continued drinking for that long, you would drink far more than you need. The body monitors swallowing and detects the distension of the stomach and upper part of the small intestine. Those messages limit drinking to not much more than you need at a given time (Stricker & Hoffmann, 2007).

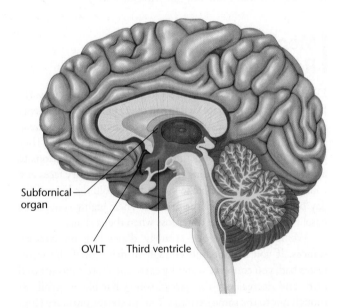

Subfornical organ

OVLT   Third ventricle

FIGURE 10.8 The brain's receptors for osmotic pressure and blood volume
These neurons are in areas surrounding the third ventricle of the brain, where no blood–brain barrier prevents blood-borne chemicals from entering the brain. (Based in part on DeArmond, Fusco, & Dewey, 1974; Weindl, 1973)

STOP & CHECK

8. Would adding salt to the body's extracellular fluids increase or decrease osmotic thirst?

ANSWER

8. Adding salt to the extracellular fluids would increase osmotic thirst because it would draw water from the cells into the extracellular spaces.

Hypovolemic Thirst and Sodium-Specific Hunger

Suppose you lose a significant amount of body fluid by bleeding, diarrhea, or sweating. Although your body's osmotic pressure stays the same, you need fluid. Your heart has trouble pumping blood to the head, and nutrients do not flow as easily as usual into your cells. Your body will react with hormones that constrict blood vessels—vasopressin and *angiotensin II*. When blood volume drops, the kidneys release the enzyme *renin*, which splits a portion off angiotensinogen, a large protein in the blood, to form angiotensin I, which other enzymes convert to **angiotensin II**. Like vasopressin, angiotensin II constricts the blood vessels, compensating for the drop in blood pressure (Figure 10.9).

Angiotensin II also helps trigger thirst, in conjunction with receptors that detect blood pressure in the large veins. However, this thirst is different from osmotic thirst, because you need to restore lost salts and not just water. This kind of thirst is known as **hypovolemic** (HI-po-vo-LEE-mik) **thirst**, meaning thirst based on low volume. When angiotensin II reaches the brain, it stimulates neurons in areas adjoining the third ventricle (Fitts, Starbuck, & Ruhf, 2000; Mangiapane & Simpson, 1980; Tanaka et al., 2001). Those neurons send axons to the hypothalamus, where they release angiotensin II as their neurotransmitter (Tanaka, Hori, & Nomura, 2001). That is, the neurons surrounding the third ventricle both respond to angiotensin II and release it. As in many other cases, the connection between a neurotransmitter and its function is not arbitrary. The brain uses a chemical that was already performing a related function elsewhere in the body.

Whereas an animal with osmotic thirst needs water, one with hypovolemic thirst can't drink much pure water. If it did, it would dilute its body fluids. It therefore increases its preference for slightly salty water (Stricker, 1969). If the animal is offered both water and salt, it alternates between them to yield an appropriate mixture. It shows a strong craving for salty tastes. This preference, known as **sodium-specific hunger**, develops automatically as soon as the need exists (Richter, 1936). In contrast, specific hungers for other vitamins and minerals have to be learned by trial and error (Rozin & Kalat, 1971). You may have noticed this phenomenon yourself. A woman around the time of menstruation, or anyone who has sweated heavily, finds that salty snacks taste especially good.

Sodium-specific hunger depends partly on hormones (Schulkin, 1991). When the body's sodium reserves are low, the adrenal glands produce the hormone **aldosterone** (al-DOSS-ter-one), which causes the kidneys, salivary glands, and sweat glands to retain salt (Verrey & Beron, 1996). Aldosterone and angiotensin II together change the properties of taste receptors on the tongue, neurons in the nucleus of the tractus solitarius (part of the taste system), and neurons elsewhere in the brain to increase salt intake (Krause & Sakal, 2007). Note that aldosterone indicates low sodium and angiotensin II indicates low blood volume. Either one by itself produces only a small effect on salt intake, but their combined effect is a massive increase in a preference for salt, sometimes producing a preference for salt over sugar or anything else (Geerling & Loewy, 2008). Table 10.1 summarizes the differences between osmotic thirst and hypovolemic thirst.

STOP & CHECK

9. Who would drink more pure water—someone with osmotic thirst or someone with hypovolemic thirst?

ANSWER

9. Someone with osmotic thirst would drink more water. Someone with hypovolemic thirst would drink more of a solution containing salts.

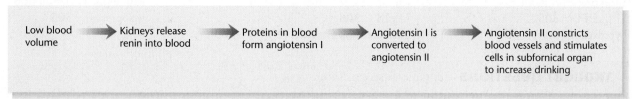

Low blood volume → Kidneys release renin into blood → Proteins in blood form angiotensin I → Angiotensin I is converted to angiotensin II → Angiotensin II constricts blood vessels and stimulates cells in subfornical organ to increase drinking

FIGURE 10.9 Hormonal response to hypovolemia *(© Cengage Learning 2013)*

TABLE 10.1   Osmotic and Hypovolemic Thirst

Type of Thirst	Stimulus	Best Relieved by Drinking	Receptor Location	Hormone Influences
Osmotic	High solute concentration outside cells causes loss of water from cells	Water	OLVT, a brain area adjoining the third ventricle	Accompanied by vasopressin secretion to conserve water
Hypovolemic	Low blood volume	Water containing solutes	1. Receptors measuring blood pressure in the veins 2. Subfornical organ, a brain area adjoining the third ventricle	Increased by angiotension II

The Psychology and Biology of Thirst

You may have thought that temperature regulation happens automatically and that water regulation depends on your behavior. You can see now that the distinction is not entirely correct. You control your body temperature partly by automatic means, such as sweating or shivering, but also partly by behavioral means, such as choosing a warm or cool place. You control your body water partly by the behavior of drinking but also by hormones that alter kidney activity. If your kidneys cannot regulate your water and sodium adequately, your brain gets signals to change your drinking or sodium intake. In short, keeping your body's chemical reactions going depends on both skeletal and autonomic controls.

SUMMARY

1. Different mammalian species have evolved different ways of maintaining body water, ranging from frequent drinking (beavers) to extreme conservation of fluids (gerbils). Humans alter their strategy depending on the availability of acceptable fluids.   **305**

2. An increase in the osmotic pressure of the blood draws water out of cells, causing osmotic thirst. Neurons in the OVLT, an area adjoining the third ventricle, detect changes in osmotic pressure and send information to hypothalamic areas responsible for vasopressin secretion and drinking.   **305**

3. Loss of blood volume causes hypovolemic thirst. Animals with hypovolemic thirst drink more water containing solutes than pure water.   **307**

4. Hypovolemic thirst is triggered by the hormone angiotensin II, which increases when blood pressure falls.   **307**

5. Loss of sodium salts from the body triggers sodium-specific cravings.   **307**

KEY TERMS

Terms are defined in the module on the page number indicated. They're also presented in alphabetical order with definitions in the book's Subject Index/Glossary, which begins on page 561. Interactive flashcards and crossword puzzles are among the online resources available to help you learn these terms and the concepts they represent.

aldosterone   **307**

angiotensin II   **307**

antidiuretic hormone (ADH)   **305**

hypovolemic thirst   **307**

lateral preoptic area   **306**

osmotic pressure   **305**

osmotic thirst   **305**

OVLT   **306**

paraventricular nucleus (PVN)   **306**

sodium-specific hunger   **307**

subfornical organ (SFO)   **306**

supraoptic nucleus   **306**

vasopressin   **305**

THOUGHT QUESTIONS

1. An injection of concentrated sodium chloride triggers osmotic thirst, but an injection of equally concentrated glucose does not. Why not?

2. If all the water you drank leaked out through a tube connected to the stomach, how would your drinking change?

3. Many women crave salt during pregnancy. Why?

Hunger

Different species use different eating strategies. A snake or crocodile might have a huge meal and then eat nothing more for months (Figure 10.10). Bears eat as much as they can whenever they can. It is a sensible strategy because bears' main foods—fruits and nuts—are available in large quantities for only short times. Bears' occasional feasts tide them over through times of starvation. You might think of it as survival of the fattest. (Sorry about that one.)

A small bird, at the other extreme, eats only what it needs at the moment. The advantage of restraint is that low weight helps it fly away from predators and even a few extra milligrams might make a difference (Figure 10.11). However, in some climates, a bird needs to store a substantial amount to get through the night. Tiny chickadees manage to survive through Alaska winters. Every night, a chickadee finds a hollowed tree or other nesting site that provides as much insulation as possible, and it lowers its body temperature into a state almost like hibernation. Still, it has to shiver throughout the night to prevent its body from freezing, and all that shivering requires energy. During Alaskan winters, a chickadee eats enough

each day to increase its body weight by 10% and then loses that amount at night (Harrison, 2008; Sharbaugh, 2001). For comparison, imagine a 50 kg (110 lb) person gaining 5 kg (11 lb) during the day and then shivering it off at night.

Humans eat more than we need for today, unlike small birds, but we do not stuff ourselves like bears—not as a rule, anyway. Choosing which food to eat and how much is an important decision. We use a wide array of learned and unlearned mechanisms to help in the process.

▌ Digestion and Food Selection

Examine the digestive system, as diagrammed in Figure 10.12. Its function is to break food into smaller molecules that the cells can use. Digestion begins in the mouth, where enzymes in the saliva break down carbohydrates. Swallowed food travels down the esophagus to the stomach, where it mixes with hydrochloric acid and enzymes that digest proteins. The stomach stores food for a time, and then a round sphincter muscle opens at the end of the stomach to release food to the small intestine.

FIGURE 10.10 A python swallowing a gazelle
The gazelle weighed about 50% more than the snake. Many reptiles eat huge but infrequent meals. Their total intake over a year is far less than that of a mammal. We mammals need far more fuel because we use so much more energy, mainly for maintaining basal metabolism.

FIGURE 10.11 A great tit, a small European bird
Ordinarily, when food is abundant, tits eat just what they need each day and maintain very low fat reserves. When food is harder to find, they eat all they can and live off fat reserves between meals. During an era when their predators were scarce, tits started putting on more fat regardless of the food supplies.

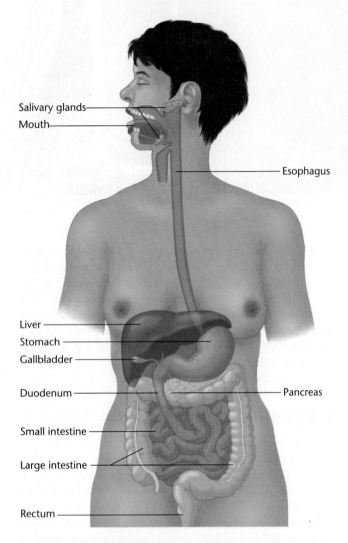

Salivary glands
Mouth
Esophagus
Liver
Stomach
Gallbladder
Duodenum
Pancreas
Small intestine
Large intestine
Rectum

FIGURE 10.12 The human digestive system (© Cengage Learning 2013)

The small intestine has enzymes that digest proteins, fats, and carbohydrates. It is also the site for absorbing digested materials into the bloodstream. The blood carries those chemicals to body cells that either use them or store them for later use. The large intestine absorbs water and minerals and lubricates the remaining materials to pass as feces.

Consumption of Dairy Products

Newborn mammals survive at first on mother's milk. As they grow older, they stop nursing for several reasons: The milk supply declines, the mother pushes them away, and they begin to eat other foods. Most mammals at about the age of weaning lose the intestinal enzyme **lactase**, which is necessary for metabolizing **lactose**, the sugar in milk. From then on, milk consumption causes stomach cramps and gas (Rozin & Pelchat, 1988). Adult mammals can drink a little milk, as you may have noticed with a pet dog, but generally not much. The declining level of lactase may be an evolved mechanism to encourage weaning at the appropriate time.

Humans are a partial exception to this rule. Many adults have enough lactase levels to consume milk and other dairy products throughout life. However, nearly all the people in China and surrounding countries lack the gene that enables adults to metabolize lactose, as do varying numbers of people in other parts of the world (Flatz, 1987). People who are lactose intolerant can consume a little milk, and larger amounts of cheese and yogurt, which are easier to digest. If they overeat dairy products, the result depends on the type of bacteria they have in their digestive system, but it often includes diarrhea, cramps, and gas pains (Ingram, Mulcare, Itan, Thomas, & Swallow, 2009). Most such people learn to limit their intake of dairy products. Figure 10.13 shows the worldwide distribution of lactose tolerance.

Within Africa, the distribution of ability to digest lactose varies in a patchy way from place to place. Whereas Europeans who can digest lactose in adulthood all have variants of the same gene, people in different parts of Africa have genes different from one another and different from Europeans, indicating that the genes for lactose digestion evolved independently in different places, probably within the last few thousand years, in response to the domestication of cattle (Tishkoff et al., 2006). When cow's milk became available, the selective pressure was strong in favor of genes enabling people to digest it.

> **STOP & CHECK**
>
> 10. What genetic difference is most important for variants in the likelihood of drinking milk in adulthood?
>
> **ANSWER**
>
> **10.** The likelihood of drinking milk in adulthood depends largely on a gene that controls the ability to digest lactose, the main sugar in milk.

Food Selection and Behavior

Does your food selection change your behavior? Many people have unsubstantiated beliefs in this regard. Many people, including physicians, believe that eating sugar makes children hyperactive. The best way to test this claim is to have children eat snacks with sugar on some days, and artificially sweetened snacks on other days, so that neither they nor their parents and teachers know when the child has eaten sugar. Studies of this type have found no significant effect of sugar on children's activity level, play behaviors, or school performance (Ells et al., 2008; Milich & Pelham, 1986). Presumably the belief that sugar causes hyperactivity is an illusion based on people's tendency to remember the observations that fit their expectation and disregard the others.

Another common misconception is that eating turkey increases the body's supply of tryptophan, which enables the brain to make chemicals that make you sleepy. That idea probably originated from the observation that many people in the United States feel sleepy after eating a turkey dinner on Thanksgiving. That sleepiness comes from overeating, not from turkey itself, which has only an average amount

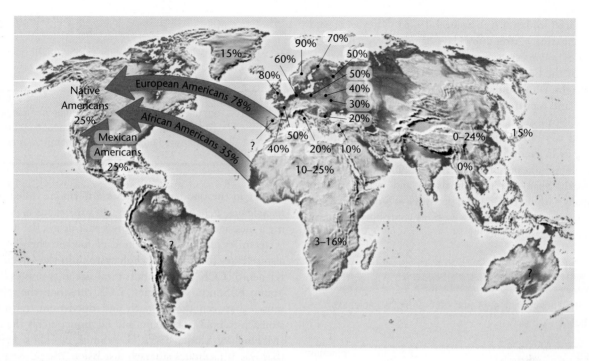

FIGURE 10.13 Percentage of adults who are lactose tolerant
People in areas with high lactose tolerance (e.g., Scandinavia) are likely to enjoy milk and other dairy products throughout their lives. Adults in areas with low tolerance (including much of Southeast Asia) drink less milk, if any. *(© Cengage Learning 2013. Based on Flatz, 1987; Rozin & Pelchat, 1988)*

of tryptophan. However, the rest of that idea is correct: Increasing tryptophan does help the brain produce melatonin, which induces sleepiness. Other than taking tryptophan pills, the most reliable way to increase tryptophan in the brain is to eat a diet high in carbohydrates. Here is the explanation: Tryptophan enters the brain by an active-transport protein that it shares with phenylalanine and other large amino acids. When you eat carbohydrates, your body reacts by increasing secretion of insulin, which moves sugars into storage and also moves phenylalanine into storage (in liver cells and elsewhere). By reducing the competition from phenylalanine, this process makes it easier for tryptophan to reach the brain, inducing sleepiness (Silber & Schmitt, 2010). In short, it's mainly the dessert at your big meal that induces sleepiness.

On the other hand, one old belief, long dismissed as nonsense, may turn out to be partly true. That belief is that fish is brain food. Many fish, including salmon, contain oils that are helpful for brain functioning, and several research studies have found that eating more fish helps some people improve their memory and reasoning abilities (Ells et al., 2008).

Short- and Long-Term Regulation of Feeding

Eating is far too important to be entrusted to just one mechanism. Your brain gets messages from your mouth, stomach, intestines, fat cells, and elsewhere to regulate your eating.

Oral Factors

You're a busy person, right? If you could get all the nutrition you need by swallowing a pill, would you do it? Once in a while you might, but not often. People like to eat. In fact, many people like to taste and chew even when they are not hungry. Figure 10.14 shows a piece of 6,500-year-old chewing gum made from birch–bark tar. The small tooth marks indicate that a child or teenager chewed it. Anthropologists don't know how the ancient people removed the sap to make the gum, and they aren't sure why anyone would chew something that tasted as bad as this gum probably did (Battersby, 1997). Clearly, the urge to chew is strong.

If necessary, could you become satiated without tasting your food? In one experiment, college students consumed lunch five days a week by swallowing one end of a rubber tube and then pushing a button to pump a liquid diet into

FIGURE 10.14 Chewing gum from about 4500 B.C.
The gum, made from birch–bark tar, has small tooth marks, indicating that a child or adolescent chewed it. *(Reprinted by permission from Macmillan Publishers Ltd: Nature, Plus c'est le meme chews, Stephen Battersby, 1997)*

the stomach (Jordan, 1969; Spiegel, 1973). (They were paid for participating.) After a few days of practice, each person established a consistent pattern of pumping in a constant volume of the liquid each day and maintaining a constant body weight. Most found the untasted meals unsatisfying, however, and reported a desire to taste or chew something (Jordan, 1969).

Could you be satisfied if you tasted something without ingesting it? In **sham-feeding** experiments, everything an animal swallows leaks out of a tube connected to the esophagus or stomach. Sham-feeding animals eat and swallow almost continually without becoming satiated (G. P. Smith, 1998). In short, taste and other mouth sensations contribute to satiety, but they are not sufficient.

> **STOP & CHECK**

11. What evidence indicates that taste is not sufficient for satiety?

ANSWER

11. It is not sufficient, because sham-feed chew and taste their food but do not become satiated.

The Stomach and Intestines

Ordinarily, we end a meal before the food reaches the blood, much less the muscles and other cells. Usually, the main signal to end a meal is distension of the stomach. In one experiment, researchers attached an inflatable cuff at the connection between the stomach and small intestine (Deutsch, Young, & Kalogeris, 1978). When they inflated the cuff, food could not pass from the stomach to the duodenum. They carefully ensured that the cuff was not traumatic to the animal and did not interfere with feeding. The key result was that, with the cuff inflated, an animal ate a normal-size meal and then stopped. Evidently, stomach distension is sufficient to produce satiety.

The stomach conveys satiety messages to the brain via the vagus nerve and the splanchnic nerves. The **vagus nerve** (cranial nerve X) conveys information about the stretching of the stomach walls, providing a major basis for satiety. The **splanchnic** (SPLANK-nik) **nerves** convey information about the nutrient contents of the stomach (Deutsch & Ahn, 1986).

However, people who have had their stomach surgically removed (because of stomach cancer or other disease) still report satiety, so stomach distension is not necessary for satiety. Later researchers found that meals end after distension of either the stomach or the duodenum (Seeley, Kaplan, & Grill, 1995). The **duodenum** (DYOU-oh-DEE-num or dyuh-ODD-ehn-uhm) is the part of the small intestine adjoining the stomach. It is the first digestive site that absorbs a significant amount of nutrients.

> **STOP & CHECK**

12. What is the evidence that stomach distension is sufficient for satiety?

ANSWER

12. If a cuff is attached to the junction between the stomach and duodenum so that food cannot leave the stomach, an animal becomes satiated when the stomach is full.

Fat in the duodenum releases a hormone called *oleoyle-thanolamide* (OEA), which stimulates the vagus nerve, sending a message to the hypothalamus that delays the next meal (Gaetani et al., 2010). Any kind of food in the duodenum also releases the hormone **cholecystokinin** (ko-leh-SIS-teh-KI-nehn) **(CCK)**, which limits meal size in two ways (Gibbs, Young, & Smith, 1973). First, CCK constricts the sphincter muscle between the stomach and duodenum, causing the stomach to hold its contents and fill more quickly than usual (McHugh & Moran, 1985; G. P. Smith & Gibbs, 1998). In that way it facilitates stomach distension, the primary signal for ending a meal. Second, CCK stimulates the vagus nerve to send signals to the hypothalamus, causing cells there to release a neurotransmitter that is a shorter version of the CCK molecule itself (Kobett et al., 2006; G. J. Schwartz, 2000). The process is something like sending a fax: The CCK in the intestines can't cross the blood–brain barrier, but it stimulates cells to release something almost like it. As in the case of angiotensin and thirst, the body uses the same chemical in the periphery and in the brain for closely related functions.

Given that CCK helps to end a meal, could we use it to help people who are trying to lose weight? Unfortunately, no. CCK produces short-term effects only. It limits the size of the meal, but an animal that has eaten a smaller than usual meal compensates by overeating at the next meal (Cummings & Overduin, 2007).

> **STOP & CHECK**

13. What are two mechanisms by which CCK increases satiety?

ANSWER

13. When the duodenum is distended, it releases CCK, which closes the sphincter muscle between the stomach and duodenum. CCK therefore increases the rate at which the stomach distends. Also, neural signals from the intestines cause certain cells in the hypothalamus to release CCK as a neurotransmitter, and at its receptors, it triggers decreased feeding.

Glucose, Insulin, and Glucagon

Much digested food enters the bloodstream as glucose, an important source of energy throughout the body and nearly the only fuel of the brain. When the blood's glucose level is high, liver cells convert some of the excess into glycogen, and fat cells convert some of it into fat. When the blood's glucose level starts to fall, the liver converts some of its glycogen back into glucose. In this way blood glucose levels stay fairly steady for most people most of the time.

However, the glucose in the blood is not equally available to the cells at all times. Two pancreatic hormones, insulin and glucagon, regulate the flow of glucose. **Insulin** enables glucose to enter the cells, except for brain cells, where glucose does not need insulin to enter. When insulin levels are high, glucose enters cells easily. When someone is getting ready for a meal, insulin levels rise, letting some of the blood glucose enter the cells in preparation for the rush of additional glucose about to enter the blood. Insulin continues to increase during and after a meal. In general, high levels of insulin decrease appetite, because the insulin enables so much glucose to enter the cells. When much glucose is already entering the cells, you don't need to eat more.

As time passes after a meal, the blood glucose level falls. Therefore, insulin levels drop, glucose enters the cells more slowly, and hunger increases (Pardal & López-Barneo, 2002)

(Figure 10.15). **Glucagon** stimulates the liver to convert some of its stored glycogen to glucose to replenish low supplies in the blood.

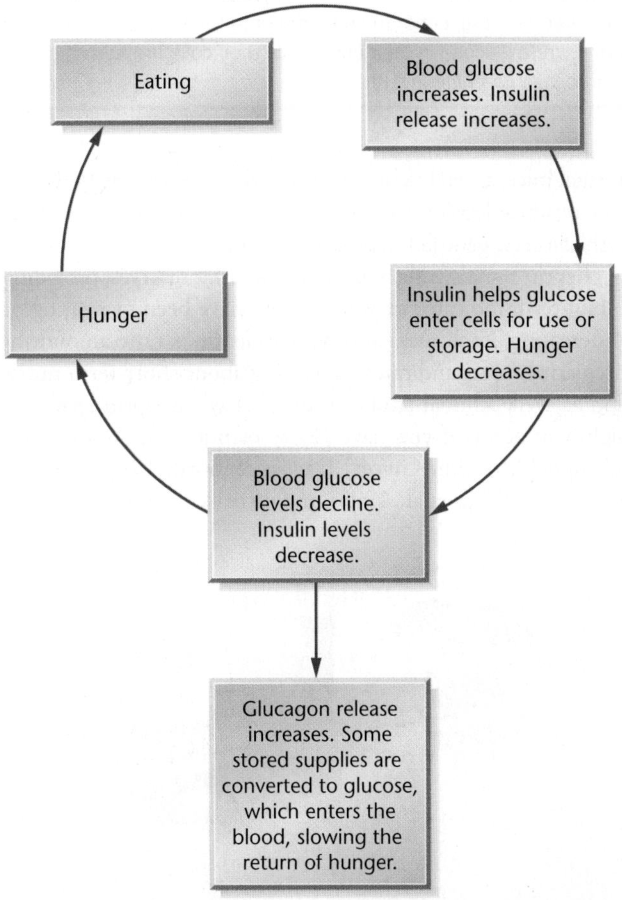

If the insulin level stays constantly high, the body continues moving blood glucose into the cells, including the liver cells and fat cells, long after a meal. Before too long, blood glucose drops, because glucose is leaving the blood without any new glucose entering. In this case, despite the high insulin level, hunger increases. In autumn, animals that are preparing for hibernation have constantly high insulin levels. They rapidly deposit much of each meal as fat and glycogen, grow hungry again, and continue gaining weight (Figure 10.16). That weight gain is a valuable preparation for a season when the animal will have to survive off its fat reserves. Most humans also eat more in autumn than in other seasons, as shown in Figure 10.17 (de Castro, 2000). In the United States, we tend to blame our autumn weight gain on the Halloween and Thanksgiving holidays, but the real reason may be an evolved drive to increase our reserves in preparation for winter. (Our ancestors didn't have good food year-round, as we do.)

If the insulin level remains constantly low, as in people with diabetes, blood glucose levels may be three or more times the normal level, but little of it enters the cells (Figure 10.18). People and animals with diabetes eat more food than normal because their cells are starving (Lindberg, Coburn, & Stricker, 1984), but they excrete most of their glucose, and they lose weight. Note that either prolonged high or prolonged low insulin levels increase eating, but for different reasons and with different effects on body weight.

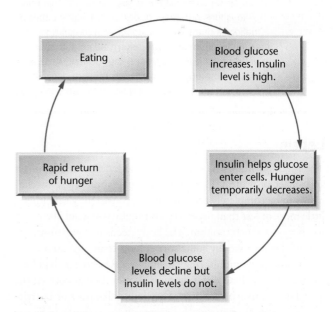

FIGURE 10.15 Insulin and glucagon feedback system
When glucose levels rise, the pancreas releases the hormone insulin, which causes cells to store the excess glucose as fats and glycogen. The entry of glucose into cells suppresses hunger and decreases eating, thereby lowering the glucose level. (© Cengage Learning 2013)

FIGURE 10.16 Effects of steady high insulin levels on feeding
Constantly high insulin causes blood glucose to be stored as fats and glycogen. Because it becomes difficult to mobilize the stored nutrients, hunger returns soon after each meal. (© Cengage Learning 2013)

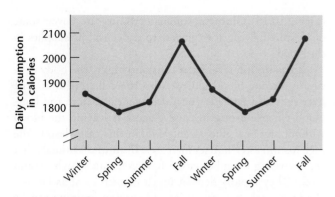

FIGURE 10.17 People eat more in fall than in other seasons
Mean intake increases by more than 10%, on average, according to people's eating diaries. *(Modified from de Castro, J. M. (2000). Eating behavior: Lessons from the real world of humans. Nutrition, 16, 800–813.)*

STOP & CHECK

14. Why do people with very low insulin levels eat so much? Why do people with constantly high levels eat so much?

15. What would happen to someone's appetite if insulin levels and glucagon levels were both high?

ANSWERS

14. Those with very low levels, as in diabetes, cannot get glucose to enter their cells, and therefore, they are constantly hungry. They pass much of their nutrition in the urine and feces. Those with constantly high levels deposit much of their glucose into fat and glycogen, so within a short time after a meal, the supply of blood glucose drops. 15. When glucagon levels rise, stored glycogen is converted to glucose, which enters the blood. If insulin levels are high also, the glucose entering the blood is free to enter all the cells. So the result would be decreased appetite.

Leptin

The mechanisms we have considered so far regulate the onset and offset of a meal. However, we can't expect those mechanisms to be completely accurate. If you consistently eat either a little more or less than necessary, eventually, you would be much too heavy or much too thin. The body needs to compensate for day-to-day mistakes by some sort of long-term regulation.

It does so by monitoring fat supplies. Researchers had long suspected some kind of fat monitoring, but they discovered the actual mechanism by accident. They found that mice of a particular genetic strain consistently become obese, as shown in Figure 10.19 (Y. Zhang et al., 1994). After researchers identified the responsible gene, they found the peptide it makes, a previously unrecognized substance that they named **leptin**, from the Greek word *leptos*, meaning "slender" (Halaas et al., 1995). Unlike insulin, which is so evolutionarily ancient that we find it throughout the animal kingdom, leptin is limited to vertebrates (Morton, Cummings, Baskin, Barsh, & Schwartz, 2006). In genetically

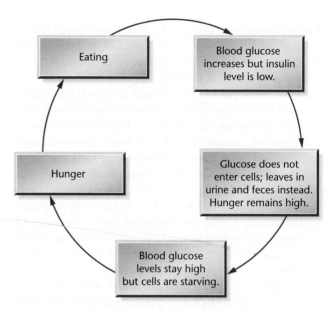

FIGURE 10.18 People with untreated diabetes eat much but lose weight
Because of their low insulin levels, the glucose in their blood cannot enter the cells, either to be stored or to be used. Consequently, they excrete glucose in their urine while their cells are starving. *(© Cengage Learning 2013)*

normal mice, as well as humans and other species, the body's fat cells produce leptin: The more fat cells, the more leptin. Mice with the *obese* gene fail to produce leptin.

Leptin signals your brain about your fat reserves, providing a long-term indicator of whether you have been overeating or undereating. Each meal also releases leptin, so the amount of circulating leptin indicates something about short-term nutrition as well. Animal studies show that when leptin levels are high, you act as if you have plenty of nutrition. You eat less (Campfield, Smith, Guisez, Devos, & Burn, 1995), become more active (Elias et al., 1998), and increase the activity of your

FIGURE 10.19 The effects of the obese gene on body weight
Mice with this gene eat more, move around less, and gain weight. *(Reprinted by permission from Macmillan Publishers Ltd.: Nature, "Positional cloning of the mouse obese gene and its human homologue," Zhang et al., 1994)*

immune system (Lord et al., 1998). (If you have enough fat supplies, you can afford to devote energy to your immune system. If you have no fat, you are starving and you have to conserve energy wherever you can.) In adolescence, a certain level of leptin triggers the onset of puberty. If your fat supply is too low to provide for your own needs, you don't have enough energy to provide for a baby. On average, thinner people enter puberty later.

Because a mouse with the *obese* gene does not make leptin, its brain reacts as if its body has no fat stores and must be starving. The mouse eats as much as possible, conserves its energy by not moving much, and fails to enter puberty. Injections of leptin reverse these symptoms: The mouse then eats less, becomes more active, and enters puberty (Pellymounter et al., 1995).

As you might imagine, news of this research inspired pharmaceutical companies to hope they could make a fortune by selling leptin. After all, the body makes leptin all the time, so it should not have unpleasant side effects. However, researchers soon discovered that almost all overweight people already produce plenty of leptin (Considine et al., 1996). The problem is that they have become less sensitive to it. Leptin sensitivity declines during pregnancy and in animals preparing for hibernation. In those cases, increased intake makes sense. Unfortunately, leptin sensitivity also declines as a result of obesity (Ernst et al., 2009; Tups, 2009). When consistent overeating leads to obesity, it damages the endoplasmic reticulum (a cell constituent) in neurons of the hypothalamus, setting in motion a series of outcomes that lead to decreased leptin sensitivity. So far, the only known way to undo that effect is physical exercise, which increases production of certain chemicals of the immune system. Those chemicals help repair the endoplasmic reticulum (Ropelle et al., 2010). We now see another reason, among several, why exercise helps people lose weight.

16. Why are leptin injections less helpful for most overweight people than for mice with the *obese* gene?

ANSWER

16. Nearly all overweight people produce leptin in proportion to body fat. However, they have low sensitivity to it.

I Brain Mechanisms

How does your brain decide when you should eat and how much? Hunger depends on the contents of your stomach and intestines, the availability of glucose to the cells, and your body's fat supplies, as well as your health and body temperature. Also, your appetite depends on more than your need for food. Just seeing a picture of highly appealing food increases your appetite (Harmon-Jones & Gable, 2009). You eat with friends and family just to be sociable. Somehow, the brain combines many kinds of information to decide when to eat, and how much. The key brain areas include several nuclei of the hypothalamus (Figure 10.6).

As shown in Figure 10.20, many kinds of information impinge onto two kinds of cells in the arcuate nucleus of the hypothalamus, which is regarded as the "master area" for control of appetite (Mendieta-Zéron, López, & Diéguez, 2008). Axons extend from the arcuate nucleus to other areas of the hypothalamus. This figure is tentative and incomplete, as feeding depends on many transmitters and mechanisms. Even in this simplified form, the figure may be intimidating. Nevertheless, it highlights some of the key mechanisms. Let's go through them step by step.

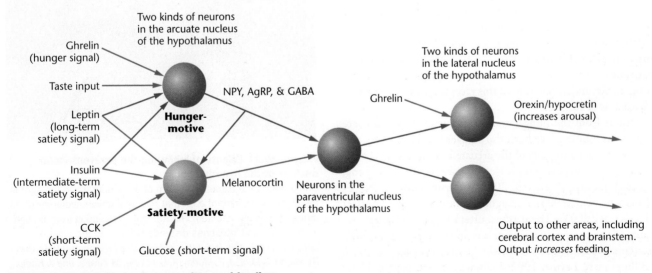

FIGURE 10.20 Hypothalamic transmitters of feeding
Hunger signals increase feeding by inhibiting inhibitory messages to the lateral hypothalamus. *(Based on reviews by Horvath, 2005; Minokoshi et al., 2004)*

The Arcuate Nucleus and Paraventricular Hypothalamus

The **arcuate nucleus** of the hypothalamus has one set of neurons sensitive to hunger signals and a second set sensitive to satiety signals. In Figure 10.20, excitatory paths are noted in green, and inhibitory paths are in red. The hunger-sensitive cells receive input from the taste pathway, and you have surely noticed that good-tasting food stimulates your hunger. Another input to the hunger-sensitive cells comes from axons releasing the neurotransmitter *ghrelin* (GRELL-in). This odd-looking word takes its name from the fact that it binds to the same receptors as growth-hormone releasing hormone (GHRH). The stomach releases **ghrelin** during a period of food deprivation, where it triggers stomach contractions. Ghrelin also acts on the hypothalamus to decrease appetite and acts on the hippocampus to enhance learning (Diano et al., 2006). Whereas the digestive system secretes several hormones that signal satiety, ghrelin is the only known hunger hormone.

Signals of both short- and long-term satiety provide input to the satiety-sensitive cells of the arcuate nucleus. Distension of the intestines triggers neurons to release the neurotransmitter CCK, a short-term signal (Fan et al., 2004). Blood glucose (a short-term signal) directly stimulates satiety cells in the arcuate nucleus (Parton et al., 2007) and leads to increased secretion of insulin, which also stimulates the satiety cells. Body fat (a long-term signal) releases leptin, which provides an additional input (Münzberg & Myers, 2005).

Much of the output from the arcuate nucleus goes to the paraventricular nucleus of the hypothalamus. The paraventricular nucleus (PVN) inhibits the lateral hypothalamus, an area important for eating. So the paraventricular nucleus is important for satiety. Rats with damage in the paraventricular nucleus eat larger than normal meals, indicating insensitivity to the usual signals for ending a meal (Leibowitz, Hammer, & Chang, 1981).

Axons from the satiety-sensitive cells of the arcuate nucleus deliver an excitatory message to the paraventricular nucleus, releasing the neuropeptide α-melanocyte stimulating hormone (αMSH), which is a type of chemical called a **melanocortin** (Ellacott & Cone, 2004). Melanocortin receptors in the paraventricular nucleus are important for limiting food intake, and deficiencies of this receptor lead to overeating (Balthasar et al., 2005).

Input from the hunger-sensitive neurons of the arcuate nucleus is inhibitory to both the paraventricular nucleus and the satiety-sensitive cells of the arcuate nucleus itself. The inhibitory transmitters here are a combination of GABA (Tong, Jones, Elmquist, & Lowell, 2008), **neuropeptide Y (NPY)** (Stephens et al., 1995), and **agouti-related peptide (AgRP)** (Kas et al., 2004). These transmitters block the satiety actions of the paraventricular nucleus, in some cases provoking extreme overeating, as tastelessly illustrated in Figure 10.21 (Billington & Levine, 1992; Leibowitz & Alexander, 1991; Morley, Levine, Grace, & Kneip, 1985). Conversely, a loss of NPY leads to decreased eating (Yang et al., 2009).

An additional pathway leads to cells in the lateral hypothalamus that release orexin, also known as hypocretin (L.-Y. Fu, Acuna-Goycolea, & van den Pol, 2004). We encountered these neurons in Chapter 9 because a deficiency of orexin leads to narcolepsy. In addition to its role in wakefulness, orexin has two roles in feeding. First, it increases animals' persistence in seeking food (G. Williams, Cai, Elliott, & Harrold, 2004). Second, orexin responds to incentives or reinforcement in general. If orexin receptors are blocked, an animal becomes less active and less likely to work for reinforcement of any kind (Borgland et al., 2009). Stimulation of orexin receptors increases activity and motivation. When you eagerly eat a hot-fudge sundae, in spite of not feeling hungry, the pleasant taste activates orexin receptors that override satiety messages from other receptors (Zheng, Patterson, & Berthoud, 2007).

In addition to the chemicals in Figure 10.20, several others contribute to the control of appetite. One consequence of control by so many chemicals is that the control of feeding can go wrong in many ways. However, when an error occurs in one way, the brain has many other mechanisms to compensate for it. A closely related point is that researchers could develop drugs to control appetite by working on many routes—leptin, insulin, NPY, and so forth—but changing any one circuit might be ineffective because of compensations by the others. One of the most promising hopes for drug researchers is the melanocortin receptors. As shown in Figure 10.20, many

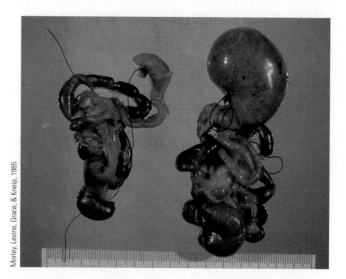

Morley, Levine, Grace, & Kneip, 1985

FIGURE 10.21 **Effects of inhibiting the paraventricular nucleus of the hypothalamus**
On the left is the digestive system of a normal rat. On the right is the digestive system of a rat that had its paraventricular hypothalamus chemically inhibited. The rat continued eating even though its stomach and intestines distended almost to the point of bursting. *(Yeah, this is a little bit disgusting.)* *(Reprinted from Brain Research, 341/1, J. E. Morley, A. S. Levine, M. Grace, and J. Kneip, "Peptide YY (PYY) a potently orexigenic agent," 200–203, 1985, with permission of Elsevier)*

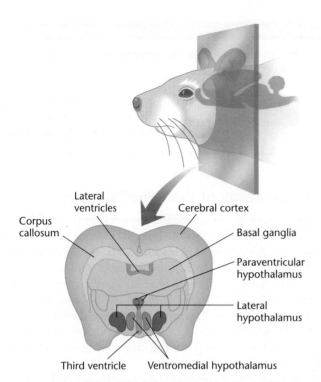

Corpus callosum

Lateral ventricles

Cerebral cortex

Basal ganglia

Paraventricular hypothalamus

Lateral hypothalamus

Third ventricle

Ventromedial hypothalamus

FIGURE 10.22 The lateral hypothalamus, ventromedial hypothalamus, and paraventricular hypothalamus The side view above indicates the plane of the coronal section of the brain below. *(After Hart, 1976)*

kinds of input converge onto the cells of the arcuate nucleus, but the input to the paraventricular nucleus is more limited. Insulin, diet drugs, and other procedures affect eating largely by altering input to the melanocortin receptors (Benoit et al., 2002; Heisler et al., 2002).

▶ **STOP & CHECK**

17. Name three hormones that increase satiety and one that increases hunger.

18. Which neuropeptide from the arcuate nucleus to the paraventricular nucleus is most important for satiety?

ANSWERS

17. Insulin, CCK, and leptin increase satiety. Ghrelin increases hunger. **18.** Melanocortin (or α-melanocyte stimulating hormone).

The Lateral Hypothalamus

Output from the paraventricular nucleus acts on the **lateral hypothalamus** (Figure 10.22), which includes so many neuron clusters and passing axons that it has been compared to a crowded train station (Leibowitz & Hoebel, 1998). The lateral hypothalamus controls insulin secretion, alters taste responsiveness, and facilitates feeding in other ways. An animal with damage in this area refuses food and water, averting its head as if the food were distasteful. The animal may starve to death unless it is force-fed, but if kept alive, it gradually recovers much of its ability to eat (Figure 10.23). In contrast, stimulation of the lateral hypothalamus increases the drive to eat.

Many axons containing dopamine pass through the lateral hypothalamus, so damage to the lateral hypothalamus interrupts these fibers. To separate the roles of hypothalamic cells from those of passing fibers, experimenters used chemicals that damage only the cell bodies, or induced lesions in very young rats, before the dopamine axons reached the lateral hypothalamus. The result was a major loss of feeding with-

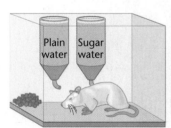

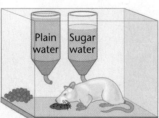

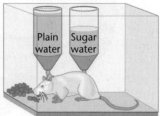

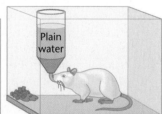

Stage 1. *Aphagia and adipsia.* Rat refuses all food and drink; must be force-fed to keep it alive.

Stage 2. *Anorexia.* Rat eats a small amount of palatable foods and drinks sweetened water. It still does not eat enough to stay alive.

Stage 3. *Adipsia.* The rat eats enough to stay alive, though at a lower-than-normal body weight. It still refuses plain water.

Stage 4. *Near-recovery.* The rat eats enough to stay alive, though at a lower-than-normal body weight. It drinks plain water, but only at mealtimes to wash down its food. Under slightly stressful conditions, such as in a cold room, the rat will return to an earlier stage of refusing food and water.

FIGURE 10.23 Recovery after damage to the lateral hypothalamus
At first, the rat refuses all food and drink. If kept alive for several weeks or months by force-feeding, it gradually recovers its ability to eat and drink enough to stay alive. However, even at the final stage of recovery, its behavior is not the same as that of normal rats. *(Based on Teitelbaum & Epstein, 1962)*

out loss of arousal and activity (Almli, Fisher, & Hill, 1979; Grossman, Dacey, Halaris, Collier, & Routtenberg, 1978; Stricker, Swerdloff, & Zigmond, 1978).

The lateral hypothalamus contributes to feeding in several ways (Leibowitz & Hoebel, 1998) (Figure 10.24):

- Axons from the lateral hypothalamus to the NTS (nucleus of the tractus solitarius), part of the taste pathway, alter the taste sensation and the salivation response to the tastes. When the lateral hypothalamus detects hunger, it sends messages to make the food taste better.
- Axons from the lateral hypothalamus extend into several parts of the cerebral cortex, facilitating ingestion and swallowing and causing cortical cells to increase their response to the taste, smell, or sight of food (Critchley & Rolls, 1996).
- The lateral hypothalamus increases the pituitary gland's secretion of hormones that increase insulin secretion.
- The lateral hypothalamus sends axons to the spinal cord, controlling autonomic responses such as digestive secretions (van den Pol, 1999). An animal with damage to the lateral hypothalamus has trouble digesting foods.

STOP & CHECK

19. In what ways does the lateral hypothalamus facilitate feeding?

ANSWER   **19.** Activity of the lateral hypothalamus improves taste, enhances cortical responses to food, and increases secretions of insulin and digestive juices.

Medial Areas of the Hypothalamus

Output from the **ventromedial hypothalamus (VMH)** inhibits feeding (Chee, Myers, Price, & Colmers, 2010), and therefore damage to this nucleus leads to overeating and weight gain (Figure 10.22). Some people with a tumor in that area have gained more than 10 kg (22 lb) per month (Al-Rashid, 1971; Killeffer & Stern, 1970; Reeves & Plum, 1969). Rats with similar damage sometimes double or triple their weight (Figure 10.25). Eventually, body weight levels off at a stable but high set point, and total food intake declines to nearly normal levels.

Although these symptoms have been known as the *ventromedial hypothalamic syndrome*, damage limited to just the ventromedial hypothalamus does not consistently increase eating

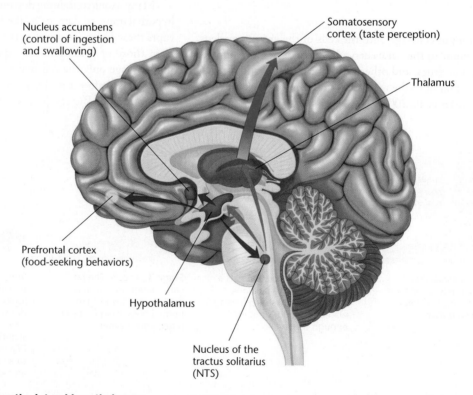

Nucleus accumbens (control of ingestion and swallowing)

Somatosensory cortex (taste perception)

Thalamus

Prefrontal cortex (food-seeking behaviors)

Hypothalamus

Nucleus of the tractus solitarius (NTS)

FIGURE 10.24 Pathways from the lateral hypothalamus
Axons from the lateral hypothalamus modify activity in several other brain areas, changing the response to taste, facilitating ingestion and swallowing, and increasing food-seeking behaviors. Also (not shown), the lateral hypothalamus controls stomach secretions. (*© Cengage Learning 2013*)

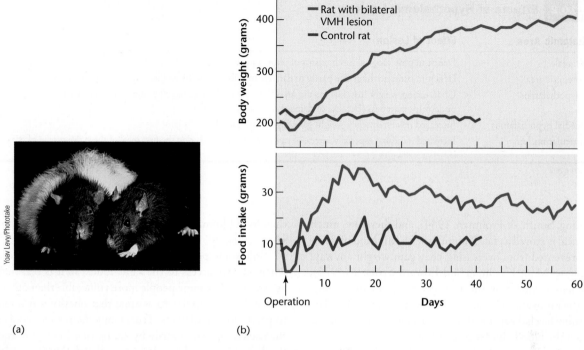

FIGURE 10.25 **Effects of damage to the ventromedial hypothalamus**
(a) On the right is a normal rat. On the left is a rat after damage to the ventromedial hypothalamus. A brain-damaged rat may weigh up to three times as much as a normal rat. (b) Weight and eating after damage to the ventromedial hypothalamus. Within a few days after the operation, the rat begins eating much more than normal. *(Reprinted by permission of the University of Nebraska Press from "Disturbances in feeding and drinking behavior after hypothalamic lesions," by P. Teitelbaum, pp. 39–69, in M. R. Jones, Ed., 1961, Nebraska Symposium on Motivation. Copyright © 1961 by the University of Nebraska Press. Copyright © renewed 1988 by the University of Nebraska Press.)*

or body weight. To produce a large effect, the lesion must extend outside the ventromedial nucleus to invade nearby axons, especially the ventral noradrenergic bundle (Figure 10.26) (Ahlskog & Hoebel, 1973; Ahlskog, Randall, & Hoebel, 1975; Gold, 1973).

Rats with damage in and around the ventromedial hypothalamus show an increased appetite compared to undamaged rats of the same weight (B. M. King, 2006; Peters, Sensenig, & Reich, 1973). Recall that rats with damage to the paraventricular nucleus eat large meals. In contrast, those with damage in the ventromedial area eat normal-size meals, but they eat more frequently (Hoebel & Hernandez, 1993). One reason is that they have increased stomach motility and secretions, and their stomachs empty faster than normal. The faster the stomach empties, the sooner the animal is ready for its next meal. Another reason for their frequent meals is that the damage increases insulin production

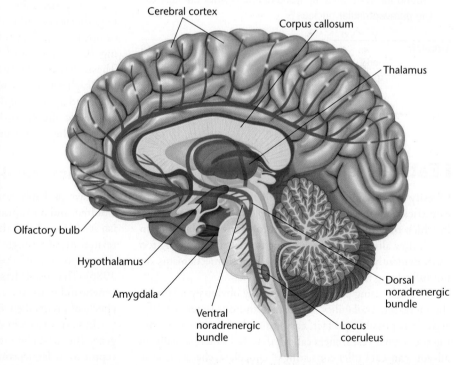

FIGURE 10.26 **Norepinephrine pathways in the human brain**
Damage to the ventral noradrenergic bundle leads to overeating and weight gain. *(Based on Valzelli, 1980)*

TABLE 10.2	Effects of Hypothalamic Lesions
Hypothalamic Area	**Effect of Lesion**
Preoptic area	Deficit in physiological mechanisms of temperature regulation
Lateral preoptic area	Deficit in osmotic thirst due partly to damage to cells and partly to interruption of passing axons
Lateral hypothalamus	Undereating, weight loss, low insulin level (because of damage to cell bodies); underarousal, underresponsiveness (because of damage to passing axons)
Ventromedial hypothalamus	Increased meal frequency, weight gain, high insulin level
Paraventricular nucleus	Increased meal size, especially increased carbohydrate intake during the first meal of the active period of the day

© Cengage Learning 2013

(B. M. King, Smith, & Frohman, 1984), and therefore, much of each meal is stored as fat. If animals with this kind of damage are prevented from overeating, they gain weight anyway! According to Mark Friedman and Edward Stricker (1976), the problem is not that the rat gets fat from overeating. Rather, the rat overeats because it is storing so much fat. The high insulin levels keep moving blood glucose into storage, even when the blood glucose level is low.

Table 10.2 summarizes the effects of lesions in several areas of the hypothalamus.

> **STOP & CHECK**

20. In what way does eating increase after damage in and around the ventromedial hypothalamus? After damage to the paraventricular nucleus?

ANSWER

20. Animals with damage to the ventromedial hypothalamus eat more frequent meals. Animals with damage to the paraventricular nucleus of the hypothalamus eat larger meals.

Eating Disorders

Obesity has become a serious problem in more and more countries. Simultaneously, other people suffer from anorexia, in which they refuse to eat enough to survive, or bulimia, in which they alternate between eating too much and eating too little. Evidently, our homeostatic or allostatic mechanisms are not fully doing their job.

The increasing prevalence of obesity obviously relates to the increased availability of our diet and our sedentary lifestyle. It is possible (in fact, easy) to make rats obese by giving them what researchers call a "cafeteria," which is really an all-you-can-eat buffet consisting of chocolate, cheese, salami, peanut butter, marshmallows, and other tasty, high-calorie foods (Geiger et al., 2009). It is hard for rats to pass up these treats, and hard for us, too. When rats become obese on this regimen, they tend to lose interest in rewards other than food (Johnson & Kenny, 2010). Many people show the same tendency.

Still, some people become obese and others do not, even when all have access to the same foods, so it is reasonable to ask what makes some people more vulnerable than others. For a time, it was popular to assume that obesity was a reaction to psychological distress. True, many distressed people cheer themselves up temporarily by eating rich foods. However, in the long run mood has only a weak relationship to weight gain. One study found obesity in 19% of people with a history of depression and in 15% of those who had never suffered depression (McIntyre, Konarski, Wilkins, Soczynska, & Kennedy, 2006).

Another possible factor is prenatal environment. A study in rats found that if a mother consumed a high-fat diet during pregnancy, her babies developed a larger than average lateral hypothalamus and produced more than the average amount of orexin and other transmitters that facilitate increased eating (Chang, Gasinskaya, Karatayev, & Leibowitz, 2008). These changes persisted throughout life. In short, exposure to a high-fat diet before birth predisposes the offspring to increased appetite and body weight. This example illustrates epigenetic effects, as described in Chapter 1: An experience can alter the expression of the genes.

Genetics and Body Weight

You have probably noticed that most thin parents have thin children, and most heavy parents have heavy children. A Danish study found that the weights of 540 adopted children correlated more strongly with that of their biological relatives than with that of their adoptive relatives (Stunkard et al., 1986). That result has generally been taken as evidence for a genetic influence, but it could just as easily be evidence for the effects of prenatal environment.

In some cases, obesity can be traced to the effects of a single gene. The most common of these is a mutated gene for the receptor to melanocortin, one of the neuropeptides responsible for hunger. People with a mutation in that gene overeat and become obese from childhood onward (Mergen, Mergen, Ozata, Oner, & Oner, 2001). People with a variant form of one gene called *FTO* weigh 3 kg (6–7 lb) more than other people, on average, and have about a two-thirds greater probability of becoming obese (Frayling et al., 2007). However, these single-gene mutations are uncommon, accounting for only a small percentage of obesity cases (Mutch & Clément, 2006).

Syndromal obesity is obesity that results from a medical condition. Some people with severe, early-onset obesity have deletions of part of a chromosome. If the deletion includes genes for leptin receptors, insulin receptors, or other key elements in regulation of eating, the outcome includes obesity as well as other problems (Bochukova et al., 2010). Prader-Willi syndrome is a genetic condition marked by mental retardation, short stature, and obesity. People with this syndrome have blood levels of ghrelin four to five times higher than average (Cummings et al., 2002). Ghrelin, you will recall, is a peptide related to food deprivation. The fact that people with Prader-Willi syndrome overeat and still produce high ghrelin levels suggests that their problem relates to an inability to turn off ghrelin release.

Most cases of obesity relate to the combined influences of many genes and the environment. Consider the Native American Pima of Arizona and Mexico. Most are seriously overweight, apparently because of several genes (Norman et al., 1998). However, obesity was uncommon among them in the early 1900s, when their diet consisted of desert plants that ripen in the brief rainy season. The Pima apparently evolved a strategy of eating all they could when food was available because it would have to carry them through periods of scarcity. They also evolved a tendency to conserve energy by limiting their activity. Now, with a more typical U.S. diet that is equally available at all times, the strategy of overeating and inactivity is maladaptive. In short, their weight depends on the combination of genes and environment. Neither one by itself has this effect.

How might genes affect weight gain? Differences in hunger or digestion are one possibility, but exercise is another. One study found that mildly obese people spent more time sitting and less time moving about, both while they were obese and after they had lost weight (J. A. Levine et al., 2005). Evidently, their sedentary habits were a lifelong trait, perhaps genetic in origin, rather than a reaction to being overweight.

![STOP & CHECK]

21. Why did the Pima begin gaining weight in the mid-1900s?

ANSWER

21. They shifted from a diet of local plants that were seasonally available to a calorie-rich diet that is available throughout the year.

Weight Loss

In the United States, obesity is now officially classified as a disease, and never mind the fact that we don't have a clear definition of what we mean by *disease*. One positive conse-

quence is that people are relieved from thinking of themselves as morally guilty for being overweight. A possible negative consequence is that some may decide to give up. The most practical consequence is that insurance companies will now pay treatment providers to help obese patients . . . if the providers have evidence that their treatment is safe and effective.

Dieting by itself is not reliably effective, largely because most people don't stick to the diet for long. You will hear advocates of a particular diet plan state that many people on their plan lost a significant amount of weight. That statement may be true, but it means little unless we know how many other people tried that plan and failed to lose weight. We also need to know how many people who lost weight gained it back. According to one review of the literature, about as many people gain weight on a diet as lose, and few maintain a significant weight loss for years (Mann et al., 2007). Many psychologists now recommend small changes in diet ("eat a little less than usual") on the expectation that more people will stick to this diet, and making a small change is better than failing to make a large change (Stroebele et al., 2008).

The most successful treatments require a change of lifestyle, including increased exercise as well as decreased eating. That combination does help people lose weight, although only 20%–40% keep the weight off for at least 2 years (Powell, Calvin, & Calvin, 2007).

Particularly important advice is to reduce or eliminate the intake of soft drinks. Researchers have found that people who consume at least one soft drink per day are more likely than others to be overweight, and if they are not already overweight, they are more likely than others to become overweight (Dhingra et al., 2007; Liebman et al., 2006). One reason is that nearly all soft drinks are sweetened with fructose, a sugar that does not increase insulin or leptin nearly as much as other sugars do (Teff et al., 2004). Therefore, if you drink something with fructose, you gain calories without feeling satiety.

Diet soft drinks do not contain fructose, but they pose a different problem. In one study, rats mostly ate the usual laboratory diet, but sometimes one group ate naturally sweetened yogurt while the other group ate yogurt sweetened with saccharin (noncaloric). Overall, the rats eating the noncaloric ("diet") yogurt gained *more* weight. The interpretation is complex: Ordinarily, rats, like people, learn to calibrate the calories in their food. They learn that when they eat sweets, they gain a good deal of energy, and so they learn either to limit their intake of sweets or to compensate by eating less of something else. Rats that consumed noncaloric sweeteners lost this tendency. They learned that taste is a poor predictor of energy, and so they overate other foods and stopped compensating afterward. They also became less active (Swithers & Davidson, 2008).

If diet and exercise fail to help someone lose weight, another option is weight-loss drugs. For years, the most effective combination was "fen–phen": *Fenfluramine* increases the release of serotonin and blocks its reuptake. *Phentermine* blocks reuptake of norepinephrine and dopamine and therefore prolongs their activity. The fen–phen combination produces brain effects similar to those of a completed meal (Rada & Hoebel, 2000). Unfortunately, fenfluramine often produces medical complications, so it has been withdrawn from use. A replacement drug, *sibutramine* (Meridia), which blocks reuptake of serotonin and norepinephrine, decreases meal size and binge eating (Appolinario et al., 2003). The drug *orlistat* (Xenical) prevents the intestines from absorbing up to 30% of fats in the diet. Approximately half of people using orlistat have at least 5% weight loss 2 years later (Powell et al., 2007). A side effect is intestinal discomfort from the large globs of undigested fats. Also, the bowel movements are thick with fat.

Finally, if someone with extreme obesity fails to respond to other treatments, an option is gastric bypass surgery, in which part of the stomach is removed or sewed off so that food cannot enter. Remember that stomach distension is a major contributor to satiety. By decreasing stomach size, the surgery makes it possible for a smaller meal to produce satiety. The most common result is that someone goes from being "morbidly obese" to just "obese," and that is a meaningful benefit. However, 10%–20% of people experience serious side effects, including infections, bowel obstruction, leakage of food, and nutritional deficiencies (Powell et al., 2007). Surgery is worth considering only in severe cases of obesity.

> **STOP & CHECK**

22. In one study, rats eating the less-caloric yogurt gained more weight than those eating the more-caloric type. What explanation was proposed?

ANSWER   **22.** The rats unlearned their usual calibration that more sweets mean more energy and therefore stopped compensating after eating other sweets.

Bulimia Nervosa

Bulimia nervosa is a condition in which people alternate between binges of overeating and periods of strict dieting. Many, but not all, induce themselves to vomit. About 95% of people with bulimia also suffer from depression, anxiety, or other emotional problems (Hudson et al., 2007). In the United States, about 1.5% of women and 0.5% of men develop bulimia at some time in life. It has become more common over the years. That is, bulimia is more common among young people today than it ever was in their parents' generation and more common in their parents' generation than in their grandparents'. The increase is presumably due to the ready availability of large quantities of very tasty high-calorie foods that were less abundant in previous eras.

On average, people with bulimia show a variety of biochemical abnormalities, including increased production of ghrelin, a hormone associated with increased appetite (Monteleone, Serritella, Scognamiglio, & Maj, 2010). The biochemistry is probably a result of the binges and purges, rather than a cause. After therapy that decreases the symptoms of bulimia, the ghrelin and other body chemicals return toward normal levels (Tanaka et al., 2006).

In important ways bulimia resembles drug addiction (Hoebel, Rada, Mark, & Pothos, 1999). Eating tasty foods activates the same brain areas as addictive drugs, such as the nucleus accumbens. Drug addicts who cannot get drugs sometimes overeat as a substitute, and food-deprived people or animals become more likely than others to use drugs.

Researchers examined rats that were food deprived for 12 hours a day, including the first 4 hours of their wakeful period, and then offered a very sweet, syrupy sugar solution. Over several weeks on this regimen, the rats drank more and more each day, especially during the first hour of availability each day. The intake released dopamine and opioid (opiate-like) compounds in the brain, similar to the effects of highly addictive drugs (Colantuoni et al., 2001, 2002). It also increased the levels of dopamine type 3 receptors in the brain—again, a trend resembling that of rats that receive morphine (Spangler et al., 2004). If they were then deprived of this sweet liquid, they showed withdrawal symptoms, including head shaking, teeth chattering, and tremors. An injection of morphine relieved these symptoms. In short, the rats showed clear indications of an addiction to big doses of sugar (Avena, Rada, & Hoebel, 2008). Similarly, we can regard bulimic cycles of dieting and binge eating as an addiction.

> **STOP & CHECK**

23. Researchers have found that people with bulimia nervosa have elevated ghrelin levels. Why are those levels probably not the cause of bulimia?

24. What evidence from rats suggests that bulimia resembles an addiction?

ANSWERS   **23.** As people recover from bulimia, the ghrelin returns toward normal levels. If their genetics or other factors produced constantly high ghrelin, it should remain high regardless of current diet. **24.** Rats that alternate between food deprivation and a very sweet diet gradually eat more and more, and they react to deprivation of the sweet diet with head shaking and teeth chattering, like the symptoms of morphine withdrawal.

MODULE 10.3 ■ IN CLOSING

The Multiple Controls of Hunger

The brain areas that control eating monitor blood glucose, stomach distension, duodenal contents, body weight, fat cells, hormones, and more. Because the system is so complex, it can produce errors in many ways. However, the complexity of the system also provides a kind of security: If one part of the system makes a mistake, another part can counteract it. We notice people who choose a poor diet or eat the wrong amount. Perhaps we should be even more impressed by how many people eat appropriately. The regulation of eating succeeds not in spite of its complexity but because of it.

SUMMARY

1. The ability to digest a food is one major determinant of preference for that food. For example, people who cannot digest lactose generally do not like to eat dairy products.   **309**

2. Widespread beliefs that sugar causes hyperactivity and that turkey causes sleepiness are unfounded. However, research does support the idea that eating fish enhances some people's memory and reasoning.   **310**

3. People and animals eat partly for the sake of taste. However, a sham-feeding animal, which tastes its foods but does not absorb them, eats far more than normal.   **311**

4. Factors controlling hunger include distension of the stomach and intestines, secretion of CCK by the duodenum, and the availability of glucose and other nutrients to the cells.   **312**

5. Appetite depends partly on the availability of glucose and other nutrients to the cells. The hormone insulin increases the entry of glucose to the cells, including cells that store nutrients for future use. Glucagon mobilizes stored fuel and converts it to glucose in the blood. Thus, the combined influence of insulin and glucagon determines how much glucose is available at any time.   **312**

6. Fat cells produce a peptide called leptin, which provides the brain with a signal about weight loss or gain and therefore corrects day-to-day errors in the amount of feeding. Deficiency of leptin production leads to obesity and inactivity. However, leptin deficiency is rare among humans.   **314**

7. The arcuate nucleus of the hypothalamus receives signals of both hunger and satiety. Good-tasting foods and the transmitter ghrelin stimulate neurons that promote hunger. Glucose, insulin, leptin, and CCK stimulate neurons that promote satiety.   **315**

8. Axons from the two kinds of neurons in the arcuate nucleus send competing messages to the paraventricular nucleus, releasing neuropeptides that are specific to the feeding system. The paraventricular nucleus inhibits the lateral nucleus of the hypothalamus.   **316**

9. The lateral nucleus of the hypothalamus facilitates feeding by axons that enhance taste responses elsewhere in the brain and increase the release of insulin and digestive juices.   **316**

10. The ventromedial nucleus of the hypothalamus and the axons passing by it influence eating by regulating stomach emptying time and insulin secretion. Animals with damage in this area eat more frequently than normal because they store much of each meal as fat and then fail to mobilize their stored fats for current use.   **318**

11. Obesity is partly under genetic control, although no single gene accounts for many cases of obesity. The effects of genes depend on what foods are available. Genes also influence activity levels.   **320**

12. Dieting is seldom an effective means of long-term weight loss. Dieting combined with exercise is more effective, although at best it helps less than half of people. Reducing consumption of soft drinks is highly recommended. In more severe cases of obesity, people consider weight-loss drugs or surgery.   **321**

13. Bulimia nervosa is characterized by alternation between undereating and overeating. It has been compared to addictive behaviors.   **322**

KEY TERMS

Terms are defined in the module on the page number indicated. They're also presented in alphabetical order with definitions in the book's Subject Index/Glossary, which begins on page 561. Interactive flashcards and crossword puzzles are among the online resources available to help you learn these terms and the concepts they represent.

agouti-related peptide (AgRP)   316

arcuate nucleus   316

bulimia nervosa   322

cholecystokinin (CCK)   312

duodenum   312

ghrelin   316

glucagon   313

insulin   313

lactase   310

lactose   310

lateral hypothalamus   317

leptin   314

melanocortin   316

neuropeptide Y (NPY)   316

sham-feeding   312

splanchnic nerves   312

vagus nerve   312

ventromedial hypothalamus (VMH)   318

THOUGHT QUESTION

For most people, insulin levels tend to be higher during the day than at night. Use this fact to explain why people grow hungry a few hours after a daytime meal but not so quickly at night.

CHAPTER 10 Interactive Exploration and Study

The **Psychology CourseMate** for this text brings chapter topics to life with interactive learning, study, and exam preparation tools, including quizzes and flashcards for the Key Concepts that appear throughout each module, as well as an interactive media-rich eBook version of the text that is fully searchable and includes highlighting and note taking capabilities and interactive versions of the book's **Stop & Check** quizzes and **Try It Yourself Online** activities. The site also features **Virtual Biological Psychology Labs, videos,** and **animations** to help you better understand concepts—logon and learn more at **www.cengagebrain.com**, which is your gateway to all of this text's complimentary and premium resources, including the following:

Virtual Biological Psychology Labs

Explore the experiments that led to modern-day understanding of biopsychology with the Virtual Biological Psychology Labs, featuring a realistic lab environment that allows you to conduct experiments and evaluate data to better understand how scientists came to the conclusions presented in your text. The labs cover a range of topics, including perception, motivation, cognition, and more. You may purchase access at **www.cengagebrain.com**, or login at **login.cengagebrain.com** if an access card was included with your text.

Videos

Profile of Bulimia Nervosa

Animations

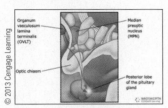

Thirst

Also available—

- Hypothalamic Control of Feeding
- Pathways from the Lateral Hypothalamus

Suggestions for Further Exploration

Books

Gisolfi, C. V., & Mora, F. (2000). *The hot brain: Survival, temperature, and the human body.* Cambridge, MA: MIT Press. Discusses research on temperature regulation.

Widmaier, E. P. (1998). *Why geese don't get obese (and we do).* New York: Freeman. Lighthearted and often entertaining discussion of the physiology of eating, thirst, and temperature regulation.

Websites

The Psychology CourseMate for this text provides regularly updated links to relevant online resources for this chapter, including sites concerning the hypothalamus and sugar addiction.

Reproductive Behaviors

11

CHAPTER OUTLINE

MAIN IDEAS

1. Sex chromosomes influence development mainly, but not entirely, by controlling production of sex hormones such as testosterone and estradiol.

2. Sex hormones exert organizing and activating effects on the genitals and the brain. Organizing effects occur during a sensitive period and last indefinitely. Activating effects are temporary.

3. In mammals, organizing effects of hormones influence the external genitals and the hypothalamus. The difference between masculine and feminine appearance of the external genitals depends on the amount of testosterone during an early sensitive period.

4. Parental behavior depends on both hormones and experience.

5. Much about men's and women's sexual behavior, including mate choice, could be the product of evolutionary selection. However, current data do not enable us to determine how much is built-in and how much is determined by our experiences.

6. Hormones contribute to the development of sexual identity and orientation.

OPPOSITE: Humans may be the only species that plans parenthood, but all species have a strong biological drive that leads to parenthood.

What good is sex? Well, yes, of course: We enjoy it. Presumably we evolved to enjoy it because sexual activity sometimes leads to reproduction, which passes on the genes. You evolved from a long line of ancestors who engaged in sexual activity at least once.

But why did we evolve to reproduce sexually instead of individually? In some species of reptiles, a female sometimes has offspring by herself, using only her own genes and none from a male (Booth, Johnson, Moore, Schal, & Vargo, 2011). In many ways, reproduction would be easier without sex. What advantage does sex provide?

You might suggest the advantage of having a partner while you rear children. In humans, that kind of cooperation is usually helpful. However, many species reproduce sexually even though the male doesn't help at all with the young, and in some fish species, *neither* sex cares for the young—they just release their sperm and eggs in the same place and then depart.

Biologists' explanation is that sexual reproduction increases variation and thereby enables quick evolutionary adaptations to changes in the environment. Certain invertebrates reproduce sexually when they live in a complex and changing environment, but reproduce nonsexually when they live in a constant environment (Becks & Agrawal, 2010). Sex also corrects errors: If you have a disadvantageous mutation in one gene and your mate has a disadvantageous mutation in a different gene, your children could have a normal copy of both genes.

In this chapter, we consider many questions about sexual reproduction that we often ignore or take for granted. We also consider some of the ways in which being biologically male or female influences our behavior.

Sex and Hormones

Being male or female influences many aspects of your life. For humans and other mammals, it all begins with your genes. Females have two X chromosomes, whereas males have an X and a Y chromosome. Biologists used to believe that the chromosomes determine sexual differentiation entirely through hormones. Let's examine that story, and then see how it is incomplete.

Male and female mammals start with the same anatomy during an early stage of prenatal development. Both have a set of **Müllerian ducts** (precursors to female internal structures) and a set of Wolffian ducts (precursors to male internal structures), as well as undifferentiated gonads that are on their way to becoming either testes or ovaries. The male's Y chromosome includes the **SRY** (sex-determining region on the Y chromosome) **gene**, which causes those primitive gonads to develop into **testes**, the sperm-producing organs. The developing testes produce **androgens** (hormones that

are more abundant in males) that increase the growth of the testes, causing them to produce more androgens and so forth. That positive feedback cannot go on forever, but it lasts for a period of early development. Androgens also cause the primitive **Wolffian ducts**, precursors for other male reproductive structures, to develop into *seminal vesicles* (saclike structures that store semen) and the *vas deferens* (a duct from the testis into the penis). The testes also produce *Müllerian inhibiting hormone (MIH)*, which causes the Müllerian ducts to degenerate. The final result is the development of a penis and scrotum. Because females do not have the SRY gene, their gonads develop into **ovaries** instead of testes, and their Wolffian ducts degenerate. Because their ovaries do not produce MIH, females' Müllerian ducts develop and mature into oviducts, uterus, and the upper vagina. Figure 11.1 shows how the primitive unisex structures develop into male or female external genitals.

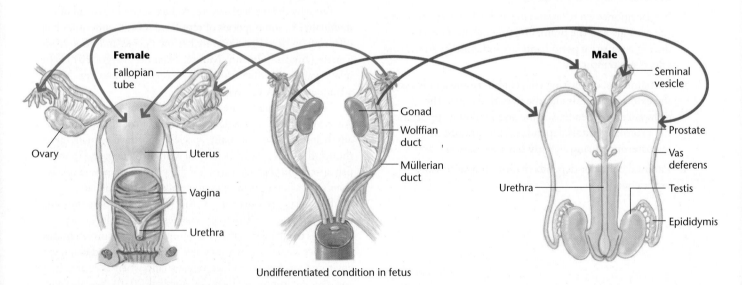

FIGURE 11.1 Differentiation of human genitals
We begin life with undifferentiated structures, as shown in the center. The gonad shown in blue for the fetus develops into either the ovaries, as shown on the left, or the testes, as shown on the right. The Müllerian ducts of the fetus develop into a female's uterus, oviducts, and the upper part of the vagina. The Wolffian ducts of the fetus develop into a male's seminal vesicles (which store semen) and vas deferens, a duct from the testis into the penis. The Müllerian ducts degenerate in males, and the Wolffian ducts degenerate in females. *(Based on Netter, 1983)*

From then on, the male's testes produce more androgens than **estrogens** (hormones that are more abundant in females). The female's ovaries produce more estrogens than androgens. Androgens and estrogens are **steroid hormones**, containing four carbon rings, derived from cholesterol, as in Figure 11.2. We are often warned about the risks of excessive cholesterol, but a moderate amount is necessary for generating these important hormones. Steroids exert their effects in three ways (Nadal, Díaz, & Valverde, 2001). First, they bind to membrane receptors, like neurotransmitters, exerting rapid effects. Second, they enter cells and activate certain kinds of proteins in the cytoplasm. Third, they bind to receptors that bind to chromosomes, where they activate or inactivate certain genes (Figure 11.3).

Androgens and estrogens are categories of chemicals; neither androgen nor estrogen is a specific chemical itself. The most widely known androgen is **testosterone**. The most prominent type of estrogen is **estradiol**. **Progesterone**, another predominantly female hormone, prepares the uterus for the implantation of a fertilized ovum and promotes the maintenance of pregnancy.

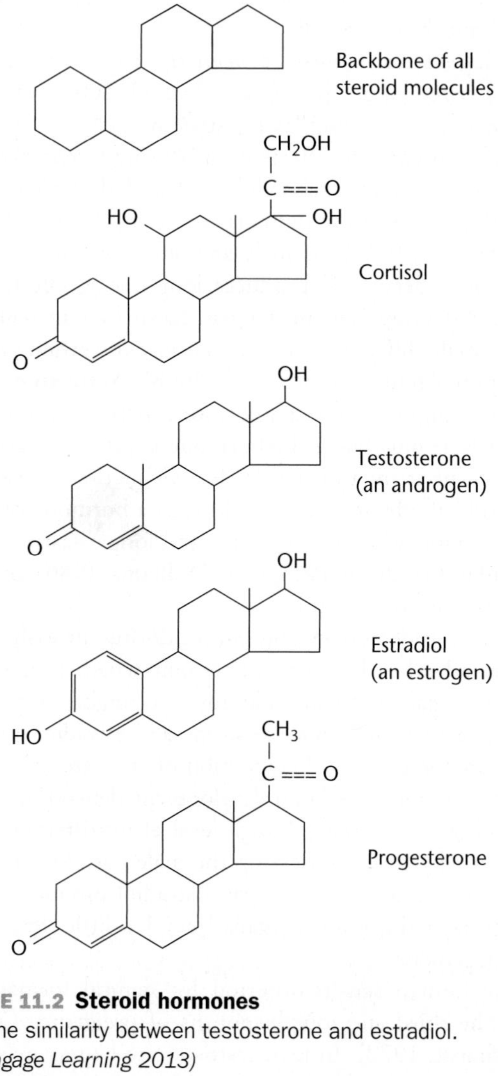

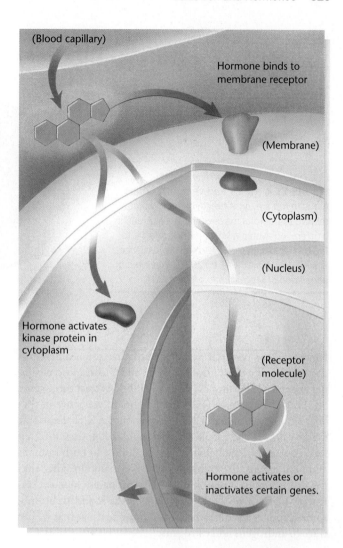

FIGURE 11.3 Routes of action for steroid hormones
Steroid hormones such as estrogens and androgens bind to membrane receptors, activate proteins in the cytoplasm, and activate or inactivate certain genes. *(Revised from Starr & Taggart, 1989)*

Backbone of all steroid molecules

Cortisol

Testosterone (an androgen)

Estradiol (an estrogen)

Progesterone

FIGURE 11.2 Steroid hormones
Note the similarity between testosterone and estradiol.
(© Cengage Learning 2013)

Androgens promote the development of typically masculine features, such as facial hair. Estrogens promote typically female features, such as breast development. Androgens and estrogens also influence activity in many brain areas and alter the pattern of which neurons survive during early development (Forger et al., 2004; Morris, Jordan, & Breedlove, 2004). Certain brain areas are relatively larger in men, on average, and others relatively larger in women, as Figure 11.4 shows (Cahill, 2006; J. M. Goldstein et al., 2001). These differences relate to gender and not to brain size. When researchers compare men and women who have the same overall brain volume, many of the patterns shown in Figure 11.4 still emerge (Luders, Gaser, Narr, & Toga, 2009). However, remember that these are averages. Most individuals show male-typical patterns in some ways and female-typical patterns in others.

For many years, biologists assumed that hormones account for all the biological differences between males and

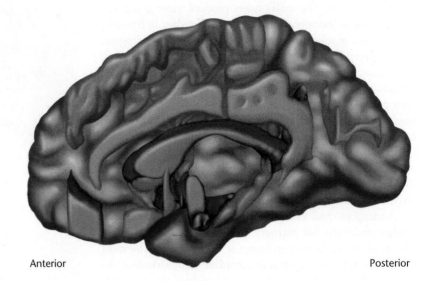

FIGURE 11.4 Men's and women's brains
Areas in red are, on average, larger in women relative to the total mass of the brain. Areas in blue are, on average, larger in men relative to the total mass. *(Nature Reviews Neuroscience, 7, 477–484, from Cahill, L. (2006). Reprinted by permission of Macmillan Publishing Ltd.)*

Anterior   Posterior

females. Later research demonstrated that some differences depend directly on control by the X and Y chromosomes independently of hormones (Arnold, 2009). At least three genes on the Y chromosome (found only in men) are active in specific brain areas, and at least one gene on the X chromosome is active only in the female brain (Arnold, 2004; Carruth, Reisert, & Arnold, 2002; Vawter et al., 2004). In both humans and nonhumans, the Y chromosome has many sites that alter the expression of genes on other chromosomes (Lemos, Araripe, & Hartl, 2008). In short, genes on the X and Y chromosomes produce sex differences in addition to those that we can trace to androgens and estrogens.

> **STOP & CHECK**

1. What does the SRY gene do?

2. How do sex hormones affect neurons?

ANSWERS

1. The SRY gene (sex-determining region on the Y chromosome) causes the undifferentiated gonad of a mammal to develop into a testis, which then produces testosterone and MIH to direct development toward the male pattern. 2. Sex hormones, which are steroids, bind to receptors on the membrane, activate certain proteins in the cell's cytoplasm, and activate or inactivate particular genes.

Organizing Effects of Sex Hormones

If we injected estrogens into adult males and androgens into adult females, could we make males act like females or females act like males? Researchers of the mid-1900s, working with a variety of mammals and birds, were surprised to find that the answer was almost always *no*. But hormones injected early in life have much stronger effects.

Biologists distinguish between the organizing and activating effects of sex hormones (Arnold, 2009). **Organizing effects** produce long-lasting structural effects. The most prominent organizing effects occur during a sensitive stage of early development—shortly before and after birth in rats and well before birth in humans—determining whether the body develops female or male anatomy. The surge of hormones at puberty also produces long-lasting effects, such as breast development in women, facial hair in men, and male–female differences in the anatomy of certain parts of the hypothalamus (Ahmed et al., 2008). **Activating effects** are more temporary, when a hormone increases some activity that lasts only while the hormone is present. Activating effects occur at any time in life. The distinction between the two kinds of effects is not absolute, as a hormone can produce a combination of temporary and longer-lasting effects (Arnold & Breedlove, 1985; C. L. Williams, 1986). Still, the distinction is often useful.

Let's consider organizing effects during an early **sensitive period**, when hormones determine whether an embryo develops a male or female anatomy. You might imagine that testosterone produces male anatomy and estradiol produces female anatomy. No. Differentiation of the external genitals and several aspects of brain development depend mainly on the level of testosterone. A high level of testosterone causes the external genitals to develop the male pattern, and a low level leads to the female pattern. Estradiol produces important effects on the internal organs, but it has little effect on the external genitals.

The human sensitive period for genital formation is about the third and fourth months of pregnancy (Money & Ehrhardt, 1972). In rats, testosterone begins masculinizing the external genitals during the last several days of pregnancy and first few days after birth and then continues masculinizing them at a declining rate for the next month (Bloch & Mills, 1995; Bloch, Mills, & Gale, 1995; E. C. Davis, Shryne, & Gorski, 1995; Rhees, Shryne, & Gorski, 1990). A female rat that is injected with testosterone shortly before or after birth is partly masculinized, just as if her own body had produced the testosterone (I. L. Ward & Ward, 1985). Her clitoris grows larger than normal, and her behavior is partly masculinized. She approaches sexually receptive females (Woodson & Balleine, 2002), mounts them, and makes copulatory thrusting movements rather than arching her back and allowing males to mount her. In short, early testosterone promotes the male pattern and inhibits the female pattern (Gorski, 1985; J. D. Wilson, George, & Griffin, 1981).

Injecting a genetic male with estrogens produces little effect on his external anatomy. However, he develops the female-typical pattern of anatomy and behavior if he genetically lacks androgen receptors, if he is castrated (deprived of his testes), or if he is exposed to substances that block testosterone effects. Drugs that tend to feminize or demasculinize early development include alcohol, marijuana, haloperidol (an antipsychotic drug), phthalates (chemicals common in many manufactured products), and cocaine (Ahmed, Shryne, Gorski, Branch, & Taylor, 1991; Dalterio & Bartke, 1979; Hull, Nishita, Bitran, & Dalterio, 1984; Raum, McGivern, Peterson, Shryne, & Gorski, 1990; Swan et al., 2010). To a slight extent, even aspirin interferes with the male pattern of development (Amateau & McCarthy, 2004). Although estradiol does not significantly alter a male's external anatomy, estradiol and several related compounds do produce abnormalities of the prostate gland—the gland that stores sperm and releases it during intercourse. Some of those estradiol-like compounds are now prevalent in the linings of plastic bottles and cans, so almost everyone is exposed to them (Timms, Howdeshell, Barton, Richter, & vom Saal, 2005). In short, male development is vulnerable to many sources of interference.

The overall mechanism of early sexual differentiation has been described by saying that nature's "default setting" is to make every mammal a female. Add early testosterone and the individual becomes a male; without testosterone, it develops as a female, regardless of the amount of estradiol or other estrogens. That generalization is an overstatement. A genetic female that lacks estradiol during the early sensitive period develops approximately normal female external anatomy but does not develop normal sexual behavior. Even if she is given estradiol injections as an adult, she shows little sexual response toward either male or female partners (Bakker, Honda, Harada, & Balthazart, 2002). So estradiol contributes to female development, including certain aspects of brain differentiation, even if it is not important for external anatomy.

3. What would be the genital appearance of a mammal exposed to high levels of both androgens and estrogens during early development? What if it were exposed to low levels of both?

4. From the standpoint of protecting a male fetus's sexual development, what are some drugs that a pregnant woman should avoid?

ANSWERS

3. A mammal exposed to high levels of both male and female hormones will appear male. One exposed to low levels of both will appear female. Genital development depends mostly on the presence or absence of androgens and is nearly independent of estradiol levels. **4.** Pregnant women should avoid alcohol, marijuana, haloperidol, phthalates, and cocaine because these drugs interfere with male sexual development. Even aspirin and the chemicals lining bottles and cans produce mild abnormalities. Obviously, the results depend on both quantities and timing of exposure to these chemicals.

Sex Differences in the Hypothalamus

In addition to controlling differences in the external genitals, sex hormones early in life influence development in parts of the hypothalamus, amygdala, and other brain areas (Shah et al., 2004). For example, one area in the anterior hypothalamus, known as the **sexually dimorphic nucleus**, is larger in males than in females and contributes to control of male sexual behavior. Parts of the female hypothalamus generate a cyclic pattern of hormone release, as in the human menstrual cycle. The male hypothalamus cannot, and neither can the hypothalamus of a female who was exposed to extra testosterone early in life. Typical female rats have a characteristic way of holding food and dodging from other rats that might try to take it away. A female rat that was either deprived of estrogens or exposed to extra testosterone in infancy pivots around the midpoint of her trunk, like males, instead of around her pelvis, like other females (Field, Whishaw, Forgie, & Pellis, 2004).

In rodents, testosterone exerts much of its organizing effect through a surprising route: After it enters a neuron in early development, it is converted to estradiol! Testosterone and estradiol are chemically very similar, as you can see in Figure 11.2. In organic chemistry, a ring of six carbon atoms containing three double bonds is an *aromatic* compound. An enzyme found in the brain can *aromatize* testosterone into estradiol. Other androgens that cannot be aromatized into estrogens are less effective in masculinizing the hypothalamus. Drugs that prevent testosterone from being aromatized to estradiol block the organizing effects of testosterone on sexual development and thereby impair male sexual behavior and fertility (Gerardin & Pereira, 2002; Rochira et al., 2001).

Why, then, does a female rodent's own estradiol fail to masculinize her hypothalamus? During the early sensitive period, immature mammals have a protein called **alpha-fetoprotein,** which is not present in adults (Gorski, 1980; MacLusky & Naftolin, 1981). Alpha-fetoprotein in rodents binds with estradiol and prevents it from entering cells, where it could produce masculinizing effects. Because testosterone does not bind to alpha-fetoprotein, it can enter neurons, where enzymes convert it into estradiol. That is, testosterone is a way of getting estradiol to its receptors when estradiol circulating in the blood is inactivated.

This explanation of testosterone's effects makes sense of an otherwise puzzling fact: Injecting a large amount of estradiol actually masculinizes a female rodent's development. The reason is that normal amounts are bound to alpha-fetoprotein, but a larger amount exceeds the capacity of alpha-fetoprotein and therefore enters the cells and masculinizes them.

> **STOP & CHECK**

5. How would the external genitals appear on a genetic female rat that lacked alpha-fetoprotein?

ANSWER   **5.** A female that lacked alpha-fetoprotein would be masculinized by her own estradiol, as researchers have in fact demonstrated (Bakker et al., 2006).

Sex Differences in Childhood Behavior

As prenatal hormones influence the structure of the male or female brain, do they also contribute to differences in behavior? In the second module of this chapter we shall consider influences on sexual behavior and sexual orientation, but at this point let's consider possible influences on childhood behavior.

Typically, most boys play mostly with "boys' toys" such as balls and toy cars, whereas most girls play mostly with "girls' toys"

such as dolls and toy tea sets. Some children have a stronger preference for boys' or girls' toys than others do, and their preferences tend to be consistent over time. Those who show the greatest preference for boys' toys and activities at age 3½ usually show the greatest amount of typical boys' activities at age 8, and they tend to be the most physically active at age 12. Similarly, those with the greatest preference for girls' toys and activities at 3½ usually show the greatest preference for typical girls' activities at later ages (Golombok et al., 2008; Mattocks et al., 2010).

Much of this pattern results from socialization, as most parents give their sons and daughters different sets of toys. However, socialization need not be the whole story. Indeed, it may be that parents give those toys because previous generations found that boys and girls typically differ in their interests from the start. In one study, infants 3–8 months old (too young to walk, crawl, or do much with a toy) sat in front of pairs of toys, where researchers could monitor eye movements. The girls looked at dolls more than they looked at toy trucks. The boys looked at both about equally (Alexander, Wilcox, & Woods, 2009). (Note that the children had not seen the trucks move, so at this point the trucks were simply unknown objects.) This study suggests a predisposition for boys and girls to prefer different types of toys, although we should consider an alternative explanation: Girls mature faster than boys, and perhaps it was harder for boys at this age to show a preference, whatever that preference may have been.

In two studies male monkeys played with balls and toy cars more than female monkeys did, whereas the females played more with dolls (Alexander & Hines, 2002; Hassett, Siebert, & Wallen, 2008). Figure 11.5 summarizes the results from one of those studies. Monkeys' preferences were not as strong as most children's, but it is noteworthy that the sexes differed at all in their first encounters with these toys. Other studies found that prenatal injections of testosterone into female monkey fetuses led to increased masculine-type play after they were born. In those cases the focus was on spontaneous, rough-and-tumble play rather than playing with toys, but the idea is similar (Wallen, 2005).

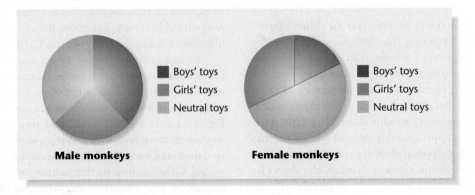

FIGURE 11.5 Toy choices by male and female monkeys
Male monkeys spent more time than female monkeys did with "boys' toys" and the females spent more time than the males with "girls' toys." *(Based on data from G. M. Alexander & M. Hines (2002). "Sex differences in response to children's toys in nonhuman primates"* (Cercopithecus aethiops sabaeus). Evolution and Human Behavior, 23, 467–479.)

Finally, two studies correlated chemicals in the mother's blood during pregnancy with their children's choices of toys years later. Researchers took blood samples from pregnant women, measuring testosterone (some of which would enter the fetus). When the daughters reached age 3½, researchers observed their toy play. The girls who had been exposed to higher testosterone levels in prenatal life showed slightly elevated preferences for boys' toys (Hines et al., 2002). These girls were anatomically normal, and we have no reason to believe that the parents treated girls differently based on how much testosterone had been present in prenatal life. In another study, researchers measured phthalate levels in pregnant women. Phthalates inhibit testosterone production. U.S. law bans phthalates from children's toys, but pregnant women are exposed to phthalates from other sources, including perfumes, hair spray, and food packaging. Researchers measured phthalate levels in pregnant women's urine samples and compared results to the sons' toy use at ages 3 to 6. On average, sons of women with high phthalate levels showed less interest in typical boys' toys and more interest in typical girls' toys (Swan et al., 2010). In summary, these studies suggest that prenatal hormones, especially testosterone, alter the brain in ways that influence differences between boys and girls in their activities and interests.

Do these studies imply that prenatal hormones determine toy preferences, regardless of rearing? No. Prenatal hormones combine forces with rearing experiences. When a child shows a preference for a certain kind of toy, even if it is just a small preference, parents tend to provide more of that kind of toy and more opportunities to strengthen that preference. Psychologists call this a "multiplier effect" (Dickens & Flynn, 2001). Furthermore, if most boys in the past have preferred one kind of toy and most girls preferred another, parents start with this presupposition and provide those toys from the start.

> **STOP & CHECK**

6. What evidence most directly links children's toy play to prenatal hormones?

ANSWER

6. Girls whose mothers had higher testosterone levels during pregnancy tend to play with boys' toys more than the average for other girls. Boys whose mothers had higher phthalate exposure tend to play with boys' toys less than the average for other boys.

Activating Effects of Sex Hormones

At any time in life, not just during a sensitive period, current levels of testosterone or estradiol exert activating effects, temporarily modifying behavior. Changes in hormonal secretions influence sexual behavior within 15 minutes (Taziaux, Keller, Bakker, & Balthazart, 2007). Behaviors can also influence hormonal secretions. For example, when doves court each other, each stage of their behavior initiates hormonal changes that alter the birds' readiness for the next sequence of behaviors (C. Erickson & Lehrman, 1964; Lehrman, 1964; Martinez-Vargas & Erickson, 1973).

Rodents

For rodents, as for other mammals, sex hormones facilitate sexual activity. Testosterone is essential for male sexual arousal (Hull & Dominguez, 2007). A combination of estradiol and progesterone is the most effective combination for females (Matuszewich, Lorrain, & Hull, 2000). Arousal also depends on previous experience. Sexually experienced rats are aroused more easily because the effects of previous experience sensitize the response to future stimuli (Dominguez, Brann, Gil, & Hull, 2006).

Sex hormones activate sexual behavior partly by enhancing sensations. Estrogens increase the sensitivity of the *pudendal nerve*, which transmits tactile stimulation from the vagina and cervix to the brain (Komisaruk, Adler, & Hutchison, 1972). Testosterone increases sensitivity in the penis (Etgen, Chu, Fiber, Karkanias, & Morales, 1999). Sex hormones also bind to receptors that increase responses in parts of the hypothalamus, including the ventromedial nucleus, the medial preoptic area (MPOA), and the anterior hypothalamus.

Erection depends partly on the fact that testosterone increases the release of nitric oxide (NO), which increases blood flow to the penis. (As mentioned in Chapter 3, nitric oxide also increases blood flow in the brain.) The drug sildenafil (Viagra) increases male sexual ability by prolonging the effects of nitric oxide (Rowland & Burnett, 2000).

Testosterone and estradiol prime the MPOA and several other brain areas to release dopamine. MPOA neurons release dopamine strongly during sexual activity, and the more dopamine they release, the more likely the male is to copulate (Putnam, Du, Sato, & Hull, 2001). Castrated male rats produce normal amounts of dopamine in the MPOA, but they do not release it in the presence of a receptive female, and they do not attempt to copulate (Hull, Du, Lorrain, & Matuszewich, 1997).

In moderate concentrations, dopamine stimulates mostly type D_1 and D_5 receptors, which facilitate erection of the penis in the male (Hull et al., 1992) and sexually receptive postures in the female (Apostolakis et al., 1996). In higher concentrations, dopamine stimulates type D_2 receptors, which leads to orgasm (Giuliani & Ferrari, 1996; Hull et al., 1992). The sudden burst of dopamine in several brain areas at the time of orgasm resembles the "rush" that addictive drugs produce (Holstege et al., 2003). Whereas dopamine stimulates sexual activity, the neurotransmitter serotonin inhibits it, in part by blocking dopamine release (Hull et al., 1999). Many popular antidepressant drugs increase serotonin activity, and one of their side effects is to decrease sexual arousal and orgasm.

Researchers found what appeared to be a major difference between male and female rats in their sexual motivation: After rats have had sexual relations in a particular cage, males work hard to return to that cage, but females generally do not. Then the researchers varied the procedure. A male rat was confined to that cage, but the female was free to enter or leave at any time. She could therefore control the timing of when their sexual activity started and stopped. Under these conditions, females developed a clear preference for that cage (Paredes & Vazquez, 1999). Evidently, female rats find sex reinforcing only if they get to decide when it occurs. (The rumor is that the same trend may be true for other species as well.)

7. By what mechanism do testosterone and estradiol affect the hypothalamic areas responsible for sexual behavior?

ANSWER

7. Testosterone and estradiol prime hypothalamic cells to be ready to release dopamine. They also increase sensitivity in the genital area.

Humans

Although humans are less dependent on current sex hormone levels than other species are, hormones do alter people's sexual arousal. They also affect brain systems with functions not directly related to sex. For example, testosterone decreases pain and anxiety, and estrogens probably do, too (Edinger & Frye, 2004). Decreases of sex hormones—for example, in men being treated for prostate cancer—lead to impairments of memory (Bussiere, Beer, Neiss, & Janowsky, 2005). Estrogens directly stimulate parts of the prefrontal cortex that are important for working memory—that is, memory for what one is doing at the moment (Wang, Hara, Janssen, Rapp, & Morrison, 2010). In short, sex hormones serve functions that go beyond sexual behavior itself.

Testosterone

Among men, levels of testosterone correlate positively with sexual arousal and the drive to seek sexual partners. Researchers found that, on average, married men and men living with a woman in a committed relationship have lower testosterone levels than single, unpaired men of the same age (M. McIntyre et al., 2006). The apparently obvious interpretation was that once a man established a lasting relationship, he no longer needed to work so hard to seek a sexual partner, and his testosterone levels dropped. However, that study did not tell us which came first, the committed relationship or the lower testosterone level. Another study found that men's testosterone levels did not change after marriage. Instead, men with lower testosterone levels were more likely to marry than were men with high testosterone levels (van Anders & Watson, 2006). Similar studies found that single women had higher testosterone levels than women with a long-term partner, either homosexual or heterosexual (van Anders & Goldey, 2010; van

Anders & Watson, 2006). Also, both men and women with high testosterone levels are more likely than average to seek additional sex partners, even after they marry or establish a long-term relationship (M. McIntyre et al., 2006; van Anders, Hamilton, & Watson, 2007).

Overall, these results say that high testosterone levels are associated with seeking multiple partners, to some extent for both men and women. It is tempting to assume that testosterone causes the drive for multiple partners, but the data are correlational, and we should hesitate about a cause and effect conclusion. The alternative interpretation is that some other influence leads to an interest in multiple partners, and the variety of partners increases testosterone production. It has been shown that when women think about sex or anticipate having sex, their testosterone levels increase temporarily (van Anders, Brotto, Farrell, & Yule, 2009; van Anders, Hamilton, Schmidt, & Watson, 2007). So, the relationship between testosterone and sexual interest may go both directions.

Decreases in testosterone levels generally decrease male sexual activity. For example, castration (removal of the testes) generally decreases a man's sexual interest and activity (Carter, 1992). However, low testosterone is not the usual basis for **impotence**, the inability to have an erection. The most common cause is impaired blood circulation, especially in older men. Other common causes include neurological problems, reactions to drugs, and psychological tension (Andersson, 2001).

Testosterone reduction has sometimes been tried as a means of controlling sex offenders, including exhibitionists, rapists, child molesters, and those who commit incest. One major practical problem is getting sex offenders to continue taking drugs that block testosterone (Hughes, 2007). Another drawback is the side effects of testosterone deprivation, including weight gain, diabetes, and depression (Giltay & Gooren, 2009).

8. What is the explanation for why married men tend to have lower testosterone levels than single men of the same age?

ANSWER

8. Men with lower testosterone levels are more likely to get married than are men with higher testosterone levels.

Estradiol and Related Hormones

A woman's hypothalamus and pituitary interact with the ovaries to produce the **menstrual cycle**, a periodic variation in hormones and fertility over the course of about 28 days (Figure 11.6). After the end of a menstrual period, the anterior pituitary releases **follicle-stimulating hormone (FSH)**, which promotes the growth of a follicle in the ovary. The follicle nurtures the *ovum* (egg cell) and produces several types of estrogen, including estradiol. Toward the middle of the menstrual cycle, the follicle builds up more and more receptors to FSH, so even though the actual concentration of FSH in the blood is decreasing, its effects on the follicle increase. As a result, the follicle produces increasing amounts of estradiol. The increased release of estradiol causes an increased release of FSH as well as a sudden surge in the release of **luteinizing hormone (LH)** from the anterior pituitary (see the top graph in Figure 11.6). FSH and LH combine to cause the follicle to release an ovum.

The remnant of the follicle (now called the *corpus luteum*) releases the hormone progesterone, which prepares the uterus for the implantation of a fertilized ovum. Progesterone also

inhibits the further release of LH. Toward the end of the menstrual cycle, the levels of LH, FSH, estradiol, and progesterone all decline. If the ovum is not fertilized, the lining of the uterus is cast off (menstruation), and the cycle begins again. If the ovum is fertilized, the levels of estradiol and progesterone increase gradually during pregnancy. One consequence of high estradiol and progesterone levels is fluctuating activity at the serotonin 3 ($5HT_3$) receptor, which is responsible for nausea (Rupprecht et al., 2001). Pregnant women often experience nausea because of the heightened activity of that receptor. Figure 11.7 summarizes the interactions between the pituitary and the ovary. Increased sensitivity to nausea may be an evolved adaptation to minimize the risk of eating something harmful to the fetus.

Birth-control pills prevent pregnancy by interfering with the usual feedback cycle between the ovaries and the pituitary.

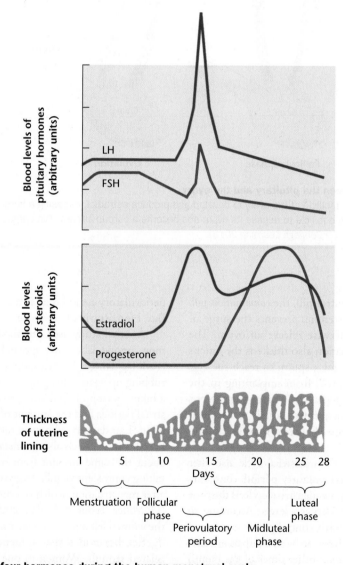

FIGURE 11.6 Blood levels of four hormones during the human menstrual cycle
Note that estrogen and progesterone are both at high levels during the midluteal phase but drop sharply at menstruation. (© Cengage Learning 2013)

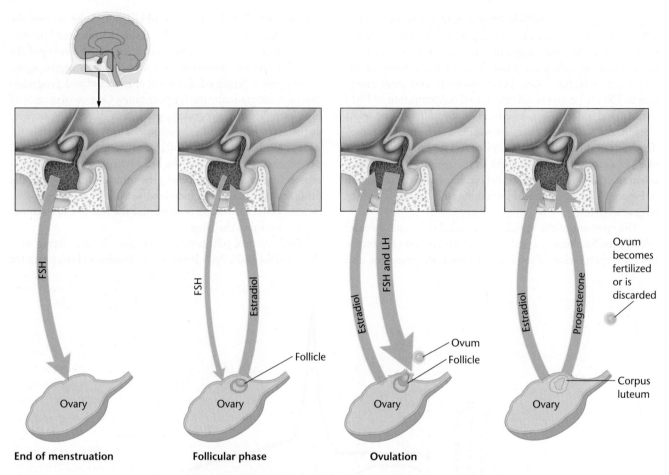

FIGURE 11.7 Interactions between the pituitary and the ovary
FSH from the pituitary stimulates a follicle of the ovary to develop and produce estradiol, releasing a burst of FSH and LH from the pituitary. Those hormones cause the follicle to release its ovum and become a corpus luteum. The corpus luteum releases progesterone while the ovary releases estradiol. *(© Cengage Learning 2013)*

The most widely used birth-control pill, the *combination pill*, containing estrogen and progesterone, prevents the surge of FSH and LH that would otherwise release an ovum. The estrogen–progesterone combination also thickens the mucus of the cervix, making it harder for a sperm to reach the egg, and prevents an ovum, if released, from implanting in the uterus. Thus, the pill prevents pregnancy in many ways. Note, however, that it does not protect against sexually transmitted diseases such as AIDS or syphilis. "Safe sex" must go beyond the prevention of pregnancy.

Changes in hormones over the menstrual cycle also alter women's sexual interest. The **periovulatory period**, consisting of the days around the middle of the menstrual cycle, is the time of maximum fertility and high estrogen levels. According to two studies, women not taking birth-control pills initiate more sexual activity (either with a partner or by masturbation) during the periovulatory period than at other times of the month (D. B. Adams, Gold, & Burt, 1978; Udry & Morris, 1968) (Figure 11.8). According to another study, women rate an erotic video as more pleasant and arousing if they watch it during the periovulatory period than if they watch it at other times (Slob, Bax, Hop, Rowland, & van der Werff ten Bosch, 1996).

Another study used a method that is, shall we say, not common among laboratory researchers. The researchers studied erotic lap dancers, who earn tips by dancing between a man's legs, rubbing up against his groin, while wearing, in most cases, just a bikini bottom. Lap dancers recorded the times of their menstrual periods and the amount of tip income they received each night. Lap dancers who were taking contraceptive pills (which keep hormone levels about constant through the month) earned about the same amount from one day to another. Those not taking contraceptive pills received the largest tips 9 to 15 days after menstruation, which is a time of increasing estrogen levels (G. Miller, Tybur, & Jordan, 2007). A likely hypothesis is that the women felt and acted sexier at this time.

Sex hormones also influence women's attention to sex-related stimuli. Women in one study were asked to look at facial photos on a screen and classify each as male or female as quickly as possible. They made the classifications more quickly when they were in their periovulatory period than at

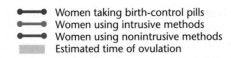

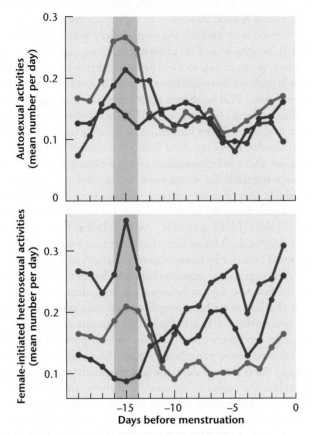

FIGURE 11.8 Female-initiated sexual activities
The top graph shows autosexual activities (masturbation and sexual fantasies); the bottom graph shows female-initiated activities with a male partner. "Intrusive" birth-control methods are diaphragm, foam, and condom; "nonintrusive" methods are IUD and vasectomy. Women other than pill users initiate sex more often when their estrogen levels peak. *(Adams, Gold, & Burt, 1978)*

with fertility move women's mate preferences toward men who look and act more masculine.

9. At what time in a woman's menstrual cycle do her estradiol levels increase? When are they lowest?

ANSWER 9. Estrogen levels increase during the days leading up to the middle of the menstrual cycle. They are lowest during and just after menstruation.

Oxytocin

In addition to the sex hormones, the pituitary hormone **oxytocin** is also important for reproductive behavior. Oxytocin stimulates contractions of the uterus during delivery of a baby, and it stimulates the mammary gland to release milk.

Sexual pleasure also releases oxytocin, especially at orgasm (M. R. Murphy, Checkley, Seckl, & Lightman, 1990). People typically experience a state of relaxation shortly after orgasm as a result of oxytocin release. In animal studies, rats show increased exploration of potentially dangerous places—that is, decreased anxiety—after orgasm. Blocking the release of oxytocin prevents that effect, so oxytocin is apparently responsible for the calmness and lack of anxiety after orgasm (Waldherr & Neumann, 2007). Strong release of oxytocin facilitates formation of pair bonds between mating partners (Kosfeld, Heinrichs, Zak, Fischbacher, & Fehr, 2005). It is also apparently related to the formation of a pair bond between mother and infant. A study found that women who had the highest oxytocin levels during pregnancy spent the most time gazing at, vocalizing to, touching, and pleasurably interacting with their infants after delivery (Feldman, Welle, Zagoory-Sharon, & Levine, 2007).

Oxytocin also facilitates other social behaviors. When people inhale a nasal spray containing oxytocin, as compared to a placebo, they become more accurate at recognizing familiar faces (Rimmele, Hediger, Heinrichs, & Klaver, 2009). They are also quicker to recognize blurry words on a screen, if those words refer to pleasant social relationship words, such as *love* or *kissing* (Unkelbach, Guastella, & Forgas, 2008).

Also consider effects on the "Trust Game." If you are playing this game, someone hands you some money. You can give some or all of it to another person, and if so the amount you give triples in value. That person can then return to you whatever amount he or she chooses. So you have to decide how much you trust that person. What effect would you expect from oxytocin? It depends. People who are given oxytocin give more money to people who seem trustworthy, but not to people who seem competitive and aggressive (Mikolajczak et al., 2010). People sometimes call oxytocin a "love hormone," but as you can see, that term is misleading. It might enhance your attraction toward someone you already love, but it doesn't make you love or trust everyone. Testosterone, incidentally, *decreases* trust (Bos, Terburg, & van Honk, 2010).

other times of the cycle (Macrae, Alnwick, Milne, & Schloerscheidt, 2002). In another study, women were presented with a computer that enabled them to modify pictures of men's faces to make each one look more feminine or more masculine. When they were asked specifically to show the face of the man they would prefer for a "short-term sexual relationship," women preferred more masculine-looking faces around the time of ovulation than they did at other times (Penton-Voak et al., 1999). When women were asked to view videotapes of two men and choose one for a short-term relationship, women around the time of ovulation were more likely to choose a man who seemed athletic, competitive, and assertive and who did *not* describe himself as having a "nice personality" (Gangestad, Simpson, Cousins, Garver-Apgar, & Christensen, 2004). In short, the hormones associated

STOP & CHECK

10. What behavioral change occurs after orgasm, and which hormone is responsible?

ANSWER

10. Anxiety decreases after orgasm because of release of the pituitary hormone oxytocin.

▌Parental Behavior

A female mammal's behavior changes in many ways when she becomes a mother. In addition to nursing and caring for the young, she eats and drinks more than usual, and becomes less fearful and more aggressive, especially in defense of her young. Although the role of hormones is less central for humans, it is critical for maternal behavior in other species. After a mother rat delivers her babies, she increases her secretion of estradiol and prolactin, while decreasing production of progesterone (Numan & Woodside, 2010). Prolactin is necessary for milk production and certain aspects of maternal behavior, such as retrieving the young when they wander away from the nest (Lucas, Ormandy, Binart, Bridges, & Kelly, 1998). It also inhibits sensitivity to leptin, enabling the mother to eat far more than usual.

In addition to secreting hormones, the female changes her pattern of hormone receptors. Late in pregnancy, her brain increases its sensitivity to estradiol in the areas responsible for maternal behavior (Rosenblatt, Olufowobi, & Siegel, 1998). The hormonal changes increase the mothers' attention to their young after delivery. Hormones increase activity in the medial preoptic area and anterior hypothalamus (Featherstone, Fleming, & Ivy, 2000), areas that are necessary for rats' maternal behavior (J. R. Brown, Ye, Bronson, Dikkes, & Greenberg, 1996) (Figure 11.9). We have already encountered the preoptic area/anterior hypothalamus, or POA/AH, because of its importance for temperature regulation, thirst, and sexual behavior. It's a busy little area.

Another key hormone is vasopressin, synthesized by the hypothalamus and secreted by the posterior pituitary gland. Vasopressin is important for social behavior in many species, partly by facilitating olfactory recognition of other individuals (Tobin et al., 2010). Male prairie voles, which secrete much vasopressin, establish long-term pair bonds with females and help rear their young. A male meadow vole, with much lower vasopressin levels, mates with a female and then virtually ignores her (Figure 11.10). Imagine a male meadow vole in a long, narrow cage. At one end, he can sit next to a female with which he has just mated. (She is confined there.) At the other end, he can sit next to a different female. Will he choose his recent mate (showing loyalty) or the new female (seeking variety)? The answer: neither. He sits right in the middle, by himself, as far away as he can get from both females. However, these little social isolates changed their behavior after researchers found a way to increase activity of the genes responsible for vasopressin in the voles' hypothalamus. Suddenly, they showed a strong preference for a recent mate and, if placed into the same cage, they even helped her take care of her babies (M. M. Lim et al., 2004). Whether the female was surprised, we don't know. This result is a strong example of altering social behavior by manipulating the activity of a single gene.

Although rodent maternal behavior depends on hormones for the first few days, it becomes less dependent later. If a female that has never been pregnant is left with some baby rats, she ignores them at first but gradually becomes more attentive. (Because the babies cannot survive without parental care, the experimenter must periodically replace them with new, healthy babies.) After about 6 days, the adoptive mother builds a nest, assembles the babies in the nest, licks them, and does everything else that normal mothers do, except nurse them. This experience-dependent behavior does not require hormonal changes and occurs even in rats that had their ovaries removed (Mayer & Rosenblatt, 1979; Rosenblatt, 1967). That is, humans are not the only species in which a mother can adopt young without first going through pregnancy.

An important influence from being with babies is that the mother becomes accustomed to their odors. Infant rats release chemicals that stimulate the mother's vomeronasal organ, which responds to pheromones (see Chapter 7). We might imagine that

FIGURE 11.9 Brain development and maternal behavior in mice
The mouse on the left shows normal maternal behavior. The one on the right has a genetic mutation that impairs the development of the preoptic area and anterior hypothalamus. *(Reprinted from Cell, 86/2, Brown, J. R., Ye, H., Bronson, R. T., Dikkes, P., & Greenberg, M. E., "A defect in nurturing in mice lacking the immediate early gene fosB," 297–309, 1996, with permission of Elsevier.)*

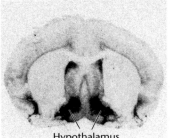

(a)

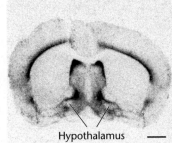

Hypothalamus

Hypothalamus

(b)

FIGURE 11.10 **Effects of vasopressin on social and mating behaviors**
Prairie voles (top) form long-term pair bonds. Staining of their brain shows much expression of the hormone vasopressin in the hypothalamus. A closely related species, meadow voles (bottom), show no social attachments. Their brains have lower vasopressin levels, as indicated by less staining in the hypothalamus. *(Reprinted by permission from "Enhanced partner preference in a promiscuous species by manipulating the expression of a single gene," by Lim, M. M., Wang, Z., Olazabal, D. E., Ren, X., Terwilliger, E. F., & Young, L. J., Nature, 429, 754–757. Copyright 2004 Nature Publishing Group/Macmillan Magazines Ltd.)*

evolution would have equipped infants with pheromones that elicit maternal behavior, but actually, their pheromones stimulate aggressive behaviors that *interfere* with maternal behavior (Sheehan, Cirrito, Numan, & Numan, 2000). For a mother that has just gone through pregnancy, this interference does not matter because her hormones primed her medial preoptic area so strongly that it overrides competing impulses. A female without hormonal priming, however, rejects the young until she has become familiar with their smell (Del Cerro et al., 1995).

Why do mammals need two mechanisms for maternal behavior—one hormone-dependent and one not? In the early phase, hormones compensate for the mother's lack of familiarity with the young. In the later phase, experience maintains the maternal behavior even though the hormones start to decline (Rosenblatt, 1970).

Are hormones important for human parental behavior? Hormonal changes are necessary for a woman to nurse a baby, and oxytocin levels correlate with several aspects of motherly at-

tention to an infant. However, hormonal changes are not necessary for human parental behavior. After all, many people adopt children and become excellent parents.

STOP & CHECK

11. What factors are responsible for maternal behavior shortly after rats give birth? What factors become more important in later days?

ANSWER

11. The early stage of rats' maternal behavior depends on a surge in the release of the hormones prolactin and estradiol. A few days later, her experience with the young decreases the vomeronasal responses that would tend to make her reject them. Experience with the young maintains maternal behavior after the hormone levels begin to drop.

MODULE 11.1 ■ **IN CLOSING**

Reproductive Behaviors and Motivations

A mother rat licks her babies all over shortly after their birth, and that stimulation is essential for their survival. Why does she do it? Presumably, she does not understand that licking will help them. She licks because they are covered with a salty fluid that tastes good to her. If she has access to other salty fluids, she stops licking her young (Gubernick & Alberts, 1983). Analo-

gously, sexual behavior in general serves the function of passing on our genes, but we engage in sexual behavior just because it feels good. We evolved a tendency to enjoy the sex act. The same principle holds for hunger, thirst, and other motivations: We evolved tendencies to enjoy acts that have, in general, increased our ancestors' probability of surviving and reproducing.

SUMMARY

1. Male and female behaviors differ because of sex hormones that activate particular genes. Also, certain genes on the X and Y chromosomes exert direct effects on brain development.   328

2. Organizing effects of a hormone, exerted during a sensitive period, produce relatively permanent alterations in anatomy and physiology.   330

3. In the absence of sex hormones, an infant mammal develops female-looking external genitals. The addition of testosterone shifts development toward the male pattern. Extra estradiol, within normal limits, does not determine whether the individual looks male or female. However, estradiol and other estrogens modify development of the brain and internal sexual organs.   330

4. During early development in rodents, testosterone is converted within certain brain cells to estradiol, which actually masculinizes their development. Estradiol in the blood does not masculinize development because it is bound to proteins in the blood.   331

5. In adulthood, sex hormones activate sex behaviors, partly by facilitating activity in the medial preoptic area and anterior hypothalamus. The hormones prime cells to release dopamine in response to sexual arousal.   333

6. A woman's menstrual cycle depends on a feedback cycle that increases and then decreases the release of several hormones. Although women can respond sexually at any time in their cycle, on average, they show increased sexual interest when estrogen levels are increasing.   334

7. The pituitary hormone oxytocin is important for sexual pleasure, delivery of a baby, and milk production. Its release after orgasm decreases anxiety. It also increases attention to anything associated with favorable social or sexual relationships.   337

8. Hormones released around the time of giving birth facilitate maternal behavior in females of many mammalian species. Prolonged exposure to young also induces parental behavior. Hormonal facilitation is not necessary for human parental behavior.   338

KEY TERMS

Terms are defined in the module on the page number indicated. They're also presented in alphabetical order with definitions in the book's Subject Index/Glossary, which begins on page 561. Interactive flashcards and crossword puzzles are among the online resources available to help you learn these terms and the concepts they represent.

activating effects 330	luteinizing hormone (LH) 335	sensitive period 330
alpha-fetoprotein 332	menstrual cycle 334	sexually dimorphic
androgens 328	Müllerian ducts 328	nucleus 331
estradiol 329	organizing effects 330	SRY gene 328
estrogens 329	ovaries 328	steroid hormones 329
follicle-stimulating hormone	oxytocin 337	testis 328
(FSH) 335	periovulatory period 336	testosterone 329
impotence 334	progesterone 329	Wolffian ducts 328

THOUGHT QUESTIONS

1. The pill RU-486 produces abortions by blocking the effects of progesterone. Why would blocking progesterone interfere with pregnancy?

2. The presence or absence of testosterone determines whether a mammal will differentiate as a male or a female. In birds, the story is the opposite: The presence or absence of estrogen is critical (Adkins & Adler, 1972). What problems would sex determination by estrogen create if that were the mechanism for mammals? Why do those problems not arise in birds? (Hint: Think about the difference between live birth and hatching from an egg.)

3. Antipsychotic drugs, such as haloperidol and chlorpromazine, block activity at dopamine synapses. What side effects might they have on sexual behavior?

Variations in Sexual Behavior

P eople vary considerably in their frequency of sexual activity, preferred types of sexual activity, and sexual orientation. In this module, we explore some of that diversity, but first we consider a few differences between men and women in general. Do men's and women's mating behaviors make biological sense? If so, should we interpret these behaviors as products of evolution? These questions have proved to be difficult and controversial.

Evolutionary Interpretations of Mating Behavior

Part of Charles Darwin's theory of evolution by natural selection was that individuals whose genes help them survive will produce more offspring, and therefore the next generation will resemble those with these favorable genes. A second part of his theory, not so widely accepted at first, was **sexual selection**: Genes that make an individual more appealing to the other sex will increase the probability of reproduction, and therefore the next generation will resemble those who had these favorable genes.

Sexual selection can go only so far, however, if it starts to interfere with survival. A male deer with large antlers attracts females, but being impressive wouldn't help if the weight became so great that it interfered with the deer's movement. A bird's bright colors attract potential mates, but they also run the risk of attracting a predator's attention. In many bird species, the male is brightly colored, but the female is not, presumably because she sits on the nest and needs to be less conspicuous. In a few species, such as phalaropes, the female is more brightly colored, but in those species, the female lays the egg and deserts it, leaving the dull-colored male to sit on the nest. In species where the male and female share the nesting duties, such as pigeons and doves, the male and female look alike, and neither is especially gaudy.

In humans, too, some of the differences between men and women may be results of sexual selection. That is, to some extent women evolved based on what appeals to men, and men evolved based on what appeals to women. Certain aspects of behavior may also reflect different evolutionary pressures for men and women. Evolutionary psychologists cite several pos-

Phalaropes are shore birds, in which the female is brilliantly colored and the male is drabber. The female lays eggs and deserts the nest, leaving the male to attend to it.

sible examples, although each has been controversial (Buss, 2000). Let's examine the evidence and reasoning.

Interest in Multiple Mates

More men than women seek opportunities for casual sexual relationships with many partners. Why? From the evolutionary standpoint of spreading one's genes, men can succeed by either of two strategies (Gangestad & Simpson, 2000): Be loyal to one woman and devote your energies to helping her and her babies, or mate with many women and hope that some of them can raise your babies without your help. No one needs to be conscious of these strategies, of course. The idea is that men who acted these ways in the past propagated their genes, and today's men might have inherited genes that promote these behaviors. In contrast, a woman can have no more than one pregnancy per 9 months, regardless of her number of sex partners. So evolution may have predisposed men, or at least some men, to be more interested in multiple mates than women are.

341

One objection is that a woman does sometimes gain from having multiple sex partners (Hrdy, 2000). If her husband is infertile, mating with another man could be her only way of reproducing. Also, another sexual partner may provide aid of various sorts to her and her children. In addition, she has the possibility of "trading up," abandoning her first mate for a better one. So the prospect of multiple mates may be more appealing to men, but it has advantages for women, too. Human cultures vary substantially in how well they tolerate women having multiple sexual partners.

Another objection is that researchers have no direct evidence that genes influence people's preferences for one mate or many. We shall return to this issue later.

What Men and Women Seek in a Mate

Almost all people seeking a romantic partner prefer someone who is healthy, intelligent, honest, and physically attractive. Typically, women have some additional interests that are less common for men. In particular, women are more likely than men are to prefer a mate who is likely to be a good provider (Buss, 2000). As you might guess, that tendency is strongest in societies where women have no income of their own. According to evolutionary theorists, the reason is this: While a woman is pregnant or taking care of a small child, she needs help getting food and other requirements. Evolution would have favored any gene that caused women to seek good providers. Related to this tendency, most women tend to be cautious during courtship. Even if a man seems interested in her, a woman waits before concluding that he has a strong commitment to her (Buss, 2001). She would not want a man who acts interested briefly and then leaves when she needs him.

A woman is also much more likely to reject a man because of his smell than a man is to reject a woman because of her smell (Herz & Inzlicht, 2002). One possible reason is that body odor relates to some of the same genes that control the immune system, known as the *major histocompatibility complex.* Research has found that a woman tends to be less sexually responsive to a man whose immune genes, and therefore body odor, are too similar to her own (Garver-Apgar, Gangestad, Thornhill, Miller, & Olp, 2006). Avoiding a man of similar odor may be a way to avoid inbreeding.

Men tend to have a stronger preference for a young partner. An evolutionary explanation is that young women are likely to remain fertile longer than older women are, so a man can have more children by pairing with a young woman. Curiously, male chimpanzees show no preference for young females, perhaps because chimpanzee mating does not entail a long-term commitment. In fact, male chimps usually prefer older (but still fertile) females, who tend to have a higher social rank than younger females do (Muller, Thompson, & Wrangham, 2006).

Men remain fertile into old age, so a woman has less need to insist on youth. Women do prefer young partners when possible, but in many societies, only older men have enough financial resources to get married.

Differences in Jealousy

Traditionally, in most cultures, men have been more jealous of women's infidelities than women have been of men's infidelities. From an evolutionary standpoint, why might men be more jealous than women? If a man is to pass on his genes—the key point in evolution—he needs to be sure that the children he supports are his own. An unfaithful wife threatens that certainty. A woman knows that any children she bears are her own, so she does not have the same worry.

One way to test this interpretation of jealousy is to compare cultures. Some cultures consider sexual infidelity acceptable for both husband and wife; some prohibit it completely for both; and some consider it more acceptable for the husband than for the wife. However, no known society considers it more acceptable for the wife. Should we be more impressed that jealousy is always at least as strong for men as for women, and usually more, or should we be more impressed that jealousy varies among cultures? The answer is not obvious.

Which would upset you more: if your partner had a brief sexual affair with someone else, or if he or she became emotionally close to someone else? According to several studies, men say they would be more upset by the sexual infidelity, whereas women would be more upset by the emotional infidelity (Shakelford, Buss, & Bennett, 2002). However, those studies dealt with hypothetical situations. Most men and women who have actually dealt with an unfaithful partner say they were more upset by their partner's becoming emotionally close to someone else than by the sexual affair (C. H. Harris, 2002).

Evolved or Learned?

If a behavior has clear advantages for survival or reproduction and is similar across most or all cultures, can we conclude that it developed by evolution? Not necessarily. Of course, the brain evolved, just like any other organ, and of course, our behavioral tendencies are a product of evolution. But the key question is whether evolution has micromanaged our behavior down to such details as whether to look for a mate with high earning potential or how jealous to be of an unfaithful mate.

Cross-cultural similarity is not necessarily good evidence for an evolved tendency. For example, people throughout the world agree that $2 + 2 = 4$, but we don't assume that they have a gene for that belief. To establish that we evolved a tendency to act in some way, the most decisive evidence would be to demonstrate genes that affect the relevant behaviors. For example, if most men have genes influencing them to prefer young women, then presumably, we should be able to find some men with a mutation in that gene causing them to lose that preference. Although this example may not be the best, the point is that we need to be cautious about inferring what is a product of our evolution and what is learned.

Conclusions

Discussing these issues is difficult. Ideally, we would like to consider the evidence and logical arguments entirely on their scientific merits. However, when someone describes how evolutionary selection may have led men to be interested in multiple sex partners or to be more jealous than women are, it sometimes sounds like a justification for men to act that way. No gene forces men or women to behave in any particular way.

Even leaving aside the social implications as far as we can, no firm scientific consensus emerges. We need more data, especially about the effects of particular genes, before we draw a firm conclusion.

> **STOP & CHECK**

12. What evolutionary advantage is suggested for why women are more interested in men's wealth and success than men are interested in women's wealth?

ANSWER

12. During pregnancy and early child care, a female is limited in her ability to get food and therefore prefers a male partner who can provide for her. A healthy male is not similarly dependent on a female.

Gender Identity and Gender-Differentiated Behaviors

The coral goby is a species of fish in which the male and female tend their eggs and young together. If one of them dies, the survivor looks for a new partner. But it does not look far. This is a very stay-at-home kind of fish. If it cannot easily find a partner of the opposite sex but does find an unmated member of its own sex—oh, well—it simply changes sex and mates with the neighbor. Male-to-female and female-to-male switches are equally common (Nakashima, Kuwamura, & Yogo, 1995).

People do not have the same flexibility as coral gobies, but we do have variations in sexual development. Sexual development is a sensitive issue, so let us specify from the start: "Different" does not mean "wrong." People differ naturally in their sexual development just as they do in anything else.

Gender identity is how we identify sexually and what we call ourselves. The biological differences between males and females are *sex differences*, whereas the differences that result from people's thinking about themselves as male or female are *gender differences*. To maintain this useful distinction, we should resist the trend to speak of the "gender" of dogs, fruit flies, and so forth. Gender identity is a human characteristic.

In most cases people accept the gender identity that matches their external appearance, which matches the way they were reared. However, some are dissatisfied with their assigned gender, and many would describe themselves as being masculine in some ways and feminine in others. Psychologists have long assumed that gender depends mainly or entirely on the way people rear their children. However, several kinds of evidence suggest that biological factors, especially prenatal hormones, are important also.

Intersexes

Some people have anatomies intermediate between male and female (Haqq & Donahoe, 1998). Individuals who appear to be a mixture of male and female are referred to as **hermaphrodites** (from Hermes and Aphrodite in Greek mythology). For example, some people are born with an XX chromosome pattern but an SRY gene that translocated from the father's Y chromosome onto another chromosome. Despite their XX chromosomes, they have either an ovary and a testis, or two testes, or a mixture of testis and ovary tissue on each side.

Others develop an intermediate appearance because of an atypical hormone pattern. Recall that testosterone masculinizes the genitals and the hypothalamus during early development. A genetic male with low levels of testosterone or a deficiency of testosterone receptors may develop a female or intermediate appearance (Misrahi et al., 1997). A genetic female who is exposed to more testosterone than the average female can be partly masculinized.

The most common cause of this condition is **congenital adrenal hyperplasia (CAH)**, meaning overdevelopment of the adrenal glands from birth. Ordinarily, the adrenal gland has a negative feedback relationship with the pituitary gland. The pituitary secretes adrenocorticotropic hormone (ACTH), which stimulates the adrenal gland. Cortisol, one of the hormones from the adrenal gland, feeds back to decrease the release of ACTH.

Accord Alliance

This group of intersexed people gathered to provide mutual support and to protest against the early surgical treatments they received. They requested that their names be used to emphasize that their intersexuality should not be considered shameful. From left to right: Martha Coventry, Max Beck, David Vandertie, Kristi Bruce, and Angela Moreno.

Some people have a genetic limitation in their ability to produce cortisol. Because the pituitary fails to receive much cortisol as a feedback signal, it continues secreting more ACTH, causing the adrenal gland to secrete larger amounts of its other hormones, including testosterone. In a genetic male, the extra testosterone causes no apparent difficulty. However, genetic females with this condition develop various degrees of masculinization of their external genitals. (The ovaries and other internal organs are less affected.) Figure 11.11 shows a structure that appears intermediate between clitoris and penis and swellings that appear intermediate between labia and scrotum. After birth, these children are given medical treatments to bring their adrenal hormones within normal levels. Some are also given surgery to alter their external genital appearance, as we shall discuss later.

People whose sexual development is intermediate, as in Figure 11.11, are called **intersexes**. How common are intersexes? An estimated 1 child in 100 in the United States is born with some degree of genital ambiguity, and 1 in 2,000 has enough ambiguity to make its male or female status uncertain (Blackless et al., 2000). However, the accuracy of these estimates is doubtful, as hospitals and families keep the information private. Maintaining confidentiality is of course important, but an unfortunate consequence is that intersexed people have trouble finding others like themselves. For more information, consult the website of the Intersex Society of North America (ISNA): http://www.isna.org/.

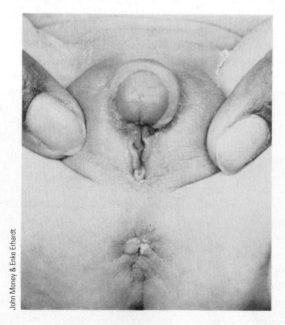

FIGURE 11.11 **External genitals of a genetic female, age 3 months**
The genitals were masculinized by excess androgens from the adrenal gland before birth. *(From Money, John and Ehrhardt, Anke A., Man and Woman, Boy and Girl: Differentiation and Dimorphism of Gender Identity from Conception to Maturity, p. 115, Figure 6.2. © 1972 The Johns Hopkins University Press. Reprinted by permission of The Johns Hopkins University Press.)*

STOP & CHECK

13. What is a common cause for a genetic female (XX) to develop a partly masculinized anatomy?

ANSWER 13. If a genetic female is genetically deficient in her ability to produce cortisol, the pituitary gland does not receive negative feedback signals and therefore continues stimulating the adrenal gland. The adrenal gland then produces large amounts of other hormones, including testosterone, which masculinizes development.

Interests and Preferences of CAH Girls

For many years, the policy was to raise most intersexed people as girls, on the assumption that surgery could make them look like normal girls, and they would develop behaviors corresponding to the way they were reared. However, their brains were exposed to higher than normal testosterone levels during prenatal and early postnatal life compared to other girls. Was their behavior masculinized? As discussed in the first module of this chapter, prenatal levels of testosterone correlate with girls' toy choices. The same idea applies here. In several studies, girls with CAH were observed in a room full of toys—including some that were girl typical (dolls, plates and dishes, cosmetics kits), some that were boy typical (toy car, tool set, gun), and some that were neutral (puzzles, crayons, board games). Figure 11.12 shows the results from one such study (Pasterski et al., 2005). Note how girls with CAH were intermediate between the preferences of boys and girls without CAH. When the children tested with a parent present, again the girls with CAH were intermediate between the other two groups.

Other studies have reported similar results and have found that the girls exposed to the largest amount of testosterone in early development showed the largest preference for boys' toys (Berenbaum, Duck, & Bryk, 2000; Nordenström, Servin, Bohlin, Larsson, & Wedell, 2002). You might wonder whether the parents, knowing that these girls had been partly masculinized in appearance, might have encouraged "tomboyish" activities. Psychologists' observations suggest the opposite: The parents encouraged the girls with CAH any time they played with girl-typical toys (Pasterski et al., 2005). A study of CAH girls in adolescence found that, on average, their interests are intermediate between those of typical male and female adolescents. For example, they read more sports magazines and fewer style and glamour magazines than the average for other teenage girls (Berenbaum, 1999). In adulthood, they show more physical aggression than most other women do, and less interest in infants (Mathews, Fane, Conway, Brook, & Hines, 2009). They are more interested in rough sports and more likely than average to be in heavily male-dominated occupations such as auto mechanic and truck driver (Frisén et al., 2009).

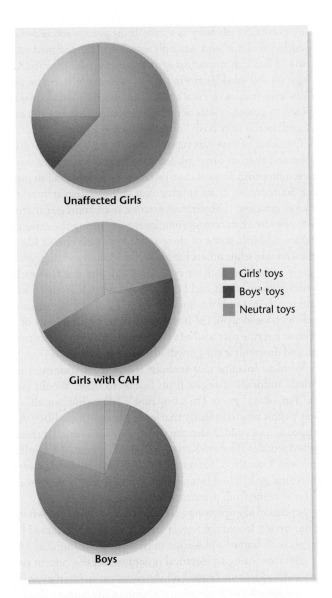

Girls' toys
Boys' toys
Neutral toys

Unaffected Girls

Girls with CAH

Boys

FIGURE 11.12 Toy preferences by CAH girls, unaffected girls, and unaffected boys
CAH girls were intermediate between unaffected girls and boys. These data show results when the children played alone. Results changed slightly when the mother or father was present, but in each case, the CAH girls were intermediate between the other groups. *(Based on data of Byne et al., 2001)*

STOP & CHECK

14. If a genetic female is exposed to extra testosterone during prenatal development, what behavioral effect is likely?

ANSWER

14. A girl who is exposed to extra testosterone during prenatal development is more likely than most other girls to prefer boy-typical toys.

Testicular Feminization

Certain individuals with an XY chromosome pattern have the genital appearance of a female. This condition is known as **androgen insensitivity**, or **testicular feminization**. Although such individuals produce normal amounts of androgens (including testosterone), they lack the receptor that enables androgen to activate genes in a cell's nucleus. Consequently, the cells are insensitive to androgens, and development proceeds as if the level of testosterone and similar hormones was low. This condition occurs in various degrees, resulting in anatomy that ranges from a smaller than average penis to genitals like those of a normal female. In some cases, no one has any reason to suspect the person is anything other than a normal female, until puberty. Then, in spite of breast development and broadening of the hips, menstruation does not begin because the body has internal testes instead of ovaries and a uterus. (The vagina is short and leads to nothing but skin.) Also, pubic hair is sparse or absent, because it depends on androgens in females as well as males.

STOP & CHECK

15. What would cause a genetic male (XY) to develop a partly feminized external anatomy?

ANSWER

15. A genetic male with a gene that prevents testosterone from binding to its receptors will develop an appearance that partly or completely resembles a female.

Issues of Gender Assignment and Rearing

Many girls with CAH and related conditions are born with a nearly normal appearance, but some look as much male as female and presumably were exposed to high levels of prenatal testosterone. Some genetic males are born with a very small penis because of a condition called *cloacal exstrophy*, a defect of pelvis development (Reiner & Gearhart, 2004). Despite their genital anatomy, they had typical male levels of testosterone in prenatal development.

How should children with either of these conditions be reared? Beginning in the 1950s, medical doctors began recommending that all intersexed people be reared as girls, using surgery if necessary to make their genitals look more feminine (Dreger, 1998). The reason was that it is easier to reduce an enlarged clitoris to normal size than expand it to penis size. If necessary, surgeons can build an artificial vagina or lengthen a short one. After the surgery, the child looks female. Physicians and psychologists assumed that any child who was consistently reared as a girl would fully accept that identity.

And she lives happily ever after, right? Not necessarily. Of those with cloacal exstrophy who are reared as girls, all develop typical male interests, many or most eventually demand reassignment as males, and nearly all develop sexual attraction toward women, not men (Reiner & Gearhart, 2004).

Girls with the CAH history also have a difficult adjustment, especially if they were subjected to clitoris-reduction surgery. A surgically created or lengthened vagina may be satisfactory to a male partner, but it provides no sensation to the woman and requires almost daily attention to prevent it from scarring over. Nearly all women with a history of CAH have significant sexual difficulties, including lack of orgasm. Many report no sexual partner ever, little or no interest in sex, and little or no romantic attraction to men (Frisén et al., 2009; Meyer-Bahlburg, Dolezal, Baker, & New, 2008; Minto, Liao, Woodhouse, Ransley, & Creighton, 2003; Nordenström et al., 2010; Zucker et al., 1996).

Many intersexes wish they had their original "abnormal" enlarged clitoris instead of the mutilated, insensitive structure left to them by a surgeon. Moreover, intersexes resent being deceived. Historian Alice Dreger (1998) describes the case of one intersex:

> As a young person, [she] was told she had "twisted ovaries" that had to be removed; in fact, her testes were removed. At the age of twenty, "alone and scared in the stacks of a [medical] library," she discovered the truth of her condition. Then "the pieces finally fit together. But what fell apart was my relationship with both my family and physicians. It was not learning about chromosomes or testes that caused enduring trauma, it was discovering that I had been told lies. I avoided all medical care for the next 18 years.... [The] greatest source of anxiety is not our gonads or karyotype. It is shame and fear resulting from an environment in which our condition is so unacceptable that caretakers lie." (p. 192)

How should such a child be reared? A growing number of specialists follow these recommendations (Diamond & Sigmundson, 1997):

- Be completely honest with the intersexed person and the family, and do nothing without their informed consent.
- Identify the child as male or female based mainly on the predominant external appearance. That is, there should be no bias toward calling every intersex a female. Those born with masculinized external genitals seldom make a successful adaptation to a female gender assignment (Houk & Lee, 2010).
- Rear the child as consistently as possible, but be prepared that the person might later be sexually oriented toward males, females, both, or neither.
- Do not perform surgery to reduce the ambiguous penis/clitoris to the size of a normal clitoris. Such surgery impairs the person's erotic sensation and is at best premature, as no one knows how the child's sexual orientation will develop. If the intersexed person makes an informed request for such surgery in adulthood, then it is appropriate, but otherwise it should be avoided.

Discrepancies of Sexual Appearance

The evidence from intersexes does not indisputably resolve the roles of rearing and hormones in determining gender identity. From a scientific viewpoint, the most decisive way to settle the issue would be to raise a normal male baby as a female or to raise a normal female baby as a male. If the process succeeded in producing an adult who was fully satisfied in the assigned role, we would know that upbringing determines gender identity. Although no one would perform such an experiment intentionally, we can learn from accidental events. In some cases, someone was exposed to a more-or-less normal pattern of male hormones before and shortly after birth but then reared as a girl.

One kind of case was reported first in the Dominican Republic and then in other places, usually in communities with much inbreeding. In each case, certain genetic males fail to produce 5α-*reductase* 2, an enzyme that converts testosterone to *dihydrotestosterone*. Dihydrotestosterone is an androgen that is more effective than testosterone for masculinizing the external genitals. At birth, some of these individuals look almost like a typical female, while others have a swollen clitoris and somewhat "lumpy" labia. Nearly all are considered girls and reared as such. However, their brains had been exposed to male levels of testosterone during early development. At puberty, the testosterone levels increase sharply, the body makes increased amounts of a different enzyme that converts testosterone to dihydrotestosterone, and the result is the growth of a penis and scrotum.

Women: Imagine that at about age 12 years, your external genitals suddenly changed from female to male. Would you say, "Yep, okay, I guess I'm a boy now"? Most (but not all) of these people reacted exactly that way. The girl-turned-boy developed a male gender identity and directed his sexual interest toward females (Cohen-Kettenis, 2005; Imperato-McGinley, Guerrero, Gautier, & Peterson, 1974). Remember, these were not typical girls. Their brains had been exposed to male levels of testosterone from prenatal life onward.

A particularly upsetting case is that of one infant boy whose penis foreskin would not retract enough for easy urination. His parents took him to a physician to circumcise the foreskin, but the physician, using an electrical procedure, set the current too high and accidentally burned off the entire penis. On the advice of respected and well-meaning authorities, the parents elected to rear the child as a female, with the appropriate surgery. What makes this case especially interesting is that the child had a twin brother (whom the parents did not let the physician try to circumcise). If both twins developed satisfactory gender identities, one as a girl and the other as a boy, the results would say that rearing was decisive in gender identity.

Initial reports claimed that the child reared as a girl had a female gender identity, though she also had strong tomboyish tendencies (Money & Schwartz, 1978). However, by about age 10, she had figured out that something was wrong and that "she" was really a boy. She had preferred boys' activities and played only with boys' toys. She even tried urinating in a standing position, despite always making a mess. By age 14, she insisted that she wanted to live as a boy. At that time, her (now his) father tearfully explained the earlier events. The child changed names and became known as a boy. At age 25, he married a somewhat older woman and adopted her children. Clearly, a biological predisposition had won out over the family's attempts to rear the child as a girl (Colapinto, 1997; Diamond & Sigmundson, 1997). Some years later, the story ended tragically with this man's suicide.

We should not draw universal conclusions from a single case. However, the point is that it was a mistake to impose surgery and hormonal treatments to try to force this child to become female. When the prenatal hormone pattern of the brain is in conflict with a child's appearance, no one can be sure how that child will develop psychologically. Hormones don't have complete control, but rearing patterns don't, either.

STOP & CHECK

16. When "girls" reached puberty and grew a penis and scrotum, what happened to their gender identity?

ANSWER

16. Most changed their gender identity from female to male.

Sexual Orientation

Contrary to what biologists once assumed, homosexual behavior occurs in many animal species, and not just in captive animals, those that cannot find a member of the opposite sex, or those with hormonal abnormalities (Bagemihl, 1999). If "natural" means "occurs in nature," then homosexuality is natural.

What accounts for differences in sexual orientation? Many influences appear to be important, including genetics, prenatal environment, and as-yet unidentified aspects of experience. The explanations will probably be different for different people, and in general different for men than for women. Whereas most men discover their sexual orientation early, many women are slower. Feminine-type behaviors in childhood and adolescence correlate strongly with homosexual orientation in adulthood for men (Cardoso, 2009; Alanko et al., 2010), but early masculine-type behaviors are poor predictors of sexual orientation in women (Udry & Chantala, 2006). A higher percentage of women than men experience at least some physical attraction to both males and females (Chivers, Rieger, Latty, & Bailey, 2004; Lippa, 2006), and some women switch—once or more—between homosexual and heterosexual orientations (Diamond, 2007). Switches in sexual orientation are rare in men. Although we shall note certain biological correlates of female homosexuality, the case for a biological predisposition seems stronger for men.

Behavioral and Anatomical Differences

On average, homosexual and heterosexual people differ anatomically in several ways. On average, heterosexual men are slightly taller and heavier than homosexual men (Bogaert, 2010). However, let's emphasize that term "slightly": The difference on average is only 1.5 cm (about half an inch). Despite the stereotype, a fair number of homosexual men are tall, athletic, and masculine in appearance.

On average, people who differ in sexual orientation also differ in several behaviors that are not directly related to sex. More men than women give directions in terms of distances and north, south, east, or west. Women are more likely to describe landmarks. Gay men also tend to use landmarks and are better than heterosexual men at remembering landmarks (Hassan & Rahman, 2007). Consider this task: Experimenters repeatedly present a loud noise and measure the startle response. On some trials, they present a weaker noise just before the loud noise; the first noise decreases the startle response to the louder one. The decrease is called "prepulse inhibition." Prepulse inhibition is ordinarily stronger in men than in women. In this regard, homosexual women are slightly shifted in the male direction compared to heterosexual women (Rahman, Kumari, & Wilson, 2003).

Genetics

Studies of the genetics of sexual orientation have focused mainly on twins. Early studies of the genetics of human sexual orientation began by advertising in gay or lesbian publications for homosexual people with twins. Then they contacted the other twin to fill out a questionnaire. The questionnaire included diverse items to conceal the fact that the real interest was sexual orientation. The results showed a stronger concordance for monozygotic than dizygotic twins (Bailey & Pillard, 1991; Bailey, Pillard, Neale, & Agyei, 1993). That is, if one twin is homosexual, the probability for the other to be homosexual is fairly high for a monozygotic twin, and less high for a dizygotic twin. However, the kind of person who answers an ad in a gay or lesbian magazine may not be representative of others. A later study examined the data from all the twins in Sweden between ages 20 and 47 (Långström, Rahman, Carlström, & Lichtenstein, 2010). The Swedish study differed not only in the breadth of the sample but also in the behavioral criterion. Instead of asking about sexual orientation, the researchers asked whether someone had ever had a same-sex partner. Figure 11.13 compares the data from the two studies. The results do not indicate total number of people with homosexual activity or orientation. Rather, they indicate concordance—the probability of homosexual activity or orientation in one twin, given that the other twin had already indicated such activity. Although both sets of results show a higher concordance for monozygotic than dizygotic twins, note the huge difference between the studies. From these data it is reasonable to infer a genetic contribution to sexual orientation, but we can't be sure about the size of that contribution.

Several studies reported a higher incidence of homosexuality among the maternal than paternal relatives of homosexual men (Camperio-Ciani, Corna, & Capiluppi, 2004; Hamer, Hu, Magnuson, Hu, & Pattatucci, 1993). For example, uncles and cousins on the mother's side were more likely to be homosexual than uncles and cousins on the father's side. These results suggest a gene on the X chromosome, which a man necessarily receives from his mother. However, other studies have not replicated these results, and the current status is inconclusive (Bailey et al., 1999; Rice, Anderson, Risch, & Ebers, 1999).

An Evolutionary Question

If certain genes promote a homosexual orientation, why hasn't evolution selected strongly against those genes, which de-

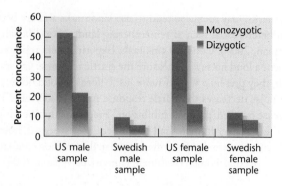

FIGURE 11.13 Twin concordance for homosexuality
The concordance for homosexual orientation (U.S. study) or homosexual activity (Swedish study) was higher for monozygotic twins than for dizygotic twins. *(Based on the data of Bailey & Pillard, 1991; Bailey, Pillard, Neale, & Agyei, 1993; Långström, Rahman, Carlström, & Lichtenstein, 2010)*

crease the probability of reproduction? Several possibilities are worth considering (Gavrilets & Rice, 2006). One is that genes for homosexuality are maintained by kin selection, as discussed in Chapter 1. That is, even if homosexual people do not have children themselves, they might do a wonderful job of helping their brothers and sisters rear children. Survey data in the United States indicate that homosexual men are no more likely than heterosexuals, and perhaps less likely, to help support their relatives (Bobrow & Bailey, 2001). However, observations in Samoa found that homosexual men are more helpful than average toward their nephews and nieces (Vasey & VanderLaan, 2010). It is difficult to know what might have been the usual pattern through human existence.

According to a second hypothesis, genes that produce homosexuality in males produce advantageous effects in their sisters and other female relatives, increasing their probability of reproducing and spreading the genes. The results of one study support this hypothesis. Homosexual men's mothers and aunts had a greater than average number of children (Camperio-Ciani et al., 2004). However, a common estimate is that the average homosexual man has one fifth as many children as the average heterosexual man. Could his female relatives have enough children to compensate for this decrease? It seems unlikely.

A third hypothesis is that certain genes lead to homosexuality in men homozygous for the gene but produce reproductive advantages in men heterozygous for the gene (Rahman & Wilson, 2003). A closely related idea is that several genes produce advantages for survival or reproduction, but a combination of them leads to homosexuality.

A fourth idea is that homosexuality relates to the activation or inactivation of genes (Bocklandt, Horvath, Vilain, & Hamer, 2006). As mentioned in Chapter 1, it is possible for environmental events to attach a methyl group (CH_3) to a gene and inactivate it. A parent can pass the inactivation of a gene to the next generation. Conceivably, this mechanism might produce a significant amount of homosexuality without relying on the spread of a gene that promotes homosexuality.

▶ STOP & CHECK

17. For which kind of twin pair is the concordance for sexual orientation greatest?

18. It seems difficult to explain how a gene could remain at a moderately high frequency in the population if most men with the gene do not reproduce. How would the hypothesis about inactivation by a methyl group help with the explanation?

ANSWERS

17. Monozygotic twins have higher concordance than dizygotic twins. Note the importance of stating this point correctly: Do *not* say that homosexuality is more common in monozygotic than dizygotic twins. It is the *concordance* that is greater—that is, the probability that both twins have the same sexual orientation. **18.** According to this hypothesis, some unknown event in the environment can attach a methyl group to some unidentified gene, inactivating the gene. That gene could be passed to the next generation, producing evidence for a hereditary effect, even though there is no "gene for homosexuality." If this event of attaching a methyl group to that gene happens often enough, the result could be a moderately high prevalence of homosexuality, even if men with the inactivated gene seldom reproduce.

Prenatal Influences

Adult hormone levels do *not* explain sexual orientation. On average, homosexual and heterosexual men have nearly the same hormone levels, and most lesbian women have about the same hormone levels as heterosexual women. However, it is possible that sexual orientation depends on testosterone levels during a sensitive period of brain development (Ellis & Ames, 1987). Animal studies have shown that prenatal or early postnatal hormones can produce organizing effects on both anatomy and sexual behavior. External anatomy develops at a different time from brain anatomy, and so it is possible for hormones to alter one differently from the other.

The mother's immune system may exert prenatal effects. Several studies (though not all) report that the probability of a homosexual orientation is slightly higher among men who have older brothers. Younger brothers make no difference, nor do younger or older sisters (Bogaert, 2003b; Purcell, Blanchard, & Zucker, 2000). Furthermore, what matters is the number of *biological* older brothers. Growing up with older stepbrothers or adopted brothers has no apparent influence. Having a biological older brother has an influence, even if the brothers were reared separately (Bogaert, 2006). In short, the influence does not stem from social experiences. The key is how many previous times the mother gave birth to a son. The most prominent hypothesis is that a mother's immune system sometimes reacts against a protein in a son and then attacks subsequent sons enough to alter their development. That hypothesis fits with the observation that later-born homosexual men tend to be shorter than average (Bogaert, 2003a).

Another aspect of prenatal environment relates to stress on the mother during pregnancy. Research has shown that prenatal stress alters sexual development in laboratory animals. In several experiments, rats in the final week of pregnancy had the stressful experience of confinement in tight Plexiglas tubes for more than 2 hours each day under bright lights. In some cases, they were given alcohol as well. These rats' daughters looked and acted approximately normal. The sons, however, had normal male anatomy but in adulthood often responded to the presence of another male by arching their backs in the typical rat female posture for sex (I. L. Ward, Ward, Winn, & Bielawski, 1994). Most males that were subjected to either prenatal stress or alcohol developed male sexual behavior in addition to these female sexual behaviors, but those that were subjected to both stress and alcohol had decreased male sexual behaviors (I. L. Ward, Bennett, Ward, Hendricks, & French, 1999).

Prenatal stress and alcohol may alter brain development through several routes. Stress releases endorphins, which can antagonize the effects of testosterone on the hypothalamus (O. B. Ward, Monaghan, & Ward, 1986). Stress also elevates levels of the adrenal hormone corticosterone, which decreases testosterone release (O. B. Ward, Ward, Denning, French, & Hendricks, 2002; M. T. Williams, Davis, McCrea, Long, & Hennessy, 1999). The long-term effects of either prenatal stress or alcohol include several changes in the structure of the nervous system, making the affected males' anatomy closer to that of females (Nosenko & Reznikov, 2001; I. L. Ward, Romeo, Denning, & Ward, 1999).

Although the relevance of these results to humans is uncertain, they prompted investigators to examine possible effects of prenatal stress on humans. One approach is to ask the mothers of homosexual men whether they experienced any unusual stress during pregnancy. Three surveys compared mothers of homosexual sons to mothers of heterosexual sons. In two of the three, the mothers of homosexual sons recalled more than average stressful experiences during their pregnancies (Bailey, Willerman, & Parks, 1991; Ellis, Ames, Peckham, & Burke, 1988; Ellis & Cole-Harding, 2001). However, these studies relied on women's memories of pregnancies more than 20 years earlier. A better but more difficult procedure would be to measure stress during pregnancy and examine the sexual orientation of the sons many years later.

STOP & CHECK

19. By what route might having an older brother increase the probability of male homosexuality?

20. How might stress to a pregnant rat alter the sexual orientation of her male offspring?

ANSWERS **19.** Having an older brother might increase the probability of male homosexuality by altering the mother's immune system in the prenatal environment. The effect of the older brother does not depend on growing up in the same home. **20.** Evidently, stress increases the release of endorphins in the hypothalamus, and very high endorphin levels can block the effects of testosterone.

Brain Anatomy

Do brains also differ as a function of sexual orientation? The results are complex. On average, homosexual men are shifted partly in the female-typical direction for some brain structures but not others. Similarly, on average, homosexual women's brains are slightly shifted in the male direction in some ways but not others (Rahman & Wilson, 2003). Several of the reported differences have no clear relationship to sexuality itself, although they may relate to other behavioral differences between heterosexual and homosexual people.

On average, the left and right hemispheres of the cerebral cortex are of nearly equal size in heterosexual females, whereas the right hemisphere is a few percent larger in heterosexual males. Homosexual males resemble heterosexual females in this regard, and homosexual females are intermediate between heterosexual females and males. Also, in heterosexual females the left amygdala has more widespread connections than the right amygdala, whereas in heterosexual males the right amygdala has more widespread connections. Again, homosexual males resemble heterosexual females in this regard, and homosexual females are intermediate (Savic & Lindström, 2008). The anterior commissure (Figures 4.13 and 14.5) is, on average, larger in heterosexual women than in heterosexual men. In homosexual men, it is at least as large as in women, perhaps even slightly larger (Gorski & Allen, 1992). The suprachiasmatic nucleus (SCN) is also larger in homosexual men than in heterosexual men (Swaab & Hofman, 1990). However, when interpreting these and other reported differences, we should remember two cautions (Kaiser, Haller, Schmitz, & Nitsch, 2009): First, we don't know whether these brain differences are causes or effects of sexual orientation. Brain differences can predispose to different behaviors, but it is also true, as discussed in Chapter 5, that persistent behaviors can change brain anatomy. Second, it is relatively easy to publish results showing a difference between two groups, such as homosexual and heterosexual people, even if the difference was unpredicted, small, and hard to explain. It is less easy to publish results showing no difference. Thus it is possible that the published papers overstate certain anatomical differences.

The most widely cited research concerns the third interstitial nucleus of the anterior hypothalamus (INAH-3), which is generally more than twice as large in heterosexual men as in women. This area has more cells with androgen receptors in men than in women (Shah et al., 2004) and probably plays a role in sexual behavior, although the exact role is uncertain. Simon LeVay (1991) examined INAH-3 in 41 people who had died between the ages of 26 and 59. Of these, 16 were heterosexual men, 6 were heterosexual women, and 19 were homosexual men. All of the homosexual men, 6 of the 16 heterosexual men, and 1 of the 6 women had died of AIDS. LeVay found that the mean volume of INAH-3 was larger in heterosexual men than in heterosexual women or homosexual men, who were about equal in this regard. Figure 11.14 shows typical cross-sections for a heterosexual man and a homosexual man. Figure 11.15 shows the distribution of volumes for the three

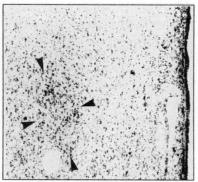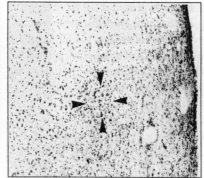

FIGURE 11.14 Typical sizes of interstitial nucleus 3 of the anterior hypothalamus
On average, the volume of this structure was more than twice as large in a sample of heterosexual men (left) than in a sample of homosexual men (right), for whom it was about the same size as in women. *(From "A difference in hypothalamic structure between heterosexual and homosexual men," S. LeVay, Science, 253, pp. 1034–1037. Copyright 1991. Reprinted by permission from AAAS.)*

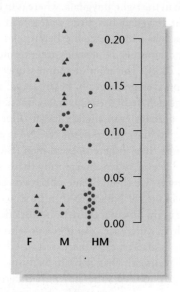

FIGURE 11.15 Volumes of the interstitial nucleus 3 of the anterior hypothalamus (INAH-3)
Samples are females (F), heterosexual males (M), and homosexual males (HM). Each filled circle represents a person who died of AIDS, and each triangle represents a person who died from other causes. The one open circle represents a bisexual man who died of AIDS. *(Reprinted by permission from "A difference in hypothalamic structure between heterosexual and homosexual men," by S. LeVay, Science, 253, pp. 1034–1037. Copyright © 1991 American Association for the Advancement of Science.)*

man's INAH-3, you could make a reasonable guess about sexual orientation, but you could not be confident.

A later study partly replicated these trends. Researchers found that the INAH-3 nucleus was slightly larger in heterosexual than homosexual men, although in this study the homosexual men's INAH-3 nucleus was larger than that of heterosexual women (Byne et al., 2001). Among heterosexual men or women, the INAH-3 nucleus was larger in those who were HIV negative than those who were HIV positive, but even if we look only at HIV+ men, we still find a difference in the hypothalamus between heterosexual and homosexual men. Figure 11.16 displays the means for the five groups. On microscopic examination of the INAH-3, researchers found that heterosexual men had larger neurons than homosexual men but about the same number. (Neither this study nor LeVay's earlier study included homosexual females.) Still another study found INAH-3 to be larger in heterosexual males than in male-to-female transsexuals—that is, people

groups. Note that the difference between heterosexual men and the other two groups is fairly large, on average, and that the cause of death (AIDS versus other) has no clear relationship to the results. LeVay (1993) later examined the hypothalamus of a homosexual man who died of lung cancer; he had a small INAH-3, like the homosexual men who died of AIDS. In Figure 11.15, note also the substantial amount of difference among individuals. If you could examine some

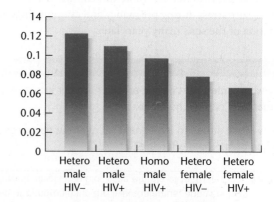

FIGURE 11.16 Another comparison of INAH-3
In this study, the mean volume for homosexual men was larger than that of women but smaller than that of heterosexual men. *(Based on data of Byne et al., 2001)*

born as males who changed their identities to female (Garcia-Falgueras & Swaab, 2008).

The meaning of these results is not clear. Do differences in the hypothalamus influence sexual orientation, or does sexual activity influence the size of hypothalamic neurons? Some brain areas do grow or shrink in adults because of hormones or behavioral activities (Cooke, Tabibnia, & Breedlove, 1999). Studies of nonhumans offer suggestive results. About 8% of rams (male sheep) direct their sexual behavior toward other males. One area of the anterior hypothalamus was larger in female-oriented rams than in male-oriented rams and larger in them than in females (Roselli, Larkin, Resko, Stellflug, & Stormshak, 2004). (Whether this area corresponds to human INAH-3 is uncertain.) This area becomes larger in male than female sheep before birth as a result of prenatal testosterone levels (Roselli, Stadelman, Reeve, Bishop, & Stormshak, 2007). In sheep, at least, an anatomical difference appears before any sexual behavior, and so it is more likely a cause than a result. The same may or may not be true in humans.

> **STOP & CHECK**

21. In LeVay's study, what evidence argues against the idea that INAH-3 volume depends on AIDS rather than sexual orientation?

ANSWER 21. The average size of INAH-3 was about the same for heterosexual men who died of AIDS and those who died of other causes. One homosexual man who died of other causes had about the same size INAH-3 as heterosexual men who died of AIDS.

MODULE 11.2 ■ IN CLOSING

We Are Not All the Same

When Alfred Kinsey conducted the first massive surveys of human sexual behavior, he found that most of the people he interviewed considered their own behavior "normal," whatever it was. Many believed that sexual activity much more frequent than their own was excessive and abnormal and might even lead to insanity (Kinsey, Pomeroy, & Martin, 1948; Kinsey, Pomeroy, Martin, & Gebhard, 1953).

How far have we come since then? People today are more aware of sexual diversity than they were in Kinsey's time and generally more accepting. Still, intolerance remains common. Biological research will not tell us how to treat one another, but it can help us understand how we come to be so different.

SUMMARY

1. In many species, males and females evolve different appearances and behaviors because of sexual selection. That is, they evolve in ways that make them more appealing to the other sex. **341**

2. Many of the mating habits of people can be interpreted in terms of increasing the probability of passing on our genes. However, it is hard to know how many of the differences between men and women are evolutionary adaptations and how many are learned. **341**

3. People can develop ambiguous genitals or genitals that don't match their chromosomal sex for several reasons. One is congenital adrenal hyperplasia, in which a genetic defect in cortisol production leads to overstimulation of the adrenal gland and therefore extra testosterone production. When that condition occurs in a female fetus, she becomes partly masculinized. **343**

4. On average, girls with a history of congenital adrenal hyperplasia show more interest in boy-typical toys than other girls do, and during adolescence and young adulthood, they continue to show partly masculinized interests. **344**

5. Testicular feminization, or androgen insensitivity, is a condition in which someone with an XY chromosome pattern is partly or fully insensitive to androgens and therefore develops a female external appearance. **345**

6. People born with intermediate or ambiguous genitals are called intersexes. For many years, physicians recommended surgery to make these people look more feminine. However, many intersexed people do not develop an unambiguous female identity, and many protest against the imposed surgery. **345**

7. Some children have a gene that decreases their early production of dihydrotestosterone. Such a child looks female at birth and is considered a girl but develops a penis at adolescence. Most of these people then accept a male gender identity. **346**

8. On average, homosexual people differ from heterosexual people in several anatomical and physiological regards, although the averages do not apply to every individual. **347**

9. Plausible biological explanations for homosexual orientation include genetics, prenatal hormones, and (in males)

reactions to the mother's immune system. Hormone levels in adulthood are within the normal range.   **347**

10. Several hypotheses have been offered for how genes promoting homosexuality could remain at moderate frequencies in the population when most homosexual people do not have children.   **347**

11. On average, certain aspects of brain anatomy differ between homosexual and heterosexual men, although it is not certain whether these differences are causes or effects of the behavior.   **349**

KEY TERMS

Terms are defined in the module on the page number indicated. They're also presented in alphabetical order with definitions in the book's Subject Index/Glossary, which begins on page 561. Interactive flashcards and crossword puzzles are among the online resources available to help you learn these terms and the concepts they represent.

androgen insensitivity   **345**

congenital adrenal
   hyperplasia   **343**

gender identity   **343**

hermaphrodite   **343**

intersex   **344**

sexual selection   **341**

testicular feminization   **345**

THOUGHT QUESTION

1. On average, intersexes have IQ scores in the 110 to 125 range, well above the mean for the population (Dalton, 1968; Ehrhardt & Money, 1967; Lewis, Money, & Epstein, 1968). One possible interpretation is that a hormonal pattern intermediate between male and female promotes great intellectual development. Another possibility is that intersexuality may be more common in intelligent families than in less intelligent ones or that the more intelligent families are more likely to bring their intersexed children to an investi-gator's attention. What kind of study would be best for deciding among these hypotheses? (For one answer, see Money & Lewis, 1966.)

2. Recall LeVay's study of brain anatomy in heterosexual and homosexual men. Certain critics have suggested that one or more of the men classified as "heterosexual" might actually have been homosexual or bisexual. If so, would that fact strengthen or weaken the overall conclusions?

CHAPTER 11 Interactive Exploration and Study

The **Psychology CourseMate** for this text brings chapter topics to life with interactive learning, study, and exam preparation tools, including quizzes and flashcards for the Key Concepts that appear throughout each module, as well as an interactive media-rich eBook version of the text that is fully searchable and includes highlighting and note taking capabilities and inter-active versions of the book's **Stop & Check** quizzes and **Try It Yourself Online** activities. The site also features **Virtual Biological Psychology Labs, videos,** and **animations** to help you better understand concepts—logon and learn more at **www.cengagebrain.com**, which is your gateway to all of this text's complimentary and premium resources, including the following:

Virtual Biological Psychology Labs

Explore the experiments that led to modern-day understanding of biopsychology with the Virtual Biological Psychology Labs, featuring a realistic lab environment that allows you to conduct experiments and evaluate data to better understand how scientists came to the conclu-sions presented in your text. The labs cover a range of topics, including perception, motivation, cognition, and more. You may purchase access at **www.cengagebrain.com**, or login at **login.cengagebrain.com** if an access card was included with your text.

Videos

Erectile Dysfunction

Animations

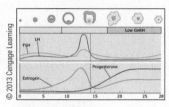

Menstrual Cycle

Suggestions for Further Exploration

Books

Colapinto, J. (2000). *As nature made him: The boy who was raised as a girl.* New York: HarperCollins. Describes the boy whose penis was accidentally removed.

Diamond, J. (1997). *Why is sex fun?* New York: Basic Books. Human sexual behavior differs from that of other species in many ways and therefore raises many evolutionary issues, which this book addresses. For example, why do humans have sex at times when the woman cannot become pregnant? Why do women have menopause? Why don't men breast-feed their babies? And what good are men, anyway? If you haven't thought about such questions before, you should read this book.

LeVay, S. (2011). *Gay, straight, and the reason why.* New York: Oxford University Press. A scientific discussion of the research concerning the factors that influence sexual orientation.

Websites

The Psychology CourseMate for this text provides regularly updated links to relevant online resources for this chapter, such as **The Endocrine Society** and the **Intersex Society of America**.

Emotional Behaviors

MAIN IDEAS

1. Emotions include cognitions, actions, and feelings. Several kinds of evidence support the theory that emotional feelings result from actions of the muscles or organs.

2. Many brain areas contribute to emotions. It is not clear that different emotions are localized differently in the brain.

3. Aggressive and fearful behaviors represent the combined outcome of many biological and environmental influences.

4. The amygdala responds quickly to emotional stimuli. Damage to the amygdala interferes with attention to information that is relevant to emotions.

OPPOSITE: People express emotions by facial expressions, gestures, and postures.

5. Stressful events arouse the sympathetic nervous system and later the adrenal cortex. Prolonged or severe stress produces many of the same bodily responses that illness does.

We know the meaning [of consciousness] so long as no one asks us to define it.

William James (1892/1961, p. 19)

Unfortunately, one of the most significant things ever said about emotion may be that everyone knows what it is until they are asked to define it.

Joseph LeDoux (1996, p. 23)

Suppose researchers have discovered a new species—let's call it species X—and psychologists begin testing its abilities. They place food behind a green card and nothing behind a red card and find that after a few trials, X always goes to the green card. So we conclude that X shows learning, memory, and hunger. Then researchers offer X a green card and a variety of gray cards; X still goes to the green, so it must have color vision and not just brightness discrimination. Next they let X touch a blue triangle that is extremely hot. X makes a loud sound and backs away. Someone picks up the blue triangle (with padded gloves) and starts moving with it rapidly toward X. As soon as X sees this happening, it makes the same sound, turns, and starts moving rapidly away. Shall we conclude that it feels fear?

If you said yes, now let me add: I said this was a new species, and so it is, but it's a new species of robot, not animal. Do you still think X feels fear? Most people are willing to talk about artificial learning, memory, intelligence, and motivation, but not emotion.

If such behavior isn't adequate evidence for emotion in a robot, is it adequate evidence for an animal? Emotion is a difficult topic because it implies conscious feelings that we cannot observe. Biological researchers therefore concentrate mostly on emotional *behaviors*, which are observable, even if the emotional feelings are not. Still, most of us eventually hope to learn something about the emotional experiences themselves.

What Is Emotion?

By one definition, emotion includes "cognitive evaluations, subjective changes, autonomic and neural arousal, and impulses to action" (Plutchik, 1982, p. 551). That sounds okay, but by that definition, don't hunger and thirst count as emotions? One definition of motivation is "an internal process that modifies the way an organism responds to a certain class of external stimuli" (Numan & Woodside, 2010). By that definition, don't happiness, sadness, fear, and anger count as motivations? Distinguishing between motivation and emotion is difficult, and possibly not worth the effort. Still, the term *emotion* provides a convenient category to discuss some important, interesting topics.

Regardless of how we word the definition, or whether we define it at all, psychologists generally agree that emotion has three components—cognitions ("This is a dangerous situation"), feelings ("I feel frightened"), and actions ("Run for the nearest exit"). Of these, feelings are the most central to our concept of emotion. If someone reports feeling frightened, we attribute emotion to that person at once. However, if someone coolly calculates, "This is a dangerous situation," but feels no tenseness or arousal, we would be less inclined to attribute emotion. What are emotional feelings, what causes them, and what function do they serve?

Emotions, Autonomic Arousal, and the James-Lange Theory

Emotional situations arouse the autonomic nervous system, which has two branches—the sympathetic and the parasympathetic (Figure 12.1). Walter Cannon was the first to understand that the sympathetic nervous system prepares the body for brief, vigorous "fight-or-flight" responses. The parasympathetic nervous system increases digestion and other processes that save energy and prepare for later events. However, each situation evokes its own special mixture of sympathetic and parasympathetic arousal (Wolf, 1995). For example, nausea is associated with sympathetic stimulation of the stomach (decreasing its contractions and secretions) and parasympathetic stimulation of the intestines and salivary glands.

How does the autonomic nervous system relate to emotions? Common sense holds that first you feel an emotion,

Walter B. Cannon (1871–1945)

As a matter of routine I have long trusted unconscious processes to serve me.... [One] example I may cite was the interpretation of the significance of bodily changes which occur in great emotional excitement, such as fear and rage. These changes—the more rapid pulse, the deeper breathing, the increase of sugar in the blood, the secretion from the adrenal glands—were very diverse and seemed unrelated. Then, one wakeful night, after a considerable collection of these changes had been disclosed, the idea flashed through my mind that they could be nicely integrated if conceived as bodily preparations for supreme effort in flight or in fighting.

which then changes your heart rate and prompts other responses. In contrast, according to the **James-Lange theory** (James, 1884), the autonomic arousal and skeletal actions come first. What you experience as an emotion is the label you give to your responses: You feel afraid *because* you run away; you feel angry *because* you attack.

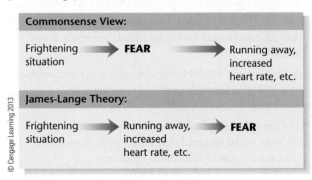

You might object, "How would I know to run away before I was scared?" In a later paper, William James (1894) clarified his position. An emotion has three components: cognitions, actions, and feelings. The cognitive aspect comes first. You quickly appraise something as good, bad, frightening, or whatever. Your appraisal of the situation leads to an appropriate

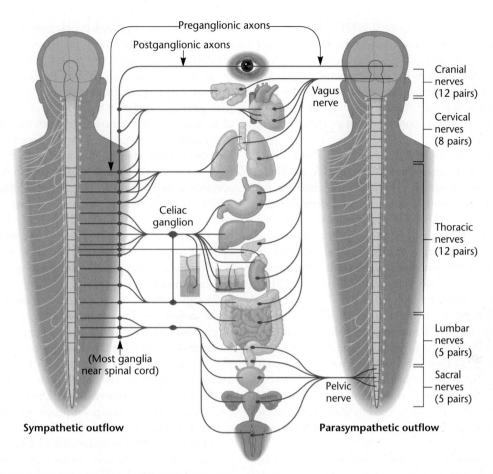

FIGURE 12.1 The sympathetic and parasympathetic nervous systems
Review Chapter 4 for more information. (© Cengage Learning 2013)

action, such as running away, attacking, or sitting motionless with your heart racing. When William James said that arousal and actions led to emotions, he meant the *feeling* aspect of an emotion. That is,

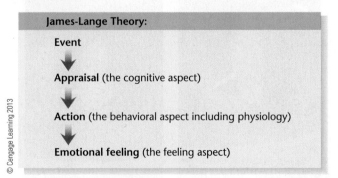

James-Lange Theory:

Event
↓
Appraisal (the cognitive aspect)
↓
Action (the behavioral aspect including physiology)
↓
Emotional feeling (the feeling aspect)

If a feeling is a kind of sensation, it is hard to know where the sensation would come from if not from some change in the body. Nevertheless, we want to test the idea. The James-Lange theory leads to two predictions: People with weak autonomic or skeletal responses should feel less emotion, and causing or increasing someone's responses should enhance an emotion. Let's consider the evidence.

Is Physiological Arousal *Necessary* for Emotions?

People with damage to the spinal cord are paralyzed from the level of the damage downward. People who cannot move their arms and legs certainly cannot attack or run away. Most of them report that they feel emotions about the same as before their injury (Cobos, Sánchez, Pérez, & Vila, 2004). This finding indicates that emotions do not require feedback from muscle movements. However, paralysis does not affect the autonomic nervous system, so it remains possible that emotional feelings depend on feedback from autonomic responses.

In people with an uncommon condition called **pure autonomic failure**, output from the autonomic nervous system to the body fails, either completely or almost completely. Heartbeat and other organ activities continue, but the nervous system no longer regulates them. Someone with this condition does not react to stressful experiences with changes in heart rate, blood pressure, or sweating. According to the James-Lange theory, we would expect such people to report no emotions. In fact, they report "having" the same emotions as anyone else. They have little difficulty identifying what emotion a character in a story would probably experience (Heims,

Critchley, Dolan, Mathias, & Cipolotti, 2004). However, they say they *feel* their emotions much less intensely than before (Critchley, Mathias, & Dolan, 2001). Presumably, when they report emotions, they refer to the cognitive aspect: "Yes, I'm angry, because this is a situation that calls for anger." But they do not *feel* the anger, or if they do, they feel it weakly. Their decreased emotional feeling is consistent with predictions from the James-Lange theory.

Here is another example: Botulinum toxin ("BOTOX") blocks transmission at synapses and nerve-muscle junctions. Physicians sometimes use it to paralyze the muscles for frowning and thereby remove frown lines on people's faces. One result is that people become slightly slower at reading unhappy sentences. Ordinarily, when people read something unpleasant, they frown just a bit. Evidently an inability to frown interferes with processing unpleasant information (Havas, Glenberg, Gutowski, Lucarelli, & Davidson, 2010). A related study examined people with BOTOX injections that temporarily paralyzed all the facial muscles. These people reported weaker than usual emotional responses when they watched short videos (Davis, Senghas, Brandt, & Ochsner, 2010). Another study found that people with brain damage that prevents voluntary facial movements have trouble recognizing other people's emotional expressions, especially expressions of fear (Pistoia et al., 2010). The implication of all these studies is that feeling a body change is important for feeling an emotion.

Evidence pointing away from this conclusion comes from a study of people with two kinds of brain damage. People with damage to the right somatosensory cortex had normal autonomic responses to emotional music but reported little subjective experience. People with damage to part of the prefrontal cortex had weak autonomic responses but normal subjective responses (Johnson, Tranel, Lutgendorf, & Adolphs, 2009). However, it was not clear whether people's reports of their "emotional experience" accurately recorded the feeling aspect of emotion, as opposed to the cognitive aspect.

Is Physiological Arousal *Sufficient* for Emotions?

According to the James-Lange theory, emotional feelings result from the body's actions. If your heart started racing and you started sweating and breathing rapidly, would you feel an emotion? Well, it depends. If you had those responses because you ran a mile, you would attribute your feelings to the exercise, not emotion. However, if they occurred spontaneously, you might indeed interpret your increased sympathetic nervous system arousal as fear. Rapid breathing in particular makes people worry that they are suffocating, and they experience a **panic attack**, marked by extreme sympathetic nervous system arousal (Klein, 1993).

What about other emotions? For example, if you find yourself smiling, do you become happier? To test this hypothesis, how could we get people to smile? Yes, of course, we could tell them to smile. However, if we tell people to smile and then

ask whether they are happy, people guess what the experiment is about and say what they think we want to hear. Clever researchers found a way to get people to smile while concealing the purpose of the study. It is a method you could easily try yourself: Hold a pen in your mouth, either with your teeth or with your lips, as shown in Figure 12.2. Now examine a page of newspaper comic strips. Mark each one + for very funny, ✓ for somewhat funny, or − for not funny. Most people rate cartoons funnier when holding a pen with their teeth—which forces a smile—than when holding it with their lips—which prevents a smile (Strack, Martin, & Stepper, 1988). That is, the sensation of smiling increases happiness, although only slightly. (Telling a depressed person to cheer up and smile does not help.)

Researchers also found a clever way to ask people to frown without saying so. They said they wanted to test people's ability to do a cognitive task and a motor task at the same time. The cognitive task was to examine photographs and rate their pleasantness or unpleasantness. For the motor task, researchers attached golf tees to each of the person's eyebrows and said to try to keep the tips of the golf tees touching each other. The only way to do that was to frown. People given this instruction rated the photographs as more unpleasant than the average for people who were not induced to frown (Larsen, Kasimatis, & Frey, 1992).

However, although smiles and frowns slightly alter happiness, smiles are not *necessary* for happiness. People with a rare condition called *Möbius syndrome* cannot move their facial muscles to make a smile, as shown in Figure 12.3. They nevertheless experience happiness and amusement, although they have trouble making friends because other people react to the lack of smiling. The girl shown in the figure underwent surgery to give her an artificial smile (G. Miller, 2007b).

FIGURE 12.2 Effect of facial expression on emotion
People who hold a pen in their teeth, and who are therefore forced to smile, are more likely to report amusement than are people with a pen in their lips, who therefore cannot smile.

Courtesy of Lori Thomas

FIGURE 12.3 Möbius syndrome
People with this condition cannot move their facial muscles to smile. This girl went through surgery to give her an artificial smile, as shown. The lack of a smile before surgery did not rob her of happiness or a sense of humor, although it interfered with her ability to make friends.

Overall, the results suggest that our perceptions of the body's actions contribute to our emotional feelings, as the James-Lange theory proposed. Many psychologists therefore refer to emotions as "embodied"—that is, they depend on responses of the body. The theory does not insist that we can tell one emotion apart from another by our physiological responses.

> **STOP & CHECK**

1. According to the James-Lange theory, what kind of person should feel no emotions?

2. How did researchers get people to smile or frown without using those words?

ANSWERS 1. Someone who had no muscle movements and no perceivable changes in any organ should feel no emotions. However, such a person might still recognize the cognitive aspects of emotion. ("This is a sad situation.") 2. They got people to smile by telling them to hold a pen between their teeth. They got people to frown by attaching golf tees to their eyebrows and then telling them to keep the two tees touching each other.

Brain Areas Associated with Emotion

Do different emotions activate different brain areas? Moreover, which brain areas react most strongly to emotions?

Attempts to Localize Specific Emotions

Traditionally, the **limbic system**—the forebrain areas surrounding the thalamus—has been regarded as critical for emotion (Figure 12.4). We consider one part of it, the amygdala, in more detail later in this chapter. Much of the cerebral cortex also reacts to emotional situations.

Whereas many brain areas respond to emotion in one way or another, it is theoretically important to know whether different brain areas respond to different emotions. For example, does one brain area respond during happiness and another during sadness? Many researchers have used PET or fMRI techniques to identify the cortical areas that respond while people look at emotional pictures or listen to emotional stories. In Figure 12.5, each dot represents one research study that found significant activation of a particular cortical area associated with happiness, sadness, disgust, fear, or anger (Phan,

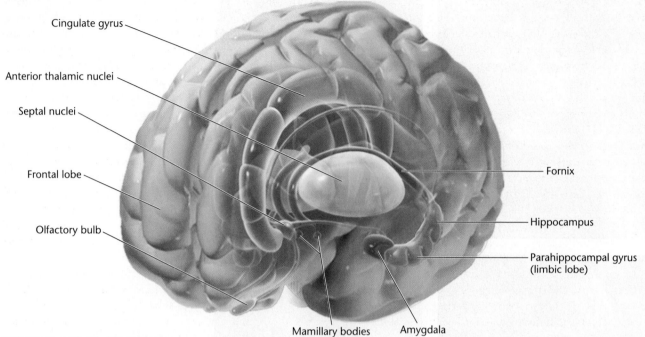

FIGURE 12.4 The limbic system
The limbic system is a group of stuctures in the interior of the brain. Here you see them as if the exterior of the brain were transparent. (© *Argosy Publishing Inc.*)

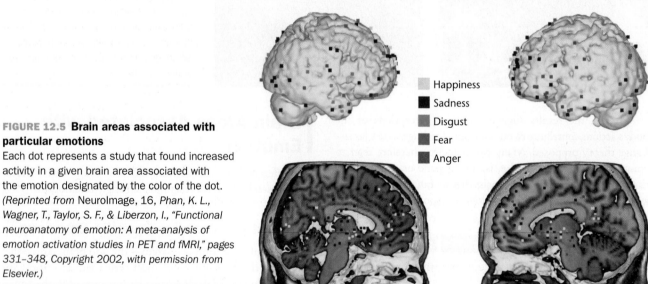

FIGURE 12.5 Brain areas associated with particular emotions
Each dot represents a study that found increased activity in a given brain area associated with the emotion designated by the color of the dot. (*Reprinted from NeuroImage, 16, Phan, K. L., Wagner, T., Taylor, S. F., & Liberzon, I., "Functional neuroanatomy of emotion: A meta-analysis of emotion activation studies in PET and fMRI," pages 331–348, Copyright 2002, with permission from Elsevier.*)

Wager, Taylor, & Liberzon, 2002). The frontal and temporal cortices show many dots, and other kinds of research also point to these areas as important for emotions (Kringelbach, 2005). However, the most salient point of this figure is the variability of location for each emotion. The results apparently depend more on the details of procedure than on which emotion was targeted.

Sometimes, physicians insert electrodes directly into the brains of patients with epilepsy to monitor their responses over time. In one study, researchers used these implanted electrodes to record responses to emotional pictures. They did find partic-

ular cells that responded mainly to pleasant pictures and others that responded mainly to unpleasant pictures (Kawasaki et al., 2005). However, no one has demonstrated cells that respond only to a particular unpleasant emotion, such as sadness or fear.

Of all emotions, only disgust seems to be associated with the response of a particular brain area. The *insular cortex*, or *insula*, is strongly activated if you see a disgusting picture (F. C. Murphy, Nimmo-Smith, & Lawrence, 2003; M. L. Phillips et al., 1997) or the facial expression of someone who is feeling disgusted (Wicker et al., 2003). That is, if you see someone who looks disgusted, you feel disgusted, too. In fact, different parts of the insula respond to different types of disgusting scenes, such as a video of a surgical operation and a video of someone vomiting (Harrison, Gray, Gianaros, & Critchley, 2010).

Locating disgust in the insula is interesting because that is the primary taste cortex (Figure 7.21). *Disgust* is literally *disgust*, or bad taste. To react with disgust is to react as if something tasted bad; we want to spit it out. One man with damage to his insular cortex not only failed to experience disgust in daily life but also had trouble recognizing other people's disgust expressions. When he heard a retching sound, he did not recognize that it meant nausea or vomiting. How disgusted would you be if you found a cockroach in your soup? What if you saw someone whose intestines were spilling out through a hole in the abdomen? What if you saw people with feces on their hands and faces? To questions like these, this patient gave much lower ratings than other people do (Calder, Keane, Manes, Antoun, & Young, 2000).

However, the insula also responds to frightening pictures (Schienle et al., 2002) and pictures of angry faces (Fusar-Poli et al., 2009), not just to items suggesting disgust. Therefore, we should not too closely equate the insula with disgust.

STOP & CHECK

3. The insula is important for which kind of emotion, and which kind of sensation?

ANSWER

3. The insula is important for disgust and taste.

Contributions of the Left and Right Hemispheres

Another hypothesis relates the two hemispheres of the brain to different categories of emotion. Activity of the left hemisphere, especially its frontal and temporal lobes, relates to what Jeffrey Gray (1970) called the **Behavioral Activation System (BAS)**, marked by low to moderate autonomic arousal and a tendency to approach, which could characterize either happiness or anger. Increased activity of the frontal and temporal lobes of the right hemisphere is associated with the **Behavioral Inhibition System (BIS)**, which increases attention and arousal, inhibits action, and stimulates emotions such as fear and disgust (Davidson & Fox, 1982; Davidson & Henriques, 2000; F. C. Murphy et al., 2003; Reuter-Lorenz & Davidson, 1981).

The difference between the hemispheres relates to personality: On average, people with greater activity in the frontal cortex of the left hemisphere tend to be happier, more outgoing, and more fun-loving. People with greater right-hemisphere activity tend to be socially withdrawn, less satisfied with life, and prone to unpleasant emotions (Knyazev, Slobodskaya, & Wilson, 2002; Schmidt, 1999; Shackman, McMenamin, Maxwell, Greischar, & Davidson, 2009; Urry et al., 2004).

The right hemisphere appears to be more responsive to emotional stimuli than the left. For example, listening to either laughter or crying activates the right amygdala more than the left (Sander & Scheich, 2001). When people look at faces, drawing their attention to the emotional expression increases the activity in the right temporal cortex (Narumoto, Okada, Sadato, Fukui, & Yonekura, 2001). People with damage to the right temporal cortex have trouble identifying other people's emotional expressions or even saying whether two people are expressing the same emotion or different ones (H. J. Rosen et al., 2002).

In one fascinating study, people watched videotapes of 10 people. All 10 described themselves honestly during one speech and completely dishonestly during another. The task of the observers was to guess which of the two interviews was the honest one. The task is more difficult than it might sound, and most people are no more correct than chance (about 5 of 10). The only group tested that performed better than chance was a group of people with left-hemisphere brain damage (Etcoff, Ekman, Magee, & Frank, 2000). They got only 60% correct—not great, but at least better than chance. Evidently, the right hemisphere is better not only at expressing emotions but also at detecting other people's emotions. With the left hemisphere out of the way, the right hemisphere was free to do what it does best.

In another study, 11 patients went through a procedure in which one hemisphere at a time was anesthetized by drug injection into one of the carotid arteries, which provide blood to the head. (This procedure, called the Wada procedure, is sometimes used before certain kinds of brain surgery.) All 11 patients had left-hemisphere language, so they could not be interviewed with the left hemisphere inactivated. When they were tested with the right hemisphere inactivated, something fascinating happened: They could still describe any of the sad, frightening, or irritating events they had experienced in life, but they remembered only the facts, not the emotion. For example, one patient remembered a car wreck, another remembered visiting his mother while she was dying, and another remembered a time his wife threatened to kill him. But they denied they had felt any significant fear, sadness, or anger. When they described the same events with both hemispheres active, they remembered strong emotions. So evidently, when the right hemisphere is inactive, people do not experience strong emotions and do not even remember feeling them (Ross, Homan, & Buck, 1994).

STOP & CHECK

4. What are the contributions of the right hemisphere to emotional behaviors and interpreting other people's emotions?

ANSWER

4. Activation of the right hemisphere is associated with withdrawal from events and social contact. The right hemisphere is also more specialized than the left for interpreting other people's expressions of emotions.

▌The Functions of Emotions

If we evolved the capacity to experience and express emotions, emotions must have been adaptive for our ancestors, and probably for us as well. What good do emotions do?

For certain emotions, the answer is clear. Fear alerts us to escape from danger. Anger directs us to attack an intruder. Disgust tells us to avoid something that might cause illness. The adaptive value of happiness, sadness, embarrassment, and other emotions is less obvious, although researchers have suggested some plausible possibilities.

Also, emotions provide a useful guide when we need to make a quick decision. Sometimes, your "gut feeling" is useful. In one study, college students viewed a series of slides of snakes and spiders, each presented for just 10 ms, followed by a masking stimulus—a random array of unrecognizable patterns. Under these conditions, people cannot identify whether they saw a snake or a spider. For each participant, one kind of stimulus—either the snakes or the spiders—was always followed by a mild shock 5.6 seconds later. Most of those shocked after spider pictures developed a bigger heart rate increase after

spider pictures, and people shocked after snake pictures learned an increased heart rate after snake pictures, even though neither group could consciously identify the pictures. On certain trials, participants were asked to report any perceived changes in their heart rate, which were compared to measurements of their actual heart rate. On other trials, after the stimulus, they guessed whether a shock was forthcoming. In general, those who were most accurate at reporting their heart rate increases were the most accurate at predicting whether they were about to get a shock (Katkin, Wiens, & Öhman, 2001). The interpretation is that people who are good at detecting their autonomic responses may have valid gut feelings about dangers that they cannot identify consciously.

Emotions and Moral Decisions

We base many important decisions partly on emotional considerations—how we think one outcome or another will make us feel. Consider the following moral dilemmas, of which Figure 12.6 illustrates three.

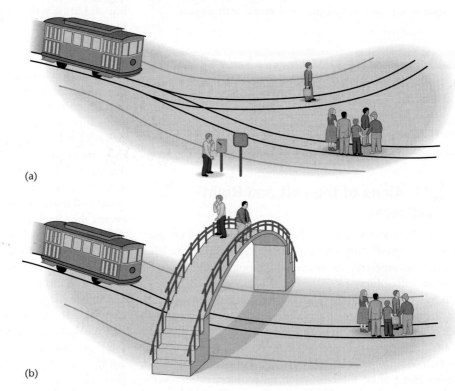

(a)

(b)

FIGURE 12.6 Three moral dilemmas

(a) Would you divert a runaway train so it kills one person instead of five? (b) Would you push someone off a footbridge so a runaway train kills him instead of five others? (c) Would you push someone off a sinking lifeboat to save yourself and four others?
(© Cengage Learning 2013)

(c)

The Trolley Dilemma. A runaway trolley is headed toward five people on a track. The only way you can prevent their death is to switch the trolley onto another track, where it will kill one person. Would it be right to pull the switch?

The Footbridge Dilemma. You are standing on a footbridge overlooking a trolley track. A runaway trolley is headed toward five people on a track. The only way you can prevent their death is to push a heavy-set stranger off the footbridge and onto the track so that he will block the trolley. Would it be right to push him?

The Lifeboat Dilemma. You and six other people are on a lifeboat in icy waters, but it is overcrowded and starting to sink. If you push one of the people off the boat, the boat will stop sinking and the rest of you will survive. Would it be right to push someone off?

The Hospital Dilemma. You are a surgeon, and five of your patients will die soon unless they get organ transplants. Each needs the transplant of a different organ. You haven't been able to find organ donors for any of them. Then a nurse bursts into your office: "Good news! A visitor to the hospital has just arrived, who has exactly the same tissue type as all five of your patients! We can kill this visitor and use the organs to save the five others!" Would it be right to do so?

In each of these dilemmas, you can save five people (including yourself in the lifeboat case) by killing one person. However, although that may be true logically, the decisions do not feel the same. Most people (though not all) say it is right to pull the switch in the trolley dilemma. Fewer say yes in the footbridge and lifeboat dilemmas. Almost no one endorses killing one person to save five others in the hospital dilemma. Brain scans show that contemplating the footbridge or lifeboat dilemma activates brain areas known to respond to emotions, including parts of the prefrontal cortex and cingulate gyrus (Greene, Sommerville, Nystrom, Darley, & Cohen, 2001). Responses in the amygdala are also important. We don't want to act to harm someone, because we identify with that other person and begin to feel the pain that our actions might cause that other person (Pfaff, 2007). In short, when we are making a decision about right and wrong, we seldom work it out rationally. One decision or the other immediately "feels" right. After we have already decided, we try to think of a logical justification (Haidt, 2001).

Decision Making After Brain Damage that Impairs Emotions

Damage to parts of the prefrontal cortex blunts people's emotions in most regards, except for an occasional outburst of anger. It also impairs decision making. People with such damage often make impulsive decisions without pausing to consider the consequences, including how they will feel after a possible mistake. When given a choice, they frequently make a quick decision and then immediately sigh or wince, knowing that

they have made the wrong choice (Berlin, Rolls, & Kischka, 2004). You might think of impulsive decisions as emotional, but these people's decisions often seem unemotional. For example, if confronted with the trolley car dilemma or the other dilemmas we just discussed, people with prefrontal damage are more likely than average to choose the utilitarian option of killing one to save five, even in situations where most people find the choice emotionally unacceptable (Koenigs et al., 2007). And they make that utilitarian decision quickly and calmly.

The most famous case of a person with prefrontal damage is that of Phineas Gage. In 1848, an explosion sent an iron rod through Gage's prefrontal cortex. Amazingly, he survived. During the next few months, his behavior was impulsive and he made poor decisions. These are common symptoms of prefrontal damage. However, the reports about his behavior provide little detail. Over the years, with multiple retellings, people elaborated and exaggerated the meager facts available (Kotowicz, 2007).

We know more about a modern case. Antonio Damasio (1994) examined a man with prefrontal cortex damage who expressed almost no emotions. Nothing angered him. He was never very sad, even about his own brain damage. Nothing gave him much pleasure, not even music. Far from being brilliantly rational, he frequently made bad decisions that cost him his job, his marriage, and his savings. When tested in the laboratory, he successfully predicted the probable outcomes of various decisions. For example, when asked what would happen if he cashed a check and the bank teller handed him too much money, he knew the probable consequences of returning it or walking away with it. But he admitted, "I still wouldn't know what to do" (A. R. Damasio, 1994, p. 49). He knew that one action would win him approval and another would get him in trouble, but he apparently did not anticipate that approval would feel good and trouble would feel bad. In a sense, any choice requires consideration of values and emotions—how we think one outcome or another will make us feel. In Damasio's words, "Inevitably, emotions are inseparable from the idea of good and evil" (A. Damasio, 1999, p. 55).

After damage to a particular part of the prefrontal cortex—the ventromedial prefrontal cortex—people seem deficient in their sense of guilt, both in everyday life and in laboratory situations. Consider two economic games: In the one-shot Dictator game, you are the Dictator, and you are given some money to divide between yourself and another person, whatever way you choose. Most people split it evenly or almost evenly, keeping a little more than half for themselves. People with ventromedial prefrontal damage keep about 90%, on average. In the Trust game (also mentioned in Chapter 11), one person gets some money and has the option of giving some of it to a Trustee. If so, the amount given triples in value, and the Trustee can return any amount of it, such as half, to the first person. People with ventromedial prefrontal damage give less, showing decreased trust. If they are in the position of Trustee, they keep all or nearly all of the money instead of returning it (Krajbich, Adolphs, Tranel, Denburg, &

Camerer, 2009). In short, they show less than normal concern for others. If most people didn't show a reasonable amount of concern for others, civilization would fall apart.

Here is an experiment to explore further the role of emotions in decisions. In the Iowa Gambling Task, people can draw one card at a time from four piles. They always win $100 in play money from decks A and B, or $50 from C and D. However, some of the cards also have penalties:

© Cengage Learning 2013

| Gain $100; one-half of all cards also have penalties averaging $250 | Gain $100; one-tenth of all cards also have penalties of $1250 | Gain $50; one-half of all cards also have penalties averaging $50 | Gain $50; one-tenth of all cards also have penalties of $250 |

When you see all the payoffs laid out, you can easily determine that the best strategy is to pick cards from decks C and D. In the experiment, however, people have to discover the payoffs by trial and error. Ordinarily, as people sample from all four decks, they gradually start showing signs of nervous tension whenever they draw a card from A or B, and they start shifting their preference toward C and D. People with damage to either the prefrontal cortex or the amygdala (part of the temporal lobe) are slow in processing emotional information. In this experiment, they show no nervous tension when drawing from decks A and B, and they continue choosing those decks (Bechara, Damasio, Damasio, & Lee, 1999). In short, failure to anticipate the unpleasantness of likely outcomes leads to bad decisions.

Of course, it is also true that emotions sometimes interfere with good decisions. If you were driving and suddenly started skidding on a patch of ice, what would you do? A patient with damage to his prefrontal cortex who happened to face this situation calmly followed the advice he had always heard: Take your foot off the accelerator and steer in the direction of the skid (Shiv, Loewenstein, Bechara, Damasio, & Damasio, 2005). Most people in this situation panic, hit the brakes, and steer away from the skid, making a bad situation worse.

> **STOP & CHECK**
>
> 5. If brain damage impairs someone's emotions, what happens to the person's decision making?

ANSWER

5. After brain damage that impairs emotion, people make impulsive decisions, evidently because they do not quickly imagine how bad a poor decision might make them feel.

MODULE 12.1 ■ IN CLOSING

Emotions and the Nervous System

Although we regard emotions as nebulous internal states, they are fundamentally biological. As William James observed in the early days of psychology, emotions are "embodied"—an emotional feeling requires some action and a perception of that action.

Biological research sheds light on many of the central questions about the psychology of emotions. For example, one issue is whether people have a few "basic" emotions or continuous dimensions along which emotions vary. If researchers found that different emotions depended on different brain areas or different neurotransmitters, that evidence would strongly support the idea of basic emotions. However, so far, researchers have found no evidence that each emotion has a specific physiology, with the possible exception of disgust.

Studies of people with brain damage also shed light on the functions of emotion, particularly with relation to moral behavior and decision making. Far from being an impediment to intelligent behavior, emotional reactions are often a useful quick guide to appropriate actions. In short, understanding emotions and understanding their biology go hand in hand.

SUMMARY

1. According to the James-Lange theory, the feeling aspect of an emotion results from feedback from actions of the muscles and organs. **356**

2. Consistent with the James-Lange theory, people who have impaired autonomic responses have weaker emotional feelings, although they continue to identify the cognitive aspects of emotion. **357**

3. Feedback from facial movements or other actions can strengthen an emotional feeling, but they are not necessary for such feelings. **358**

4. Emotional experiences arouse many brain areas, as measured by fMRI scans or EEG recordings. So far, the research does not convincingly assign different emotions to different brain areas, with the possible exception of disgust. **359**

5. Activation of the frontal and temporal areas of the left hemisphere is associated with approach and the Behavioral Activation System. The corresponding areas of the right hemisphere are associated with withdrawal, decreased activity, and the Behavioral Inhibition System. The right hemisphere is more effective than the left for recognizing emotional expressions. **361**

6. Brain damage that impairs emotional feelings and responses also impairs decision making. One interpreta-tion is that people decide badly because they do not quickly imagine their emotional reactions to possible consequences. **362**

7. People with damage to the ventromedial prefrontal cortex show little concern for other people. They apparently lack a normal sense of guilt. **363**

KEY TERMS

Terms are defined in the module on the page number indicated. They're also presented in alphabetical order with definitions in the book's Subject Index/Glossary, which begins on page 561. Interactive flashcards and crossword puzzles are among the online resources available to help you learn these terms and the concepts they represent.

Behavioral Activation System (BAS) **361**

Behavioral Inhibition System (BIS) **361**

James-Lange theory **356**

limbic system **359**

panic attack **358**

pure autonomic failure **357**

THOUGHT QUESTION

According to the James-Lange theory, we should expect people with pure autonomic failure to experience weaker than average emotions. What kind of people might experience stronger than average emotions?

Attack and Escape Behaviors

Have you ever watched a cat play with a rat or mouse before killing it? It might kick, bat, toss, pick up, shake, and carry the rodent. Is the cat sadistically tormenting its prey? No. Most of what we call its "play" behaviors are a compromise between attack and escape: When the rodent is facing away, the cat approaches; if the rodent turns around and bares its teeth to the cat, the cat bats it or kicks it defensively (Pellis et al., 1988). A cat usually goes for a quick kill if the rodent is small and inactive or if the cat has been given drugs that lower its anxiety. The same cat withdraws altogether if confronted with a large, menacing rodent. "Play" occurs in intermediate situations (Adamec, Stark-Adamec, & Livingston, 1980; Biben, 1979; Pellis et al., 1988).

Most of the vigorous emotional behaviors we observe in animals fall into the categories of attack and escape, and it is no coincidence that we describe the sympathetic nervous system as the fight-or-flight system. These behaviors and their corresponding emotions—anger and fear—are closely related both behaviorally and physiologically.

▌Attack Behaviors

Attack behavior depends on the individual as well as the situation. If a hamster intrudes into another hamster's territory, the home hamster sniffs the intruder and eventually attacks, but usually not at once. Suppose the intruder leaves, and a little later, another hamster intrudes. The home hamster attacks faster and more vigorously than before. The first attack increases the probability of a second attack against any intruder for the next 30 minutes or more (Potegal, 1994). It is as if the first attack gets the hamster in the mood to attack again. During that period, activity builds up in the corticomedial area of the amygdala (Figure 12.7), and as it does so, it increases the hamster's probability of attacking (Potegal, Ferris, Hebert, Meyerhoff, & Skaredoff, 1996; Potegal, Hebert, DeCoster, & Meyerhoff, 1996). Something similar happens in people, although we can only speculate about whether the brain mechanism is the same: If you hold a toddler's arm to prevent him or her from playing with a toy, the result is sometimes screaming and other signs of anger. If you pause 30 seconds and then do

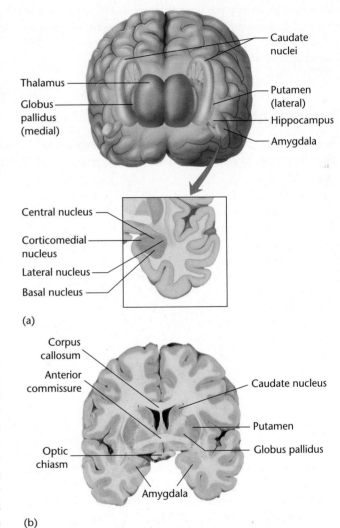

(a)

(b)

FIGURE 12.7 Location of amygdala in the human brain
The amygdala, located in the interior of the temporal lobe, receives input from many cortical and subcortical areas. Part (a) shows several nuclei of the amygdala. *([a] After Hanaway, Woolsey, Gado, & Roberts, 1998; Nieuwenhuys, Voogd, & vanHuijzen, 1988; [b] Photo courtesy of Dr. Dana Copeland)*

it again, the anger is more rapid and more intense (Potegal, Robison, Anderson, Jordan, & Shapiro, 2007).

The same is true for adults. You may have noticed times when one person annoys you and a few minutes later you get angry with someone else. You have probably been told, "If you become angry, count to 10 before you act." Counting to a few thousand would work better, but the idea is correct. Lying on your back is another way to decrease anger. Research has shown that it is easier to feel angry while standing (and therefore in a position to attack) than while lying in a more helpless position (Harmon-Jones & Peterson, 2009). As in several cases in the first module, this finding supports the idea that emotion is embodied: What you are doing or about to do affects how you feel.

Heredity and Environment in Violence

Why do some people turn to violence more readily than others do? Some environmental factors are easy to identify. Certainly people who were abused in childhood, people who witnessed violent abuse between their parents, and people who live in a violent neighborhood are at greater risk of violence themselves. Another environmental factor is exposure to lead, which is harmful to developing brains. Since the banning of lead-based paints and the rise of unleaded gasoline, the prevalence of violent crime has declined, possibly as a result of the decreased lead in the environment (Nevin, 2007).

What about heredity? Monozygotic twins resemble each other more closely than dizygotic twins do with regard to violent and criminal behaviors, and adopted children resemble their biological parents more closely than their adoptive parents (Rhee & Waldman, 2002). However, various kinds of aggressive behavior occur under different circumstances, and we cannot expect to find a single gene or set of genes that will account for all the variations (Yeh, Coccaro, & Jacobson, 2010). For example, researchers found one gene linked to aggressive behavior that is common only among people of Finnish ancestry (Bevilacqua et al., 2010).

After researchers repeatedly failed to find a strong link between any single gene and aggressive behavior, they explored the possibility of interactions between heredity and environment. Several studies have found that violence is particularly enhanced in people with both a genetic predisposition *and* a troubled early environment (Cadoret, Yates, Troughton, Woodworth, & Stewart, 1995; Caspi et al., 2002; Enoch, Steer, Newman, Gibson, & Goldman, 2010; Widom & Brzustowicz, 2006). Figure 12.8 illustrates the effects of genetic differences in production of the enzyme *monoamine oxidase A* (*MAO*$_A$). This enzyme breaks down the neurotransmitters dopamine, norepinephrine, and serotonin, thus lowering the available amounts. Researchers find little difference in aggressive or other antisocial behavior, on average, between people with high or low amounts of MAO$_A$. However, the effects of this gene apparently interact with childhood experience. As the figure shows, the rate of antisocial behavior was low among people who were treated well in childhood, regardless

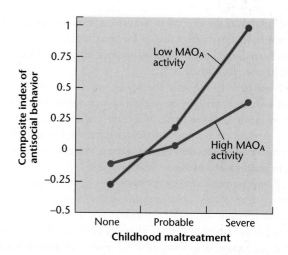

FIGURE 12.8 Genes, environment, and antisocial behavior in men
The y axis represents a complex score combining several types of measurement. Higher scores indicate more aggressive behaviors. *(From "Role of genotype in the cycle of violence in maltreated children," from Caspi, A., et al., Science, 297, 851–854. © 2002 AAAS.)*

of their MAO$_A$ levels. In those who endured a small amount of mistreatment in childhood, the rate of antisocial behavior increased, but their MAO$_A$ levels did not make much difference. However, among those who were seriously maltreated in childhood, the rate of antisocial behavior was significantly higher for those with low MAO$_A$ activity (Caspi et al., 2002). This result is fascinating because of its apparent demonstration of an interaction between genetics and environment. However, from a theoretical standpoint, it is not clear why decreased MAO$_A$ should be linked to increased aggression, or why the effect of this gene should depend on the environment. We can look forward to more detailed investigations of this relationship.

STOP & CHECK

6. What relationship did Caspi et al. (2002) report between the enzyme MAO$_A$ and antisocial behavior?

ANSWER

6. Overall, people with genes for high or low production of MAO$_A$ do not differ significantly in their probability of antisocial behavior. However, among those who suffered serious maltreatment during childhood, people with lower levels of the enzyme showed higher rates of antisocial behavior.

Hormones

Most fighting in the animal kingdom is by males competing for mates or females defending their young. Male aggressive behavior depends heavily on testosterone, which is highest for adult males in the reproductive season. Even in species that do not have a particular season for breeding, testosterone increases are linked with increased striving for social dominance (Beehner et al., 2009).

Similarly, throughout the world, men fight more often than women, commit more violent crimes, shout more insults at one another, and so forth. Moreover, young adult men, who have the highest testosterone levels, have the highest rate of aggressive behaviors and violent crimes. Women's violent acts are in most cases less severe (Archer, 2000).

If we compare men of the same age, do men with higher testosterone levels also commit more violent behavior? Yes, on average, although the effects are often smaller than most people expect (Archer, Birring, & Wu, 1998; Archer, Graham-Kevan, & Davies, 2005). Figure 12.9 shows one set of results. Note that high testosterone levels were more common among men convicted of violent crimes than for those convicted of less violent crimes, but also note that the differences are small. According to the "triple imbalance hypothesis," the reason testosterone's effects are unimpressive is that violence depends on other chemicals as well, especially cortisol and serotonin (van Honk, Harmon-Jones, Morgan, & Schutter, 2010). Cortisol, which increases under stressful conditions, increases fear, and a decrease in cortisol is associated with loss of inhibitions. Therefore, aggression tends to be highest when testosterone levels are high and cortisol levels low. Men with high levels of both testosterone and cortisol are likely to inhibit their violent impulses. Serotonin also tends to inhibit violent impulses.

To test the effects of testosterone, correlational studies are not ideal, because men with high testosterone levels may be unusual in other regards besides testosterone. Several studies used the idea of temporarily increasing testosterone levels in women. Because most women start with low testosterone levels, researchers can readily measure the effects of an increase. In one study, women received either testosterone or placebo and then played the Ultimatum game. In this game, the first person is given $10 and then must propose how to split it with a second person—$5 each, or $7 for me and $3 for you, or whatever. The second person can then accept the offer, or veto it, in which case neither person receives anything. We might expect that giving testosterone to the first person would lead to a greedy offer, but in fact the women receiving testosterone offered their partner a bit *more* money, on average, than did those receiving a placebo (Eisenegger, Naef, Snozzi, Heinrichs, & Fehr, 2010). That reaction doesn't make sense in terms of aggression, although it might make sense in terms of enhancing one's status. That is, someone who offers the other person a good share of the money is saying, "I'm so successful that I can afford to be generous with you."

In another study, the women's task was to examine photos of faces and try to identify the expressed emotions among six choices: anger, disgust, fear, happiness, sadness, and surprise. The photos were morphed from 0% (neutral expression) to 100% expression of an emotion. Figure 12.10 shows the example for anger.

The result was that after women received testosterone, most became less accurate at recognizing facial expressions of anger (van Honk & Schutter, 2007). Meanwhile, other research shows that testosterone *increases* responses of the amygdala to photos showing angry expressions (Hermans, Ramsey, & van Honk, 2008). Evidently, testosterone affects certain brain areas differently, increasing the responses of emotion-related areas, while decreasing the ability of the cerebral cortex to identify the emotion consciously. We can speculate that the result might be increased emotional arousal and decreased ability to regulate that emotion deliberately.

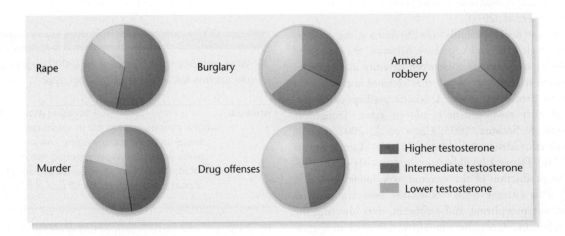

FIGURE 12.9 Testosterone levels for male prisoners
Testosterone levels are higher, on average, for men convicted of murder or rape than for those convicted of burglary or drug offenses.
(Based on Dabbs, Carr, Frady, & Riad, 1995)

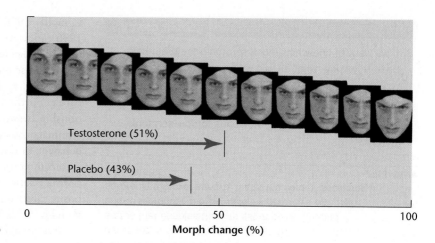

FIGURE 12.10 Stimuli to measure people's ability to identify emotion
For each of six emotions, researchers prepared views ranging from 0% to 100% expression of the emotion. In this case, the emotion is anger. Women identified the expression more quickly, on average, after a placebo injection than after a testosterone injection. *(From van Honk, J., & Schutter, D. J. L. G. "Testosterone reduces conscious detection of signals serving social correction," Psychological Science, 18, 663–667. Used by permission of Blackwell Publishing.)*

Testosterone (51%)

Placebo (43%)

0   50   100
Morph change (%)

STOP & CHECK

7. How does testosterone influence emotional and cognitive responses to a facial expression of anger?

ANSWER

7. It decreases the ability to recognize the expression consciously but increases the responses in emotion-related areas of the brain.

Serotonin Synapses and Aggressive Behavior

Several lines of evidence link aggressive behavior to low serotonin release. Let's examine some of this evidence.

Nonhuman Animals

Much of the earliest evidence came from studies on mice. Luigi Valzelli (1973) found that isolating male mice for 4 weeks increased their aggressive behavior and decreased their serotonin *turnover*. When neurons release serotonin, they reabsorb most of it and synthesize enough to replace the amount that washed away. Thus, the amount present in neurons remains fairly constant, and if we examine that amount, we have little idea how much the neurons have been releasing. However, if we measure the serotonin metabolites in body fluids, we gauge the **turnover**, which is the amount that neurons released and replaced. Researchers estimate serotonin turnover from the concentration of **5-hydroxyindoleacetic acid (5-HIAA)**, serotonin's main metabolite, in the cerebrospinal fluid (CSF). Measuring the amount in the blood or urine is a simpler but less accurate alternative.

Comparing different genetic strains of mice, Valzelli and his colleagues found that social isolation lowered serotonin turnover by the greatest amount in the genetic strains that reacted with the greatest amount of fighting after social isolation (Valzelli & Bernasconi, 1979). Social isolation does not decrease serotonin turnover in female mice in any genetic strain, and it does not make the females aggressive.

That is, serotonin's effects combine with those of testosterone, as in the triple imbalance hypothesis mentioned previously. Serotonin activity is lower in juvenile rodents than in adults, and aggressive behavior is higher in the juveniles (Taravosh-Lahn, Bastida, & Delville, 2006). Serotonin release is also below average in highly aggressive hamsters (Cervantes & Delville, 2009).

In a fascinating study, investigators measured 5-HIAA levels in 2-year-old male monkeys living in a natural environment and then observed their behavior closely. The monkeys in the lowest quartile for 5-HIAA, and therefore the lowest serotonin turnover, were the most aggressive, had the greatest probability of attacking larger monkeys, and incurred the most injuries. Most of them died by age 6. In contrast, monkeys with high serotonin turnover survived (Higley et al., 1996). Female monkeys with low 5-HIAA levels are also likely to get injured and die young (Westergaard, Cleveland, Trenkle, Lussier, & Higley, 2003).

If most monkeys with low turnover die young, why hasn't natural selection eliminated the genes for low serotonin turnover? One possibility is that evolution selects for an intermediate amount of aggression and anxiety (Trefilov, Berard, Krawczak, & Schmidtke, 2000). The most fearless animals get into fights and die young, but those with too much fear have other problems. We could say the same about humans: People with too little fear take excessive risks—wrestling alligators, bungee jumping with a frayed cord, things like that. Those with too much fear are withdrawn and unlikely to succeed (Nettle, 2006).

We can also see aggressiveness as a high-risk, high-payoff strategy: A monkey with low 5-HIAA starts many fights and probably dies young. However, a monkey who wins enough of those fights survives and achieves a dominant status within the group (Howell et al., 2007). In female monkeys, too, those with low 5-HIAA levels tend to achieve higher status in the troop (Riddick et al., 2009). Under some circumstances, taking aggressive risks to achieve a dominant status might be a reasonable gamble.

8. If we want to know how much serotonin the brain has been releasing, what should we measure?

9. Given that monkeys with low serotonin turnover pick many fights and in most cases die young, what keeps natural selection from eliminating the genes for low serotonin turnover?

ANSWERS

8. We can measure the concentration of 5-HIAA, a serotonin metabolite, in the cerebrospinal fluid or other body fluids. The more 5-HIAA, the more serotonin has been released and presumably resynthesized. **9.** Although most monkeys with low serotonin turnover die young, many of the survivors achieve a dominant status that enables them to get more of the food and to reproduce more frequently. Monkeys with high serotonin turnover survive, but at the cost of accepting a low status.

Humans

Many studies have found low serotonin turnover in people with a history of violent behavior, including people convicted of arson and other violent crimes (Virkkunen, Nuutila, Goodwin, & Linnoila, 1987) and people who attempt suicide by violent means, as illustrated in Figure 12.11 (G. L. Brown et al., 1982; Edman, Åsberg, Levander, & Schalling, 1986; Mann, Arango, & Underwood, 1990; Pandey et al., 1995; Roy, DeJong, & Linnoila, 1989; Sher et al., 2006; Spreux-Varoquaux et al., 2001). Follow-up studies on people released from prison have found that those with lower serotonin turnover had a greater probability of further convictions for violent crimes (Virkkunen, DeJong, Bartko, Goodwin, &

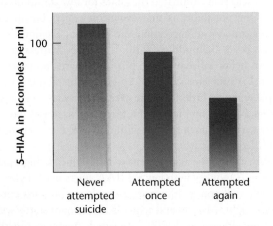

FIGURE 12.11 Levels of 5-HIAA in the CSF of depressed people
Measurements for the suicide-attempting groups were taken after the first attempt. Low levels of 5-HIAA indicate low serotonin turnover. (*Based on results of Roy, DeJong, & Linnoila, 1989*)

Linnoila, 1989; Virkkunen, Eggert, Rawlings, & Linnoila, 1996). However, although each of these relationships is statistically reliable, the effects are not sufficiently powerful that we could use blood tests to make important decisions about individuals, such as which prisoners should be eligible for parole. Furthermore, although the research points to a relationship between low serotonin turnover and highly violent criminal or suicidal acts, the results are less clear for aggressive behavior in the normal population (where extreme violence is uncommon). In the normal population, studies often find a weak relationship, and sometimes a relationship in the opposite direction—that is, somewhat *less* aggression by people with low 5-HIAA (Coccaro & Lee, 2010).

It is possible to alter serotonin synthesis by changes in diet. Neurons synthesize serotonin from tryptophan, an amino acid found in small amounts in proteins. Tryptophan crosses the blood–brain barrier by an active transport channel that it shares with phenylalanine and other large amino acids. Thus, a diet high in other amino acids impairs the brain's ability to synthesize serotonin. One study found that many young men on such a diet showed an increase in aggressive behavior a few hours after eating (Moeller et al., 1996). Considering these results, it would seem prudent for anyone with aggressive or suicidal tendencies to reduce consumption of aspartame (NutraSweet, which is 50% phenylalanine) and maize (American corn), which is high in phenylalanine and low in tryptophan (Lytle, Messing, Fisher, & Phebus, 1975).

Much of the variation in serotonin activity, and therefore violence, relates to genetics. People vary in the gene that controls *tryptophan hydroxylase*, the enzyme that converts tryptophan into serotonin. People with less active forms of this enzyme are more likely than average to report frequent anger and aggression (Hennig, Reuter, Netter, Burk, & Landt, 2005; Rujescu et al., 2002) and more likely to make violent suicide attempts (Abbar et al., 2001).

How Do We Explain Serotonin Effects?

If some treatment suddenly lowered your serotonin level, would you at once become violent? When researchers have used drugs or diet to suppress serotonin levels, some people felt depressed, others became more aggressive or impulsive, and those with previous drug problems reported a craving for drugs (Kaplan, Muldoon, Manuck, & Mann, 1997; Van der Does, 2001; S. N. Young & Leyton, 2002). In short, serotonin's role is not specific to aggression. A better hypothesis is that high levels of serotonin inhibit a variety of impulses, and low levels remove inhibitions. Then the resulting behavior depends on what had been inhibited, which varies from one person to another. In an interesting study that illustrated inhibition, people ate a diet rich in other amino acids but lacking tryptophan. That diet temporarily reduced their serotonin levels. Then they had to learn a response to avoid a loud buzzing noise and a loss of money. People low in serotonin learned the response, but they differed from the placebo group in this regard: Ordinarily, when people receive punishments, such as a loss of money, they become inhibited. They become inactive or slow to respond in a variety of situations. The people low in serotonin failed to show that kind of generalized inhibition (Crockett, Clark, & Robbins, 2009).

The serotonin-aggression relationship is complex in another way also: Although most studies imply that serotonin inhibits aggressive behavior, the brain releases serotonin during aggressive behavior (van der Vegt et al., 2003). Apparently, a low level of serotonin activity prior to aggravation magnifies the response when serotonin is suddenly released at the start of an aggressive encounter (Nelson & Trainor, 2007).

STOP & CHECK

10. What change in diet can alter the production of serotonin?

ANSWER

10. To raise production of serotonin, increase consumption of tryptophan or decrease consumption of proteins high in phenylalanine and other large amino acids that compete with tryptophan for entry to the brain.

Fear and Anxiety

What is the "right" amount of anxiety? It depends. If you are sitting with family or friends at a restaurant, a low level of anxiety is appropriate. If you are walking alone at night and you hear footsteps approaching you, it is time to turn up your anxiety level.

Nevertheless, even among people in the same situation, some show much more anxiety than others do, partly for genetic reasons (Aleman, Swart, & van Rijn, 2008; Chen et al., 2006; Lonsdorf et al., 2009, 2010; Wray et al., 2009). Both experiences and genetics modify activity in the amygdala, one of the main areas for regulating anxiety.

Fear, Anxiety, and the Amygdala

Do we have any built-in, unlearned fears? Yes, at least one: Even newborns are frightened by loud noises. The response to an unexpected loud noise, known as the **startle reflex**, is extremely fast: Auditory information goes first to the cochlear nucleus in the medulla and from there directly to an area in the pons that commands tensing the muscles, especially the neck muscles. Tensing the neck muscles is important because the neck is so vulnerable to injury. (Chapter 5 discussed how woodpeckers protect their necks while pecking a tree.) Information reaches the pons within 3 to 8 ms after a loud noise, and the full startle reflex occurs in less than two tenths of a second (Yeomans & Frankland, 1996).

Although you don't have to learn to fear loud noises, your current mood or situation modifies your reaction. Your startle reflex is more vigorous if you are already tense. People with

People's choices of activities depend in part on how easily they develop anxiety.

post-traumatic stress disorder, who are certainly known for their intense anxiety, show a much enhanced startle reflex (Grillon, Morgan, Davis, & Southwick, 1998).

Studies of Rodents

Psychologists measure variations in the startle reflex as a gauge of fear or anxiety. In research with nonhumans, psychologists first measure the normal response to a loud noise. Then they repeatedly pair a stimulus, such as a light, with shock. Finally, they present the light just before the loud noise and determine how much the light increases the startle response. A control group is tested with a stimulus that has not been paired with shock. Results of such studies consistently show that after animals have learned to associate a stimulus with shock, that stimulus becomes a fear signal, and presenting the fear signal just before a sudden loud noise enhances the startle response. Conversely, a stimulus previously associated with pleasant stimuli or the absence of danger becomes a safety signal that decreases the startle reflex (Schmid, Koch, & Schnitzler, 1995).

Investigators have determined that the amygdala (Figures 12.7 and 12.12) is important for enhancing the startle reflex. Many cells in the amygdala, especially in the basolateral and central nuclei, get input from pain fibers as well as vision or hearing, so the circuitry is well suited to establishing conditioned fears (Uwano, Nishijo, Ono, & Tamura, 1995). Some cells in the amygdala respond strongly to rewards, others to punishments, and still others to surprises in either direction (Belova, Paton, Morrison, & Salzman, 2007).

Output from the amygdala to the hypothalamus controls autonomic fear responses, such as increased blood pressure. The amygdala also has axons to areas of the prefrontal cortex that control approach and avoidance responses (Garcia, Vouimba, Baudry, & Thompson, 1999; Lacroix, Spinelli, Heidbreder, & Feldon, 2000). Additional axons extend to midbrain areas that relay information to the pons to control the startle reflex (LeDoux, Iwata, Cicchetti, & Reis, 1988; Zhao & Davis, 2004). Figure 12.12 shows the connections.

If a rat has damage to the amygdala, it still shows a normal startle reflex, but signals before the noise do not modify the reflex. In one study, rats were repeatedly exposed to a light followed by shock and then tested for their responses to a loud noise. Intact rats showed a moderate startle reflex to the loud noise and an enhanced response if the light preceded the noise. In contrast, rats with damage in the path from the amygdala to the hindbrain showed the same startle reflex with or without the light (Hitchcock & Davis, 1991).

Do these results indicate that amygdala damage destroys fear? Not necessarily. An alternative explanation is that the rats have trouble interpreting or understanding stimuli with emotional consequences. The same issue arises with humans, as we shall see.

An odd parasite has evolved a way to exploit the consequences of amygdala damage (Berdoy, Webster, & Macdonald, 2000). *Toxoplasma gondii* is a protozoan that infects many mammals but reproduces only in cats. Cats excrete the parasite's eggs in their feces, thereby releasing them into the ground. Rats that burrow in the ground can become infected with the parasite. When the parasite enters a rat, it migrates to the brain where it apparently damages the amygdala. The rat then fearlessly approaches a cat, guaranteeing that the cat will eat the rat and that the parasite will find its way back into a cat!

The amygdala is important for learning what to fear (Antoniadis, Winslow, Davis, & Amaral, 2007; Kwon & Choi, 2009; Wilensky, Schafe, Kristensen, & LeDoux, 2006). That is not the only type of fear conditioning. If a rat has received shocks after a particular stimulus in a particular cage, it learns to fear the stimulus (by changes in the amygdala) but it also learns to fear the cage… and new cages… and new situations. The same

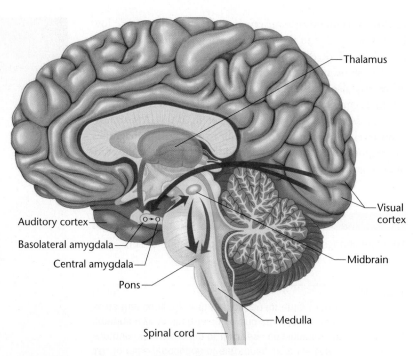

FIGURE 12.12 Amygdala and learned fears
The central amygdala receives sensory input from the lateral and basolateral amygdala. It sends output to the central gray area of the midbrain, which relays information to a nucleus in the pons responsible for the startle reflex. Damage anywhere along the route from amygdala to pons interferes with learned fears that modify the startle reflex. (© Cengage Learning 2013)

is true for humans. If you are attacked or if you have other traumatic experiences, you become more fearful in a wide variety of situations. It is as if your brain has decided, "This is a dangerous world. I need to be alert for new threats." This long-term, generalized emotional arousal depends on a brain area called the **bed nucleus of the stria terminalis** (Duvarci, Bauer, & Paré, 2009; Toufexis, 2007). The stria terminalis is a set of axons that connect this nucleus to the amygdala, as shown in Figure 12.13.

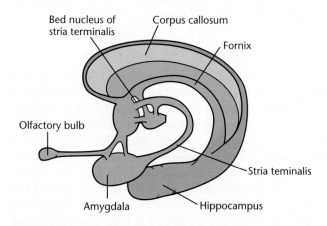

FIGURE 12.13 The bed nucleus of the stria terminalis
The bed nucleus is critical for long-term adjustments of anxiety, whereas the amygdala is responsible for fear of individual items. The stria terminalis is a set of axons connecting its bed nucleus to the amygdala. (© Cengage Learning 2013)

11. What brain mechanism enables the startle reflex to be so fast?

12. How could a researcher use the startle reflex to determine whether some stimulus causes fear?

ANSWERS **11.** Loud noises activate a path from the cochlea to cells in the pons that trigger a tensing of neck muscles. **12.** Present the stimulus before giving a loud noise. If the stimulus increases the startle reflex beyond its usual level, then the stimulus produced fear.

Studies of Monkeys

The effect of amygdala damage in monkeys was described in classic studies early in the 1900s and is known as the *Klüver-Bucy syndrome*, from the names of the primary investigators. Monkeys showing this syndrome are tame and placid. They attempt to pick up lighted matches and other objects that they ordinarily avoid. They display less than the normal fear of snakes or of larger, more dominant monkeys (Kalin, Shelton, Davidson, & Kelley, 2001).

However, not all monkeys with amygdala damage react with the full Klüver-Bucy syndrome. The most prominent effect is an alteration of monkeys' social behaviors, although the exact results vary depending on the age of the monkeys, the social situation, and the exact location of the damage. Some monkeys with damage to the amygdala are withdrawn and fearful, but others are friendly and fearless (Bauman, Toscano, Mason, Lavenex, & Amaral, 2006; Emery et al., 2001; Kalin, Shelton, & Davidson, 2004; Machado et al., 2008; Rosvold, Mirsky, & Pribram, 1954). Among intact monkeys, those with a more vigorously reactive amygdala tend to show the greatest fear in response to a noise or an intruder (Oler et al., 2010).

Response of the Human Amygdala to Visual Stimuli

Studies using fMRI show that the human amygdala responds strongly when people look at photos that arouse fear or photos of faces showing fear. To a lesser extent it also responds to faces showing happiness or sadness (Fusar-Poli et al., 2009). Instructing people to pay attention to pleasant stimuli increases the amygdala's responses to them (Cunningham, Van Bavel & Johnsen, 2008).

Contrary to what we might guess, the amygdala responds most strongly when a facial expression is a bit ambiguous or difficult to interpret. Consider angry and frightened faces. As a rule, it is easy to interpret an angry face looking straight at you, but a fearful face looking straight at you is more puzzling. Frightened people almost always stare at whatever is frightening them, and so you will almost never see someone stare at you with a fearful expres-

sion unless the person is afraid of *you*! Consequently, you recognize an angry expression faster if it is directed toward you and a fearful expression faster if it is directed to the side (Adams & Kleck, 2005). The amygdala, however, responds more strongly to a fearful face directed toward you (Adams et al., 2003) (Figure 12.14). That is, the amygdala responds more strongly to the expression that is harder to interpret. Presumably the arousal indicates that it is working harder to make sense of the stimulus.

Individual Differences in Amygdala Response and Anxiety

Most people's tendency toward anxiety generally remains fairly consistent over time. Most infants with an "inhibited" temperament develop into shy, fearful children and then into shy adults who show an enhanced amygdala response to the sight of any unfamiliar face (Beaton et al., 2008; Schwartz, Wright, Shin, Kagan, & Rauch, 2003). One study found a strong relationship between amygdala activation and fearfulness. College students carried a beeper for 28 days. It beeped at unpredictable times each day, calling for the student to record his or her emotional state at the moment. A year later the students came into a laboratory for the second part of the study, in which an fMRI recorded their amygdala response to very brief presentations of frightening pictures. The amygdala responses correlated highly with the number of unpleasant emotions they had recorded the previous year (Barrett, Bliss-Moreau, Duncan, Rauch, & Wright, 2007). Presumably they recorded so many unpleasant emotions because they were biologically predisposed to react strongly.

In a study of Israeli soldiers, researchers first measured their amygdala responses to briefly flashed unpleasant photos, at the

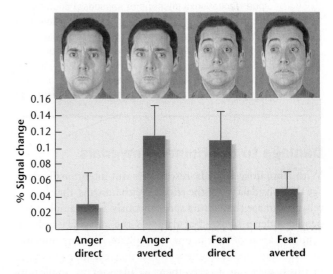

FIGURE 12.14 Amygdala response and direction of gaze
The amygdala responds more strongly to an angry face directed away from the viewer and to a frightened face directed toward the viewer. (*From Adams, R. B. et al. "Effects of gaze on amygdala sensitivity to anger and fear faces," Science, 2003, 300:1536. Reprinted with permission from AAAS/Science Magazine.*)

time of the soldiers' induction into the army. Later they measured the soldiers' responses to combat stress. Those with the greatest amygdala response at the start reported the greatest amount of combat stress (Admon et al., 2009). Again, it appears that amygdala response is closely related to fear reactivity.

Fear reactivity, in turn, affects much of life—even, according to one study, political attitudes. People were asked a series of questions about their support for use of military force, police powers, the death penalty, gun ownership, and so forth. Researchers also measured each person's responses to sudden loud noises, repeated numerous times. As shown in Figure 12.15, those showing high support for military and police action showed a greater startle response to the loud noises, which we know indicates amygdala activity (Oxley et al., 2008). The interpretation is that people with a highly reactive amygdala are likely to perceive dangers, and therefore to support strong protection against those dangers. (This relationship, of course, says nothing about whether the high support or low support group is *correct*. It just indicates that when we are arguing about policy, our brain physiology influences our decision, just as facts and logic do.)

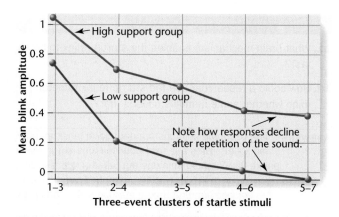

FIGURE 12.15 **Fear responses and political attitudes** On average, people who show a stronger startle response to loud noises tend to favor greater reliance on military and police powers. *(From Oxley, D. R., Smith, K. B., Alford, J. R., Hibbing, M. V., Miller, J. L., Scalora, M., et al. (2008). Political attitudes vary with physiological traits.* Science, 321, 1667–1670. *Reprinted by permission from the American Association for the Advancement of Science.)*

STOP & CHECK

13. What evidence indicates that amygdala activity corresponds to the effort needed for interpreting emotional information?

14. What can we predict about someone if we know the strength of that person's amygdala responses to upsetting pictures or loud noises?

ANSWERS
13. The amygdala responds more strongly to a fearful face directed at the viewer, rather than a similar face looking to the side. People usually find it easier to understand a fearful face looking to the side. 14. People with a highly reactive amygdala are likely to report many negative emotional experiences during a day, to show strong responses to stressful experiences, and to favor strong reliance on military and police power.

Damage to the Human Amygdala

With laboratory animals, researchers can intentionally damage the amygdala to see the effects. With humans, they have to rely on damage that occurs spontaneously. For example, some people suffer a stroke that damages the amygdala and surrounding areas, at least in one hemisphere. They are impaired in some ways and not others. When they examine emotional pictures, they can classify them as pleasant vs. unpleasant about as well as anyone else. However, they experience little arousal from viewing unpleasant pictures (Berntson, Bechara, Damasio, Tranel, & Cacioppo, 2007). That is, they continue to experience the cognitive aspect of unpleasant emotions, but not the feeling aspect.

It is possible to study damage limited to the amygdala only in people with the rare genetic disorder *Urbach-Wiethe disease*. They suffer skin lesions, and many also accumulate calcium in the amygdala until it wastes away. Much of the research on this condition deals with a woman known by her initials, SM. SM describes herself as fearless, and she certainly acts that way. When she viewed 10 clips from the scariest movies the researchers could find, she reported feeling only excitement, no fear. Researchers took her to an exotic pet store. In spite of insisting that she hates snakes and spiders, she was happy to hold a snake (Figure 12.16), and the staff repeatedly had to restrain her from touching or poking the tarantulas and venomous snakes they had. When the researchers took her to a "haunted house," she led the way without hesitation, venturing down dark hallways. When people dressed as monsters jumped out, other people in the group screamed, but SM laughed, started poking one of the monsters out of curiosity, and scared the monster! Her fearlessness is dangerous to her. She has been held up at gun point and knife point and has been physically assaulted repeatedly. Evidently she plunges into dangerous situations without the caution other people would show. When she describes these events, she remembers feeling angry, but not afraid (Feinstein, Adolphs, Damasio, & Tranel, 2011).

Here is another example of her fearlessness: Suppose you are standing, and a person you don't know approaches you, face to face. How close could that person come before you began to feel uncomfortable? Most people stand about 0.7 m (2 feet) away from another person, but SM's preferred distance is about half that. When a man unknown to her, instructed by the experimenters, approached her so close that their noses touched, with eye-to-eye contact, she showed and reported no discomfort (Kennedy, Gläscher, Tyszka, & Adolphs, 2009).

FIGURE 12.16 SM, a woman with amygdala damage, holds a snake at an exotic pet store
Although she said she hates snakes, she was curious to hold this one and wanted to touch the others, including venomous ones. *(From Feinstein, J. S., Adolphs, R., Damasio, A., & Tranel, D. (2011). The human amygdala and the induction and experience of fear. Current Biology, 21, 34–38 with permission from Elsevier)*

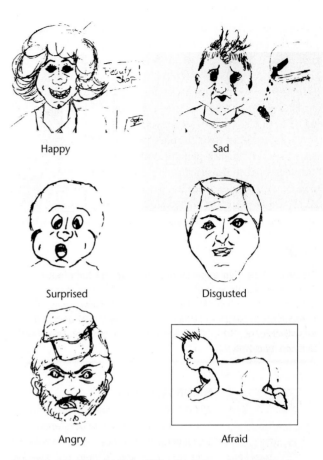

FIGURE 12.17 Drawings by SM, who has a damaged amygdala
She at first declined to draw a fearful expression because, she said, she could not imagine it. When urged to try, she remembered that frightened people are often depicted with their hair on end, at least in cartoons. *(From "Fear and the human amygdala," by R. Adolphs, D. Tranel, H. Damasio, and A. Damasio, Journal of Neuroscience, 15, pp. 5879–5891. Copyright © 1995 by Oxford University Press. Reprinted by permission.)*

SM and other people with Urbach-Wiethe disease often fail to recognize the emotional expressions in faces, especially expressions of fear or disgust (Boucsein, Weniger, Mursch, Steinhoff, & Irle, 2001). Even when they recognize an expression as fear or disgust, they rate it as less intense than other people do, and they are less likely than average to remember a photo of an emotional expression if they see the same photo an hour later (Siebert, Markowitsch, & Bartel, 2003).

When SM was asked to draw faces showing certain emotions (Figure 12.17), she made good drawings of most expressions but had trouble drawing a fearful expression, saying that she did not know what such a face would look like. When the researcher urged her to try, she drew someone crawling away with hair on end, as cartoonists often indicate fear (Adolphs, Tranel, Damasio, & Damasio, 1995).

Why do SM and others with amygdala damage have trouble identifying facial expressions of fear? At first, the assumption was that someone with amygdala damage doesn't feel fear and therefore can't understand it in others. But then Ralph Adolphs and his colleagues observed that SM focuses almost entirely on the nose and mouth of each photograph. Also, in everyday life, she seldom makes eye contact, looking at the mouth instead (Spezio, Huang, Castelli, & Adolphs, 2007). Suppose you are looking at a computer screen, and a face is flashed briefly on the screen, located such that your eyes are fixated on the mouth. Almost instantaneously, you would move your gaze to focus on the eyes, and you would be especially impelled to do so if you saw at first glance that the face was showing fear (Gamer & Büchel, 2009). She has no reluctance to make eye contact, but someone's eyes simply don't attract her attention the way they do for other people (Kennedy & Adolphs, 2010). When researchers asked her to look at the eyes, she quickly recognized fearful expressions (Adolphs et al., 2005). Seeing the eyes is particularly important for recognizing fear. People express happiness with the mouth, but fear mainly with the eyes (Morris, deBonis, & Dolan, 2002; Vuilleumier, 2005). Figure 12.18 shows only the whites of the eyes of people expressing fear (left) and happiness (right). Most people recognize the fear expression from the eyes alone, but not the happy expression (Whalen et al., 2004).

These observations suggest an alternative interpretation of the function of the amygdala. Instead of being responsible for *feeling* fear or other emotions, perhaps it is responsible for detecting emotional information and directing other brain areas to pay attention to it in the proper way. The distinction between these interpretations is difficult to test. As is often the case, good research points the way for further research.

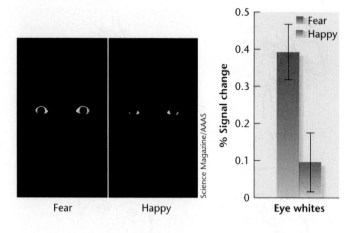

Fear   Happy   Eye whites

FIGURE 12.18 Eye expressions for fear and happiness
The eye whites alone enable most people to guess that the
person on the left was feeling afraid. *(From "Human amygdala
responsivity to masked fearful eye whites," by P. J. Whalen et al.
(2004). Science, 306, 2061. Reprinted by permission from AAAS/
Science magazine.)*

Ralph Adolphs

*Will a better understanding of the social
brain lead to a better understanding of
social behavior? And can such knowledge
ultimately be used to help our species
negotiate and survive in the vastly complex social world it has helped create? To
approach such questions, social neuroscientists will need to establish dialogues
with other disciplines in the social and behavioral sciences,
and to be highly sensitive to the public consequences of the
data they generate. (Adolphs, personal communication)*

STOP & CHECK

15. Why do people with amygdala damage have trouble recognizing expressions of fear?

ANSWER **15.** They focus their vision on the nose and mouth. Expressions of fear depend almost entirely on the eyes.

▌Anxiety Disorders

Most psychological disorders include increased anxiety as one
of the symptoms. In generalized anxiety disorder, phobia, and
panic disorder, the only major symptom is increased anxiety.
Panic disorder is characterized by frequent periods of anxiety
and occasional attacks of rapid breathing, increased heart rate,
sweating, and trembling—that is, extreme arousal of the sympathetic nervous system. It is more common in women than in
men and far more common in adolescents and young adults
than in older adults (Shen et al., 2007; Swoboda, Amering,

Windhaber, & Katschnig, 2003). Twin studies suggest a genetic predisposition, although no single gene has been identified
(Hettema, Neale, & Kendler, 2001; Kim, Lee, Yang, Hwang,
& Yoon, 2009). Curiously, panic disorder occurs in about 15%
of people with *joint laxity*, commonly known as being "double-
jointed" (able to bend the fingers backward farther than usual).
Even when people with joint laxity do not have panic disorder,
they tend to have stronger fears than most other people do
(Bulbena et al., 2004; Bulbena, Gago, Sperry, & Bergé, 2006).

The research so far links panic disorder to some abnormalities in the hypothalamus and not necessarily the amygdala. Panic disorder is associated with decreased activity of
the neurotransmitter GABA and increased levels of orexin.
Orexin, as discussed in Chapters 9 and 10, is associated with
maintaining wakefulness and activity. We might not have
guessed that it would also be associated with anxiety, but
apparently it is, and drugs that block orexin receptors block
panic responses (Johnson et al., 2010).

Pharmacological Relief from Anxiety

People with excessive anxiety sometimes seek relief through
medications. A variety of studies indicate that anxiety is increased by the transmitters orexin and CCK (cholecystokinin) in the amygdala or hippocampus (C. Becker et al., 2001;
Frankland, Josselyn, Bradwejn, Vaccarino, & Yeomans, 1997).
So far, no drugs based on orexin or CCK have been approved.
However, many drugs are available to increase activity of the
transmitter GABA, which inhibits anxiety.

The most common anti-anxiety drugs ("anxiolytic drugs")
are the **benzodiazepines** (BEN-zo-die-AZ-uh-peens), such
as diazepam (trade name Valium), chlordiazepoxide (Lib-
rium), and alprazolam (Xanax). Benzodiazepines bind to the
GABA$_A$ receptor, which includes a site that binds GABA as
well as sites that modify the sensitivity of the GABA site (Figure 12.19). (The brain also has other kinds of GABA receptors, such as GABA$_B$, with different behavioral effects.)

At the center of the GABA$_A$ receptor is a chloride channel. When open, it permits chloride ions (Cl$^-$) to cross the
membrane into the neuron, hyperpolarizing the cell. (That is,
the synapse is inhibitory.) Surrounding the chloride channel
are four units, each containing one or more sites sensitive to
GABA. Benzodiazepines bind to additional sites on three of
those four units (labeled α in Figure 12.19). When a benzodiazepine molecule attaches, it neither opens nor closes the
chloride channel but twists the receptor so that the GABA
binds more easily (Macdonald, Weddle, & Gross, 1986). Benzodiazepines thus facilitate the effects of GABA.

Benzodiazepines exert their anti-anxiety effects in the
amygdala, hypothalamus, midbrain, and several other areas. A
minute amount of benzodiazepines injected directly into a rat's
amygdala decreases learned shock-avoidance behaviors (Pesold
& Treit, 1995), relaxes the muscles, and increases social approaches to other rats (S. K. Sanders & Shekhar, 1995). Benzodiazepines also decrease the responses in a rat's brain to the
smell of a cat. Ordinarily, that smell triggers an apparently built-
in fear (McGregor, Hargreaves, Apfelbach, & Hunt, 2004).

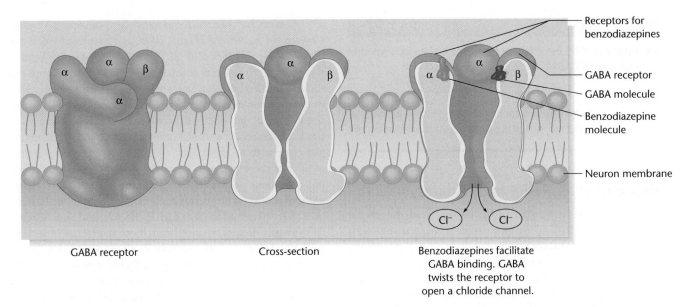

GABA receptor   Cross-section   Benzodiazepines facilitate GABA binding. GABA twists the receptor to open a chloride channel.

FIGURE 12.19 The GABA$_A$ receptor complex
Of its four receptor sites sensitive to GABA, the three α sites are also sensitive to benzodiazepines. *(Based on Guidotti, Ferrero, Fujimoto, Santi, & Costa, 1986)*

Benzodiazepines produce a variety of additional effects, including the possibility of addiction (Tan et al., 2010). When they reach the thalamus and cerebral cortex, they induce sleepiness, block epileptic convulsions, and impair memory (Rudolph et al., 1999). The mixture of effects is a problem. For example, you might want to reduce your anxiety without becoming sleepy, and presumably, you don't want to impair your memory. Researchers hope to develop drugs with more specific and limited effects (Korpi & Sinkkonen, 2006).

APPLICATIONS AND EXTENSIONS

Alcohol as an Anxiety Reducer

Alcohol promotes the flow of chloride ions through the GABA$_A$ receptor complex by binding strongly at a special site found on only certain kinds of GABA$_A$ receptors (Glykys et al., 2007). Alcohol influences the brain in other ways as well, but the effects on GABA are responsible for alcohol's anti-anxiety and intoxicating effects. Drugs that block the effects of alcohol on the GABA$_A$ receptor complex also block most of alcohol's behavioral effects. One experimental drug, known as Ro15-4513, is particularly effective in this regard (Suzdak et al., 1986). Besides affecting the GABA$_A$ receptor complex, Ro15-4513 blocks the effects of alcohol on motor coordination, its depressant action on the brain, and its ability to reduce anxiety (H. C. Becker, 1988; Hoffman, Tabakoff, Szabó, Suzdak, & Paul, 1987; Ticku & Kulkarni, 1988) (Figure 12.20).

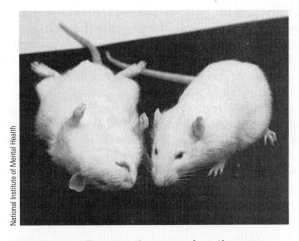

FIGURE 12.20 Two rats that were given the same amount of alcohol
The rat on the right was later given the experimental drug Ro15-4513. Within 2 minutes, its performance and coordination improved significantly.

Could Ro15-4513 be useful as a "sobering-up" pill or as a treatment to help people who want to stop drinking alcohol? Hoffman-LaRoche, the company that discovered it, concluded that the drug would be too risky. People who relied on the pill might think they were sober and try to drive home when they were still impaired. Furthermore, giving such a pill to alcoholics would probably backfire. Because alcoholics drink to get drunk, a pill that decreased their feeling of intoxication would probably increase their drinking. Ro15-4513 reduces but does not eliminate alcohol's effects, especially with large amounts of alcohol (Poling, Schlinger, & Blakely, 1988). ∎

16. What would be the effect of benzodiazepines on someone who had no GABA?

ANSWER

16. Benzodiazepines facilitate the effects of GABA, so a person without GABA would have no response to benzodiazepines.

Relearning as Relief from Anxiety

To the extent that anti-anxiety drugs provide relief, the relief is temporary. If you have a long-term problem of excessive anxiety, you probably shouldn't try to solve it with daily benzodiazepines. If your fear is based on a particular traumatic experience, an alternative is to try to extinguish the learned fear. Suppose, for sake of illustration, that you once almost drowned in the ocean, and now you are terribly afraid to go near it. A reasonable approach is to expose you to your feared object, perhaps a little at a time, in hopes of extinction (in the classical-conditioning sense). First you wade through a puddle, then set foot into a pond, then a bigger pond, and you work up through lakes until you are ready to face the ocean. Clinical psychologists generally use that approach to relieve phobias, with good success. The problem is, extinction training suppresses original learning or overhangs it with new learning, but does not eliminate it. Young children sometimes fully extinguish a learned reaction, but adults seldom do, and the original fear might return, especially after a time of stress (Gogolla, Caroni, Lüthi, & Herry, 2009).

How could we extinguish a learned fear more fully? In general, it is easier to extinguish a learned response immediately after original learning than it is later. After time has passed, the learning becomes stronger. Psychologists say it has *consolidated*. Ordinarily, if you have a traumatic experience, no one is there to extinguish the learning in the next few minutes. However, if an event strongly revives the original experience, that connection again becomes temporarily labile (unconsolidated) and available for either reconsolidation or highly effective extinction.

This process has been demonstrated for both rats (Monfils, Cowansage, Klann, & LeDoux, 2009) and humans. Here is the human study (Schiller et al., 2010): Imagine you watch as a series of red squares and blue squares appear. When you see a red square, nothing happens, but when you see a blue square, 38% of the time you receive a mildly painful shock. Before long, you show distinct signs of anxiety at the sight of that blue square. A day later, you return to the laboratory and you see a blue square, just once, with no shock, just enough to give you a strong reminder of the experience. Later you undergo extinction training, with many presentations of both the red and blue squares, without shock. If you get this extinction training about 10 minutes after the reminder, it is highly effective, and your learned fear virtually disappears, long term. If you receive the extinction training 6 hours after the reminder, or after no reminder, the extinction suppresses the fear temporarily, but it may return later.

A related approach uses *propanolol*, a drug that interferes with protein synthesis at certain synapses in the amygdala. Suppose you learn a fear of some stimulus. Later you are exposed to that stimulus under the influence of propanolol. Exposure awakens the memory and makes the memory trace labile, but propanolol evidently blocks the reconsolidation. The result is a much weaker emotional response, although you can still describe the experience in words (Kindt, Soeter, & Vervliet, 2009). Psychiatrists have successfully applied this method to post-traumatic stress disorder by asking people to describe their traumatic experience under the influence of propanolol. The result was a persisting decrease in fear intensity (Brunet et al., 2008).

17. Why is extinction more effective a few minutes after a brief reminder of the original learning?

ANSWER

17. The reminder brings the representation of the learning into a labile state from which it can be reconsolidated or extinguished.

MODULE 12.2 ■ IN CLOSING

Doing Something About Emotions

It is hard to foresee future developments, but suppose researchers make sudden advances in linking emotional behaviors to physiological measurements. Imagine if we could take a blood sample—measuring 5-HIAA or whatever—plus an fMRI scan and a few other measurements and then predict which people will commit violent crime. What would we want to do with that information, if anything?

And what about anxiety? Suppose research enables us to modulate people's anxiety precisely without undesirable side effects. Would it be a good idea to use these methods to assure that everyone had the "right" anxiety level—not too much, not too little? Future research will give us new options and opportunities. Deciding what to do with them is another matter.

SUMMARY

1. An experience that gradually provokes an attack leaves the individual more ready than usual to attack again.   **366**

2. Aggressive behavior relates to both genetic and environmental influences. Some studies indicate that one gene increases aggressive behavior mainly among people who had abusive experiences in childhood.   **367**

3. Differences in testosterone levels correlate weakly with variations in aggressive behavior. Aggressive behavior depends on a combination of chemicals, with testosterone increasing the probability and both cortisol and serotonin decreasing it.   **367**

4. Low serotonin turnover is associated with an increased likelihood of impulsive behavior, sometimes including violence. Monkeys with low serotonin turnover get into many fights and in most cases die young. However, those that survive have a high probability of achieving a dominant status.   **369**

5. Researchers measure enhancement of the startle reflex as an indication of anxiety or learned fears.   **371**

6. The amygdala is critical for increasing or decreasing the startle reflex on the basis of learned information.   **372**

7. According to studies using fMRI, the human amygdala responds strongly to fear stimuli and any other stimuli that evoke strong emotional processing. It responds most strongly when the processing is effortful.   **373**

8. People with damage to the amygdala fail to focus their attention on stimuli with important emotional content. One woman with damage limited to the amygdala seems almost entirely fearless.   **374**

9. Damage to the amygdala impairs recognition of fear expressions largely because of lack of attention to the eyes.   **375**

10. Panic disorder is associated with increased orexin release and decreased GABA release in the hippocampus.   **376**

11. Anti-anxiety drugs decrease fear by facilitating the binding of the neurotransmitter GABA to the GABA$_A$ receptors, especially in the amygdala.   **376**

12. A behavioral approach to reducing anxiety is to reawaken a learned fear and then apply extinction procedures while the memory is in a labile state.   **378**

KEY TERMS

Terms are defined in the module on the page number indicated. They're also presented in alphabetical order with definitions in the book's Subject Index/Glossary, which begins on page 561. Interactive flashcards and crossword puzzles are among the online resources available to help you learn these terms and the concepts they represent.

bed nucleus of the stria terminalis   **372**
benzodiazepines   **376**
GABA$_A$ receptor   **376**
5-hydroxyindoleacetic acid (5-HIAA)   **369**
panic disorder   **376**
startle reflex   **371**
turnover   **369**

THOUGHT QUESTIONS

1. Much of the play behavior of a cat can be analyzed into attack and escape components. Is the same true for children's play?

2. People with amygdala damage approach other people indiscriminately instead of trying to choose people who look friendly and trustworthy. What might be a possible explanation?

Stress and Health

In the early days of scientific medicine, physicians made little allowance for the relation of personality or emotions to health and disease. If someone became ill, the cause had to be structural, like a virus or bacterium. Today, **behavioral medicine** emphasizes the effects on health of diet, smoking, exercise, stressful experiences, and other behaviors. We accept the idea that emotions and other experiences influence people's illnesses and patterns of recovery. This view does not imply mind-body dualism. Stress and emotions are brain activities, after all.

Concepts of Stress

The term *stress*, like the term *emotion*, is hard to define or quantify. Hans Selye (1979) defined **stress** as the nonspecific response of the body to any demand made upon it. When Selye was in medical school, he noticed that patients with a wide variety of illnesses have much in common: They develop a fever, they lose their appetite, they become inactive, they are sleepy most of the day, and their immune systems become more active. Later, when doing laboratory research, he found that rats exposed to heat, cold, pain, confinement, or the sight of a cat responded to these dissimilar stimuli in similar ways, including increased heart rate, breathing rate, and adrenal secretions. Selye inferred that any threat to the body, in addition to its specific effects, activated a generalized response to stress, which he called the **general adaptation syndrome**. The initial stage, which he called *alarm*, is characterized by increased activity of the sympathetic nervous system, readying the body for brief emergency activity. During the second stage, *resistance*, the sympathetic response declines, but the adrenal cortex secretes **cortisol** and other hormones that enable the body to maintain prolonged alertness, fight infections, and heal wounds. After intense, prolonged stress, the body enters the third stage, *exhaustion*. During this stage, the individual is tired, inactive, and vulnerable because the nervous system and immune systems no longer have the energy to sustain their heightened responses (Sapolsky, 1998).

Stress-related illnesses and psychiatric problems are widespread in industrial societies, possibly because of changes in the type of stresses that we face. As Robert Sapolsky (1998) has argued, many of our crises are prolonged, such as advancing in a career, paying a mortgage, or caring for a relative with a chronic health problem. If a long-term, almost inescapable issue activates the general adaptation syndrome, the result can be exhaustion.

Selye's concept of stress included any *change* in one's life, such as either getting fired from your job or getting promoted. Bruce McEwen (2000, p. 173) proposed an alternative definition that is better for most purposes: "events that are interpreted as threatening to an individual and which elicit physiological and behavioral responses." Although this definition differs from Selye's, the idea remains that many kinds of events can be stressful, and the body reacts to all kinds of stress in similar ways.

Stress and the Hypothalamus-Pituitary-Adrenal Cortex Axis

Stress activates two body systems. One is the sympathetic nervous system, which prepares the body for brief emergency responses—"fight or flight." The other is the **HPA axis**—the hypothalamus, pituitary gland, and adrenal cortex. Activation of the hypothalamus induces the anterior pituitary gland to secrete **adrenocorticotropic hormone (ACTH)**, which in turn stimulates the human adrenal cortex to secrete cortisol, which enhances metabolic activity and elevates blood levels of sugar and other nutrients (Figure 12.21). Many researchers refer to cortisol as a "stress hormone" and use measurements of cortisol level as an indication of someone's recent stress level. Compared to the autonomic nervous system, the HPA axis reacts more slowly, but it becomes the dominant response to prolonged stressors, such as living with an abusive parent or spouse.

Stress that releases cortisol helps the body mobilize its energies to fight a difficult situation, but the effects depend on amount and duration. Brief or moderate stress improves attention and memory formation (Krugers, Hoogenraad, & Groc, 2010). It improves performance on relatively simple tasks, although it impairs performance that requires complex, flexible thinking (Arnsten, 2009). Stress also enhances activity of the immune system, helping it fight illnesses (Benschop

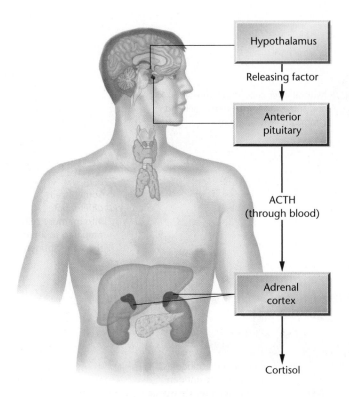

FIGURE 12.21 The hypothalamus-pituitary-adrenal cortex axis
Prolonged stress increases secretion of the adrenal hormone cortisol, which elevates blood sugar and increases metabolism. These changes help the body sustain prolonged activity but at the expense of decreased immune system activity. (© Cengage Learning 2013)

et al., 1995). However, prolonged stress impairs memory and immune activity. To see why, we start with an overview of the immune system.

The Immune System

The **immune system** consists of cells that protect the body against viruses, bacteria, and other intruders. The immune system is like a police force: If it is too weak, the "criminals" (viruses and bacteria) run wild and create damage. If it becomes too strong and unselective, it starts attacking "law-abiding citizens" (the body's own cells). When the immune system attacks normal cells, we call the result an *autoimmune disease*. Myasthenia gravis and rheumatoid arthritis are examples of autoimmune diseases.

Leukocytes

The most important elements of the immune system are the **leukocytes**, commonly known as white blood cells (Kiecolt-Glaser & Glaser, 1993; O'Leary, 1990).

We distinguish several types of leukocytes, including B cells, T cells, and natural killer cells (Figure 12.22):

- *B cells,* which mature mostly in the bone marrow, secrete **antibodies**, which are Y-shaped proteins that attach to particular kinds of antigens, just as a key fits a lock. Every cell has surface proteins called **antigens** (antibody-generator molecules), and your body's antigens are as unique as your fingerprints. The B cells recognize the "self" antigens, but when they find an unfamiliar antigen, they attack the cell. This kind of attack defends the body against viruses and bacteria. It also causes rejection of organ transplants, unless physicians take special steps to minimize the attack. After the body has made antibodies against a particular intruder, it "remembers" the intruder and quickly builds more of the same kind of antibody if it encounters that intruder again.

- *T cells* mature in the thymus gland. Several kinds of T cells attack intruders directly (without secreting antibodies), and some help other T cells or B cells to multiply.

- *Natural killer cells,* another kind of leukocytes, attack tumor cells and cells that are infected with viruses. Whereas each B or T cell attacks a particular kind of foreign antigen, natural killer cells attack all intruders.

In response to an infection, leukocytes and other cells produce small proteins called **cytokines** (e.g., interleukin-1, or IL-1) that combat infections and also communicate with the brain to elicit appropriate behaviors (Maier & Watkins, 1998). Cytokines are the immune system's way of telling the brain that the body is ill. They trigger the hypothalamus to produce fever, sleepiness, lack of energy, lack of appetite, and loss of sex drive. The immune system also reacts to infection by increased production of *prostaglandins*, additional chemicals that promote sleepiness. In other words, cytokines and prostaglandins are responsible for what Selye called the general adaptation syndrome.

Note also that what we usually consider symptoms are actually part of the body's way of fighting the illness. Most people think of fever and sleepiness as something the illness did to them, but in fact, fever and sleepiness are strategies that evolved for fighting the illness. As discussed in Chapter 10, a moderate fever helps fight many infections. Sleep and inactivity are ways of conserving energy so that the body can devote more energy to its immune attack against the intruders.

STOP & CHECK

18. What kind of cell releases cytokines?

19. What behavioral changes do cytokines stimulate?

ANSWERS 18. Leukocytes, which are part of the immune system, release cytokines. 19. Cytokines stimulate neurons to produce fever, decreased hunger, decreased sex drive, and increased sleepiness.

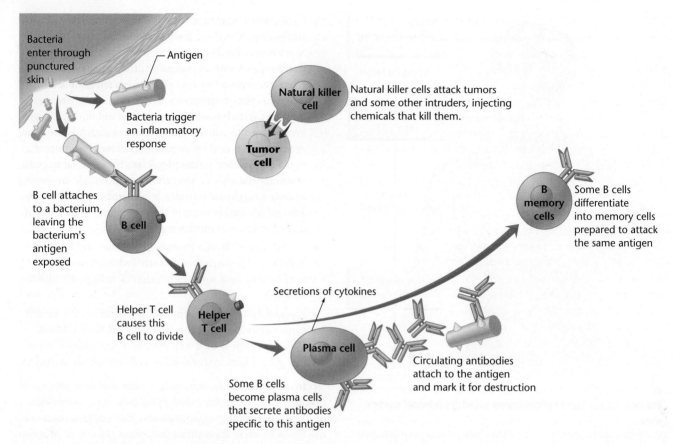

Bacteria enter through punctured skin

Antigen

Bacteria trigger an inflammatory response

Natural killer cell

Natural killer cells attack tumors and some other intruders, injecting chemicals that kill them.

Tumor cell

B cell attaches to a bacterium, leaving the bacterium's antigen exposed

B cell

B memory cells

Some B cells differentiate into memory cells prepared to attack the same antigen

Helper T cell causes this B cell to divide

Helper T cell

Secretions of cytokines

Plasma cell

Circulating antibodies attach to the antigen and mark it for destruction

Some B cells become plasma cells that secrete antibodies specific to this antigen

FIGURE 12.22 Immune system responses to a bacterial infection
B cells bind to bacteria and produce antibodies against the bacteria. When a helper T cell attaches to the B cell, it stimulates the B cell to generate copies of itself, called B memory cells, that immunize the body against future invasions by the same kind of bacteria. (© Cengage Learning 2013)

Effects of Stress on the Immune System

The nervous system has more control than we might have guessed over the immune system. The study of this relationship, called **psychoneuroimmunology**, deals with the ways experiences alter the immune system and how the immune system in turn influences the central nervous system (Ader, 2001).

Stress affects the immune system in several ways. In response to a stressful experience, the nervous system activates the immune system to increase its production of natural killer cells and the secretion of cytokines (Segerstrom & Miller, 2004). The immune system evolved to protect against the stress you might get from an injury, but in prosperous countries today it responds more often to such events as taking exams in college (L. Y. Liu et al., 2002), giving a public lecture (Dickerson, Gable, Irwin, Aziz, & Kemeny, 2009), or seeing photos of sick or injured people (Schaller, Miller, Gervais, Yager, & Chen, 2010).

The elevated cytokine levels help combat infections, but they also trigger the brain to produce the same symptoms as if one were ill. Rats subjected to inescapable shocks show symptoms resembling illness, including fever, sleepiness, and decreased appetite. The same is true for people who are under great stress (Maier & Watkins, 1998). Many of the symptoms of depression, such as loss of interest and loss of appetite, are similar to those of illness and are probably related to the increased cytokines found in depressed people (Dantzer, O'Connor, Freund, Johnson, & Kelley, 2008). In short, if you have been under much stress and start to feel ill, one possibility is that your symptoms are reactions to the stress itself.

A prolonged stress response is as draining on the body as a prolonged illness would be (Segerstrom & Miller, 2004; Zorrilla et al., 2001). A likely hypothesis is that prolonged increase of cortisol directs energy toward increasing metabolism and therefore detracts energy from synthesizing proteins, including the proteins of the immune system. For example, in 1979 at the Three Mile Island nuclear power plant, a major accident was barely contained. The people who continued to live in the vicinity during the next year had lower than normal levels of B cells, T cells, and natural killer cells. They also complained of emotional distress and showed impaired performance on a proofreading task (A. Baum, Gatchel, & Schaeffer, 1983; McKinnon, Weisse, Reynolds, Bowles, & Baum,

1989). A study of research scientists in Antarctica found that a 9-month period of cold, darkness, and social isolation reduced T cell functioning to about half of normal levels (Tingate, Lugg, Muller, Stowe, & Pierson, 1997).

In one study, 276 volunteers filled out an extensive questionnaire about stressful life events before being injected with a moderate dose of common cold virus. (The idea was that those with the strongest immune responses could fight off the cold, but others would succumb.) People who reported brief stressful experiences were at no more risk for catching a cold than were people who reported no stress. However, for people who reported stress lasting longer than a month, the longer it lasted, the greater the risk of illness (S. Cohen et al., 1998).

Prolonged stress can also harm the hippocampus. Stress releases cortisol, and cortisol enhances metabolic activity throughout the body. When metabolic activity is high in the hippocampus, its cells become more vulnerable. Toxins or overstimulation are then more likely than usual to damage or kill neurons in the hippocampus (Sapolsky, 1992). Rats exposed to high stress—such as being restrained in a mesh wire retainer for 6 hours a day for 3 weeks—show shrinkage of dendrites in the hippocampus and impairments in the kinds of memory that depend on the hippocampus (Kleen, Sitomer, Killeen, & Conrad, 2006). They also show atrophy of other brain areas (Dias-Ferreira et al., 2009). High cortisol levels may also be responsible for the deterioration of the hippocampus and decline of memory that occur in many older people (Cameron & McKay, 1999).

> **STOP & CHECK**
>
> **20.** How do the effects of prolonged stress mimic the effects of illness?
>
> **21.** How does prolonged stress damage the hippocampus?

ANSWERS

20. Prolonged stress increases release of cytokines. Cytokines tell the brain to initiate responses to combat illness, such as fever, inactivity, and loss of appetite. **21.** Stress increases the release of cortisol, which enhances metabolic activity throughout the body. When neurons in the hippocampus have high metabolic activity, they become more vulnerable to damage by toxins or overstimulation.

Stress Control

Individuals vary in their reactions to a stressful experience. Studies with mice have identified genes that relate to being more vulnerable or more resilient (Krishnan et al., 2007). Individual differences also relate to life circumstances. In baboon troops, the entry of a new adult male into a troop is stressful to females, because he may attack either them or their babies. However, a female who has a male "friend" to defend her (possibly the father of her babies) shows less stress response

(Beehner, Bergman, Cheney, Seyfarth, & Whitten, 2005). In humans, resilience in the face of stress correlates with stronger connections between the amygdala and the prefrontal cortex (Kim & Whalen, 2009; St. Jacques, Colcos, & Cabeza, 2009).

People have found many ways to control their stress responses. Possibilities include special breathing routines, exercise, meditation, and distraction, as well as, of course, trying to deal with the problem that caused the stress. Social support is one of the most powerful methods of coping with stress, and researchers have demonstrated its effectiveness by brain measurements as well as people's self-reports. In one study, happily married women were given moderately painful shocks to their ankles. On various trials, they held the hand of their husband, a man they did not know, or no one. Holding the husband's hand reduced the response indicated by fMRI in several brain areas, including the prefrontal cortex. Holding the hand of an unknown man reduced the response a little, on average, but not as much as holding the husband's hand (Coan, Schaefer, & Davidson, 2006). In short, as expected, brain responses correspond to people's self-reports that social support from a loved one helps reduce stress.

Post-traumatic Stress Disorder

People have long recognized that many soldiers returning from battle are prone to continuing anxieties and distress. In the past, people called this condition *battle fatigue* or *shell shock*. Today, they call it **post-traumatic stress disorder (PTSD)**. PTSD occurs in some people who have endured terrifying experiences, such as a life-threatening attack or watching someone get killed. The symptoms, lasting at least a month after the event, include frequent distressing recollections (flashbacks) and nightmares about the traumatic event, avoidance of reminders of it, and vigorous reactions to noises and other stimuli (Yehuda, 2002).

However, not all people who endure traumas develop PTSD. For example, investigators in one study examined 218 people admitted to a hospital emergency ward after severe automobile accidents. All showed about similar stress responses at the time and 1 week later, but the responses declined over time in some and increased in others so that about one sixth of them met the criteria for PTSD 4 months after the accident (Shalev et al., 2000). The ones developing PTSD had not been in consistently worse wrecks than the others. Evidently, they were more vulnerable to PTSD. Other studies have confirmed that the people showing the greatest distress shortly after a traumatic event are not necessarily the ones who later develop PTSD (Harvey & Bryant, 2002).

What accounts for differences in vulnerability? Most PTSD victims have a smaller than average hippocampus (Stein, Hanna, Koverola, Torchia, & McClarty, 1997). It might seem natural to assume that severe stress elevated the cortisol secretion and that the high cortisol levels damaged the hippocampus. However, PTSD victims show *lower* than normal cortisol levels both immediately after the traumatic event and weeks later (Delahanty, Raimonde, & Spoonster, 2000; Yehuda, 1997). The low levels suggest another hypothesis: Perhaps people with low cortisol levels are ill-equipped to combat stress and therefore more vulnerable to the damaging effects of stress and more prone than other people to PTSD.

To determine whether certain people are predisposed to PTSD, investigators examined men who developed PTSD during war. First, they confirmed earlier reports that most PTSD victims had a smaller than average hippocampus. Then they found cases in which the PTSD victim had an identical twin who had not been in battle and who did not have PTSD. The results showed that the twin without PTSD *also* had a smaller than average hippocampus (Gilbertson et al., 2002). Presumably, both twins had a smaller than average hippocampus from the start, which increased their susceptibility to PTSD.

One further point about PTSD: A study compared Vietnam War veterans who suffered injuries that produced various kinds of brain damage. Of those whose damage included the amygdala, *none* suffered PTSD. Of those with damage elsewhere in the brain, 40% suffered PTSD (Koenigs et al.,

2008). Apparently, the amygdala, which is so important for emotional processing, is essential for the extreme emotional impact that produces PTSD.

> **STOP & CHECK**

22. How do the cortisol levels of PTSD victims compare to those of other people?

23. What evidence indicates that a smaller than average hippocampus makes people more vulnerable to PTSD?

ANSWERS

22. People with PTSD have lower than normal cortisol levels in contrast to most people, who show elevated cortisol levels in response to stress. **23.** On average, PTSD victims have a smaller than average hippocampus. For those who have an identical twin, the twin also has a smaller than average hippocampus, even if he or she does not have PTSD.

MODULE 12.3 ■ IN CLOSING

Emotions and Body Reactions

Research on stress and health provides an interesting kind of closure. Decades ago, Hans Selye argued that any stressful event leads to the general adaptation syndrome, marked by fever and other signs of illness. We now see why: The body reacts to prolonged stress by activating the adrenal cortex and the immune system, and the resulting increase in cytokines produces the

same reactions that an infection would. Research has also improved our understanding of the predispositions behind posttraumatic stress disorder and makes it possible to foresee a new era of advances in psychosomatic medicine. Emotional states, which once seemed too ephemeral for scientific study, are now part of mainstream biology.

SUMMARY

1. Hans Selye introduced the idea of the general adaptation syndrome, which is the way the body responds to all kinds of illness and stress. **380**

2. Brief stress activates the sympathetic nervous system. More prolonged stress activates the hypothalamus-pituitary-adrenal cortex axis. The adrenal cortex releases cortisol, which increases metabolism. **380**

3. Although brief stress enhances the immune response and facilitates memory formation, prolonged stress drains the body of the resources it needs for other purposes. **382**

4. Stress activates the immune system, helping to fight viruses and bacteria. The immune system releases cytokines, which stimulate the hypothalamus to initiate activities to combat illness. **382**

5. Because stress causes release of cytokines, it can lead to fever, sleepiness, and other symptoms that resemble those of illness. **382**

6. The high cortisol levels associated with prolonged stress damage cells in the hippocampus, thereby impairing memory. **383**

7. Successful methods of coping with stress, such as social support, produce measurable effects in brain responses as well as in people's self-reports. **383**

8. After a severely trying event, some people but not others develop post-traumatic stress disorder (PTSD). Evidently, people with a smaller than average hippocampus and lower than average cortisol levels are predisposed to PTSD. **383**

KEY TERMS

Terms are defined in the module on the page number indicated. They're also presented in alphabetical order with definitions in the book's Subject Index/Glossary, which begins on page 561. Interactive flashcards and crossword puzzles are among the online resources available to help you learn these terms and the concepts they represent.

adrenocorticotropic hormone (ACTH)   **380**

antibody   **381**

antigen   **381**

behavioral medicine   **380**

cortisol   **380**

cytokine   **381**

general adaptation syndrome   **380**

HPA axis   **380**

immune system   **381**

leukocyte   **381**

post-traumatic stress disorder (PTSD)   **383**

psychoneuroimmunology   **382**

stress   **380**

THOUGHT QUESTION

If someone were unable to produce cytokines, what would be the consequences?

CHAPTER 12   Interactive Exploration and Study

The **Psychology CourseMate** for this text brings chapter topics to life with interactive learning, study, and exam preparation tools, including quizzes and flashcards for the Key Concepts that appear throughout each module, as well as an interactive media-rich eBook version of the text that is fully searchable and includes highlighting and note taking capabilities and interactive versions of the book's **Stop & Check** quizzes and **Try It Yourself Online** activities. The site also features **Virtual Biological Psychology Labs, videos,** and **animations** to help you better understand concepts—logon and learn more at **www.cengagebrain.com**, which is your gateway to all of this text's complimentary and premium resources, including the following:

Virtual Biological Psychology Labs

© 2013 Cengage Learning

Explore the experiments that led to modern-day understanding of biopsychology with the Virtual Biological Psychology Labs, featuring a realistic lab environment that allows you to conduct experiments and evaluate data to better understand how scientists came to the conclusions presented in your text. The labs cover a range of topics, including perception, motivation, cognition, and more. You may purchase access at **www.cengagebrain.com**, or login at **login.cengagebrain.com** if an access card was included with your text.

Videos

© 2013 Cengage Learning

Facial Analysis

Also available—

- Emotional Memory
- Suspicion and Trust
- Health and Stress
- The Limbic System

Animations

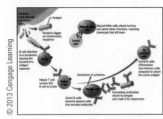

© 2013 Cengage Learning

Cells of the Immune System

Also available—

- Sympathetic and Parasympathetic Nervous System
- Amygdala and Fear Conditioning
- GABA Synapse
- CNS Depressants
- Hypothalamus and Pituitary

Suggestions for Further Exploration

Books

Damasio, A. (1999). *The feeling of what happens.* New York: Harcourt Brace. A neurologist's account of the connection between emotion and consciousness, full of interesting examples.

McEwen, B. S., with Lasley, E. N. (2002). *The end of stress as we know it.* Washington, DC: Joseph Henry Press. Readable review by one of the leading researchers.

Pfaff, D. W. (2007). *The neuroscience of fair play.* New York: Dana Press. Exploration of how the physiology of emotions, especially the amygdala, relates to moral behavior.

Websites

The Psychology CourseMate for this text provides regularly updated links to relevant online resources for this chapter, such as one concerning stress.

The Biology of Learning and Memory

13

CHAPTER OUTLINE

MAIN IDEAS

1. To understand the physiology of learning, we must answer two questions: What changes occur in a single cell during learning, and how do changed cells work together to produce adaptive behavior?

2. Psychologists distinguish among several types of memory, dependent on different brain areas.

3. Learning requires changes that facilitate or decrease the activity at particular synapses.

Suppose you type something on your computer and then save it. A year later, you come back, click the correct filename, and retrieve what you wrote. How did the computer remember what to do?

That question has two parts. First, how do the physical properties of silicon chips enable them to alter their properties when you type certain keys? Second, how does the wiring diagram take the changes in individual silicon chips and convert them into a useful activity?

Similarly, when we try to explain how you remember some experience, we deal with two questions. First, how does a pattern of sensory information alter the properties of certain neurons? Second, after neurons change their properties, how does the nervous system produce the behavioral changes that we call learning or memory?

We begin this chapter by considering how the various brain areas interact to produce learning and memory. In the second module, we turn to the detailed physiology of how experience changes neurons and synapses.

OPPOSITE: Learning produces amazingly complex behaviors.

Learning, Memory, Amnesia, and Brain Functioning

Suppose you lost your ability to form long-lasting memories. You remember what just happened but nothing earlier. You feel as if you awakened from a long sleep only a second ago. So you write on a sheet of paper, "Just now, for the first time, I have suddenly become conscious!" A little later, you forget this experience, too. As far as you can tell, you have just now emerged into consciousness after a long sleeplike period. You look at this sheet of paper on which you wrote about becoming conscious, but you don't remember writing it. How odd! You must have written it when in fact you were not conscious! Irritated, you cross off that statement and write anew, "*NOW* I am for the first time conscious!" And a minute later, you cross that one off and write it again. Eventually, someone finds this sheet of paper on which you have repeatedly written and crossed out statements about suddenly feeling conscious for the first time.

Sound far-fetched? It really happened to a patient who developed severe memory impairments after encephalitis damaged his temporal cortex (B. A. Wilson, Baddeley, & Kapur, 1995). Life without memory means no sense of existing across time. Your memory is almost synonymous with your sense of "self."

Localized Representations of Memory

What happens in the brain during learning and memory? One early idea was that a connection grew between two brain areas. Russian physiologist Ivan Pavlov pioneered the investigation of what we now call **classical conditioning** (Figure 13.1a), in which pairing two stimuli changes the response to one of them (Pavlov, 1927). The experimenter starts by presenting a **conditioned stimulus (CS)**, which initially elicits no response of note, and then presents the **unconditioned stimulus (UCS)**, which automatically elicits the **unconditioned response (UCR)**. After some pairings of the CS and the UCS (perhaps just one or two, perhaps many), the individual begins making a new, learned response to the CS, called a **conditioned response (CR)**. In his original experiments, Pavlov presented a dog with a sound (CS) followed by meat (UCS),

which stimulated the dog to salivate (UCR). After many such pairings, the sound alone (CS) stimulated the dog to salivate (CR). In that case and many others, the CR resembles the UCR, but in some cases, it does not. For example, if a rat experiences a CS paired with shock, the shock elicits screaming and jumping, but the CS elicits a freezing response.

In **instrumental conditioning** (also known as operant conditioning), an individual's response leads to a reinforcer or punishment (Figure 13.1b). A **reinforcer** is any event that increases the future probability of the response. A **punishment** is an event that suppresses the frequency of the response. For example, when a rat enters one arm of a maze and finds Froot Loops cereal (a potent reinforcer for a rat), its probability of entering that arm again increases. If it receives a shock instead, the probability decreases. The primary difference between classical and instrumental conditioning is that in instrumental conditioning the individual's response determines the outcome (reinforcer or punishment), whereas in classical conditioning the CS and UCS occur at certain times regardless of the individual's behavior. (The behavior is useful, however, in preparing for the UCS.)

Some cases of learning are difficult to label as classical or instrumental. For example, after a male songbird hears the song of his own species during his first few months, he imitates it the following year. The song that he heard was not paired with any other stimulus, so it doesn't look like classical conditioning. He learned the song without reinforcers or punishments, so we can't call it instrumental conditioning either. That is, animals have specialized methods of learning other than classical and instrumental conditioning. Also, the way animals (including people) learn varies from one situation to another. For example, in most situations, learning occurs only if the CS and UCS, or response and reinforcer, occur close together in time. But if you eat something, especially something unfamiliar, and get sick later, you learn a strong aversion to the taste of that food, even if taste and illness are separated by hours (Rozin & Kalat, 1971; Rozin & Schull, 1988).

Lashley's Search for the Engram

Pavlov proposed that classical conditioning reflects a strengthened connection between a CS center and a UCS center in the

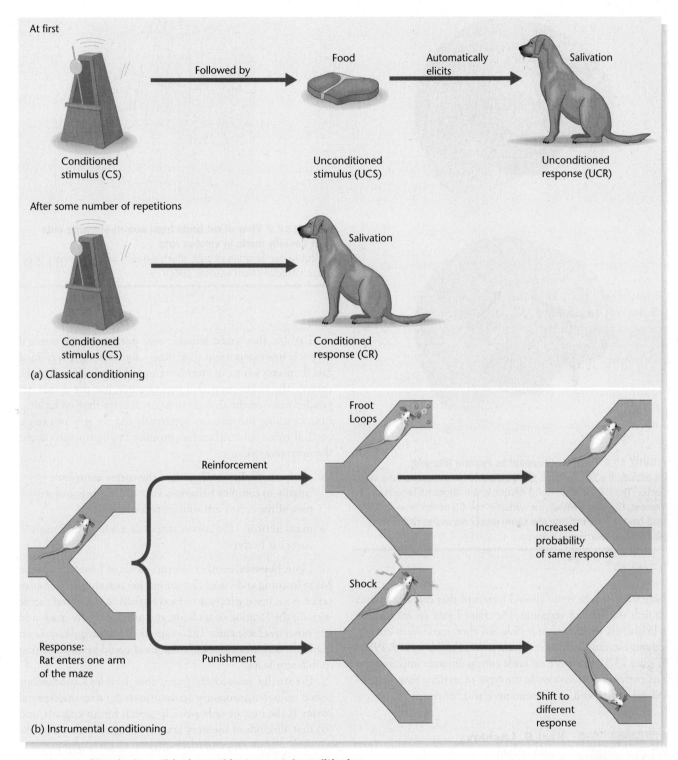

FIGURE 13.1 Classical conditioning and instrumental conditioning
(a) In classical conditioning, two stimuli (CS and UCS) are presented at certain times regardless of what the learner does. (b) In instrumental conditioning, the learner's behavior controls the presentation of reinforcer or punishment. *(© Cengage Learning 2013)*

brain. That strengthened connection lets any excitation of the CS center flow to the UCS center, evoking the unconditioned response (Figure 13.2). Karl Lashley set out to test this hypothesis. Lashley was searching for the **engram**—the physical representation of what has been learned. (A connection between two brain areas would be a possible example of an engram.)

Lashley reasoned that if learning depends on new or strengthened connections between two brain areas, a knife cut

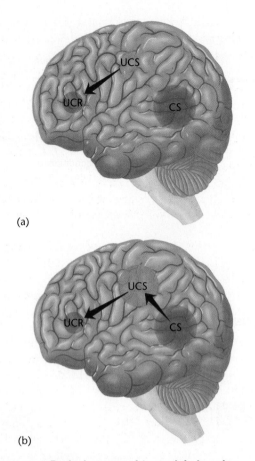

(a)

(b)

FIGURE 13.2 Pavlov's proposal to explain learning
(a) Initially, the UCS excites the UCS center, which excites the UCR center. The CS excites the CS center, which elicits no response of interest. (b) After training, excitation in the CS center flows to the UCS center, thus eliciting the same response as the UCS.
(© Cengage Learning 2013)

somewhere in the brain should interrupt that connection and abolish the learned response. He trained rats on mazes and a brightness discrimination task and then made deep cuts in varying locations in their cerebral cortices (Lashley, 1929, 1950) (Figure 13.3). However, no knife cut significantly impaired the rats' performances. Evidently, the types of learning that he studied did not depend on connections across the cortex.

Karl S. Lashley
(1890–1958)
Psychology is today a more fundamental science than neurophysiology. By this I mean that the latter offers few principles from which we may predict or define the normal organization of behavior, whereas the study of psychological processes furnishes a mass of factual material to which the laws of nervous action in behavior must conform. (Lashley, 1930, p. 24)

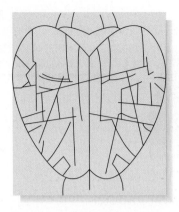

FIGURE 13.3 View of rat brain from above, showing cuts that Lashley made in various rats
No cut or combination of cuts interfered with a rat's memory of a maze. *(Adapted from Lashley, 1950)*

Lashley also tested whether any portion of the cerebral cortex is more important than others for learning. He trained rats on mazes before or after he removed large portions of the cortex. The lesions impaired performance, but the deficit depended more on the amount of brain damage than on its location. Learning and memory apparently did not rely on a single cortical area. Lashley therefore proposed two principles about the nervous system:

- **equipotentiality**—all parts of the cortex contribute equally to complex behaviors such as learning, and any part of the cortex can substitute for any other.

- **mass action**—the cortex works as a whole, and more cortex is better.

Note, however, another interpretation of Lashley's results: Maze learning and visual discrimination learning are complex tasks. A rat finding its way to food attends to visual and tactile stimuli, the location of its body, the position of its head, and any other available cues. This example of learning depends on many cortical areas, but different areas could be contributing in different ways.

Eventually, researchers found that Lashley's conclusions rested on two unnecessary assumptions: (a) that the cerebral cortex is the best or only place to search for an engram, and (b) that all kinds of memory are physiologically the same. As we shall see, investigators who discarded these assumptions reached different conclusions.

The Modern Search for the Engram

Richard F. Thompson and his colleagues used a simpler task than Lashley's and sought the engram of memory not in the cerebral cortex but in the cerebellum. Thompson and colleagues studied classical conditioning of eyelid responses in rabbits. They presented first a tone (CS) and then a puff of air (UCS) to the cornea of the rabbit's eye. At first, a rabbit blinked at the airpuff but not at the tone. After repeated pairings, classical conditioning occurred and the rabbit blinked at the tone also. Investigators recorded the activity in various brain cells to determine which ones changed their responses during learning.

Thompson set out to determine the location of learning. Imagine a sequence of brain areas from the sensory receptors to the motor neurons controlling the muscles:

© Cengage Learning 2013

If we damage any one of those areas, learning will be impaired, but we can't be sure that learning occurred in the damaged area. For example, if the learning occurs in area D, damage in A, B, or C will prevent learning by blocking the input to D. Damage in E or F will prevent learning by blocking the output from D. Thompson and colleagues reasoned as follows: Suppose the learning occurs in D. If so, then D has to be active at the time of the learning, and so do all the areas leading up to D (A, B, and C). However, learning should not require areas E and beyond. If area E were blocked, nothing would relay information to the muscles, so we would see no response, but learning could occur nevertheless, and we could see evidence of it later.

Thompson identified one nucleus of the cerebellum, the **lateral interpositus nucleus (LIP)**, as essential for learning. At the start of training, those cells showed little response to the tone, but as learning proceeded, their responses increased (R. F. Thompson, 1986). When the investigators temporarily suppressed that nucleus in an untrained rabbit, either by cooling the nucleus or by injecting a drug into it, and then presented the CSs and UCSs, the rabbit showed no responses during the training. Then they waited for the LIP to recover and continued training. At that point, the rabbit began to learn, but it learned *at the same speed as animals that had received no previous training*. Evidently, while the LIP was suppressed, the training had no effect.

But does learning actually occur *in* the LIP, or does this area just relay the information to a later area where learning occurs? In the next experiments, investigators suppressed activity in the red nucleus, a midbrain motor area that receives input from the cerebellum. When the red nucleus was suppressed, the rabbits again showed no responses during training. However, as soon as the red nucleus had recovered from the cooling or drugs, the rabbits showed strong learned responses to the tone (R. E. Clark & Lavond, 1993; Krupa, Thompson, & Thompson, 1993). In other words, suppressing the red nucleus temporarily prevented the response but did not prevent learning. Evidently, learning did not require activity in the red nucleus or any area after it. The researchers concluded, therefore, that the learning occurred in the LIP. Figure 13.4 summarizes these experiments.

How did they know that learning didn't depend on some area *before* the LIP? If it did, then suppressing the LIP would not have prevented learning. Still, one could imagine that learning occurred in the LIP *and* an earlier area. That is, we have no reason to insist that learning occur in one location alone. However, consider the results of this study: Single-cell recordings found that classical conditioning of the eyeblink response was accompanied by increased responses in both the LIP and the *medial geniculate nucleus* (the auditory portion of the thalamus), which provides a major input to the LIP. However, after an auditory conditioned stimulus, the activity increased in the LIP 10–20 ms before it increased in the medial geniculate nucleus (Halverson, Lee, & Freeman, 2010). Evidently the increased activity in the medial geniculate nucleus represents feedback from the LIP, and learning itself must rely on the LIP alone.

The mechanisms for this type of conditioning are probably similar in humans. According to PET scans on young adults, when pairing a stimulus with an airpuff produces a conditioned eyeblink, activity increases in the cerebellum, red nucleus, and several other areas (Logan & Grafton, 1995). People who have damage in the cerebellum have weaker conditioned eyeblinks, and the blinks are less accurately timed relative to the onset of the airpuff (Gerwig et al., 2005). The cerebellum is critical for many other instances of classical conditioning also, but only if the delay between the onset of the CS and the onset of the UCS is short (Pakaprot, Kim, & Thompson, 2009). As mentioned in Chapter 8, the cerebellum is specialized for timing brief intervals, on the order of a couple of seconds or less. Also, the results differ in the case of *trace conditioning*, in which the CS (such as a tone) ends before the onset of the UCS, and the animal has to associate a memory trace of the CS with the UCS. In that case, learning depends on the basal ganglia as well as the cerebellum (Flores & Disterhoft, 2009).

▶▶▶▶▶ **STOP & CHECK**

1. Thompson found a localized engram, whereas Lashley did not. What key differences in procedures or assumptions were probably responsible for their different results?

2. What evidence indicates that the red nucleus is necessary for performance of a conditioned response but not for learning the response?

ANSWERS

1. Thompson studied a different, simpler type of learning. Also, he looked in the cerebellum instead of the cerebral cortex. **2.** If the red nucleus is inactivated during training, the animal makes no conditioned responses during the training, so the red nucleus is necessary for the response. However, as soon as the red nucleus recovers, the animal can show conditioned responses at once, without any further training, so learning occurred while the red nucleus was inactivated.

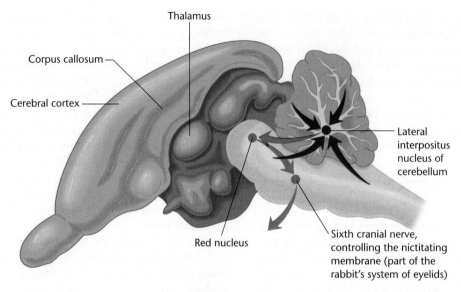

Thalamus

Corpus callosum

Cerebral cortex

Lateral interpositus nucleus of cerebellum

Red nucleus

Sixth cranial nerve, controlling the nictitating membrane (part of the rabbit's system of eyelids)

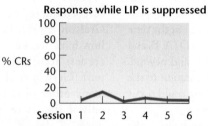

Responses while LIP is suppressed

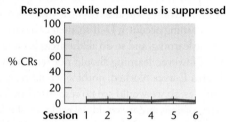

Responses while red nucleus is suppressed

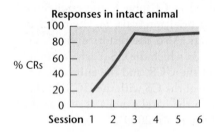

Responses in intact animal

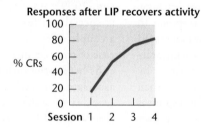

Responses after LIP recovers activity

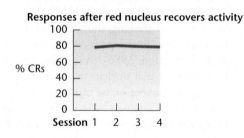

Responses after red nucleus recovers activity

FIGURE 13.4 Localization of an engram
Temporarily inactivating the lateral interpositus nucleus blocked all indications of learning. After the inactivation wore off, the rabbits learned as slowly as rabbits with no previous training. Temporarily inactivating the red nucleus blocked responses during the period of inactivation, but the learned response appeared as soon as the red nucleus recovered. *(Based on the results of Clark & Lavond, 1993; Krupa, Thompson, & Thompson, 1993)*

▌Types of Memory

Decades ago, psychologists expected to find laws of learning or memory that would apply to all situations. Gradually, they became aware of important differences among types of learning and memory. Researchers continue to explore exactly what are the best distinctions to draw, and studies of brain damage make important contributions to this pursuit.

Short-Term and Long-Term Memory

Donald Hebb (1949) reasoned that no one mechanism could account for all the phenomena of learning. You can immediately repeat something you just heard, so it is clear that some

memories form quickly. Old people can recall events from their childhood, so we also see that some memories last a lifetime. Hebb could not imagine a chemical process that is fast enough to account for immediate memory yet stable enough to provide permanent memory. He therefore proposed a distinction between **short-term memory** of events that have just occurred and **long-term memory** of events from further back. Several types of evidence supported this idea:

- Short-term memory and long-term memory differ in their capacity. If you hear a series of numbers or letters, such as DZLAUV, you can probably repeat no more than about seven of them, and with other kinds of material, your maximum is even less. Long-term memory has a vast, difficult-to-estimate capacity.

- Short-term memory depends on rehearsal. For example, if you read the letter sequence DZLAUV and then something distracts you, your chance of repeating the letters declines rapidly (Peterson & Peterson, 1959). You can recall long-term memories that you haven't thought about in years.

- With short-term memory, once you have forgotten something, it is lost. With long-term memory, a hint might help you reconstruct something you thought you had forgotten. For example, try naming all your high school teachers. After you have named all you can, you can name still more if someone shows you photos and tells you the teachers' initials.

Based on these distinctions, researchers proposed that all information initially entered a short-term storage, where it stayed until the brain had time to **consolidate** it into long-term memory. If anything interrupted the rehearsal before consolidation took place, the information was simply lost.

Our Changing Views of Consolidation

Later studies made the distinction between short-term and long-term memory increasingly problematic. First, many short-term memories are not simply temporary stores on their way to being long-term memories. When you watch a soccer or hockey match, you remember the score until it changes, perhaps an hour later. Rehearsing that score for an hour doesn't turn it into a long-term memory.

Furthermore, consolidation isn't what we used to think it was. The original idea was that the brain held onto something in short-term memory for whatever time it needed to do what it had to do in order to establish a long-term memory—mainly, synthesize new proteins (Canal & Gold, 2007). Once formed, the long-term memory was supposed to be permanent. This idea failed in two ways. First, the time needed for consolidation varies enormously. If you are trying to memorize facts that you consider boring, you might have to work at it for hours. But if your romantic partner whispers something emotionally exciting to you, or if someone warns you about the venomous snake that got loose in your dormitory, how long will it take you to establish that memory? Emotionally significant memories form quickly. Why? Remember from Chapter 12 that stressful or emotionally exciting experiences increase the secretion of epinephrine (adrenaline) and cortisol. Small to moderate amounts of cortisol activate the amygdala and hippocampus, where they enhance the storage and consolidation of recent experiences (Cahill & McGaugh, 1998). The amygdala in turn stimulates the hippocampus and cerebral cortex, which are both important for memory storage. However, prolonged stress, which releases even more cortisol, impairs memory (deQuervain, Roozendaal, & McGaugh, 1998; Newcomer et al., 1999). The main point here is that consolidation can be fast or slow,

James L. McGaugh

Memory is perhaps the most critical capacity that we have as humans. Memory is not simply a record of experiences; it is the basis of our knowledge of the world, our skills, our hopes and dreams and our ability to interact with others and thus influence our destinies. Investigation of how the brain enables us to bridge our present existence with our past and future is thus essential for understanding human nature. Clearly, the most exciting challenge of science is to determine how brain cells and systems create our memories.

and it certainly depends on more than the time necessary to synthesize some new proteins.

The second problem is that a "consolidated" memory is not solid forever. As mentioned in Chapter 12, a memory reawakened by a reminder becomes labile—that is, changeable or vulnerable. If the reminder is followed by a similar experience, the memory is **reconsolidated**—that is, strengthened again—by a process that requires protein synthesis. Giving a reminder and then administering a drug that blocks protein synthesis substantially weakens the memory (Nader & Hardt, 2009). New experiences during the reconsolidation process can modify the memory, also. Suppose someone says, "Remember the time we went to Disneyland?" You reply, "Oh, yes." If the other person then elaborates on one part of your Disneyland experience, you update and modify your memory to highlight that aspect, probably at the expense of other details that might fade in your memory.

> **STOP & CHECK**

3. How do epinephrine and cortisol enhance memory storage?

ANSWER

3. Epinephrine and cortisol both enhance emotional memories by stimulating the amygdala and hippocampus.

Working Memory

To replace the concept of short-term memory, A. D. Baddeley and G. J. Hitch introduced the term **working memory** to refer to the way we store information while we are working with it. A common test of working memory is the **delayed response task**, which requires responding to something that you saw or heard a short while ago. For example, imagine that while you stare at a central fixation point, a light flashes briefly at some point toward the periphery, in any direction. You have to continue staring at that central point for a few seconds until you hear a beep, and then look toward the place where you remember seeing the light. This task can be modified for use with monkeys and other species. During the delay, the learner has to store a representation of the stimulus, and much research points to the prefrontal cortex as an important location for this storage. During the delay, certain cells in the prefrontal cortex as well as the parietal cortex increase their activity, and different cells become active depending on the direction the eye movement will need to take (Chafee & Goldman-Rakic, 1998). The increase in activity does not necessarily take the form of repeated action potentials; another possibility is that cells store extra calcium, increasing their readiness to respond to new signals when the time comes (Mongillo, Barak, & Tsodyks, 2008).

Damage to the prefrontal cortex impairs performance, and the deficit can be amazingly precise, depending on the exact location of the damage. For example, after damage in a particular spot, a monkey might be unable to remember that the light had been directly to the left of fixation, despite being able to see that location and despite being able to remember a light in any other location. After damage in a different spot, a monkey might not be able to remember light in some other location (Sawaguchi & Iba, 2001).

Many older people have impairments of working memory, probably because of changes in the prefrontal cortex. Studies on aged monkeys find decreases in the number of neurons and the amount of input in certain parts of the prefrontal cortex (D. E. Smith, Rapp, McKay, Roberts, & Tuszynski, 2004). Older humans with declining memory show declining activity in the prefrontal cortex, but those with intact memory show *greater* activity than young adults (A. C. Rosen et al., 2002; Rossi et al., 2004). Presumably, the increased activity means that the prefrontal cortex is working harder in these older adults to compensate for impairments elsewhere in the brain. Furthermore, stimulant drugs that enhance activity in the prefrontal cortex improve the memory of aged monkeys (Castner & Goldman-Rakic, 2004). Such treatments have potential for treating people with failing memory.

STOP & CHECK

4. What is the primary brain location for working memory, and what is one hypothesis for how it stores temporary information?

ANSWER

4. The prefrontal cortex is the primary location. According to one hypothesis, it stores temporary information by elevated calcium levels, which potentiate later responses.

▌The Hippocampus

Amnesia is memory loss. One patient ate lunch and, 20 minutes later, ate a second lunch, apparently having forgotten the first meal. Another 20 minutes later, he started on a

third lunch and ate most of it. A few minutes later, he said he would like to "go for a walk and get a good meal" (Rozin, Dow, Moscovitch, & Rajaram, 1998). Other patients with amnesia also forget that they have just eaten, although when they start to eat again, they remark on not enjoying the food as much as usual (Higgs, Williamson, Rotshtein, & Humphreys, 2008).

However, even in severe cases, no one loses all kinds of memory equally. A patient who forgets that he ate lunch a few minutes ago still remembers how to eat with a knife and fork, for example, and what different foods taste like, and how to cook them. Studies on amnesia help clarify the distinctions among different kinds of memory and enable us to explore the mechanisms of memory.

People with Hippocampal Damage

In 1953, Henry Molaison, known in most research reports as H. M., was suffering about 10 minor epileptic seizures per day and a major seizure about once a week, despite trying every available antiepileptic drug. Eventually, he agreed to try a desperate measure. A surgeon who had experimented with various forms of lobotomy for mental illness had come to believe that removing the medial temporal lobe would relieve epilepsy. (Although it does in occasional cases, the surgeon was wrong to believe this was a general rule.) The neurosurgeon removed the hippocampus and some nearby structures of the medial temporal cortex from both of H. M.'s hemispheres. Researchers knew almost nothing about the hippocampus at the time, and no one knew what to expect after the surgery. We now know that various parts of the hippocampus are active during both the formation of memories and later recall (Eldridge, Engel, Zeineh, Bookheimer, & Knowlton, 2005). Although the operation reduced H. M.'s epilepsy to no more than two major seizures per year, he suffered a severe memory impairment (Milner, 1959; Penfield & Milner, 1958; Scoville & Milner, 1957). Figure 13.5 shows the normal anatomy of the hippocampus and the damage in H. M.

Anterograde and Retrograde Amnesia

After the surgery, H. M.'s intellect and language abilities remained intact, and his personality remained the same except for emotional placidity (Eichenbaum, 2002). However, he suffered massive **anterograde amnesia** (inability to form memories for events that happened after brain damage). He also suffered a **retrograde amnesia** (loss of memory for events that occurred before the brain damage). Initially, researchers said his retrograde amnesia was confined to 1 to 3 years before the surgery. Later, they found it was more extensive. H. M. is representative of many people who have suffered amnesia after damage to the hippocampus and surrounding structures of the medial temporal lobe. All show both anterograde and retrograde amnesia, with the retrograde amnesia being most severe for the time leading up to the damage. For example, amnesic patients can usually tell where they lived as a child and where they lived as a teenager but might not be able to say where they lived 3 years ago (Bayley, Hopkins, & Squire, 2006).

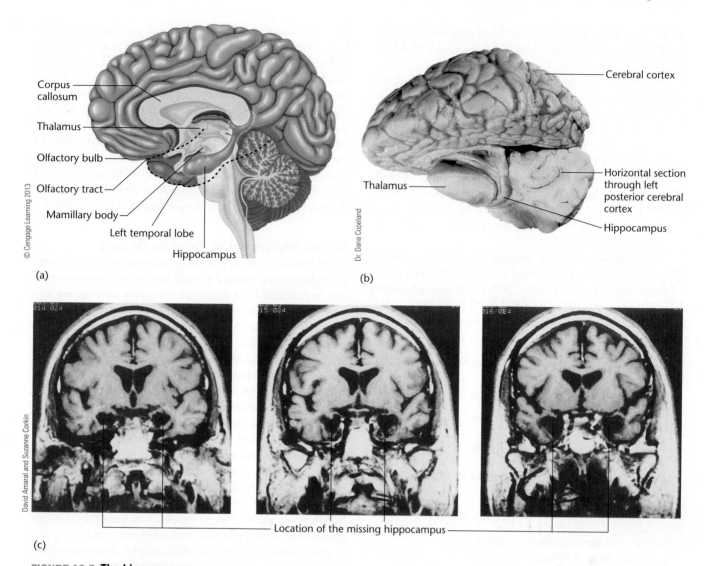

FIGURE 13.5 The hippocampus

(a) Location of the hippocampus in the interior of the temporal lobe. The left hippocampus is closer to the viewer than the rest of this plane; the right hippocampus is behind the plane. The dashed line marks the location of the temporal lobe, which is not visible in the midline. (b) Photo of a human brain from above. The top part of the left hemisphere has been cut away to show how the hippocampus loops over (dorsal to) the thalamus, posterior to it, and then below (ventral to) it. (c) MRI scan of H. M.'s brain, showing absence of the hippocampus. The three views show coronal planes at successive locations, anterior to posterior.

Intact Working Memory

Despite H. M.'s huge deficits in forming long-term memories, his short-term or working memory remained intact. In one test, Brenda Milner (1959) asked him to remember the number 584. After a 15-minute delay without distractions, he recalled it correctly, explaining, "It's easy. You just remember 8. You see, 5, 8, and 4 add to 17. You remember 8, subtract it from 17, and it leaves 9. Divide 9 in half and you get 5 and 4, and there you are, 584. Easy." A moment later, after his attention had shifted to another subject, he had forgotten both the number and the complicated line of thought he had associated with it. Most other patients with severe amnesia also show normal working memory, given a lack of distraction (Shrager, Levy, Hopkins, & Squire, 2008).

Impaired Storage of Long-Term Memory

Although H. M. showed normal working memory, as soon as he was distracted, the memory was gone. For several years after his operation, whenever he was asked his age and the date, he answered "27" and "1953." After a few years, he started guessing wildly, generally underestimating his age by 10 years or more and missing the date by as many as 43 years (Corkin, 1984). He could read the same magazine repeatedly without losing interest. Often, he told someone about a childhood incident and then, a minute or two later, told the same person the same story again (Eichenbaum, 2002). In 1980, he moved to a nursing home. Four years later, he could not say where he lived or who cared for him. Although he watched the news on television every night, he could recall only a few fragments of events since 1953. Over the years, many new words entered the English language, such as *jacuzzi* and *granola*. H. M. regarded them as nonsense (Corkin, 2002).

You might wonder whether he was surprised at his own appearance in a photo or mirror. Yes and no. When asked his age or whether his hair turned gray, he replied that he did not know. When shown a photo of himself with his mother, taken long after his surgery, he recognized his mother but not himself. However, when he saw himself in the mirror, he showed no surprise (Corkin, 2002). He had, of course, seen himself daily in the mirror over all these years. He also had the context of knowing that the person in the mirror must be himself, whereas the person in the photo could be anyone.

H. M. formed a few weak semantic (factual) memories for new information he encountered repeatedly (Corkin, 2002; O'Kane, Kensinger, & Corkin, 2004). For example, when he was given first names and asked to fill in appropriate last names, his replies included some who became famous after 1953, such as these:

H. M.'s Answer

Elvis	Presley
Martin Luther	King
Billy	Graham
Fidel	Castro
Lyndon	Johnson

He provided even more names when he was given additional information:

H. M.'s Answer

Famous artist, born in Spain...	Pablo Picasso

One study found an interesting qualification to the usual rule that patients with amnesia cannot learn new information. The investigators showed a series of shapes with unrelated labels, as shown in Figure 13.6. As expected, amnesic patients made no progress toward learning the labels for each shape.

Then the researchers let the patients devise their own labels. Each patient had to look at one shape at a time and describe it so that another person, who was looking at the 12 shapes unlabeled, would know which one the patient was looking at. At first, the descriptions were slow and uninformative. For the shape at the upper right of Figure 13.6, one patient said, "The next one looks almost . . . the opposite of somebody kind uh . . . slumped down, on the ground, with the same type of . . ." Eventually, he said it looked like someone sleeping with his knees bent. By the fourth trial, he quickly labeled that shape as "the siesta guy," and he continued saying the same thing from then on, even in later sessions on later days (Duff, Hengst, Tranel, & Cohen, 2006).

Severe Impairment of Episodic Memory

H. M. had severe impairment of **episodic memories**, memories of single personal events. He could not describe any experience that he had after his surgery. His retrograde amnesia was also greatest for episodic memories. Although he could describe facts that he learned before his operation, he could relate few personal experiences. Another patient, K. C., suffered widespread brain damage after a motorcycle accident, with scattered damage in the hippocampus and other locations, leading to an apparently complete loss of episodic memories. He cannot describe a single event from any time of his life, although he remembers many facts that he knew before the damage. When he looks at old family pictures in a photo album, he identifies the people and sometimes the places, but he cannot remember anything about the events that happened in the photos (Rosenbaum et al., 2005). Although his brain damage is so diffuse that we cannot be sure which part of the damage is responsible for his memory loss, the observations do tell us that the brain treats episodic memories differently from other memories.

How would memory loss affect people's ability to imagine the future? If you try to imagine a future event, you call upon your memory of similar experiences and modify them. Studies using fMRI show that describing past events and imagining future events activate mostly the same areas, including the hippocampus (Addis, Wong, & Schacter, 2007). People with amnesia are just as impaired at imagining the future as they are at describ-

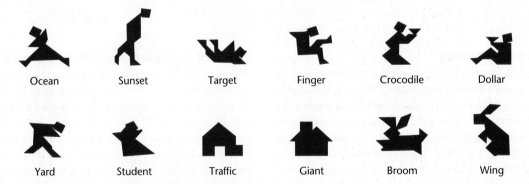

Ocean	Sunset	Target	Finger	Crocodile	Dollar
Yard	Student	Traffic	Giant	Broom	Wing

FIGURE 13.6 Displays for a Memory Test of Amnesic Patients
Although they could not remember the arbitrary labels that an experimenter gave to each object (as shown), they did remember the descriptions that they devised themselves. *(From Duff, M. C., Hengst, J., Tranel, D., & Cohen, N. J. (2006). Development of shared information in communication despite hippocampal amnesia.* Nature Neuroscience, 9, *140–146. Used by permission, Macmillan Publishing Ltd.)*

ing the past. For example, here is part of one patient's attempt to imagine a visit to a museum, with prompts by a psychologist (Hassabis, Kumaran, Vann, & Maguire, 2007, p. 1727):

> Patient: [pause] There's not a lot, as it happens.
> Psychologist: So what does it look like in your imagined scene?
> Patient: Well, there's big doors. The openings would be high, so the doors would be very big with brass handles, the ceiling would be made of glass, so there's plenty of light coming through. Huge room, exit on either side of the room, there's a pathway and map through the center and on either side there'd be the exhibits. [pause] I don't know what they are. There'd be people. [pause] To be honest there's not a lot coming. . . . My imagination isn't . . . well, I'm not imagining it, let's put it that way. . . . I'm not picturing anything at the moment.

Better Implicit than Explicit Memory

Nearly all patients with amnesia show better *implicit* than *explicit* memory. **Explicit memory** is deliberate recall of information that one recognizes as a memory, also known as **declarative memory**. If you have an explicit or declarative memory of something, you can state it in words. **Implicit memory** is an influence of experience on behavior, even if you do not recognize that influence. For example, you might be talking to someone about sports while other people nearby are carrying on a conversation about the latest movies. If asked, you could not say what the others were talking about, but suddenly, you comment for no apparent reason, "I wonder what's on at the movies?" To experience implicit memory, try the Online Try It Yourself exercise "Implicit Memories."

TRY IT YOURSELF ➔ **ONLINE**

Another example of implicit memory: As an experiment, three hospital workers agreed to act in special ways toward a patient with amnesia. One was as pleasant as possible. The second was neutral. The third was stern, refused all requests, and made the patient perform boring tasks. After 5 days, the patient was asked to look at photos of the three workers and try to identify them or say anything he knew about them. He said he did not recognize any of them. Then he was asked which one he would approach as a possible friend or which one he would ask for help. He was asked this question repeatedly—it was possible to ask repeatedly because he never remembered being asked before—and he usually chose the photo of the "friendly" person and never chose the "unfriendly" person in spite of the fact that the unfriendly person was a beautiful woman, smiling in the photograph (Tranel & Damasio, 1993). He could not say why he chose to avoid her.

Intact Procedural Memory

Procedural memory, the development of motor skills and habits, is a special kind of implicit memory. As with other examples of implicit memory, you might not be able to describe

a motor skill or habit in words, and you might not even recognize it as a memory. For example, H. M. learned to read words written backward, as they would be seen in a mirror, although he was surprised at this skill, as he did not remember having tried it before (Corkin, 2002). Patient K. C. has a part-time job at a library and has learned to use the Dewey decimal system in sorting books, although he does not remember when or where he learned it (Rosenbaum et al., 2005).

Here is another example of procedural memory: In the video game Tetris, geometrical forms such as ⊞ and ⊟ fall from the top, and the player must move and rotate them to fill available spaces at the bottom of the screen. Normal people improve their skill over a few hours and readily describe the game and its strategy. After playing the same number of hours, patients with amnesia cannot describe the game and say they don't remember playing it. Nevertheless, they improve, slowly. Moreover, when they are about to fall asleep, they report seeing images of little piles of blocks falling and rotating (Stickgold, Malia, Maguire, Roddenberry, & O'Connor, 2000). They are puzzled and wonder what these images mean!

In summary, people with amnesia, including H. M., generally show the following pattern:

- Normal working memory
- Severe anterograde amnesia for declarative memory—that is, difficulty forming new declarative memories, especially episodic memories.
- Some degree of retrograde amnesia—that is, loss of old memories—mainly limited to episodic memories.
- Better implicit than explicit memory.
- Nearly intact procedural memory.

➔ **STOP & CHECK**

5. What is the difference between anterograde and retrograde amnesia?

6. Which types of memory are least impaired in people with amnesia?

ANSWERS

5. Retrograde amnesia is forgetting events before brain damage; anterograde amnesia is failing to store memories of events after brain damage. **6.** People with amnesia are generally least impaired on working memory, implicit memory, and procedural memory.

Theories of the Function of the Hippocampus

Exactly how does the hippocampus contribute to memory? Some of the research comes from patients with damage to the hippocampus, but to get better control over both the anatomy and the environment, researchers also conduct research on laboratory animals.

The Hippocampus and Declarative Memory

Although patients with hippocampal damage acquire new skills, they have enormous trouble learning new facts. Larry Squire (1992) proposed that the hippocampus is critical for declarative memory, especially episodic memory. How could we test this hypothesis with nonhumans, who cannot "declare" anything? What could they do that would be the equivalent of declarative or episodic memory? Researchers have developed many clever approaches (Crystal, 2009). Here is one example: A rat digs food out of five piles of sand, each with a different odor. Then it gets a choice between two of the odors and is rewarded if it goes toward the one it smelled first. Intact rats learn to respond correctly, apparently demonstrating memory of not only what they smelled but also when they smelled it. Memory of a specific event qualifies as episodic, at least by a broad definition. Rats with hippocampal damage do poorly on this task (Fortin, Agster, & Eichenbaum, 2002; Kesner, Gilbert, & Barua, 2002).

In the **delayed matching-to-sample task**, an animal sees an object (the sample) and then, after a delay, gets a choice between two objects, from which it must choose the one that matches the sample. In the **delayed nonmatching-to-sample task**, the procedure is the same except that the animal must choose the object that is different from the sample (Figure 13.7). In both cases, the animal must remember which object was present on this occasion, thereby showing what we might call a declarative memory, perhaps an episodic memory. Hippocampal damage strongly impairs performance in most cases (Zola et al., 2000).

The Hippocampus and Spatial Memory

A second hypothesis focuses on spatial memories. Electrical recordings indicate that many neurons in a rat's hippocampus are tuned to particular spatial locations, responding best when an animal is in a particular place (O'Keefe & Burgess, 1996) or looking in a particular direction (Dudchenko & Taube, 1997; Rolls, 1996). When people perform spatial tasks, such as imagining the best route between one house and another, fMRI results show enhanced activity in the hippocampus (Kumaran & Maguire, 2005). An fMRI study with college students recorded their responses to photos of familiar campus sights. Buildings close to each other on campus produced more similar hippocampal responses than did those that are

Larry R. Squire

Memory is personal and evocative, intertwined with emotion, and it provides us with a sense of who we are.... There has been a revolution in our understanding of what memory is and what happens in the brain when we learn and remember. At the beginning of the 21st century, one has the sense that memory may be the first mental faculty that will be understandable in terms of molecules, cells, brain systems, and behavior. Yet, even with all the progress, there can be no doubt that the study of the brain is still a young science, rich with opportunity for the student and beginning scientist. This is a good time to hear about the promise and excitement of neuroscience. The best is yet to come. (Squire, personal communication)

farther apart (Morgan, MacEvoy, Aguirre, & Epstein, 2011). All of these results suggest a major role for the hippocampus in spatial memory.

Researchers conducted PET scans on the brains of London taxi drivers as they answered questions such as, "What's the shortest legal route from the Carlton Tower Hotel to the Sherlock Holmes Museum?" (London taxi drivers are well trained and answer with impressive accuracy.) Answering these route questions activated their hippocampus much more than did answering nonspatial questions. MRI scans also revealed that the taxi drivers have a larger than average posterior hippocampus and that the longer they had been taxi drivers, the larger their posterior hippocampus (Maguire et al., 2000). This surprising result suggests actual growth of the adult human hippocampus in response to spatial learning experiences.

Consider a couple of ways to test spatial memory in nonhumans. From a central point, a **radial maze** has several arms—typically eight—some or all of which have a bit of food at the end (Figure 13.8). A rat's best strategy is to explore each arm once and only once, remembering where it has already gone. In a variation of the task, a rat might have to learn that the arms with a rough floor never have food or that the arms pointing toward the window never have food. Thus, a rat can make a mistake either by entering a never-correct arm or by entering a correct arm twice.

Rats with damage to the hippocampus gradually learn not to enter the never-correct arms, but even after much training they often enter a correct arm twice. That is, they forget which arms they have already tried (Jarrard, Okaichi, Steward, & Goldschmidt, 1984; Olton & Papas, 1979; Olton, Walker, & Gage, 1978). With people, psychological researchers use a virtual radial maze that the person can navigate on a com-

Monkey lifts sample object to get food.

Food is under the new object.

FIGURE 13.7   A delayed nonmatching-to-sample task *(© Cengage Learning 2013)*

FIGURE 13.8 **A radial maze**
A rat that reenters one arm before trying other arms has made an error of spatial working memory.

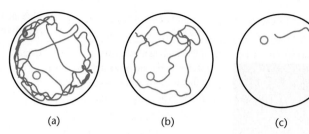

(a)   (b)   (c)

FIGURE 13.9 **The Morris water maze**
An intact rat learns by trial and error. In each case the line traces the path a rat took to the platform, marked by a circle. On the fifth trial (A), the rat stayed mainly near the edge and never found the platform. On the 34th trial (B), it found the platform in 35 seconds. On the 71st trial (C), it went directly to the platform in 6 seconds. (de Bruin, J. P. C., Winkels, W. A. M., & de Brabander, J. M. (1997). Response learning of rats in a Morris water maze: Involvement of the medial prefrontal cortex. Behavioral Brain Research, 85, 47–55.)

puter screen. On this task, people with damage to the hippocampus are slow to learn which arms are never correct, and they frequently visit one arm several times before trying all the others (Goodrich-Hunsaker & Hopkins, 2010). That is, the human data resemble those of rats.

Another test of spatial memory is the **Morris water maze**, in which a rat swims through murky water to find a rest platform that is just under the surface (Figure 13.9). (Rats swim as little as they can. Humans are among the very few land mammals that swim recreationally.) A rat with hippocampal damage slowly learns to find the platform if it always starts from the same place and the rest platform is always in the same place. However, if it has to start from a different location or if the rest platform occasionally moves from one location to another, the rat is disoriented (Eichenbaum, 2000; P. Liu & Bilkey, 2001).

If a rat already learned to find the platform before damage to the hippocampus, the damage leaves the rat exploring the water haphazardly, like a rat that had never been in the water maze before. It ignores landmarks, including a beacon of light pointing to the platform. Researchers observed that the rat acts as if it not only forgot where the platform was but also forgot that there even was a platform (R. E. Clark, Broadbent, & Squire, 2007).

As with the radial maze, researchers sometimes test people with a virtual water maze that they navigate on a computer. People with a rare condition called *acute transient global amnesia* have a temporary dysfunction of the hippocampus. If they are tested soon after onset of the condition, they are slow to learn the correct route in a virtual water maze (Bartsch et al., 2010).

Interesting evidence for the role of the hippocampus in spatial memory comes from comparisons of closely related species that differ in their spatial memory. Clark's nutcracker, a member of the jay family, lives at high altitudes in western North America. During the summer and fall, it buries seeds in thousands of locations and then digs them up to survive

the winter, when other food is unavailable. Pinyon jays live at lower elevations, bury less food, and depend on it less to survive the winter. Scrub jays and Mexican jays, living at still lower altitudes, depend even less on stored food. Of these four species, the Clark's nutcrackers have the largest hippocampus and perform best on tests of spatial memory. Pinyon jays are second best in both respects. On nonspatial tasks, such as color memory, size of hippocampus does not correlate with performance (Basil, Kamil, Balda, & Fite, 1996; Olson, Kamil, Balda, & Nims, 1995) (Figure 13.10). In short, species comparisons show a link between the hippocampus and spatial memory.

Hippocampus and Contextual Memory

A third hypothesis relates to learning about context. You could try this yourself: Describe something that you experienced yesterday or today. Then describe something you experienced months or years ago. How do your two narratives differ? Your recent narrative probably includes more detail about where you were, who else was there, where people were sitting, perhaps what some of them were wearing, exactly what certain people said, maybe the weather outside, and other important and not so important details. When you describe something from long ago, you remember the highlights or "gist" of the event but fewer details.

TRY IT YOURSELF

The hippocampus is important for remembering details and context. A recent memory, which generally depends on the hippocampus, includes much detail. As time passes, memory becomes less detailed, less dependent on the hippocampus, and more dependent on the cerebral cortex (Takehara-Nishiuchi & McNaughton, 2008). The same is true of rats: When rats are trained to do something, and then tested again after a short delay, they remember the response best if they are tested in the same location. That is, their memory depends on the context. As time passes, the context matters less and less, and to the extent that rats remember the response, they remember it equally

	Habitat	Size of Hippocampus Relative to Rest of Brain	Spatial Memory	Color Memory
Clark's nutcracker 	Lives high in mountains; stores food in summer and relies on finding it to survive the winter.	Largest	Best	Slightly worse
Pinyon jay 	Lives at fairly high altitude; depends on stored food to survive the winter.	Second largest	Second best	Slightly better
Scrub jay 	Stores some food but less dependent on it.	Smaller	Less good	Slightly worse
Mexican jay 	Stores some food but less dependent on it.	Smaller	Less good	Slightly better

FIGURE 13.10 Hippocampus and spatial memory in jays
Of four related species, the species that relies most heavily on stored food to get through the winter has the largest hippocampus and performs best on laboratory tests of spatial memory. Size of hippocampus does not relate consistently to nonspatial memory. *(Based on results of Basil, Kamil, Balda, & Fite, 1996; Olson, Kamil, Balda, & Nims, 1995) (© Tom Vezo/The Wildlife Collection)*

well in a different location. Rats with damage to the hippocampus, if they learn something at all, show no difference between testing in the familiar place and some other place. Their memory doesn't depend on context, presumably because they do not remember it (Winocur, Moscovitch, & Sekeres, 2007).

In humans, recalling a recent memory (which usually includes details and context) activates the hippocampus. Recalling an old factual memory may or may not activate the hippocampus, but episodic memories, because they necessarily include some context details, do activate the hippocampus. This hypothesis is well suited to dealing with the observation that people with hippocampal damage have particular trouble with episodic memories.

Single-cell recordings in rats confirm the idea that the hippocampus responds to context. In one study, rats learned that when they were in room A, they had to dig in flowerpot X instead of Y to find food, but in room B they had to dig in flowerpot Y instead of X, regardless of location of the flowerpots within each room. As already described, most cells in the hippocampus become active only in a particular location within a room or other setting. In this experiment, most of those "place" cells responded much more strongly to their preferred place if the correct kind of flowerpot was in that place (Komorowski, Manns, & Eichenbaum, 2009).

We have considered three hypotheses of the role of the hippocampus and found evidence to support each. The views are not necessarily in conflict, as the hippocampus probably contributes in more than one way. It is also possible that researchers will find a way to combine all three hypotheses into one.

7. Suppose a rat is in a radial maze in which six arms have food once per day, and two other arms never have food. What kind of mistake does a rat with hippocampal damage make?

8. According to the context hypothesis, why does hippocampal damage impair episodic memory?

ANSWERS

7. Although it learns not to enter the arms that are never correct, it seems to forget which arms it has entered today, and it enters a single arm repeatedly. 8. The hippocampus is especially important for remembering context, and episodic memory necessarily includes some context and detail.

The Basal Ganglia

The hippocampus is not responsible for all learning and memory. It is most important for episodic memory—the kind of memory that develops from a single experience. After damage to the hippocampus, learning still occurs, but it occurs gradually over repeated experiences, and it is often the kind of memory that is hard to put into words.

For example, imagine the following: You are playing basketball, guarding player #22, who sometimes shoots from the outside and sometimes tries to drive around you to the basket. You could guard more effectively if you knew that player's likely choice at this moment. If you play against this player long enough, you learn what to expect. He or she might be more likely to shoot from the outside when behind on the score, less likely if the last outside shot missed, more likely late in the game, less likely if player #31 is also in the lineup, and so forth. None of these cues by itself is an accurate predictor. That is, an episodic memory won't help, because whether your opponent shot from the inside or outside on one play doesn't provide you with reliable information. However, you might gradually pick up a pattern. When you do, you might say afterward that you just had a "hunch" your opponent was going to shoot from outside, and you guarded accordingly—and therefore won the game, let's suppose.

Gradual learning like that depends on the basal ganglia. We could call it implicit learning or habit learning. Let's consider another example, one that many researchers have used. On each trial, you are given three or four pieces of information, typically pictures (Figure 13.11), and your task is to use that information to predict the weather to be either sunny or rainy. By trial and error, you quickly discover that none of the pictures is completely accurate, but each is partly accurate. (This task resembles the actual task of weather forecasting.) For example, perhaps when the first picture is a light bulb instead of a candle, it usually rains. A butterfly instead of a fish in the second position, and a sailboat instead of a plane in the third position also indicate probable rain. By paying attention

FIGURE 13.11 The "weather" task of probabilistic learning Each picture provides information that enables a partly accurate prediction, but together they are highly accurate. (© Cengage Learning 2013)

to any one picture, you could guess correctly most of the time, but by attending to all three, you could increase your accuracy.

On this task, most normal people quickly adopt a strategy of responding based on one of the pictures, and therefore getting the correct answer most of the time but not always. We detect this strategy by the pattern of errors. That strategy is based on declarative memory—quickly noticing, for example, that a light bulb in the first position usually indicates rain. However, after many repetitions, gradually people start doing better, eventually approaching 100% correct, without necessarily being able to say what strategy they are following. Gradually the basal ganglia learned the pattern and established a habit. If we test people with Parkinson's disease, who have impairments of the basal ganglia, many of them perform about the same as normal people at first, because they have an intact hippocampus. However, even after many trials, they continue basing their answers on one picture, and they do not show the gradual improvement that requires the basal ganglia. On other kinds of complex learning tasks, if they don't form an explicit, declarative memory, they don't improve at all (Moody, Chang, Vanek, & Knowlton, 2010). That is, they don't learn habits and implicit memories.

People with amnesia from hippocampal damage perform randomly on the weather task for many trials, because they form no declarative memories and they cannot remember that any particular symbol is usually a signal for one type of weather or the other. In fact, even after many trials, they cannot describe the task or the instructions. However, if they continue long enough, they show gradual improvement, based on habits supported by the basal ganglia (Bayley, Frascino, & Squire, 2005; Shohamy, Myers, Kalanithi, & Gluck, 2008). If the signals switch, so that the signal that formerly predicted a high chance of rain now predicts a high chance of sun, they are very slow to switch their responses (Shohamy, Myers, Hopkins, Sage, & Gluck, 2009). When normal people try to learn a complex task under conditions of extreme distraction, they too learn slowly, like people with a damaged hippocampus. Their gradual learning under these conditions depends on the basal ganglia (Foerde, Knowlton, & Poldrack, 2006).

Together, these results do suggest that the hippocampus is more important for declarative memory and the basal ganglia more important for procedural memory. However, psychologists no longer believe in a strict separation between hippocampal tasks and basal ganglia tasks. Nearly all tasks activate both areas (Albouy et al., 2008), and it is possible to shift from one type of memory to the other, even on the same task.

> **STOP & CHECK**

9. If you learn a skill (e.g., predicting the weather) as a procedural habit, instead of learning the same skill as a declarative memory, how will the outcome differ?

ANSWER

9. If you learn it as a procedural habit (based on the basal ganglia), you will learn more slowly and probably be unable to describe what you have learned. However, if the task requires simultaneous attention to a variety of cues, you might reach a higher level of accurate performance than someone learning a declarative memory.

▌Other Types of Amnesia

Different kinds of brain damage produce different types of amnesia. Here we briefly consider two more examples: Korsakoff's syndrome and Alzheimer's disease.

Korsakoff's Syndrome

Korsakoff's syndrome, also known as *Wernicke-Korsakoff syndrome*, is brain damage caused by prolonged thiamine deficiency. Severe thiamine deficiency occurs mostly in chronic alcoholics who go for weeks at a time on a diet of nothing but alcoholic beverages, lacking in vitamins. The brain needs thiamine (vitamin B_1) to metabolize glucose, its primary fuel. Prolonged thiamine deficiency leads to a loss or shrinkage of neurons throughout the brain. One of the areas most affected is the dorsomedial thalamus, the main source of input to the prefrontal cortex. The symptoms of Korsakoff's syndrome are similar to those of people with damage to the prefrontal cortex, including apathy, confusion, and memory loss. They also overlap those of hippocampal damage, with major impairment of episodic memory and sparing of implicit memory.

A distinctive symptom of Korsakoff's syndrome is **confabulation**, in which patients fill in memory gaps with guesses. They seldom confabulate on semantic questions such as "What is the capital of Russia?" or nonsense questions such as "Who is Princess Lolita?" They confabulate mainly on questions about episodic memory, such as "What did you do last weekend?" (Borsutzky, Fujiwara, Brand, & Markowitsch, 2008; Schnider, 2003). Usually, the confabulated answer was true at some time in the past but not now, such as, "I went dancing," or "I visited with my children." Most of the confabulated answers are more pleasant than the currently true answers (Fotopoulou, Solms, & Turnbull, 2004). That tendency may reflect the patient's attempt to maintain pleasant emo-

tions or merely the fact that the patient's past life was, on the whole, more pleasant than the present.

The tendency to confabulate produces a fascinating influence on the strategies for studying. Suppose you have to learn a long list of three-word sentences such as: "Medicine cured hiccups" and "Tourist desired snapshot." Would you simply reread the list many times? Or would you alternate between reading the list and testing yourself?

Medicine cured _____.
Tourist desired _____.

Almost everyone learns better the second way. Completing the sentences forces you to be more active and calls your attention to the items you have not yet learned. Korsakoff's patients, however, learn much better the first way, by reading the list over and over. The reason is, when they test themselves, they confabulate. ("*Medicine cured headache. Tourist desired passport.*") Then they remember their confabulation instead of the correct answer (Hamann & Squire, 1995).

> **STOP & CHECK**

10. On what kind of question is someone with Korsakoff's syndrome most likely to confabulate?

ANSWER

10. Patients with Korsakoff's syndrome confabulate on questions for which they would expect to know the answer, such as questions about themselves. Their confabulations are usually statements that were true at one time.

Alzheimer's Disease

Another cause of memory loss is **Alzheimer's** (AHLTZ-hime-ers) **disease**. Daniel Schacter (1983) reported playing golf with an Alzheimer's patient who remembered the rules and jargon of the game correctly but kept forgetting how many strokes he took. On five occasions, he teed off, waited for the other player to tee off, and then teed off again, having forgotten his first shot. As with other amnesic patients, Alzheimer's patients have better procedural than declarative memory. They learn new skills but then surprise themselves with their good performance because they don't remember doing it before (Gabrieli, Corkin, Mickel, & Growdon, 1993). Their memory and alertness vary substantially from time to time, suggesting that many of their problems result from malfunctioning neurons, rather than the death of neurons (Palop, Chin, & Mucke, 2006). Increased arousal improves memory, and people who drink 3 to 5 cups of coffee per day are less likely than average to develop Alzheimer's (Eskelinen, Ngandu, Tuomilehto, Soininen, & Kivipelto, 2009).

Alzheimer's disease gradually progresses to more serious memory loss, confusion, depression, restlessness, hallucinations, delusions, sleeplessness, and loss of appetite. It occasionally strikes people younger than age 40 but becomes more common

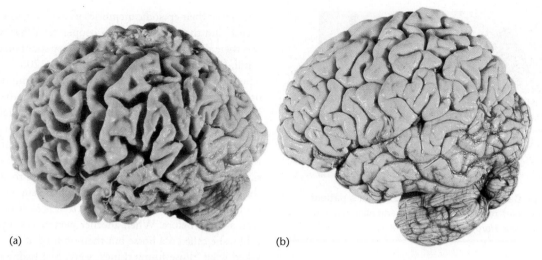

(a)   (b)

FIGURE 13.12 Brain atrophy in Alzheimer's disease
A patient with Alzheimer's (a) has gyri that are clearly shrunken in comparison with those of a normal person (b). *(Dr. Robert D. Terry, Department of Neurosciences, School of Medicine, University of California at San Diego)*

with age, affecting almost 5% of people between ages 65 and 74 and almost 50% of people over 85 (Evans et al., 1989).

The first major clue to the cause of Alzheimer's was the fact that people with *Down syndrome* (a type of mental retardation) almost invariably get Alzheimer's disease if they survive into middle age (Lott, 1982). People with Down syndrome have three copies of chromosome 21 rather than the usual two. That fact led investigators to examine chromosome 21, where they found a gene linked to many cases of early-onset Alzheimer's disease (Goate et al., 1991; Murrell, Farlow, Ghetti, & Benson, 1991). Later researchers found two more genes linked to early-onset Alzheimer's. For cases with onset of symptoms after age 60 to 65 (vastly more common than early-onset cases), one gene has a significant influence, and several other genes appear to be related in one population or another (Bertram & Tanzi, 2008). However, the genes linked to the late-onset variety increase the risk only slightly, as opposed to the genes for early onset that increase it strongly. About half of all patients with late-onset Alzheimer's disease have no known relatives with the disease (St George-Hyslop, 2000).

Although genes do not completely control Alzheimer's disease, understanding the genes shed light on the disease itself. The genes controlling early-onset Alzheimer's disease cause a protein called **amyloid-β** to accumulate both inside and outside neurons (LaFerla, Green, & Oddo, 2007). The impact varies among cells (Abramov et al., 2009; Busche et al., 2008), but the net effect is to damage dendritic spines, decrease synaptic input, and decrease plasticity (Wei, Nguyen, Kessels, Hagiwara, Sisodia, & Malinow, 2010).

As amyloid damages axons and dendrites, the damaged structures cluster into structures called plaques (Selkoe, 2000). As the plaques accumulate, the cerebral cortex, hippocampus, and other areas atrophy (waste away), as Figures 13.12 and 13.13 show.

In addition to amyloid-β, a second problem relates to the **tau protein** in the intracellular support structure of axons (Davies, 2000). High levels of amyloid-β cause more phos-

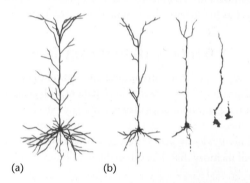

(a)   (b)

FIGURE 13.13 Neuronal degeneration in Alzheimer's disease
(a) A cell in the prefrontal cortex of a normal human; (b) cells from the same area of cortex in Alzheimer's disease patients at various stages of deterioration. *(© Cengage Learning 2013. After "Dendritic changes," by A. B. Scheibel, p. 70. In B. Reisberg, Ed.,* Alzheimer's Disease, *1983. Free Press.)*

phate groups to attach to tau proteins. The altered tau can't bind to its usual targets within axons, and so it starts spreading into the cell body and dendrites. The attack of tau from within dendrites adds to the attack by amyloid-β, magnifying the damage. Researchers hypothesize that altered tau also increases the production of amyloid-β, causing a vicious cycle (Ittner & Götz, 2011). The altered tau is principally responsible for tangles, structures formed from degeneration within neurons (Figure 13.14). The pattern of amyloid, tau, and other chemicals varies from one Alzheimer's patient to another, and it may be useful to distinguish several subtypes of patients (Iqbal & Grundke-Iqbal, 2010).

At this point, no drug is highly effective for Alzheimer's disease, although many new possibilities are under investigation (Roberson & Mucke, 2006). The most common treatment is to give drugs that stimulate acetylcholine receptors or prolong acetylcholine release. The result is increased arousal.

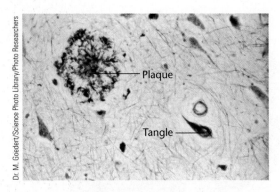

FIGURE 13.14 Cerebral cortex of an Alzheimer's patient
Plaques and tangles result from amyloid-β and abnormal tau protein. *(From Taylor, Hardy, & Fischbeck, 2002)*

An interesting possibility is *curcumin*, a component of turmeric, a spice in Indian curries. Research with animals shows that curcumin inhibits amyloid-β deposits and phosphate attachment to tau proteins. Research on possible human applications has just begun (Hamaguchi, Ono, & Tamada, 2010).

What Patients with Amnesia Teach Us

The study of patients with amnesia reveals that people do not lose all aspects of memory equally. A patient with great difficulty establishing new memories may remember events from long ago, and someone with greatly impaired factual memory may learn new skills. Evidently, people have several somewhat independent kinds of memory that depend on different brain areas.

> **STOP & CHECK**

11. How does amyloid-β relate to tau?

ANSWER 11. The protein amyloid-β accumulates both inside and outside neurons. Within neurons, it increases phosphate attachment to tau proteins. The altered tau proteins no longer attach to their usual sites, and therefore they spread to cell bodies and dendrites, where they add to the damage that amyloid-β caused.

▮ Other Brain Areas in Memory

Most of this module has focused on the hippocampus and the basal ganglia. Chapter 12 mentioned the importance of the amygdala for fear memories. Other brain areas are important for learning and memory, too. In fact, most of the brain contributes in one way or another.

Investigators asked two patients with parietal lobe damage to describe various events from their past. When tested this way, their episodic memory appeared sparse, almost devoid of details. However, the investigators asked follow-up questions, such as, "Where were you?" and "Who else was there at the time?" Then these patients answered in reasonable detail, indi-

cating that their episodic memories were intact, as well as their speech and their willingness to cooperate. What was lacking was their ability to elaborate on a memory spontaneously (Berryhill, Phuong, Picasso, Cabeza, & Olson, 2007). Ordinarily, when most of us recall an event, one thing reminds us of another, and we start adding one detail after another, until we have said all that we know. In people with parietal lobe damage, that process of associating one piece with another is impaired.

People with damage in the anterior and inferior regions of the temporal lobe suffer **semantic dementia**, a loss of semantic memory. One patient while riding down a road saw some sheep and asked what they were. The problem wasn't that he couldn't remember the word *sheep*. It was as if he had never seen a sheep before. When another person saw a picture of a zebra, she called it a horse but then pointed at the stripes and asked what "those funny things" were. She hadn't merely lost the word *zebra* but had lost the concept of zebra. Such patients cannot remember the typical color of common fruits and vegetables or the appearance of various animals. Don't think of the anterior and inferior temporal lobe as the sole point of storage for semantic memory. These areas store some of the information and serve as a "hub" for communicating with other brain areas to bring together a full concept (Patterson, Nestor, & Rogers, 2007). Serious deficits in semantic memory occur only after bilateral damage. People with damage to the temporal cortex in just one hemisphere perform approximately normally (Ralph, Cipoloti, Manes, & Patterson, 2010).

Parts of the prefrontal cortex, shown in Figure 13.15, are important for learning about rewards and punishments. The basal ganglia also learn about the reward values of various actions, but they learn slowly, based on the average reward over a long period of time. The prefrontal cortex responds more quickly, based on the most recent events. If you are confronted with an opportunity to make a response, cells in the ventromedial prefrontal cortex respond based on the reward to be expected, based on past experience. Cells in the orbitofrontal cortex respond based on how that reward compares to other possible choices. For example, a $2 reward might be good or bad depending on whether other choices offer a $1 or $5 reward (Frank & Claus, 2006). Cells in the orbitofrontal cortex are also important for "self control." If you have a choice between a small reward now and a larger one later, you try to restrain your impulse to take the immediate reward. If the orbitofrontal cortex is damaged or temporarily inactivated, you become more likely to take the immediate reward (Figner et al., 2010; Sellitto, Ciaramelli, & De Pellegrino, 2010). Children have trouble restraining their impulses, because the prefrontal cortex is slow to mature.

> **STOP & CHECK**

12. Which brain area records the expected gains and losses associated with possible actions?

ANSWER 12. The prefrontal cortex.

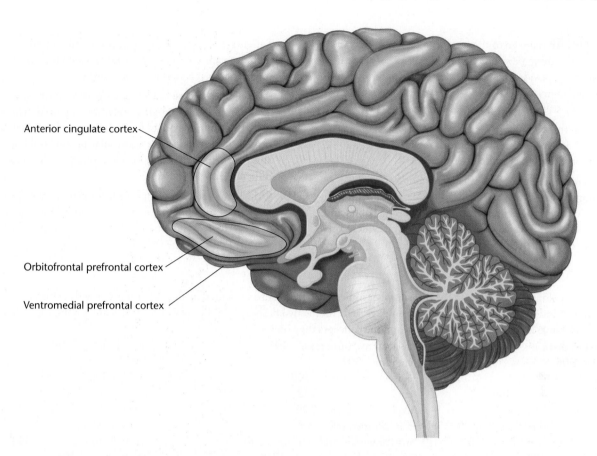

FIGURE 13.15 Three areas important for making decisions
These areas respond to the expected outcome of a decision relative to other possible outcomes and to discrepancies between actual and expected outcomes. The orbitofrontal cortex gets its name because it is close to the orbit of the eye. *(© Cengage Learning 2013)*

MODULE 13.1 ■ IN CLOSING

Different Types of Memory

"Overall intelligence," as measured by an IQ test, is a convenient fiction. It is convenient because, under most circumstances, people who are good at one kind of intellectual task are also good at other kinds, so an overall test score makes useful predictions. However, it is a fiction because different kinds of abilities rely on different brain processes, and it is possible to damage one but not another. Even memory is composed of separate abilities, and it is possible to lose one type or aspect of memory without impairing others. The study of amnesia shows how the brain operates as a series of partly independent mechanisms serving specific purposes.

SUMMARY

1. Ivan Pavlov suggested that learning depends on the growth of a connection between two brain areas. Karl Lashley showed that learning does *not* depend on new connections across the cerebral cortex. **390**

2. Richard Thompson found that some instances of classical conditioning take place in small areas of the cerebellum. **392**

3. Psychologists distinguish between short-term memory and long-term memory. Short-term memory holds only a small amount of information and retains it only briefly unless it is constantly rehearsed. **394**

4. Working memory, a modern alternative to the concept of short-term memory, stores information that one is currently using. **395**

5. People with damage to the hippocampus have great trouble forming new long-term declarative memories, especially episodic memories. However, they still show implicit memory, they still store short-term memories, and they still form new procedural memories.   **396**

6. Several theories about the hippocampus focus on its role in declarative memory, spatial memory, and memory for details and context.   **399**

7. Whereas the hippocampus is important for rapid storage of an event, the basal ganglia learn gradually. Gradual learning is important for developing habits and for seeing complex patterns that may not be evident on a single trial.   **403**

8. Patients with Korsakoff's syndrome often fill in their memory gaps with confabulations, which they then remember as if they were true.   **404**

9. Alzheimer's disease is a progressive disease, most common in old age, characterized by impaired memory and attention. It is related to deposition of amyloid-β protein in the brain. The accumulating amyloid leads to abnormalities of the tau protein, causing additional difficulties.   **404**

10. Other brain areas are important for elaborating episodic memories, for semantic memories, and for memories of the reward or punishment values of various possible actions.   **406**

KEY TERMS

Terms are defined in the module on the page number indicated. They're also presented in alphabetical order with definitions in the book's Subject Index/Glossary, which begins on page 561. Interactive flashcards and crossword puzzles are among the online resources available to help you learn these terms and the concepts they represent.

THOUGHT QUESTION

Lashley sought to find the engram, the physiological representation of learning. In general terms, how would you recognize an engram if you saw one? That is, what would someone have to demonstrate before you could conclude that a particular change in the nervous system was really an engram?

Storing Information in the Nervous System

I f you walk through a field, are the footprints that you leave "memories"? How about the mud that you pick up on your shoes? If the police wanted to know who walked across that field, a forensics expert could check your shoes to answer the question. And yet we would not call these physical traces memories in the usual sense.

Similarly, when a pattern of activity passes through the brain, it leaves a path of physical changes, but not every change is a memory. The task of finding how the brain stores memories is a little like searching for the proverbial needle in a haystack, and researchers have explored many avenues that seemed promising for a while but now seem fruitless.

APPLICATIONS AND EXTENSIONS

Blind Alleys and Abandoned Mines

Textbooks, this one included, concentrate mostly on successful research that led to our current understanding of a field. You may get the impression that science progresses smoothly, with each investigator contributing to the body of knowledge. However, if you look at old journals or textbooks, you will find discussions of many "promising" or "exciting" findings that we disregard today. Scientific research does not progress straight from ignorance to enlightenment. It explores one direction after another, a little like a rat in a complex maze, abandoning the dead ends and pursuing arms that lead further.

The problem with the maze analogy is that an investigator seldom runs into a wall that clearly identifies the end of a route. A better analogy is a prospector digging for gold, never certain whether to abandon an unprofitable spot or to keep digging just a little longer. Many once-exciting lines of research in the physiology of learning are now of little more than historical interest. Here are three examples.

1. Wilder Penfield sometimes performed brain surgery for severe epilepsy on conscious patients who had only scalp anesthesia. When he applied a brief, weak electrical stimulus to part of the brain, the patient could describe the experience that the stimulation evoked. Stimulation of the temporal cortex sometimes evoked vivid descriptions such as:

I feel as though I were in the bathroom at school.
I see myself at the corner of Jacob and Washington in South Bend, Indiana.
I remember myself at the railroad station in Vanceburg, Kentucky; it is winter and the wind is blowing outside, and I am waiting for a train.

Penfield (1955; Penfield & Perot, 1963) suggested that each neuron stores a particular memory, like a videotape of one's life. However, brain stimulation rarely elicited a memory of a specific event. Usually, it evoked vague sights and sounds, or recollections of common experiences such as "seeing a bed" or "hearing a choir sing 'White Christmas.'" Stimulation almost never elicited memories of doing anything—just of seeing and hearing. Also, some patients reported events that they had never actually experienced, such as being chased by a robber or seeing Christ descend from the sky. In short, the stimulation produced something more like a dream than a memory.

2. G. A. Horridge (1962) apparently demonstrated that decapitated cockroaches can learn. First he cut the connections between a cockroach's head and the rest of its body. Then he suspended the cockroach so that its legs dangled just above a surface of water. An electrical circuit was arranged as in Figure 13.16 so that the roach's leg received a shock whenever it touched the water. Each experimental roach was paired with a control roach that got a leg shock whenever the first roach did. Only the experimental roach had any control over the shock, however. This kind of experiment is known as a "yoked-control" design.

Over 5 to 10 minutes, roaches in the experimental group increased a response of tucking the leg under the body to avoid shocks. Roaches in the control group did not, on average, change their leg position as a result of the shocks. Thus, the changed response apparently qualifies as learning and not as an accidental byproduct of the shocks.

These experiments initially seemed a promising way to study learning in a simple nervous system (Eisenstein & Cohen, 1965). Unfortunately, decapitated cockroaches learn slowly, and the results vary sharply from one individ-

409

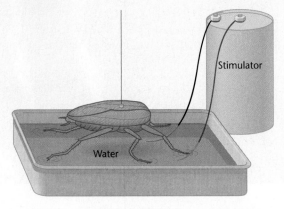

FIGURE 13.16 Learning in a headless cockroach?
The decapitated cockroach, suspended just above the water, receives a shock whenever its hind leg touches the water. A cockroach in the control group gets a shock whenever the first roach does regardless of its own behavior. According to some reports, the experimental roach learned to keep its leg out of the water. *(From G. A. Horridge, "Learning of Leg Position by the Ventral Nerve Cord in Headless Insects." Proceedings of the Royal Society of London, B, 157, 1962, 33–52. Copyright © 1962 The Royal Society of London. Reprinted by permission of the Royal Society of London and G. A. Horridge.)*

ual to another, limiting the usefulness of the results. After a handful of studies, interest in this line of research faded.

3. In the 1960s and early 1970s, several investigators proposed that each memory is coded as a specific molecule, probably RNA or protein. The boldest test of that hypothesis was an attempt to transfer memories chemically from one individual to another. James McConnell (1962) reported that, when planaria (flatworms) cannibalized other planaria that had been classically conditioned to respond to a light, they apparently "remembered" what the cannibalized planaria had learned. At least they learned the response faster than planaria generally do.

Inspired by that report, other investigators trained rats to approach a clicking sound for food (Babich, Jacobson, Bubash, & Jacobson, 1965). After the rats were well trained, the experimenters ground up their brains, extracted RNA, and injected it into untrained rats. The recipient rats learned to approach the clicking sound faster than rats in the control group did.

That report led to a wealth of studies on the transfer of training by brain extracts. In some of these experiments, rats that received brain extracts from a trained group showed apparent memory of the task, whereas those that received extracts from an untrained group did not (Dyal, 1971; Fjerdingstad, 1973). The results were inconsistent and unreplicable, however, even within a single laboratory (L. T. Smith, 1975). Many laboratories failed to find any hint of a transfer effect. By the mid-1970s, most biological psychologists saw no point in continuing this research. ∎

Mary Ellen Hebb

Donald O. Hebb
(1904–1985)

Modern psychology takes completely for granted that behavior and neural function are perfectly correlated.... There is no separate soul or life force to stick a finger into the brain now and then and make neural cells do what they would not otherwise.... It is quite conceivable that some day the assumption will have to be rejected. But it is important also to see that we have not reached that day yet.... One cannot logically be a determinist in physics and chemistry and biology, and a mystic in psychology. (Hebb, 1946, p. xiii)

Learning and the Hebbian Synapse

Research on the physiology of learning began with Ivan Pavlov's concept of classical conditioning. Although, as we considered earlier, that theory led Karl Lashley to an unsuccessful search for connections in the cerebral cortex, it also stimulated Donald Hebb to propose a mechanism for change at a synapse.

Hebb suggested that when the axon of neuron A "repeatedly or persistently takes part in firing [cell B], some growth process or metabolic change takes place in one or both cells" that increases the subsequent ability of axon A to excite cell B (Hebb, 1949, p. 62). In other words, an axon that has successfully stimulated cell B in the past becomes even more successful in the future.

Consider how this process relates to classical conditioning. Suppose axon A initially excites cell B slightly, and axon C excites B more strongly. If A and C fire together, their combined effect on B may produce an action potential. You might think of axon A as the CS and axon C as the UCS. Pairing activity in axons A and C increases the future effect of A on B.

A synapse that increases in effectiveness because of simultaneous activity in the presynaptic and postsynaptic neurons is called a **Hebbian synapse**. In Chapter 6, we encountered examples of this type of synapse. In the development of the visual system, if an axon from the left eye consistently fires at the same time as one from the right eye, a neuron in the visual cortex increases its response to both of them. Such synapses may also be critical for many kinds of associative learning. Neuroscientists have discovered much about the mechanisms of Hebbian synapses.

▶ **STOP & CHECK**

13. How can a Hebbian synapse account for the basic phenomena of classical conditioning?

ANSWER

13. In a Hebbian synapse, pairing the activity of a weaker (CS) axon with a stronger (UCS) axon produces an action potential and in the process strengthens the response of the cell to the CS axon. On later trials, it will produce a bigger depolarization of the postsynaptic cell, which we can regard as a conditioned response.

Single-Cell Mechanisms of Invertebrate Behavior Change

If we are going to look for a needle in a haystack, a good strategy is to look in a small haystack. Therefore, many researchers have turned to studies of invertebrates. Vertebrate and invertebrate nervous systems are organized differently, but the chemistry of the neuron, the principles of the action potential, and the neurotransmitters and their receptors are the same. If we identify the physical basis of learning and memory in an invertebrate, we have at least a hypothesis of what *might* work in vertebrates. (Biologists have long used this strategy for studying genetics, embryology, and other biological processes.)

Aplysia as an Experimental Animal

Aplysia, a marine invertebrate related to the common slug, has been a popular animal for studies of the physiology of learning (Figure 13.17). Compared to vertebrates, it has fewer neurons, many of which are large and easy to study. Moreover, unlike vertebrates, *Aplysia* neurons are virtually identical from one individual to another so that different investigators can study the properties of the same neuron.

One commonly studied behavior is the withdrawal response: If someone touches the siphon, mantle, or gill of an *Aplysia* (Figure 13.18), the animal vigorously withdraws the irritated structure. Investigators have traced the neural path from the touch receptors through other neurons to the motor neurons that direct the response. Using this neural pathway, investigators have studied changes in behavior as a result of experience. In 2000, Eric Kandel won a Nobel prize for this work.

Habituation in *Aplysia*

Habituation is a decrease in response to a stimulus that is presented repeatedly and accompanied by no change in other stimuli. For example, if your clock chimes every hour, you gradually respond less and less. If we repeatedly stimulate an

Eric R. Kandel

The questions posed by higher cognitive processes such as learning and memory are formidable, and we have only begun to explore them. Although elementary aspects of simple forms of learning have been accessible to molecular analysis in invertebrates, we are only now beginning to know a bit about the genes and proteins involved in more complex, hippocampus based learning processes of mammals.

Aplysia's gills with a brief jet of seawater, it withdraws at first, but after many repetitions, it stops responding. The decline in response is not due to muscle fatigue because, even after habituation has occurred, direct stimulation of the motor neuron produces a full-size muscle contraction (Kupfermann, Castellucci, Pinsker, & Kandel, 1970). We can also rule out changes in the sensory neuron. The sensory neuron still gives a full, normal response to stimulation; it merely fails to excite the motor neuron as much as before (Kupfermann et al., 1970). We are therefore left with the conclusion that habituation in *Aplysia* depends on a change in the synapse between the sensory neuron and the motor neuron (Figure 13.19).

Sensitization in *Aplysia*

If you experience an unexpected, intense pain, you temporarily react more strongly than usual to other strong, sudden stimuli. This phenomenon is **sensitization**, an increase in response to mild stimuli as a result of exposure to more intense stimuli. Similarly, a strong stimulus almost anywhere on *Aplysia*'s skin intensifies a later withdrawal response to a touch.

Researchers traced sensitization to changes at identified synapses (Cleary, Hammer, & Byrne, 1989; Dale, Schacher, & Kandel, 1988; Kandel & Schwartz, 1982). Strong stimulation

FIGURE 13.17 *Aplysia*, **a marine mollusk**
A full-grown animal is a little larger than the average human hand.

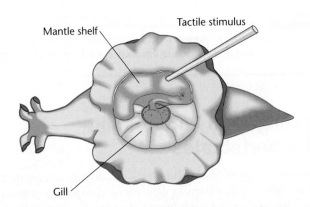

FIGURE 13.18 **Touching an** *Aplysia* **causes a withdrawal response**
The sensory and motor neurons controlling this reaction have been identified and studied. (© *Cengage Learning 2013*)

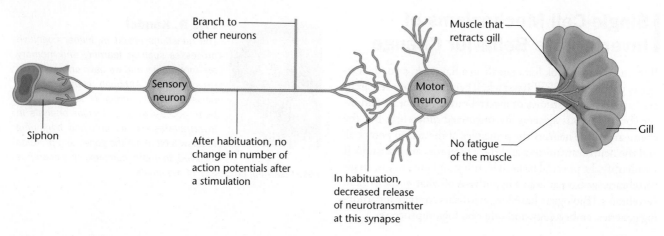

FIGURE 13.19 Habituation of the gill-withdrawal reflex in *Aplysia*
Touching the siphon causes gill withdrawal. After many repetitions, the response habituates (declines) because of decreased transmission at the synapse between the sensory neuron and the motor neuron. *(Redrawn from "Neuronal Mechanisms of Habituation and Dishabituation of the Gill-Withdrawal Reflex in Aplysia," by V. Castellucci, H. Pinsker, I. Kupfermann, and E. Kandel,* Science, 167, *pp. 1745–1748. Copyright © 1970 by AAAS. Used by permission of AAAS and V. Castellucci.)*

on the skin excites a *facilitating interneuron* that releases serotonin (5-HT) onto the presynaptic terminals of many sensory neurons. Serotonin blocks potassium channels in these membranes. The result is that after later action potentials, the membrane takes longer than usual to repolarize (because potassium is slow to flow out of the cell). Therefore, the presynaptic neuron continues releasing its neurotransmitter for longer than usual. Repeating this process causes the sensory neuron to synthesize new proteins that produce long-term sensitization (C. H. Bailey, Giustetto, Huang, Hawkins, & Kandel, 2000). This research shows how it is possible to explain one example of behavioral plasticity in terms of molecular events. Later studies explored mechanisms of classical and instrumental conditioning in *Aplysia*.

> **STOP & CHECK**

14. When serotonin blocks potassium channels on the presynaptic terminal, what is the effect on transmission?

ANSWER
14. Blocking potassium channels prolongs the action potential and therefore prolongs the release of neurotransmitters, producing an increased response.

Long-Term Potentiation in Vertebrates

Since the work of Sherrington and Cajal, most neuroscientists have assumed that learning depends on changes at synapses, and the work on *Aplysia* supports that idea. The first evidence for a similar process among vertebrates came from studies of neurons in the rat hippocampus (Bliss & Lømo, 1973). The phenomenon, known as **long-term potentiation (LTP)**, is

this: One or more axons connected to a dendrite bombard it with a rapid series of stimuli. The burst of intense stimulation leaves some of the synapses potentiated (more responsive to new input of the same type) for minutes, days, or weeks.

LTP shows three properties that make it an attractive candidate for a cellular basis of learning and memory:

- **specificity**—If some of the synapses onto a cell have been highly active and others have not, only the active ones become strengthened.

- **cooperativity**—Nearly simultaneous stimulation by two or more axons produces LTP much more strongly than does repeated stimulation by just one axon.

- **associativity**—Pairing a weak input with a strong input enhances later response to the weak input, as illustrated in Figure 13.20. In this regard, LTP matches what we would expect of Hebbian synapses. In some cases, a synapse that was almost completely inactive before LTP becomes effective afterward (Kerchner & Nicoll, 2008).

The opposite change, **long-term depression (LTD)**, a prolonged decrease in response at a synapse, occurs for axons that have been less active than others, such as axon 3 in Figure 13.20 (Collingridge, Peineau, Howland, & Wang, 2010). You can think of this as a compensatory process. As one synapse strengthens, another weakens (Royer & Paré, 2003). If learning produced only a strengthening of synapses, then every time you learned something, your brain would get more and more active, burning more and more fuel!

Biochemical Mechanisms

Determining how LTP or LTD occurs has been a huge research challenge because each neuron has many tiny synapses, sometimes in the tens of thousands. Isolating the chemical

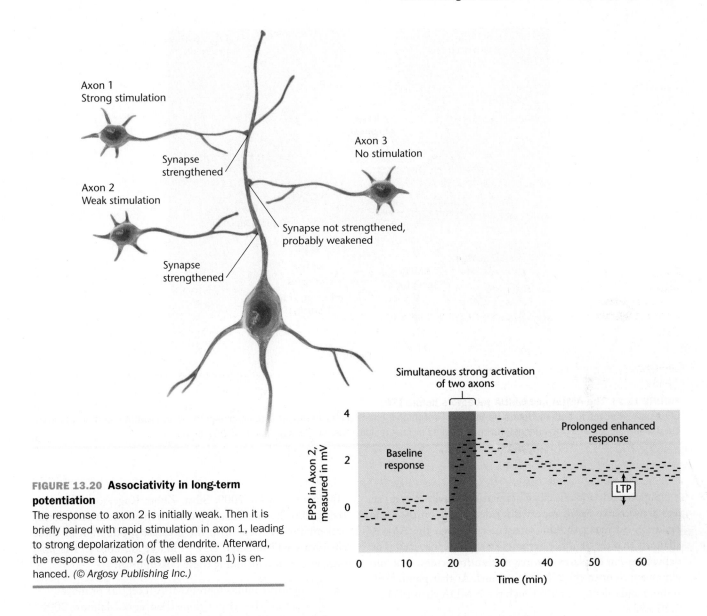

FIGURE 13.20 Associativity in long-term potentiation
The response to axon 2 is initially weak. Then it is briefly paired with rapid stimulation in axon 1, leading to strong depolarization of the dendrite. Afterward, the response to axon 2 (as well as axon 1) is enhanced. (© Argosy Publishing Inc.)

changes at any one synapse takes an enormous amount of creative research. We shall discuss LTP in the hippocampus, where it occurs most readily and where its mechanisms have been most extensively studied.

AMPA and NMDA Synapses

In a few cases, LTP depends on changes at GABA synapses (Nugent, Penick, & Kauer, 2007), but in most cases, it depends on changes at glutamate synapses. The brain has several types of receptors for glutamate, its most abundant transmitter. Neuroscientists identify different dopamine receptors by number, such as D_1 and D_2, and different GABA receptors by letter, such as $GABA_A$. For glutamate, they named the different receptors after certain drugs that stimulate them. Here we are interested in two types of glutamate receptors, called AMPA and NMDA. The **AMPA receptor** is excited by the neurotransmitter glutamate, but it can also respond to a drug called α-amino-3-hydroxy-5-methyl-4-isoxazolepropionic acid (abbreviated AMPA). The **NMDA receptor** is also ordinarily excited only by glutamate, but it can respond to a drug called N-methyl-D-aspartate (abbreviated NMDA).

Both are ionotropic receptors. That is, when they are stimulated, they open a channel to let ions enter the postsynaptic cell. The AMPA receptor is a typical ionotropic receptor that opens sodium channels. The NMDA receptor, however, is different: Its response to the transmitter glutamate *depends on the degree of polarization across the membrane*. When glutamate attaches to an NMDA receptor while the membrane is at its resting potential, the ion channel is usually blocked by magnesium ions. (Magnesium ions, positively charged, are attracted to the negative charge inside the cells but do not fit through the NMDA channel.) The NMDA channel opens only if the magnesium leaves, and the surest way to detach the magnesium is to depolarize the membrane, decreasing the negative charge that attracts it (Figure 13.21).

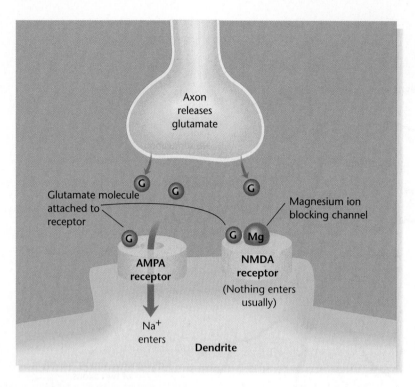

FIGURE 13.21 The AMPA and NMDA receptors before LTP
Glutamate attaches to both receptors. At the AMPA receptor, it opens a channel to let sodium ions enter. At the NMDA receptor, it binds but usually fails to open the channel, which is blocked by magnesium ions. (© *Cengage Learning 2013*)

Suppose an axon releases glutamate repeatedly. Better yet, let's activate two axons repeatedly, side by side on the same dendrite. So many sodium ions enter through the AMPA channels that the dendrite becomes strongly depolarized. The depolarization displaces the magnesium molecules, enabling glutamate to open the NMDA channel. At that point, both sodium and calcium enter through the NMDA channel (Figure 13.22).

The entry of calcium is the key to maintaining LTP. When calcium enters through the NMDA channel, it activates a protein called CaMKII (α-calcium-calmodulin-dependent protein kinase II) (Lisman, Schulman, & Cline, 2002; Otmakhov et al., 2004). CaMKII sets in motion a series of reactions leading to release of a protein called CREB—cyclic adenosine monophosphate responsive element-binding protein. (You can see why it's almost always abbreviated.) CREB goes to the nucleus of the cell and regulates the expression of several genes. In some cases, the altered gene expression lasts for months or years, long enough to account for long-term memory (Miller et al., 2010). The effects of CaMKII and CREB are magnified by **BDNF**—brain-derived neurotrophic factor, a neurotrophin similar to nerve growth factor that Chapter 5 discussed. Persisting activity at synapses leads to action potentials that start in axons but back-propagate into the dendrites, which then release BDNF. The formation and maintenance of LTP depends on all these chemicals—CaMKII, CREB, and BDNF (Kuczewski et al.,

2008; Minichiello, 2009; Silva, Zhou, Rogerson, Shobe, & Balaji, 2009), as well as others. When neurons are repeatedly activated, only those with the greatest production of these chemicals will undergo LTP (Han et al., 2007). The final outcome varies, including these possibilities:

- The dendrite builds more AMPA receptors or moves old ones into better positions (Poncer & Malinow, 2001; Takahashi, Svoboda, & Malinow, 2003).

- The dendrite may make more branches and spines, thus forming additional synapses with the same axon (Engert & Bonhoeffer, 1999; Toni, Buchs, Nikonenko, Bron, & Muller, 1999; Xu et al., 2009) (Figure 13.23). Recall from Chapter 5 that enriched experience also leads to increased dendritic branching.

- Phosphate groups attach to certain AMPA receptors to make them more responsive than before.

- In some cases, the neuron makes more NMDA receptors (Grosshans, Clayton, Coultrap, & Browning, 2002).

Let's summarize: When glutamate massively stimulates AMPA receptors, the resulting depolarization enables glutamate to stimulate nearby NMDA receptors also. Stimulation of the NMDA receptors lets calcium enter the cell, where it sets into motion a series of changes that potentiate the dendrite's future responsiveness to glutamate at AMPA receptors. After LTP occurs, NMDA receptors revert to their original condition.

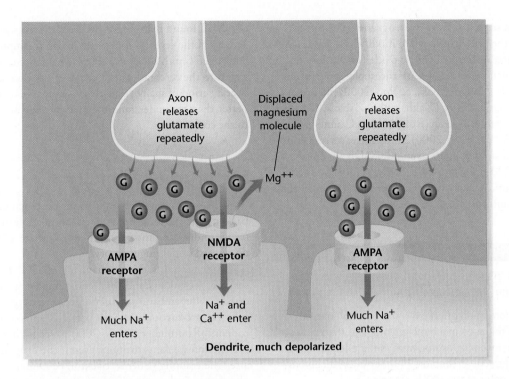

FIGURE 13.22 The AMPA and NMDA receptors during LTP
If one or more AMPA receptors have been repeatedly stimulated, enough sodium enters to largely depolarize the dendrite's membrane. Doing so displaces the magnesium ions and enables glutamate to open the NMDA receptor, through which sodium and calcium enter. *(© Cengage Learning 2013)*

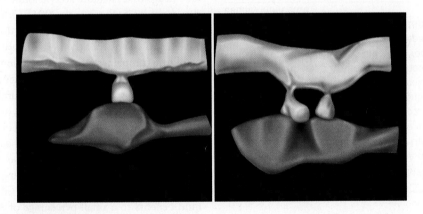

FIGURE 13.23 One way in which LTP occurs
In some cases, the dendrite makes new branches to the same axon, increasing the overall stimulation. *(Based on Toni, Buchs, Nikonenko, Bron, & Muller, 1999)*

Once LTP has been established, it no longer depends on NMDA synapses. Drugs that block NMDA synapses prevent the *establishment* of LTP, but they do not interfere with the *maintenance* of LTP that was already established (Gustafsson & Wigström, 1990; Uekita & Okaichi, 2005). In other words, once LTP occurs, the AMPA receptors stay potentiated, regardless of what happens to the NMDAs.

This question might occur to you: LTP depends on chemicals that alter gene expression, but LTP occurs only at the synapses that were highly activated. So how do the genes know which synapses to strengthen? The answer is that during the period of heavy bombardment at a synapse, chemical changes at that synapse mark it for later identification by chemicals circulating through the cell (Redondo & Morris, 2011; Wang et al., 2009).

Presynaptic Changes

The changes just described occur in the postsynaptic neuron. In many cases, LTP depends on changes in the presynaptic neuron instead or in addition. Extensive stimulation of a postsynaptic cell causes it to release a **retrograde transmitter** that travels back to the presynaptic cell to modify it. In many cases, that retrograde transmitter is nitric oxide (NO). As a result, a presynaptic neuron decreases its threshold for producing action potentials (Ganguly, Kiss, & Poo, 2000), increases its release of neurotransmitter (Zakharenko, Zablow, & Siegelbaum, 2001), expands its axon (Routtenberg, Cantallops, Zaffuto, Serrano, & Namgung, 2000), and releases its transmitter from additional sites along its axon (Reid, Dixon, Takahashi, Bliss, & Fine, 2004). In short, LTP reflects increased activity by the presynaptic neuron as well as increased responsiveness by the postsynaptic neuron.

> **STOP & CHECK**

15. Before LTP: In the normal state, what is the effect of glutamate at the AMPA receptors? At the NMDA receptors?

16. During the formation of LTP: When a burst of intense stimulation releases much more glutamate than usual at two or more incoming axons, what is the effect of the glutamate at the AMPA receptors? At the NMDA receptors? Which ions enter at the NMDA receptors?

17. After the neuron has gone through LTP: What is now the effect of glutamate at the AMPA receptors? At the NMDA receptors?

ANSWERS

15. Before LTP glutamate stimulates AMPA receptors but usually has little effect at the NMDA receptors because magnesium blocks them. 16. During the formation of LTP the massive glutamate input strongly stimulates the AMPA receptors, thus depolarizing the dendrite. This depolarization enables glutamate to excite the NMDA receptors also. Both calcium and sodium enter there. 17. After LTP has been established, glutamate stimulates the AMPA receptors more than before, mainly because of an increased number of AMPA receptors. At the NMDA receptors, it is again usually ineffective.

Consolidation, Revisited

Earlier in the chapter, we encountered the concept that a short-term memory can be consolidated into a long-term memory. Long-term potentiation in the hippocampus is important for certain types of learning, but as time passes and learning proceeds, the memory becomes less dependent on the hippocampus and more dependent on the cerebral cortex (Sacco & Sacchetti, 2010). This process is gradual over varying periods of time. In one study, fMRI showed that after people learned some associations, they showed more activity in the hippocampus after 15 minutes, and more activity in the cerebral cortex after 24 hours (Takashima et al., 2009). In another study, people aged 51–64 answered detailed questions about news events of the previous 30 years—the kind of events you might remember only if you were attending to news events at the time. Measurements us-

ing fMRI found that progressively older events produced more activity in the cerebral cortex and less in the hippocampus and amygdala (Smith & Squire, 2009). That is, we can demonstrate a shift to the cerebral cortex both over a period of one day and over a period of many years! At this point we understand LTP better than we understand the gradual shift of representation to the cortex.

Improving Memory

Most biological research on learning and memory focuses on basic mechanisms, in hopes of practical applications later, after we understand the process better. Is there anything we can do toward improving memory?

Understanding the mechanisms of LTP may enable researchers to understand what could impair or improve memory. LTP depends on production of several proteins, and enhancing production of these proteins enhances memory in rodents (Routtenberg et al., 2000). Drugs that inhibit their production weakens memory, even if the drugs are given days after the training (Shema, Sacktor, & Dudai, 2007). Several pharmaceutical companies are investigating drugs that might improve learning by enhancing LTP (Farah et al., 2004).

Moderate doses of stimulant drugs enhance learning by increasing arousal. Caffeine is one example, and methylphenidate (Ritalin) is another. Many patients with Alzheimer's disease take drugs that facilitate acetylcholine by blocking the enzyme that degrades it (Farah et al., 2004). Other drugs recommended for memory improvement have more doubtful effects. You may have heard claims that the herb *Ginkgo biloba* improves memory. Drug companies face stiff regulation by the Food and Drug Administration before they can market a new drug, but a company marketing an herb or other naturally occurring substance does not have to do any research at all, provided that the label or advertisement does not claim medical benefits. You may see advertisements for vitamin pills or other supplements that brag of containing *Ginkgo biloba*. You may also notice that the ads generally leave it to your imagination what good, if any, this supplement does. Some early research on Ginkgo biloba suggested mild benefits to a small percentage of Alzheimer's patients or other older adults with impaired blood flow to the brain. However, a more extensive study of more than 3,000 people tested in many ways over six years found that the substance has no benefits (Snitz et al., 2009).

Researchers using biotechnological methods have found ways to alter gene expression in mice, enhancing memory in certain ways. However, so far the benefits come with a cost (Lehrer, 2009). Mice with increased expression of a gene that enhances NMDA receptors show faster learning, but also chronic pain. Mice with another variant gene learn complex mazes faster than usual, but are worse than average at learning simple mazes. Another type of mouse learns quickly, at the cost of learning fears quickly and failing to unlearn the fears. Chemically improving memory does not appear to be a simple matter.

By far the best way to improve learning is by the old-fashioned way of studying better in the first place. Still, researchers have found the biological basis for why one kind of study technique works. Suppose someone tells you a miscellaneous series of facts. Later you would remember a few of them. You would remember more if someone engages your curiosity first by asking questions. For example, do you know which musical instrument was invented to sound like human singing? Take a guess. How sure are you? How curious are you to find out whether your guess was right? If you rate your curiosity high, you will remember the correct answer (violin) much better than if someone had told you that fact without first asking you to guess. The research finds that activity increases in several brain areas while you are waiting for the answer, especially if you rate your curiosity high. Activity also increases greatly in several other areas when you hear the correct answer, especially if your guess had been wrong (Kang et al., 2009). Exactly how this in-

creased brain activity improves memory remains uncertain, but at least we know where to look. Furthermore, it confirms the importance of stirring someone's curiosity, as a study technique.

➤ **STOP & CHECK**

18. At this point, what type of drug or chemical is most clearly shown to improve memory without unacceptable side effects?

ANSWER

18. Caffeine and other stimulants produce benefits. Other drugs may become helpful, but the evidence does not support their use at this time.

MODULE 13.2 ■ IN CLOSING

The Physiology of Memory

In this module, we examined biochemical changes at synapses. After we understand these mechanisms more completely, what can we do with the information? Presumably, we will help people overcome or prevent memory deterioration. We can expect much better therapies for Alzheimer's disease and so forth. Should we also look forward to improving memory for normal people? Would you like to have a supermemory?

Maybe, but let's be cautious. Even though you could add memory chips to your computer to store ever-larger quantities

of information, you don't want or need to keep everything forever. Similarly, you might not want your brain to retain every experience, even if it had unlimited storage capacity. The ideal memory would not just record more information. It would faithfully record the important information and discard the rest. If we improve memory in any way, we will still want to maintain that selectivity.

SUMMARY

1. A Hebbian synapse is one that is strengthened by being repeatedly active when the postsynaptic neuron produces action potentials. **410**

2. Habituation of the gill-withdrawal reflex in *Aplysia* depends on a mechanism that decreases the release of transmitter from a particular presynaptic neuron. **411**

3. Sensitization of the gill-withdrawal reflex in *Aplysia* occurs when serotonin blocks potassium channels in a presynaptic neuron and thereby prolongs the release of transmitter from that neuron. **411**

4. Long-term potentiation (LTP) is an enhancement of response at certain synapses because of a brief but intense series of stimuli delivered to a neuron, generally by two or more axons delivering simultaneous inputs. **412**

5. If axons are active at a very slow rate, their synapses may decrease in responsiveness—a process known as long-term depression (LTD). **412**

6. LTP in hippocampal neurons occurs as follows: Repeated glutamate excitation of AMPA receptors depolarizes the

membrane. The depolarization removes magnesium ions that had been blocking NMDA receptors. Glutamate is then able to excite the NMDA receptors, opening a channel for calcium ions to enter the neuron. **413**

7. When calcium enters through the NMDA-controlled channels, it activates a protein that sets in motion a series of events that build more AMPA receptors and increase the growth of dendritic branches. These changes increase the later responsiveness of the dendrite to incoming glutamate at AMPA receptors. **414**

8. At many synapses, LTP relates to increased release of transmitter from the presynaptic neuron, in addition to or instead of changes in the postsynaptic neuron. **415**

9. Although researchers hope to develop drugs or procedures to improve memory, at this point no such procedure is safe and effective, with the exception of mild stimulants such as caffeine. **416**

KEY TERMS

Terms are defined in the module on the page number indicated. They're also presented in alphabetical order with definitions in the book's Subject Index/Glossary, which begins on page 561. Interactive flashcards and crossword puzzles are among the online resources available to help you learn these terms and the concepts they represent.

AMPA receptor **413**	habituation **411**	NMDA receptor **413**
associativity **412**	Hebbian synapse **410**	retrograde transmitter **416**
BDNF **414**	long-term depression (LTD) **412**	sensitization **411**
cooperativity **412**	long-term potentiation (LTP) **412**	specificity **412**

THOUGHT QUESTIONS

1. If a synapse has already developed LTP once, should it be easier or more difficult to get it to develop LTP again? Why?

2. Dopamine facilitates activity at many AMPA synapses (Tye et al., 2010). How might this fact help explain how methylphenidate (Ritalin) improves learning?

CHAPTER 13 Interactive Exploration and Study

The **Psychology CourseMate** for this text brings chapter topics to life with interactive learning, study, and exam preparation tools, including quizzes and flashcards for the Key Concepts that appear throughout each module, as well as an interactive media-rich eBook version of the text that is fully searchable and includes highlighting and note-taking capabilities and interactive versions of the book's **Stop & Check** quizzes and **Try It Yourself Online** activities. The site also features **Virtual Biological Psychology Labs**, **videos**, and **animations** to help you better understand concepts—logon and learn more at **www.cengagebrain.com**, which is your gateway to all of this text's complimentary and premium resources, including the following:

Virtual Biological Psychology Labs

Explore the experiments that led to modern-day understanding of biopsychology with the Virtual Biological Psychology Labs, featuring a realistic lab environment that allows you to conduct experiments and evaluate data to better understand how scientists came to the conclusions presented in your text. The labs cover a range of topics, including perception, motivation, cognition, and more. You may purchase access at **www.cengagebrain.com**, or login at **login.cengagebrain.com** if an access card was included with your text.

Videos

Neural Networks and Memory

Also available—

- Mike, an Amnesic Patient
- Tom, a Patient with Alzheimer's
- Brain Food
- Boosting your Memory

Animations

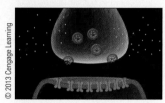

Habituation

Also available—

- Learning Module: Classical Conditioning

Try It Yourself Online

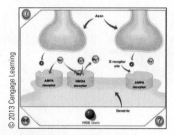

Long-Term Potentiation

Suggestions for Further Exploration

Books

Eichenbaum, H. (2002). *The cognitive neuroscience of memory.* New York: Oxford University Press. Thoughtful treatment of both the behavioral and physiological aspects of memory.

Schnider, A. (2008). *The confabulating mind: How the brain creates reality.* New York: Oxford. A study of people with Korsakoff's syndrome and other conditions that lead to confident but false memory reports.

Websites

The Psychology CourseMate for this text provides regularly updated links to relevant online resources for this chapter, such as one about Alzheimer's disease and another about memory loss.

Cognitive Functions

14

CHAPTER OUTLINE

MAIN IDEAS

1. The left and right hemispheres of the brain communicate primarily through the corpus callosum, although other smaller commissures also exchange some information between the hemispheres. After damage to the corpus callosum, each hemisphere has access to information only from the opposite half of the body and from the opposite visual field.

2. For most people, the left hemisphere is specialized for language and analytical processing. The right hemisphere is specialized for certain complex visuospatial tasks and synthetic processing.

3. The language specializations of the human brain are enormous elaborations of features that are present in other primates.

4. Abnormalities of the left hemisphere can lead to a great variety of specific language impairments.

5. Stimuli become conscious when corresponding brain activity reaches a high enough level, spreading through much of the cerebral cortex.

OPPOSITE: Language may have evolved from our tendency to make gestures.

Biological explanations of vision, hearing, and movement are fairly detailed. Research progresses, mainly because researchers can measure the stimuli and behaviors reasonably well. Language, thought, and attention are harder to measure, and therefore harder to study. Nevertheless, they have been integral topics for neuroscience since its earliest days, beginning with Paul Broca's report in the 1860s that speech depends on part of the left frontal cortex.

Although research on the biology of cognition is difficult, many of the results are fascinating. After damage to the corpus callosum, which connects the two hemispheres, people act as if they have two fields of awareness—separate "minds," you might say. With damage to certain areas of the left hemisphere, people lose their language abilities, while remaining unimpaired in other ways. People with damage to parts of the right hemisphere ignore the left side of their body and the left side of the world. Studies of such people offer clues about how the brain operates and raise stimulating questions.

Lateralization of Function

S ymmetry is common in nature. The sun, stars, and planets are nearly symmetrical, as are most animals and plants. When an atom undergoes radioactive decay, it emits identical rays in exactly opposite directions. However, the human brain is asymmetrical. The left hemisphere has somewhat different functions from the right hemisphere. Why? Presumably, assigning different functions to the two hemispheres provides some advantage. This module explores the distinctions between hemispheres.

▮ The Left and Right Hemispheres

The left hemisphere of the cerebral cortex is connected to skin receptors and muscles mainly on the right side of the body. The right hemisphere is connected to skin receptors and muscles mainly on the left side. As an exception to this rule, both hemispheres control the trunk muscles and facial muscles. The left hemisphere sees only the right half of the world. The right hemisphere sees only the left half of the world. Each hemisphere gets auditory information from both ears but slightly stronger information from the contralateral ear. Taste and smell, however, are uncrossed. Each hemisphere gets taste information from its own side of the tongue (Aglioti, Tassinari, Corballis, & Berlucchi, 2000; Pritchard, Macaluso, & Eslinger, 1999) and smell information from the nostril on its own side (Herz, McCall, & Cahill, 1999; Homewood & Stevenson, 2001).

Why all vertebrates (and many invertebrates) evolved so that each hemisphere controls the contralateral (opposite) side of the body, no one knows. At any rate, the left and right hemispheres of the cerebral cortex exchange information through a set of axons called the **corpus callosum** (Figure 14.1; see also Figures 4.10 and 4.13) and through the anterior commissure, the hippocampal commissure, and a couple of other small commissures. Information that initially enters one hemisphere crosses quickly so that both hemispheres have access to the information.

The two hemispheres are not mirror images of each other. In most humans, the left hemisphere is specialized for language. The functions of the right hemisphere are more difficult to summarize, as we shall see later. Such division of labor between the

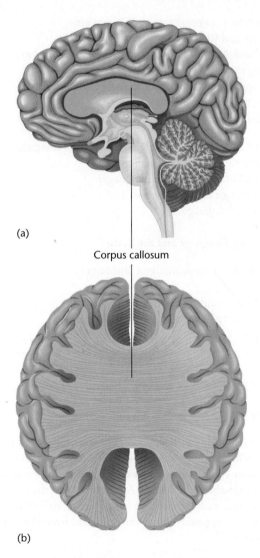

(a)

Corpus callosum

(b)

FIGURE 14.1 Two views of the corpus callosum
The corpus callosum is a large set of axons conveying information between the two hemispheres. (a) A sagittal section through the human brain. (b) A dissection (viewed from above) in which gray matter has been removed to expose the corpus callosum.
(© Cengage Learning 2013)

two hemispheres is known as **lateralization**. If you had no corpus callosum, your left hemisphere could react only to information from the right side of your body, and your right hemisphere could react only to information from the left. Because of the corpus callosum, however, each hemisphere receives information from both sides. Only after damage to the corpus callosum (or to one hemisphere) do we see clear evidence of lateralization.

Visual and Auditory Connections to the Hemispheres

Before we can discuss lateralization in any detail, let's consider how the eyes connect to the brain. The hemispheres connect to the eyes such that each hemisphere gets input from the opposite half of the visual world. That is, the left hemisphere sees the right side of the world, and the right hemisphere sees

the left side. In rabbits and other species with eyes far to the side of the head, the left eye connects to the right hemisphere, and the right eye connects to the left. *Human eyes are not connected to the brain in this way.* Both of your eyes face forward. You see the left side of the world almost as well with your right eye as with your left eye.

Figure 14.2 illustrates the connections from the eyes to the human brain. Light from the right half of the **visual field** (what is visible at any moment) strikes the left half of *each* retina, and light from the left visual field strikes the right half of each retina. The left half of each retina connects to the left hemisphere, which therefore sees the right visual field. Similarly, the right half of each retina connects to the right hemisphere, which sees the left visual field. A small vertical strip down the center of each retina, covering about 5 degrees of visual arc, connects to both hemispheres (Innocenti, 1980; Lavidor & Walsh, 2004). In Figure 14.2, note how half of the

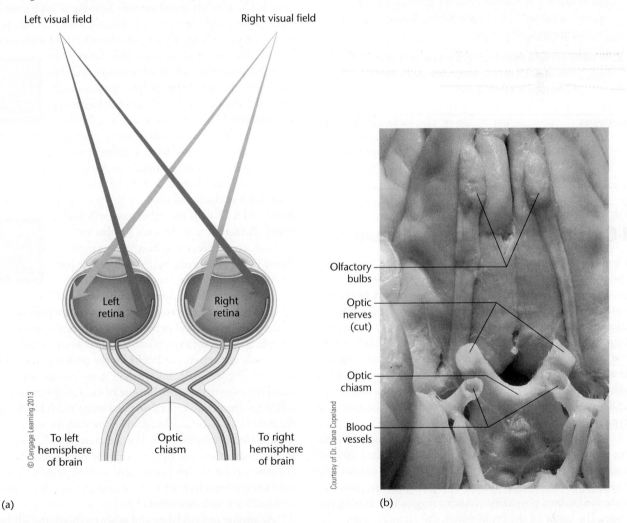

Left visual field   Right visual field

Left retina   Right retina

© Cengage Learning 2013

To left hemisphere of brain   Optic chiasm   To right hemisphere of brain

(a)

Olfactory bulbs

Optic nerves (cut)

Optic chiasm

Blood vessels

Courtesy of Dr. Dana Copeland

(b)

FIGURE 14.2 Connections from the eyes to the human brain
(a) The left hemisphere connects to the left half of each retina and thus gets visual input from the right half of the world. The opposite is true of the right hemisphere. (b) At the optic chiasm, axons from the right half of the left retina cross to the right hemisphere, and axons from the left half of the right retina cross to the left hemisphere.

axons from each eye cross to the opposite side of the brain at the **optic chiasm** (literally, the "optic cross").

Right visual field ⇒ left half of each retina ⇒ left hemisphere

Left visual field ⇒ right half of each retina ⇒ right hemisphere

The auditory system is organized differently. Each ear sends the information to both sides of the brain, because any brain area that contributes to localizing sounds must compare input from both ears. However, each hemisphere does pay more attention to the ear on the opposite side (Hugdahl, 1996).

STOP & CHECK

1. The left hemisphere of the brain is connected to the right eye in rabbits. In humans, the left hemisphere is connected to the left half of each retina. Explain the reason for this species difference.

2. In humans, light from the right visual field strikes the _____ half of each retina, which sends its axons to the _____ hemisphere of the brain.

ANSWERS 1. In rabbits, the right eye is far to the side of the head and sees only the right visual field. In humans, the eyes point straight ahead and half of each eye sees the right visual field. 2. left . . . left.

Cutting the Corpus Callosum

Damage to the corpus callosum prevents the two hemispheres from exchanging information. Occasionally, surgeons sever the corpus callosum as a treatment for severe **epilepsy**, a condition characterized by repeated episodes of excessive synchronized neural activity. Epilepsy can result from a mutation in a gene controlling the GABA receptor (Baulac et al., 2001), from trauma or infection in the brain, brain tumors, or exposure to toxic substances. Often, the cause is not known. About 1% to 2% of all people have epilepsy. The symptoms vary depending on the location and type of brain abnormality.

Antiepileptic drugs block sodium flow across the membrane or enhance the effects of GABA. More than 90% of epileptic patients respond well enough to live a normal life. However, if someone continues having frequent seizures despite medication, physicians consider surgically removing the **focus**, the point in the brain where the seizures begin. The location of the focus varies from one person to another.

Removing the focus is not an option if someone has several foci. Therefore, the idea arose to cut the corpus callosum to prevent epileptic seizures from crossing from one hemisphere to the other. One benefit is that, as predicted, the person's epileptic seizures affect only half the body. (The abnormal activity cannot cross the corpus callosum, so it remains within one hemisphere.) A surprising bonus is that the seizures become less frequent. Evidently, epileptic activity rebounds back and forth between the hemispheres and prolongs seizures. If it can't bounce back and forth across the corpus callosum, a seizure may not develop at all.

How does severing the corpus callosum affect other aspects of behavior? People who have undergone surgery to the corpus callosum, referred to as **split-brain people**, maintain their intellect and motivation, and they still walk without difficulty. They also use the two hands together on familiar tasks such as tying shoes. However, if they are asked to pretend they are hitting a golf ball, threading a needle, or attaching a fishhook to a line, they struggle with any task that is not familiar to them (Franz, Waldie, & Smith, 2000).

Split-brain people can use their two hands independently in a way that other people cannot. For example, try drawing ∪ with your left hand while simultaneously drawing ⊃ with your right hand. Most people find this task difficult, but split-brain people do it with ease. Or try drawing circles with both hands simultaneously, but one of them just a little faster than the other (not twice as fast). Most people find this task difficult; split-brain people spontaneously draw the circles at different speeds (Kennerley, Diedrichsen, Hazeltine, Semjen, & Ivry, 2002).

The difficulty of simultaneously moving your left hand one way and your right hand a different way reflects a cognitive difficulty more than a motor limitation. It is hard to draw a ∪ with one hand and a ⊃ with the other, but if you carefully draw both of them and then try to *trace over* the ∪ with one hand and a ⊃ with the other, you will find it easier. Evidently, it is difficult to plan two actions at once unless you have clear targets to direct your movements. Split-brain people have no trouble planning two actions at once.

Research by Roger Sperry and his students (Nebes, 1974) revealed behavioral effects when stimuli were limited to one side of the body. In a typical experiment, a split-brain person stared straight ahead as the experimenter flashed words or pictures on either side of a screen, too briefly for the person to move his or her eyes (Figure 14.3). Information going to one hemisphere could not cross to the other, because of the damage to the corpus callosum. The person could then point with the left hand to what the right hemisphere saw and could point with the right hand to what the left hemisphere saw. The person could talk about what the left hemisphere saw, but not what the right hemisphere saw. (In most people the left hemisphere controls speech.) The two halves of the brain had different information, and they could not communicate with each other.

According to fMRI data and other methods, the left hemisphere is dominant for speech production in more than 95% of right-handers and nearly 80% of left-handers (McKeever, Seitz, Krutsch, & Van Eys, 1995). Not many left-handers have complete right-hemisphere dominance for speech. A more common pattern is mixed left- and right-hemisphere dominance. In contrast to speech production, speech comprehension is more

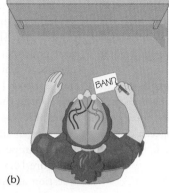

(a) (b) (c)

FIGURE 14.3 Effects of damage to the corpus callosum
(a) When the word *hatband* is flashed on a screen, (b) a woman with a split brain can report only what her left hemisphere saw—"band."
(c) However, with her left hand, she can point to a hat, which is what the right hemisphere saw. *(© Cengage Learning 2013)*

equally divided. The left hemisphere understands speech better than the right hemisphere, but for most people, the right hemisphere understands speech reasonably well, except with complex grammar (Beeman & Chiarello, 1998).

A split-brain person can name an object after viewing it briefly in the right visual field and therefore the left hemi-

sphere. The same person viewing a display in the left visual field (right hemisphere) usually cannot name or describe it. However, a small amount of information travels between the hemispheres through several smaller commissures, as shown in Figure 14.4, and some split-brain people get enough information to describe objects in part (Berlucchi, Mangun,

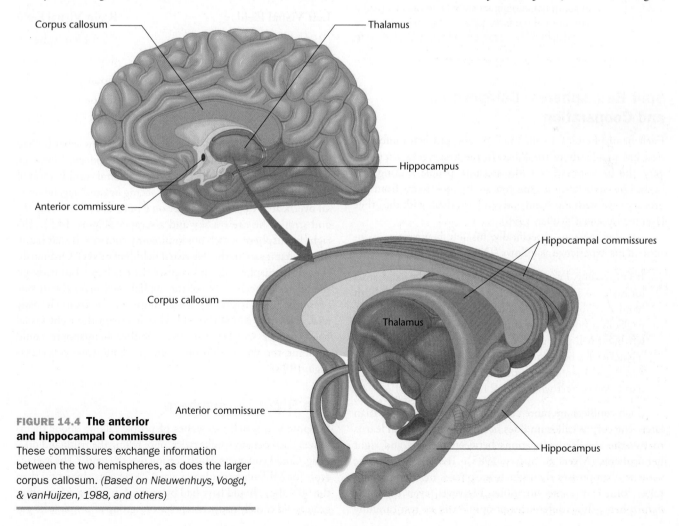

FIGURE 14.4 The anterior and hippocampal commissures
These commissures exchange information between the two hemispheres, as does the larger corpus callosum. *(Based on Nieuwenhuys, Voogd, & vanHuijzen, 1988, and others)*

& Gazzaniga, 1997; Forster & Corballis, 2000). A patient who cannot name something points to it correctly with the left hand, even while saying, "I don't know what it was." (Of course, a split-brain person who watches the left hand point out an object can then name it.)

Is it an advantage for just one hemisphere to control speech? Possibly. Many people who have bilateral control of speech stutter (Fox et al., 2000), although not all people who stutter have bilateral control of speech. Perhaps having two speech centers produces competing messages to the speech muscles.

> **STOP & CHECK**

3. Can a split-brain person name an object after feeling it with the right hand? With the left hand? Explain.

4. After a split-brain person sees something in the left visual field, how can he or she identify the object?

ANSWERS   **3.** A split-brain person can describe something after feeling it with the right hand but not with the left. The right hand sends its information to the left hemisphere, which is dominant for language in most people. The left hand sends its information to the right hemisphere, which cannot speak. **4.** After seeing something in the left visual field, a split-brain person could point to the correct answer with the left hand.

Split Hemispheres: Competition and Cooperation

Each hemisphere of a split-brain person processes information independently of the other. In the first weeks after surgery, the hemispheres act like separate people sharing one body. One split-brain person repeatedly took items from the grocery shelf with one hand and returned them with the other (Reuter-Lorenz & Miller, 1998).

Another person—specifically, his left hemisphere—described his experience as follows (Dimond, 1979):

> If I'm reading, I can hold the book in my right hand; it's a lot easier to sit on my left hand, than to hold it with both hands. . . . You tell your hand—I'm going to turn so many pages in a book—turn three pages—then somehow the left hand will pick up two pages and you're at page 5, or whatever. It's better to let it go, pick it up with the right hand, and then turn to the right page. With your right hand, you correct what the left has done. (p. 211)

Such conflicts are more common soon after surgery than later. The corpus callosum does not heal, but the brain learns to use the smaller connections between the left and right hemispheres (Myers & Sperry, 1985). The left hemisphere somehow suppresses the right hemisphere's interference and takes control in some situations. However, even then, the hemispheres show differences of opinion if we test carefully

enough. In one study, researchers asked a split-brain person to identify photos after viewing them briefly in one visual field or the other. They formed photos by morphing pictures of the split-brain person himself, and pictures of another familiar person. When he saw a picture in the right visual field (left hemisphere), he was more likely to say it was himself. When he saw it in the left visual field (right hemisphere), he usually thought it was the other person (Turk et al., 2002).

In other situations, the hemispheres learn to cooperate. A split-brain person who was tested with the apparatus shown in Figure 14.3 used an interesting strategy to answer a yes–no question about what he saw in the left visual field. Suppose an experimenter flashes a picture in the left visual field and asks, "Was it green?" The left (speaking) hemisphere takes a guess: "Yes." That guess might be correct. If not, the right hemisphere, which knows the correct answer, makes the face frown. (Both hemispheres control facial muscles on both sides of the face.) The left hemisphere, feeling the frown, says, "Oh, I'm sorry, I meant 'no.'"

In another experiment, a split-brain person saw two words flashed at once, one on each side. He was then asked to draw a picture of what he had read. Each hemisphere saw a full word, but the two words could combine to make a different word. For example,

Left Visual Field	**Right Visual Field**
(Right Hemisphere)	(Left Hemisphere)
hot	dog
honey	moon
sky	scraper
rain	bow

With the right hand, he almost always drew what he had seen in the right visual field, such as *dog* or *moon*. However, with the left hand, he sometimes drew a literal combination of the two words. For example, after seeing *hot* and *dog*, he drew an overheated dog, not a wiener on a bun, and after seeing *sky* and *scraper*, he drew a sky and a scraper (Figure 14.5). The right hemisphere, which predominantly controls the left hand, drew what it saw in the left visual field (*hot* or *sky*). Ordinarily, the left hemisphere doesn't control the left hand, but through the bilateral mechanisms of the medial corticospinal pathway (described in Chapter 8), it can move the left hand clumsily and, evidently, enough to add what it saw in the right visual field (*dog* or *scraper*). However, neither hemisphere could combine the words into one concept (Kingstone & Gazzaniga, 1995).

The Right Hemisphere

Suppose you watch videotapes of people talking about themselves. Each person speaks twice, once telling the truth and once lying. Could you guess which version was the truth? The average score for MIT undergraduates was 47% correct, a bit worse than the 50% they should have had by random guessing. Most other groups did equally badly, except for one group of people who got

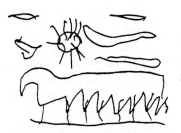

SCRAPER-SKY

FIGURE 14.5 A split-brain person draws with the left hand
He saw the word *sky* in the left visual field and *scraper* in the right
visual field. His left hemisphere controlled the left hand enough
to draw a scraper, and his right hemisphere controlled it enough
to draw a sky. *(From "Subcortical Transfer of Higher Order Information: More Illusory Than Real?" by A. Kingstone and M. S. Gazzaniga,
1995. Neuropsychology, 9, pp. 321–328. Copyright © 1995 American Psychological Association. Reprinted by permission.)*

Jerre Levy

*Despite the quite amazing progress
of the last half century in neuroscien-
tific understanding, we are still, in my
view, as distant now as ever in knowing what questions to ask about how
and why brains make minds. It is simply evading the issue to say, as some
philosophers do, that our mental experiences are just the inside view of
the stuff we measure on the outside. Why is the inside view
so utterly different from our external measurements? Even if
we specified all the critical spatiotemporal neural dynamics
that were necessary and sufficient for a given mental experience, this would not tell us why those dynamics give rise to
any experience at all… Nature will answer if we ask the right
questions. (Levy, personal communication)*

60% correct—still not a great score, but at least better than random (Etcoff, Ekman, Magee, & Frank, 2000). Who do you suppose they were? They were people with left-hemisphere brain
damage! They only poorly understood the speech, but they were
adept at reading gestures and facial expressions. As mentioned
in Chapter 12, the right hemisphere is better than the left at perceiving the emotions in people's gestures and tone of voice, such
as happiness or sadness (Adolphs, Damasio, & Tranel, 2002). If
the left hemisphere is damaged (and therefore prevented from
interfering with the right hemisphere), the right hemisphere is
free to make reliable judgments. In contrast, people with damage
in parts of the right hemisphere
speak in a monotone voice,
do not understand other people's emotional expressions, and
usually fail to understand humor and sarcasm (Beeman &
Chiarello, 1998).

The right hemisphere is
dominant for recognizing emotions in others, including both
pleasant and unpleasant emotions (Narumoto, Okada, Sadato, Fukui, & Yonekura, 2001).
In a split-brain person, the right
hemisphere does better than
the left at recognizing whether
two photographs show the
same or different emotions
(Stone, Nisenson, Eliassen, &
Gazzaniga, 1996). Moreover,
according to Jerre Levy and her
colleagues' studies of brain-in-
tact people, when the left and
right hemispheres perceive different emotions in someone's
face, the response of the right
hemisphere dominates. For ex-

ample, examine the faces in Figure 14.6. Each of these combines
half of a smiling face with half of a neutral face. Which looks
happier to you: face (a) or face (b)? Most people choose face (a),
with the smile on the viewer's left (Heller & Levy, 1981; Hoptman & Levy, 1988; Levy, Heller, Banich, & Burton, 1983). Similarly, a frown on the viewer's left looks sadder than
a frown on the viewer's right (Sackeim, Putz, Vingiano, Coleman, & McElhiney, 1988). Remember, what you see in your left visual field stimulates your right hemisphere first.

TRY IT YOURSELF

(a)   (b)

FIGURE 14.6 Half of a smiling face combined with half of a neutral face
Which looks happier to you—(a) the one with a smile on your left or (b) the one with a smile on
your right? Your answer suggests which hemisphere of your brain is dominant for interpreting
emotional expressions. *(Reprinted from Brain and Cognition, 2/4, Levy, J., Heller, W., Banich,
M. T., Burton, L. A., "Asymmetry of perception in free viewing of chimeric faces," 404–419, 1983,
with permission from Elsevier.)*

The right hemisphere also appears more adept than the left at comprehending spatial relationships. For example, one young woman with damage to her posterior right hemisphere had trouble finding her way around, even in familiar areas. To reach a destination, she needed directions with specific visual details, such as, "Walk to the corner where you see a building with a statue in front of it. Then turn left and go to the corner that has a flagpole and turn right. . . ." Each of these directions had to include an unmistakable feature. If the instruction was "go to the city government building—that's the one with a tower," she might go to a different building that happened to have a tower (Clarke, Assal, & de Tribolet, 1993).

How can we best describe the difference in functions between the hemispheres?

According to Robert Ornstein (1997), the left hemisphere focuses more on details and the right hemisphere more on overall patterns. For example, in one study, people with intact brains examined visual stimuli such as the one in Figure 14.7, in which many repetitions of a small letter compose a different large letter. When they were asked to identify the small letters (in this case, B), activity increased in the left hemisphere, but when they were asked to identify the large overall letter (H), activity increased in the right hemisphere (Fink et al., 1996).

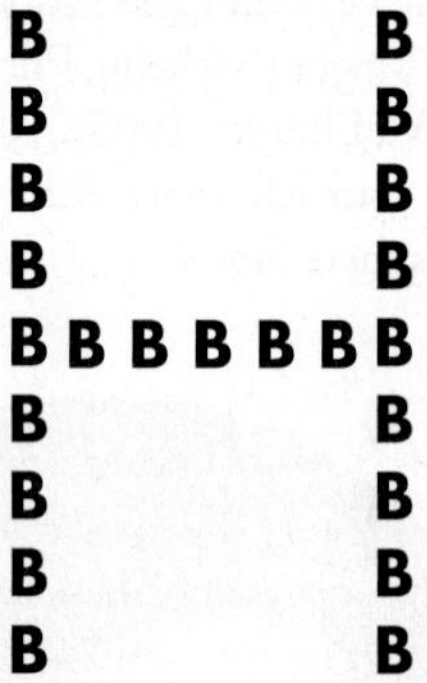

B B
B B
B B
B B
B B B B B B B
B B
B B
B B
B B

FIGURE 14.7 Analytical vs. holistic perception
When people are told to name the large composite letter, they have more activity in the right hemisphere. When told to name the small component letters, they have more activity in the left hemisphere. *(Based on Fink, Halligan, et al., 1996)*

Hemispheric Specializations in Intact Brains

Even in people without brain damage, careful testing demonstrates differences between the hemispheres. Suppose you smell something with just one nostril, so the information goes primarily to one hemisphere (in this case, the ipsilateral one). Further suppose that it's an unfamiliar odor that you can't name. Twelve seconds later you smell something again with either the same nostril or the other one, and you have to say whether it is the same as the previous smell. You will be more accurate if you smelled the two substances with the same nostril, and therefore the same hemisphere (Yeshurun, Dudai, & Sobel, 2008). (Yes, you're right, this is the kind of thing that seldom happens in everyday life.)

Another task, and again it's a laboratory task with little obvious application to everyday life: On each trial in this experiment, you respond to a signal with a handgrip. Right before the signal, a picture flashes very briefly on one side of the screen or the other, so briefly (subliminally) that you can't identify it consciously. This subliminal signal indicates whether you can earn a large or a small reward with your handgrip on this trial. Even though the signal is subliminal, you will grasp more strongly when it signals a large reward... but only if it flashes to the same hemisphere that controls the hand you are using on this trial (Schmidt, Palminteri, Lafargue, & Pessiglione, 2010).

Here is something you can try yourself: Tap with your right hand as many times as you can in a short period of time. Rest and repeat with your left hand. Then repeat with each hand while talking. The Online Try It Yourself activity "Hemisphere Control" will keep track of your totals. For most right-handers and many left-handers, talking decreases the tapping rate with the right hand more than with the left hand (Kinsbourne & McMurray, 1975). Evidently, it is more difficult to do two things at once when both activities depend on the same hemisphere.

STOP & CHECK

5. Which hemisphere is dominant for the following in most people: speech, emotional inflection of speech, interpreting other people's emotional expressions, spatial relationships, perceiving overall patterns?

ANSWER 5. The left hemisphere is dominant for speech. The right hemisphere is dominant for all the other items listed.

Development of Lateralization and Handedness

Because most people's language depends primarily on the left hemisphere, it is natural to ask whether the hemispheres differ anatomically. If so, do they differ before speech develops? How does handedness relate to hemispheric dominance for speech?

Anatomical Differences Between the Hemispheres

The human brain is specialized to attend to language sounds. If you listen to a repeated syllable ("*pack pack pack pack . . .*") and then suddenly the vowel sound changes (". . . *pack pack pack peck . . .*"), the change catches your attention and evokes larger electrical responses measured on your scalp. Changing from *pack* to *peck* also increases the evoked response from a baby, even a premature infant (Cheour-Luhtanen et al., 1996). Evidently, humans attend to language sounds from the start.

Do the hemispheres differ from the start? Norman Geschwind and Walter Levitsky (1968) found that one section

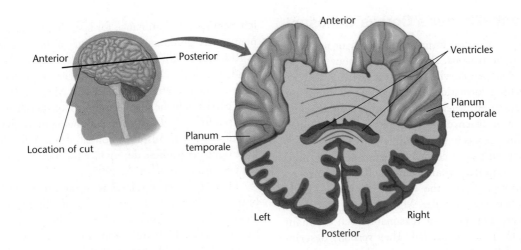

FIGURE 14.8 Horizontal section through a human brain
This cut, just above the surface of the temporal lobe, shows the planum temporale, an area critical for speech comprehension. It is larger in the left hemisphere than in the right hemisphere. *(From "Human Brain: Left-Right Asymmetries in Temporal Speech Region," by N. Geschwind and W. Levitsky, 1968, Science, 161, pp. 186–187. Copyright © 1968 by AAAS and N. Geschwind. Reprinted by permission.)*

of the temporal cortex, called the **planum temporale** (PLAY-num tem-poh-RAH-lee), is larger in the left hemisphere for 65% of people (Figure 14.8). Sandra Witelson and Wazir Pallie (1973) examined the brains of infants who died before age 3 months and found that the left planum temporale was larger in 12 of 14.

Smaller but still significant differences are found between left and right hemispheres of chimpanzees, bonobos, and gorillas (Hopkins, 2006). Chimpanzees with a larger left than right planum temporale generally show a preference for using their right hand, as most humans do (Hopkins, Russell, & Cantalupo, 2007). Evidently, the specialization we see in the human brain built upon specializations already present in our apelike ancestors of long ago.

Maturation of the Corpus Callosum

The corpus callosum gradually grows and thickens as myelin increases around certain axons during childhood and adolescence (Luders, Thompson, & Toga, 2010). The corpus callosum also matures by discarding many axons. At an early stage, the brain generates far more axons than it will have at maturity (Ivy & Killackey, 1981; Killackey & Chalupa, 1986). The reason is that any two neurons connected by the corpus callosum need to have corresponding functions. For example, a neuron in the left hemisphere that responds to light in the center of the fovea should be connected to a right-hemisphere neuron that responds to light in the same location. During early embryonic development, the genes cannot specify exactly where those two neurons will be. Therefore, many connections are made across the corpus callosum, but only those axons that happen to connect very similar cells survive (Innocenti & Caminiti, 1980).

Because the connections take years to develop their mature adult pattern, certain behaviors of young children resemble those of split-brain adults. In one study, 3- and 5-year-old children were asked to feel two fabrics, either with one hand at two times or with two hands at the same time, and

say whether the materials felt the same or different. The 5-year-olds did equally well with one hand or with two. The 3-year-olds made 90% more errors with two hands than with one (Galin, Johnstone, Nakell, & Herron, 1979). The likely interpretation is that the corpus callosum matures sufficiently between ages 3 and 5 to facilitate the comparison of stimuli between the two hands.

Other kinds of tasks show continuing maturation of the corpus callosum in 5- and 6-year-olds. Did you ever play with an Etch-A-Sketch toy? You can rotate two wheels, one with each hand. One wheel moves a line up or down, and the other moves it left or right. Five- and six-year-olds have great trouble with this toy, partly because their corpus callosum is not mature enough to integrate the actions of the two hands. In contrast, consider the task of tapping keys with one hand or two whenever a stimulus appears on the screen. Adults and older children are slower to respond with two hands than with one, presumably because the message to one hand interferes with the message to the other hand. Children younger than 6 years respond just as fast with two hands as with one, again suggesting that they do not yet have a mature corpus callosum (Franz & Fahey, 2007).

Etch-A-Sketch toy

Development Without a Corpus Callosum

Rarely, the corpus callosum forms incompletely or not at all, possibly for genetic reasons. People born without a corpus callosum are unlike people who have it cut later in life. First, whatever prevented formation of the corpus callosum undoubtedly affects brain development in other ways. Second, the absence or near absence of the corpus callosum induces the remaining brain areas to develop differently.

People born without a corpus callosum perform more slowly or less accurately than average on tasks that require cooperation between the two hemispheres—Etch-A-Sketch, for example (Mueller, Marion, Paul, & Brown, 2009). However, they perform reasonably well on many tasks where split-brain people fail. They verbally describe what they feel with either hand and what they see in either visual field. They also feel objects with the two hands and say whether they are the same or different (Paul et al., 2007). How do they do so? They do not use their right hemisphere for speech (Lassonde, Bryden, & Demers, 1990). Rather, each hemisphere develops pathways connecting it to both sides of the body, enabling the left (speaking) hemisphere to feel both the left and right hands. Also, the brain's other commissures become larger than usual, including the **anterior commissure** (Figures 4.12 and 14.4), which connects the anterior parts of the cerebral cortex, and the *hippocampal commissure*, which connects the left and right hippocampi (Figure 14.4). The extra development of these other commissures partly compensates for the lack of a corpus callosum. However, the amount of information they convey varies from one person to another, and so do the behavioral deficits.

> **STOP & CHECK**
>
> 6. A child born without a corpus callosum can name something felt with the left hand, but an adult who suffered damage to the corpus callosum cannot. What are two likely explanations?

ANSWER

6. In children born without a corpus callosum, the left hemisphere develops more than the usual connections with the left hand, and the anterior commissure and other commissures grow larger than usual.

Hemispheres, Handedness, and Language Dominance

For more than 95% of right-handed people, the left hemisphere is strongly dominant for speech (McKeever et al., 1995). Left-handers are more variable. Most left-handers have left-hemisphere dominance for speech, but some have right-hemisphere dominance or a mixture of left and right (Basso & Rusconi, 1998). The same is true for people who were left-handed in early childhood but forced to switch to writing right-handed (Siebner et al., 2002). Many left-handers who have partial right-hemisphere control of speech are also partly reversed for spatial perception, showing more than the usual amount of left-hemisphere contribution. A few left-handers have right-hemisphere dominance for both language and spatial perception (Flöel et al., 2001).

Hand preference relates to some other asymmetries in brain and behavior. Suppose you are hiking through the woods when you come to a fork in the path. Other things being equal, which direction do you choose? You might imagine that you choose randomly, but most people show a tendency to pick one direction more than the other. In one study, people wore a device on their belt that counted the number of times they turned left or right over 3 days. On average, right-handers turned mostly to the left, and left-handers turned mostly to the right (Mohr, Landis, Bracha, & Brugger, 2003).

Might this tendency relate to some other observations? In most races—car races, horse races, ice skating races, and so forth—the track is set up for turning to the left (counterclockwise). In baseball, players run the bases to the left (counterclockwise). Watch little children when they run around in circles on a playground. Do you see most of them running counterclockwise?

∎ Avoiding Overstatements

The research on left-brain/right-brain differences is exciting, but it sometimes leads to unscientific assertions. Occasionally, you may hear a person say something like, "I don't do well in science because it is a left-brain subject and I am a right-brain person." That kind of statement is based on two reasonable premises and a doubtful one. The scientific ideas are that (a) the hemispheres are specialized for different functions and (b) certain tasks evoke greater activity in one hemisphere or the other. The doubtful premise is that any individual habitually relies mostly on one hemisphere.

What evidence do you suppose someone has for believing, "I am a right-brain person"? Did he or she undergo an MRI or PET scan to determine which hemisphere was larger or more active? Not likely. Generally, when people say, "I am right-brained," their only evidence is that they perform well on creative tasks or poorly on logical tasks. (Saying, "I am right-brained" sometimes implies that *because* I do poorly on logical tasks, *therefore*, I am creative. Unfortunately, illogical is not the same as creative.) In fact, you use both hemispheres for all but the simplest tasks. Most tasks require cooperation by both hemispheres.

MODULE 14.1 ■ IN CLOSING

One Brain, Two Hemispheres

Imagine you are a split-brain person. Someone asks you—that is, your left hemisphere, the talking side of you—a question to which you honestly reply that you do not know. Meanwhile, your left hand points to the correct answer. It must be an unsettling experience.

Now imagine life from the standpoint of that right hemisphere. You sit there mute, while that other hemisphere is jabbering away. Sometimes, you disagree with what that hemisphere is saying or wish it would just shut up for a while. This must be an unsettling experience, too.

Do split-brain people really have two minds, two consciousnesses? At times, they seem to. At least, there are times when one side answers a question and the other cannot. We cannot get into someone else's head to know what it is like. Indeed, each hemisphere does not know what, if anything, the other hemisphere is experiencing.

SUMMARY

1. The corpus callosum is a set of axons connecting the two hemispheres of the brain. **422**

2. The left hemisphere controls speech in most people, and each hemisphere controls mostly the hand on the opposite side, sees the opposite side of the world, and feels the opposite side of the body. **422**

3. In humans, the left visual field projects onto the right half of each retina, which sends axons to the right hemisphere. The right visual field projects onto the left half of each retina, which sends axons to the left hemisphere. **423**

4. After damage to the corpus callosum, each hemisphere answers questions about the information that reaches it directly. Each slowly answers a few questions about information on the other side if it crosses the anterior commissure or one of the other small commissures. **424**

5. Although the two hemispheres of a split-brain person are sometimes in conflict, they find ways to cooperate and cue each other. **426**

6. The right hemisphere is dominant for the emotional inflections of speech and for interpreting other people's emotional expressions in either speech or facial expression. In vision, it attends mostly to overall patterns in contrast to the left hemisphere, which is better for details. **426**

7. The left and right hemispheres differ anatomically even during infancy. Young children have some trouble comparing information from the left and right hands because the corpus callosum is not fully mature. **428**

8. A child born without a corpus callosum does not show all the same deficits as an adult who sustains damage to the corpus callosum. **430**

9. The brain of a left-handed person is not simply a mirror image of a right-hander's brain. Most left-handers have left-hemisphere or mixed dominance for speech; few have strong right-hemisphere dominance for speech. **430**

KEY TERMS

Terms are defined in the module on the page number indicated. They're also presented in alphabetical order with definitions in the book's Subject Index/Glossary, which begins on page 561. Interactive flashcards and crossword puzzles are among the online resources available to help you learn these terms and the concepts they represent.

anterior commissure **430**
corpus callosum **422**
epilepsy **424**

focus **424**
lateralization **423**
optic chiasm **424**

planum temporale **429**
split-brain people **424**
visual field **423**

THOUGHT QUESTION

When a person born without a corpus callosum moves the fingers of one hand, he or she also is likely to move the fingers of the other hand involuntarily. What possible explanation can you suggest?

Evolution and Physiology of Language

Nearly all animals communicate through visual, auditory, tactile, or chemical (pheromonal) displays. Human language stands out from other forms of communication because of its **productivity**—its ability to improvise new combinations of signals to represent new ideas. Did we evolve this ability out of nothing or from a precursor already present in other species? Why did we evolve language, whereas other species did not? And what brain specializations make language possible?

Nonhuman Precursors of Language

Evolution rarely creates something totally new. Bat wings are modified arms, and porcupine quills are modified hairs. We would expect human language to be a modification of something we can detect in our closest relatives, chimpanzees.

Common Chimpanzees

After many unsuccessful attempts to teach chimpanzees to speak, researchers achieved better results by teaching them American Sign Language or other visual systems (B. T. Gardner & Gardner, 1975; Premack & Premack, 1972) (Figure 14.9). In one version, chimps learned to press keys bearing symbols to type messages on a computer (Rumbaugh, 1977), such as "Please machine give apple" or to another chimpanzee, "Please share your chocolate."

Is the use of symbols really language? Not everything that we can translate as a series of words is really language. For example, when you insert your ATM card and enter your four-digit PIN, you don't really understand those four digits to mean, "Please machine give money." Similarly, when a chimpanzee presses four symbols on a machine, it may not understand them to mean, "Please machine give apple." The chimps' use of symbols had features that raised doubts about calling it language (Rumbaugh, 1990; Terrace, Petitto, Sanders, & Bever, 1979):

- The chimpanzees seldom used symbols in new, original combinations. That is, their symbol use was short on *productivity*.

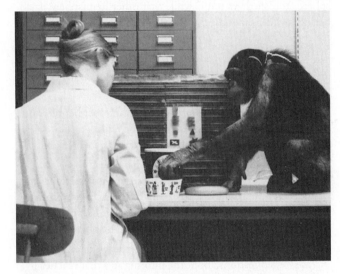

FIGURE 14.9 An attempt to teach chimpanzees language
One of the Premacks's chimps, Elizabeth, reacts to colored plastic chips that read "Not Elizabeth banana insert—Elizabeth apple wash." *(Photo courtesy of Ann Premack)*

- The chimpanzees used their symbols mainly to request, seldom to describe.

Nevertheless, the chimpanzees showed at least moderate understanding. For example, the chimp Washoe, trained in sign language, usually answered "Who" questions with names, "What" questions with objects, and "Where" questions with places, even when she used the wrong symbol for a name, object, or place (Van Cantfort, Gardner, & Gardner, 1989).

Bonobos

Amid widespread skepticism about chimpanzee language, surprising results emerged from studies of an endangered species, *Pan paniscus*, known as the bonobo or the pygmy chimpanzee (a misleading name because they are practically the same size as common chimpanzees).

Bonobos' social order resembles humans' in several regards. Males and females form strong, sometimes lasting, personal attachments. They often copulate face to face. The female is sexually responsive on almost any day and not just during her fertile period. The males contribute significantly to infant care. Adults often share food. They stand comfortably on their hind legs. In short, they resemble humans more than other primates do.

In the mid-1980s, Sue Savage-Rumbaugh, Duane Rumbaugh, and their associates tried to teach a female bonobo named Matata to press symbols that lit when touched. Each symbol represents a word (Figure 14.10). Although Matata made little progress, her infant son Kanzi learned just by watching her. When given a chance to use the symbol board, he quickly excelled. Later, researchers noticed that Kanzi understood a fair amount of spoken language. For example, whenever anyone said the word "light," Kanzi would flip the light switch. By age 5½, he understood about 150 English words and responded to such unfamiliar spoken commands as "Throw your ball in the river"

FIGURE 14.10 Language tests for Kanzi, a bonobo (Pan paniscus)
He listens to questions through earphones and points to answers on a board. The experimenter with him does not hear the questions. *(From Georgia State University's Language Research Center, operated with the Yerkes Primate Center of Emory. Photo courtesy of Duane Rumbaugh.)*

and "Go to the refrigerator and get out a tomato" (Savage-Rumbaugh, 1990; Savage-Rumbaugh, Sevcik, Brakke, & Rumbaugh, 1992). Kanzi and his younger sister developed language comprehension comparable to that of a typical 2- to 2½-year-old child (Savage-Rumbaugh et al., 1993):

- They understand more than they can produce.
- They use symbols to name and describe objects even when they are not requesting them.
- They request items that they do not see, such as "bubbles" (I want to play with the bubble-blower).
- They occasionally use the symbols to describe past events. Kanzi once pressed the symbols "Matata bite"

to explain the cut that he had received on his hand an hour earlier.

- They frequently make original, creative requests, such as asking one person to chase another.

Why have Kanzi and Mulika developed more impressive skills than other chimpanzees? Perhaps bonobos have more language potential than common chimpanzees. A second explanation is that Kanzi and Mulika began language training when young. A third reason pertains to the method of training: Perhaps learning by observation and imitation promotes better understanding than the formal training methods of previous studies (Savage-Rumbaugh et al., 1992).

Duane Rumbaugh, Sue Savage-Rumbaugh, and chimpanzee Austin

Chimpanzees and bonobos are outstanding teachers of psychology. They never presume that we, as their students, know a damn thing about who they are. And they certainly aren't impressed with our degrees. Consequently, they are able to teach all manner of important things about what it means to be human and to be ape—that is, if we as students are quiet, listen carefully, and let them tell us as only they can.

STOP & CHECK

7. What are three likely explanations for why bonobos made more language progress than common chimpanzees?

ANSWER

7. Bonobos may be more predisposed to language than common chimpanzees. The bonobos started training at an earlier age. They learned by imitation instead of formal training techniques.

Nonprimates

What about nonprimate species? Spectacular results have been reported for Alex, an African gray parrot (Figure 14.11). Parrots are, of course, famous for imitating sounds. Irene Pepperberg was the first to argue that parrots can use sounds meaningfully. She kept Alex in a stimulating environment and taught him by saying a word many times and offering rewards if Alex approximated the same sound. Here is an excerpt early in training (Pepperberg, 1981, p. 142):

> Pepperberg: Pasta! (*Takes pasta.*) Pasta! (*Alex stretches from his perch, appears to reach for pasta.*)
>
> Alex: Pa!
>
> Pepperberg: Better . . . what is it?
>
> Alex: Pah-ah.
>
> Pepperberg: Better!
>
> Alex: Pah-ta.
>
> Pepperberg: Okay, here's the pasta. Good try.

Although pasta was used in this example, Pepperberg generally used toys. For example, if Alex said "paper," "wood," or "key," she would give him what he asked for. In no case did she reward him with food for saying "paper" or "wood."

In one test, Alex viewed a tray of 12 objects and correctly answered 39 of 48 questions such as "What color is the key?" (answer: "green") and "What object is gray?" (answer: "circle"). Many of his incorrect answers were almost correct. In one case, he was asked the color of the block and he responded with the color of the rock (Pepperberg, 1993). He also answered questions of the form "How many blue keys?" in which he had to count the blue keys among objects of two shapes and two colors (Pepperberg, 1994).

Relying on language is not always helpful. Pepperberg put Alex and three other gray parrots on perches; each had a chain of large plastic links from the perch to an almond on the bottom. (Almonds are favorite foods for parrots.) The parrots untrained in language used their claws to pull up the chain until they reached the almond. Alex and another language-trained parrot repeatedly told the experimenter, "Want nut." When she declined to bring it to them, they gave up (Pepperberg, 2004) (Figure 14.12).

What do we learn from studies of nonhuman language abilities? At a practical level, we gain insights into how best to teach language to those who do not learn it easily, such as people with brain damage or children with autism. At a more theoretical level, these studies indicate that human language evolved from precursors present in other species. These studies also point out the ambiguity of our concept: We cannot decide whether chimpanzees or parrots have language unless we define language more precisely.

How Did Humans Evolve Language?

Although a few other species can learn a little language after much training, humans stand out by learning it easily. How did we evolve this ability? Most theories fall into two categories: (a) we evolved it as a byproduct of overall brain development or (b) we evolved it as a specialization.

Language: Byproduct of Intelligence, or Specialized Adaptation?

The simplest view is that as humans evolved big brains, language developed as an accidental byproduct of intelligence. In its simplest form, this hypothesis faces serious problems.

FIGURE 14.11 Language tests for Alex
Alex conversed about objects in simple English—for example, answering, "What color is the circle?" He received no food rewards. (*Courtesy of Irene Pepperburg/The Alex Foundation*)

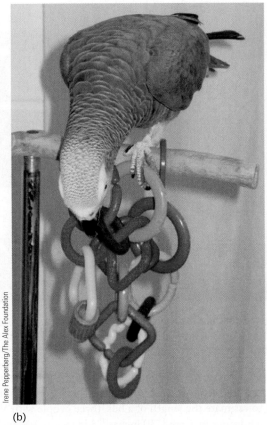

(a)   (b)

FIGURE 14.12 A gray parrot with a reasoning task
Two parrots not trained in language pulled up chain links to reach the treat. Two with language training persisted in saying, "Want nut," apparently expecting help.

People with Normal Intelligence but Impaired Language

If language is a product of overall brain size, then anyone with a full-size brain and normal overall intelligence should have normal language. However, not all do. In one family, 16 of 30 people over three generations show severe language deficits despite normal intelligence in other regards. Because of a particular dominant gene, the affected people have serious troubles in pronunciation and many other aspects of language (Fisher, Vargha-Khadem, Watkins, Monaco, & Pembrey, 1998; Gopnik & Crago, 1991; Lai, Fisher, Hurst, Vargha-Khadem, & Monaco, 2001). When they speak, their brains show activity in posterior regions instead of the frontal cortex, as in other people (Vargha-Khadem, Gadian, Copp, & Mishkin, 2005).

They have trouble with even simple grammatical rules, as shown in the following dialogue about making plurals:

Experimenter	Respondent
This is a wug; these are ...	How should I know?
	[Later] These are wug.
This is a zat; these are ...	These are zacko.
This is a sas; these are ...	These are sasss.
	[Not sasses]

In another test, experimenters presented sentences and asked whether each sentence was correct and, if not, how to improve it. They made many errors and odd corrections. For example:

Original Item	Attempted Correction
The boy eats three cookie.	The boys eat four cookie.

Despite the language difficulties, these people behave normally and intelligently in most regards. Evidently, language requires more than just a large brain and overall intelligence.

People with Mental Retardation but Relatively Spared Language

What about the reverse? Could someone with mental retardation have good language? Psychologists would have answered "no," until they discovered **Williams syndrome**, affecting about 1 person in 20,000. Despite mental retardation in most regards, many people with Williams syndrome speak grammatically and fluently. The cause is a deletion of several genes from chromosome 7 (Korenberg et al., 2000), leading to decreased gray matter, especially in visual processing areas (Kippenhan et al., 2005; Meyer-Lindenberg et al., 2004; Reiss et al., 2004). Affected people are poor at tasks re-

People with Williams syndrome have a characteristic appearance, as well as a special set of behavioral strengths and weaknesses.

lated to numbers, visuospatial skills (e.g., copying a drawing), and spatial perception (e.g., finding their way home). When asked to estimate the length of a bus, three people with Williams syndrome answered "30 inches," "3 inches or 100 inches maybe," and "2 inches, 10 feet" (Bellugi, Lichtenberger, Jones, Lai, & St George, 2000). Throughout life, they require constant supervision and cannot hold even simple jobs.

In spite of overall mental retardation, with a mean IQ score around 50–60, many people with Williams syndrome perform well, or at least close to normal, in certain regards. One is music, such as the ability to clap a complex rhythm and memorize songs (Levitin & Bellugi, 1998). Another is friendliness and the ability to interpret facial expressions, such as relaxed or worried, serious or playful, flirtatious or uninterested (Tager-Flusberg, Boshart, & Baron-Cohen, 1998). Their fascination with faces probably relates to the fact that their fusiform cortex—an area sensitive to faces (as described in Chapter 6)—is about twice as large as normal (Golarai et al., 2010). However, many also have bouts of severe anxiety or quarrelsome irritability that interfere with social relationships (Martens, Wilson, & Reutens, 2008).

Their most surprising skill is language. Although their language abilities develop more slowly than average, some individuals have remarkably good language, considering their impairments in other regards. Figure 14.13 shows the result when a young woman with Williams syndrome was asked to draw an elephant and describe it. Contrast her almost poetic description to the unrecognizable drawing.

Let's not overstate the case. People with Williams syndrome do not handle language perfectly (Martens, Wilson, & Reutens, 2008; Meyer-Lindenberg, Mervis, & Berman, 2006). Their grammar is awkward, like that of someone who learned a second language late in life (Clahsen & Almazen, 1998; Karmiloff-Smith et al., 1998). If shown a picture of an unfamiliar object and told its name, they are as likely to think the name refers to part of the object as to the object itself (Stevens & Karmiloff-Smith, 1997). They use fancy words when a common word would work better, such as "I have to evacuate the glass" instead of "empty" or "pour out" the glass (Bellugi et al., 2000). Still, observations of Williams syndrome indicate that language is not simply a byproduct of overall intelligence.

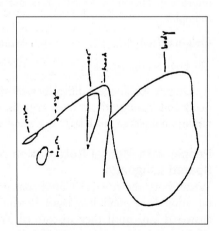

And what an elephant is, it is one of the animals. And what the elephant does, it lives in the jungle. It can also live in the zoo. And what it has, it has long gray ears, fan ears, ears that can blow in the wind. It has a long trunk that can pick up grass, or pick up hay . . . If they're in a bad mood it can be terrible . . . If the elephant gets mad it could stomp; it could charge, like a bull can charge. They have long big tusks. They can damage a car . . . it could be dangerous. When they're in a pinch, when they're in a bad mood it can be terrible. You don't want an elephant as a pet. You want a cat or a dog or a bird . . .

FIGURE 14.13 A young woman with Williams syndrome draws and describes an elephant
The investigator added the labels on the drawing based on what the woman said she was drawing. *(From "Williams Syndrome: An Unusual Neuropsychological Profile," by U. Bellugi, P. O. Wang, and T. L. Jernigan, S. H. Broman and J. Grafman, Eds.,* Atypical Cognitive Deficits in Developmental Disorders. *Copyright © 1994 Lawrence Erlbaum. Reprinted by permission.)*

Language as a Specialization

If language is not just a byproduct of overall intelligence, it must have evolved as a specialized brain mechanism. Noam Chomsky (1980) and Steven Pinker (1994) proposed that humans have a **language acquisition device**, a built-in mechanism for acquiring language. Most children develop language so quickly and easily that it seems they must have been biologically "prepared" for this learning. Also, deaf children quickly learn sign language, and if no one teaches them a sign language, they invent one of their own and teach it to one another (Goldin-Meadow, McNeill, & Singleton, 1996; Goldin-Meadow & Mylander, 1998).

Researchers have begun to explore the genetic basis of this preparation for language. Remember that family whose members have such trouble with pronunciation and basic grammar? Their problem stems from a mutation in a gene designated *FOXP2* (Lai et al., 2001). Although both humans and chimpanzees have that gene, it differs in two places, resulting in proteins with different amino acids at two sites. That gene produces a multitude of effects, partly on brain development, but also on structures of the jaw and throat that are important for speech (Konopka et al., 2009). If researchers altered this gene in chimpanzees, what would happen? Presumably language depends on more than just one gene, but the result would be interesting. That study hasn't been done, but researchers did alter the *FOXP2* gene in mice. The effects included changes in vocalizations and increased dendritic branching and synaptic plasticity in the basal ganglia (Enard et al., 2009).

So back to the original question: How and why did humans evolve language? The fossil record cannot answer a question like this, and we are left with speculations. One is that language relates to the long period of dependency in childhood. Social interactions among people, including those between parents and children, favored the evolution of language, and overall intelligence may be a byproduct of language development more than language is a byproduct of intelligence (Deacon, 1992, 1997).

> **STOP & CHECK**

8. What evidence argues against the hypothesis that language evolution depended simply on the overall evolution of brain and intelligence?

9. Describe tasks that people with Williams syndrome do poorly and those that they do well.

ANSWERS   9. Relatively good: language, interpretation of facial expressions, social behaviors, some aspects of music. Poor: numbers, visual-motor skills, and spatial perception. 8. Some people have normal brain size but very poor language. Also, some people are mentally retarded but nevertheless develop nearly normal language.

A Sensitive Period for Language Learning

If humans are specially adapted to learn language, perhaps we are adapted to learn best during a sensitive period early in life, just as sparrows learn their song best during an early period. One way to test this hypothesis is to see whether people learn a second language best if they start young. The consistent result is that adults are better than children at memorizing the vocabulary of a second language, but children have a great advantage on learning the pronunciation and grammar. There is no sharp cutoff for learning a second language; starting at age 2 is better than 4, 4 is better than 6, and 13 is better than 16 (Hakuta, Bialystok, & Wiley, 2003; Harley & Wang, 1997; Weber-Fox & Neville, 1996). However, people who start learning a second language beyond age 12 or so almost never reach the level of a true native speaker (Abrahamsson & Hyltenstam, 2009). Also, learning a second language from the start is very different from learning one later. The first module of this chapter noted that the left hemisphere is dominant for language. People who grow up in a bilingual home, speaking two languages from the start, are an exception. In most cases, they show substantial bilateral activity during speech, for both languages. Also, the language areas of their temporal and frontal cortex grow thicker than average (Mechelli et al., 2004). People who learn a second language after age 6 or so activate just the left hemisphere for both languages (Hull & Vaid, 2007). Many people guess that a bilingual person might rely on the left hemisphere for one language and the right hemisphere for the other. That guess is wrong, as the second language depends on the same brain areas as the first (Perani & Abutalebi, 2005).

Another way to test the sensitive-period idea is to study people who learned no language during early childhood. The clearest data come from studies of deaf children whose parents concentrated unsuccessfully on teaching them spoken language and lip-reading, and then eventually gave up on this effort and introduced sign language. Children who began while still young learned sign language much better than those who started later (Harley & Wang, 1997). A child who learns English early can learn sign language later, and a deaf child who learns sign language early can learn English later (except for poor pronunciation), but a child who learns no language while young is permanently impaired at learning any kind of language (Mayberry, Lock, & Kazmi, 2002). This observation strongly supports the importance of learning language in early childhood.

> **STOP & CHECK**

10. What is the strongest evidence in favor of a sensitive period for language learning?

ANSWER   10. Deaf children who are not exposed to sign language either while they were young) do not become proficient at it.

▌Brain Damage and Language

Another way to study specializations for language is to examine the role of various brain areas. Much of our knowledge has come from studies of people with brain damage.

Broca's Aphasia (Nonfluent Aphasia)

In 1861, French surgeon Paul Broca treated the gangrene of a patient who had been mute for 30 years. When the man died 5 days later, Broca did an autopsy and found a lesion in the left frontal cortex. Over the next few years, Broca examined the brains of additional patients with **aphasia** (language impairment). In nearly all cases, he found damage that included this same area, which is now known as **Broca's area** (Figure 14.14). The usual cause was a stroke (an interruption of blood flow to part of the brain). Broca published his results in 1865, slightly later than papers by other French physicians, Marc and Gustave Dax, who also pointed to the left hemisphere as the seat of language abilities (Finger & Roe, 1996). Broca received the credit, however, because his description was more detailed and more convincing. This discovery, the first demonstration of the function of a particular brain area, paved the way for modern neurology.

We now know that speaking activates much of the brain, mostly in the left hemisphere, and not just Broca's area (Wallesch, Henriksen, Kornhuber, & Paulson, 1985) (Figure 14.15). Damage limited to Broca's area produces only minor or brief language impairment. Serious deficits result from extensive damage that extends into other areas as well. Most cases result from a stroke, but similar deficits result from diseases causing gradual atrophy to Broca's area and surrounding areas (S. M. Wilson et al., 2010).

When people with brain damage suffer impaired language production, we call it **Broca's aphasia**, or **nonfluent aphasia**, regardless of the exact location of damage. People with Broca's aphasia also have comprehension deficits when the meaning of a sentence depends on prepositions, word endings, or unusual word order—in short, when the sentence structure is complicated.

Difficulty in Language Production

People with Broca's aphasia are slow and awkward with all forms of expression, including speaking, writing, and gesturing, as well as sign language for the deaf (Cicone, Wapner, Foldi, Zurif, & Gardner, 1979; Neville et al., 1998; Petitto et al., 2000). So Broca's aphasia relates to language, not just the vocal muscles.

When people with Broca's aphasia speak, they omit most pronouns, prepositions, conjunctions, auxiliary (helping) verbs, quantifiers, and tense and number endings. At least, those are the results for people speaking English. People with aphasia use more word endings if they speak German, Italian, or other languages in which word endings are more critical than they are in English (Blackwell & Bates, 1995). Prepositions, conjunctions, helping verbs, and so forth are known as the *closed class* of grammatical forms because a language rarely adds new prepositions, conjunctions, and the like. In contrast, new nouns and verbs (the *open class*)

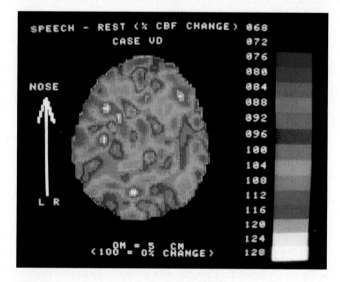

FIGURE 14.15 Brain activity during speech for a normal adult

This study inferred brain activity from patterns of blood flow. Red indicates the highest level of activity, followed by yellow, green, and blue. The areas in red showed the greatest increase in activity during speech. Note the increased activity in many brain areas, especially on the left side. *(Reprinted from* Brain and Language, *25/2, Wallesch, Henriksen, Kornhuber, & Paulson, "Observations on regional cerebral blood flow in cortical and subcortical structures during language production in normal man," pp. 224–233, 1985, with permission from Elsevier.)*

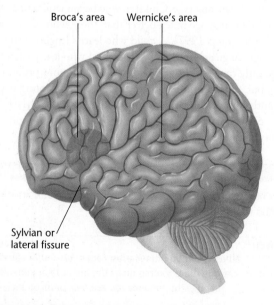

Broca's area   Wernicke's area

Sylvian or lateral fissure

FIGURE 14.14 Two areas important for language
(© Cengage Learning 2013)

enter a language frequently. People with Broca's aphasia seldom use the closed-class words. They find it difficult to repeat a phrase such as "No ifs, ands, or buts," although they can successfully repeat, "The general commands the army." Furthermore, patients who cannot read aloud "To be or not to be" can read "Two bee oar knot two bee" (H. Gardner & Zurif, 1975). Clearly, the trouble is with the word meanings, not just pronunciation.

Why do people with Broca's aphasia omit the grammatical words and endings? Perhaps they have suffered damage to a "grammar area" in the brain, but here is another possibility: When speaking is a struggle, people leave out the weakest elements. Many people who are in great pain speak as if they have Broca's aphasia (Dick et al., 2001).

Problems in Comprehending Grammatical Words and Devices

People with Broca's aphasia have trouble understanding the same kinds of words that they omit when speaking, such as prepositions and conjunctions. They often misunderstand sentences with complex grammar, such as "The girl that the boy is chasing is tall" (Zurif, 1980). However, most English sentences follow the subject-verb-object order, and their meaning is clear even without the prepositions and conjunctions. You can demonstrate this for yourself by taking a paragraph and deleting its prepositions, conjunctions, articles, helping verbs, pronouns, and word endings to see how it might appear to someone with Broca's aphasia. Here is an example, taken from earlier in this section. Note how understandable it is despite the deletions:

In 1861, ~~the~~ French surgeon Paul Broca treat~~ed~~ ~~the~~ gangrene ~~of a~~ patient ~~who had~~ been mute ~~for~~ 30 years. ~~When the~~ man die~~d~~ 5 day~~s~~ later, Broca did ~~an~~ autopsy ~~and~~ found ~~a~~ lesion ~~in the~~ left frontal cortex. ~~Over the~~ next few year~~s~~, Broca examined ~~the~~ brain~~s of~~ additional patient~~s~~ ~~with~~ aphasia (language impairment). ~~In~~ nearly all case~~s~~, ~~he~~ found damage ~~that~~ included ~~this~~ same area, ~~which~~ is now know~~n~~ ~~as~~ Broca's area. ~~The~~ usual cause was ~~a~~ stroke (~~an~~ interruption ~~of~~ blood flow ~~to~~ part ~~of the~~ brain).

Still, people with Broca's aphasia have not totally lost their knowledge of grammar. For example, they generally recognize that something is wrong with the sentence "He written has songs," even if they cannot say how to improve it (Wulfeck & Bates, 1991). In many ways, their comprehension resembles that of normal people who are distracted. If you listen to someone speaking rapidly with a heavy accent in a noisy room, while you are trying to do something else at the same time, you catch bits and pieces of what the speaker says and try to guess the rest. Even when we hear a sentence clearly, we sometimes ignore the grammar. If you hear "The dog was bitten by the man," you might assume it was the dog that did the biting (Ferreira, Bailey, & Ferraro, 2002). Patients with Broca's aphasia just rely on inferences more often than others do.

Broca's Area One Step at a Time

Brain damage studies give us only general information about what Broca's area does. More detailed information comes from the rare opportunities to record from individual cells. Occasionally physicians expose someone's brain to explore options for treating severe epilepsy. Although the scalp is anesthetized, the brain is awake. In a few cases, researchers implanted electrodes to record activity in Broca's area while the person listened to sentences or processed them in other ways. The cells that responded first made the same response regardless of what, if anything, the person was supposed to do with the word. Evidently these cells had something to do with understanding the word. A second group of cells responded a bit later, and responded more strongly if the instruction was to change the tense (walk → walked) or number (rock → rocks). A third group, with the latest response, was active in preparation for saying the word. Those cells responded most strongly to long words that required more effort to speak (Sahin, Pinker, Cash, Schomer, & Halgren, 2009). These results suggest that cells in Broca's area go through at least three stages in controlling speech.

STOP & CHECK

11. What kind of words are Broca's patients least likely to use?

12. What kind of words do Broca's patients have the most trouble understanding?

ANSWERS

11. They have the greatest trouble with "closed-class" words that are meaningful only in the context of a sentence, such as prepositions, conjunctions, and helping verbs. 12. They have the most trouble understanding the same kind of words they have trouble producing—the closed-class words.

Wernicke's Aphasia (Fluent Aphasia)

In 1874, Carl Wernicke (pronounced WER-nih-kee by most English speakers, although the German pronunciation is VAYR-nih-keh), a 26-year-old junior assistant in a German hospital, discovered that damage in part of the left temporal cortex produced a different kind of language impairment. Although patients could speak and write, their language comprehension was poor. Damage in and around **Wernicke's area** (Figure 14.14), located near the auditory cortex, produces **Wernicke's aphasia**, characterized by poor language comprehension and impaired ability to remember the names of objects. It is also known as **fluent aphasia** because the person can still speak smoothly. As with Broca's aphasia, the symptoms and brain damage vary. We use the term Wernicke's aphasia, or fluent aphasia, to describe a certain pattern of behavior, independent of the location of damage.

The typical characteristics of Wernicke's aphasia are as follows:

1. *Articulate speech.* In contrast to people with Broca's aphasia, those with Wernicke's aphasia speak fluently, except when pausing to try to think of the name of something.

2. *Difficulty finding the right word.* People with Wernicke's aphasia have **anomia** (ay-NOME-ee-uh), difficulty recalling the names of objects. They make up names (e.g., "thingamajig"), substitute one name for another, and use roundabout expressions such as "the thing that we used to do with the thing that was like the other one." When they do manage to find some of the right words, they arrange them improperly, such as, "The Astros listened to the radio tonight" (instead of "I listened to the Astros on the radio tonight") (R. C. Martin & Blossom-Stach, 1986).

3. *Poor language comprehension.* People with Wernicke's aphasia have trouble understanding spoken and written speech and—in the case of deaf people—sign language (Petitto et al., 2000). Although many sentences are clear enough without the prepositions, word endings, and grammar that confuse Broca's aphasics, few sentences make sense without nouns and verbs (which trouble Wernicke's patients).

The following conversation is between a woman with Wernicke's aphasia and a speech therapist trying to teach her the names of some objects. (The Duke University Department of Speech Pathology and Audiology provided this dialogue.)

> **Therapist:** (*Holding picture of an apron*) Can you name that one?
>
> **Woman:** Um . . . you see I can't, I can I can barely do; he would give me sort of umm. . .
>
> **T:** A clue?
>
> **W:** That's right . . . just a like, just a . . .
>
> **T:** You mean, like, "You wear that when you wash dishes or when you cook a meal . . ."?

> **W:** Yeah, something like that.
>
> **T:** Okay, and what is it? You wear it around your waist, and you cook . . .
>
> **W:** Cook. Umm, umm, see I can't remember.
>
> **T:** It's an apron.
>
> **W:** Apron, apron, that's it, apron.
>
> **T:** (*Holding another picture*) That you wear when you're getting ready for bed after a shower.
>
> **W:** Oh, I think that he put under different, something different. We had something, you know, umm, you know.
>
> **T:** A different way of doing it?
>
> **W:** No, umm . . . umm . . . (*Pause*)
>
> **T:** It's actually a bathrobe.
>
> **W:** Bathrobe. Uh, we didn't call it that, we called it something else.
>
> **T:** Smoking jacket?
>
> **W:** No, I think we called it, uh . . .
>
> **T:** Lounging . . .?
>
> **W:** No, no, something, in fact, we called it just . . . (*Pause*)
>
> **T:** Robe?
>
> **W:** Robe. Or something like that.

The patient still knows the names of objects and recognizes them when she hears them; she just has trouble finding them for herself. In some ways, her speech resembles that of a student called upon to speak in a foreign language class after poorly studying the vocabulary list.

Although Wernicke's area and surrounding areas are important, language comprehension also depends on the connections to other brain areas. For example, reading the word *lick* activates not only Wernicke's area but also the part of the motor cortex responsible for tongue movements. Reading *throw* activates the part of the premotor cortex controlling hand movements (Willems, Hagoort, & Casasanto, 2010). Apparently when you think about an action word, you imagine doing it. Table 14.1 contrasts Broca's aphasia and Wernicke's aphasia.

TABLE 14.1	Broca's Aphasia and Wernicke's Aphasia		
Type	**Pronunciation**	**Content of Speech**	**Comprehension**
Broca's aphasia	Poor	Mostly nouns and verbs; omits prepositions and other grammatical connectives	Impaired if the meaning depends on complex grammar
Wernicke's aphasia	Unimpaired	Grammatical but often nonsensical; has trouble finding the right word, especially names of objects	Seriously impaired

13. Describe the speech production of people with Wernicke's aphasia.

14. Describe the speech comprehension of people with Wernicke's aphasia.

ANSWERS

13. People with Wernicke's aphasia speak fluently and grammatically but omit most nouns and verbs and therefore make little sense. **14.** People with Wernicke's aphasia understand little speech.

Music and Language

Language occurs in every human culture, and no other species develops language as we know it. Exactly the same could be said for music. Language and music have many parallels, including the ability of both to evoke strong emotions. Broca's area is strongly activated when orchestral musicians sight-read music, as well as when they perform difficult visuospatial tasks (Sluming, Brooks, Howard, Downes, & Roberts, 2007). The parallels between language and music are sufficient to suggest that they arose together. That is, whatever evolutionary processes helped us develop language also enabled us to develop music.

Consider some of the parallels (Patel, 2008):

- Trained musicians and music students tend to be better than average at learning a second language.

- In both language and music, we alter the timing and volume to add emphasis or to express emotion.

- English speakers average about 0.5 to 0.7 seconds between one stressed syllable and another in speech and prefer music with about 0.5 to 0.7 seconds between beats.

- Greek and Balkan languages have less regular rhythms than English, and much of the music written by speakers of those languages has irregularly spaced beats.

- English usually stresses the first syllable of a word or phrase, whereas French more often stresses the final syllable. Similarly, French composers more often than English composers make the final note of a phrase longer than the others.

- English vowels vary in duration more than French vowels do. For example, compare the vowels in *tourist* or *pirate*. English composers, on average, have more variation in note length from one note to the next.

These similarities and others suggest that we use the language areas of the brain when we compose music, and we prefer music that resembles our language in rhythms and tones (Ross, Choi, & Purves, 2007). You could think of music as an alternative method of communication.

15. In what way do musical compositions vary depending on the language spoken by the composer?

ANSWER

15. Musical compositions tend to follow the same rhythms that are common in the language spoken by the composer.

Dyslexia

Dyslexia is a specific impairment of reading in someone with adequate vision, adequate motivation, and adequate overall cognitive skills. It is more common in boys than girls and has been linked to at least four genes that produce deficits in hearing or cognition (Galaburda, LoTurco, Ramus, Fitch, & Rosen, 2006). Dyslexia is especially common in English because it has so many words with odd spellings. (Consider *phlegm, bivouac, khaki, yacht, choir, physique*, and *gnat*.) However, dyslexia occurs in all languages and always pertains to a difficulty converting symbols into sounds (Ziegler & Goswami, 2005). A study comparing readers of English and Chinese found that normal readers activated somewhat different brain areas, presumably because English letters represent sounds, whereas a Chinese symbol represents a whole syllable or word. However, English-speaking dyslexics and Chinese-speaking dyslexics were remarkably similar in showing decreased activation in several brain areas while reading (Hu, et al., 2010).

As a rule, people with dyslexia are more likely to have a bilaterally symmetrical cerebral cortex, whereas in other people, the planum temporale and certain other areas are larger in the left hemisphere (Galaburda, Sherman, Rosen, Aboitiz, & Geschwind, 1985; Hynd & Semrud-Clikeman, 1989; Jenner, Rosen, & Galaburda, 1999). Several brain areas in the parietal and temporal cortex have less than average gray matter in children with dyslexia and show less arousal during reading (Hoeft et al., 2006; Gabrieli, 2009). Similar differences are apparent in 5- and 6-year-olds who have a family history of dyslexia (Raschle, Chang, & Gaab, 2011). Evidently these brain features represent a predisposition toward dyslexia rather than a result of failure to read.

Reading is a complicated skill that requires seeing subtle differences as *abode* vs. *adobe*, hearing subtle differences as *symphony* vs. *sympathy*, and connecting the sound patterns to the visual symbols. In fact, even understanding spoken language requires a combination of vision and hearing. Non-deaf people do far more lip-reading than they realize. Consider your experience when you see a foreign film that is dubbed badly or a film in which the soundtrack is slightly off from the picture.

In the often confusing literature about dyslexia, one point that stands out is that different people have different kinds of reading problems, and no one explanation works for all. Most (but not all) have auditory problems, a smaller number have impaired control of eye movements, and some have both (Judge, Caravolas, & Knox, 2006). Some researchers distinguish between *dysphonetic dyslexics* and *dyseidetic dyslexics* (Flynn & Boder, 1991), although many people with dyslexia do not fit neatly into either category (Farmer & Klein, 1995). Dysphonetic dyslexics have trouble sounding out words, so they try to memorize each word as a whole, and when they don't recognize a word, they guess based on context. For example, they might read the word *laugh* as "funny." Dyseidetic readers sound out words well enough, but they fail to recognize a word as a whole. They read slowly and have particular trouble with irregularly spelled words.

The most severe cases of dyseidetic dyslexia result from brain damage that restricts the field of vision. People who see only one letter at a time have many short eye movements, very slow reading, and particular difficulty with long words. In one study, normal people viewed words on a computer screen while a device monitored their eye movements and blurred every letter on the screen except the one the viewer focused on. The result was very slow reading (Rayner & Johnson, 2005).

Most but not all people with dyslexia have auditory problems (Caccappolo-van Vliet, Miozzo, & Stern, 2004). Brain scans have shown that dyslexics' brains, on average, show less than normal responses to speech sounds, especially consonants (Helenius, Salmelin, Richardson, Leinonen, & Lyytinen, 2002; McCrory, Frith, Brunswick, & Price, 2000). Many people with dyslexia have particular trouble detecting the temporal order of sounds, such as noticing the difference between beep-click-buzz and beep-buzz-click (Farmer & Klein, 1995; Kujala et al., 2000; Nagarajan et al., 1999). They also have much difficulty making Spoonerisms—that is, trading the first consonants of two words, such as listening to "dear old queen" and saying "queer old dean" or hearing "way of life" and replying "lay of wife" (Paulesu et al., 1996). Doing so, of course, requires close attention to sounds and their order. Many people with dyslexia have trouble with other temporal order tasks as well, such as tapping a regular rhythm with the fingers (Wolff, 1993).

However, the problem cannot be simply impaired hearing. Many deaf or partly deaf people can read, and people with dyslexia have no trouble carrying on a conversation (which would be difficult if their hearing were seriously impaired). The problem must be something more specific, such as paying attention to certain aspects of sound or connecting sound to vision. In one study, dyslexics performed normally at watching nonsense words flashed on the screen and saying whether they were the same or different. (For example, *brap-brap* would be the same and *sond-snod* would be different.) They were also normal at listening to two non-sense words and saying whether they were the same. They were impaired only when they had to look at a nonsense word on the screen and then say whether it was the same as a nonsense word they heard (Snowling, 1980).

Many people with dyslexia also have abnormalities in their attention (Facoetti, Corradi, Ruffino, Gori, & Zorzi, 2010). Here is a demonstration. Fixate your eyes on the central dot in each display below and, without moving your eyes left or right, try to read the middle letter of each three-letter display:

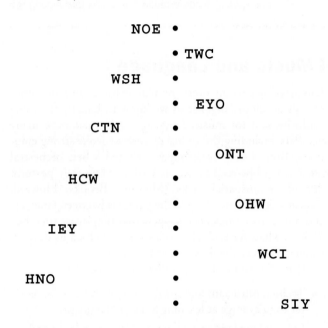

Most people find it easier to read the letters close to the fixation point, but some people with dyslexia are unusually adept at identifying letters well to the right of their fixation point. When they focus on a word, they are worse than average at reading it but better than average at perceiving letters 5 to 10 degrees to the right of it (Geiger, Lettvin, & Zegarra-Moran, 1992; Lorusso et al., 2004). That kind of attentional focus could certainly confuse attempts at reading (De Luca, Di Page, Judica, Spinelli, & Zoccolotti, 1999). Figure 14.16 shows the mean results for normal readers and for people with dyslexia.

For people with this abnormality, an effective treatment might be to teach them to attend to just one word at a time. Some children and adults with dyslexia have been told to place over the page that they are reading a sheet of paper with a window cut out of it that is large enough to expose just one word. In 3 months, 15 dyslexic children improved their reading skills by 1.22 grade levels (Geiger, Lettvin, & Fahle, 1994). Four dyslexic adults also made spectacular progress; one advanced from a third-grade to a tenth-grade reading level in 4 months (Geiger et al., 1992). After about the first 3 weeks of practice, they no longer needed the special cutout sheet of paper.

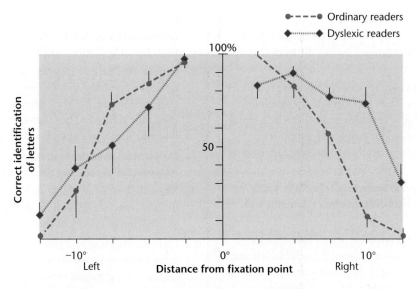

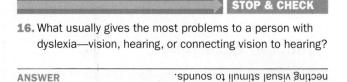

FIGURE 14.16 Identification of letters at various distances from the fixation point
Normal readers identify a letter most accurately when it is closest to the fixation point, and their accuracy drops for letters farther away. Many people with dyslexia are more accurate than normal readers are in identifying letters 5 to 10 degrees to the right of fixation. *(Reprinted from "Task-Determined Strategies of Visual Process," by G. Geiger, J. Y. Lettvin, & U. Zagarra-Moran, 1992, Cognitive Brain Research, 1, pp. 39–52, 1992, with kind permission of Elsevier Science-NL, Sara Burgerhartstraat 25, 1055 KV Amsterdam, The Netherlands.)*

One final twist: Of the four adults with dyslexia who went through this process, three decided that they would rather return to being dyslexic! While dyslexic, they could attend to several tasks at once, such as talking to someone, listening to news on the radio, creating a work of art, and so forth. When they learned to read one word at a time, they found themselves able to perform only one task at a time, and they missed their old way of life. In short, their reading skills were tied to their overall attentional strategies.

STOP & CHECK

16. What usually gives the most problems to a person with dyslexia—vision, hearing, or connecting vision to hearing?

ANSWER

16. Generally, the greatest problem arises with connecting visual stimuli to sounds.

MODULE 14.2 ■ IN CLOSING

Language and the Brain

Perhaps the best summary of dyslexia is also the best summary of language impairments in general: Language and reading are sufficiently complicated that people can become impaired in many ways for many reasons. Language is not simply a byproduct of overall intelligence, but it is hardly independent of other intellectual functions either.

SUMMARY

1. Chimpanzees can learn to communicate through gestures or nonvocal symbols, although their output does not closely resemble human language. Bonobos have made more language progress than common chimpanzees because of species differences, early onset of training, and different training methods. **432**

2. An African gray parrot has shown surprising language abilities, with a brain organized differently from that of primates. **434**

3. The hypothesis that language emerged as a byproduct of overall intelligence or brain size faces major problems: Some people have full-size brains and otherwise normal intelligence but impaired language, and people with Williams syndrome have nearly normal language despite mental retardation. **434**

4. People are specialized to learn language easily, partly because of one gene that differs between humans and chimpanzees. **437**

5. The best evidence for a sensitive period for language development is the observation that deaf children learn sign language much better if they start early than if their first opportunity comes later in life. Also, learning a second language in early childhood differs in many ways from learning it later. **437**

6. People with Broca's aphasia (nonfluent aphasia) have difficulty speaking and writing. They find prepositions, conjunctions, and other grammatical connectives especially difficult. They also fail to understand speech when its meaning depends on complex grammar. **438**

7. People with Wernicke's aphasia have trouble understanding speech and recalling the names of objects. **439**

8. Music has many parallels with language. Composers usually write music with rhythm patterns that resemble the rhythm of speech in their own language. **441**

9. Dyslexia (reading impairment) has many forms. The main problem is usually in converting visual signals into auditory information or attending to the right aspects of a visual display. **441**

KEY TERMS

Terms are defined in the module on the page number indicated. They're also presented in alphabetical order with definitions in the book's Subject Index/Glossary, which begins on page 561. Interactive flashcards and crossword puzzles are among the online resources available to help you learn these terms and the concepts they represent.

anomia **440**

aphasia **438**

Broca's aphasia (nonfluent aphasia) **438**

Broca's area **438**

dyslexia **441**

language acquisition device **437**

productivity **432**

Wernicke's aphasia (fluent aphasia) **439**

Wernicke's area **439**

Williams syndrome **435**

THOUGHT QUESTIONS

1. Most people with Broca's aphasia suffer from partial paralysis on the right side of the body. Most people with Wernicke's aphasia do not. Why?

2. In a syndrome called *word blindness*, a person loses the ability to read (even single letters), although the person can still see and speak. What is a possible neurological explanation? That is, can you imagine a pattern of brain damage that might produce this result?

Conscious and Unconscious Processes and Attention

In Chapter 1, we introduced the mind–body problem: In a universe composed of matter and energy, why is there such a thing as consciousness? And how does it relate to the brain? Now armed with more understanding of the brain, it is time to return to those questions (even if we can't answer them).

The Mind–Brain Relationship

Suppose you say, "I became frightened because I saw a man with a gun." A neuroscientist says, "You became frightened because of increased electrochemical activity in the central amygdala of your brain." If both statements are right, what is the connection between them?

Biological explanations of behavior raise the **mind–body** or **mind–brain problem:** What is the relationship between the mind and the brain? The most widespread view among nonscientists is, no doubt, **dualism**, the belief that mind and body are different kinds of substance that exist independently. The French philosopher René Descartes defended dualism but recognized the vexing issue of how a mind that is not made of material could influence a physical brain. He proposed that mind and brain interact at a single point in space, which he suggested was the pineal gland, the smallest unpaired structure he could find in the brain (Figure 1.5).

Although we credit Descartes with the first explicit defense of dualism, he hardly originated the idea. Our experiences seem so different from the physical actions of the brain that most people take it for granted that mind and brain are different. However, nearly all current philosophers and neuroscientists reject dualism. The decisive objection is that dualism conflicts with one of the cornerstones of physics, known as the law of the conservation of matter and energy: So far as we can tell, the total amount of matter and energy in the universe has been fixed since the Big Bang that originated it all. Matter can transform into energy or energy into matter, but neither one emerges from nothing or disappears into nothing. Because matter alters its course only when other matter or energy acts upon it, a mind that is not composed of matter or energy could not make anything happen, including muscle movements.

The alternative to dualism is **monism**, the belief that the universe consists of only one kind of substance. Various forms of monism are possible, grouped into the following categories:

- **materialism:** the view that everything that exists is material, or physical. According to one version of this view ("eliminative materialism"), mental events don't exist at all, and any folk psychology based on minds and mental activity is fundamentally mistaken. However, most of us find it difficult to believe that our minds are figments of our imagination! A more plausible version is that we will eventually find a way to explain all psychological experiences in purely physical terms.

- **mentalism:** the view that only the mind really exists and that the physical world could not exist unless some mind were aware of it. It is not easy to test this idea—go ahead and try!—but few philosophers or scientists take it seriously.

- **identity position:** the view that mental processes and certain kinds of brain processes are the same thing, described in different terms. By analogy, one could describe the *Mona Lisa* as an extraordinary painting, or one could list the exact color and brightness of each point on the painting. Although the two descriptions appear entirely different, they refer to the same object.

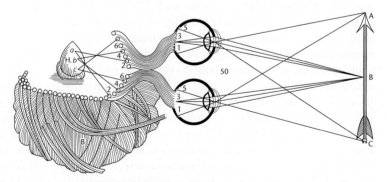

FIGURE 14.17 René Descartes's conception of brain and mind
Descartes understood how light from an object (the arrow) reached the retinas at the back of the eyes. The letters and numbers represent pathways that he imagined from the retinas to the pineal gland. (His guesses about those pathways were wrong.) *(From Descartes' Treatises on Man)*

The identity position does not say that the mind is the brain. It says the mind is brain *activity*. Just as fire is not a "thing," but what happens to something, mental activity is what happens in the brain. The identity position also does not say brain activity "causes consciousness." Brain activity does not cause consciousness any more than consciousness causes brain activity. Each is the same as the other.

Can we be sure that monism is correct? No. However, researchers adopt it as the most reasonable working hypothesis, to see how much progress they can make on that assumption. As you have seen throughout this text, experiences and brain activities appear inseparable. Stimulation of any brain area provokes an experience, and any experience evokes brain activity, and damage to any brain area leads to loss of some mental function. As far as we can tell, you cannot have mental activity without brain activity. If you use terms like *mind* to mean a ghostlike something that is neither matter nor energy, don't underestimate the scientific and philosophical arguments that can be marshaled against you (Dennett, 1991).

(Does a belief in monism mean that we are lowering our evaluation of minds? Maybe not. Maybe we are elevating our concept of the material world.)

> **STOP & CHECK**

17. Why do nearly all scientists and philosophers reject the idea of dualism?

ANSWER

17. Dualism contradicts the law of the conservation of matter and energy. According to that law, the only way to influence matter and energy, including that of your body, is to act on it with other matter and energy.

David Chalmers (1995) distinguished between what he calls the easy problems and the hard problem of consciousness. The easy problems pertain to such questions as the difference between wakefulness and sleep and what brain activity occurs during consciousness. These issues are difficult scientifically but not philosophically. In contrast, the **hard problem** concerns why consciousness exists at all. As Chalmers (1995, p. 203) put it, "Why doesn't all this information-processing go on 'in the dark,' free of any inner feel?" Why does brain activity *feel* like anything at all? Many scientists (Crick & Koch, 2004) and philosophers (Chalmers, 2004) agree that we cannot answer that question, at least at present. We don't even have a clear hypothesis to test. The best we can do is determine what brain activity is necessary or sufficient for consciousness. Maybe research on subordinate questions will some day lead us to a breakthrough on the hard question, or maybe not. But starting with the "easy" questions seems the best strategy.

> **STOP & CHECK**

18. What is meant by the "hard problem"?

ANSWER

18. The hard problem is why minds exist at all in a physical world. Why is there such a thing as consciousness?

Brain Activity Associated with Consciousness

Although we don't have even a good hypothesis about *why* brain activity is (sometimes) conscious, we might be able to discover which types of brain activity are conscious (Crick & Koch, 2004). Once we answer that question, we might be better at identifying signs of consciousness in nonhuman animals, infants, or brain-damaged people. Already researchers tentatively use brain measurements for that purpose. Researchers used fMRI to record brain activity in a young woman who was in a persistent vegetative state following a brain injury in a traffic accident. She had neither spoken nor made any other purposive movements. However, when she was told to imagine playing tennis, the fMRI showed increased activity in motor areas of her cortex, similar to what healthy volunteers showed. When she was told to imagine walking through her house, a different set of brain areas became active, again similar to those of healthy volunteers (Owen et al., 2006). Follow-up studies found another patient in a vegetative state whose brain showed similar responses to instructions, although several other patients did not (K. Smith, 2007). Do these results mean that certain patients in a vegetative state are actually conscious? The answer is not certain, but the possibilities are exciting.

One of the main problems in research is that we cannot observe consciousness. Even defining it is treacherously difficult. For practical purposes, researchers use this operational definition: If a cooperative person reports awareness of one stimulus and not another, then he or she was **conscious** of the first and not the second. With individuals who cannot speak—such as infants, people with Broca's aphasia, or nonhuman animals—this definition doesn't apply. We might infer consciousness based on other criteria, but we won't use such individuals for research.

Using this definition, the next step is to present a given stimulus under two conditions. In one condition we expect the observer to be conscious of it, and in the other condition we expect the observer to be unconscious of it. In both cases the stimulus excites receptors that send a message to the brain, but once the message reaches the brain presumably something different happens for conscious vs. unconscious processing.

How could we present a stimulus while preventing consciousness? Researchers have developed clever approaches, mostly based on interference. Suppose you clearly see a yellow dot. Then, although the dot remains on the screen, other dots around it flash on and off. While they are flashing you may be unable to see the stationary dot. This procedure is called "flash suppression" (Kreiman, Fried, & Koch, 2002). Similarly, suppose you see a yellow dot, and then some blue dots all around it start moving rapidly. They grab your attention so strongly that you have trouble seeing the yellow dot. In fact, it seems to disappear for a few seconds, reappear for a few seconds, disappear again, and so forth (Bonneh, Cooperman, & Sagi, 2001).

Experiments Using Masking

Many studies use **masking**: a brief visual stimulus is preceded and followed by longer interfering stimuli. In many cases, just the later stimulus is presented, in which case it is called **backward masking**. In one study, researchers flashed a word on a screen for 29 milliseconds (ms). On some trials, it was preceded and followed by a blank screen:

In these cases, people identified the word almost 90% of the time. On other trials, the researchers flashed a word for the same 29 ms but preceded and followed it with masking patterns:

 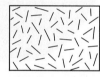

In the masking condition, people usually say they saw no word at all, and almost never identify it. Using fMRI and evoked potentials, the researchers found that the stimulus initially activates the primary visual cortex for both the conscious and unconscious conditions but activates it more strongly in the conscious condition (because of less interference). Also, in the conscious condition, the activity spreads to additional brain areas (Dehaene et al., 2001), including the prefrontal cortex and parietal cortex. Those areas apparently amplify the signal. For people with damage to the prefrontal cortex, a visual stimulus has to last longer before it becomes conscious, relative to other people (Del Cul, Dehaene, Reyes, Bravo, & Slachevsky, 2009).

A conscious stimulus also synchronizes responses for neurons in various brain areas (Eckhorn et al., 1988; Gray, König, Engel, & Singer, 1989; Melloni et al., 2007; Womelsdorf et al., 2007). When you see something and recognize it, it evokes activity precisely synchronized in several brain areas, in the frequency of about 30–50 Hz (cycles per second), known as *gamma waves*. (Doesburg, Green, McDonald, & Ward, 2009; Fisch et al., 2009). One consequence of synchronized action potentials is that their synaptic inputs arrive simultaneously at their target cells, producing maximal summation (Fell & Axmacher, 2011).

Overall, the data imply that consciousness of a stimulus depends on the amount and spread of brain activity. Conscious stimuli also produce more consistent responses from one trial to another than do similar but unconscious stimuli (Schurger, Pereira, Treisman, & Cohen, 2010). Becoming conscious of something means that its information takes over more of your brain's activity.

STOP & CHECK

19. In the experiment by Dehaene et al., how were the conscious and unconscious stimuli similar? How were they different?

20. In this experiment, how did the brain's responses differ between the conscious and unconscious stimuli?

ANSWERS

19. The conscious and unconscious stimuli were physically the same (a word flashed on the screen for 29 ms). The difference was that a stimulus did not become conscious if it was preceded and followed by an interfering pattern. **20.** If a stimulus became conscious, it activated the same brain areas as an unconscious stimulus but more strongly, and then the activity spread to additional areas. Also, brain responses become synchronized when a pattern is conscious.

Experiments Using Binocular Rivalry

Here is another way to make a stimulus unconscious. Look at Figure 14.18, but hold it so close to your eyes that your nose touches the page, right between the two circles. Better yet, look at the two parts through a pair of tubes, such as the tubes inside rolls of paper towels or toilet paper. You will see red and black vertical stripes with your left eye and green and black horizontal stripes with your right eye. (Close one eye and then the other to make sure you see completely different patterns with the two eyes.) Seeing something requires seeing *where* it is, and the red vertical stripes cannot be in the same place as the green horizontal stripes. Because your brain cannot perceive both patterns in the same location, your perception alternates. For a while, you see the red and black stripes, and then gradually, the green and black invade your consciousness. Then your perception shifts back to the red and black. For the average person, each perception lasts about 2 seconds before switching to the other, but some people switch faster or slower. These shifts, known as **binocular rivalry**, are gradual, sweeping from one side to another. The two images do not necessarily divide your attention time equally. Some people see with one eye longer than the other. Also, an emotionally charged image, such as a picture of a happy face, holds attention longer than a neutral image (Yoon, Hong, Joormann, & Kang, 2009).

TRY IT YOURSELF

The stimulus seen by each eye evokes a brain response that researchers can measure with fMRI or similar methods. As the first perception fades and the stimulus seen by the other eye replaces it, the first pattern of brain activity fades also, and a different pattern replaces it. Each shift in perception is accompanied by a shift in the activity over a large portion of the brain (Lee, Blake, & Heeger, 2005).

Both the red–black and green–black patterns you just experienced were stationary. To make the brain responses easier to distinguish, researchers presented to one eye a stationary stimulus and to the other eye a pattern that pulsated in size and brightness, as shown in Figure 14.19. Then they recorded brain activity in several areas. At times when people reported consciousness of the pulsating stimulus, pulsating activity at the same rhythm was prominent in much of the brain, as shown in Figure 14.20. When people reported consciousness of the stationary stimulus, the pulsating activity was weak (Cosmelli et al., 2004). Again, the conclusion is that a conscious stimulus strongly activates much of the brain, virtually taking over brain activity. When the same stimulus is unconscious, it produces weaker and less widespread activity.

> **STOP & CHECK**
>
> **21.** How could someone use fMRI to determine which of two patterns in binocular rivalry is conscious at a given moment?
>
> **ANSWER**
> **21.** Make one stimulus pulsate at a given rhythm and look for brain areas showing that rhythm of activity. The rhythm takes over widespread areas of the brain when that pattern is conscious.

FIGURE 14.18 Binocular rivalry
If possible, look at the two circles through tubes, such as those from inside rolls of toilet paper or paper towels. Otherwise, touch your nose to the paper between the two parts so that your left eye sees one pattern while your right eye sees the other. The two views will compete for your consciousness, and your perception will alternate between them. (© Cengage Learning 2013)

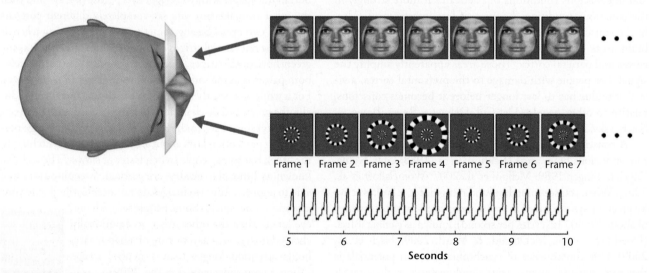

Frame 1   Frame 2   Frame 3   Frame 4   Frame 5   Frame 6   Frame 7

5   6   7   8   9   10
Seconds

FIGURE 14.19 Stimuli for a study of binocular rivalry
The pattern in one eye was stationary. The one in the other eye pulsated a few times per second. Researchers could then examine brain activity to find cells that followed the rhythm of the pulsating stimulus. (Reprinted from NeuroImage, 23/1, Cosmelli et al. "Waves of consciousness: Ongoing cortical patterns during binocular rivalry," 128–140, 2004, with permission from Elsevier.)

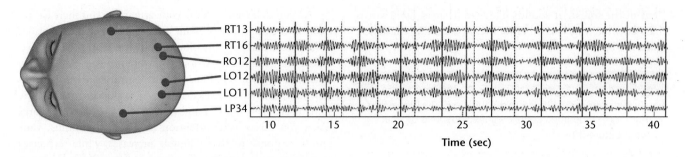

FIGURE 14.20 Brain activity during binocular rivalry
When the person reported seeing the pulsating stimulus, neurons throughout much of the brain responded vigorously at the same rhythm as the stimulus. When the person reported the stationary stimulus, the rhythmic activity subsided. *(Reprinted from* NeuroImage, 23/1, *Cosmelli et al. "Waves of consciousness: Ongoing cortical patterns during binocular rivalry," 128–140, 2004, with permission from Elsevier.)*

The Fate of an Unattended Stimulus

Let's further consider binocular rivalry. While you are attending to, say, the green and black stripes, your brain does not completely discard information from the red and black stripes in your other eye. Certainly, if a bright stimulus suddenly flashed in that eye, it would capture your attention. More interestingly, suppose a word fades onto the screen slowly, and you are to report the time when your attention shifts to the previously unattended eye. The word will capture your attention, causing you to shift your attention faster than you would have otherwise. Moreover, if it is a word from your own language, or better yet your own name, it captures your attention faster than if it were a word from a language you do not understand (Jiang, Costello, & He, 2007). If a meaningful stimulus captures your attention faster than a meaningless stimulus, somehow your brain had to know it was meaningful *before* it became conscious! The conclusion is that much of brain activity is unconscious, and even unconscious activity can influence behavior.

	STOP & CHECK

22. If someone is aware of the stimulus on the right in a case of binocular rivalry, what evidence indicates that the brain is also processing the stimulus on the left?

ANSWER

22. If a stimulus gradually appears on the left side, attention shifts to the left faster if that stimulus is a meaningful word than if it is a word from an unfamiliar language.

Consciousness as a Threshold Phenomenon

In binocular rivalry, you might be aware of a pattern in one part of your visual field and another pattern in another part, but each point in the visual field sees just one or the other. Is that a general principle, or do occasions arise when you are partly conscious of one stimulus and partly conscious of another? Does consciousness come in degrees?

This is not an easy question to answer, but one study suggests that consciousness is a yes–no phenomenon. Researchers flashed blurry words on a screen for brief fractions of a second and asked people to identify each word, if possible, and rate *how* conscious they were of the word on a scale from 0 to 100. People almost always rated a word either 0 or 100. They almost never said they were partly conscious of something (Sergent & Dehaene, 2004). These results suggest that consciousness is a threshold phenomenon. When a stimulus activates enough neurons to a sufficient extent, the activity reverberates, magnifies, and extends over much of the brain. If a stimulus fails to reach that level, the pattern fades away.

The Timing of Consciousness

Are you conscious of events instant by instant as they happen? It certainly seems that way, but if there were a delay between an event and your consciousness of it, how would you know? You wouldn't. Perhaps you sometimes construct a conscious experience after the event.

Consider the **phi phenomenon** that perceptual researchers noted long ago: If you see a dot in one position alternating with a similar dot nearby, it will seem that the dot is moving back and forth. Considering just the simplest case, imagine what happens if you see a dot in one position and then another: ◆ → ◆. You see a dot in one position, it appears to move, and you see it in the second position. Okay, but *when* did you see it move? When you saw it in the first position, you didn't know it was going to appear in the second position. You could not perceive it as moving until *after* it appeared in the second position. Evidently, you perceived it as moving from one position to the second after it appeared in the second position! In other words, the second position changed your perception of what occurred before it.

Another example: Suppose you hear a recorded word that is carefully engineered to sound halfway between *dent* and *tent*. We'll call it **ent*. If you hear it in the phrase "**ent* in the fender," it sounds like *dent*. If you hear it in the phrase "*ent in the forest," it sounds like *tent*. That is, later words changed what you heard before them (Connine, Blasko, & Hall, 1991).

STOP & CHECK

23. In what way does the phi phenomenon imply that a new stimulus sometimes changes consciousness of what went before it?

ANSWER

23. Someone who sees a dot on the left and then a dot on the right perceives the dot as moving from left to right. The perceived movement would have occurred before the dot on the right, but the person had no reason to infer that movement until after the dot appeared on the right.

Attention

Attention is closely aligned with consciousness. Of all that your eyes see at any instant, you are conscious of only those few to which you direct your attention (Huang, Treisman, & Pashler, 2007). For example, consider **inattentional blindness** or *change blindness*: If something in a complex scene changes slowly, or changes while you blink your eyes, you probably will not notice it unless you are paying attention to the particular item that changes (Henderson & Hollingworth, 2003; Rensink, O'Regan, & Clark, 1997). You can experience this phenomenon with the Online Try It Yourself exercise "Change Blindness."

TRY IT YOURSELF ONLINE

Brain Areas Controlling Attention

Psychologists distinguish bottom-up from top-down attention. A bottom-up process is a reaction to a stimulus. If you are sitting on a park bench, gazing off into the distance, when suddenly a deer runs past you, it grabs your attention. A top-down process is intentional. You might be looking for someone you know in a crowd, and you have to check one face after another to find the one you want.

You can control your attention (top-down) even without moving your eyes. To illustrate, keep your eyes fixated on the central *x* in the following display. Then attend to the G at the right and gradually shift your attention clockwise around the circle. Notice how you become aware of different parts of the circle without moving your eyes.

As you deliberately shift your attention, you increase activity in the appropriate brain area. Another demonstration: What is the current sensation in your left foot? Chances are, before you read this question, you were not conscious of *any* sensation in your left foot. When you directed your attention to it, activity increased in the corresponding part of the somatosensory cortex (Lambie & Marcel, 2002). Similarly, when you direct your attention to a visual stimulus, your brain's response to that stimulus increases, while responses to other stimuli decrease (Kamitani & Tong, 2005; Wegener, Freiwald, & Kreiter, 2004).

One of psychologists' favorite ways to study attention is the **Stroop effect**, the difficulty of ignoring words and saying the color of ink. In the following display, say aloud the color of ink of each word, ignoring the words themselves:

RED BLUE GREEN GREEN BROWN BLUE RED PURPLE GREEN RED

After all your years of learning to read words, it is hard to suppress that habit and respond to the color instead. However, when people successfully do so, they enhance the activity in the color–vision areas of the cortex and decrease the activity in the areas responsible for identifying words (Polk, Drake, Jonides, Smith, & Smith, 2008).

Directing your attention toward something requires increasing activity in some neurons and decreasing it in others. Suppose, for example, you are looking for a friend in a crowd, but it's a carnival crowd. Some people are dressed as clowns or wearing other gaudy attire, but your friend is wearing a plain shirt and blue jeans. You need to suppress the attention and activity that the highly unusual items would ordinarily attract (Mevorach, Hodsoll, Allen, Shalev, & Humphreys, 2010). Deliberate, top-down direction of attention depends on parts of the prefrontal cortex and parietal cortex (Buschman & Miller, 2007; Rossi, Bichot, Desimone, & Ungerleider, 2007). Here is an experiment demonstrating that point: On each trial, a participant viewed a display similar to Figure 14.21, visible for half a second. A square appeared in the center of the screen, indicating the color to which the observer should attend. On the right were several lines differing in color and orientation. The task was to identify the line of the indicated color and then indicate whether or not it was vertical. If the central square directed attention to the same color for many trials in a row—green, for example—the task was fairly easy. But when the color switched from one trial to the next, the participant had to alter attention, and the result was increased activity in parts of the prefrontal cortex and parietal cortex. Furthermore, monkeys with damage to the prefrontal cortex performed this task at near-normal levels when the central cue stayed the same color many times in a row, but they suffered severely if the color changed frequently from trial to trial (Rossi, Pessoa, Desimone, & Ungerleider, 2009).

Your ability to resist distraction on tasks like this fluctuates. That is, you might pay close attention for a while and then get distracted. In another experiment, people viewed displays like that in Figure 14.22. The task was to report the orientation (vertical or horizontal) of the line inside the

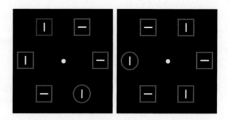

FIGURE 14.22 Example stimulus for experiment on distraction
The task required attending to the circle, wherever it was. On some trials one of the squares was red. Although irrelevant to the task, it often attracted attention and slowed performance. *(From Leber, A. B. (2010). Neural predictors of within-subject fluctuations in attentional control. 11458–11465.)*

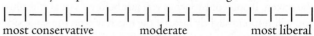

STOP & CHECK

24. What brain response was related to people's ability to resist distraction from an irrelevant red square among the green squares and circle?

ANSWER

24. Resistance to distraction related to the amount of activity in part of the prefrontal cortex before the presentation of stimuli.

Unilateral Neglect

Spectacular failure of attention often occurs in people with damage to the right hemisphere. Many such people show **spatial neglect**—a tendency to ignore the left side of the body or the left side of objects. (Damage in the left hemisphere seldom produces significant neglect of the right side.) They also generally ignore much of what they hear in the left ear and feel in the left hand, especially if they simultaneously feel something in the right hand. They may put clothes on only the right side of the body.

If asked to point "straight ahead," most patients with neglect point to the right of center. If a patient with neglect is shown a long horizontal line and asked to divide it in half, generally the person picks a spot well to the right of center, as if part of the left side wasn't there (Richard, Honoré, Bernati, & Rousseaux, 2004).

People with intact brains generally do not hit the center of the line but veer 2% to 3% to the left of center. Also, if they are asked to indicate a rating of something along a scale from left to right, they show a slight tendency to prefer the left side (Nicholls, Orr, Okubo, & Loftus, 2006). For example, on the questions that follow, most people would rate their political views slightly more conservative on the first question than on the second:

1. Rate your political views on the following scale:

|—|—|—|—|—|—|—|—|—|—|—|—|—|—|—|—|
most conservative   moderate   most liberal

2. Rate your political views on the following scale:

|—|—|—|—|—|—|—|—|—|—|—|—|—|—|—|—|
most liberal   moderate   most conservative

FIGURE 14.21 Example stimulus for experiment on controlling attention
The square in the center of the visual field indicated the color to attend on the right. The participant indicated whether that line was or was not vertical. *(© Cengage Learning 2013)*

green circle, ignoring the five green squares. On some trials, one of the squares was red instead of green. Anything that is different attracts attention, and on average, people responded a bit more slowly on trials with a red square present. However, the amount of delay varied from trial to trial. On trials when activity was enhanced in the middle frontal gyrus (part of the prefrontal cortex) at the *start* of the trial (before seeing the stimuli), the red square produced the least distraction (Leber, 2010). This result confirms the importance of the prefrontal cortex in directing attention and suppressing distraction.

The ability to resist distraction also varies among individuals. People with attention-deficit disorder are notorious for their vulnerability to distraction. In general, people who habitually play action video games perform above average on many tests of attention, because of greatly enhanced top-down control (Mishra, Zinni, Bavelier, & Hillyard, 2011). It seems likely that years of playing video games improves attention, although the alternative possibility remains that people who start with better attention abilities are the most likely to persist at video games. One experiment found that 21 hours of playing action video games was not enough to produce a major effect (Boot, Kramer, Simons, Fabiani, & Gratton, 2008). In addition to video games, one study found that three months of intensive training at meditation also improves certain aspects of attention (Lutz et al., 2009).

You might try the following demonstration. Try marking the center of the line below. Then measure it to see how close you came. Most people miss slightly to the left. Curiously, people with extensive musical training usually get within 1% of the exact center (Patston, Corballis, Hogg, & Tippett, 2006).

TRY IT YOURSELF

Some patients with neglect also show deviations when estimating the midpoint of a numerical range. For example, what is halfway between 11 and 19? The correct answer is, of course, 15, but some people with neglect say "17." Evidently, they discount the lower numbers as if they were on the left side (Doricchi, Guariglia, Gasparini, & Tomaiuolo, 2005; Zorzi, Priftis, & Umiltà, 2002). At least in Western society, many people visualize the numbers as a line stretching to the right, as in the *x* axis of a graph.

All of these results vary, depending on the amount and location of right hemisphere damage (Buxbaum, 2006). People with damage to the inferior right parietal cortex tend to neglect everything to the left of their own body. People with damage to the right superior temporal cortex neglect the left side of objects, even if they are on the right side of the body (Hillis et al., 2005). After damage to an axon pathway called the right *superior longitudinal fasciculus*, connecting the right posterior parietal cortex to the prefrontal cortex, people neglect the left side almost always. After damage that spares this pathway, people neglect the left side only when distracted by something on the right side (Ptak & Schnider, 2010).

Although some neglect patients have sensory losses, in many cases, the main problem is loss of attention rather than impaired sensation. One patient was shown a letter E, composed of small Hs, as in Figure 14.23(c). She identified it as a big E composed of small Hs, indicating that she saw the whole figure. However, when she was then asked to cross off all the Hs, she crossed off only the ones on the right. When she was shown the figures in Figure 14.23(e), she identified them as an O composed of little Os and an X composed of little Xs. Again, she could see both halves of both figures, but when she was asked to cross off all the elements, she crossed off only the ones on the right. The researchers summarized by saying she saw the forest but only half the trees (Marshall & Halligan, 1995).

Several procedures increase attention to the neglected side. Simply telling the person to pay attention to the left side helps temporarily. So does having the person look left while at the same time feeling an object with the left hand (Vaishnavi, Calhoun, & Chatterjee, 2001) or hearing a sound from the left side of the world (Frassinetti, Pavani, & Làdavas, 2002). Something similar is true for unimpaired people also. Suppose you are staring straight ahead and an experimenter is flashing stimuli on the left and right sides. Your task is to identify something about each stimulus, such as whether it was on the top or bottom half of the screen. If someone touches you just before a visual stimulus, you will respond slightly faster if the touch was on the same side of the body as the visual stimulus (Kennett, Eimer, Spence, & Driver, 2001). That is, a touch stimulus briefly increases attention to one side of the body or the other.

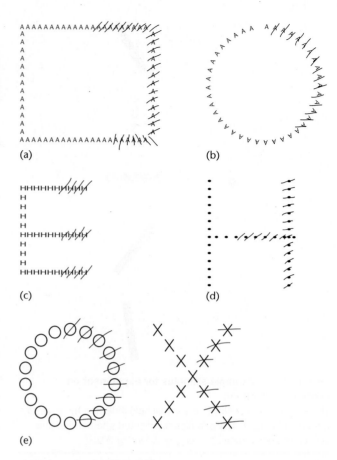

FIGURE 14.23 Spatial neglect
A patient with neglect identified the overall figures as E, O, and X, indicating that she saw the whole figures. However, when asked to cross off the elements that composed them, she crossed off only the parts on the right. *(From J. C. Marshall and P. W. Halligan, "Seeing the forest but only half the trees?" Nature, 373, pp. 521–523, Figure 1 [parts C and E]. © 1995 Nature.)*

Other manipulations also shift the attention. For example, some patients with neglect usually report feeling nothing with the left hand, especially if the right hand feels something at the time. However, if you cross one hand over the other as shown in Figure 14.24, the person is more likely to report feeling the left hand, which is now on the right side of the body (Aglioti, Smania, & Peru, 1999). Also, the person ordinarily has trouble pointing to anything in the left visual field but has somewhat better success if the hand was so far to the left that he or she would have to move it to the right to point to the object (Mattingley, Husain, Rorden, Kennard, & Driver, 1998). Again, the conclusion is that neglect is not due to a loss of sensation but a difficulty in directing attention to the left side.

Many patients with neglect also have deficits in spatial working memory (Malhotra et al., 2005) and in shifting attention, even when location is irrelevant. For example, one patient could not listen to two sounds and say which one came first, unless the sounds were very prolonged (Cusack, Carlyon, & Robertson, 2000). In short, the problems associated with neglect extend to many kinds of attention, not just the left–right dimension.

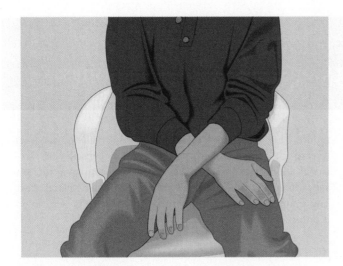

FIGURE 14.24 A way to reduce sensory neglect
Ordinarily, someone with right hemisphere damage neglects the left arm. However, if the left arm crosses over or under the right, attention to the left arm increases. *(© Cengage Learning 2013)*

24. What is the evidence that spatial neglect is a problem in attention, not just sensation?

25. What are several procedures that increase attention to the left side in a person with spatial neglect?

ANSWERS

24. When a patient with neglect sees a large letter composed of small letters, he or she can identify the large letter but then neglects part of it when asked to cross off all the small letters. Also, someone who neglects the left hand pays attention to it when it is crossed over the right hand. 25. Simply telling the person to attend to something on the left helps temporarily. Having the person look to the left while feeling something on the left side increases attention to the left object. Crossing the left hand over the right increases attention to the left hand. Moving a hand far to the left makes it easier for the person to point to something in the left visual field because the hand will move toward the right to point at the object.

Attending to Attention and Being Conscious of Consciousness

Before the 1970s, many psychological researchers, especially those studying learning in rats, were not convinced that the concept of attention was useful at all. Today, the concept of attention is well established in cognitive psychology, although some still doubt that consciousness is a scientifically useful concept. Research in this area is difficult because we cannot observe consciousness itself, and we have no access to it beyond what people report. Most researchers agree that we have made no progress toward answering the hard problem of why consciousness exists at all. Still, progress continues at an encouraging rate on subordinate questions, such as finding the brain activities most important for consciousness and attention. How far we can go is uncertain, but the only way to find out is to try.

SUMMARY

1. Dualism—the belief in a nonmaterial mind that exists separately from the body and influences it—conflicts with the conservation of matter and energy, one of the best-established principles of physics. Nearly all neuroscientists and philosophers accept some version of monism, the idea that mental activity is inseparable from brain activity. **445**

2. The hard problem is the question of why consciousness exists at all. Most researchers agree that we cannot answer this question, at least at present. **446**

3. Researchers sometimes use brain recordings to infer whether someone is conscious. More confident inferences should become possible after we better understand what aspects of brain functioning are necessary for consciousness. **446**

4. To identify the brain activities associated with consciousness, researchers present the same stimulus under conditions when an observer probably will or probably will not identify it consciously. **447**

5. When someone is conscious of a stimulus, the representation of that stimulus spreads over a large portion of the brain. **447**

6. Many stimuli influence our behavior without being conscious. Even before a stimulus becomes conscious, the brain processes the information enough to identify something as meaningful or meaningless. **449**

7. People almost never say they were partly conscious of something. It may be that consciousness is a threshold phenomenon: We become conscious of anything that exceeds a certain level of brain activity, and we are not conscious of other events. **449**

8. We are not always conscious of events instantaneously as they occur. Sometimes, a later event modifies our conscious perception of a stimulus that went before it. **449**

9. Attention to a stimulus is almost synonymous with being conscious of it. Because attention is limited, people often fail to notice changes in a scene that occur gradually or between one glance and another. **450**

10. It is possible to direct attention toward one stimulus and away from another deliberately. **450**

11. Deliberate, top-down attention depends on activity in the prefrontal cortex and parietal cortex. **450**

12. Attention and resistance to distraction vary across time and vary among individuals. Long-term players of action video games generally show above-average performance on attention tasks. Prolonged meditation training may also enhance attention. **451**

13. Damage to parts of the right hemisphere produce spatial neglect for the left side of the body or the left side of objects. **451**

14. Neglect results from a deficit in attention, not sensation. For example, someone with neglect can see an entire letter enough to say what it is, even though that same person ignores the left half when asked to cross out all the elements that compose it. **452**

15. People with sensory neglect also have difficulties with working memory and with shifting attention from one stimulus to another, even when the stimuli do not vary from left to right. **452**

KEY TERMS

Terms are defined in the module on the page number indicated. They're also presented in alphabetical order with definitions in the book's Subject Index/Glossary, which begins on page 561. Interactive flashcards and crossword puzzles are among the online resources available to help you learn these terms and the concepts they represent.

backward masking   447

binocular rivalry   447

conscious   446

dualism   445

hard problem   446

identity position   445

inattentional blindness   450

masking   447

materialism   445

mentalism   445

mind–brain problem   445

monism   445

phi phenomenon   449

spatial neglect   451

Stroop effect   450

THOUGHT QUESTIONS

1. Could a computer be conscious? What evidence, if any, would convince you that it was conscious?

2. The operational definition of consciousness applies only to people willing and able to report that they are conscious of some events and not others. Research using this definition has determined certain brain correlates of consciousness. Could we now use those brain correlates to infer consciousness or its absence in newborn infants, brain-damaged people, or nonhuman animals?

CHAPTER 14 Interactive Exploration and Study

The **Psychology CourseMate** for this text brings chapter topics to life with interactive learning, study, and exam preparation tools, including quizzes and flashcards for the Key Concepts that appear throughout each module, as well as an interactive media-rich eBook version of the text that is fully searchable and includes highlighting and note-taking capabilities and interactive versions of the book's **Stop & Check** quizzes and **Try It Yourself Online** activities. The site also features **Virtual Biological Psychology Labs**, **videos**, and **animations** to help you better understand concepts—logon and learn more at **www.cengagebrain.com**, which is your gateway to all of this text's complimentary and premium resources, including the following:

Virtual Biological Psychology Labs

© 2013 Cengage Learning

Explore the experiments that led to modern-day understanding of biopsychology with the Virtual Biological Psychology Labs, featuring a realistic lab environment that allows you to conduct experiments and evaluate data to better understand how scientists came to the conclusions presented in your text. The labs cover a range of topics, including perception, motivation, cognition, and more. You may purchase access at **www.cengagebrain.com**, or login at **login.cengagebrain.com** if an access card was included with your text.

Videos

Evaluating Patients with Brain Damage

Also available—

+ Corpus Callosum
+ Situated Cognition

Animations

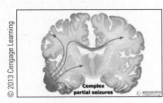

Seizure Pathways

Also available—

■ Hemisphere Lateralization
■ Learning Module: Wernicke-Geschwind Model
■ Capture of Attention by a Meaningful Stimulus

Try It Yourself Online

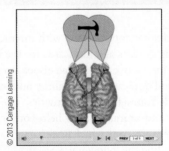

Split Brain

Also available—

■ McGurk Effect
■ Phi Phenomenon
■ Binocular Rivalry
■ Change Blindness

*Look for these and additional **animations** and **Try It Yourself Online** activities, which are also available among the media resources for Chapter 14:*

Suggestions for Further Exploration

Books

Baars, B. J., & Gage, N. M. (Eds.). (2007). *Cognition, brain, and consciousness.* San Diego, CA: Elsevier. Review of research on brain mechanisms of attention and consciousness.

Dehaene, S. (2009). *Reading in the brain.* New York: Viking. Review of research on biological bases of language, especially as they relate to reading.

Ornstein, R. (1997). *The right mind.* New York: Harcourt Brace. Very readable description of split-brain research and the differences between the left and right hemispheres.

Websites

The Psychology CourseMate for this text provides regularly updated links to relevant online resources for this chapter, including ones on language training in bonobos, aphasia, and dyslexia.

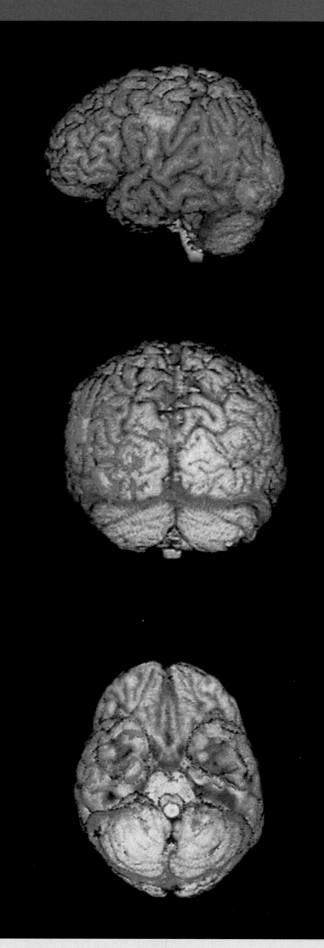

Mood Disorders and Schizophrenia

15

CHAPTER OUTLINE

MAIN IDEAS

1. Psychological disorders result from a combination of environmental and biological influences, including genetics.

2. The effectiveness of certain drugs provides a clue as to the underlying basis of depression and schizophrenia, but many questions remain about how these drugs exert their effects.

3. Schizophrenia may be the result of genetic or other problems that impair early development of the brain.

OPPOSITE: PET scans show the brain areas that increase their activation during visual and auditory hallucinations by a patient with schizophrenia.

Are mental illnesses really *illnesses*, analogous to tuberculosis or influenza? Or are they normal reactions to abnormal experiences? They are not exactly either. They are outcomes that combine biological predispositions with experiences. To control them, we need a good understanding of both aspects.

Abnormal behavior comes in many varieties. *The Diagnostic and Statistical Manual of Mental Disorders, fourth edition* (American Psychiatric Association, 1994) lists hundreds of disorders. This chapter deals with mood disorders—depression and bipolar disorder—and schizophrenia. These disorders have been the focus of a huge amount of biological research. Chapter 12 discussed anxiety disorders and Chapter 3 had a section about addictions.

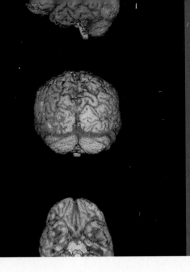

Mood Disorders

Different people can get to the same place by different routes. For example, the people in a room at any moment may have started from different cities or different parts of a city and traveled in different ways, although they all reached the same destination. Similarly, people can become depressed through different routes, including genetics, traumatic experiences, hormonal problems, substance abuse, head injuries, brain tumors, and other illnesses. Despite having different causes, or combinations of causes, these people all look and act depressed (Figure 15.1). In this module, we explore some of the many factors that contribute to depression.

▌ Major Depressive Disorder

Many people say they feel "depressed" when they feel sad or discouraged. Major depression is much more intense and prolonged. According to the *DSM-IV* (American Psychiatric Association, 1994), people with a **major depression** feel sad and helpless every day for weeks at a time. They have little energy, feel worthless, contemplate suicide, have trouble sleeping, cannot concentrate, find little pleasure, and can hardly even imagine being happy again.

Absence of happiness is a more reliable symptom than increased sadness. In one study, people carried a beeper that sounded at unpredictable times to signal them to describe their emotional reactions at the moment. People with depression reported only an average number of unpleasant experiences but far below the average number of pleasant ones (Peters, Nicolson, Berkhof, Delespaul, & deVries, 2003). In other studies, people examined photographs or films as researchers recorded their reactions. Individuals with depression reacted normally to sad or frightening depictions but seldom smiled at the comedies or pleasant pictures (Rottenberg, Kasch, Gross, & Gotlib, 2002; Sloan, Strauss, & Wisner, 2001). Additional studies found that people with depression show a decreased response to happy facial expressions (Monk et al., 2008) and a decreased response to a likely reward (McFarland & Klein, 2009).

A survey reported that about 5% of adults in the United States have a "clinically significant" depression (i.e., serious

FIGURE 15.1 The face of depression
Depression shows in a person's face, walk, voice, and mannerisms.

enough to warrant attention) within a given year, and more than 10% do at some point in life (Narrow, Rae, Robins, & Regier, 2002). Reported one-year prevalence rates vary among countries and ethnic groups, from less than 5% among Chinese-Canadians to more than 15% in India (Murali, 2001; Tiwari & Wang, 2006). It is hard to know how seriously to take these numbers. Standards for diagnosis inevitably vary from place to place, and psychiatrists have no laboratory tests to confirm a diagnosis.

Childhood depression is about equally common for boys and girls, but beyond about age 14, depression is more common in females (Twenge & Nolen-Hoeksema, 2002). Various hypotheses have been advanced to explain this tendency, but none is well established.

Although some people suffer from long-term depression (Klein, 2010), it is more common to have episodes of depression separated by periods of normal mood. The first episode is special in certain regards. The first episode is generally longer than most of the later ones, and most patients can identify a highly stressful event that triggered the first episode. For later episodes, people are less and less likely to identify a triggering event (Post, 1992). It is as if the brain learns how to be depressed and gets better at it (Monroe & Harkness, 2005). In that regard it is like epilepsy and migraine headaches: The more often you have had an episode, the easier it is to start another one (Post & Silberstein, 1994).

Genetics

Studies of twins and adopted children indicate a moderate degree of heritability for depression (Shih, Belmonte, & Zandi, 2004). However, although researchers have identified several genes linked to depression, none of the genes by itself has a large effect (Camp et al., 2005; Holmans et al., 2007).

One reason why no gene shows a strong link to depression is that when we talk about depression, we are probably lumping together at least two distinguishable syndromes. People with early-onset depression (before age 30) have a high probability of other relatives with depression (Bierut et al., 1999; Kendler, Gardner, & Prescott, 1999; Lyons et al., 1998), as well as relatives with anxiety disorders, attention-deficit disorder, alcohol or marijuana abuse, obsessive-compulsive disorder, bulimia, migraine headaches, and irritable bowel syndrome (Q. Fu et al., 2002; Hudson et al., 2003). People with late-onset depression (especially after age 45 to 50) have a high probability of relatives with circulatory problems (Kendler, Fiske, Gardner, & Gatz, 2009). Distinguishing between early-onset and late-onset cases may lead to progress in identifying genes, and perhaps in selecting effective therapies.

Still, given the difficulty so far in identifying any gene strongly linked to depression, another hypothesis arose: Perhaps the effect of a gene varies with the environment. One gene controls the serotonin transporter, a protein that regulates the ability of axons to reabsorb serotonin after its release, to recycle it for further use. Investigators examined the serotonin transporter genes of 847 young adults, identifying two types: the "short" type and the "long" type. They also asked each participant to report certain stressful events over five years, including financial setbacks, loss of job, divorce, and so forth. Figure 15.2 shows the results. For people with two short forms of the gene, increasing numbers of stressful experiences led to a big increase in the probabil-

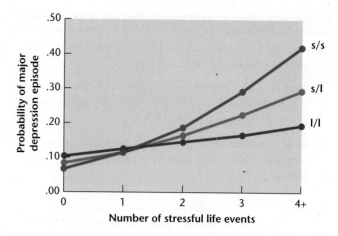

FIGURE 15.2 Genetics, stress, and depression
The effect of the serotonin transporter gene depends on the amount of stress. (*Reprinted by permission from A. Caspi, et al., "Influence of life stress on depression: Moderation by a polymorphism in the 5-HTT gene,"* Science, 301, pp. 386–389. © 2003 AAAS.)

ity of depression. For those with two long forms, stressful events only slightly increased the risk of depression. Those with one short and one long gene were intermediate. In other words, the short form of the gene by itself did not lead to depression, but it might magnify the reaction to stressful events (Caspi et al., 2003).

This report provoked a great deal of excitement. However, since then most researchers have failed to replicate the result, finding no significant relationship between depression and the serotonin transporter gene itself and no interaction between effects of the gene and stress (Munafo, Durrant, Lewis, & Flint, 2009; Risch et al., 2009).

When a result in psychology, medicine, or any other field cannot be replicated, the obvious interpretation is that the first report was wrong. Given the huge number of researchers collecting studies, occasionally a random fluctuation in data suggests a relationship between variables that are in fact unrelated. However, here is another possibility: If a study finds no significant correlation between two variables, perhaps one or both of the variables was poorly measured. (We can't expect a poorly measured variable to correlate with anything else.) Our measurements of depression are probably good enough, but the measurements of stress are more doubtful. Generally researchers ask people how many stressful events they have experienced, and simply count them. Losing a job can be extremely stressful or hardly stressful at all, depending on how easily someone found an equal or better job. Similarly, divorce is much more stressful to some people than others. Also, the biochemical methods used to measure short vs. long forms of the gene have been inaccurate in many cases (Wray et al., 2009). We should await more research with more careful measurements before we draw a firm conclusion.

1. What evidence suggests two types of depression influenced by different genes?

2. What did Caspi and colleagues report to be the relationship between depression and the gene controlling the serotonin transporter protein?

3. What should we conclude from the fact that most researchers have not been able to replicate Caspi et al.'s finding?

ANSWERS

1. Relatives of people with early-onset depression have a high risk of depression and many other psychological disorders. Relatives of people with late-onset depression have a high probability of circulatory problems. 2. People with the short form of the gene are more likely than other people to react to stressful experiences by becoming depressed. However, in the absence of stressful experiences, their probability is not increased. 3. Either variation in this gene is not really related to depression, or the studies so far have been hampered by inaccurate measurement.

Other Biological Influences

Genetic differences partly explain why some people are more vulnerable to depression than others are, but other factors contribute also. A few cases of depression are linked to viral infections. Borna disease, a viral infection of farm animals, produces periods of frantic activity alternating with periods of inactivity (Figure 15.3). In 1985, investigators tested 370 people for possible exposure to this virus (Amsterdam et al.,

1985). Only 12 people tested positive for Borna disease virus, but all 12 were suffering from major depression or bipolar disorder. These 12 were a small percentage of the 265 depressed people tested; still, *none* of the 105 nondepressed people had the virus.

Since then, thousands of people have been tested in Europe, Asia, and North America. The Borna virus is found in about 5% of normal people and about one-third of people with severe depression or schizophrenia (Bode, Ferszt, & Czech, 1993; Bode, Riegel, Lange, & Ludwig, 1992; Nunes et al., 2008; Terayama et al., 2003). The role of this virus in psychiatric disorders remains uncertain, but the results so far suggest that viruses might be a predisposing factor in some cases.

Hormones may be another trigger for depression. Stress is accepted as an important factor in depression, and stress increases release of cortisol, as discussed in Chapter 12. About 20% of women report some degree of **postpartum depression**—that is, depression after giving birth—and many researchers suspect that hormonal fluctuations are a contributing factor. Stress hormones reach a peak late in pregnancy, and ovarian hormones go through major changes around the time of delivery. One study found that after a drug-induced drop in estradiol and progesterone levels, women with a history of postpartum depression suddenly show new symptoms of depression, whereas other women do not (M. Bloch et al., 2000). Among older men, a declining level of the hormone testosterone is associated with increased probability of depression (Almeida, Yeap, Hankey, Jamrozik, & Flicker, 2008). However, few studies have been done that directly link hormones to depression, and the relationship remains uncertain (Brummelte & Galea, 2010). We do know that the risk of postpartum depression increases in women with previous bouts of depres-

FIGURE 15.3 Symptoms of Borna disease
Animals infected with Borna disease have periods of frantic activity alternating with inactivity, much like a person with bipolar disorder. (left) Horse with Borna disease. (right) Same horse after recovery. *(Figure 2, page 174, from Bode L. and Ludwig H., (1997). "Clinical similarities and close genetic relationship of human and animal Borna disease virus." Archives of Virology (Supplement 13), 167–182. Springer-Verlag. Photo scan by Kevin J. Nolte.)*

sion, stressful life events, and a lack of social support—that is, the same factors linked to major depression at any other time of life (O'Hara, 2009).

Abnormalities of Hemispheric Dominance

Studies of normal people have found a fairly strong relationship between happy mood and increased activity in the left prefrontal cortex (Jacobs & Snyder, 1996). Most people with depression have decreased activity in the left and increased activity in the right prefrontal cortex, and this imbalance is stable over years despite changes in symptoms of depression (Davidson, 1984; Pizzagalli et al., 2002; Vuga et al., 2006). Here's something you can try: Ask someone to solve a cognitive problem, such as, "See how many words you can think of that start with *hu-*" or "Try to remember all the ingredients you've ever seen on a pizza." Then unobtrusively watch the person's eye movements to see whether they gaze right or left. Most people gaze to the right during verbal tasks, but most individuals with depression gaze to the left, suggesting right-hemisphere dominance (Lenhart & Katkin, 1986).

TRY IT YOURSELF

STOP & CHECK

4. Some people offer to train you to use the right hemisphere of your brain more strongly, allegedly to increase creativity. If they were successful, can you see any disadvantage?

ANSWER

4. People with predominant right-hemisphere activity and decreased left-hemisphere activity show an increased tendency toward depression.

▌Antidepressant Drugs

You might assume that investigators first determine the causes of a psychological disorder and then develop medications based on the causes. The opposite order has been more common: First investigators find a drug that seems helpful, and then they try to figure out how it works. Like many other psychiatric drugs, the early antidepressants were discovered by accident.

APPLICATIONS AND EXTENSIONS

Accidental Discoveries of Psychiatric Drugs

Nearly all of the earliest psychiatric drugs were discovered by accident. Disulfiram, for example, was originally used in the manufacture of rubber. Someone noticed that workers in a certain rubber factory avoided alcohol and traced the cause to disulfiram, which had altered the workers' metabolism so they became ill after drinking al-

cohol. Disulfiram became the drug Antabuse, sometimes prescribed for people who are trying to avoid alcohol.

The use of bromides to control epilepsy was originally based on a theory that was all wrong (Friedlander, 1986; Levitt, 1975). Many people in the 1800s believed that masturbation caused epilepsy and that bromides reduced sexual drive. Therefore, they reasoned, bromides should reduce epilepsy. It turns out that bromides do relieve epilepsy but for different reasons.

Iproniazid, the first antidepressant drug, was originally marketed to treat tuberculosis, until physicians noticed that it relieved depression. Similarly, chlorpromazine, the first antipsychotic drug, was originally used for other purposes, until physicians noticed its ability to alleviate schizophrenia. For decades, researchers sought new drugs entirely by trial and error. Today, researchers evaluate new potential drugs in test tubes or tissue samples until they find one with a potential for stronger or more specific effects on neurotransmission. The result is the use of fewer laboratory animals. ■

Types of Antidepressants

Antidepressant drugs fall into several categories, including tricyclics, selective serotonin reuptake inhibitors, monoamine oxidase inhibitors, and atypical antidepressants (Figure 15.4). The **tricyclics** (e.g., imipramine, trade name Tofranil) operate by blocking the transporter proteins that reabsorb serotonin, dopamine, and norepinephrine into the presynaptic neuron after their release. The result is to prolong the presence of the neurotransmitters in the synaptic cleft, where they continue stimulating the postsynaptic cell. However, the tricyclics also block histamine receptors, acetylcholine receptors, and certain

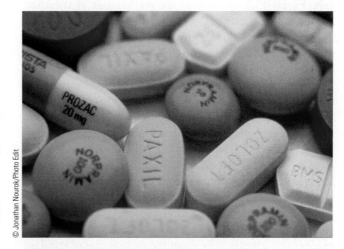

© Jonathan Nourok/Photo Edit

FIGURE 15.4 Antidepressant pills
Tricyclic drugs block the reuptake of catecholamines and serotonin by presynaptic terminals. Selective serotonin reuptake inhibitors, such as Prozac, have similar effects but are limited to serotonin. MAOIs block an enzyme that breaks down catecholamines and serotonin.

sodium channels (Horst & Preskorn, 1998). As mentioned in Chapter 9, blocking histamine produces drowsiness. Blocking acetylcholine leads to dry mouth and difficulty urinating. Blocking sodium channels causes heart irregularities, among other problems. People have to limit their use of tricyclic drugs to minimize these side effects.

The **selective serotonin reuptake inhibitors (SSRIs)** are similar to tricyclics but specific to the neurotransmitter serotonin. For example, fluoxetine (trade name Prozac) blocks the reuptake of serotonin. SSRIs produce milder side effects than the tricyclics, but their effectiveness is about the same. Other common SSRIs include sertraline (Zoloft), fluvoxamine (Luvox), citalopram (Celexa), and paroxetine (Paxil or Seroxat). Several newer drugs are **serotonin norepinephrine reuptake inhibitors (SNRIs)**, such as duloxetine (Cymbalta) and venlafaxine (Effexor). As you might guess, they block reuptake of serotonin and norepinephrine.

The **monoamine oxidase inhibitors (MAOIs)** (e.g., phenelzine, trade name Nardil) block the enzyme monoamine oxidase (MAO), a presynaptic terminal enzyme that metabolizes catecholamines and serotonin into inactive forms. When MAOIs block this enzyme, the presynaptic terminal has more of its transmitter available for release. Generally, physicians prescribe tricyclics or SSRIs first and then try MAOIs with people who did not respond to the other drugs (Thase, Trivedi, & Rush, 1995). People taking MAOIs must avoid foods containing tyramine—including cheese, raisins, and many others—because a combination of tyramine and MAOIs increases blood pressure. Figure 15.5 summarizes the mechanisms of tricyclics, SSRIs, and MAOIs.

The **atypical antidepressants** are a miscellaneous group—everything other than the types just discussed (Horst & Preskorn, 1998). One example is bupropion (Wellbutrin), which inhibits reuptake of dopamine and to some extent norepinephrine but not serotonin.

In addition, many people use St. John's wort, an herb. Because it is marketed as a nutritional supplement instead of a drug, the U.S. Food and Drug Administration does not regulate it, and its purity varies from one bottle to another. It has the advantage of being less expensive than antidepressant drugs. An advantage or disadvantage, depending on your point of view, is that it is available without prescription. People can get it easily but often take inappropriate amounts. Its effectiveness appears to be about the same as that of standard antidepressant drugs (Kasper, Caraci, Forti, Drago, & Aguglia, 2010). However, it has a potentially dangerous side effect: All mammals have a liver enzyme that breaks down plant toxins. St. John's wort increases the effectiveness of that enzyme. Increasing the breakdown of toxins sounds like a good thing, but the enzyme also breaks down most medicines. Therefore,

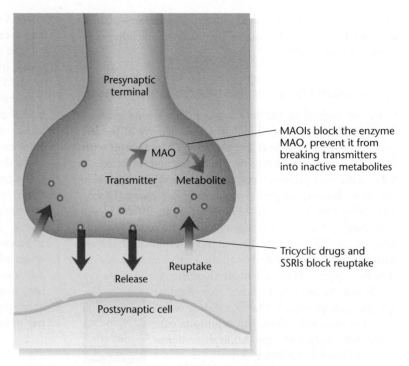

FIGURE 15.5 Routes of action of antidepressants
Tricyclics block the reuptake of dopamine, norepinephrine, and serotonin. SSRIs specifically block the reuptake of serotonin. SNRIs block reuptake of serotonin and norepinephrine. MAOIs block the enzyme MAO, which converts dopamine, norepinephrine, or serotonin into inactive chemicals. *(© Cengage Learning 2013)*

taking St. John's wort decreases the effectiveness of other drugs you might be taking—including other antidepressant drugs, cancer drugs, and AIDS drugs (He, Yang, Li, Du, & Zhou, 2010; Moore et al., 2000).

> **STOP & CHECK**

5. What are the effects of tricyclic drugs?

6. What are the effects of SSRIs?

7. What are the effects of MAOIs?

ANSWERS

5. Tricyclic drugs block reuptake of serotonin and catecholamines. They also block histamine receptors, acetylcholine receptors, and certain sodium channels, thereby producing unpleasant side effects. 6. SSRIs selectively inhibit the reuptake of serotonin. 7. MAOIs block the enzyme MAO, which breaks down catecholamines and serotonin. The result is increased availability of these transmitters.

How Do Antidepressants Work?

Understanding how antidepressants work should shed some light on the causes of depression. The commonly used antidepressants increase the presence of serotonin or other neurotransmitters at the synapse, and so it might seem that the problem in depression is too little of the neurotransmitters. However, the story is not that simple. So far as we can tell from blood metabolites, people with depression have approximately normal levels of release of neurotransmitters. In fact, some studies show that people with depression have an *increase* in serotonin release (Barton et al., 2008). Furthermore, it is possible to decrease serotonin levels suddenly by consuming all the amino acids except tryptophan, the precursor to serotonin. For most people, this decrease in serotonin does not provoke any feelings of depression (Neumeister et al., 2004, 2006).

Furthermore, given that different drugs act in different ways on different neurotransmitters, wouldn't you expect some of them to be more effective than others? So far as we can tell, all of them are about equal in effectiveness (Montgomery et al., 2007). Two studies examined patients who failed to respond to an antidepressant drug within a few weeks. In one study the psychiatrists added a second drug, and in the other study they switched patients from one drug to the other. The result was that some patients who did not respond to the first drug did respond after a few weeks on the new regimen (Rush et al., 2006; Trivedi et al., 2006). Should we conclude, as the researchers did, that adding a drug or switching drugs helped? No. Unfortunately, neither study included a control group that stayed on the first drug for the additional time. In short, we have no clear evidence that any antidepressant drug produces any different effects from any other.

The time course of effects poses an additional threat to any explanation in terms of neurotransmitters: Antidepressant drugs produce their effects on neurotransmitters in the synapses within minutes to hours, depending on the drug, but people need to take the drugs for 2 or more weeks before they experience any mood elevation (Stewart et al., 1998). This delay of benefits strongly suggests that increasing the levels of neurotransmitters at synapses does not explain the benefits of the drugs. Perhaps the neurotransmitter effects are not even relevant.

Today, much research attention focuses on neurotrophins. As discussed in Chapter 5, neurotrophins aid in the survival, growth, and connections of neurons. Most people with depression have lower than average levels of a neurotrophin called *brain-derived neurotrophic factor* (BDNF) that is important for synaptic plasticity, learning, and proliferation of new neurons in the hippocampus (Martinowich, Manji, & Lu, 2007; Sen, Duman, & Sanacora, 2008). As a result of low BDNF, most people with depression have a smaller than average hippocampus, impaired learning, and reduced production of new hippocampal neurons. Prolonged use of antidepressant drugs generally increases BDNF production and improves learning and formation of new neurons. This process takes weeks (Drzyzga, Marcinowska, & Obuchowicz, 2009; Vetencourt et al., 2008). That is, the time course for BDNF and changes in the hippocampus matches the time course for behavioral recovery. Procedures that block neuron production also block the behavioral benefits of antidepressant drugs (Airan et al., 2007).

Apparently BDNF by itself does not automatically elevate mood, but it helps by facilitating new learning that builds new synapses and removes many old ones. That mode of action explains why antidepressants help people in depression—who might profit from substituting new thoughts for old ones—but fail to elevate mood for normal people (Castrén & Rantamäki, 2010).

Although this story may seem convincing, the conclusion remains tentative, as a few antidepressant drugs improve mood without demonstrable effects on BDNF (Basterzi et al., 2008; Matrisciano et al., 2009). Perhaps antidepressants work in more than one way.

STOP & CHECK

8. In what way does the time course of antidepressants conflict with the idea that they improve mood by increasing neurotransmitter levels?

9. As opposed to an interpretation in terms of neurotransmitter levels, what is an alternative explanation for the benefits of antidepressant drugs?

ANSWERS 8. Antidepressants produce their effects on serotonin and other neurotransmitters quickly, but their behavioral benefits develop gradually over 2 to 3 weeks. 9. Antidepressant drugs increase production of BDNF, which gradually promotes growth of new neurons, new synapses, and new learning in the hippocampus.

How Effective Are Antidepressants?

So far we have considered explanations of how antidepressants work. How sure are we that they *do* work? Not everyone is convinced (Kirsch, 2010), and at least we have to say that the effectiveness is limited.

In most cases, depression occurs in episodes. That is, even without treatment, many people recover within a few months. Furthermore, giving someone a medication produces an expectation of improvement, thereby enhancing the probability of recovery, even if the medication itself is ineffective. To test the effectiveness of an antidepressant drug, researchers need to compare its effects to those of a placebo (a pharmacologically inactive substance).

Figure 15.6 summarizes the results of many experiments in which people were randomly assigned to receive antidepressant drugs or placebos. The horizontal axis represents the mean amount of improvement on the Hamilton Depression Rating Scale. The pink triangles represent patients receiving the drug in a study, and the gray circles represent patients receiving a placebo. The size of the triangle or circle is proportional to the number of patients in a group. Many people respond well on placebos, either because of spontaneous recovery over time or because of the expectation that a pill induced. Younger patients are particularly likely to respond to placebos (Bridge, Birmaher, Iyengar, Barbe, & Brent, 2009). For patients with mild to moderate depression, the results for placebo groups overlap those for drug groups, and the differences between the groups are, on average, too small to be of much clinical significance. Only for people with severe depression do the drugs show a meaningful advantage (Kirsch et al., 2008). Another independent analysis of the research confirmed that the drugs show no clear benefit over placebos for people with mild to moderate depression (Fournier et al., 2010). Furthermore, even at the most severe levels of depression, antidepressants help some people and not others (Uhr et al., 2008).

An alternative to antidepressant drugs is psychotherapy. Reviews of the research literature find that antidepressant drugs and psychotherapy are about equally effective for treating all levels of depression, from mild to severe, with three exceptions: First, the drugs work better for *dysthymia*, a long-term, almost life-long condition of unhappy mood. Nearly all of the research studies examined short-term therapies, and it may be that brief psychotherapy is ineffective for such a long-term condition. Second, antidepressants are generally ineffective for patients who had suffered abuse or neglect during early childhood or patients with multiple psychological disorders. Those patients usually respond better to psychotherapy (Asarnow et al., 2009; Nemeroff et al., 2003). Third, psychotherapy is more likely to have long-term benefits, reducing the likelihood of a relapse months or years after the end of treatment (Bortolotti, Menchetti, Bellini, Montaguti, & Berardi, 2008; Imel, Malterer, McKay & Wampold, 2008).

Would a combination of antidepressant drugs and psychotherapy work better than either one alone? On average, people who improve while receiving both treatments improve more than people receiving either one alone. However, the percentage of people showing improvement increases only slightly with combined treatment (de Maat et al., 2008; Hollon et al., 2005). That is, it is not the case that many people respond better to one treatment than the other. Evidently, many people with mild to moderate depression improve with only a placebo, another group improves with either antidepressants or psychotherapy, a few respond better to one or the other, and the remainder—one-third to one-half, by most estimates—do not respond well to either one (Friedman et al., 2009; Hollon, Thase, & Markowitz, 2002; Thase et al., 1997).

The effects of antidepressants and those of psychotherapy overlap more than we might have guessed. Brain scans show that antidepressants and psychotherapy increase metabolism in the same brain areas (Brody et al., 2001; S. D. Martin et al., 2001). That similarity should not be terribly surprising if we accept the mind–body monism position. If mental activity is the same thing as brain activity, then changing someone's thoughts should indeed change brain chemistry.

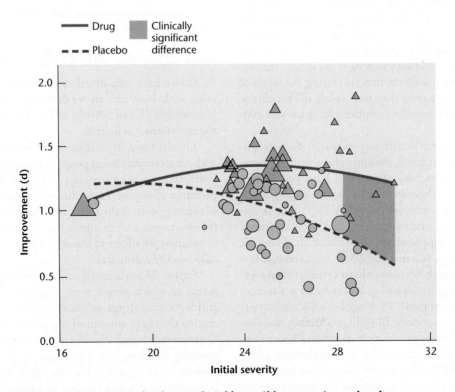

FIGURE 15.6 Mean improvement from depression by people taking antidepressants or placebos
Pink triangles represent people taking medications in a particular study. Gray circles represent people taking placebos. The size of the triangle or circle is proportional to the number of people in the study. *(From Kirsch, 2008)*

→ STOP & CHECK

10. As depression becomes more severe, what happens to the percentage of patients showing improvement while taking antidepressant drugs or placebos?

11. What is an advantage of psychotherapy over antidepressant drugs?

ANSWERS

10. For more severe cases, the percentage of patients who improve remains about the same for patients taking antidepressant drugs, but fewer patients taking placebos show improvement. **11.** People who respond well to psychotherapy have a lower risk of later relapse than people who respond to antidepressant drugs. Also, antidepressant drugs produce unpleasant side effects and appear to be less effective for people with multiple disorders or people who suffered abuse or neglect in childhood.

Electroconvulsive Therapy (ECT)

Many people with depression do not respond well to either drugs or psychotherapy. What options are available for them? One possibility, despite its stormy history, is treatment through an electrically induced seizure, known as **electroconvulsive therapy (ECT)**. ECT originated with the observation that for people with both epilepsy and schizophrenia, as symptoms of one disorder increase, symptoms of the other often decrease (Trimble & Thompson, 1986). In the 1930s, Ladislas Meduna tried to relieve schizophrenia by inducing convulsions. Soon, other physicians were doing the same, inducing seizures with a large dose of insulin. Insulin shock is a dreadful experience, however, and difficult to control. An Italian physician, Ugo Cerletti, after years of experimentation with animals, developed a method of inducing seizures with an electric shock through the head (Cerletti & Bini, 1938). Electroconvulsive therapy is quick, and most patients awaken calmly without remembering it.

When ECT proved to be not very effective with schizophrenia, you might guess that psychiatrists would abandon it. Instead, they tried it for other mental hospital patients, despite having no theoretical basis. ECT did indeed relieve depression in many cases. However, its misuse during the 1950s earned it a bad reputation, as some patients were given ECT hundreds of times without their consent.

When antidepressant drugs became available in the late 1950s, the use of ECT declined abruptly. However, it made a partial comeback in the 1970s. ECT today is used only with informed consent, usually for patients with severe depression who have not responded to antidepressant drugs (Reisner, 2003). It is usually applied every other day for about 2 weeks. Patients are given muscle relaxants or anesthetics to minimize discomfort and the possibility of injury (Figure 15.7).

The most common side effect of ECT is memory loss, but limiting the shock to the right hemisphere reduces the memory loss. In any case, the memory impairment lasts no more than a few months, not forever (Reisner, 2003). Besides the threat of

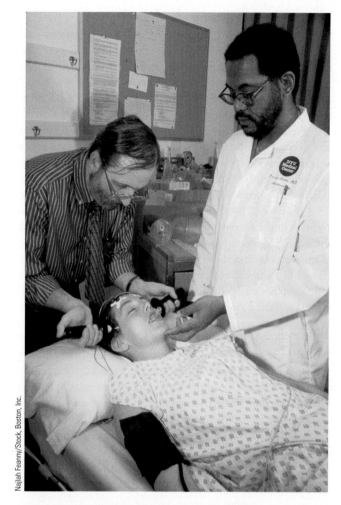

Najiah Feamy/Stock, Boston, Inc.

FIGURE 15.7 Electroconvulsive therapy (ECT)
In contrast to an earlier era, ECT today is administered with muscle relaxants or anesthetics to minimize discomfort and only if the patient gives informed consent.

memory loss, the other serious drawback to ECT is the high risk of relapsing into another episode of depression within a few months (Riddle & Scott, 1995). After ECT has relieved depression, the usual strategy is to try to prevent a relapse by means of drugs, psychotherapy, or periodic ECT treatments (Swoboda, Conca, König, Waanders, & Hansen, 2001).

More than half a century after the introduction of ECT, no one is yet sure how it relieves depression, but like antidepressant drugs, ECT increases the proliferation of new neurons in the hippocampus (Perera et al., 2007). It also alters the expression of at least 120 genes in the hippocampus and frontal cortex alone (Altar et al., 2004).

A similar treatment is repetitive transcranial magnetic stimulation. An intense magnetic field is applied to the scalp, stimulating the axons near the surface of the brain. This procedure is moderately effective against depression, although its mechanism of behavioral effect is not known (Ridding & Rothwell, 2007).

Altered Sleep Patterns

Almost everyone with depression has sleep problems, and the sleep problems generally precede the mood changes. One study identified teenagers who reported almost daily problems in falling asleep or staying asleep. Within the next 6 to 7 years, more than half of these young people developed depression (Roane & Taylor, 2008).

The usual sleep pattern for a depressed person resembles the sleep of healthy people who travel a couple of time zones west and have to go to bed later than usual: They fall asleep but awaken early, unable to get back to sleep, and they enter REM sleep within 45 minutes after going to sleep, as Figure 15.8 illustrates. In addition, people who are depressed have more than the average number of eye movements per minute during REM sleep. Many of their relatives show these same sleep patterns, and the relatives who show these patterns are more likely to become depressed themselves than are relatives who sleep normally (Modell, Ising, Holsboer, & Lauer, 2005). In short, altered sleep is a lifelong trait of people who are predisposed to depression.

Surprisingly, although most people feel worse after a sleepless night, a night of total sleep deprivation is the quickest known method of relieving depression (Ringel & Szuba, 2001). However, the benefit is brief, as the depression usually returns after the next night's sleep. Also, while sleep deprivation helps alleviate depression, it increases sensitivity to pain (Kundermann, Hemmeter-Spernal, Huber, Krieg, & Lautenbacher, 2008).

A more practical solution is to alter the sleep schedule, going to bed earlier than usual. The person might still awaken in the very early morning, but by that time he or she would have received seven or eight hours of sleep. This procedure relieves depression for at least a week in most patients and often longer (Riemann et al., 1999).

Researchers cannot yet explain how sleep deprivation or rescheduling produces mood benefits. A better understanding might lead to other treatments for depression.

STOP & CHECK

12. How can one decrease the memory loss associated with ECT?

13. What change in sleep habits sometimes relieves depression?

ANSWERS **12.** ECT over just the right hemisphere produces less memory loss. **13.** Getting people with depression to go to bed earlier sometimes relieves depression.

Other Therapies

Each of the currently available treatments for depression has its pros and cons, and some people with depression do not respond well to any of them. The search continues for new and improved treatments.

One promising possibility is a program of regular, nonstrenuous exercise, such as brisk walking for half an hour or more per day (Leppämäki, Partonen, & Lönnqvist, 2002).

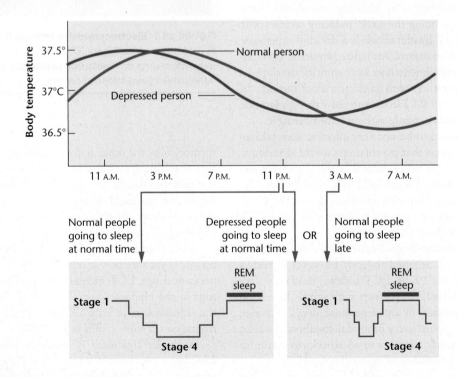

FIGURE 15.8 Circadian rhythms and depression
Most people with depression have their circadian rhythms advanced by several hours. They sleep as if they had gone to bed later than they actually did. *(Bottom graphs from* Sleep *by J. Allan Hobson, ©1989, 1995 by J. Allan Hobson. Reprinted by permission of Henry Holt and Company, LLC.)*

Many studies have shown that active people are less likely than sedentary people to become depressed. However, most of these studies are correlational in nature and do not support a cause-and-effect conclusion. A few controlled experiments have yielded inconclusive results (Teychenne, Ball, & Salmon, 2010). Still, exercise increases blood flow to the brain and provides other benefits, without the costs or risks of other treatments (Hillman, Erickson, & Kramer, 2008; Hunsberger et al., 2007). More research is necessary, but in the meantime, exercise is a good recommendation.

Bipolar Disorder

Depression can be either unipolar or bipolar. People with **unipolar disorder** vary between normality and one pole—depression. People with **bipolar disorder**, formerly known as *manic-depressive disorder*, alternate between two poles—depression and its opposite, mania. **Mania** is characterized by restless activity, excitement, laughter, self-confidence, rambling speech, and loss of inhibitions. People with mania become dangerous to themselves and others. Figure 15.9 shows the brain's increase in glucose use during mania and its decrease during depression (Baxter et al., 1985).

People who have full-blown episodes of mania are said to have **bipolar I disorder**. People with **bipolar II disorder** have milder manic phases, called hypomania, characterized by agitation or anxiety. In addition to the mood swings, most people with bipolar disorder have attention deficits, poor impulse control, and impairments of verbal memory (Quraishi & Frangou, 2002). Diagnoses of bipolar disorder have been increasing since the 1990s, especially among teenagers and young adults (Moreno et al., 2007). It is now estimated that about 1% of people will have bipolar I disorder at some time in life, another 1% will have bipolar II disorder, and 2% to 3% will have "subthreshold" bipolar disorder—a minor case not quite strong enough for a diagnosis of bipolar disorder (Merikangas et al., 2007).

Genetics

A genetic predisposition for bipolar disorder is supported by the usual types of evidence—twin studies and adoption studies. In addition, researchers have located two genes that appear to increase the probability of bipolar II disorder (Nwulia et al., 2007). They have also demonstrated that some of the same genes that predispose to major depression also predispose to bipolar disorder (Liu et al., 2011). However, the genes merely increase the risk. None of the genes shows a strong relationship to the disorder.

Treatments

The first successful treatment for bipolar disorder, and still the most common one, is **lithium** salts. Lithium's benefits were discovered accidentally by an Australian investigator, J. F. Cade, who believed uric acid might relieve mania and depression. Cade mixed uric acid (a component of urine) with a lithium salt to help it dissolve and then gave the solution to

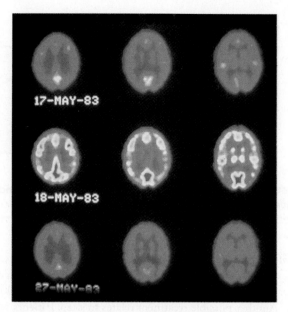

FIGURE 15.9 **PET scans for a patient with bipolar disorder** Horizontal planes through three levels of the brain are shown for each day. On May 17 and May 27, when the patient was depressed, brain metabolic rates were low. On May 18, when the patient was in a cheerful, hypomanic mood, the brain metabolic rate was high. Red indicates the highest metabolic rate, followed by yellow, green, and blue. *(Reprinted by permission from Macmillan Publishers Ltd: Nature, A functional neuroanatomy of hallucinations in schizophrenia, Silbersweig et al., 1995.)*

patients. It was indeed helpful, although investigators eventually realized that lithium was the effective agent, not uric acid.

Lithium stabilizes mood, preventing a relapse into either mania or depression. The dose must be regulated carefully, as a low dose is ineffective and a high dose is toxic (Schou, 1997). Two other effective drugs are valproate (trade names Depakene, Depakote, and others) and carbamazepine. If these drugs are not fully effective, physicians sometimes supplement them with antidepressant drugs or antipsychotic drugs—the ones also prescribed for schizophrenia. Antidepressant drugs are risky, as they sometimes provoke a switch from depression to mania. Antipsychotic drugs can be helpful, but they also produce unpleasant side effects.

Lithium, valproate, and carbamazepine have many effects on the brain. A good research strategy is to assume that they relieve bipolar disorder because of some effect they have in common. One effect they share is that they decrease the number of AMPA type glutamate receptors in the hippocampus (Du et al., 2008). Excessive glutamate activity is responsible for some aspects of mania. Also, the drugs that are effective against bipolar disorder block the synthesis of a brain chemical called *arachidonic acid*, which is produced during brain inflammation (S. I. Rapoport & Bosetti, 2002). Bipolar patients show an increased expression of genes associated with inflammation (Padmos et al., 2008). The effects of arachidonic acid are also counteracted by omega-3 fatty acids, such as those in

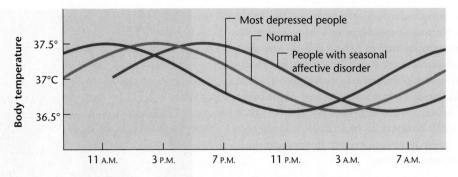

FIGURE 15.10 Circadian rhythms for major depression and seasonal affective disorder (SAD)
Patients with SAD are phase-delayed whereas most other patients with depression are phase-advanced. *(© Cengage Learning 2013)*

seafood, and epidemiological studies suggest that people who eat at least a pound (0.45 kg) of seafood per week have a decreased risk of bipolar disorder (Noaghiul & Hibbeln, 2003).

Another possible treatment relates to sleep. Patients with bipolar disorder during the depressed phase tend to stay in bed for many hours. During the manic phase, they awaken early, reach their activity peak earlier in the day than most people, and get relatively little sleep (Salvatore et al., 2008). Preliminary studies suggest that getting people to maintain a consistent sleeping schedule in a dark, quiet room reduces the intensity of mood swings (Wehr et al., 1998).

STOP & CHECK

14. What are two common treatments for bipolar disorder?

ANSWER

14. The common treatments for bipolar disorder are lithium salts and certain anticonvulsant drugs—valproate and carbamazepine.

▌Seasonal Affective Disorder

One more form of depression is **seasonal affective disorder (SAD)**—depression that recurs during a particular season, such as winter. SAD is most prevalent near the poles, where the winter nights are long (Haggarty et al., 2002).

SAD differs from other types of depression in many ways. For example, patients with SAD have phase-delayed sleep and temperature rhythms—becoming sleepy and wakeful later than normal—unlike most other patients with depression, whose rhythms are phase-advanced (Teicher et al., 1997) (Figure 15.10). Also, SAD is seldom as severe as major depression. Many people with SAD have a mutation in one of the genes responsible for regulating the circadian rhythm, as discussed in Chapter 9 (Johansson et al., 2003).

It is possible to treat SAD with very bright lights (e.g., 2,500 lux) for an hour or more each day. The bright light treatment is effective in the morning, afternoon, or evening (Eastman, Young, Fogg, Liu, & Meaden, 1998; Lewy et al., 1998; Terman, Terman, & Ross, 1998). Although its benefits are as yet unexplained, they are substantial. Bright light is less expensive than the other antidepressant therapies and produces its benefits more rapidly, often within 1 week (Kripke, 1998).

STOP & CHECK

15. What are the advantages of bright light treatment compared to antidepressant drugs?

ANSWER

15. It is cheaper, has no side effects, and produces its benefits more quickly.

MODULE 15.1 ▪ IN CLOSING

Biology of Mood Swings

There is nothing abnormal about feeling sad or happy if something unusually bad or good has just happened to you. For people with major depression or bipolar disorder, mood becomes largely independent of events. A traumatic experience might trigger a bout of depression, but once someone has become depressed, the mood persists for months, and even the best of news provides little cheer. A bipolar patient in a manic state has boundless energy and self-confidence that no contradiction can deter. Studying these states has great potential to inform us about the brain states that correspond to moods.

SUMMARY

1. People with major depression find that almost nothing makes them happy. In most cases, depression occurs as a series of episodes. **460**

2. Depression has a genetic predisposition, but no one gene has a strong effect by itself. **461**

3. Uncommonly, depression can be a reaction to a virus, or possibly to hormonal changes. **462**

4. Depression is associated with decreased activity in the left hemisphere of the cortex. **463**

5. Several kinds of antidepressant drugs are in wide use. Tricyclics block reuptake of serotonin and catecholamines. SSRIs block reuptake of serotonin. SNRIs block reuptake of both serotonin and norepinephrine. MAOIs block an enzyme that breaks down catecholamines and serotonin. Atypical antidepressants are a miscellaneous group with diverse effects. **463**

6. Antidepressants alter synaptic activity quickly, but their effects on behavior require at least 2 weeks. Although different drugs affect different neurotransmitters, they all appear to be about equally effective. It is possible that their well-known effects on neurotransmitters are not the main reason for their effects on behavior. **464**

7. Most people with depression have a deficiency of the neurotrophin BDNF, which promotes development of new neurons, synapses, and learning in the hippocampus. Most antidepressant drugs produce a gradual increase in BDNF, and therefore enhance synaptic plasticity in the hippocampus. The effects on BDNF may be the main reason for the drugs' benefits. **465**

8. Antidepressant drugs are ineffective for many people. For depressed patients with mild to moderate depression, antidepressants are not significantly more effective than placebos. **465**

9. Psychotherapy is about as effective as antidepressant drugs for patients with all levels of severity. Psychotherapy is more likely than antipsychotic drugs to produce long-lasting benefits that prevent or delay a relapse after the end of treatment. **466**

10. Other therapies for depression include electroconvulsive therapy, altered sleep patterns, and exercise. **467**

11. People with bipolar disorder alternate between depression and mania. Effective therapies include lithium salts and certain other drugs. A consistent sleep schedule is also recommended. **469**

12. Seasonal affective disorder is marked by recurrent depression during one season of the year. Exposure to bright lights is usually effective in treating it. **470**

KEY TERMS

Terms are defined in the module on the page number indicated. They're also presented in alphabetical order with definitions in the book's Subject Index/Glossary, which begins on page 561. Interactive flashcards and crossword puzzles are among the online resources available to help you learn these terms and the concepts they represent.

atypical antidepressants **464**
bipolar disorder **469**
bipolar I disorder **469**
bipolar II disorder **469**
electroconvulsive therapy (ECT) **467**
lithium **469**
major depression **460**
mania **469**
monoamine oxidase inhibitors (MAOIs) **464**
postpartum depression **462**
seasonal affective disorder (SAD) **470**
selective serotonin reuptake inhibitors (SSRIs) **464**
serotonin norepinephrine reuptake inhibitors (SNRIs) **464**
tricyclics **463**
unipolar depression **469**

THOUGHT QUESTIONS

1. Some people have suggested that ECT relieves depression by causing people to forget the events that caused it. What evidence opposes this hypothesis?

2. Certain people suffer from what they describe as "post-Christmas depression," a feeling of letdown after all the excitement of the holiday season. What other explanation can you offer?

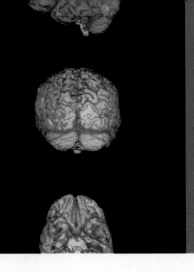

Schizophrenia

Here is a conversation between two people diagnosed with schizophrenia (Haley, 1959, p. 321):

A: Do you work at the air base?

B: You know what I think of work. I'm 33 in June, do you mind?

A: June?

B: 33 years old in June. This stuff goes out the window after I live this, uh—leave this hospital. So I can't get my vocal cords back. So I lay off cigarettes. I'm in a spatial condition, from outer space myself. . . .

A: I'm a real spaceship from across.

B: A lot of people talk that way, like crazy, but "Believe It or Not," by Ripley, take it or leave it—alone—it's in the *Examiner*, it's in the comic section, "Believe It or Not," by Ripley, Robert E. Ripley, believe it or not, but we don't have to believe anything, unless I feel like it. Every little rosette—too much alone.

A: Yeah, it could be possible.

B: I'm a civilian seaman.

A: Could be possible. I take my bath in the ocean.

B: Bathing stinks. You know why? 'Cause you can't quit when you feel like it. You're in the service.

People with schizophrenia say and do things that other people (including other people with schizophrenia) find difficult to understand. The causes of the disorder are not well understood, but they include a large biological component.

▌ Diagnosis

Schizophrenia was originally called *dementia praecox*, which is Latin for "premature mental deterioration." In 1911, Eugen Bleuler introduced the term *schizophrenia*. Although the term is Greek for "split mind," it is *not* related to *dissociative identity disorder* (previously known as *multiple personality disorder*), in which someone alternates among different personalities. What Bleuler meant by *schizophrenia* was a split between the emotional and intellectual aspects of experience: The person's emotional expression or lack of it seems unconnected with current experiences. For example, someone might giggle or cry for no apparent reason or show no reaction to bad news. Not all patients show this detachment of emotion from intellect, but the term lives on.

Diagnosis of schizophrenia is difficult. In most areas of medicine, a physician can confirm a diagnosis with a lab test of some sort. Psychiatry has no dependable lab tests. Psychiatrists rely on behavioral observations, and many cases leave room for uncertainty.

According to the *DSM-IV* (American Psychiatric Association, 1994), to be diagnosed with **schizophrenia**, someone must have deteriorated in everyday functioning (work, interpersonal relations, self care, etc.) for at least 6 months, and must show at least two of the following, that are not attributable to other disorders:

- **Delusions** (unjustifiable beliefs, such as "Beings from outer space are controlling my actions")
- **Hallucinations** (false sensory experiences, such as hearing voices when alone)
- Disorganized speech (rambling or incoherent)
- Grossly disorganized behavior
- Weak or absent signs of emotion, speech, and socialization

Each of these is a judgment call. Sometimes a statement that appears to be a delusion ("People are persecuting me") is actually true, or at least defensible. Many healthy people have heard a voice when they knew they were alone, at least once or twice. The term "grossly disorganized behavior" encompasses a wide variety of possibilities. The symptoms vary so greatly that you could easily find several people diagnosed with schizophrenia who have almost nothing in common (Andreasen, 1999).

The first four items on the list—delusions, hallucinations, disorganized speech, and disorganized behavior—are called **positive symptoms** (behaviors that are present that should be absent). Weak or absent emotion, speech, and socialization are **negative symptoms** (behaviors that are absent that should

Nancy Andreason

Nancy C. Andreasen

Being a scientist and a clinician is a double privilege. We actually get paid to spend our time asking both scientific and clinical questions that everyone would like to ask and have answered, and people grant us the trust of sharing their most intimate thoughts and experiences with us.

be present). Negative symptoms are usually stable over time and difficult to treat.

It is also useful to distinguish *cognitive* symptoms. The cognitive symptoms are limitations of thought and reasoning that are common in schizophrenia, even if they are not central to the diagnosis. Overall intelligence varies considerably, but on average, IQ scores are a few points below those of the rest of the population (Woodberry, Giuliano, & Seidman, 2008). The most typical type of thought disorder of schizophrenia is a difficulty understanding and using abstract concepts. Related symptoms include deficits in attention and working memory (Hanlon et al., 2005).

Which of the various symptoms, if any, is the primary problem? According to Nancy Andreasen (1999), a leading investigator of schizophrenia, the main problem is disordered thoughts that result from abnormal interactions between the cortex and the thalamus and cerebellum. The disordered thinking may lead to the hallucinations, delusions, and other symptoms.

One way to test this idea is to see whether we could make normal, healthy people talk or behave in incoherent ways if we overtaxed their working memory. Imagine yourself in the following study. The researcher shows a series of pictures for 30 seconds each, and you are supposed to tell a short story about each one. If you see the same picture a second time, you should tell a totally new story about it, unlike your first one. Furthermore, on some trials, you have an additional task to burden your memory while you are trying to tell a story: A series of letters appears on the screen, one at a time. You should pay attention to every second letter. Whenever it is the same as the last letter that you paid attention to, you should press a key. For example,

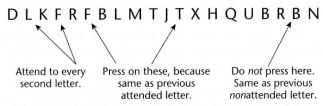

D L K F R F B L M T J T X H Q U B R B N

Attend to every second letter. Press on these, because same as previous attended letter. Do *not* press here. Same as previous *non*attended letter.

Most people's speech becomes less clear when they perform this memory task while trying to tell a story. If it is the second presentation of a picture, requiring them to avoid what they said the first time and tell a totally new story, the memory task causes even greater interference, and their speech becomes incoherent, somewhat like schizophrenic speech (Kerns, 2007). The implication is that memory impairment could be the central symptom.

16. Why are hallucinations considered a positive symptom?

ANSWER

16. Hallucinations are considered a positive symptom because they are present when they should be absent. A "positive" symptom is not a "good" symptom.

APPLICATIONS AND EXTENSIONS

Differential Diagnosis of Schizophrenia

In the rules for diagnosing schizophrenia, did you notice the expression "not attributable to other disorders"? Even if someone's symptoms match the description of schizophrenia perfectly, it is important to make a **differential diagnosis**—that is, one that rules out other conditions with similar symptoms. Here are a few conditions that sometimes resemble schizophrenia:

- *Mood disorder with psychotic features:* People with depression frequently have delusions, especially delusions of guilt or failure. Some report hallucinations also.

- *Substance abuse:* Many of the positive symptoms of schizophrenia can develop from prolonged use of amphetamine, methamphetamine, cocaine, LSD, or phencyclidine ("angel dust"). Someone who stops taking the drugs is likely, though not certain, to recover from these symptoms. Substance abuse is more likely than schizophrenia to produce visual hallucinations.

- *Brain damage:* Damage or tumors in the temporal or prefrontal cortex often produce some of the symptoms of schizophrenia.

- *Undetected hearing deficits:* Sometimes, someone who is starting to have trouble hearing thinks that everyone else is whispering and starts to worry, "They're whispering about me!" Delusions of persecution can develop.

- *Huntington's disease:* The symptoms of Huntington's disease include hallucinations, delusions, and disordered thinking, as well as motor symptoms. An uncommon type of schizophrenia, catatonic schizophrenia, includes motor abnormalities, so a mixture of psychological and motor symptoms could represent either schizophrenia or Huntington's disease.

- *Nutritional abnormalities:* Niacin deficiency can produce hallucinations and delusions (Hoffer, 1973), and so can a deficiency of vitamin C or an allergy to milk proteins (not the same as lactose intolerance). Some people who cannot tolerate wheat gluten or other proteins react with hallucinations and delusions (Reichelt, Seim, & Reichelt, 1996). ■

Demographic Data

Worldwide, about 1% of people suffer from schizophrenia at some point in life (Narrow et al., 2002; Perälä et al., 2007). The estimate rises or falls depending on how many mild cases we include. Since the mid-1900s, the reported prevalence of schizophrenia has been declining in many countries (Suvisaari, Haukka, Tanskanen, & Lönnqvist, 1999; Torrey & Miller, 2001). Is schizophrenia actually less common, or are psychiatrists just diagnosing it differently? This is not an easy question to answer. However, even when it is diagnosed today, it appears to be less severe than it often used to be. Perhaps our society is doing something to prevent schizophrenia without knowing what.

Schizophrenia occurs in all ethnic groups and all parts of the world. However, it is significantly more common in cities than in rural areas, for reasons unknown (Kelly et al., 2010). Also it is 10 to 100 times more common in the United States and Europe than in most Third World countries (Torrey, 1986). Part of that discrepancy could be due to differences in recordkeeping, but other possibilities exist, including social support and diet. A diet high in sugar and saturated fat, as is common in prosperous countries, aggravates schizophrenia, whereas a diet rich in fish alleviates it (Peet, 2004). Omega-3 fatty acids, abundant in seafood, increase production of BDNF, increase production of new cells in the hippocampus, and block apoptosis and other neural damage (V. R. King et al., 2006; Venna, 2008).

Lifetime prevalence of schizophrenia is more common for men than women by a ratio of about 7:5. On average, it is also more severe in men and has an earlier onset—usually in the teens or early 20s for men and the mid to late 20s for women (Aleman, Kahn, & Selten, 2003).

Researchers have documented several unexplained oddities about schizophrenia. The points that follow do not fit neatly into any currently prominent theory. They indicate how many mysteries remain:

- Schizophrenia is significantly less common than average among people with type 1 (juvenile-onset) diabetes, although it is more common than average in people with type 2 (adult-onset) diabetes (Juvonen et al., 2007).

- People with schizophrenia have an increased risk of colon cancer but below average probability of respiratory cancer or brain cancer (Hippisley-Cox, Vinogradova, Coupland, & Parker, 2007; Roppel, 1978).

- People with schizophrenia seldom develop rheumatoid arthritis or allergies (Goldman, 1999; Rubinstein, 1997).

- Women who have a schizophrenic breakdown during pregnancy usually give birth to daughters. However, those who have a breakdown shortly after giving birth usually give birth to sons (M. A. Taylor, 1969).

- Many people with schizophrenia have a characteristic body odor, attributed to the chemical *trans*-3-methyl-2-hexenoic acid, and decreased ability to smell that

chemical themselves (Brewer et al., 2007; K. Smith, Thompson, & Koster, 1969).

- Most people with schizophrenia and many of their unaffected relatives have deficits in pursuit eye movements—the ability to keep their eyes on a moving target (Keefe et al., 1997; Sereno & Holzman, 1993).

> **STOP & CHECK**

17. Has the reported prevalence of schizophrenia been increasing, decreasing, or staying the same?

ANSWER

17. Schizophrenia has been decreasing in reported prevalence.

▌Genetics

Huntington's disease (Chapter 8) can be called a genetic disease: By examining part of chromosome 4, one can predict with almost perfect accuracy who will develop the disease and who will not. At one time, many researchers believed that schizophrenia might be a genetic disease in the same sense. However, accumulating evidence indicates that although schizophrenia has a genetic basis, it does not depend on any single gene.

Twin Studies

The more closely you are biologically related to someone with schizophrenia, the greater your own probability of schizophrenia, as shown in Figure 15.11 (Gottesman, 1991). One of the most important points in Figure 15.11, confirmed by other studies (Cardno et al., 1999), is that monozygotic twins have a much higher **concordance** (agreement) for schizophrenia than do dizygotic twins. Furthermore, twin pairs who are really monozygotic, but thought they weren't, are more concordant than twin pairs who thought they were, but really aren't (Kendler, 1983). That is, *being* monozygotic is more critical than *being treated as* monozygotic.

The high concordance for monozygotic twins has long been taken as strong evidence for a genetic influence. However, note two limitations:

- Monozygotic twins have only about 50% concordance, not 100%. Monozygotic twins could differ because a gene is activated in one individual and suppressed in another (Tsujita et al., 1998), or they could differ because of environmental influences.

- In Figure 15.11, note the greater similarity between dizygotic twins than between siblings. Dizygotic twins have the same genetic resemblance as siblings but greater environmental similarity, including prenatal environment.

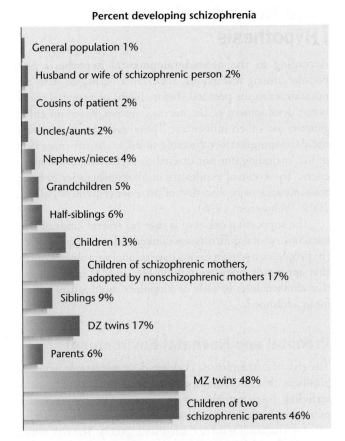

Percent developing schizophrenia

General population 1%

Husband or wife of schizophrenic person 2%

Cousins of patient 2%

Uncles/aunts 2%

Nephews/nieces 4%

Grandchildren 5%

Half-siblings 6%

Children 13%

Children of schizophrenic mothers, adopted by nonschizophrenic mothers 17%

Siblings 9%

DZ twins 17%

Parents 6%

MZ twins 48%

Children of two schizophrenic parents 46%

FIGURE 15.11 **Probabilities of developing schizophrenia**
People with a closer genetic relationship to someone with schizophrenia have a higher probability of developing it themselves. *(Based on data from Gottesman, 1991)*

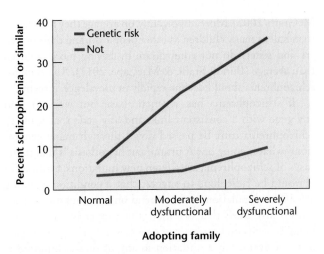

FIGURE 15.12 **Probability of schizophrenia or similar conditions in adopted children**
The probability was higher for children of a mother with schizophrenia, but growing up in a dysfunctional family magnified that risk. *(Based on data from Wynne et al., 2006)*

Adopted Children Who Develop Schizophrenia

When an adopted child develops schizophrenia, the disorder is more common in the person's biological relatives than adopting relatives. One Danish study found schizophrenia in 12.5% of the immediate biological relatives and none of the adopting relatives (Kety et al., 1994). Note in Figure 15.11 that children of a mother with schizophrenia have a moderately high probability of schizophrenia, even if adopted by mentally healthy parents.

These results suggest a genetic basis, but they are also consistent with a prenatal influence. Consider a pregnant woman with schizophrenia. True, she passes her genes to her child, but she also provides the prenatal environment. Many women with schizophrenia smoke, drink, use other drugs, and eat a less than desirable diet during pregnancy. A disproportionate number have complications during pregnancy and delivery (Jablensky, Morgan, Zubrick, Bower, & Yellachich, 2005). If some of their children develop schizophrenia, we cannot be sure that the influence is genetic.

Studies on adopted children also support a role for environmental influences. A study of adopted children in Fin-

land found a high probability of schizophrenia or related conditions among children who had a biological mother with schizophrenia *and* a severely disordered adopting family. The genetic risk itself or the disordered family itself had less effect, as shown in Figure 15.12 (Wynne et al., 2006).

Efforts to Locate a Gene

The strongest evidence for a genetic influence would be to locate a gene that is consistently linked with schizophrenia. Researchers working with various populations have identified more than a dozen genes that appear to be more common in people with schizophrenia. One that has attracted much interest, called *DISC1* (*disrupted in schizophrenia 1*), controls production of dendritic spines (Hayashi-Takagi et al., 2010) and the generation of new neurons in the hippocampus (Duan et al., 2007). Other genes linked to schizophrenia in several studies are important for brain development (Hall et al., 2006; Stefansson et al., 2009), control of transmission at glutamate synapses (Dickman & Davis, 2009), and connections between the hippocampus and the prefrontal cortex (Esslinger et al., 2009). However, researchers have not had great success at replicating the results from one population to another. A study of nearly 2,000 patients with schizophrenia and a control group found no statistically significant relationship between schizophrenia and any of the 14 genes that previous studies identified as linked to schizophrenia (Sanders et al., 2008).

In a way, these results should not be surprising. If schizophrenia depended on a single gene, it would be hard for that gene to remain in 1% of the population, given the natural selection pressures against it. People with schizophrenia die younger than other people, on average (Saha, Chant, &

McGrath, 2007). More importantly, on average they have fewer than half as many children as other people do, and their brothers and sisters do not compensate by having more children than average (Bundy, Stahl, & MacCabe, 2011). Any gene for schizophrenia should decline rapidly in prevalence, it seems.

If schizophrenia has a genetic basis but we can't find any gene with a consistent link, and any gene that leads to schizophrenia can't be passed down through many generations, what is going on? A prominent hypothesis is that many cases of schizophrenia arise from new mutations. Ordinarily, it would be ridiculous to suggest that a condition affecting 1% of the population could depend on new mutations. Mutations just aren't that common. But proper brain development depends on hundreds of genes. A mutation in one gene is a rare event, but a mutation in any of several hundred is not so rare. An even more likely possibility is deletion of a gene, a fairly common error in reproduction (International Schizophrenia Consortium, 2009). Researchers examined the chromosomes of people with and without schizophrenia and found genetic *microdeletions* and *microduplications* (i.e., elimination or duplication of parts of a gene) in 5% of the control group, 15% of people with schizophrenia, and 20% of people with onset of schizophrenia before age 18 (Walsh et al., 2008). Those microdeletions and microduplications were distributed over a great many genes. Thus, the hypothesis is that a new mutation or deletion of any of a large number of genes disrupts brain development and increases the probability of schizophrenia. As fast as natural selection weeds out those mutations or deletions, new ones arise to replace them.

One observation supporting this idea is that schizophrenia is somewhat more common among children of older fathers (Byrne, Agerbo, Ewald, Eaton, & Mortensen, 2003; Malaspina et al., 2002). Women are born with all the eggs they will ever have, but men continue making new sperm throughout life, and the possibility of mutations accumulates over time.

We need not assume that all cases of schizophrenia have a genetic predisposition. Others may depend on prenatal environment or other influences on brain development.

> **STOP & CHECK**

18. The fact that adopted children who develop schizophrenia usually have biological relatives with schizophrenia implies a probable genetic basis. What other interpretation is possible?

19. Does the hypothesis of new mutations conflict with the results showing that an aberrant form of the gene *DISC1* is often linked to schizophrenia?

ANSWERS **18.** A biological mother can influence her child's development through prenatal environment as well as genetics, even if the child is adopted early. **19.** No. Although mutations in many genes can, according to the hypothesis, lead to schizophrenia, the *DISC1* gene could be one where the mutation is more certain to cause schizophrenia.

The Neurodevelopmental Hypothesis

According to the **neurodevelopmental hypothesis** now popular among researchers, schizophrenia begins with abnormalities in the prenatal (before birth) or neonatal (newborn) development of the nervous system, based on either genetics or other influences. These early problems leave the developing brain vulnerable to other disturbances later in life, including but not limited to highly stressful experiences. The eventual results are mild abnormalities in brain anatomy and major disorders of behavior (Fatemi & Folsom, 2009; Weinberger, 1996).

The supporting evidence is that (a) several kinds of prenatal or neonatal difficulties are linked to later schizophrenia; (b) people with schizophrenia have minor brain abnormalities that apparently originate early in life; and (c) it is plausible that abnormalities of early development could impair behavior in adulthood.

Prenatal and Neonatal Environment

The risk of schizophrenia is elevated among people who had problems that could have affected their brain development, including poor nutrition of the mother during pregnancy, premature birth, low birth weight, and complications during delivery (Ballon, Dean, & Cadenhead, 2007). The risk is also elevated if the mother was exposed to extreme stress, such as the sudden death of a close relative, early in her pregnancy (Khashau et al., 2008). None of these influences by itself accounts for many cases of schizophrenia, although together their influence is greater (Cannon, Jones, & Murray, 2002). Schizophrenia has also been linked to head injuries in early childhood (AbdelMalik, Husted, Chow, & Bassett, 2003), although we do not know whether the head injuries led to schizophrenia or early symptoms of schizophrenia increased the risk of head injuries.

If a mother is Rh-negative and her baby is Rh-positive, the baby's Rh-positive blood factor may trigger an immunological rejection by the mother. The response is weak with the woman's first Rh-positive baby but stronger in later pregnancies, and it is more intense with boy than girl babies. Second- and later-born boy babies with Rh incompatibility have an increased risk of hearing deficits, mental retardation, and several other problems, and about twice the usual probability of schizophrenia (Hollister, Laing, & Mednick, 1996).

Another suggestion of prenatal influences comes from the **season-of-birth effect:** the tendency for people born in winter to have a slightly (5% to 8%) greater probability of developing schizophrenia than people born at other times of the year. This tendency is particularly pronounced in latitudes far from the equator (Davies, Welham, Chant, Torrey, & McGrath, 2003; Torrey, Miller, et al., 1997).

What might account for this effect? One possibility is complications of delivery or early nutrition (Jablensky et al., 2005). Another is viral infection. Influenza and other viral epidemics are most common in the fall. Therefore, the reasoning goes, many pregnant women become infected in the fall with a virus that impairs a crucial stage of brain development in a baby who will be born in the winter. A virus that affects the mother might or might not cross the placenta into the fetus's brain, but the mother's cytokines do cross, and excessive cytokines can impair brain development (Zuckerman, Rehavi, Nachman, & Weiner, 2003). Animal studies show that some of the effects of cytokines on brain development appear mild at first but gradually impair brain development as the individual approaches adulthood (Vuillermot, Weber, Feldon, & Meyer, 2010). The mother's infection also causes a fever, which can damage the fetal brain. A fever of just 38.5° C (101° F) slows the division of fetal neurons (Laburn, 1996). (Exercise during pregnancy does *not* overheat the abdomen and is not dangerous to the fetus. Hot baths and saunas may be risky, however.) When mice are infected with influenza during pregnancy, their offspring develop a number of behavioral abnormalities, including deficient exploration and deficient social reactions to other mice (Shi, Fatemi, Sidwell, & Patterson, 2003).

Researchers examined the records of tens of thousands of people in Scotland, England, and Denmark over several decades. They found increased schizophrenia rates among people born 2 to 3 months after major influenza epidemics, such as the one in the autumn of 1957 (Adams, Kendell, Hare, & Munk-Jørgensen, 1993). Other studies retrieved blood samples that hospitals had taken from pregnant women and stored for decades. Researchers found increased incidence of influenza virus among mothers whose children eventually developed schizophrenia (A. S. Brown et al., 2004; Buka et al., 2001). Rates of schizophrenia are also increased among offspring of mothers who had rubella (German measles), herpes, and other infections during pregnancy (A. S. Brown et al., 2001; Buka et al., 2008).

Certain childhood infections may also relate to schizophrenia. The parasite *Toxoplasma gondii* (discussed also in Chapter 12 in the context of anxiety and the amygdala) reproduces only in cats, but it can infect humans and other species also. If it infects the brain of an infant or child, it impairs brain development and leads to memory disorder, hallucinations, and delusions (Torrey & Yolken, 2005). People who develop schizophrenia in adulthood are more likely than other people to have had a pet cat in childhood (Torrey, Rawlings, & Yolken, 2000). Blood tests have found antibodies to the Toxoplasma parasite in a higher percentage of people with schizo-

phrenia than in the general population (Leweke et al., 2004; Niebuhr et al., 2008; Yolken et al., 2001).

In short, some cases of schizophrenia may develop as a result of infections. This mechanism is an alternative or supplement to genetics and other influences. Evidently, a variety of influences can lead to similar outcomes in schizophrenia.

STOP & CHECK

20. What does the season-of-birth effect suggest about a possible cause of schizophrenia?

ANSWER

20. The season-of-birth effect is the observation that schizophrenia is slightly more common among people who were born in the winter. One interpretation is that influenza or other infections of the mother during the fall impair brain development of a baby born in the winter.

Mild Brain Abnormalities

In accord with the neurodevelopmental hypothesis, some (though not all) people with schizophrenia show mild abnormalities of brain anatomy that vary from one individual to another. On average, people with schizophrenia have less than average gray matter and white matter, and larger than average ventricles—the fluid-filled spaces within the brain (Meyer-Lindenberg, 2010; Wolkin et al., 1998; Wright et al., 2000) (Figure 15.13)

Figure 15.14 summarizes 15 studies, including a total of 390 people with schizophrenia. Brain areas marked in yellow showed decreased volume in the most studies, those in various shades of red showed decreases in fewer studies, and those in gray appeared normal in all studies (Honea, Crow,

Ventricles

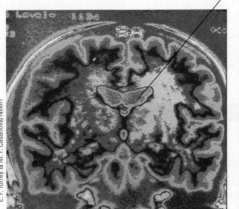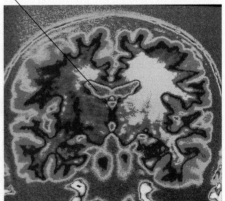

FIGURE 15.13 Coronal sections for identical twins
The twin on the left has schizophrenia; the twin on the right does not. The ventricles (near the center of each brain) are larger in the twin with schizophrenia.

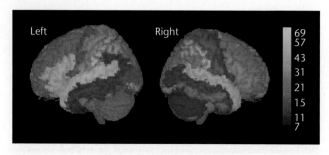

FIGURE 15.14 Cortical areas showing decreased volume in patients with schizophrenia
Areas in yellow showed decreased volume in the largest percentage of studies. Those in various shades of red showed decreases in fewer studies. *(From "Regional deficits in brain volume in schizophrenia: A meta-analysis of voxel-based morphometry studies," by R. Honea, T. J., Crow, D., Passingham, and C. E. Mackay,* American Journal of Psychiatry, *162, 2233–2245. Reprinted by permission from the* American Journal of Psychiatry, *Copyright (2005) American Psychiatric Association.)*

Passingham, & Mackay, 2005). Note that the strongest deficits were in the left temporal and frontal areas of the cortex. Note also that most cortical areas showed mild abnormalities in at least one or two studies. The thalamus, which is in the interior of the brain and therefore not shown in Figure 15.14, is also smaller than average for people with schizophrenia (Harms et al., 2007).

The areas with consistent signs of abnormality include some that mature slowly, such as the dorsolateral prefrontal cortex (Berman, Torrey, Daniel, & Weinberger, 1992; Fletcher et al., 1998; Gur, Cowell, et al., 2000). The abnormalities include weaker than average connections from the dorsolateral prefrontal cortex to other brain areas, and less than normal activity in this area during tasks requiring attention and memory (Lynall et al., 2010; van den Heuvel, Mandl, Stam, Kahn, & Pol, 2010; Weiss et al., 2009). As you might predict, people with schizophrenia perform poorly at tasks that depend on the prefrontal cortex (Goldberg, Weinberger, Berman, Pliskin, & Podd, 1987; Spindler, Sullivan, Menon, Lim, & Pfefferbaum, 1997). Most patients with schizophrenia show deficits of memory and attention similar to those of people with damage to the temporal or pre-

frontal cortex (Park, Holzman, & Goldman-Rakic, 1995) (Methods 15.1).

At a microscopic level, the most reliable finding is that cell bodies are smaller than normal, especially in the hippocampus and prefrontal cortex (Pierri, Volk, Auh, Sampson, & Lewis, 2001; Rajkowska, Selemon, & Goldman-Rakic, 1998; Selemon, Rajkowska, & Goldman-Rakic, 1995; Weinberger, 1999).

Lateralization also differs from the normal pattern. In most people, the left hemisphere is slightly larger than the right, especially in the planum temporale of the temporal lobe, but in people with schizophrenia, the right planum temporale is equal or larger (Kasai et al., 2003; Kwon et al., 1999). People with schizophrenia have lower than normal overall activity in the left hemisphere (Gur & Chin, 1999) and are more likely than other people to be left-handed (Satz & Green, 1999). All these results suggest a subtle change in brain development.

The reasons behind the brain abnormalities are not certain. Most researchers have been careful to limit their studies to patients with schizophrenia who have never taken, or who have not recently taken, antipsychotic drugs, so the deficits are not a result of treatments for schizophrenia. However, many people with schizophrenia use alcohol, marijuana, and other drugs, and it is likely that some of the brain abnormalities result from heavy drug use (Rais et al., 2008; Sullivan et al., 2000).

The results are inconsistent as to whether the brain damage associated with schizophrenia is *progressive*—that is, whether it increases over time. The brain damage associated with Parkinson's disease, Huntington's disease, and Alzheimer's disease gets worse as the person ages. Brain abnormalities are found in young people shortly after a diagnosis of schizophrenia (Lieberman et al., 2001), and many studies find that the brain abnormalities are no greater in older patients (Andreasen et al., 1990; Censits, Ragland, Gur, & Gur, 1997; Russell, Munro, Jones, Hemsley, & Murray, 1997; Selemon et al., 1995). However, other studies show a moderate degree of increased brain loss as patients age (Cahn et al., 2002; Hulshoff et al., 2001; Mathalon, Sullivan, Lim, & Pfefferbaum, 2001; Rais et al., 2008). Nevertheless, the brains of people with schizophrenia do not show the signs that accompany neuron death—proliferation of glia cells and activation of the genes responsible for repair after injury (Arnold, 2000; Benes, 1995; K. O. Lim et al., 1998). Possibly, the neurons are shrinking without dying.

METHODS | 15.1

The Wisconsin Card Sorting Task

Neuropsychologists use many behavioral tests to measure the functioning of the prefrontal cortex. One is the Wisconsin Card Sorting Task. A person is handed a shuffled deck of cards that differ in number, color, and shape of objects—for example, three red circles, five blue triangles, four green squares. First the person is asked to sort them by one rule, such as separate them by color. Then the rule changes, and

the person is supposed to sort them by a different rule, such as number. Shifting to a new rule requires suppressing the old one and evokes activity in the prefrontal cortex (Konishi et al., 1998). People with damage to the prefrontal cortex can sort by whichever rule is first, but then they have trouble shifting to a new rule. People with schizophrenia have the same difficulty. (So do children.)

In any case, most of the damage is apparent early, and later changes are relatively small.

Early Development and Later Psychopathology

One question may have struck you. How can we reconcile the idea of abnormalities in early development with the fact that the disorder is usually diagnosed after age 20? The time course may not be as puzzling as it seems at first (Weinberger, 1996). Most of the people who develop schizophrenia in adulthood had shown other problems since childhood, including deficits in attention, memory, and impulse control (Keshavan, Diwadkar, Montrose, Rajarethinam, & Sweeney, 2005). Furthermore, the prefrontal cortex, an area that shows consistent signs of deficit in schizophrenia, is one of the slowest brain areas to mature. In one study, researchers damaged this area in infant monkeys and tested the monkeys later. At age 1 year, the monkeys' behavior was nearly normal, but by age 2 years, it had deteriorated markedly (P. S. Goldman, 1971, 1976). That is, the effects of the brain damage grew worse over age. Presumably, the effects of brain damage were minimal at age 1 year because the dorsolateral prefrontal cortex doesn't do much at that age anyway. Later, when it should begin assuming important functions, the damage begins to make a difference (Figure 15.15).

STOP & CHECK

21. If schizophrenia is due to abnormal brain development, why do behavioral symptoms not become apparent until later in life?

ANSWER

21. Parts of the prefrontal cortex are very slow to reach maturity; therefore, early disruption of this area's development might not produce any symptoms early in life, when the prefrontal cortex is contributing little anyway.

Treatments

Before antipsychotic drugs became available in the mid-1950s, most people with schizophrenia were confined to mental hospitals with little hope of recovery. Today, mental hospitals are far less crowded because of drugs and outpatient treatment.

Antipsychotic Drugs and Dopamine

In the 1950s, psychiatrists discovered that **chlorpromazine** (trade name Thorazine) relieves the positive symptoms of schizophrenia for most, though not all, patients. Researchers later discovered other **antipsychotic**, or **neuroleptic**, **drugs** (drugs that tend to relieve schizophrenia and similar conditions) in two chemical families: the **phenothiazines** (FEE-no-THI-uh-zeens), which include chlorpromazine, and the **butyrophenones** (BYOO-tir-oh-FEE-noans), which include haloperidol (trade name Haldol). Behavioral benefits of any of these drugs develop gradually over a month or more. Symptoms generally return after cessation of treatment.

As Figure 15.16 illustrates, each of these drugs blocks dopamine synapses. For each drug, researchers determined the mean dose prescribed for patients with schizophrenia (displayed along the horizontal axis) and the amount needed to block dopamine receptors (displayed along the vertical axis). As the figure shows, the drugs that are most effective against schizophrenia (and therefore used in the smallest doses) are the most effective at blocking dopamine receptors (Seeman, Lee, Chau-Wong, & Wong, 1976).

That finding inspired the **dopamine hypothesis of schizophrenia**, which holds that schizophrenia results from excess activity at dopamine synapses in certain brain areas. Although the concentration of dopamine in the brain is no higher than normal, the turnover is elevated, especially in the basal ganglia (Kumakura et al., 2007). That is, neurons release dopamine at a faster than average rate and synthesize more to replace the molecules that they do not reabsorb. Elevated dopamine release also occurs in people showing the first symptoms of schizophrenia (Howes et al., 2009).

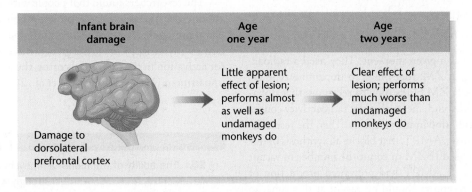

FIGURE 15.15 Delayed effects of brain damage in infant monkeys
After damage to the dorsolateral prefrontal cortex, monkeys are unimpaired at age 1 year but impaired later, when this area ordinarily matures. Researchers speculate that similar damage in humans might produce behavioral deficits not apparent until adulthood. *(Based on P. S. Goldman, 1976)*

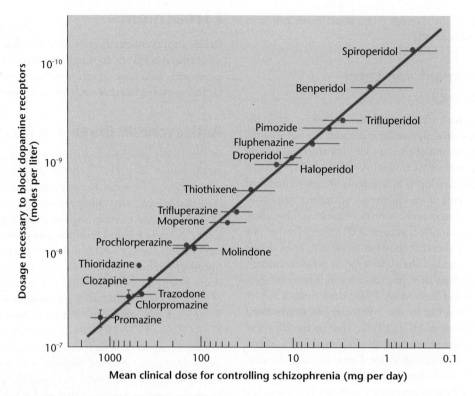

FIGURE 15.16 Dopamine-blocking effects of antipsychotic drugs
Drugs are arranged along the horizontal axis in terms of the average daily dose prescribed for patients with schizophrenia. (Horizontal lines indicate common ranges.) *Larger doses* are to the left and *smaller* doses are to the right so that *more effective* drugs are to the right. Along the vertical axis is a measurement of the amount of each drug required to achieve a certain degree of blockage of postsynaptic dopamine receptors. *Larger doses* are toward the bottom and *smaller* doses are toward the top so that the drugs on top are *more effective*. *(From "Antipsychotic Drug Doses and Neuroleptic/Dopamine Receptors," by P. Seeman, T. Lee, M. Chau-Wong, and K. Wong, Nature, 261, 1976, pp. 717–719. Copyright © 1976 Macmillan Magazines Limited. Reprinted by permission of Nature and Phillip Seeman.)*

Further support for the dopamine hypothesis comes from the fact that large, repeated use of amphetamine, methamphetamine, or cocaine induces **substance-induced psychotic disorder**, characterized by hallucinations and delusions, the positive symptoms of schizophrenia. Each of these drugs increases or prolongs the activity at dopamine synapses. LSD, which also produces psychotic symptoms, is best known for its effects on serotonin synapses, but it also stimulates dopamine synapses.

Researchers set out to measure the number of dopamine receptors occupied at a given moment. They used a radioactively labeled drug, IBZM, that binds to dopamine type D_2 receptors. Because IBZM binds only to receptors that dopamine did not already bind, measuring the radioactivity counts the number of vacant dopamine receptors. Then the researchers used a second drug, AMPT, that blocks all synthesis of dopamine and again used IBZM to count the number of vacant D_2 receptors. Because AMPT had prevented production of dopamine, *all* D_2 receptors should be vacant at this time, so the researchers got a count of the total. Then they subtracted the first count from the second count, yielding the number of D_2 receptors occupied by dopamine at the first count:

- First count: IBZM binds to all D_2 receptors not already attached to dopamine.

- Second count: IBZM binds to all D_2 receptors (because AMPT eliminated production of dopamine).

- Second count minus first count equals the number of D_2 receptors bound to dopamine at the first count.

The researchers found that people with schizophrenia had about twice as many D_2 receptors occupied as normal (Abi-Dargham et al., 2000). Another study found that among patients with schizophrenia, the greater the amount of D_2 receptor activation in the prefrontal cortex, the greater the cognitive impairment (Meyer-Lindenberg et al., 2002).

> **STOP & CHECK**

23. The ability of traditional antipsychotic drugs to relieve schizophrenia correlates strongly with what effect on neurotransmitters?

ANSWER

22. Their ability to relieve schizophrenia correlates strongly with how well they block activity at dopamine synapses.

Role of Glutamate

Abnormalities of dopamine transmission need not be the whole story for schizophrenia. According to the **glutamate hypothesis of schizophrenia**, the problem relates in part to deficient activity at glutamate synapses, especially in the prefrontal cortex. In many brain areas, dopamine inhibits glutamate release, or glutamate stimulates neurons that inhibit dopamine release. Therefore, increased dopamine would produce the same effects as decreased glutamate. The antipsychotic effects of drugs that block dopamine are compatible with either the excess-dopamine hypothesis or the deficient-glutamate hypothesis.

Schizophrenia is associated with lower than normal release of glutamate and fewer than normal receptors in the prefrontal cortex and hippocampus (Akbarian et al., 1995; Ibrahim et al., 2000; Tsai et al., 1995). Similar abnormalities occur in people known to be at high risk for developing schizophrenia, because of their family background and early behaviors (Valli et al., 2011). Mice with a deficiency of glutamate receptors show some abnormal behaviors, including increased anxiety, impaired memory, and impaired social behaviors (Belforte et al., 2010).

Further support for the glutamate hypothesis comes from the effects of **phencyclidine (PCP)** ("angel dust"), a drug that inhibits the NMDA glutamate receptors. At low doses, it produces intoxication and slurred speech. At larger doses, it produces both positive and negative symptoms of schizophrenia, including hallucinations, thought disorder, loss of emotions, and memory loss. PCP is an interesting model for schizophrenia in other regards also (Farber, Newcomer, & Olney, 1999; Olney & Farber, 1995):

- PCP and the related drug *ketamine* produce little if any psychotic response in preadolescents. Just as the symptoms of schizophrenia usually begin to emerge well after puberty, so do the psychotic effects of PCP and ketamine.

- LSD, amphetamine, and cocaine produce temporary schizophrenic symptoms in almost anyone, and the effects are not much worse in people with a history of schizophrenia than in anyone else. However, PCP produces severe effects for someone who has recovered from schizophrenia, including a long-lasting relapse.

It might seem that the best test of the glutamate hypothesis would be to administer glutamate itself. However, recall from Chapter 5 that strokes kill neurons by overstimulating glutamate synapses. Increasing overall brain glutamate would be risky. However, drugs that stimulate particular kinds of metabotropic glutamate receptors have shown much promise in treating schizophrenia (González-Maeso et al., 2008; Patil et al., 2007).

Furthermore, the NMDA glutamate receptor has a primary site that is activated by glutamate and a secondary site that is activated by glycine (Figure 15.17). Glycine by itself does not activate the receptor, but it increases the effectiveness of glutamate. Thus, an increase in glycine can increase the activity at NMDA synapses without overstimulating glutamate throughout the brain. Although glycine is not an effective an-

tipsychotic drug by itself, it increases the effects of other antipsychotic drugs, especially with regard to negative symptoms (Heresco-Levy et al., 1999; Heresco-Levy & Javitt, 2004). Studies on laboratory mice found that extra glycine decreases the behavioral responses to phencyclidine (Yee et al., 2006).

23. What drugs induce mainly the positive symptoms of schizophrenia? What drug can induce both positive and negative symptoms?

24. Why are the effects of antipsychotic drugs equally compatible with the dopamine hypothesis and the glutamate hypothesis?

ANSWERS

23. Repeated use of amphetamine, cocaine, or LSD induces positive symptoms, such as hallucinations and delusions. Phencyclidine induces both positive and negative symptoms. **24.** Dopamine inhibits glutamate cells in many areas, and glutamate stimulates neurons that inhibit dopamine. Therefore, the effects of increasing dopamine are similar to those of decreasing glutamate.

New Drugs

The brain has several dopamine pathways with different functions. The drugs that block dopamine synapses produce their benefits by acting on neurons in the **mesolimbocortical system**, a set of neurons that project from the midbrain tegmentum to the limbic system. However, the drugs also block dopamine neurons in the *mesostriatal system* that projects to the basal ganglia (Figure 15.18). The effect on the basal ganglia produces **tardive dyskinesia** (TARD-eev dis-kih-NEE-zhee-uh), characterized by tremors and other involuntary movements that develop gradually and to varying degrees among different patients (Kiriakakis, Bhatia, Quinn, & Marsden, 1998).

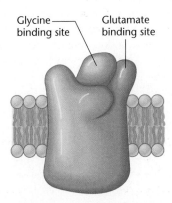

Glycine binding site   Glutamate binding site

FIGURE 15.17 An NMDA glutamate receptor
NMDA glutamate receptors have a primary binding site for glutamate and a secondary binding site for glycine. Glycine increases the effect of glutamate. (© Cengage Learning 2013)

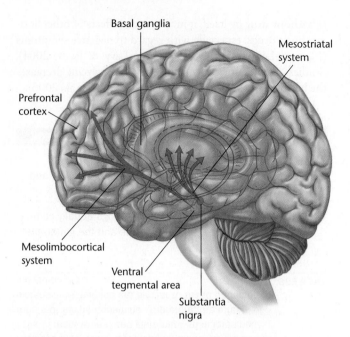

FIGURE 15.18 Two major dopamine pathways
Overactivity of the mesolimbocortical system is linked to the symptoms of schizophrenia. The path to the basal ganglia is associated with tardive dyskinesia, a movement disorder. *(Adapted from Valzelli, 1980)*

Once tardive dyskinesia emerges, it can last long after someone quits the drug (Kiriakakis et al., 1998). Consequently, the best strategy is to prevent it from starting. Certain new drugs called **second-generation antipsychotics**, or atypical antipsychotics, alleviate schizophrenia without producing movement problems (Figure 15.19). The most common of these drugs are clozapine, amisulpride, risperidone, olanzapine, and aripiprazole. They are more effective than older drugs at treating the negative symptoms of schizophrenia, and they are now used more widely (J. M. Davis, Chen, & Glick, 2003; Edlinger et al., 2005). Unfortunately, although

they avoid tardive dyskinesia, they produce other side effects, including weight gain and impairment of the immune system. All things considered, the atypical antipsychotics do not improve overall quality of life more than the older drugs (Crossley & Constante, 2010; P. B. Jones et al., 2006).

Compared to drugs like haloperidol, the second-generation antipsychotics have less effect on dopamine type D_2 receptors but more strongly antagonize serotonin type $5\text{-}HT_2$ receptors (Kapur et al., 2000; Meltzer, Matsubara, & Lee, 1989; Mrzljak et al., 1996; Roth, Willins, Kristiansen, & Kroeze, 1999). They also increase the release of glutamate (Melone et al., 2001). In short, schizophrenia is neither a one-gene disorder nor a one-neurotransmitter disorder.

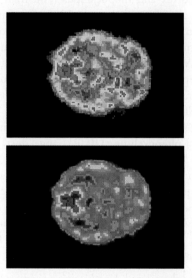

FIGURE 15.19 PET scans of a patient with schizophrenia
These PET scans of a patient with schizophrenia (a) taking clozapine and (b) during a period off the drug demonstrate that clozapine increases brain activity in many brain areas. Red indicates the highest activity, followed by yellow, green, and blue. *(Hank Morgan/Science Source/Photo Researchers)*

Many Remaining Mysteries

A great deal about abnormal psychology remains unknown. One of the most fundamental questions is whether it even makes sense to distinguish among different disorders. Some of the drugs originally approved for schizophrenia are often effective in relieving depression or bipolar disorder. Antidepressant drugs help relieve anxiety disorders. Drugs intended for bipolar disorder help many people with attention-deficit disorder. If the same treatments work for different disorders, maybe those disorders are not so different after all (Dean, 2011). Another major mystery is why concordance for schizophrenia in monozygotic twins is only about 50%. If they share their genes and presumably nearly the same environment, why isn't concordance nearly

100%? Also, why are the treatments for both depression and schizophrenia highly successful for some people and not at all for others? Perhaps you can name additional puzzles.

Research is a little like reading a good mystery novel that presents a mixture of important clues and irrelevant information. In research on schizophrenia, we have an enormous amount of information, but also major gaps and occasional points that don't seem to fit. The final chapter of our mystery novel on schizophrenia isn't complete. However, although researchers have not yet solved the mystery, it should also be clear that they have made progress. It will be fascinating to see what develops in future research.

SUMMARY

1. Positive symptoms of schizophrenia (behaviors that are not present in most other people) include hallucinations, delusions, inappropriate emotions, bizarre behaviors, and thought disorder. **472**

2. Negative symptoms (normal behaviors absent that should be present) include deficits of social interaction, emotional expression, and speech. **472**

3. Studies of twins and adopted children imply a genetic predisposition to schizophrenia. However, the adoption studies do not distinguish between the roles of genetics and prenatal environment. **474**

4. So far, researchers have not located any gene that is strongly linked with schizophrenia in general. A promising hypothesis is that schizophrenia results from new mutations or deletions of any of the hundreds of genes that are important for brain development. **475**

5. According to the neurodevelopmental hypothesis, either genes or difficulties early in life impair brain development in ways that increase vulnerability to later insults and predispose to behavioral abnormalities beginning in early adulthood. **476**

6. The probability of schizophrenia is slightly higher than average for those who were subjected to difficulties before or at the time of birth or during early infancy. **476**

7. Some people with schizophrenia show mild abnormalities of brain development, especially in the temporal

and frontal lobes. They also show cognitive deficits that make sense if their frontal and temporal lobes are less than fully functional. **477**

8. Parts of the prefrontal cortex are very slow to mature. It is plausible that early disruption of those areas might produce behavioral symptoms that become manifest as schizophrenia in young adults. **479**

9. According to the dopamine hypothesis, schizophrenia is due to excess dopamine activity. Drugs that block dopamine synapses reduce the positive symptoms of schizophrenia, and drugs that increase dopamine activity induce the positive symptoms. **479**

10. According to the glutamate hypothesis, part of the problem is deficient glutamate activity. Phencyclidine, which blocks NMDA glutamate synapses, produces both positive and negative symptoms of schizophrenia, especially in people predisposed to schizophrenia. **481**

11. Prolonged use of antipsychotic drugs may produce tardive dyskinesia, a movement disorder. Second-generation antipsychotic drugs relieve both positive and negative symptoms without producing tardive dyskinesia. However, these drugs apparently do not improve overall quality of life any better than the original drugs do. **481**

KEY TERMS

Terms are defined in the module on the page number indicated. They're also presented in alphabetical order with definitions in the book's Subject Index/Glossary, which begins on page 561. Interactive flashcards and crossword puzzles are among the online resources available to help you learn these terms and the concepts they represent.

THOUGHT QUESTION

On average, people who use much marijuana are more likely than others to develop schizophrenia. However, over the last several decades, the use of marijuana has increased substantially while the prevalence of schizophrenia has remained steady or decreased. What would be a reasonable conclusion about the relationship between marijuana use and schizophrenia?

CHAPTER 15   Interactive Exploration and Study

The **Psychology CourseMate** for this text brings chapter topics to life with interactive learning, study, and exam preparation tools, including quizzes and flashcards for the Key Concepts that appear throughout each module, as well as an interactive media-rich eBook version of the text that is fully searchable and includes highlighting and note-taking capabilities and interactive versions of the book's **Stop & Check** quizzes and **Try It Yourself Online** activities. The site also features **Virtual Biological Psychology Labs**, **videos**, and **animations** to help you better understand concepts—logon and learn more at **www.cengagebrain.com**, which is your gateway to all of this text's complimentary and premium resources, including the following:

Virtual Biological Psychology Labs

Explore the experiments that led to modern-day understanding of biopsychology with the Virtual Biological Psychology Labs, featuring a realistic lab environment that allows you to conduct experiments and evaluate data to better understand how scientists came to the conclusions presented in your text. The labs cover a range of topics, including perception, motivation, cognition, and more. You may purchase access at **www.cengagebrain.com**, or login at **login.cengagebrain.com** if an access card was included with your text.

Videos

Emilie, a Portrait of Bipolar

Also available—
- Magnetic Stimulation to the Brain
- Andre, a Portrait of Schizophrenia

Animations

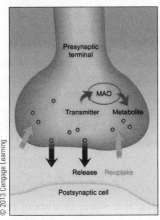

Presynaptic
terminal

MAO

Transmitter   Metabolite

Release   Reuptake

Postsynaptic cell

Antidepressants

Also available—
- Saccades and Schizophrenia   **xxx**

Suggestions for Further Exploration

Books

Andreasen, N. C. (2001). *Brave new brain.* New York: Oxford University Press. Excellent discussion of biological research on psychiatric disorders by one of the leading researchers dealing with schizophrenia.

Kirsch, I. (2010). *The Emperor's New Drugs.* New York: Basic Books. A highly skeptical discussion of the effectiveness or ineffectiveness of antidepressant drugs.

Websites

The Psychology CourseMate for this text provides regularly updated links to relevant online resources for this chapter concerning depression and schizophrenia.

Brief, Basic Chemistry

MAIN IDEAS

1. All matter is composed of a limited number of elements that combine in endless ways.
2. Atoms, the component parts of an element, consist of protons, neutrons, and electrons. Most atoms can gain or lose electrons, or share them with other atoms.
3. The chemistry of life is predominantly the chemistry of carbon compounds.

▌ Introduction

To understand certain aspects of biological psychology, particularly the action potential and the molecular mechanisms of synaptic transmission, you need to know a little about chemistry. If you have taken a high school or college course and remember the material reasonably well, you should have no trouble with the chemistry in this text. If your knowledge of chemistry is pretty hazy, this appendix will help. (If you plan to take other courses in biological psychology, you should study as much biology and chemistry as possible.)

▌ Elements and Compounds

If you look around, you will see an enormous variety of materials—dirt, water, wood, plastic, metal, cloth, glass, your own body. Every object is composed of a small number of basic building blocks. If a piece of wood catches fire, it breaks down into ashes, gases, and water vapor. The same is true of your body. An investigator could take those ashes, gases, and water and break them down by chemical and electrical means into carbon, oxygen, hydrogen, nitrogen, and a few other materials. Eventually, however, the investigator arrives at a set of materials that cannot be broken down further: Pure carbon or pure oxygen, for example, cannot be converted into anything simpler, at least not by ordinary chemical means. (High-power bombardment with subatomic particles is another story.) The matter we see is composed of **elements** (materials that cannot be broken down into other materials) and **compounds** (materials made up by combining elements).

Chemists have found 92 elements in nature, and they have constructed more in the laboratory. (Actually, one of the 92—technetium—is so rare as to be virtually unknown

in nature.) Figure A.1, the periodic table, lists each of these elements. Of these, only a few are important for life on Earth. Table A.1 shows the elements commonly found in the human body.

Note that each element has a one- or two-letter abbreviation, such as O for oxygen, H for hydrogen, and Ca for calcium. These are internationally accepted symbols that facilitate communication among chemists who speak different languages. For example, element number 19 is called potassium in English, potassio in Italian, kālijs in Latvian, and draslík in Czech. But chemists in all countries use the symbol K (from *kalium*, the Latin word for "potassium"). Similarly, the symbol for sodium is Na (from *natrium*, the Latin word for "sodium"), and the symbol for iron is Fe (from the Latin word *ferrum*).

A compound is represented by the symbols for the elements that compose it. For example, NaCl stands for sodium chloride (common table salt). H_2O, the symbol for water, indicates that water consists of two parts of hydrogen and one part of oxygen.

TABLE A.1	The Elements That Compose Almost All of the Human Body	
Element	**Symbol**	**Percentage by Weight in Human Body**
Oxygen	O	65
Carbon	C	18
Hydrogen	H	10
Nitrogen	N	3
Calcium	Ca	2
Phosphorus	P	1.1
Potassium	K	0.35
Sulfur	S	0.25
Sodium	Na	0.15
Chlorine	Cl	0.15
Magnesium	Mg	0.05
Iron	Fe	Trace
Copper	Cu	Trace
Iodine	I	Trace
Fluorine	F	Trace
Manganese	Mn	Trace
Zinc	Zn	Trace
Selenium	Se	Trace
Molybdenum	Mo	Trace

Periodic Table of the Elements

Period	1 IA (Alkali Metals)	2 IIA (Alkaline Earth Metals)	3 IIIB (Transition Elements)	4 IVB	5 VB	6 VIB	7 VIIB	8 VIIIB	9 VIIIB	10 VIIIB	11 IB	12 IIB	13 IIIA	14 IVA	15 VA	16 VIA	17 VIIA (Halogens)	18 VIIA (Noble Gases)
1	1 H hydrogen 1.008																	2 He helium 4.003
2	3 Li lithium 6.941	4 Be beryllium 9.012											5 B boron 10.81	6 C carbon 12.011	7 N nitrogen 14.007	8 O oxygen 16.0	9 F fluorine 18.999	10 Ne neon 20.179
3	11 Na sodium 22.99	12 Mg magnesium 24.305											13 Al aluminum 26.982	14 Si silicon 28.085	15 P phosphorous 30.974	16 S sulfur 32.060	17 Cl chlorine 35.453	18 Ar argon 39.948
4	19 K potassium 39.098	20 Ca calcium 40.08	21 Sc scandium 44.955	22 Ti titanium 47.90	23 V vanadium 50.941	24 Cr chromium 51.996	25 Mn manganese 54.938	26 Fe iron 55.847	27 Co cobalt 58.933	28 Ni nickel 58.70	29 Cu copper 63.546	30 Zn zinc 65.38	31 Ga gallium 69.72	32 Ge germanium 72.59	33 As arsenic 74.922	34 Se selenium 78.96	35 Br bromine 79.904	36 Kr krypton 83.80
5	37 Rb rubidium 85.468	38 Sr strontium 87.62	39 Y yttrium 88.906	40 Zr zirconium 91.22	41 Nb niobium 92.906	42 Mo molybdenum 95.940	43 Tc technetium (97)	44 Ru ruthenium 101.07	45 Rh rhodium 102.905	46 Pd palladium 106.40	47 Ag silver 107.868	48 Cd cadmium 112.41	49 In indium 114.82	50 Sn tin 118.69	51 Sb antimony 121.75	52 Te tellurium 127.60	53 I iodine 126.904	54 Xe xenon 131.30
6	55 Cs cesium 132.905	56 Ba barium 137.33	57 La lanthanum 138.906 †	72 Hf hafnium 178.49	73 Ta tantalum 180.948	74 W tungsten 183.85	75 Re rhenium 186.207	76 Os osmium 190.20	77 Ir iridum 192.22	78 Pt platinum 195.09	79 Au gold 196.967	80 Hg mercury 200.59	81 Tl thallium 204.37	82 Pb lead 207.20	83 Bi bismuth 208.980	84 Po polonium (209)	85 At astatine (210)	86 Rn radon (222)
7	87 Fr francium (223)	88 Ra radium 226.025	89 Ac actinium (227) ‡	104 Rf rutherfordium (261)	105 Db dubnium (262)	106 Sg seaborgium (266)	107 Bh bohrium (264)	108 Hs hassium (269)	109 Mt meitnerium (268)	110 Ds darmstadtium (271)	111 Rg roentgenium (272)	112 Cn copernicium (285)	113 Uut ununtrium (284)	114 Uuq ununquadium (289)	115 Uup ununpentium (288)	116 Uuh ununhexium (292)	117 Uus ununseptium (?)	118 Uuo ununoctium (?)

Inner Transition Elements

† Lanthanides 6	58 Ce cerium 140.12	59 Pr praseodymium 140.908	60 Nd neodymium 144.24	61 Pm prometheum (145)	62 Sm samarium 150.40	63 Eu europium 151.96	64 Gd gadolinium 157.25	65 Tb terbium 158.925	66 Dy dysprosium 162.50	67 Ho holmium 164.93	68 Er erbium 167.26	69 Tm thulium 168.934	70 Yb ytterbium 173.04	71 Lu lutetium 174.97
‡ Actinides 7	90 Th thorium 232.038	91 Pa protactinium 231.036	92 U uranium 238.029	93 Np neptunium (237)	94 Pu plutonium (244)	95 Am americium (243)	96 Cm curium (247)	97 Bk berkelium (247)	98 Cf californium (251)	99 Es einsteinium (254)	100 Fm fermium (257)	101 Md mendelevium (258)	102 No nobelium (255)	103 Lr lawrencium (260)

Key: atomic number — 1; symbol of element — H; element name — hydrogen; atomic weight — 1.008

FIGURE A.1 The periodic table of chemistry

It is called "periodic" because certain properties show up at periodic intervals. For example, the column from lithium down consists of metals that readily form salts. The column at the far right consists of gases that do not readily form compounds. Elements 112–118 have only tentative names and symbols.

Atoms and Molecules

A block of iron can be chopped finer and finer until it is divided into tiny pieces that cannot be broken down any further. These pieces are called **atoms**. Every element is composed of atoms. A compound, such as water, can also be divided into tinier and tinier pieces. The smallest possible piece of a compound is called a **molecule**. A molecule of water can be further decomposed into two atoms of hydrogen and one atom of oxygen, but when that happens the compound is broken and is no longer water. A molecule is the smallest piece of a compound that retains the properties of the compound.

An atom is composed of subatomic particles, including protons, neutrons, and electrons. A proton has a positive electrical charge, a neutron has a neutral charge, and an electron has a negative charge. The nucleus of an atom—its center—contains one or more protons plus a number of neutrons. Electrons are found in the space around the nucleus. Because an atom has the same number of protons as electrons, the electrical charges balance out. (Ions, which we will soon consider, have an imbalance of positive and negative charges.)

The difference between one element and another is in the number of protons in the nucleus of the atom. Hydrogen has just one proton, for example, and oxygen has eight. The number of protons is the **atomic number** of the element; in the periodic table it is recorded at the top of the square for each element. The number at the bottom is the element's **atomic weight**, which indicates the weight of an atom relative to the weight of one proton. A proton has a weight of one unit, a neutron has a weight just trivially greater than one, and an electron has a weight just trivially greater than zero. The atomic weight of the element is the number of protons in the atom plus the average number of neutrons. For example, most hydrogen atoms have one proton and no neutrons; a few atoms per thousand have one or two neutrons, giving an average atomic weight of 1.008. Sodium ions have 11 protons; most also have 12 neutrons, and the atomic weight is slightly less than 23. (Can you figure out the number of neutrons in the average potassium atom? Refer to Figure A.1.)

Ions and Chemical Bonds

An atom that has gained or lost one or more electrons is called an **ion**. For example, if sodium and chloride come together, the sodium atoms readily lose one electron each and the chloride atoms gain one each. The result is a set of positively charged sodium ions (indicated Na^+) and negatively charged chloride ions (Cl^-). Potassium atoms, like sodium atoms, tend to lose an electron and to become positively charged ions (K^+); calcium ions tend to lose two electrons and gain a double positive charge (Ca^{++}).

Because positive charges attract negative charges, sodium ions attract chloride ions. When dry, sodium and chloride form a crystal structure, as Figure A.2 shows. (In water solution, the two kinds of ions move about haphazardly, occasionally attracting one another but then pulling apart.) The attraction of positive ions for negative ions forms an **ionic bond**. In other cases, instead of transferring an electron from one atom to another,

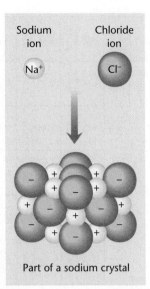

FIGURE A.2 The crystal structure of sodium chloride
Each sodium ion is surrounded by chloride ions, and each chloride ion is surrounded by sodium ions; no ion is bound to any other single ion in particular.

some pairs of atoms share electrons with each other, forming a **covalent bond**. For example, two hydrogen atoms bind, as shown in Figure A.3, and two hydrogen atoms bind with an oxygen atom, as shown in Figure A.4. Atoms that are attached by a covalent bond cannot move independently of one another.

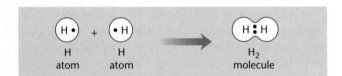

FIGURE A.3 Structure of a hydrogen molecule
A hydrogen atom has one electron; in the compound the two atoms share the two electrons equally.

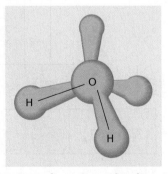

FIGURE A.4 Structure of a water molecule
The oxygen atom shares a pair of electrons with each hydrogen atom. Oxygen holds the electrons more tightly, making the oxygen part of the molecule more negatively charged than the hydrogen part of the molecule.

Reactions of Carbon Atoms

Living organisms depend on the enormously versatile compounds of carbon. Because of the importance of these compounds for life, the chemistry of carbon is known as organic chemistry.

Carbon atoms form covalent bonds with hydrogen, oxygen, and a number of other elements. They also form covalent bonds with other carbon atoms. Two carbon atoms may share from one to three pairs of electrons. Such bonds can be indicated as follows:

C—C   Two atoms share one pair of electrons.
C=C   Two atoms share two pairs of electrons.
C≡C   Two atoms share three pairs of electrons.

Each carbon atom ordinarily forms four covalent bonds, either with other carbon atoms, with hydrogen atoms, or with other atoms. Many biologically important compounds include long chains of carbon compounds linked to one another, such as:

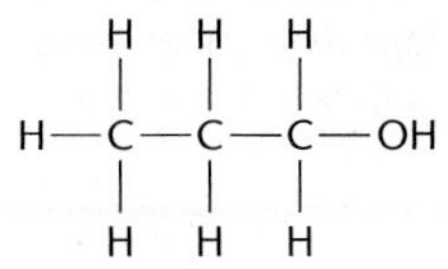

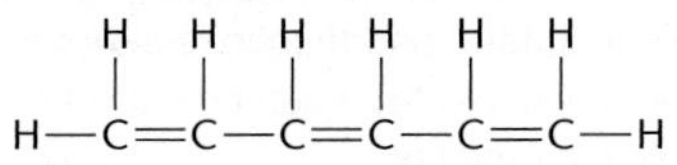

Note that each carbon atom has a total of four bonds, counting each double bond as two. In some molecules, the carbon chain loops around to form a ring:

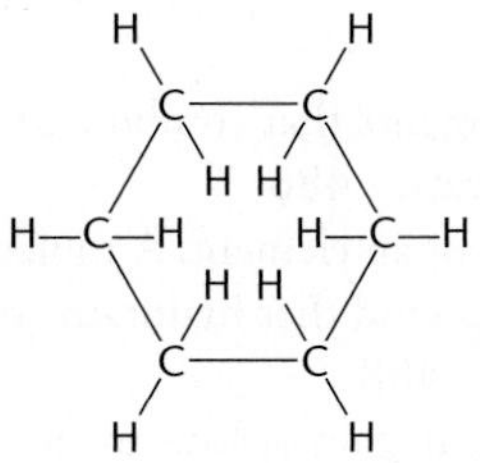

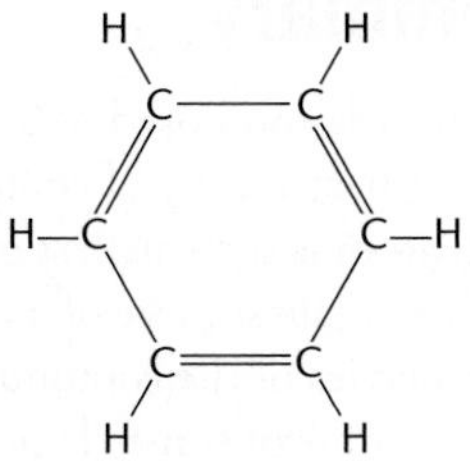

Ringed structures are common in organic chemistry. To simplify the diagrams chemists often omit the hydrogen atoms. You can simply assume that each carbon atom in the diagram has four covalent bonds and that all the bonds not shown are with hydrogen atoms. To further simplify the diagrams, chemists often omit the carbon atoms themselves, showing only the carbon-to-carbon bonds. For example, the two molecules shown in the previous diagram might be rendered as follows:

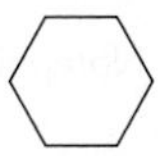

If a particular carbon atom has a bond with some atom other than hydrogen, the diagram shows the exception. For example, in each of the two molecules diagrammed below, one carbon has a bond with an oxygen atom, which in turn has a bond with a hydrogen atom. All the bonds that are not shown are carbon–hydrogen bonds.

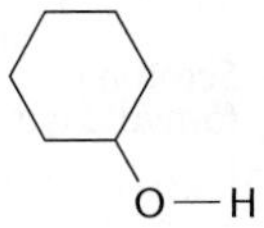

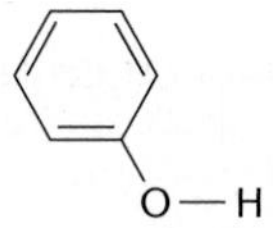

Figure A.5 illustrates some carbon compounds that are critical for animal life. Purines and pyrimidines form the central structure of DNA and RNA, the chemicals responsible for heredity. Proteins, fats, and carbohydrates are the primary types of fuel that the body uses. Figure A.6 displays the chemical structures of seven neurotransmitters that are extensively discussed in this text.

Chemical Reactions in the Body

A living organism is an immensely complicated, coordinated set of chemical reactions. Life requires that the rate of each reaction be carefully regulated. In many cases one reaction

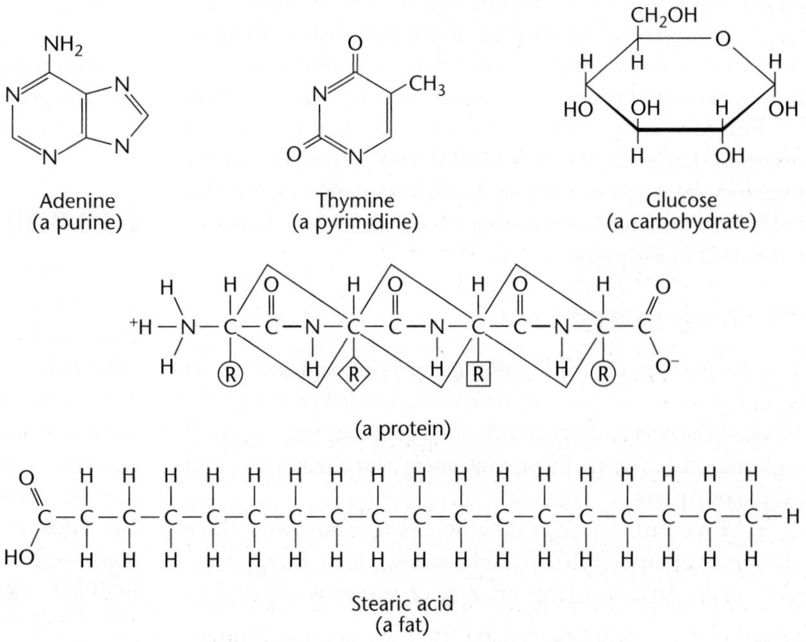

Adenine
(a purine)

Thymine
(a pyrimidine)

Glucose
(a carbohydrate)

(a protein)

FIGURE A.5 Structures of some important biological molecules
The R in the protein represents a point of attachment for various chains that differ from one amino acid to another. Actual proteins are much longer than the chemical shown here.

Stearic acid
(a fat)

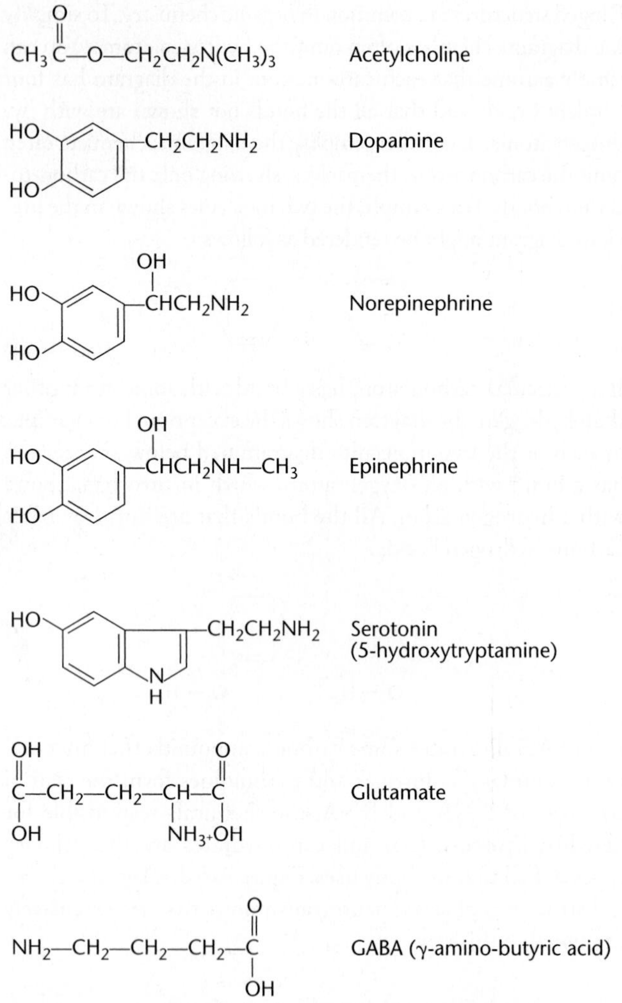

$$CH_3 \overset{\overset{O}{\|}}{C} - O - CH_2CH_2N(CH_3)_3 \qquad \text{Acetylcholine}$$

Dopamine — $HO-\langle\rangle-CH_2CH_2NH_2$

Norepinephrine — $HO-\langle\rangle-\overset{\overset{OH}{|}}{C}HCH_2NH_2$

Epinephrine — $HO-\langle\rangle-\overset{\overset{OH}{|}}{C}HCH_2NH-CH_3$

Serotonin (5-hydroxytryptamine) — $CH_2CH_2NH_2$

Glutamate

GABA (γ-amino-butyric acid) — $NH_2-CH_2-CH_2-CH_2-\overset{\overset{O}{\|}}{C}-OH$

FIGURE A.6 Chemical structures of seven abundant neurotransmitters

produces a chemical that enters into another reaction, which produces another chemical that enters into another reaction, and so forth. If any one of those reactions is too rapid compared to the others, the chemical it produces will accumulate to possibly harmful levels. If a reaction is too slow, it will not produce enough product and the next reaction will be stalled.

Enzymes are proteins that control the rate of chemical reactions. Each reaction is controlled by a particular enzyme. Enzymes are a type of catalyst. A catalyst is any chemical that facilitates a reaction among other chemicals without being altered itself in the process.

The Role of ATP

The body relies on **ATP (adenosine triphosphate)** as its main way of sending energy where it is needed (Figure A.7). Much of the energy derived from food goes into forming ATP molecules that eventually provide energy for the muscles and other body parts.

ATP consists of adenosine bound to ribose and three phosphate groups (PO_3). Phosphates form high-energy covalent bonds. That is, a large amount of energy is required to

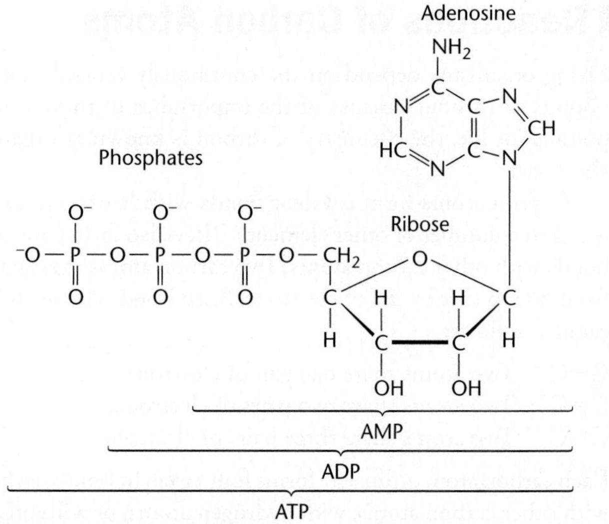

FIGURE A.7 ATP, composed of adenosine, ribose, and three phosphates
ATP can lose one phosphate group to form ADP (adenosine diphosphate) and then lose another one to form AMP (adenosine monophosphate). Each time it breaks off a phosphate group, it releases energy.

form the bonds and a large amount of energy is released when they break. ATP can break off one or two of its three phosphates to provide energy.

▌Summary

1. Matter is composed of 92 elements that combine to form an endless variety of compounds. **486**
2. An atom is the smallest piece of an element. A molecule is the smallest piece of a compound that maintains the properties of the compound. **488**
3. The atoms of some elements can gain or lose an electron, thus becoming ions. Positively charged ions attract negatively charged ions, forming an ionic bond. In some cases two or more atoms may share electrons, thus forming a covalent bond. **488**
4. The principal carrier of energy in the body is a chemical called ATP. **490**

▌Terms

atom 488
atomic number 488
atomic weight 488
ATP (adenosine triphosphate) 490
compound 486
covalent bond 488
element 486
enzyme 490
ion 488
ionic bond 488
molecule 488

Society for Neuroscience Policies on the Use of Animals and Human Subjects in Neuroscience Research

Policy on the Use of Animals in Neuroscience Research

The Policy on the Use of Animals in Neuroscience Research affects a number of the Society for Neuroscience's functions that involve making decisions about animal research conducted by individual members. These include the scheduling of scientific presentations at the Annual Meeting, the review and publication of original research papers in *The Journal of Neuroscience*, and the defense of members whose ethical use of animals in research is questioned by antivivisectionists. The responsibility for implementing the policy in each of these areas will rest with the relevant administrative body (Program Committee, Publications Committee, Editorial Board, and Committee on Animals in Research, respectively), in consultation with Council.

Introduction

The Society for Neuroscience, as a professional society for basic and clinical researchers in neuroscience, endorses and supports the appropriate and responsible use of animals as experimental subjects. Knowledge generated by neuroscience research on animals has led to important advances in the understanding of diseases and disorders that affect the nervous system and in the development of better treatments that reduce suffering in humans and animals. This knowledge also makes a critical contribution to our understanding of ourselves, the complexities of our brains, and what makes us human. Continued progress in understanding how the brain works and further advances in treating and curing disorders of the nervous system require investigation of complex functions at all levels in the living nervous system. Because no adequate alternatives exist, much of this research must be done on animal subjects. The Society takes the position that neuroscientists have an obligation to contribute to this progress through responsible and humane research on animals.

Several functions of the Society are related to the use of animals in research. A number of these involve decisions about research conducted by individual members of the Society, including the scheduling of scientific presentations at the Annual Meeting, the review and publication of original research papers in *The Journal of Neuroscience*, and the defense of members whose ethical use of animals in research is questioned by antivivisectionists. Each of these functions, by establishing explicit support of the Society for the research of individual members, defines a relationship between the Society and its members. The purpose of this document is to outline the policy that guides that relationship. Compliance with the following policy will be an important factor in determining the suitability of research for presentation at the Annual Meeting or for publication in *The Journal of Neuroscience*, and in situations where the Society is asked to provide public and active support for a member whose use of animals in research has been questioned.

General Policy

Neuroscience research uses complicated, often invasive methods, each of which is associated with different problems, risks, and specific technical considerations. An experimental method that would be deemed inappropriate for one kind of research may be the method of choice for another kind of research. It is therefore impossible for the Society to define specific policies and procedures for the care and use of all research animals and for the design and conduct of every neuroscience experiment.

The U.S. *Public Health Service Policy on Humane Care and Use of Laboratory Animals* (PHS Policy) and the *Guide for the Care and Use of Laboratory Animals* (the Guide) describe a set of general policies and procedures designed to ensure the humane and appropriate use of live vertebrate animals in all forms of biomedical research. The Society finds the policies and procedures set forth in the PHS Policy and the Guide to be both necessary and sufficient to ensure a high standard of animal care and use and adopts them as its official "Policy on the Use of Animals in Neuroscience Research" (Society Policy). All Society members are expected to conduct their animal research in compliance with the Society Policy and are required to verify that they have done so when submitting abstracts for presentation at the Annual Meeting or manuscripts for publication in *The Journal of Neuroscience*. Adherence to the Society Policy is also an important step toward receiving help from the Society in responding to questions about a member's use of animals in research. A complete description of the Society's policy and procedures for defending members whose research comes under attack is given in the Society's *Handbook for the Use of Animals in Neuroscience Research*.

Local Committee Review

An important element of the Society Policy is the establishment of a local committee that is charged with reviewing and approving all proposed animal care and use procedures. In addition to scientists experienced in research involving animals and a veterinarian, the membership of this local committee should include an individual who is not affiliated with the member's institution in any other way. In reviewing a proposed use of animals, the committee should evaluate the adequacy of institutional policies, animal husbandry, veterinary care, and the physical plant. Specific attention should be paid to proposed procedures for animal procurement, quarantine and stabilization, separation by species, disease diagnosis and treatment, anesthesia and analgesia, surgery and postsurgical care, and euthanasia. The review committee also should ensure that procedures involving live vertebrate animals are designed and performed with due consideration of their relevance to human or animal health, the advancement of knowledge, or the good of society. This review and approval of a member's use of live vertebrate animals in research by a local committee is an essential component of the Society Policy. Assistance in developing appropriate animal care and use procedures and establishing a local review committee can be obtained from the documents listed here and from the Society.

Other Laws, Regulations, and Policies

In addition to complying with the policy described above, Regular Members (i.e., North American residents) of the Society must also adhere to all relevant national, state, or local laws and/or regulations that govern their use of animals in neuroscience research. Thus, U.S. members must observe the U.S. Animal Welfare Act (as amended in 1985) and its implementing regulations from the U.S. Department of Agriculture. Canadian members must abide by the *Guide to the Care and Use of Experimental Animals,* and members in Mexico must comply with the *Reglamento de la Ley General de Salud en Materia de Investigacion para la Salud* of the Secretaria de Salud (published on Jan. 6, 1987). Similarly, in addition to complying with the laws and regulations of their home countries, Foreign Members of the Society should adhere to the official Society Policy outlined here.

Recommended References

"Anesthesia and paralysis in experimental animals." (1984). *Visual Neuroscience, 1,* 421–426.

The Biomedical Investigator's Handbook for Researchers Using Animal Models. (1987). Foundation for Biomedical Research, 818 Connecticut Ave., N.W., Suite 303, Washington, D.C. 20006.

Guide for the Care and Use of Laboratory Animals (7th ed. 1996). NRC (National Research Council), Institute of Laboratory Animal Resources, National Academy of Sciences, 2101 Constitution Ave., N.W., Washington, D.C. 20418.

Guide to the Care and Use of Experimental Animals (2nd ed., vol. 1). (1993). Canadian Council on Animal Care, 350 Albert St., Suite 315, Ottawa, Ontario, Canada K1R 1B1.

Handbook for the Use of Animals in Neuroscience Research. (1991). Society for Neuroscience, 11 Dupont Circle, N.W., Suite 500, Washington, D.C. 20036.

OPRR Public Health Service Policy on Humane Care and Use of Laboratory Animals (revised Sept. 1986). Office for Protection from Research Risks, NIH, 6100 Executive Blvd., Suite 3B01-MSC 7507, Rockville, MD 20892-7507.

Preparation and Maintenance of Higher Mammals During Neuroscience Experiments. Report of a National Institutes of Health Workshop. (March 1991). NIH Publication No. 91-3207, National Eye Institute, Bldg. 31, Rm. 6A47, Bethesda, MD 20892.

Seventh Title of the Regulations of the General Law of Health, Regarding Health Research. In: *Laws and Codes of Mexico.* (1995). Published in the Porrua Collection (12th updated ed., pp. 430–431). Porrua Publishers, Mexico.

The following principles, based largely on the PHS Policy, can be a useful guide in the design and implementation of experimental procedures involving laboratory animals.

Animals selected for a procedure should be of an appropriate species and quality and the minimum number required to obtain valid results.

Proper use of animals, including the avoidance or minimization of discomfort, distress, and pain, when consistent with sound scientific practices, is imperative.

Procedures with animals that may cause more than momentary or slight pain or distress should be performed with appropriate sedation, analgesia, or anesthesia. Surgical or other painful procedures should not be performed on unanesthetized animals paralyzed by chemical agents.

Postoperative care of animals shall be such as to minimize discomfort and pain and, in any case, shall be equivalent to accepted practices in schools of veterinary medicine.

Animals that would otherwise suffer severe or chronic pain or distress that cannot be relieved should be painlessly killed at the end of the procedure or, if appropriate, during the procedure. If the study requires the death of the animal, the animal must be killed in a humane manner.

Living conditions should be appropriate for the species and contribute to the animals' health and comfort. Normally, the housing, feeding, and care of all animals used for biomedical purposes must be directed by a veterinarian or other scientist trained and experienced in the proper care, handling, and use of the species being maintained or studied. In any case, appropriate veterinary care shall be provided.

Exceptions to these principles require careful consideration and should only be made by an appropriate review group such as an institutional animal care and use committee.

Policy on the Use of Human Subjects in Neuroscience Research

Experimental procedures involving human subjects must have been conducted in conformance with the policies and principles contained in the Federal Policy for the Protection of

Human Subjects (United States Office of Science and Technology Policy) and in the Declaration of Helsinki. When publishing a paper in *The Journal of Neuroscience* or submitting an abstract for presentation at the Annual Meeting, authors must sign a statement of compliance with this policy.

Recommended References

Declaration of Helsinki. (Adopted in 1964 by the 18th World Medical Assembly in Helsinki, Finland, and revised by the 29th World Medical Assembly in Tokyo in 1975.) (1984). In A.C. Varga (Ed.), *The Main Issue in Bioethics Revised Edition.* New York: Paulist Press, 1984.

Federal Policy for the Protection of Human Subjects; Notices and Rules. (June 18, 1991). *Federal Register.* 56 (117) 28002–28007.

http://www.apa.org/science/anguide.html
This Website presents the ethical guidelines adopted by the American Psychological Association. They are largely similar to those of the Neuroscience Society.

References

Numbers in parentheses following entries indicate the chapter in which a reference is cited.

Abbar, M., Couret, P., Bellivier, F., Leboyer, M., Boulenger, J. P., Castelhau, D., et al. (2001). Suicide attempts and the tryptophan hydroxylase gene. *Molecular Psychiatry, 6,* 268–273. (12)

Abbott, N. J., Rönnback, L., & Hansson, E. (2006). Astrocyte-endothelial interactions at the blood–brain barrier. *Nature Reviews Neuroscience, 7,* 41–53. (2)

AbdelMalik, P., Husted, J., Chow, E. W. C., & Bassett, A. S. (2003). Childhood head injury and expression of schizophrenia in multiply affected families. *Archives of General Psychiatry, 60,* 231–236. (15)

Abi-Dargham, A., Rodenhiser, J., Printz, D., Zea-Ponce, Y., Gil, R., Kegeles, L. S., et al. (2000). Increased baseline occupancy of D2 receptors by dopamine in schizophrenia. *Proceedings of the National Academy of Sciences, USA, 97,* 8104–8109. (15)

Abrahamsen, B., Zhao, J., Asante, C. O., Cendan, C. M., Marsh, S., Martinez-Barbera, J. P., et al. (2008). The cell and molecular basis of mechanical, cold, and inflammatory pain. *Science, 321,* 702–705. (7)

Abrahamsson, N., & Hyltenstam, K. (2009). Age of onset and nativelikeness in a second language: Listener perception versus linguistic scrutiny. *Language Learning, 59,* 249–306. (14)

Abramov, E., Dolev, I., Fogel, H., Ciccotosto, G. D., Ruff, E., & Slutsky, I. (2009). Amyloid-β as a positive endogenous regulator of release probability at hippocampal synapses. *Nature Neuroscience, 12,* 1567–1576. (13)

Adamec, R. E., Stark-Adamec, C., & Livingston, K. E. (1980). The development of predatory aggression and defense in the domestic cat (*Felis catus*): 3. Effects on development of hunger between 180 and 365 days of age. *Behavioral and Neural Biology, 30,* 435–447. (12)

Adams, D. B., Gold, A. R., & Burt, A. D. (1978). Rise in female-initiated sexual activity at ovulation and its suppression by oral contraceptives. *New England Journal of Medicine, 299,* 1145–1150. (11)

Adams, R. B., Jr., Gordon, H. L., Baird, A. A., Ambady, N., & Kleck, R. E. (2003). Effects of gaze on amygdala sensitivity to anger and fear faces. *Science, 300,* 1536. (12)

Adams, R. B., Jr., & Kleck, R. E. (2005). Effects of direct and averted gaze on the perception of facially communicated emotion. *Emotion, 5,* 3–11. (12)

Adams, W., Kendell, R. E., Hare, E. H., & Munk-Jørgensen, P. (1993). Epidemiological evidence that maternal influenza contributes to the aetiology of schizophrenia. *British Journal of Psychiatry, 163,* 522–534. (15)

Addis, D. R., Wong, A. T., & Schacter, D. L. (2007). Remembering the past and imagining the future: Common and distinct neural substrates during event construction and elaboration. *Neuropsychologia, 45,* 1363–1377. (13)

Ader, R. (2001). Psychoneuroimmunology. *Current Directions in Psychological Science, 10,* 94–98. (12)

Adkins, E. K., & Adler, N. T. (1972). Hormonal control of behavior in the Japanese quail. *Journal of Comparative and Physiological Psychology, 81,* 27–36. (11)

Adler, E., Hoon, M. A., Mueller, K. L., Chandrashekar, J., Ryba, N. J. P., & Zuker, C. S. (2000). A novel family of mammalian taste receptors. *Cell, 100,* 693–702. (7)

Admon, R., Lubin, G., Stern, O., Rosenberg, K., Sela, L., Ben-Ami, H., et al. (2009). Human vulnerability to stress depends on amygdala's predisposition and hippocampal plasticity. *Proceedings of the National Academy of Sciences (U.S.A.), 106,* 14120–14125. (12)

Adolphs, R., Damasio, H., & Tranel, D. (2002). Neural systems for recognition of emotional prosody: A 3-D lesion study. *Emotion, 2,* 23–51. (14)

Adolphs, R., Tranel, D., & Buchanan, T. W. (2005). Amygdala damage impairs emotional memory for gist but not details of complex stimuli. *Nature Neuroscience, 8,* 512–518. (12)

Adolphs, R., Tranel, D., Damasio, H., & Damasio, A. (1995). Fear and the human amygdala. *Journal of Neuroscience, 15,* 5879–5891. (12)

Agarwal, N., Pacher, P., Tegeder, I., Amaya, F., Constantin, C. E., Brenner, G. J., et al. (2007). Cannabinoids mediate analgesia largely via peripheral type 1 cannabinoid receptors in nociceptors. *Nature Neuroscience, 10,* 870–879. (7)

Aglioti, S., Smania, N., Atzei, A., & Berlucchi, G. (1997). Spatio-temporal properties of the pattern of evoked phantom sensations in a left index amputee patient. *Behavioral Neuroscience, 111,* 867–872. (5)

Aglioti, S., Smania, N., & Peru, A. (1999). Frames of reference for mapping tactile stimuli in brain-damaged patients. *Journal of Cognitive Neuroscience, 11,* 67–79. (14)

Aglioti, S., Tassinari, G., Corballis, M. C., & Berlucchi, G. (2000). Incomplete gustatory localization as shown by analysis of taste discrimination after callosotomy. *Journal of Cognitive Neuroscience, 12,* 238–245. (7, 14)

Ahlskog, J. E., & Hoebel, B. G. (1973). Overeating and obesity from damage to a noradrenergic system in the brain. *Science, 182,* 166–169. (10)

Ahlskog, J. E., Randall, P. K., & Hoebel, B. G. (1975). Hypothalamic hyperphagia: Dissociation from hyperphagia following destruction of noradrenergic neurons. *Science, 190,* 399–401. (10)

Ahmed, E. I., Zehr, J. L., Schulz, K. M., Lorenz, B. H., DonCarlos, L. L., & Sisk, C. L (2008). Pubertal hormones modulate the addition of new cells to sexually dimorphic brain regions. *Nature Neuroscience, 11,* 995–997. (11)

Ahmed, I. I., Shryne, J. E., Gorski, R. A., Branch, B. J., & Taylor, A. N. (1991). Prenatal ethanol and the prepubertal sexually dimorphic nucleus of the preoptic area. *Physiology & Behavior, 49,* 427–432. (11)

Aimone, J. B., Wiles, J., & Gage, F. H. (2006). Potential role for adult neurogenesis in the encoding of time in new memories. *Nature Neuroscience, 9,* 723–727. (5)

Airaksinen, M. S., & Saarma, M. (2002). The GDNF family: Signalling, biological functions and therapeutic value. *Nature Reviews Neuroscience, 3,* 383–394. (5)

Airan, R. D., Meltzer, L. A., Roy, M., Gong, Y., Chen, H., & Deisseroth, K. (2007). High-speed imaging reveals neurophysiological links to behavior in an animal model of depression. *Science, 317,* 819–823. (15)

Akbarian, S., Kim, J. J., Potkin, S. G., Hagman, J. O., Tafazzoli, A., Bunney, W. E., Jr., et al. (1995). Gene expression for glutamic acid decarboxylase is reduced without loss of neurons in prefrontal cortex of schizophrenics. *Archives of General Psychiatry, 52,* 258–266. (15)

Alanko, K., Santtila, P., Harlaar, N., Witting, K., Varjonen, M., Jern, P., et al. (2010). Common genetic effects of gender atypical behavior in childhood and sexual orientation in adulthood: A study of Finnish twins. *Archives of Sexual Behavior, 39,* 81–92. (11)

Albanese, M.-C., Duerden, E. G., Rainville, P., & Duncan, G. H. (2007). Memory traces of pain in human cortex. *Journal of Neuroscience, 27,* 4612–4620. (7)

Albouy, G., Sterpenich, V., Balteau, E., Vandewalle, G., Desseilles, M., Dang-Vu, T., et al. (2008). Both the hippocampus and striatum are involved in consolidation of motor sequence memory. *Neuron, 58,* 261–272. (13)

Albright, T. D., Jessell, T. M., Kandel, E. R., & Posner, M. I. (2001). Progress in the neural sciences in the century after Cajal (and the mysteries that remain). *Annals of the New York Academy of Sciences, 929,* 11–40. (2)

Aldrich, M. S. (1998). Diagnostic aspects of narcolepsy. *Neurology, 50*(Suppl. 1), S2–S7. (9)

Aleman, A., Kahn, R. S., & Selten, J. P. (2003). Sex differences in the risk of schizophrenia. *Archives of General Psychiatry, 60,* 565–571. (15)

Aleman, A., Swart, M., & van Rijn, S. (2008). Brain imaging, genetics and emotion. *Biological Psychology, 79,* 58–69. (12)

Alexander, G. M., & Hines, M. (2002). Sex differences in response to children's toys in nonhuman primates (*Cercopithecus aethiops sebaeus*). *Evolution and Human Behavior, 23,* 467–479. (11)

Alexander, G. M., Wilcox, T., & Woods, R. (2009). Sex differences in infants' visual interest in toys. *Archives of Sexual Behavior, 38,* 427–433. (11)

Allen, H. L., Estrada, K., Lettre, G., Berndt, S. I., Weedon, M. N., Rivadeneira, F., et al. (2010). Hundreds of variants clustered in genomic loci and biological pathways affect human height. *Nature, 467,* 832–838. (1)

Allen, J. S., Damasio, H., Grabowski, T. J., Bruss, J., & Zhang, W. (2003). Sexual dimorphism and asymmetries in the gray-white composition of the human cerebrum. *NeuroImage, 18,* 880–894. (4)

Alleva, E., & Francia, N. (2009). Psychiatric vulnerability: Suggestions from animal models and role of neurotrophins. *Neuroscience and Biobehavioral Reviews, 33,* 525–536. (5)

Allison, T., & Cicchetti, D. V. (1976). Sleep in mammals: Ecological and constitutional correlates. *Science, 194,* 732–734. (9)

Almeida, O. P., Yeap, B. B., Hankey, G. J., Jamrozik, K., & Flicker, L. (2008). Low free testosterone concentration as a potentially treatable cause of depressive symptoms in older men. *Archives of General Psychiatry, 65,* 283–289. (15)

Almli, C. R., Fisher, R. S., & Hill, D. L. (1979). Lateral hypothalamus destruction in infant rats produces consummatory deficits without sensory neglect or attenuated arousal. *Experimental Neurology, 66,* 146–157. (10)

Al-Rashid, R. A. (1971). Hypothalamic syndrome in acute childhood leukemia. *Clinical Pediatrics, 10,* 53–54. (10)

Altar, C. A., Laeng, P., Jurata, L. W., Brockman, J. A., Lemire, A., Bullard, J., et al. (2004). Electroconvulsive seizures regulate gene expression of distinct neurotrophic signaling pathways. *Journal of Neuroscience, 24,* 2667–2677. (15)

Alter, M. D., Rubin, D. B., Ramsey, K., Halpern, R., Stephan, D. A., Abbott, L. F., et al. (2008). Variation in the large-scale organization of gene expression levels in the hippocampus relates to stable epigenetic variability in behavior. *PLoS ONE, 3,* e3344. (1)

Alto, L. T., Howton, L. A., Conner, J. M., Hollis, E. R. III, Blesch, A., & Tuszynski, M. H. (2009). Chemotropic guidance facilitates axonal regeneration and synapse formation after spinal cord injury. *Nature Neuroscience, 12,* 1106–1113. (5)

Amateau, S. K., & McCarthy, M. M. (2004). Induction of PGE2 by estradiol mediates developmental masculinization of sex behavior. *Nature Neuroscience, 7,* 643–650. (11)

American Psychiatric Association. (1994). *Diagnostic and statistical manual of mental disorders* (4th ed.). Washington, DC: Author. (15)

Amiry-Moghaddam, M., & Ottersen, O. P. (2003). The molecular basis of water transport in the brain. *Nature Reviews Neuroscience, 4,* 991–1001. (2)

Amsterdam, J. D., Winokur, A., Dyson, W., Herzog, S., Gonzalez, F., Rott, R., et al. (1985). Borna disease virus. *Archives of General Psychiatry, 42,* 1093–1096. (15)

Anaclet, C., Parmentier, R., Ouk, K., Guidon, G., Buda, C., Sastre, J.-P., et al. (2009). Orexin/hypocretin and histamine: Distinct roles in the control of wakefulness demonstrated using knock-out mouse models. *Journal of Neuroscience, 29,* 14423–14438. (9)

Andersen, J. L., Klitgaard, H., & Saltin, B. (1994). Myosin heavy chain isoforms in single fibres from m. vastus lateralis of sprinters: Influence of training. *Acta Physiologica Scandinavica, 151,* 135–142. (8)

Andersen, T. S., Tiippana, K., & Sams, M. (2004). Factors influencing audiovisual fission and fusion illusions. *Cognitive Brain Research, 21,* 301–308. (4)

Andersson, K.-E. (2001). Pharmacology of penile erection. *Pharmacological Reviews, 53,* 417–450. (11)

Andreasen, N. C. (1988). Brain imaging: Applications in psychiatry. *Science, 239,* 1381–1388. (4)

Andreasen, N. C. (1999). A unitary model of schizophrenia. *Archives of General Psychiatry, 56,* 781–787. (15)

Andreasen, N. C., Swayze, V. W., II, Flaum, M., Yates, W. R., Arndt, S., & McChesney, C. (1990). Ventricular enlargement in schizophrenia evaluated with computed tomographic scanning. *Archives of General Psychiatry, 47,* 1008–1015. (15)

Andresen, J. M., Gayán, J., Cherny, S. S., Brocklebank, D., Alkorta-Aranburu, G., Addis, E. A., et al. (2007). Replication of twelve association studies for Huntington's disease residual age of onset in large Venezuelan kindreds. *Journal of Medical Genetics, 44,* 45–50. (8)

Andrew, D., & Craig, A. D. (2001). Spinothalamic lamina I neurons selectively sensitive to histamine: A central neural pathway for itch. *Nature Neuroscience, 4,* 72–77. (7)

Andrews, T. J., Halpern, S. D., & Purves, D. (1997). Correlated size variations in human visual cortex, lateral geniculate nucleus, and optic tract. *Journal of Neuroscience, 17,* 2859–2868. (6)

Angulo, M. C., Kozlov, A. S., Charpak, S., & Audinat, E. (2004). Glutamate released from glial cells synchronizes neuronal activity in the hippocampus. *Journal of Neuroscience, 24,* 6920–6927. (2)

Ankney, C. D. (1992). Sex differences in relative brain size: The mismeasure of women, too? *Intelligence, 16,* 329–336. (4)

Antanitus, D. S. (1998). A theory of cortical neuron-astrocyte interaction. *Neuroscientist, 4,* 154–159. (2)

Antoniadis, E. A., Winslow, J. T., Davis, M., & Amaral, D. G. (2007). Role of the primate amygdala in fear-potentiated startle. *Journal of Neuroscience, 27,* 7386–7396. (12)

Apostolakis, E. M., Garai, J., Fox, C., Smith, C. L., Watson, S. J., Clark, J. H., et al. (1996). Dopaminergic regulation of progesterone receptors: Brain D5 dopamine receptors mediate induction of lordosis by D1-like agonists in rats. *Journal of Neuroscience, 16,* 4823–4834. (11)

Appolinario, J. C., Bacaltchuk, J., Sichieri, R., Claudino, A. M., Godoy-Matos, A., Morgan, C., et al. (2003). A randomized, double-blind, placebo-controlled study of sibutramine in the treatment of binge-eating disorder. *Archives of General Psychiatry, 60,* 1109–1116. (10)

Araneda, R. C., Kini, A. D., & Firestein, S. (2000). The molecular receptive range of an odorant receptor. *Nature Neuroscience, 3,* 1248–1255. (7)

Archer, J. (2000). Sex differences in aggression between heterosexual partners: A meta-analytic review. *Psychological Bulletin, 126,* 651–680. (12)

Archer, J., Birring, S. S., & Wu, F. C. W. (1998). The association between testosterone and aggression in young men: Empirical findings and a meta-analysis. *Aggressive Behavior, 24,* 411–420. (12)

Archer, J., Graham-Kevan, N., & Davies, M. (2005). Testosterone and aggression: A reanalysis of Book, Starzyk, and Quinsey's (2001) study. *Aggression and Violent Behavior, 10,* 241–261. (12)

Arnold, A. P. (2004). Sex chromosomes and brain gender. *Nature Reviews Neuroscience, 5,* 701–708. (1, 11)

Arnold, A. P. (2009). The organizational-activational hypothesis as the foundation for a unified theory of sexual differentiation of all mammalian tissues. *Hormones and Behavior, 55,* 570–578. (11)

Arnold, A. P., & Breedlove, S. M. (1985). Organizational and activational effects of sex steroids on brain and behavior: A reanalysis. *Hormones and Behavior, 19,* 469–498. (11)

Arnold, S. E. (2000). Cellular and molecular neuropathology of the parahippocampal region in schizophrenics. *Annals of the New York Academy of Sciences, 911,* 275–292. (15)

Arnsten, A. F. T. (2009). Stress signaling pathways that impair prefrontal cortex structure and function. *Nature Reviews Neuroscience, 10,* 410–422. (12)

Arvidson, K., & Friberg, U. (1980). Human taste: Response and taste bud number in fungiform papillae. *Science, 209,* 807–808. (7)

Asarnow, J. R., Emslie, G., Clarke, G., Wagner, K. D., Spirito, A., Vitiello, B., et al. (2009). Treatment of selective serotonin reuptake inhibitor-resistant depression in adolescents: Predictors and moderators of treatment response. *Journal of the American Academy of Child & Adolescent Psychiatry, 48,* 330–339. (15)

Ascherio, A., Weisskopf, M. G., O'Reilly, E. J., McCullough, M., Calle, E. E., Rodriguez, C., et al. (2004). Coffee consumption, gender, and Parkinson's disease mortality in the cancer prevention study II cohort: The modifying effects of estrogen. *American Journal of Epidemiology, 160,* 977–984. (8)

Aserinsky, E., & Kleitman, N. (1955). Two types of ocular motility occurring in sleep. *Journal of Applied Physiology, 8,* 1–10. (9)

Ashmore, L. J., & Sehgal, A. (2003). A fly's eye view of circadian entrainment. *Journal of Biological Rhythms, 18,* 206–216. (9)

Aston-Jones, G., Chen, S., Zhu, Y., & Oshinsky, M. L. (2001). A neural circuit for circadian regulation of arousal. *Nature Neuroscience, 4,* 732–738. (9)

Athos, E. A., Levinson, B., Kistler, A., Zemansky, J., Bostrom, A., Freimer, N., et al. (2007). Dichotomy and perceptual distortions in absolute pitch ability. *Proceedings of the National Academy of Sciences, USA, 104,* 14795–14800. (7)

Avena, N. M., Rada, P., & Hoebel, B. G. (2008). Evidence for sugar addiction: Behavioral and neurochemical effects of intermittent, excessive sugar intake. *Neuroscience and Biobehavioral Reviews, 32,* 20–39. (10)

Avissar, M., Furman, A. C., Saunders, J. C., & Parsons, T. D. (2007). Adaptation reduces spike-count reliability, but not spike-timing precision, of auditory nerve responses. *Journal of Neuroscience, 27,* 6461–6472. (7)

Azrin, N. H., Sisson, R. W., Meyers, R., & Godley, M. (1982). Alcoholism treatment by disulfiram and community reinforcement therapy. *Journal of Behavior Therapy and Experimental Psychiatry, 13*, 105–112. (3)

Babich, F. R., Jacobson, A. L., Bubash, S., & Jacobson, A. (1965). Transfer of a response to naive rats by injection of ribonucleic acid extracted from trained rats. *Science, 149*, 656–657. (13)

Babiloni, C., Brancucci, A., Pizzella, V., Romani, G. L., Tecchio, F., Torquati, K., et al. (2005). Contingent negative variation in the parasylvian cortex increases during expectancy of painful sensorimotor events: A magnetoencephalographic study. *Behavioral Neuroscience, 119*, 491–502. (7)

Babkoff, H., Caspy, T., Mikulincer, M., & Sing, H. C. (1991). Monotonic and rhythmic influences: A challenge for sleep deprivation research. *Psychological Bulletin, 109*, 411–428. (9)

Backlund, E.-O., Granberg, P.-O., Hamberger, B., Sedvall, G., Seiger, A., & Olson, L. (1985). Transplantation of adrenal medullary tissue to striatum in Parkinsonism. In A. Björklund & U. Stenevi (Eds.), *Neural grafting in the mammalian CNS* (pp. 551–556). Amsterdam: Elsevier. (8)

Bäckman, J., & Alerstam, T. (2001). Confronting the winds: Orientation and flight behavior of roosting swifts, *Apus apus. Proceedings of the Royal Society of London. Series B—Biological Sciences, 268*, 1081–1087. (9)

Baddeley, A. D., & Hitch, G. J. (1994). Developments in the concept of working memory. *Neuropsychology, 8*, 485–493. (13)

Baer, J. S., Sampson, P. D., Barr, H. M., Connor, P. D., & Streissguth, A. P. (2003). A 21-year longitudinal analysis of the effects of prenatal alcohol exposure on young adult drinking. *Archives of General Psychiatry, 60*, 377–385. (3)

Bagemihl, B. (1999). *Biological exuberance.* New York: St. Martin's Press. (11)

Baghdoyan, H. A., Spotts, J. L., & Snyder, S. G. (1993). Simultaneous pontine and basal fore brain microinjections of carbachol suppress REM sleep. *Journal of Neuroscience, 13*, 229–242. (9)

Bailey, C. H., Giustetto, M., Huang, Y.-Y., Hawkins, R. D., & Kandel, E. R. (2000). Is heterosynaptic modulation essential for stabilizing Hebbian plasticity and memory? *Nature Reviews Neuroscience, 1*, 11–20. (13)

Bailey, J. M., & Pillard, R. C. (1991). A genetic study of male sexual orientation. *Archives of General Psychiatry, 48*, 1089–1096. (11)

Bailey, J. M., Pillard, R. C., Dawood, K., Miller, M. B., Farrer, L. A., Trivedi, S., et al. (1999). A family history study of male sexual orientation using three independent samples. *Behavior Genetics, 29*, 79–86. (11)

Bailey, J. M., Pillard, R. C., Neale, M. C., & Agyei, Y. (1993). Heritable factors influence sexual orientation in women. *Archives of General Psychiatry, 50*, 217–223. (11)

Bailey, J. M., Willerman, L., & Parks, C. (1991). A test of the maternal stress theory of human male homosexuality. *Archives of Sexual Behavior, 20*, 277–293. (11)

Bakker, J., De Mees, C., Douhard, Q., Balthazart, J., Gabant, P., Szpirer, J., et al. (2006). Alpha-fetoprotein protects the developing female mouse brain from masculinization and defeminization by estrogens. *Nature Neuroscience, 9*, 220–226. (11)

Bakker, J., Honda, S.-I., Harada, N., & Balthazart, J. (2002). The aromatase knock-out mouse provides new evidence that estradiol is required during development in the female for the expression of sociosexual behaviors in adulthood. *Journal of Neuroscience, 22*, 9104–9112. (11)

Ballard, P. A., Tetrud, J. W., & Langston, J. W. (1985). Permanent human Parkinsonism due to 1-methyl-4-phenyl-1,2,3,6-tetrahydropyridine (MPTP). *Neurology, 35*, 949–956. (8)

Ballon, J. S., Dean, K. A., & Cadenhead, K. S. (2007). Obstetrical complications in people at risk for developing schizophrenia. *Schizophrenia Research, 98*, 307–311. (15)

Balthasar, N., Dalgaard, L. T., Lee, C. E., Yu, J., Funahashi, H., Williams, T., et al. (2005). Divergence of melanocortin pathways in the control of food intake and energy expenditure. *Cell, 123*, 493–505. (10)

Banks, W. P., & Isham, E. A. (2009). We infer rather than perceive the moment we decided to act. *Psychological Science, 20*, 17–21. (8)

Barbour, D. L., & Wang, X. (2003). Contrast tuning in auditory cortex. *Science, 299*, 1073–1075. (7)

Bargary, G., Barnett, K. J., Mitchell, K. J., & Newell, F. N. (2009). Colored-speech synaesthesia is triggered by multisensory, not unisensory, perception. *Psychological Science, 20*, 529–533. (7)

Barinaga, M. (1996). Finding new drugs to treat stroke. *Science, 272*, 664–664. (5)

Barnea, G., O'Donnell, S., Mancia, F., Sun, X., Nemes, A., Mendelsohn, M., et al. (2004). Odorant receptors on axon termini in the brain. *Science, 304*, 1468. (7)

Barnes, B. M. (1996, September/October). Sang froid. *The Sciences, 36*(5), 13–14. (9)

Barnett, K. J., Finucane, C., Asher, J. E., Bargary, G., Corvin, A. P., Newell, F. N., et al. (2008). Familial patterns and the origins of individual differences in synaesthesia. *Cognition, 106*, 871–893. (7)

Barrett, L. F., Bliss-Moreau, E., Duncan, S. L., Rauch, S. L., & Wright, C. I. (2007). The amygdala and the experience of affect. *Social Cognitive & Affective Neuroscience, 2*, 73–83. (12)

Barton, D. A., Esler, M. D., Dawood, T., Lambert, E. A., Haikerwal, D., Brenchley, C., et al. (2008). Elevated brain serotonin turnover in patients with depression. *Archives of General Psychiatry, 65*, 38–46. (15)

Barton, R. A., & Harvey, P. H. (2000). Mosaic evolution of brain structure in mammals. *Nature, 405*, 1055–1058. (4)

Bartoshuk, L. M. (1991). Taste, smell, and pleasure. In R. C. Bolles (Ed.), *The hedonics of taste* (pp. 15–28). Hillsdale, NJ: Erlbaum. (7)

Bartoshuk, L. M., Gentile, R. L., Moskowitz, H. R., & Meiselman, H. L. (1974). Sweet taste induced by miracle fruit (*Synsephalum dulcificum*). *Physiology & Behavior, 12*, 449–456. (7)

Bartsch, T., Schönfeld, R., Müller, F. J., Alfke, K., Leplow, B., Aldenhoff, J., et al. (2010). Focal lesions of human hippocampal CA1 neurons in transient global amnesia impair place memory. *Science, 328*, 1412–1415. (13)

Basil, J. A., Kamil, A. C., Balda, R. P., & Fite, K. V. (1996). Differences in hippocampal volume among food storing corvids. *Brain, Behavior and Evolution, 47*, 156–164. (13)

Basso, A., & Rusconi, M. L. (1998). Aphasia in left-handers. In P. Coppens, Y. Lebrun, & A. Basso (Eds.), *Aphasia in atypical populations* (pp. 1–34). Mahwah, NJ: Erlbaum. (14)

Basterzi, A. D., Yazici, K., Aslan, E., Delialioglu, B. T., Acar, S. T., & Yazici, A. (2008). Effects of fluoxetine and venlafaxine on serum brain derived neurotrophic factor levels in depressed patients. *Progress in Neuro-psychopharmacology & biological psychiatry, 33*, 281–285. (15)

Battersby, S. (1997). Plus c'est le même chews. *Nature, 385*, 679. (10)

Baulac, S., Huberfeld, G., Gourfinkel-An, I., Mitropoulou, G., Beranger, A., Prud'homme, J.-F., et al. (2001). First genetic evidence of GABAA receptor dysfunction in epilepsy: A mutation in the γ2-subunit gene. *Nature Genetics, 28*, 46–48. (14)

Baum, A., Gatchel, R. J., & Schaeffer, M. A. (1983). Emotional, behavioral, and physiological effects of chronic stress at Three Mile Island. *Journal of Consulting and Clinical Psychology, 51*, 565–582. (12)

Bauman, M. D., Toscano, J. E., Mason, W. A., Lavenex, P., & Amaral, D. G. (2006). The expression of social dominance following neonatal lesions of the amygdala or hippocampus in rhesus monkeys (*Macaca mulatta*). *Behavioral Neuroscience, 120*, 749–760. (12)

Bautista, D. M., Siemens, J., Glazer, J. M., Tsuruda, P. R., Basbaum, A. I., Stucky, C. L., et al. (2007). The menthol receptor TRPM8 is the principal detector of environmental cold. *Nature, 448*, 204–208. (7)

Bautista, D. M., Sigal, Y. M., Milstein, A. D., Garrison, J. L., Zorn, J. A., Tsuruda, P. R., et al. (2008). Pungent agents from Szechuan peppers excite sensory neurons by inhibiting two-pore potassium channels. *Nature Neuroscience, 11*, 772–779. (7)

Baxter, L. R., Phelps, M. E., Mazziotta, J. C., Schwartz, J. M., Gerner, R. H., Selin, C. E., et al. (1985). Cerebral metabolic rates for glucose in mood disorders. *Archives of General Psychiatry, 42*, 441–447. (15)

Bayley, P. J., Frascino, J. C., & Squire, L. R. (2005). Robust habit learning in the absence of awareness and independent of the medial temporal lobe. *Nature, 436*, 550–553. (13)

Bayley, P. J., Hopkins, R. O., & Squire, L. R. (2006). The fate of old memories after medial temporal lobe damage. *Journal of Neuroscience, 26*, 13311–13317. (13)

Baylis, G. C., & Driver, J. (2001). Shape-coding in IT cells generalizes over contrast and mirror reversal but not figure-ground reversal. *Nature Neuroscience, 4*, 937–942. (6)

Bean, B. P. (2007). The action potential in mammalian central neurons. *Nature Reviews Neuroscience, 8*, 451–465. (2)

Beaton, E. A., Schmidt, L. A., Schulkin, J., Antony, M. M., Swinson, R. P., & Hall, G. B. (2008). Different neural responses to stranger and personally familiar faces in shy and bold adults. *Behavioral Neuroscience, 122*, 704–709. (12)

Beauchamp, M. S., & Ro, T. (2008). Neural substrates of sound-touch synesthesia after a thalamic lesion. *Journal of Neuroscience, 28*, 13696–13702. (7)

Bechara, A., Damasio, H., Damasio, A. R., & Lee, G. P. (1999). Different contributions of the human amygdala and ventromedial prefrontal cortex to decision-making. *Journal of Neuroscience, 19*, 5473–5481. (12)

Beck, S., Richardson, S. P., Shamin, E. A., Dang, N., Schubert, M., & Hallett, M. (2008). Short intracortical and surround inhibition are selectively reduced during movement initiation in focal hand dystonia. *Journal of Neuroscience, 28*, 10363–10369. (5)

Becker, C., Thiébot, M.-H., Touitou, Y., Hamon, M., Cesselin, F., & Benoliel, J.-J. (2001). Enhanced cortical extracellular levels of cholecystokinin-like material in a model of anticipation of social defeat in the rat. *Journal of Neuroscience, 21*, 262–269. (12)

Becker, H. C. (1988). Effects of the imidazobenzodiazepine Ro15-4513 on the stimulant and depressant actions of ethanol on spontaneous locomotor activity. *Life Sciences, 43*, 643–650. (12)

Becks, L., & Agrawal, A. F. (2010). Higher rates of sex evolve in spatially heterogeneous environments. *Nature, 468*, 89–92. (11)

Beebe, D. W., & Gozal, D. (2002). Obstructive sleep apnea and the prefrontal cortex: Towards a comprehensive model linking nocturnal upper airway obstruction to daytime cognitive and behavioral deficits. *Journal of Sleep Research, 11*, 1–16. (9)

Beehner, J. C., Bergman, T. J., Cheney, D. L., Seyfarth, R. M., & Whitten, P. L. (2005). The effect of new alpha males on female stress in free-ranging baboons. *Animal Behaviour, 69*, 1211–1221. (12)

Beehner, J. C., Gesquirere, L., Seyfarth, R. M., Cheney, D. L., Alberts, S. C., & Altmann, J. (2009). Testosterone related to age and life-history stages in male baboons and geladas. *Hormones and Behavior, 56*, 472–480. (12)

Beeman, M. J., & Chiarello, C. (1998). Complementary right- and left-hemisphere language comprehension. *Current Directions in Psychological Science, 7*, 2–8. (14)

Behl, C. (2002). Oestrogen as a neuroprotective hormone. *Nature Reviews Neuroscience, 3*, 433–442. (14)

Behrens, M., Foerster, S., Staehler, F., Raguse, J.-D., & Meyerhof, W. (2007). Gustatory expression pattern of the human TAS2R bitter receptor gene family reveals a heterogenous population of bitter responsive taste receptor cells. *Journal of Neuroscience, 27*, 12630–12640. (7)

Békésy, G.—See von Békésy, G.

Belforte, J. E., Zsiros, V., Sklar, E. R., Jiang, Z., Yu, G., Li, Y., et al. (2010). Postnatal NMDA receptor ablation in corticolimbic interneurons confers schizophrenia-like phenotypes. *Nature Neuroscience, 13*, 76–83. (15)

Bella, S. D., Giguere, J. F., & Peretz, I. (2009). Singing in congenital amusia. *Journal of the Acoustical Society of America, 126*, 414–424. (7)

Bellugi, U., Lichtenberger, L., Jones, W., Lai, Z., & St George, M. (2000). I. The neurocognitive profile of Williams syndrome: A complex pattern of strengths and weaknesses. *Journal of Cognitive Neuroscience, 12*(Suppl.), 7–29. (14)

Belova, M. A., Paton, J. J., Morrison, S. E., & Salzman, C. D. (2007). Expectation modulates neural responses to pleasant and aversive stimuli in primate amygdala. *Neuron, 55*, 970–984. (12)

Benedetti, F., Amanzio, M., Vighetti, S., & Asteggiano, G. (2006). The biochemical and neuroendocrine bases of the hyperalgesic nocebo effect. *Journal of Neuroscience, 26*, 12014–12022. (7)

Benedetti, F., Arduino, C., & Amanzio, M. (1999). Somatotopic activation of opioid systems by target-directed expectations of analgesia. *Journal of Neuroscience, 19*, 3639–3648. (7)

Benes, F. M. (1995). Is there a neuroanatomic basis for schizophrenia? An old question revisited. *The Neuroscientist, 1*, 104–115. (15)

Benes, F. M., Turtle, M., Khan, Y., & Farol, P. (1994). Myelination of a key relay zone in the hippocampal formation occurs in the human brain during childhood, adolescence, and adulthood. *Archives of General Psychiatry, 51*, 477–484. (5)

Benoit, S. C., Air, E. L., Coolen, L. M., Strauss, R., Jackman, A., Clegg, D. J., et al. (2002). The catabolic action of insulin in the brain is mediated by melanocortins. *Journal of Neuroscience, 22*, 9048–9052. (10)

Benschop, R. J., Godaert, G. L. R., Geenen, R., Brosschot, J. F., DeSmet, M. B. M., Olff, M., et al. (1995). Relationships between cardiovascular and immunologic changes in an experimental stress model. *Psychological Medicine, 25*, 323–327. (12)

Berdoy, M., Webster, J. P., & Macdonald, D. W. (2000). Fatal attraction in rats infected with *Toxoplasma gondii. Proceedings of the Royal Society of London, B, 267*, 1591–1594. (12)

Berenbaum, S. A. (1999). Effects of early androgens on sex-typed activities and interests in adolescents with congenital adrenal hyperplasia. *Hormones and Behavior, 35*, 102–110. (11)

Berenbaum, S. A., Duck, S. C., & Bryk, K. (2002). Behavioral effects of prenatal versus postnatal androgen excess in children with 21-hydroxylase-deficient congenital adrenal hyperplasia. *Journal of Clinical Endocrinology & Metabolism, 85*, 727–733. (11)

Berger, R. J., & Phillips, N. H. (1995). Energy conservation and sleep. *Behavioural Brain Research, 69*, 65–73. (9)

Berger-Sweeney, J., & Hohmann, C. F. (1997). Behavioral consequences of abnormal cortical development: Insights into developmental disabilities. *Behavioural Brain Research, 86*, 121–142. (5)

Bergmann, O., Bhardwaj, R. D., Bernard, S., Zdunek, S., Barnabé-Heider, F., Walsh, S., et al. (2009). Evidence for cardiomyocyte renewal in humans. *Science, 324*, 98–102. (5)

Berlin, H. A., Rolls, E. T., & Kischka, U. (2004). Impulsivity, time perception, emotion and reinforcement sensitivity in patients with orbitofrontal cortex lesions. *Brain, 127*, 1108–1126. (12)

Berlucchi, G., Mangun, G. R., & Gazzaniga, M. S. (1997). Visuospatial attention and the split brain. *News in Physiological Sciences, 12*, 226–231. (14)

Berman, K. F., Torrey, E. F., Daniel, D. G., & Weinberger, D. R. (1992). Regional cerebral blood flow in monozygotic twins discordant and concordant for schizophrenia. *Archives of General Psychiatry, 49*, 927–934. (15)

Bernal, D., Donley, J. M., Shadwick, R. E., & Syme, D. A. (2005). Mammal-like muscles power swimming in a cold-water shark. *Science, 437*, 1349–1352. (10)

Bernstein, J. J., & Gelderd, J. B. (1970). Regeneration of the long spinal tracts in the goldfish. *Brain Research, 20*, 33–38. (5)

Berntson, G. G., Bechara, A., Damasio, H., Tranel, D., & Cacioppo, J. T. (2007). Amygdala contribution to selective dimensions of emotion. *Social Cognitive & Affective Neuroscience, 2*, 123–129. (12)

Berridge, C. W., Stellick, R. L., & Schmeichel, B. E. (2005). Wake-promoting actions of medial basal forebrain β_2 receptor stimulation. *Behavioral Neuroscience, 119*, 743–751. (9)

Berridge, K. C., & Robinson, T. E. (1995). The mind of an addicted brain: Neural sensitization of wanting versus liking. *Current Directions in Psychological Science, 4*, 71–76. (3)

Berridge, K. C., & Robinson, T. E. (1998). What is the role of dopamine in reward: Hedonic impact, reward learning, or incentive salience? *Brain Research Reviews, 28*, 309–369. (3)

Berryhill, M. E., Phuong, L., Picasso, L., Cabeza, R., & Olson, I. R. (2007). Parietal lobe and episodic memory: Bilateral damage causes impaired free recall of autobiographical memory. *Journal of Neuroscience, 27*, 14415–14423. (13)

Berson, D. M., Dunn, F. A., & Takao, M. (2002). Phototransduction by retinal ganglion cells that set the circadian clock. *Science, 295*, 1070–1073. (9)

Bertram, L., & Tanzi, R. E. (2008). Thirty years of Alzheimer's disease genetics: The implications of systematic meta-analyses. *Nature Reviews Neuroscience, 9*, 768–778. (13)

Beuming, T., Kniazeff, J., Bergmann, M. L., Shi, L., Gracia, L., Raniszewska, K., et al. (2008). The binding sites for cocaine and dopamine in the dopamine transporter overlap. *Nature Neuroscience, 11*, 780–789. (3)

Bevilacqua, L., Doly, S., Kaprio, J., Yuan, Q., Tikkanen, R., Paunio, T., et al. (2010). A population-specific *HTR2B* stop codon predisposes to severe impulsivity. *Nature, 468*, 1061–1066. (12)

Biben, M. (1979). Predation and predatory play behaviour of domestic cats. *Animal Behaviour, 27*, 81–94. (12)

Biernaskie, J., Chernenko, G., & Corbett, D. (2004). Efficacy of rehabilitative experience declines with time after focal ischemic brain injury. *Journal of Neuroscience, 24*, 1245–1254. (5)

Bierut, L. J., Heath, A. C., Bucholz, K. K., Dinwiddie, S. H., Madden, P. A. F., Statham, D. J., et al. (1999). Major depressive disorder in a community-based twin sample. *Archives of General Psychiatry, 56*, 557–563. (15)

Bilgüvar, K., Öztürk, A. K., Louvi, A., Kwan, K. Y., Choi, M., Tatli, B., et al. (2010). Whole-exome sequencing identifies recessive *WDR62* mutations in severe brain malformations. *Nature, 467*, 207–210. (5)

Billington, C. J., & Levine, A. S. (1992). Hypothalamic neuropeptide Y regulation of feeding and energy metabolism. *Current Opinion in Neurobiology, 2,* 847–851. (10)

Bimler, D., & Kirkland, J. (2009). Colour-space distortion in women who are heterozygous for colour deficiency. *Vision Research, 49,* 536–543. (6)

Binder, G. K., & Griffin, D. E. (2001). Interferon-g-mediated site-specific clearance of alphavirus from CNS neurons. *Science, 293,* 303–306. (2)

Bird, A. (2007). Perceptions of epigenetics. *Nature, 447,* 396–398. (1)

Björnsdotter, M., Löken, L., Olausson, H., Vallbo, Å., & Wessberg, J. (2009). Somatotopic organization of gentle touch processing in the posterior insular cortex. *Journal of Neuroscience, 29,* 9314–9320. (7)

Blackless, M., Charuvastra, A., Derryck, A., Fausto-Sterling, A., Lauzanne, K., & Lee, E. (2000). How sexually dimorphic are we? Review and synthesis. *American Journal of Human Biology, 12,* 151–166. (11)

Blackwell, A., & Bates, E. (1995). Inducing agrammatic profiles in normals: Evidence for the selective vulnerability of morphology under cognitive resource limitation. *Journal of Cognitive Neuroscience, 7,* 228–257. (14)

Blake, R., & Hirsch, H. V. B. (1975). Deficits in binocular depth perception in cats after alternating monocular deprivation. *Science, 190,* 1114–1116. (6)

Blake, R., Palmeri, T. J., Marois, R., & Kim, C.-Y. (2005). On the perceptual reality of synesthetic color. In L. C. Robertson & N. Sagiv (Eds.), *Synesthesia* (pp. 47–73). Oxford, England: Oxford University Press. (7)

Blakemore, S.-J., Wolpert, D. M., & Frith, C. D. (1998). Central cancellation of self-produced tickle sensation. *Nature Neuroscience, 1,* 635–640. (7)

Blankenburg, F., Ruff, C. C., Deichmann, R., Rees, G., & Driver, J. (2006). The cutaneous rabbit illusion affects human primary sensory cortex somatotopically. *PLoS Biology, 4,* 459–466. (7)

Bliss, T. V. P., & Lømo, T. (1973). Long-lasting potentiation of synaptic transmission in the dentate area of the anaesthetized rabbit following stimulation of the perforant path. *Journal of Physiology (London), 232,* 331–356. (13)

Bloch, G. J., & Mills, R. (1995). Prepubertal testosterone treatment of neonatally gonadectomized male rats: Defeminization and masculinization of behavioral and endocrine function in adulthood. *Neuroscience and Biobehavioral Reviews, 59,* 187–200. (11)

Bloch, G. J., Mills, R., & Gale, S. (1995). Prepubertal testosterone treatment of female rats: Defeminization of behavioral and endocrine function in adulthood. *Neuroscience and Biobehavioral Reviews, 19,* 177–186. (11)

Bloch, M., Schmidt, P. J., Danaceau, M., Murphy, J., Nieman, L., & Rubinow, D. R. (2000). Effects of gonadal steroids in women with a history of postpartum depression. *American Journal of Psychiatry, 157,* 924–930. (15)

Bobrow, D., & Bailey, J. M. (2001). Is male homosexuality maintained via kin selection? *Evolution and Human Behavior, 22,* 361–368. (11)

Bochukova, E. G., Huang, N., Keogh, J., Henning, E., Purmann, C., Blaszczyk, K., et al. (2010). Large, rare chromosomal deletions associated with severe early-onset obesity. *Nature, 463,* 666–670. (10)

Bocklandt, S., Horvath, S., Vilain, E., & Hamer, D. H. (2006). Extreme skewing of X chromosome inactivation in mothers of homosexual men. *Human Genetics, 118,* 691–694. (11)

Bode, L., Ferszt, R., & Czech, G. (1993). Borna disease virus infection and affective disorders in man. *Archives of Virology (Suppl. 7),* 159–167. (15)

Bode, L., & Ludwig, H. (1997). Clinical similarities and close genetic relationship of human and animal Borna disease virus. *Archives of Virology (Suppl. 13),* 167–182. (15)

Bode, L., Riegel, S., Lange, W., & Ludwig, H. (1992). Human infections with Borna disease virus: Seroprevalence in patients with chronic diseases and healthy individuals. *Journal of Medical Virology, 36,* 309–315. (15)

Boettiger, C. A., Mitchell, J. M., Tavares, V. C., Robertson, M., Joslyn, G., D'Esposito, M., et al. (2007). Immediate reward bias in humans: Fronto-parietal networks and a role for the catechol-O-methyltransferase 158$^{val/val}$ genotype. *Journal of Neuroscience, 27,* 14383–14391. (3)

Bogaert, A. F. (2003a). The interaction of fraternal birth order and body size in male sexual orientation. *Behavioral Neuroscience, 117,* 381–384. (11)

Bogaert, A. F. (2003b). Number of older brothers and sexual orientation: New tests and the attraction/behavior distinction in two national probability samples. *Journal of Personality and Social Psychology, 84,* 644–652. (11)

Bogaert, A. F. (2006). Biological versus nonbiological older brothers and men's sexual orientation. *Proceedings of the National Academy of Sciences, USA, 103,* 10771–10774. (11)

Bogaert, A. F. (2010). Physical development and sexual orientation in men and women: An analysis of NATSAL-2000. *Archives of Sexual Behavior, 39,* 110–116. (11)

Boivin, D. B., Duffy, J. F., Kronauer, R. E., & Czeisler, C. A. (1996). Dose-response relationships for resetting of human circadian clock by light. *Nature, 379,* 540–542. (9)

Bonath, B., Noesselt, T., Martinez, A., Mishra, J., Schwiecker, K., Heinze, H.-J., et al. (2007). Neural basis of the ventriloquist illusion. *Current Biology, 17,* 1697–1703. (4)

Bonifati, V., Rizzu, P., van Baren, M. J., Schaap, O., Breedlove, G. J., Krieger, E., et al. (2003). Mutations in the *DJ-x* gene associated with autosomal recessive early-onset Parkinsonism. *Science, 299,* 256–259. (8)

Bonneh, Y. S., Cooperman, A., & Sagi, D. (2001). Motion-induced blindness in normal observers. *Nature, 411,* 798–801. (14)

Boot, W. R., Kramer, A. F., Simons, D. J., Fabiani, M., & Gratton, G. (2008). The effects of video game playing on attention, memory, and executive control. *Acta Psychologia, 129,* 387–398. (514)

Booth, F. W., & Neufer, P. D. (2005, January/February). Exercise controls gene expression. *American Scientist, 93,* 28–35. (8)

Booth, W., Johnson, D. H., Moore, S., Schal, C., & Vargo, E. L. (2011). Evidence for viable, nonclonal but fatherless Boa constrictors. *Biology Letters, 7,* 253–256. (11)

Borgland, S. L., Chang, S.-J., Bowers, M. S., Thompson, J. L., Vittoz, N., Floresco, S. B., et al. (2009). Orexin A/hypocretin-1 selectively promotes motivation for positive reinforcers. *Journal of Neuroscience, 29,* 11215–11225. (10)

Borodinsky, L. N., Root, C. M., Cronin, J. A., Sann, S. B., Gu, X., & Spitzer, N. C. (2004). Activity-dependent homeostatic specification of transmitter expression in embryonic neurons. *Nature, 429,* 523–530. (3)

Borsutzky, S., Fujiwara, E., Brand, M., & Markowitsch, H. J. (2008). Confabulations in alcoholic Korsakoff patients. *Neuropsychologia, 46,* 3133–3143. (13)

Bortolotti, B., Menchetti, M., Bellini, F., Montaguti, M. B., & Berardi, D. (2008). Psychological interventions for major depression in primary care: A meta-analytic review of randomized controlled trials. *General Hospital Psychiatry, 30,* 293–302. (15)

Bos, P. A., Terburg, D., & van Honk, J. (2010). Testosterone decreases trust in socially naïve humans. *Proceedings of the National Academy of Sciences (U.S.A.), 107,* 9991–9995. (11)

Bouchard, T. J., Jr., & McGue, M. (2003). Genetic and environmental influences on human psychological differences. *Journal of Neurobiology, 54,* 4–45. (1)

Boucsein, K., Weniger, G., Mursch, K., Steinhoff, B. J., & Irle, E. (2001). Amygdala lesion in temporal lobe epilepsy subjects impairs associative learning of emotional facial expressions. *Neuropsychologia, 39,* 231–236. (12)

Bourque, C. W. (2008). Central mechanisms of osmosensation and systemic osmoregulation. *Nature Reviews Neuroscience, 9,* 519–531. (10)

Boutrel, B., Franc, B., Hen, R., Hamon, M., & Adrien, J. (1999). Key role of 5-HT1B receptors in the regulation of paradoxical sleep as evidenced in 5-HT1B knock-out mice. *Journal of Neuroscience, 19,* 3204–3212. (9)

Bowles, S. (2006). Group competition, reproductive leveling, and the evolution of human altruism. *Science, 314,* 1569–1572. (1)

Bowles, S., & Posel, B. (2005). Genetic relatedness predicts South African migrant workers' remittances to their families. *Nature, 434,* 380–383. (1)

Bowmaker, J. K. (1998). Visual pigments and molecular genetics of color blindness. *News in Physiological Sciences, 13,* 63–69. (6)

Bowmaker, J. K., & Dartnall, H. J. A. (1980). Visual pigments of rods and cones in a human retina. *Journal of Physiology (London), 298,* 501–511. (6)

Branco, T., Clark, B. A., & Häusser, M. (2010). Dendritic discrimination of temporal input sequences in cortical neurons. *Science, 329,* 1671–1675. (3)

Brandt, T. (1991). Man in motion: Historical and clinical aspects of vestibular function. *Brain, 114,* 2159–2174. (7)

Brans, R. G. H., Kahn, R. S., Schnack, H. G., van Baal, G. C. M., Posthuma, D., van Haren, N. E.

M., et al. (2010). Brain plasticity and intellectual ability are influenced by shared genes. *Journal of Neuroscience, 30*, 5519–5524. (5)

Brasted, P. J., Watts, C., Robbins, T. W., & Dunnett, S. B. (1999). Associative plasticity in striatal transplants. *Proceedings of the National Academy of Sciences, USA, 96*, 10524–10529. (8)

Braun, A. R., Balkin, T. J., Wesensten, N. J., Guadry, F., Carson, R. E., Varga, M., et al. (1998). Dissociated pattern of activity in visual cortices and their projections during human rapid eye movement sleep. *Science, 279*, 91–95. (8, 9)

Braus, H. (1960). Anatomie des Menschen, 3. Band: Periphere Leistungsbahnen II. Centrales Nervensystem, Sinnesorgane. 2. Auflage [Human anatomy: Vol. 3. Peripheral pathways II. Central nervous system, sensory organs (2nd ed.)]. Berlin: Springer-Verlag. (4)

Breiter, H. C., Aharon, I., Kahneman, D., Dale, A., & Shizgal, P. (2001). Functional imaging of neural responses to expectancy and experience of monetary gains and losses. *Neuron, 30*, 619–639. (3)

Bremmer, F., Kubischik, M., Hoffmann, K.-P., & Krekelberg, B. (2009). Neural dynamics of saccadic suppression. *Journal of Neuroscience, 29*, 12374–12383. (6)

Brewer, W. J., Wood, S. J., Pantelis, C., Berger, G. E., Copolov, D. L., & McGorry, P. D. (2007). Olfactory sensitivity through the course of psychosis: Relationships to olfactory identification, symptomatology and the schizophrenia odour. *Psychiatry Research, 149*, 97–104. (15)

Breysse, N., Carlsson, T., Winkler, C., Björklund, A., & Kirik, D. (2007). The functional impact of the intrastriatal dopamine neuron grafts in Parkinsonian rats is reduced with advancing disease. *Journal of Neuroscience, 27*, 5849–5856. (8)

Bridge, H., Thomas, O., Jbabdi, S., & Cowey, A. (2008). Changes in connectivity after visual cortical brain damage underlie altered visual function. *Brain, 131*, 1433–1444. (6)

Bridge, J. A., Birmaher, B., Iyengar, S., Barbe, R. P., & Brent, D. A. (2009). Placebo response in randomized controlled trials of antidepressants for pediatric major depressive disorder. *American Journal of Psychiatry, 166*, 42–49. (15)

Bridgeman, B., & Staggs, D. (1982). Plasticity in human blindsight. *Vision Research, 22*, 1199–1203. (6)

Brisbare-Roch, C., Dingemanse, J., Koberstein, R., Hoever, P., Aissoui, H., Flores, S., et al. (2007). Promotion of sleep by targeting the orexin system in rats, dogs and humans. *Nature Medicine, 13*, 150–155. (9)

Brody, A. L., Saxena, S., Stoesssel, P., Gillies, L. A., Fairbanks, L. A., Alborzian, S., et al. (2001). Regional brain metabolic changes in patients with major depression treated with either paroxetine or interpersonal therapy. *Archives of General Psychiatry, 58*, 631–640. (15)

Brooks, D. C., & Bizzi, E. (1963). Brain stem electrical activity during deep sleep. *Archives Italiennes de Biologie, 101*, 648–665. (9)

Brouwer, G. J., & Heeger, D. J. (2009). Decoding and reconstructing color from responses in human visual cortex. *Journal of Neuroscience, 29*, 13992–14003. (6)

Brown, A. S., Begg, M. D., Gravenstein, S., Schaefer, C. A., Wyatt, R. J., Bresnahan, M., et al. (2004). Serologic evidence of prenatal influenza in the etiology of schizophrenia. *Archives of General Psychiatry, 61*, 774–780. (15)

Brown, A. S., Cohen, P., Harkavy-Friedman, J., Babulas, V., Malaspina, D., Gorman, J. M., et al. (2001). Prenatal rubella, premorbid abnormalities, and adult schizophrenia. *Biological Psychiatry, 49*, 473–486. (15)

Brown, C. E., Li, P., Boyd, J. D., Delaney, K. R., & Murphy, T. H. (2007). Extensive turnover of dendritic spines and vascular remodeling in cortical tissues recovering from stroke. *Journal of Neuroscience, 27*, 4101–4109. (5)

Brown, G. L., Ebert, M. H., Goyer, P. F., Jimerson, D. C., Klein, W. J., Bunney, W. E., et al. (1982). Aggression, suicide, and serotonin: Relationships of CSF amine metabolites. *American Journal of Psychiatry, 139*, 741–746. (12)

Brown, J., Babor, T. F., Litt, M. D., & Kranzler, H. R. (1994). The type A/type B distinction. *Annals of the New York Academy of Sciences, 708*, 23–33. (3)

Brown, J. R., Ye, H., Bronson, R. T., Dikkes, P., & Greenberg, M. E. (1996). A defect in nurturing in mice lacking the immediate early gene *fos B*. *Cell, 86*, 297–309. (11)

Brown, T. P., Rumsby, P. C., Capleton, A. C., Rushton, L., & Levy, L. S. (2006). Pesticides and Parkinson's disease—Is there a link? *Environmental Health Perspectives, 114*, 156–164. (8)

Bruck, M., Cavanagh, P., & Ceci, S. J. (1991). Forty-something: Recognizing faces at one's 25th reunion. *Memory & Cognition, 19*, 221–228. (6)

Brummelte, S., & Galea, L. A. M. (2010). Depression during pregnancy and postpartum: Contribution of stress and ovarian hormones. *Progress in Neuropsychopharmacology & Biological Psychiatry, 34*, 766–776. (15)

Brunet, A., Orr, S. P., Tremblay, J., Robertson, K., Nader, K., & Pitman, R. K. (2008). Effect of post-retrieval propanolol on psychophysiologic responding during subsequent script-driven traumatic imagery in post-traumatic stress disorder. *Journal of Psychiatric Research, 42*, 503–506. (12)

Bruno, R. M., & Sakmann, B. (2006). Cortex is driven by weak but synchronously active thalamocortical synapses. *Science, 312*, 1622–1627. (3)

Buchen, L. (2010). Illuminating the brain. *Nature, 465*, 26–28. (4)

Buck, L., & Axel, R. (1991). A novel multigene family may encode odorant receptors: A molecular basis for odor recognition. *Cell, 65*, 175–187. (7)

Buckholtz, J. W., Treadway, M. T., Cowan, R. L., Woodward, N. D., Li, R., Ansari, M. S., et al. (2010). Dopaminergic network differences in human impulsivity. *Science, 329*, 532. (3)

Buell, S. J., & Coleman, P. D. (1981). Quantitative evidence for selective dendritic growth in normal human aging but not in senile dementia. *Brain Research, 214*, 23–41. (5)

Buka, S. L., Cannon, T. D., Torrey, E. F., Yolken, R. H., & Collaborative Study Group on the Prenatal Origins of Severe Psychiatric Disorders. (2008). Maternal exposure to herpes simplex vi-

rus and risk of psychosis among adult offspring. *Biological Psychiatry, 63*, 809–815. (15)

Buka, S. L., Tsuang, M. T., Torrey, E. F., Klebanoff, M. A., Bernstein, D., & Yolken, R. H. (2001). Maternal infections and subsequent psychosis among offspring. *Archives of General Psychiatry, 58*, 1032–1037. (15)

Bulbena, A., Gago, J., Martin-Santos, R., Porta, M., Dasquens, J., & Berrios, G. E. (2004). Anxiety disorder & joint laxity: A definitive link. *Neurology, Psychiatry and Brain Research, 11*, 137–140. (12)

Bulbena, A., Gago, J., Sperry, L., & Bergé, D. (2006). The relationship between frequency and intensity of fears and a collagen condition. *Depression and Anxiety, 23*, 412–417. (12)

Bundgaard, M. (1986). Pathways across the vertebrate blood–brain barrier: Morphological viewpoints. *Annals of the New York Academy of Sciences, 481*, 7–19. (2)

Bundy, H., Stahl, B. H., & MacCabe, J. H. (2011). A systematic review and meta-analysis of the fertility of patients with schizophrenia and their unaffected relatives. *Acta Psychiatrica Scandinavica, 123*, 98–106. (15)

Burman, D. D., Lie-Nemeth, T., Brandfonbrener, A. G., Parisi, T., & Meyer, J. R. (2009). Altered finger representations in sensorimotor cortex of musicians with focal dystonia: Precentral cortex. *Brain Imaging and Behavior, 3*, 10–23. (5)

Burr, D. C., Morrone, M. C., & Ross, J. (1994). Selective suppression of the magnocellular visual pathway during saccadic eye movements. *Nature, 371*, 511–513. (6)

Burrell, B. (2004). *Postcards from the brain museum*. New York: Broadway Books. (4)

Burton, H., Snyder, A. Z., Conturo, T. E., Akbudak, E., Ollinger, J. M., & Raichle, M. E. (2002). Adaptive changes in early and late blind: A fMRI study of Braille reading. *Journal of Neurophysiology, 87*, 589–607. (5)

Burton, R. F. (1994). *Physiology by numbers*. Cambridge, England: Cambridge University Press. (10)

Busche, M. A., Eichhoff, G., Adelsberger, H., Abramowski, D., Wiederhold, K.-H., Haass, C., et al. (2008). Clusters of hyperactive neurons near amyloid plaques in a mouse model of Alzheimer's disease. *Science, 321*, 1686–1689. (13)

Buschman, T. J., & Miller, E. K. (2007). Top-down versus bottom-up control of attention in the prefrontal and posterior parietal cortices. *Science, 315*, 1860–1862. (14)

Buss, D. M. (1994). The strategies of human mating. *American Scientist, 82*, 238–249. (1)

Buss, D. M. (2000). Desires in human mating. *Annals of the New York Academy of Sciences, 907*, 39–49. (11)

Buss, D. M. (2001). Cognitive biases and emotional wisdom in the evolution of conflict between the sexes. *Current Directions in Psychological Science, 10*, 219–223. (11)

Bussiere, J. R., Beer, T. M., Neiss, M. B., & Janowsky, J. S. (2005). Androgen deprivation impairs memory in older men. *Behavioral Neuroscience, 119*, 1429–1437. (11)

Butler, M. P., Turner, K. W., Park, J. H., Schoomer, E. E., Zucker, I., & Gorman, M. R. (2010). Seasonal regulation of reproduction: Altered role of melatonin under naturalistic conditions in hamsters. *Proceedings of the Royal Society B, 277,* 2867–2874. (9)

Buxbaum, L. J. (2006). On the right (and left) track: Twenty years of progress in studying hemispatial neglect. *Cognitive Neuropsychology, 23,* 184–201. (14)

Byl, N. N., McKenzie, A., & Nagarajan, S. S. (2000). Differences in somatosensory hand organization in a healthy flutist and a flutist with focal hand dystonia: A case report. *Journal of Hand Therapy, 13,* 302–309. (5)

Byne, W., Tobet, S., Mattiace, L. A., Lasco, M. S., Kemether, E., Edgar, M. A., et al. (2001). The interstitial nuclei of the human anterior hypothalamus: An investigation of variation with sex, sexual orientation, and HIV status. *Hormones and Behavior, 40,* 86–92. (11)

Byrne, M., Agerbo, E., Ewald, H., Eaton, W. W., & Mortensen, P. B. (2003). Parental age and risk of schizophrenia. *Archives of General Psychiatry, 60,* 673–678. (15)

Cabeza, R., Anderson, N. D., Locantore, J. K., & McIntosh, A. R. (2002). Aging gracefully: Compensatory brain activity in high-performing older adults. *NeuroImage, 17,* 1394–1402. (5)

Caccappolo-van Vliet, E., Miozzo, M., & Stern, Y. (2004). Phonological dyslexia: A test case for reading models. *Psychological Science, 15,* 583–590. (14)

Cadoret, R. J., Yates, W. R., Troughton, E., Woodworth, G., & Stewart, M. A. (1995). Genetic-environmental interaction in the genesis of aggressivity and conduct disorders. *Archives of General Psychiatry, 52,* 916–924. (12)

Cahill, L. (2006). Why sex matters for neuroscience. *Nature Reviews Neuroscience, 7,* 477–484. (11)

Cahill, L., & McGaugh, J. L. (1998). Mechanisms of emotional arousal and lasting declarative memory. *Trends in Neurosciences, 21,* 294–299. (13)

Cahn, W., Hulshoff, H. E., Lems, E. B. T. E., van Haren, N. E. M., Schnack, H. G., van der Linden, J. A., et al. (2002). Brain volume changes in first-episode schizophrenia. *Archives of General Psychiatry, 59,* 1002–1010. (15)

Cai, D. J., Mednick, S. A., Harrison, E. M., Kanady, J. C., & Mednick, S. C. (2009). REM, not incubation, improves creativity by priming associative networks. *Proceedings of the National Academy of Sciences (U.S.A.), 106,* 10130–10134. (9)

Cai, D. J., & Rickard, T. C. (2009). Reconsidering the role of sleep for motor memory. *Behavioral Neuroscience, 123,* 1153–1157. (9)

Cai, D. J., Shuman, T., Gorman, M. R., Sage, J. R., & Anagnostaras, S. G. (2009). Sleep selectively enhances hippocampus-dependent memory in mice. *Behavioral Neuroscience, 123,* 713–719. (9)

Cajal, S. R. (1937). *Recollections of my life. Memoirs of the American Philosophical Society, 8.* (Original work published 1901–1917) (2)

Caldara, R., & Seghier, M. L. (2009). The fusiform face area responds automatically to statistical regularities optimal for face categorization. *Human Brain Mapping, 30,* 1615–1625. (6)

Calder, A. J., Keane, J., Manes, F., Antoun, N., & Young, A. W. (2000). Impaired recognition and experience of disgust following brain injury. *Nature Neuroscience, 3,* 1077–1078. (12)

Caldwell, J. A., Mu, Q., Smith, J. K., Mishory, A., Caldwell, J. L., Peters, G., et al. (2005). Are individual differences in fatigue vulnerability related to baseline differences in cortical activation? *Behavioral Neuroscience, 119,* 694–707. (9)

Calignano, A., LaRana, G., Giuffrida, A., & Piomelli, D. (1998). Control of pain initiation by endogenous cannabinoids. *Nature, 394,* 277–281. (3)

Cameron, H. A., & McKay, R. D. G. (1999). Restoring production of hippocampal neurons in old age. *Nature Neuroscience, 2,* 894–897. (12)

Cameron, N. M., Champagne, F. A., Parent, C., Fish, E. W., Ozaki-Kuroda, K., & Meaney, M. J. (2005). The programming of individual differences in defensive responses and reproductive strategies in the rat through variations in maternal care. *Neuroscience and Biobehavioral Reviews, 29,* 843–865. (5)

Camp, N. J., Lowry, M. R., Richards, R. L., Plenk, A. M., Carter, C., Hensel, C. H., et al. (2005). Genome-wide linkage analyses of extended Utah pedigrees identifies loci that influence recurrent, early-onset major depression and anxiety disorders. *American Journal of Medical Genetics Part B: Neuropsychiatric Genetics, 135B,* 85–93. (15)

Campbell, S. S., & Tobler, I. (1984). Animal sleep: A review of sleep duration across phylogeny. *Neuroscience and Biobehavioral Reviews, 8,* 269–300. (9)

Camperio-Ciani, A., Corna, F., & Capiluppi, C. (2004). Evidence for maternally inherited factors favouring male homosexuality and promoting female fecundity. *Proceedings of the Royal Society of London, B, 271,* 2217–2221. (11)

Campfield, L. A., Smith, F. J., Guisez, Y., Devos, R., & Burn, P. (1995). Recombinant mouse OB protein: Evidence for a peripheral signal linking adiposity and central neural networks. *Science, 269,* 546–552. (10)

Canal, C. E., & Gold, P. E. (2007). Different temporal profiles of amnesia after intra-hippocampus and intra-amygdala infusions of anisomycin. *Behavioral Neuroscience, 121,* 732–741. (13)

Canepari, M., Rossi, R., Pellegrino, M. A., Orell, R. W., Cobbold, M., Harridge, S., et al. (2005). Effects of resistance training on myosin function studies by the in vitro motility assay in young and older men. *Journal of Applied Physiology, 98,* 2390–2395. (8)

Cannon, M., Jones, P. B., & Murray, R. M. (2002). Obstetric complications and schizophrenia: Historical and meta-analytic review. *American Journal of Psychiatry, 159,* 1080–1092. (15)

Cannon, W. B. (1929). Organization for physiological homeostasis. *Physiological Reviews, 9,* 399–431. (10)

Cannon, W. B. (1945). *The way of an investigator.* New York: Norton. (inside cover)

Cao, M., & Guilleminault, C. (2010). Families with sleepwalking. *Sleep Medicine, 11,* 726–734. (9)

Cao, Y. Q., Mantyh, P. W., Carlson, E. J., Gillespie, A.-M., Epstein, C. J., & Basbaum, A. I. (1998). Primary afferent tachykinins are required to experience moderate to intense pain. *Nature, 392,* 390–394. (7)

Capela, J. P., Carmo, H., Remião, F., Bastos, M. L., Meisel, A., & Carvalho, F. (2009). Molecular and cellular mechanisms of ecstasty-induced neurotoxicity: An overview. *Molecular Neurobiology, 39,* 210–271. (3)

Cardno, A. G., Marshall, E. J., Coid, B., Macdonald, A. M., Ribchester, T. R., Davies, N. J., et al. (1999). Heritability estimates for psychotic disorders. *Archives of General Psychiatry, 56,* 162–168. (15)

Cardoso, F. L. (2009). Recalled sex-typed behavior in childhood and sports' preferences in adulthood of heterosexual, bisexual, and homosexual men from Brazil, Turkey, and Thailand. *Archives of Sexual Behavior, 38,* 726–736. (11)

Carlsson, A. (2001). A paradigm shift in brain research. *Science, 294,* 1021–1024. (3)

Carpenter, G. A., & Grossberg, S. (1984). A neural theory of circadian rhythms: Aschoff's rule in diurnal and nocturnal mammals. *American Journal of Physiology, 247,* R1067–R1082. (9)

Carreiras, M., Seghier, M. L., Baquero, S., Estévez, A., Lozano, A., Devlin, J. T., et al. (2009). An anatomical signature for literacy. *Nature, 461,* 983–986. (5)

Carruth, L. L., Reisert, I., & Arnold, A. P. (2002). Sex chromosome genes directly affect brain sexual differentiation. *Nature Neuroscience, 5,* 933–934. (11)

Carter, C. S. (1992). Hormonal influences on human sexual behavior. In J. B. Becker, S. M. Breedlove, & D. Crews (Eds.), *Behavioral endocrinology* (pp. 131–142). Cambridge, MA: MIT Press. (11)

Cash, S. S., Halgren, E., Dehghani, N., Rosssetti, A. O., Thesen, T., Wang, C. M., et al. (2009). The human K-complex represents an isolated cortical down-state. *Science, 324,* 1084–1087. (9)

Caspi, A., McClay, J., Moffitt, T. E., Mill, J., Martin, J., Craig, I. W., et al. (2002). Role of genotype in the cycle of violence in maltreated children. *Science, 297,* 851–854. (12)

Caspi, A., Sugden, K., Moffitt, T. E., Taylor, A., Craig, I. W., Harrington, H., et al. (2003). Influence of life stress on depression: Moderation by a polymorphism in the 5-HTT gene. *Science, 301,* 386–389. (15)

Cassia, V. M., Turati, C., & Simion, F. (2004). Can a nonspecific bias toward top-heavy patterns explain newborns' face preference? *Psychological Science, 15,* 379–383. (6)

Castellucci, V. F., Pinsker, H., Kupfermann, I., & Kandel, E. (1970). Neuronal mechanisms of habituation and dishabituation of the gill-withdrawal reflex in *Aplysia. Science, 167,* 1745–1748. (13)

Castner, S. A., & Goldman-Rakic, P. S. (2004). Enhancement of working memory in aged monkeys by a sensitizing regimen of dopamine D1 receptor stimulation. *Journal of Neuroscience, 24,* 1446–1450. (13)

Castrén, E., & Rantamäki, T. (2010). The role of BDNF and its receptors in depression and antidepressant drug action: Reactivation of developmental plasticity. *Developmental Neurobiology, 70,* 289–296. (15)

Catalano, S. M., & Shatz, C. J. (1998). Activity-dependent cortical target selection by thalamic axons. *Science, 281,* 559–562. (5)

Catania, K. C. (2006). Underwater "sniffing" by semi-aquatic mammals. *Nature, 444*, 1024–1025. (7)

Catchpole, C. K., & Slater, P. J. B. (1995). *Bird song: Biological themes and variations*. Cambridge, England: Cambridge University Press. (1)

Catmur, C., Walsh, V., & Heyes, C. (2007). Sensorimotor learning configures the human mirror system. *Current Biology, 17*, 1527–1531. (8)

Catterall, W. A. (1984). The molecular basis of neuronal excitability. *Science, 223*, 653–661. (2)

Censits, D. M., Ragland, J. D., Gur, R. C., & Gur, R. E. (1997). Neuropsychological evidence supporting a neurodevelopmental model of schizophrenia: A longitudinal study. *Schizophrenia Research, 24*, 289–298. (15)

Cepeda-Benito, A., Davis, K. W., Reynoso, J. T., & Harraid, J. H. (2005). Associative and behavioral tolerance to the analgesic effects of nicotine in rats: Tail-flick and paw-lick assays. *Psychopharmacology, 180*, 224–233. (3)

Cerletti, U., & Bini, L. (1938). L'Elettro-shock. *Archivio Generale di Neurologia e Psichiatria e Psicoanalisi, 19*, 266–268. (15)

Cervantes, M. C., & Delville, Y. (2009). Serotonin 5-HT_{1A} and 5-HT_3 receptors in an impulsive-aggressive phenotype. *Behavioral Neuroscience, 123*, 589–598. (12)

Chabris, C. F., & Glickman, M. E. (2006). Sex differences in intellectual performance: Analysis of a large cohort of competitive chess players. *Psychological Science, 17*, 1040–1046. (4)

Chafee, M. V., & Goldman-Rakic, P. S. (1998). Matching patterns of activity in primate prefrontal area 8a and parietal area 7ip neurons during a spatial working memory task. *Journal of Neurophysiology, 79*, 2919–2940. (13)

Chalmers, D. J. (1995). Facing up to the problem of consciousness. *Journal of Consciousness Studies, 2*, 200–219. (1, 14)

Chalmers, D. L. (2004). How can we construct a science of consciousness? In M. S. Gazzaniga (Ed.), *The cognitive neurosciences* (3rd ed.) (pp. 1111–1119). Cambridge, MA: MIT Press. (14)

Chalmers, D. (2007). Naturalistic dualism. In M. Velmans & S. Schneider (Eds.), *The Blackwell companion to consciousness* (pp. 359–368). Malden, MA: Blackwell. (1)

Chan, C. S., Guzman, J. N., Ilijic, E., Mercer, J. N., Rick, C., Tkatch, T., et al. (2007). "Rejuvenation" protects neurons in mouse models of Parkinson's disease. *Nature, 447*, 1081–1086. (8)

Chang, E. F., & Merzenich, M. M. (2003). Environmental noise retards auditory cortical development. *Science, 300*, 498–502. (7)

Chang, G.-Q., Gaysinskaya, V., Karatayev, O., & Leibowitz, S. F. (2008). Maternal high-fat diet and fetal programming: Increased proliferation of hypothalamic peptide-producing neurons that increase risk for overeating and obesity. *Journal of Neuroscience, 28*, 12107–12119. (10)

Changeux, J.-P. (2010). Nicotine addiction and nicotinic receptors: Lessons from genetically modified mice. *Nature Reviews Neuroscience, 11*, 389–401. (3)

Chao, M. V. (2010). A conversation with Rita Levi-Montalcini. *Annual Review of Physiology, 72*, 1–13. (5)

Chaudhari, N., Landin, A. M., & Roper, S. D. (2000). A metabotropic glutamate receptor variant functions as a taste receptor. *Nature Neuroscience, 3*, 113–119. (7)

Chaudhri, N., Sahuque, L. L., & Janak, P. H. (2009). Ethanol seeking triggered by environmental context is attenuated by blocking dopamine D1 receptors in the nucleus accumbens core and shell in rats. *Psychopharmacology, 207*, 303–314. (3)

Chee, M. J. S., Myers, M. G. Jr., Price, C. J., & Colmers, W. F. (2010). Neuropeptide Y suppresses anorexigenic output from the ventromedial nucleus of the hypothalamus. *Journal of Neuroscience, 30*, 3380–3390. (10)

Chee, M. W. L., Tan, J. C., Zheng, H., Parimal, S., Weissman, D. H., Zagorodnov, V., et al. (2008). Lapsing during sleep deprivation is associated with distributed changes in brain activation. *Journal of Neuroscience, 28*, 5519–5528. (9)

Cheer, J. F., Wassum, K. M., Heien, M. L. A. V., Phillips, P. E. M., & Wightman, R. M. (2004). Cannabinoids enhance subsecond dopamine release in the nucleus accumbens of awake rats. *Journal of Neuroscience, 24*, 4393–4400. (3)

Chen, L. M., Friedman, R. M., & Roe, A. W. (2003). Optical imaging of a tactile illusion in area 3b of the primary somatosensory cortex. *Science, 302*, 881–885. (7)

Chen, Z.-Y., Jing, D., Bath, K. G., Ieraci, A., Khan, T., Siao, C.-J., et al. (2006). Genetic variant BDNF (Val66Met) polymorphism alters anxiety-related behavior. *Science, 314*, 140–143. (12)

Cheour-Luhtanen, M., Alho, K., Sainio, K., Rinne, T., Reinikainen, K., Pohjavuoir, M., et al. (1996). The ontogenetically earliest discriminative response of the human brain. *Psychophysiology, 33*, 478–481. (14)

Chiang, M.-C., Barysheva, M., Shattuck, D. W., Lee, A. D., Madsen, S. K., Avedissian, C., et al. (2009). Genetics of brain fiber architecture and intellectual performance. *Journal of Neuroscience, 29*, 2212–2224. (4)

Chiueh, C. C. (1988). Dopamine in the extrapyramidal motor function: A study based upon the MPTP-induced primate model of Parkinsonism. *Annals of the New York Academy of Sciences, 515*, 226–248. (8)

Chivers, M. L., Rieger, G., Latty, E., & Bailey, J. M. (2004). A sex difference in the specificity of sexual arousal. *Psychological Science, 15*, 736–744. (11)

Cho, K. (2001). Chronic "jet lag" produces temporal lobe atrophy and spatial cognitive deficits. *Nature Neuroscience, 4*, 567–568. (9)

Choi, D.-S., Cascini, M.-G., Mailliard, W., Young, H., Paredes, P., McMahon, T., et al. (2004). The type I equilibrative nucleoside transporter regulates ethanol intoxication and preference. *Nature Neuroscience, 7*, 855–861. (3)

Chomsky, N. (1980). *Rules and representations*. New York: Columbia University Press. (14)

Chuang, H., Prescott, E. D., Kong, H., Shields, S., Jordt, S.-E., Basbaum, A. I., et al. (2001). Bradykinin and nerve growth factor release the capsaicin receptor from PtdIns(4, 5)P2-mediated inhibition. *Nature, 411*, 957–962. (7)

Churchland, P. S. (1986). *Neurophilosophy*. Cambridge, Massachusetts: MIT Press. (1)

Cicone, N., Wapner, W., Foldi, N. S., Zurif, E., & Gardner, H. (1979). The relation between gesture and language in aphasic communication. *Brain and Language, 8*, 342–349. (14)

Clahsen, H., & Almazen, M. (1998). Syntax and morphology in Williams syndrome. *Cognition, 68*, 167–198. (14)

Clark, D. A., Mitra, P. P., & Wang, S. S.-H. (2001). Scalable architecture in mammalian brains. *Nature, 411*, 189–193. (4)

Clark, R. E., Broadbent, N. J., & Squire, L. R. (2007). The hippocampus and spatial memory: Findings with a novel modification of the water maze. *Journal of Neuroscience, 27*, 6647–6654. (13)

Clark, R. E., & Lavond, D. G. (1993). Reversible lesions of the red nucleus during acquisition and retention of a classically conditioned behavior in rabbits. *Behavioral Neuroscience, 107*, 264–270. (13)

Clark, W. S. (2004). Is the zone-tailed hawk a mimic? *Birding, 36*, 494–498. (1)

Clarke, S., Assal, G., & deTribolet, N. (1993). Left hemisphere strategies in visual recognition, topographical orientation and time planning. *Neuropsychologia, 31*, 99–113. (14)

Clarkson, A. N., Huang, B. S., MacIsaac, S. E., Mody, I., & Carmichael, S. T. (2010). Reducing excessive GABA-mediated tonic inhibition promotes functional recovery after a stroke. *Nature, 468*, 305–309. (5)

Clayton, E. C., & Williams, C. L. (2000). Glutamatergic influences on the nucleus paragigantocellularis: Contribution to performance in avoidance and spatial memory tasks. *Behavioral Neuroscience, 114*, 707–712. (9)

Cleary, L. J., Hammer, M., & Byrne, J. H. (1989). Insights into the cellular mechanisms of short-term sensitization in *Aplysia*. In T. J. Carew & D. B. Kelley (Eds.), *Perspectives in neural systems and behavior* (pp. 105–119). New York: Liss. (13)

Cleary, M., Moody, A. D., Buchanan, A., Stewart, H., & Dutton, G. N. (2009). Assessment of a computer-based treatment for older amblyopes: The Glasgow Pilot Study. *Eye, 23*, 124–131. (6)

Clelland, C. D., Choi, M., Romberg, C., Clemenson, G. D. Jr., Fragniere, A., Tyers, P., et al. (2009). A functional role for adult hippocampal neurogenesis in spatial pattern separation. *Science, 325*, 210–213. (5)

Clutton-Brock, T. (2009). Cooperation between non-kin in animal societies. *Nature, 462*, 51–57. (1)

Clutton-Brock, T. H., O'Riain, M. J., Brotherton, P. N. M., Gaynor, D., Kansky, R., Griffin, A. S., et al. (1999). Selfish sentinels in cooperative mammals. *Science, 284*, 1640–1644. (1)

Coan, J. A., Schaefer, H. S., & Davidson, R. J. (2006). Lending a hand: Social regulation of the neural response to threat. *Psychological Science, 17*, 1032–1039. (12)

Cobos, P., Sánchez, M., Pérez, N., & Vila, J. (2004). Effects of spinal cord injuries on the subjective component of emotions. *Cognition and Emotion, 18*, 281–287. (12)

Coccaro, E. F., & Lee, R. (2010). Cerebrospinal fluid 5-hydroxyindolacetic acid and homovanillic acid:

Reciprocal relationships with impulsive aggression in human subjects. *Journal of Neural Transmission, 117,* 241–248. (12)

Coderre, T. J., Katz, J., Vaccarino, A. L., & Melzack, R. (1993). Contribution of central neuroplasticity to pathological pain: Review of clinical and experimental evidence. *Pain, 52,* 259–285. (7)

Cohen, D., & Nicolelis, M. A. L. (2004). Reduction of single-neuron firing uncertainty by cortical ensembles during motor skill learning. *Journal of Neuroscience, 24,* 3574–3582. (8)

Cohen, L. G., Celnik, P., Pascual-Leone, A., Corwell, B., Faiz, L., Dambrosia, J., et al. (1997). Functional relevance of cross-modal plasticity in blind humans. *Nature, 389,* 180–183. (5)

Cohen, S., Frank, E., Doyle, W. J., Skoner, D. P., Rabin, B. S., & Swaltney, J. M., Jr. (1998). Types of stressors that increase susceptibility to the common cold in healthy adults. *Health Psychology, 17,* 214–223. (12)

Cohen-Kettenis, P. T. (2005). Gender change in 46, XY persons with 5α-reductase-2 deficiency and 17β-hydroxysteroid dehydrogenase-3 deficiency. *Archives of Sexual Behavior, 34,* 399–410. (11)

Cohen-Tannoudji, M., Babinet, C., & Wassef, M. (1994). Early determination of a mouse somatosensory cortex marker. *Nature, 368,* 460–463. (5)

Colantuoni, C., Rada, P., McCarthy, J., Patten, C., Avena, N. M., Chadeayne, A., et al. (2002). Evidence that intermittent, excessive sugar intake causes endogenous opioid dependence. *Obesity Research, 10,* 478–488. (10)

Colantuoni, C., Schwenker, J., McCarthy, J., Rada, P., Ladenheim, B., Cadet, J.-L., et al. (2001). Excessive sugar intake alters binding to dopamine and mu-opioid receptors in the brain. *NeuroReport, 12,* 3549–3552. (10)

Colapinto, J. (1997, December 11). The true story of John/Joan. *Rolling Stone,* pp. 54–97. (11)

Collingridge, G. L., Peineau, S., Howland, J. G., & Wang, Y. T. (2010). Long-term depression in the CNS. *Nature Reviews Neuroscience, 11,* 459–473. (13)

Colom, R., Haier, R. J., Head, K., Álvarez-Linera, J., Quiroga, M. A., Shih, P. C., et al. (2009). Gray matter correlates of fluid, crystallized, and spatial intelligence: Testing the P-FIT model. *Intelligence, 37,* 124–135. (4)

Conn, P. M., & Parker, J. V. (2008). Winners and losers in the animal-research war. *American Scientist, 96,* 184–186. (1)

Connine, C. M., Blasko, D. G., & Hall, M. (1991). Effects of subsequent sentence context in auditory word recognition: Temporal and linguistic constraints. *Journal of Memory and Language, 30,* 234–250. (14)

Considine, R. V., Sinha, M. K., Heiman, M. L., Kriauciunas, A., Stephens, T. W., Nyce, M. R., et al. (1996). Serum immunoreactive-leptin concentrations in normal-weight and obese humans. *New England Journal of Medicine, 334,* 292–295. (10)

Cooke, B. M., Tabibnia, G., & Breedlove, S. M. (1999). A brain sexual dimorphism controlled by adult circulating androgens. *Proceedings of the National Academy of Sciences, USA, 96,* 7538–7540. (11)

Coppola, D. M., Purves, H. R., McCoy, A. N., & Purves, D. (1998). The distribution of oriented contours in the real world. *Proceedings of the National Academy of Sciences, USA, 95,* 4002–4006. (6)

Corcoran, A. J., Barber, J. R., & Conner, W. E. (2009). Tiger moth jams bat sonar. *Science, 325,* 325–327. (7)

Corkin, S. (1984). Lasting consequences of bilateral medial temporal lobectomy: Clinical course and experimental findings in H. M. *Seminars in Neurology, 4,* 249–259. (13)

Corkin, S. (2002). What's new with the amnesic patient H. M.? *Nature Reviews Neuroscience, 3,* 153–159. (13)

Corkin, S., Rosen, T. J., Sullivan, E. V., & Clegg, R. A. (1989). Penetrating head injury in young adulthood exacerbates cognitive decline in later years. *Journal of Neuroscience, 9,* 3876–3883. (5)

Cosmelli, D., David, O., Lachaux, J.-P., Martinerie, J., Garnero, L., Renault, B., et al. (2004). Waves of consciousness: Ongoing cortical patterns during binocular rivalry. *NeuroImage, 23,* 128–140. (14)

Coss, R. G., Brandon, J. G., & Globus, A. (1980). Changes in morphology of dendritic spines on honeybee calycal interneurons associated with cumulative nursing and foraging experiences. *Brain Research, 192,* 49–59. (5)

Costa, M., Braun, C., & Birbaumer, N. (2003). Gender differences in response to pictures of nudes: A magnetoencephalography study. *Biological Psychology, 63,* 129–147. (4)

Costa, V. D., Lang, P. J., Sabatinelli, D., Versace, F., & Bradley, M. M. (2010). Emotional imagery: Assessing pleasure and arousal in the brain's reward circuitry. *Human Brain Mapping, 31,* 1446–1457. (3)

Courchesne, E., Townsend, J., Akshoomoff, N. A., Saitoh, O., Yeung-Courchesne, R., Lincoln, A. J., et al. (1994). Impairment in shifting attention in autistic and cerebellar patients. *Behavioral Neuroscience, 108,* 848–865. (4)

Cowart, B. J. (2005, Spring). Taste, our body's gustatory gatekeeper. *Cerebrum, 7(2),* 7–22. (7)

Cowey, A., & Stoerig, P. (1995). Blindsight in monkeys. *Nature, 373,* 247–249. (6)

Cox, J. J., Reimann, F., Nicholas, A. K., Thornton, G., Roberts, E., Springell, K., et al. (2006). An *SCNxA* channelopathy causes congenital inability to experience pain. *Nature, 304,* 115–117. (7)

Craig, A. D., Krout, K., & Andrew, D. (2001). Quantitative response characteristics of thermoreceptive and nociceptive lamina I spinothalamic neurons in the cat. *Journal of Neurophysiology, 86,* 1459–1480. (7)

Craig, A. M., & Boudin, H. (2001). Molecular heterogeneity of central synapses: Afferent and target regulation. *Nature Neuroscience, 4,* 569–578. (3)

Crair, M. C., Gillespie, D. C., & Stryker, M. P. (1998). The role of visual experience in the development of columns in cat visual cortex. *Science, 279,* 566–570. (6)

Crair, M. C., & Malenka, R. C. (1995). A critical period for long-term potentiation at thalamocortical synapses. *Nature, 375,* 325–328. (6)

Cravchik, A., & Goldman, D. (2000). Neurochemical individuality. *Archives of General Psychiatry, 57,* 1105–1114. (3)

Cremers, C. W. R. J., & van Rijn, P. M. (1991). Acquired causes of deafness in childhood. *Annals of the New York Academy of Sciences, 630,* 197–202. (7)

Crick, F. C., & Koch, C. (2004). A framework for consciousness. In M. S. Gazzaniga (Ed.), *The cognitive neurosciences* (3rd ed., pp. 1133–1143). Cambridge, MA: MIT Press. (14)

Crick, F., & Mitchison, G. (1983). The function of dream sleep. *Nature, 304,* 111–114. (9)

Critchley, H. D., Mathias, C. J., & Dolan, R. J. (2001). Neuroanatomical basis for first- and second-order representations of bodily states. *Nature Neuroscience, 4,* 207–212. (12)

Critchley, H. D., & Rolls, E. T. (1996). Hunger and satiety modify the responses of olfactory and visual neurons in the primate orbito-frontal cortex. *Journal of Neurophysiology, 75,* 1673–1686. (10)

Crockett, M. J., Clark, L., & Robbins, T. W. (2009). Reconciling the role of serotonin in behavioral inhibition and aversion: Acute tryptophan depletion abolishes punishment-induced inhibition in humans. *Journal of Neuroscience, 29,* 11993–11999. (12)

Crossin, K. L., & Krushel, L. A. (2000). Cellular signaling by neural cell adhesion molecules of the immunoglobulin family. *Developmental Dynamics, 218,* 260–279. (5)

Crossley, N. A., & Constante, M. (2010). Efficacy of atypical v. typical antipsychotics in the treatment of early psychosis: meta-analysis. *British Journal of Psychiatry, 196,* 434–439. (15)

Crystal, J. D. (2009). Elements of episodic-like memory in animal models. *Behavioural Processes, 80,* 269–277. (13)

Cummings, D. E., Clement, K., Purnell, J. Q., Vaisse, C., Foster, K. E., Frayo, R. S., et al. (2002). Elevated plasma ghrelin levels in Prader-Willi syndrome. *Nature Medicine, 8,* 643–644. (10)

Cummings, D. E., & Overduin, J. (2007). Gastrointestinal regulation of food intake. *Journal of Clinical Investigation, 117,* 13–23. (10)

Cunningham, W. A., Van Bavel, J. J., & Johnsen, I. R. (2008). Adaptive flexibility: Evaluative processing goals shape amygdala activity. *Psychological Science, 19,* 152–160. (12)

Cusack, R., Carlyon, R. P., & Robertson, I. H. (2000). Neglect between but not within auditory objects. *Journal of Cognitive Neuroscience, 12,* 1056–1065. (14)

Cutler, W. B., Preti, G., Krieger, A., Huggins, G. R., Garcia, C. R., & Lawley, H. J. (1986). Human axillary secretions influence women's menstrual cycles: The role of donor extract from men. *Hormones and Behavior, 20,* 463–473. (7)

Cuzon, V. C., Yeh, P. W. L., Yanagawa, Y., Obata, K., & Yeh, H. H. (2008). Ethanol consumption during early pregnancy alters the disposition of tangentially migrating GABAergic interneurons in the fetal cortex. *Journal of Neuroscience, 28,* 1854–1864. (5)

Czeisler, C. A., Johnson, M. P., Duffy, J. F., Brown, E. N., Ronda, J. M., & Kronauer, R. E. (1990).

Exposure to bright light and darkness to treat physiologic maladaptation to night work. *New England Journal of Medicine, 322,* 1253–1259. (9)

Czeisler, C. A., Weitzman, E. D., Moore-Ede, M. C., Zimmerman, J. C., & Knauer, R. S. (1980). Human sleep: Its duration and organization depend on its circadian phase. *Science, 210,* 1264–1267. (9)

Dabbs, J. M., Jr., Carr, T. S., Frady, R. L., & Riad, J. K. (1995). Testosterone, crime, and misbehavior among 692 male prison inmates. *Personality and Individual Differences, 18,* 627–633. (12)

Dale, N., Schacher, S., & Kandel, E. R. (1988). Long-term facilitation in *Aplysia* involves increase in transmitter release. *Science, 239,* 282–285. (13)

Dale, P. S., Harlaar, N., Haworth, C. M. A., & Plomin, R. (2010). Two by two: A twin study of second-language acquisition. *Psychological Science, 21,* 635–640. (1)

Dalterio, S., & Bartke, A. (1979). Perinatal exposure to cannabinoids alters male reproductive function in mice. *Science, 205,* 1420–1422. (11)

Dalton, K. (1968). Ante-natal progesterone and intelligence. *British Journal of Psychiatry, 114,* 1377–1382. (11)

Dalton, P., Doolittle, N., & Breslin, P. A. (2002). Gender-specific induction of enhanced sensitivity to odors. *Nature Neuroscience, 5,* 199–200. (7)

Damasio, A. (1999). *The feeling of what happens.* New York: Harcourt Brace. (12)

Damasio, A. R. (1994). *Descartes' error.* New York: Putnam's Sons. (12)

Damsma, G., Pfaus, J. G., Wenkstern, D., Phillips, A. G., & Fibiger, H. C. (1992). Sexual behavior increases dopamine transmission in the nucleus accumbens and striatum of male rats: A comparison with novelty and locomotion. *Behavioral Neuroscience, 106,* 181–191. (3)

Dantzer, R., O'Connor, J. C., Freund, G. G., Johnson, R. W., & Kelley, K. W. (2008). From inflammation to sickness and depression: When the immune system subjugates the brain. *Nature Reviews Neuroscience, 9,* 46–57. (12)

Darwin, C. (1859). *The origin of species.* New York: D. Appleton. (1)

Davalos, D., Grutzendler, J., Yang, G., Kim, J. V., Zuo, Y., Jung, S., et al. (2005). ATP mediates rapid microglial response to local brain injury *in vivo. Nature Neuroscience, 8,* 752–758. (2)

Davidson, R. J. (1984). Affect, cognition, and hemispheric specialization. In C. E. Izard, J. Kagan, & R. B. Zajonc (Eds.), *Emotions, cognition, & behavior* (pp. 320–365). Cambridge, England: Cambridge University Press. (15)

Davidson, R. J., & Fox, N. A. (1982). Asymmetrical brain activity discriminates between positive and negative affective stimuli in human infants. *Science, 218,* 1235–1237. (12)

Davidson, R. J., & Henriques, J. (2000). Regional brain function in sadness and depression. In J. C. Borod (Ed.), *The neuropsychology of emotion* (pp. 269–297). London: Oxford University Press. (12)

Davidson, S., Zhang, X., Khasabov, S. G., Simone, D. A., & Giesler, G. J. Jr. (2009). Relief of itch by scratching: State-dependent inhibition of primate spinothalamic tract neurons. *Nature Neuroscience, 12,* 544–546. (7)

Davidson, S., Zhang, X., Yoon, C. H., Khasabov, S. G., Simone, D. A., & Giesler, G. J., Jr. (2007). The itch-producing agents histamine and cowhage activate separate populations of primate spinothalamic tract neurons. *Journal of Neuroscience, 27,* 10007–10014. (7)

Davies, G., Welham, J., Chant, D., Torrey, E. F., & McGrath, J. (2003). A systematic review and meta-analysis of Northern hemisphere season of birth effects in schizophrenia. *Schizophrenia Bulletin, 29,* 587–593. (15)

Davies, P. (2000). A very incomplete comprehensive theory of Alzheimer's disease. *Annals of the New York Academy of Sciences, 924,* 8–16. (13)

Davies, P. (2006). *The Goldilocks enigma.* Boston, MA: Houghton Mifflin. (1)

Davis, E. C., Shryne, J. E., & Gorski, R. A. (1995). A revised critical period for the sexual differentiation of the sexually dimorphic nucleus of the preoptic area in the rat. *Neuroendocrinology, 62,* 579–585. (11)

Davis, J. I., Senghas, A., Brandt, F., & Ochsner, K. N. (2010). The effects of BOTOX injections on emotional experience. *Emotion, 10,* 433–440. (12)

Davis, J. M., Chen, N., & Glick, I. D. (2003). A meta-analysis of the efficacy of second-generation antipsychotics. *Archives of General Psychiatry, 60,* 553–564. (15)

Davis, K. D., Kiss, Z. H. T., Luo, L., Tasker, R. R., Lozano, A. M., & Dostrovsky, J. O. (1998). Phantom sensations generated by thalamic microstimulation. *Nature, 391,* 385–387. (5)

Dawkins, R. (1989). *The selfish gene* (new ed.). Oxford, England: Oxford University Press. (1)

Dawson, T. M., & Dawson, V. L. (2003). Molecular pathways of neurodegeneration in Parkinson's disease. *Science, 302,* 819–822. (8)

Dawson, T. M., Gonzalez-Zulueta, M., Kusel, J., & Dawson, V. L. (1998). Nitric oxide: Diverse actions in the central and peripheral nervous system. *The Neuroscientist, 4,* 96–112. (3)

Day, S. (2005). Some demographic and sociocultural aspects of synesthesia. In L. C. Robertson & N. Sagiv (Eds.), *Synesthesis* (pp. 11–33). Oxford, England: Oxford University Press. (7)

de Bruin, J. P. C., Winkels, W. A. M., & de Brabander, J. M. (1997). Response learning of rats in a Morris water maze: Involvement of the medial prefrontal cortex. *Behavioral Brain Research, 85,* 47–55. (13)

de Castro, J. M. (2000). Eating behavior: Lessons from the real world of humans. *Nutrition, 16,* 800–813. (10)

de Jong, W. W., Hendriks, W., Sanyal, S., & Nevo, E. (1990). The eye of the blind mole rat (*Spalax ehrenbergi*): Regressive evolution at the molecular level. In E. Nevo & O. A. Reig (Eds.), *Evolution of subterranean mammals at the organismal and molecular levels* (pp. 383–395). New York: Liss. (9)

de la Rocha, J., Marchetti, C., Schiff, M., & Reyes, A. D. (2008). Linking the response properties of cells in auditory cortex with network architecture: Cotuning versus lateral inhibition. *Journal of Neuroscience, 28,* 9151–9163. (7)

De Luca, M., Di Page, E., Judica, A., Spinelli, D., & Zoccolotti, P. (1999). Eye movement patterns in linguistic and non-linguistic tasks in developmental surface dyslexia. *Neuropsychologia, 37,* 1407–1420. (14)

de Maat, S., Dekker, J., Schoevers, R., van Aalst, G., Gijsbers-van Wijk, C., Hendriksen, M., et al. (2008). Short psychodynamic supportive psychotherapy, antidepressants, and their combination in the treatment of major depression: A mega-analysis based on three randomized clinical trials. *Depression and Anxiety, 25,* 565–574. (15)

De Wall, C. N., Mac Donald, G., Webster, G. D., Masten, C. L., Baumeister, R. F., Powell, C., et al. (2010). Acetaminophen reduces social pain: Behavioral and neural evidence. *Psychological Science, 21,* 931–937. (7)

Deacon, T. W. (1992). Brain-language coevolution. In J. A. Hawkins & M. Gell-Mann (Eds.), *The evolution of human languages* (pp. 49–83). Reading, MA: Addison-Wesley. (14)

Deacon, T. W. (1997). *The symbolic species.* New York: Norton. (4, 14)

Deadwyler, S. A., Porrino, L., Siegel, J. M., & Hampson, R. E. (2007). Systemic and nasal delivery of orexin-A (hypocretin-1) reduces the effects of sleep deprivation on cognitive performance in nonhuman primates. *Journal of Neuroscience, 27,* 14239–14247. (9)

Dean, C. E. (2011). Psychopharmacology: A house divided. *Progress in Neuro-Psychopharmacology & Biological Psychiatry, 35,* 1–10. (15)

DeArmond, S. J., Fusco, M. M., & Dewey, M. M. (1974). *Structure of the human brain.* New York: Oxford University Press. (10)

DeCoursey, P. (1960). Phase control of activity in a rodent. *Cold Spring Harbor symposia on quantitative biology, 25,* 49–55. (9)

DeFelipe, C., Herrero, J. F., O'Brien, J. A., Palmer, J. A., Doyle, C. A., Smith, A. J. H., et al. (1998). Altered nociception, analgesia and aggression in mice lacking the receptor for substance P. *Nature, 392,* 394–397. (7)

Dehaene, S., Naccache, L., Cohen, L., LeBihan, D., Mangin, J.-F., Poline, J.-B., et al. (2001). Cerebral mechanisms of word masking and unconscious repetition priming. *Nature Neuroscience, 4,* 752–758. (14)

Del Cerro, M. C. R., Perez Izquierdo, M. A., Rosenblatt, J. S., Johnson, B. M., Pacheco, P., & Komisaruk, B. R. (1995). Brain 2-deoxyglucose levels related to maternal behavior-inducing stimuli in the rat. *Brain Research, 696,* 213–220. (11)

Del Cul, A., Dehaene, S., Reyes, P., Bravo, E., & Slachevsky, A. (2009). Causal role of prefrontal cortex in the threshold for access to consciousness. *Brain, 132,* 2531–2540. (14)

Delahanty, D. L., Raimonde, A. J., & Spoonster, E. (2000). Initial posttraumatic urinary cortisol levels predict subsequent PTSD symptoms in motor vehicle accident victims. *Biological Psychiatry, 48,* 940–947. (12)

Deliagina, T. G., Orlovsky, G. N., & Pavlova, G. A. (1983). The capacity for generation of rhythmic oscillations is distributed in the lumbosacral spinal cord of the cat. *Experimental Brain Research, 53*, 81–90. (8)

Dement, W. (1972). *Some must watch while some must sleep.* San Francisco: Freeman. (9)

Dement, W., & Kleitman, N. (1957a). Cyclic variations in EEG during sleep and their relation to eye movements, body motility, and dreaming. *Electroencephalography and Clinical Neurophysiology, 9*, 673–690. (9)

Dement, W., & Kleitman, N. (1957b). The relation of eye movements during sleep to dream activity: An objective method for the study of dreaming. *Journal of Experimental Psychology, 53*, 339–346. (9)

Dement, W. C. (1990). A personal history of sleep disorders medicine. *Journal of Clinical Neurophysiology, 7*, 17–47. (9)

Dennett, D. C. (1991). *Consciousness explained.* Boston, MA: Little, Brown. (1, 14)

deQuervain, D. J.-F., Roozendaal, B., & McGaugh, J. L. (1998). Stress and glucocorticoids impair retrieval of long-term spatial memory. *Nature, 394*, 787–790. (13)

Derégnaucourt, S., Mitra, P. P., Fehér, O., Pytte, C., & Tchernichovski, O. (2005). How sleep affects the developmental learning of bird song. *Nature, 433*, 710–716. (9)

DeSimone, J. A., Heck, G. L., & Bartoshuk, L. M. (1980). Surface active taste modifiers: A comparison of the physical and psycho-physical properties of gymnemic acid and sodium lauryl sulfate. *Chemical Senses, 5*, 317–330. (7)

DeSimone, J. A., Heck, G. L., Mierson, S., & DeSimone, S. K. (1984). The active ion transport properties of canine lingual epithelia in vitro. *Journal of General Physiology, 83*, 633–656. (7)

Desmurget, M., Reilly, K. T., Richard, N., Szathmari, A., Mottolese, C., & Sirigu, A. (2009). Movement intention after parietal cortex stimulation in humans. *Science, 324*, 811–813. (8)

Detre, J. A., & Floyd, T. F. (2001). Functional MRI and its applications to the clinical neurosciences. *Neuroscientist, 7*, 64–79. (4)

Deutsch, D., Henthorn, T., Marvin, E., & Xu, H. S. (2006). Absolute pitch among American and Chinese conservatory students: Prevalence differences, and evidence for a speech-related critical period. *Journal of the Acoustical Society of America, 119*, 719–722. (7)

Deutsch, J. A., & Ahn, S. J. (1986). The splanchnic nerve and food intake regulation. *Behavioral and Neural Biology, 45*, 43–47. (10)

Deutsch, J. A., Young, W. G., & Kalogeris, T. J. (1978). The stomach signals satiety. *Science, 201*, 165–167. (10)

DeValois, R. L., Albrecht, D. G., & Thorell, L. G. (1982). Spatial frequency selectivity of cells in macaque visual cortex. *Vision Research, 22*, 545–559. (6)

Devane, W. A., Dysarz, F. A., III, Johnson, M. R., Melvin, L. S., & Howlett, A. C. (1988). Determination and characterization of a cannabinoid receptor in rat brain. *Molecular Pharmacology, 34*, 605–613. (3)

Devor, E. J., Abell, C. W., Hoffman, P. L., Tabakoff, B., & Cloninger, C. R. (1994). Platelet MAO activity in Type I and Type II alcoholism. *An-nals of the New York Academy of Sciences, 708*, 119–128. (3)

Devor, M. (1996). Pain mechanisms. *The Neuroscientist, 2*, 233–244. (7)

DeYoe, E. A., Felleman, D. J., Van Essen, D. C., & McClendon, E. (1994). Multiple processing streams in occipitotemporal visual cortex. *Nature, 371*, 151–154. (6)

Dhingra, R., Sullivan, L., Jacques, P. F., Wang, T. J., Fox, C. S., Meigs, J. B., et al. (2007). Soft drink consumption and risk of developing cardiometabolic risk factors and the metabolic syndrome in middle-aged adults in the community. *Circulation, 116*, 480–488. (10)

Di Lorenzo, P. M., Chen, J.-Y., & Victor, J. D. (2009). Quality time: Representation of a multidimensional sensory domain through temporal coding. *Journal of Neuroscience, 29*, 9227–9238. (7)

Di Lorenzo, P. M., Leshchinskiy, S., Moroney, D. N., & Ozdoba, J. M. (2009). Making time count: Functional evidence for temporal coding of taste sensation. *Behavioral Neuroscience, 123*, 14–25. (2)

Diamond, L. M. (2007). A dynamical systems approach to the development and expression of female same-sex sexuality. *Perspectives on Psychological Science, 2*, 142–161. (11)

Diamond, M., & Sigmundson, H. K. (1997). Management of intersexuality: Guidelines for dealing with persons with ambiguous genitalia. *Archives of Pediatrics and Adolescent Medicine, 151*, 1046–1050. (11)

Diamond, M. C., Scheibel, A. B., Murphy, G. M., & Harvey, T. (1985). On the brain of a scientist: Albert Einstein. *Experimental Neurology, 88*, 198–204. (4)

Diano, S., Farr, S. A., Benoit, S. C., McNay, E. C., da Silva, I., Horvath, B., et al. (2006). Ghrelin controls hippocampal spine synapse density and memory performance. *Nature Neuroscience, 9*, 381–388. (10)

Dias-Ferreira, E., Sousa, J. C., Melo, I., Morgado, P., Mesquita, A. R., Cerqueira, J. J., et al. (2009). Chronic stress causes frontostriatal reorganization and affects decision making. *Science, 325*, 621–625. (12)

Dichgans, J. (1984). Clinical symptoms of cerebellar dysfunction and their topodiagnostic significance. *Human Neurobiology, 2*, 269–279. (8)

Dick, D. M., Johnson, J. K., Viken, R. J., & Rose, R. J. (2000). Testing between-family associations in within-family comparisons. *Psychological Science, 11*, 409–413. (3)

Dick, F., Bates, E., Wulfeck, B., Utman, J. A., Dronkers, N., & Gernsbacher, M. A. (2001). Language deficits, localization, and grammar: Evidence for a distributive model of language breakdown in aphasic patients and neurologically intact individuals. *Psychological Review, 108*, 759–788. (14)

Dickens, W. T., & Flynn, J. R. (2001). Heritability estimates versus large environmental effects: The IQ paradox resolved. *Psychological Review, 108*, 346–369. (11)

Dickerson, S. S., Gable, S. L., Irwin, M. R., Aziz, N., & Kemeny, M. E. (2009). Social-evaluative threat and proinflammatory cytokine regulation. *Psychological Science, 20*, 1237–1244. (12)

Dierks, T., Linden, D. E. J., Jandl, M., Formisano, E., Goebel, R., Lanfermann, H., et al. (1999). Activation of Heschl's gyrus during auditory hallucinations. *Neuron, 22*, 615–621. (4)

Dijk, D.-J., & Archer, S. N. (2010). *PERIOD3*, circadian phenotypes, and sleep homeostasis. *Sleep Medicine Reviews, 14*, 151–160. (9)

Dijk, D.-J., & Cajochen, C. (1997). Melatonin and the circadian regulation of sleep initiation, consolidation, structure, and the sleep EEG. *Journal of Biological Rhythms, 12*, 627–635. (9)

Dijk, D.-J., Neri, D. F., Wyatt, J. K., Ronda, J. M., Riel, E., Ritz-deCecco, A., et al. (2001). Sleep, performance, circadian rhythms, and light-dark cycles during two space shuttle flights. *American Journal of Physiology: Regulatory, Integrative, and Comparative Physiology, 281*, R1647–R1664. (9)

Dilks, D. D., Serences, J. T., Rosenau, B. J., Yantis, S., & McCloskey, M. (2007). Human adult cortical reorganization and consequent visual distortion. *Journal of Neuroscience, 27*, 9585–9594. (5)

Diller, L., Packer, O. S., Verweij, J., McMahon, M. J., Williams, D. R., & Dacey, D. M. (2004). L and M cone contributions to the midget and parasol ganglion cell receptive fields of macaque monkey retina. *Journal of Neuroscience, 24*, 1079–1088. (6)

DiMarzo, V., Fontana, A., Cadas, H., Schinelli, S., Cimino, G., Schwartz, J.-C., et al. (1994). Formation and inactivation of endogenous cannabinoid anandamide in central neurons. *Nature, 372*, 686–691. (3)

Dimond, S. J. (1979). Symmetry and asymmetry in the vertebrate brain. In D. A. Oakley & H. C. Plotkin (Eds.), *Brain, behaviour, and evolution* (pp. 189–218). London: Methuen. (14)

Dinstein, I., Hasson, U., Rubin, N., & Heeger, D. J. (2007). Brain areas selective for both observed and executed movements. *Journal of Neurophysiology, 98*, 1415–1427. (8)

Dinstein, I., Thomas, C., Humphreys, K., Minshew, N., Behrmann, M., & Heeger, D. J. (2010). Normal movement selectivity in autism. *Neuron, 66*, 461–469. (8)

Doesburg, S. M., Green, J. J., McDonald, J. J., & Ward, L. M. (2009). Rhythms of consciousness: Binocular rivalry reveals large-scale oscillatory network dynamics mediating visual perception. *PLoS ONE, 4*, e6142. (14)

Domhoff, G. W. (in press). The neural substrate for dreaming: Is it a subsystem of the default network? *Consciousness and Cognition.* (90)

Dominguez, J. M., Brann, J. H., Gil, M., & Hull, E. M. (2006). Sexual experience increases nitric oxide synthase in the medial preoptic area of male rats. *Behavioral Neuroscience, 120*, 1389–1394. (11)

Doricchi, F., Guariglia, P., Gasparini, M., & Tomaiuolo, F. (2005). Dissociation between physical and mental number line bisection in right hemisphere brain damage. *Nature Neuroscience, 8*, 1663–1665. (14)

Doty, R. L., Applebaum, S., Zusho, H., & Settle, R. G. (1985). Sex differences in odor identification ability: A cross-cultural analysis. *Neuropsychologia, 23*, 667–672. (7)

Dowling, J. E. (1987). *The retina*. Cambridge, MA: Harvard University Press. (6)

Dowling, J. E., & Boycott, B. B. (1966). Organization of the primate retina. *Proceedings of the Royal Society of London, B, 166*, 80–111. (6)

Downar, J., Mikulis, D. J., & Davis, K. D. (2003). Neural correlates of the prolonged salience of painful stimulation. *NeuroImage, 20*, 1540–1551. (7)

Downing, P. E., Chan, A. W.-Y., Peelen, M. V., Dodds, C. M., & Kanwisher, N. (2005). Domain specificity in visual cortex. *Cerebral Cortex, 16*, 1453–1461. (6)

Doyon, J., Korman, M., Morin, A., Dostie, V., Tahar, A. H., Benali, H., et al. (2009). Contribution of night and day sleep vs. simple passage of time to the consolidation of motor sequence and visuomotor adaptation learning. *Experimental Brain Research, 195*, 15–26. (9)

Dreger, A. D. (1998). *Hermaphrodites and the medical invention of sex*. Cambridge, MA: Harvard University Press. (11)

Drewnowski, A., Henderson, S. A., Shore, A. B., & Barratt-Fornell, A. (1998). Sensory responses to 6-*n*-propylthiouracil (PROP) or sucrose solutions and food preferences in young women. *Annals of the New York Academy of Sciences, 855*, 797–801. (7)

Drzyzga, L. R., Marcinowska, A., & Obuchowicz, E. (2009). Antiapoptotic and neurotrophic effects of antidepressants: A review of clinical and experimental studies. *Brain Research Bulletin, 79*, 248–257. (15)

Du, J., Creson, T. K., Wu, L.-J., Ren, M., Gray, N. A., Falke, C., et al. (2008). The role of hippocampal GluR1 and GluR2 receptors in manic-like behavior. *Journal of Neuroscience, 28*, 68–79. (15)

Duan, X., Chang, J. H., Ge, S., Faulkner, R. L., Kim, J. Y., Kitabatake, Y., et al. (2007). Disrupted-in-schizophrenia 1 regulated integration of newly generated neurons in the adult brain. *Cell, 130*, 1146–1158. (15)

Ducci, F., & Goldman, D. (2008). Genetic approaches to addiction: Genes and alcohol. *Addiction, 103*, 1414–1428. (3)

Ducommun, C. Y., Michel, C. M., Clarke, S., Adriani, M., Seeck, M., Landis, T., et al. (2004). Cortical motion deafness. *Neuron, 43*, 765–777. (7)

Dudchenko, P. A., & Taube, J. S. (1997). Correlation between head direction cell activity and spatial behavior on a radial arm maze. *Behavioral Neuroscience, 111*, 3–19. (13)

Duelli, R., & Kuschinsky, W. (2001). Brain glucose transporters: Relationship to local energy demand. *News in Physiological Sciences, 16*, 71–76. (2)

Duff, M. C., Hengst, J., Tranel, D., & Cohen, N. J. (2006). Development of shared information in communication despite hippocampal amnesia. *Nature Neuroscience, 9*, 140–146. (13)

Dunbar, G. L., Sandstrom, M. I., Rossignol, J., & Lescaudron, L. (2006). Neurotrophic enhancers as therapy for behavioral deficits in rodent models of Huntington's disease: Use of gangliosides, substituted pyrimidines, and mesenchymal stem cells. *Behavioral and Cognitive Neuroscience Reviews, 5*, 63–79. (8)

Duvarci, S., Bauer, E. P., & Paré, D. (2009). The bed nucleus of the stria terminalis mediates inter-individual variations in anxiety and fear. *Journal of Neuroscience, 29*, 10357–10361. (12)

Dyal, J. A. (1971). Transfer of behavioral bias: Reality and specificity. In E. J. Fjerdingstad (Ed.), *Chemical transfer of learned information* (pp. 219–263). New York: American Elsevier. (13)

Earnest, D. J., Liang, F.-Q., Ratcliff, M., & Cassone, V. M. (1999). Immortal time: Circadian clock properties of rat suprachiasmatic cell lines. *Science, 283*, 693–695. (9)

Eastman, C. I., Hoese, E. K., Youngstedt, S. D., & Liu, L. (1995). Phase-shifting human circadian rhythms with exercise during the night shift. *Physiology & Behavior, 58*, 1287–1291. (9)

Eastman, C. I., Young, M. A., Fogg, L. F., Liu, L., & Meaden, P. M. (1998). Bright light treatment of winter depression. *Archives of General Psychiatry, 55*, 883–889. (15)

Eaves, L. J., Martin, N. G., & Heath, A. C. (1990). Religious affiliation in twins and their parents: Testing a model of cultural inheritance. *Behavior Genetics, 20*, 1–22. (1)

Eccles, J. C. (1964). *The physiology of synapses*. Berlin: Springer-Verlag. (3)

Ecker, A. S., Berens, P., Keliris, G. A., Bethge, M., Logothetis, N. K., & Tolias, A. S. (2010). Decorrelated neuronal firing in cortical microcircuits. *Science, 327*, 584–587. (6)

Eckhorn, R., Bauer, R., Jordan, W., Brosch, M., Kruse, W., Munk, M., et al. (1988). Coherent oscillations: A mechanism of feature linking in the visual cortex? *Biological Cybernetics, 60*, 121–130. (14)

Edelman, G. M. (1987). *Neural Darwinism*. New York: Basic Books. (5)

Edinger, J. D., McCall, W. V., Marsh, G. R., Radtke, R. A., Erwin, C. W., & Lininger, A. (1992). Periodic limb movement variability in older DIMS patients across consecutive nights of home monitoring. *Sleep, 15*, 156–161. (9)

Edinger, K. L., & Frye, C. A. (2004). Testosterone's analgesic, anxiolytic, and cognitive-enhancing effects may be due in part to actions of its 5α-reduced metabolites in the hippocampus. *Behavioral Neuroscience, 118*, 1352–1364. (11)

Edlinger, M., Hausmann, A., Kemmler, G., Kurz, M., Kurzhaler, I., Walch, T., et al. (2005). Trends in the pharmacological treatment of patients with schizophrenia over a 12 year observation period. *Schizophrenia Research, 77*, 25–34. (15)

Edman, G., Åsberg, M., Levander, S., & Schalling, D. (1986). Skin conductance habituation and cerebrospinal fluid 5-hydroxy-indoleacetic acid in suicidal patients. *Archives of General Psychiatry, 43*, 586–592. (12)

Ehrhardt, A. A., & Money, J. (1967). Progestin-induced hermaphroditism: IQ and psychosexual identity in a study of ten girls. *Journal of Sex Research, 3*, 83–100. (11)

Ehrlich, P. R., Dobkin, D. S., & Wheye, D. (1988). *The birder's handbook*. New York: Simon & Schuster. (10)

Eichenbaum, H. (2000). A cortical-hippocampal system for declarative memory. *Nature Reviews Neuroscience, 1*, 41–50. (13)

Eichenbaum, H. (2002). *The cognitive neuroscience of memory*. New York: Oxford University Press. (13)

Eidelberg, E., & Stein, D. G. (1974). Functional recovery after lesions of the nervous system. *Neurosciences Research Program Bulletin, 12*, 191–303. (5)

Eippert, F., Finsterbusch, J., Binget, U., & Büchel, C. (2009). Direct evidence for spinal cord involvement in placebo analgesia. *Science, 326*, 404. (7)

Eisenberger, N. I., Lieberman, M. D., & Williams, K. D. (2003). Does rejection hurt? An fMRI study of social exclusion. *Science, 302*, 290–292. (7)

Eisenegger, C., Naef, M., Snozzi, R., Heinrichs, M., & Fehr, E. (2010). Prejudice and truth about the effect of testosterone on human bargaining. *Nature, 463*, 356–359. (12)

Eisenstein, E. M., & Cohen, M. J. (1965). Learning in an isolated prothoracic insect ganglion. *Animal Behaviour, 13*, 104–108. (13)

Ek, M., Engblom, D., Saha, S., Blomqvist, A., Jakobsson, P.-J., & Ericsson-Dahlstrand, A. (2001). Pathway across the blood–brain barrier. *Nature, 410*, 430–431. (10)

Elbert, T., Candia, V., Altenmüller, E., Rau, H., Sterr, A., Rockstroh, B., et al. (1998). Alteration of digital representations in somatosensory cortex in focal hand dystonia. *Neuroreport, 9*, 3571–3575. (5)

Elbert, T., Pantev, C., Wienbruch, C., Rockstroh, B., & Taub, E. (1995). Increased cortical representation of the fingers of the left hand in string players. *Science, 270*, 305–307. (5)

Eldridge, L. L., Engel, S. A., Zeineh, M. M., Bookheimer, S. Y., & Knowlton, B. J. (2005). A dissociation of encoding and retrieval processes in the human hippocampus. *Journal of Neuroscience, 25*, 3280–3286. (13)

Elias, C. F., Lee, C., Kelly, J., Aschkenazi, C., Ahima, R. S., Couceyro, P. R., et al. (1998). Leptin activates hypothalamic CART neurons projecting to the spinal cord. *Neuron, 21*, 1375–1385. (10)

Ellacott, K. L. J., & Cone, R. D. (2004). The central melanocortin system and the integration of short- and long-term regulators of energy homeostasis. *Recent Progress in Hormone Research, 59*, 395–408. (10)

Elliott, T. R. (1905). The action of adrenalin. *Journal of Physiology (London), 32*, 401–467. (3)

Ellis, L., & Ames, M. A. (1987). Neurohormonal functioning and sexual orientation: A theory of homosexuality–heterosexuality. *Psychological Bulletin, 101*, 233–258. (11)

Ellis, L., Ames, M. A., Peckham, W., & Burke, D. (1988). Sexual orientation of human offspring may be altered by severe maternal stress during pregnancy. *Journal of Sex Research, 25*, 152–157. (11)

Ellis, L., & Cole-Harding, S. (2001). The effects of prenatal stress, and of prenatal alcohol and nicotine exposure, on human sexual orientation. *Physiology & Behavior, 74*, 213–226. (11)

Ellis-Behnke, R. G., Liang, Y.-X., You, S.-W., Tay, D. K. C., Zhang, S., So, K.-F., et al. (2006). Nano neuro knitting: Peptide nanofiber scaffold for brain repair and axon regeneration with functional return of vision. *Proceedings of the National Academy of Sciences, USA, 103*, 5054–5059. (5)

Ells, L. J., Hillier, F. C., Shucksmith, J., Crawley, H., Harbige, L., Shield, J., et al. (2008). A systematic review of the effect of dietary exposure that could be achieved through normal dietary intake on learning and performance of school-aged children of relevance to UK schools. *British Journal of Nutrition, 100,* 927–936. (10)

Elston, G. N. (2000). Pyramidal cells of the frontal lobe: All the more spinous to think with. *Journal of Neuroscience, 20,* RC95: 1–4. (4)

Emery, N. J., Capitanio, J. P., Mason, W. A., Machado, C. J., Mendoza, S. P., & Amaral, D. G. (2001). The effects of bilateral lesions of the amygdala on dyadic social interactions in rhesus monkeys (*Macaca mulatta*). *Behavioral Neuroscience, 115,* 515–544. (12)

Emmorey, K., Allen, J. S., Bruss, J., Schenker, N., & Damasio, H. (2003). A morphometric analysis of auditory brain regions in congenitally deaf adults. *Proceedings of the National Academy of Sciences, USA, 100,* 10049–10054. (7)

Enard, W., Gehre, S., Hammerschmidt, K., Hölter, S. M., Blass, T., Somel, M., et al. (2009). A humanized version of Foxp2 affects cortico-basal ganglia circuits in mice. *Cell, 137,* 961–971. (14)

Eng, M. Y., Schuckit, M. A., & Smith, T. L. (2005). The level of response to alcohol in daughters of alcoholics and controls. *Drug and Alcohol Dependence, 79,* 83–93. (3)

Engert, F., & Bonhoeffer, T. (1999). Dendritic spine changes associated with hippocampal long-term synaptic plasticity. *Nature, 399,* 66–70. (13)

Enoch, M.-A., Steer, C. D., Newman, T. K., Gibson, N., & Goldman, D. (2010). Early life stress, *MAOA,* and gene–environment interactions predict behavioral disinhibition in children. *Genes, Brain, and Behavior, 9,* 65–74. (12)

Epping-Jordan, M. P., Watkins, S. S., Koob, G. F., & Markou, A. (1998). Dramatic decreases in brain reward function during nicotine withdrawal. *Nature, 393,* 76–79. (3)

Erickson, C., & Lehrman, D. (1964). Effect of castration of male ring doves upon ovarian activity of females. *Journal of Comparative and Physiological Psychology, 58,* 164–166. (11)

Erickson, K. I., Prakash, R. S., Voss, M. W., Chaddock, L., Heo, S., McLaren, M., et al. (2010). Brain-derived neurotrophic factor is associated with age-related decline in hippocampal volume. *Journal of Neuroscience, 30,* 5368–5375. (5)

Erickson, R. P. (1982). The across-fiber pattern theory: An organizing principle for molar neural function. *Contributions to Sensory Physiology, 6,* 79–110. (7)

Erickson, R. P., diLorenzo, P. M., & Woodbury, M. A. (1994). Classification of taste responses in brain stem: Membership in fuzzy sets. *Journal of Neurophysiology, 71,* 2139–2150. (7)

Ernst, M. B., Wunderlich, C. M., Hess, S., Paehler, M., Mesaros, A., Koralov, S. B., et al. (2009). Enhanced stat3 activation in POMC neurons provokes negative feedback inhibition of leptin and insulin signaling in obesity. *Journal of Neuroscience, 29,* 11582–11593. (10)

Eschenko, O., Mölle, M., Born, J., & Sara, S. J. (2006). Elevated sleep spindle density after learning or after retrieval in rats. *Journal of Neurophysiology, 26,* 12914–12920. (9)

Eskelinen, M. H., Ngandu, T., Tuomilehto, J., Soininen, H., & Kivipelto, M. (2009). Midlife coffee and tea drinking and the risk of late-life dementia: A population-based CAIDE study. *Journal of Alzheimer's Disease, 16,* 85–91. (13)

Esser, S. K., Hill, S., & Tononi, G. (2009). Breakdown of effective connectivity during slow wave sleep: Investigating the mechanism underlying a cortical gate using large-scale modeling. *Journal of Neurophysiology, 102,* 2096–2111. (9)

Esslinger, C., Walter, H., Kirsch, P., Erk, S., Schnell, K., Arnold, C., et al. (2009). Neural mechanisms of a genome-wide supported psychosis variant. *Science, 324,* 605. (15)

Etcoff, N. L., Ekman, P., Magee, J. J., & Frank, M. G. (2000). Lie detection and language comprehension. *Nature, 405,* 139. (12, 14)

Etgen, A. M., Chu, H.-P., Fiber, J. M., Karkanias, G. B., & Morales, J. M. (1999). Hormonal integration of neurochemical and sensory signals governing female reproductive behavior. *Behavioural Brain Research, 105,* 93–103. (11)

Euston, D. R., Tatsuno, M., & McNaughton, B. L. (2007). Fast-forward playback of recent memory sequences in prefrontal cortex during sleep. *Science, 318,* 1147–1150. (9)

Evans, D. A., Funkenstein, H. H., Albert, M. S., Scherr, P. A., Cook, N. R., Chown, M. J., et al. (1989). Prevalence of Alzheimer's disease in a community population of older persons. *Journal of the American Medical Association, 262,* 2551–2556. (13)

Evarts, E. V. (1979). Brain mechanisms of movement. *Scientific American, 241*(3), 164–179. (8)

Evenson, K. R., Foraker, R. E., Morris, D. L., & Rosamond, W. D. (2009). A comprehensive review of prehospital and in-hospital delay times in acute stroke care. *International Journal of Stroke, 4,* 187–199. (5)

Eyre, J. A., Taylor, J. P., Villagra, F., Smith, M., & Miller, S. (2001). Evidence of activity-dependent withdrawal of corticospinal projections during human development. *Neurology, 57,* 1543–1554. (8)

Facoetti, A., Corradi, N., Ruffino, M., Gori, S., & Zorzi, M. (2010). Visual spatial attention and speech segmentation are both impaired in preschoolers at familial risk for developmental dyslexia. *Dyslexia, 16,* 22–239. (14)

Fadda, F. (2000). Tryptophan-free diets: A physiological tool to study brain serotonin function. *News in Physiological Sciences, 15,* 260–264. (3)

Fadool, D. A., Tucker, K., Perkins, R., Fasciani, G., Thompson, R. N., Parsons, A. D.. et al. (2004). Kv1.3 channel gene-targeted deletion produces "super-smeller mice" with altered glomeruli, interacting scaffolding proteins, and biophysics. *Neuron, 41,* 389–404. (7)

Fagen, Z. M., Mitchum, R., Vezina, P., & McGehee, D. S. (2007). Enhanced nicotinic receptor function and drug abuse vulnerability. *Journal of Neuroscience, 27,* 8771–8778. (3)

Falleti, M. G., Maruff, P., Collie, A., Darby, D. G., & McStephen, M. (2003). Qualitative similarities in cognitive impairment associated with 24 h of sustained wakefulness and a blood alcohol concentration of 0.05%. *Journal of Sleep Research, 12,* 265–274. (9)

Fan, P. (1995). Cannabinoid agonists inhibit the activation of 5-HT3 receptors in rat nodose ganglion neurons. *Journal of Neurophysiology, 73,* 907–910. (3)

Fan, W., Ellacott, K. L. J., Halatchev, I. G., Takahashi, K., Yu, P., & Cone, R. D. (2004). Cholecystokinin-mediated suppression of feeding involves the brainstem melanocortin system. *Nature Neuroscience, 7,* 335–336. (10)

Fantz, R. L. (1963). Pattern vision in newborn infants. *Science, 140,* 296–297. (6)

Farah, M. J. (1990). *Visual agnosia.* Cambridge, MA: MIT Press. (6)

Farah, M. J., Illes, J., Cook-Deegan, R., Gardner, H., Kandel, E., King, P., et al. (2004). Neurocognitive enhancement: What can we do and what should we do? *Nature Reviews Neuroscience, 5,* 421–425. (13)

Farah, M. J., Wilson, K. D., Drain, M., & Tanaka, J. N. (1998). What is "special" about face perception? *Psychological Review, 105,* 482–498. (6)

Farber, N. B., Newcomer, J. W., & Olney, J. W. (1999). Glycine agonists: What can they teach us about schizophrenia? *Archives of General Psychiatry, 56,* 13–17. (15)

Farivar, R. (2009). Dorsal-ventral integration in object recognition. *Brain Research Reviews, 61,* 144–153. (6)

Farmer, M. E., & Klein, R. M. (1995). The evidence for a temporal processing deficit linked to dyslexia: A review. *Psychonomic Bulletin & Review, 2,* 460–493. (14)

Fatemi, S. H., & Folsom, T. D. (2009). The neurodevelopmental hypothesis of schizophrenia, revisited. *Schizophrenia Bulletin, 35,* 528–548. (15)

Featherstone, R. E., Fleming, A. S., & Ivy, G. O. (2000). Plasticity in the maternal circuit: Effects of experience and partum condition on brain astrocyte number in female rats. *Behavioral Neuroscience, 114,* 158–172. (11)

Feeney, D. M., & Sutton, R. L. (1988). Catecholamines and recovery of function after brain damage. In D. G. Stein & B. A. Sabel (Eds.), *Pharmacological approaches to the treatment of brain and spinal cord injury* (pp. 121–142). New York: Plenum Press. (5)

Feeney, D. M., Sutton, R. L., Boyeson, M. G., Hovda, D. A., & Dail, W. G. (1985). The locus coeruleus and cerebral metabolism: Recovery of function after cerebral injury. *Physiological Psychology, 13,* 197–203. (5)

Feinstein, J. S., Adolphs, R., Damasio, A., & Tranel, D. (2011). The human amygdala and the induction and experience of fear. *Current Biology, 21,* 34–38. (12)

Feldman, R., Weller, A., Zagoory-Sharon, O., & Levine, A. (2007). Evidence for a neuroendocrinological foundation of human affiliation. *Psychological Science, 18,* 965–970. (11)

Fell, J., & Axmacher, N. (2011). The role of phase synchronization in memory processes. *Nature Reviews Neuroscience, 12,* 105–118. (14)

Feller, G. (2010). Protein stability and enzyme activity at extreme biological temperatures. *Journal* of *Physics—Condensed Matter, 22,* article 323101. (10)

Fendrich, R., Wessinger, C. M., & Gazzaniga, M. S. (1992). Residual vision in a scotoma: Implications for blindsight. *Science, 258,* 1489–1491. (6)

Feng, J., Fouse, S., & Fan, G. (2007). Epigenetic regulation of neural gene expression and neuronal function. *Pediatric Research, 61* (5), Part 2, 58R–63R. (1)

Feng, J., Spence, I., & Pratt, J. (2007). Playing an action video game reduces gender differences in spatial cognition. *Psychological Science, 18,* 850–855. (4)

Fentress, J. C. (1973). Development of grooming in mice with amputated forelimbs. *Science, 179,* 704–705. (8)

Ferreira, F., Bailey, K. G. D., & Ferraro, V. (2002). Good-enough representations in language comprehension. *Current Directions in Psychological Science, 11,* 11–15. (14)

Fettiplace, R. (1990). Transduction and tuning in auditory hair cells. *Seminars in the Neurosciences, 2,* 33–40. (7)

Field, E. F., Whishaw, I. Q., Forgie, M. L., & Pellis, S. M. (2004). Neonatal and pubertal, but not adult, ovarian steroids are necessary for the development of female-typical patterns of dodging to protect a food item. *Behavioral Neuroscience, 118,* 1293–1304. (11)

Figner, B., Knoch, D., Johnson, E. J., Krosch, A. R., Lisanby, S. H., Fehr, E., et al. (2010). Lateral prefrontal cortex and self-control in intertemporal choice. *Nature Neuroscience, 13,* 538–539. (13)

Filosa, J. A., Bonev, A. D., Straub, S. V., Meredith, A. L., Wilkerson, M. K., Aldrich, R. W., et al. (2006). Local potassium signaling couples neuronal activity to vasodilation in the brain. *Nature Neuroscience, 9,* 1397–1403. (2)

Fils-Aime, M.-L., Eckardt, M. J., George, D. T., Brown, G. L., Mefford, I., & Linnoila, M. (1996). Early-onset alcoholics have lower cerebrospinal fluid 5-hydroxyindoleacetic acid levels than late-onset alcoholics. *Archives of General Psychiatry, 53,* 211–216. (3)

Finch, C. E. (2009). Update on slow aging and negligible senescence—A mini-review. *Gerontology, 55,* 307–313. (1)

Fine, I., Smallman, H. S., Doyle, P., & MacLeod, D. I. A. (2002). Visual function before and after the removal of bilateral congenital cataracts in adulthood. *Vision Research, 42,* 191–210. (6)

Fine, I. Wade, A. R., Brewer, A. A., May, M. G., Goodman, D. F., Boynton, G. M., et al. (2003). Long-term deprivation affects visual perception and cortex. *Nature Neuroscience, 6,* 915–916. (6)

Finger, S., & Roe, D. (1996). Gustave Dax and the early history of cerebral dominance. *Archives of Neurology, 53,* 806–813. (14)

Fink, G., Sumner, B. E. H., Rosie, R., Grace, O., & Quinn, J. P. (1996). Estrogen control of central neurotransmission: Effect on mood, mental state, and memory. *Cellular and Molecular Neurobiology, 16,* 325–344. (14)

Fink, G. R., Halligan, P. W., Marshall, J. C., Frith, C. D., Frackowiak, R. S. J., & Dolan, R. J. (1996). Where in the brain does visual attention select the forest and the trees? *Nature, 382,* 626–628. (14)

Fisch, L, Privman, E., Ramot, M., Harel, M., Nir, Y., Kipervasser, S., et al. (2009). Neural "ignition": Enhanced activation linked to perceptual awareness in human ventral stream visual cortex. *Neuron, 64,* 562–574. (14)

Fisher, S. E., Vargha-Khadem, F., Watkins, K. E., Monaco, A. P., & Pembrey, M. E. (1998). Localisation of a gene implicated in a severe speech and language disorder. *Nature Genetics, 18,* 168–170. (14)

Fitts, D. A., Starbuck, E. M., & Ruhf, A. (2000). Circumventricular organs and ANGII-induced salt appetite: Blood pressure and connectivity. *American Journal of Physiology, 279,* R2277–R2286. (10)

Fitzgerald, P. B., Brown, T. L., & Daskalakis, Z. J. (2002). The application of transcranial magnetic stimulation in psychiatry and neurosciences research. *Acta Psychiatrica Scandinavica, 105,* 324–340. (4)

Fjell, A. M., Walhovd, K. B., Fennema-Notestine, C., McEvoy, L. K., Hagler, D. J., Holland, D., et al. (2009). One-year brain atrophy evident in healthy aging. *Journal of Neuroscience, 29,* 15223–15231. (5)

Fjerdingstad, E. J. (1973). Transfer of learning in rodents and fish. In W. B. Essman & S. Nakajima (Eds.), *Current biochemical approaches to learning and memory* (pp. 73–98). Flushing, NY: Spectrum. (13)

Flatz, G. (1987). Genetics of lactose digestion in humans. *Advances in Human Genetics, 16,* 1–77. (10)

Fleet, W. S., & Heilman, K. M. (1986). The fatigue effect in hemispatial neglect. *Neurology, 36*(Suppl. 1), 258. (5)

Fletcher, P. C., McKenna, P. J., Frith, C. D., Grasby, P. M., Friston, K. J., & Dolan, R. J. (1998). Brain activations in schizophrenia during a graded memory task studied with functional neuroimaging. *Archives of General Psychiatry, 55,* 1001–1008. (15)

Fletcher, R., & Voke, J. (1985). *Defective colour vision.* Bristol, England: Hilger. (6)

Flöel, A., Knecht, S., Lohmann, H., Deppe, M., Sommer, J., Dräger, B., et al. (2001). Language and spatial attention can lateralize to the same hemisphere in healthy humans. *Neurology, 57,* 1018–1024. (14)

Flor, H., Elbert, T., Knecht, S., Wienbruch, C., Pantev, C., Birbaumer, N., et al. (1995). Phantom-limb pain as a perceptual correlate of cortical reorganization following arm amputation. *Nature, 375,* 482–484. (5)

Florence, S. L., & Kaas, J. H. (1995). Large-scale reorganization at multiple levels of the somatosensory pathway follows therapeutic amputation of the hand in monkeys. *Journal of Neuroscience, 15,* 8083–8095. (5)

Flores, L. C., & Disterhoft, J. F. (2009). Caudate nucleus is critically involved in trace eyeblink conditioning. *Journal of Neuroscience, 29,* 14511–14520. (13)

Flynn, J. M., & Boder, E. (1991). Clinical and electrophysiological correlates of dysphonetic and dyseidetic dyslexia. In J. F. Stein (Ed.), *Vision and visual dyslexia* (pp. 121–131). Vol. 13 of J. R. Cronly-Dillon (Ed.), *Vision and visual dysfunction.* Boca Raton, FL: CRC Press. (14)

Foerde, K., Knowlton, B. J., & Poldrack, R. A. (2006). Modulation of competing memory systems by distraction. *Proceedings of the National Academy of Sciences, USA, 103,* 11778–11783. (13)

Fogel, S. M., Nader, R., Cote, K. A., & Smith, C. T. (2007). Sleep spindles and learning potential. *Behavioral Neuroscience, 121,* 1–10. (9)

Földy, C., Neu, A., Jones, M. V., & Soltesz, I. (2006). Presynaptic activity-dependent modulation of cannabinoid type 1 receptor-mediated inhibition of GABA release. *Journal of Neuroscience, 26,* 1465–1469. (3)

Foltz, E. I., & White, L. E. Jr. (1962). Pain "relief" by frontal cingulumotomy. *Journal of Neurosurgery, 19,* 89–100. (7)

Foo, H., & Mason, P. (2009). Analgesia accompanying food consumption requires ingestion of hedonic foods. *Journal of Neuroscience, 29,* 13053–13062. (7)

Forger, N. G., & Breedlove, S. M. (1987). Motoneuronal death during human fetal development. *Journal of Comparative Neurology, 234,* 118–122. (5)

Forger, N. G., Rosen, G. J., Waters, E. M., Jacob, D., Simerly, R. B., & de Vries, G. J. (2004). Deletion of *Bax* eliminates sex differences in the mouse forebrain. *Proceedings of the National Academy of Sciences, USA, 101,* 13666–13671. (11)

Foroni, F., & Semin, G. R. (2009). Language that puts you in touch with your bodily feelings. *Psychological Science, 20,* 974–980. (8)

Forster, B., & Corballis, M. C. (2000). Interhemispheric transfer of colour and shape information in the presence and absence of the corpus callosum. *Neuropsychologia, 38,* 32–45. (14)

Forsyth, R. J., Salorio, C. F., & Christensen, J. R. (2010). Modeling early recovery patterns after paediatric traumatic brain injury. *Archives of Disease in Childhood, 95,* 266–270. (4)

Fortin, N. J., Agster, K. L., & Eichenbaum, H. B. (2002). Critical role of the hippocampus in memory for sequences of events. *Nature Neuroscience, 5,* 458–462. (13)

Fotopoulou, A., Solms, M., & Turnbull, O. (2004). Wishful reality distortions in confabulation: A case report. *Neuropsychologia, 47,* 727–744. (13)

Fournier, J. C., DeRubeis, R. J., Hollon, S. D., Dimidjian, S., Amsterdam, J., Shelton, R. C., et al. (2010). Antidepressant drug effects and depression severity. *Journal of the American Medical Association, 303,* 47–53. (15)

Fox, P. T., Ingham, R. J., Ingham, J. C., Zamarripa, F., Xiong, J.-H., & Lancaster, J. L. (2000). Brain correlates of stuttering and syllable production: A PET performance-correlation analysis. *Brain, 123,* 1985–2004. (14)

Frangou, S., Chitins, X., & Williams, S. C. R. (2004). Mapping IQ and gray matter density in healthy young people. *NeuroImage, 23,* 800–805. (4)

Frank, M. J., & Claus, E. D. (2006). Anatomy of a decision: Striato-orbitofrontal interactions in reinforcement learning, decision making, and reversal. *Psychological Review, 113,* 300–326. (13)

Frank, M. J., Samanta, J., Moustafa, A. A., & Sherman, S. J. (2007). Hold your horses: Impulsivity, deep brain stimulation, and medication in Parkinsonism. *Science, 318,* 1309–1312. (8)

Frank, R. A., Mize, S. J. S., Kennedy, L. M., de los Santos, H. C., & Green, S. J. (1992). The effect of *Gymnema sylvestre* extracts on the sweetness of eight sweeteners. *Chemical Senses, 17,* 461–479. (7)

Frankland, P. W., Josselyn, S. A., Bradwejn, J., Vaccarino, F. J., & Yeomans, J. S. (1997). Activation of amygdala cholecystokinin B receptors potentiates the acoustic startle response in the rat. *Journal of Neuroscience, 17,* 1838–1847. (12)

Franz, E. A., & Fahey, S. (2007). Developmental change in interhemispheric communication. *Psychological Science, 18,* 1030–1031. (14)

Franz, E. A., Waldie, K. E., & Smith, M. J. (2000). The effect of callosotomy on novel versus familiar bimanual actions: A neural dissociation between controlled and automatic processes? *Psychological Science, 11,* 82–85. (14)

Frassinetti, F., Pavani, F., & Làdavas, E. (2002). Acoustical vision of neglected stimuli: Interaction among spatially converging audiovisual inputs in neglect patients. *Journal of Cognitive Neuroscience, 14,* 62–69. (14)

Frayling, T. M., Timpson, N. J., Weedon, M. N., Zeggini, E., Freathy, R. M., Lindgren, C. M., et al. (2007). A common variant in the *FTO* gene is associated with body mass index and predisposes to childhood and adult obesity. *Science, 316,* 889–894. (10)

Freed, C. R., Greene, P. E., Breeze, R. E., Tsai, W.-Y., DuMouchel, W., Kao, R., et al. (2001). Transplantation of embryonic dopamine neurons for severe Parkinson's disease. *New England Journal of Medicine, 344,* 710–719. (8)

Freedman, M. S., Lucas, R. J., Soni, B., von Schantz, M., Muñoz, M., David-Gray, Z., et al. (1999). Regulation of mammalian circadian behavior by non-rod, non-cone, ocular photoreceptors. *Science, 284,* 502–504. (9)

Frese, M., & Harwich, C. (1984). Shiftwork and the length and quality of sleep. *Journal of Occupational Medicine, 26,* 561–566. (9)

Frey, S. H., Bogdanov, S., Smith, J. C., Watrous, S., & Breidenbach, W. C. (2008). Chronically deafferented sensory cortex recovers a grossly typical organization after allogenic hand transplantation. *Current Biology, 18,* 1530–1534. (5)

Fried, S., Münch, T. A., & Werblin, F. S. (2002). Mechanisms and circuitry underlying directional selectivity in the retina. *Nature, 420,* 411–414. (6)

Friedlander, W. J. (1986). Who was "the father of bromide treatment of epilepsy"? *Archives of Neurology, 43,* 505–507. (15)

Friedman, E. S., Thase, M. E., Wisniewski, S. R., Trivedi, M. H., Biggs, M. M., Fava, M., et al. (2009). Cognitive therapy augmentation versus CT switch treatment: A STAR*D report. *International Journal of Cognitive Therapy, 2,* 66–87. (15)

Friedman, M. I., & Stricker, E. M. (1976). The physiological psychology of hunger: A physiological perspective. *Psychological Review, 83,* 409–431. (10)

Frisén, L., Nordenström, A., Falhammar, H., Filipsson, H., Holmdahl, G., Janson, P. O., et al. (2009). Gender role behavior, sexuality, and psychosocial adaptation in women with congenital adrenal hyperplasia due to CYP21A2 deficiency. *Journal of Clinical Endocrinology & Metabolism, 94,* 3432–3439. (11)

Fritsch, G., & Hitzig, E. (1870). Über die elektrische Erregbarkeit des Grosshirns [Concerning the electrical stimulability of the cerebrum]. *Archiv für Anatomie Physiologie und Wissenschaftliche Medicin, 300*–332. (8)

Fu, L.-Y., Acuna-Goycolea, C., & van den Pol, A. N. (2004). Neuropeptide Y inhibits hypocretin/orexin neurons by multiple presynaptic and postsynaptic mechanisms: Tonic depression of the hypothalamic arousal system. *Journal of Neuroscience, 24,* 8741–8751. (10)

Fu, Q., Heath, A. C., Bucholz, K. K., Nelson, E., Goldberg, J., Lyons, M. J., et al. (2002). Shared genetic risk of major depression, alcohol dependence, and marijuana dependence. *Archives of General Psychiatry, 59,* 1125–1132. (15)

Fu, W., Sugai, T., Yoshimura, H., & Onoda, N. (2004). Convergence of olfactory and gustatory connections onto the endopiriform nucleus in the rat. *Neuroscience, 126,* 1033–1041. (7)

Fuchs, T., Haney, A., Jechura, T. J., Moore, F. R., & Bingman, V. P. (2006). Daytime naps in night-migrating birds: Behavioural adaptation to seasonal sleep deprivation in the Swainson's thrush, *Catharus ustulatus. Animal Behaviour, 72,* 951–958. (9)

Fuller, R. K., & Roth, H. P. (1979). Disulfiram for the treatment of alcoholism: An evaluation in 128 men. *Annals of Internal Medicine, 90,* 901–904. (3)

Fusar-Poli, P., Placentino, A., Carletti, F., Landi, P., Allen, P., Surguladze, S., et al. (2009). Functional atlas of emotional faces processing: A voxel-based meta-analysis of 105 functional magnetic resonance imaging studies. *Journal of Psychiatry and Neuroscience, 34,* 418–432. (12)

Fuster, J. M. (1989). *The prefrontal cortex* (2nd ed.). New York: Raven Press. (4)

Gabrieli, J. D. E. (2009). Dyslexia: A new synergy between education and cognitive neuroscience. *Science, 325,* 280–283. (14)

Gabrieli, J. D. E., Corkin, S., Mickel, S. F., & Growdon, J. H. (1993). Intact acquisition of mirror-tracing skill in Alzheimer's disease and in global amnesia. *Behavioral Neuroscience, 107,* 899–910. (13)

Gaetani, S., Fu, J., Cassano, T., Dipasquale, P., Romano, A., Righetti, L., et al. (2010). The fat-induced satiety factor oleoylethanolamide suppresses feeding through central release of oxytocin. *Journal of Neuroscience, 30,* 8096–8101. (10)

Gage, F. H. (2000). Mammalian neural stem cells. *Science, 287,* 1433–1438. (5)

Gais, S., Plihal, W., Wagner, U., & Born, J. (2000). Early sleep triggers memory for early visual discrimination skills. *Nature Neuroscience, 3,* 1335–1339. (9)

Galaburda, A. M., LoTurco, J., Ramus, F., Fitch, R. H., & Rosen, G. D. (2006). From genes to behavior in developmental dyslexia. *Nature Neuroscience, 9,* 1213–1217. (14)

Galaburda, A. M., Sherman, G. F., Rosen, G. D., Aboitiz, F., & Geschwind, N. (1985). Developmental dyslexia: Four consecutive patients with cortical anomalies. *Annals of Neurology, 18,* 222–233. (14)

Galin, D., Johnstone, J., Nakell, L., & Herron, J. (1979). Development of the capacity for tactile information transfer between hemispheres in normal children. *Science, 204,* 1330–1332. (14)

Gallese, V., Fadiga, L., Fogassi, L., & Rizzolatti, G. (1996). Action recognition in the premotor cortex. *Brain, 119,* 593–609. (8)

Gamer, M., & Büchel, C. (2009). Amygdala activation predicts gaze toward fearful eyes. *Journal of Neuroscience, 29,* 9123–9126. (12)

Gan, W.-B., Kwon, E., Feng, G., Sanes, J. R., & Lichtman, J. W. (2003). Synaptic dynamism measured over minutes to months: Age-dependent decline in an autonomic ganglion. *Nature Neuroscience, 6,* 956–960. (5)

Gangestad, S. W., & Simpson, J. A. (2000). The evolution of human mating: Trade-offs and strategic pluralism. *Behavioral and Brain Sciences, 23,* 573–644. (11)

Gangestad, S. W., Simpson, J. A., Cousins, A. J., Garver-Apgar, C. E., & Christensen, P. N. (2004). Women's preferences for male behavioral displays change across the menstrual cycle. *Psychological Science, 15,* 203–207. (11)

Ganguly, K., Kiss, L., & Poo, M. (2000). Enhancement of presynaptic neuronal excitability by correlated presynaptic and postsynaptic spiking. *Nature Neuroscience, 3,* 1018–1026. (13)

Gao, J.-H., Parsons, L. M., Bower, J. M., Xiong, J., Li, J., & Fox, P. T. (1996). Cerebellum implicated in sensory acquisition and discrimination rather than motor control. *Science, 272,* 545–547. (8)

Gao, X., Martin, E. R., Liu, Y., Mayhew, G., Vance, J. M., & Scott, W. K. (2009). Genome-wide linkage screen in familial Parkinson disease identifies loci on chromosomes 3 and 18. *American Journal of Human Genetics, 84,* 499–504. (8)

Garcia, R., Vouimba, R.-M., Baudry, M., & Thompson, R. F. (1999). The amygdala modulates prefrontal cortex activity relative to conditioned fear. *Nature, 402,* 294–296. (12)

Garcia-Falgueras, A., & Swaab, D. F. (2008). A sex difference in the hypothalamic uncinate nucleus: Relationship to gender identity. *Brain, 131,* 3132–3146. (11)

Gardner, B. T., & Gardner, R. A. (1975). Evidence for sentence constituents in the early utterances of child and chimpanzee. *Journal of Experimental Psychology: General, 104,* 244–267. (14)

Gardner, H., & Zurif, E. B. (1975). Bee but not be: Oral reading of single words in aphasia and alexia. *Neuropsychologia, 13,* 181–190. (14)

Garver-Apgar, C. E., Gangestad, S. W., Thornhill, R., Miller, R. D., & Olp, J. J. (2006). Major histocompatibility complex alleles, sexual responsivity, and unfaithfulness in romantic couples. *Psychological Science, 17,* 830–835. (11)

Gaser, C., & Schlaug, G. (2003). Brain structures differ between musicians and non-musicians. *Journal of Neuroscience, 23,* 9240–9245. (5)

Gavrilets, S., & Rice, W. R. (2006). Genetic models of homosexuality: Generating testable predictions. *Proceedings of the Royal Society, B, 273,* 3031–3038. (11)

Ge, S., Yang, C.-h., Hsu, K.-s., Ming, G.-l., & Song, H. (2007). A critical period for enhanced synaptic plasticity in newly generated neurons of the adult brain. *Neuron, 54*, 559–566. (5)

Geerling, J. C., & Loewy, A. D. (2008). Central regulation of sodium appetite. *Experimental Physiology, 93*, 177–209. (10)

Geier, C. F., Terwilliger, R., Teslovich, T., Velanova, K., & Luna, B. (2010). Immaturities in reward processing and its influence on inhibitory control in adolescence. *Cerebral Cortex, 20*, 1613–1629. (5)

Geiger, B. M., Haburcak, M., Avena, N. M., Moyer, M. C., Hoebel, B. G., & Pothos, E. N. (2009). Deficits of mesolimbic dopamine neurotransmission in rat dietary obesity. *Neuroscience, 159*, 1193–1199. (10)

Geiger, G., Lettvin, J. Y., & Fahle, M. (1994). Dyslexic children learn a new visual strategy for reading: A controlled experiment. *Vision Research, 34*, 1223–1233. (14)

Geiger, G., Lettvin, J. Y., & Zegarra-Moran, O. (1992). Task-determined strategies of visual process. *Cognitive Brain Research, 1*, 39–52. (14)

Gerardin, D. C. C., & Pereira, O. C. M. (2002). Reproductive changes in male rats treated perinatally with an aromatase inhibitor. *Pharmacology Biochemistry and Behavior, 71*, 309–313. (11)

Gerwig, M., Hajjar, K., Dimitrova, A., Maschke, M., Kolb, F. P., Frings, M., et al. (2005). Timing of conditioned eyeblink responses is impaired in cerebellar patients. *Journal of Neuroscience, 25*, 3919–3931. (13)

Geschwind, N., & Levitsky, W. (1968). Human brain: Left–right asymmetries in temporal speech region. *Science, 161*, 186–187. (14)

Ghashghaei, H. T., Lai, C., & Anton, E. S. (2007). Neuronal migration in the adult brain: Are we there yet? *Nature Reviews Neuroscience, 8*, 141–151. (5)

Ghosh, A., Sydekum, E., Haiss, F., Peduzzi, S., Schneider, R., Baltes, C., et al. (2009). Functional and anatomical reorganization of the sensory-motor cortex after incomplete spinal cord injury in adult rats. *Journal of Neuroscience, 29*, 12210–12219. (5)

Gibbs, F. P. (1983). Temperature dependence of the hamster circadian pacemaker. *American Journal of Physiology, 244*, R607–R610. (9)

Gibbs, J., Young, R. C., & Smith, G. P. (1973). Cholecystokinin decreases food intake in rats. *Journal of Comparative and Physiological Psychology, 84*, 488–495. (10)

Gilbert, S. J., Henson, R. N. A., & Simons, J. S. (2010). The scale of functional specialization within human prefrontal cortex. *Journal of Neuroscience, 30*, 1233–1237. (4)

Gilbertson, M. W., Shenton, M. E., Ciszewski, A., Kasai, K., Lasko, N. B., Orr, S. P., et al. (2002). Smaller hippocampal volume predicts pathological vulnerability to psychological trauma. *Nature Neuroscience, 5*, 1242–1247. (12)

Gillette, M. U., & McArthur, A. J. (1996). Circadian actions of melatonin at the suprachiasmatic nucleus. *Behavioural Brain Research, 73*, 135–139. (9)

Gilman, J. M., Ramchandani, V. A., Davis, M. B., Bjork, J. M., & Hommer, D. W. (2008). Why we like to drink: A functional magnetic resonance imaging study of the rewarding and anxiolytic effects of alcohol. *Journal of Neuroscience, 28*, 4583–4591. (3)

Gilmore, J. H., Lin, W., Prastawa, M. W., Looney, C. B., Vetsa, Y. S. K., Knickmeyer, R. C., et al. (2007). Regional gray matter growth, sexual dimorphism, and cerebral asymmetry in the neonatal brain. *Journal of Neuroscience, 27*, 1255–1260. (4)

Gilmour, D., Knaut, H., Maischein, H.-M., & Nüsslein-Volhard, C. (2004). Towing of sensory axons by their migrating target cells *in vivo. Nature Neuroscience, 7*, 491–492. (4)

Giltay, E. J., & Gooren, L. J. G. (2009). Potential side effects of androgen deprivation treatment in sex offenders. *Journal of the American Academy of Psychiatry and the Law, 37*, 53–58. (11)

Ginsberg, M. D. (2008). Neuroprotection for ischemic stroke: Past, present and future. *Neuropharmacology, 55*, 363–389. (5)

Giraux, P., Sirigu, A., Schneider, F., & Dubernard, J.-M. (2001). Cortical reorganization in motor cortex after graft of both hands. *Nature Neuroscience, 4*, 691–692. (5)

Giuliani, D., & Ferrari, F. (1996). Differential behavioral response to dopamine D2 agonists by sexually naive, sexually active, and sexually inactive male rats. *Behavioral Neuroscience, 110*, 802–808. (11)

Glendenning, K. K., Baker, B. N., Hutson, K. A., & Masterton, R. B. (1992). Acoustic chiasm V: Inhibition and excitation in the ipsilateral and contralateral projections of LSO. *Journal of Comparative Neurology, 319*, 100–122. (7)

Gloria, R., Angelos, L., Schaefer, H. S., Davis, J. M., Majeskie, M., Richmond, B. S., et al. (2009). An fMRI investigation of the impact of withdrawal on regional brain activity during nicotine anticipation. *Psychophysiology, 46*, 681–693. (3)

Glykys, J., Peng, Z., Chandra, D., Homanics, G. E., Houser, C. R., & Mody, I. (2007). A new naturally occurring GABAA receptor subunit partnership with high sensitivity to ethanol. *Nature Neuroscience, 10*, 40–48. (12)

Goard, M., & Dan, Y. (2009). Basal forebrain activation enhances cortical coding of natural scenes. *Nature Neuroscience, 12*, 1444–1449. (9)

Goate, A., Chartier-Harlin, M. C., Mullan, M., Brown, J., Crawford, F., Fidani, L., et al. (1991). Segregation of a missense mutation in the amyloid precursor protein gene with familial Alzheimer's disease. *Nature, 349*, 704–706. (13)

Godfrey, K. M., Lillycrop, K. A., Burdge, G. C., Gluckman, P. D., & Hanson, M. A. (2007). Epigenetic mechanisms and the mismatch concept of the developmental origins of health and disease. *Pediatric Research, 61 (5), Part 2*, 5R–10R. (1)

Gogolla, N., Caroni, P., Lüthi, A., & Herry, C. (2009). Perineuronal nets protect fear memories from erasure. *Science, 325*, 1258–1261. (12)

Gogos, J. A., Osborne, J., Nemes, A., Mendelsohn, M., & Axel, R. (2000). Genetic ablation and restoration of the olfactory topographic map. *Cell, 103*, 609–620. (5)

Golarai, G., Hong, S., Haas, B. W., Galaburda, A. M., Mills, D. L., Bellugi, U., et al. (2010). The fusiform face area is enlarged in Williams syndrome. *Journal of Neuroscience, 30*, 6700–6712. (14)

Gold, R. M. (1973). Hypothalamic obesity: The myth of the ventromedial hypothalamus. *Science, 182*, 488–490. (10)

Goldberg, T. E., Weinberger, D. R., Berman, K. F., Pliskin, N. H., & Podd, M. H. (1987). Further evidence for dementia of the prefrontal type in schizophrenia? *Archives of General Psychiatry, 44*, 1008–1014. (15)

Golden, S. M. (2009). Does childhood use of stimulant medication as a treatment or ADHD affect the likelihood of future drug abuse and dependence? A literature review. *Journal of Child & Adolescent Substance Abuse, 18*, 343–358. (3)

Goldin-Meadow, S., McNeill, D., & Singleton, J. (1996). Silence is liberating: Removing the handcuffs on grammatical expression in the manual modality. *Psychological Review, 103*, 34–55. (14)

Goldin-Meadow, S., & Mylander, C. (1998). Spontaneous sign systems created by deaf children in two cultures. *Nature, 391*, 279–281. (14)

Goldman, L. S. (1999). Medical illness in patients with schizophrenia. *Journal of Clinical Psychiatry, 60*(Suppl 21), 10–15. (15)

Goldman, P. S. (1971). Functional development of the prefrontal cortex in early life and the problem of neuronal plasticity. *Experimental Neurology, 32*, 366–387. (15)

Goldman, P. S. (1976). The role of experience in recovery of function following orbital prefrontal lesions in infant monkeys. *Neuropsychologia, 14*, 401–412. (15)

Goldman-Rakic, P. S. (1988). Topography of cognition: Parallel distributed networks in primate association cortex. *Annual Review of Neuroscience, 11*, 137–156. (4)

Goldstein, A. (1980). Thrills in response to music and other stimuli. *Physiological Psychology, 8*, 126–129. (7)

Goldstein, J. M., Seidman, L. J., Horton, N. J., Makris, N., Kennedy, D. N., Caviness, V. S., Jr., et al. (2001). Normal sexual dimorphism of the adult human brain assessed by in vivo magnetic resonance imaging. *Cerebral Cortex, 11*, 490–497. (11)

Golestani, N., Molko, N., Dehaene, S., LeBihan, D., & Pallier, C. (2006). Brain structure predicts the learning of foreign speech sounds. *Cerebral Cortex, 17*, 575–582. (4)

Golestani, N., Price, C. J., & Scott, S. K. (2011). Born with an ear for dialects? Structural plasticity in the expert phonetician brain. *Journal of Neuroscience, 31*, 4213–4220. (5)

Golombok, S., Rust, J., Zervoulis, K., Croudace, T., Golding, J., & Hines, M. (2008). Developmental trajectories of sex-typed behavior in boys and girls: A longitudinal general population study of children aged 2.5–8 years. *Child Development, 79*, 1583–1593. (11)

Gonzalez Andino, S. L., de Peralta Menendez, R. G., Khateb, A., Landis, T., & Pegna, A. J. (2009). Electrophysiological correlates of affective blindsight. *NeuroImage, 44*, 581–589. (6)

González-Maeso, J., Ang, R. L., Yuen, T., Chan, P., Weisstaub, N. V., López-Giménez, J. F., et al. (2008). Identification of a serotonin/glutamate receptor complex implicated in psychosis. *Nature, 452*, 93–97. (15)

Goodale, M. A. (1996). Visuomotor modules in the vertebrate brain. *Canadian Journal of Physiology and Pharmacology, 74,* 390–400. (6, 8)

Goodale, M. A., Milner, A. D., Jakobson, L. S., & Carey, D. P. (1991). A neurological dissociation between perceiving objects and grasping them. *Nature, 349,* 154–156. (6, 8)

Goodrich-Hunsaker, N. J., & Hopkins, R. O. (2010). Spatial memory deficits in a virtual radial arm maze in amnesic participants with hippocampal damage. *Behavioral Neuroscience, 124,* 405–413. (13)

Gooley, J. J., Rajaratnam, S. M. W., Brainard, G. C., Kronauer, R. E., Czeisler, C. A., & Lockley, S. W. (2010). Spectral responses of the human circadian system depend on the irradiance and duration of exposure to light. *Science Translational Medicine, 2,* 31ra33. (9)

Gopnik, M., & Crago, M. B. (1991). Familial aggregation of a developmental language disorder. *Cognition, 39,* 1–50. (14)

Gorski, R. A. (1980). Sexual differentiation of the brain. In D. T. Krieger & J. C. Hughes (Eds.), *Neuroendocrinology* (pp. 215–222). Sunderland, MA: Sinauer. (11)

Gorski, R. A. (1985). The 13th J. A. F. Stevenson memorial lecture. Sexual differentiation of the brain: Possible mechanisms and implications. *Canadian Journal of Physiology and Pharmacology, 63,* 577–594. (11)

Gorski, R. A., & Allen, L. S. (1992). Sexual orientation and the size of the anterior commissure in the human brain. *Proceedings of the National Academy of Sciences, USA, 89,* 7199–7202. (11)

Gottesman, I. I. (1991). *Schizophrenia genesis.* New York: Freeman. (15)

Gougoux, F., Belin, P., Voss, P., Lepore, F., Lassonde, M., & Zatorre, R. J. (2009). Voice perception in blind persons: A functional magnetic resonance imaging study. *Neuropsychologia, 47,* 2967–2974. (5)

Granados-Fuentes, D., Tseng, A., & Herzog, E. D. (2006). A circadian clock in the olfactory bulb controls olfactory responsivity. *Journal of Neuroscience, 26,* 12219–12225. (9)

Gray, C. M., König, P., Engel, A. K., & Singer, W. (1989). Oscillatory responses in cat visual cortex exhibit inter-columnar synchronization which reflects global stimulus properties. *Nature, 338,* 334–337. (14)

Gray, J. A. (1970). The psychophysiological basis of introversion–extraversion. *Behavioural Research Therapy, 8,* 249–266. (12)

Graziadei, P. P. C., & deHan, R. S. (1973). Neuronal regeneration in frog olfactory system. *Journal of Cell Biology, 59,* 525–530. (5)

Graziano, M. S. A., Taylor, C. S. R., & Moore, T. (2002). Complex movements evoked by microstimulation of precentral cortex. *Neuron, 34,* 841–851. (4, 8)

Greene, J. D., Sommerville, R. B., Nystrom, L. E., Darley, J. M., & Cohen, J. D. (2001). An fMRI investigation of emotional engagement in moral judgment. *Science, 293,* 2105–2108. (12)

Greengard, P. (2001). The neurobiology of slow synaptic transmission. *Science, 294,* 1024–1030. (3)

Greenough, W. T. (1975). Experiential modification of the developing brain. *American Scientist, 63,* 37–46. (5)

Griffin, D. R., Webster, F. A., & Michael, C. R. (1960). The echolocation of flying insects by bats. *Animal Behaviour, 8,* 141–154. (7)

Griffiths, T. D., Uppenkamp, S., Johnsrude, I., Josephs, O., & Patterson, R. D. (2001). Encoding of the temporal regularity of sound in the human brainstem. *Nature Neuroscience, 4,* 633–637. (7)

Grillon, C., Morgan, C. A., III, Davis, M., & Southwick, S. M. (1998). Effect of darkness on acoustic startle in Vietnam veterans with PTSD. *American Journal of Psychiatry, 155,* 812–817. (12)

Gritton, H. J., Sutton, B. C., Martinez, V., Sarter, M., & Lee, T. M. (2009). Interactions between cognition and circadian rhythms: Attentional demands modify circadian entrainment. *Behavioral Neuroscience, 123,* 937–948. (9)

Gross, C. G. (1999). The fire that comes from the eye. *The Neuroscientist, 5,* 58–64. (6)

Gross, C. G., & Graziano, M. S. A. (1995). Multiple representations of space in the brain. *The Neuroscientist, 1,* 43–50. (4)

Grosshans, D. R., Clayton, D. A., Coultrap, S. J., & Browning, M. D. (2002). LTP leads to rapid surface expression of NMDA but not AMPA receptors in adult rat CA1. *Nature Neuroscience, 5,* 27–33. (13)

Grossman, S. P., Dacey, D., Halaris, A. E., Collier, T., & Routtenberg, A. (1978). Aphagia and adipsia after preferential destruction of nerve cell bodies in hypothalamus. *Science, 202,* 537–539. (10)

Grueter, M., Grueter, T., Bell, V., Horst, J., Laskowski, W., Sperling, K., et al. (2007). Hereditary prosopagnosia: The first case series. *Cortex, 43,* 734–749. (6)

Grutzendler, J., Kasthuri, N., & Gan, W.-B. (2002). Long-term dendritic spine stability in the adult cortex. *Nature, 420,* 812–816. (5)

Gubernick, D. J., & Alberts, J. R. (1983). Maternal licking of young: Resource exchange and proximate controls. *Physiology & Behavior, 31,* 593–601. (11)

Guérit, J.-M. (2005). Neurophysiological patterns of vegetative and minimally conscious states. *Neuropsychological Rehabilitation, 15,* 357–371. (9)

Guidotti, A., Ferrero, P., Fujimoto, M., Santi, R. M., & Costa, E. (1986). Studies on endogenous ligands (endocoids) for the benzodiazepine/beta carboline binding sites. *Advances in Biochemical Pharmacology, 41,* 137–148. (12)

Guidotti, A., Forchetti, C. M., Corda, M. G., Konkel, D., Bennett, C. D., & Costa, E. (1983). Isolation, characterization, and purification to homogeneity of an endogenous polypeptide with agonistic action on benzodiazepine receptors. *Proceedings of the National Academy of Sciences, USA, 80,* 3531–3535. (12)

Guillery, R. W., Feig, S. L., & Lozsádi, D. A. (1998). Paying attention to the thalamic reticular nucleus. *Trends in Neurosciences, 21,* 28–32. (4, 9)

Guillery, R. W., Feig, S. L., & van Lieshout, D. P. (2001). Connections of higher order visual relays in the thalamus: A study of corticothalamic pathways in cats. *Journal of Comparative Neurology, 438,* 66–85. (6)

Guiso, L., Monte, F., Sapienza, P., & Zingales, L. (2008). Culture, gender, and math. *Science, 320,* 1164–1165. (4)

Güler, A. D., Ecker, J. L., Lall, G. S., Haq, S., Altimus, C. M., Liao, H.-W., et al. (2008). Melanopsin cells are the principal conduits for rod-cone input to non-image-forming vision. *Nature, 453,* 102–105. (9)

Gunn, S. R., & Gunn, W. S. (2007). Are we in the dark about sleepwalking's dangers? In C. A. Read (Ed.), *Cerebrum 2007: Emerging ideas in brain science* (pp. 71–84). New York: Dana Press. (9)

Guo, S.-W., & Reed, D. R. (2001). The genetics of phenylthiocarbamide perception. *Annals of Human Biology, 28,* 111–142. (7)

Gupta, A. S., van der Meer, M. A. A., Touretzky, D. S., & Redish, A. D. (2010). Hippocampal replay is not a simple function of experience. *Neuron, 65,* 695–705. (9)

Gur, R. E., & Chin, S. (1999). Laterality in functional brain imaging studies of schizophrenia. *Schizophrenia Bulletin, 25,* 141–156. (15)

Gur, R. E., Cowell, P. E., Latshaw, A., Turetsky, B. I., Grossman, R. I., Arnold, S. E., et al. (2000). Reduced dorsal and orbital prefrontal gray matter volumes in schizophrenia. *Archives of General Psychiatry, 57,* 761–768. (15)

Gusella, J. F., & MacDonald, M. E. (2000). Molecular genetics: Unmasking polyglutamine triggers in neurodegenerative disease. *Nature Reviews Neuroscience, 1,* 109–115. (8)

Gustafsson, B., & Wigström, H. (1990). Basic features of long-term potentiation in the hippocampus. *Seminars in the Neurosciences, 2,* 321–333. (13)

Gutschalk, A., Patterson, R. D., Scherg, M., Uppenkamp, S., & Rupp, A. (2004). Temporal dynamics of pitch in human auditory cortex. *NeuroImage, 22,* 755–766. (7)

Gvilia, I., Turner, A., McGinty, D., & Szymusiak, R. (2006). Preoptic area neurons and the homeostatic regulation of rapid eye movement sleep. *Journal of Neuroscience, 26,* 3037–3044. (9)

Gwinner, E. (1986). Circannual rhythms in the control of avian rhythms. *Advances in the Study of Behavior, 16,* 191–228. (9)

Haas, H., & Panula, P. (2003). The role of histamine and the tuberomamillary nucleus in the nervous system. *Nature Reviews Neuroscience, 4,* 121–130. (9)

Hadjikhani, N., Liu, A. K., Dale, A. M., Cavanagh, P., & Tootell, R. B. H. (1998). Retinotopy and color sensitivity in human visual cortical area V8. *Nature Neuroscience, 1,* 235–241. (6)

Hagenbuch, B., Gao, B., & Meier, P. J. (2002). Transport of xenobiotics across the blood–brain barrier. *News in Physiological Sciences, 17,* 231–234. (2)

Haggarty, J. M., Cernovsky, Z., Husni, M., Minor, K., Kermean, P., & Merskey, H. (2002). Seasonal affective disorder in an Arctic community. *Acta Psychiatrica Scandinavica, 105,* 378–384. (15)

Haidt, J. (2001). The emotional dog and its rational tail: A social intuitionist approach to moral judgment. *Psychological Review, 108,* 814–834. (12)

Haier, R. J., Colom, R., Schroeder, D. H., Condon, C. A., Tang, C., Eaves, E., et al. (2009). Gray matter and intelligence factors: Is there a neuro-*g*? *Intelligence, 37*, 136–144. (4)

Haier, R. J., Jung, R. E., Yeo, R. A., Head, K., & Alkire, M. T. (2004). Structural brain variation and general intelligence. *NeuroImage, 23*, 425–433. (4)

Haimov, I., & Arendt, J. (1999). The prevention and treatment of jet lag. *Sleep Medicine Reviews, 3*, 229–240. (9)

Haimov, I., & Lavie, P. (1996). Melatonin—A soporific hormone. *Current Directions in Psychological Science, 5*, 106–111. (9)

Hains, B. C., Everhart, A. W., Fullwood, S. D., & Hulsebosch, C. E. (2002). Changes in serotonin, serotonin transporter expression and serotonin denervation supersensitivity: Involvement in chronic central pain after spinal hemisection in the rat. *Experimental Neurology, 175*, 347–362. (5)

Hakuta, K., Bialystok, E., & Wiley, E. (2003). Critical evidence: A test of the critical-period hypothesis for second-language acquisition. *Psychological Science, 14*, 31–38. (14)

Halaas, J. L, Gajiwala, K. S., Maffei, M., Cohen, S. L., Chait, B. T., Rabinowitz, D., et al. (1995). Weight-reducing effects of the plasma protein encoded by the obese gene. *Science, 269*, 543–546. (10)

Halaschek-Wiener, J., Amirabbasi-Beik, M., Monfared, N., Pieczyk, M., Sailer, C., Kollar, A., et al. (2009). Genetic variation in healthy oldest-old. *PLoS ONE, 4*, e6641. (1)

Haley, J. (1959). An interactional description of schizophrenia. *Psychiatry, 22*, 321–332. (15)

Hall, J., Whalley, H. C., Job, D. E., Baig, B. J., McIntosh, A. M., Evans, K. L., et al. (2006). A neuregulin 1 variant associated with abnormal cortical function and psychotic symptoms. *Nature Neuroscience, 9*, 1477–1478. (15)

Hallem, E. A., Fox, A. N., Zwiebel, L. J., & Carlson, J. R. (2004). Mosquito receptor for human-sweat odorant. *Nature, 427*, 212–213. (7)

Hallmayer, J., Faraco, J., Lin, L., Hesselson, S., Winkelmann, J., Kawashima, M., et al. (2009). Narcolepsy is strongly associated with the T-cell receptor alpha locus. *Nature Genetics, 41*, 708–711. (9)

Halpern, S. D., Andrews, T. J., & Purves, D. (1999). Interindividual variation in human visual performance. *Journal of Cognitive Neuroscience, 11*, 521–534. (6)

Halverson, H. E., Lee, I., & Freeman, J. H. (2010). Associative plasticity in the medial auditory thalamus and cerebellar interpositus nucleus during eyeblink conditioning. *Journal of Neuroscience, 30*, 8787–8796. (13)

Hamaguchi, T., Ono, K., & Yamada, M. (2010). Curcumin and Alzheimer's disease. *CNS Neuroscience & Therapeutics, 16*, 285–297. (13)

Hamann, S. B., & Squire, L. R. (1995). On the acquisition of new declarative knowledge in amnesia. *Behavioral Neuroscience, 109*, 1027–1044. (13)

Hamer, D. H., Hu, S., Magnuson, V. L., Hu, N., & Pattatucci, A. M. L. (1993). A linkage between DNA markers on the X chromosome and male sexual orientation. *Science, 261*, 321–327. (11)

Hamilton, N. B., & Attwell, D. (2010). Do astrocytes really exocytose neurotransmitters? *Nature Reviews Neuroscience, 11*, 227–238. (2)

Hamilton, W. D. (1964). The genetical evolution of social behavior (I and II). *Journal of Theoretical Biology, 7*, 1–16, 17–52. (1)

Han, C. J., & Robinson, J. K. (2001). Cannabinoid modulation of time estimation in the rat. *Behavioral Neuroscience, 115*, 243–246. (3)

Han, J.-H., Kushner, S. A., Yiu, A. P., Cole, C. J., Matynia, A., Brown, R. A., et al. (2007). Neuronal competition and selection during memory formation. *Science, 316*, 457–460. (13)

Hanada, R., Leibbrandt, A., Hanada, T., Kitaoka, S., Furuyashiki, T., Fujihara, H., et al. (2009). Central control of fever and female body temperature by RANKL/RANK. *Nature, 462*, 515–509. (10)

Hanaway, J., Woolsey, T. A., Gado, M. H., & Roberts, M. P., Jr. (1998). *The brain atlas.* Bethesda, MD: Fitzgerald Science Press. (12)

Hanlon, F. M., Weisend, M. P., Yeo, R. A., Huang, M., Lee, R. R., Thoma, R. J., et al. (2005). A specific test of hippocampal deficit in schizophrenia. *Behavioral Neuroscience, 119*, 863–875. (15)

Hannibal, J., Hindersson, P., Knudsen, S. M., Georg, B., & Fahrenkrug, J. (2001). The photopigment melanopsin is exclusively present in pituitary adenylate cyclase-activating polypeptide-containing retinal ganglion cells of the retinohypothalamic tract. *Journal of Neuroscience, 21*, RC191: 1–7. (9)

Hanson, K. L., & Luciana, M. (2010). Neurocognitive impairments in MDMA and other drug users: MDMA alone may not be a cognitive risk factor. *Journal of Clinical and Experimental Neuropsychology, 32*, 337–349. (3)

Haqq, C. M., & Donahoe, P. K. (1998). Regulation of sexual dimorphism in mammals. *Physiological Reviews, 78*, 1–33. (11)

Hara, J., Beuckmann, C. T., Nambu, T., Willie, J. T., Chemelli, R. M., Sinton, C. M., et al. (2001). Genetic ablation of orexin neurons in mice results in narcolepsy, hypophagia, and obesity. *Neuron, 30*, 345–354. (9)

Hargreaves, R. (2007). New migraine and pain research. *Headache, 47*(Suppl 1), S26–S43. (4)

Hari, R. (1994). Human cortical functions revealed by magnetoencephalography. *Progress in Brain Research, 100*, 163–168. (4)

Harley, B., & Wang, W. (1997). The critical period hypothesis: Where are we now? In A. M. B. deGroot & J. F. Knoll (Eds.), *Tutorials in bilingualism* (pp. 19–51). Mahwah, NJ: Erlbaum. (14)

Harmon-Jones, E., & Gable, P. A. (2009). Neural activity underlying the effect of approach-motivated positive affect on narrowed attention. *Psychological Science, 20*, 406–49. (10)

Harmon-Jones, E., & Peterson, C. K. (2009). Supine body position reduces neural response to anger evocation. *Psychological Science, 20*, 1209–1210. (12)

Harms, M. P., Wang, L., Mamah, D., Barch, D. M., Thompson, P. A., & Csernansky, J. G. (2007). Thalamic shape abnormalities in individuals with schizophrenia and their nonpsychotic siblings. *Journal of Neuroscience, 27*, 13835–13842. (15)

Harper, L. V. (2005). Epigenetic inheritance and the intergenerational transfer of experience. *Psychological Bulletin, 131*, 340–360. (1)

Harper, S. Q., Staber, P. D., He, X., Eliason, S. L., Martino, I. H., Mao, Q., et al. (2005). RNA interference improves motor and neuropathological abnormalities in a Huntington's disease mouse model. *Proceedings of the National Academy of Sciences, USA, 102*, 5820–5825. (8)

Harris, C. H. (2002). Sexual and romantic jealousy in heterosexual and homosexual adults. *Psychological Science, 13*, 7–12. (11)

Harris, C. R. (1999, July/August). The mystery of ticklish laughter. *American Scientist, 87*(4), 344–351. (7)

Harris, K. M., & Stevens, J. K. (1989). Dendritic spines of CA1 pyramidal cells in the rat hippocampus: Serial electron microscopy with reference to their biophysical characteristics. *Journal of Neuroscience, 9*, 2982–2997. (2)

Harrison, G. H. (2008, January). How chickadees weather winter. *National Wildlife, 46*(1), 14–15. (10)

Harrison, N. A., Gray, M. A., Gianaros, P. J., & Critchley, H. D. (2010). The embodiment of emotional feelings in the brain. *Journal of Neuroscience, 30*, 12878–12884. (12)

Hart, B. L. (Ed.). (1976). *Experimental psychobiology.* San Francisco: Freeman. (10)

Hartline, H. K. (1949). Inhibition of activity of visual receptors by illuminating nearby retinal areas in the limulus eye. *Federation Proceedings, 8*, 69. (6)

Harvey, A. G., & Bryant, R. A. (2002). Acute stress disorder: A synthesis and critique. *Psychological Bulletin, 128*, 886–902. (12)

Hassabis, D., Kumaran, D., Vann, S. D., & Maguire, E. A. (2007). Patients with hippocampal amnesia cannot imagine new experiences. *Proceedings of the National Academy of Sciences, USA, 104*, 1726–1731. (13)

Hassan, B., & Rahman, Q. (2007). Selective sexual orientation-related differences in object location memory. *Behavioral Neuroscience, 121*, 625–633. (11)

Hassani, O. K., Lee, M. G., Henny, P., & Jones, B. E. (2009). Discharge profiles of identified GABAergic in comparison to cholinergic and putative glutamatergic basal forebrain neurons across the sleep-wake cycle. *Journal of Neuroscience, 29*, 11828–11840. (9)

Hassett, J. M., Siebert, E. R., & Wallen, K. (2008). Sex differences in rhesus monkey toy preferences parallel those of children. *Hormones and Behavior, 54*, 359–364. (11)

Hatcher, J. M., Pennell, K. D., & Miller, G. W. (2008). Parkinson's disease and pesticides: A toxicological perspective. *Trends in Pharmacological Science, 29*, 322–329. (8)

Haueisen, J., & Knösche, T. R. (2001). Involuntary motor activity in pianists evoked by music perception. *Journal of Cognitive Neuroscience, 13*, 786–792. (8)

Havas, D. A., Glenberg, A. M., Gutowski, K. A., Lucarelli, M. J., & Davidson, R. J. (2010). Cosmetic use of botulinum toxin-A affects processing of emotional language. *Psychological Science, 21*, 895–900. (12)

Havlicek, J., & Roberts, S. C. (2009). MHC-correlated mate choice in humans: A review. *Psychoneuroendocrinology, 34*, 497–512. (7)

Hayashi-Takagi, A., Takaki, M., Graziane, N., Seshadri, S., Murdoch, H., Dunlop, A. J., et al. (2010). Disrupted-in-schizophrenia 1(*DISC-1*) regulates spines of the glutamate synapse via Rac1. *Nature Neuroscience, 13*, 327–332. (15)

Haydon, P. G. (2001). Glia: Listening and talking to the synapse. *Nature Reviews Neuroscience, 2*, 185–193. (2)

Hayes, J. E., Bartoshuk, L. M., Kidd, J. R., & Duffy, V. B. (2008). Supertasting and PROP bitterness depends on more than the *TAS2R38* gene. *Chemical Senses, 33*, 255–265. (7)

Haynes, J.-D., Katsuyuki, S., Rees, G., Gilbert, S., Frith, C., & Passingham, R. E. (2007). Reading hidden intentions in the human brain. *Current Biology, 17*, 323–328. (4)

He, S. M., Yang, A. K., Li, X. T., Du, Y. M., & Zhou, S. F. (2010). Effects of herbal products on the metabolism and transport of anticancer agents. *Expert Opinion on Drug Metabolism & Toxicity, 6*, 1195–1213. (15)

He, W., Yasumatsu, K., Varadarajan, V., Yamada, A., Lem, J., Ninomiya, Y., et al. (2004). Umami taste receptors are mediated by a-transducin and a-gustducin. *Journal of Neuroscience, 24*, 7674–7680. (7)

Hebb, D. O. (1949). *Organization of behavior.* New York: Wiley. (13)

Hegdé, J., & Van Essen, D. C. (2000). Selectivity for complex shapes in primate visual area V2. *Journal of Neuroscience, 20*, RC61: 1–6. (6)

Heims, H. C., Critchley, H. D., Dolan, R., Mathias, C. J., & Cipolotti, L. (2004). Social and motivational functioning is not critically dependent on feedback of autonomic responses: Neuropsychological evidence from patients with pure autonomic failure. *Neuropsychologia, 42*, 1979–1988. (12)

Heisler, L. K., Cowley, M. A., Tecott, L. H., Fan, W., Low, M. J., Smart, J. L., et al. (2002). Activation of central melanocortin pathways by fenfluramine. *Science, 297*, 609–611. (10)

Helenius, P., Salmelin, R., Richardson, U., Leinonen, S., & Lyytinen, H. (2002). Abnormal auditory cortical activation in dyslexia 100 msec after speech onset. *Journal of Cognitive Neuroscience, 14*, 603–617. (14)

Heller, W., & Levy, J. (1981). Perception and expression of emotion in right-handers and left-handers. *Neuropsychologia, 19*, 263–272. (14)

Henderson, J. M., & Hollingworth, A. (2003). Global transsaccadic change blindness during scene perception. *Psychological Science, 14*, 493–497. (14)

Hendry, S. H. C., & Reid, R. C. (2000). The koniocellular pathway in primate vision. *Annual Review of Neuroscience, 23*, 127–153. (6)

Hennig, J., Reuter, M., Netter, P., Burk, C., & Landt, O. (2005). Two types of aggression are differentially related to serotonergic activity and the A779C *TPH* polymorphism. *Behavioral Neuroscience, 119*, 16–25. (12)

Hennig, R., & Lømo, T. (1985). Firing patterns of motor units in normal rats. *Nature, 314*, 164–166. (8)

Herdener, M., Esposito, F., di Salle, F., Boller, C., Hilti, C. C., Habermeyer, B., et al. (2010). Musi-

cal training induces functional plasticity in human hippocampus. *Journal of Neuroscience, 30*, 1377–1384. (5)

Heresco-Levy, U., & Javitt, D. C. (2004). Comparative effects of glycine and D-cycloserine on persistent negative symptoms in schizophrenia: A retrospective analysis. *Schizophrenia Research, 66*, 89–96. (15)

Heresco-Levy, U., Javitt, D. C., Ermilov, M., Mordel, C., Silipo, G., & Lichtenstein, M. (1999). Efficacy of high-dose glycine in the treatment of enduring negative symptoms of schizophrenia. *Archives of General Psychiatry, 56*, 29–36. (15)

Herkenham, M. (1992). Cannabinoid receptor localization in brain: Relationship to motor and reward systems. *Annals of the New York Academy of Sciences, 654*, 19–32. (3)

Herkenham, M., Lynn, A. B., de Costa, B. R., & Richfield, E. K. (1991). Neuronal localization of cannabinoid receptors in the basal ganglia of the rat. *Brain Research, 547*, 267–274. (3)

Hermans, E. J., Ramsey, N. F., & van Honk, J. (2008). Exogenous testosterone enhances responsiveness to social threat in the neural circuitry of social aggression in humans. *Biological Psychiatry, 63*, 263–270. (12)

Herrero, S. (1985). *Bear attacks: Their causes and avoidance.* Piscataway, NJ: Winchester. (7)

Hertzog, C., Kramer, A. F., Wilson, R. S., & Lindenberger, U. (2009). Enrichment effects on adult cognitive development. *Psychological Science in the Public Interest, 9*, 1–65. (5)

Herz, R. S., & Inzlicht, M. (2002). Sex differences in response to physical and social factors involved in human mate selection: The importance of smell for women. *Evolution and Human Behavior, 23*, 359–364. (7, 11)

Herz, R. S., McCall, C., & Cahill, L. (1999). Hemispheric lateralization in the processing of odor pleasantness versus odor names. *Chemical Senses, 24*, 691–695. (14)

Hess, B. J. M. (2001). Vestibular signals in self-orientation and eye movement control. *News in Physiological Sciences, 16*, 234–238. (7)

Hesse, M. D., Thiel, C. M., Stephan, K. E., & Fink, G. R. (2006). The left parietal cortex and motor intention: An event-related functional magnetic resonance imaging study. *Neuroscience, 140*, 1209–1221. (8)

Hettema, J. M., Neale, M. C., & Kendler, K. S. (2001). A review and meta-analysis of the genetic epidemiology of anxiety disorders. *American Journal of Psychiatry, 158*, 1568–1578. (12)

Heyes, C. (2010). Where do mirror neurons come from? *Neuroscience and Biobehavioral Reviews, 34*, 575–583. (8)

Higgs, S., Williamson, A. C., Rotshtein, P., & Humphreys, G. W. (2008). Sensory-specific satiety is intake in amnesics who eat multiple meals. *Psychological Science, 19*, 623–628. (13)

Higley, J. D., Mehlman, P. T., Higley, S. B., Fernald, B., Vickers, J., Lindell, S. G., et al. (1996). Excessive mortality in young free-ranging male nonhuman primates with low cerebrospinal fluid 5-hydroxyindoleacetic acid concentrations. *Archives of General Psychiatry, 53*, 537–543. (12)

Hill, S. Y., De Bellis, M. D., Keshavan, M. S., Lowers, L., Shen, S., Hall, J., et al. (2001). Right amygdala volume in adolescents and young adult offspring from families at high risk for developing alcoholism. *Biological Psychiatry, 49*, 894–905. (3)

Hillis, A. E., Newhart, M., Heidler, J., Barker, P. B., Herskovits, E. H., & Degaonkar, M. (2005). Anatomy of spatial attention: Insights from perfusion imaging and hemispatial neglect in acute stroke. *Journal of Neuroscience, 25*, 3161–3167. (14)

Hillman, C. H., Erickson, K. I., & Kramer, A. F. (2008). Be smart, exercise your heart: Exercise effects on brain and cognition. *Nature Reviews Neuroscience, 9*, 58–65. (15)

Hines, M., Golombok, S., Rust, J., Johnston, K. J., Golding, J., & the Avon Longitudinal Study of Parents and Children Study Team. (2002). Testosterone during pregnancy and gender role behavior of preschool children: A longitudinal, population study. *Child Development, 73*, 1678–1687. (11)

Hippisley-Cox, J., Vinogradova, Y., Coupland, C., & Parker, C. (2007). Risk of malignancy in patients with schizophrenia or bipolar disorder. *Archives of General Psychiatry, 64*, 1368–1376. (15)

Hitchcock, J. M., & Davis, M. (1991). Efferent pathway of the amygdala involved in conditioned fear as measured with the fear-potentiated startle paradigm. *Behavioral Neuroscience, 105*, 826–842. (12)

Hiyama, T. Y., Watanabe, E., Okado, H., & Noda, M. (2004). The subfornical organ is the primary locus of sodium-level sensing by Nax sodium channels for the control of salt-intake behavior. *Journal of Neuroscience, 24*, 9276–9281. (10)

Hnasko, T. S., Sotak, B. N., & Palmiter, R. D. (2005). Morphine reward in dopamine-deficient mice. *Nature, 438*, 854–857. (3)

Hobson, J. A. (1989). *Sleep.* New York: Scientific American Library. (15)

Hobson, J. A. (2009). REM sleep and dreaming: Towards a theory of protoconsciousness. *Nature Reviews Neuroscience, 10*, 803–813. (9)

Hobson, J. A., & McCarley, R. W. (1977). The brain as a dream state generator: An activation-synthesis hypothesis of the dream process. *American Journal of Psychiatry, 134*, 1335–1348. (9)

Hobson, J. A., Pace-Schott, E. F., & Stickgold, R. (2000). Dreaming and the brain: Toward a cognitive neuroscience of conscious states. *Behavioral and Brain Sciences, 23*, 793–1121. (9)

Hochberg, L. R., Serruya, M. D., Friehs, G. M., Mukand, J. A., Saleh, M., Caplan, A. H., et al. (2006). Neuronal ensemble control of prosthetic devices by a human with tetraplegia. *Nature, 442*, 164–171. (8)

Hoebel, B. G., & Hernandez, L. (1993). Basic neural mechanisms of feeding and weight regulation. In A. J. Stunkard & T. A. Wadden (Eds.), *Obesity: Theory and therapy* (2nd ed., pp. 43–62). New York: Raven Press. (10)

Hoebel, B. G., Rada, P. V., Mark, G. P., & Pothos, E. (1999). Neural systems for reinforcement and inhibition of behavior: Relevance to eating, addiction, and depression. In D. Kahneman, E. Diener, & N. Schwartz (Eds.), *Well-being: Foun-*

dations of hedonic psychology (pp. 560–574). New York: Russell Sage Foundation. (10)

Hoeft, F., Hernandez, A., McMillon, G., Taylor-Hill, H., Martindale, J. L., Meyler, A., et al. (2006). Neural basis of dyslexia: A comparison between dyslexic and nondyslexic children equated for reading ability. *Journal of Neuroscience, 26,* 10700–10708. (14)

Hoffer, A. (1973). Mechanism of action of nicotinic acid and nicotinamide in the treatment of schizophrenia. In D. Hawkins & L. Pauling (Eds.), *Orthomolecular psychiatry* (pp. 202–262). San Francisco: Freeman. (15)

Hoffman, P. L., Tabakoff, B., Szabó, G., Suzdak, P. D., & Paul, S. M. (1987). Effect of an imidazobenzodiazepine, Ro15-4513, on the incoordination and hypothermia produced by ethanol and pento-barbital. *Life Sciences, 41,* 611–619. (12)

Hoffmann, F., & Curio, G. (2003). REM-Schlaf und rezidivierende Erosio corneae—eine Hypothese. [REM sleep and recurrent corneal erosion—A hypothesis.] *Klinische Monatsblatter für Augenheilkunde, 220,* 51–53. (9)

Hökfelt, T., Johansson, O., & Goldstein, M. (1984). Chemical anatomy of the brain. *Science, 225,* 1326–1334. (3)

Holcombe, A. O., & Cavanagh, P. (2001). Early binding of feature pairs for visual perception. *Nature Neuroscience, 4,* 127–128. (4)

Hollister, J. M., Laing, P., & Mednick, S. A. (1996). Rhesus incompatibility as a risk factor for schizophrenia in male adults. *Archives of General Psychiatry, 53,* 19–24. (15)

Hollon, S. D., Jarrett, R. B., Nierenberg, A. A., Thase, M. E., Trivedi, M., & Rush, A. J. (2005). Psychotherapy and medication in the treatment of adult and geriatric depression: Which monotherapy or combined treatment? *Journal of Clinical Psychiatry, 66,* 455–468. (15)

Hollon, S. D., Thase, M. E., & Markowitz, J. C. (2002). Treatment and prevention of depression. *Psychological Science in the Public Interest, 3,* 39–77. (15)

Holmans, P., Weissman, M. M., Zubenko, G. S., Scheftner, W. A., Crowe, R. R., DePaulo, J. R. Jr., et al. (2007). Genetics of recurrent early-onset major depression (GenRED): Final genome scan report. *American Journal of Psychiatry, 164,* 248–258. (15)

Holstege, G., Georgiadis, J. R., Paans, A. M. J., Meiners, L. C., van der Graaf, F. H. C. E., & Reinders, A. A. T. S. (2003). Brain activation during human male ejaculation. *Journal of Neuroscience, 23,* 9185–9193. (11)

Holy, T. E., Dulac, C., & Meister, M. (2000). Responses of vomeronasal neurons to natural stimuli. *Science, 289,* 1569–1572. (7)

Homewood, J., & Stevenson, R. J. (2001). Differences in naming accuracy of odors presented to the left and right nostrils. *Biological Psychology, 58,* 65–73. (14)

Honea, R., Crow, T. J., Passingham, D., & Mackay, C. E. (2005). Regional deficits in brain volume in schizophrenia: A meta-analysis of voxel-based morphometry studies. *American Journal of Psychiatry, 162,* 2233–2245. (15)

Hoover, J. E., & Strick, P. L. (1993). Multiple output channels in the basal ganglia. *Science, 259,* 819–821. (8)

Hopkins, W. D. (2006). Comparative and familial analysis of handedness in great apes. *Psychological Bulletin, 132,* 538–559. (14)

Hopkins, W. D., Russell, J. L., & Cantalupo, C. (2007). Neuroanatomical correlates of handedness for tool use in chimpanzees (*Pan troglodytes*). *Psychological Science, 18,* 971–977. (14)

Hoptman, M. J., & Levy, J. (1988). Perceptual asymmetries in left- and right-handers for cartoon and real faces. *Brain and Cognition, 8,* 178–188. (14)

Horne, J. A. (1992). Sleep and its disorders in children. *Journal of Child Psychology & Psychiatry & Allied Disciplines, 33,* 473–487. (9)

Horne, J. A., & Minard, A. (1985). Sleep and sleepiness following a behaviourally "active" day. *Ergonomics, 28,* 567–575. (9)

Horridge, G. A. (1962). Learning of leg position by the ventral nerve cord in headless insects. *Proceedings of the Royal Society of London, B, 157,* 33–52. (13)

Horst, W. D., & Preskorn, S. H. (1998). Mechanisms of action and clinical characteristics of three atypical antidepressants: Venlafaxine, nefazodone, bupropion. *Journal of Affective Disorders, 51,* 237–254. (15)

Horvath, T. L. (2005). The hardship of obesity: A soft-wired hypothalamus. *Nature Neuroscience, 8,* 561–565. (10)

Hoshi, E., & Tanji, J. (2000). Integration of target and body-part information in the premotor cortex when planning action. *Nature, 408,* 466–470. (8)

Houk, C. P., & Lee, P. A. (2010). Approach to assigning gender in 46,XX congenital adrenal hyperplasia with male external genitalia: Replacing dogmatism with pragmatism. *Journal of Clinical Endocrinology & Metabolism, 95,* 4501–4508. (11)

Hovda, D. A., & Feeney, D. M. (1989). Amphetamine-induced recovery of visual cliff performance after bilateral visual cortex ablation in cats: Measurements of depth perception thresholds. *Behavioral Neuroscience, 103,* 574–584. (5)

Howard, J. D., Plailly, J., Grueschow, M., Haynes, J.-D., & Gottfried, J. A. (2009). Odor quality coding and categorization in human posterior piriform cortex. *Nature Neuroscience, 12,* 932–938. (7)

Howell, S., Westergaard, G., Hoos, B., Chavanne, T. J., Shoaf, S. E., Cleveland, A., et al. (2007). Serotonergic influences on life-history outcomes in free-ranging male rhesus macaques. *American Journal of Primatology, 69,* 851–865. (12)

Howes, O. D., Montgomery, A. J., Asselin, M.-C., Murray, R. M., Valli, I., Tabraham, P., et al. (2009). Elevated striatal dopamine function linked to prodromal signs of schizophrenia. *Archives of General Psychiatry, 66,* 13–20. (15)

Hrdy, S. B. (2000). The optimal number of fathers. *Annals of the New York Academy of Sciences, 907,* 75–96. (11)

Hróbjartsson, A., & Gøtzsche, P. C. (2001). Is the placebo powerless? *New England Journal of Medicine, 344,* 1594–1602. (7)

Hsieh, P.-J., Vul, E., & Kanwisher, N. (2010). Recognition alters the spatial pattern of fMRI activa-tion in early retinotopic cortex. *Journal of Neurophysiology, 103,* 1501–1507. (6)

Hu, P., Stylos-Allan, M., & Walker, M. P. (2006). Sleep facilitates consolidation of emotional declarative memory. *Psychological Science, 17,* 891–898. (9)

Hu, W., Lee, H. L., Zhang, Q., Liu, T., Geng, L. B., Seghier, M. L., et al. (2010). Developmental dyslexia in Chinese and English populations: Dissociating the effect of dyslexia from language differences. *Brain, 133,* 1694–1706. (14)

Hua, J. Y., & Smith, S. J. (2004). Neural activity and the dynamics of central nervous system development. *Nature Neuroscience, 7,* 327–332. (5)

Huang, A. L., Chen, X., Hoon, M. A., Chandrashekar, J., Guo, W., Tränker, D., et al. (2006). The cells and logic for mammalian sour taste detection. *Nature, 442,* 934–938. (7)

Huang, L., Treisman, A., & Pashler, H. (2007). Characterizing the limits of human visual awareness. *Science, 317,* 823–825. (14)

Huang, Y.-J., Maruyama, Y., Lu, K.-S., Pereira, E., Plonsky, I., Baur, J. E., et al. (2005). Mouse taste buds use serotonin as a neurotransmitter. *Journal of Neuroscience, 25,* 843–847. (3)

Hubbard, E. M., Piazza, M., Pinel, P., & Dehaene, S. (2005). Interactions between number and space in parietal cortex. *Nature Reviews Neuroscience, 6,* 435–448. (4)

Hubel, D. H. (1963, November). The visual cortex of the brain. *Scientific American, 209*(5), 54–62. (6)

Hubel, D. H., & Wiesel, T. N. (1959). Receptive fields of single neurons in the cat's striate cortex. *Journal of Physiology, 148,* 574–591. (6)

Hubel, D. H., & Wiesel, T. N. (1965). Binocular interaction in striate cortex of kittens reared with artificial squint. *Journal of Neurophysiology, 28,* 1041–1059. (6)

Hubel, D. H., & Wiesel, T. N. (1977). Functional architecture of macaque monkey visual cortex. *Proceedings of the Royal Society of London, B, 198,* 1–59. (6)

Hubel, D. H., & Wiesel, T. N. (1998). Early exploration of the visual cortex. *Neuron, 20,* 401–412. (6)

Huber, R., Ghilardi, M. F., Massimini, M., & Tononi, G. (2004). Local sleep and learning. *Nature, 430,* 78–81. (9)

Hudson, J. I., Hiripi, E., Pope, H. G., Jr., & Kessler, R. C. (2007). The prevalence and correlates of eating disorders in the National Comorbidity Survey Replication. *Biological Psychiatry, 61,* 348–358. (10)

Hudson, J. I., Mangweth, B., Pope, H. G., Jr., De Col, C., Hausmann, A., Gutweniger, S., et al. (2003). Family study of affective spectrum disorder. *Archives of General Psychiatry, 60,* 170–177. (15)

Hudspeth, A. J. (1985). The cellular basis of hearing: The biophysics of hair cells. *Science, 230,* 745–752. (7)

Huey, E. D., Garcia, C., Wassermann, E. M., Tierney, M. C., & Grafman, J. (2008). Stimulant treatment of frontotemporal dementia in 8 patients. *Journal of Clinical Psychiatry, 69,* 1981–1982. (5)

Hugdahl, K. (1996). Brain laterality—Beyond the basics. *European Psychologist, 1,* 206–220. (14)

Hughes, J. C., & Cook, C. C. H. (1997). The efficacy of disulfiram: A review of outcome studies. *Addiction, 92,* 381–395. (3)

Hughes, J. R. (2007). Review of medical reports on pedophilia. *Clinical Pediatrics, 46,* 667–682. (11)

Hull, E. M., & Dominguez, J. M. (2007). Sexual behavior in male rodents. *Hormones and Behavior, 52,* 45–55. (11)

Hull, E. M., Du, J., Lorrain, D. S., & Matuszewich, L. (1997). Testosterone, preoptic dopamine, and copulation in male rats. *Brain Research Bulletin, 44,* 327–333. (11)

Hull, E. M., Eaton, R. C., Markowski, V. P., Moses, J., Lumley, L. A., & Loucks, J. A. (1992). Opposite influence of medial preoptic D_1 and D_2 receptors on genital reflexes: Implications for copulation. *Life Sciences, 51,* 1705–1713. (11)

Hull, E. M., Lorrain, D. S., Du, J., Matuszewich, L., Lumley, L. A., Putnam, S. K., et al. (1999). Hormone-neurotransmitter interactions in the control of sexual behavior. *Behavioural Brain Research, 105,* 105–116. (11)

Hull, E. M., Nishita, J. K., Bitran, D., & Dalterio, S. (1984). Perinatal dopamine-related drugs demasculinize rats. *Science, 224,* 1011–1013. (11)

Hull, R., & Vaid, J. (2007). Bilingual language lateralization: A meta-analytic tale of two hemispheres. *Neuropsychologia, 45,* 1987–2008. (14)

Hulshoff, H. E., Schnack, H. G., Mandl, R. C. W., van Haren, N. E. M., Koning, H., Collins, L., et al. (2001). Focal gray matter density changes in schizophrenia. *Archives of General Psychiatry, 58,* 1118–1125. (15)

Hunsberger, J. G., Newton, S. S., Bennett, A. H., Duman, C. H., Russell, D. S., Salton, S. R., et al. (2007). Antidepressant actions of the exercise-regulated gene VGF. *Nature Medicine, 13,* 1476–1482. (15)

Hunt, S. P., & Mantyh, P. W. (2001). The molecular dynamics of pain control. *Nature Reviews Neuroscience, 2,* 83–91. (7)

Hunter, W. S. (1923). *General psychology* (Rev. ed.). Chicago: University of Chicago Press. (4)

Huntington's Disease Collaborative Research Group. (1993). A novel gene containing a trinucleotide repeat that is expanded and unstable on Huntington's disease chromosomes. *Cell, 72,* 971–983. (8)

Hurovitz, C. S., Dunn, S., Domhoff, G. W., & Fiss, H. (1999). The dreams of blind men and women: A replication and extension of previous findings. *Dreaming, 9,* 183–193. (6)

Hurvich, L. M., & Jameson, D. (1957). An opponent-process theory of color vision. *Psychological Review, 64,* 384–404. (6)

Hutcheson, D. M., Everitt, B. J., Robbins, T. W., & Dickinson, A. (2001). The role of withdrawal in heroin addiction: Enhances reward or promotes avoidance? *Nature Neuroscience, 4,* 943–947. (3)

Hutchison, K. E., LaChance, H., Niaura, R., Bryan, A., & Smolen, A. (2002). The DRD4 VNTR polymorphism influences reactivity to smoking cues. *Journal of Abnormal Psychology, 111,* 134–143. (3)

Hutchison, K. E., McGeary, J., Smolen, A., & Bryan, A. (2002). The DRD4 VNTR polymorphism moderates craving after alcohol consumption. *Health Psychology, 21,* 139–146. (3)

Hyde, J. (2005). The gender similarities hypothesis. *American Psychologist, 60,* 581–592. (4)

Hyde, J. S., Lindberg, S. M., Linn, M. C., Ellis, A. B., & Williams, C. C. (2008). Gender similarities characterize math performance. *Science, 321,* 494–495. (4)

Hyde, K. L., Lerch, J., Norton, A., Forgeard, M., Winner, E., Evans, A. C., et al. (2009a). Musical training shapes structural brain development. *Journal of Neuroscience, 29,* 3019–3025. (5)

Hyde, K. L., Lerch, J., Norton, A., Forgeard, M., Winner, E., Evans, A. C., et al. (2009b). The effects of musical training on structural brain development: A longitudinal study. *Annals of the New York Academy of Sciences, 1169,* 182–186. (5)

Hyde, K. L., Lerch, J. P., Zatorre, R. J., Griffiths, T. D., Evans, A. C., & Peretz, I. (2007). Cortical thickness in congenital amusia: When less is better than more. *Journal of Neuroscience, 27,* 13028–13032. (7)

Hyde, K. L., & Peretz, I. (2004). Brains that are out of tune but in time. *Psychological Science, 15,* 356–360. (7)

Hynd, G. W., & Semrud-Clikeman, M. (1989). Dyslexia and brain morphology. *Psychological Bulletin, 106,* 447–482. (14)

Ibrahim, H. M., Hogg, A. J., Jr., Healy, D. J., Haroutunian, V., Davis, K. L., & Meador-Woodruff, J. H. (2000). Ionotropic glutamate receptor binding and subunit mRNA expression in thalamic nuclei in schizophrenia. *American Journal of Psychiatry, 157,* 1811–1823. (15)

Iggo, A., & Andres, K. H. (1982). Morphology of cutaneous receptors. *Annual Review of Neuroscience, 5,* 1–31. (7)

Ikeda, H., Stark, J., Fischer, H., Wagner, M., Drdla, R., Jäger, T., et al. (2006). Synaptic amplifier of inflammatory pain in the spinal dorsal horn. *Science, 312,* 1659–1662. (7)

Ikonomidou, C., Bittigau, P. Ishimaru, M. J., Wozniak, D. F., Koch, C., Genz, K., et al. (2000). Ethanol-induced apoptotic neurodegeneration and fetal alcohol syndrome. *Science, 287,* 1056–1060. (5)

Imamura, K., Mataga, N., & Mori, K. (1992). Coding of odor molecules by mitral/tufted cells in rabbit olfactory bulb: I. Aliphatic compounds. *Journal of Neurophysiology, 68,* 1986–2002. (7)

Imayoshi, I., Sakamoto, M., Ohtsuka, T., Takao, K., Miyakawa, T., Yamaguchi, M., et al. (2008). Roles of continuous neurogenesis in the structural and functional integrity of the adult forebrain. *Nature Neuroscience, 11,* 1153–1161. (5)

Imel, Z. E., Malterer, M. B., McKay, K. M., & Wampold, B. E. (2008). A meta-analysis of psychotherapy and medication in unipolar depression and dysthymia. *Journal of Affective Disorders, 110,* 197–206. (15)

Imperato-McGinley, J., Guerrero, L., Gautier, T., & Peterson, R. E. (1974). Steroid 5 alpha-reductase deficiency in man: An inherited form of male pseudohermaphroditism. *Science, 186,* 1213–1215. (11)

Ingram, C. J. E., Mulcare, C. A., Itan, Y., Thomas, M. G., & Swallow, D. M. (2009). Lactose digestion and the evolutionary genetics of lactase persistence. *Human Genetics, 124,* 579–591. (10)

Innocenti, G. M. (1980). The primary visual pathway through the corpus callosum: Morphological and functional aspects in the cat. *Archives Italiennes de Biologie, 118,* 124–188. (14)

Innocenti, G. M., & Caminiti, R. (1980). Postnatal shaping of callosal connections from sensory areas. *Experimental Brain Research, 38,* 381–394. (14)

Inouye, S. T., & Kawamura, H. (1979). Persistence of circadian rhythmicity in a mammalian hypothalamic "island" containing the suprachiasmatic nucleus. *Proceedings of the National Academy of Sciences, USA, 76,* 5962–5966. (9)

International Schizophrenia Consortium. (2009). Common polygenic variation contributes to risk of schizophenia and bipolar disorder. *Nature, 460,* 748–752. (15)

Iqbal, K., & Grundke-Iqbal, I. (2010). Alzheimer's disease, a multifactorial disorder seeking multitherapies. *Alzheimers & Dementia, 6,* 420–424. (13)

Isoda, M., & Hikosaka, O. (2007). Switching from automatic to controlled action by monkey medial frontal cortex. *Nature Neuroscience, 10,* 240–248. (8)

Ito, M. (1984). *The cerebellum and neural control.* New York: Raven Press. (8)

Ittner, L. M., & Götz, J. (2011). Amyloid-β and tau—a toxic *pas de deux* in Alzheimer's disease. *Nature Reviews Neuroscience, 12,* 67–72. (13)

Ivry, R. B., & Diener, H. C. (1991). Impaired velocity perception in patients with lesions of the cerebellum. *Journal of Cognitive Neuroscience, 3,* 355–366. (8)

Ivy, G. O., & Killackey, H. P. (1981). The ontogeny of the distribution of callosal projection neurons in the rat parietal cortex. *Journal of Comparative Neurology, 195,* 367–389. (14)

Iwema, C. L., Fang, H., Kurtz, D. B., Youngentob, S. L., & Schwob, J. E. (2004). Odorant receptor expression patterns are restored in lesion-recovered rat olfactory epithelium. *Journal of Neuroscience, 24,* 356–369. (7)

Jablensky, A. V., Morgan, V., Zubrick, S. R., Bower, C., & Yellachich, L.-A. (2005). Pregnancy, delivery, and neonatal complications in a population cohort of women with schizophrenia and major affective disorders. *American Journal of Psychiatry, 162,* 79–91. (15)

Jacobs, B., & Scheibel, A. B. (1993). A quantitative dendritic analysis of Wernicke's area in humans: I. Lifespan changes. *Journal of Comparative Neurology, 327,* 83–96. (5)

Jacobs, G. D., & Snyder, D. (1996). Frontal brain asymmetry predicts affective style in men. *Behavioral Neuroscience, 110,* 3-6. (15)

Jacobs, G. H., Williams, G. A., Cahill, H., & Nathans, J. (2007). Emergence of novel color vision in mice engineered to express a human cone photopigment. *Science, 315,* 1723–1725. (6)

James, W. (1884). What is an emotion? *Mind, 9,* 188–205. (12)

James, W. (1894). The physical basis of emotion. *Psychological Review, 1,* 516–529. (12)

James, W. (1961). *Psychology: The briefer course.* New York: Harper. (Original work published 1892) (12)

Jameson, K. A., Highnote, S. M., & Wasserman, L. M. (2001). Richer color experience in observers with multiple photopigment opsin genes. *Psychonomic Bulletin & Review, 8,* 244–261. (6)

Jäncke, L., Beeli, G., Eulig, C., & Hänggi, J. (2009). The neuroanatomy of grapheme-color synesthesia. *European Journal of Neuroscience, 29,* 1287–1293. (7)

Jarrard, L. E., Okaichi, H., Steward, O., & Goldschmidt, R. B. (1984). On the role of hippocampal connections in the performance of place and cue tasks: Comparisons with damage to hippocampus. *Behavioral Neuroscience, 98,* 946–954. (13)

Jenner, A. R., Rosen, G. D., & Galaburda, A. M. (1999). Neuronal asymmetries in primary visual cortex of dyslexic and nondyslexic brains. *Annals of Neurology, 46,* 189–196. (14)

Jerison, H. J. (1985). Animal intelligence as encephalization. *Philosophical Transactions of the Royal Society of London, B, 308,* 21–35. (4)

Ji, D., & Wilson, M. A. (2007). Coordinated memory replay in the visual cortex and hippocampus during sleep. *Nature Neuroscience, 10,* 100–107. (9)

Jiang, J., Zhu, W., Shi, F., Liu, Y., Qin, W., Li, K., et al. (2009). Thick visual cortex in the early blind. *Journal of Neuroscience, 29,* 2205–2211. (5)

Jiang, Y., Costello, P., & He, S. (2007). Processing of invisible stimuli. *Psychological Science, 18,* 349–355. (14)

Jin, X., & Costa, R. M. (2010). Start/stop signals emerge in nigrostriatal circuits during sequence learning. *Nature, 466,* 457–462. (8)

Johanek, L. M., Meyer, R. A., Hartke, T., Hobelmann, J. G., Maine, D. N., LaMotte, R. H., et al. (2007). Psychophysical and physiological evidence for parallel afferent pathways mediating the sensation of itch. *Journal of Neuroscience, 27,* 7490–7497. (7)

Johansson, C., Willeit, M., Smedh, C., Ekholm, J., Paunio, T., Kieseppä, T., et al. (2003). Circadian clock-related polymorphisms in seasonal affective disorder and their relevance to diurnal preference. *Neuropsychopharmacology, 28,* 734–739. (15)

Johnson, E. L., Tranel, D., Lutgendorf, S., & Adolphs, R. (2009). A neuroanatomical dissociation for emotion induced by music. *International Journal of Psychophysiology, 72,* 24–33. (12)

Johnson, L. C. (1969). Physiological and psychological changes following total sleep deprivation. In A. Kales (Ed.), *Sleep: Physiology & pathology* (pp. 206–220). Philadelphia: Lippincott. (9)

Johnson, M. T. V., Kipnis, A. N., Coltz, J. D., Gupta, A., Silverstein, P., Zwiebel, F., et al. (1996). Effects of levodopa and viscosity on the velocity and accuracy of visually guided tracking in Parkinson's disease. *Brain, 119,* 801–813. (8)

Johnson, P. M., & Kenny, P. J. (2010). Dopamine D2 receptors in addiction-like reward dysfunction and compulsive eating in obese rats. *Nature Neuroscience, 13,* 635–641. (10)

Jonas, P., Bischofberger, J., & Sandkühler, J. (1998). Corelease of two fast neurotransmitters at a central synapse. *Science, 281,* 419–424. (3)

Jones, A. R., & Shusta, E. V. (2007). Blood–brain barrier transport of therapeutics via receptor-mediation. *Pharmaceutical Research, 24,* 1759–1771. (2)

Jones, C. R., Campbell, S. S., Zone, S. E., Cooper, F., DeSano, A., Murphy, P. J., et al. (1999). Familial advanced sleep-phase syndrome: A short-period circadian rhythm variant in humans. *Nature Medicine, 5,* 1062–1065. (9)

Jones, E. G., & Pons, T. P. (1998). Thalamic and brainstem contributions to large-scale plasticity of primate somatosensory cortex. *Science, 282,* 1121–1125. (5)

Jones, H. S., & Oswald, I. (1968). Two cases of healthy insomnia. *Electroencephalography and Clinical Neurophysiology, 24,* 378–380. (9)

Jones, P. B., Barnes, T. R. E., Davies, L., Dunn, G., Lloyd, H., Hayhurst, K. P., et al. (2006). Randomized controlled trial of the effect on quality of life of second- vs. first-generation antipsychotic drugs in schizophrenia. *Archives of General Psychiatry, 63,* 1079–1087. (15)

Jordan, H. A. (1969). Voluntary intragastric feeding. *Journal of Comparative and Physiological Psychology, 62,* 237–244. (10)

Jouvet, M. (1960). Telencephalic and rhombencephalic sleep in the cat. In G. E. W. Wolstenholme & M. O'Connor (Eds.), *CIBA Foundation symposium on the nature of sleep* (pp. 188–208). Boston: Little, Brown. (9)

Joyner, A. L., & Guillemot, F. (1994). Gene targeting and development of the nervous system. *Current Opinion in Neurobiology, 4,* 37–42. (4)

Judge, J., Caravolas, M., & Knox, P. C. (2006). Smooth pursuit eye movements and phonological processing in adults with dyslexia. *Cognitive Neuropsychology, 23,* 1174–1189. (14)

Jueptner, M., & Weiller, C. (1998). A review of differences between basal ganglia and cerebellar control of movements as revealed by functional imaging studies. *Brain, 121,* 1437–1449. (8)

Juvonen, H., Reunanen, A., Haukka, J., Muhonen, M., Suvisari, J., Arajärvi, R., et al. (2007). Incidence of schizophrenia in a nationwide cohort of patients with type 1 diabetes mellitus. *Archives of General Psychiatry, 64,* 894–899. (15)

Kaas, J. H. (1983). What, if anything, is SI? Organization of first somatosensory area of cortex. *Physiological Reviews, 63,* 206–231. (7)

Kaas, J. H., Merzenich, M. M., & Killackey, H. P. (1983). The reorganization of somatosensory cortex following peripheral nerve damage in adult and developing mammals. *Annual Review of Neuroscience, 6,* 325–356. (5)

Kaas, J. H., Nelson, R. J., Sur, M., Lin, C.-S., & Merzenich, M. M. (1979). Multiple representations of the body within the primary somatosensory cortex of primates. *Science, 204,* 521–523. (4)

Kaiser, A., Haller, S., Schmitz, S., & Nitsch, C. (2009). On sex/gender related similarities and differences in fMRI language research. *Brain Research Reviews, 61,* 49-59. (11)

Kales, A., Scharf, M. B., & Kales, J. D. (1978). Rebound insomnia: A new clinical syndrome. *Science, 201,* 1039–1041. (9)

Kalin, N. H., Shelton, S. E., & Davidson, R. J. (2004). The role of the central nucleus of the amygdala in mediating fear and anxiety in the primate. *Journal of Neuroscience, 24,* 5506–5515. (12)

Kalin, N. H., Shelton, S. E., Davidson, R. J., & Kelley, A. E. (2001). The primate amygdala mediates acute fear but not the behavioral and physiological components of anxious temperament. *Journal of Neuroscience, 21,* 2067–2074. (12)

Kamitani, Y., & Tong, F. (2005). Decoding the visual and subjective contents of the human brain. *Nature Neuroscience, 8,* 679–685. (14)

Kandel, E. R., & Schwartz, J. H. (1982). Molecular biology of learning: Modulation of transmitter release. *Science, 218,* 433–443. (13)

Kang, M. J., Hsu, M., Krajbich, I. M., Loewenstein, G., Mcclure, S. M., Wang, J. T., et al. (2009). The wick in the candle of learning. *Psychological Science, 8,* 963–973. (13)

Kanwisher, N. (2010). Functional specificity in the human brain: A window into the functional architecture of the mind. *Proceedings of the National Academy of Sciences, 107,* 11163–11170. (6)

Kanwisher, N., & Yovel, G. (2006). The fusiform face area: A cortical region specialized for the perception of faces. *Philosophical Transactions of the Royal Society, B, 361,* 2109–2128. (6)

Kaplan, J. R., Muldoon, M. F., Manuck, S. B., & Mann, J. J. (1997). Assessing the observed relationship between low cholesterol and violence-related mortality. *Annals of the New York Academy of Sciences, 836,* 57–80. (12)

Kapur, S., Zipusky, R., Jones, C., Shammi, C. S., Remington, G., & Seeman, P. (2000). A positron emission tomography study of quetiapine in schizophrenia. *Archives of General Psychiatry, 57,* 553–559. (15)

Karama, S., Ad-Dab'bagh, Y., Haier, R. J., Deary, I. J., Lyttelton, O. C., Lepage, C., et al. (2009). Positive association between cognitive ability and cortical thickness in a representative US sample of healthy 6 to 18 year olds. *Intelligence, 37,* 145–155. (4)

Kargo, W. J., & Nitz, D. A. (2004). Improvements in the signal-to-noise ratio of motor cortex cells distinguish early versus late phases of motor skill learning. *Journal of Neuroscience, 24,* 5560–5569. (8)

Karlsson, M., & Frank, L. M. (2009). Awake replay of remote experiences in the hippocampus. *Nature Neuroscience, 12,* 913–918. (9)

Karmiloff-Smith, A., Tyler, L. K., Voice, K., Sims, K., Udwin, O., Howlin, P., et al. (1998). Linguistic dissociations in Williams syndrome: Evaluating receptive syntax in on-line and off-line tasks. *Neuropsychologia, 36,* 343–351. (14)

Karnath, H. O., Rüter, J., Mandler, A., & Himmelbach, M. (2009). The anatomy of object recognition: Visual form agnosia caused by nedial occipitotemporal stroke. *Journal of Neuroscience, 29,* 5854–5862. (6)

Karrer, T., & Bartoshuk, L. (1991). Capsaicin desensitization and recovery on the human tongue. *Physiology & Behavior, 49,* 757–764. (7)

Kas, M. J. H., Tiesjema, B., van Dijk, G., Garner, K. M., Barsh, G. S., Ter Brake, O., et al. (2004). Induction of brain region-specific forms of obesity by agouti. *Journal of Neuroscience, 24,* 10176–10181. (10)

Kasai, K., Shenton, M. E., Salisbury, D. F., Hirayasu, Y., Onitsuka, T., Spencer, M. H., et al. (2003). Progressive decrease of left Heschl gyrus and planum temporale gray matter volume in first-episode schizophrenia. *Archives of General Psychiatry, 60,* 766–775. (15)

Kasper, S., Caraci, F., Forti, B., Drago, F., & Aguglia, E. (2010). Efficacy and tolerability of Hypericum extract for the treatment of mild to moderate depression. *European Neuropsychopharmacology, 20,* 747–765. (15)

Katkin, E. S., Wiens, S., & Öhman, A. (2001). Nonconscious fear conditioning, visceral perception, and the development of gut feelings. *Psychological Science, 12,* 366–370. (12)

Kavanau, J. L. (1998). Vertebrates that never sleep: Implications for sleep's basic function. *Brain Research Bulletin, 46,* 269–279. (9)

Kawasaki, H., Adolphs, R., Oya, H., Kovach, C., Damasio, H., Kaufman, O., et al. (2005). Analysis of single-unit responses to emotional scenes in human ventromedial prefrontal cortex. *Journal of Cognitive Neuroscience, 17,* 1509–1518. (12)

Kay, K. N., Naselaris, T., Prenger, R. J., & Gallant, J. L. (2008). Identifying natural images from human brain activity. *Nature, 452,* 352–355. (4)

Kee, N., Teixeira, C. M., Wang, A. H., & Frankland, P. W. (2007). Preferential incorporation of adult-generated granule cells into spatial memory networks in the dentate gyrus. *Nature Neuroscience, 10,* 355–362. (5)

Keefe, R. S. E., Silverman, J. M., Mohs, R. C., Siever, L. J., Harvey, P. D., Friedman, L., et al. (1997). Eye tracking, attention, and schizotypal symptoms in nonpsychotic relatives of patients with schizophrenia. *Archives of General Psychiatry, 54,* 169–176. (15)

Keele, S. W., & Ivry, R. (1990). Does the cerebellum provide a common computation for diverse tasks? *Annals of the New York Academy of Sciences, 608,* 179–207. (8)

Kelly, B. D., O'Callaghan, E., Waddington, J. L., Feeney, L., Browne, S., Scully, P. J., et al. (2010). Schizophrenia and the city: A review of literature and prospective study of psychosis and urbanicity in Ireland. *Schizophrenia Research, 116,* 75–89. (15)

Kelly, T. L., Neri, D. F., Grill, J. T., Ryman, D., Hunt, P. D., Dijk, D.-J., et al. (1999). Nonentrained circadian rhythms of melatonin in submariners scheduled to an 18-hour day. *Journal of Biological Rhythms, 14,* 190–196. (9)

Kendler, K. S. (1983). Overview: A current perspective on twin studies of schizophrenia. *American Journal of Psychiatry, 140,* 1413–1425. (15)

Kendler, K. S. (2001). Twin studies of psychiatric illness. *Archives of General Psychiatry, 58,* 1005–1014. (1)

Kendler, K. S., Fiske, A., Gardner, C. O., & Gatz, M. (2009). Delineation of two genetic pathways to major depression. *Biological Psychiatry, 65,* 808–811. (15)

Kendler, K. S., Gardner, C. O., & Prescott, C. A. (1999). Clinical characteristics of major depression that predict risk of depression in relatives. *Archives of General Psychiatry, 56,* 322–327. (15)

Kennard, C., Lawden, M., Morland, A. B., & Ruddock, K. H. (1995). Colour identification and colour constancy are impaired in a patient with incomplete achromatopsia associated with prestriate cortical lesions. *Proceedings of the Royal Society of London, B, 260,* 169–175. (6)

Kennaway, D. J., & Van Dorp, C. F. (1991). Free-running rhythms of melatonin, cortisol, electrolytes, and sleep in humans in Antarctica. *American Journal of Physiology, 260,* R1137–R1144. (9)

Kennedy, D. P., & Adolphs, R. (2010). Impaired fixation to eyes following amygdala damage arises from abnormal bottom-up attention. *Neuropsychologia, 48,* 3392–3398. (12)

Kennedy, D. P., Gläscher, J., Tyszka, J. M., & Adolphs, R. (2009). Personal space regulation by the human amygdala. *Nature Neuroscience, 12,* 1226–1227. (12)

Kennerley, S. W., Diedrichsen, J., Hazeltine, E., Semjen, A., & Ivry, R. B. (2002). Callosotomy patients exhibit temporal uncoupling during continuous bimanual movements. *Nature Neuroscience, 5,* 376–381. (14)

Kennett, S., Eimer, M., Spence, C., & Driver, J. (2001). Tactile-visual links in exogenous spatial attention under different postures: Convergent evidence from psychophysics and ERPs. *Journal of Cognitive Neuroscience, 13,* 462–478. (14)

Kenny, P. J., Chen, S. A., Kitamura, O., Markou, A., & Koob, G. F. (2006). Conditioned withdrawal drives heroin consumption and decreases reward sensitivity. *Journal of Neuroscience, 26,* 5894–5900. (3)

Kerchner, G. A., & Nicoll, R. A. (2008). Silent synapses and the emergence of a postsynaptic mechanism for LTP. *Nature Reviews Neuroscience, 9,* 813–825. (13)

Kerns, J. G. (2007). Experimental manipulation of cognitive control processes causes an increase in communication disturbances in healthy volunteers. *Psychological Medicine, 37,* 995–1004. (15)

Kerr, J. N. D., & Denk, W. (2008). Imaging *in vivo*: Watching the brain in action. *Nature Reviews Neuroscience, 9,* 195–205. (4)

Keshavan, M. S., Diwadkar, V. A., Montrose, D. M., Rajarethinam, R., & Sweeney, J. A. (2005). Premorbid indicators and risk for schizophrenia: A selective review and update. *Schizophrenia Research, 79,* 45–57. (15)

Kesner, R. P., Gilbert, P. E., & Barua, L. A. (2002). The role of the hippocampus in meaning for the temporal order of a sequence of odors. *Behavioral Neuroscience, 116,* 286–290. (13)

Kety, S. S., Wender, P. H., Jacobson, B., Ingraham, L. J., Jansson, L., Faber, B., et al. (1994). Mental illness in the biological and adoptive relatives of schizophrenic adoptees. *Archives of General Psychiatry, 51,* 442–455. (15)

Keverne, E. B. (1999). The vomeronasal organ. *Science, 286,* 716–720. (7)

Khashau, A. S., Abel, K. M., McNamee, R., Pedersen, M. G., Webb, R. T., Baker, P. N., et al. (2008). Higher risk of offspring schizophrenia following antenatal maternal exposure to severe adverse life events. *Archives of General Psychiatry, 65,* 146–152. (15)

Kiecolt-Glaser, J. K., & Glaser, R. (1993). Mind and immunity. In D. Goleman & J. Gurin (Eds.), *Mind/body medicine* (pp. 39–61). Yonkers, NY: Consumer Reports Books. (12)

Kilgour, A. R., de Gelder, B., & Lederman, S. J. (2004). Haptic face recognition and prosopagnosia. *Neuropsychologia, 42,* 707–712. (6)

Killackey, H. P., & Chalupa, L. M. (1986). Ontogenetic change in the distribution of callosal projection neurons in the postcentral gyrus of the fetal rhesus monkey. *Journal of Comparative Neurology, 244,* 331–348. (14)

Killeffer, F. A., & Stern, W. E. (1970). Chronic effects of hypothalamic injury. *Archives of Neurology, 22,* 419–429. (10)

Kilner, J. M., Neal, A., Weiskopf, N., Friston, K. J., & Frith, C. D. (2009). Evidence of mirror neurons in human inferior frontal gyrus. *Journal of Neuroscience, 29,* 10153–10159. (8)

Kim, M. J., & Whalen, P. J. (2009). The structural integrity of an amygdala-prefrontal pathway predicts trait anxiety. *Journal of Neuroscience, 29,* 11614–11618. (12)

Kim, U., Jorgenson, E., Coon, H., Leppert, M., Risch, N., & Drayna, D. (2003). Positional cloning of the human quantitative trait locus underlying taste sensitivity to phenylthiocarbamide. *Science, 299,* 1221–1225. (7)

Kim, Y.-K., Lee, H.-J., Yang, J.-C., Hwang, J.-A., & Yoon, H.-K. (2009). A tryptophan hydroxylase 2 gene polymorphism is associated with panic disorder. *Behavior Genetics, 39,* 170–175. (12)

Kindt, M., Soeter, M., & Vervliet, B. (2009). Beyond extinction: Erasing human fear responses and preventing the return of fear. *Nature Neuroscience, 12,* 256–258. (12)

King, B. M. (2006). The rise, fall, and resurrection of the ventromedial hypothalamus in the regulation of feeding behavior and body weight. *Physiology & Behavior, 87,* 221–244. (10)

King, B. M., Smith, R. L., & Frohman, L. A. (1984). Hyperinsulinemia in rats with ventromedial hypothalamic lesions: Role of hyperphagia. *Behavioral Neuroscience, 98,* 152–155. (10)

King, V. R., Huang, W. L., Dyall, S. C., Curran, O. E., Priestley, J. V., & Michael-Titus, A. T. (2006). Omega-3 fatty acids improve recovery, whereas omega-6 fatty acids worsen outcome after spinal cord injury in the adult rat. *Journal of Neuroscience, 26,* 4672–4680. (15)

Kingstone, A., & Gazzaniga, M. S. (1995). Subcortical transfer of higher order information: More illusory than real? *Neuropsychology, 9,* 321–328. (14)

Kinnamon, J. C. (1987). Organization and innervation of taste buds. In T. E. Finger & W. L. Silver (Eds.), *Neurobiology of taste and smell* (pp. 277–297). New York: Wiley. (7)

Kinomura, S., Larsson, J., Gulyás, B., & Roland, P. E. (1996). Activation by attention of the human reticular formation and thalamic intralaminar nuclei. *Science, 271,* 512–515. (9)

Kinsbourne, M., & McMurray, J. (1975). The effect of cerebral dominance on time sharing between speaking and tapping by preschool children. *Child Development, 46*, 240–242. (14)

Kinsey, A. C., Pomeroy, W. B., & Martin, C. E. (1948). *Sexual behavior in the human male.* Philadelphia: Saunders. (11)

Kinsey, A. C., Pomeroy, W. B., Martin, C. E., & Gebhard, P. H. (1953). *Sexual behavior in the human female.* Philadelphia: Saunders. (11)

Kippenhan, J. S., Olsen, R. K., Mervis, C. B., Morris, C. A., Kohn, P., Meyer-Lindenberg, A., et al. (2005). Genetic contributions to human gyrification: Sulcal morphometry in Williams syndrome. *Journal of Neuroscience, 25*, 7840–7846. (14)

Kiriakakis, V., Bhatia, K. P., Quinn, N. P., & Marsden, C. D. (1998). The natural history of tardive dyskinesia: A long-term follow-up study of 107 cases. *Brain, 121*, 2053–2066. (15)

Kirkpatrick, P. J., Smielewski, P., Czosnyka, M., Menon, D. K., & Pickard, J. D. (1995). Near-infrared spectroscopy in patients with head injury. *Journal of Neurosurgery, 83*, 963–970. (5)

Kirsch, I. (2010). *The Emperor's New Drugs.* New York: Basic Books. (15)

Kirsch, I., Deacon, B. J., Huedo-Medina, T. B., Scoboria, A., Moore, T. J., & Johnson, B. T. (2008). Initial severity and antidepressant benefits: A meta-analysis of data submitted to the Food and Drug Administration. *PLoS Medicine, 5*, e45. (15)

Kleen, J. K., Sitomer, M. T., Killeen, P. R., & Conrad, C. D. (2006). Chronic stress impairs spatial memory and motivation for reward without disrupting motor ability and motivation to explore. *Behavioral Neuroscience, 120*, 842–851. (12)

Klein, D. F. (1993). False suffocation alarms, spontaneous panics, and related conditions. *Archives of General Psychiatry, 50*, 306–317. (11)

Klein, D. N. (2010). Chronic depression: Diagnosis and classification. *Current Directions in Psychological Science, 19*, 96–100. (15)

Kleitman, N. (1963). *Sleep and wakefulness* (Rev. ed.). Chicago: University of Chicago Press. (9)

Kluger, M. J. (1991). Fever: Role of pyrogens and cryogens. *Physiological Reviews, 71*, 93–127. (10)

Klüver, H., & Bucy, P. C. (1939). Preliminary analysis of functions of the temporal lobes in monkeys. *Archives of Neurology and Psychiatry, 42*, 979–1000. (4)

Knabl, J., Witschi, R., Hösl, K., Reinold, H., Zeilhofer, U. B., Ahmadi, S., et al. (2008). Reversal of pathological pain through specific spinal GABA_A receptor subtypes. *Nature, 451*, 330–334. (7)

Knoll, J. (1993). The pharmacological basis of the beneficial effects of (2) deprenyl (selegiline) in Parkinson's and Alzheimer's diseases. *Journal of Neural Transmission* (Suppl. 40), 69–91. (8)

Knyazev, G. G., Slobodskaya, H. R., & Wilson, G. D. (2002). Psychophysiological correlates of behavioural inhibition and activation. *Personality and Individual Differences, 33*, 647–660. (12)

Ko, C.-H., Liu, G.-C., Hsiao, S., Yen, J.-Y., Yang, M.-J., Lin, W.-C., et al. (2009). Brain activities associated with gaming urge of online gaming addiction. *Journal of Psychiatric Research, 43*, 739–747. (3)

Kobayakawa, K., Kobayakawa, R., Matsumoto, H., Oka, Y., Imai, T., Ikawa, M., et al. (2007). Innate versus learned odour processing in the mouse olfactory bulb. *Nature, 450*, 503–508. (7)

Kobett, P., Paulitsch, S., Goebel, M., Stengel, A., Schmidtmann, M., van der Voort, I. R., et al. (2006). Peripheral injection of CCK-8S induces Fos expression in the dorsomedial hypothalamic nucleus in rats. *Brain Research, 1117*, 109–117. (10)

Kodituwakku, P. W. (2007). Defining the behavioral phenotype in children with fetal alcohol spectrum disorders: A review. *Neuroscience & Biobehavioral Reviews, 31*, 192–201. (5)

Koenigs, M., Huey, E. D., Raymont, V., Cheon, B., Solomon, J., Wassermann, E. M., et al. (2008). Focal brain damage protects against post-traumatic stress disorder in combat veterans. *Nature Neuroscience, 11*, 232–237. (12)

Koenigs, M., Young, L., Adolphs, R., Tranel, D., Cushman, F., Hauser, M., et al. (2007). Damage to the prefrontal cortex increases utilitarian moral judgments. *Nature, 446*, 908–911. (12)

Koepp, M. J., Gunn, R. N., Lawrence, A. D., Cunningham, V. J., Dagher, A., Jones, T., et al. (1998). Evidence for striatal dopamine release during a video game. *Nature, 393*, 266–268. (3)

Kohler, E., Keysers, C., Umiltà, M. A., Fogassi, L., Gallese, V., & Rizzolatti, G. (2002). Hearing sounds, understanding actions: Action representation in mirror neurons. *Science, 297*, 846–848. (8)

Kohn, M. (2008). The needs of the many. *Nature, 456*, 296–299. (1)

Komisaruk, B. R., Adler, N. T., & Hutchison, J. (1972). Genital sensory field: Enlargement by estrogen treatment in female rats. *Science, 178*, 1295–1298. (11)

Komorowski, R. W., Manns, J. R., & Eichenbaum, H. (2009). Robust conjunctive item-lace coding by hippocampal neurons parallels learning what happens where. *Journal of Neuroscience, 29*, 9918–9929. (13)

Komura, Y., Tamura, R., Uwano, T., Nishijo, H., Kaga, K., & Ono, T. (2001). Retrospective and prospective coding for predicted reward in the sensory thalamus. *Nature, 412*, 546–549. (4)

Kondo, I., Marvizon, J. C. G., Song, B., Salgado, F., Codeluppi, S., Hua, X.-Y., et al. (2005). Inhibition by spinal m- and d-opioid agonists of afferent-evoked substance P release. *Journal of Neuroscience, 25*, 3651–3660. (7)

Kong, J., Shepel, P. N., Holden, C. P., Mackiewicz, M., Pack, A. I., & Geiger, J. D. (2002). Brain glycogen decreases with increased periods of wakefulness: Implications for homeostatic drive to sleep. *Journal of Neuroscience, 22*, 5581–5587. (9)

Konishi, S., Nakajima, K., Uchida, I., Kameyama, M., Nakahara, K., Sekihara, K., et al. (1998). Transient activation of inferior prefrontal cortex during cognitive set shifting. *Nature Neuroscience, 1*, 80–84. (15)

Konopka, G., Bomar, J. M., Winden, K., Coppola, G., Jonsson, Z. O., Gao, F., et al. (2009). Human specific transcriptional regulation of CNS development genes by *FOXP2. Nature, 462*, 213–217. (1, 14)

Korenberg, J. R., Chen, X.-N., Hirota, H., Lai, Z., Bellugi, U., Burian, D., et al. (2000). VI. Genome structure and cognitive map of Williams syndrome. *Journal of Cognitive Neuroscience, 12*(Suppl.), 89–107. (14)

Korman, M., Doyon, J., Doljansky, J., Carrier, J., Dagan, Y., & Karni, A. (2007). Daytime sleep condenses the time course of motor memory consolidation. *Nature Neuroscience, 10*, 1206–1213. (9)

Kornhuber, H. H. (1974). Cerebral cortex, cerebellum, and basal ganglia: An introduction to their motor functions. In F. O. Schmitt & F. G. Worden (Eds.), *The neurosciences: Third study program* (pp. 267–280). Cambridge, MA: MIT Press. (8)

Korpi, E. R., & Sinkkonen, S. T. (2006). GABAA receptor subtypes as targets for neuropsychiatric drug development. *Pharmacology & Therapeutics, 109*, 12–32. (12)

Kosfeld, M., Heinrichs, M., Zak, P. J., Fischbacher, U., & Fehr, E. (2005). Oxytocin increases trust in humans. *Nature, 435*, 673–676. (11)

Kosslyn, S. M., Ganis, G., & Thompson, W. L. (2001). Neural foundations of imagery. *Nature Reviews Neuroscience, 2*, 635–642. (6)

Kosslyn, S. M., & Thompson, W. L. (2003). When is early visual cortex activated during visual mental imagery? *Psychological Bulletin, 129*, 723–746. (6)

Kostrzewa, R. M., Kostrzewa, J. P., Brown, R. W., Nowak, P., & Brus, R. (2008). Dopamine receptor supersensitivity: Development, mechanisms, presentation, and clinical applicability. *Neurotoxicity Research, 14*, 121–128. (5)

Kotowicz, Z. (2007). The strange case of Phineas Gage. *History of the Human Sciences, 20*, 115–131. (12)

Kourtzi, Z., & Kanwisher, N. (2000). Activation in human MT/MST by static images with implied motion. *Journal of Cognitive Neuroscience, 12*, 48-55. (6)

Kraemer, D. J. M., Macrae, C. N., Green, A. E., & Kelley, W. M. (2005). Sound of silence activates auditory cortex. *Nature, 434*, 158. (7)

Krajbich, I., Adolphs, R., Tranel, D., Denburg, N. L., & Camerer, C. F. (2009). Economic games quantify diminished sense of guilt in patients with damage to the prefrontal cortex. *Journal of Neuroscience, 29*, 2188–2192. (12)

Krakauer, A. H. (2005). Kin selection and cooperative courtship in wild turkeys. *Nature, 434*, 69–72. (1)

Krause, E. G., & Sakal, R. R. (2007). Richter and sodium appetite: From adrenalectomy to molecular biology. *Appetite, 49*, 353–367. (10)

Kreek, M. J., Nielsen, D. A., Butelman, H. R., & LaForge, K. S. (2005). Genetic influences on impulsivity, risk taking, stress responsivity and vulnerability to drug abuse and addiction. *Nature Neuroscience, 8*, 1450–1457. (3)

Kreiman, G., Fried, I., & Koch, C. (2002). Single-neuron correlates of subjective vision in the human medial temporal lobe. *Proceedings of the National Academy of Sciences (U.S.A.), 99*, 8378–8383. (14)

Kreitzer, A. C., & Malenka, R. C. (2007). Endocannabinoid-mediated rescue of striatal LTD and motor deficits in Parkinson's disease models. *Nature, 445*, 643–647. (8)

Kreitzer, A. C., & Regehr, W. G. (2001). Retrograde inhibition of presynaptic calcium influx by endogenous cannabinoids at excitatory synapses onto Purkinje cells. *Neuron, 29,* 717–727. (3)

Kriegeskorte, N., Formisano, E., Sorger, B., & Goebel, R. (2007). Individual faces elicit distinct response patterns in human anterior temporal cortex. *Proceedings of the National Academy of Sciences (U.S.A.), 104,* 20600–20605. (6)

Kringelbach, M. L. (2005). The human orbitofrontal cortex: Linking reward to hedonic experience. *Nature Reviews Neuroscience, 6,* 691–702. (12)

Kripke, D. F. (1998). Light treatment for nonseasonal depression: Speed, efficacy, and combined treatment. *Journal of Affective Disorders, 49,* 109–117. (15)

Krishnan, V., Han, M.-H., Graham, D. L., Berton, O., Renthal, W., Russo, S. J., et al. (2007). Molecular adaptations underlying susceptibility and resistance to social defeat in brain reward regions. *Cell, 131,* 391–404. (12)

Krishnan-Sarin, S., Krystal, J. H., Shi, J., Pittman, B., & O'Malley, S. S. (2007). Family history of alcoholism influences naloxone-induced reduction in alcohol drinking. *Biological Psychiatry, 62,* 694–697. (3)

Krueger, J. M., Rector, D. M., Roy, S., Van Dongen, H. P. A., Belenky, G., & Panksepp, J. (2008). Sleep as a fundamental property of neuronal assemblies. *Nature Reviews Neuroscience, 9,* 910–919. (9)

Krugers, H. J., Hoogenraad, C. C., & Groc, L. (2010). Stress hormones and AMPA receptor trafficking in synaptic plasticity and memory. *Nature Reviews Neuroscience, 11,* 675–681. (12)

Krupa, D. J., Thompson, J. K., & Thompson, R. F. (1993). Localization of a memory trace in the mammalian brain. *Science, 260,* 989–991. (13)

Kuba, H., Ishii, T. M., & Ohmori, H. (2006). Axonal site of spike initiation enhances auditory coincidence detection. *Nature, 444,* 1069–1072. (2)

Kubista, H., & Boehm, S. (2006). Molecular mechanisms underlying the modulation of exocytotic noradrenaline release via presynaptic receptors. *Pharmacology & Therapeutics, 112,* 213–242. (3)

Kuczewski, N., Porcer, C., Ferrand, N., Fiorentino, H., Pellegrino, C., Kolarow, R., et al. (2008). Backpropagating action potentials trigger dendritic release of BDNF during spontaneous network activity. *Journal of Neuroscience, 28,* 7013–7023. (13)

Kujala, T., Myllyviita, K., Tervaniemi, M., Alho, K., Kallio, J., & Näätänen, R. (2000). Basic auditory dysfunction in dyslexia as demonstrated by brain activity measurements. *Psychophysiology, 37,* 262–266. (14)

Kujawa, S. G., & Liberman, M. C. (2009). Adding insult to injury: Cochlear nerve degeneration after "temporary" noise-induced hearing loss. *Journal of Neuroscience, 29,* 14077–14085. (7)

Kullmann, D. M., & Lamsa, K. P. (2007). Long-term synaptic plasticity in hippocampal interneurons. *Nature Reviews Neuroscience, 8,* 687–699. (3)

Kumakura, Y., Cumming, P., Vernaleken, I., Buchholz, H.-G., Siessmeier, T., Heinz, A., et al. (2007). Elevated [18F]fluorodopamine turnover in brains of patients with schizophrenia. *Journal of Neuroscience, 27,* 8080–8087. (15)

Kumaran, D., & Maguire, E. A. (2005). The human hippocampus: Cognitive maps or relational memory? *Journal of Neuroscience, 25,* 7254–7259. (13)

Kumpik, D. P., Kacelnik, O., & King, A. J. (2010). Adaptive reweighting of auditory localization cues in response to chronic unilateral earplugging in humans. *Journal of Neuroscience, 30,* 4883–4894. (7)

Kundermann, B., Hemmeter-Spernal, J., Huber, M. T., Krieg, J.-C., & Lautenbacher, S. (2008). Effects of total sleep deprivation in major depression: Overnight improvement of mood is accompanied by increased pain sensitivity and augmented pain complaints. *Psychosomatic Medicine, 70,* 92–101. (15)

Kupfermann, I., Castellucci, V., Pinsker, H., & Kandel, E. (1970). Neuronal correlates of habituation and dishabituation of the gill withdrawal reflex in *Aplysia. Science, 167,* 1743–1745. (13)

Kusunoki, M., Moutoussis, K., & Zeki, S. (2006). Effect of background colors on the tuning of color-selective cells in monkey area V4. *Journal of Neurophysiology, 95,* 3047–3059. (6)

Kuypers, H. G. J. M. (1989). Motor system organization. In G. Adelman (Ed.), *Neuroscience year* (pp. 107–110). Boston: Birkhäuser. (8)

Kwon, J. S., McCarley, R. W., Hirayasu, Y., Anderson, J. E., Fischer, I. A., Kikinis, R., et al. (1999). Left planum temporale volume reduction in schizophrenia. *Archives of General Psychiatry, 56,* 142–148. (15)

Kwon, J.-T., & Choi, J. S. (2009). Cornering the fear engram: Long-term synaptic changes in the lateral nucleus of the amygdala after fear conditioning. *Journal of Neuroscience, 29,* 9700–9703. (12)

Laburn, H. P. (1996). How does the fetus cope with thermal challenges? *News in Physiological Sciences, 11,* 96–100. (5, 15)

Lacroix, L., Spinelli, S., Heidbreder, C. A., & Feldon, J. (2000). Differential role of the medial and lateral prefrontal cortices in fear and anxiety. *Behavioral Neuroscience, 114,* 1119–1130. (12)

Laeng, B., & Caviness, V. S. (2001). Prosopagnosia as a deficit in encoding curved surfaces. *Journal of Cognitive Neuroscience, 13,* 556–576. (6)

Laeng, B., Svartdal, F., & Oelmann, H. (2004). Does color synesthesia pose a paradox for early-selection theories of attention? *Psychological Science, 15,* 277–281. (7)

LaFerla, F. M., Green, K. N., & Oddo, S. (2007). Intracellular amyloid-b in Alzheimer's disease. *Nature Reviews Neuroscience, 8,* 499–509. (13)

Lahti, T. A., Leppämäki, S., Ojanen, S.-M., Haukka, J., Tuulio-Henriksson, A., Lönnqvist, J., et al. (2006). Transition into daylight saving time influences the fragmentation of the rest–activity cycle. *Journal of Circadian Rhythms, 4,* 1. (9)

Lai, C. S. L., Fisher, S. E., Hurst, J. A., Vargha-Khadem, F., & Monaco, A. P. (2001). A forkhead-domain gene is mutated in a severe speech and language disorder. *Nature, 413,* 519–523. (14)

Lake, R. I. E., Eaves, L. J., Maes, H. H. M., Heath, A. C., & Martin, N. G. (2000). Further evidence against the environmental transmission of individual differences in neuroticism from a collabora-

tive study of 45,850 twins and relatives on two continents. *Behavior Genetics, 30,* 223–233. (1)

Lalancette-Hébert, M., Gowing, G., Simard, A., Weng, Y. C., & Kriz, J. (2007). Selective ablation of proliferating microglial cells exacerbates ischemic injury in the brain. *Journal of Neuroscience, 30,* 2596–2605. (5)

Lambie, J. A., & Marcel, A. J. (2002). Consciousness and the varieties of emotion experience: A theoretical framework. *Psychological Review, 109,* 219–259. (14)

Land, E. H., Hubel, D. H., Livingstone, M. S., Perry, S. H., & Burns, M. M. (1983). Colour-generating interactions across the corpus callosum. *Nature, 303,* 616–618. (6)

Landis, D. M. D. (1987). Initial junctions between developing parallel fibers and Purkinje cells are different from mature synaptic junctions. *Journal of Comparative Neurology, 260,* 513–525. (3)

Långström, N., Rahman, Q., Carlström, E., & Lichtenstein, P. (2010). Genetic and environmental effects on same-sex sexual behavior: A population study of twins in Sweden. *Archives of Sexual Behavior, 39,* 75–80. (11)

Lara, A. H., Kennerley, S. W., & Wallis, J. D. (2009). Encoding of gustatory working memory by orbitofrontal neurons. *Journal of Neuroscience, 29,* 765–774. (7)

Larsen, R. J., Kasimatis, M., & Frey, K. (1992). Facilitating the furrowed brow—An unobtrusive test of the facial feedback hypothesis applied to unpleasant affect. *Cognition & Emotion, 6,* 321–338. (12)

Lashley, K. S. (1929). *Brain mechanisms and intelligence.* Chicago: University of Chicago Press. (13)

Lashley, K. S. (1930). Basic neural mechanisms in behavior. *Psychological Review, 37,* 1–24. (13)

Lashley, K. S. (1950). In search of the engram. *Symposia of the Society for Experimental Biology, 4,* 454–482. (13)

Lassonde, M., Bryden, M. P., & Demers, P. (1990). The corpus callosum and cerebral speech lateralization. *Brain and Language, 38,* 195–206. (14)

Lau, H. C., Rogers, R. D., Haggard, P., & Passingham, R. E. (2004). Attention to intention. *Science, 303,* 1208–1210. (8)

Laurent, J.-P., Cespuglio, R., & Jouvet, M. (1974). Dèlimitation des voies ascendantes de l'activité ponto-géniculo-occipitale chez le chat [Demarcation of the ascending paths of ponto-geniculo-occipital activity in the cat]. *Brain Research, 65,* 29–52. (9)

Lavidor, M., & Walsh, V. (2004). The nature of foveal representation. *Nature Reviews Neuroscience, 5,* 729–735. (14)

Lazarus, M., Yoshida, K., Coppair, R., Bass, C. E., Mochizuki, T., Lowell, B. B., et al. (2007). EP3 prostaglandin receptors in the median preoptic nucleus are critical for fever responses. *Nature Neuroscience, 10,* 1131–1133. (10)

Lè, A. D., Li, Z., Funk, D., Shram, M., Li, T. K., & Shaham, Y. (2006). Increased vulnerability to nicotine self-administration and relapse in alcohol-naïve offspring of rats selectively bred for high alcohol intake. *Journal of Neuroscience, 26,* 1872–1879. (3)

Le Grand, R., Mondloch, C. J., Maurer, D., & Brent, H. P. (2001). Early visual experience and face processing. *Nature, 410,* 809. (6)

Leber, A. B. (2010). Neural predictors of within-subject fluctuations in attentional control. *Journal of Neuroscience, 30,* 11458–11465. (14)

LeDoux, J. (1996). *The emotional brain.* New York: Simon & Schuster. (12)

LeDoux, J. E., Iwata, J., Cicchetti, P., & Reis, D. J. (1988). Different projections of the central amygdaloid nucleus mediate autonomic and behavioral correlates of conditioned fear. *Journal of Neuroscience, 8,* 2517–2529. (12)

Lee, K. M., Skoe, E., Kraus, N., & Ashley, R. (2009). Selective subcortical enhancement of musical intervals in musicians. *Journal of Neuroscience, 29,* 5832–5840. (5)

Lee, M. G., Hassani, O. K., & Jones, B. E. (2005). Discharge of identified orexin/hypocretin neurons across the sleep-waking cycle. *Journal of Neuroscience, 25,* 6716–6720. (9)

Lee, S.-H., Blake, R., & Heeger, D. J. (2005). Traveling waves of activity in primary visual cortex during binocular rivalry. *Nature Neuroscience, 8,* 22–23. (14)

Legrand, L. N., Iacono, W. G., & McGue, M. (2005, March/April). Predicting addiction. *American Scientist, 93,* 140–147. (3)

Lehky, S. R. (2000). Deficits in visual feature binding under isoluminant conditions. *Journal of Cognitive Neuroscience, 12,* 383–392. (4)

Lehrman, D. S. (1964). The reproductive behavior of ring doves. *Scientific American, 211*(5), 48–54. (11)

Lehrer, J. (2009). Small, furry... and smart. *Nature, 461,* 862–864. (13)

Leibniz, G. (1714). *The Principles of Nature and Grace, Based on Reason.* (1)

Leibowitz, S. F., & Alexander, J. T. (1991). Analysis of neuropeptide Y-induced feeding: Dissociation of Y$_1$ and Y$_2$ receptor effects on natural meal patterns. *Peptides, 12,* 1251–1260. (10)

Leibowitz, S. F., Hammer, N. J., & Chang, K. (1981). Hypothalamic paraventricular nucleus lesions produce overeating and obesity in the rat. *Physiology & Behavior, 27,* 1031–1040. (10)

Leibowitz, S. F., & Hoebel, B. G. (1998). Behavioral neuroscience of obesity. In G. A. Bray, C. Bouchard, & P. T. James (Eds.), *Handbook of obesity* (pp. 313–358). New York: Dekker. (10)

Lein, E. S., & Shatz, C. J. (2001). Neurotrophins and refinement of visual circuitry. In W. M. Cowan, T. C. Südhof, & C. F. Stevens (Eds.), *Synapses* (pp. 613–649). Baltimore: Johns Hopkins University Press. (6)

Leinders-Zufall, T., Lane, A. P., Puche, A. C., Ma, W., Novotny, M. V., Shipley, M. T., et al. (2000). Ultrasensitive pheromone detection by mammalian vomeronasal neurons. *Nature, 405,* 792–796. (7)

Lemos, B., Araripe, L. O., & Hartl, D. L. (2008). Polymorphic Y chromosomes harbor cryptic variation with manifold functional consequences. *Science, 319,* 91–93. (11)

Lenggenhager, B., Tadi, T., Metzinger, T., & Blanke, O. (2007). Video ergo sum: Manipulating bodily self-consciousness. *Science, 317,* 1096–1099. (4)

Lenhart, R. E., & Katkin, E. S. (1986). Psychophysiological evidence for cerebral laterality effects in a high-risk sample of students with subsyndromal bipolar depressive disorder. *American Journal of Psychiatry, 143,* 602–607. (15)

Lenz, F. A., & Byl, N. N. (1999). Reorganization in the cutaneous core of the human thalamic principal somatic sensory nucleus (ventral caudal) in patients with dystonia. *Journal of Neurophysiology, 82,* 3204–3212. (5)

Leon, L. R. (2002). Invited review: Cytokine regulation of fever: Studies using gene knockout mice. *Journal of Applied Physiology, 92,* 2648–2655. (10)

Leopold, D. A., Bondar, I. V., & Giese, M. A. (2006). Norm-based face encoding by single neurons in the monkey inferotemporal cortex. *Nature, 442,* 572–575. (6)

Leppämäki, S., Partonen, T., & Lönnqvist, J. (2002). Bright-light exposure combined with physical exercise elevates mood. *Journal of Affective Disorders, 72,* 572–575. (15)

Leriche, L., Björklund, T., Breysse, N., Besret, L., Grégoire, M.-C., Carlsson, T., et al. (2009). Positron emission tomography imaging demonstrates correlation between behavioral recovery and correction of dopamine neurotransmission after gene therapy. *Journal of Neuroscience, 29,* 1544–1553. (8)

LeVay, S. (1991). A difference in hypothalamic structure between heterosexual and homosexual men. *Science, 253,* pp. 1034–1037. (11)

LeVay, S. (1993). *The sexual brain.* Cambridge, MA: MIT Press. (11)

Levenson, R. W., Oyama, O. N., & Meek, P. S. (1987). Greater reinforcement from alcohol for those at risk: Parental risk, personality risk, and sex. *Journal of Abnormal Psychology, 96,* 242–253. (3)

LeVere, T. E. (1975). Neural stability, sparing and behavioral recovery following brain damage. *Psychological Review, 82,* 344–358. (5)

LeVere, T. E., & Morlock, G. W. (1973). Nature of visual recovery following posterior neodecortication in the hooded rat. *Journal of Comparative and Physiological Psychology, 83,* 62–67. (5)

Levi-Montalcini, R. (1987). The nerve growth factor 35 years later. *Science, 237,* 1154–1162. (5)

Levi-Montalcini, R. (1988). *In praise of imperfection.* New York: Basic Books. (5)

Levin, E. D., & Rose, J. E. (1995). Acute and chronic nicotine interactions with dopamine systems and working memory performance. *Annals of the New York Academy of Sciences, 757,* 245–252. (3)

Levine, J. A., Lannngham-Foster, L. M., McCrady, S. K., Krizan, A. C., Olson, L. R., Kane, P. H., et al. (2005). Interindividual variation in posture allocation: Possible role in human obesity. *Science, 307,* 584–586. (10)

Levine, J. D., Fields, H. L., & Basbaum, A. I. (1993). Peptides and the primary afferent nociceptor. *Journal of Neuroscience, 13,* 2273–2286. (3)

Levitin, D. J., & Bellugi, U. (1998). Musical abilities in individuals with Williams syndrome. *Music Perception, 15,* 357–389. (14)

Levitt, R. A. (1975). *Psychopharmacology.* Washington, DC: Hemisphere. (15)

Levitzki, A. (1988). From epinephrine to cyclic AMP. *Science, 241,* 800–806. (3)

Levy, J., Heller, W., Banich, M. T., & Burton, L. A. (1983). Asymmetry of perception in free viewing of chimeric faces. *Brain and Cognition, 2,* 404–419. (14)

Leweke, F. M., Gerth, C. W., Koethe, D., Klosterkötter, J., Ruslanova, I., Krivogorsky, B., et al. (2004). Antibodies to infectious agents in individuals with recent onset schizophrenia. *European Archives of Psychiatry and Clinical Neuroscience, 254,* 4–8. (15)

Lewis, D. A. (1997). Development of the prefrontal cortex during adolescence: Insights into vulnerable neural circuits in schizophrenia. *Neuropsychopharmacology, 16,* 385–398. (5, 15)

Lewis, E. R., Everhart, T. E., & Zeevi, Y. Y. (1969). Studying neural organization in *Aplysia* with the scanning electron microscope. *Science, 165,* 1140–1143. (3)

Lewis, T. L., & Maurer, D. (2005). Multiple sensitive periods in human visual development: Evidence from visually deprived children. *Developmental Psychobiology, 46,* 163–183. (6)

Lewis, V. G., Money, J., & Epstein, R. (1968). Concordance of verbal and nonverbal ability in the adrenogenital syndrome. *Johns Hopkins Medical Journal, 122,* 192–195. (11)

Lewy, A. J., Bauer, V. K., Cutler, N. L., Sack, R. L., Ahmed, S., Thomas, K. H., et al. (1998). Morning vs. evening light treatment of patients with winter depression. *Archives of General Psychiatry, 55,* 890–896. (15)

Li, N., & DiCarlo, J. J. (2008). Unsupervised natural experience rapidly alters invariant object representation in visual cortex. *Science, 321,* 1502–1507. (6)

Li, R., Polat, U., Makous, W., & Bavelier, D. (2009). Enhancing the contrast sensitivity function through action video game training. *Nature Neuroscience, 12,* 549–551. (6)

Liberles, S. D., & Buck, L. B. (2006). A second class of chemosensory receptors in the olfactory epithelium. *Nature, 442,* 645–650. (7)

Libet, B., Gleason, C. A., Wright, E. W., & Pearl, D. K. (1983). Time of conscious intention to act in relation to onset of cerebral activities (readiness potential): The unconscious initiation of a freely voluntary act. *Brain, 106,* 623–642. (8)

Lieberman, J., Chakos, M., Wu, H., Alvir, J., Hoffman, E., Robinson, D., et al. (2001). Longitudinal study of brain morphology in first episode schizophrenia. *Biological Psychiatry, 49,* 487–499. (15)

Liebman, M., Pelican, S., Moore, S. A., Holmes, B., Wardlaw, M. K., Melcher, L. M., et al. (2006). Dietary intake-, eating behavior-, and physical activity-related determinants of high body mass index in the 2003 Wellness IN the Rockies cross-sectional study. *Nutrition Research, 26,* 111–117. (10)

Lim, K. O., Adalsteinsson, E., Spielman, D., Sullivan, E. V., Rosenbloom, M. J., & Pfefferbaum, A. (1998). Proton magnetic resonance spectroscopic imaging of cortical gray and white matter in schizophrenia. *Archives of General Psychiatry, 55,* 346–352. (15)

Lim, M. M., Wang, Z., Olazábal, D. E., Ren, X., Terwilliger, E. F., & Young, L. J. (2004). Enhanced partner preference in a promiscuous species by manipulating the expression of a single gene. *Nature, 429,* 754–757. (11)

Lin, D. Y., Shea, S. D., & Katz, L. C. (2006). Representation of natural stimuli in the rodent main olfactory bulb. *Neuron, 50*, 937–949. (7)

Lin, J.-S., Hou, Y., Sakai, K., & Jouvet, M. (1996). Histaminergic descending inputs to the mesopontine tegmentum and their role in the control of cortical activation and wakefulness in the cat. *Journal of Neuroscience, 16*, 1523–1537. (9)

Lin, L., Faraco, J., Li, R., Kadotani, H., Rogers, W., Lin, X., et al. (1999). The sleep disorder canine narcolepsy is caused by a mutation in the hypocretin (orexin) receptor 2 gene. *Cell, 98*, 365–376. (9)

Lindberg, N. O., Coburn, C., & Stricker, E. M. (1984). Increased feeding by rats after subdiabetogenic streptozotocin treatment: A role for insulin in satiety. *Behavioral Neuroscience, 98*, 138–145. (10)

Lindemann, B. (1996). Taste reception. *Physiological Reviews, 76*, 719–766. (7)

Lindholm, P., Voutilainen, M. H., Laurén, J., Peränen, V.-M., Leppänen, V.-M., Andressoo, J.-O., et al. (2007). Novel neurotrophic factor CDNF protects and rescues midbrain dopamine neurons *in vivo*. *Nature, 448*, 73–77. (8)

Lindner, A., Iyer, A., Kagan, I., & Andersen, R. A. (2010). Human posterior parietal cortex plans where to reach and what to avoid. *Journal of Neuroscience, 30*, 11715–11725. (8)

Lindsay, P. H., & Norman, D. A. (1972). *Human information processing*. New York: Academic Press. (7)

Liou, Y.-C., Tocilj, A., Davies, P. L., & Jia, Z. (2000). Mimicry of ice structure by surface hydroxyls and water of a b-helix antifreeze protein. *Nature, 406*, 322–324. (10)

Lippa, R. A. (2006). Is high sex drive associated with increased sexual attraction to both sexes? *Psychological Science, 17*, 46–52. (11)

Lisman, J., Schulman, H., & Cline, H. (2002). The molecular basis of CaMKII function in synaptic and behavioural memory. *Nature Reviews Neuroscience, 3*, 175–190. (13)

Lisman, J. E., Raghavachari, S., & Tsien, R. W. (2007). The sequence of events that underlie quantal transmission at central glutamatergic synapses. *Nature Reviews Neuroscience, 8*, 597–609. (3)

Litt, A., Khan, U., & Shiv, B. (2010). Lusting while loathing: Parallel counterdriving of wanting and liking. *Psychological Science, 21*, 118–125. (3)

Liu, F., Wollstein, A., Hysi, P. G., Ankra-Badu, G. A., Spector, T. D., Park, D., et al. (2010). Digital quantification of human eye color highlights genetic association of three new loci. *PLoS Genetics, 6*, e1000934. (1)

Liu, G., & Tsien, R. W. (1995). Properties of synaptic transmission at single hippocampal synaptic boutons. *Nature, 375*, 404–408. (3)

Liu, K., Lu, Y., Lee, J. K., Samara, R., Willenberg, R., Sears-Kraxberger, I., et al. (2010). PTEN deletion enhances the regenerative ability of adult corticospinal neurons. *Nature Neuroscience, 13*, 1075–1081. (5)

Liu, L. Y., Coe, C. L., Swenson, C. A., Kelly, E. A., Kita, H., & Busse, W. W. (2002). School examinations enhance airway inflammation to antigen challenge. *American Journal of Respiratory and Critical Care Medicine, 165*, 1062–1067. (12)

Liu, P., & Bilkey, D. K. (2001). The effect of excitotoxic lesions centered on the hippocampus or perirhinal cortex in object recognition and spatial memory tasks. *Behavioral Neuroscience, 115*, 94–111. (13)

Liu, X., Zwiebel, L. J., Hinton, D., Benzer, S., Hall, J. C., & Rosbash, M. (1992). The period gene encodes a predominantly nuclear protein in adult Drosophila. *Journal of Neuroscience, 12*, 2735–2744. (9)

Liu, Y., Blackwood, D. H., Caesar, S., de Geus, E. J. C., Farmer, A., Ferreira, M. A. R., et al. (2011). Meta-analysis of genome-wide association data of bipolar disorder and major depressive disorder. *Molecular Psychiatry, 16*, 2–4. (15)

Liu, Z.-W., Faraguna, U., Cirelli, C., Tononi, G., & Gao, X.-B. (2010). Direct evidence for wake-related increases and sleep-related decreases in synaptic strength in rodent cortex. *Journal of Neuroscience, 30*, 8671–8675. (9)

Livingstone, M. S. (1988, January). Art, illusion and the visual system. *Scientific American, 258*(1), 78–85. (6)

Livingstone, M. S., & Hubel, D. (1988). Segregation of form, color, movement, and depth: Anatomy, physiology, and perception. *Science, 240*, 740–749. (6)

Ljungberg, M. C., Stern, G., & Wilkin, G. P. (1999). Survival of genetically engineered, adult-derived rat astrocytes grafted into the 6-hydroxydopamine lesioned adult rat striatum. *Brain Research, 816*, 29–37. (8)

Lockwood, A. H., Salvi, R. J., Coad, M. L., Towsley, M. L., Wack, D. S., & Murphy, B. W. (1998). The functional neuroanatomy of tinnitus: Evidence for limbic system links and neural plasticity. *Neurology, 50*, 114–120. (7)

Loe, I. M., Feldman, H. M., Yasui, E., & Luna, B. (2009). Oculomotor performance identifies underlying cognitive deficits in attention-deficit/hyperactivity disorder. *Journal of the American Academy of Child and Adolescent Psychiatry, 48*, 431–440. (5)

Loewenstein, W. R. (1960, August). Biological transducers. *Scientific American, 203*(2), 98–108. (7)

Loewi, O. (1960). An autobiographic sketch. *Perspectives in Biology, 4*, 3–25. (3)

Logan, C. G., & Grafton, S. T. (1995). Functional anatomy of human eyeblink conditioning determined with regional cerebral glucose metabolism and positron-emission tomography. *Proceedings of the National Academy of Sciences, USA, 92*, 7500–7504. (13)

Löken, L. S., Wessberg, J., Morrison, I., McGlone, F., & Olausson, H. (2009). Coding of pleasant touch by unmyelinated afferents in humans. *Nature Neuroscience, 12*, 547–548. (7)

Lomber, S. G., & Malhotra, S. (2008). Double dissociation of "what" and "where" processing in auditory cortex. *Nature Neuroscience, 11*, 609–617. (7)

Long, M. A., Jutras, M. J., Connors, B. W., & Burwell, R. D. (2005). Electrical synapses coordinate activity in the suprachiasmatic nucleus. *Nature Neuroscience, 8*, 61–66. (9)

Lonsdorf, T. B., Weike, A. I., Golkar, A., Schalling, M., Hamm, A. O., & Öhman, A. (2010). Amygdala-dependent fear conditioning in humans is modulated by the *BDNF* val66met polymorphism. *Behavioral Neuroscience, 124*, 9–15. (12)

Lord, G. M., Matarese, G., Howard, J. K., Baker, R. J., Bloom, S. R., & Lechler, R. I. (1998). Leptin modulates the T-cell immune response and reverses starvation-induced immunosuppression. *Nature, 394*, 897–901. (10)

Lorincz, A., & Nusser, Z. (2010). Molecular identity of dendritic voltage-gated sodium channels. *Science, 328*, 906–909. (2)

Lorrain, D. S., Riolo, J. V., Matuszewich, L., & Hull, E. M. (1999). Lateral hypothalamic serotonin inhibits nucleus accumbens dopamine: Implications for sexual refractoriness. *Journal of Neuroscience, 19*, 7648–7652. (3)

Lorusso, M. L., Facoetti, A., Pesenti, S., Cattaneo, C., Molteni, M., & Geiger, G. (2004). Wider recognition in peripheral vision common to different subtypes of dyslexia. *Vision Research, 44*, 2413–2424. (14)

Lott, I. T. (1982). Down's syndrome, aging, and Alzheimer's disease: A clinical review. *Annals of the New York Academy of Sciences, 396*, 15–27. (13)

Lotto, R. B., & Purves, D. (2002). The empirical basis of color perception. *Consciousness and Cognition, 11*, 609–629. (6)

Lotze, M., Grodd, W., Birbaumer, N., Erb, M., Huse, E., & Flor, H. (1999). Does use of a myoelectric prosthesis prevent cortical reorganization and phantom limb pain? *Nature Neuroscience, 2*, 501–502. (5)

Loui, P., Alsop, D., & Schlaug, G. (2009). Tone deafness: A new disconnection syndrome? *Journal of Neuroscience, 29*, 10215–10220. (7)

Lucas, B. K., Ormandy, C. J., Binart, N., Bridges, R. S. & Kelly, P. A. (1998). Null mutation of the prolactin receptor gene produces a defect in maternal behavior. *Endocrinology, 139*, 4102–4107. (11)

Lucas, R. J., Douglas, R. H., & Foster, R. G. (2001). Characterization of an ocular photopigment capable of driving pupillary constriction in mice. *Nature Neuroscience, 4*, 621–626. (9)

Lucas, R. J., Freedman, M. S., Muñoz, M., Garcia-Fernández, J.-M., & Foster, R. G. (1999). Regulation of the mammalian pineal by non-rod, non-cone ocular photoreceptors. *Science, 284*, 505–507. (9)

Luczak, S. E., Glatt, S. J., & Wall, T. L. (2006). Meta-analysis of *ALDHx* and *ADHIB* with alcohol dependence in Asians. *Psychological Bulletin, 132*, 607–621. (3)

Luders, E., Gaser, C., Narr, K. L., & Toga, A. W. (2009). Why sex matters: Brain size independent differences in gray matter distributions between men and women. *Journal of Neuroscience, 29*, 14265–14270. (11)

Luders, E., Narr, K. L., Thompson, P. M., Rex, D. E., Jancke, L., Steinmetz, H., et al. (2004). Gender differences in cortical complexity. *Nature Neuroscience, 7*, 799–800. (4)

Luders, E., Thompson, P. M., & Toga, A. W. (2010). The development of the corpus callosum in the healthy human brain. *Journal of Neuroscience, 30*, 10985–10990. (14)

Ludwig, M., & Leng, G. (2006). Dendritic peptides release and peptide-dependent behaviours. *Nature Reviews Neuroscience, 7,* 126–136. (3)

Luna, B., Padmanabhan, A., & O'Hearn, K. (2010). What has fMRI told us about the development of cognitive control through adolescence? *Brain and Cognition, 72,* 101–113. (5)

Lund, R. D., Lund, J. S., & Wise, R. P. (1974). The organization of the retinal projection to the dorsal lateral geniculate nucleus in pigmented and albino rats. *Journal of Comparative Neurology, 158,* 383–404. (6)

Lutz, A., Slagter, H. A., Rawlings, N. B., Francis, A. D., Greischar, L. L., & Davidson, R. J. (2009). Mental training enhances attentional stability: Neural and behavioral evidence. *Journal of Neuroscience, 29,* 13418–13427. (14)

Lyman, C. P., O'Brien, R. C., Greene, G. C., & Papafrangos, E. D. (1981). Hibernation and longevity in the Turkish hamster *Mesocricetus brandti. Science, 212,* 668–670. (9)

Lynall, M.-E., Bassett, D. S., Kerwin, R., McKenna, P. J., Kitzbichler, M., Muller, U., et al. (2010). Functional connectivity and brain networks in schizophrenia. *Journal of Neuroscience, 30,* 9477–9487. (15)

Lyons, M. J., Eisen, S. A., Goldberg, J., True, W., Lin, N., Meyer, J. M., et al. (1998). A registry-based twin study of depression in men. *Archives of General Psychiatry, 55,* 468–472. (15)

Lytle, L. D., Messing, R. B., Fisher, L., & Phebus, L. (1975). Effects of long-term corn consumption on brain serotonin and the response to electric shock. *Science, 190,* 692–694. (12)

Macdonald, R. L., Weddle, M. G., & Gross, R. A. (1986). Benzodiazepine, ß-carboline, and barbiturate actions on GABA responses. *Advances in Biochemical Psychopharmacology, 41,* 67–78. (12)

Macey, P. M., Henderson, L. A., Macey, K. E., Alger, J. R., Frysinger, R. C., Woo, M. A., et al. (2002). Brain morphology associated with obstructive sleep apnea. *American Journal of Respiratory & Critical Care Medicine, 166,* 1382–1387. (9)

MacFarlane, J. G., Cleghorn, J. M., & Brown, G. M. (1985a, September). *Circadian rhythms in chronic insomnia.* Paper presented at the World Congress of Biological Psychiatry, Philadelphia. (9)

MacFarlane, J. G., Cleghorn, J. M., & Brown, G. M. (1985b). Melatonin and core temperature rhythms in chronic insomnia. In G. M. Brown & S. D. Wainwright (Eds.), *The pineal gland: Endocrine aspects* (pp. 301–306). New York: Pergamon Press. (9)

MacFarquhar, L. (2009, July 27). The kindest cut. *The New Yorker, 85*(22), 38–51. (1)

Machado, C. J., Emery, N. J., Capitanio, J. P., Mason, W. A., Mendoza, S. P., & Amaral, D. G. (2008). Bilateral neurotoxic amygdala lesions in rhesus monkeys (*Macaca mulatta*): Consistent pattern of behavior across different social contexts. *Behavioral Neuroscience, 122,* 251–266. (12)

MacLean, P. D. (1949). Psychosomatic disease and the "visceral brain": Recent developments bearing on the Papez theory of emotion. *Psychosomatic Medicine, 11,* 338–353. (12)

MacLusky, N. J., & Naftolin, F. (1981). Sexual differentiation of the central nervous system. *Science, 211,* 1294–1303. (11)

Macphail, E. M. (1985). Vertebrate intelligence: The null hypothesis. *Philosophical Transactions of the Royal Society of London, B, 308,* 37–51. (4)

Macrae, C. N., Alnwick, K. A., Milne, A. B., & Schloerscheidt, A. M. (2002). Person perception across the menstrual cycle. *Psychological Science, 13,* 532–536. (11)

Maffei, A., Nataraj, K., Nelson, S. B., & Turrigiano, G. G. (2006). Potentiation of cortical inhibition by visual deprivation. *Nature, 443,* 81–84. (6)

Maguire, E. A., Gadian, D. G., Johnsrude, I. S., Good, C. D., Ashburner, J., Frackowiak, R. S. J., et al. (2000). Navigation-related structural change in the hippocampi of taxi drivers. *Proceedings of the National Academy of Sciences, USA, 97,* 4398–4403. (13)

Maier, S. F., & Watkins, L. R. (1998). Cytokines for psychologists: Implications of bidirectional immune-to-brain communication for understanding behavior, mood, and cognition. *Psychological Review, 105,* 83–107. (12)

Malaspina, D., Corcoran, C., Fahim, C., Berman, A., Harkavy-Friedman, J., Yale, S., et al. (2002). Paternal age and sporadic schizophrenia: Evidence for de novo mutations. *American Journal of Medical Genetics, 114,* 299–303. (15)

Malhotra, P., Jäger, H. R., Parton, A., Greenwood, R., Playford, E. D., Brown, M. M., et al. (2005). Spatial working memory capacity in unilateral neglect. *Brain, 128,* 424–435. (14)

Mallis, M. M., & DeRoshia, C. W. (2005). Circadian rhythms, sleep, and performance in space. *Aviation, Space, and Environmental Medicine, 76*(Suppl. 6), B94–B107. (9)

Malmberg, A. B., Chen, C., Tonegawa, S., & Basbaum, A. I. (1997). Preserved acute pain and reduced neuropathic pain in mice lacking PKCγ. *Science, 278,* 279–283. (7)

Mameli, M., Halbout, B., Creton, C., Engblom, D., Parkitna, J. R., Spanagel, R., et al. (2009). Cocaine-evoked synaptic plasticity: Persistence in the VTA triggers adaptations in the NAc. *Nature Neuroscience, 12,* 1036–1041. (3)

Mancuso, K., Hauswirth, W. W., Li, Q., Connor, T. B., Kuchenbecker, J. A., Mauck, M. C., et al. (2009). Gene therapy for red-green colour blindness. *Nature, 461,* 784–787. (6)

Manfredi, M., Stocchi, F., & Vacca, L. (1995). Differential diagnosis of Parkinsonism. *Journal of Neural Transmission* (Suppl. 45), 1–9. (8)

Mangan, M. A. (2004). A phenomenology of problematic sexual behavior. *Archives of Sexual Behavior, 33,* 287–293. (9)

Mangiapane, M. L., & Simpson, J. B. (1980). Subfornical organ: Forebrain site of pressor and dipsogenic action of angiotensin II. *American Journal of Physiology, 239,* R382–R389. (10)

Mann, J. J., Arango, V., & Underwood, M. D. (1990). Serotonin and suicidal behavior. *Annals of the New York Academy of Sciences, 600,* 476–485. (12)

Mann, T., Tomiyama, A. J., Westling, E., Lew, A.-M., Samuels, B., & Chatman, J. (2007). Medicare's search for effective obesity treatments. *American Psychologist, 62,* 220–233. (10)

Maquet, P., Laureys, S., Peigneux, P., Fuchs, S., Petiau, C., Phillips, C., et al. (2000). Experience-dependent changes in cerebral activation during human REM sleep. *Nature Neuroscience, 3,* 831–836. (9)

Maquet, P., Peters, J.-M., Aerts, J., Delfiore, G., Degueldre, C., Luxen, A., et al. (1996). Functional neuroanatomy of human rapid-eye-movement sleep and dreaming. *Nature, 383,* 163–166. (8, 9)

Maraganore, D. M., deAndrade, M., Lesnick, T. G., Strain, K. J., Farrer, M. J., Rocca, W. A., et al. (2005). High-resolution whole-genome association study of Parkinson disease. *American Journal of Human Genetics, 77,* 685–693. (8)

Marcar, V. L., Zihl, J., & Cowey, A. (1997). Comparing the visual deficits of a motion blind patient with the visual deficits of monkeys with area MT removed. *Neuropsychologia, 35,* 1459–1465. (6)

March, S. M., Abate, P., Spear, N. E., & Molina, J. C. (2009). Fetal exposure to moderate ethanol doses: Heightened operant responsiveness elicited by ethanol-related reinforcers. *Alcoholism: Clinical and Experimental Research, 33,* 1981–1993. (3)

Maricich, S. M., Wellnitz, S. A., Nelson, A. M., Lesniak, D. R., Gerling, G. J., Lumpkin, E. A., et al. (2009). Merkel cells are essential for light-touch responses. *Science, 324,* 1580–1582. (7)

Mariño, G., Fernández, A. F., Cabrera, S., Lundberg, Y. W., Cabanillas, R., Rodríguez, F., et al. (2010). Autophagy is essential for mouse sense of balance. *Journal of Clinical Investigation, 120,* 2331–2344. (7)

Marris, E. (2006). Grey matters. *Nature, 444,* 808–810. (1)

Marshall, J. C., & Halligan, P. W. (1995). Seeing the forest but only half the trees? *Nature, 373,* 521–523. (14)

Marshall, J. F. (1985). Neural plasticity and recovery of function after brain injury. *International Review of Neurobiology, 26,* 201–247. (5)

Martens, M. A., Wilson, S. J., & Reutens, D. C. (2008). Research review: Williams syndrome: A critical review of the cognitive, behavioral, and neuroanatomical phenotype. *Journal of Child Psychology and Psychiatry, 49,* 576–608. (14)

Martin, E. R., Scott, W. K., Nance, M. A., Watts, R. L., Hubble, J. P., Koller, W. C., et al. (2001). Association of single-nucleotide polymorphisms of the tau gene with late-onset Parkinson disease. *Journal of the American Medical Association, 286,* 2245–2250. (8)

Martin, G., Rojas, L. M., Ramírez, Y., & McNeil, R. (2004). The eyes of oilbirds (*Steatornis caripensis*): Pushing at the limits of sensitivity. *Naturwissenschaften, 91,* 26–29. (6)

Martin, P. R., Lee, B. B., White, A. J. R., Solomon, S. G., & Rütiger, L. (2001). Chromatic sensitivity of ganglion cells in the peripheral primate retina. *Nature, 410,* 933–936. (6)

Martin, R. C., & Blossom-Stach, C. (1986). Evidence of syntactic deficits in a fluent aphasic. *Brain and Language, 28,* 196–234. (14)

Martin, S. D., Martin, E., Rai, S. S., Richardson, M. A., Royall, R., & Eng, C. (2001). Brain blood flow changes in depressed patients treated with interpersonal psychotherapy or venlafaxine hydrochloride. *Archives of General Psychiatry, 58,* 641–648. (15)

Martindale, C. (2001). Oscillations and analogies: Thomas Young, MD, FRS, genius. *American Psychologist, 56,* 342–345. (6)

Martinez-Vargas, M. C., & Erickson, C. J. (1973). Some social and hormonal determinants of nest-building behaviour in the ring dove (*Streptopelia risoria*). *Behaviour, 45,* 12–37. (11)

Martinowich, K., Manji, H., & Lu, B. (2007). New insights into BDNF function in depression and anxiety. *Nature Neuroscience, 10,* 1089–1093. (15)

Masland, R. H. (2001). The fundamental plan of the retina. *Nature Neuroscience, 4,* 877–886. (6)

Mason, M. F., Norton, M. I., Van Horn, J. D., Wegner, D. M., Grafton, S. T., & Macrae, C. N. (2007). Wandering minds: The default network and stimulus-independent thought. *Science, 315,* 393–395. (4)

Massa, F., Mancini, G., Schmidt, H., Steindel, F., Mackie, K., Angioni, C., et al. (2010). Alterations in the hippocampal endocannabinoid system in diet-induced obese mice. *Journal of Neuroscience, 30,* 6273–6281. (3)

Massimini, M., Ferrarelli, F., Huber, R., Esser, S. K., Singh, H., & Tononi, G. (2005). Breakdown of cortical effective connectivity during sleep. *Science, 309,* 2228–2232. (9)

Mathalon, D. H., Sullivan, E. V., Lim, K. O., & Pfefferbaum, A. (2001). Progressive brain volume changes and the clinical course of schizophrenia in men. *Archives of General Psychiatry, 58,* 148–157. (15)

Mathews, G. A., Fane, B. A., Conway, G. S., Brook, C. G. D., & Hines, M. (2009). Personality and congenital adrenal androgen exposure. *Hormones and Behavior, 55,* 285–291. (11)

Matrisciano, F., Bonaccorso, S., Ricciardi, A., Scaccianoce, S., Panaccione, I., Wang, L., et al. (2009). Changes in BDNF serum levels in patients with major depression disorder (MDD) after 6 months treatment with sertraline, escitalopram, or venlafaxine. *Journal of Psychiatric Research, 43,* 247–254. (15)

Matsumoto, Y., Mishima, K., Satoh, K., Tozawa, T., Mishima, Y., Shimizu, T., et al. (2001). Total sleep deprivation induces an acute and transient increase in NK cell activity in healthy young volunteers. *Sleep, 24,* 804–809. (9)

Matsunami, H., Montmayeur, J.-P., & Buck, L. B. (2000). A family of candidate taste receptors in human and mouse. *Nature, 404,* 601–604. (7)

Mattingley, J. B., Husain, M., Rorden, C., Kennard, C., & Driver, J. (1998). Motor role of human inferior parietal lobe revealed in unilateral neglect patients. *Nature, 392,* 179–182. (14)

Mattocks, C., Hines, M., Ness, A., Leary, S., Griffiths, A., Tilling, K., et al. (2010). Associations between sex-typed behaviour at age 3½ and levels and patterns of physical activity at age 12: The Avon Longitudinal Study of Parents and Children. *Archives of Disease in Childhood, 95,* 509–512. (11)

Matuszewich, L., Lorrain, D. S., & Hull, E. M. (2000). Dopamine release in the medial preoptic area of female rats in response to hormonal ma-

nipulation and sexual activity. *Behavioral Neuroscience, 114,* 772–782. (11)

Maurice, D. M. (1998). The Von Sallmann lecture of 1996: An ophthalmological explanation of REM sleep. *Experimental Eye Research, 66,* 139–145. (9)

May, P. R. A., Fuster, J. M., Haber, J., & Hirschman, A. (1979). Woodpecker drilling behavior: An endorsement of the rotational theory of impact brain injury. *Archives of Neurology, 36,* 370–373. (5)

Mayberry, R. I., Lock, E., & Kazmi, H. (2002). Linguistic ability and early language exposure. *Nature, 417,* 38. (14)

Mayer, A. D., & Rosenblatt, J. S. (1979). Hormonal influences during the ontogeny of maternal behavior in female rats. *Journal of Comparative and Physiological Psychology, 93,* 879–898. (11)

Maze, I., Covington, H. E. III, Dietz, D. M., La Plant, Q., Renthal, W., Russo, S. J., et al. (2010). Essential role of the histone methyltransferase G9a in cocaine-induced plasticity. *Science, 327,* 213–216. (3)

McAllen, R. M., Tanaka, M., Ootsuka, Y., & McKinley, M. J. (2010). Multiple thermoregulatory effectors with independent central controls. *European Journal of Applied Physiology, 109,* 27–33. (10)

McBurney, D. H., & Bartoshuk, L. M. (1973). Interactions between stimuli with different taste qualities. *Physiology & Behavior, 10,* 1101–1106. (7)

McCarley, R. W., & Hoffman, E. (1981). REM sleep, dreams, and the activation-synthesis hypothesis. *American Journal of Psychiatry, 138,* 904–912. (9)

McCarthy, G., Puce, A., Gore, J. C., & Allison, T. (1997). Face-specific processing in the human fusiform gyrus. *Journal of Cognitive Neuroscience, 9,* 605–610. (6)

McClintock, M. K. (1971). Menstrual synchrony and suppression. *Nature, 229,* 244–245. (7)

McConnell, J. V. (1962). Memory transfer through cannibalism in planarians. *Journal of Neuropsychiatry, 3*(Suppl. 1), 42–48. (13)

McConnell, S. K. (1992). The genesis of neuronal diversity during development of cerebral cortex. *Seminars in the Neurosciences, 4,* 347–356. (5)

McCrory, E., Frith, U., Brunswick, N., & Price, C. (2000). Abnormal functional activation during a simple word repetition task: A PET study of adult dyslexics. *Journal of Cognitive Neuroscience, 12,* 753–762. (14)

McDaniel, M. A. (2005). Big-brained people are smarter: A meta-analysis of the relationship between *in vivo* brain volume and intelligence. *Intelligence, 33,* 337–346. (4)

McEwen, B. S. (2000). The neurobiology of stress: From serendipity to clinical relevance. *Brain Research, 886,* 172–189. (10, 12)

McFarland, B. R., & Klein, D. N. (2009). Emotional reactivity in depression: Diminished responsiveness to anticipated reward but not to anticipated punishment or to nonreward or avoidance. *Depression and Anxiety, 26,* 117–122. (15)

McGowan, P. O., Sasaki, A., D'Alessio, A. C., Dymov, S., Labonté, B., Szyf, M., et al. (2009). Epigenetic regulation of the glucocorticoid receptor

in human brain associates with childhood abuse. *Nature Neuroscience, 12,* 342–348. (1)

McGregor, I. S., Hargreaves, G. A., Apfelbach, R., & Hunt, G. E. (2004). Neural correlates of cat odor-induced anxiety in rats: Region-specific effects of the benzodiazepine midazolam. *Journal of Neuroscience, 24,* 4134–4144. (12)

McGuire, S., & Clifford, J. (2000). Genetic and environmental contributions to loneliness in children. *Psychological Science, 11,* 487–491. (1)

McHugh, P. R., & Moran, T. H. (1985). The stomach: A conception of its dynamic role in satiety. *Progress in Psychobiology and Physiological Psychology, 11,* 197–232. (10)

McIntyre, M., Gangestad, S. W., Gray, P. B., Chapman, J. F., Burnham, T. C., O'Rourke, M. T., et al. (2006). Romantic involvement often reduces men's testosterone levels—But not always: The moderating effect of extrapair sexual interest. *Journal of Personality and Social Psychology, 91,* 642–651. (11)

McIntyre, R. S., Konarski, J. Z., Wilkins, K., Soczynska, J. K., & Kennedy, S. H. (2006). Obesity in bipolar disorder and major depressive disorder: Results from a National Community Health Survey on Mental Health and Well-Being. *Canadian Journal of Psychiatry, 51,* 274–280. (10)

McKeever, W. F., Seitz, K. S., Krutsch, A. J., & Van Eys, P. L. (1995). On language laterality in normal dextrals and sinistrals: Results from the bilateral object naming latency task. *Neuropsychologia, 33,* 1627–1635. (14)

McKemy, D. D., Neuhausser, W. M., & Julius, D. (2002). Identification of a cold receptor reveals a general role for TRP channels in thermosensation. *Nature, 416,* 52–58. (7)

McKinnon, W., Weisse, C. S., Reynolds, C. P., Bowles, C. A., & Baum, A. (1989). Chronic stress, leukocyte-subpopulations, and humoral response to latent viruses. *Health Psychology, 8,* 839–402. (12)

Mechelli, A., Crinion, J. T., Noppeney, U., O'Doherty, J., Ashburner, J., Frackowiak, R. S., et al. (2004). Structural plasticity in the bilingual brain. *Nature, 431,* 757. (14)

Meddis, R., Pearson, A. J. D., & Langford, G. (1973). An extreme case of healthy insomnia. *EEG and Clinical Neurophysiology, 35,* 213–214. (9)

Meister, M., Wong, R. O. L., Baylor, D. A., & Shatz, C. J. (1991). Synchronous bursts of action potentials in ganglion cells of the developing mammalian retina. *Science, 252,* 939–943. (5)

Melloni, L., Molina, C., Pena, M., Torres, D., Singer, W., & Rodriguez, E. (2007). Synchronization of neural activity across cortical areas correlates with conscious perception. *Journal of Neuroscience, 27,* 2858–2865. (14)

Melone, M., Vitellaro-Zuccarello, L., Vallejo-Illarramendi, A., Pérez-Samartin, A., Matute, C., Cozzi, A., et al. (2001). The expression of glutamate transporter GLT-1 in the rat cerebral cortex is down-regulated by the antipsychotic drug clozapine. *Molecular Psychiatry, 6,* 380–386. (15)

Meltzer, H. Y., Matsubara, S., & Lee, J.-C. (1989). Classification of typical and atypical antipsychotic drugs on the basis of dopamine D-1, D-2 and serotonin2 pKi values. *Journal of Pharmacology and Experimental Therapeutics, 251,* 238–246. (15)

Meltzoff, A. N., & Moore, M. K. (1977). Imitation of facial and manual gestures by human neonates. *Science, 198,* 75–78. (8)

Melzack, R., & Wall, P. D. (1965). Pain mechanisms: A new theory. *Science, 150,* 971–979. (7)

Mendieta-Zéron, H., López, M., & Diéguez, C. (2008). Gastrointestinal peptides controlling body weight homeostasis. *General and Comparative Endocrinology, 155,* 481–495. (10)

Merabet, L. B., Hamilton, R., Schlaug, G., Swisher, J. D., Kiriakopoulos, E. T., Pitskel, N. B., et al. (2008). Rapid and reversible recruitment of early visual cortex for touch. *PLoS ONE, 3,* e3046. (5)

Mergen, M., Mergen, H., Ozata, M., Oner, R., & Oner, C. (2001). A novel melanocortin 4 receptor (MC4R) gene mutation associated with morbid obesity. *Journal of Clinical Endocrinology & Metabolism, 86,* 3448–3451. (10)

Merikangas, K. R., Akiskal, H. S., Angst, J., Greenberg, P. E., Hirschfeld, R. M. A., Petukhova, M., et al. (2007). Lifetime and 12-month prevalence of bipolar spectrum disorder in the National Comorbidity Survey Replication. *Archives of General Psychiatry, 64,* 543–552. (15)

Merton, P. A. (1972). How we control the contraction of our muscles. *Scientific American, 226*(5), 30–37. (8)

Merzenich, M. M., Nelson, R. J., Stryker, M. P., Cynader, M. S., Schoppman, A., & Zook, J. M. (1984). Somatosensory cortical map changes following digit amputation in adult monkeys. *Journal of Comparative Neurology, 224,* 591–605. (5)

Meshi, D., Drew, M. R., Saxe, M., Ansorge, M. S., David, D., Santarelli, L., et al. (2006). Hippocampal neurogenesis is not required for behavioral effects of environmental enrichment. *Nature Neuroscience, 9,* 729–731. (5)

Mesulam, M.-M. (1995). Cholinergic pathways and the ascending reticular activating system of the human brain. *Annals of the New York Academy of Sciences, 757,* 169–179. (4, 9)

Mevorach, C., Hodsoll, J., Allen, H., Shalev, L., & Humphreys, G. (2010). Ignoring the elephant in the room: A neural circuit to downregulate salience. *Journal of Neuroscience, 30,* 6072–6079. (14)

Meyer, K., Kaplan, J. T., Essex, R., Webber, C., Damasio, H., & Damasio, A. (2010). Predicting visual stimuli on the basis of activity in auditory cortices. *Nature Neuroscience, 13,* 667–671. (7)

Meyer-Bahlburg, H. F. L., Dolezal, C., Baker, S. W., & New, M. I. (2008). Sexual orientation in women with classical or non-classical congenital adrenal hyperplasia as a function of degree of prenatal androgen excess. *Archives of Sexual Behavior, 37,* 85–99. (11)

Meyer-Lindenberg, A. (2010). From maps to mechanisms through neuroimaging of schizophrenia. *Nature, 468,* 194–202. (15)

Meyer-Lindenberg, A., Kohn, P., Mervis, C. B., Kippenhan, J. S., Olsen, R. K., Morris, C. A., et al. (2004). Neural basis of genetically determined visuospatial construction deficit in Williams syndrome. *Neuron, 43,* 623–631. (14)

Meyer-Lindenberg, A., Mervis, C. B., & Berman, K. F. (2006). Neural mechanisms in Williams syndrome: A unique window to genetic influences on cognition and behaviour. *Nature Reviews Neuroscience, 7,* 380–393. (14)

Meyer-Lindenberg, A., Miletich, R. S., Kohn, P. D., Esposito, G., Carson, R. E., Quarantelli, M., et al. (2002). Reduced prefrontal activity predicts exaggerated striatal dopaminergic function in schizophrenia. *Nature Neuroscience, 5,* 267–271. (15)

Mezzanotte, W. S., Tangel, D. J., & White, D. P. (1992). Waking genioglossal electromyogram in sleep apnea patients versus normal controls (a neuromuscular compensatory mechanism). *Journal of Clinical Investigation, 89,* 1571–1579. (9)

Michel, F., & Anderson, M. (2009). Using the antisaccade task to investigate the relationship between the development of inhibition and the development of intelligence. *Developmental Science, 12,* 272–288. (5)

Mihalcescu, I., Hsing, W., & Leibler, S. (2004). Resilient circadian oscillator revealed in individual cyanobacteria. *Nature, 430,* 81–85. (9)

Mikolajczak, M., Gross, J. J., Lane, A., Corneille, O., de Timary, P., & Luminet, O. (2010). Oxytocin makes people trusting, not gullible. *Psychological Science, 21,* 1072–1074. (11)

Miles, F. A., & Evarts, E. V. (1979). Concepts of motor organization. *Annual Review of Psychology, 30,* 327–362. (8)

Milich, R., & Pelham, W. E. (1986). Effects of sugar ingestion on the classroom and playgroup behavior of attention deficit disordered boys. *Journal of Consulting and Clinical Psychology, 54,* 714–718. (10)

Miller, C. A., Gavin, C. F., White, J. A., Parrish, R. R, Honasoge, A., Yancey, C. R., et al. (2010). Cortical DNA methylation maintains remote memory. *Nature Neuroscience, 13,* 664–666. (13)

Miller, E. (2000). The prefrontal cortex and cognitive control. *Nature Reviews Neuroscience, 1,* 59–65. (4)

Miller, G. (2007a). Animal extremists get personal. *Science, 318,* 1856–1585. (1)

Miller, G. (2007b). The mystery of the missing smile. *Science, 316,* 826–827. (12)

Miller, G., Tybur, J. M., & Jordan, B. D. (2007). Ovulatory cycle effects on tip earnings by lap dancers: Economic evidence for human estrus? *Evolution and Human Behavior, 28,* 375–381. (11)

Miller, S. L., & Maner, J. K. (2010). Scent of a woman: Men's testosterone responses to olfactory ovulation cues. *Psychological Science, 21,* 276–283. (7)

Milner, B. (1959). The memory defect in bilateral hippocampal lesions. *Psychiatric Research Reports, 11,* 43–58. (13)

Minichiello, L. (2009). TrkB signaling pathways in LTP and learning. *Nature Reviews Neuroscience, 10,* 850–860. (13)

Minokoshi, Y., Alquier, T., Furukawa, N., Kim, Y.-B., Lee, A., Xue, B., et al. (2004). AMP-kinase regulates food intake by responding to hormonal and nutrient signals in the hypothalamus. *Nature, 428,* 569–574. (10)

Minto, C. L., Liao, L.-M., Woodhouse, C. R. J., Ransley, P. G., & Creighton, S. M. (2003). The effect of clitoral surgery in individuals who have intersex conditions with ambiguous genitalia: A cross-sectional study. *Lancet, 361,* 1252–1257. (11)

Mishra, J., Zinni, M., Bavelier, D., & Hillyard, S. A. (2011). Neural basis of superior performance of action videogame players in an attention-demanding task. *Journal of Neuroscience, 31,* 992–998. (14)

Misrahi, M., Meduri, G., Pissard, S., Bouvattier, C., Beau, I., Loosfelt, H., et al. (1997). Comparison of immunocytochemical and molecular features with the phenotype in a case of incomplete male pseudohermaphroditism associated with a mutation of the luteinizing hormone receptor. *Journal of Clinical Endocrinology & Metabolism, 82,* 2159–2165. (11)

Mistlberger, R. E., & Skene, D. J. (2004). Social influences on mammalian circadian rhythms: Animal and human studies. *Biological Rhythms, 79,* 533–556. (9)

Mitchell, D. E. (1980). The influence of early visual experience on visual perception. In C. S. Harris (Ed.), *Visual coding and adaptability* (pp. 1–50). Hillsdale, NJ: Erlbaum. (6)

Miyazawa, A., Fujiyoshi, Y., & Unwin, N. (2003). Structure and gating mechanism of the acetylcholine receptor pore. *Nature, 423,* 949–955. (3)

Mochizuki, T., Crocker, A., McCormack, S., Yanagisawa, M., Sakurai, T., & Scammell, T. E. (2004). Behavioral state instability in orexin knock-out mice. *Journal of Neuroscience, 24,* 6291–6300. (9)

Modell, S., Ising, M., Holsboer, F., & Lauer, C. J. (2005). The Munich vulnerability study on affective disorders: Premorbid polysomnographic profile of affected high-risk probands. *Biological Psychiatry, 58,* 694–699. (15)

Moeller, F. G., Dougherty, D. M., Swann, A. C., Collins, D., Davis, C. M., & Cherek, D. R. (1996). Tryptophan depletion and aggressive responding in healthy males. *Psychopharmacology, 126,* 97–103. (12)

Mohr, C., Landis, T., Bracha, H. S., & Brugger, P. (2003). Opposite turning behavior in right-handers and non-right-handers suggests a link between handedness and cerebral dopamine asymmetries. *Behavioral Neuroscience, 117,* 1448–1452. (14)

Mondloch, C. J., Maurer, D., & Ahola, S. (2006). Becoming a face expert. *Psychological Science, 17,* 930–934. (6)

Money, J. (1967). Sexual problems of the chronically ill. In C. W. Wahl (Ed.), *Sexual problems: Diagnosis and treatment in medical practice* (pp. 266–287). New York: Free Press. (8)

Money, J., & Ehrhardt, A. A. (1972). *Man & woman, boy & girl.* Baltimore: Johns Hopkins University Press. (11)

Money, J., & Lewis, V. (1966). IQ, genetics and accelerated growth: Adrenogenital syndrome. *Bulletin of the Johns Hopkins Hospital, 118,* 365–373. (11)

Money, J., & Schwartz, M. (1978). Biosocial determinants of gender identity differentiation and development. In J. B. Hutchison (Ed.), *Biological determinants of sexual behaviour* (pp. 765–784). Chichester, England: Wiley. (11)

Monfils, M.-H., Cowansage, K. K., Klann, E., & LeDoux, J. E. (2009). Extinction-reconsolidation boundaries: Key to persistent attenuation of fear memories. *Science, 324*, 951–955. (12)

Mongillo, G., Barak, O., & Tsodyks, M. (2008). Synaptic theory of working memory. *Science, 319*, 1543–1546. (13)

Monk, C. S., Klein, R. G., Telzer, E. H., Schroth, E. A., Mannuzza, S., Moulton, J. L., III, et al. (2008). Amygdala and nucleus accumbens activation to emotional facial expressions in children and adolescents at risk for major depression. *American Journal of Psychiatry, 165*, 90–98. (15)

Monk, T. H., & Aplin, L. C. (1980). Spring and autumn daylight time changes: Studies of adjustment in sleep timings, mood, and efficiency. *Ergonomics, 23*, 167–178. (9)

Monroe, S. M., & Harkness, K. L. (2005). Life stress, the "kindling" hypothesis, and the recurrence of depression. *Psychological Review, 112*, 417–445. (15)

Monteleone, P., Serritella, C., Scognamiglio, P., & Maj, M. (2010). Enhanced ghrelin secretion in the cephalic phase of food ingestion in women with bulimia nervosa. *Psychoneuroendocrinology, 35*, 284–288. (10)

Montgomery, K. J., Seeherman, K. R., & Haxby, J. V. (2009). The well-tempered social brain. *Psychological Science, 20*, 1211–1213. (8)

Montgomery, S. A., Baldwin, D. S., Blier, P., Fineberg, N. A., Kasper, S., Lader, M., et al. (2007). Which antidepressants have demonstrated superior efficacy? A review of the evidence. *International Clinical Psychopharmacology, 22*, 323–329. (15)

Monti-Bloch, L., Jennings-White, C., & Berliner, D. L. (1998). The human vomeronasal system: A review. *Annals of the New York Academy of Sciences, 855*, 373–389. (7)

Monti-Bloch, L., Jennings-White, C., Dolberg, D. S., & Berliner, D. L. (1994). The human vomeronasal system. *Psychoneuroendocrinology, 19*, 673–686. (7)

Moody, T. D., Chang, G. Y., Vanek, Z. F., & Knowlton, B. J. (2010). Concurrent discrimination learning in Parkinson's disease. *Behavioral Neuroscience, 124*, 1–8. (13)

Moore, L. B., Goodwin, B., Jones, S. A., Wisely, G. B., Serabjit-Singh, C. J., Willson, T. M., et al. (2000). St. John's wort induces hepatic drug metabolism through activation of the pregnane X receptor. *Proceedings of the National Academy of Sciences, USA, 97*, 7500–7502. (15)

Moore, T., Rodman, H. R., Repp, A. B., & Gross, C. G. (1995). Localization of visual stimuli after striate cortex damage in monkeys: Parallels with human blindsight. *Proceedings of the National Academy of Sciences, USA, 92*, 8215–8218. (6)

Moore-Ede, M. C., Czeisler, C. A., & Richardson, G. S. (1983). Circadian timekeeping in health and disease. *New England Journal of Medicine, 309*, 469–476. (9)

Morand, S. M., Grosbras, M.-H., Caldara, R., & Harvey, M. (2010). Looking away from faces: Influence of high-level visual processes on sac-

cade programming. *Journal of Vision, 10*(3), article 16. (5)

Moreno, C., Laje, G., Blanco, C., Jiang, H., Schmidt, A. B., & Olfson, M. (2007). National trends in the outpatient diagnosis and treatment of bipolar disorder in youth. *Archives of General Psychiatry, 64*, 1032–1039. (15)

Morfini, G. A., You, Y.-M., Pollema, S. L., Kaminska, A., Liu, K., Yoshioka, K., et al. (2009). Pathogenic huntingtin inhibits fast axonal transport by activating JNK3 and phosphorylating kinesin. *Nature Neuroscience, 12*, 864–871. (8)

Morgan, L. K., MacEvoy, S. P., Aguirre, G. K., & Epstein, R. A. (2011). Distances between real-world locations are represented in the human hippocampus. *Journal of Neuroscience, 31*, 1238–1245. (13)

Mori, K., Mataga, N., & Imamura, K. (1992). Differential specificities of single mitral cells in rabbit olfactory bulb for a homologous series of fatty acid odor molecules. *Journal of Neurophysiology, 67*, 786–789. (7)

Moritz, C. T., Perlmutter, S. I., & Fetz, E. E. (2008). Direct control of paralysed muscles by cortical neurons. *Nature, 456*, 639–643. (8)

Morley, J. E., Levine, A. S., Grace, M., & Kneip, J. (1985). Peptide YY (PYY), a potent orexigenic agent. *Brain Research, 341*, 200–203. (10)

Morris, J. A., Jordan, C. L., & Breedlove, S. M. (2004). Sexual differentiation of the vertebrate nervous system. *Nature Neuroscience, 7*, 1034–1039. (11)

Morris, J. S., deBonis, M., & Dolan, R. J. (2002). Human amygdala responses to fearful eyes. *NeuroImage, 17*, 214–222. (12)

Morris, M., Lack, L., & Dawson, D. (1990). Sleep-onset insomniacs have delayed temperature rhythms. *Sleep, 13*, 1–14. (9)

Morrison, A. R., Sanford, L. D., Ball, W. A., Mann, G. L., & Ross, R. J. (1995). Stimulus-elicited behavior in rapid eye movement sleep without atonia. *Behavioral Neuroscience, 109*, 972–979. (9)

Morton, A. J., Wood, N. I., Hastings, M. H., Hurelbink, C., Barker, R. A., & Maywood, E. S. (2005). Disintegration of the sleep–wake cycle and circadian timing in Huntington's disease. *Journal of Neuroscience, 25*, 157–163. (9)

Morton, G. J., Cummings, D. E., Baskin, D. G., Barsh, G. S., & Schwartz, M. W. (2006). Central nervous system control of food intake and body weight. *Nature, 443*, 289–295. (10)

Moruzzi, G., & Magoun, H. W. (1949). Brain stem reticular formation and activation of the EEG. *Electroencephalography and Clinical Neurophysiology, 1*, 455–473. (9)

Moss, C. F., & Simmons, A. M. (1986). Frequency selectivity of hearing in the green treefrog, *Hyla cinerea*. *Journal of Comparative Physiology, A, 159*, 257–266. (7)

Moss, S. J., & Smart, T. G. (2001). Constructing inhibitory synapses. *Nature Reviews Neuroscience, 2*, 240–250. (3)

Mrosovsky, N. (1990). *Rheostasis: The physiology of change.* New York: Oxford University Press. (10)

Mrzljak, L., Bergson, C., Pappy, M., Huff, R., Levenson, R., & Goldman-Rakic, P. S. (1996). Localization of dopamine D4 receptors in GAB-

Aergic neurons of the primate brain. *Nature, 381*, 245–248. (15)

Mueller, K. L. O., Marion, S. D., Paul, L. K., & Brown, W. S. (2009). Bimanual motor coordination in agenesis of the corpus callosum. *Behavioral Neuroscience, 123*, 1000–1011. (14)

Muller, M. N., Thompson, M. E., & Wrangham, R. W. (2006). Male chimpanzees prefer mating with old females. *Current Biology, 16*, 2234–2238. (11)

Mulligan, S. J., & MacVicar, B. A. (2004). Calcium transients in astrocyte end feet cause cerebrovascular constrictions. *Nature, 431*, 195–199. (2)

Munafo, M. R., Durrant, C., Lewis, G., & Flint, J. (2009). Gene x environment interactions at the serotonin transporter locus. *Biological Psychiatry, 65*, 211–219. (15)

Munk, M. H. J., Roelfsema, P. R., König, P., Engel, A. K., & Singer, W. (1996). Role of reticular activation in the modulation of intracortical synchronization. *Science, 272*, 271–274. (9)

Munoz, D. P., & Everling, S. (2004). Look away: The anti-saccade task and the voluntary control of eye movement. *Nature Reviews Neuroscience, 5*, 218–228. (5, 8)

Münzberg, H., & Myers, M. G., Jr. (2005). Molecular and anatomical determinants of central leptin resistance. *Nature Neuroscience, 8*, 566–570. (10)

Murali, M. S. (2001). Epidemiological study of prevalence of mental disorders in India. *Indian Journal of Community Medicine, 26*, 198. (15)

Murphy, D. L., Fox, M. A., Timpano, K. R., Moya, P. R., Ren-Patterson, R., Andrews, A. M., et al. (2008). How the serotonin story is being rewritten by new gene-based discoveries principally related to *SLC6A4*, the serotonin transporter gene, which functions to influence all cellular serotonin systems. *Neuropharmacology, 55*, 932–960. (3)

Murphy, F. C., Nimmo-Smith, I., & Lawrence, A. D. (2003). Functional neuroanatomy of emotions: A meta-analysis. *Cognitive, Affective, & Behavioral Neuroscience, 3*, 207–233. (12)

Murphy, M. R., Checkley, S. A., Seckl, J. R., & Lightman, S. L. (1990). Naloxone inhibits oxytocin release at orgasm in man. *Journal of Clinical Endocrinology & Metabolism, 71*, 1056–1058. (11)

Murray, G., Nicholas, C. L., Kleiman, J., Dwyer, R., Carrington, M. J., Allen, N. B., et al. (2009). Nature's clocks and human mood: The circadian system modulates reward motivation. *Emotion, 9*, 705–716. (9)

Murrell, J., Farlow, M., Ghetti, B., & Benson, M. D. (1991). A mutation in the amyloid precursor protein associated with hereditary Alzheimer's disease. *Science, 254*, 97–99. (13)

Musacchia, G., Sams, M., Skoe, E., & Kraus, N. (2007). Musicians have enhanced subcortical auditory and audiovisual processing of speech and music. *Proceedings of the National Academy of Sciences, USA, 104*, 15894–15898. (5)

Mutch, D. M., & Clément, K. (2006). Unraveling the genetics of human obesity. *PLoS Genetics, 2*, e188. (10)

Myers, J. J., & Sperry, R. W. (1985). Interhemispheric communication after section of the forebrain commissures. *Cortex, 21*, 249–260. (14)

Nadal, A., Díaz, M., & Valverde, M. A. (2001). The estrogen trinity: Membrane, cytosolic, and nuclear effects. *News in Physiological Sciences, 16,* 251–255. (11)

Nadarajah, B., & Parnavelas, J. G. (2002). Modes of neuronal migration in the developing cerebral cortex. *Nature Reviews Neuroscience, 3,* 423–432. (5)

Nader, K., & Hardt, O. (2009). A single standard for memory: The case for reconsolidation. *Nature Reviews Neuroscience, 10,* 224–241. (13)

Nagarajan, S., Mahncke, H., Salz, T., Tallal, P., Roberts, T., & Merzenich, M. M. (1999). Cortical auditory signal processing in poor readers. *Proceedings of the National Academy of Sciences, USA, 96,* 6483–6488. (14)

Nakashima, Y., Kuwamura, T., & Yogo, Y. (1995). Why be a both-ways sex changer? *Ethology, 101,* 301–307. (11)

Nakata, H., Yoshie, M., Miura, A., & Kudo, K. (2010). Characteristics of the athletes' brain: Evidence from neurophysiology and neuroimaging. *Brain Research Reviews, 62,* 197–211. (6)

Narr, K. L., Woods, R. P., Thompson, P. M., Szeszko, P., Robinson, D., Dimtcheva, T., et al. (2007). Relationships between IQ and regional cortical gray matter thickness in healthy adults. *Cerebral Cortex, 17,* 2163–2171. (4)

Narrow, W. E., Rae, D. S., Robins, L. N., & Regier, D. A. (2002). Revised prevalence estimates of mental disorders in the United States. *Archives of General Psychiatry, 59,* 115–123. (15)

Narumoto, J., Okada, T., Sadato, N., Fukui, K., & Yonekura, Y. (2001). Attention to emotion modulates fMRI activity in human right superior temporal sulcus. *Cognitive Brain Research, 12,* 225–231. (12, 14)

Nassi, J. J., & Callaway, E. M. (2006). Multiple circuits relaying primate parallel visual pathways to the middle temporal cortex. *Journal of Neuroscience, 26,* 12789–12798. (6)

Nassi, J. J., & Callaway, E. M. (2009). Parallel processing strategies of the primate visual system. *Nature Reviews Neuroscience, 10,* 360–372. (6)

Nathans, J., Davenport, C. M., Maumenee, I. H., Lewis, R. A., Hejtmancik, J. F., Litt, M., et al. (1989). Molecular genetics of human blue cone monochromacy. *Science, 245,* 831–838. (6)

Naumer, M. J., & van den Bosch, J. J. F. (2009). Touching sounds: Thalamocortical plasticity and the neural basis of multisensory integration. *Journal of Neurophysiology, 102,* 7–8. (7)

Nebes, R. D. (1974). Hemispheric specialization in commissurotomized man. *Psychological Bulletin, 81,* 1–14. (14)

Nef, P. (1998). How we smell: The molecular and cellular bases of olfaction. *News in Physiological Sciences, 13,* 1–5. (7)

Neitz, M., Kraft, T. W., & Neitz, J. (1998). Expression of L cone pigment gene subtypes in females. *Vision Research, 38,* 3221–3225. (6)

Nelson, C. A., Wewerka, S., Thomas, K. M., Tribby-Walbridge, S., deRegnier, R., & Georgieff, M. (2000). Neurocognitive sequelae of infants of diabetic mothers. *Behavioral Neuroscience, 114,* 950–956. (5)

Nelson, D. O., & Prosser, C. L. (1981). Intracellular recordings from thermosensitive preoptic neurons. *Science, 213,* 787–789. (10)

Nelson, R. J., & Trainor, B. C. (2007). Neural mechanisms of aggression. *Nature Reviews Neuroscience, 8,* 536–546. (12)

Nemeroff, C. B., Heim, C. M., Thase, M. E., Klein, D. N., Rush, J., Shatzberg, A. F., et al. (2003). Differential responses to psychotherapy versus pharmacotherapy in patients with chronic forms of major depression and childhood trauma. *Proceedings of the National Academy of Sciences, USA, 100,* 14293–14296. (15)

Netter, F. H. (1983). *CIBA collection of medical illustrations: Vol. 1. Nervous system.* New York: CIBA. (11)

Nettle, D. (2006). The evolution of personality variation in humans and other animals. *American Psychologist, 61,* 622–631. (12)

Neumeister, A., Hu, X.-Z., Luckenbaugh, D. A., Schwarz, M., Nugent, A. C., Bonne, O., et al. (2006). Differential effects of *x*-HTTLPR genotypes on the behavioral and neural responses to tryptophan depletion in patients with major depression and controls. *Archives of General Psychiatry, 63,* 978–986. (15)

Neumeister, A., Nugent, A. C., Waldeck, T., Geraci, M., Schwarz, M., Bonne, O., et al. (2004). Neural and behavioral responses to tryptophan depletion in unmedicated patients with remitted major depressive disorder and controls. *Archives of General Psychiatry, 61,* 765–773. (15)

Neville, H. J., Bavelier, D., Corina, D., Rauschecker, J., Karni, A., Lalwani, A., et al. (1998). Cerebral organization for language in deaf and hearing subjects: Biological constraints and effects of experience. *Proceedings of the National Academy of Sciences, USA, 95,* 922–929. (14)

Nevin, R. (2007). Understanding international crime trends: The legacy of preschool lead exposure. *Environmental Research, 104,* 315–336. (12)

Newcomer, J. W., Selke, G., Melson, A. K., Hershey, T., Craft, S., Richards, K., et al. (1999). Decreased memory performance in healthy humans induced by stress-level cortisol treatment. *Archives of General Psychiatry, 56,* 527–533. (13)

Nicholas, M. K., & Arnason, B. G. W. (1992). Immunologic responses in central nervous system transplantation. *Seminars in the Neurosciences, 4,* 273–283. (8)

Nicholls, M. E. R., Orr, C. A., Okubo, M., & Loftus, A. (2006). Satisfaction guaranteed: The effect of spatial biases on responses to Likert scales. *Psychological Science, 17,* 1027–1028. (4)

Nicklas, W. J., Saporito, M., Basma, A., Geller, H. M., & Heikkila, R. E. (1992). Mitochondrial mechanisms of neurotoxicity. *Annals of the New York Academy of Sciences, 648,* 28–36. (8)

Nicolelis, M. A. L., Ghazanfar, A. A., Stambaugh, C. R., Oliveira, L. M. O., Laubach, M., Chapin, J. K., et al. (1998). Simultaneous encoding of tactile information by three primate cortical areas. *Nature Neuroscience, 1,* 621–630. (4)

Niebuhr, D. W., Millikan, A. M., Cowan, D. N., Yolken, R., Li, Y., & Weber, N. S. (2008). Selected infectious agents and risk of schizophrenia among U.S. military personnel. *American Journal of Psychiatry, 165,* 99–106. (15)

Niessing, J., & Friedrich, R. W. (2010). Olfactory pattern classification by discrete neuronal network states. *Nature, 465,* 47–52. (7)

Nieuwenhuys, R., Voogd, J., & vanHuijzen, C. (1988). *The human central nervous system* (3rd Rev. ed.). Berlin: Springer-Verlag. (4, 10, 12, 14)

Nilsson, G. E. (1999, December). The cost of a brain. *Natural History, 108,* 66–73. (4)

Nir, Y., & Tononi, G. (2010). Dreaming and the brain: From phenomenology to neurophysiology. *Trends in Cognitive Sciences, 14,* 88–100. (9)

Nishimaru, H., Restrepo, C. E., Ryge, J., Yanagawa, Y., & Kiehn, O. (2005). Mammalian motor neurons corelease glutamate and acetylcholine at central synapses. *Proceedings of the National Academy of Sciences, USA, 102,* 5245–5249. (3)

Nishimura, Y., Onoe, H., Morichika, Y., Perfiliev, S., Tsukada, H., & Isa, T. (2007). Time-dependent central compensatory mechanisms of finger dexterity after spinal cord injury. *Science, 318,* 1150–1155. (5)

Nitabach, M. N., & Taghert, P. H. (2008). Organization of the *Drosophila* circadian control circuit. *Current Biology, 18,* R84–R93. (9)

Noaghiul, S., & Hibbeln, J. R. (2003). Cross-national comparisons of seafood consumption and rates of bipolar disorders. *American Journal of Psychiatry, 160,* 2222–2227. (15)

Noonan, M. A., Bulin, S. E., Fuller, D. C., & Eisch, A. J. (2010). Reduction of adult hippocampal neurogenesis confers vulnerability in an animal model of cocaine addiction. *Journal of Neuroscience, 30,* 304–315. (3)

Nordenström, A., Frisén, L., Falhammar, H., Filipsson, H., Holmdahl, G., Janson, P. O., et al. (2010). Sexual function and surgical outcome in women with congenital adrenal hyperplasia due to CYP21A2 deficiency: Clinical perspective and the patients' perception. *Journal of Clinical Endocrinology & Metabolism, 95,* 3633–3640. (11)

Nordenström, A., Servin, A., Bohlin, G., Larsson, A., & Wedell, A. (2002). Sex-typed toy play behavior correlates with the degree of prenatal androgen exposure assessed by CYP21 genotype in girls with congenital adrenal hyperplasia. *Journal of Clinical Endocrinology & Metabolism, 87,* 5119–5124. (11)

Norman, R. A., Tataranni, P. A., Pratley, R., Thompson, D. B., Hanson, R. L., Prochazka, M., et al. (1998). Autosomal genomic scan for loci linked to obesity and energy metabolism in Pima Indians. *American Journal of Human Genetics, 62,* 659–668. (10)

North, R. A. (1989). Neurotransmitters and their receptors: From the clone to the clinic. *Seminars in the Neurosciences, 1,* 81–90. (3)

North, R. A. (1992). Cellular actions of opiates and cocaine. *Annals of the New York Academy of Sciences, 654,* 1–6. (3)

Noseda, R., Kainz, V., Jakubowski, M., Gooley, J. J., Saper, C. B., Digre, K., et al. (2010). A neural mechanism for exacerbation of headache by light. *Nature Neuroscience, 13,* 239–245. (9)

Nosenko, N. D., & Reznikov, A. G. (2001). Prenatal stress and sexual differentiation of monoaminergic brain systems. *Neurophysiology, 33*, 197–206. (11)

Nottebohm, F. (2002). Why are some neurons replaced in adult brain? *Journal of Neuroscience, 22*, 624–628. (5)

Nowak, M. A., & Sigmund, K. (2005). Evolution of indirect reciprocity. *Science, 437*, 1291–1298. (1)

Nugent, F. S., Penick, S. C., & Kauer, J. A. (2007). Opioids block long-term potentiation of inhibitory synapses. *Nature, 446*, 1086–1090. (13)

Numan, M., & Woodside, B. (2010). Maternity: Neural mechanisms, motivational processes, and physiological adaptations. *Behavioral Neuroscience, 124*, 715–741. (11, 12)

Nunes, S. O. V., Itano, E. N., Amarante, M. K., Reiche, E. M. V., Miranda, H. C., de Oliveira, C. E. C., et al. (2008). REN from Borna disease virus in patients with schizophrenia, schizoaffective patients, and in their biological relatives. *Journal of Clinical Laboratory Analysis, 22*, 314–320. (15)

Nwulia, E. A., Miao, K., Zandi, P. P., Mackinnon, D. F., DePaulo, J. R., Jr., & McInnis, M. G. (2007). Genome-wide scan of bipolar II disorder. *Bipolar Disorders, 9*, 580–588. (15)

Ó Scalaidhe, S. P., Wilson, F. A. W., & Goldman-Rakic, P. S. (1997). Areal segregation of face-processing neurons in prefrontal cortex. *Science, 278*, 1135–1138. (6)

O'Dowd, B. F., Lefkowitz, R. J., & Caron, M. G. (1989). Structure of the adrenergic and related receptors. *Annual Review of Neuroscience, 12*, 67–83. (3)

O'Hara, M. W. (2009). Postpartum depression: What we know. *Journal of Clinical Psychology, 65*, 1258–1269. (15)

Ohira, K., Furuta, T., Hioki, H., Nakamura, K. C., Kuramoto, E., Tanaka, Y., et al. (2010). Ischemia-induced neurogenesis of neocortical layer 1 progenitor cells. *Nature Neuroscience, 13*, 173–179. (5)

Oka, Y., Omura, M., Kataoka, H., & Touhara, K. (2004). Olfactory receptor antagonism between odorants. *The EMBO Journal, 23*, 120–126. (7)

O'Kane, G., Kensinger, E. A., & Corkin, S. (2004). Evidence for semantic learning in profound amnesia: An investigation with patient H. M. *Hippocampus, 14*, 417–425. (13)

O'Keefe, J., & Burgess, N. (1996). Geometric determinants of the place fields of hippocampal neurons. *Nature, 381*, 425–434. (13)

Oláh, S., Füle, M., Komlósi, G., Varga, S., Báldi, R., Barzó, P., et al. (2009). Regulation of microcircuits by unitary GABA-mediated volume transmission. *Nature, 461*, 1278–1281. (3)

Olanow, C. W., Goetz, C. G., Kordower, J. H., Stoessl, A. J., Sossi, V., Brin, M. F., et al. (2003). A double-blind controlled trial of bilateral fetal nigral transplantation in Parkinson's disease. *Annals of Neurology, 54*, 403–414. (8)

Olds, J. (1958). Satiation effects in self-stimulation of the brain. *Journal of Comparative and Physiological Psychology, 51*, 675–678. (3)

Olds, J., & Milner, P. (1954). Positive reinforcement produced by electrical stimulation of the septal area and other regions of the rat brain. *Journal of Comparative and Physiological Psychology, 47*, 419–428. (3)

O'Leary, A. (1990). Stress, emotion, and human immune function. *Psychological Bulletin, 108*, 363–382. (12)

Oler, J. A., Fox, A. S., Shelton, S. E., Rogers, J., Dyer, T. D., Davidson, R. J., et al. (2010). Amygdalar and hippocampal substrates of anxious temperament differ in their heritability. *Nature, 466*, 864–868. (12)

Oliet, S. H. R., Baimouknametova, D. V., Piet, R., & Bains, J. S. (2007). Retrograde regulation of GABA transmission by the tonic release of oxytocin and endocannabinoids governs postsynaptic firing. *Journal of Neuroscience, 27*, 1325–1333. (3)

Olney, J. W., & Farber, N. B. (1995). Glutamate receptor dysfunction and schizophrenia. *Archives of General Psychiatry, 52*, 998–1007. (15)

Olson, D. J., Kamil, A. C., Balda, R. P., & Nims, P. J. (1995). Performance of four seed-caching corvid species in operant tests of nonspatial and spatial memory. *Journal of Comparative Psychology, 109*, 173–181. (13)

Olson, E. J., Boeve, B. F., & Silber, M. H. (2000). Rapid eye movement sleep behaviour disorder: Demographic, clinical and laboratory findings in 93 cases. *Brain, 123*, 331–339. (9)

Olton, D. S., & Papas, B. C. (1979). Spatial memory and hippocampal function. *Neuropsychologia, 17*, 669–682. (13)

Olton, D. S., Walker, J. A., & Gage, F. H. (1978). Hippocampal connections and spatial discrimination. *Brain Research, 139*, 295–308. (13)

Ono, M., Igarashi, T., Ohno, E., & Sasaki, M. (1995). Unusual thermal defence by a honeybee against mass attack by hornets. *Nature, 377*, 334–336. (10)

Ornstein, R. (1997). *The right mind*. New York: Harcourt Brace. (14)

Ostrovsky, Y., Meyers, E., Ganesh, S., Mathur, U., & Sinha, P. (2009). Visual parsing after recovery from blindness. *Psychological Science, 20*, 1484–1491. (6)

Otmakhov, N., Tao-Cheng, J.-H., Carpenter, S., Asrican, B., Dosemici, A., & Reese, T. S. (2004). Persistent accumulation of calcium/calmodulin-dependent protein kinase II in dendritic spines after induction of NMDA receptor-dependent chemical long-term potentiation. *Journal of Neuroscience, 25*, 9324–9331. (13)

Ouchi, Y., Yoshikawa, E., Okada, H., Futatsubashi, M., Sekine, Y., Iyo, M., et al. (1999). Alterations in binding site density of dopamine transporter in the striatum, orbitofrontal cortex, and amygdala in early Parkinson's disease: Compartment analysis for ß-CFT binding with positron emission tomography. *Annals of Neurology, 45*, 601–610. (8)

Owen, A. M., Coleman, M. R., Boly, M., Davis, M. H., Laureys, S., & Pickard, J. D. (2006). Detecting awareness in the vegetative state. *Science, 313*, 1402. (14)

Owen, A. M., Hampshire, A., Grahn, J. A., Stenton, R., Dajani, S., Burns, A. S., et al. (2010). Putting brain training to the test. *Nature, 465*, 775–778. (5)

Oxley, D. R., Smith, K. B., Alford, J. R., Hibbing, M. V., Miller, J. L., Scalora, M., et al. (2008). Political attitudes vary with physiological traits. *Science, 321*, 1667–1670. (12)

Padmos, R. C., Hillegers, M. H. J., Knijff, E. M., Vonk, R., Bouvy, A., Staal, F. J. T., et al. (2008). A discriminating messenger RNA signature for bipolar disorder formed by an aberrant expression of inflammatory genes in monocytes. *Archives of General Psychiatry, 65*, 395–407. (15)

Pakaprot, N., Kim, S., & Thompson, R. F. (2009). The role of the cerebellar interpositus nucleus in short and long term memory for trace eyeblink conditioning. *Behavioral Neuroscience, 123*, 54–61. (13)

Palinkas, L. A. (2003). The psychology of isolated and confined environments. *American Psychologist, 58*, 353–363. (9)

Pallier, P. N., Maywood, E. S., Zheng, Z., Chesham, J. E., Inyushkin, A. N., Dyball, R., et al. (2007). Pharmacological imposition of sleep slows cognitive decline and reverses dysregulation of circadian gene expression in a transgenic mouse model of Huntington's disease. *Journal of Neuroscience, 27*, 7869–7878. (8)

Palop, J. J., Chin, J., & Mucke, L. (2006). A network dysfunction perspective on neurodegenerative diseases. *Nature, 443*, 768–773. (13)

Palva, S., Linkenkaer-Hansen, K., Näätänen, R., & Palva, J. M. (2005). Early neural correlates of conscious somatosensory perception. *Journal of Neuroscience, 25*, 5248–5258. (7)

Pandey, G. N., Pandey, S. C., Dwivedi, Y., Sharma, R. P., Janicak, P. G., & Davis, J. M. (1995). Platelet serotonin-2A receptors: A potential biological marker for suicidal behavior. *American Journal of Psychiatry, 152*, 850–855. (12)

Pandey, S. C., Zhang, H., Ugale, R., Prakash, A., Xu, T., & Misra, K. (2008). Effector intermediate-early gene Arc in the amygdala plays a critical role in alcoholism. *Journal of Neuroscience, 28*, 2589–2600. (3)

Panov, A. V., Gutekunst, C.-A., Leavitt, B. R., Hayden, M. R, Burke, J. R., Strittmatter, W. J., et al. (2002). Early mitochondrial calcium defects in Huntington's disease are a direct effect of polyglutamines. *Nature Neuroscience, 5*, 731–736. (8)

Pardal, R., & López-Barneo, J. (2002). Low glucose-sensing cells in the carotid body. *Nature Neuroscience, 5*, 197–198. (10)

Paré, M., Smith, A. M., & Rice, F. L. (2002). Distribution and terminal arborizations of cutaneous mechanoreceptors in the glabrous finger pads of the monkey. *Journal of Comparative Neurology, 445*, 347–359. (7)

Paredes, R. G., & Vazquez, B. (1999). What do female rats like about sex? Paced mating. *Behavioural Brain Research, 105*, 117–127. (11)

Parent, M. B., Habib, M. K., & Baker, G. B. (1999). Task-dependent effects of the antidepressant/antipanic drug phenelzine on memory. *Psychopharmacology, 142*, 280–288. (9)

Park, I.-H., Zhao, R., West, J. A., Yabuuchi, A., Huo, H., Ince, T. A., et al. (2008). Reprogramming of human somatic cells to pluripotency with defined factors. *Nature, 451*, 141–146. (8)

Park, I. S., Lee, K. J., Han, J. W., Lee, N. J., Lee, W. T., Park, K. A., et al. (2009). Experience-dependent plasticity of cerebellar vermis in basketball players. *Cerebellum, 8,* 334–339. (8)

Park, S., Holzman, P. S., & Goldman-Rakic, P. S. (1995). Spatial working memory deficits in the relatives of schizophrenic patients. *Archives of General Psychiatry, 52,* 821–828. (15)

Parker, G. H. (1922). *Smell, taste, and allied senses in the vertebrates.* Philadelphia: Lippincott. (7)

Parr-Brownlie, L. C., & Hyland, B. I. (2005). Bradykinesia induced by dopamine D$_2$ receptor blockade is associated with reduced motor cortex activity in the rat. *Journal of Neuroscience, 25,* 5700–5709. (8)

Parton, L. E., Ye, C. P., Coppari, R., Enriori, P. J., Choi, B., Zhang, C.-Y., et al. (2007). Glucose sensing by POMC neurons regulates glucose homeostasis and is impaired in obesity. *Nature, 449,* 228–232. (10)

Pascalis, O., Scott, L. S., Kelly, D. J., Shannon, R. W., Nicholson, E., Coleman, M., et al. (2005). Plasticity of face processing in infancy. *Proceedings of the National Academy of Sciences, USA, 102,* 5297–5300. (6)

Pascual, A., Hidalgo-Figueroa, M., Piruat, J. I., Pintado, C. O., Gómez-Díaz, R., & López-Barneo, J. (2008). Absolute requirement of GDNF for adult catecholaminergic neuron survival. *Nature Neuroscience, 11,* 755–761. (5)

Pasterski, V. L., Geffner, M. E., Brain, C., Hindmarsh, P., Brook, C., & Hines, M. (2005). Prenatal hormones and postnatal socialization by parents as determinants of male-typical toy play in girls with congenital adrenal hyperplasia. *Child Development, 76,* 264–278. (12)

Patel, A. D. (2008). *Music, language, and the brain.* New York: Oxford University Press. (14)

Patil, S. T., Zhang, L., Martenyi, F., Lowe, S. L., Jackson, K. A., Andreev, B. V., et al. (2007). Activation of mGlu 2/3 receptors as a new approach to treat schizophrenia: A randomized phase 2 clinical trial. *Nature Medicine,* 1102–1107. (15)

Patston, L. L. M., Corballis, M. C., Hogg, S. L., & Tippet, L. J. (2006). The neglect of musicians: Line bisection reveals an opposite bias. *Psychological Science, 17,* 1029–1031. (14)

Patterson, K., Nestor, P. J., & Rogers, T. T. (2007). Where do you know what you know? The representation of semantic knowledge in the human brain. *Nature Reviews Neuroscience, 8,* 976–987. (13)

Paul, L. K., Brown, W. S., Adolphs, R., Tyszka, J. M., Richards, L. J., Mukherjee, P., et al. (2007). Agenesis of the corpus callosum: Genetic, developmental and functional aspects of connectivity. *Nature Reviews Neuroscience, 8,* 287–299. (14)

Paulesu, E., Frith, U., Snowling, M., Gallagher, A., Morton, J., Frackowiak, R. S. J., et al. (1996). Is developmental dyslexia a disconnection syndrome? *Brain, 119,* 143–157. (14)

Paus, T., Marrett, S., Worsley, K. J., & Evans, A. C. (1995). Extraretinal modulation of cerebral blood flow in the human visual cortex: Implications for saccadic suppression. *Journal of Neurophysiology, 74,* 2179–2183. (6)

Pavlov, I. P. (1927). *Conditioned reflexes.* Oxford, England: Oxford University Press. (13)

Pearson, H. (2006). Freaks of nature? *Nature, 444,* 1000–1001. (8)

Peet, M. (2004). Nutrition and schizophrenia: Beyond omega-3 fatty acids. *Prostaglandins, Leukotrienes and Essential Fatty Acids, 70,* 417–422. (15)

Peeters, R., Simone, L., Nelissen, K., Fabbri-Desstro, M., Vanduffel, W., Rizzolatti, G., & Orban, G. A. (2009). The representation of tool use in humans and monkeys: Common and uniquely human features. *Journal of Neuroscience, 29,* 11523–11539. (1)

Peigneux, P., Laureys, S., Fuchs, S., Collette, F., Perrin, F., Reggers, J., et al. (2004). Are spatial memories strengthened in the human hippocampus during slow wave sleep? *Neuron, 44,* 535–545. (9)

Peleg, G., Katzir, G., Peleg, O., Kamara, M., Brodsky, L., Hel-or, H., et al. (2006). Hereditary family signature of facial expressions. *Proceedings of the National Academy of Sciences, USA, 103,* 15921–15926. (1)

Pelli, D. G., & Tillman, K. A. (2008). The uncrowded window of object recognition. *Nature Neuroscience, 11,* 1129–1135. (6)

Pellis, S. M., O'Brien, D. P., Pellis, V. C., Teitelbaum, P., Wolgin, D. L., & Kennedy, S. (1988). Escalation of feline predation along a gradient from avoidance through "play" to killing. *Behavioral Neuroscience, 102,* 760–777. (12)

Pellymounter, M. A., Cullen, M. J., Baker, M. B., Hecht, R., Winters, D., Boone, T., et al. (1995). Effects of the obese gene product on body weight regulation in *ob/ob* mice. *Science, 269,* 540–543. (10)

Penagos, H., Melcher, J. R., & Oxenham, A. J. (2004). A neural representation of pitch salience in nonprimary human auditory cortex revealed with functional magnetic resonance imaging. *Journal of Neuroscience, 24,* 6810–6815. (7)

Penfield, W. (1955). The permanent record of the stream of consciousness. *Acta Psychologica, 11,* 47–69. (13)

Penfield, W., & Milner, B. (1958). Memory deficit produced by bilateral lesions in the hippocampal zone. *Archives of Neurology and Psychiatry, 79,* 475–497. (13)

Penfield, W., & Perot, P. (1963). The brain's record of auditory and visual experience. *Brain, 86,* 595–696. (13)

Penfield, W., & Rasmussen, T. (1950). *The cerebral cortex of man.* New York: Macmillan. (4, 8)

Penton-Voak, I. S., Perrett, D. I., Castles, D. L., Kobayashi, T., Burt, D. M., Murray, L. K., et al. (1999). Menstrual cycle alters face preference. *Nature, 399,* 741–742. (11)

Pepperberg, I. M. (1981). Functional vocalizations by an African grey parrot. *Zeitschrift für Tierpsychologie, 55,* 139–160. (14)

Pepperberg, I. M. (1993). Cognition and communication in an African grey parrot (*Psittacus erithacus*): Studies on a nonhuman, nonprimate, nonmammalian subject. In H. L. Roitblat, L. M. Herman, & P. E. Nachtigall (Eds.), *Language and communication: Comparative perspectives* (pp. 221–248). Hillsdale, NJ: Erlbaum. (14)

Pepperberg, I. M. (1994). Numerical competence in an African gray parrot (*Psittacus erithacus*). *Journal of Comparative Psychology, 108,* 36–44. (14)

Pepperberg, I. M. (2004). "Insightful" string-pulling in grey parrots (*Psittacus erithacus*) is affected by vocal competence. *Animal Cognition, 7,* 263–266. (14)

Perälä, J., Suvisaari, J., Saarni, S. I., Kuoppasalmi, K., Isometsä, E., Pirkola, S., et al. (2007). Lifetime prevalence of psychotic and bipolar I disorders in a general population. *Archives of General Psychiatry, 64,* 19–28. (15)

Perani, D., & Abutalebi, J. (2005). The neural basis of first and second language processing. *Current Opinion in Neurobiology, 15,* 202–206. (14)

Perera, T. D., Coplan, J. D., Lisanby, S. H., Lipira, C. M., Arif, M., Carpio, C., et al. (2007). Antidepressant-induced neurogenesis in the hippocampus of adult nonhuman primates. *Journal of Neuroscience, 27,* 4894–4901. (15)

Peretz, I., Cummings, S., & Dube, M. P. (2007). The genetics of congenital amusia (tone deafness): A family-aggregation study. *American Journal of Human Genetics, 81,* 582–588. (7)

Perlow, M. J., Freed, W. J., Hoffer, B. J., Seiger, A., Olson, L., & Wyatt, R. J. (1979). Brain grafts reduce motor abnormalities produced by destruction of nigrostriatal dopamine system. *Science, 204,* 643–647. (8)

Pernía-Andrade, A. J., Kato, A., Witschi, R., Nyilas, R., Katona, I., Freund, T. F., et al. (2009). Spinal endocannabinoids and CB$_1$ receptors mediate C-fiber-induced heterosynaptic pain sensitization. *Science, 325,* 760–764. (7)

Perrone, J. A., & Thiele, A. (2001). Speed skills: Measuring the visual speed analyzing properties of primate MT neurons. *Nature Neuroscience, 4,* 526–532. (6)

Pert, C. B. (1997). *Molecules of emotion.* New York: Touchstone. (7)

Pert, C. B., & Snyder, S. H. (1973). The opiate receptor: Demonstration in nervous tissue. *Science, 179,* 1011–1014. (3, 7)

Pesold, C., & Treit, D. (1995). The central and basolateral amygdala differentially mediate the anxiolytic effect of benzodiazepines. *Brain Research, 671,* 213–221. (12)

Peters, F., Nicolson, N. A., Berkhof, J., Delespaul, P., & deVries, M. (2003). Effects of daily events on mood states in major depressive disorder. *Journal of Abnormal Psychology, 112,* 203–211. (15)

Peters, R. H., Sensenig, L. D., & Reich, M. J. (1973). Fixed-ratio performance following ventromedial hypothalamic lesions in rats. *Physiological Psychology, 1,* 136–138. (10)

Peters, R. M., Hackeman, E., & Goldreich, D. (2009). Diminutive digits discern delicate details: Fingertip size and the sex difference in tactile spatial acuity. *Journal of Neuroscience, 29,* 15756–15761. (7)

Peterson, L. R., & Peterson, M. J. (1959). Short-term retention of individual verbal items. *Journal of Experimental Psychology, 58,* 193–198. (13)

Petitto, L. A., Zatorre, R. J., Gauna, K., Nikelski, E. J., Dostie, D., & Evans, A. C. (2000). Speech-like cerebral activity in profoundly deaf people processing signed languages: Implications for the neural basis of human language. *Proceedings of the National Academy of Sciences, USA, 97,* 13961–13966. (14)

Petrovic, P., Kalso, E., Petersson, K. M., & Ingvar, M. (2002). Placebo and opioid analgesia—Imaging a shared neuronal network. *Science, 295,* 1737–1740. (7)

Pfaff, D. W. (2007). *The neuropsychology of fair play.* New York: Dana Press. (12)

Phan, K. L., Wager, T., Taylor, S. F., & Liberzon, I. (2002). Functional neuroanatomy of emotion: A meta-analysis of emotion activation studies in PET and fMRI. *NeuroImage, 16,* 331–348. (12)

Phelps, M. E., & Mazziotta, J. C. (1985). Positron emission tomography: Human brain function and biochemistry. *Science, 228,* 799–809. (4)

Phillips, M. L., Young, A. W., Senior, C., Brammer, M., Andrew, C., Calder, A. J., et al. (1997). A specific neural substrate for perceiving facial expressions of disgust. *Nature, 389,* 495–498. (12)

Pich, E. M., Pagliusi, S. R., Tessari, M., Talabot-Ayer, D., van Huijsduijnen, R. H., & Chiamulera, C. (1997). Common neural substrates for the addictive properties of nicotine and cocaine. *Science, 275,* 83–86. (3)

Pierri, J. N., Volk, C. L. E., Auh, S., Sampson, A., & Lewis, D. A. (2001). Decreased somal size of deep layer 3 pyramidal neurons in the prefrontal cortex of subjects with schizophrenia. *Archives of General Psychiatry, 58,* 466–473. (15)

Pietropaolo, S., Feldon, J., Alleva, E., Cirulli, F., & Yee, B. K. (2006). The role of voluntary exercise in enriched rearing: A behavioral analysis. *Behavioral Neuroscience, 120,* 787–803. (5)

Pillon, B., Ertle, S., Deweer, B., Sarazin, M., Agid, Y., & Dubois, B. (1996). Memory for spatial location is affected in Parkinson's disease. *Neuropsychologia, 34,* 77–85. (8)

Pinker, S. (1994). *The language instinct.* New York: HarperCollins. (14)

Pinto, L., & Götz, M. (2007). Radial glial cell heterogeneity: The source of diverse progeny in the CNS. *Progress in Neurobiology, 83,* 2–23. (2)

Pistoia, F., Conson, M., Trojano, L., Grossi, D., Ponari, M., Colonnese, C., et al. (2010). Impaired conscious recognition of negative facial expressions in patients with locked-in syndrome. *Journal of Neuroscience, 30,* 7838–7844. (12)

Pizzagalli, D. A., Holmes, A. J., Dillon, D. G., Goetz, E. L., Birk, J. L., Bogdan, R., et al. (2009). Reduced caudate and nucleus accumbens response to rewards in unmedicated individuals with major depressive disorder. *American Journal of Psychiatry, 166,* 702–710. (3)

Pizzagalli, D. A., Nitschke, J. B., Oakes, T. R., Hendrick, A. M., Horras, K. A., Larson, C. L., et al. (2002). Brain electrical tomography in depression: The importance of symptom severity, anxiety, and melancholic features. *Biological Psychiatry, 52,* 73–85. (15)

Pizzorusso, T., Medini, P., Berardi, N., Chierzi, S., Fawcett, J. W., & Maffei, L. (2002). Reactivation of ocular dominance plasticity in the adult visual cortex. *Science, 298,* 1248–1251. (6)

Plihal, W., & Born, J. (1997). Effects of early and late nocturnal sleep on declarative and procedural memory. *Journal of Cognitive Neuroscience, 9,* 534–547. (9)

Plomin, R., Corley, R., DeFries, J. C., & Fulker, D. (1990). Individual differences in television viewing in early childhood: Nature as well as nurture. *Psychological Science, 1,* 371–377. (1)

Ploner, M., Gross, J., Timmerman, L., & Schnitzler, A. (2006). Pain processing is faster than tactile processing in the human brain. *Journal of Neuroscience, 26,* 10879–10882. (7)

Plutchik, R. (1982). A psychoevolutionary theory of emotions. *Social Science Information, 21,* 529–553. (12)

Poduslo, S. E., Huang, R., & Spiro, A. III (2009). A genome screen of successful aging without cognitive decline identifies LRP1B by haplotype analysis. *American Journal of Medical Genetics, B, 153B,* 114–119. (1)

Poldrack, R. A., Sabb, F. W., Foerde, K., Tom, S. M., Asarnow, R. F., Bookheimer, S. Y., et al. (2005). The neural correlates of motor skill automaticity. *Journal of Neuroscience, 25,* 5356–5364. (8)

Poling, A., Schlinger, H., & Blakely, E. (1988). Failure of the partial inverse benzodiazepine agonist Ro15-4513 to block the lethal effects of ethanol in rats. *Pharmacology, 31,* 945–947. (12)

Polk, T. A., Drake, R. M., Jonides, J. J., Smith, M. R., & Smith, E. E. (2008). Attention enhances the neural processing of relevant features and suppresses the processing of irrelevant features in humans: A functional magnetic resonance imaging study of the Stroop task. *Journal of Neuroscience, 28,* 13786–13792. (14)

Poncer, J. C., & Malinow, R. (2001). Postsynaptic conversion of silent synapses during LTP affects synaptic gain and transmission dynamics. *Nature Neuroscience, 4,* 989–996. (13)

Pons, T. P., Garraghty, P. E., Ommaya, A. K., Kaas, J. H., Taub, E., & Mishkin, M. (1991). Massive cortical reorganization after sensory deafferentation in adult macaques. *Science, 252,* 1857–1860. (5)

Pontieri, F. E., Tanda, G., Orzi, F., & DiChiara, G. (1996). Effects of nicotine on the nucleus accumbens and similarity to those of addictive drugs. *Nature, 382,* 255–257. (3)

Poo, M.-m. (2001). Neurotrophins as synaptic modulators. *Nature Reviews Neuroscience, 2,* 24–32. (5)

Pope, H. G., Jr., Gruber, A. J., Hudson, J. I., Huestis, M. A., & Yurgelun-Todd, D. (2001). Neuropsychological performance in long-term cannabis users. *Archives of General Psychiatry, 58,* 909–915. (3)

Poremba, A., Saunders, R. C., Crane, A. M., Cook, M., Sokoloff, L., & Mishkin, M. (2003). Functional mapping of the primate auditory system. *Science, 299,* 568–572. (7)

Porter, J., Craven, B., Khan, R. M., Chang, S.-J., Kang, I., Judkewicz, B., et al. (2007). Mechanisms of scent-tracking in humans. *Nature Neuroscience, 10,* 27–29. (7)

Posner, S. F., Baker, L., Heath, A., & Martin, N. G. (1996). Social contact, social attitudes, and twin similarity. *Behavior Genetics, 26,* 123–133. (1)

Post, R. M. (1992). Transduction of psychological stress into the neurobiology of recurrent affective disorder. *American Journal of Psychiatry, 149,* 999–1010. (15)

Post, R. M., & Silberstein, S. D. (1994). Shared mechanisms in affective illness, epilepsy, and migraine. *Neurology, 44*(Suppl 7), S37–S47. (15)

Potegal, M. (1994). Aggressive arousal: The amygdala connection. In M. Potegal & J. F. Knutson (Eds.), *The dynamics of aggression* (pp. 73–111). Hillsdale, NJ: Erlbaum. (12)

Potegal, M., Ferris, C., Hebert, M., Meyerhoff, J. M., & Skaredoff, L. (1996). Attack priming in female Syrian golden hamsters is associated with a *c-fos* coupled process within the corticomedial amygdala. *Neuroscience, 75,* 869–880. (12)

Potegal, M., Hebert, M., DeCoster, M., & Meyerhoff, J. L. (1996). Brief, high-frequency stimulation of the corticomedial amygdala induces a delayed and prolonged increase of aggressiveness in male Syrian golden hamsters. *Behavioral Neuroscience, 110,* 401–412. (12)

Potegal, M., Robison, S., Anderson, F., Jordan, C., & Shapiro, E. (2007). Sequence and priming in 15 month-olds' reactions to brief arm restraint: Evidence for a hierarchy of anger responses. *Aggressive Behavior, 33,* 508–518. (12)

Poulsen, P., Esteller, M., Vaag, A., & Fraga, M. F. (2007). The epigenetic basis of twin discordance in age-related diseases. *Pediatric Research, 61*(5), Part 2, 38R–42R. (1)

Powell, L. H., Calvin, J. E., III, & Calvin, J. E., Jr. (2007). Effective obesity treatments. *American Psychologist, 62,* 234–246. (10)

Premack, A. J., & Premack, D. (1972). Teaching language to an ape. *Scientific American, 227*(4), 92–99. (14)

Preti, G., Cutler, W. B., Garcia, C. R., Huggins, G. R., & Lawley, H. J. (1986). Human axillary secretions influence women's menstrual cycles: The role of donor extract of females. *Hormones and Behavior, 20,* 474–482. (7)

Price, M. P., Lewin, G. R., McIlwrath, S. L., Cheng, C., Xie, J., Heppenstall, P. A., et al. (2000). The mammalian sodium channel BNC1 is required for normal touch sensation. *Nature, 407,* 1007–1011. (7)

Pritchard, T. C., Hamilton, R. B., Morse, J. R., & Norgren, R. (1986). Projections of thalamic gustatory and lingual areas in the monkey, *Macaca fascicularis. Journal of Comparative Neurology, 244,* 213–228. (7)

Pritchard, T. C., Macaluso, D. A., & Eslinger, P. J. (1999). Taste perception in patients with insular cortex lesions. *Behavioral Neuroscience, 113,* 663–671. (7, 14)

Prober, D. A., Rihel, J., Onah, A. A., Sung, R.-J., & Schier, A. F. (2006). Hypocretin/orexin overexpression induces an insomnia-like phenotype in zebrafish. *Journal of Neuroscience, 26,* 13400–13410. (9)

Provine, R. R. (1979). "Wing-flapping" develops in wingless chicks. *Behavioral and Neural Biology, 27,* 233–237. (8)

Provine, R. R. (1981). Wing-flapping develops in chickens made flightless by feather mutations. *Developmental Psychobiology, 14,* 48 B 1–486. (8)

Provine, R. R. (1984). Wing-flapping during development and evolution. *American Scientist, 72,* 448–455. (8)

Provine, R. R. (1986). Yawning as a stereotyped action pattern and releasing stimulus. *Ethology, 72,* 109–122. (8)

Prutkin, J., Duffy, V. B., Etter, L., Fast, K., Gardner, E., Lucchina, L. A., et al. (2000). Genetic variation and inferences about perceived taste intensity in mice and men. *Physiology & Behavior, 69,* 161–173. (7)

Ptak, R., & Schnider, A. (2010). The dorsal attention network mediates orienting toward behaviorally relevant stimuli in spatial neglect. *Journal of Neuroscience, 30,* 12557–12565. (14)

Puca, A. A., Daly, M. J., Brewster, S. J., Matise, T. C., Barrett, J., Shea-Drinkwater, M., et al. (2001). A genome-wide scan for linkage to human exceptional longevity identifies a locus on chromosome 4. *Proceedings of the National Academy of Sciences (U.S.A.), 98,* 10505–10508. (1)

Purcell, D. W., Blanchard, R., & Zucker, K. J. (2000). Birth order in a contemporary sample of gay men. *Archives of Sexual Behavior, 29,* 349–356. (11)

Purves, D., & Hadley, R. D. (1985). Changes in the dendritic branching of adult mammalian neurones revealed by repeated imaging *in situ. Nature, 315,* 404–406. (5)

Purves, D., & Lotto, R. B. (2003). *Why we see what we do: An empirical theory of vision.* Sunderland, MA: Sinauer Associates. (6)

Purves, D., Shimpi, A., & Lotto, R. B. (1999). An empirical explanation of the Cornsweet effect. *Journal of Neuroscience, 19,* 8542–8551. (6)

Putnam, S. K., Du, J., Sato, S., & Hull, E. M. (2001). Testosterone restoration of copulatory behavior correlates with medial preoptic dopamine release in castrated male rats. *Hormones and Behavior, 39,* 216–224. (11)

Queen, T. L., & Hess, T. M. (2010). Age differences in the effects of conscious and unconscious thought in decision making. *Psychology and Aging, 25,* 251–261. (5)

Quraishi, S., & Frangou, S. (2002). Neuropsychology of bipolar disorder: A review. *Journal of Affective Disorders, 72,* 209–226. (15)

Rada, P. V., & Hoebel, B. G. (2000). Supraadditive effect of Δ-fenfluramine plus phentermine on extracellular acetylcholine in the nucleus accumbens: Possible mechanism for inhibition of excessive feeding and drug abuse. *Pharmacology Biochemistry and Behavior, 65,* 369–373. (10)

Radoeva, P. D., Prasad, S., Brainard, D. H., & Aguirre, G. K. (2008). Neural activity within area V1 reflects unconscious visual performance in a case of blindsight. *Journal of Cognitive Neuroscience, 20,* 1927–1939. (6)

Ragsdale, D. S., McPhee, J. C., Scheuer, T., & Catterall, W. A. (1994). Molecular determinants of state-dependent block of Na1 channels by local anesthetics. *Science, 265,* 1724–1728. (2)

Rahman, Q., Kumari, V., & Wilson, G. D. (2003). Sexual orientation-related differences in prepulse inhibition of the human startle response. *Behavioral Neuroscience, 117,* 1096–1102. (11)

Rahman, Q., & Wilson, G. D. (2003). Born gay? The psychobiology of human sexual orientation. *Personality and Individual Differences, 34,* 1337–1382. (11)

Rainville, P., Duncan, G. H., Price, D. D., Carrier, B., & Bushnell, M. C. (1997). Pain affect encoded in human anterior cingulate but not somatosensory cortex. *Science, 277,* 968–971. (7)

Rais, M., Cahn, W., Van Haren, N., Schnack, H., Caspers, E., Hulshoff, H., et al. (2008). Excessive brain volume loss over time in cannabis-using first-episode schizophrenia patients. *American Journal of Psychiatry, 165,* 490–496. (15)

Raj, A., Rifkin, S. A., Andersen, E., & van Oudenaarden, A. (2010). Variability in gene expression underlies incomplete penetrance. *Nature, 463,* 913–918. (1)

Rajkowska, G., Selemon, L. D., & Goldman-Rakic, P. S. (1998). Neuronal and glial somal size in the prefrontal cortex. *Archives of General Psychiatry, 55,* 215–224. (15)

Rakic, P. (1998). Cortical development and evolution. In M. S. Gazzaniga & J. S. Altman (Eds.), *Brain and mind: Evolutionary perspectives* (pp. 34–40). Strasbourg, France: Human Frontier Science Program. (5)

Rakic, P. (2008). Interview. *Nature Reviews Neuroscience, 9,* 893–894. (5)

Rakic, P., & Lidow, M. S. (1995). Distribution and density of monoamine receptors in the primate visual cortex devoid of retinal input from early embryonic stages. *Journal of Neuroscience, 15,* 2561–2574. (6)

Ralph, M. A. L., Cipolotti, L., Manes, F., & Patterson, K. (2010). Taking both sides: Do unilateral anterior temporal lobe lesions disrupt semantic memory? *Brain, 133,* 3243–3255. (13)

Ralph, M. R., Foster, R. G., Davis, F. C., & Menaker, M. (1990). Transplanted suprachiasmatic nucleus determines circadian period. *Science, 247,* 975–978. (9)

Ralph, M. R., & Menaker, M. (1988). A mutation of the circadian system in golden hamsters. *Science, 241,* 1225–1227. (9)

Ramachandran, V. S. (2003, May). Hearing colors, tasting shapes. *Scientific American, 288*(5), 52–59. (7)

Ramachandran, V. S., & Blakeslee, S. (1998). *Phantoms in the brain.* New York: Morrow. (5)

Ramachandran, V. S., & Hirstein, W. (1998). The perception of phantom limbs: The D. O. Hebb lecture. *Brain, 121,* 1603–1630. (5)

Ramirez, J. J. (2001). The role of axonal sprouting in functional reorganization after CNS injury: Lessons from the hippocampal formation. *Restorative Neurology and Neuroscience, 19,* 237–262. (5)

Ramirez, J. J., Bulsara, K. R., Moore, S. C., Ruch, K., & Abrams, W. (1999). Progressive unilateral damage of the entorhinal cortex enhances synaptic efficacy of the crossed entorhinal afferent to dentate granule cells. *Journal of Neuroscience, 19:* RC42, 1–6. (5)

Ramirez, J. J., Campbell, D., Poulton, W., Barton, C., Swails, J., Geghman, K., et al. (2007). Bilateral entorhinal cortex lesions impair acquisition of delayed spatial alternation in rats. *Neurobiology of Learning and Memory, 87,* 264–268. (5)

Ramirez, J. J., McQuilkin, M., Carrigan, T., MacDonald, K., & Kelley, M. S. (1996). Progressive entorhinal cortex lesions accelerate hippocampal sprouting and spare spatial memory in rats. *Proceedings of the National Academy of Sciences, USA, 93,* 15512–15517. (5)

Ramirez-Amaya, V., Marrone, D. F., Gage, F. H., Worley, P. F., & Barnes, C. A. (2006). Integration of new neurons into functional neural networks. *Journal of Neuroscience, 26,* 12237–12241. (5)

Ramón y Cajal, S. *see* Cajal, S. R.

Ranson, S. W., & Clark, S. L. (1959). *The anatomy of the nervous system: Its development and function* (10th ed.). Philadelphia: Saunders. (4)

Rapoport, S. I., & Bosetti, F. (2002). Do lithium and anticonvulsants target the brain arachidonic acid cascade in bipolar patients? *Archives of General Psychiatry, 59,* 592–596. (15)

Rapoport, S. I., & Robinson, P. J. (1986). Tight-junctional modification as the basis of osmotic opening of the blood–brain barrier. *Annals of the New York Academy of Sciences, 481,* 250–267. (2)

Rasch, B., Pommer, J., Diekelmann, & Born, J. (2009). Pharmacological REM sleep suppression paradoxically improves rather than impairs skill memory. *Nature Neuroscience, 12,* 396–397. (9)

Raschle, N. M., Chang, M., & Gaab, N. (2011). Structural brain alterations associated with dyslexia predate reading onset. *NeuroImage, 57,* 742–749. (14)

Rattenborg, N. C., Amlaner, C. J., & Lima, S. L. (2000). Behavioral, neurophysiological and evolutionary perspectives on unihemispheric sleep. *Neuroscience and Biobehavioral Reviews, 24,* 817–842. (9)

Rattenborg, N. C., Mandt, B. H., Obermeyer, W. H., Winsauer, P. J., Huber, R., Wikelski, M., et al. (2004). Migratory sleeplessness in the white-crowned sparrow (*Zonotrichia leucophrys gambelii*). *PLoS Biology, 2,* 924–936. (9)

Raum, W. J., McGivern, R. F., Peterson, M. A., Shryne, J. H., & Gorski, R. A. (1990). Prenatal inhibition of hypothalamic sex steroid uptake by cocaine: Effects on neurobehavioral sexual differentiation in male rats. *Developmental Brain Research, 53,* 230–236. (11)

Rauskolb, S., Zagrebelsky, M., Dreznjak, A., Deogracias, R., Matsumoto, T., Wiese, S., et al. (2010). Global deprivation of brain-derived neurotrophic factor in the CNS reveals an area-specific requirement for dendritic growth. *Journal of Neuroscience, 30,* 1739–1749. (5)

Rayner, K., & Johnson, R. L. (2005). Letter-by-letter acquired dyslexia is due to the serial encoding of letters. *Psychological Science, 16,* 530–534. (14)

Redmond, D. E., Jr., Bjugstad, K. B., Teng, Y. D., Ourednik, V., Ourednik, J., Wakeman, D. R., et al. (2007). Behavioral improvement in a primate Parkinson's model is associated with multiple homeostatic effects of human neural stem cells. *Proceedings of the National Academy of Sciences, USA, 104,* 12175–12180. (8)

Redondo, R. L., & Morris, R. G. M. (2011). Making memories last: The synaptic tagging and capture hypothesis. *Nature Reviews Neuroscience, 12,* 17–30. (13)

Reeves, A. G., & Plum, F. (1969). Hyperphagia, rage, and dementia accompanying a ventromedial hypothalamic neoplasm. *Archives of Neurology, 20,* 616–624. (10)

Refinetti, R. (2000). *Circadian physiology.* Boca Raton, FL: CRC Press. (9)

Refinetti, R., & Carlisle, H. J. (1986). Complementary nature of heat production and heat intake during behavioral thermoregulation in the rat. *Behavioral and Neural Biology, 46,* 64–70. (10)

Refinetti, R., & Menaker, M. (1992). The circadian rhythm of body temperature. *Physiology & Behavior, 51,* 613–637. (9)

Regan, T. (1986). The rights of humans and other animals. *Acta Physiologica Scandinavica, 128*(Suppl. 554), 33–40. (1)

Reichelt, K. L., Seim, A. R., & Reichelt, W. H. (1996). Could schizophrenia be reasonably explained by Dohan's hypothesis on genetic interaction with a dietary peptide overload? *Progress in Neuro-Psychopharmacology & Biological Psychiatry, 20,* 1083–1114. (15)

Reichling, D. B., Kwiat, G. C., & Basbaum, A. I. (1988). Anatomy, physiology, and pharmacology of the periaqueductal gray contribution to antinociceptive controls. In H. L. Fields & J.-M. Besson (Eds.), *Progress in brain research* (Vol. 77, pp. 31–46). Amsterdam: Elsevier. (7)

Reick, M., Garcia, J. A., Dudley, C., & McKnight, S. L. (2001). NPAS2: An analog of clock operative in the mammalian forebrain. *Science, 293,* 506–509. (9)

Reid, C. A., Dixon, D. B., Takahashi, M., Bliss, T. V. P., & Fine, A. (2004). Optical quantal analysis indicates that long-term potentiation at single hippocampal mossy fiber synapses is expressed through increased release probability, recruitment of new release sites, and activation of silent synapses. *Journal of Neuroscience, 24,* 3618–3626. (13)

Reiner, W. G., & Gearhart, J. P. (2004). Discordant sexual identity in some genetic males with cloacal exstrophy assigned to female sex at birth. *New England Journal of Medicine, 350,* 333–341. (11)

Reisner, A. D. (2003). The electroconvulsive therapy controversy: Evidence and ethics. *Neuropsychology Review, 13,* 199–219. (15)

Reiss, A. L., Eckert, M. A., Rose, F. E., Karchemskiy, A., Kesler, S., Chang, M., et al. (2004). An experiment of nature: Brain anatomy parallels cognition and behavior in Williams syndrome. *Journal of Neuroscience, 24,* 5009–5015. (14)

Rennaker, R. L., Chen, C.-F. F., Ruyle, A. M., Sloan, A. M., & Wilson, D. A. (2007). Spatial and temporal distribution of odorant-evoked activity in the piriform cortex. *Journal of Neuroscience, 27,* 1534–1542. (7)

Rensch, B. (1977). Panpsychic identism and its meaning for a universal evolutionary picture. *Scientia, 112,* 337–349. (1)

Rensink, R. A., O'Regan, J. K., & Clark, J. J. (1997). To see or not to see: The need for attention to perceive changes in scenes. *Psychological Science, 8,* 368–373. (14)

Reuter-Lorenz, P., & Davidson, R. J. (1981). Differential contributions of the two cerebral hemispheres to the perception of happy and sad faces. *Neuropsychologia, 19,* 609–613. (12)

Reuter-Lorenz, P. A., & Miller, A. C. (1998). The cognitive neuroscience of human laterality: Lessons from the bisected brain. *Current Directions in Psychological Science, 7,* 15–20. (14)

Revusky, S. (2009). Chemical aversion treatment of alcoholism. In S. Reilly & T. R. Schachtman (Eds.), *Conditioned taste aversion* (pp. 445–472). New York: Oxford University Press. (3)

Reyna, V. F., & Farley, F. (2006). Risk and rationality in adolescent decision making. *Psychological Science in the Public Interest, 7,* 1–44. (5)

Rhee, S. H., & Waldman, I. D. (2002). Genetic and environmental influences on antisocial behavior: A meta-analysis of twin and adoption studies. *Psychological Bulletin, 128,* 490–529. (12)

Rhees, R. W., Shryne, J. E., & Gorski, R. A. (1990). Onset of the hormone-sensitive perinatal period for sexual differentiation of the sexually dimorphic nucleus of the preoptic area in female rats. *Journal of Neurobiology, 21,* 781–786. (11)

Rhodes, J. S., van Praag, H., Jeffrey, S., Girard, I., Mitchell, G. S., Garland, T., Jr., et al. (2003). Exercise increases hippocampal neurogenesis to high levels but does not improve spatial learning in mice bred for increased voluntary wheel running. *Behavioral Neuroscience, 117,* 1006–1016. (5)

Ricciardi, E., Bonino, D., Sani, L., Vecchi, T., Guazzelli, M., Haxby, J. V., et al. (2009). Do we really need vision? How blind people "see" the actions of others. *Journal of Neuroscience, 29,* 9719–9724. (8)

Rice, G., Anderson, C., Risch, N., & Ebers, G. (1999). Male homosexuality: Absence of linkage to microsatellite markers at Xq28. *Science, 284,* 665–667. (11)

Richard, C., Honoré, J., Bernati, T., & Rousseaux, M. (2004). Straight-ahead pointing correlates with long-line bisection in neglect patients. *Cortex, 40,* 75–83. (14)

Richter, C. P. (1922). A behavioristic study of the activity of the rat. *Comparative Psychology Monographs, 1,* 1–55. (9)

Richter, C. P. (1936). Increased salt appetite in adrenalectomized rats. *American Journal of Physiology, 115,* 155–161. (10)

Richter, C. P. (1950). Taste and solubility of toxic compounds in poisoning of rats and humans. *Journal of Comparative and Physiological Psychology, 43,* 358–374. (7)

Richter, C. P. (1967). Psychopathology of periodic behavior in animals and man. In J. Zubin & H. F. Hunt (Eds.), *Comparative psychopathology* (pp. 205–227). New York: Grune & Stratton. (9)

Richter, C. P. (1975). Deep hypothermia and its effect on the 24-hour clock of rats and hamsters. *Johns Hopkins Medical Journal, 136,* 1–10. (9)

Richter, C. P., & Langworthy, O. R. (1933). The quill mechanism of the porcupine. *Journal für Psychologie und Neurologie, 45,* 143–153. (4)

Riddick, N. V., Czoty, P. W., Gage, H. D., Kaplan, J. R., Nader, S. H., Icenhower, M., et al. (2009). Behavioral and neurobiological characteristics influencing social hierarchy formation in female cynomolgus monkeys. *Neuroscience, 158,* 1257–1265. (12)

Ridding, M. C., & Rothwell, J. C. (2007). Is there a future for therapeutic use of transcranial magnetic stimulation? *Nature Reviews Neuroscience, 8,* 559–567. (15)

Riddle, W. J. R., & Scott, A. I. F. (1995). Relapse after successful electroconvulsive therapy: The use and impact of continuation antidepressant drug treatment. *Human Psychopharmacology, 10,* 201–205. (15)

Riemann, D., König, A., Hohagen, F., Kiemen, A., Voderholzer, U., Backhaus, J., et al. (1999). How to preserve the antidepressive effect of sleep deprivation: A comparison of sleep phase advance and sleep phase delay. *European Archives of Psychiatry and Clinical Neuroscience, 249,* 231–237. (15)

Rigori, D., Brass, M., & Sartori, G. (2010). Post-action determinants of the reported time of conscious intentions. *Frontiers in Human Neuroscience, 4,* article 38. (8)

Rimmele, U., Hediger, K., Heinrichs, M., & Klaver, P. (2009). Oxytocin makes a face in memory familiar. *Journal of Neuroscience, 29,* 38–42. (11)

Ringel, B. L., & Szuba, M. P. (2001). Potential mechanisms of the sleep therapies for depression. *Depression and Anxiety, 14,* 29–36. (15)

Rinn, W. E. (1984). The neuropsychology of facial expression: A review of the neurological and psychological mechanisms for producing facial expressions. *Psychological Bulletin, 95,* 52–77. (8)

Risch, N., Herrell, R., Lehner, T., Liang, K.-Y., Eaves, L., Hoh, J., et al. (2009). Interaction between the serotonin transporter gene (5-HTTLPR), stressful life events, and risk of depression. *Journal of the American Medical Association, 301,* 2462–2471. (15)

Rittenhouse, C. D., Shouval, H. Z., Paradiso, M. A., & Bear, M. F. (1999). Monocular deprivation induces homosynaptic long-term depression in visual cortex. *Nature, 397,* 347–350. (6)

Ritz, B., Ascherio, A., Checkoway, H., Marder, K. S., Nelson, L. M., Rocca, W. A., et al. (2007). Pooled analysis of tobacco use and risk of Parkinson's disease. *Archives of Neurology, 64,* 990–997. (8)

Rizzolatti, G., & Sinigaglia, C. (2010). The functional role of the parieto-frontal mirror circuit: Interpretations and misinterpretations. *Nature Reviews Neuroscience, 11,* 264–274. (8)

Ro, T., Shelton, D., Lee, O. L., & Chang, E. (2004). Extrageniculate mediation of unconscious vision in transcranial magnetic stimulation-induced blindsight. *Proceedings of the National Academy of Sciences, USA, 101,* 9933–9935. (4)

Roane, B. M., & Taylor, D. J. (2008). Adolescent insomnia as a risk factor for early adult depression and substance abuse. *Sleep, 31,* 1351–1356. (15)

Robbins, T. W., & Everitt, B. J. (1995). Arousal systems and attention. In M. S. Gazzaniga (Ed.), *The cognitive neurosciences* (pp. 703–720). Cambridge, MA: MIT Press. (9)

Roberson, E. D., & Mucke, E. (2006). 100 years and counting: Prospects for defeating Alzheimer's disease. *Science, 314,* 781–784. (13)

Roberts, L. E., Eggermont, J. J., Caspary, D. M., Shore, S. E., Melcher, J. R., & Kaltenbach, J. A. (2010). Ringing ears: The neuroscience of tinnitus. *Journal of Neuroscience, 30,* 14972–14979. (7)

Roberts, S. C., Gosling, L. M., Carter, V., & Petrie, M. (2008). MHC-correlated odour preferences in humans and the use of oral contraceptives. *Proceedings of the Royal Society B, 275,* 2715–2722. (7)

Robertson, I. H. (2005, Winter). The deceptive world of subjective awareness. *Cerebrum, 7*(1), 74–83. (4)

Robertson, L., Treisman, A., Friedman-Hill, S., & Grabowecky, M. (1997). The interaction of spatial and object pathways: Evidence from Balint's syndrome. *Journal of Cognitive Neuropsychology, 9,* 295–317. (4)

Robillard, T. A. J., & Gersdorff, M. C. H. (1986). Prevention of pre- and perinatal acquired hearing defects: Part I. Study of causes. *Journal of Auditory Research, 26,* 207–237. (7)

Robins Wahlin, T.-B., Lundin, A., & Dear, K. (2007). Early cognitive deficits in Swedish gene carriers of Huntington's disease. *Neuropsychology, 21,* 31–44. (8)

Rochira, V., Balestrieri, A., Madeo, B., Baraldi, E., Faustini-Fustini, M., Granata, A. R. M., et al. (2001). Congenital estrogen deficiency: In search of the estrogen role in human male reproduction. *Molecular and Cellular Endocrinology, 178,* 107–115. (11)

Rodriguez, I., Greer, C. A., Mok, M. Y., & Mombaerts, P. A. (2000). A putative pheromone receptor gene expressed in human olfactory mucosa. *Nature Genetics, 26,* 18–19. (7)

Roenneberg, T., Kuehnle, T., Pramstaller, P. P., Ricken, J., Havel, M., Ricken, J., et al. (2004). A marker for the end of adolescence. *Current Biology, 14,* R1038–R1039. (9)

Roenneberg, T., Kumar, C. J., & Merrow, M. (2007). The human circadian clock entrains to sun time. *Current Biology, 17,* R44–R45. (9)

Roffwarg, H. P., Muzio, J. N., & Dement, W. C. (1966). Ontogenetic development of human sleep-dream cycle. *Science, 152,* 604–609. (9)

Roitman, M. F., Wheeler, R. A., Wightman, R. M., & Carelli, R. M. (2008). Real-time chemical responses in the nucleus accumbens differentiate rewarding and aversive stimuli. *Nature Neuroscience, 11,* 1376–1377. (3)

Rokers, B., Cormack, L. K., & Huk, A. C. (2009). Disparity- and velocity-based signals for three-dimensional motion perception in human MT+. *Nature Neuroscience, 12,* 1050–1055. (6)

Rolls, A., Shechter, R., & Schwartz, M. (2009). The bright side of the glial scar in CNS repair. *Nature Reviews Neuroscience, 10,* 235–241. (5)

Rolls, E. T. (1995). Central taste anatomy and neurophysiology. In R. L. Doty (Ed.), *Handbook of olfaction and gustation* (pp. 549–573). New York: Dekker. (7)

Rolls, E. T. (1996) The representation of space in the primate hippocampus, and its relation to memory. In K. Ishikawa, J. L. McGaugh, & H. Sakata (Eds.), *Brain processes and memory* (pp. 203–227). Amsterdam: Elsevier. (13)

Rome, L. C., Loughna, P. T., & Goldspink, G. (1984). Muscle fiber activity in carp as a function of swimming speed and muscle temperature. *American Journal of Psychiatry, 247,* R272–R279. (8)

Romer, A. S. (1962). *The vertebrate body.* Philadelphia: Saunders. (5)

Romero, E., Cha, G.-H., Verstreken, P., Ly, C. V., Hughes, R. E., Bellen, H. J., et al. (2007). Suppression of neurodegeneration and increased neurotransmission caused by expanded full-length huntingtin accumulating in the cytoplasm. *Neuron, 57,* 27–40. (8)

Rommel, S. A., Pabst, D. A., & McLellan, W. A. (1998). Reproductive thermoregulation in marine mammals. *American Scientist, 86,* 440–448. (10)

Roorda, A., & Williams, D. R. (1999). The arrangement of the three cone classes in the living human eye. *Nature, 397,* 520–522. (6)

Ropelle, E. R., Flores, M. B., Cintra, D. E., Rocha, G. Z., Pauli, J. R., Morar, J., et al. (2010). IL-6 and IL-10 anti-inflammatory activity links exercise to hypothalamic insulin and leptin sensitivity through IKKβ and ER stress inhibition. *PLoS Biology, 8,* e1000465. (10)

Roppel, R. M. (1978). Cancer and mental illness. *Science, 201,* 398. (15)

Rosano, C., Venkatraman, V. K., Guralnik, J., Newman, A. B., Glynn, N. W., Launer, L., et al. (2010). Psychomotor speed and functional brain MRI 2 years after completing a physical activity treatment. *Journals of Gerontology Series A-Biological Sciences and Medical Sciences, 65,* 639–647. (5)

Rose, J. E., Brugge, J. F., Anderson, D. J., & Hind, J. E. (1967). Phase-locked response to low-frequency tones in single auditory nerve fibers of the squirrel monkey. *Journal of Neurophysiology, 30,* 769–793. (7)

Roselli, C. E., Larkin, K., Resko, J. A., Stellflug, J. N., & Stormshak, F. (2004). The volume of a sexually dimorphic nucleus in the ovine medial preoptic area/anterior hypothalamus varies with sexual partner preference. *Endocrinology, 145,* 478–483. (11)

Roselli, C. E., Stadelman, H., Reeve, R., Bishop, C. V., & Stormshak, F. (2007). The ovine sexually dimorphic nucleus of the medial preoptic area is organized prenatally by testosterone. *Endocrinology, 148,* 4450–4457. (11)

Rosen, A. C., Prull, M. W., O-Hara, R., Race, E. A., Desmond, J. E., Glover, G. H., et al. (2002). Variable effects of aging on frontal lobe contributions to memory. *NeuroReport, 13,* 2425–2428. (13)

Rosen, H. J., Perry, R. J., Murphy, J., Kramer, J. H., Mychack, P., Schuff, N., et al. (2002). Emotion comprehension in the temporal variant of frontotemporal dementia. *Brain, 125,* 2286–2295. (12)

Rosenbaum, R. S., Köhler, S., Schacter, D. L., Moscovitch, M., Westmacott, R., Black, S. E., et al. (2005). The case of K. C.: Contributions of a memory-impaired person to memory theory. *Neuropsychologia, 43,* 989–1021. (13)

Rosenblatt, J. S. (1967). Nonhormonal basis of maternal behavior in the rat. *Science, 156,* 1512–1514. (11)

Rosenblatt, J. S. (1970). Views on the onset and maintenance of maternal behavior in the rat. In L. R. Aronson, E. Tobach, D. S. Lehrman, & J. S. Rosenblatt (Eds.), *Development and evolution of behavior* (pp. 489–515). San Francisco: Freeman. (11)

Rosenblatt, J. S., Olufowobi, A., & Siegel, H. I. (1998). Effects of pregnancy hormones on maternal responsiveness, responsiveness to estrogen stimulation of maternal behavior, and the lordosis response to estrogen stimulation. *Hormones and Behavior, 33,* 104–114. (11)

Rosenkranz, K., Butler, K., Williamson, A., & Rothwell, J. C. (2009). Regaining motor control in musician's dystonia by restoring sensorimotor organization. *Journal of Neuroscience, 29,* 14627–14636. (5)

Rosenzweig, M. R., & Bennett, E. L. (1996). Psychobiology of plasticity: Effects of training and experience on brain and behavior. *Behavioural Brain Research, 78,* 57–65. (5)

Ross, D., Choi, J., & Purves, D. (2007). Musical intervals in speech. *Proceedings of the National Academy of Sciences, USA, 104,* 9852–9857. (14)

Ross, E. D., Homan, R. W., & Buck, R. (1994). Differential hemispheric lateralization of primary and social emotions. *Neuropsychiatry, Neuropsychology, and Behavioral Neurology, 7,* 1–19. (12)

Rossi, A. F., Bichot, N. P., Desimone, R., & Ungerleider, L. G. (2007). Top-down attentional deficits in macaques with lesions of lateral prefrontal cortex. *Journal of Neuroscience, 27,* 11306–11314. (14)

Rossi, A. F., Pessoa, L., Desimone, R., & Ungerleider, L. G. (2009). The prefrontal cortex and the executive control of attention. *Experimental Brain Research, 192,* 489–497. (14)

Rossi, D. J., Oshima, T., & Attwell, D. (2000). Glutamate release in severe brain ischaemia is mainly by reversed uptake. *Nature, 403,* 316–321. (5)

Rossi, E. A., & Roorda, A. (2010). The relationship between visual resolution and cone spacing in the human fovea. *Nature Neuroscience, 13,* 156–157. (6)

Rossi, S., Miniussi, C., Pasqualetti, P., Babiloni, C., Rossini, P. M., & Cappa, S. F. (2004). Age-related functional changes of prefrontal cortex in long-term memory: A repetitive transcranial magnetic stimulation study. *Journal of Neuroscience, 24,* 7939–7944. (13)

Rosvold, H. E., Mirsky, A. F., & Pribram, K. H. (1954). Influence of amygdalectomy on social behavior in monkeys. *Journal of Comparative and Physiological Psychology, 47,* 173–178. (12)

Roth, B. L., Willins, D. L., Kristiansen, K., & Kroeze, W. K. (1999). Activation is hallucinogenic and antagonism is therapeutic: Role of 5-HT2A receptors in atypical antipsychotic drug actions. *Neuroscientist, 5,* 254–262. (15)

Rottenberg, J., Kasch, K. L., Gross, J. J., & Gotlib, I. H. (2002). Sadness and amusement reactivity differentially predict concurrent and prospective functioning in major depressive disorder. *Emotion, 2,* 135–146. (15)

Routtenberg, A., Cantallops, I., Zaffuto, S., Serrano, P., & Namgung, U. (2000). Enhanced learning after genetic overexpression of a brain growth protein. *Proceedings of the National Academy of Sciences, USA, 97,* 7657–7662. (13)

Rouw, R., & Scholte, H. S. (2007). Increased structural connectivity in grapheme-color synesthesia. *Nature Neuroscience, 10,* 792–797. (7)

Rovainen, C. M. (1976). Regeneration of Müller and Mauthner axons after spinal transection in larval lampreys. *Journal of Comparative Neurology, 168,* 545–554. (5)

Rowland, D. L., & Burnett, A. L. (2000). Pharmacotherapy in the treatment of male sexual dysfunction. *Journal of Sex Research, 37,* 226–243. (11)

Roy, A., DeJong, J., & Linnoila, M. (1989). Cerebrospinal fluid monoamine metabolites and suicidal behavior in depressed patients. *Archives of General Psychiatry, 46,* 609–612. (12)

Royer, S., & Paré, D. (2003). Conservation of total synaptic weight through balanced synaptic depression and potentiation. *Nature, 422,* 518–522. (13)

Rozin, P., Dow, S., Moscovitch, M., & Rajaram, S. (1998). What causes humans to begin and end a meal? A role for memory for what has been eaten, as evidenced by a study of multiple meal eating in amnesic patients. *Psychological Science, 9,* 392–396. (13)

Rozin, P., & Kalat, J. W. (1971). Specific hungers and poison avoidance as adaptive specializations of learning. *Psychological Review, 78,* 459–486. (10, 13)

Rozin, P., & Pelchat, M. L. (1988). Memories of mammaries: Adaptations to weaning from milk. *Progress in Psychobiology and Physiological Psychology, 13,* 1–29. (10)

Rozin, P., & Schull, J. (1988). The adaptive-evolutionary point of view in experimental psychology. In R. C. Atkinson, R. J. Herrnstein, G. Lindzey, & R. D. Luce (Eds.), *Stevens' handbook of experimental psychology* (2nd ed.): Vol. 1. *Perception and motivation* (pp. 503–546). New York: Wiley (13)

Rubens, A. B., & Benson, D. F. (1971). Associative visual agnosia. *Archives of Neurology, 24,* 305–316. (6)

Rubin, B. D., & Katz, L. C. (2001). Spatial coding of enantiomers in the rat olfactory bulb. *Nature Neuroscience, 4,* 355–356. (7)

Rubinow, M. J., Arseneau, L. M., Beverly, J. L., & Juraska, J. M. (2004). Effect of the estrous cycle on water maze acquisition depends on the temperature of the water. *Behavioral Neuroscience, 118,* 863–868. (10)

Rubinstein, G. (1997). Schizophrenia, rheumatoid arthritis and natural resistance genes. *Schizophrenia Research, 25,* 177–181. (15)

Rudolph, U., Crestani, F., Benke, D., Brünig, I., Benson, J. A., Fritschy, J.-M., et al. (1999). Benzodiazepine actions mediated by specific γ-aminobutyric acidA receptor subtypes. *Nature, 401,* 796–800. (12)

Rudoy, J. D., Voss, J. L., Westerberg, C. E., & Paller, K. A. (2009). Strengthening individual memories by reactivating them during sleep. *Science, 326,* 1079. (9)

Rujescu, D., Giegling, I., Bondy, B., Gietl, A., Zill, P., & Möller, H.-J. (2002). Association of anger-related traits with SNPs in the TPH gene. *Molecular Psychiatry, 7,* 1023–1029. (12)

Rumbaugh, D. M. (Ed.). (1977). *Language learning by a chimpanzee: The Lana Project.* New York: Academic Press. (14)

Rumbaugh, D. M. (1990). Comparative psychology and the great apes: Their competency in learning, language, and numbers. *Psychological Record, 40,* 15–39. (14)

Rupprecht, R., di Michele, F., Hermann, B., Ströhle, A., Lancel, M., Romeo, E., et al. (2001). Neuroactive steroids: Molecular mechanisms of action and implications for neuro-psychopharmacology. *Brain Research Reviews, 37,* 59–67. (11)

Rusak, B., & Zucker, I. (1979). Neural regulation of circadian rhythms. *Physiological Reviews, 59,* 449–526. (9)

Rush, A. J., Trivedi, M. H., Wisniewski, S. R., Stewart, J. W., Nierenberg, A. A., Thase, M. E., et al. (2006). Bupropion-SR, sertraline, or venlaxine-XR after failure of SSRIs for depression. *New England Journal of Medicine, 354,* 1231–1242. (15)

Russell, A. J., Munro, J. C., Jones, P. B., Hemsley, D. R., & Murray, R. M. (1997). Schizophrenia and the myth of intellectual decline. *American Journal of Psychiatry, 154,* 635–639. (15)

Russell, M. J., Switz, G. M., & Thompson, K. (1980). Olfactory influences on the human menstrual cycle. *Pharmacology, Biochemistry, and Behavior, 13,* 737–738. (7)

Rüttiger, L., Braun, D. I., Gegenfurtner, K. R., Petersen, D., Schönle, P., & Sharpe, L. T. (1999). Selective color constancy deficits after circumscribed unilateral brain lesions. *Journal of Neuroscience, 19,* 3094–3106. (6)

Saad, W. A., Luiz, A. C., Camargo, L. A. A., Renzi, A., & Manani, J. V. (1996). The lateral preoptic area plays a dual role in the regulation of thirst in the rat. *Brain Research Bulletin, 39,* 171–176. (10)

Sabel, B. A. (1997). Unrecognized potential of surviving neurons: Within-systems plasticity, recovery of function, and the hypothesis of minimal residual structure. *The Neuroscientist, 3,* 366–370. (5)

Sabo, K. T., & Kirtley, D. D. (1982). Objects and activities in the dreams of the blind. *International Journal of Rehabilitation Research, 5,* 241–242. (4)

Sacco, T., & Sacchetti, B. (2010). Role of secondary sensory cortices in emotional memory storage and retrieval in rats. *Science, 329,* 649–656. (13)

Sack, R. L., & Lewy, A. J. (2001). Circadian rhythm sleep disorders: Lessons from the blind. *Sleep Medicine Reviews, 5,* 189–206. (9)

Sackeim, H. A., Putz, E., Vingiano, W., Coleman, E., & McElhiney, M. (1988). Lateralization in the processing of emotionally laden information: I. Normal functioning. *Neuropsychiatry, Neuropsychology, and Behavioral Neurology, 1,* 97–110. (14)

Sacks, O. (2010, August 30). Face-blind. *The New Yorker, 86*(31), 36–43. (6)

Sadato, N., Pascual-Leone, A., Grafman, J., Deiber, M.-P., Ibañez, V., & Hallett, M. (1998). Neural networks for Braille reading by the blind. *Brain, 121,* 1213–1229. (5)

Sadato, N., Pascual-Leone, A., Grafman, J., Ibañez, V., Deiber, M.-P., Dold, G., et al. (1996). Activation of the primary visual cortex by Braille reading in blind subjects. *Nature, 380,* 526–528. (5)

Sadri-Vakili, G., Kumaresan, V., Schmidt, H. D., Famous, K. R., Chawla, P., Vassoler, F. M., et al. (2010). Cocaine-induced chromatin remodeling increases brain-derived neurotrophic factor transcription in the rat medial prefrontal cortex, which alters the reinforcing efficacy of cocaine. *Journal of Neuroscience, 30,* 11735–11744. (1)

Saha, S., Chant, D., & McGrath, J. (2007). A systematic review of mortality in schizophrenia. *Archives of General Psychiatry, 64,* 1123–1131. (15)

Sahin, N. T., Pinker, S., Cash, S. S., Schomer, D., & Halgren, E. (2009). Sequential processing of lexical, grammatical, and phonological information within Broca's area. *Science, 326,* 445–449. (14)

Sakurai, T. (2007). The neural circuit of orexin (hypocretin): Maintaining sleep and wakefulness. *Nature Reviews Neuroscience, 8,* 171–181. (9)

Salmelin, R., Hari, R., Lounasmaa, O. V., & Sams, M. (1994). Dynamics of brain activation during picture naming. *Nature, 368,* 463–465. (4)

Salthouse, T. A. (2006). Mental exercise and mental aging. *Perspectives on Psychological Science, 1,* 68–87. (5)

Salvatore, P., Ghidini, S., Zita, G., De Panfilis, C., Lambertino, S., Maggini, C., et al. (2008). Circadian activity rhythm abnormalities in ill and recovered bipolar I disorder patients. *Bipolar Disorders, 10,* 256–265. (15)

Sánchez, I., Mahlke, C., & Yuan, J. (2003). Pivotal role of oligomerization in expanded polyglutamine neurodegenerative disorders. *Nature, 421,* 373–379. (8)

Sander, K., & Scheich, H. (2001). Auditory perception of laughing and crying activates human amygdala regardless of attentional state. *Cognitive Brain Research, 12,* 181–198. (12)

Sanders, A. R., Duan, J., Levinson, D. F., Shi, J., He, D., Hou, C., et al. (2008). No significant association of 14 candidate genes with schizophrenia in a large European ancestry sample: Implications for psychiatric genetics. *American Journal of Psychiatry, 165,* 497–506. (15)

Sanders, S. K., & Shekhar, A. (1995). Anxiolytic effects of chlordiazepoxide blocked by injection of GABA$_A$ and benzodiazepine receptor antagonists in the region of the anterior basolateral amygdala of rats. *Biological Psychiatry, 37,* 473–476. (12)

Sanes, J. N., Donoghue, J. P., Thangaraj, V., Edelman, R. R., & Warach, S. (1995). Shared neural substrates controlling hand movements in human motor cortex. *Science, 268,* 1775–1777. (8)

Sanes, J. R. (1993). Topographic maps and molecular gradients. *Current Opinion in Neurobiology, 3,* 67–74. (5)

Sanger, T. D., Pascual-Leone, A., Tarsy, D., & Schlaug, G. (2001). Nonlinear sensory cortex response to simultaneous tactile stimuli in writer's cramp. *Movement Disorders, 17,* 105–111. (5)

Sanger, T. D., Tarsy, D., & Pascual-Leone, A. (2001). Abnormalities of spatial and temporal sensory discrimination in writer's cramp. *Movement Disorders, 16,* 94–99. (5)

Sapolsky, R. M. (1992). *Stress, the aging brain, and the mechanisms of neuron death.* Cambridge, MA: MIT Press. (12)

Sapolsky, R. M. (1998). *Why zebras don't get ulcers.* New York: Freeman. (12)

Satinoff, E. (1964). Behavioral thermoregulation in response to local cooling of the rat brain. *American Journal of Physiology, 206,* 1389–1394. (10)

Satinoff, E. (1991). Developmental aspects of behavioral and reflexive thermoregulation. In H. N. Shanir, G. A. Barr, & M. A. Hofer (Eds.), *Developmental psychobiology: New methods and changing concepts* (pp. 169–188). New York: Oxford University Press. (10)

Satinoff, E., McEwen, G. N., Jr., & Williams, B. A. (1976). Behavioral fever in newborn rabbits. *Science, 193,* 1139–1140. (10)

Satinoff, E., & Rutstein, J. (1970). Behavioral thermoregulation in rats with anterior hypothalamic lesions. *Journal of Comparative and Physiological Psychology, 71,* 77–82. (10)

Sato, M., & Stryker, M. P. (2008). Distinctive features of adult ocular dominance plasticity. *Journal of Neuroscience, 28,* 10278–10286. (6)

Satz, P., & Green, M. F. (1999). Atypical handedness in schizophrenia: Some methodological and theoretical issues. *Schizophrenia Bulletin, 25,* 63–78. (15)

Savage-Rumbaugh, E. S. (1990). Language acquisition in a nonhuman species: Implications for the innateness debate. *Developmental Psychobiology, 23,* 599–620. (14)

Savage-Rumbaugh, E. S., Murphy, J., Sevcik, R. A., Brakke, K. E., Williams, S. L., & Rumbaugh, D. M. (1993). Language comprehension in ape and child. *Monographs of the Society for Research in Child Development, 58*(Serial no. 233). (14)

Savage-Rumbaugh, E. S., Sevcik, R. A., Brakke, K. E., & Rumbaugh, D. M. (1992). Symbols: Their communicative use, communication, and combination by bonobos (*Pan paniscus*). In L. P. Lipsitt & C. Rovee-Collier (Eds.), *Advances in infancy research* (Vol. 7, pp. 221–278). Norwood, NJ: Ablex. (14)

Savic, I., Berglund, H., Gulyas, B., & Roland, P. (2001). Smelling of odorous sex hormone-like compounds causes sex-differentiated hypothalamic activations in humans. *Neuron, 31,* 661–668. (7)

Savic, I., & Lindström, P. (2008). PET and MRI show differences in cerebral asymmetry and functional connectivity between homo- and heterosexual subjects. *Proceedings of the National Academy of Sciences, USA, 105,* 9403–9408. (11)

Sawaguchi, T., & Iba, M. (2001). Prefrontal cortical representation of visuospatial working memory in monkeys examined by local inactivation with muscimol. *Journal of Neurophysiology, 86,* 2041–2053. (13)

Sawamoto, N., Honda, M., Hanakawa, T., Fukuyama, H., & Shibasaki, H. (2002). Cognitive slowing in Parkinson's disease: A behavioral evaluation independent of motor slowing. *Journal of Neuroscience, 22,* 5198–5203. (8)

Schacter, D. L. (1983). Amnesia observed: Remembering and forgetting in a natural environment. *Journal of Abnormal Psychology, 92,* 236–242. (13)

Schaller, M., Miller, G. E., Gervais, W. M., Yager, S., & Chen, E. (2010). Mere visual perception of other people's disease symptoms facilitates a more aggressive immune response. *Psychological Science, 21,* 649–652. (12)

Scheer, F. A. J. L., Wright, K. P., Jr., Kronauer, R. E., & Czeisler, C. A. (2007). Plasticity of the intrinsic period of the human circadian timing system. *PLoS ONE, 8,* e721. (9)

Scheibel, A. B. (1983). Dendritic changes. In B. Reisberg (Ed.), *Alzheimer's Disease* (pp. 69–73). New York: Free Press. (13)

Schenck, C. H., & Mahowald, M. W. (1996). Long-term, nightly benzodiazepine treatment of injurious parasomnias and other disorders of disrupted nocturnal sleep in 170 adults. *American Journal of Medicine, 100,* 333–337. (9)

Schenk, T. (2006). An allocentric rather than perceptual deficit in patient D. F. *Nature Neuroscience, 9,* 1369–1370. (6)

Schenk, T., Mai, N., Ditterich, J., & Zihl, J. (2000). Can a motion-blind patient reach for moving objects? *European Journal of Neuroscience, 12,* 3351–3360. (6)

Scherer, S. S. (1986). Reinnervation of the extraocular muscles in goldfish is nonselective. *Journal of Neuroscience, 6,* 764–773. (5)

Scherrer, G., Imamachi, N., Cao, Y.-Q., Contet, C., Mennicken, F., O'Donnell, D., et al. (2009). Dissociation of the opioid receptor mechanisms that control mechanical and heat pain. *Cell, 137,* 1148–1159. (7)

Schienle, A., Stark, R., Walter, B., Blecker, C., Ott, U., Kirsch, P., et al. (2002). The insula is not specifically involved in disgust processing: An fMRI study. *NeuroReport, 13,* 2023–2026. (12)

Schiff, N. D., Giacino, J. T., Kalmar, K., Victor, J. D., Baker, K., Gerber, M., et al. (2007). Behavioural improvements with thalamic stimulation after severe traumatic brain injury. *Nature, 448,* 600–603. (5)

Schiffman, S. S. (1983). Taste and smell in disease. *New England Journal of Medicine, 308,* 1275–1279, 1337–1343. (7)

Schiffman, S. S., & Erickson, R. P. (1971). A psychophysical model for gustatory quality. *Physiology & Behavior, 7,* 617–633. (7)

Schiffman, S. S., & Erickson, R. P. (1980). The issue of primary tastes versus a taste continuum. *Neuroscience and Biobehavioral Reviews, 4,* 109–117. (7)

Schiffman, S. S., Lockhead, E., & Maes, F. W. (1983). Amiloride reduces the taste intensity of Na1 and Li1 salts and sweeteners. *Proceedings of the National Academy of Sciences, USA, 80,* 6136–6140. (7)

Schiffman, S. S., McElroy, A. E., & Erickson, R. P. (1980). The range of taste quality of sodium salts. *Physiology & Behavior, 24,* 217–224. (7)

Schiller, D., Monfils, M.-H., Raio, C. M., Johnson, D. C., LeDoux, J. E., & Phelps, E. A. (2010). Preventing the return of fear in humans using reconsolidation update mechanisms. *Nature, 463,* 49–53. (12)

Schlack, A., Krekelberg, B., & Albright, T. D. (2007). Recent history of stimulus speeds affects the speed tuning of neurons in area MT. *Journal of Neuroscience, 27,* 11009–11018. (6)

Schlinger, H. D., Jr. (1996). How the human got its spots. *Skeptic, 4,* 68–76. (1)

Schmid, A., Koch, M., & Schnitzler, H.-U. (1995). Conditioned pleasure attenuates the startle response in rats. *Neurobiology of Learning and Memory, 64,* 1–3. (12)

Schmid, M. C., Mrowka, S. W., Turchi, J., Saunders, R. C., Wilke, M., Peters, A. J., et al. (2010). Blindsight depends on the lateral geniculate nucleus. *Nature, 466,* 373–377. (6)

Schmidt, L., Palminteri, S., Lafargue, G., & Pessiglione, M. (2010). Splitting motivation: Unilateral effects of subliminal incentives. *Psychological Science, 21,* 977–983. (14)

Schmidt, L. A. (1999). Frontal brain electrical activity in shyness and sociability. *Psychological Science, 10,* 316–320. (12)

Schmidt-Hieber, C, Jonas, P., & Bischofberger, J. (2004). Enhanced synaptic plasticity in newly generated granule cells of the adult hippocampus. *Nature, 429,* 184–187. (5)

Schmitt, K. C., & Reith, M. E. A. (2010). Regulation of the dopamine transporter. *Annals of the New York Academy of Sciences, 1187,* 316–340. (3)

Schneider, B. A., Trehub, S. E., Morrongiello, B. A., & Thorpe, L. A. (1986). Auditory sensitivity in preschool children. *Journal of the Acoustical Society of America, 79,* 447–452. (7)

Schneider, P., Scherg, M., Dosch, G., Specht, H. J., Gutschalk, A., & Rupp, A. (2002). Morphology of Heschl's gyrus reflects enhanced activation in the auditory cortex of musicians. *Nature Neuroscience, 5,* 688–694. (5)

Schnider, A. (2003). Spontaneous confabulation and the adaptation of thought to ongoing reality. *Nature Reviews Neuroscience, 4,* 662–671. (13)

Schomacher, M., Müller, H. D., Sommer, C., Schwab, S., & Schäbitz, W.-R. (2008). Endocannabinoids mediate neuroprotection after transient focal cerebral ischemia. *Brain Research, 1240,* 213–220. (5)

Schou, M. (1997). Forty years of lithium treatment. *Archives of General Psychiatry, 54,* 9–13. (15)

Schroeder, J. A., & Flannery-Schroeder, E. (2005). Use of herb *Gymnema sylvestre* to illustrate the principles of gustatory sensation: An undergraduate neuroscience laboratory exercise. *Journal of Undergraduate Neuroscience Education, 3,* A59–A62. (7)

Schuckit, M. A., & Smith, T. L. (1996). An 8-year follow-up of 450 sons of alcoholic and control subjects. *Archives of General Psychiatry, 53,* 202–210. (3)

Schuckit, M. C., & Smith, T. L. (1997). Assessing the risk for alcoholism among sons of alcoholics. *Journal of Studies on Alcohol, 58,* 141–145. (3)

Schulkin, J. (1991). *Sodium hunger: The search for a salty taste.* Cambridge, England: Cambridge University Press. (10)

Schurger, A., Pereira, F., Treisman, A., & Cohen, J. D. (2010). Reproducibility distinguishes conscious from nonconscious neural representations. *Science, 327,* 97–99. (14)

Schwab, M. E. (1998). Regenerative nerve fiber growth in the adult central nervous system. *News in Physiological Sciences, 13,* 294–298. (5)

Schwartz, C. E., Wright, C. I., Shin, L. M., Kagan, J., & Rauch, S. L. (2003). Inhibited and uninhibited infants "grown up": Adult amygdalar response to novelty. *Science, 300,* 1952–1953. (12)

Schwartz, G. J. (2000). The role of gastrointestinal vagal afferents in the control of food intake: Current prospects. *Nutrition, 16,* 866–873. (10)

Schwartz, L., & Tulipan, L. (1933). An outbreak of dermatitis among workers in a rubber manufacturing plant. *Public Health Reports, 48,* 809–814. (3)

Schwartz, M. F. (1995). Re-examining the role of executive functions in routine action production.

Annals of the New York Academy of Sciences, 769, 321–335. (8)

Schwartz, W. J., & Gainer, H. (1977). Suprachiasmatic nucleus: Use of 14C-labeled deoxyglucose uptake as a functional marker. *Science, 197,* 1089–1091. (9)

Schweinhardt, P., Seminowicz, D. A., Jaeger, E., Duncan, G. H., & Bushnell, M. C. (2009). The anatomy of the mesolimbic reward system: A link between personality and the placebo analgesic response. *Journal of Neuroscience, 29,* 4882–4887. (7)

Scott, S. H. (2004). Optimal feedback control and the neural basis of volitional motor control. *Nature Reviews Neuroscience, 5,* 532–544. (8)

Scott, W. K., Nance, M. A., Watts, R. L., Hubble, J. P., Koller, W. C., Lyons, K., et al. (2001). Complete genomic screen in Parkinson disease. *Journal of the American Medical Association, 286,* 2239–2244. (8)

Scoville, W. B., & Milner, B. (1957). Loss of recent memory after bilateral hippocampal lesions. *Journal of Neurology, Neurosurgery, and Psychiatry, 20,* 11–21. (13)

Seal, R. P., Wang, X., Guan, Y., Raja, S., Woodbury, C. J., Basbaum, A. I., et al. (2009). Injury-induced mechanical hypersensitivity requires C-low threshold mechanoreceptors. *Nature, 462,* 651–655. (7)

Seeley, R. J., Kaplan, J. M., & Grill, H. J. (1995). Effect of occluding the pylorus on intraoral intake: A test of the gastric hypothesis of meal termination. *Physiology & Behavior, 58,* 245–249. (10)

Seeman, P., Lee, T., Chau-Wong, M., & Wong, K. (1976). Antipsychotic drug doses and neuroleptic/dopamine receptors. *Nature, 261,* 717–719. (15)

Segal, N. L. (2000). Virtual twins: New findings on within-family environmental influences on intelligence. *Journal of Educational Psychology, 92,* 442–448. (1)

Segerstrom, S. C., & Miller, G. E. (2004). Psychological stress and the human immune system: A meta-analytic study of 30 years of inquiry. *Psychological Bulletin, 130,* 610–630. (12)

Sehgal, A., Ousley, A., Yang, Z., Chen, Y., & Schotland, P. (1999). What makes the circadian clock tick: Genes that keep time? *Recent Progress in Hormone Research, 54,* 61–85. (9)

Sejnowski, T. J., & Destexhe, A. (2000). Why do we sleep? *Brain Research, 886,* 208–223. (9)

Selemon, L. D., Rajkowska, G., & Goldman-Rakic, P. S. (1995). Abnormally high neuronal density in the schizophrenic cortex. *Archives of General Psychiatry, 52,* 805–818. (15)

Selkoe, D. J. (2000). Toward a comprehensive theory for Alzheimer's disease. *Annals of the New York Academy of Sciences, 924,* 17–25. (13)

Sellitto, M., Ciaramelli, E., & de Pellegrino, G. (2010). Myopic discounting of future rewards after medial orbitofrontal damage in humans. *Journal of Neuroscience, 30,* 16429–16436. (13)

Selye, H. (1979). Stress, cancer, and the mind. In J. Taché, H. Selye, & S. B. Day (Eds.), *Cancer, stress, and death* (pp. 11–27). New York: Plenum Press. (12)

Selzer, M. E. (1978). Mechanisms of functional recovery and regeneration after spinal cord transection in larval sea lamprey. *Journal of Physiology, 277,* 395–408. (5)

Semendeferi, K., Lu, A., Schenker, N., & Damasio, H. (2002). Humans and great apes share a large frontal cortex. *Nature Neuroscience, 5,* 272–276. (4)

Sen, S., Duman, R., & Sanacora, G. (2008). Serum brain-derived neurotrophic factor, depression, and antidepressant medications: Meta-analyses and implications. *Biological Psychiatry, 64,* 527–532. (15)

Sereno, A. B., & Holzman, P. S. (1993). Express saccades and smooth pursuit eye movement function in schizophrenic, affective disorder, and normal subjects. *Journal of Cognitive Neuroscience, 5,* 303–316. (15)

Sergent, C., & Dehaene, S. (2004). Is consciousness a gradual phenomenon? *Psychological Science, 15,* 720–728. (14)

Serino, A., Pizzoferrato, F., & Làdavas, E. (2008). Viewing a face (especially one's own face) being touched enhances tactile perception on the face. *Psychological Science, 19,* 434–438. (7)

Shackman, A. J., McMenamin, B. W., Maxwell, J. S., Greischar, L. L., & Davidson, R. J. (2009). Right dorsolateral prefrontal cortical activity and behavioral inhibition. *Psychological Science, 20,* 1500–1506. (12)

Shah, B., Shine, R., Hudson, S., & Kearney, M. (2003). Sociality in lizards: Why do thick-tailed geckos (*Nephrurus milii*) aggregate? *Behaviour, 140,* 1039–1052. (10)

Shah, N. M., Pisapia, D. J., Maniatis, S., Mendelsohn, M. M., Nemes, A., & Axel, R. (2004). Visualizing sexual dimorphism in the brain. *Neuron, 43,* 313–319. (11)

Shakelford, T. K., Buss, D. M., & Bennett, K. (2002). Forgiveness or breakup: Sex differences in responses to a partner's infidelity. *Cognition and Emotion, 16,* 299–307. (11)

Shalev, A. Y., Peri, T., Brandes, D., Freedman, S., Orr, S. P., & Pitman, R. K. (2000). Auditory startle response in trauma survivors with posttraumatic stress disorder: A prospective study. *American Journal of Psychiatry, 157,* 255–261. (12)

Shapiro, C. M., Bortz, R., Mitchell, D., Bartel, P., & Jooste, P. (1981). Slow-wave sleep: A recovery period after exercise. *Science, 214,* 1253–1254. (9)

Sharbaugh, S. M. (2001). Seasonal acclimatization to extreme climatic conditions by black-capped chickadees (*Poecile atricapilla*) in interior Alaska (64° N). *Physiological and Biochemical Zoology, 74,* 568–575. (10)

Sharma, J., Angelucci, A., & Sur, M. (2000). Induction of visual orientation modules in auditory cortex. *Nature, 404,* 841–847. (5)

Shatz, C. J. (1992, September). The developing brain. *Scientific American, 267*(9), 60–67. (5)

Shatz, C. J. (1996). Emergence of order in visual-system development. *Proceedings of the National Academy of Sciences, USA, 93,* 602–608. (6)

Shaughnessy, M. F. (2009). An interview with Christian Ambler: Traumatic brain injury in sports. *North American Journal of Psychology, 11,* 297–308. (5)

Sheehan, T. P., Cirrito, J., Numan, M. J., & Numan, M. (2000). Using *c-Fos* immunocytochemistry to identify forebrain regions that may inhibit maternal behavior in rats. *Behavioral Neuroscience, 114,* 337–352. (11)

Shema, R., Sacktor, T. C., & Dudai, Y. (2007). Rapid erasure of long-term memory associations in the cortex by an inhibitor of PKMz. *Science, 317,* 951–953. (13)

Shen, H., Gong, Q. H., Aoki, C., Yuan, M., Ruderman, Y., Dattilo, M., et al. (2007). Reversal of neurosteroid effects at α(β(δ GABA_A receptors triggers anxiety at puberty. *Nature Neuroscience, 10,* 469–477. (12)

Sher, L., Carballo, J. J., Grunebaum, M. F., Burke, A. K., Zalsman, G., Huang, Y.-Y., et al. (2006). A prospective study of the association of cerebrospinal fluid monoamine metabolite levels with lethality of suicide attempts in patients with bipolar disorder. *Bipolar Disorder, 8,* 543–550. (12)

Sherrington, C. S. (1906). *The integrative action of the nervous system* (2nd ed.). New York: Scribner's. New Haven, CT: Yale University Press, 1947. (3)

Sherrington, C. S. (1941). *Man on his nature.* New York: Macmillan. (3)

Shettleworth, S. J. (2009). The evolution of comparative cognition: Is the snark still a boojum? *Behavioural Processes, 80,* 210–217. (1)

Shi, L., Fatemi, S. H., Sidwell, R. W., & Patterson, P. H. (2003). Maternal influenza infection causes marked behavioral and pharmacological changes in the offspring. *Journal of Neuroscience, 23,* 297–302. (15)

Shih, R. A., Belmonte, P. L., & Zandi, P. P. (2004). A review of the evidence from family, twin and adoption studies for a genetic contribution to adult psychiatric disorders. *International Review of Psychiatry, 16,* 260–283. (15)

Shima, K., Isoda, M., Mushiake, H., & Tanji, J. (2007). Categorization of behavioural sequences in the prefrontal cortex. *Nature, 445,* 315–318. (8)

Shimojo, S., Kamitani, Y., & Nishida, S. (2001). Afterimage of perceptually filled-in surface. *Science, 293,* 1677–1680. (6)

Shimura, H., Schlossmacher, M. G., Hattori, N., Frosch, M. P., Trockenbacher, A., Schneider, R., et al. (2001). Ubiquitination of a new form of a-synuclein by parkin from human brain: Implications for Parkinson's disease. *Science, 293,* 263–269. (8)

Shine, R., Phillips, B., Waye, H., LeMaster, M., & Mason, R. T. (2001). Benefits of female mimicry in snakes. *Nature, 414,* 267. (10)

Shiv, B., Loewenstein, G., Bechara, A., Damasio, H., & Damasio, A. R. (2005). Investment behavior and the negative side of emotion. *Psychological Science, 16,* 435–439. (12)

Shohamy, D., Myers, C. E., Hopkins, R. O., Sage, J., & Gluck, M. A. (2009). Distinct hippocampal and basal ganglia contributions to probabilistic learning and reversal. *Journal of Cognitive Neuroscience, 21,* 1821–1833. (13)

Shohamy, D., Myers, C. E., Kalanithi, J., & Gluck, M. A. (2008). Basal ganglia and dopamine contributions to probabilistic category learning. *Neuroscience and Biobehavioral Reviews, 32,* 219–236. (13)

Shoulson, I. (1990). Huntington's disease: Cognitive and psychiatric features. *Neuropsychiatry, Neuropsychology, and Behavioral Neurology, 3,* 15–22. (8)

Shrager, Y., Levy, D. A., Hopkins, R. O., & Squire, L. R. (2008). Working memory and the organization of brain systems. *Journal of Neuroscience, 28,* 4818–4822. (13)

Shubin, N., Tabin, C., & Carroll, S. (2009). Deep homology and the origins of evolutionary novelty. *Nature, 457,* 818–823. (1)

Shutts, D. (1982). *Lobotomy: Resort to the knife.* New York: Van Nostrand Reinhold. (4)

Siderowf, A., & Stern, M. (2003). Update on Parkinson disease. *Annals of Internal Medicine, 138,* 651–658. (4, 8)

Siebert, M., Markowitsch, H. J., & Bartel, P. (2003). Amygdala, affect and cognition: Evidence from 10 patients with Urbach-Wiethe disease. *Brain, 126,* 2627–2637. (12)

Siebner, H. R., Limmer, C., Peinemann, A., Drzezga, A., Bloom, B. R., Schwaiger, M., et al. (2002). Long-term consequences of switching handedness: A positron emission tomography study on handwriting in "converted" left-handers. *Journal of Neuroscience, 22,* 2816–2825. (14)

Siegel, J. M. (1995). Phylogeny and the function of REM sleep. *Behavioural Brain Research, 69,* 29–34. (9)

Siegel, J. M. (2009). Sleep viewed as a state of adaptive inactivity. *Nature Reviews Neuroscience, 10,* 747–753. (9)

Siegel, S. (1983). Classical conditioning, drug tolerance, and drug dependence. *Research Advances in Alcohol and Drug Problems, 9,* 279–314. (3)

Siegel, S. (1987). Alcohol and opiate dependence: Reevaluation of the Victorian perspective. *Research Advances in Alcohol and Drug Problems, 9,* 279–314. (3)

Silber, B. Y., & Schmitt, J. A. J. (2010). Effects of tryptophan loading on human cognition, mood, and sleep. *Neuroscience and Biobehavioral Reviews, 34,* 387–407. (10)

Silbersweig, D. A., Stern, E., Frith, C., Cahill, C., Holmes, A., Grootoonk, S., et al. (1995). A functional neuroanatomy of hallucinations in schizophrenia. *Nature, 378,* 176–179. (15)

Silk, J. B., Brosnan, S. F., Vonk, J., Henrich, J., Povinelli, D. J., Richardson, A. S., et al. (2005). Chimpanzees are indifferent to the welfare of unrelated group members. *Nature, 437,* 1357–1359. (1)

Silva, A. J., Zhou, Y., Rogerson, T., Shobe, J., & Balaji, J. (2009). Molecular and cellular approaches to memory allocation in neural circuits. *Science, 326,* 391–395. (13)

Silver, R. A. (2010). Neuronal arithmetic. *Nature Reviews Neuroscience, 11,* 474–489. (3)

Simner, J., Harrold, J., Creed, H., Monro, L., & Foulkes, L. (2009). Early detection of markers for synaesthesia in childhood populations. *Brain, 132,* 57–64. (7)

Simner, J., & Ward, J. (2006). The taste of words on the tip of the tongue. *Nature, 444,* 438. (7)

Simon, E. (2000). Interface properties of circumventricular organs in salt and fluid balance. *News in Physiological Sciences, 15,* 61–67. (10)

Sincich, L. C., Park, K. F., Wohlgemuth, M. J., & Horton, J. C. (2004). Bypassing V1: A direct geniculate input to area MT. *Nature Neuroscience, 7,* 1123–1128. (6)

Sinclair, J. R., Jacobs, A. L., & Nirenberg, S. (2004). Selective ablations of a class of amacrine cells alters spatial processing in the retina. *Journal of Neuroscience, 24,* 1459–1467. (6)

Singer, T., Seymour, B., O'Doherty, J., Kaube, H., Dolan, R. J., & Frith, C. D. (2004). Empathy for pain involves the affective but not sensory components of pain. *Science, 303,* 1157–1162. (7)

Singh, S., & Mallic, B. N. (1996). Mild electrical stimulation of pontine tegmentum around locus coeruleus reduces rapid eye movement sleep in rats. *Neuroscience Research, 24,* 227–235. (9)

Singleton, A. B., Farrer, M., Johnson, J., Singleton, A., Hague, S., Kachergus, J., et al. (2003). a-synuclein locus triplication causes Parkinson's disease. *Science, 302,* 841. (8)

Sirigu, A., Grafman, J., Bressler, K., & Sunderland, T. (1991). Multiple representations contribute to body knowledge processing. Evidence from a case of autopagnosia. *Brain, 114,* 629–642. (7)

Sirotin, Y. B., Hillman, E. M. C., Bordier, C., & Das, A. (2009). Spatiotemporal precision and hemodynamic mechanism of optical point spreads in alert primates. *Proceedings of the National Academy of Sciences, 106,* 18390–18395. (4)

Sjöström, M., Friden, J., & Ekblom, B. (1987). Endurance, what is it? Muscle morphology after an extremely long distance run. *Acta Physiologica Scandinavica, 130,* 513–520. (8)

Skitzki, J. J., Chen, Q., Wang, W. C., & Evans, S. S. (2007). Primary immune surveillance: Some like it hot. *Journal of Molecular Medicine, 85,* 1361–1367. (10)

Sloan, D. M., Strauss, M. E., & Wisner, K. L. (2001). Diminished response to pleasant stimuli by depressed women. *Journal of Abnormal Psychology, 110,* 488–493. (15)

Slob, A. K., Bax, C. M., Hop, W. C. J., Rowland, D. L., & van der Werff ten Bosch, J. J. (1996). Sexual arousability and the menstrual cycle. *Psychoneuroendocrinology, 21,* 545–558. (11)

Sluming, V., Brooks, J., Howard, M., Downes, J. J., & Roberts, N. (2007). Broca's area supports enhanced visuospatial cognition in orchestral musicians. *Journal of Neuroscience, 27,* 3799–3806. (14)

Smith, C. N., & Squire, L. R. (2009). Medial temporal lobe activity during retrieval of semantic memory is related to the age of the memory. *Journal of Neuroscience, 29,* 930–938. (13)

Smith, D. E., Rapp, P. R., McKay, H. M., Roberts, J. A., & Tuszynski, M. H. (2004). Memory impairment in aged primates is associated with focal death of cortical neurons and atrophy of subcortical neurons. *Journal of Neuroscience, 24,* 4373–4381. (13)

Smith, G. P. (1998). Pregastric and gastric satiety. In G. P. Smith (Ed.), *Satiation: From gut to brain* (pp. 10–39). New York: Oxford University Press. (10)

Smith, G. P., & Gibbs, J. (1998). The satiating effects of cholecystokinin and bombesin-like peptides. In G. P. Smith (Ed.), *Satiation: From gut to*

brain (pp. 97–125). New York: Oxford University Press. (10)

Smith, K. (2007). Looking for hidden signs of consciousness. *Nature, 446,* 355. (14)

Smith, K., Thompson, G. F., & Koster, H. D. (1969). Sweat in schizophrenic patients: Identification of the odorous substance. *Science, 166,* 398–399. (15)

Smith, L. T. (1975). The interanimal transfer phenomenon: A review. *Psychological Bulletin, 81,* 1078–1095. (13)

Smith, M. A., Brandt, J., & Shadmehr, R. (2000). Motor disorder in Huntington's disease begins as a dysfunction in error feedback control. *Nature, 403,* 544–549. (8)

Smith, P. J., Blumenthal, J. A., Hoffman, B. M., Cooper, H., Strauman, T. A., Welsh-Bohmer, K., et al. (2010). Aerobic exercise and neurocognitive performance: A meta-analytic review of randomized controlled trials. *Psychosomatic Medicine, 72,* 239–252. (5)

Smulders, T. V., Shiflett, M. W., Sperling, A. J., & DeVoogd, T. J. (2000). Seasonal changes in neuron numbers in the hippocampal formation of a food-hoarding bird: The black-capped chickadee. *Journal of Neurobiology, 44,* 414–422. (5)

Snitz, B. E., O'Meara, E. S., Carlson, M. C., Arnold, A. M., Ives, D. G., Rapp, S. R., et al. (2009). *Ginkgo biloba* for preventing cognitive decline in older adults: A randomized trial. *Journal of the American Medical Association, 302,* 2663–2670. (13)

Snowling, M. J. (1980). The development of grapheme-phoneme correspondence in normal and dyslexic readers. *Journal of Experimental Child Psychology, 29,* 294–305. (14)

Snyder, L. H., Grieve, K. L., Brotchie, P., & Andersen, R. A. (1998). Separate body- and world-referenced representations of visual space in parietal cortex. *Nature, 394,* 887–891. (8)

Solms, M. (1997). *The neuropsychology of dreams.* Mahwah, NJ: Erlbaum. (9)

Solms, M. (2000). Dreaming and REM sleep are controlled by different brain mechanisms. *Behavioral and Brain Sciences, 23,* 843–850. (9)

Solomon, S. G., & Lennie, P. (2007). The machinery of colour vision. *Nature Reviews Neuroscience, 8,* 276–286. (6)

Somjen, G. G. (1988). Nervenkitt: Notes on the history of the concept of neuroglia. *Glia, 1,* 2–9. (2)

Song, H., Stevens, C. F., & Gage, F. H. (2002). Neural stem cells from adult hippocampus develop essential properties of functional CNS neurons. *Nature Neuroscience, 5,* 438–445. (5)

Soon, C. S., Brass, M., Heinze, H.-J., & Haynes, J.-D. (2008). Unconscious determinants of free decisions in the human brain. *Nature Neuroscience, 11,* 543–545. (8)

Sowell, E. R., Thompson, P. M., Holmes, C. J., Jernigan, T. L., & Toga, A. W. (1999). In vivo evidence for post-adolescent brain maturation in frontal and striatal regions. *Nature Neuroscience, 6,* 309–315. (5)

Spalding, K. L., Bhardwaj, R. D., Buchholz, B. A., Druid, H., & Frisén, J. (2005). Retrospective birth dating of cells in humans. *Cell, 122,* 133–143. (5)

Spangler, R., Wittkowski, K. M., Goddard, N. L., Avena, N. M., Hoebel, B. G., & Leibowitz, S. F.

(2004). Opiate-like effects of sugar on gene expression in reward areas of the rat brain. *Molecular Brain Research, 124,* 134–142. (10)

Speer, N. K., Reynolds, J. R., Swallow, K. M., & Zacks, J. M. (2009). Reading stories activates neural representations of visual and motor experiences. *Psychological Science, 20,* 989–999. (8)

Spelke, E. S. (2005). Sex differences in intrinsic aptitude for mathematics and science? *American Psychologist, 60,* 950–958. (4)

Spencer, R. M. C., Zelaznik, H. N., Diedrichsen, J., & Ivry, R. B. (2003). Disrupted timing of discontinuous but not continuous movements by cerebellar lesions. *Science, 300,* 1437–1439. (8)

Sperry, R. W. (1943). Visuomotor coordination in the newt (*Triturus viridescens*) after regeneration of the optic nerve. *Journal of Comparative Neurology, 79,* 33–55. (5)

Sperry, R. W. (1975). In search of psyche. In F. G. Worden, J. P. Swazey, & G. Adelman (Eds.), *The neurosciences: Paths of discovery* (pp. 425–434). Cambridge, MA: MIT Press. (5)

Spezio, M. L., Huang, P.-Y. S., Castelli, F., & Adolphs, R. (2007). Amygdala damage impairs eye contact during conversations with real people. *Journal of Neuroscience, 27,* 3994–3997. (12)

Spiegel, T. A. (1973). Caloric regulation of food intake in man. *Journal of Comparative and Physiological Psychology, 84,* 24–37. (10)

Spindler, K. A., Sullivan, E. V., Menon, V., Lim, K. O., & Pfefferbaum, A. (1997). Deficits in multiple systems of working memory in schizophrenia. *Schizophrenia Research, 27,* 1–10. (15)

Spreux-Varoquaux, O., Alvarez, J.-C., Berlin, I., Batista, G., Despierre, P.-G., Gilton, A., et al. (2001). Differential abnormalities in plasma 5-HIAA and platelet serotonin concentrations in violent suicide attempters. *Life Sciences, 69,* 647–657. (12)

Spurzheim, J. G. (1908). *Phrenology* (Rev. ed.) Philadelphia: Lippincott. (4)

Squire, L. R. (1992). Memory and the hippocampus: A synthesis from findings with rats, monkeys, and humans. *Psychological Review, 99,* 195–231. (13)

Squires, T. M. (2004). Optimizing the vertebrate vestibular semicircular canal: Could we balance any better? *Physical Review Letters, 93,* 198106. (7)

St George-Hyslop, P. H. (2000). Genetic factors in the genesis of Alzheimer's disease. *Annals of the New York Academy of Sciences, 924,* 1–7. (13)

St. Jacques, P. L., Dolcos, F., & Cabeza, R. (2009). Effects of aging on functional connectivity of the amygdala for subsequent memory of negative pictures. *Psychological Science, 20,* 74–84. (12)

Stalnaker, T. A., Roesch, M. R., Franz, T. M., Calu, D. J., Singh, T., & Schoenbaum, G. (2007). Cocaine-induced decision-making deficits are mediated by miscoding in basolateral amygdala. *Nature Neuroscience, 10,* 949–951. (3)

Stanford, L. R. (1987). Conduction velocity variations minimize conduction time differences among retinal ganglion cell axons. *Science, 238,* 358–360. (2)

Starr, C., & Taggart, R. (1989). *Biology: The unity and diversity of life.* Pacific Grove, CA: Brooks/Cole. (3, 4, 7, 8, 11)

Steeves, J., Dricot, L., Goltz, H. C., Sorger, B., Peters, J., Milner, A. D., et al. (2009). Abnormal face identity coding in the middle fusiform gyrus of two brain-damaged prosopagnosic patients. *Neuropsychologia, 47,* 2584–2592. (6)

Stefansson, H., Rujescu, D., Cichon, S., Pietiläinen, O. P. H., Ingason, A., Steinberg, S., et al. (2008). Large recurrent microdeletions associated with schizophrenia. *Nature, 455,* 232–236. (1)

Stein, M. B., Hanna, C., Koverola, C., Torchia, M., & McClarty, B. (1997). Structural brain changes in PTSD. *Annals of the New York Academy of Sciences, 821,* 76–82. (12)

Steinberg, L., Graham, S., O'Brien, L., Woolard, J., Cauffman, E., & Banich, M. (2009). Age differences in future orientation and delay discounting. *Child Development, 80,* 28–44. (5)

Steiner, T., Ringleb, P., & Hacke, W. (2001). Treatment options for large hemispheric stroke. *Neurology, 57*(Suppl. 2), S61–S68. (5)

Stella, N., Schweitzer, P., & Piomelli, D. (1997). A second endogenous cannabinoid that modulates long-term potentiation. *Nature, 382,* 677–678. (3)

Stephens, T. W., Basinski, M., Bristow, P. K., Bue-Valleskey, J. M., Burgett, S. G., Craft, L., et al. (1995). The role of neuropeptide Y in the anti-obesity action of the obese gene product. *Nature, 377,* 530–532. (10)

Sterpenich, V., D'Argembeau, A., Desseilles, M., Balteau, E., Albouy, G., Vandewalle, G., et al. (2006). The locus coeruleus is involved in the successful retrieval of emotional memories in humans. *Journal of Neuroscience, 26,* 7416–7423. (9)

Stevens, C. F. (2001). An evolutionary scaling law for the primate visual system and its basis in cortical function. *Nature, 411,* 193–195. (6)

Stevens, M., & Cuthill, I. C. (2007). Hidden messages: Are ultraviolet signals a special channel in avian communication? *Bioscience, 57,* 501–507. (6)

Stevens, T., & Karmiloff-Smith, A. (1997). Word learning in a special population: Do individuals with Williams syndrome obey lexical constraints? *Journal of Child Language, 24,* 737–765. (14)

Stewart, J. W., Quitkin, F. M., McGrath, P. J., Amsterdam, J., Fava, M., Fawcett, J., et al. (1998). Use of pattern analysis to predict differential relapse of remitted patients with major depression during 1 year of treatment with fluoxetine or placebo. *Archives of General Psychiatry, 55,* 334–343. (15)

Stickgold, R., Malia, A., Maguire, D., Roddenberry, D., & O'Connor, M. (2000). Replaying the game: Hypnagogic images in normals and amnesics. *Science, 290,* 350–353. (13)

Stocco, A., Lebiere, C., & Anderson, J. R. (2010). Conditional routing of information to the cortex: A model of the basal ganglia's role in cognitive coordination. *Psychological Review, 117,* 541–574. (4)

Stockman, A., & Sharpe, L. T. (1998). Human cone spectral sensitivities: A progress report. *Vision Research, 38,* 3193–3206. (6)

Stokes, M., Thompson, R., Cusack, R., & Duncan, J. (2009). Top-down activation of shape-specific population codes in visual cortex during mental imagery. *Journal of Neuroscience, 29,* 1565–1572. (6)

Stone, V. E., Nisenson, L., Eliassen, J. C., & Gazzaniga, M. S. (1996). Left hemisphere representations of emotional facial expressions. *Neuropsychologia, 34,* 23–29. (14)

Storey, K. B., & Storey, J. M. (1999, May/June). Lifestyles of the cold and frozen. *The Sciences, 39*(3), 33–37. (10)

Stout, A. K., Raphael, H. M., Kanterewicz, B. I., Klann, E., & Reynolds, I. J. (1998). Glutamate-induced neuron death requires mitochondrial calcium uptake. *Nature Neuroscience, 1,* 366–373. (5)

Strack, F., Martin, L. L., & Stepper, S. (1988). Inhibiting and facilitating conditions of the human smile: A nonobtrusive test of the facial feedback hypothesis. *Journal of Personality and Social Psychology, 54,* 768–777. (12)

Stricker, E. M. (1969). Osmoregulation and volume regulation in rats: Inhibition of hypovolemic thirst by water. *American Journal of Physiology, 217,* 98–105. (10)

Stricker, E. M., & Hoffmann, M. L. (2007). Presystemic signals in the control of thirst, salt appetite, and vasopressin secretion. *Physiology & Behavior, 91,* 404–412. (10)

Stricker, E. M., Swerdloff, A. F., & Zigmond, M. J. (1978). Intrahypothalamic injections of kainic acid produce feeding and drinking deficits in rats. *Brain Research, 158,* 470–473. (10)

Strickland, T. L., Miller, B. L., Kowell, A., & Stein, R. (1998). Neurobiology of cocaine-induced organic brain impairment: Contributions from functional neuroimaging. *Neuropsychology Review, 8,* 1–9. (3)

Striemer, C. L., Chapman, C. S., & Goodale, M. A. (2009). "Real-time" obstacle avoidance in the absence of primary visual cortex. *Proceedings of the National Academy of Sciences (U.S.A.), 106,* 15996–16001. (6)

Stroebele, N., de Castro, J. M., Stuht, J., Catenacci, V., Wyatt, H. R., & Hill, J. O. (2008). A small-changes approach reduces energy intake in free-living humans. *Journal of the American College of Nutrition, 28,* 63–68. (10)

Strotmann, J., Levai, O., Fleischer, J., Schwarzenbacher, K., & Breer, H. (2004). Olfactory receptor proteins in axonal processes of chemosensory neurons. *Journal of Neuroscience, 224,* 7754–7761. (7)

Stryker, M. P., & Sherk, H. (1975). Modification of cortical orientation selectivity in the cat by restricted visual experience: A reexamination. *Science, 190,* 904–906. (6)

Stryker, M. P., Sherk, H., Leventhal, A. G., & Hirsch, H. V. B. (1978). Physiological consequences for the cat's visual cortex of effectively restricting early visual experience with oriented contours. *Journal of Neurophysiology, 41,* 896–909. (6)

Studer, L., Tabar, V., & McKay, R. D. G. (1998). Transplantation of expanded mesencephalic precursors leads to recovery in Parkinsonian rats. *Nature Neuroscience, 1,* 290–295. (8)

Stunkard, A. J., Sorensen, T. I. A., Hanis, C., Teasdale, T. W., Chakraborty, R., Schull, W. J., et al.

(1986). An adoption study of human obesity. *New England Journal of Medicine, 314,* 193–198. (10)

Stuss, D. T., & Benson, D. F. (1984). Neuropsychological studies of the frontal lobes. *Psychological Bulletin, 95,* 3–28. (4)

Sullivan, E. V., Deshmukh, A., Desmond, J. E., Mathalon, D. H., Rosenbloom, M. J., Lim, K. O., et al. (2000). Contribution of alcohol abuse to cerebellar volume deficits in men with schizophrenia. *Archives of General Psychiatry, 57,* 894–902. (15)

Sun, H.-S., Jackson, M. F., Martin, L. J., Jansen, K., Teves, L., Cui, H., et al. (2009). Suppression of hippocampal TRPM7 protein prevents delayed neuronal death in brain ischemia. *Nature Neuroscience, 12,* 1300–1307. (5)

Sun, Y.-G., & Chen, Z.-F. (2007). A gastrin-releasing peptide receptor mediates the itch sensation in the spinal cord. *Nature, 448,* 700–703. (7)

Sun, Y.-G., Zhao, Z.-Q., Meng, X.-L., Yin, J., Liu, X.-Y., & Chen, Z. F. (2009). Cellular basis of itch sensation. *Science, 325,* 1531–1534. (7)

Sunaert, S., Van Hecke, P., Marchal, G., & Orban, G. A. (1999). Motion-responsive regions of the human brain. *Experimental Brain Research, 127,* 355–370. (6)

Sur, M., & Leamey, C. A. (2001). Development and plasticity of cortical areas and networks. *Nature Reviews Neuroscience, 2,* 251–262. (6)

Sutton, L. C., Lea, E., Will, M. J., Schwartz, B. A., Hartley, C. E., Poole, J. C., et al. (1997). Inescapable shock-induced potentiation of morphine analgesia. *Behavioral Neuroscience, 111,* 1105–1113. (7)

Sutton, R. L., Hovda, D. A., & Feeney, D. M. (1989). Amphetamine accelerates recovery of locomotor function following bilateral frontal cortex ablation in rats. *Behavioral Neuroscience, 103,* 837–841. (5)

Suvisaari, J. M., Haukka, J. K., Tanskanen, A. J., & Lönnqvist, J. K. (1999). Decline in the incidence of schizophrenia in Finnish cohorts born from 1954 to 1965. *Archives of General Psychiatry, 56,* 733–740. (15)

Suzdak, P. D., Glowa, J. R., Crawley, J. N., Schwartz, R. D., Skolnick, P., & Paul, S. M. (1986). A selective imidazobenzodiazepine antagonist of ethanol in the rat. *Science, 234,* 1243–1247. (12)

Swaab, D. F., & Hofman, M. A. (1990). An enlarged suprachiasmatic nucleus in homosexual men. *Brain Research, 537,* 141–148. (11)

Swan, S. H., Liu, F., Hines, M., Kruse, R. L., Wang, C., Redmon, J. B., et al. (2010). Prenatal phthalate exposure and reduced masculine play in boys. *International Journal of Andrology, 33,* 259–269. (11)

Swithers, S. E., & Davidson, T. L. (2008). A role for sweet taste: Calorie predictive relations in energy regulation by rats. *Behavioral Neuroscience, 122,* 161–173. (10)

Swoboda, E., Conca, A., König, P., Waanders, R., & Hansen, M. (2001). Maintenance electroconvulsive therapy in affective and schizoaffective disorders. *Neuropsychobiology, 43,* 23–28. (15)

Swoboda, H., Amering, M., Windhaber, J., & Katschnig, H. (2003). The long-term course of

panic disorder—an 11 year follow-up. *Journal of Anxiety Disorders, 17,* 223–232. (12)

Syken, J., GrandPre, T., Kanold, P. O., & Shatz, C. J. (2006). PirB restricts ocular-dominance plasticity in visual cortex. *Science, 313,* 1795–1800. (6)

Szymusiak, R. (1995). Magnocellular nuclei of the basal forebrain: Substrates of sleep and arousal regulation. *Sleep, 18,* 478–500. (9)

Tabrizi, S. J., Cleeter, M. W. J., Xuereb, J., Taanman, J.-W., Cooper, J. M., & Schapira, A. H. V. (1999). Biochemical abnormalities and excitotoxicity in Huntington's disease brain. *Annals of Neurology, 45,* 25–32. (8)

Taddese, A., Nah, S. Y., & McCleskey, E. W. (1995). Selective opioid inhibition of small nociceptive neurons. *Science, 270,* 1366–1369. (7)

Tagawa, Y., Kanold, P. O., Majdan, M., & Shatz, C. J. (2005). Multiple periods of functional ocular dominance plasticity in mouse visual cortex. *Nature Neuroscience, 8,* 380–388. (6)

Tager-Flusberg, H., Boshart, J., & Baron-Cohen, S. (1998). Reading the windows to the soul: Evidence of domain-specific sparing in Williams syndrome. *Journal of Cognitive Neuroscience, 10,* 631–639. (14)

Taillard, J., Philip, P., Coste, O., Sagaspe, P., & Bioulac, B. (2003). The circadian and homeostatic modulation of sleep pressure during wakefulness differs between morning and evening chronotypes. *Journal of Sleep Research, 12,* 275–282. (9)

Takahashi, K., Lin, J.-S., & Sakai, K. (2006). Neuronal activity of histaminergic tuberomammillary neurons during wake–sleep states in the mouse. *Journal of Neuroscience, 26,* 10292–10298. (9)

Takahashi, T., Svoboda, K., & Malinow, R. (2003). Experience strengthening transmission by driving AMPA receptors into synapses. *Science, 299,* 1585–1588. (13)

Takano, T., Tian, G.-F., Peng, W., Lou, N., Libionka, W., Han, X., et al. (2006). Astrocyte-mediated control of cerebral blood flow. *Nature Neuroscience, 9,* 260–267. (2)

Takashima, A., Nieuwenhuis, I. L. C., Jensen, O., Talamini, L. M., Rijpkema, M., & Fernández, G. (2009). Shift from hippocampal to neocortical centered retrieval network with consolidation. *Journal of Neuroscience, 29,* 10087–10093. (13)

Takatsuru, Y., Fukumoto, D., Yoshitomo, M., Nemoto, T., Tsukada, H., & Nabekura, J. (2009). Neuronal circuit remodeling in the contralateral cortical hemisphere during functional recovery from cerebral infarction. *Journal of Neuroscience, 29,* 10081–10086. (5)

Takehara-Nishiuchi, K., & McNaughton, B. L. (2008). Spontaneous changes of neocortical code for associative memory during consolidation. *Science, 322,* 960–963. (13)

Tamietto, M., Castelli, L., Vighetti, S., Perozzo, P., Geminiani, G., Weiskrantz, L., et al. (2009). Unseen facial and bodily expressions trigger fast emotional reactions. *Proceedings of the National Academy of Sciences (U.S.A.), 106,* 17661–17666. (6)

Tan, K. R., Brown, M., Laboèbe, G., Yvon, C., Creton, C., Fritschy, J.-M., et al. (2010). Neural bases

for addictive properties of benzodiazepines. *Nature, 463,* 769–774. (12)

Tanaka, J., Hayashi, Y., Nomura, S., Miyakubo, H., Okumura, T., & Sakamaki, K. (2001). Angiotensinergic and noradrenergic mechanisms in the hypothalamic paraventricular nucleus participate in the drinking response induced by activation of the subfornical organ in rats. *Behavioural Brain Research, 118,* 117–122. (10)

Tanaka, J., Hori, K., & Nomura, M. (2001). Dipsogenic response induced by angiotensinergic pathways from the lateral hypothalamic area to the subfornical organ in rats. *Behavioural Brain Research, 118,* 111–116. (10)

Tanaka, K., Sugita, Y., Moriya, M., & Saito, H.-A. (1993). Analysis of object motion in the ventral part of the medial superior temporal area of the macaque visual cortex. *Journal of Neurophysiology, 68,* 128–142. (6)

Tanaka, M., Nakahara, T., Muranaga, T., Kojima, S., Yasuhara, D., Ueno, H., et al. (2006). Ghrelin concentrations and cardiac vagal tone are decreased after pharmacologic and cognitive-behavioral treatment in patients with bulimia nervosa. *Hormones and Behavior, 50,* 261–265. (10)

Tanaka, Y., Kamo, T., Yoshida, M., & Yamadori, A. (1991). "So-called" cortical deafness. *Brain, 114,* 2385–2401. (7)

Tandon, S., Kambi, N., Lazar, L., Mohammed, H., & Jain, N. (2009). Large-scale expansion of the face representation in somatosensory areas of the lateral sulcus after spinal cord injuries in monkeys. *Journal of Neuroscience, 29,* 12009–12019. (5)

Tanji, J., & Shima, K. (1994). Role for supplementary motor area cells in planning several movements ahead. *Nature, 371,* 413–416. (8)

Tanner, C. M., Ottman, R., Goldman, S. M., Ellenberg, J., Chan, P., Mayeux, R., et al. (1999). Parkinson disease in twins: An etiologic study. *Journal of the American Medical Association, 281,* 341–346. (8)

Taravosh-Lahn, K., Bastida, C., & Delville, Y. (2006). Differential responsiveness to fluoxetine during puberty. *Behavioral Neuroscience, 120,* 1084–1092. (12)

Tarr, M. J., & Gauthier, I. (2000). FFA: A flexible fusiform area for subordinate-level visual processing automatized by experience. *Nature Neuroscience, 3,* 764–769. (6)

Tashiro, A., Makino, H., & Gage, F. H. (2007). Experience-specific functional modification of the dentate gyrus through adult neurogenesis: A critical period during an immature stage. *Journal of Neuroscience, 27,* 3252–3259. (5)

Tattersall, G. J., Andrade, D. V., & Abe, A. S. (2009). Heat exchange from the toucan bill reveals a controllable vascular thermal radiator. *Science, 325,* 468–470. (10)

Taub, E., & Berman, A. J. (1968). Movement and learning in the absence of sensory feedback. In S. J. Freedman (Ed.), *The neuropsychology of spatially oriented behavior* (pp. 173–192). Homewood, IL: Dorsey. (5)

Taylor, J. P., Hardy, J., & Fischbeck, K. H. (2002). Toxic proteins in neurodegenerative disease. *Science, 296,* 1991–1995. (13)

Taylor, M. A. (1969). Sex ratios of newborns: Associated with prepartum and postpartum schizophrenia. *Science, 164,* 723–721. (15)

Taziaux, M., Keller, M., Bakker, J., & Balthazart, J. (2007). Sexual behavior activity tracks rapid changes in brain estrogen concentrations. *Journal of Neuroscience, 27,* 6563–6572. (11)

Teff, K. L., Elliott, S. S., Tschöp, M., Kieffer, T. J., Rader, D., Heiman, M., et al. (2004). Dietary fructose reduces circulating insulin and leptin, attenuates postprandial suppression of ghrelin, and increases triglycerides in women. *Journal of Clinical Endocrinology & Metabolism, 89,* 2963–2972. (10)

Teicher, M. H., Glod, C. A., Magnus, E., Harper, D., Benson, G., Krueger, K., et al. (1997). Circadian rest–activity disturbances in seasonal affective disorder. *Archives of General Psychiatry, 54,* 124–130. (15)

Teitelbaum, P. (1961). Disturbances in feeding and drinking behavior after hypothalamic lesions. In M. R. Jones (Ed.), *Nebraska Symposia on Motivation 1961* (pp. 39–69). Lincoln: University of Nebraska Press. (10)

Teitelbaum, P., & Epstein, A. N. (1962). The lateral hypothalamic syndrome. *Psychological Review, 69,* 74–90. (10)

Teitelbaum, P., Pellis, V. C., & Pellis, S. M. (1991). Can allied reflexes promote the integration of a robot's behavior? In J. A. Meyer & S. W. Wilson (Eds.), *From animals to animats: Simulation of animal behavior* (pp. 97–104). Cambridge, MA: MIT Press/Bradford Books. (8)

Temel, Y., Boothman, L. J., Blokland, A., Magill, P. J., Steinbusch, H. W. M., Visser-Vandewalle, V., et al. (2007). Inhibition of 5-HT neuron activity and induction of depressive-like behavior by high-frequency stimulation of the subthalamic nucleus. *Proceedings of the National Academy of Sciences, USA, 104,* 17087–17092. (8)

Terayama, H., Nishino, Y., Kishi, M., Ikuta, K., Itoh, M., & Iwahashi, K. (2003). Detection of anti-Borna virus (BDV) antibodies from patients with schizophrenia and mood disorders in Japan. *Psychiatry Research, 120,* 201–206. (15)

Terman, M., Terman, J. S., & Ross, D. C. (1998). A controlled trial of timed bright light and negative air ionization for treatment of winter depression. *Archives of General Psychiatry, 55,* 875–882. (15)

Terrace, H. S., Petitto, L. A., Sanders, R. J., & Bever, T. G. (1979). Can an ape create a sentence? *Science, 206,* 891–902. (14)

Tetrud, J. W., Langston, J. W., Garbe, P. L., & Ruttenber, A. J. (1989). Mild Parkinsonism in persons exposed to 1-methyl-4-phenyl-1,2,3,6-tetrahydropyridine (MPTP). *Neurology, 39,* 1483–1487. (8)

Teychenne, M., Ball, K., & Salmon, J. (2010). Sedentary behavior and depression among adults: A review. *International Journal of Behavioral Medicine, 17,* 246–254. (15)

Thalemann, R., Wölfling, K., & Grüsser, S. M. (2007). Specific cue reactivity on computer game-related cues in excessive gamers. *Behavioral Neuroscience, 121,* 614–618. (3)

Thanickal, T. C., Moore, R. Y., Nienhuis, R., Ramanathan, L., Gulyani, S., Aldrich, M., et al. (2000). Reduced number of hypocretin neurons in human narcolepsy. *Neuron, 27,* 469–474. (9)

Thapar, A., Fowler, T., Rice, F., Scourfield, J., van den Bree, M., Thomas, H., et al. (2003). Maternal smoking during pregnancy and attention deficit hyperactivity disorder symptoms in offspring. *American Journal of Psychiatry, 160,* 1985–1989. (5)

Thase, M. E., Greenhouse, J. B., Frank, E., Reynolds, C. F., III, Pilkonis, P. A., Hurley, K., et al. (1997). Treatment of major depression with psychotherapy or psychotherapy-psychopharmacology combinations. *Archives of General Psychiatry, 54,* 1009–1015. (15)

Thase, M. E., Trivedi, M. H., & Rush, A. J. (1995). MAOIs in the contemporary treatment of depression. *Neuropsychopharmacology, 12,* 185–219. (15)

Theusch, E., Basu, A., & Gitschier, J. (2009). Genome-wide study of families with absolute pitch reveals linkage to 8q24.21 and locus heterogeneity. *American Journal of Human Genetics, 85,* 112–119. (7)

Thiele, A., Henning, P., Kubischik, K.-P., & Hoffman, K.-P. (2002). Neural mechanisms of saccadic suppression. *Science, 295,* 2460–2462. (6)

Thier, P., Dicke, P. W., Haas, R., & Barash, S. (2000). Encoding of movement time by populations of cerebellar Purkinje cells. *Nature, 405,* 72–76. (8)

Thomas, C., Avidan, G., Humphreys, K., Jung, K., Gao, F., & Behrmann, M. (2009). Reduced structural connectivity in ventral visual cortex in congenital prosopagnosia. *Nature Neuroscience, 12,* 29–31. (6)

Thompson, B. L., Levitt, P., & Stanwood, G. D. (2009). Prenatal exposure to drugs: Effects on brain development and implications for policy and education. *Nature Reviews Neuroscience, 10,* 303–312. (5)

Thompson, R. F. (1986). The neurobiology of learning and memory. *Science, 233,* 941–947. (13)

Ticku, M. K., & Kulkarni, S. K. (1988). Molecular interactions of ethanol with GABAergic system and potential of Ro15-4513 as an ethanol antagonist. *Pharmacology Biochemistry and Behavior, 30,* 501–510. (12)

Timms, B. G., Howdeshell, K. L., Barton, L., Richter, C. A., & vom Saal, F. S. (2005). Estrogenic chemicals in plastic and oral contraceptives disrupt development of the fetal mouse prostate and urethra. *Proceedings of the National Academy of Sciences, USA, 102,* 7014–7019. (11)

Tinbergen, N. (1951). *The study of instinct.* Oxford, England: Oxford University Press. (1)

Tinbergen, N. (1973). The search for animal roots of human behavior. In N. Tinbergen (Ed.), *The animal in its world* (Vol. 2, pp. 161–174). Cambridge, MA: Harvard University Press. (1)

Tingate, T. R., Lugg, D. J., Muller, H. K., Stowe, R. P., & Pierson, D. L. (1997). Antarctic isolation: Immune and viral studies. *Immunology and Cell Biology, 75,* 275–283. (12)

Tishkoff, S. A., Reed, F. A., Ranciaro, A., Voight, B. F., Babbitt, C. C., Silverman, J. S., et al. (2006). Convergent adaptation of human lactase persistence in Africa and Europe. *Nature Genetics, 39,* 31–40. (10)

Tiwari, S. K., & Wang, J. L. (2006). The epidemiology of mental and substance use-related disorders among White, Chinese, and other Asian populations in Canada. *Canadian Journal of Psychiatry, 51,* 904–912. (15)

Tobin, V. A., Hashimoto, H., Wacker, D. W., Takayanagi, Y., Langnaese, K., Caquíneau, C., et al. (2010). An intrinsic vasopressin system in the olfactory bulb is involved in social recognition. *Nature, 464,* 413–417. (11)

Toh, K. L., Jones, C. R., He, Y., Eide, E. J., Hinz, W. A., Virshup, D. M., et al. (2001). An hPer2 phosphorylation site mutation in familial advanced sleep phase syndrome. *Science, 291,* 1040–1043. (9)

Toien, Ø., Blake, J., Edgar, D. M., Grahn, D. A., Heller, H. C., & Barnes, B. M. (2011). Hibernation in black bears: Independence of metabolic suppression from body temperature. *Science, 331,* 906–909. (9)

Tokizawa, K., Yasuhara, S., Nakamura, M., Uchida, Y., Crawshaw, L. I., & Nagashma, K. (2010). Mild hypohydration induced by exercise in the heat attenuates autonomic thermoregulatory responses to the heat, but not thermal pleasantness in humans. *Physiology & Behavior, 100,* 340–345. (10)

Tomchik, S. M., Berg, S., Kim, J. W., Chaudhari, N., & Roper, S. D. (2007). Breadth of tuning and taste coding in mammalian taste buds. *Journal of Neuroscience, 27,* 10840–10848. (7)

Tominaga, M., Caterina, M. J., Malmberg, A. B., Rosen, T. A., Gilbert, H., Skinner, K., et al. (1998). The cloned capsaicin receptor integrates multiple pain-producing stimuli. *Neuron, 21,* 531–543. (7)

Tomo, I., de Monvel, J. B., & Fridberger, A. (2007). Sound-evoked radial strain in the hearing organ. *Biophysical Journal, 93,* 3279–3284. (7)

Tong, Q., Ye, C.-P., Jones, J. E., Elmquist, J. K., & Lowell, B. B. (2008). Synaptic release of GABA by AgRP neurons is required for normal regulation of energy balance. *Nature Neuroscience, 11,* 998–1000. (10)

Toni, N., Buchs, P.-A., Nikonenko, I., Bron, C. R., & Muller, D. (1999). LTP promotes formation of multiple spine synapses between a single axon terminal and a dendrite. *Nature, 402,* 421–425. (13)

Toomey, R., Lyons, M. J., Eisen, S. A., Xian, H., Chantarujikapong, S., Seidman, L. J., et al. (2003). A twin study of the neuropsychological consequences of stimulant abuse. *Archives of General Psychiatry, 60,* 303–310. (3)

Torrey, E. F. (1986). Geographic variations in schizophrenia. In C. Shagass, R. C. Josiassen, W. H. Bridger, K. J. Weiss, D. Stoff, & G. M. Simpson (Eds.), *Biological psychiatry 1985* (pp. 1080–1082). New York: Elsevier. (15)

Torrey, E. F., & Miller, J. (2001). *The invisible plague: The rise of mental illness from 1750 to the present.* New Brunswick, NJ: Rutgers University Press. (15)

Torrey, E. F., Miller, J., Rawlings, R., & Yolken, R. H. (1997). Seasonality of births in schizophrenia and bipolar disorder: A review of the literature. *Schizophrenia Research, 28,* 1–38. (15)

Torrey, E. F., Rawlings, R., & Yolken, R. H. (2000). The antecedents of psychosis: A case-control study of selected risk factors. *Schizophrenia Research, 46,* 17–23. (15)

Torrey, E. F., & Yolken, R. H. (2005). *Toxoplasma gondii* as a possible cause of schizophrenia. *Biological Psychiatry, 57,* 128S. (15)

Toufexis, D. (2007). Region- and sex-specific modulation of anxiety behaviours in the rat. *Journal of Neuroendocrinology, 19,* 461–473. (12)

Townsend, J., Courchesne, E., Covington, J., Westerfield, M., Harris, N. S., Lyden, P., et al. (1999). Spatial attention deficits in patients with acquired or developmental cerebellar abnormality. *Journal of Neuroscience, 19,* 5632–5643. (8)

Tran, P. B., & Miller, R. J. (2003). Chemokine receptors: Signposts to brain development and disease. *Nature Reviews Neuroscience, 4,* 444–455. (5)

Tranel, D., & Damasio, A. (1993). The covert learning of affective valence does not require structures in hippocampal system or amygdala. *Journal of Cognitive Neuroscience, 5,* 79–88. (13)

Travers, S. P., Pfaffmann, C., & Norgren, R. (1986). Convergence of lingual and palatal gustatory neural activity in the nucleus of the solitary tract. *Brain Research, 365,* 305–320. (7)

Trefilov, A., Berard, J., Krawczak, M., & Schmidtke, J. (2000). Natal dispersal in rhesus macaques is related to serotonin transporter gene promoter variation. *Behavior Genetics, 30,* 295–301. (12)

Treisman, A. (1999). Feature binding, attention and object perception. In G. W. Humphreys, J. Duncan, & A. Treisman (Eds.), *Attention, space, and action* (pp. 91–111). Oxford, England: Oxford University Press. (4)

Trevena, J. A., & Miller, J. (2002). Cortical movement preparation before and after a conscious decision to move. *Consciousness and Cognition, 11,* 162–190. (8)

Trim, R. S., Schuckit, M. A., & Smith, T. L. (2009). The relationships of the level of response to alcohol and additional characteristics to alcohol use disorders across adulthood: A discrete-time survival analysis. *Alcoholism—Clinical and Experimental Research, 33,* 1562–1570. (3)

Trimble, M. R., & Thompson, P. J. (1986). Neuropsychological and behavioral sequelae of spontaneous seizures. *Annals of the New York Academy of Sciences, 462,* 284–292. (15)

Trinh, K., Andrews, L., Krause, J., Hanak, T., Lee, D., Gelb, M., et al. (2010). Decaffeinated coffee and nicotine-free tobacco provide neuroprotection in *Drosophila* models of Parkinson's disease through an NRF2-dependent mechanism. *Journal of Neuroscience, 30,* 5525–5532. (8)

Trivedi, M. H., Fava, M., Wisniewski, S. R., Thase, M. E., Quitlein, F., Warden, D., et al. (2006). Medication augmentation after failure of SSRIs for depression. *New England Journal of Medicine, 354,* 1243–1252. (15)

Trivers, R. L. (1985). *Social evolution.* Menlo Park, CA: Benjamin/Cummings. (1)

Trudel, E., & Bourque, C. W. (2010). Central clock excites vasopressin neurons by waking osmosensory afferents during late sleep. *Nature Neuroscience, 13,* 467–474. (10)

Tsai, G., Passani, L. A., Slusher, B. S., Carter, R., Baer, L., Kleinman, J. E., et al. (1995). Abnormal excitatory neurotransmitter metabolism in schizophrenic brains. *Archives of General Psychiatry, 52,* 829–836. (15)

Tsai, G. E., Ragan, P., Chang, R., Chen, S., Linnoila, M. I., & Coyle, J. T. (1998). Increased glutamatergic neurotransmission and oxidative stress after alcohol withdrawal. *American Journal of Psychiatry, 155,* 726–732. (3)

Tsankova, N., Renthal, W., Kumar, A., & Nestler, E. J. (2007). Epigenetic regulation in psychiatric disorders. *Nature Reviews Neuroscience, 8,* 355–367. (1)

Ts'o, D. Y., & Roe, A. W. (1995). Functional compartments in visual cortex: Segregation and interaction. In M. S. Gazzaniga (Ed.), *The cognitive neurosciences* (pp. 325–337). Cambridge, MA: MIT Press. (6)

Tsujita, T., Niikawa, N., Yamashita, H., Imamura, A., Hamada, A., Nakane, Y., et al. (1998). Genomic discordance between monozygotic twins discordant for schizophrenia. *American Journal of Psychiatry, 155,* 422–424. (15)

Tu, Y., Kroener, S., Abernathy, K., Lapish, C., Seamans, J., Chandler, L. J., et al. (2007). Ethanol inhibits persistent activity in prefrontal cortical neurons. *Journal of Neuroscience, 27,* 4765–4775. (3)

Tucker, D. M., Luu, P., & Pribram, K. H. (1995). Social and emotional self-regulation. *Annals of the New York Academy of Sciences, 769,* 213–239. (8)

Tups, A. (2009). Physiological models of leptin resistance. *Journal of Neuroendocrinology, 21,* 961–971. (10)

Turk, D. J., Heatherton, T. F., Kelley, W. M., Funnell, M. G., Gazzaniga, M. S., & Macrae, C. N. (2002). Mike or me? Self-recognition in a split-brain patient. *Nature Neuroscience, 5,* 841–842. (14)

Turner, R. S., & Anderson, M. E. (2005). Context-dependent modulation of movement-related discharge in the primate globus pallidus. *Journal of Neuroscience, 25,* 2965–2976. (8)

Twenge, J. M., & Nolen-Hoeksema, S. (2002). Age, gender, race, socioeconomic status, and birth cohort differences on the children's depression inventory: A meta-analysis. *Journal of Abnormal Psychology, 111,* 578–588. (15)

Tye, K. M., Tye, L. D., Cone, J. J., Hekkelman, E. F., Janak, P. H., & Bonci, A. (2010). Methylphenidate facilitates learning-induced amygdala plasticity. *Nature Neuroscience, 13,* 475–481. (13)

Uchida, N., Takahashi, Y. K., Tanifuji, M., & Mori, K., (2000). Odor maps in the mammalian olfactory bulb: Domain organization and odorant structural features. *Nature Neuroscience, 3,* 1035–1043. (7)

Udry, J. R., & Chantala, K. (2006). Masculinity–femininity predicts sexual orientation in men but not in women. *Journal of Biosocial Science, 38,* 797–809. (11)

Udry, J. R., & Morris, N. M. (1968). Distribution of coitus in the menstrual cycle. *Nature, 220,* 593–596. (11)

Uekita, T., & Okaichi, H. (2005). NMDA antagonist MK-801 does not interfere with the use of spatial representation in a familiar environment. *Behavioral Neuroscience, 119,* 548–556. (13)

Uhr, M., Tontsch, A., Namendorf, C., Ripke, S., Lucae, S., Ising, M., et al. (2008). Polymorphisms in the drug transporter gene *ABCBx* predict antidepressant treatment response in depression. *Neuron, 57,* 203–209. (15)

Unkelbach, C., Guastella, A. J., & Forgas, J. P. (2008). Oxytocin selectively facilitates recognition of positive sex and relationship words. *Psychological Science, 19,* 1092–1094. (11)

Unterberg, A. W., Stover, J., Kress, B., & Kiening, K. L. (2004). Edema and brain trauma. *Neuroscience, 129,* 1021–1029. (5)

Urry, H. L., Nitschke, J. B., Dolski, I., Jackson, D. C., Dalton, K. M., Mueller, C. J., et al. (2004). Making a life worth living: Neural correlates of well-being. *Psychological Science, 15,* 367–372. (12)

U.S.–Venezuela Collaborative Research Project. (2004). Venezuelan kindreds reveal that genetic and environmental factors modulate Huntington's disease age of onset. *Proceedings of the National Academy of Sciences, USA, 101,* 3498–3503. (8)

Uwano, T., Nishijo, H., Ono, T., & Tamura, R. (1995). Neuronal responsiveness to various sensory stimuli, and associative learning in the rat amygdala. *Neuroscience, 68,* 339–361. (12)

Vaishnavi, S., Calhoun, J., & Chatterjee, A. (2001). Binding personal and peripersonal space: Evidence from tactile extinction. *Journal of Cognitive Neuroscience, 13,* 181–189. (14)

Valente, E. M., Abou-Sleiman, P. M., Caputo, V., Muquit, M. M. K., Harvey, K., Gispert, S., et al. (2004). Hereditary early-onset Parkinson's disease caused by mutations in *PINKx. Science, 304,* 1158–1160. (8)

Valli, I., Stone, J., Mechelli, A., Bhattacharyya, S., Raffin, M., Allen, P., et al. (2011). Altered medial temporal activation related to local glutamate levels in subjects with prodromal signs of psychosis. *Biological Psychiatry, 69,* 97–99. (15)

Vallines, I., & Greenlee, M. W. (2006). Saccadic suppression of retinotopically localized blood oxygen level-dependent responses in human primary visual area V1. *Journal of Neuroscience, 26,* 5965–5969. (6)

Valzelli, L. (1973). The "isolation syndrome" in mice. *Psychopharmacologia, 31,* 305–320. (12)

Valzelli, L. (1980). *An approach to neuroanatomical and neurochemical psychophysiology.* Torino, Italy: C. G. Edizioni Medico Scientifiche. (10, 15)

Valzelli, L., & Bernasconi, S. (1979). Aggressiveness by isolation and brain serotonin turnover changes in different strains of mice. *Neuropsychobiology, 5,* 129–135. (12)

van Anders, S. M., Brotto, L., Farrell, J., & Yule, M. (2009). Associations among physiological and subjective sexual response, sexual desire, and salivary steroid hormones in healthy premenopausal women. *Journal of Sex Medicine, 6,* 739–751. (11)

van Anders, S. M., & Goldey, K. L. (2010). Testosterone and parnering are linked via relationship status for women and "relationship orientation" for men. *Hormones and Behavior, 58,* 820–826. (11)

van Anders, S. M., Hamilton, L. D., Schmidt, N., & Watson N. V. (2007). Associations between testosterone secretin and sexual activity in women. *Hormones and Behavior, 51,* 477–482. (11)

van Anders, S. M., Hamilton, L. D., & Watson, N. V. (2007). Multiple partners are associated with higher testosterone in North American men and women. *Hormones and Behavior, 51,* 454–459. (11)

van Anders, S. M., & Watson, N. V. (2006). Relationship status and testosterone in North American heterosexual and non-heterosexual men and women: Cross-sectional and longitudinal data. *Psychoneuroendocrinology, 31,* 715–723. (11)

Van Cantfort, T. E., Gardner, B. T., & Gardner, R. A. (1989). Developmental trends in replies to Wh- questions by children and chimpanzees. In R. A. Gardner, B. T. Gardner, & T. E. Van Cantfort (Eds.), *Teaching sign language to chimpanzees* (pp. 198–239). Albany: State University of New York Press. (14)

van den Heuvel, M. P., Mandl, R. C. W., Stam, C. J., Kahn, R. S., & Pol, H. E. H. (2010). Aberrant frontal and temporal complex network structure in schizophrenia: A graph theoretical analysis. *Journal of Neuroscience, 30,* 15915–15926. (15)

van den Pol, A. N. (1999). Hypothalamic hypocretin (orexin): Robust innervation of the spinal cord. *Journal of Neuroscience, 19,* 3171–3182. (10)

Van der Borght, K., Havekes, R., Bos, T., Eggen, B. J. L., & Van der Zee, E. A. (2007). Exercise improves memory acquisition and retrieval in the Y-maze task: Relationship with hippocampal neurogenesis. *Behavioral Neuroscience, 121,* 324–334. (5)

Van der Does, A. J. W. (2001). The effects of tryptophan depletion on mood and psychiatric symptoms. *Journal of Affective Disorders, 64,* 107–119. (12)

van der Vegt, B. J., Lieuwes, N., van de Wall, E. H. E. M., Kato, K., Moya-Albiol, L., Martínez-Sanchis, W., et al. (2003). Activation of serotonergic neurotransmission during the performance of aggressive behavior in rats. *Behavioral Neuroscience, 117,* 667–674. (12)

Van Essen, D. C., & DeYoe, E. A. (1995). Concurrent processing in the primate visual cortex. In M. S. Gazzaniga (Ed.), *The cognitive neurosciences* (pp. 383–400). Cambridge, MA: MIT Press. (6)

van Honk, J., Harmon-Jones, E., Morgan, B. E., & Schutter, D. J. L. G. (2010). Socially explosive minds: The triple imbalance hypothesis of reactive aggression. *Journal of Personality, 78,* 69–94. (12)

van Honk, J., & Schutter, D. J. L. G. (2007). Testosterone reduces conscious detection of signals serving social correction. *Psychological Science, 18,* 663–667. (12)

van Leeuwen, M., Peper, J. S., van den Berg, S. M., Brouwer, R. M., Pol, H. E. H., Kahn, R. S., et al. (2009). A genetic analysis of brain volumes and IQ in children. *Intelligence, 37,* 181–191. (4)

van Meer, M. P. A., van der Marel, K., Wang, K., Otte, W. M., el Bouzati, S., Roeling, T. A. P., et al. (2010). Recovery of sensorimotor function after experimental stroke correlates with restoration of resting-state interhemispheric functional activity. *Journal of Neuroscience, 30,* 3964–3972. (5)

van Praag, H., Kempermann, G., & Gage, F. H. (1999). Running increases cell proliferation and neurogenesis in the adult mouse dentate gyrus. *Nature Neuroscience, 2,* 266–270. (5)

van Praag, H., Schinder, A. F., Christie, B. R., Toni, N., Palmer, T. D., & Gage, F. H. (2002). Functional neurogenesis in the adult hippocampus. *Nature, 415,* 1030–1034. (5)

Van Wanrooij, M. M., & Van Opstal, A. J. (2004). Contribution of head shadow and pinna cues to chronic monaural sound localization. *Journal of Neuroscience, 24,* 4163–4171. (7)

Van Wanrooij, M. M., & Van Opstal, A. J. (2005). Relearning sound localization with a new ear. *Journal of Neuroscience, 25,* 5413–5424. (7)

Van Zoeren, J. G., & Stricker, E. M. (1977). Effects of preoptic, lateral hypothalamic, or dopamine-depleting lesions on behavioral thermoregulation in rats exposed to the cold. *Journal of Comparative and Physiological Psychology, 91,* 989–999. (10)

Vanduffel, W., Fize, D., Mandeville, J. B., Nelissen, K., Van Hecke, P., Rosen, B. R., et al. (2001). Visual motion processing investigated using contrast agent-enhanced fMRI in awake behaving monkeys. *Neuron, 32,* 565–577. (6)

Vargas-Irwin, C. E., Shakhnarovich, G., Yadollahpour, P., Mislow, J. M. K., Black, M. J., & Donoghue, J. P. (2010). Decoding complete reach and grasp actions from local primary motor cortex populations. *Journal of Neuroscience, 30,* 9659–9669. (8)

Vargha-Khadem, F., Gadian, D. G., Copp, A., & Mishkin, M. (2005). *FOXP*x and the neuroanatomy of speech and language. *Nature Reviews Neuroscience, 6,* 131–138. (14)

Vasey, P. L., & VanderLaan, D. P. (2010). An adaptive cognitive dissociation between willingness to help kin and nonkin in Samoan *Fa'afafine*. *Psychological Science, 21,* 292–297. (11)

Vawter, M. P., Evans, S., Choudary, P., Tomita, H., Meador-Woodruff, J., Molnar, M., et al. (2004). Gender-specific gene expression in post-mortem human brain. Localization to sex chromosomes. *Neuropsychopharmacology, 29,* 373–384. (11)

Velanova, K., Wheeler, M. E., & Luna, B. (2009). The maturation of task set-related activation supports late developmental improvements in inhibitory control. *Journal of Neuroscience, 29,* 12558–12567. (8)

Velliste, M., Perel, S., Spalding, M. C., Whitford, A. S., & Schwartz, A. B. (2008). Cortical control of a prosthetic arm for self-feeding. *Nature, 453,* 1098–1101. (8)

Venna, V. R., Deplanque, D., Allet, C., Belarbi, K., Hamdane, M., & Bordet, R. (2008). PUFA induce antidepressant-like effects in parallel to structural and molecular changes in the hippocampus. *Psychoneuroendocrinology, 34,* 199–211. (15)

Verhage, M., Maia, A. S., Plomp, J. J., Brussard, A. B., Heeroma, J. H., Vermeer, H., et al. (2000). Synaptic assembly of the brain in the absence of neurotransmitter secretion. *Science, 287,* 864–869. (5)

Verrey, F., & Beron, J. (1996). Activation and supply of channels and pumps by aldosterone. *News in Physiological Sciences, 11,* 126–133. (10)

Vessal, M., & Darian-Smith, C. (2010). Adult neurogenesis occurs in primate sensorimotor cortex following cervical dorsal rhizotomy. *Journal of Neuroscience, 30,* 8613–8623. (5)

Vetencourt, J. F. M., Sale, A., Viegi, A., Baroncelli, L., DePasquale, R., O'Leary, O. F., et al. (2008). The antidepressant fluoxetine restores plasticity in the adult visual cortex. *Science, 320,* 385–388. (15)

Virkkunen, M., DeJong, J., Bartko, J., Goodwin, F. K., & Linnoila, M. (1989). Relationship of psychobiological variables to recidivism in violent offenders and impulsive fire setters. *Archives of General Psychiatry, 46,* 600–603. (12)

Virkkunen, M., Eggert, M., Rawlings, R., & Linnoila, M. (1996). A prospective follow-up study of alcoholic violent offenders and fire setters. *Archives of General Psychiatry, 53,* 523–529. (12)

Virkkunen, M., Nuutila, A., Goodwin, F. K., & Linnoila, M. (1987). Cerebrospinal fluid monoamine metabolite levels in male arsonists. *Archives of General Psychiatry, 44,* 241–247. (12)

Virkkunen, M., Rawlings, R., Tokola, R., Poland, R. E., Guidotti, A., Nemeroff, C., et al. (1994). CSF biochemistries, glucose metabolism, and diurnal activity rhythms in alcoholic, violent offenders, fire setters, and healthy volunteers. *Archives of General Psychiatry, 51,* 20–27. (3)

Visser, E. K., Beersma, G. M., & Daan, S. (1999). Melatonin suppression by light in humans is maximal when the nasal part of the retina is illuminated. *Journal of Biological Rhythms, 14,* 116–121. (9)

Viswanathan, A., & Freeman, R. D. (2007). Neurometabolic coupling in cerebral cortex reflects synaptic more than spiking activity. *Nature Neuroscience, 10,* 1308–1312. (4)

Vliegen, J., Van Grootel, T. J., & Van Opstal, A. J. (2004). Dynamic sound localization during rapid eye–head gaze shifts. *Journal of Neuroscience, 24,* 9291–9302. (7)

Vocci, F. J., Acri, J., & Elkashef, A. (2005). Medication development for addictive disorders: The state of the science. *American Journal of Psychiatry, 162,* 1432–1440. (3)

Volavka, J., Czobor, P., Goodwin, D. W., Gabrielli, W. F., Penick, E. C., Mednick, S. A., et al. (1996). The electroencephalogram after alcohol administration in high-risk men and the development of alcohol use disorders 10 years later. *Archives of General Psychiatry, 53,* 258–263. (3)

Volkow, N. D., Fowler, J. S., Wang, G.-J., Telang, F., Logan, J., Jayne, M., et al. (2010). Cognitive control of drug craving inhibits brain reward regions in cocaine abusers. *NeuroImage, 49,* 2536–2543. (3)

Volkow, N. D., Wang, G.-J., Telang, F., Fowler, J. S., Logan, J., Childress, A.-R., et al. (2006). Cocaine cues and dopamine in dorsal striatum: Mechanism of craving in cocaine addiction. *Journal of Neuroscience, 26,* 6583–6588. (3)

von Békésy, G. (1956). Current status of theories of hearing. *Science, 123,* 779–783. (7)

von der Ohe, C. G., Darian-Smith, C., Garner, C. C., & Heller, H. C. (2006). Ubiquitous and temperature-dependent neural plasticity in hibernators. *Journal of Neuroscience, 26,* 10590–10598. (9)

von Gall, C., Garabette, M. L., Kell, C. A., Frenzel, S., Dehghani, F., Schumm-Draeger, P. M., et al. (2002). Rhythmic gene expression in pituitary depends on heterologous sensitization by the neurohormone melatonin. *Nature Neuroscience*, 5, 234–238. (9)

von Melchner, L., Pallas, S. L., & Sur, M. (2000). Visual behaviour mediated by retinal projections directed to the visual pathway. *Nature*, 404, 871–876. (5)

Vrba, E. S. (1998). Multiphasic growth models and the evolution of prolonged growth exemplified by human brain evolution. *Journal of Theoretical Biology*, 190, 227–239. (5)

Vuga, M., Fox, N. A., Cohn, J. F., George, C. J., Levenstein, R. M., & Kovacs, M. (2006). Long-term stability of frontal electroencephalographic asymmetry in adults with a history of depression and controls. *International Journal of Psychophysiology*, 59, 107–115. (15)

Vuillermot, S., Weber, L., Feldon, J., & Meyer, U. (2010). A longitudinal examination of the neurodevelopmental impact of prenatal immune activation in mice reveals primary defects in dopaminergic development relevant to schizophrenia. *Journal of Neuroscience*, 30, 1270–1287. (15)

Vuilleumier, P. (2005). Cognitive science: Staring fear in the face. *Nature*, 433, 22–23. (12)

Vyazovskiy, V. V., Cirelli, C., Pfister-Genskow, M., Faraguna, U., & Tononi, G. (2008). Molecular and electrophysiological evidence for net synaptic potentiation in wake and depression in sleep. *Nature Neuroscience*, 11, 200–208. (9)

Wager, T. D., Rilling, J. K., Smith, E. E., Sokolik, A., Casey, K. L., Davidson, R. J., et al. (2004). Placebo-induced changes in fMRI in the anticipation and experience of pain. *Science*, 303, 1162–1167. (7)

Wager, T. D., Scott, D. J., & Zubieta, J.-K. (2007). Placebo effects on human m-opioid activity during pain. *Proceedings of the National Academy of Sciences, USA*, 104, 11056–11061. (7)

Wagner, E. L., & Gleeson, T. T. (1997). Postexercise thermoregulatory behavior and recovery from exercise in desert iguanas. *Physiology & Behavior*, 61, 175–180. (10)

Wagner, U., Gais, S., Haider, H., Verleger, R., & Born, J. (2004). Sleep inspires insight. *Nature*, 427, 352–355. (9)

Waisbren, S. R., Brown, M. J., de Sonneville, L. M. J., & Levy, H. L. (1994). Review of neuropsychological functioning in treated phenylketonuria: An information-processing approach. *Acta Paediatrica*, 83(Suppl. 407), 98–103. (1)

Waldherr, M., & Neumann, I. D. (2007). Centrally released oxytocin mediates mating-induced anxiolysis in male rats. *Proceedings of the National Academy of Sciences, USA*, 104, 16681–16684. (11)

Waldvogel, J. A. (1990). The bird's eye view. *American Scientist*, 78, 342–353. (6)

Wallen, K. (2005). Hormonal influences on sexually differentiated behavior in nonhuman primates. *Frontiers in Neuroendocrinology*, 26, 7–26. (11)

Wallesch, C.-W., Henriksen, L., Kornhuber, H. H., & Paulson, O. B. (1985). Observations on regional cerebral blood flow in cortical and subcortical structures during language production in normal man. *Brain and Language*, 25, 224–233. (14)

Wallman, J., & Pettigrew, J. D. (1985). Conjugate and disjunctive saccades in two avian species with contrasting oculomotor strategies. *Journal of Neuroscience*, 5, 1418–1428. (6)

Walsh, T., McClellan, J. M., McCarthy, S. E., Addington, A. M., Pierce, S. B., & Cooper, G. M. (2008). Rare structural variants disrupt multiple genes in neurodevelopmental pathways in schizophrenia. *Science*, 320, 539–543. (15)

Walsh, V., & Cowey, A. (2000). Transcranial magnetic stimulation and cognitive neuroscience. *Nature Reviews Neuroscience*, 1, 73–79. (4)

Walters, E. T., (2009). Chronic pain, memory, and injury: Evolutionary clues from snail and rat nociceptors. *International Journal of Comparative Psychology*, 22, 127–140. (7)

Wan, C. Y., Wood, A. G., Reutens, D. C., & Wilson, S. J. (2010). Early but not late-blindness leads to enhanced auditory perception. *Neuropsychologia*, 48, 344–348. (5)

Wang, A., Liang, Y., Fridell, R. A., Probst, F. J., Wilcox, E. R., Touchman, J. W., et al. (1998). Associations of unconventional myosin *MYO15* mutations with human nonsyndromic deafness *DFNB3*. *Science*, 280, 1447–1451. (7)

Wang, A. C. J., Hara, Y., Janssen, W. G. M., Rapp, P. R., & Morrison, J. H. (2010). Synaptic estrogen receptor-α levels in prefrontal cortex in female rhesus monkeys and their correlation with cognitive performance. *Journal of Neuroscience*, 30, 12770–12776. (11)

Wang, D. O., Kim, S. M., Zhao, Y., Hwang, H., Miura, S. K., Sossin, W. S., et al. (2009). Synapse- and stimulus-specific local translation during long-term neuronal plasticity. *Science*, 324, 1536–1540. (13)

Wang, Q., Schoenlein, R. W., Peteanu, L. A., Mathies, R. A., & Shank, C. V. (1994). Vibrationally coherent photochemistry in the femtosecond primary event of vision. *Science*, 266, 422–424. (6)

Wang, T., Okano, Y., Eisensmith, R., Huang, S. Z., Zeng, Y. T., Wilson, H. Y. L., et al. (1989). Molecular genetics of phenylketonuria in Orientals: Linkage disequilibrium between a termination mutation and haplotype 4 of the phenylalanine hydroxylase gene. *American Journal of Human Genetics*, 45, 675–680. (1)

Wang, X., Lu, T., Snider, R. K., & Liang, L. (2005). Sustained firing in auditory cortex evoked by preferred stimuli. *Nature*, 435, 341–346. (7)

Warach, S. (1995). Mapping brain pathophysiology and higher cortical function with magnetic resonance imaging. *The Neuroscientist*, 1, 221–235. (4)

Ward, I. L., Bennett, A. L., Ward, O. B., Hendricks, S. E., & French, J. A. (1999). Androgen threshold to activate copulation differs in male rats prenatally exposed to alcohol, stress, or both factors. *Hormones and Behavior*, 36, 129–140. (11)

Ward, I. L., Romeo, R. D., Denning, J. H., & Ward, O. B. (1999). Fetal alcohol exposure blocks full masculinization of the dorsolateral nucleus in rat spinal cord. *Physiology & Behavior*, 66, 571–575. (11)

Ward, I. L., Ward, B., Winn, R. J., & Bielawski, D. (1994). Male and female sexual behavior potential of male rats prenatally exposed to the influence of alcohol, stress, or both factors. *Behavioral Neuroscience*, 108, 1188–1195. (11)

Ward, I. L., & Ward, O. B. (1985). Sexual behavior differentiation: Effects of prenatal manipulations in rats. In N. Adler, D. Pfaff, & R. W. Goy (Eds.), *Handbook of behavioral neurobiology* (Vol. 7, pp. 77–98). New York: Plenum Press. (11)

Ward, O. B., Monaghan, E. P., & Ward, I. L. (1986). Naltrexone blocks the effects of prenatal stress on sexual behavior differentiation in male rats. *Pharmacology Biochemistry and Behavior*, 25, 573–576. (11)

Ward, O. B., Ward, I. L., Denning, J. H., French, J. A., & Hendricks, S. E. (2002). Postparturitional testosterone surge in male offspring of rats stressed and/or fed ethanol during late pregnancy. *Hormones and Behavior*, 41, 229–235. (11)

Ward, R., Danziger, S., Owen, V., & Rafal, R. (2002). Deficits in spatial coding and feature binding following damage to spatiotopic maps in the human pulvinar. *Nature Neuroscience*, 5, 99–100. (4)

Warren, R. M. (1999). *Auditory perception*. Cambridge, England: Cambridge University Press. (7)

Wässle, H. (2004). Parallel processing in the mammalian retina. *Nature Neuroscience*, 5, 747–757. (6)

Watanabe, D., Savion-Lemieux, T., & Penhune, V. B. (2007). The effect of early musical training on adult motor performance: Evidence for a sensitive period in motor learning. *Experimental Brain Research*, 176, 332–340. (5)

Watanabe, M., & Munoz, D. P. (2010). Presetting basal ganglia for volitional actions. *Journal of Neuroscience*, 30, 10144–10157. (8)

Wattendorf, E., Welge-Lüssen, A., Fiedler, K., Bilecen, D., Wolfensberger, M., Fuhr, P., et al. (2009). Olfactory impairment predicts brain atrophy in Parkinson's disease. *Journal of Neuroscience*, 29, 15410–15413. (8)

Waxman, S. G., & Ritchie, J. M. (1985). Organization of ion channels in the myelinated nerve fiber. *Science*, 228, 1502–1507. (2)

Weaver, I. C. G., Cervoni, N., Champagne, F. A., D'Alessio, A. C., Sharma, S., Seckl, J. R., et al. (2004). Epigenetic programming by maternal behavior. *Nature Neuroscience*, 7, 847–854. (1)

Webb, W. B. (1974). Sleep as an adaptive response. *Perceptual and Motor Skills*, 38, 1023–1027. (9)

Weber-Fox, C. M., & Neville, H. J. (1996). Maturational constraints on functional specializations for language processing: ERP and behavioral evidence in bilingual speakers. *Journal of Cognitive Neuroscience*, 8, 231–256. (14)

Wegener, D., Freiwald, W. A., & Kreiter, A. K. (2004). The influence of sustained selective attention on stimulus selectivity in macaque visual area MT. *Journal of Neuroscience*, 24, 6106–6114. (14)

Wehr, T. A., Turner, E. H., Shimada, J. M., Lowe, C. H., Barker, C., & Leinbenluft, E. (1998). Treatment of a rapidly cycling bipolar patient by using extended bed rest and darkness to stabilize the timing and duration of sleep. *Biological Psychiatry*, 43, 822–828. (15)

Wei, W., Nguyen, L. N., Kessels, H. W., Hagiwara, H., Sisodia, S., & Malinow, R. (2010). Amyloid beta from axons and dendrites reduces local spine number and plasticity. *Nature Neuroscience*, *13*, 190–196. (13)

Weidensaul, S. (1999). *Living on the wind*. New York: North Point Press. (10)

Weinberger, D. R. (1996). On the plausibility of "the neurodevelopmental hypothesis" of schizophrenia. *Neuropsychopharmacology*, *14*, 1S–11S. (15)

Weinberger, D. R. (1999). Cell biology of the hippocampal formation in schizophrenia. *Biological Psychiatry*, *45*, 395–402. (15)

Weindl, A. (1973). Neuroendocrine aspects of circumventricular organs. In W. F. Ganong & L. Martini (Eds.), *Frontiers in neuroendocrinology 1973* (pp. 3–32). New York: Oxford University Press. (10)

Weinshenker, D., & Schroeder, J. P. (2007). There and back again: A tale of norepinephrine and drug addiction. *Neuropsychopharmacology*, *32*, 1433–1451. (3)

Weiskrantz, L., Warrington, E. K., Sanders, M. D., & Marshall, J. (1974). Visual capacity in the hemianopic field following a restricted occipital ablation. *Brain*, *97*, 709–728. (6)

Weiss, A. P., Ellis, C. B., Roffman, J. L., Stufflebeam, S., Hamalainen, M. S., Duff, M., et al. (2009). Aberrant frontoparietal function during recognition memory in schizophrenia: A multimodal neuroimaging investigation. *Journal of Neuroscience*, *29*, 11347–11359. (15)

Weiss, P. (1924). Die funktion transplantierter amphibienextremitäten. Aufstellung einer resonanztheorie der motorischen nerventätigkeit auf grund abstimmter endorgane [The function of transplanted amphibian limbs. Presentation of a resonance theory of motor nerve action upon tuned end organs]. *Archiv für Mikroskopische Anatomie und Entwicklungsmechanik*, *102*, 635–672. (5)

Weiss, P. H., & Fink, G. R. (2009). Grapheme-colour synaesthetes show increased grey matter volumes of parietal and fusiform cortex. *Brain*, *132*, 65–70. (7)

Weissman, D. H., Roberts, K. C., Visscher, K. M., & Woldorff, M. G. (2006). The neural bases of momentary lapses in attention. *Nature Neuroscience*, *9*, 971–978. (4)

Welchman, A. E., Stanley, J., Schomers, M. R., Miall, C., & Bülthoff, H. H. (2010). The quick and the dead: When reaction beats intention. *Proceedings of the Royal Society, B*, *277*, 1667–1674. (8)

Weller, L., Weller, A., Koresh-Kamin, H., & Ben-Shoshan, R. (1999). Menstrual synchrony in a sample of working women. *Psychoneuroendocrinology*, *24*, 449–459. (7)

Weller, L., Weller, A., & Roizman, S. (1999). Human menstrual synchrony in families and among close friends: Examining the importance of mutual exposure. *Journal of Comparative Psychology*, *113*, 261–268. (7)

Wessinger, C. M., VanMeter, J., Tian, B., Van Lare, J., Pekar, J., & Rauschecker, J. P. (2001). Hierarchical organization of the human auditory cortex revealed by functional magnetic resonance imaging. *Journal of Cognitive Neuroscience*, *13*, 1–7. (7)

Westergaard, G. C., Cleveland, A., Trenkle, M. K., Lussier, I. D., & Higley, J. D. (2003). CSF 5-HIAA concentration as an early screening tool for predicting significant life history outcomes in female specific-pathogen-free (SPF) rhesus macaques (*Macaca mulatta*) maintained in captive breeding groups. *Journal of Medical Primatology*, *32*, 95–104. (12)

Whalen, P. J., Kagan, J., Cook, R. G., Davis, F. C., Kim, H., Polis, S., et al. (2004). Human amygdala responsivity to masked fearful eye whites. *Science*, *306*, 2061. (12)

Wheeler, M. E., & Treisman, A. (2002). Binding in short-term visual memory. *Journal of Experimental Psychology: General*, *131*, 48–64. (4)

White, L. E., Coppola, D. M., & Fitzpatrick, D. (2001). The contribution of sensory experience to the maturation of orientation selectivity in ferret visual cortex. *Nature*, *411*, 1049–1052. (6)

Whitman, B. W., & Packer, R. J. (1993). The photic sneeze reflex: Literature review and discussion. *Neurology*, *43*, 868–871. (8)

Whyte, J., Katz, D., Long, D., DiPasquale, M. C., Polansky, M., Kalmar, K., et al. (2005). Predictors of outcome in prolonged posttraumatic disorders of consciousness and assessment of medication effects: A multicenter study. *Archives of Physical Medicine and Rehabilitation*, *86*, 453–462. (5)

Wichmann, T., Vitek, J. L., & DeLong, M. R. (1995). Parkinson's disease and the basal ganglia: Lessons from the laboratory and from neurosurgery. *The Neuroscientist*, *1*, 236–244. (8)

Wicker, B., Keysers, C., Plailly, J., Royet, J.-P., Gallese, V., & Rizzolatti, G. (2003). Both of us disgusted in *my* insula: The common neural basis of seeing and feeling disgust. *Neuron*, *40*, 655–664. (8, 12)

Widom, C. S., & Brzustowicz, L. M. (2006). MAOI and the "cycle of violence": Childhood abuse and neglect, MAOA genotype, and risk of violent and antisocial behavior. *Biological Psychiatry*, *60*, 684–689. (12)

Wiesel, T. N. (1982). Postnatal development of the visual cortex and the influence of environment. *Nature*, *299*, 583–591. (6)

Wiesel, T. N., & Hubel, D. H. (1963). Single-cell responses in striate cortex of kittens deprived of vision in one eye. *Journal of Neurophysiology*, *26*, 1003–1017. (6)

Wild, H. M., Butler, S. R., Carden, D., & Kulikowski, J. J. (1985). Primate cortical area V4 important for colour constancy but not wavelength discrimination. *Nature*, *313*, 133–135. (6)

Wilensky, A. E., Schafe, G. E., Kristensen, M. P., & LeDoux, J. E. (2006). Rethinking the fear circuit. *Journal of Neuroscience*, *26*, 12387–12396. (12)

Willems, R. M., Hagoort, P., & Casasanto, D. (2010). Body-specific representations of action verbs: Neural evidence from right- and left-handers. *Psychological Science*, *21*, 67–74. (14)

Willerman, L., Schultz, R., Rutledge, J. N., & Bigler, E. D. (1991). In vivo brain size and intelligence. *Intelligence*, *15*, 223–228. (4)

Williams, C. L. (1986). A reevaluation of the concept of separable periods of organizational and activational actions of estrogens in development of brain and behavior. *Annals of the New York Academy of Sciences*, *474*, 282–292. (11)

Williams, G., Cai, X. J., Elliott, J. C., & Harrold, J. A. (2004). Anabolic neuropeptides. *Physiology & Behavior*, *81*, 211–222. (10)

Williams, M. T., Davis, H. N., McCrea, A. E., Long, S. J., & Hennessy, M. B. (1999). Changes in the hormonal concentrations of pregnant rats and their fetuses following multiple exposures to a stressor during the third trimester. *Neurotoxicology and Teratology*, *21*, 403–414. (11)

Williams, R. W., & Herrup, K. (1988). The control of neuron number. *Annual Review of Neuroscience*, *11*, 423–453. (2, 8)

Willingham, D. B., Koroshetz, W. J., & Peterson, E. W. (1996). Motor skills have diverse neural bases: Spared and impaired skill acquisition in Huntington's disease. *Neuropsychology*, *10*, 315–321. (8)

Wilson, B. A., Baddeley, A. D., & Kapur, N. (1995). Dense amnesia in a professional musician following herpes simplex virus encephalitis. *Journal of Clinical and Experimental Neuropsychology*, *17*, 668–681. (13)

Wilson, J. D., George, F. W., & Griffin, J. E. (1981). The hormonal control of sexual development. *Science*, *211*, 1278–1284. (11)

Wilson, R. I., & Nicoll, R. A. (2002). Endocannabinoid signaling in the brain. *Science*, *296*, 678–682. (3)

Wilson, S. M., Dronkers, N. F., Ogar, J. M., Jang, J., Growdon, M. E., Agosta, F., et al. (2010). Neural correlates of syntactic processing in the nonfluent variant of primary progressive aphasia. *Journal of Neuroscience*, *30*, 16845–16854. (14)

Winer, G. A., Cottrell, J. F., Gregg, V., Fournier, J. S., & Bica. L. A. (2002). Fundamentally misunderstanding visual perception: Adults' belief in visual emissions. *American Psychologist*, *57*, 417–424. (2)

Winfree, A. T. (1983). Impact of a circadian clock on the timing of human sleep. *American Journal of Physiology*, *245*, R497–R504. (9)

Winocur, G., & Hasher, L. (1999). Aging and time-of-day effects on cognition in rats. *Behavioral Neuroscience*, *113*, 991–997. (9)

Winocur, G., & Hasher, L. (2004). Age and time-of-day effects on learning and memory in a non-matching-to-sample test. *Neurobiology of Aging*, *25*, 1107–1115. (9)

Winocur, G., Moscovitch, M., & Sekeres, M. (2007). Memory consolidation or transformation: Context manipulation and hippocampal representations of memory. *Nature Neuroscience*, *10*, 555–557. (13)

Wirdefeldt, K., Gatz, M., Pawitan, Y., & Pedersen, N. L. (2005). Risk and protective factors for Parkinson's disease: A study in Swedish twins. *Annals of Neurology*, *57*, 27–33. (8)

Wirz-Justice, A., Werth, E., Renz, C., Müller, S., & Kräuchi, K. (2002). No evidence for a phase delay in human circadian rhythms after a single morning melatonin administration. *Journal of Pineal Research*, *32*, 1–5. (9)

Wise, R. A. (1996). Addictive drugs and brain stimulation reward. *Annual Review of Neuroscience*, *19*, 319–340. (3)

Wissman, A. M., & Brenowitz, E. A. (2009). The role of neurotrophins in the seasonal-like growth of the avian song control system. *Journal of Neuroscience*, *29*, 6461–6471. (5)

Witelson, S. F., Beresh, H., & Kigar, D. L. (2006). Intelligence and brain size in 100 postmortem brains: Sex, lateralization and age factors. *Brain, 129*, 386–398. (4)

Witelson, S. F., Kigar, D. L., & Harvey, T. (1999). The exceptional brain of Albert Einstein. *Lancet, 353*, 2149–2153. (4)

Witelson, S. F., & Pallie, W. (1973). Left hemisphere specialization for language in the newborn: Neuroanatomical evidence of asymmetry. *Brain, 96*, 641–646. (14)

Wolf, S. (1995). Dogmas that have hindered understanding. *Integrative Physiological and Behavioral Science, 30*, 3–4. (12)

Wolff, P. H. (1993). Impaired temporal resolution in developmental dyslexia. *Annals of the New York Academy of Sciences, 682*, 87–103. (14)

Wolkin, A., Rusinek, H., Vaid, G., Arena, L., Lafargue, T., Sanfilipo, M., et al. (1998). Structural magnetic resonance image averaging in schizophrenia. *American Journal of Psychiatry, 155*, 1064–1073. (15)

Wolpert, L. (1991). *The triumph of the embryo.* Oxford, England: Oxford University Press. (5)

Womelsdorf, T., Schoffelen, J.-M., Oostenveld, R., Singer, W., Desimone, R., Engel, A. K., et al. (2007). Modulation of neuronal interactions through neuronal synchronization. *Science, 316*, 1609–1612. (14)

Wong, P. C. M., Skoe, E., Russo, N. M., Dees, T., & Kraus, N. (2007). Musical experience shapes human brainstem encoding of linguistic pitch perception. *Nature Neuroscience, 10*, 420–422. (5)

Wong, P. C. M., Warrier, C. M., Penhune, V. B., Roy, A. K., Sadehh, A., Parrish, T. B., et al. (2007). Volume of left Heschl's gyrus and linguistic pitch learning. *Cerebral Cortex, 18*, 828–836. (4)

Wong-Riley, M. T. T. (1989). Cytochrome oxidase: An endogenous metabolic marker for neuronal activity. *Trends in Neurosciences, 12*, 94–101. (2)

Woodberry, K. A., Giuliano, A. J., & Seidman, L. J. (2008). Premorbid IQ in schizophrenia: A meta-analytic review. *American Journal of Psychiatry, 165*, 579–587. (15)

Wooding, S., Kim, U., Bamshad, M J., Larsen, J., Jorde, L. B., & Drayna, D. (2004). Natural selection and molecular evolution in *PTC,* a bitter-taste receptor gene. *American Journal of Human Genetics, 74*, 637–646. (1)

Woodson, J. C., & Balleine, B. W. (2002). An assessment of factors contributing to instrumental performance for sexual reward in the rat. *Quarterly Journal of Experimental Psychology, 55B*, 75–88. (11)

Woodworth, R. S. (1934). *Psychology* (3rd ed.). New York: Holt. (2)

Woolf, N. J. (1996). Global and serial neurons form a hierarchically arranged interface proposed to underlie memory and cognition. *Neuroscience, 74*, 625–651. (9)

Wray, N. R., James, M. R., Gordon, S. D., Dumenil, T., Ryan, L., Coventry, W. L., et al. (2009). Accurate, large-scale genotyping of 5HTTLPR and flanking single nucleotide polymorphisms in an association study of depression, anxiety, and per-

sonality measures. *Biological Psychiatry, 66*, 468–476. (12, 15)

Wright, I. C., Rabe-Hesketh, S., Woodruff, P. W. R., David, A. S., Murray, R. M., & Bullmore, E. T. (2000). Meta-analysis of regional brain volumes in schizophrenia. *American Journal of Psychiatry, 157*, 16–25. (15)

Wu, S. S., & Frucht, S. J. (2005). Treatment of Parkinson's disease: What's on the horizon? *CNS Drugs, 19*, 723–743. (8)

Wulfeck, B., & Bates, E. (1991). Differential sensitivity to errors of agreement and word order in Broca's aphasia. *Journal of Cognitive Neuroscience, 3*, 258–272. (14)

Wulff, K., Gatti, S., Wettstein, J. G., & Foster, R. G. (2010). Sleep and circadian rhythm disruption in psychiatric and neurodegenerative disease. *Nature Neuroscience, 11*, 589–599. (9)

Wurtman, J. J. (1985). Neurotransmitter control of carbohydrate consumption. *Annals of the New York Academy of Sciences, 443*, 145–151. (3)

Wyart, C., Webster, W. W., Chen, J. H., Wilson, S. R., McClary, A., Khan, R. M., et al. (2007). Smelling a single component of male sweat alters levels of cortisol in women. *Journal of Neuroscience, 27*, 1261–1265. (7)

Wynne, C. D. L. (2004). The perils of anthropomorphism. *Nature, 428*, 606. (1)

Wynne, L. C., Tienari, P., Nieminen, P., Sorri, A., Lahti, I., Moring, J., et al. (2006). Genotype-environment interaction in the schizophrenia spectrum: Genetic liability and global family ratings in the Finnish adoption study. *Family Process, 45*, 419–434. (15)

Xu, H.-T., Pan, F., Yang, G., & Gan, W.-B. (2007). Choice of cranial window type for *in vivo* imaging affects dendritic spine turnover in the cortex. *Nature Neuroscience, 10*, 549–551. (5)

Xu, T., Yu, X., Perlik, A. J., Tobin, W. F., Zweig, J. A., Tennant, K., et al. (2009). Rapid formation and selective stabilization of synapses for enduring motor memories. *Nature, 462*, 915–919. (13)

Xu, Y., Padiath, Q. S., Shapiro, R. E., Jones, C. R., Wu, S. C., Saigoh, N., et al. (2005). Functional consequences of a *CKxd* mutation causing familial advanced sleep phase syndrome. *Nature, 434*, 640–644. (9)

Yamaguchi, S., Isejima, H., Matsuo, T., Okura, R., Yagita, K., Kobayashi, M., et al. (2003). Synchronization of cellular clocks in the suprachiasmatic nucleus. *Science, 302*, 1408–1412. (9)

Yamamoto, S., & Kitazawa, S. (2001). Reversal of subjective temporal order due to arm crossing. *Nature Neuroscience, 4*, 759–765. (2)

Yamamoto, T. (1984). Taste responses of cortical neurons. *Progress in Neurobiology, 23*, 273–315. (7)

Yanagisawa, K., Bartoshuk, L. M., Catalanotto, F. A., Karrer, T. A., & Kveton, J. F. (1998). Anesthesia of the chorda tympani nerve and taste phantoms. *Physiology & Behavior, 63*, 329–335. (7)

Yang, G., Pan, F., & Gan, W.-B. (2009). Stably maintained dendritic spines are associated with lifelong memories. *Nature, 462*, 920–924. (5)

Yang, L., Scott, K. A., Hyun, J., Tamashiro, K. L., Tray, N., Moran, T. H., et al. (2009). Role of dorsomedial hypothalamic neuropeptide Y in mod-

ulating food intake and energy balance. *Journal of Neuroscience, 29*, 179–190. (10)

Yavich, L., Forsberg, M. M., Karayiorgou, M., Gogos, J. A., & Männistö, P. T. (2007). Site-specific role of catechol-o-methyltransferase in dopamine overflow within prefrontal cortex and dorsal striatum. *Journal of Neuroscience, 27*, 10196–10202. (3)

Yee, B. K., Balic, E., Singer, P., Schwerdel, C., Grampp, T., Gabernet, L., et al. (2006). Disruption of glycine transporter 1 restricted to forebrain neurons is associated with a precognitive and antipsychotic phenotypic profile. *Journal of Neuroscience, 26*, 3169–3181. (15)

Yeh, M. T., Coccaro, E. F., & Jacobson, K. C. (2010). Multivariate behavior genetic analyses of aggressive behavior subtypes. *Behavior Genetics, 40*, 603–617. (12)

Yehuda, R. (1997). Sensitization of the hypothalamic-pituitary-adrenal axis in posttraumatic stress disorder. *Annals of the New York Academy of Sciences, 821*, 57–75. (12)

Yehuda, R. (2002). Post-traumatic stress disorder. *New England Journal of Medicine, 346*, 108–114. (12)

Yeomans, J. S., & Frankland, P. W. (1996). The acoustic startle reflex: Neurons and connections. *Brain Research Reviews, 21*, 301–314. (12)

Yeshurun, Y., Dudai, Y., & Sobel, N. (2008). Working memory across nostrils. *Behavioral Neuroscience, 122*, 1031–1037. (14)

Yin, H. H., & Knowlton, B. J. (2006). The role of the basal ganglia in habit formation. *Nature Reviews Neuroscience, 7*, 464–476. (8)

Yiu, G., & He, Z. (2006). Glial inhibition of CNS axon regeneration. *Nature Reviews Neuroscience, 7*, 617–627. (5)

Yolken, R. H., Bachmann, S., Rouslanova, I., Lillehoj, E., Ford, G., Torrey, E. F., et al. (2001). Antibodies to *Toxoplasma gondii* in individuals with first-episode schizophrenia. *Clinical Infectious Diseases, 32*, 842–844. (15)

Yoo, S.-S., Hu, P. T., Gujar, N., Jolesz, F. A., & Walker, M. P. (2007). A deficit in the ability to form new human memories without sleep. *Nature Neuroscience, 10*, 385–392. (9)

Yoon, K. L., Hong, S. W., Joormann, J., & Kang, P. (2009). Perception of facial expressions of emotion during binocular rivalry. *Emotion, 9*, 172–182. (14)

Yoshida, J., & Mori, K. (2007). Odorant category profile selectivity of olfactory cortex neurons. *Journal of Neuroscience, 27*, 9105–9114. (7)

Yoshida, K., Li, X., Cano, G., Lazarus, M., & Saper, C. B. (2009). Parallel preoptic pathways for thermoregulation. *Journal of Neuroscience, 29*, 11954–11964. (10)

Young, A. B. (1995). Huntington's disease: Lessons from and for molecular neuroscience. *The Neuroscientist, 1*, 51–58. (8)

Young, S. N., & Leyton, M. (2002). The role of serotonin in human mood and social interaction: Insight from altered tryptophan levels. *Pharmacology, Biochemistry and Behavior, 71*, 857–865. (12)

Yousem, D. M., Maldjian, J. A., Siddiqi, F., Hummel, T., Alsop, D. C., Geckle, R. J., et al. (1999). Gender effects on odor-stimulated functional magnetic resonance imaging. *Brain Research, 818,* 480–487. (7)

Yu, T. W., & Bargmann, C. I. (2001). Dynamic regulation of axon guidance. *Nature Neuroscience Supplement, 4,* 1169–1176. (5)

Zadra, A., & Pilon, M. (2008). Polysomnographic diagnosis of sleepwalking: Effects of sleep deprivation. *Annals of Neurology, 63,* 513–519. (9)

Zakharenko, S. S., Zablow, L., & Siegelbaum, S. A. (2001). Visualization of changes in presynaptic function during long-term synaptic plasticity. *Nature Neuroscience, 4,* 711–717. (13)

Zatorre, R. J., Bouffard, M., & Belin, P. (2004). Sensitivity to auditory object features in human temporal neocortex. *Journal of Neuroscience, 24,* 3637–3642. (7)

Zeevalk, G. D., Manzino, L., Hoppe, J., & Sonsalla, P. (1997). In vivo vulnerability of dopamine neurons to inhibition of energy metabolism. *European Journal of Pharmacology, 320,* 111–119. (8)

Zeitzer, J. M., Buckmaster, C. L., Parker, K. J., Hauck, C. M., Lyons, D. M., & Mignot, E. (2003). Circadian and homeostatic regulation of hypocretin in a primate model: Implications for the consolidation of wakefulness. *Journal of Neuroscience, 23,* 3555–3560. (9)

Zeki, S. (1980). The representation of colours in the cerebral cortex. *Nature, 284,* 412–418. (6)

Zeki, S. (1983). Colour coding in the cerebral cortex: The responses of wavelength-selective and colour-coded cells in monkey visual cortex to changes in wavelength composition. *Neuroscience, 9,* 767–781. (6)

Zeki, S., McKeefry, D. J., Bartels, A., & Frackowiak, R. S. J. (1998). Has a new color area been discovered? *Nature Neuroscience, 1,* 335. (6)

Zeki, S., & Shipp, S. (1988). The functional logic of cortical connections. *Nature, 335,* 311–317. (6)

Zhang, T. Y., Hellstrom, I. C., Bagot, R. C., Wen, X. L., Dioro, J., & Meaney, M. J. (2010). Maternal care and DNA methylation of a glutamic acid decarboxylase 1 promoter in rat hippocampus. *Journal of Neuroscience, 30,* 13130–13137. (1)

Zhang, X., & Firestein, S. (2002). The olfactory receptor gene superfamily of the mouse. *Nature Neuroscience, 5,* 124–133. (7)

Zhang, X., Smith, D. L., Meriin, A. B., Engemann, S., Russel, D. E., Roark, M., et al. (2005). A potent small molecule inhibits polyglutamine aggregation in Huntington's disease neurons and suppresses neurodegeneration *in vivo. Proceedings of the National Academy of Sciences, USA, 102,* 892–897. (8)

Zhang, Y., Proenca, R., Maffei, M., Barone, M., Leopold, L., & Friedman, J. M. (1994). Positional cloning of the mouse obese gene and its human homologue. *Nature, 372,* 425–432. (10)

Zhao, Y., Terry, D., Shi, L., Weinstein, H., Blanchard, S. C., & Javitch, J. A. (2010). Single-molecule dynamics of gating in a neurotransmitter transporter homologue. *Nature, 465,* 188–193. (3)

Zhao, Z., & Davis, M. (2004). Fear-potentiated startle in rats is mediated by neurons in the deep layers of the superior colliculus/deep mesencephalic nucleus of the rostral midbrain through the glutamate non-NMDA receptors. *Journal of Neuroscience, 24,* 10326–10334. (12)

Zheng, B., Larkin, D. W., Albrecht, U., Sun, Z. S., Sage, M., Eichele, G., et al. (1999). The mPer2 gene encodes a functional component of the mammalian circadian clock. *Nature, 400,* 169–173. (9)

Zheng, H., Patterson, L. M., & Berthoud, H.-R. (2007). Orexin signaling in the ventral tegmental area is required for high-fat appetite induced by opioid stimulation of the nucleus accumbens. *Journal of Neuroscience, 27,* 11075–11082. (10)

Zhou, F., Zhu, X., Castellani, R. J., Stimmelmayr, R., Perry, G., Smith, M. A., et al. (2001). Hibernation, a model of neuroprotection. *American Journal of Pathology, 158,* 2145–2151. (9)

Zhu, Y., Fenik, P., Zhen, G., Mazza, E., Kelz, M., Aston-Jones, G., et al. (2007). Selective loss of catecholaminergic wake-active neurons in a murine sleep apnea model. *Journal of Neuroscience, 27,* 10060–10071. (9)

Ziegler, J. C., & Goswami, U. (2005). Reading acquisition, developmental dyslexia, and skilled reading across languages: A psycholinguistic grain size theory. *Psychological Bulletin, 131,* 3–29. (14)

Zihl, J., von Cramon, D., & Mai, N. (1983). Selective disturbance of movement vision after bilateral brain damage. *Brain, 106,* 313–340. (6)

Zipser, B. D., Johanson, C. E., Gonzalez, L., Berzin, T. M., Tavares, R., Hulette, C. M., et al. (2006). Microvascular injury and blood–brain barrier leakage in Alzheimer's disease. *Neurobiology of Aging, 28,* 977–986. (2)

Zola, S. M., Squire, L. R., Teng, E., Stefanacci, L., Buffalo, E. A., & Clark, R. E. (2000). Impaired recognition memory in monkeys after damage limited to the hippocampal region. *Journal of Neuroscience, 20,* 451–463. (13)

Zorrilla, E. P., Luborsky, L., McKay, J. R., Rosenthal, R., Houldin, A., Tax, A., et al. (2001). The relationship of depression and stressors to immunological assays: A meta-analytic review. *Brain, Behavior, and Immunity, 15,* 199–226. (12)

Zorzi, M., Priftis, K., & Umiltà, C. (2002). Neglect disrupts the mental number line. *Nature, 417,* 138. (14)

Zucker, K. J., Bradley, S. J., Oliver, G., Blake, J., Fleming, S., & Hood, J. (1996). Psychosexual development of women with congenital adrenal hyperplasia. *Hormones and Behavior, 30,* 300–318. (11)

Zuckerman, L, Rehavi, M., Nachman, R., & Weiner, I. (2003). Immune activation during pregnancy in rats leads to a post-pubertal emergence of disrupted latent inhibition, dopaminergic hyperfunction, and altered limbic morphology in the offspring: A novel neurodevelopmental model of schizophrenia. *Neuropsychopharmacology, 28,* 1778–1789. (15)

Zurif, E. B. (1980). Language mechanisms: A neuropsychological perspective. *American Scientist, 68,* 305–311. (14)

Name Index

Subject Index/Glossary

Note: Italicized page numbers refer to figures, illustrations, and tables.

Abducens nerve, *92*

Ablation removal of a brain area, generally with a surgical knife, 109

Absolute pitch, 197

Absolute refractory period a time when the membrane is unable to produce an action potential, 43

Accessory nerves, *92*

Acetaldehyde, 80

Acetyl groups, *12, 13*

Acetylcholine a chemical similar to an amino acid, except that it includes an N(CH₃)₃ group instead of an NH₂, group 60, *60*
 Alzheimer's disease and, 405
 excitatory, 63
 motor neurons and, 62
 as a neurotransmitter, 61
 postganglionic axons and, 91
 receptor, 63, *63*
 skeletal muscles and, 232
 wakefulness and sleep, 281, 282

Across-fiber principle idea that each receptor responds to a wide range of stimuli and contributes to the perception of every stimulus in its system, 215

ACTH. *See* Adrenocorticotropic hormone (ACTH)

Action potentials messages sent by axons, 40
 all-or-none law and, 41
 auditory neurons and, *196*, 197
 local neurons and, 45, 46
 molecular basis of, 41, *42*
 movements of ions during, 41, *42*
 myelin sheath and, 44, 45
 neurotransmitter and, 60
 presynaptic terminal and, 60
 propagation of, 43, *44*
 refractory period and, 42, 43
 SCN and, 271
 temporal pattern and, 217
 touch receptors and, 204

Activating effect temporary effect of a hormone, which occurs at any time in life while the hormone is present, 330

Activation-synthesis hypothesis idea that a dream represents the brain's effort to make sense of sparse and distorted information, 292

Active transport a protein-mediated process that expends energy to enable a molecule to cross a membrane, 34, 35

Acute transient global amnesia, 401

Adaptation decreased response to a stimulus as a result of recent exposure to it, 217

Addictions
 behavior and, 78–80, 81
 benzodiazepines and, 377
 brain reorganization and, 79
 explanation for, 79
 opiate drugs and, 74
 Ritalin and, 74

Adenosine, 61

ADHD (attention deficit disorder), 74, 131, 138

Adrenal cortex, 67

Adrenal medulla, 67

Adrenaline, 59

Adrenocorticotropic hormone (ACTH) chemical released from the anterior pituitary gland, which enhances metabolic activity and elevates blood levels of sugar, 66, *67*, *68*, 343, 380

Aerobic requiring the use of oxygen during movements, 234

Afferent axon axon that brings information into a structure, 32, *32*

Affinities, 71

Age
 circadian rhythms and, *267, 267, 268*, 269
 sleep patterns and, 291, *291*

Agonist a drug that mimics or increases the effects of a neurotransmitter, 71

Agouti-related peptide (AgRP) inhibitory transmitter that blocks the satiety actions of the paraventricular nucleus, 316

AgRP. *See* Agouti-related peptide (AgRP)

AIDS, 336, 349, 350

Alarm (stress stage), 380

Alcohol, 77
 anxiety and, 377, 378
 brain damage recovery behavior and, 149
 brain development and, 131
 demasculinization of early development, 331
 disulfiram (Antabuse) and, 463
 fetal alcohol syndrome and, 131, *131*
 genetics and, 77
 heritability and, 14
 medications to combat, 80, 81
 risk factors of, 77, 78, *78*
 Ro15-4513 and, 377
 sexual orientation and prenatal, 349
 thiamine deficiency and, 35, 404
 water regulation during, 305

Alcohol dependence (alcoholism) the habitual use of alcohol despite medical or social harm, 77

Alcoholics Anonymous, 80

Aldosterone adrenal hormone that causes the body to retain salt, *67*, 307

Allied reflexes, 237

All-or-none law principle that the amplitude and velocity of an action potential are independent of the stimulus that initiated it, 42

Allostasis the adaptive way in which the body changes its set points depending on the situation, 299

Alpha waves a steady series of brain waves at a frequency of 8 to 12 per second that are characteristic of relaxation, 276, *277*

Alpha-fetoprotein protein that binds with estradiol in the bloodstream of immature mammals, 332

Altruistic behavior an action that benefits someone other than the actor, 17

Alzheimer's disease condition characterized by memory loss, confusion, depression, restlessness, hallucinations, delusions, sleeplessness, and loss of appetite, 404
 brain atrophy and, *405*
 brain damage and, 141
 Ginkgo biloba and, 416
 neuronal degeneration and, *405*
 nucleus basalis and, 97

Amacrine cells, 155, 168

American Sign Language, 432

Amino acids acids containing an amine group (NH₂), 60, 61, *61*
 brain and, 34, 35
 DNA/RNA and, 10
 PKU diet and, 14

Amisulpride, 482

Amnesia memory loss, 396
 Alzheimer's disease and, 404, 405
 basal ganglia and, 403, 404
 Korsakoff's syndrome and, 404
 results and patients with, 406
 types of, 396–398, 399

AMPA receptor a glutamate receptor that can respond to α-amino-3-hydrozy-5-methyl-4-isoxazolepropionic acid (AMPA), 413–416, *414, 415*

Amphetamine a drug that blocks reuptake of dopamine and other neurotransmitters, 73, 74, 76

Amplitude the intensity of a sound wave, 194

AMPT (radioactively labeled drug), 480

Amputated limb, 146–147

Amusia, 197

Amygdala
 anxiety and, 371
 damage to, 372, 374–375, 376
 emotions and, 359, 360, 361
 fear and, 374–375
 learned fears and, 372, *372*
 location of, *366*
 PTSD and, 384
 responses and, 363, 373, *373*
 visual stimuli and, 373

Amyloid-β a protein that accumulates to higher than normal levels in the brains of people with Alzheimer's disease, 405, *406*

Amyotrophic lateral sclerosis, 246

Anaerobic proceeding without using oxygen at the time of a reaction, 234

Anandamide chemical that binds to cannabinoid receptors, 69, 75

Anatomical directions, 87

Androgen insensitivity. *See* Testicular feminization

Androgens testes-produced hormones that are more abundant in males, 67, 328
 steroid hormones and, 329

Angel dust, 481

Anger, *360, 361, 362*, 370

Angiotensin II hormone that constricts the blood vessels, compensating for the drop in blood pressure; triggers thirst, 307

Animal Defense League, 23

Anomia difficulty recalling the names of objects, 440

Antabuse (disulfram) drug that antagonizes the effects of acetaldehyde dehydrogenase by binding to its copper ion, 80

Antagonist a drug that blocks a neurotransmitter, 71

Antagonistic muscles opposing sets of muscles that are required to move a leg or arm back and forth, 232, *233*

Anterior, 88

Anterior cingulate cortex, 407

Anterior commissure bundle of axons that connects the two hemispheres of the cerebral cortex, 430
 corpus callosum and, *95*, 100
 hemispheres and, *425*